CENTRAL STATISTICAL OFFICE

Annual Abstract of Statistics

No 126
1990 Edition

Editor: Geoff Dennis

London: Her Majesty's Stationery Office

First published 1990

ISBN 0 11 620395 1

Her Majesty's Stationery Office

Standing order service

Placing a standing order with HMSO BOOKS enables a customer to receive future editions of this title automatically as published.

This saves the time, trouble and expense of placing individual orders and avoids the problem of knowing when to do so.

For details please write to HMSO BOOKS (PC 13A/1), Publications Centre, PO Box 276, London SW8 5DT and quoting reference X02.02.51.

The standing order service also enables customers to receive automatically as published all material of their choice which additionally saves extensive catalogue research. The scope and selectivity of the service has been extended by new techniques, and there are more than 3,500 classifications to choose from. A special leaflet describing the service in detail may be obtained on request.

Introduction

The *Annual Abstract of Statistics* for the United Kingdom is prepared by the Central Statistical Office in collaboration with statistics divisions of other Government departments. The name of the department or organisation providing the statistics is given under each table. Some of the statistics provided by government departments are actually collected by other organisations such as the national associations. The assistance provided by these organisations is gratefully acknowledged.

In addition, an Index of Sources is given on pages 328 to 334, which sets out the official publications or other sources from which tables in this issue contain the latest statistics available, even though they may not yet have appeared in departmental publications.

Most of the tables in this *Abstract of Statistics* give annual figures, so far as they are available, for each of the years 1978 to 1988 and some include figures for the early months of 1989. Current data for many of the series appearing in the *Abstract* are contained in *Economic Trends,* the *Monthly Digest of Statistics* and in *Financial Statistics,* all prepared by the Central Statistical Office. Regional information, supplementary to the national figures in this *Abstract,* is published in *Regional Trends* also prepared by the Central Statistical Office. These publications are available from Her Majesty's Stationery Office at the address given on the back cover.

Definitions

Area covered. Except where otherwise stated all statistics relate to the United Kingdom of Great Britain and Northern Ireland.

Time series. So far as possible annual totals are given throughout, but quarterly or monthly figures are given where these are more suitable to the type of series. Except where it is stated to the contrary all statistics are for calendar years ended 31 December.

For some series, weekly data are collected and not figures for calendar years. In such cases the figures appearing for particular years are cumulative totals for 52 or 53 weeks and attention to this is drawn by the footnotes to the tables. Since the series have not been adjusted to make them equivalent to a calendar year, care must be taken in making comparisons between annual figures for periods of differing numbers of weeks.

Explanatory notes. Several sections of the *Abstract* are preceded by explanatory notes which should be read in conjunction with the tables. Definitions of many of the terms occurring in the *Abstract* and the *Monthly Digest of Statistics* are given in the *Supplement of Definitions and Explanatory Notes* to the *Monthly Digest,* published annually. Detailed notes on items which appear in both the *Abstract* and *Financial Statistics* are given in an annual supplement to the latter entitled *Financial Statistics: Explanatory Handbook.* The original sources listed in the Index of Sources may also be consulted.

Consumption and stocks. Statistics of consumption and stocks should be used with care. The terms 'consumption', 'disposals' and 'stocks' are defined in details given in the *Supplement* to the *Monthly Digest of Statistics.* The stocks figures given may often relate to only part of the total stocks in the country.

Standard Industrial Classification

The Standard Industrial Classification has been prepared as a means of securing uniformity and comparability in the statistics published by government departments in the United Kingdom. It is a system of classification according to industry; it does not relate to commodities or occupations for which other systems of classification have been devised. It was compiled to conform with the organisation and structure of industry within the United Kingdom.

A revised Classification, which replaces the 1968 Classification was published in 1979 and came into general use in 1983. One of the principal objectives of this revision is to eliminate such differences, as the structure of British industry allows, between the activity classification of the European Community, ('Nomenclature Generale des Activites Economiques dans les Communautes Europeennes (NACE)') and the 1968 Classification. The 1980 Classification is a different structure from its predecessor with 10 Divisions, 60 Classes, 22 Groups and 334 activity Headings. Full details are available from *Standard Industrial Classification revised 1980* (HMSO 1979, price £4.25 net) and *Indexes to the Standard Industrial Classification Revised 1980* (HMSO 1981, price £12.95 net). A detailed reconciliation between the 1980 and the 1968 Classifications is available only from the Central Statistical Office, Branch A3, Millbank Tower, Millbank, London SW1P 4QU, price £2.00.

Revisions and changes in content

Revisions. The scope of the *Abstract* is revised from time to time to include new statistical information as it becomes available. Some of the figures, particularly for the latest year, are provisional and are revised in a subsequent issue of the *Abstract.*

New tables. The following new tables have been added:

Chapter 3 — 3.23
3.24 Income Support
3.25

Chapter 2 — Has been reviewed and some tables renumbered, and new tables introduced.

Deletions.

Table 2.4 — Age distribution of the resident population: mid-year estimates.

Table 2.7 — Projected resident population at mid-year.

Table 3.26 — Supplementary benefit recipients of regular weekly payments.

Symbols and conventions used

Change of basis. Where consecutive figures have been compiled on different bases and are not strictly comparable, a fotnote is added indicating the nature of the difference.

Units of measurement. A table showing the various units of measurement used in this *Abstract* and, where appropriate, their metric equivalents, is given on the inside back cover.

Rounding of figures. In tables where figures have been rounded to the nearest final digit, there may be an apparent slight discrepancy between the sums of the constituent items and the total as shown.

Symbols. The following symbols have been used throughout:

. . = not available
— = nil or neglible (less than half the final digit shown)
nei = not elsewhere included
nes = not elsewhere specified

Central Statistical Office
Great George Street
London SW1P 3AQ

November 1989

Contents

*New or revised in this issue of the Annual Abstract

Contents *(contd)* Page

Contents *(contd)*

Contents *(contd)*

Page

Contents *(contd)* Page

Contents *(contd)* Page

1 Area and Climate

1.1 Area of the United Kingdom
at 31 March 1981

	Total	Land	Inland water[1]	Total	Land	Inland water[1]
Metric measure	Thousand hectares			Square kilometres		
United Kingdom	24 410	24 088	322	244 100	240 882	3 218
Great Britain	22 998	22 740	258	229 979	227 399	2 580
England and Wales	15 121	15 032	89	151 207	150 319	888
England	13 044	12 968	76	130 439	129 681	758
Wales	2 077	2 064	13	20 768	20 638	130
Scotland	7 877	7 708	169	78 772	77 080	1 692
Northern Ireland[2]	1 412	1 348	64	14 121	13 483	638
Imperial measure	Thousand acres			Square miles		
United Kingdom	60 318	59 524	794	94 247	93 005	1 242
Great Britain	58 829	56 192	637	88 795	87 799	996
England and Wales	37 361	37 145	219	58 381	58 038	343
England	32 232	32 045	187	50 363	50 070	293
Wales	5 132	5 100	32	8 018	7 968	50
Scotland	19 465	19 047	418	30 414	29 761	653
Northern Ireland[2]	3 489	3 332	157	5 452	5 206	246

Standard regions	Thousand Square Kilometres
United Kingdom	244.1
North	15.4
Yorkshire & Humberside	15.4
East Midlands	15.6
East Anglia	12.6
South East	27.2
South West	23.9
West Midlands	13.0
North West	7.3
Wales	20.8
Scotland	78.8
Northern Ireland	14.0

1 Excluding tidal water.

2 Excluding certain tidal waters that are parts of statutory areas in Northern Ireland.

Sources *Ordnance Survey; Ordnance Survey of Northern Ireland; Central Statistical Office*

1.2 Mean daily air temperature at sea level

Degrees celsius[1]

	Average 1951 – 80	1978	1979	1980	1981	1982	1983	1984	1985	1986	1987	1988
England and Wales												
Annual mean	9.8	9.8	9.3	9.9	9.7	10.4	10.4	10.0	9.2	9.1	9.5	10.2
January	4.0	3.9	0.9	3.1	5.2	3.6	7.0	3.8	1.3	4.1	1.4	5.8
February	4.1	3.1	1.9	6.3	3.7	5.5	2.6	3.5	2.8	−0.4	4.1	5.2
March	5.9	7.2	5.3	5.4	8.3	6.6	7.0	4.6	5.0	5.4	4.6	6.6
April	8.2	6.8	8.1	9.0	8.2	8.9	7.3	8.5	8.7	6.1	10.3	8.5
May	11.3	11.5	10.3	11.3	11.6	11.9	10.6	10.1	11.0	11.3	10.3	12.0
June	14.3	14.0	14.3	14.3	13.8	15.7	14.6	14.7	12.9	14.8	13.1	14.6
July	16.0	15.1	16.5	15.0	16.0	16.8	19.2	16.6	16.4	16.1	16.2	15.1
August	15.9	15.4	15.4	16.3	16.6	16.4	17.6	17.8	15.0	14.1	16.0	15.7
September	14.0	14.5	13.9	15.2	15.1	14.8	14.2	14.1	14.9	11.9	14.2	13.8
October	11.0	12.4	11.9	9.6	8.9	10.7	11.0	11.7	11.4	11.4	10.3	11.1
November	7.1	9.0	7.3	7.0	8.1	8.5	8.1	8.6	4.7	8.3	7.2	6.2
December	5.1	4.8	6.3	6.0	1.4	4.9	6.3	5.7	6.7	6.4	6.1	7.7
Scotland												
Annual mean	8.5	8.6	7.9	8.7	8.4	8.9	9.1	8.3	7.6	7.9	8.2	9.0
January	3.5	2.8	0.8	2.8	4.3	2.9	5.6	1.5	1.6	2.9	2.0	4.2
February	3.4	1.9	1.9	4.9	3.9	5.5	2.7	2.8	3.4	0.5	3.5	4.5
March	5.1	5.9	3.6	4.2	6.0	5.6	6.2	4.1	4.2	5.0	3.8	5.0
April	7.1	6.1	6.7	8.3	7.3	8.2	5.8	7.2	7.2	5.2	8.5	7.2
May	9.9	10.9	8.3	10.4	10.6	9.9	9.0	9.1	9.7	9.9	9.3	10.5
June	12.7	12.5	12.8	12.7	12.9	12.8	12.2	12.5	11.4	13.0	11.0	13.6
July	13.9	13.2	13.8	13.5	13.9	15.1	16.0	14.6	14.1	13.8	14.3	13.7
August	13.9	13.9	13.2	14.1	14.7	14.3	15.5	15.5	13.2	12.1	13.8	13.9
September	12.2	12.6	11.9	13.3	13.1	12.2	13.3	11.8	11.9	10.7	11.9	12.3
October	9.8	11.0	10.6	8.1	6.7	9.6	9.4	9.8	10.3	9.8	8.2	9.3
November	6.0	7.6	5.9	6.3	6.3	6.6	7.2	7.4	3.5	7.1	6.4	6.0
December	4.5	4.2	4.7	5.5	0.8	3.9	6.1	5.6	4.9	4.7	5.2	7.3
Northern Ireland												
Annual mean	9.0	9.3	8.4	9.2	9.2	9.4	9.8	8.4	8.6	8.3	8.9	9.4
January	4.0	3.6	0.9	2.7	5.6	4.0	5.8	2.2	1.3	3.6	3.2	4.5
February	4.2	3.4	2.6	5.4	4.4	5.6	3.2	2.3	4.2	1.3	4.2	4.8
March	5.7	6.3	4.3	4.9	7.3	6.2	7.0	4.5	5.0	5.4	4.9	6.4
April	7.7	6.7	6.9	8.7	8.2	9.0	6.0	7.3	8.3	5.4	9.3	8.5
May	10.3	11.4	8.6	11.3	10.9	10.8	9.8	8.5	9.8	10.0	10.0	10.7
June	13.1	12.7	13.1	12.8	13.1	14.1	13.2	12.9	12.0	13.8	11.6	14.2
July	14.4	14.1	15.10	13.8	14.5	15.6	17.5	14.7	14.5	14.3	15.1	13.8
August	14.3	14.4	13.8	15.1	15.4	12.9	16.7	16.1	13.3	12.1	14.6	14.0
September	12.6	13.6	12.4	13.9	13.6	12.9	14.5	12.6	13.6	11.3	12.2	12.5
October	10.2	11.9	10.9	8.9	7.2	10.3	10.1	10.0	10.7	10.1	8.3	9.9
November	6.4	8.4	6.9	6.7	7.5	6.5	7.8	6.3	4.3	7.1	7.0	6.0
December	5.1	4.5	6.9	5.7	2.2	4.4	6.8	5.4	5.9	5.5	6.1	7.8

1 To convert degrees celsius into degrees fahrenheit: multiply by 9, divide by 5, and add 32.

Source Meteorological Office

1.3 Rainfall

Millimetres[1]

	Average 1941 – 70	1978	1979	1980	1981	1982	1983	1984	1985	1986	1987	1988
England and Wales												
Annual total	912	905	1 002	979	998	973	879	899	885	992	914	931
January	86	111	86	78	58	72	92	144	72	120	30	154
February	65	86	66	93	52	44	42	57	29	17	58	63
March	59	78	125	104	153	101	67	59	66	80	83	94
April	58	52	68	18	64	23	108	11	70	84	66	42
May	67	47	124	32	91	46	117	59	65	85	48	60
June	61	70	42	128	49	129	37	43	94	43	102	37
July	73	89	33	74	55	39	40	27	73	54	77	138
August	90	71	94	96	48	90	33	57	117	117	72	92
September	83	54	38	67	141	78	101	116	46	27	67	66
October	83	19	78	131	124	125	78	100	48	98	171	92
November	97	54	87	87	69	126	53	145	77	124	81	49
December	90	174	161	71	94	100	111	81	128	143	59	44
Scotland												
Annual total	1 431	1 419	1 531	1 533	1 523	1 675	1 456	1 473	1 505	1 642	1 353	1 637
January	137	158	120	120	157	154	220	223	85	192	70	193
February	104	104	38	95	91	107	59	111	47	21	95	149
March	92	166	178	113	152	153	149	103	95	169	142	159
April	90	52	96	20	33	46	74	60	111	80	76	85
May	91	40	102	18	87	92	115	24	73	176	77	55
June	92	69	75	150	103	72	86	66	84	63	101	33
July	112	90	105	125	92	57	43	55	167	87	120	202
August	129	110	143	146	52	156	51	50	224	120	126	187
September	137	177	112	172	235	200	172	166	200	66	160	156
October	149	99	152	187	218	196	230	216	85	159	165	177
November	142	198	204	181	216	229	49	233	141	232	107	91
December	156	156	206	206	87	213	208	166	193	277	114	150
Northern Ireland												
Annual total	1 095	1 077	1 142	1 159	1 209	1 165	952	1 037	1 114	1 173	993	1 234
January	104	134	96	115	100	107	117	180	76	155	49	167
February	75	74	29	104	68	90	51	111	38	5	63	112
March	70	113	98	113	128	112	113	72	86	115	99	132
April	68	32	82	19	47	24	59	30	76	106	50	42
May	73	31	96	37	141	65	83	22	74	124	42	43
June	79	57	54	118	88	123	53	57	74	46	100	49
July	93	68	51	81	78	21	20	49	118	74	82	145
August	103	80	137	84	43	92	35	71	183	141	133	135
September	107	112	75	118	175	99	111	104	156	10	133	116
October	107	54	138	148	154	126	132	112	49	106	96	147
November	102	117	163	88	94	167	39	114	86	131	80	54
December	114	205	123	134	93	139	139	115	98	160	66	92

1 1 millimetre = 0.0394 inches.

Source Meteorological Office

1.4 Mean daily sunshine

Hours

	Average 1951 – 80	1978	1979	1980	1981	1982	1983	1984	1985	1986	1987	1988
England and Wales												
Annual mean	4.05	3.66	3.90	3.89	3.64	4.09	3.90	4.29	3.95	4.14	3.74	4.05
January	1.61	1.62	1.92	2.00	1.64	1.85	1.62	2.18	1.71	1.85	1.69	1.74
February	2.35	1.90	2.09	1.63	2.48	1.98	2.70	2.14	2.87	2.73	2.35	3.74
March	3.60	3.81	2.94	2.78	2.13	4.87	2.79	2.09	3.75	4.00	3.28	3.10
April	5.06	3.79	4.27	5.64	4.37	5.90	4.73	7.42	4.54	4.45	5.30	4.60
May	6.31	6.50	5.99	7.32	4.61	7.32	4.35	5.58	5.54	6.31	6.25	6.50
June	6.70	5.50	5.70	5.50	5.23	5.43	5.84	7.03	5.70	6.83	4.09	5.83
July	5.91	4.65	5.70	5.00	5.00	5.59	7.41	7.89	6.32	5.35	5.61	4.91
August	5.55	4.71	5.43	4.77	6.08	5.43	6.90	6.53	5.22	4.61	5.05	5.83
September	4.59	4.93	5.42	4.66	5.28	4.93	3.68	3.84	4.45	5.69	5.05	4.77
October	3.26	2.96	3.41	3.58	3.71	2.31	3.64	3.31	3.39	3.68	3.42	3.29
November	2.10	2.44	2.19	1.92	1.71	1.99	1.53	1.73	2.69	2.50	1.76	2.96
December	1.47	1.12	1.68	1.75	1.48	1.46	1.68	1.73	1.19	1.69	1.07	1.32
Scotland												
Annual mean	3.51	3.20	3.37	3.17	3.49	3.53	3.14	3.37	3.26	3.53	3.30	3.40
January	1.33	1.47	1.53	1.26	1.19	1.19	1.02	1.21	1.55	1.14	1.22	1.38
February	2.42	2.50	3.04	1.52	2.53	2.16	2.40	1.62	2.79	2.95	2.20	2.20
March	3.29	3.16	3.42	2.69	3.19	3.74	2.18	2.21	3.33	3.68	3.49	3.09
April	5.00	3.84	3.94	5.54	6.18	4.84	4.42	5.97	3.84	4.30	4.05	4.15
May	5.74	6.37	5.28	7.40	5.45	6.89	3.67	6.75	5.42	5.05	5.68	6.49
June	5.88	5.44	5.62	4.57	4.92	5.27	5.50	4.78	5.64	6.53	4.59	6.12
July	4.86	4.28	3.56	3.70	4.14	6.01	5.87	5.54	3.79	4.18	3.89	4.08
August	4.56	3.32	4.03	3.36	4.79	4.39	5.02	4.71	3.97	4.51	4.20	4.15
September	3.65	3.08	4.56	2.93	3.52	3.34	2.89	2.79	3.03	4.31	4.93	3.87
October	2.68	2.46	2.40	2.81	3.24	2.05	2.40	2.54	3.15	3.16	2.74	2.37
November	1.66	1.66	1.85	1.45	1.56	1.45	1.52	1.23	1.69	1.64	1.49	2.07
December	1.07	0.86	1.21	0.86	1.13	0.98	0.80	1.09	0.93	0.88	1.10	0.88
Northern Ireland												
Annual mean	3.41	3.11	3.28	3.08	3.04	3.56	3.04	3.45	3.02	3.46	3.16	3.31
January	1.47	1.84	1.66	1.46	1.15	1.53	1.30	1.40	1.80	1.22	1.47	1.73
February	2.31	2.50	2.52	1.81	1.94	2.19	2.35	1.60	2.32	2.63	2.38	2.40
March	3.23	3.22	3.49	2.96	2.66	4.73	1.90	2.26	2.78	3.62	2.52	2.52
April	5.01	3.91	4.21	4.91	5.51	5.16	5.30	5.79	4.17	5.16	3.36	4.56
May	5.70	5.47	5.10	7.26	4.43	5.78	4.12	7.64	4.86	4.90	5.93	5.87
June	5.60	4.28	4.80	3.31	4.28	4.51	4.05	4.81	5.54	5.15	3.70	5.94
July	4.25	4.05	3.18	3.62	3.31	5.75	5.80	5.19	3.27	2.68	3.53	3.83
August	4.37	2.89	4.38	3.20	4.02	4.02	4.38	3.69	3.23	4.06	3.67	3.67
September	3.50	3.08	3.76	3.01	3.72	3.65	2.61	3.35	2.73	5.32	4.97	3.43
October	2.56	2.98	2.95	2.66	3.11	2.58	2.77	3.10	2.60	3.35	3.64	2.87
November	1.81	1.74	2.05	1.83	1.52	1.54	1.17	1.64	1.85	2.37	1.70	1.97
December	1.11	1.42	1.30	0.91	0.82	1.25	0.80	0.89	1.14	1.11	1.03	0.97

Source Meteorological Office

2 Population and Vital Statistics

This section begins with a summary of population figures for the United Kingdom and constituent countries from 1851 to 2031 and for Great Britain from 1801 (Table 2.1). Table 2.2 analyses the elements of population change. Tables 2.3–2.4 give details of the national sex and age structure for years up to the present date. The marital condition of the population is given in Tables 2.6 and 2.7. Table 2.5 gives projections of the population by sex and age up to the year 2031. The distribution of population at local and regional level is summarised in Tables 2.8 and 2.9.

In the main, historical series relate to census information while mid-year estimates which make allowance for underenumeration and absences abroad in the latest census are given for the recent past and the present.

Population *(Tables 2.1–2.4).*

Figures shown in these tables relate to the population enumerated at successive censuses, mid-year estimates and population projections.

Definition of resident population

The estimated population of an area includes all those usually resident in the area, whatever their nationality. Members of HM and non-UK Armed Forces are taken to be resident at their stationed address. Students are taken to be resident at their term-time address.

The current series of estimates are updated annually, starting with those derived from the 1981 Census of Population and then allowing for births, deaths and migration.

Projected resident population of the United Kingdom and constituent countries *(Tables 2.1, 2.2 and 2.5).*

These projections are prepared by the Government Actuary, in consultation with the Registrars General, as a common framework for use in national planning in a number of different fields. A single principal projection is made periodically on a set of assumptions which seems most appropriate on the basis of the statistical evidence available at the time. In addition every few years variant projections are made on assumptions differing from those of the principal projection.

The population projections in Tables 2.1, 2.2 and 2.5 are 1988 based. The base population is as estimated for mid-1988 by the Registrars General, and the assumptions for mortality, fertility and migration reflect statistical evidence up to mid-1988.

Geographical distribution of the enumerated population: census figures *(Table 2.8).*

The urban and rural districts and the conurbations shown in the table are based on local government administrative areas as they were prior to reorganisation in England and Wales in 1974 and in Scotland in 1975. Preliminary population counts from the 1981 Census were prepared for these areas in England and Wales, but it was not possible to continue the series to 1981 in Scotland or in Northern Ireland.

A new study of urban land and population based on the 1981 Census of Population has been made in Great Britain and the results published in *1981 Census, Key Statistics for Urban Areas, Great Britain.* This gives the total population in Great Britain in urban areas in 1981 as 48 655 thousand and the population in remaining rural areas as 5 630 thousand, indicating that the division by administrative areas underestimated the urban population. However, it is not possible to give statistics of population in earlier years for the new urban areas, so the series based on administrative areas is given in Table 2.8.

Migration into and out of the United Kingdom *(Tables 2.10 and 2.11).*

A migrant into the United Kingdom is defined as a person who has resided abroad for a year or more and on entering has declared the intention to reside here for a year or more; and *vice versa* for a migrant from the United Kingdom. Estimates are derived from the International Passenger Survey (IPS), a sample survey covering the principal air and sea routes between the United Kingdom and overseas but excluding routes to and from the Irish Republic. The figures include British citizens as well as people subject to immigration control.

In Table 2.11, type of occupation is that followed prior to migration.

Acceptances for settlement in the United Kingdom *(Table 2.12).*

This table presents in geographic regions the statistics of individual nationalities, arranged alphabetically within each region. The figures are on a different basis to those derived from the IPS (Tables 2.10 and 2.11) and relate only to people subject to immigration control. It should be noted that information is not separately available for all nationalities and countries and therefore the group sub-totals shown are simply the totals of the countries listed.

Divorces *(Tables 2.14, 2.15).*

Table 2.14 gives figures for dissolutions and annulments by duration of marriage and age of wife. Scottish figures prior to 1979 relate only to marriages which took place in Scotland. Data in Table 2.15 give petitions filed for divorce, divorces by fact proven (grounds) and separations.

Births *(Tables 2.16, 2.17 and 2.18).*

For Scotland and Northern Ireland the number of births relate to those registered during the year. For England and Wales the figures up to and including 1930–32 are for those registered while later figures relate to births occurring in each year.

Deaths *(Tables 2.19–2.22).*

The figures relate to the number of deaths registered during the calendar year, the normal time lag between occurrence and registration being a matter of days only.

Life tables *(Table 2.23).*

The interim life tables are constructed from the estimated Home population in 1984–86 and the total deaths registered in those years.

2.1 Population summary

Thousands

	United Kingdom			England and Wales			Wales	Scotland			Northern Ireland		
	Persons	Males	Females	Persons	Males	Females	Persons	Persons	Males	Females	Persons	Males	Females
Enumerated population: census figures													
1801	..	..	..	8 893	4 255	4 638	587	1 608	739	869	..	..	..
1851	22 259	10 855	11 404	17 928	8 781	9 146	1 163	2 889	1 376	1 513	1 442	698	745
1901	38 237	18 492	19 745	32 528	15 729	16 799	2 013	4 472	2 174	2 298	1 237	590	647
1911	42 082	20 357	21 725	36 070	17 446	18 625	2 421	4 761	2 309	2 452	1 251	603	648
1921[1]	44 027	21 033	22 994	37 887	18 075	19 811	2 656	4 882	2 348	2 535	1 258	610	648
1931[1]	46 038	22 060	23 978	39 952	19 133	20 819	2 593	4 843	2 326	2 517	1 243	601	642
1951	50 225	24 118	26 107	43 758	21 016	22 742	2 599	5 096	2 434	2 662	1 371	668	703
1961	52 709	25 481	27 228	46 105	22 304	23 801	2 644	5 179	2 483	2 697	1 425	694	731
1966[2]	53 788	26 044	27 745	47 136	22 841	24 295	2 663	5 168	2 479	2 689	1 485	724	761
1971	55 515	26 952	28 562	48 750	23 683	25 067	2 731	5 229	2 515	2 714	1 536	755	781
1981	55 848	27 104	28 742	49 155	23 873	25 281	2 792	5 131	2 466	2 664	1 533[4]	750	783
Usually resident													
1981	55 089	26 803	28 286	48 522	23 625	24 897	2 750	5 035	2 428	2 607	1 532	749	783
Resident population: mid-year estimates													
1958	51 652	24 887	26 765	45 109	21 744	23 365	2 615	5 141	2 460	2 682	1 402	684	719
1959	51 956	25 043	26 913	45 386	21 885	23 501	2 623	5 163	2 472	2 690	1 408	686	722
1960	52 372	25 271	27 102	45 775	22 097	23 678	2 629	5 178	2 482	2 696	1 420	692	728
1961	52 807	25 528	27 279	46 196	22 347	23 849	2 635	5 184	2 485	2 698	1 427	696	732
1962	53 292	25 826	27 465	46 657	22 631	24 026	2 652	5 198	2 495	2 703	1 437	700	737
1963	53 625	25 992	27 633	46 973	22 787	24 186	2 664	5 205	2 500	2 705	1 447	705	741
1964	53 991	26 191	27 800	47 324	22 978	24 346	2 677	5 208	2 501	2 707	1 458	711	747
1965	54 350	26 368	27 982	47 671	23 151	24 521	2 693	5 210	2 501	2 709	1 468	716	752
1966	54 643	26 511	28 132	47 966	23 296	24 671	2 702	5 201	2 496	2 704	1 476	719	757
1967	54 959	26 673	28 286	48 272	23 451	24 821	2 710	5 198	2 496	2 702	1 489	726	763
1968	55 214	26 784	28 429	48 511	23 554	24 957	2 715	5 200	2 498	2 702	1 503	733	770
1969	55 461	26 908	28 553	48 738	23 666	25 072	2 722	5 208	2 503	2 706	1 514	739	776
1970	55 632	26 992	28 641	48 891	23 738	25 153	2 729	5 214	2 507	2 707	1 527	747	781
1971	55 928	27 167	28 761	49 152	23 897	25 255	2 740	5 236	2 516	2 720	1 540	755	786
1972	56 097	27 259	28 837	49 327	23 989	25 339	2 755	5 231	2 513	2 717	1 539	758	782
1973	56 223	27 332	28 891	49 459	24 061	25 399	2 773	5 234	2 515	2 719	1 530	756	774
1974	56 236	27 349	28 887	49 468	24 075	25 393	2 785	5 241	2 519	2 722	1 527	755	772
1975	56 226	27 361	28 865	49 470	24 091	25 378	2 795	5 232	2 516	2 716	1 524	753	770
1976	56 216	27 360	28 856	49 459	24 089	25 370	2 799	5 233	2 517	2 716	1 524	754	770
1977	56 190	27 345	28 845	49 440	24 076	25 364	2 801	5 226	2 515	2 711	1 523	754	769
1978	56 178	27 330	28 849	49 443	24 067	25 375	2 804	5 212	2 509	2 704	1 523	754	770
1979	56 240	27 373	28 867	49 508	24 113	25 395	2 810	5 204	2 505	2 699	1 530	755	773
1980	56 330	27 411	28 919	49 603	24 156	25 448	2 816	5 194	2 501	2 693	1 533	755	778
1981	56 352	27 409	28 943	49 634	24 160	25 474	2 814	5 180	2 495	2 685	1 538	754	784
1982	56 306	27 386	28 920	49 601	24 143	25 459	2 807	5 167	2 490	2 677	1 538	754	784
1983	56 347	27 417	28 931	49 654	24 176	25 478	2 808	5 153	2 488	2 665	1 543	756	788
1984	56 460	27 487	28 973	49 764	24 244	25 519	2 807	5 146	2 484	2 662	1 551	760	791
1985	56 618	27 574	29 044	49 924	24 330	25 594	2 812	5 137	2 481	2 656	1 558	763	795
1986	56 763	27 647	29 116	50 075	24 403	25 672	2 821	5 121	2 475	2 646	1 567	768	798
1987	56 930	27 737	29 193	50 243	24 493	25 750	2 836	5 112	2 471	2 641	1 575	773	802
1988	57 065	27 813	29 253	50 393	24 576	25 817	2 857	5 094	2 462	2 632	1 578	774	804
Resident population: projections (mid-year)[3]													
1991	57 533	28 087	29 446	50 878	24 853	26 024	2 896	5 061	2 450	2 610	1 595	783	811
1996	58 462	28 618	29 845	51 801	25 372	26 429	2 944	5 037	2 447	2 590	1 625	799	826
2001	59 201	29 043	30 157	52 551	25 796	26 755	2 978	4 999	2 435	2 564	1 651	813	838
2006	59 648	29 323	30 325	53 050	26 094	26 956	2 994	4 930	2 407	2 523	1 667	822	845
2011	59 989	29 545	30 443	53 472	26 350	27 122	3 005	4 843	2 369	2 474	1 673	826	847
2021	60 823	30 031	30 792	54 499	26 922	27 576	3 032	4 653	2 283	2 370	1 672	826	845
2031	61 200	30 237	30 964	55 081	27 226	27 856	3 019	4 450	2 185	2 265	1 669	826	844

1 Figures for Northern Ireland are estimated. The population at the census of 1926 was 1 257 thousand (608 thousand males and 649 thousand females).

2 Except for Northern Ireland, where a full census was taken, figures are based on the 10 per cent sample census.

3 These projections are 1988 based. More detail given in Table 2.5.

4 The figures include 44 500 non-enumerated persons.

Sources *Office of Population Censuses and Surveys; General Register Office (Scotland); General Register Office (Northern Ireland); Government Actuary's Department*

2.2 Population changes

Thousands

	Population at beginning of period[1]	Average annual change					
		Total increase or decrease(–)	Births	Deaths[2]	Excess of births over deaths	Net civilian migration	Other adjustments[3]
United Kingdom							
1901–1911	38 237	385	1 091	624	467	–82	
1911–1921	42 082	195	975	689	286	–92	
1921–1931	44 027	201	824	555	268	–67	
1931–1951	46 038	213	793	603	190	+22	
1951–1961	50 290	252	839	593	246	–7	+13
1961–1971	52 807	310	962	638	324	–32	+18
1971–1981	55 928	42	736	666	69	–44	+17
1981–1988	56 352	102	745	656	89	+10	+4
1988–1991	57 065	156	801	646	156	0	
1991–2001	57 533	167	818	651	167	0	
2001–2011	59 201	79	734	655	79	0	
2011–2021	59 989	83	760	677	83	0	
England and Wales							
1901–1911	32 528	354	929	525	404	–50	
1911–1921	36 070	182	828	584	244	–62	
1921–1931	37 887	207	693	469	224	–17	
1931–1951	39 952	193	673	518	155	+38	
1951–1961	43 815	238	714	516	197	+30	+10
1961–1971	46 196	296	832	560	272	+7	+16
1971–1981	49 152	48	638	585	53	–18	+13
1981–1988	49 634	108	651	578	74	+31	+4
1988–1991	50 393	161	707	568	138	23	
1991–2001	50 878	167	722	575	147	20	
2001–2011	52 551	92	652	579	72	20	
2011–2021	53 472	103	682	599	83	20	
Scotland							
1901–1911	4 472	29	131	76	54	–25	
1911–1921	4 761	12	118	82	36	–24	
1921–1931	4 882	–4	100	65	35	–39	
1931–1951	4 843	13	92	67	25	–11	–1
1951–1961	5 102	8	95	62	34	–28	+2
1961–1971	5 184	3	97	63	34	–32	+2
1971–1981	5 236	–6	70	64	6	–15	+4
1981–1988	5 180	–12	66	63	3	–16	1
1988–1991	5 094	–11	66	61	5	–16	
1991–2001	5 061	–6	67	60	7	–13	
2001–2011	4 999	–16	57	60	–3	–13	
2011–2021	4 843	–19	55	61	–6	–13	
Northern Ireland							
1901–1911	1 237	1	31	23	8	–6	
1911–1921	1 251	1	29	22	7	–6	
1921–1931	1 258	–2	30	21	9	–11	
1931–1951	1 243	6	28	18	10	–4	
1951–1961	1 373	5	30	15	15	–9	–
1961–1971	1 427	11	33	16	17	–7	+1
1971–1981	1 540	0	28	17	11	–11	–
1981–1988	1 538	6	28	16	12	–5	0
1988–1991	1 578	5	28	16	12	–7	
1991–2001	1 595	6	28	16	13	–7	
2001–2011	1 651	2	25	16	9	–7	
2011–2021	1 673	0	23	17	7	–7	

1 Census enumerated population up to 1951; mid-year estimates of resident population from 1951 to 1988 and mid-1988 based projections of resident population thereafter.

2 Including deaths of non-civilians and merchant seamen who died outside the country. These numbered 577 000 in 1911–1921 and 240 000 in 1931–1951 for England and Wales; 74 000 in 1911–1921 and 34 000 in 1931–1951 for Scotland; and 10 000 in 1911–1926 for Northern Ireland.

3 For England and Wales, changes in Armed Forces, in visitor balance and other adjustments.

Sources *Office of Population Censuses and Surveys; General Register Office (Scotland); General Register Office (Northern Ireland); Government Actuary's Department*

2.3 Age distribution of the enumerated population: census figures
United Kingdom

	1901	1931[1]	1951	1971	1981[2, 3]
Persons: all ages	38 237	46 038	50 225	55 515	55 089
Under 5	4 381	3 531	4 326	4 505	3 349
Under 16	..	..	11 975	14 168	12 384
Under 18	..	..	13 248	15 705	14 272
5–14	8 040	7 643	6 999	8 882	8 106
15–29	10 808	11 853	10 328	11 678	12 409
30–44	7 493	9 717	11 125	9 759	10 760
45–64	5 706	9 877	11 980	13 384	12 296
65–74	1 278	2 461	3 689	4 713	5 049
75 and over	531	957	1 777	2 594	3 120
Pensionable age aggregate	2 387	4 421	6 828	9 015	9 680
Under 1	938	712	773	891	713
1 and under 2	857	699	805	878	714
2–4	2 586	2 119	2 748	2 736	1 923
5–9	4 106	3 897	3 689	4 670	3 685
10–14	3 934	3 746	3 310	4 213	4 420
15–19	3 826	3 989	3 175	3 832	4 611
20–24	3 674	4 024	3 393	4 237	4 081
25–29	3 308	3 841	3 761	3 610	3 717
30–34	2 833	3 494	3 515	3 259	4 114
35–39	2 494	3 195	3 786	3 169	3 485
40–44	2 165	3 028	3 825	3 331	3 162
45–49	1 837	2 901	3 603	3 544	3 051
50–54	1 566	2 713	3 209	3 273	3 151
55–59	1 236	2 365	2 746	3 360	3 242
60–64	1 067	1 897	2 422	3 206	2 852
65–69	743	1 455	2 069	2 707	2 730
70–74	535	1 005	1 620	2 005	2 318
75–79	313	581	1 049	1 331	1 635
80–84	157	263	506	790	920
85 and over	61	113	224	473	565
Males: all ages	18 492	22 060	24 118	26 952	26 803
Under 5	2 190	1 784	2 215	2 312	1 717
Under 16	..	..	6 110	7 275	6 352
Under 18	..	..	6 753	8 064	7 318
5–14	4 024	3 859	3 566	4 561	4 159
15–29	5 191	5 804	5 073	5 915	6 294
30–44	3 597	4 495	5 461	4 909	5 401
45–64	2 705	4 647	5 554	6 452	6 003
65–74	565	1 099	1 561	1 976	2 210
75 and over	219	372	687	828	1 019
Pensionable age aggregate	785	1 471	2 247	2 804	3 228
Under 1	471	361	397	457	364
1 and under 2	429	353	412	451	366
2–4	1 290	1 070	1 406	1 404	987
5–9	2 052	1 967	1 885	2 395	1 893
10–14	1 972	1 892	1 681	2 166	2 266
15–19	1 898	1 987	1 564	1 961	2 356
20–24	1 737	1 958	1 648	2 132	2 067
25–29	1 556	1 860	1 861	1 822	1 871
30–34	1 349	1 636	1 725	1 652	2 065
35–39	1 200	1 462	1 856	1 598	1 750
40–44	1 048	1 397	1 881	1 659	1 586
45–49	886	1 348	1 764	1 750	1 528
50–54	747	1 274	1 495	1 591	1 556
55–59	582	1 131	1 234	1 614	1 577
60–64	490	894	1 061	1 497	1 342
65–69	332	663	885	1 196	1 234
70–74	233	436	675	779	976
75–79	133	237	428	461	608
80–84	63	98	189	244	278
85 and over	23	36	70	124	133

1 Figures included for Northern Ireland are estimated.
2 The figures for Northern Ireland have been revised using a new estimate of 44 500 non-enumerated persons in the 1981 Census.
3 1981 data cover the 'usually resident' population and are not strictly comparable with other data.

Sources *Office of Population Censuses and Surveys; General Register Office (Scotland); General Register Office (Northern Ireland)*

2.3 Age distribution of the enumerated population: census figures
United Kingdom

(continued)

Thousands

	1901	1931[1]	1951	1971	1981[2,3]
Females: all ages	19 745	23 978	26 107	28 562	28 286
Under 5	2 190	1 747	2 111	2 194	1 632
Under 16	..	..	5 864	6 893	6 032
Under 18	..	..	6 495	7 641	6 954
5–14	4 016	3 784	3 433	4 321	3 946
15–29	5 618	6 049	5 255	5 764	6 115
30–44	3 895	5 222	5 663	4 850	5 359
45–64	3 001	5 229	6 425	6 931	6 293
65–74	713	1 361	2 128	2 737	2 839
75 and over	312	586	1 091	1 765	2 102
Pensionable age aggregate	1 601	2 950	4 580	6 211	6 451
Under 1	466	351	376	434	349
1 and under 2	428	347	393	428	348
2–4	1 296	1 050	1 342	1 332	936
5–9	2 054	1 930	1 804	2 274	1 793
10–14	1 962	1 854	1 629	2 047	2 154
15–19	1 928	2 002	1 611	1 872	2 255
20–24	1 938	2 066	1 744	2 105	2 014
25–29	1 752	1 981	1 900	1 700	1 846
30–34	1 484	1 858	1 790	1 607	2 049
35–39	1 294	1 733	1 930	1 572	1 735
40–44	1 117	1 631	1 943	1 672	1 575
45–49	951	1 553	1 839	1 794	1 523
50–54	819	1 439	1 714	1 683	1 594
55–59	654	1 234	1 512	1 746	1 665
60–64	577	1 003	1 361	1 709	1 510
65–69	411	792	1 183	1 511	1 497
70–74	302	569	944	1 226	1 342
75–79	180	344	620	870	1 028
80–84	94	165	317	546	642
85 and over	38	77	154	349	432

1 Figures included for Northern Ireland are estimated.
2 The figures for Northern Ireland have been revised using a new estimate of 44 500 non-enumerated persons in the 1981 Census.
3 1981 data cover the 'usually resident' population and are not strictly comparable with other data.

Sources *Office of Population Censuses and Surveys; General Register Office (Scotland); General Register Office (Northern Ireland)*

2.4 Age distribution of the enumerated population: census figures
Constituent countries

Thousands

	England and Wales				Scotland				Northern Ireland			
	1951	1961	1971	1981[1]	1951	1961	1971	1981[1]	1951	1961	1971	1981[1,2]
Persons: all ages	43 758	46 105	48 750	48 522	5 096.4	5 179.3	5 229.0	5 035.3	1 370.9	1 425.0	1 536.1	1 532.2
Under 5	3 718	3 597	3 905	2 910	470.8	469.2	444.3	308.4	137.8	146.5	156.2	130.8
Under 16	10 243	11 233	12 246	10 773	1 331.4	1 413.9	1 438.1	1 167.0	400.7	437.0	483.9	443.3
Under 18	11 323	12 576	13 574	12 418	1 481.4	1 567.5	1 596.7	1 350.8	443.6	487.5	534.9	502.9
5–14	5 974	6 987	7 671	7 053	784.5	869.9	910.5	769.6	240.9	265.6	300.8	283.1
15–29	8 912	8 925	10 236	10 859	1 107.3	1 034.1	1 099.2	1 183.1	308.9	299.2	343.2	366.9
30–44	9 767	9 263	8 593	9 541	1 083.8	1 000.3	912.7	947.2	274.4	262.5	253.4	272.4
45–64	10 563	11 836	11 849	10 884	1 143.0	1 256.9	1 217.9	1 116.3	273.9	307.3	316.5	295.2
65–74	3 257	3 520	4 178	4 488	343.6	358.4	426.5	444.3	87.9	92.3	108.2	116.2
75 and over	1 568	1 976	2 318	2 786	163.5	190.5	217.9	266.5	47.0	51.6	57.8	67.8
Pensionable age aggregate	6 029	6 858	8 007	8 611	633.7	695.3	803.7	847.6	165.1	180.1	204.9	220.6
Under 1	659	764	774	619	87.6	97.8	86.0	66.1	26.7	30.8	31.1	27.1
1 and under 2	689	725	761	622	89.0	94.3	86.4	65.0	27.1	29.8	30.9	27.4
2–4	2 370	2 107	2 370	1 669	294.2	277.1	271.9	177.3	84.1	86.0	94.2	76.2
5–9	3 162	3 262	4 044	3 207	397.9	420.7	468.4	344.4	129.2	132.4	157.1	134.3
10–14	2 812	3 725	3 627	3 846	386.6	449.1	442.1	425.2	111.7	133.2	143.7	148.8
15–19	2 704	3 201	3 314	4 020	361.9	374.1	392.3	446.6	108.5	120.2	126.4	144.5
20–24	2 927	2 878	3 731	3 564	364.2	333.0	390.4	394.3	100.9	93.8	114.9	122.3
25–29	3 280	2 846	3 191	3 275	381.2	327.0	316.4	342.2	99.5	85.2	101.9	99.9
30–34	3 079	2 984	2 871	3 656	345.0	332.5	300.6	358.7	91.2	86.5	86.7	98.7
35–39	3 323	3 242	2 786	3 092	368.6	347.3	300.8	300.3	94.1	90.9	82.4	92.5
40–44	3 365	3 037	2 935	2 792	370.2	320.5	311.3	288.1	89.1	85.1	84.3	81.2
45–49	3 172	3 229	3 135	2 689	349.6	342.6	322.8	285.7	80.8	87.0	86.0	76.1
50–54	2 825	3 221	2 897	2 785	308.0	342.2	295.8	289.6	76.3	82.0	80.0	76.0
55–59	2 423	2 928	2 976	2 877	260.7	312.5	306.3	289.8	62.2	72.5	78.5	75.1
60–64	2 143	2 458	2 841	2 533	224.7	259.5	293.0	251.3	54.5	65.7	72.0	68.0
65–69	1 829	1 979	2 400	2 426	192.2	204.6	247.2	240.8	47.4	52.2	60.3	63.4
70–74	1 428	1 542	1 778	2 062	151.4	153.9	179.3	203.5	40.5	40.1	47.9	52.8
75–79	924	1 069	1 185	1 458	97.8	105.4	115.2	142.5	27.2	27.0	29.9	34.6
80–84	446	605	707	821	45.9	57.9	65.6	78.3	13.7	16.2	17.5	20.5
85 and over	198	302	425	507	19.8	27.2	37.2	45.6	6.1	8.4	10.4	12.7
Males: all ages	21 016	22 304	23 683	23 625	2 434.4	2 482.7	2 514.6	2 428.5	667.8	694.2	754.7	749.5
Under 5	1 904	1 846	2 003	1 492	241.0	240.1	228.5	158.3	70.6	75.4	80.3	66.8
Under 16	5 228	5 756	6 288	5 526	677.4	723.5	737.9	598.3	204.7	224.4	249.0	227.6
Under 18	5 774	6 440	6 971	6 368	752.9	800.7	818.7	691.9	226.4	249.8	275.2	258.3
5–14	3 045	3 578	3 940	3 619	398.2	445.2	466.7	394.5	123.0	136.2	154.9	145.6
15–29	4 388	4 502	5 184	5 506	532.8	507.8	554.4	599.7	152.0	148.8	176.0	187.9
30–44	4 804	4 612	4 337	4 794	523.7	486.5	446.9	471.2	133.2	127.1	124.9	135.8
45–64	4 902	5 663	5 728	5 331	523.7	588.6	573.5	531.9	128.3	145.5	151.2	140.3
65–74	1 372	1 419	1 755	1 971	148.9	143.7	174.5	188.9	39.9	40.0	45.9	50.0
75 and over	600	684	737	912	65.8	71.0	70.3	83.9	20.8	21.3	21.4	23.0
Pensionable age aggregate	1 972	2 102	2 492	2 882	214.7	214.6	244.8	272.8	60.7	61.3	67.4	73.0
Under 1	338	393	397	317	45.0	49.9	44.2	33.8	13.8	15.9	15.9	13.8
1 and under 2	353	372	390	319	45.6	48.4	44.5	33.4	13.9	15.4	15.9	14.1
2–4	1 213	1 080	1 215	857	150.4	141.8	139.8	91.0	42.9	44.1	48.5	38.9
5–9	1 616	1 671	2 074	1 647	202.5	215.1	240.1	176.3	66.1	68.1	81.1	69.3
10–14	1 429	1 907	1 865	1 972	195.7	230.1	226.5	218.2	56.9	68.1	73.7	76.4
15–19	1 335	1 622	1 696	2 054	173.2	187.4	199.4	227.8	55.4	60.3	65.1	74.4
20–24	1 427	1 434	1 876	1 805	172.4	159.4	196.6	199.8	48.7	46.9	59.3	62.5
25–29	1 626	1 446	1 612	1 648	187.2	161.0	158.3	172.2	47.9	41.6	51.6	51.0
30–34	1 514	1 502	1 460	1 835	166.1	162.8	148.1	180.5	44.6	41.6	43.5	49.7
35–39	1 633	1 616	1 410	1 554	177.6	170.5	147.4	149.5	45.5	43.9	40.7	46.1
40–44	1 658	1 494	1 467	1 405	180.0	153.2	151.4	141.3	43.0	41.6	40.7	40.0
45–49	1 556	1 584	1 552	1 351	168.7	163.9	157.0	139.5	38.8	42.1	41.7	37.1
50–54	1 318	1 575	1 412	1 381	141.3	164.3	139.6	139.6	36.1	39.6	39.1	36.3
55–59	1 089	1 408	1 434	1 403	115.8	147.3	143.2	138.4	28.9	34.4	37.4	35.5
60–64	939	1 096	1 330	1 196	97.9	113.2	133.7	114.4	24.4	29.4	33.1	31.4
65–69	781	819	1 063	1 100	83.2	83.4	106.6	105.7	21.6	23.0	26.4	28.2
70–74	591	600	692	871	65.7	60.2	67.9	83.2	18.3	17.0	19.5	21.8
75–79	375	389	410	544	41.6	40.2	39.4	50.9	12.4	11.3	11.6	12.8
80–84	165	205	217	248	17.8	21.7	20.5	22.5	6.0	6.7	6.4	6.7
85 and over	61	90	110	119	6.4	9.0	10.4	10.5	2.4	3.2	3.5	3.5

See footnotes page 11.

2.4 (*continued*) **Age distribution of the enumerated population: census figures**

Constituent countries

Thousands

	England and Wales				Scotland				Northern Ireland			
	1951	1961	1971	1981[1]	1951	1961	1971	1981[1]	1951	1961	1971	1981[1,2]
Females: all ages	22 742	23 801	25 067	24 897	2 661.4	2 696.6	2 714.3	2 606.8	703.1	730.8	781.4	782.7
Under 5	1 814	1 751	1 902	1 418	229.8	229.1	215.8	150.1	67.2	71.2	75.9	64.0
Under 16	5 015	5 477	5 958	5 248	653.9	690.5	700.2	568.6	196.0	212.6	234.8	215.7
Under 18	5 550	6 136	6 603	6 050	728.4	766.9	778.0	658.9	217.2	237.8	259.7	244.6
5–14	2 929	3 410	3 732	3 434	386.1	424.8	443.8	375.1	117.9	129.4	145.9	137.5
15–29	4 523	4 423	5 052	5 353	574.4	526.4	544.8	583.4	156.9	150.4	167.2	178.8
30–44	4 963	4 651	4 256	4 747	559.7	513.8	465.7	475.9	141.2	135.4	128.5	136.6
45–64	5 660	6 172	6 122	5 554	619.2	668.3	644.4	584.4	145.6	161.9	165.3	154.9
65–74	1 885	2 102	2 423	2 517	194.5	214.8	252.0	255.4	48.0	52.3	62.2	66.2
75 and over	967	1 292	1 581	1 875	97.7	119.5	147.7	182.5	26.2	30.3	36.4	44.8
Pensionable age aggregate	4 057	4 756	5 515	5 729	419.0	480.7	559.0	574.8	104.3	118.9	137.5	147.5
Under 1	321	371	377	303	42.6	47.9	41.8	32.3	12.9	14.9	15.1	13.4
1 and under 2	337	353	371	303	43.4	45.9	41.9	31.6	13.2	14.4	15.0	13.3
2–4	1 157	1 027	1 154	812	143.8	135.3	132.1	86.2	41.2	41.9	45.8	37.3
5–9	1 546	1 592	1 970	1 560	195.3	205.7	228.3	168.1	63.1	64.3	76.0	65.0
10–14	1 383	1 818	1 762	1 875	190.8	219.1	215.5	207.0	54.8	65.0	69.9	72.4
15–19	1 369	1 579	1 618	1 966	188.7	186.7	192.9	218.8	53.1	60.0	61.2	70.1
20–24	1 500	1 444	1 855	1 760	191.7	173.7	193.8	194.6	52.2	46.9	55.6	59.8
25–29	1 654	1 400	1 579	1 627	194.0	166.0	158.1	170.0	51.6	43.6	50.3	48.9
30–34	1 565	1 483	1 411	1 822	178.8	169.7	152.4	178.3	46.6	44.9	43.2	49.0
35–39	1 691	1 626	1 376	1 538	190.8	176.9	153.4	150.8	48.6	47.0	41.7	46.4
40–44	1 707	1 543	1 468	1 387	190.1	167.2	159.9	146.9	46.0	43.4	43.6	41.2
45–49	1 616	1 645	1 584	1 338	180.9	178.8	165.8	146.2	42.0	44.9	44.4	39.0
50–54	1 507	1 646	1 485	1 404	166.6	177.9	156.2	150.1	40.3	42.5	41.0	39.7
55–59	1 334	1 520	1 542	1 474	144.9	165.2	163.1	151.3	33.3	38.2	41.1	39.6
60–64	1 204	1 362	1 511	1 337	126.8	146.4	159.3	136.8	30.1	36.3	39.0	36.6
65–69	1 049	1 160	1 336	1 326	108.9	121.1	140.6	135.1	25.8	29.2	33.8	35.2
70–74	837	942	1 086	1 191	85.6	93.7	111.4	120.3	22.2	23.1	28.4	31.0
75–79	549	680	776	914	56.2	65.2	75.8	91.6	14.8	15.7	18.3	21.8
80–84	281	401	490	573	28.0	36.2	45.1	55.8	7.7	9.4	11.1	13.8
85 and over	137	212	315	388	13.5	18.2	26.8	35.1	3.7	5.2	6.9	9.2

1 1981 data cover the 'usually resident' population and are not strictly comparable with earlier data.

2 The figures for Northern Ireland have been revised using a new estimate of 44 500 non-enumerated persons in the 1981 Census.

Sources *Office of Population Censuses and Surveys; General Register Office (Scotland); General Register Office (Northern Ireland)*

2.5 Age distribution of the resident population: mid-year estimates and projections[1,2]
United Kingdom

Thousands

	1971	1976	1981	1986	1988 Base	1991	1996	2001	2011	2021	2031
Persons all ages	55 928	56 216	56 352	56 763	57 065	57 533	58 462	59 201	59 989	60 823	61 200
0–4	4 553	3 721	3 455	3 642	3 747	3 914	4 136	3 973	3 594	3 837	3 740
5–9	4 684	4 483	3 677	3 467	3 619	3 656	3 918	4 140	3 686	3 708	3 852
10–14	4 232	4 693	4 470	3 690	3 394	3 484	3 666	3 928	3 987	3 610	3 844
15–19	3 862	4 244	4 735	4 479	4 250	3 707	3 499	3 681	4 164	3 712	3 722
20–24	4 282	3 881	4 284	4 784	4 728	4 496	3 724	3 517	3 960	4 019	3 628
25–29	3 686	4 239	3 828	4 237	4 495	4 746	4 469	3 700	3 675	4 157	3 721
30–34	3 284	3 629	4 182	3 787	3 892	4 200	4 702	4 430	3 458	3 899	3 972
35–39	3 187	3 225	3 589	4 158	3 847	3 771	4 170	4 669	3 643	3 619	4 099
40–44	3 325	3 136	3 185	3 561	4 005	4 132	3 742	4 133	4 379	3 420	3 858
45–49	3 532	3 262	3 090	3 142	3 209	3 518	4 079	3 691	4 585	3 586	3 566
50–54	3 304	3 423	3 179	3 023	3 055	3 080	3 450	3 997	4 014	4 265	3 333
55–59	3 365	3 151	3 271	3 055	3 000	2 919	2 980	3 339	3 519	4 389	3 433
60–64	3 222	3 131	2 935	3 055	2 940	2 873	2 756	2 817	3 681	3 719	3 956
65–69	2 736	2 851	2 801	2 641	2 865	2 759	2 614	2 516	2 913	3 091	3 867
70–74	2 029	2 260	2 393	2 364	2 166	2 267	2 379	2 272	2 263	2 988	3 041
75–79	1 356	1 499	1 708	1 837	1 860	1 853	1 817	1 920	1 798	2 118	2 259
80–84	803	849	968	1 132	1 196	1 265	1 306	1 313	1 354	1 374	1 825
85 and over	485	538	602	709	796	894	1 056	1 166	1 315	1 313	1 484
Males all ages	27 167	27 360	27 409	27 647	27 813	28 087	28 618	29 043	29 545	30 031	30 237
0–4	2 336	1 912	1 772	1 867	1 920	2 011	2 129	2 045	1 851	1 976	1 924
5–9	2 401	2 302	1 889	1 780	1 856	1 876	2 015	2 133	1 900	1 911	1 984
10–14	2 175	2 409	2 295	1 897	1 744	1 790	1 883	2 022	2 057	1 863	1 982
15–19	1 976	2 167	2 424	2 296	2 179	1 903	1 797	1 890	2 147	1 914	1 922
20–24	2 161	1 979	2 172	2 431	2 409	2 294	1 903	1 797	2 029	2 064	1 866
25–29	1 863	2 144	1 931	2 138	2 269	2 403	2 272	1 883	1 871	2 127	1 907
30–34	1 667	1 837	2 104	1 907	1 957	2 112	2 372	2 245	1 754	1 984	2 029
35–39	1 612	1 632	1 807	2 081	1 923	1 890	2 087	2 344	1 843	1 831	2 087
40–44	1 659	1 582	1 602	1 791	2 010	2 064	1 868	2 058	2 208	1 726	1 954
45–49	1 747	1 623	1 549	1 574	1 606	1 763	2 028	1 832	2 287	1 805	1 796
50–54	1 607	1 684	1 572	1 506	1 523	1 534	1 718	1 973	1 980	2 136	1 671
55–59	1 616	1 513	1 590	1 496	1 473	1 442	1 471	1 647	1 723	2 166	1 711
60–64	1 507	1 466	1 376	1 458	1 411	1 384	1 342	1 369	1 778	1 802	1 947
65–69	1 209	1 276	1 261	1 198	1 310	1 277	1 226	1 193	1 385	1 465	1 849
70–74	790	927	1 003	1 002	918	979	1 053	1 023	1 035	1 364	1 397
75–79	468	522	630	698	716	721	729	795	773	921	981
80–84	248	253	290	362	392	423	451	474	522	544	724
85 and over	126	133	141	166	196	223	275	319	404	434	508
Females all ages	28 761	28 856	28 943	29 116	29 253	29 446	29 845	30 157	30 443	30 792	30 964
0–4	2 217	1 808	1 682	1 775	1 827	1 903	2 007	1 927	1 744	1 862	1 816
5–9	2 283	2 181	1 788	1 687	1 763	1 781	1 903	2 007	1 786	1 797	1 868
10–14	2 057	2 284	2 175	1 793	1 650	1 694	1 783	1 905	1 930	1 747	1 862
15–19	1 887	2 078	2 311	2 183	2 071	1 804	1 702	1 791	2 017	1 797	1 801
20–24	2 121	1 903	2 112	2 353	2 318	2 202	1 821	1 720	1 931	1 956	1 762
25–29	1 824	2 095	1 897	2 099	2 226	2 343	2 197	1 816	1 804	2 030	1 814
30–34	1 617	1 792	2 078	1 881	1 935	2 089	2 331	2 185	1 704	1 915	1 944
35–39	1 575	1 593	1 782	2 077	1 924	1 881	2 083	2 324	1 800	1 789	2 012
40–44	1 667	1 554	1 583	1 770	1 996	2 068	1 874	2 075	2 171	1 694	1 903
45–49	1 785	1 639	1 541	1 569	1 603	1 755	2 051	1 859	2 299	1 781	1 770
50–54	1 697	1 739	1 608	1 516	1 532	1 547	1 732	2 025	2 034	2 129	1 663
55–59	1 749	1 638	1 681	1 559	1 527	1 477	1 510	1 692	1 796	2 223	1 723
60–64	1 715	1 665	1 559	1 598	1 529	1 489	1 414	1 448	1 903	1 917	2 009
65–69	1 527	1 575	1 540	1 443	1 555	1 482	1 388	1 322	1 528	1 626	2 018
70–74	1 238	1 333	1 390	1 361	1 247	1 288	1 326	1 249	1 229	1 624	1 645
75–79	888	977	1 078	1 138	1 144	1 132	1 088	1 125	1 025	1 197	1 278
80–84	555	597	677	770	804	842	855	839	832	830	1 101
85 and over	359	405	461	543	600	671	781	847	911	879	976

1 The assumptions on which these projections are made are described in the introductory note on page 5.
2 Data have been rounded individually and may not sum exactly.

Sources *Government Actuary's Department; Office of Population Censuses and Surveys; the General Register Office (Scotland); General Register Office (Northern Ireland).*

2.5 Age distribution of the resident population: mid year estimates and projections[1,2]

(continued)

Thousands

Age	1971	1976	1981	1986	1988 Base	1991	1996	2001	2011	2021	2031
England and Wales											
Persons all ages	49 152	49 459	49 634	50 075	50 393	50 878	51 801	52 551	53 472	54 499	55 081
0–4	3 951	3 226	3 006	3 183	3 288	3 450	3 656	3 512	3 205	3 452	3 375
5–9	4 056	3 895	3 196	3 025	3 164	3 206	3 460	3 666	3 275	3 332	3 476
10–14	3 649	4 071	3 889	3 214	2 957	3 047	3 221	3 475	3 538	3 232	3 467
15–19	3 344	3 681	4 130	3 911	3 717	3 237	3 067	3 241	3 700	3 310	3 353
20–24	3 773	3 395	3 744	4 203	4 155	3 950	3 273	3 103	3 530	3 594	3 260
25–29	3 267	3 758	3 372	3 724	3 966	4 203	3 952	3 277	3 281	3 739	3 350
30–34	2 897	3 220	3 715	3 341	3 430	3 709	4 180	3 932	3 091	3 517	3 585
35–39	2 804	2 845	3 185	3 700	3 414	3 336	3 689	4 157	3 249	3 254	3 707
40–44	2 932	2 763	2 811	3 163	3 573	3 683	3 314	3 661	3 899	3 069	3 489
45–49	3 126	2 879	2 723	2 776	2 837	3 130	3 639	3 273	4 090	3 205	3 212
50–54	2 925	3 034	2 809	2 667	2 699	2 725	3 072	3 569	3 562	3 804	2 996
55–59	2 982	2 795	2 901	2 703	2 651	2 578	2 640	2 977	3 127	3 922	3 075
60–64 Males	1 337	1 304	1 227	1 299	1 256	1 232	1 192	1 218	1 593	1 607	1 743
60–64 Females	1 516	1 473	1 380	1 415	1 351	1 313	1 245	1 279	1 700	1 701	1 792
65–69	2 428	2 530	2 490	2 351	2 555	2 453	2 320	2 229	2 604	2 753	3 465
70–74	1 801	2 010	2 129	2 107	1 929	2 024	2 124	2 023	2 016	2 685	2 716
75–79	1 208	1 334	1 524	1 640	1 661	1 658	1 628	1 720	1 603	1 905	2 023
80–84	718	759	865	1 015	1 073	1 134	1 174	1 182	1 214	1 233	1 657
85 and over	438	486	541	639	719	808	955	1 056	1 192	1 186	1 347
Scotland											
Persons all ages	5 236	5 233	5 180	5 121	5 094	5 061	5 037	4 999	4 843	4 653	4 450
0–4	443	357	318	323	323	326	339	324	271	271	254
5–9	469	438	348	313	322	317	322	335	287	265	263
10–14	444	466	433	344	311	309	315	320	317	265	265
15–19	393	432	459	424	394	339	306	311	329	281	262
20–24	388	374	415	446	436	410	329	295	306	304	258
25–29	318	378	355	396	407	416	389	308	281	298	262
30–34	300	315	368	346	358	379	401	375	261	271	276
35–39	301	296	310	361	338	337	371	393	287	260	280
40–44	311	295	293	306	337	355	332	365	363	250	262
45–49	322	304	291	287	289	299	348	326	382	279	253
50–54	298	311	295	282	281	279	291	339	350	349	241
55–59	306	282	295	280	277	270	267	279	306	360	263
60–64 Males	134	128	118	126	124	121	118	118	147	153	155
60–64 Females	160	154	142	145	142	129	134	133	160	166	164
65–69	249	258	248	230	247	242	234	227	238	263	310
70–74	181	202	211	204	188	192	203	198	194	240	253
75–79	116	131	149	157	158	155	149	159	154	164	188
80–84	66	71	83	95	100	104	105	104	111	111	138
85 and over	38	42	49	57	62	70	83	89	99	102	108
Northern Ireland											
Persons all ages	1 540	1 524	1 538	1 567	1 578	1 595	1 625	1 651	1 673	1 672	1 669
0–4	158	137	131	136	137	138	141	137	118	115	110
5–9	160	150	133	130	133	133	136	139	125	111	112
10–14	139	156	148	132	126	128	131	133	132	113	111
15–19	126	131	146	144	139	130	126	129	134	121	108
20–24	121	112	125	136	137	136	122	118	124	122	109
25–29	102	103	101	117	122	126	128	114	113	119	109
30–34	88	94	99	100	104	112	121	123	106	111	112
35–39	82	84	94	97	95	98	109	118	107	106	112
40–44	83	79	81	92	95	94	95	107	118	101	107
45–49	84	79	76	79	83	90	92	93	113	102	102
50–54	81	78	76	74	75	77	87	89	101	112	96
55–59	78	74	75	72	72	71	73	83	86	106	96
60–64 Males	36	34	32	32	31	31	31	32	38	43	50
60–64 Females	39	38	37	37	37	36	35	36	42	49	53
65–69	59	63	63	60	64	62	60	59	71	74	91
70–74	47	48	53	52	49	51	52	51	53	63	73
75–79	32	33	35	40	41	40	39	41	41	49	52
80–84	18	19	21	22	24	26	27	27	29	30	36
85 and over	17	10	13	14	15	16	19	21	24	25	29

1 The assumptions on which these projections are made are described in the introductory note on page 5.
2 Data have been rounded individually and may not sum exactly.

Sources *Government Actuary's Department; Office of Population Censuses and Surveys; General Register Office (Scotland); General Register Office (Northern Ireland).*

2.6 Marital condition: census figures

Thousands

	United Kingdom						England and Wales					
	Males			Females			Males			Females		
	1961	1971	1981[1]	1961	1971	1981[1]	1961	1971	1981[1]	1961	1971	1981[1]
All ages:												
Single	11 340	12 014	11 860	10 829	11 055	10 585	9 738	10 399	10 363	9 242	9 513	9 199
Married	13 279	13 976	13 563	13 355	14 050	13 630	11 813	12 433	12 042	11 860	12 488	12 093
Widowed	760	762	749	2 860	3 139	3 182	658	666	657	2 528	2 773	2 808
Divorced	102	200	606	185	318	863	94	185	563	170	293	797
Age groups												
0 – 14: Single	6 321	6 873	5 861	6 015	6 515	5 564	5 424	5 942	5 111	5 160	5 633	4 852
15 – 19: Single	1 850	1 921	2 328	1 709	1 713	2 152	1 605	1 661	2 031	1 475	1 477	1 878
Married	20	40	26	116	159	101	17	35	22	104	140	88
Widowed	–	–	–	–	–	–	–	–	–	–	–	–
Divorced	–	–	–	–	–	1	–	–	–	–	–	1
20 – 24: Single	1 139	1 350	1 536	719	848	1 080	990	1 186	1 350	607	737	945
Married	501	779	517	941	1 244	896	444	687	443	834	1 107	782
Widowed	–	–	1	2	2	2	–	–	1	1	2	2
Divorced	1	3	12	2	10	34	1	3	11	2	9	31
25 – 34: Single	799	703	973	461	374	534	688	617	866	382	320	471
Married	2 537	2 727	2 802	2 808	2 940	3 113	2 243	2 414	2 469	2 466	2 597	2 753
Widowed	4	4	5	15	14	15	4	3	4	13	12	13
Divorced	14	41	154	24	67	230	13	38	143	22	61	212
35 – 44: Single	439	363	346	371	247	195	374	315	304	308	206	167
Married	3 032	2 828	2 806	3 104	2 868	2 836	2 692	2 502	2 487	2 748	2 525	2 505
Widowed	19	15	13	74	57	48	17	13	11	63	48	41
Divorced	29	51	169	53	72	230	27	47	157	49	66	212
45 – 54: Single	346	325	288	447	298	200	291	278	251	375	248	167
Married	3 126	2 913	2 617	2 973	2 885	2 577	2 783	2 593	2 319	2 642	2 565	2 276
Widowed	63	53	44	258	218	176	54	46	38	221	187	149
Divorced	33	50	134	57	75	164	31	46	124	53	69	151
55 – 59: Single	145	140	148	251	177	127	120	118	128	210	148	105
Married	1 373	1 397	1 326	1 201	1 290	1 259	1 225	1 248	1 184	1 074	1 151	1 124
Widowed	60	56	53	251	246	214	52	48	46	217	213	186
Divorced	12	21	50	20	33	65	11	20	47	19	30	60
60 – 64: Single	106	125	115	234	207	125	87	105	98	196	173	104
Married	1 042	1 268	1 120	926	1 095	1 018	931	1 135	1 003	830	982	911
Widowed	84	87	72	370	380	316	72	75	62	323	330	274
Divorced	7	16	35	14	27	51	7	15	33	13	25	47
65 – 74: Single	130	158	183	381	392	305	106	130	154	322	328	254
Married	1 232	1 550	1 732	1 015	1 242	1 403	1 105	1 391	1 558	917	1 122	1 266
Widowed	235	253	252	961	1 075	1 062	203	220	220	852	948	934
Divorced	5	15	41	12	27	67	5	14	38	11	26	62
75 and over: Single	66	58	82	241	285	304	53	47	69	206	243	257
Married	415	474	616	269	326	426	373	428	558	246	298	389
Widowed	294	294	310	929	1 148	1 348	257	259	276	837	1 034	1 208
Divorced	1	3	10	2	7	22	1	2	9	2	6	20

1 1981 data cover the 'usually resident' population and are not strictly comparable with earlier data.

Sources *Office of Population Censuses and Surveys; General Register Office (Scotland); General Register Office (Northern Ireland)*

2.6 Marital condition: census figures

(continued)

Thousands

	Scotland						Northern Ireland					
	Males			Females			Males			Females		
	1961	1971	1981[1]	1961	1971	1981[1]	1961	1971	1981[1]	1961	1971	1981[1]
All ages:												
Single	1 206.0	1 197.6	1 113.0	1 205.9	1 153.8	1 034.2	396.0	417.5	384.7	381.1	388.5	352.3
Married	1 187.7	1 225.9	1 201.5	1 209.2	1 241.8	1 211.3	278.0	317.6	319.3	284.9	320.4	318.1
Widowed	82.4	78.0	74.4	268.0	295.2	301.5	19.7	18.5	17.3	63.6	70.4	73.0
Divorced	6.6	13.2	39.6	13.5	23.6	59.9	0.5	1.1	3.9	1.2	2.0	6.2
Age groups												
0 – 14: Single	685.3	695.1	552.8	653.8	659.7	525.1	211.6	235.2	197.2	200.6	221.8	187.1
15 – 19: Single	185.2	194.8	224.2	175.9	177.6	207.8	59.9	64.3	72.3	58.0	58.2	66.1
Married	2.2	4.6	3.6	10.8	15.2	10.9	0.4	0.9	0.8	2.0	3.0	2.7
Widowed	–	–	–	–	–	–	–	–	–	–	–	–
Divorced	–	–	–	–	–	–	–	–	–	–	–	–
20 – 24: Single	112.2	121.2	140.2	83.6	81.5	101.7	37.0	42.3	45.9	28.7	29.7	33.1
Married	47.1	75.0	58.3	89.6	111.2	89.8	9.8	17.0	15.5	18.1	25.9	24.8
Widowed	–	–	–	0.2	0.2	0.3	–	–	–	–	–	–
Divorced	–	0.4	1.2	0.2	1.0	2.7	–	–	0.1	–	–	0.2
25 – 34: Single	80.4	60.7	80.7	56.0	37.0	47.4	30.6	25.0	26.4	22.9	16.2	15.7
Married	242.1	242.6	261.1	276.1	266.8	282.8	52.4	69.8	71.4	65.1	76.5	76.6
Widowed	0.5	0.4	0.6	1.8	1.6	1.7	0.1	0.1	0.1	0.4	0.4	0.6
Divorced	0.9	2.8	10.4	1.8	5.2	16.5	0.1	0.2	1.0	0.1	0.4	1.6
35 – 44: Single	46.4	34.9	30.9	46.1	29.6	20.0	18.7	13.5	10.9	16.5	11.3	7.7
Married	273.2	259.0	247.4	284.9	271.3	256.1	66.1	67.2	71.9	71.4	71.8	73.1
Widowed	2.3	1.6	1.6	8.9	6.8	5.6	0.5	0.4	0.5	2.2	1.7	1.9
Divorced	1.8	3.3	11.0	4.3	5.6	16.0	0.2	0.3	1.1	0.4	0.5	1.7
45 – 54: Single	40.2	33.7	27.7	55.1	37.3	24.5	15.0	13.6	10.0	17.2	13.2	8.9
Married	278.3	253.8	237.2	268.1	254.4	239.6	64.8	65.4	60.4	62.9	65.3	60.6
Widowed	7.5	5.9	5.2	29.7	24.6	20.5	1.7	1.4	1.2	7.0	6.2	5.7
Divorced	2.2	3.2	8.8	3.8	5.7	11.6	0.2	0.3	0.9	0.3	0.6	1.2
55 – 59: Single	17.9	15.7	14.8	31.8	22.0	16.3	6.2	6.2	5.4	8.7	7.2	5.7
Married	121.4	119.9	114.6	104.5	111.9	108.1	26.5	29.6	28.8	23.3	27.1	26.3
Widowed	7.2	6.4	5.9	27.6	27.1	22.4	1.5	1.5	1.4	6.1	6.5	6.2
Divorced	0.8	1.3	3.2	1.4	2.2	4.5	0.1	0.1	0.3	0.1	0.2	0.5
60 – 64: Single	13.5	14.7	11.7	29.7	26.0	15.7	5.3	5.6	4.9	8.6	7.9	5.8
Married	89.6	108.2	92.9	77.5	91.6	84.7	21.8	25.3	24.3	18.5	21.4	20.8
Widowed	9.6	9.7	7.7	38.3	39.9	33.2	2.3	2.1	1.9	9.1	9.4	8.6
Divorced	0.5	1.0	2.0	1.0	1.8	3.3	–	0.1	0.2	0.1	0.2	0.4
65 – 74: Single	16.4	19.5	20.6	46.3	49.8	38.2	7.7	8.2	7.9	12.7	14.4	12.3
Married	101.3	127.6	140.2	79.2	97.4	109.9	26.3	31.7	34.7	19.0	23.4	25.8
Widowed	25.6	26.4	25.7	88.4	103.2	103.4	6.0	6.0	5.9	20.6	24.2	24.8
Divorced	0.4	1.0	2.3	0.9	1.7	3.9	–	0.1	0.3	0.1	0.2	0.4
75 and over: Single	8.7	7.2	9.6	27.5	33.3	37.5	3.9	3.7	3.8	7.4	8.6	9.9
Married	32.6	35.3	46.2	18.5	22.2	29.4	9.8	10.7	12.2	4.7	5.9	7.8
Widowed	29.6	27.5	27.7	73.3	91.8	114.4	7.5	7.0	6.3	18.3	21.9	25.1
Divorced	0.1	0.2	0.6	0.2	0.4	1.2	–	–	–	–	–	0.1

1 1981 data for Scotland and Northern Ireland relate to the enumerated 'usually resident' population and are not strictly comparable with earlier data.

Sources *General Register Office (Scotland); General Register Office (Northern Ireland)*

2.7 Marital condition of the resident population: mid-year estimates and projections
United Kingdom

Thousands

	Males			Females		
	1981	1985	2001	1981	1985	2001[1]
All ages						
Single	11 476	11 969	13 293	10 233	10 572	11 410
Married	13 244	13 150	12 503	13 305	13 236	12 590
Widowed	732	775	855	3 109	3 263	3 149
Divorced	602	917	1 509	857	1 179	1 971
Age groups:						
0 – 14: Single	5 664	5 388	5 961	5 377	5 109	5 616
15 – 19: Single	2 256	2 239	1 797	2 086	2 079	1 680
Married	25	14	4	99	64	26
Widowed	–	–	–	–	–	–
Divorced	–	–	–	1	–	–
20 – 24: Single	1 490	1 924	1 580	1 047	1 469	1 265
Married	501	403	129	872	769	360
Widowed	1	–	–	2	1	–
Divorced	12	14	4	33	32	12
25 – 34: Single	947	1 228	2 057	518	743	1 426
Married	2 730	2 425	1 745	3 036	2 761	2 165
Widowed	5	4	2	15	11	8
Divorced	153	209	164	229	278	237
35 – 44: Single	335	418	958	187	226	675
Married	2 735	2 984	2 930	2 761	3 057	3 035
Widowed	13	13	12	47	45	41
Divorced	168	289	408	228	349	511
45 – 54: Single	278	263	413	191	166	243
Married	2 556	2 519	2 840	2 515	2 474	2 832
Widowed	43	39	41	170	151	151
Divorced	133	208	438	162	239	536
55 – 59: Single	142	133	132	121	104	75
Married	1 298	1 222	1 261	1 232	1 159	1 196
Widowed	51	46	42	208	188	155
Divorced	50	70	172	65	83	212
60 – 64: Single	110	126	101	120	122	64
Married	1 096	1 203	1 045	996	1 091	951
Widowed	70	81	63	308	328	230
Divorced	35	53	124	50	73	157
65 – 74: Single	175	161	169	292	246	142
Married	1 698	1 662	1 627	1 376	1 359	1 367
Widowed	246	240	224	1 038	1 018	807
Divorced	41	56	143	66	88	197
75 and over: Single	78	89	125	295	308	224
Married	604	718	922	418	502	658
Widowed	304	352	471	1 322	1 521	1 757
Divorced	9	18	56	21	37	109

1 The numbers for 2001 are from the mid-1985 based marital conditions projections and are not comparable with the total projected numbers shown on Tables 2.1, 2.2 and 2.5.

Sources *Office of Population Censuses and Surveys; General Register Office (Scotland); Government Actuary's Department*

2.8 Geographical distribution of the enumerated population: census figures[1]

Thousands

	Area in square kilometres[2]	1911	1931	1951	1961	1971	1981[3]
Urban and rural districts							
England and Wales:							
Urban areas	21 765	28 163	31 952	35 336	36 872	38 151	37 324
Rural districts	129 360	7 908	8 000	8 422	9 233	10 598	11 687
Scotland:							
Cities and burghs	1 300	3 140	3 362	3 563	3 646	3 705	5 131
Landward areas	75 879	1 620	1 481	1 534	1 533	1 524	
Northern Ireland:							
Urban areas	240	587	678[4]	728	770	846	1 532
Rural districts	13 330	664	602[4]	643	655	690	
Standard regions of England and Wales							
England		33 650	37 359	41 159	43 461	46 018	46 363
North	19 349	2 815	3 038	3 137	3 250	3 296	3 104
Yorkshire and Humberside	14 196	3 877	4 285	4 522	4 635	4 799	4 060
East Midlands	12 179	2 263	2 531	2 893	3 100	3 390	3 819
East Anglia	12 565	1 192	1 232	1 382	1 470	1 669	1 872
South East	27 408	11 744	13 539	15 127	16 271	17 230	16 796
South West	23 660	2 687	2 794	3 229	3 411	3 781	4 349
West Midlands	13 013	3 277	3 743	4 423	4 758	5 110	5 148
North West	7 993	5 796	6 197	6 447	6 567	6 743	6 414
Wales	20 763	2 421	2 593	2 599	2 644	2 731	2 792
Conurbations							
Greater London	1 580	7 160	8 110	8 197	7 992	7 452	6 696
West Midlands	678	1 651	1 951	2 260	2 378	2 372	2 244
West Yorkshire	1 255	1 590	1 655	1 693	1 704	1 728	1 682
South East Lancashire	983	2 328	2 427	2 423	2 428	2 393	2 245
Merseyside	394	1 157	1 347	1 386	1 384	1 267	1 127
Tyneside	235	761	827	836	856	805	738
Central Clydeside	778	..	1 690	1 759	1 802	1 728	1 718
Cities							
Birmingham	209	526	1 003	1 113	1 107	1 015	1 007
Liverpool	113	746	856	789	746	610	510
Manchester	110	714	766	703	662	544	449
Sheffield	184	455	512	513	494	520	538
Leeds	164	446	483	505	511	496	705
Bristol	110	357	397	443	437	427	391
Coventry	81	106	167	258	306	335	314
Nottingham	74	260	269	306	312	301	272
Bradford	103	288	298	292	296	294	457
Kingston-upon-Hull	71	278	314	299	303	286	270
Leicester	73	227	239	285	273	284	280
Cardiff	80	182	224	244	257	279	274
Wolverhampton	69	95	133	163	151	269	255
Stoke-on-Trent	93	235	277	275	265	265	253
Glasgow	157	784	1 088	1 090	1 055	897	766
Edinburgh	135	320	439	467	468	454	437
Dundee	50	165	176	177	183	182	180
Aberdeen	50	164	167	183	185	182	204
Belfast	73	387	438[4]	444	416	362	314

1 Populations of urban and rural districts and cities are for the administrative areas as constituted at the time of each census from 1911 to 1981. So some changes in population may be the result of changes in the constitutions of the areas; details can be found in the reports of the censuses. The cities shown do not include all urban areas with populations of 182 000 or more in 1981. Populations of Standard Regions and conurbations relate to approximately the same area throughout the period 1911 to 1981.

2 The statistics of area in square kilometres is for areas as constituted in 1971. The areas of urban and rural districts and of conurbations have not been measured since 1971, but there have been some changes in the areas of standard regions and cities.

3. Figures for urban and rural districts in England and Wales and for the conurbations are from the *Census 1981 Preliminary Report for Towns.*
Figures for Scotland, standard regions, and cities (administrative districts) are persons present on census night from *Census 1981, Key Statistics for Local Authorities, Great Britain.*
In Northern Ireland it is estimated that some 44 500 persons were not enumerated. These are included in the above figures.

4 Figures for Northern Ireland and the City of Belfast relate to the 1937 Census.

Source Office of Population Censuses and Surveys

2.9 Geographical distribution of resident population: mid-year estimates

Thousands

	1978	1979	1980	1981	1982	1983	1984	1985	1986	1987	1988
England and Wales	49 443	49 508	49 603	49 634	49 601	49 654	49 764	49 924	50 075	50 243	50 393
Scotland	5 212	5 204	5 194	5 180	5 167	5 150	5 146	5 137	5 121	5 112	5 094
Northern Ireland	1 523	1 528	1 533	1 538[1]	1 538[1]	1 543[1]	1 550[1]	1 558	1 567	1 575	1 578
Standard regions of England and Wales											
North	3 134	3 130	3 128	3 118	3 107	3 100	3 093	3 086	3 080	3 077	3 071
Yorkshire and Humberside	4 920	4 921	4 923	4 918	4 910	4 908	4 904	4 903	4 899	4 900	4 913
East Midlands	3 798	3 818	3 838	3 853	3 852	3 860	3 874	3 897	3 920	3 942	3 970
East Anglia	1 842	1 864	1 882	1 895	1 911	1 925	1 940	1 965	1 992	2 014	2 034
South East	16 939	16 952	16 993	17 010	17 006	17 042	17 112	17 192	17 265	17 318	17 344
Greater London	*6 947*	*6 888*	*6 851*	*6 806*	*6 766*	*6 754*	*6 756*	*6 768*	*6 775*	*6 770*	*6 735*
South West	4 313	4 335	4 361	4 381	4 398	4 424	4 461	4 501	4 543	4 588	4 634
West Midlands	5 175	5 179	5 185	5 186	5 180	5 176	5 176	5 183	5 181	5 198	5 207
North West	6 517	6 498	6 477	6 460	6 431	6 410	6 396	6 386	6 374	6 370	6 364
Wales	2 804	2 810	2 816	2 814	2 807	2 808	2 807	2 812	2 821	2 836	2 857
Metropolitan counties											
Tyne and Wear	1 172	1 166	1 162	1 155	1 150	1 145	1 142	1 140	1 135	1 136	1 131
South Yorkshire	1 318	1 316	1 316	1 317	1 313	1 310	1 305	1 303	1 298	1 296	1 293
West Yorkshire	2 074	2 072	2 069	2 067	2 063	2 059	2 056	2 053	2 053	2 052	2 057
West Midlands	2 710	2 694	2 684	2 673	2 666	2 658	2 647	2 642	2 632	2 624	2 617
Greater Manchester	2 654	2 641	2 628	2 619	2 605	2 598	2 588	2 583	2 579	2 580	2 578
Merseyside	1 556	1 543	1 531	1 522	1 510	1 501	1 491	1 481	1 468	1 457	1 448
London boroughs and county districts (with about 275 000 or more population)											
Tyne and Wear											
Newcastle-upon-Tyne	292	290	288	284	281	281	281	282	281	283	280
Sunderland	296	296	297	297	300	299	299	299	298	297	296
South Yorkshire											
Sheffield	555	551	549	548	546	543	540	539	534	532	528
Doncaster	288	288	290	291	289	290	288	289	289	290	292
West Yorkshire											
Leeds	730	726	721	718	716	714	712	711	711	709	710
Bradford	463	462	463	465	465	464	464	464	463	462	464
Kirklees	376	377	377	377	377	377	378	377	377	376	375
Wakefield	311	313	314	314	314	312	311	310	309	310	312
Greater London											
Croydon	325	324	322	321	322	321	319	319	319	319	317
Barnet	297	296	295	295	295	294	298	301	305	306	301
Bromley	299	298	298	298	298	299	298	298	297	298	298
Ealing	291	288	283	282	282	284	289	292	296	297	297
West Midlands											
Birmingham	1 037	1 029	1 025	1 021	1 017	1 013	1 009	1 008	1 004	998	994
Coventry	328	326	323	319	317	316	314	312	310	309	306
Sandwell	314	312	310	310	309	307	305	303	301	298	296
Dudley	299	299	300	301	301	301	301	301	301	303	304
Greater Manchester											
Manchester	477	470	465	463	459	458	455	451	451	450	446
Wigan	312	311	310	310	309	308	307	307	307	307	308
Stockport	291	292	291	290	290	289	289	291	290	291	291
Merseyside											
Liverpool	534	527	521	517	510	502	497	492	483	476	470
Wirral	343	341	341	341	339	338	338	337	335	335	335
Sefton	304	303	302	300	299	300	299	298	298	297	298
Avon											
Bristol	409	405	402	401	400	399	397	394	391	384	378
Leicestershire											
Leicester	280	280	281	283	282	282	282	283	281	280	279
South Glamorgan											
Cardiff	283	282	282	281	280	280	281	279	280	281	284
City of Glasgow local government district	815	800	788	774	762	751	744	734	725	716	703
City of Edinburgh local government district	454	452	449	446	444	441	440	440	438	439	433
Belfast	354	351	346	315[1]	310[1]	306[1]	304[1]	302	304	304	300

1 The figures for Northern Ireland have been revised using a new estimate of 44 500 non-enumerated persons in the 1981 Census.

Sources *Office of Population Censuses and Surveys; General Register Office (Scotland); General Register Office (Northern Ireland)*

2.10 Migration into and out of the United Kingdom[1]

Analysis by citizenship and country of last or next residence

Thousands

	All migrants	British citizens						Commonwealth citizens					
		Country of last/next residence						Country of last/next residence					
	Total	Total	European[2] Community	Old Commonwealth	New Commonwealth	United States of America	Other countries	Total	Australia	Canada	New Zealand	Bangladesh, India, Sri Lanka	African Commonwealth
Inflow													
1975	197	85	12	25	25	6	18	53	10	3	5	9	7
1976	191	87	15	24	21	6	20	50	9	3	3	13	6
1977	163	73	8	21	17	5	22	39	8	2	3	9	5
1978	187	73	11	18	16	6	23	50	8	3	5	17	5
1979	195	78	9	16	20	4	29	57	7	2	5	15	7
1980	174	67	13	10	16	6	20	43	6	3	4	10	6
1981	153	60	11	9	17	6	17	40	5	2	3	14	5
1982	202	98	37	10	17	8	25	41	5	1	3	14	7
1983	202	94	20	20	19	11	24	46	6	2	4	10	7
1984	201	95	22	13	18	6	36	43	7	2	5	12	7
1985	232	110	32	12	19	11	34	47	8	3	7	10	5
1986	250	120	36	14	21	10	39	44	7	2	6	11	5
1987	212	99	32	13	14	12	27	47	7	3	8	12	5
1988	216	89	26	15	14	8	26	48	11	2	7	9	4
Outflow													
1975	238	169	15	65	18	11	60	27	7	4	3	2	3
1976	210	137	17	49	16	10	45	28	8	3	3	3	3
1977	209	144	17	44	23	10	50	29	9	3	2	2	4
1978	192	126	19	37	15	14	42	25	5	2	4	3	3
1979	189	126	21	37	14	15	39	28	6	2	4	2	4
1980	229	150	17	50	21	18	45	30	7	3	4	2	3
1981	233	164	14	66	15	13	56	29	6	3	3	2	4
1982	259	187	29	61	21	15	62	32	6	3	4	3	4
1983	185	122	20	31	17	16	37	26	5	1	3	2	4
1984	164	103	21	19	17	12	34	24	6	1	2	2	2
1985	174	108	22	21	16	12	38	26	5	3	4	1	3
1986	213	132	47	34	14	13	24	31	9	3	4	2	3
1987	210	130	40	39	12	18	21	29	9	5	4	2	2
1988	237	143	41	48	15	15	24	34	6	2	3	3	5
Balance													
1975	−41	−84	−4	−40	+6	−5	−42	+26	+4	−2	+2	+7	+5
1976	−19	−51	−2	−25	+5	−4	−26	+21	+2	–	+1	+11	+3
1977	−46	−71	−10	−23	−6	−4	−27	+11	−1	−1	+1	+6	+1
1978	−5	−53	−8	−19	+1	−8	−19	+24	+3	–	+1	+14	+1
1979	+6	−48	−11	−22	+7	−11	−10	+29	+1	–	+2	+12	+2
1980	−55	−84	−4	−40	−4	−11	−25	+12	–	−1	–	+9	+3
1981	−79	−104	−3	−56	+2	−7	−39	+11	–	–	−1	+13	+1
1982	−57	−89	+8	−50	−4	−6	−36	+9	−1	−2	−1	+12	+3
1983	+17	−27	–	−11	+2	−5	−13	+19	–	+1	+1	+8	+3
1984	+37	−7	+1	−6	+2	−6	+3	+19	+1	+1	+3	+9	+5
1985	+59	+1	+10	−8	+3	−1	−3	+22	+3	–	+4	+9	+3
1986	+37	−12	−11	−19	+7	−3	+15	+13	−2	−1	+2	+9	+2
1987	+2	−32	−8	−26	+3	−6	+6	+18	−2	−2	+4	+10	+3
1988	−21	−54	−15	−33	−1	−7	+2	+14	+5	–	+4	+6	–

1 From 1988, emigrants with last residence in Channel Islands or Isle of Man, and immigrants intending to reside in those places, are excluded from the figures in this table.
2 Greece is included in the European Community from 1981.
Spain and Portugal are included in the European Community from 1986.

Source Office of Population Censuses and Surveys

2.10 Migration into and out of the United Kingdom[1]

Analysis by citizenship and country of last or next residence

(continued)

Thousands

Commonwealth citizens *(continued)* — Country of last/next residence *(continued)*: Caribbean Common-wealth	Other Common-wealth	Other countries	European Community citizens[2] (excl. British) — Country of last/next residence: Total	European[2] Com-munity	Other Europe	Other countries	Other Foreign citizens — Country of last/next residence: Total	European[2] Com-munity	Other Europe	United States of America	Pakistan	Other countries	
													Inflow
3	14	2	12	10	–	1	47	1	9	10	4	23	1975
2	12	2	12	9	–	3	43	–	9	9	9	16	1976
3	8	2	10	9	–	2	40	1	6	7	10	16	1977
2	10	1	12	11	–	1	52	1	8	9	16	18	1978
3	14	3	14	11	–	2	46	2	6	8	11	19	1979
2	10	2	11	9	–	2	54	1	12	10	9	22	1980
2	7	1	10	10	–	–	43	2	4	10	7	21	1981
1	6	2	16	15	–	1	47	1	6	11	8	22	1982
3	13	1	11	9	–	3	50	2	4	14	8	22	1983
1	8	–	15	13	–	2	47	2	6	16	7	17	1984
1	11	2	20	17	1	2	55	4	10	11	7	24	1985
2	9	2	35	31	–	3	51	1	6	14	6	24	1986
1	9	2	25	21	1	2	41	1	3	14	6	18	1987
1	10	3	26	24	1	1	53	1	7	14	5	26	1988
													Outflow
2	4	3	11	9	–	2	30	2	6	10	–	12	1975
1	4	4	15	13	1	1	30	1	7	10	1	12	1976
2	3	4	11	8	–	3	25	2	4	10	1	8	1977
–	5	3	11	9	–	2	29	2	6	10	1	11	1978
1	5	3	10	6	2	2	25	1	4	9	1	11	1979
1	7	4	17	15	1	1	31	1	6	10	–	14	1980
1	7	4	13	11	–	3	26	3	4	8	–	10	1981
2	8	3	10	7	–	3	30	–	5	14	–	11	1982
1	8	3	8	7	–	1	28	1	5	14	–	8	1983
1	6	2	8	5	–	3	30	–	4	14	1	10	1984
1	8	1	10	7	–	3	30	1	5	11	2	11	1985
1	7	3	10	8	–	1	41	1	8	20	–	12	1986
1	4	3	19	16	–	3	31	2	4	13	1	12	1987
2	9	5	22	16	3	3	38	–	6	14	2	16	1988
													Balance
+1	+11	−2	–	+1	–	–	+17	−1	+3	–	+4	+11	1975
–	+8	−2	−3	−4	−1	+1	+13	–	+2	−1	+8	+4	1976
+1	+4	−2	−1	–	–	−1	+15	−1	+2	−3	+9	+7	1977
+1	+5	−2	+1	+2	–	−1	+23	−1	+2	−1	+16	+7	1978
+3	+9	−1	+4	+5	−1	+1	+21	+1	+2	−1	+10	+8	1979
+1	+3	−2	−6	−6	−1	–	+22	–	+6	–	+9	+8	1980
+1	–	−2	−3	−1	–	−3	+17	−1	−1	+1	+6	+11	1981
−1	−2	–	+6	+8	–	−2	+17	–	+1	−3	+8	+11	1982
+2	+6	−2	+3	+2	–	+1	+22	+1	−1	–	+8	+14	1983
–	+2	−2	+7	+8	–	−1	+17	+2	+2	+2	+5	+6	1984
–	+3	+1	+10	+10	+1	−1	+26	+3	+5	–	+5	+13	1985
+1	+3	−1	+25	+23	–	+2	+11	+1	−2	−5	+5	+12	1986
–	+5	−1	+6	+5	+1	−1	+10	–	−1	+1	+5	+6	1987
−1	+1	−2	+4	+8	−2	−2	+14	+1	+1	−1	+3	+10	1988

1 From 1988, emigrants with last residence in Channel Islands or Isle of Man, and immigrants intending to reside in those places, are excluded from the figures in this table.

2 Greece is included in the European Community from 1981.
Spain and Portugal are included in the European Community from 1986.

Source *Office of Population Censuses and Surveys*

2.11 Migration into and out of the United Kingdom[1]

Analysis by occupation and sex

Thousands

	Total			Professional and managerial			Manual and clerical			Not gainfully employed[2]		
	Persons	Males	Females	Persons	Males	Females	Persons	Males	Females	Persons	Males	Females
Inflow												
1975	197	102	95	49	28	20	50	31	19	98	42	56
1976	191	100	91	52	37	15	41	23	18	98	40	58
1977	163	88	74	43	29	14	37	22	15	82	37	46
1978	187	96	91	46	33	13	33	19	14	109	44	64
1979	195	103	91	53	36	16	35	21	14	107	46	61
1980	174	92	82	44	32	12	32	19	14	97	41	56
1981	153	83	71	45	32	13	24	14	10	85	37	48
1982	202	100	101	44	35	9	38	18	20	120	48	73
1983	202	107	95	55	40	15	36	21	15	111	46	64
1984	201	102	99	59	41	18	32	15	17	111	46	64
1985	232	99	133	65	38	27	32	16	16	134	44	90
1986	250	121	130	76	52	24	46	21	25	128	47	81
1987	212	105	108	63	44	18	48	21	27	101	39	62
1988	216	109	107	07	44	23	44	26	18	105	40	66
Outflow												
1975	238	126	112	60	43	18	73	44	29	104	39	65
1976	210	118	93	70	50	20	56	36	20	84	31	53
1977	209	117	91	66	49	17	62	39	23	81	30	51
1978	192	108	85	56	39	16	56	36	20	81	33	48
1979	189	106	82	58	43	15	52	30	22	79	34	45
1980	229	134	95	65	49	16	62	42	20	102	43	59
1981	233	133	100	67	50	17	60	38	22	105	44	61
1982	259	135	124	67	48	19	66	37	29	126	50	76
1983	185	90	95	51	32	18	36	19	16	99	38	60
1984	164	80	84	51	32	19	34	16	19	79	32	47
1985	174	91	83	51	36	15	36	18	17	87	36	50
1986	213	107	106	77	55	21	38	17	22	98	35	63
1987	210	108	102	64	38	26	57	29	28	90	41	49
1988	237	125	113	68	44	23	52	25	27	118	55	63
Balance												
1975	−41	−24	−17	−12	−14	+2	−23	−13	−10	−6	+3	−9
1976	−19	−18	−1	−18	−13	−5	−15	−13	−1	+14	+9	+5
1977	−46	−29	−17	−23	−20	−3	−24	−16	−8	+1	+7	−6
1978	−5	−12	+6	−10	−7	−3	−24	−17	−7	+28	+12	+16
1979	+6	−3	+9	−5	−6	+1	−17	−9	−8	+28	+12	+16
1980	−55	−42	−14	−20	−16	−4	−30	−23	−6	−5	−2	−3
1981	−79	−50	−29	−22	−19	−4	−37	−24	−13	−20	−8	−13
1982	−57	−34	−23	−23	−13	−10	−29	−19	−10	−6	−2	−3
1983	+17	+17	−	+5	+8	−3	−	+1	−1	+12	+8	+4
1984	+37	+22	+16	+8	+8	−	−3	−1	−2	+32	+14	+18
1985	+59	+8	+51	+14	+2	+12	−3	−2	−1	+48	+8	+40
1986	+37	+13	+24	−1	−4	+3	+8	+5	+3	+30	+12	+18
1987	+2	−3	+5	−1	+7	−7	−8	−7	−1	+11	−2	+14
1988	−21	−15	−6	−1	−1	−	−8	+1	−9	−13	−16	+3

See note on page 5.

1 From 1988, emigrants with last residence in the Channel Islands or the Isle of Man, and immigrants intending to reside in those places are excluded from the figures in this table.

2 Includes housewives, students, children and retired persons.

Source *Office of Population Censuses and Surveys*

2.12 Acceptances for settlement by nationality

United Kingdom

Number of persons

Geographical region and nationality	All acceptances for settlement				
	1984	1985	1986	1987	1988
All nationalities	50 950	55 360	46 820	45 980	49 280
Europe					
European Community					
Belgium	120	100	110	60	90
Denmark	140	150	140	110	110
France	590	580	490	420	430
Germany (Federal Republic)	640	750	550	450	480
Greece	220	250	230	240	220
Italy	520	540	400	260	300
Luxembourg	–	–	–	–	–
Netherlands	540	460	410	280	220
Portugal[1]	230	230	210	230	250
Spain[1]	530	440	360	370	370
European Community	3 530	3 490	2 900	2 430	2 470
Other Western Europe					
Austria	140	120	80	100	90
Cyprus	470	420	370	380	350
Finland	100	110	110	140	130
Malta	210	180	160	120	100
Norway	210	230	170	180	160
Sweden	400	390	350	490	520
Switzerland	180	170	160	130	170
Turkey	530	480	420	460	600
Yugoslavia	130	130	130	170	190
Other Western Europe	2 370	2 240	1 950	2 160	2 310
Eastern Europe					
Bulgaria	10	20	20	10	30
Czechoslovakia	30	20	20	40	20
German Democratic Republic	10	10	–	–	10
Hungary	40	50	40	50	40
Poland	310	370	250	270	650
Romania	20	20	20	20	30
USSR	50	50	40	70	60
Eastern Europe	470	540	390	470	830
Europe	6 370	6 270	5 240	5 060	5 620
Americas					
Argentina	40	50	50	40	50
Barbados	50	60	40	60	50
Brazil	190	170	160	160	190
Canada	1 400	1 500	1 220	1 180	1 190
Chile	60	70	40	40	60
Colombia	140	170	140	160	220
Cuba	–	–	–	–	–
Guyana	190	200	140	180	200
Jamaica	290	350	490	510	620
Mexico	70	70	60	80	60
Peru	60	80	50	50	60
Trinidad and Tobago	150	160	160	140	160
USA	3 750	4 170	3 790	3 710	3 750
Uruguay	–	10	–	–	10
Venezuela	50	50	40	40	40
Americas	6 440	7 130	6 380	6 350	6 480
Africa					
Algeria	60	70	60	80	100
Egypt	350	350	260	250	300
Ethiopia	40	30	50	60	50
Ghana	690	660	520	920	1 180
Kenya	610	520	350	400	440
Libya	70	170	130	100	110

Geographical region and nationality	All acceptances for settlement				
	1984	1985	1986	1987	1988
Africa—*continued*					
Mauritius	470	410	270	300	280
Morocco	130	160	140	170	270
Nigeria	320	500	570	780	970
Sierra Leone	80	70	90	100	110
Somalia	20	20	70	70	60
South Africa	690	790	780	1 020	870
Sudan	50	110	50	70	80
Tanzania	300	330	250	210	230
Tunisia	60	40	50	30	60
Uganda	40	50	90	90	120
Zambia	110	100	120	150	180
Zimbabwe	280	320	280	350	440
Africa	4 380	4 710	4 130	5 150	5 840
Asia					
Indian Sub-Continent					
Bangladesh	4 180	5 330	4 760	3 080	2 890
India	5 140	5 500	4 210	4 610	5 020
Pakistan	5 510	6 680	5 580	3 930	4 280
Indian Sub-Continent	14 840	17 510	14 550	11 620	12 180
Middle East					
Iran	1 670	2 210	1 770	1 450	1 500
Iraq	400	550	460	450	450
Israel	290	340	340	300	240
Jordan	120	90	140	130	120
Kuwait	10	10	10	10	20
Lebanon	260	250	190	220	330
Saudi Arabia	50	30	40	30	20
Syria	70	90	80	100	120
Middle East	2 870	3 580	3 030	2 690	2 810
Remainder of Asia					
China	140	140	100	120	160
Indonesia	60	60	60	60	70
Japan	1 100	1 010	1 060	1 300	1 340
Malaysia	680	630	580	630	740
Philippines	630	780	990	1 240	1 140
Singapore	160	160	110	140	180
Sri Lanka	760	930	840	720	860
Thailand	300	340	410	470	390
BDTC Hong Kong[2]	1 040	950	880	920	1 150
Remainder of Asia	4 870	5 000	5 030	5 600	6 020
Asia	22 570	26 090	22 610	19 920	21 010
Australasia					
Australia	3 590	3 780	2 870	3 020	3 520
New Zealand	2 460	2 880	2 510	2 690	2 680
Australasia	6 040	6 660	5 380	5 710	6 190
British Overseas citizens	2 690	2 180	1 680	1 860	1 910
Other countries not elsewhere specified	860	900	750	890	960
Stateless[3]	1 600	1 420	1 550	1 040	1 270
All nationalities	50 950	55 360	47 790	45 980	49 280
Foreign	24 230	26 840	23 950	22 160	23 370
Commonwealth	26 720	28 520	23 830	23 810	25 900
Old Commonwealth	7 440	8 160	6 610	6 900	7 380
New Commonwealth and Pakistan	24 800	27 050	22 660	20 850	22 800
Foreign excluding Pakistan	18 720	20 150	18 520	18 230	19 100

1 Portugal and Spain joined the European Community on 1 January 1986.
2 British Dependent Territories citizens.
3 Includes refugees from South-East Asia.

Source Home Office

2.13 Marriages

Numbers

	1977	1978	1979	1980	1981	1982	1983	1984	1985	1986	1987	1988
United Kingdom[1]												
Marriages	403 938	416 373	416 927	418 446	397 846	387 021	389 286	395 797	393 117	393 939	397 937	394 049
Persons marrying per 1 000 resident population	*14.5*	*14.9*	*14.9*	*15.0*	*14.1*	*13.4*	*13.8*	*14.0*	*13.9*	*13.9*	*14.0*	*13.8*
Previous marital status												
Bachelors	309 307	314 463	315 137	314 849	297 589	288 408	288 713	293 645	291 171	290 144	296 290	289 493
Divorced men	76 732	84 637	85 255	87 663	85 141	84 110	86 484	88 691	88 981	91 006	89 814	92 755
Widowers	17 899	17 273	16 535	15 934	15 116	14 503	14 089	13 461	12 965	12 789	11 833	11 801
Spinsters	312 892	317 537	318 786	319 088	302 354	293 068	293 554	299 256	296 797	294 564	301 073	293 551
Divorced women	73 340	81 560	81 846	83 376	80 755	80 148	82 314	83 477	83 921	87 080	85 238	89 066
Widows	17 706	17 276	16 295	15 982	14 737	13 805	13 418	13 064	12 399	12 295	11 626	11 612
First marriage for both partners	275 424	278 177	278 993	278 608	263 209	254 868	254 620	258 997	256 594	254 237	260 459	253 150
First marriage for one partner	71 351	75 649	75 937	76 721	73 525	71 740	73 027	74 913	74 780	76 254	76 445	76 744
Remarriage for both partners	57 163	62 550	53 997	63 117	61 112	60 413	61 639	61 890	61 743	63 458	61 033	64 155
Males												
Under 21 years	59 877	58 536	55 867	52 644	46 197	41 544	37 141	33 447	30 243	25 828	24 269	20 608
21–24	137 206	139 394	140 399	141 776	133 522	127 833	127 149	127 351	123 242	119 464	118 355	109 482
25–29	92 745	95 975	97 614	98 831	96 062	96 194	99 855	105 799	109 896	114 007	119 808	120 939
30–34	41 794	45 954	47 331	48 104	46 873	45 266	45 794	47 325	47 594	49 287	51 389	53 865
35–44	33 710	36 996	37 964	39 427	39 366	41 111	43 538	45 955	46 265	48 583	48 598	51 329
45–54	18 668	19 615	19 063	19 360	18 333	18 286	18 990	19 358	19 652	20 376	19 788	21 544
55 and over	19 938	19 903	18 689	18 304	17 493	16 787	16 819	16 562	16 225	16 394	15 730	16 282
Females												
Under 21 years	138 994	137 971	133 554	127 542	114 540	104 642	96 859	90 301	82 209	72 466	68 629	59 284
21–24	119 149	124 514	128 444	133 309	129 565	128 446	132 020	136 244	137 437	138 219	140 509	134 122
25–29	61 117	63 161	64 589	65 818	65 131	66 293	70 284	76 566	80 105	85 316	90 911	95 338
30–34	29 143	32 568	33 487	34 064	32 786	31 306	32 163	32 998	33 424	35 237	36 643	39 680
35–44	26 669	29 152	29 622	30 699	30 493	31 795	33 156	34 854	35 380	37 515	36 978	39 534
45–54	15 477	15 770	14 981	15 011	14 091	13 857	14 325	14 716	14 892	15 414	15 001	16 570
55 and over	13 389	13 237	12 250	12 003	11 240	10 682	10 479	10 118	9 670	9 772	9 260	9 521
England and Wales												
Marriages	356 954	368 258	368 853	370 022	351 973	342 166	344 334	349 186	346 389	347 924	351 761	348 492
Persons marrying per 1 000 resident population	*14.4*	*14.9*	*14.9*	*14.9*	*14.2*	*13.8*	*13.9*	*14.0*	*13.9*	*13.9*	*14.0*	*13.9*[1]
Previous marital status												
Bachelors	269 046	273 719	273 986	274 140	259 106	250 999	251 845	255 469	253 296	252 953	258 750	252 780
Divorced men	71 546	78 844	79 812	81 396	79 099	78 040	79 678	81 448	81 370	83 401	82 315	84 991
Widowers	16 362	15 695	15 055	14 486	13 768	13 127	12 811	12 269	11 723	11 570	10 696	10 721
Spinsters	272 215	276 385	277 166	277 826	263 368	255 171	256 214	260 359	258 089	256 767	262 958	256 221
Divorced women	68 493	76 099	76 822	77 595	75 147	74 418	75 909	76 899	77 031	79 964	78 219	81 691
Widows	16 246	15 774	14 865	14 601	13 458	12 577	12 211	11 928	11 269	11 193	10 584	10 580
First marriage for both partners	237 961	240 512	240 744	241 001	227 713	220 427	220 949	224 015	221 927	220 372	226 308	219 791
First marriage for one partner	65 339	69 080	69 664	69 964	67 048	65 316	66 161	67 798	67 531	68 976	69 092	69 419
Remarriage for both partners	53 654	58 666	50 445	59 057	57 212	56 423	57 224	57 373	56 931	58 576	56 361	59 282
Males[2]												
Under 21 years	49 961	49 007	46 863	44 062	38 660	34 809	31 216	27 941	25 496	21 758	20 541	17 578
21–24	119 365	121 213	121 739	123 080	115 924	110 972	110 537	110 351	106 608	103 651	102 907	95 029
25–29	82 713	85 668	86 982	88 067	85 391	85 333	88 470	93 227	96 804	100 360	105 458	106 349
30–34	38 118	41 909	43 308	43 854	42 696	41 084	41 402	42 563	42 532	44 125	46 063	48 112
35–44	31 074	34 169	35 119	36 323	36 312	37 712	39 882	42 064	42 120	44 309	44 237	46 688
45–54	17 204	17 998	17 667	17 842	16 862	16 812	17 389	17 790	17 968	18 681	18 055	19 754
55 and over	18 519	18 294	17 175	16 794	16 128	15 444	15 438	15 250	14 861	15 040	14 500	14 982
Females[2]												
Under 21 years	120 091	119 535	115 709	110 288	99 246	90 669	84 125	78 026	71 394	62 831	59 705	51 717
21–24	104 152	108 758	111,964	116 618	113 149	112 314	115 641	118 928	119 707	120 769	122 999	117 239
25–29	54 774	56 617	57 851	58 767	58 183	58 932	62 288	67 567	70 495	75 224	80 062	88 833
30–34	26 710	29 908	30 852	31 259	30 122	28 510	29 194	29 917	30 055	31 658	32 932	35 609
35–44	24 500	26 786	27 374	28 258	28 011	29 240	30 381	31 969	32 296	34 375	33 818	36 135
45–54	14 251	14 464	13 771	13 709	12 842	12 596	13 007	13 401	13 549	14 054	13 690	15 173
55 and over	12 476	12 190	11 332	11 123	10 420	9 905	9 698	9 378	8 893	9 013	8 555	8 786

1 Provisional.

2 The figures for England and Wales include an assumed distribution of 'Age not stated'.

Source *Office of Population Censuses and Surveys*

2.13 Marriages
Scotland, Northern Ireland
(continued)

Numbers

	1977	1978	1979	1980	1981	1982	1983	1984	1985	1986	1987	1988
Scotland												
Marriages	37 288	37 811	37 860	38 501	36 237	34 942	34 962	36 253	36 385	35 790	35 813	35 599
Persons marrying per 1 000 population	*14.4*	*14.6*	*14.7*	*14.9*	*14.1*	*13.5*	*13.6*	*14.1*	*14.2*	*14.0*	*14.0*	*14.0*
Previous marital status												
Bachelors	31 099	31 044	31 571	31 472	29 622	28 357	27 765	28 753	28 475	27 860	28 126	27 622
Divorced men	4 863	5 419	5 016	5 777	5 462	5 416	6 111	6 488	6 876	6 890	6 740	7 062
Widowers	1 326	1 348	1 273	1 252	1 153	1 169	1 086	1 012	1 034	1 040	947	915
Spinsters	31 455	31 417	31 989	31 968	30 103	28 736	28 185	29 358	29 208	28 414	28 588	28 150
Divorced women	4 570	5 125	4 652	5 355	5 065	5 163	5 755	5 948	6 233	6 452	6 349	6 754
Widows	1 263	1 269	1 219	1 178	1 069	1 043	1 022	947	944	924	876	875
First marriage for both partners	28 528	28 260	28 967	28 692	27 012	25 752	24 991	25 951	25 674	24 968	25 147	24 628
First marriage for one partner	5 498	5 944	5 626	6 056	5 701	5 589	5 968	6 209	6 335	6 358	6 420	6 516
Remarriage for both partners	3 262	3 610	3 267	3 753	3 524	3 601	4 003	4 093	4 376	4 474	4 246	4 455
Males												
Under 21 years	7 892	7 504	7 098	6 798	5 930	5 190	4 491	4 172	3 591	3 028	2 780	2 259
21–24	13 952	13 935	14 553	14 700	13 736	12 986	12 806	12 996	12 689	12 015	11 742	10 956
25–29	7 728	7 910	8 108	8 263	8 273	8 215	8 590	9 602	9 903	10 322	10 883	11 140
30–34	2 948	3 246	3 201	3 448	3 362	3 333	3 503	3 752	4 052	4 125	4 191	4 609
35–44	2 252	2 391	2 378	2 639	2 524	2 818	3 021	3 235	3 515	3 624	3 655	3 953
45–54	1 286	1 414	1 198	1 354	1 243	1 259	1 375	1 371	1 466	1 483	1 509	1 558
55 and over	1 230	1 411	1 324	1 299	1 169	1 141	1 176	1 125	1 169	1 193	1 053	1 124
Females												
Under 21 years	14 874	14 264	13 969	13 575	12 019	10 752	9 685	9 336	8 224	7 245	6 665	5 692
21–24	11 724	12 193	12 813	13 091	12 847	12 439	12 627	13 255	13 531	13 316	13 338	12 801
25–29	4 954	5 054	5 181	5 476	5 347	5 594	6 105	6 922	7 393	7 720	8 314	8 959
30–34	1 982	2 208	2 124	2 326	2 175	2 251	2 394	2 502	2 746	2 926	3 044	3 311
35–44	1 886	2 025	1 919	2 127	2 086	2 166	2 320	2 472	2 652	2 720	2 686	2 964
45–54	1 069	1 157	1 046	1 147	1 070	1 083	1 165	1 130	1 180	1 157	1 209	1 233
55 and over	799	910	808	759	693	657	666	636	659	654	609	639
Northern Ireland[1]												
Marriages	9 696	10 304	10 214	9 923	9 636	9 913	9 990	10 358	10 343	10 225	10 363	9 958
Persons marrying per 1 000 population	*12.6*	*13.4*	*13.2*	*12.8*	*12.3*	*12.6*	*12.8*	*13.1*	*13.3*	*13.1*	*13.2*	*12.6*
Previous marital status												
Bachelors	9 162	9 700	9 580	9 237	8 861	9 052	9 103	9 423	9 400	9 331	9 414	9 091
Divorced men	323	374	427	490	580	654	695	755	735	715	759	702
Widowers	211	230	207	196	195	207	192	180	208	179	190	165
Spinsters	9 222	9 735	9 631	9 294	8 883	9 161	9 155	9 539	9 500	9 383	9 527	9 180
Divorced women	277	336	372	426	543	567	650	630	657	664	670	621
Widows	197	233	211	203	210	185	185	189	186	178	166	157
First marriage for both partners	8 935	9 405	9 282	8 915	8 484	8 689	8 680	9 031	8 993	8 897	9 004	8 731
First marriage for one partner	514	625	647	701	776	835	898	906	914	920	933	809
Remarriage for both partners	247	274	285	307	376	389	412	424	436	408	426	418
Males												
Under 21 years	2 024	2 025	1 906	1 784	1 607	1 545	1 435	1 334	1 156	1 042	948	771
21–24	3 889	4 246	4 107	3 996	3 862	3 875	3 806	4 004	3 945	3 798	3 706	3 497
25–29	2 304	2 397	2 524	2 501	2 398	2 646	2 794	2 970	3 189	3 325	3 467	3 450
30–34	728	799	822	802	815	849	889	1 010	1 010	1 037	1 135	1 144
35–44	384	436	467	465	530	581	635	656	630	650	706	688
45–54	178	203	198	164	228	215	226	197	218	212	224	232
55 and over	189	198	190	211	196	202	205	187	195	161	177	176
Females												
Under 21 years	4 029	4 172	3 876	3 679	3 275	3 221	3 050	2 939	2 591	2 390	2 259	1 875
21–24	3 273	3 563	3 667	3 600	3 569	3 693	3 751	4 061	4 199	4 134	4 172	4 082
25–29	1 389	1 490	1 557	1 575	1 601	1 767	1 891	2 077	2 217	2 372	2 535	2 546
30–34	451	452	511	479	489	545	575	579	623	653	667	760
35–44	283	341	329	314	396	389	455	413	432	420	474	435
45–54	157	149	164	155	179	178	153	185	163	151	154	164
55 and over	114	137	110	121	127	120	115	104	118	105	102	96

1 1988 data are provisional.

Sources *General Register Office (Scotland); General Register Office (Northern Ireland)*

2.14 Divorce
England and Wales, Scotland

Numbers

	1977	1978	1979	1980	1981	1982	1983	1984	1985	1986	1987	1988
England and Wales												
Decrees absolute[1], granted:												
Number[1]	129 053	143 667	138 706	148 301	145 713	146 698	147 479	144 501	160 300	153 903	151 007	152 633
Rate per 1 000 married couples	*10.4*	*11.6*	*11.2*	*12.0*	*11.9*	*12.0*	*12.2*	*12.0*	*13.4*	*12.9*	*12.7*	*12.8*[7]
Duration of marriage:												
0–4 years	23 506	25 807	25 883	28 517	28 640	30 262	31 097	30 500	45 776	38 637	35 423	35 582
5–9 years	38 790	43 228	42 190	45 152	43 808	42 499	42 041	40 866	41 537	42 187	43 150	42 617
10–14 years	24 000	27 207	26 373	28 620	28 242	28 737	28 432	27 336	27 087	26 718	26 194	26 545
15–19 years	16 061	17 918	17 124	18 541	18 499	18 855	19 103	19 108	19 460	19 547	19 576	20 132
20 years and over	26 696	29 507	27 136	27 471	26 499	26 301	26 769	26 681	26 427	26 805	26 664	27 747
Not stated					25	44	37	10	13	9	–	10
Age of wife at marriage:												
16–19 years	49 170	54 484	52 550	55 946	54 424	54 067	52 547	49 610	52 858	48 621	46 097	44 693
20–24 years	57 153	63 319	60 523	64 786	63 034	62 955	63 382	62 642	69 663	68 387	68 345	69 489
25–29 years	12 545	14 259	14 118	15 060	15 281	15 714	16 351	16 811	18 689	18 990	19 049	20 267
30–34 years	4 535	5 203	5 187	5 638	5 813	6 317	7 092	7 125	8 544	8 189	7 983	8 441
35–39 years	2 341	2 637	2 690	2 803	3 091	3 312	3 502	3 729	4 612	4 497	4 403	4 501
40–44 years	1 390	1 528	1 572	1 672	1 757	1 975	2 081	2 090	2 609	2 378	2 416	2 530
45 years and over	1 919	2 237	2 066	2 306	2 313	2 358	2 524	2 494	3 325	2 841	2 714	2 712
Age of wife at divorce:												
16–24 years	16 989	19 471	19 639	20 905	20 095	19 987	19 440	18 232	26 170	21 713	19 066	17 693
25–29 years	30 115	33 149	31 892	34 308	33 299	32 995	32 695	31 800	35 680	34 478	34 209	34 504
30–34 years	26 384	29 659	29 137	31 765	31 104	30 023	28 958	27 734	28 668	28 452	28 995	29 406
35–39 years	17 701	19 840	19 457	21 436	22 459	24 567	25 673	25 522	26 554	25 956	24 934	24 685
40–44 years	13 135	15 183	14 473	15 423	15 276	15 587	16 336	16 712	17 767	18 519	19 403	20 873
45 years and over	24 729	26 365	24 108	24 464	23 455	23 495	24 340	24 491	25 448	24 776	24 400	25 462
Not stated					25	44	37	10	13	9	–	10
Divorces in which there were:												
No children[2]	37 818	43 065	41 805	45 334	42 292	42 174	42 458	41 831	51 912	47 330	46 770	47 049
1 or more children[2]	91 235	100 602	96 901	102 967	103 421	104 524	105 021	102 670	108 388	106 573	104 237	105 584
Scotland												
Decrees absolute, granted[3, 4]:												
Number[1]	8 823	8 458	8 833	10 528	9 894	11 288	13 238	11 906	13 371	12 800	12 133	11 472
Rate per 1 000 married[5] couples	*6.9*	*6.8*	*7.2*	*8.6*	*8.0*	*9.2*	*11.0*	*9.9*	*11.2*	*10.7*	*10.2*	*9.8*
Duration of marriage:												
0–4 years	1 741	1 563	1 457	1 807	1 699	1 991	2 267	2 157	2 364	2 233	2 173	1 986
5–9 years	2 418	2 441	2 612	3 134	3 014	3 493	4 008	3 455	3 882	3 735	3 544	3 353
10–14 years	1 457	1 430	1 728	2 090	1 944	2 272	2 419	2 284	2 684	2 536	2 351	2 227
15–19 years	1 146	972	1 115	1 359	1 224	1 401	1 655	1 578	1 868	1 804	1 670	1 592
20 years and over	1 806	1 997	1 921	2 138	2 013	2 131	2 889	2 433	2 573	2 492	2 395	2 314
Age of wife at marriage:												
16–20 years	4 966	4 688	5 042	5 988	5 584	6 423	7 089	6 384	7 143	6 767	6 134	5 660
21–24 years	2 364	2 368	2 408	2 935	2 769	3 159	3 813	3 510	3 914	3 768	3 778	3 577
25–29 years	706	740	787	902	853	929	1 218	1 093	1 246	1 257	1 274	1 236
30–34 years	218	264	249	314	293	322	470	404	461	458	423	466
35–39 years	130	128	130	150	167	184	252	182	247	250	224	219
40–44 years	64	66	68	78	86	105	144	123	143	120	142	124
45 years and over	92	104	100	161	142	127	178	162	170	174	158	153
Age not stated	20	53	49			39	74	57	49	6	–	37
Age of wife at divorce:												
16–24 years	1 754	1 640	1 468	1 702	1,525	1 831	1 909	1 682	1 881	1 674	1 504	1 285
25–29 years	2 046	1 926	2 126	2 625	2 428	2 820	3 154	2 865	3 152	3 001	2 920	2 676
30–34 years	1 411	1 380	1 663	2 027	2 012	2 285	2 494	2 291	2 628	2 597	2 443	2 378
35–39 years	1 092	992	1 129	1 431	1 345	1 543	1 850	1 852	2 183	2 136	1 942	1 917
40–44 years	774	771	875	1 053	1 000	1 112	1 382	1 247	1 440	1 370	1 482	1 381
45 years and over	1 463	1 649	1 525	1 690	1 584	1 658	2 375	1 921	2 040	2 016	1 842	1 798
Age not stated	20	53	47			39	74	57	49	6	–	37
Actions[6] in which there were:												
No children	3 260	3 836	3 756	4 325	4 148	4 603	6 774	5 488	6 040	6 046	5 989	5 887
1 or more children	5 923	4 946	5 401	6 622	6 099	7 079	6 863	6 418	7 331	6 754	6 144	5 585

1 Includes decrees of divorce and of nullity.
2 Children of the family as defined by the Matrimonial Causes Act 1973.
3 For divorces under pre-1976 legislation these figures relate only to persons who were married in Scotland, and obtained their decree of divorce from the Court of Session. Also with effect from 1 May 1984 the jurisdiction of the Sheriff Courts was extended to include divorce.
4 With effect from 1984 these statistics are being collected on the basis of divorces granted only and any difference in the number of divorces brought and granted relates to nullity of marriages.
5 Rates are calculated using the average of the estimated married male and female populations.
6 These Actions relate to all persons divorced or separated in Scotland, irrespective of the country of marriage.
7 Provisional.

Sources *Office of Population Censuses and Surveys; General Register Office (Scotland); Scottish Courts Administration*

2.15 Divorce proceedings
England and Wales

Number

	1978	1979	1980	1981	1982	1983	1984	1985	1986	1987	1988
Dissolution of marriage[1]											
Petitions filed[2]	162 450	162 867	170 882	169 076	173 452	168 428	178 940	190 481	179 844	182 934	182 804
On grounds of:											
Adultery	43 260	44 090	47 920	47 250	48 010	47 130	50 720	53 330	51 730	52 780	50 250
Behaviour	56 330	60 850	64 880	66 940	72 320	69 850	73 340	81 220	81 590	85 410	88 260
Desertion	5 500	4 450	4 480	3 740	3 080	2 450	3 060	8 000	2 580	2 153	2 180
Separation (2 years and consent)	40 170	38 710	39 760	38 480	37 700	36 930	38 950	36 460	32 760	31 150	30 860
Separation (5 years)	14 960	12 960	12 510	11 690	11 390	11 320	10 780	10 210	10 200	10 420	9 830
Adultery and behaviour	1 450	1 220	890	720	710	580	1 890	970	750	760	1 000
Adultery and desertion	240	80	70	10	30	20	10	130	50	90	120
Behaviour and desertion	110	90	50	40	70	30	20	70	50	70	70
Other	440	410	320	210	140	120	170	100	140	120	240
By husbands	46 840	45 590	48 890	46 220	46 470	45 150	48 940	52 090	49 480	49 780	49 130
By wives	115 610	117 280	121 990	122 850	126 980	123 280	130 000	138 390	130 370	133 150	133 670
Decrees nisi granted	151 533	139 503	150 385	147 226	147 763	149 189	147 136	161 409	152 073	149 272	154 788
Decrees absolute granted	142 726	137 868	147 381	144 763	145 802	146 669	143 746	159 693	153 418	150 557	152 139
Nullity of marriage[3]											
Petitions filed[2]	1 117	994	1 110	1 050	921	887	1 036	574	554	542	604
By husbands	430	380	550	430	400	320	480	220	240	250	260
By wives	680	610	560	620	520	570	560	360	310	290	350
Decrees nisi granted	959	810	929	894	803	819	871	589	461	444	389
Decrees absolute granted	941	838	920	950	896	810	755	607	485	443	494
Judicial separation											
Petitions filed[2]	2 611	3 650	5 423	6 036	7 480	7 430	6 098	3 479	3 428	3 199	2 925
By husbands	240	322	480	600	840	880	1 190	350	480	360	270
By wives	2 370	3 330	4 940	5 430	6 640	6 550	4 910	3 130	2 950	2 840	2 660
Decrees granted	1 228	1 640	2 560	3 334	4 026	4 852	4 445	2 344	1 768	1 659	1 917

1 Excluding petitions in which divorce is asked for in alternative to nullity.
2 The breakdown of petitions filed is based on actual figures for The Principal Registry of the Family Division together with grossed up figures, based on a two month sample, from the county courts. Estimated figures have been rounded to tens.
3 Including cases in which dissolution is asked for in the alternative.

Source Lord Chancellor's Department

2.15 Divorce proceedings
Scotland, Northern Ireland

(continued)

Scotland

Number

	1977	1978	1979	1980	1981	1982	1983	1984	1985	1986	1987	1988[8]
Divorce[4]												
Actions in which final judgment given	9 182	8 782	9 149	10 947	10 247	11 682	13 637	11 915	13 373	13 063	12 133	..
On grounds of[5]:												
Adultery	1 590	202	57	16	6	2	–	–	–	–	..	..
Desertion	464	36	10	4	–	–	–	–	–	–	..	..
Insanity	5	–	–	–	–	–	–	–	–	–	..	..
Cruelty	2 348	392	117	32	8	2	–	–	–	–	..	..
Sodomy	–	–	–	–	–	–	–	–	–	–	..	..
On grounds of[6]:												
Adultery	942	1 342	1 533	2 013	1 749	1 926	1 844	1 415	1 760	1 610	1 531	..
Desertion	438	403	243	311	242	252	207	142	120	129	79	..
Adultery and behaviour	3	1	–	2	1	4	7	7	15	16	5	..
Behaviour	1 782	3 010	3 638	4 456	4 382	5 096	4 900	4 351	5 020	4 620	4 180	..
2 years non-cohabitation	564	1 623	1 964	2 519	2 470	2 844	4 250	4 250	4 665	4 950	4 738	..
5 years non-cohabitation	1 046	1 773	1 587	1 594	1 389	1 556	2 428	1 741	1 791	1 729	1 591	..
At instances of: Husbands	2 398	2 377	2 372	2 805	2 584	2 833	3 847	3 198	3 401	3 389	3 333	..
Wives	6 784	6 405	6 778	8 142	7 663	8 849	9 790	8 708	9 970	9 665	8 800	..
Divorce granted	8 812	8 448	8 829	10 522	9 889	11 275	13 235	11 906	13 371	13 054	12 130	..
Separation												
Action in which final judgment given	1	–	1	–	–	–	–	–	–	–	..	..
Separation granted	–	–	1	–	–	–	–	–	–	–	..	..
Duration of marriages where divorce or separation granted												
Under 1 year	14	17	8	5	9	9	3	12	42	31	31	..
1–2 years	173	142	110	149	146	173	140	158	200	202	170	..
2–5 years	1 592	1 424	1 330	1 644	1 542	1 801	2 121	1 987	2 122	2 039	1 972	..
5–10 years	2 464	2 461	2 632	3 149	3 014	3 490	4 008	3 455	3 882	3 822	3 544	..
10–20 years	2 720	2 398	2 856	3 447	3 169	3 671	4 074	3 862	4 552	4 415	4 021	..
20 years and over	1 849	2 006	1 893	2 128	2 009	2 131	2 880	2 432	2 573	2 545	2 395	..
Actions[7] in which there were:												
Children of marriage	5 923	4 946	5 399	6 622	6 099	7 079	6 863	6 418	7 331	6 910	6 144	..
No children	3 260	3 836	3 751	4 325	4 148	4 603	6 774	5 488	6 040	6 144	5 989	..

4 With effect from 1984 these statistics are being collected on the basis of divorces granted only and any difference in the number of divorces brought and granted relates to nullity of marriage.
5 Prior to the Divorce (Scotland) Act 1976.
6 The grounds given show the allegations made—divorce is granted on the grounds of irretrievable breakdown of marriage under the Divorce (Scotland) Act 1976.
7 Divorce and separation.
8 1988 figures not yet available.

Northern Ireland

Number

	1977	1978	1979	1980	1981	1982	1983	1984	1985	1986	1987	1988
Petitions filed												
Nullity of marriage	2	10	6	9	9	5	–	6	6	6	4	1
Divorce	632	714	872	1 620	1 645	1 734	1 577	1 749	1 986	1 630	1 834	2 217
Judicial separation	–	–	–	4	2	2	9	5	15	17	7	6

Sources Scottish Courts Administration; Northern Ireland Court Service

2.16 Births

Annual averages or calendar years

	Live births			Sex ratio	Rates[1]			Still-births	Still-birth rate
	Total	Male	Female		Crude birth rate[2]	General fertility rate[3]	TPFR[4]		
United Kingdom									
1900–02	1 095	558	537	1 037	28.6	115.1	..	..	..
1910–12	1 037	528	508	1 039	24.6	99.4	..	..	..
1920–22	1 018	522	496	1 052	23.1	93.0	..	..	..
1930–32	750	383	367	1 046	16.3	66.5	..	..	..
1940–42	723	372	351	1 062	15.0	..	1.89	26	..
1950–52	803	413	390	1 061	16.0	73.7	2.21	18	..
1960–62	946	487	459	1 063	17.9	90.3	2.80	18	..
1970–72	880	453	427	1 064	15.8	82.5	2.36	12	13
1980–82	735	377	358	1 053	13.0	62.5	1.83	5	7
1978	687	353	334	1 059	12.2	60.8	1.76	6	8
1979	735	378	356	1 061	13.1	64.1	1.86	6	8
1980	754	386	368	1 050	13.4	64.9	1.89	6	7
1981	731	375	356	1 054	13.0	62.2	1.81	5	7
1982	719	369	350	1 054	12.8	60.5	1.78	5	6
1983	721	370	351	1 055	12.8	60.2	1.77	4	6
1984	730	373	356	1 049	12.9	60.3	1.77	4	6
1985	751	385	366	1 053	13.3	61.4	1.80	4	6
1986	755	387	368	1 053	13.3	61.1	1.78	4	5
1987	776	398	378	1 054	13.6	62.3	1.82	4	5
1988[5]	788	403	384	1 049	13.8	63.1	1.84	4	5
England and Wales									
1900–02	932	475	458	1 037	28.6	114.7	..	..	..
1910–12	884	450	433	1 040	24.5	98.6	..	..	..
1920–22	862	442	420	1 051	22.8	91.1	..	..	..
1930–32	632	323	309	1 047	15.8	64.4	..	27	..
1940–42	607	312	295	1 057	15.6	61.3	1.81	22	..
1950–52	683	351	332	1 058	15.6	72.1	2.16	16	..
1960–62	812	418	394	1 061	17.6	88.9	2.77	16	..
1970–72	764	394	371	1 061	15.6	81.4	2.31	10	13
1980–82	639	328	311	1 053	12.9	61.8	1.81	4	7
1978	596	307	289	1 061	12.1	60.1	1.73	5	9
1979	638	328	310	1 060	12.9	63.3	1.84	5	8
1980	656	336	320	1 049	13.2	64.2	1.88	5	7
1981	635	326	309	1 055	12.8	61.3	1.80	4	7
1982	626	321	305	1 055	12.6	59.9	1.76	4	6
1983	629	323	306	1 056	12.7	59.7	1.76	4	6
1984	637	326	311	1 049	12.8	59.8	1.75	4	6
1985	656	337	320	1 054	13.1	61.0	1.78	4	6
1986	661	339	322	1 052	13.2	60.6	1.77	4	5
1987	682	350	332	1 053	13.6	62.0	1.81	3	5
1988	694	355	339	1 047	13.8	62.9	1.82	3	5

See footnotes on page 29.

2.16 Births
Annual averages or calendar years

(continued)

	Live births			Sex ratio	Rates[1]			Still-births	Still-birth rate
	Total	Male	Female		Crude birth rate[2]	General fertility rate[3]	TPFR[4]		
Scotland									
1900–02	132	67	65	1 046	29.5	120.6	..	..	..
1910–12	123	63	60	1 044	25.9	107.4	..	..	..
1920–22	125	64	61	1 046	25.6	105.9	..	..	..
1930–32	93	47	45	1 040	19.1	78.8	..	..	..
1940–42	89	46	43	1 051	18.5	73.7	..	4	..
1950–52	91	47	44	1 060	17.9	81.4	2.41	2	..
1960–62	102	53	50	1 060	19.7	97.8	2.98	2	..
1970–72	84	43	41	1 057	16.1	83.3	2.46	1	13
1980–82	68	35	33	1 051	13.1	62.2	1.80	0	6
1978	64	33	31	1 058	12.3	60.1	1.75	1	8
1979	68	35	33	1 071	13.1	63.3	1.85	0	7
1980	69	35	33	1 057	13.3	63.3	1.84	0	7
1981	69	35	34	1 045	13.3	63.1	1.83	0	6
1982	66	34	32	1 050	12.8	60.1	1.74	0	6
1983	65	34	31	1 071	12.6	59.7	1.70	0	6
1984	65	33	32	1 037	12.7	59.8	1.68	0	6
1985	67	34	33	1 048	13.0	61.0	1.71	0	6
1986	66	34	32	1 061	12.9	58.9	1.68	0	6
1987	66	34	32	1 053	13.0	58.8	1.68	0	5
1988[5]	66	34	32	1 059	13.0	59.1	1.68	0	5
Northern Ireland									
1900–02	..	..	..	..	..	..	..	..	..
1910–12	..	..	..	..	..	..	..	..	..
1920–22	31	16	15	1 048	24.2	105.9	..	..	..
1930–32	26	13	12	1 047	20.5	78.8	..	..	..
1940–42	27	14	13	1 078	20.8	73.7	..	..	..
1950–52	29	15	14	1 066	20.9	81.4	..	..	..
1960–62	31	16	15	1 068	22.5	111.5	3.47	7	23
1970–72	31	16	15	1 074	20.4	105.7	3.13	3	14
1980–82	28	14	13	1 048	18.0	87.5	2.59	0	8
1978	26	13	13	1 007	17.1	85.4	2.64	0	9
1979	28	14	14	1 058	18.3	90.4	2.80	0	9
1980	29	15	14	1 057	18.6	90.6	2.78	0	9
1981	27	14	13	1 041	17.8	86.3	2.54	0	9
1982	27	14	13	1 045	17.6	84.6	2.46	0	7
1983	27	14	13	1 068	17.7	84.0	2.44	0	7
1984	28	14	13	1 069	17.9	84.2	2.44	0	6
1985	28	14	13	1 054	17.7	83.2	2.45	0	6
1986	28	15	14	1 075	18.0	83.7	2.46	0	6
1987	28	14	14	1 056	17.7	82.2	2.41	0	6
1988[5]	28	14	14	1 055	17.5	82.0	2.39	0	5

1 Rates are based on a new series of population estimates which use a new definition and population base taking into account the 1981 Census results.
2 Rate per 1 000 population
3 Rate per 1 000 women aged 15–44.
4 Total period fertility rate is the average number of children which would be born per woman if women experienced the age-specific fertility rates of the period in question throughout their child-bearing life span. UK figures for years 1970–72 and earlier are estimates.
5 Provisional.

Sources *Office of Population Censuses and Surveys; General Register Office (Scotland); General Register Office (Northern Ireland)*

2.17 Birth occurrence inside and outside marriage by age of mother

Thousands

Year	Inside Marriage						Outside Marriage					
	All ages	Under 20	20–24	25–29	Over 30	Mean Age (Years)	All ages	Under 20	20–24	25–29	Over 30	Mean Age (Years)
United Kingdom												
1961	890	55	273	280	294	27.7	54	13	17	10	13	25.5
1971	828	70	302	271	185	26.5	74	24	25	13	12	23.8
1981	640	36	193	231	180	27.3	91	30	33	16	13	23.4
1985	609	24	169	233	183	27.7	142	42	54	27	19	23.6
1986	597	21	159	231	185	27.9	158	45	60	31	22	23.7
1987	598	18	153	235	192	28.1	178	48	68	37	26	23.9
1988	590	16	144	235	194	28.2	198	51	76	42	29	24.1
Great Britain												
1961	859	53	264	270	272	27.7	53	13	17	10	13	25.5
1971	797	68	293	261	176	26.4	73	24	25	13	12	23.8
1981	614	34	186	223	171	27.2	89	29	32	16	13	23.3
1985	584	23	162	224	175	27.7	139	41	52	27	19	22.7
1986	572	20	153	222	177	27.9	155	44	59	30	22	22.9
1987	574	17	147	227	184	28.0	174	46	66	36	25	23.4
1988	566	16	138	226	186	28.2	194	49	74	42	29	23.6

Source *Office of Population Censuses and Surveys*

2.18 Live births by age of mother

	Under 20	20–24	25–29	30–34	35–39	40–44	45 and over	All ages
All live births—Scotland								
Year								
1978	7 016	21 072	22 061	10 730	2 768	533	25	64 295
1979	7 166	22 019	23 654	11 767	3 145	585	30	68 366
1980	7 237	22 598	23 235	12 129	3 109	557	27	68 892
1981	6 880	23 050	23 170	12 134	3 238	555	27	69 054
1982	6 891	21 855	22 133	11 333	3 408	550	26	66 196
1983	6 348	21 319	22 110	11 216	3 533	530	22	65 078
1984	6 251	20 728	22 816	11 227	3 517	543	24	65 106
1985	6 528	20 809	23 511	11 600	3 692	512	24	66 676
1986	6 390	19 853	23 357	12 013	3 654	519	26	65 812
1987	6 398	19 534	23 511	12 593	3 643	542	20	66 241
1988	6 166	18 836	23 947	12 844	3 863	534	22	66 212
Age-specific fertility rates—Scotland								
Year								
1978	31.8	109.3	125.0	61.5	18.3	3.5	.2	60.3
1979	32.1	111.8	134.9	66.0	20.5	3.9	.2	63.4
1980	32.0	112.5	132.7	66.8	20.3	3.7	.2	63.3
1981	30.6	112.5	131.5	66.2	20.8	3.7	.2	63.1
1982	30.8	104.9	123.2	64.7	20.5	3.7	.2	60.1
1983	28.8	101.0	121.3	65.5	20.7	3.5	.1	58.9
1984	28.8	96.2	122.2	65.9	20.1	3.6	.2	58.4
1985	30.9	95.2	123.3	68.0	20.7	3.4	.2	59.5
1986	30.8	91.4	120.0	70.0	20.3	3.4	.2	58.5
1987	31.7	90.5	118.9	71.9	21.2	3.3	.1	58.8
1988	31.9	88.6	120.3	72.2	22.9	3.2	.1	59.1
All live births—Northern Ireland								
Year								
1978	2 127	7 641	8 362	5 371	2 184	514	40	26 239
1979	2 200	8 169	8 846	5 864	2 476	594	29	28 178
1980	2 124	8 467	9 058	5 844	2 524	524	41	28 582
1981	1 912	8 123	8 531	5 748	2 445	516	27	27 302
1982	1 913	8 023	8 457	5 598	2 519	496	22	27 028
1983	1 947	7 858	8 764	5 599	2 486	575	26	27 255
1984	2 025	8 047	8 952	5 554	2 524	568	23	27 693
1985	1 978	7 847	9 195	5 600	2 505	490	20	27 635
1986	2 096	7 832	9 497	5 690	2 493	523	21	28 152
1987	2 009	7 611	9 457	5 831	2 420	522	15	27 865
1988	2 054	7 403	9 462	6 003	2 790	536	19	27 767
Age-specific fertility rates—Northern Ireland								
Year								
1978	31.0	142.3	177.5	112.8	51.4	12.9	1.0	87.6
1979	30.9	145.4	188.6	123.2	57.1	14.7	.7	92.2
1980	29.2	143.3	191.5	122.0	56.6	12.9	1.0	91.6
1981	27.3	134.9	172.7	117.8	52.2	12.6	.7	86.3
1982	27.6	131.5	163.6	116.4	52.2	12.1	.6	84.6
1983	28.1	125.5	164.1	116.2	51.4	13.5	.7	84.0
1984	29.1	125.9	163.4	114.8	52.1	13.0	.6	84.2
1985	28.7	121.8	162.7	114.1	51.8	10.9	.5	83.1
1986	30.3	122.2	164.3	112.5	51.7	11.2	.5	83.7
1987	29.4	118.0	160.8	112.6	50.7	10.9	.4	82.2
1988	30.8	115.1	159.3	113.7	48.0	11.2	.5	82.0

Each section is headed "Age-group".

2.18 Live births by age of mother

(continued)

All live births—United Kingdom

Year	Under 20	20–24	25–29	30–34	35–39	40–44	45 and over	All ages
1978	65 217	211 293	241 021	129 178	32 889	6 766	588	686 952
1979	68 509	223 397	254 602	143 295	37 015	7 157	597	734 572
1980	70 115	232 606	255 731	147 881	39 526	7 156	693	753 708
1981	65 362	225 673	247 461	144 472	39 893	7 241	744	730 848
1982	64 239	222 200	242 495	137 689	44 919	6 932	681	719 155
1983	62 354	221 029	244 952	137 811	47 296	7 315	710	721 467
1984	62 784	220 230	249 799	139 555	48 962	7 687	600	729 617
1985	65 435	222 614	260 192	143 385	50 590	7 884	628	750 728
1986	65 892	219 749	261 889	147 190	51 612	8 075	575	754 982
1987	65 952	220 377	271 897	154 982	52 667	9 176	566	775 617
1988	66 961	219 965	276 869	159 821	53 802	9 590	548	787 566

Age-specific fertility rates—United Kingdom

Year	Under 20	20–24	25–29	30–34	35–39	40–44	45 and over	All ages
1978	29.8	108.1	124.1	64.1	20.2	4.3	.4	60.8
1979	30.5	112.3	133.0	70.0	22.2	4.5	.4	64.1
1980	30.5	113.5	134.9	71.4	23.1	4.5	.4	64.9
1981	28.3	106.8	130.4	69.5	22.4	4.6	.5	62.1
1982	27.8	102.7	127.1	69.8	23.3	4.4	.4	60.6
1983	27.1	99.5	127.0	72.1	23.6	4.5	.5	60.2
1984	27.8	96.4	126.8	74.0	24.0	4.6	.4	60.3
1985	29.6	95.3	128.2	76.7	24.5	4.6	.4	61.4
1986	30.2	93.4	124.7	78.3	24.8	4.6	.4	61.1
1987	30.9	93.9	125.5	81.3	26.6	4.8	.4	62.3
1988	32.3	94.9	124.4	82.6	28.0	4.8	.3	63.1

All live births—England and Wales

Year	Under 20	20–24	25–29	30–34	35–39	40–44	45 and over	All ages
1978	55 984	182 580	210 598	113 077	27 937	5 719	523	596 418
1979	59 143	193 209	222 102	125 664	31 394	5 978	538	638 028
1980	60 754	201 541	223 438	129 908	33 893	6 075	625	656 234
1981	56 570	194 500	215 760	126 590	34 210	6 170	690	634 492
1982	55 435	192 322	211 905	120 758	38 992	5 886	633	625 931
1983	54 059	191 852	214 078	120 996	41 277	6 210	662	629 134
1984	54 058	191 455	218 031	122 774	42 921	6 576	553	636 818
1985	56 929	193 958	227 486	126 185	44 393	6 882	584	656 417
1986	57 406	192 064	229 035	129 487	45 465	7 033	528	661 018
1987	57 545	193 232	238 929	136 558	46 604	8 112	531	681 511
1988	58 741	193 726	243 460	140 974	47 649	8 520	507	693 577

Age-specific fertility rates—England and Wales

Year	Under 20	20–24	25–29	30–34	35–39	40–44	45 and over	All ages
1978	29.4	106.9	122.6	63.1	19.5	4.2	.4	60.1
1979	30.3	111.3	131.2	69.0	21.3	4.3	.4	63.3
1980	30.4	112.7	133.6	70.5	22.3	4.3	.5	64.2
1981	28.1	105.3	129.1	68.6	21.7	4.4	.5	61.3
1982	27.4	101.6	126.4	69.1	22.8	4.2	.5	59.9
1983	26.9	98.5	126.4	71.5	23.1	4.4	.5	59.7
1984	27.4	95.5	126.2	73.6	23.6	4.5	.4	59.8
1985	29.5	94.5	127.6	76.4	24.1	4.6	.4	61.0
1986	30.1	92.7	124.0	78.1	24.6	4.5	.4	60.6
1987	30.9	93.4	125.1	81.3	26.5	4.8	.4	62.0
1988	32.4	94.9	123.8	82.7	27.9	4.8	.4	63.0

Sources *Office of Population Censuses and Surveys; General Register Office (Scotland); General Register Office (Northern Ireland)*

2.19 Deaths: analysis by age and sex

United Kingdom
Annual averages or calendar years

Number

	All ages[1]	Under 1 year	1–4	5–9	10–14	15–19	20–24	25–34	35–44	45–54	55–64	65–74	75–84	85 and over
Males														
1900–02	340 664	87 242	37 834	8 429	4 696	7 047	8 766	19 154	24 739	30 488	37 610	39 765	28 320	6 563
1910–12	303 703	63 885	29 452	7 091	4 095	5 873	6 817	16 141	21 813	28 981	37 721	45 140	29 397	7 283
1920–22	284 876	48 044	19 008	6 052	3 953	5 906	6 572	13 663	19 702	29 256	40 583	49 398	34 937	7 801
1930–32	284 249	28 840	11 276	4 580	2 890	5 076	6 495	12 327	16 326	29 376	47 989	63 804	45 247	10 022
1940–42	314 643	24 624	6 949	3 400	2 474	4 653	4 246	11 506	17 296	30 082	57 076	79 652	59 733	12 900
1950–52	307 312	14 105	2 585	1 317	919	1 498	2 289	5 862	11 074	27 637	53 691	86 435	79 768	20 131
1960–62	318 850	12 234	1 733	971	871	1 718	1 857	3 842	8 753	26 422	63 009	87 542	83 291	26 605
1970–72	335 166	9 158	1 485	1 019	802	1 778	2 104	3 590	7 733	24 608	64 898	105 058	82 905	30 027
1980–82	330 495	4 829	774	527	652	1 999	1 943	3 736	6 568	19 728	54 159	105 155	98 488	31 936
1969	337 800	9 894	1 713	998	800	1 808	1 999	3 595	8 116	25 167	68 265	104 219	82 325	28 901
1970	334 355	9 713	1 556	978	773	1 752	2 131	3 585	7 836	24 399	66 657	103 589	81 996	29 390
1971	328 537	9 366	1 439	1 055	834	1 802	2 091	3 524	7 735	24 242	63 657	102 139	81 183	29 470
1972	342 605	8 393	1 460	1 024	801	1 779	2 092	3 661	7 629	25 184	64 379	109 448	85 535	31 220
1973	338 788	7 783	1 438	978	790	1 819	2 213	3 953	7 530	25 434	61 970	108 871	85 172	30 837
1974	337 263	7 180	1 307	858	775	1 805	1 968	3 820	7 448	25 864	59 703	110 718	84 491	31 236
1975	335 006	6 392	1 139	829	842	1 871	2 018	3 845	7 006	24 630	58 581	110 126	86 653	31 074
1976	341 910	5 706	1 036	798	769	1 978	1 994	3 867	6 976	23 663	59 703	112 234	90 710	32 476
1977	329 924	5 350	918	744	702	1 892	1 947	3 864	6 752	22 787	57 214	108 677	88 569	30 508
1978	336 395	5 220	866	726	729	2 067	2 055	3 944	6 912	22 439	57 381	110 384	92 574	31 098
1979	339 568	5 447	748	708	707	2 042	1 969	4 012	6 868	21 828	56 944	110 172	96 026	32 097
1980	332 370	5 174	792	609	659	2 022	1 940	3 786	6 698	20 577	55 176	107 089	96 301	31 547
1981	329 145	4 759	771	517	666	2 008	1 919	3 761	6 544	19 740	53 770	104 950	97 881	31 859
1982	329 971	4 555	760	456	632	1 966	1 971	3 661	6 462	18 867	53 531	103 426	101 281	32 403
1983	328 824	4 230	695	469	609	1 834	1 899	3 601	6 537	18 238	54 493	100 469	103 038	32 712
1984	321 095	3 995	725	423	580	1 708	1 999	3 595	6 425	17 647	53 715	95 420	102 513	32 350
1985	331 562	4 003	728	393	583	1 612	2 031	3 452	6 728	17 316	52 502	97 458	109 241	35 515
1986	327 160	4 219	653	384	444	1 676	2 067	3 668	6 712	16 814	50 352	95 987	108 123	36 061
1987	318 282	4 105	657	377	470	1 612	2 125	3 776	6 793	15 950	47 675	93 348	105 773	35 621
1988[2]	319 119	4 110	680	433	460	1 525	2 160	3 983	6 860	16 016	46 001	91 893	107 082	37 916
Females														
1900–02	322 058	68 770	36 164	8 757	5 034	6 818	8 264	18 702	21 887	25 679	34 521	42 456	34 907	10 099
1910–12	289 608	49 865	27 817	7 113	4 355	5 683	6 531	15 676	19 647	24 481	32 813	46 453	37 353	11 828
1920–22	274 772	35 356	17 323	5 808	4 133	5 729	6 753	14 878	18 121	24 347	34 026	48 573	45 521	14 203
1930–32	275 336	21 072	9 995	3 990	2 734	4 721	5 931	12 699	15 373	24 695	39 471	59 520	56 250	18 886
1940–42	296 646	17 936	5 952	2 743	2 068	4 180	5 028	11 261	14 255	23 629	42 651	70 907	71 377	24 658
1950–52	291 597	10 293	2 098	880	625	1 115	1 717	5 018	8 989	18 875	37 075	75 220	92 848	36 844
1960–62	304 871	8 887	1 334	627	522	684	811	2 504	6 513	16 720	36 078	73 118	105 956	51 117
1970–72	322 968	6 666	1 183	654	459	718	900	2 110	5 345	15 594	36 177	75 599	109 539	68 024
1980–82[2]	330 269	3 561	585	355	425	733	772	2 099	4 360	12 206	32 052	72 618	117 760	82 743
1969	321 737	7 189	1 280	579	423	714	918	2 125	5 874	15 824	37 725	77 206	108 385	63 495
1970	321 030	7 002	1 181	648	467	662	957	2 118	5 501	15 527	36 652	76 033	108 485	65 798
1971	316 541	6 798	1 129	649	493	721	866	2 105	5 267	15 358	35 621	73 502	107 056	66 976
1972	331 333	6 198	1 238	665	416	770	878	2 107	5 267	15 897	36 260	77 261	113 076	71 300
1973	330 904	5 646	1 060	610	455	803	847	2 166	5 145	15 822	34 733	77 067	113 393	73 157
1974	330 096	5 172	981	581	503	736	805	2 070	5 038	15 972	34 342	76 929	112 492	74 475
1975	327 471	4 798	860	540	405	751	813	2 211	4 897	15 054	33 904	75 459	112 838	74 941
1976	338 889	4 070	735	516	484	724	786	2 264	4 737	14 912	34 468	76 950	118 246	79 997
1977	325 219	3 933	720	431	450	750	839	2 148	4 583	13 905	33 395	74 573	113 872	75 620
1978	330 782	3 908	715	480	497	818	823	2 343	4 719	13 914	33 353	75 433	115 730	78 049
1979	336 009	4 026	617	428	462	701	738	2 244	4 544	13 667	33 274	75 610	118 859	80 839
1980	329 149	3 938	596	409	442	771	811	2 157	4 460	12 583	32 349	73 672	116 461	80 500
1981	328 829	3 402	599	352	424	738	737	2 083	4 309	12 275	31 625	72 476	117 458	82 351
1982	332 830	3 342	561	304	410	689	767	2 057	4 312	11 759	32 183	71 705	119 362	85 379
1983	330 277	3 126	568	318	374	719	698	1 914	4 318	11 384	32 197	69 266	118 940	86 455
1984	323 823	3 005	537	304	344	665	722	1 932	4 269	10 947	32 262	66 432	116 649	85 756
1985	339 094	3 027	574	314	355	626	729	1 852	4 397	10 581	32 010	68 505	122 445	93 679
1986	333 575	2 961	561	275	307	635	769	1 882	4 387	10 211	29 954	67 313	120 663	93 657
1987	326 060	2 972	550	265	288	614	733	1 974	4 454	10 177	29 037	65 570	117 266	92 160
1988[2]	330 059	2 951	553	264	251	612	745	1 915	4 615	9 887	28 154	65 020	117 731	97 361

1 In some years the totals include a small number of persons whose age was not stated.

2 Provisional.

Sources *Office of Population Censuses and Surveys; General Register Office (Scotland); General Register Office (Northern Ireland)*

2.19 (continued) Deaths: analysis by age and sex

England and Wales

Annual averages or calendar years

Number

	All ages[1]	Under 1 year	1–4	5–9	10–14	15–19	20–24	25–34	35–44	45–54	55–64	65–74	75–84	85 and over
Males														
1900–02	288 886	76 095	32 051	7 066	3 818	5 611	7 028	15 869	21 135	26 065	31 600	33 568	23 835	5 144
1910–12	257 253	54 678	24 676	5 907	3 348	4 765	5 596	13 603	18 665	24 820	32 217	38 016	24 928	6 036
1920–22	240 605	39 796	15 565	5 151	3 314	4 901	5 447	11 551	17 004	25 073	34 639	42 025	29 685	6 455
1930–32	243 147	23 331	9 099	3 844	2 435	4 354	5 580	10 600	14 041	25 657	41 581	54 910	39 091	8 624
1940–42	268 876	19 393	5 616	2 834	2 051	3 832	3 156	9 484	14 744	25 983	50 058	68 791	51 779	11 158
1950–52	266 879	11 498	2 131	1 087	778	1 248	1 947	4 990	9 489	23 815	46 948	75 774	69 496	17 677
1960–62	278 369	10 157	1 444	812	742	1 523	1 624	3 278	7 524	22 813	54 908	77 000	73 180	23 364
1970–72	293 934	7 818	1 259	860	677	1 524	1 788	3 079	6 637	21 348	56 667	92 389	73 365	26 522
1980–82	290 352	4 168	657	452	555	1 716	1 619	3 169	5 590	16 909	47 144	92 485	87 338	28 551
1969	296 561	8 331	1 484	839	662	1 574	1 727	3 083	6 952	21 937	59 763	91 925	72 822	25 462
1970	293 053	8 269	1 315	816	649	1 551	1 836	3 089	6 717	21 162	58 099	91 037	72 625	25 888
1971	288 359	7 974	1 228	916	690	1 538	1 771	3 046	6 683	21 046	55 699	89 802	71 907	26 059
1972	300 389	7 210	1 235	847	693	1 482	1 757	3 103	6 511	21 837	56 202	96 329	75 564	27 619
1973	296 546	6 599	1 203	817	677	1 510	1 836	3 336	6 455	21 923	53 976	95 605	75 300	27 309
1974	295 315	6 137	1 095	720	649	1 582	1 666	3 241	6 222	22 388	51 883	97 331	74 770	27 631
1975	294 174	5 430	983	677	692	1 584	1 697	3 229	5 935	21 337	51 088	96 934	76 879	27 709
1976	300 058	4 879	876	676	639	1 660	1 663	3 245	5 928	20 449	52 048	98 654	80 348	28 993
1977	289 773	4 519	769	635	598	1 620	1 599	3 270	5 695	19 600	49 855	95 873	78 528	27 212
1978	295 505	4 513	739	628	619	1 776	1 761	3 325	5 849	19 307	49 976	97 194	82 067	27 751
1979	297 862	4 731	641	602	605	1 727	1 649	3 426	5 822	18 607	49 586	96 764	85 091	28 611
1980	291 869	4 471	668	517	546	1 745	1 613	3 203	5 710	17 693	48 053	94 188	85 300	28 162
1981	289 022	4 119	651	447	573	1 734	1 576	3 181	5 535	16 889	46 858	92 189	86 774	28 496
1982	290 166	3 914	652	391	546	1 669	1 668	3 122	5 526	16 144	46 521	91 079	89 940	28 994
1983	289 419	3 654	604	391	514	1 580	1 635	3 071	5 581	15 632	47 315	88 622	91 531	29 289
1984	282 357	3 443	610	348	501	1 484	1 728	3 033	5 512	15 113	46 904	83 728	90 983	28 970
1985	292 327	3 510	638	328	503	1 374	1 738	2 953	5 776	14 838	45 704	85 695	97 362	31 908
1986	287 894	3 724	573	325	380	1 429	1 746	3 104	5 767	14 370	43 637	84 437	96 201	32 201
1987	280 177	3 637	578	309	404	1 389	1 811	3 218	5 823	13 678	41 367	82 021	94 060	31 882
1988	280 931	3 649	587	374	402	1 279	1 802	3 367	5 855	13 701	39 791	80 870	95 306	33 948
Females														
1900–02	269 432	60 090	30 674	7 278	4 010	5 265	6 497	15 065	18 253	21 474	28 424	35 307	29 118	7 977
1910–12	242 079	42 642	23 335	5 883	3 519	4 522	5 256	12 742	16 363	20 611	27 571	38 489	31 363	9 782
1920–22	229 908	29 178	14 174	4 928	3 456	4 719	5 533	12 244	15 142	20 580	28 633	41 010	38 439	11 871
1930–32	233 915	16 929	8 013	3 338	2 293	3 969	5 039	10 716	13 022	21 190	33 798	50 844	48 531	16 234
1940–42	253 702	14 174	4 726	2 265	1 695	3 426	4 198	9 470	12 093	20 413	36 814	60 987	61 891	21 550
1950–52	252 176	8 367	1 727	732	520	893	1 365	4 131	7 586	16 161	31 875	65 087	81 154	32 579
1960–62	266 849	7 409	1 103	527	444	591	700	2 147	5 576	14 389	31 083	63 543	93 548	45 789
1970–72	284 181	5 677	1 020	562	396	620	806	1 814	4 585	13 417	31 222	65 817	96 952	61 293
1980–82	290 026	3 064	511	301	365	635	670	1 821	3 740	10 420	27 606	63 023	103 676	74 194
1969	282 817	6 060	1 075	498	352	634	810	1 856	5 065	13 602	32 596	67 219	96 021	57 029
1970	282 141	5 998	1 011	538	401	570	849	1 802	4 715	13 292	31 577	66 219	95 917	59 252
1971	278 903	5 746	976	568	419	631	787	1 836	4 528	13 274	30 760	64 017	94 958	60 403
1972	291 500	5 288	1 073	579	367	658	783	1 804	4 512	13 686	31 330	67 215	99 980	64 225
1973	290 932	4 808	896	510	393	681	740	1 876	4 362	13 611	29 872	67 137	100 293	65 753
1974	289 977	4 322	827	505	442	630	688	1 785	4 291	13 828	29 471	66 992	99 398	66 798
1975	288 667	4 058	716	463	354	632	711	1 921	4 180	13 053	29 192	65 822	100 000	67 565
1976	298 458	3 455	593	451	417	623	671	1 939	4 041	12 806	29 605	67 107	104 673	72 077
1977	286 155	3 322	614	373	394	616	702	1 870	3 883	11 929	28 828	64 903	100 536	68 185
1978	290 396	3 368	607	417	421	691	710	2 042	4 004	11 911	28 607	65 411	102 058	70 149
1979	295 157	3 447	527	368	386	622	635	1 938	3 868	11 671	28 624	65 646	104 807	72 618
1980	289 516	3 428	518	349	373	667	696	1 861	3 771	10 757	27 857	64 087	102 728	72 424
1981	288 868	2 902	529	302	368	650	642	1 821	3 742	10 513	27 211	62 762	103 554	73 872
1982	291 695	2 861	485	253	353	588	672	1 781	3 708	9 990	27 751	62 221	104 745	76 287
1983	290 189	2 727	489	269	332	629	597	1 655	3 708	9 786	27 792	59 913	104 844	77 448
1984	284 524	2 594	454	260	302	575	621	1 676	3 658	9 343	27 764	57 813	102 744	76 720
1985	298 407	2 631	497	260	308	544	630	1 583	3 803	9 111	27 664	59 285	108 099	83 992
1986	293 309	2 589	491	248	272	562	674	1 646	3 834	8 761	25 785	58 360	106 463	83 624
1987	286 817	2 635	489	237	246	525	639	1 708	3 897	8 774	25 000	56 858	103 354	82 455
1988	290 477	2 621	498	232	218	542	650	1 670	4 025	8 448	24 104	56 567	103 666	87 236

1 In some years the totals include a small number of persons whose age was not stated.

Source *Office of Population Censuses and Surveys*

2.19 (continued) Deaths: analysis by age and sex

Scotland

Annual averages or calendar years

Number

	All ages[1]	Under 1 year	1–4	5–9	10–14	15–19	20–24	25–34	35–44	45–54	55–64	65–74	75–84	85 and over
Males														
1900–02	40 224	9 189	4 798	1 083	672	1 069	1 292	2 506	2 935	3 591	4 597	4 531	3 117	834
1910–12	35 981	7 510	3 935	962	595	826	910	1 969	2 469	3 325	4 356	5 113	3 182	813
1920–22	34 649	6 757	2 847	710	489	747	791	1 616	2 128	3 314	4 785	5 624	3 928	911
1930–32	32 476	4 426	1 771	610	365	568	706	1 352	1 848	2 979	5 095	6 906	4 839	1 010
1940–42	36 384	3 973	1 011	449	321	668	888	1 643	2 090	3 348	5 728	8 556	6 317	1 337
1950–52	32 236	1 949	349	175	105	200	265	693	1 267	3 151	5 574	8 544	8 094	1 871
1960–62	32 401	1 578	222	121	102	146	185	456	1 013	2 986	6 682	8 505	7 980	2 425
1970–72	32 446	944	168	119	93	178	233	396	875	2 617	6 641	10 176	7 383	2 624
1980–82	31 723	451	80	56	71	206	233	423	776	2 280	5 601	10 152	8 804	2 591
1969	32 631	1 099	174	121	109	184	216	401	936	2 564	6 946	9 851	7 381	2 649
1970	32 538	1 010	186	125	90	161	232	403	891	2 604	6 923	9 987	7 266	2 660
1971	31 585	988	155	100	114	197	242	371	832	2 588	6 427	9 945	7 134	2 492
1972	33 215	833	162	133	76	176	226	413	902	2 658	6 573	10 596	7 748	2 719
1973	32 954	841	171	117	76	175	225	381	839	2 789	6 435	10 693	7 603	2 609
1974	32 722	748	148	97	83	202	183	403	953	2 739	6 205	10 757	7 505	2 699
1975	32 168	669	113	112	104	195	216	411	838	2 634	5 994	10 727	7 617	2 538
1976	32 983	568	110	84	97	204	212	448	811	2 621	6 109	10 926	8 146	2 647
1977	31 280	585	103	81	75	181	236	432	817	2 494	5 835	10 173	7 802	2 466
1978	32 432	479	87	63	78	211	210	479	854	2 508	5 888	10 734	8 299	2 542
1979	32 884	490	79	79	71	219	215	442	805	2 599	5 851	10 804	8 543	2 687
1980	31 669	481	93	65	78	190	223	421	778	2 316	5 628	10 248	8 571	2 577
1981	31 700	435	71	50	66	208	250	439	816	2 330	5 506	10 193	8 788	2 548
1982	31 801	436	77	53	69	220	225	410	733	2 195	5 669	10 015	9 052	2 647
1983	31 196	380	67	53	65	185	178	406	764	2 131	5 769	9 414	9 204	2 580
1984	30 731	389	87	53	65	172	202	429	696	2 017	5 493	9 337	9 222	2 569
1985	31 147	342	57	49	58	174	208	390	759	1 959	5 486	9 339	9 569	2 757
1986	31 111	334	66	44	49	177	238	436	757	1 967	5 354	9 169	9 574	2 946
1987	30 384	331	54	46	47	163	212	415	779	1 870	5 131	9 058	9 383	2 895
1988	30 195	324	64	39	42	181	246	475	808	1 915	4 997	8 763	9 314	3 027
Females														
1900–02	39 891	7 143	4 477	1 162	747	1 058	1 246	2 625	2 732	3 130	4 485	5 273	4 305	1 508
1910–12	36 132	5 854	3 674	981	618	836	910	2 149	2 473	2 909	3 960	5 636	4 588	1 552
1920–22	34 449	5 029	2 602	687	489	711	889	1 947	2 266	2 828	4 157	5 587	5 443	1 814
1930–32	32 377	3 319	1 602	527	339	568	666	1 508	1 812	2 731	4 380	6 630	6 178	2 117
1940–42	33 715	2 852	921	373	283	595	656	1 382	1 672	2 528	4 630	7 674	7 613	2 536
1950–52	31 525	1 432	284	115	84	185	293	714	1 127	2 188	4 204	8 157	9 310	3 431
1960–62	30 559	1 107	170	80	63	72	87	287	762	1 897	4 115	7 752	9 991	4 177
1970–72	30 978	694	118	69	46	73	74	231	608	1 769	4 036	7 823	10 112	5 324
1980–82	32 326	337	49	37	44	74	73	213	493	1 456	3 565	7 781	11 333	6 871
1969	31 190	803	156	56	58	66	85	212	647	1 817	4 168	8 014	10 003	5 105
1970	31 102	704	129	82	50	77	92	244	632	1 804	4 108	7 814	10 158	5 209
1971	30 029	734	107	64	60	64	62	214	590	1 720	4 000	7 603	9 686	5 125
1972	31 802	644	117	62	29	79	67	234	602	1 783	4 001	8 052	10 493	5 639
1973	31 591	571	105	77	46	91	80	224	604	1 796	3 890	7 930	10 355	5 822
1974	32 018	578	109	59	48	73	90	217	613	1 741	3 979	8 037	10 440	6 034
1975	30 957	499	104	56	33	84	77	228	580	1 625	3 792	7 750	10 250	5 879
1976	32 270	391	86	48	49	69	88	235	567	1 708	3 916	7 961	10 795	6 357
1977	31 014	419	73	45	41	97	100	214	557	1 578	3 671	7 761	10 628	5 830
1978	32 691	351	73	37	61	93	86	236	598	1 651	3 871	8 208	11 028	6 398
1979	32 863	388	69	37	58	59	81	247	551	1 635	3 776	8 045	11 309	6 608
1980	31 630	350	51	41	44	77	90	222	547	1 511	3 587	7 673	10 988	6 449
1981	32 128	345	46	35	43	68	69	213	453	1 414	3 556	7 935	11 144	6 807
1982	33 221	317	50	35	45	78	60	203	479	1 444	3 552	7 735	11 867	7 356
1983	32 258	266	51	33	33	67	76	201	504	1 317	3 568	7 558	11 340	7 244
1984	31 614	283	62	32	37	72	78	205	475	1 320	3 703	6 979	11 134	7 234
1985	32 820	282	55	37	34	63	76	207	481	1 179	3 563	7 449	11 604	7 790
1986	32 356	247	50	16	24	50	77	188	441	1 181	3 372	7 251	11 476	7 983
1987	31 630	232	44	21	34	60	70	195	429	1 160	3 301	7 032	11 262	7 790
1988	31 762	219	33	22	21	54	63	197	470	1 115	3 250	6 879	11 361	8 078

1 In some years the totals include a small number of persons whose age was not stated.

Source *General Register Office (Scotland)*

2.19 Deaths: analysis by age and sex
(*continued*)

Northern Ireland

Annual averages or calendar years

Number

	All ages[1]	Under 1 year	1–4	5–9	10–14	15–19	20–24	25–34	35–44	45–54	55–64	65–74	75–84	85 and over
Males														
1900–02	11 554	1 958	985	280	206	367	446	779	669	832	1 413	1 666	1 368	585
1910–12	10 469	1 697	841	222	152	282	311	569	679	836	1 148	2 011	1 287	434
1920–22	9 622	1 491	596	191	150	258	334	496	570	869	1 159	1 749	1 324	435
1930–32	8 626	1 083	406	126	90	154	209	375	437	740	1 313	1 988	1 317	388
1940–42	9 383	1 258	322	117	102	153	202	379	462	751	1 290	2 305	1 637	405
1950–52	8 197	658	105	55	36	50	77	179	318	671	1 169	2 117	2 178	583
1960–62	8 080	499	67	38	27	49	48	108	216	623	1 419	2 037	2 131	816
1970–72	8 786	396	58	40	32	76	83	115	221	643	1 590	2 493	2 157	881
1980–82	8 420	211	37	20	26	77	92	144	202	539	1 414	2 518	2 346	795
1969	8 608	464	55	38	29	50	56	111	228	666	1 556	2 443	2 122	790
1970	8 764	434	55	37	34	40	63	93	228	633	1 635	2 565	2 105	842
1971	8 593	404	56	39	30	67	78	107	220	608	1 531	2 392	2 142	919
1972	9 001	350	63	44	32	121	109	145	216	689	1 604	2 523	2 223	882
1973	9 288	343	64	44	37	134	152	236	236	722	1 559	2 573	2 269	919
1974	9 226	295	64	41	43	111	119	176	273	737	1 615	2 630	2 216	906
1975	8 664	293	43	40	46	92	105	205	233	659	1 499	2 465	2 157	827
1976	8 869	259	50	38	33	114	119	174	237	593	1 546	2 654	2 216	836
1977	8 871	246	46	28	29	91	112	162	240	693	1 524	2 631	2 239	830
1978	8 458	228	40	35	32	80	84	140	209	624	1 517	2 456	2 208	805
1979	8 822	226	28	27	31	96	105	144	241	622	1 507	2 604	2 392	799
1980	8 832	222	31	27	35	87	104	162	210	568	1 495	2 653	2 430	808
1981	8 423	205	49	20	27	66	93	141	193	521	1 406	2 568	2 319	815
1982	8 004	205	31	12	17	77	78	129	203	528	1 341	2 332	2 289	762
1983	8 209	196	24	25	30	69	86	124	192	475	1 409	2 433	2 303	843
1984	8 007	163	28	22	14	52	69	133	217	517	1 318	2 355	2 308	811
1985	8 088	151	33	16	22	64	85	109	193	519	1 312	2 424	2 310	850
1986	8 155	161	14	15	15	70	83	128	188	477	1 361	2 381	2 348	914
1987	7 721	137	25	22	19	60	102	143	191	402	1 177	2 269	2 330	844
1988[2]	7 993	137	29	20	16	65	112	141	197	400	1 213	2 260	2 462	941
Females														
1900–02	12 735	1 537	1 013	317	277	495	521	1 012	902	1 075	1 612	1 876	1 484	614
1910–12	11 397	1 369	808	249	218	325	365	785	811	961	1 282	2 328	1 402	494
1920–22	10 415	1 149	547	193	188	299	331	687	713	939	1 236	1 976	1 639	518
1930–32	9 044	824	380	125	102	184	226	475	539	774	1 293	2 046	1 541	535
1940–42	9 229	910	305	105	90	159	174	409	490	688	1 207	2 246	1 873	572
1950–52	7 896	494	87	33	21	37	59	173	276	526	996	1 976	2 384	834
1960–62	7 463	371	61	20	15	21	24	70	175	434	880	1 823	2 417	1 151
1970–72	7 809	295	45	23	17	25	20	65	152	408	919	1 959	2 475	1 407
1980–82	7 917	160	26	17	17	23	29	65	127	329	881	1 813	2 752	1 678
1969	7 730	326	49	25	13	14	23	57	162	405	961	1 973	2 361	1 361
1970	7 787	300	41	28	16	15	16	72	154	431	967	2 000	2 410	1 337
1971	7 609	318	46	17	14	26	17	55	149	364	861	1 882	2 412	1 448
1972	8 031	266	48	24	20	33	28	69	153	428	929	1 994	2 603	1 436
1973	8 381	267	59	23	16	31	27	66	179	415	971	2 000	2 745	1 582
1974	8 101	272	45	17	13	33	27	68	134	403	892	1 900	2 654	1 643
1975	7 847	241	40	21	18	35	25	62	137	376	920	1 887	2 588	1 497
1976	8 161	224	56	17	18	32	27	90	129	398	947	1 882	2 778	1 563
1977	8 050	192	33	13	15	37	37	64	143	398	896	1 909	2 708	1 605
1978	7 695	189	35	26	15	34	27	65	117	352	875	1 814	2 644	1 502
1979	7 989	191	21	23	18	20	22	59	125	361	874	1 919	2 743	1 613
1980	8 003	160	27	19	25	27	25	74	142	315	905	1 912	2 745	1 627
1981	7 833	155	24	15	13	20	26	49	114	348	858	1 779	2 760	1 672
1982	7 914	164	26	16	12	23	35	73	125	325	880	1 749	2 750	1 736
1983	7 830	133	28	16	9	23	25	58	106	281	837	1 795	2 756	1 763
1984	7 685	128	21	12	5	18	23	51	136	284	795	1 640	2 770	1 802
1985	7 867	114	22	17	13	19	23	62	113	291	783	1 771	2 742	1 897
1986	7 910	125	20	11	11	23	18	48	112	269	797	1 702	2 724	2 050
1987	7 613	105	17	7	8	29	24	71	128	243	736	1 680	2 650	1 915
1988[2]	7 820	111	22	10	12	16	32	48	120	324	800	1 574	2 704	2 047

1 In some years the totals include a small number of persons whose age was not stated.

2 Provisional.

Source *General Register Office (Northern Ireland)*

2.20 Deaths analysed by cause

England and Wales

International Statistical Classification of Diseases, Injuries and Causes of Death, Ninth Revision 1979

Number

	Code numbers	1981	1982	1983	1984[1]	1985	1986[2]	1987	1988
Infections and Total deaths		577 890	581 861	579 608	566 881	590 734	581 203	563 546	567 987
Deaths from natural causes[3]		558 102	562 251	560 599	548 046	571 725	562 449	545 723	550 051
Infections and parasitic diseases	001 – 139	2 102	2 116	2 043	2 295	2 381	2 470	2 375	2 480
Intestinal infectious diseases	001 – 009	194	206	177	193	177	176	162	164
Tuberculosis of respiratory system	010 – 012	432	454	375	376	408	376	329	384
Other tuberculosis, including late effects	013 – 018, 137	332	296	324	377	366	357	296	334
Whooping cough	033	5	14	5	1	4	3	5	–
Meningococcal infection	036	85	70	70	79	97	141	155	174
Measles	055	15	13	16	10	11	10	6	16
Malaria	084	2	10	7	4	5	3	7	6
Syphilis	090 – 097	55	46	47	68	40	38	35	29
Neoplasms	140 – 239	131 691	132 448	134 270	140 101	141 618	140 801	142 451	144 260
Malignant neoplasm of stomach	151	10 652	10 211	10 502	10 360	9 971	9 714	9 509	9 425
Malignant neoplasm of trachea, bronchus and lung	162	34 727	34 832	35 572	35 739	35 792	35 257	35 138	35 302
Malignant neoplasm of breast	174 – 175	12 597	12 492	12 759	13 409	13 592	13 746	13 840	13 723
Malignant neoplasm of uterus	179 – 182	3 537	3 512	3 464	3 381	3 494	3 466	3 377	3 418
Leukaemia	204 – 208	3 349	3 462	3 481	3 572	3 696	3 572	3 650	3 683
Benign and unspecified neoplasms	210 – 229, 239	1 240	1 532	956	1 358	1 346	1 311	1 283	1 288
Endocrine, nutritional and metabolic diseases and immunity disorders	240 – 279	6 195	5 963	6 153	8 499	9 798	10 158	9 810	10 106
Diabetes mellitus	250	4 626	4 534	4 516	6 369	7 452	7 912	7 637	7 850
Nutritional deficiencies	260 – 269	124	91	107	104	130	123	74	106
Other metabolic and immunity disorders[5]	270 – 279	849	770	914	1 077	1 270	1 253	1 368	1 376
Diseases of blood and blood-forming organs	280 – 289	1 588	1 588	1 512	2 100	2 422	2 366	2 323	2 370
Anaemias	280 – 285	1 134	1 035	949	1 363	1 522	1 409	1 329	1 245
Mental disorders	290 – 319	3 441	3 757	4 142	10 744	12 011	12 410	12 437	13 234
Diseases of nervous system and sense organs	320 – 389	6 975	7 558	7 624	10 483	11 414	11 182	10 953	11 220
Meningitis	320 – 322	266	286	281	246	306	271	260	230
Diseases of the circulatory system	390 – 459	286 258	284 246	282 815	278 849	287 054	278 749	271 061	267 927
Rheumatic heart disease	390 – 398	3 120	2 904	2 884	2 931	2 889	2 616	—	2 543
Hypertensive disease	401 – 405	5 413	5 160	4 725	4 644	4 581	4 173	3 760	3 578
Ischaemic heart disease	410 – 414	155 196	154 605	156 550	157 506	163 104	158 667	155 235	153 084
Diseases of pulmonary circulation and other forms of heart disease	415 – 429	32 751	32 259	30 529	22 425	22 835	21 930	21 112	21 202
Cerebrovascular disease	430 – 438	69 651	69 028	67 785	71 470	73 219	71 454	69 450	68 599
Diseases of the respiratory system	460 – 519	83 507	88 111	86 633	56 828	64 607	63 052	57 075	60 483
Influenza	487	626	716	796	346	662	587	190	285
Pneumonia	480 – 486	54 057	56 529	55 513	24 687	27 931	27 624	24 603	26 424
Bronchitis, emphysema	490 – 492	17 530	17 297	15 410	14 009	14 255	12 119	9 821	9 188
Asthma	493	1 603	1 577	1 645	1 764	1 972	1 990	1 898	2 006
Diseases of the digestive system	520 – 579	16 447	16 456	15 838	16 980	18 148	17 974	17 669	17 954
Ulcer of stomach and duodenum	531 – 533	4 457	4 608	4 259	4 483	4 861	4 528	4 307	4 279
Appendicitis	540 – 543	164	155	136	147	147	137	115	136
Hernia of abdominal cavity and other intestinal obstruction	550 – 553, 560	1 959	1 908	1 861	1 947	2 001	2 013	1 900	1 991
Chronic liver disease and cirrhosis	571	2 212	2 152	2 184	2 280	2 582	2 527	2 709	2 801
Diseases of the genito-urinary system	580 – 629	7 970	8 132	7 830	7 731	8 012	7 926	7 696	7 589
Nephritis, nephrotic syndrome and nephrosis	580 – 589	4 766	4 950	4 742	4 391	4 640	4 556	4 488	4 381
Hyperplasia of prostate	600	749	694	621	689	668	585	530	483
Complications of pregnancy, childbirth, etc.	630 – 676	57	42	54	52	46	45	46	41
Abortion	630 – 639	10	6	8	6	9	3	5	7
Diseases of the skin and subcutaneous tissue	680 – 709	516	493	505	601	670	743	734	772
Diseases of the musculo-skeletal system	710 – 739	3 112	3 224	3 241	4 943	5 452	5 448	5 192	5 406
Congenital anomalies	740 – 759	3 039	3 037	2 944	3 017	2 909	1 871	1 794	1 697
Certain conditions originating in the perinatal period	760 – 779	2 659	2 464	2 422	2 289	2 293	225	198	248
Birth trauma, hypoxia, birth asphyxia and other respiratory conditions	767 – 770	1 445	1 336	1 268	1 243	1 293	85	78	90
Signs, symptoms and ill-defined conditions	780 – 799[6]	2 545	2 616	2 573	2 534	2 890	3 540	3 909	4 264
Sudden infant death syndrome	798 – 0	1 085	1 156	1 133	1 118	1 195	1 315	1 375	1 422
Deaths from accidents and violence[3]	E800 – E999	19 788	19 610	19 009	18 835	19 009	18 754	17 823	17 936
All accidents	E800 – E929	..[4]	13 297	12 823	12 603	12 475	12 369	11 524	11 288
Motor vehicle accidents	E810 – E825	..[4]	5 310	5 146	5 090	4 914	4 900	4 836	4 559
Suicide and self-inflicted injury	E950 – E959	4 419	4 279	4 279	4 315	4 419	4 126	3 986	4 220
All other external causes	E930 – E949, E960 – E999	..[4]	2 034	1 907	1 917	2 115	2 259	2 313	2 428

1 Changes in OPCS coding of underlying cause of death (from 1 January 1984) have led to some differences in the pattern of causes of death for 1984 onwards as compared with previous years.

2 On 1 January 1986, a new certificate for deaths within the first 28 days of life was introduced. It is not possible to assign one underlying cause of death from this certificate. The 'cause' figures in this table for 1986 exclude all deaths at ages under 28 days.

3 Within certain main categories only selected causes of death are shown.

4 Industrial action meant that information supplied by coroners about accidental and violent deaths, except suicides, was not available.

5 Deaths assigned to AIDS & AIDS related diseases are included in ICD 270 279.

Source Office of Population Censuses and Surveys

2.20 Deaths analysed by cause
Scotland

(continued) *International Statistical Classification of Diseases, Injuries and Causes of Death, Ninth Revision, 1979*

Number

	Code numbers	1981	1982	1983	1984[1]	1985	1986	1987	1988
Total deaths		63 828	65 022	63 454	62 345	63 967	63 467	62,014	61,957
Deaths from natural causes[2]		60 749	61 940	60 612	59 519	61 148	60 562	59,328	
Infectious and parasitic diseases	001–139	284	283	279	259	278	268	250	253
Intestinal infectious diseases	001–009							7	10
Tuberculosis of respiratory system	010–012	68	50	48	46	47	41	29	41
Other tuberculosis, including late effects	013–018, 137	54	65	52	39	57	47	47	36
Whooping cough	033	1	2	–	–	–	–	–	–
Meningococcal infection	036	5	10	–	7	9	11	17	9
Measles	055	2	2	4	3	1	–	–	–
Malaria	084	–	1	–	1	–	1	1	–
Syphilis	090–097	6	2	4	2	2	3	1	2
Neoplasms	140–239	14 083	14 247	14 377	14 456	14 618	14 686	14 793	14 889
Malignant neoplasm of stomach	151	1 095	1 057	1 003	970	1 010	961	985	946
Malignant neoplasm of trachea, bronchus and lung	162	4 114	4 116	4 178	4 225	4 307	4 149	4 290	4 144
Malignant neoplasm of breast	174–175	1 182	1 236	1 271	1 248	1 264	1 326	1 245	1 268
Malignant neoplasm of uterus	179–182	328	331	359	379	353	334	327	313
Leukaemia	204–208	285	302	307	306	352	315	312	318
Benign neoplasms	210–229, 239	111	130	122	109	113	116	111	129
Endocrine, nutritional and metabolic diseases and immunity disorders	240–279	872	818	779	669	723	707	730	691
Diabetes mellitus	250	652	591	558	477	534	518	540	501
Nutritional deficiencies	260–269	30	19	16	24	21	15	12	15
Other metabolic and immunity disorders	270–279	112	138	139	106	121	116 (129)	129	126
Diseases of blood and blood-forming organs	280–289	170	162	164	149	181	167	190	175
Anaemias	280–285	106	102	94	89	83	89	89	90
Mental disorders	290–319	561	640	629	645	965	949	918	1 005
Diseases of nervous system and sense organs	320–389	749	728	801	776	810	827	788	864
Meningitis	320–322	27	25	35	25	18	20	22	25
Diseases of the circulatory system	390–459	33 214	33 279	32 243	31 489	32 319	31 424	31 057	30 511
Rheumatic heart disease	390–398	318	336	306	275	252	258	242	254
Hypertensive disease	401–405	484	498	430	411	391	372	324	304
Ischaemic heart disease	410–414	18 453	18 633	18 335	18 107	18 758	18 138	18 405	17 963
Diseases of pulmonary circulation and other forms of heart disease	415–429	2 845	2 907	2 782	2 549	2 620	2 337	2 222	2 183
Cerebrovascular disease	430–438	9 190	8 996	8 594	8 378	8 505	8 590	8 225	8 150
Diseases of the respiratory system	460–519	6 546	7 528	7 253	7 099	7 156	7 469	6 793	6 724
Influenza	487	54	235	178	59	54	121	36	25
Pneumonia	480–486	3 676	4 195	4 037	3 974	3 880	4 113	3 750	3 691
Bronchitis, emphysema	490–492	1 365	1 390	1 081	1 009	969	791	632	558
Asthma	493	143	196	163	157	146	152	159	152
Diseases of the digestive system	520–579	2 185	2 116	2 077	2 015	2 038	2 011	1 915	1 925
Ulcer of stomach and duodenum	531–533	482	491	481	475	470	448	422	359
Appendicitis	540–543	20	13	14	13	18	6	8	11
Hernia of abdominal cavity	550–553, 560	188	207	207	189	201	165	166	193
Chronic liver disease and cirrhosis	571	450	422	431	423	423	380	401	429
Diseases of the genito-urinary system	580–629	871	933	892	804	897	887	842	810
Nephritis, nephrotic syndrome and nephrosis	580–589	519	572	557	513	555	538	514	525
Hyperplasia of prostate	600	40	36	41	37	37	41	34	25
Complications of pregnancy, childbirth, etc.	630–676	13	6	8	8	9	7	2	8
Abortion	630–639	1	–	2	1	1	2	–	1
Diseases of the skin and subcutaneous tissue	680–709	43	51	57	70	89	86	79	76
Diseases of the musculo-skeletal system	710–739	264	245	262	239	269	289	252	318
Congenital anomalies	740–759	297	293	298	291	265	224	225	237
Certain conditions originating in the perinatal period	760–779	324	324	245	278	246	250	230	210
Birth trauma, hypoxia, birth asphyxia and other respiratory conditions	767–770	183	173	143	160	122	142	131	123
Signs, symptoms and ill-defined conditions	780–799[3]	273	287	248	272	285	311	264	297
Sudden infant death syndrome	798.0	157	150	127	137	139	153 (136)	136	134
Deaths from accidents and violence[2]	E800–E999	3 079	3 082	2 842	2 826	2 819	2 905	2 686	2 964
All accidents	E800–E929	2 254	2 245	2 085	2 050	1 981	2 055	1 858	2 020
Motor vehicle accidents	E810–E825	725	741	644	612	609	608	582	561
Suicide and self-inflicted injuries	E950–E959	516	561	505	519	569	568	522	598
All other external causes	E930–E949, E960–E999	309	267	252	257	269	282	306	346

1 See page 37.
3 See page 5.
2 Within certain main categories only selected causes of death are shown.

Source General Register Office (Scotland)

2.20 Deaths analysed by cause

Northern Ireland

(continued) *International Statistical Classification of Diseases, Injuries and Causes of Death, Ninth Revision, 1979*

Number

	Code numbers	1981	1982	1983	1984	1985	1986[1]	1987	1988[2]
Total deaths		16 256	15 918	16 039	15 692	15 955	16 065	15 334	15 813
Deaths from natural causes[1]		15 400	15 109	15 208	14 951	15 209	15 335	14 572	14 979
Infectious and parasitic diseases	001–139	74	72	57	42	43	38	63	45
Intestinal infectious diseases	001–009							–	3
Tuberculosis of respiratory system	010–012	18	10	12	10	16	11	13	7
Other tuberculosis, including late effects	013–018, 137	4	2	2	6	2	3	1	2
Whooping cough	033	–	–	–	–	–	–	–	–
Meningococcal infection	036	2	2	7	2	5	1	6	2
Measles	055	2	–	1	–	–	1	1	1
Malaria	084	–	–	–	–	–	–	–	–
Syphilis	090–097	1	2	1	–	1	–	–	1
Neoplasms	140–239	3 063	3 102	3 170	3 327	3 254	3 282	3 417	3 409
Malignant neoplasm of stomach	151	259	272	257	240	231	243	239	241
Malignant neoplasm of trachea, bronchus and lung	162	689	690	691	788	761	736	759	777
Malignant neoplasm of breast	174–175	296	269	284	304	308	294	312	317
Malignant neoplasm of uterus	179–182	83	89	88	67	62	78	73	64
Leukaemia	204–208	85	99	73	108	86	77	83	83
Benign neoplasms and neoplasms of unspecified nature	210–229, 239	40	28	21	22	14	40	42	47
Endocrine, nutritional and metabolic diseases	240–279	137	117	151	225	119	116	78	73
Diabetes mellitus	250	103	93	120	192	91	85	57	46
Nutritional deficiencies	260–269	3	–	–	3	2	–	1	1
Other metabolic and immunity disorders	270–279	15	15	21	22	17	22	16	19
Diseases of blood and blood-forming organs	280–289	45	30	43	42	31	24	27	18
Anaemias	280–285	30	23	26	29	16	13	14	8
Mental disorders	290–319	37	29	42	33	13	64	35	35
Diseases of nervous system and sense organs	320–389	192	189	238	221	166	163	174	152
Meningitis	320–322	10	8	7	8	8	4	4	4
Diseases of the circulatory system	390–459	8 655	8 093	8 234	8 099	8 031	8 064	7 602	7 774
Rheumatic heart disease	390–398	66	67	48	60	55	59	53	47
Hypertensive disease	401–405	121	95	95	97	57	62	69	49
Ischaemic heart disease	410–414	4 909	4 563	4 785	4 825	4 736	4 686	4 538	4 747
Diseases of pulmonary circulation and other forms of heart disease	415–429	1 068	1 028	867	784	884	874	796	834
Cerebrovascular disease	430–438	2 111	1 982	2 079	1 966	1 941	2 008	1 818	1 708
Diseases of the respiratory system	460–519	2 111	2 364	2 207	1 936	2 511	2 581	2 269	2 568
Influenza	487	24	15	42	15	28	23	2	9
Pneumonia	480–486	1 263	1 523	1 368	1 150	1 651	1 730	1 510	1 678
Bronchitis, emphysema	490–492	334	301	270	209	184	168	158	179
Asthma	493	45	48	55	43	49	64	50	55
Diseases of the digestive system	520–579	421	442	434	424	420	400	368	358
Ulcer of stomach and duodenum	531–533	121	112	103	101	96	83	77	88
Appendicitis	540–543	4	5	3	3	4	2	3	1
Hernia of abdominal cavity and other intestinal obstruction	550–553, 560	46	37	50	45	35	47	41	39
Chronic liver disease and cirrhosis	571	65	71	64	75	69	64	58	59
Diseases of the genito-urinary system	580–629	286	293	240	256	304	290	237	250
Nephritis, nephrotic syndrome and nephrosis	580–589	193	206	157	156	223	186	147	161
Hyperplasia of prostate	600	18	11	15	10	8	9	9	4
Complications of pregnancy, childbirth, etc.	630–676	1	2	4	3	–	–	1	1
Abortion	630–639	–	1	–	–	–	–	–	1
Diseases of the skin and subcutaneous tissue	680–709	14	13	11	15	12	15	28	40
Diseases of the musculo-skeletal system	710–739	48	26	58	54	36	40	46	50
Congenital anomalies	740–759	134	150	159	145	133	113	91	92
Certain conditions originating in the perinatal period	760–779	146	137	125	102	96	99	79	100
Birth trauma, hypoxia, birth asphyxia and other respiratory conditions	767–770	77	49	55	44	47	36	31	37
Signs, symptoms and ill-defined conditions	780–799[3]	36	50	35	27	40	47	57	44
Sudden infant death syndrome	798.0							16	10
Deaths from accidents and violence[1]	E800–E999	856	809	831	741	746	730	762	834
All accidents	E800–E929	600	591	572	532	527	487	542	516
Motor vehicle accidents	E810–E825	230	225	205	178	197	185	228	233
Suicide and self-inflicted injuries	E950–E959	90	93	142	109	117	145	86	153
All other external causes	E930–E949, E960–E999	166	125	117	100	102	98	134	138

1 Within certain main categories only selected causes of death are shown.
2 Provisional.
3 See page 5.

Source General Register Office (Northern Ireland)

2.21 Infant and maternal mortality

	Deaths of infants under 1 year of age per thousand live births												Maternal deaths per thousand live births[2]			
	United Kingdom			England and Wales[1]			Scotland			Northern Ireland						
	Total	Males	Females	Total	Males	Females	Total	Males	Females	Total	Males	Females	United Kingdom	England and Wales	Scotland	Northern Ireland
1900–02	142	156	128	146	160	131	124	136	111	113	123	103	4.71	4.67	4.74	6.03
1910–12	110	121	98	110	121	98	109	120	97	101	110	92	3.95	3.67	5.65	5.28
1920–22	82	92	71	80	90	69	94	106	82	86	95	77	4.37	4.03	6.36	5.62
1930–32	67	75	58	64	72	55	84	94	73	75	83	66	4.54	4.24	6.40	5.24
1940–42	59	66	51	55	62	48	77	87	66	80	89	70	3.29	2.74	4.50	3.79
1950–52	30	34	26	29	33	25	37	42	32	40	45	36	0.88	0.79	1.09	1.09
1960–62	22	25	19	22	24	19	26	30	22	27	30	24	0.36	0.36	0.37	0.43
1970–72	18	20	16	18	20	15	19	22	17	22	24	20	0.17	0.17	0.17	0.10
1980–82	12	13	10	11	13	10	12	13	10	13	15	12	0.09	0.09	0.14	0.06
1978	13.3	14.8	11.7	13.2	14.7	11.6	12.9	14.5	11.2	15.9	17.3	14.5	0.10	0.11	0.06	–
1979	12.9	14.4	11.3	12.8	14.4	11.1	12.8	13.9	11.8	14.8	15.6	13.9	0.11	0.12	0.10	0.04
1980	12.2	13.4	10.6	12.0	13.3	10.7	12.1	13.6	10.4	13.4	15.1	11.5	0.11	0.11	0.15	0.07
1981	11.2	12.7	9.5	11.1	12.6	9.4	11.3	12.3	10.2	13.2	14.7	11.6	0.09	0.09	0.19	0.04
1982	11.0	12.3	9.5	10.8	12.2	9.4	11.4	12.9	9.8	13.6	14.8	12.4	0.07	0.07	0.09	0.07
1983	10.1	11.3	8.9	10.1	11.3	8.9	9.9	11.3	8.5	12.1	13.9	10.1	0.09	0.09	0.12	0.15
1984	9.6	10.7	8.4	9.5	10.6	8.3	10.3	11.7	8.9	10.5	11.4	9.6	0.09[3]	0.08	0.12	0.11
1985	9.4	10.4	8.3	9.4	10.4	8.2	9.4	10.0	8.7	9.6	10.6	8.5	0.07[3]	0.07	0.13	–
1986	9.5	10.9	8.1	9.6	11.0	8.0	8.8	9.9	7.7	10.2	11.0	9.2	0.07	0.07	0.11	–
1987	9.1[3]	10.3[3]	7.9[3]	9.2	10.4	7.9	8.5	9.7	7.2	8.7[3]	9.6[3]	7.7[3]	0.06	0.07	0.03	0.04
1988	9.0[3]	10.2[3]	7.7[3]	9.0	10.3	7.7	8.2	9.5	6.8	8.7[3]	9.6[3]	8.2[3]	0.06	0.06	0.12	0.04

1 From 1937 to 1956 death rates are based on the births to which they relate in the current and preceding years.

2 Deaths in pregnancy and childbirth.

3 Provisional.

Sources *Office of Population Censuses and Surveys; General Register Office (Scotland); General Register Office (Northern Ireland)*

2.21 (continued)

Infant mortality
Analysis by sex and age of infant

Deaths per 1 000 live births

	1976	1977	1978	1979	1980	1981	1982	1983	1984	1985	1986	1987	1988[1]
Total													
United Kingdom:													
Still births[2]	9.7	9.5	8.5	7.9	7.2	6.6	6.2	5.8	5.7	5.5	5.3	5.0	4.9
Perinatal[2]	18.0	17.3	15.6	14.7	13.2	12.0	11.4	10.5	10.2	10.1	9.6	9.0	8.8
Neonatal	9.9	9.5	8.8	8.3	7.7	6.7	6.4	5.9	5.7	5.4	5.3	5.0	4.9
Post Neonatal	4.6	4.6	4.5	4.6	4.4	4.4	4.6	4.3	3.9	4.0	4.2	4.1	4.1
England and Wales:													
Still births[2]	9.7	9.4	8.5	8.0	7.2	6.6	6.3	5.7	5.7	5.5	5.3	5.0	4.9
Perinatal[2]	17.8	17.0	15.5	14.7	13.1	11.8	11.3	10.4	10.1	10.1	9.6	8.9	8.7
Neonatal	9.7	9.3	8.7	8.2	7.7	6.7	6.3	5.9	5.6	5.4	5.3	5.1	4.9
Post Neonatal	4.6	4.5	4.5	4.6	4.4	4.4	4.6	4.3	3.9	4.0	4.3	4.1	4.1
Scotland:													
Still births[2]	9.6	8.8	8.1	6.9	6.7	6.3	5.8	5.8	5.8	5.5	5.8	5.1	5.4
Perinatal[2]	18.3	18.3	15.4	14.1	13.1	11.6	11.5	10.6	11.0	9.8	10.2	8.9	8.9
Neonatal	10.3	11.3	8.8	8.7	7.8	6.9	7.1	5.8	6.4	5.5	5.2	4.7	4.5
Post Neonatal	4.5	4.8	4.1	4.2	4.3	4.4	4.3	4.1	3.9	3.9	3.6	3.8	3.7
Northern Ireland:													
Still births[2]	10.4	12.0	9.2	8.7	9.2	8.8	6.9	7.4	5.9	6.4	4.4	6.1	5.0
Perinatal[2]	22.3	21.1	18.1	16.6	15.6	15.3	13.3	13.1	10.8	11.1	9.5	9.8	9.3
Neonatal	13.3	10.7	10.5	9.4	8.0	8.3	7.8	7.3	6.7	5.6	6.0	4.8	5.4
Post Neonatal	5.0	6.6	5.4	5.4	5.4	4.9	5.9	4.8	3.8	4.0	4.2	3.8	3.6
Males													
United Kingdom:													
Perinatal[2]	19.4	18.3	16.5	15.7	14.3	12.8	12.3	11.3	11.1	11.2	10.4	9.7	9.5
Neonatal	11.3	10.7	9.7	9.4	8.6	7.7	7.2	6.5	6.4	5.9	6.0	5.7	5.5
Infant mortality	16.4	15.8	14.8	14.4	13.4	12.7	12.3	11.4	10.7	10.4	10.9	10.3	10.2
England and Wales:													
Perinatal[2]	19.2	18.1	16.4	15.7	14.2	12.8	12.2	11.2	11.0	11.3	10.4	9.8	9.4
Neonatal	11.1	10.4	9.6	9.4	8.5	7.7	7.1	6.5	6.3	6.0	6.0	5.7	5.5
Infant mortality	16.2	15.4	14.7	14.4	13.3	12.6	12.2	11.3	10.6	10.4	11.0	10.4	10.3
Scotland:													
Perinatal[2]	19.8	18.7	16.8	15.3	14.2	12.2	13.1	11.6	12.6	10.1	10.9	8.9	9.7
Neonatal	11.8	13.0	10.3	9.7	9.1	7.1	8.1	6.1	7.1	5.5	5.6	5.3	5.3
Infant mortality	17.0	18.3	14.5	13.9	13.6	12.3	12.9	11.3	11.7	10.0	9.9	9.7	9.5
Northern Ireland:													
Perinatal[2]	21.9	22.2	19.2	16.6	16.9	15.7	13.5	14.3	10.7	11.3	9.7	10.5	10.9
Neonatal	14.2	11.9	11.2	9.9	9.1	8.8	8.4	8.8	7.3	6.3	6.2	5.3	6.0
Infant mortality	19.1	18.7	17.3	15.6	15.1	14.7	14.8	13.9	11.4	10.6	11.0	9.6	9.6
Females													
United Kingdom:													
Perinatal[2]	16.5	16.1	14.7	13.6	12.0	11.0	10.4	9.7	9.2	9.1	8.8	8.1	8.0
Neonatal	8.4	8.2	7.7	7.1	6.8	5.8	5.6	5.2	4.9	4.8	4.6	4.3	4.3
Infant mortality	12.0	12.3	11.7	11.3	10.7	9.6	9.5	8.9	8.4	8.3	8.1	7.9	7.7
England and Wales:													
Perinatal[2]	16.2	15.8	14.7	13.5	12.0	10.9	10.3	9.6	9.1	8.9	8.7	8.0	8.0
Neonatal	8.2	8.0	7.7	7.0	6.8	5.6	5.4	5.2	4.8	4.8	4.5	4.3	4.3
Infant mortality	12.2	12.0	11.6	11.0	10.7	9.4	9.4	8.9	8.3	8.2	8.0	7.9	7.7
Scotland:													
Perinatal[2]	16.7	17.8	14.0	12.9	11.9	11.1	9.8	9.6	9.3	9.5	9.4	9.0	8.1
Neonatal	8.6	9.5	7.2	7.6	6.4	6.7	6.1	5.5	5.7	5.5	4.8	4.1	3.7
Infant mortality	12.5	13.8	11.2	11.8	10.4	10.2	9.8	8.5	8.9	8.7	7.7	7.2	6.8
Northern Ireland:													
Perinatal[2]	22.7	20.0	17.1	16.6	14.2	15.0	13.1	11.8	10.9	10.9	9.2	9.2	7.6
Neonatal	12.3	9.4	9.7	8.9	6.9	7.8	7.1	5.7	6.1	4.9	5.8	4.4	4.7
Infant mortality	17.5	15.6	14.5	13.9	11.5	11.6	12.4	10.1	9.6	8.5	9.2	7.7	8.2

1 Provisional.
2 Deaths per 1,000 live and stillbirths.

Sources *Office of Population Censuses and Surveys; General Register Office (Scotland); General Register Office (Northern Ireland)*

2.22 Death rates per 1 000 population[1]

Analysis by age and sex

United Kingdom

	All ages	0–4	5–9	10–14	15–19	20–24	25–34	35–44	45–54	55–64	65–74	75–84	85 and over
Males													
1900–02	18.4	57.0	4.1	2.4	3.7	5.0	6.6	11.0	18.6	35.0	69.9	143.6	289.6
1910–12	14.9	40.5	3.3	2.0	3.0	3.9	5.0	8.0	14.9	29.8	62.1	133.8	261.5
1920–22	13.5	33.4	2.9	1.8	2.9	3.9	4.5	6.9	11.9	25.3	57.8	131.8	259.1
1930–32	12.9	22.3	2.3	1.5	2.6	3.3	3.5	5.7	11.3	23.7	57.9	134.2	277.0
1940–42	..	..	..	..	..	..	..	..	..	..	..	..	..
1950–52	12.6	7.7	0.7	0.5	0.9	1.4	1.6	3.0	8.5	23.2	55.2	127.6	272.0
1960–62	12.5	6.4	0.5	0.4	0.9	1.1	1.1	2.5	7.4	22.2	54.4	123.4	251.0
1970–72	12.4	4.6	0.4	0.4	0.9	1.0	1.0	2.4	7.3	20.9	52.9	116.3	246.1
1980–82	12.1	3.2	0.3	0.3	0.8	0.9	0.9	1.9	6.3	18.2	46.7	107.1	224.9
1969	12.5	4.8	0.4	0.4	0.9	0.9	1.0	2.4	7.4	21.9	55.5	119.8	250.4
1970	12.3	4.8	0.4	0.4	0.9	1.0	1.0	2.3	7.2	21.4	54.0	119.0	253.4
1971	12.2	4.7	0.4	0.4	0.9	1.0	1.0	2.4	7.3	20.6	52.3	118.2	251.0
1972	12.6	4.4	0.4	0.4	0.9	1.0	1.0	2.4	7.5	21.0	53.8	119.8	248.0
1973	12.4	4.2	0.4	0.3	0.9	1.1	1.0	2.3	7.4	20.8	51.9	117.5	240.9
1974	12.3	4.2	0.4	0.3	0.9	1.0	1.0	2.3	7.4	20.6	51.6	115.3	240.3
1975	12.2	3.7	0.4	0.3	0.9	1.0	1.0	2.2	7.3	19.9	50.5	115.2	237.2
1976	12.5	3.5	0.3	0.3	0.9	1.0	1.0	2.2	7.2	20.1	51.0	117.5	246.0
1977	12.1	3.5	0.3	0.3	0.9	1.0	1.0	2.1	7.0	19.2	49.0	110.7	229.4
1978	12.3	3.4	0.3	0.3	0.9	1.0	1.0	2.1	7.0	19.3	49.3	111.8	232.0
1979	12.4	3.8	0.3	0.3	0.9	1.0	1.0	2.1	6.9	19.2	48.8	112.0	236.0
1980	12.1	3.4	0.3	0.3	0.8	0.9	0.9	2.0	6.5	18.7	47.2	108.6	227.0
1981	12.3	3.2	0.3	0.3	0.9	0.9	1.0	2.0	6.4	18.4	47.5	110.6	239.5
1982	12.0	2.9	0.3	0.3	0.8	0.9	0.9	1.8	6.1	17.9	46.4	106.4	225.0
1983	12.0	2.7	0.3	0.3	0.8	0.8	0.9	1.8	5.9	18.0	46.3	104.6	221.0
1984	11.7	2.6	0.3	0.3	0.7	0.9	0.9	1.7	5.7	17.5	44.9	100.9	212.8
1985	12.0	2.6	0.2	0.3	0.7	0.8	0.9	1.8	5.6	17.5	45.0	104.8	223.4
1986	11.8	2.6	0.2	0.2	0.7	0.9	0.9	1.7	5.5	17.0	43.6	102.0	217.1
1987[2]	11.5	2.5	0.2	0.3	0.7	0.9	0.9	1.7	5.2	16.4	42.0	97.3	194.3
1988[2]	11.5	2.5	0.2	0.3	0.7	0.9	0.9	1.7	5.1	16.0	41.2	96.6	193.9
Females													
1900–02	16.3	47.9	4.3	2.6	3.5	4.3	5.8	9.0	14.4	27.9	59.3	127.0	262.6
1910–12	13.3	34.0	3.3	2.1	2.9	3.4	4.4	6.7	11.5	23.1	50.7	113.7	234.0
1920–22	11.9	26.9	2.8	1.9	2.8	3.4	4.1	5.6	9.3	19.2	45.6	111.5	232.4
1930–32	11.5	17.7	2.1	1.5	2.4	2.9	3.3	4.6	8.3	17.6	43.7	110.1	246.3
1940–42	..	..	..	..	..	..	..	..	..	..	..	..	..
1950–52	11.2	6.0	0.5	0.4	0.7	1.0	1.4	2.3	5.3	12.9	35.5	98.4	228.8
1960–62	11.2	4.9	0.3	0.3	0.4	0.5	0.8	1.8	4.5	11.0	30.8	87.3	218.5
1970–72	11.3	3.6	0.3	0.2	0.4	0.4	0.6	1.6	4.5	10.5	27.5	76.7	196.1
1980–82	11.4	2.3	0.2	0.2	0.3	0.4	0.5	1.3	3.9	9.9	24.8	67.2	179.5
1969	11.3	3.7	0.3	0.2	0.4	0.4	0.6	1.8	4.5	10.8	29.1	78.1	203.2
1970	11.2	3.6	0.3	0.2	0.4	0.4	0.6	1.7	4.5	10.5	28.3	77.0	205.0
1971	11.1	3.6	0.3	0.2	0.4	0.4	0.6	1.6	4.4	10.4	26.9	76.6	209.1
1972	11.5	3.5	0.3	0.2	0.4	0.4	0.6	1.6	4.6	10.7	27.8	78.2	197.3
1973	11.5	3.2	0.3	0.2	0.4	0.4	0.6	1.6	4.5	10.5	27.1	76.5	192.5
1974	11.4	3.1	0.3	0.2	0.4	0.4	0.6	1.6	4.5	10.6	26.7	74.8	191.0
1975	11.3	3.0	0.2	0.2	0.4	0.4	0.6	1.5	4.4	10.4	26.0	73.4	188.3
1976	11.7	2.6	0.2	0.2	0.3	0.4	0.6	1.5	4.4	10.4	26.5	75.2	198.0
1977	11.3	2.7	0.2	0.2	0.4	0.4	0.5	1.5	4.2	10.1	25.5	71.0	183.1
1978	11.5	2.8	0.2	0.2	0.4	0.4	0.6	1.5	4.3	10.1	25.7	70.5	184.5
1979	11.6	2.8	0.2	0.2	0.3	0.4	0.6	1.4	4.3	10.2	25.6	70.8	187.1
1980	11.4	2.7	0.2	0.2	0.3	0.4	0.5	1.3	4.0	10.0	25.0	67.7	181.3
1981	11.6	2.5	0.2	0.2	0.3	0.4	0.5	1.3	3.9	10.0	25.5	70.4	190.6
1982	11.5	2.3	0.2	0.2	0.3	0.4	0.5	1.2	3.8	9.9	24.8	66.8	179.4
1983	11.4	2.1	0.2	0.2	0.3	0.3	0.5	1.2	3.6	9.8	24.7	65.1	177.2
1984	11.2	2.0	0.2	0.2	0.3	0.3	0.5	1.2	3.5	9.7	24.3	62.6	170.2
1985	11.7	2.0	0.2	0.2	0.3	0.3	0.5	1.2	3.4	9.9	24.7	64.8	178.4
1986	11.5	2.0	0.2	0.2	0.3	0.3	0.5	1.1	3.3	9.5	24.0	63.2	172.4
1987[2]	11.2	2.0	0.2	0.2	0.3	0.3	0.5	1.1	3.3	9.4	23.3	60.8	159.9
1988[2]	11.3	1.9	0.2	0.2	0.3	0.3	0.5	1.2	3.2	9.2	23.2	60.4	162.3

1 The figures 1974 to 1980 incorporate the revised intercensal estimates for England and Wales, and Northern Ireland, but the old series estimates for Scotland.

2 Provisional.

Sources *Office of Population Censuses and Surveys; General Register Office (Scotland); General Register Office (Northern Ireland)*

2.23 Life tables

United Kingdom

Age $_x$	Interim Life Table, 1985 – 87			
	Males		Females	
	l_x	$\mathring{e}_x$	l_x	$\mathring{e}_x$
0	100 000	71.9	100 000	77.6
5	98 760	67.8	99 031	73.4
10	98 654	62.9	98 947	68.5
15	98 527	57.9	98 861	63.5
20	98 179	53.1	98 720	58.6
25	97 762	48.4	98 564	53.7
30	97 366	43.5	98 375	48.8
35	96 884	38.7	98 090	43.9
40	96 238	34.0	97 663	39.1
45	95 172	29.3	96 951	34.4
50	93 324	24.9	95 742	29.8
55	90 119	20.7	93 753	25.3
60	84 654	16.8	90 457	21.2
65	75 996	13.4	85 215	17.3
70	63 897	10.5	77 639	13.7
75	48 418	8.0	66 793	10.5
80	31 224	6.0	52 113	7.8
85	15 916	4.5	34 002	5.5

England and Wales

Age $_x$	Interim Life Table, 1985 – 87			
	Males		Females	
	l_x	$\mathring{e}_x$	l_x	$\mathring{e}_x$
0	100 000	72.1	100 000	77.8
5	98 754	68.0	99 032	73.6
10	98 653	63.1	98 949	68.6
15	98 527	58.2	98 863	63.7
20	98 185	53.4	98 722	58.8
25	97 779	48.6	98 567	53.9
30	97 397	43.8	98 383	49.0
35	96 930	38.9	98 100	44.1
40	96 304	34.2	97 676	39.3
45	95 280	29.5	96 978	34.5
50	93 495	25.0	95 792	29.9
55	90 396	20.8	93 852	25.5
60	85 068	16.9	90 650	21.3
65	76 560	13.5	85 511	17.4
70	64 582	10.5	78 091	13.8
75	49 141	8.0	67 412	10.6
80	31 838	6.0	52 792	7.8
85	16 319	4.5	34 601	5.6

Scotland

Age $_x$	Interim Life Table, 1985 – 87			
	Males		Females	
	l_x	$\mathring{e}_x$	l_x	$\mathring{e}_x$
0	10 000	70.2	10 000	76.2
5	9 883	66.0	9 906	71.9
10	9 869	61.1	9 898	67.0
15	9 855	56.2	9 889	62.0
20	9 816	51.4	9 875	57.1
25	9 769	46.7	9 858	52.2
30	9 721	41.9	9 835	47.3
35	9 661	37.1	9 805	42.4
40	9 578	32.4	9 754	37.7
45	9 437	27.9	9 671	33.0
50	9 198	23.5	9 530	28.4
55	8 799	19.5	9 290	24.1
60	8 139	15.8	8 884	20.0
65	7 152	12.6	8 267	16.3
70	5 844	9.9	7 374	13.0
75	4 266	7.6	6 156	10.0
80	2 631	5.7	4 659	7.4
85	1 279	4.3	2 940	5.3

Northern Ireland

Age $_x$	Interim Life Table, 1985 – 87			
	Males		Females	
	l_x	$\mathring{e}_x$	l_x	$\mathring{e}_x$
0	10 000	70.4	10 000	76.6
5	9 872	66.3	9 893	72.5
10	9 858	61.4	9 883	67.5
15	9 846	56.4	9 876	62.6
20	9 806	51.6	9 861	57.7
25	9 751	46.9	9 845	52.8
30	9 697	42.2	9 822	47.9
35	9 638	37.4	9 795	43.0
40	9 568	32.7	9 754	38.2
45	9 730	28.1	9 676	33.5
50	9 216	23.7	9 553	28.9
55	8 809	19.7	9 336	24.5
60	8 190	16.0	8 974	20.3
65	7 226	12.7	8 425	16.5
70	5 929	9.9	7 627	12.9
75	4 376	7.6	6 455	9.8
80	2 755	5.6	4 881	7.1
85	1 316	4.0	2 997	5.0

Note Column l_x shows the number who would survive to exact age x, out of 100 000 or 10 000 born, who were subject throughout their lives to the death rates experienced in the three-year period indicated.
Column $\mathring{e}_x$ is 'the expectation of life', that is, the average future lifetime which would be lived by a person aged exactly x if likewise subject to the death rates experienced in the three-year period indicated. (See introductory note on page 5.)

Source *Government Actuary's Department*

3 Social Conditions

Government expenditure on social services and housing

The following tables of general government expenditure on the social services and housing in the United Kingdom comprise a summary table followed by separate tables for each of the social services and housing. The definition of government expenditure used in these tables follows that in Table 9.4 of *United Kingdom National Accounts 1989 Edition,* the CSO Blue Book, and covers both current and capital expenditure of the central government (including the National Insurance Fund) and local authorities. The housing table also includes the capital expenditure of public corporations concerned with housing. As in the Blue Book government expenditure is measured after deducting fees and charges for services. Expenditure on administration includes the cost of common services (accommodation, stationery and printing, superannuation, etc.) some of which is not directly borne by the departments administering each service. Transfers from one part of government to another have been eliminated to avoid double counting. The figures relate to years ended 31 March. Figures for the latest two years are the most recent estimates available and are subject to revision.

It should be noted that the figures no longer include imputed rents for the use of fixed assets owned and used by general government. In the Blue Book imputed rents have been replaced by capital consumption. Capital consumption, however, cannot be allocated to individual services and is therefore not included in these tables.

The following notes give brief descriptions of each of the main services shown in the tables.

Education
This covers expenditure by the Education Departments, local education authorities and the University Grants Committee on education in schools, training colleges, technical institutions and universities. It includes expenditure on school meals and milk.

The education statistics in Table 3.2 are provided by the Department of Education and Science. They are not normally able to provide a full set of estimates, from their sources, for the latest financial year. The CSO has in the past made estimates from a variety of sources but, following a review of their accuracy, it has been decided that they do not give a reliable guide to the final outcome and have therefore been withdrawn.

National health service
This covers expenditure by central government on hospital and community health, family practitioner and other health services. The expenditure by local authorities on the provision of health centres, health visiting, home nursing, ambulance services, vaccination and immunisation, etc., was transferred to central government on 1 April 1974. Only the net costs of providing these services are included in total government expenditure, receipts from patients being shown separately.

Personal social services
This covers local authority expenditure on the aged, handicapped and homeless, child care, care of mothers and young children, mental health, domestic help, etc. Also included are central government grants to voluntary approved schools.

Welfare foods
This covers the cost of providing welfare foods at reduced prices to children and expectant mothers. Only the net costs of providing these services are included in the total government expenditure, payments by the recipients of the services being shown separately.

Social security

This comprises both benefits under the Social Security schemes and non-contributory benefits and allowances, administered by the Department of Social Security. The analysis by type of Income Support is not exact; the estimates are derived from average numbers in receipt of benefit and average amounts paid. Unified housing benefit (rent rebates and allowances) is also included as social security expenditure and not as housing expenditure. This is now mainly administered by local authorities who receive grants from central government.

Housing
The table shows, in addition to government expenditure on housing, the capital expenditure of public corporations and the total expenditure of the public sector on housing. The government expenditure figures cover subsidies paid by the Housing Departments towards the provision of housing by local authorities, new town development corporations and housing associations; subsidies by local authorities to their housing revenue accounts; rent rebates for tenants of housing owned by local authorities and new towns; rent allowances for tenants of privately-owned housing; grants to persons for the reduction of mortgage interest payments; capital expenditure on the provision of houses for letting; capital grants to housing associations; grants by local authorities towards the cost of conversion and improvement of privately-owned houses; net lending by the central government and local authorities for private house purchase and improvement and loans for first time purchases. The public corporations' figures cover capital expenditure on the provision of houses for letting and lending by the Housing Corporation to housing associations.

Social Security

Tables 3.12 to 3.16, 3.20 to 3.28 give details of contributors and beneficiaries under the National Insurance and Industrial Injury Acts, supplementary benefits and war pensions.

There are three types of contributor:

Class 1 Employed persons, that is, persons working for employers. Their contributions are paid partly by themselves and partly by their employers. They are covered for all benefits.

Class 2 Self-employed persons, that is, persons working on their own account. They are covered for all benefits other than unemployment and industrial injuries.

Class 3 Non-employed persons, that is, persons who do not work for gain. They are covered for benefits other than unemployment, sickness, industrial injuries and maternity allowances.

Class 4 Payable, in addition to Class 2 by self-employed persons, and the amount payable is proportionate to profits or gains between a lower and upper limit in any one year.

An employer must pay a contribution for every employee whose earnings exceed a base level. Most employed persons pay the full employee's contribution, but retirement pensioners working for an employer do not and some married women and some widows who are working need not, unless they so wish, contribute except for industrial injuries benefit. Thus the total numbers in the analysis by benefit for which the contributions were payable are less than the total numbers in the analysis by class of contributor.

Sickness benefit and Invalidity (Tables 3.17 and 3.18)
The population at risk for sickness benefit is the working population apart from men over age 65 and women over age 60 who are retirement pensioners and all men over 70 and women over 65, members of the Armed Forces, mariners while at sea, most non-industrial civil servants and Post Office employees (who do not normally claim sickness benefit until an illness has lasted six months) and married women and certain widows who have chosen not to be insured for sickness benefit. The tables exclude periods of incapacity, covered by Statutory Sick Pay from 6 April 1983. In general SSP was for a maximum of 8 weeks for the tax year 1983/84 to 1985/86. From 6 April 1986 the SSP period has been extended to 28 weeks.

(continued on page 45)

Fatal injuries at work (Table 3.35)
Under the Notification of Accidents and Dangerous Occurrences Regulations, in force from 1 January 1981 to 30 March 1986, most fatal injuries at or resulting from work activities were reported to HSC enforcement authorities. From 1 April 1986 this requirement continues under the Reporting of Injuries Diseases and Dangerous Occurrences Regulations, currently in force. Prior to 1981, fatal injuries were reported on a less comprehensive basis, and are not therefore comparable with the totals given in the table. Deaths of self employed people and members of the public are included in the table. Some of these were reported voluntarily prior to 1981.

3.1 Summary of government expenditure on social services and housing
Years ended 31 March

£ million

	1978/79	1979/80	1980/81	1981/82	1982/83	1983/84	1984/85	1985/86	1986/87	1987/88	1988/89
Education[1]	9 169	10 617	13 049	14 088	15 158	16 084	16 681	17 439	19 013	20 764	–
National health service	7 835	9 195	11 944	13 267	14 385	15 383	16 312	17 344	18 621	20 489	23 062
Personal social services	1 423	1 785	2 230	2 420	2 552	2 789	2 940	3 467	3 413	3 844	3 979
Welfare foods	27	29	35	52	70	86	98	113	120	124	101
Social security benefits	17 080	20 142	24 426	29 968	33 946	37 190	40 211	43 246	47 008	48 980	50 479
Housing	4 946	6 101	6 304	4 764	4 353	4 744	4 643	4 348	3 921	3 962	2 860
Total government expenditure	40 480	47 869	57 988	64 559	70 464	76 276	80 885	85 957	92 096	98 158	–
Current expenditure	36 357	43 027	53 039	60 629	66 500	71 567	76 163	81 439	87 872	93 737	–
Capital expenditure	4 123	4 842	4 949	3 930	3 964	4 709	4 722	4 518	4 224	4 421	–
Total government expenditure	40 480	47 869	57 988	64 559	70 464	76 276	80 885	85 957	92 096	98 158	–
Central government	28 851	34 000	41 716	47 932	52 884	57 222	61 282	65 440	70 534	74 584	–
Local authorities	11 629	13 869	16 272	16 627	17 580	19 054	19 603	20 517	21 562	23 574	–
Total government expenditure	40 480	47 869	57 988	64 559	70 464	76 276	80 885	85 957	92 096	98 158	–

1 Includes school meals and milk.

Source Central Statistical Office

3.2 Government expenditure on education

Years ended 31 March

£ million

	1977/78	1978/79	1979/80	1980/81	1981/82	1982/83	1983/84	1984/85	1985/86	1986/87	1987/88[3]
Current expenditure											
Nursery schools	30	33	43	52	57	63	67	70	74	81	4 771 (nursery and primary)
Primary schools	1 833	2 030	2 321	2 840	3 093	3 255	3 377	3 483	3 705	4 157	
Secondary schools	2 320	2 609	2 956	3 695	4 143	4 435	4 675	4 850	5 066	5 583	6 027
Special schools	248	296	350	443	500	543	583	620	667	727	812
Further and adult education[1]	1 020	1 112	1 301	1 591	1 812	1 987	2 157	2 261	2 379	2 625	2 897
Training of teachers: tuition	58	56	64	78	83	93	86	93	110	142	156
Universities[1]	724	826	981	1 264	1 277	1 388	1 497	1 562	1 608	1 654	1 824
Other education expenditure	330	347	405	516	553	599	656	697	736	871	908
Related current expenditure:											
Training of teachers: residence	9	9	12	15	15	18	20	18	19	19	14
School welfare[2]	11	13	16	20	23	27	30	33	37	40	59
Meals and milk	434	467	508	479	480	499	519	527	532	559	544
Youth service and physical training	87	102	121	148	169	192	209	227	239	211	245
Maintenance grants and allowances to pupils and students	364	436	520	630	702	759	825	850	838	806	838
Transport of pupils	131	155	181	215	234	253	262	268	275	290	277
Miscellaneous expenditure	2	2	2	3	3	4	4	5	5	5	6
Value added tax paid by local authorities	95	115	212	299	293	359	400	445	477	504	525
Total current expenditure	7 696	8 608	9 993	12 288	13 437	14 475	15 367	16 009	16 767	18 274	19 903
Capital expenditure											
Nursery schools	6	5	6	6	4	4	6	7	8	7	247 (nursery and primary)
Primary schools	124	118	132	174	136	128	141	144	164	180	
Secondary schools	263	238	235	274	233	239	232	210	223	187	213
Special schools	23	15	18	26	22	21	20	14	17	23	11
Further and adult education	80	74	93	129	108	139	141	139	83	149	176
Training of teachers	1	1	3	2	2	3	2	3	3	3	3
Universities	78	84	106	117	117	116	139	121	140	156	158
Other education expenditure	3	5	7	10	10	13	14	11	11	10	32
Related capital expenditure	31	21	24	23	19	20	22	23	23	24	21
Total capital expenditure	609	561	624	761	651	683	717	672	672	739	861
Total expenditure											
Central government	1 058	1 161	1 394	1 779	1 797	2 022	2 222	2 289	2 398	2 560	2 942
Local authorities	7 247	8 008	9 223	11 270	12 291	13 136	13 862	14 392	15 041	16 453	17 822
Total government expenditure	8 305	9 169	10 617	13 049	14 088	15 158	16 084	16 681	17 439	19 013	20 764
Gross domestic product (average estimate) at market prices	150 750	173 053	207 632	236 573	259 946	284 576	308 660	330 378	361 277	385 585	425 614
Expenditure as a percentage of GDP	*5.5*	*5.3*	*5.1*	*5.5*	*5.4*	*5.4*	*5.3*	*5.1*	*4.8*	*4.9*	*4.9*

1 Including tuition fees.

2 From 1 April 1974 expenditure on the school health service is included in the National Health Service.

3 Provisional.

Sources *Department of Education and Science; Central Statistical Office*

3.3 Government expenditure on the national health service
Years ended 31 March

£ million

	1978/79	1979/80	1980/81	1981/82	1982/83	1983/84	1984/85	1985/86	1986/87	1987/88	1988/89[3]
Current expenditure											
Central government:											
Hospitals and Community health services[1]:											
Running expenses[2]	5 241	6 168	8 162	9 033	9 691	10 448	10 912	11 570	12 356	13 669	15 313
Family practitioner services:											
General medical services	463	570	754	866	973	1 049	1 192	1 291	1 373	1 514	1 703
Pharmaceutical services[2]	880	986	1 213	1 394	1 599	1 767	1 919	2 041	2 235	2 459	2 814
General dental services[2]	330	400	494	562	629	681	747	776	877	972	1 136
General ophthalmic services[2]	90	107	123	148	238	191	206	170	155	183	203
Administration	297	365	450	474	488	452	473	475	553	602	639
less Payments by patients:											
Hospital services	-34	-42	-57	-69	-72	-81	-84	-92	-99	-106	-103
Pharmaceutical services	-28	-49	-88	-107	-125	-134	-149	-158	-204	-256	-202
Dental services	-65	-78	-106	-132	-163	-179	-197	-225	-261	-290	-282
Ophthalmic services	-30	-33	-34	-38	-45	-51	-52	-14	-1	-1	–
Total	-157	-202	-285	-346	-405	-445	-482	-489	-565	-653	-587
Departmental administration	71	88	109	121	109	135	137	142	171	193	215
Other services	154	191	236	183	206	219	218	283	324	336	326
Total current expenditure	7 369	8 673	11 256	12 435	13 528	14 497	15 322	16 259	17 479	19 275	21 762
Capital expenditure											
Central government	466	522	688	832	857	886	990	1 085	1 142	1 209	1 300
Total expenditure											
Central government	7 835	9 195	11 944	13 267	14 385	15 383	16 312	17 344	18 621	20 484	23 062

1 Including the school health service.
2 Before deducting payments by patients.
3 Provisional.

Source *Central Statistical Office*

3.4 Government expenditure on welfare services[1]

Years ended 31 March

£ million

	1978/79	1979/80	1980/81	1981/82	1982/83	1983/84	1984/85	1985/86	1986/87	1987/88	1988/89
Personal social services											
Central government current expenditure	67	90	112	99	93	101	106	115	123	125	135
Local authorities current expenditure:											
Running expenses	1 284	1 601	2 004	2 212	2 372	2 595	2 725	3 229	3 163	3 593	3 725
Capital expenditure	72	94	114	109	87	93	109	123	127	126	119
Total	1 423	1 785	2 230	2 420	2 552	2 789	2 940	3 467	3 413	3 844	3 979
Welfare foods service											
Central government current expenditure on welfare foods (including administration)	27	29	35	52	70	86	98	113	120	129	101
less Receipts from the public	–	–	–	–	–	–	–	–	–	–	–
Total	27	29	35	52	70	86	98	113	120	129	101

1 School meals and milk is included in Table 3.2.

Source *Central Statistical Office*

3.5 Government expenditure on social security benefits

Years ended 31 March

£ million

	1978/79	1979/80	1980/81	1981/82	1982/83	1983/84	1984/85	1985/86	1986/87	1987/88	1988/89
Central government current expenditure											
National insurance fund:											
Retirement pensions	7 736	9 008	10 753	12 386	13 845	14 932	15 603	16 949	18 162	19 062	19 714
Lump sums to pensioners	–	98	100	103	105	106	108	108	110	109	112
Widows' benefits and guardians' allowances	525	585	663	718	753	801	815	830	857	872	946
Unemployment benefit	659	681	1 328	1 758	1 550	1 545	1 623	1 638	1 788	1 516	1 180
Sickness benefit	688	657	651	671	537	279	292	290	191	204	217
Invalidity benefit	892	1 048	1 212	1 441	1 673	1 960	2 236	2 452	2 790	3 095	3 553
Maternity benefit	126	146	155	164	157	145	167	169	174	53	28
Death grant	16	16	17	17	17	18	17	18	18	3	0
Injury benefit	53	48	47	45	48	–	–	–	–	–	–
Disablement benefit	226	255	294	329	359	383	397	424	457	469	472
Industrial death benefit	33	37	43	48	52	56	57	60	63	58	59
Statutory sick pay	–	–	–	–	–	445	523	561	854	911	971
Statutory maternity pay	–	–	–	–	–	–	–	–	–	192	251
Redundancy Fund	101	128	313	464	439	438	344	358	256	92	82
Maternity Fund	26	32	40	50	53	59	57	65	71	31	–
Non-contributory benefits:											
War pensions	341	375	424	479	504	524	544	581	589	599	603
Family benefits:											
Child benefit	1 869	2 931	3 052	3 497	3 799	4 137	4 438	4 637	4 699	4 778	4 698
One parent benefit	–	–	63	76	91	110	123	138	152	168	180
Family Credit	–	–	–	–	–	–	–	–	–	–	455
Family income supplement	27	31	48	73	103	133	137	142	175	195	–
Maternity grants	–	–	–	17	17	18	19	18	15	–	–
Income support/Supplementary benefits:											
Supplementary pensions	694	760	930	1 450	1 482	752	922	1 044	1 219	1 365	5
Supplementary allowances	1 413	1 496	2 053	3 569	5 023	5 121	5 821	6 707	7 078	6 945	23
Income support	–	–	–	–	–	–	–	–	–	–	7 998
Social Fund	–	–	–	–	–	–	–	–	–	31	181
Other non-contributory benefits:											
Old persons' pensions	40	38	41	42	43	44	42	44	48	40	39
Lump sums to pensioners	101	6	5	6	6	6	6	7	8	9	7
Attendance allowance	178	215	257	346	422	517	601	715	812	933	1 082
Invalid care allowance	4	5	6	7	9	11	12	14	107	193	168
Mobility allowance	48	81	128	177	241	310	364	431	526	609	680
Invalidity pension and severe disablement allowance	75	91	105	138	163	193	248	280	300	310	323
RPI Adjustment	–	–	–	–	–	–	–	–	–	97	3
Housing benefit[1]	479	538	655	572	1 018	2 540	2 910	3 215	3 465	3 703	3 942
Administration	730	836	1 043	1 325	1 437	1 607	1 785	1 851	2 024	2 338	2 507
Total government expenditure	17 080	20 142	24 426	29 968	33 946	37 190	40 211	43 746	47 008	48 980	50 479

1 From 1981–82 comprises expenditure by the Department of Health and Social Security under the unified housing benefit scheme.

Source *Central Statistical Office*

3.6 Government and other public sector expenditure on housing

Years ended 31 March

£ million

	1978/79	1979/80	1980/81	1981/82	1982/83	1983/84	1984/85	1985/86	1986/87	1987/88	1988/89
Government expenditure											
Current expenditure											
Central government housing subsidies:											
to local authorities	1 208	1 534	1 689	1 064	567	417	451	554	513	548	587
to public corporations	216	261	281	291	260	276	304	295	298	310	313
to housing associations	23	24	29	40	46	21	18	17	29	38	41
grants to housing associations	–	–	45	115	120	200	182	157	129	109	97
Local authorities housing subsidies	267	414	537	553	584	649	620	562	542	490	471
Grants under the option mortgage scheme	141	181	222	254	299	–	–	–	–	–	–
Administration, etc.	67	85	115	109	140	168	117	125	194	242	245
Total current expenditure	1 922	2 499	2 918	2 426	2 016	1 731	1 692	1 710	1 705	1 737	1 754
Capital expenditure											
Investment in housing by local authorities	1 724	1 788	1 432	287	61	794	1 016	1 151	948	999	– 18
Capital grants to housing associations	614	577	535	471	607	983	940	927	894	929	927
Improvement grants	109	156	178	269	561	1 214	982	641	584	585	509
Net lending for house purchase	107	516	629	807	640	– 320	– 357	– 354	– 448	– 282	– 132
Capital grants to public corporations	3	7	13	13	17	20	26	17	23	25	16
Net lending to public corporations	467	558	599	491	451	322	344	256	215	– 31	– 196
Total capital expenditure	3 024	3 602	3 386	2 338	2 337	3 013	2 951	2 638	2 216	2 225	1 106
Total expenditure											
Central government	2 672	3 142	3 413	2 739	2 367	2 239	2 265	2 223	2 101	1 928	1 785
Local authorities	2 274	2 959	2 891	2 025	1 986	2 505	2 378	2 125	1 820	2 034	1 075
Total government expenditure	4 946	6 101	6 304	4 764	4 353	4 744	4 643	4 348	3 921	3 962	2 860
Public corporations' capital expenditure											
Investment in housing	268	307	345	408	395	411	448	428	425	430	429
Net lending to private sector	12	34	47	33	– 33	– 32	– 16	– 7	– 6	– 10	– 10
Total	280	341	392	441	362	379	432	421	419	420	419
Total public sector expenditure[1]	4 759	5 884	6 097	4 714	4 264	4 801	4 731	4 513	4 125	4 413	3 475

1 Total government expenditure *less* grants and loans to public corporations *plus* public corporations' capital expenditure.

Source *Central Statistical Office*

3.7 Stock of dwellings
Great Britain

	1981[1]	1982	1983	1984	1985	1986	1987	1988[3]
Estimated annual gains and losses (Thousands)								
Gains: New construction	145.5	175.4	198.6	209.5	195.3	201.7	205.7	215.5
Other		11.4	11.9	13.7	12.8	10.8	10.8	11.2
Losses: Slum clearance	−22.9	23.2	15.2	12.2	11.0	8.8	8.4	8.6
Other		10.4	9.6	15.3	11.7	9.6	9.8	9.6
Net gain	122.6	153.2	185.5	195.6	185.4	194.1	198.3	208.5
Stock at end of year[2]	21 093	21 246	21 432	21 627	21 813	22 007	22 205	22 414
Estimated tenure distribution at end of year (percentage)								
Owner occupied	*56.5*	*58.1*	*59.4*	*60.5*	*61.5*	*62.5*	*63.6*	*64.9*
Rented: From local authorities and new towns	*30.5*	*29.4*	*28.5*	*27.8*	*27.1*	*26.5*	*25.8*	*24.7*
From housing associations	*2.2*	*2.2*	*2.3*	*2.4*	*2.5*	*2.5*	*2.6*	*2.7*
From private owners including other tenures	*10.7*	*10.2*	*9.8*	*9.3*	*8.9*	*8.5*	*8.1*	*7.7*

Note: For statistical purposes the stock estimates are expressed to the nearest thousand, but should not be regarded as accurate to the last digit.
1 April to December only.
2 Estimates are based on data from the 1971 and 1981 Censuses.
3 Provisional.

Sources *Department of the Environment; Welsh Office; Scottish Development Department*

3.8 Renovations
Great Britain

Number of dwellings

	1979	1980	1981	1982	1983	1984	1985	1986	1987	1988[5]
England										
Local authorities and new towns[1]	75 967	77 275	52 931	57 722	85 461	86 612	96 482	133 661	148 364	174 128
Housing associations[2]	17 173	14 676	11 243	17 364	14 513	18 517	11 350	12 714	10 890	11 488
Private owners: grants paid[3]	65 359	74 465	68 941	104 028	219 832	229 107	136 412	113 328	108 908	105 959
All	158 499	166 416	133 115	179 114	319 806	334 236	244 244	259 703	268 162	291 575
Wales										
Local authorities[1]	..	..	..	..	..	2 390	1 728	2 788	5 886	6 307
Housing associations[2]	218	252	694	1 009	993	760	945	907	948	867
Private owners: grants paid[3]	6 116	7 348	7 100	10 989	27 323	29 978	17 152	18 571	19 097	20 187
All	6 334	7 600	7 794	11 998	28 316	33 128	19 825	22 266	25 931	27 361
Scotland										
Local authorities and new towns[4]	34 805	22 282	26 065	51 214	41 583	33 774	58 999	71 678	87 185	62 918
Housing associations[2, 4]	2 703	2 787	1 833	3 422	2 530	1 424	1 124	1 414	1 262	1 123
Private owners: grants paid[3]	8 719	13 420	18 036	23 957	45 498	60 661	46 286	31 453	30 668	31 209
All	46 227	38 489	45 934	78 593	89 611	95 859	106 409	104 545	119 115	95 250
Great Britain										
Local authorities and new towns[1, 4]	110 772	99 557	78 996	108 936	127 044	120 386	157 209	208 127	241 435	243 353
Housing associations[2, 4]	20 094	17 715	13 770	21 795	18 036	20 701	13 419	15 035	13 100	13 478
Private owners: grants paid[3]	80 194	95 233	94 077	138 974	292 653	319 746	199 850	163 352	158 673	157 355
All	211 060	212 505	186 843	269 705	437 733	460 833	370 478	386 514	413 208	414 186

1 Work completed. Figures for new towns are not available from January 1978 to April 1980 inclusive. From 1981 including improvement for sale. Figures for Wales not available before 1984.
2 Work approved under specific housing association legislation. Figures for Wales are for work completed by Housing Corporation funded housing associations only.
3 Including grants paid to housing associations under private owner grant legislation. Figures for England and Scotland from October 1980 and Wales from April 1981 include a small number of grants to tenants in both public and private sectors.
4 Work approved in Scotland.
5 Provisional.

Sources *Department of the Environment; Welsh Office; Scottish Development Department*

3.9 Slum clearance: dwellings demolished or closed

Number

	1979	1980/81	1981/82	1982/83	1983/84	1984/85	1985/86	1986/87	1987/88[5]
England and Wales: total[1]	30 426	28 385	23 485	17 074	11 622	10 319	9 120	7 026	6 614
Demolished: In clearance areas	23 747	22 063	19 139	14 310	7 272	6 390	5 278	4 161	3 637
Elsewhere	2 472	3 248	2 414	1 944	2 450	2 142	2 439	1 663	1 588
Closed[2]	4 207	3 074	1 932	820	1 900	1 787	1 403	1 202	1 389
Scotland[3]**: total**	5 573	5 815	4 975	3 704	1 987	1 736	1 618	1 628	1 787
Unfit[4]	4 001	4 017	2 710	2 511	1 735	1 040	639	704	794
Other[2]	1 572	1 798	2 265	1 193	252	696	979	924	993

1 From 1980/81 slum clearance statistics for England are collected on a financial year basis.
2 Less dwellings included in numbers demolished which had previously been reported as closed.
3 Action under the Housing Acts, Town and Country Planning Acts and other specific statutory powers and other action. Unfit houses comprise houses failing to meet the tolerable standard introduced by the Housing (Scotland) Act 1969 and houses dealt with under earlier statutory provisions as being unfit for human habitation.
4 Figures from 1979 are for below tolerable standard.
5 Provisional.

Sources *Department of the Environment; Welsh Office; Scottish Development Department*

3.10 Permanent dwellings completed

Number

	United Kingdom				England and Wales			
	Total	For local housing authorities[1]	For private owners	Housing Associations and other[2]	Total	For local housing authorities[1]	For private owners	Housing Associations and other[2]
1966	396 009	176 871	208 647	10 491	349 480	142 430	197 502	9 548
1967	415 455	199 749	204 208	11 498	362 898	159 347	192 940	10 611
1968	425 835	187 984	226 068	11 783	371 726	148 049	213 273	10 404
1969	378 324	180 958	185 916	11 450	324 165	139 850	173 377	10 938
1970	362 226	176 926	174 342	10 958	307 266	134 874	162 084	10 308
1971	364 475	154 894	196 313	13 268	309 776	117 215	179 998	12 563
1972	330 936	120 431	200 755	9 750	287 294	93 635	184 622	9 037
1973	304 637	102 604	191 080	10 953	264 047	79 289	174 413	10 345
1974	279 582	121 017	145 177	13 388	241 173	99 423	129 626	12 124
1975	321 936	150 526	154 528	16 882	278 694	122 857	140 381	15 456
1976	324 769	151 824	155 229	17 716	278 660	124 152	138 477	16 031
1977	314 093	143 250	143 905	26 938	276 011	121 246	128 688	26 077
1978	288 603	112 340	152 166	24 097	254 001	96 752	134 578	22 671
1979	251 816	88 485	144 055	19 276	220 722	77 192	125 306	18 224
1980	241 719	87 974	131 707	22 038	214 652	78 012	115 897	20 743
1981	206 351	68 072	118 326	19 953	179 568	58 148	103 748	17 672
1982	182 248	39 921	128 539	13 788	158 807	33 386	113 404	12 017
1983	207 999	38 892	152 189	16 917	180 466	31 363	134 040	15 063
1984	219 926	37 311	164 898	17 517	190 470	31 090	144 603	14 777
1985	206 124	30 343	161 967	13 814	176 902	24 299	140 582	12 021
1986	211 866	24 800	173 940	13 126	183 142	20 033	152 046	11 063
1987	215 403	20 977	181 627	12 799	188 132	16 718	160 377	11 037
1988	225 716	20 912	192 211	12 593	197 352	16 470	170 648	10 234

	Scotland				Northern Ireland			
	Total	For local housing authorities[1]	For private owners	Housing Associations and other[2]	Total	For local housing authorities[1]	For private owners	Housing Associations and other[2]
1966	36 029	27 515	7 870	644	10 500	6 926	3 275	299
1967	41 458	33 222	7 498	738	11 099	7 180	3 770	149
1968	41 989	32 011	8 720	1 258	12 120	7 924	4 075	121
1969	42 628	33 932	8 326	370	11 531	7 176	4 213	142
1970	43 126	34 360	8 220	546	11 834	7 692	4 038	104
1971	40 783	28 577	11 614	592	13 916	9 102	4 701	113
1972	31 992	19 593	11 835	564	11 650	7 203	4 298	149
1973	30 033	17 349	12 215	469	10 557	5 966	4 452	139
1974	28 336	16 182	11 239	915	10 073	5 412	4 312	349
1975	34 323	22 784	10 371	1 168	8 919	4 885	3 776	258
1976	36 527	21 154	13 704	1 669	9 582	6 518	3 048	16
1977	27 320	14 328	12 132	860	10 762	7 676	3 085	1
1978	25 759	9 907	14 443	1 409	8 843	5 681	3 145	17
1979	23 782	7 857	15 175	750	7 312	3 436	3 574	302
1980	20 611	7 455	12 242	914	6 456	2 507	3 568	381
1981	20 015	7 065	11 021	1 929	6 768	2 859	3 557	352
1982	16 434	3 721	11 529	1 184	7 007	2 814	3 606	587
1983	17 941	3 486	13 178	1 277	9 592	4 044	4 971	577
1984	18 841	2 633	14 118	2 090	10 415	3 588	6 177	650
1985	18 421	2 811	14 445	1 165	10 801	3 233	6 940	628
1986	18 579	2 187	14 812	1 580	10 145	2 580	7 082	483
1987	17 602	2 495	13 799	1 308	9 669	1 764	7 451	454
1988	18 155	2 730	14 052	1 373	10 209	1 712	7 511	986

1 Including the Commission for the New Towns and New Towns Development Corporations, the Scottish Special Housing Association, the Northern Ireland Housing Trust and the Northern Ireland Housing Executive.

2 Dwellings provided by housing associations other than the Scottish Special Housing Association and the Northern Ireland Housing Trust and provided or authorised by government departments for the families of police, prison staffs, the armed forces and certain other services.

Sources *Department of the Environment; Welsh Office; Scottish Development Department; Department of the Environment (Northern Ireland)*

3.11 National Insurance Fund
Years ended 31 March

£ thousand

	1978/79	1979/80	1980/81	1981/82	1982/83	1983/84	1984/85	1985/86	1986/87	1987/88
Receipts										
Opening balance	3 927 423	4 197 180	4 752 533	5 177 647	4 194 593	4 164 605	4 742 324	5 165 213	5 400 988	5 858 038
Contributions	9 187 766	10 643 821	12 813 167	14 354 078	16 663 862	18 167 156	19 421 971	21 222 636	22 778 266	26 050 756
Consolidated Fund supplement	2 016 974	2 394 600	2 906 900	2 490 200	2 642 891	2 866 800	2 654 055	2 210 245	2 463 600	2 184 725
Income from investments	452 400	554 940	628 004	608 233	514 038	506 882	533 732	557 951	619 805	607 863
Other receipts	239	284	99 748	96 210	87 859	92 792	96 196	61 778	176 987	194 933
Total	15 584 802	17 790 825	21 200 352	22 726 368	24 103 243	25 798 235	27 448 278	29 217 823	31 439 646	28 207 349
Expenditure										
Total benefits[1]	10 940 284	12 534 704	15 263 350	17 676 334	19 073 084	20 220 929	21 333 736	22 929 064	24 611 284	25 442 704
Unemployment	659 960	680 622	1 328 374	1 758 436	1 550 329	1 544 676	1 623 021	1 637 596	1 787 975	1 516 649
Sickness	655 222	617 064	618 416	643 782	514 251	267 108	287 455	280 026	190 643	203 623
Invalidity	892 508	1 048 343	1 211 978	1 441 266	1 672 580	1 959 334	2 239 461	2 451 527	2 791 026	3 098 571
Maternity	125 700	146 300	172 400	180 600	157 100	145 400	166 727	169 820	174 117	53 216
Widows' pensions	523 100	582 700	660 700	715 700	751 204	798 752	812 834	829 160	854 709	869 360
Guardians' allowances[2} / Child's special allowance	2 010	2 010	2 330	2 340	2 240	2 130	1 824	1 542	1 680	1 534
Retirement pensions	7 754 282	9 003 744	10 767 868	12 387 182	13 844 825	14 932 644	15 622 324	16 949 265	18 162 400	19 057 883
Death grants	16 330	16 462	16 641	17 245	17 335	17 132	17 422	18 661	18 842	2 694
Injury	52 620	47 497	46 869	49 173	47 564	7 573	342	–	–	–
Disablement	221 132	250 279	289 173	323 517	353 326	379 730	392 235	419 054	453 052	466 658
Death	32 820	36 930	43 120	48 280	52 430	55 550	56 640	60 279	63 163	58 602
Pensioners' lump sum payments		97 953	100 381	103 413	104 500	105 500	107 600	107 618	109 660	109 690
Other benefits	4 600	4 800	5 100	5 400	5 400	5 400	5 000	4 516	4 017	4 224
Payments in lieu of benefits forgone[3]	32 749	39 946	32 312	26 223	31 176	11 569	10 825	9 775	–	–
Other payments	6 053	4 457	4 629	391	287	316	10 736	1 709	7 782	4 785
Administration	408 536	459 185	622 976	732 927	749 321	746 097	833 569	838 124	765 699	830 539
Transfers to Northern Ireland			99 438	95 900	84 770	77 000	95 000	60 000	175 000	155 000
Total	11 387 622	13 038 292	16 022 705	18 531 775	19 938 638	21 055 911	22 283 065	23 838 672	25 559 765	26 438 028
Accumulated funds	4 197 180	4 752 533	5 177 647	4 194 593	4 164 605	4 742 324	5 165 213	5 379 151	5 879 881	7 481 287

1 The total benefits figure for Northern Ireland in 1984/85 and 1985/86 includes payments in lieu of benefit forgone.
2 Including figures of Child's special allowance for Northern Ireland.
3 Payments to the Post Office, British Telecommunications, Consolidated and Trading Funds, (from 1986/7 Estains payments not shown separately and are included with Sickness Benefit together with Injury Benefit. Estains arrangements were abolished on 25.8.86).

Sources *Department of Social Security; Department of Health and Social Services (Northern Ireland)*

3.12 National Insurance Acts: persons for whom contributions were payable
Persons who paid contributions in a tax year ending April[1]

Millions

	Total			Men			Married women			Single, widowed and divorced women		
	1985	1986	1987	1985	1986	1987	1985	1986	1987	1985	1986	1987
Total[2]	23.60	24.01	24.25	14.55	14.66	14.72	5.51	5.66	5.71	3.54	3.70	3.82
Class 1 Standard rate	19.86	20.35	20.65	12.75	12.79	12.74	3.77	4.06	4.28	3.34	3.50	3.64
Contracted in	10.41	10.88	11.15	6.03	6.15	6.21	2.36	2.58	2.70	2.02	2.15	2.24
Contracted out	8.38	8.33	8.24	6.07	5.97	5.81	1.22	1.27	1.33	1.09	1.10	1.11
Mixed contracted in/out	1.07	1.14	1.26	0.65	0.67	0.72	0.19	0.21	0.25	0.23	0.25	0.29
Class 1 Reduced rate	1.69	1.50	1.30	–	–	–	1.59	1.40	1.22	0.11	0.10	0.08
Mixed Class 1 Standard and Reduced rate	0.05	0.06	0.06	–	–	–	0.05	0.05	0.05	0.01	0.01	0.01
Class 2	1.66	1.73	1.85	1.52	1.57	1.66	0.09	0.10	0.13	0.06	0.06	0.06
Mixed Class 1 and Class 2	0.25	0.26	0.29	0.22	0.23	0.25	0.02	0.02	0.02	0.02	0.02	0.02
Class 3[3]	0.09	0.11	0.10	0.07	0.07	0.07	0.01	0.02	0.02	0.01	0.01	0.01

1 The tax year commences on 6 April and ends on 5 April of the year following. The years shown at the head of the column refer to the end of the tax year. Persons who paid any contributions at any time in the tax year are shown.
2 Not all figures agree because of rounding.
3 Persons who paid a mixture of Class 3 contributions and others are not included in 'Class 3' but are shown according to the type of the additional contribution.

Source *Department of Social Security*

3.13 Weekly rates of principal social security benefits

£

	1979 Nov.	1980 Nov.	1981 Nov.	1982 Nov.	1983 Nov.	1984 Nov.	1985 Nov.	1986 July	1987 April	1988 April	1989 April
Unemployment benefit:[1]											
Men and women	18.50	20.65	22.50	25.00	27.05	28.45	30.45	30.80	31.45	32.75	34.70
Sickness benefit:[1]											
Men and women	18.50	20.65	22.50	25.00	25.95	27.25	29.15	29.45	30.05	31.30	33.20
Invalidity benefit:											
Invalidity pension	23.30	26.00	28.35	31.45	32.60	34.25	38.30	38.70	39.50	41.15	43.60
Invalidity allowance:											
High rate	4.90	5.45	6.20	6.90	7.15	7.50	8.05	8.15	8.30	8.65	9.20
Middle rate	3.10	3.45	4.00	4.40	4.60	4.80	5.10	5.20	5.30	5.50	5.80
Low rate	1.55	1.75	2.00	2.20	2.30	2.40	2.55	2.60	2.65	2.75	2.90
Increase for dependants:											
Adult	14.00	15.60	17.00	18.85	19.55	20.55	23.00	23.25	23.75	24.75	26.20
Each child	7.10	7.50		7.95	7.60	7.65	8.05	8.05	8.05	8.40	8.95
Attendance allowance:											
Higher rate	18.60	21.65	23.65	26.25	27.20	28.60	30.60	30.95	31.60	32.95	34.90
Lower rate	12.40	14.45	15.75	17.50	18.15	19.10	20.45	20.65	21.10	22.00	23.30
Mobility allowance[2]	12.00	14.50	16.50	18.30	19.00	20.00	21.40	21.65	22.10	23.05	24.40
Maternity benefit:											
Maternity allowance for insured women	18.50	20.65	22.50	25.00	25.95	27.25	29.15	29.45	30.05	31.30	33.20
Death grant[3]	30.00	30.00	30.00	30.00	30.00	30.00	30.00	30.00	30.00	–	–
Guardian's allowance	7.10	7.50	7.70	7.95	7.60	7.65	8.05	8.05	8.05	8.40	8.95
Widow's benefit:											
Widow's pension	23.30	27.15	29.60	32.85	34.05	35.80	38.30	38.70	39.50	41.15	43.60
Widowed mother's allowance	23.30	27.15	29.60	32.85	34.05	35.80	38.30	38.70	39.50	41.15	43.60
Addition for each child	7.10	7.50	7.70	7.95	7.60	7.65	8.05	8.05	8.05	8.40	8.95
Retirement pension:[4]											
Single person	23.30	27.15	29.60	32.85	34.05	35.80	38.30	38.70	39.50	41.15	43.60
Married couple	37.30	43.45	47.35	52.55	54.50	57.30	61.30	61.95	63.25	65.90	69.80
Non-contributory retirement pension:											
Man or woman	14.00	16.30	17.75	19.70	20.45	21.50	23.00	23.25	23.75	24.75	26.20
Married woman	8.40	9.80	10.65	11.80	12.25	12.85	13.75	13.90	14.20	14.80	15.65
Industrial injuries benefit:											
Injury benefit	21.25	23.40	25.25	27.75	[6]						
Disablement pension at 100 per cent rate	38.00	44.30	48.30	53.60	55.60	58.40	62.50	63.20	64.50	67.20	71.20
Widow's or widower's pension	23.85	27.70	30.15	33.40	34.60	36.35	38.85	39.25	40.05	41.15	43.60
Increase for dependants:[5]											
Adult	11.45	12.75	13.90	15.45	16.70	17.55	18.80	19.00	19.40	20.20	21.40
Each child	1.70	1.25	0.80	0.30	0.15	[7]					

1 Persons under the age of 18 are entitled to the appropriate adult rate.
2 Mobility Allowance was introduced from 1 January 1976 at the £5.00 rate.
3 Death grant is not payable in respect of the death of a person who on 4 July 1948 was aged 65 or over (man) and 60 or over (women). This benefit was abolished from April 1987 and replaced by payments from Social Fund.
4 Retirement pensioners over 80 receive 25p addition.
5 An allowance for one adult dependant is payable, where appropriate, with unemployment benefit, sickness benefit, retirement pension, injury benefit, certain disablement pensions and maternity allowance. Allowances for dependent children are payable with any of these benefits. Changes in these increases take effect from the same date as the main benefit.
6 Injury benefit ceased on 6 April 1983.
7 Child dependency addition was abolished from 24 November 1984.

Source *Department of Social Security*

3.13 Weekly rates of principal social security benefits

(continued)

£

	1978 Nov.	1979 Nov.	1980 Nov.	1981 Nov.	1982 Nov.	1983 Nov.	1984 Nov.	1985 Nov.	1986 July	1987 April	1988 April	1989 April
Child benefit:												
All children	3.00	4.00	4.75	5.25	5.85	6.50	6.85	7.00	7.10	7.25	7.25	7.25
Family Credit[8]												
(maximum awards payable):												
Families with 1 child												
Child under 11	10.50	13.50	17.00	18.50	21.00	22.00	23.00	25.00	25.30	25.85	38.15	40.90
Child 11 – 15	10.50	13.50	17.00	18.50	21.00	22.00	23.00	25.50	25.80	26.40	43.50	46.50
Child 16 and over	10.50	13.50	17.00	18.50	21.00	22.00	23.00	26.00	26.30	26.90	46.80	49.95
Child age 18	–	–	–	–	–	–	–	–	–	–	53.45	56.90
Increase for each additional child												
Child under 11	1.00	1.00	1.50	1.50	2.00	2.00	2.00	2.50	2.55	2.60	6.05	7.30
Child 11 – 15	1.00	1.00	1.50	1.50	2.00	2.00	2.00	3.00	3.05	3.15	11.40	12.90
Child 16 and over	1.00	1.00	1.50	1.50	2.00	2.00	2.00	3.50	3.55	3.65	14.70	16.35
Child age 18	–	–	–	–	–	–	–	–	–	–	21.35	23.30
War pension:												
Ex-private (100 per cent assessment)	31.90	38.00	44.30	48.30	53.60	55.60	58.40	62.50	63.20	64.50	67.20	71.20
War widow	25.30	30.20	35.30	38.45	42.70	44.25	46.55	49.80	50.30	51.35	53.50	56.65
Supplementary benefits:[10, 15]												
Weekly scale rate of requirements[11]												
Married couple[12]												
Ordinary rate	25.25	29.70	34.60	37.75	41.70	43.50	45.55	47.85	48.40	49.35	–	–
Long-term rate	31.55	37.65	43.45	47.35	52.30	54.55	57.10	60.00	60.65	61.85	–	–
Single householder:[13]												
Ordinary rate	15.55	18.30	21.30	23.25	25.70	26.80	28.05	29.50	29.80	30.40	–	–
Long-term rate	19.90	23.70	27.15	29.60	32.70	34.10	35.70	37.50	37.90	38.65	–	–
Non-householder aged:												
18 or over												
Ordinary rate	12.45	14.65	17.05	18.60	20.55	21.45	22.45	23.60	23.85	24.35	–	–
Long-term rate	15.95	18.95	21.70	23.65	26.15	27.25	28.55	30.00	30.35	30.95	–	–
16 – 17												
Ordinary rate	9.55	11.25	13.10	14.30	15.80	16.50	17.30	18.20	18.40	18.75	–	–
Long-term rate				18.15	20.05	20.90	21.90	23.00	23.25	23.70	–	–
Increase for children aged:												
13 – 15	7.95	9.35	10.90	11.90	13.15	13.70	14.35	15.10	15.30	15.60	–	–
11 – 12	6.55	7.70										
5 – 10	5.30	6.25	7.30	7.90	8.75	9.15	9.60	10.10	10.20	10.40	–	–
Under 5	4.40	5.20										
Income Support:												
Personal allowances[13]												
Single												
aged 16–17	–	–	–	–	–	–	–	–	–	–	19.40	20.80
aged 18–24	–	–	–	–	–	–	–	–	–	–	26.05	27.40
aged 25 or over	–	–	–	–	–	–	–	–	–	–	33.40	34.90
Couple												
both aged under 18	–	–	–	–	–	–	–	–	–	–	38.80	41.60
one or both 18 or over	–	–	–	–	–	–	–	–	–	–	51.45	54.80
Lone parent												
aged 16–17	–	–	–	–	–	–	–	–	–	–	19.40	20.80
aged 18 or over	–	–	–	–	–	–	–	–	–	–	33.40	34.90
Dependent children and young people												
aged under 11	–	–	–	–	–	–	–	–	–	–	10.75	11.75
aged 11–15	–	–	–	–	–	–	–	–	–	–	16.10	17.35
aged 16–17	–	–	–	–	–	–	–	–	–	–	19.40	20.80
aged 18	–	–	–	–	–	–	–	–	–	–	26.05	27.40

8 Family credit superseded Family Income Supplement from April 1988.
9 Child aged 16–17.
10 Supplementary pension is paid to people over age 65 (men) or 60 (women). Supplementary allowance is paid to people below those ages. Persons aged 80 years and over are entitled to a further 25p.
11 Scale rates for normal requirements other than rent.
12 Including couples as man and wife.
13 Including any single person who is directly responsible for rent.
14 In addition to personal allowances a claimant may also be entitled to a premium(s). The types of premium are family, lone parent, pensioner, higher pensioner, disability, severe disability and disabled child.
15 Supplementary Benefit was replaced by Income Support from April 1988.

Source Department of Social Security

3.14 National Insurance contributions

Date from	Class 1: Lower earnings limit (LEL) — No contribution liability if earnings are below: Weekly	Monthly	Upper earnings limit (UEL) — Weekly/monthly up to: Weekly	Monthly	Percentage of earnings — Standard rate[1]: Employee	Employer	Total	Reduced rate[2]: Employee	Employer	Total	Employers contribution only[3]	Others: Class 2	Class 3
	£	£	£	£	%	%[4]	%[4]	%	%[4]	%[4]	%[4]	£	£
6 April 1984													
Not contracted out	34.00	147.33	250.00	1 083.33	*9.00*	*11.45*	*20.45*	*3.85*	*11.45*	*15.30*	*11.45*		
Contracted out (i) (ii)	34.00	147.33	250.00	1 083.33									
(i) on earnings up to LEL plus					*9.00*	*11.45*	*20.45*	*3.85*	*11.45*	*15.30*	*11.45*		
(ii) on earnings between LEL and UEL					*6.85*	*7.35*	*14.20*	*3.85*	*7.35*	*11.20*	*7.35*		
Classes 2 and 3												4.60	4.50
6 April 1985													
Not contracted out	35.50	153.83	265.00	1 148.33	*9.00*	*10.45*	*19.45*	*3.85*	*10.45*	*14.30*	*10.45*		
Contracted out (i) (ii)	35.50	153.83	265.00	1 148.33									
(i) on earnings up to LEL plus					*9.00*	*10.45*	*19.45*	*3.85*	*10.45*	*14.30*	*10.45*		
(ii) on earnings between LEL and UEL					*6.85*	*6.35*	*13.20*	*3.85*	*6.35*	*10.20*	*6.35*		
Classes 2 and 3												4.75	4.65

	Class 1 — Not contracted out: Employee: Standard[1]	Employee: Reduced[2]	Employer: Standard and reduced	Employer only[3]: Standard only	Contracted out — Employee: Standard: Up to LEL[5]	Employee: Standard: Over LEL	Employee: Reduced	Employer: Standard and reduced: Up to LEL[5]	Employer: Standard and reduced: Over LEL	Employer only: Standard only: Up to LEL[5]	Employer only: Standard only: Over LEL	Others: Class 2	Class 3
	%	%	%	%	%	%	%	%	%	%	%	£	£
6 April 1987													
Weekly earnings (£)													
39.00 – 64.99	*5.0*	*3.85*	*5.0*	*5.0*	*5.0*	*2.85*	*3.85*	*5.0*	*0.9*	*5.0*	*0.9*		
65.00 – 99.99	*7.0*	*3.85*	*7.0*	*7.0*	*7.0*	*4.85*	*3.85*	*7.0*	*2.9*	*7.0*	*2.9*		
100.00 – 149.99	*9.0*	*3.85*	*9.0*	*9.0*	*9.0*	*6.85*	*3.85*	*9.0*	*4.9*	*9.0*	*4.9*		
150.00 – 295.00	*9.0*	*3.85*	*10.45*	*10.45*	*9.0*	*6.85*	*3.85*	*10.45*	*6.35*	*10.45*	*6.35*		
over 295.00	–	–	*10.45*	*10.45*	–	–	–	*10.45*	*10.45*	*10.45*	*10.45*		
Classes 2 and 3												3.85	3.75
6 April 1988													
Weekly earnings (£)													
41.00 – 69.99	*5.0*	*3.85*	*5.0*	*5.0*	*5.0*	*3.0*	*3.85*	*5.0*	*1.2*	*5.0*	*1.2*		
70.00 – 104.99	*7.0*	*3.85*	*7.0*	*7.0*	*7.0*	*5.0*	*3.85*	*7.0*	*3.2*	*7.0*	*3.2*		
105.00 – 154.99	*9.0*	*3.85*	*9.0*	*9.0*	*9.0*	*7.0*	*3.85*	*9.0*	*5.2*	*9.0*	*5.2*		
155.00 – 305.00	*9.0*	*3.85*	*10.45*	*10.45*	*9.0*	*7.0*	*3.85*	*10.45*	*6.65*	*10.45*	*6.65*		
over 305.00	–	–	*10.45*	*10.45*	–	–	–	*10.45*	*10.45*	*10.45*	*10.45*		
Classes 2 and 3												4.05	3.95
6 April 1989													
Weekly earnings (£)													
43.00 – 74.99	*5.0*	*3.85*	*5.0*	*5.0*	*5.0*	*3.0*	*3.85*	*5.0*	*1.2*	*5.0*	*1.2*		
75.00 – 114.99	*7.0*	*3.85*	*7.0*	*7.0*	*7.0*	*5.0*	*3.85*	*7.0*	*3.2*	*7.0*	*3.2*		
115.00 – 164.99	*9.0*	*3.85*	*9.0*	*9.0*	*9.0*	*7.0*	*3.85*	*9.0*	*5.2*	*9.0*	*5.2*		
165.00 – 325.00	*9.0*	*3.85*	*10.45*	*10.45*	*9.0*	*7.0*	*3.85*	*10.45*	*6.65*	*10.45*	*6.65*		
over 325.00			*10.45*	*10.45*	–	–	–	*10.45*	*10.45*	*10.45*	*10.45*		
Classes 2 and 3 men												4.25	4.15
women												4.15	–

1 For employees who are under pension age (65 men/60 women), but excluding those married women or widows who are liable for contributions at the reduced rate.

2 For employees who are married women or widows and liable for contributions at the reduced rate.

3 For all employees over pension age. Applicable also to employees who had made other arrangements to pay Class 1 contributions.

4 Includes 2 per cent National Insurance surcharge under the National Insurance Surcharge Act 1976. The employers contribution was raised by a further 1.5 per cent from 2 October 1978 when the surcharge was increased to 3.5 per cent. From 2 August 1982 the surcharge was reduced to 2 per cent, from 6 April 1983 reduced to 1.5 per cent and from 1 August 1983 reduced to 1.0 per cent and reduced to nil from 6 October 1984.

5 From 6 October 1985 LEL £35.50 a week, from 6 April 1986 LEL £38.00 a week, from 6 April 1987 LEL £39.00 a week, from 6 April 1988 LEL £41.00 a week, from 6 April 1989 LEL £43.00 a week.

Source Department of Social Security

3.15 Social Security Acts: number of persons receiving benefit

United Kingdom

At 31 December

Thousands

	1977	1978	1979	1980	1981	1982	1983	1984	1985	1986	1987	1988
Persons receiving:												
Unemployment benefit[1]	589	561	503	753	1 206[13]	1 041	987	926	901	956	811	630.2
Sickness and invalidity benefit[2, 3]	1 068	1 180	1 238	1 197	1 156	1 198	1 202	1 044	1 098	1 141	1 168	1 278
Maternity grant[4]	622	638	674	680	587[15]	670	687	662	776	715	–[17]	–[17]
Death grant[5]	581	597	607	606	604	611	14[14]	13.7[14]	615	15[16]	6.3	–
Guardians' allowances	5.0	5.0	4.9	4.6	4.4	4.1	3.9	3.3	3.2	2.9	2.7	2.6
Widows' benefits[6, 7]	500	473	467	15[8]	433	426	420	414	398	389	380	388
National Insurance retirement pensions:[7]												
Males	3 069	3 135	3 199	3 241	3 280	3 280	3 280	3 268	3 353	3 411	3 454	3 479.1
Females	5 568	5 650	5 737	5 866	6 010	6 105	6 208	6 259	6 379	6 455	6 490	6 523.5
Total	8 637	8 785	8 936	9 108	9 291	9 386	9 487	9 528	9 732	9 865	9 944	10 001.6
Non contributory retirement pensions:[7]												
Males	9	7	6	6	6	6	6	6	6	7	7	43
Females	68	62	54	50	45	42	39	38	34	36	35	32.6
Total	78	69	60	56	51	48	45	43	39	42	41	39.3
Injury benefit[3, 9]	47	51	51	43	36	36	30	–	–	–	–	–
Industrial disablement pensions[20]												
At end of statistical year	205	204	202	201	197	194	191	186	191	189	189	189.5
Child benefit[8, 10]												
Families receiving benefit	7 506	7 390	7 410	7 397	7 352	7 261	7 174	7 097	7 034	6 979	6 928	6 923
Family income supplement[11]	97	89	89	106	143	179	215	218	214	218[16]	220[19]	–
Family Credit[18]	–	–	–	–	–	–	–	–	–	–	–	298.3
Supplementary benefits[21]												
At November/December	3 106	3 048	2 970	3 247	3 873	4 432	4 524	4 788	4 771	5 158	5 088	–[20]
War pensions[12]	397	382	367	355	341	327	314	302	291	275	266	258

1 Great Britain figures are an average of the four quarters for the year and for Northern Ireland an average of the two six monthly figures. Due to industrial action and figures being unavailable, the Northern Ireland figures for 1985 relate to May only.
2 Average of twelve monthly figures commencing on the first monday in June up to 1982 and from first monday in April thereafter. For Northern Ireland average of twelve monthly figures commencing from January. A relatively small number of claims do not result in the payment of benefit but are included here because they indicate notified incapacity for work.
3 Includes overseas cases.
4 Northern Ireland figures are at 31 March. Three months figures to 5 April 1987 only when benefit was abolished and replaced by a payment from the Social Fund.
5 Grants paid in year. This benefit was abolished from April 1987 and replaced by a payment from the Social Fund. No statistics for Great Britain are available after December 1985.
6 Excluding widows' allowances paid during the first twenty-six weeks of widowhood the number of such allowances does not exceed 35 000 in a six month period. Widows allowance was replaced by widows payment on 11.4.88.
7 Northern Ireland figures are at 30 November.
8 Includes overseas cases.
9 Injury benefit was abolished from 6 April 1983 with transitional payments until 3 October 1983.
10 From April 1977 child benefit replaced family allowance.
11 Northern Ireland figures are at 1 December.
12 Great Britain only.
13 February 1981 data for Great Britain only, due to industrial action.
14 Northern Ireland only. Great Britain data not available due to industrial action.
15 Estimated.
16 Northern Ireland figure only.
17 Payments of Maternity Grant ceased in respect of babies due or born after 5 April 1987. Northern Ireland only: 1986 figures are for year ended 31 March 1987 (only 46 awards of Maternity Grant for Period 1 April 1987 – 5 April 1987).
18 Family Income Supplement was replaced by Family Credit from April 1988.
19 Great Britain figures are as at 30.4.87.
20 End of statistical year was 30 September up to 1986. After 30.9.86 statistical year ends the sunday before the first monday in April.
21 From April 1988 Supplementary Benefit was replaced by Income Support.

Sources *Department of Social Security; Department of Health and Social Services (Northern Ireland)*

3.16 Unemployed claimants analysed by benefit entitlement
United Kingdom

	1981[1]	1982[2]	1983	1984[3]	1985	1986	1987	1988
	Nov.	Nov.	Nov.	Nov.	Nov.[4]	Nov.	Nov.	Nov.
Flat-rate benefit payable—total	42	1 013	938	926	872	955	676	521.6
Flat-rate benefit only	21	742	709	723	679	768	549	402.2
Flat-rate benefit and earnings-related supplement[2]	13	–	–	–	–	–	–	–
Flat-rate benefit, earnings-related supplement and supplementary allowance[2,5]	2	–	–	–	–	–	–	–
Flat-rate benefit and supplementary allowance[5]	6	271	229	203	193	187	127	119.3
Supplementary allowance only[5]	64	1 499	1 685	1 773	1 690	1 715	1 407	1 143
No flat-rate benefit or supplementary allowance[3,5]	5	473	383	420	461	500	425	347.3
Total	111	2 985	3 006	3 119	3 023	3 170	2 508	2 012.8
Males								
Flat-rate benefit payable—total	25	702	613	577	541	596	442	328.2
Flat-rate benefit only	10	463	414	402	375	435	331	227.5
Flat-rate benefit and earnings-related supplement[2]	8	–	–	–	–	–	–	–
Flat-rate benefit, earnings-related supplement and supplementary allowance[2,5]	2	–	–	–	–	–	–	–
Flat-rate benefit and supplementary allowance[5]	5	239	199	175	166	161	111	100.7
Supplementary allowance only[5]	50	1 156	1 284	1 350	1 281	1 308	1 140	886
No flat-rate benefit or supplementary allowance[3,5]	2	324	221	234	252	275	279	209.9
Total	77	2 182	2 118	2 161	2 074	2 179	1 861	1 424.1
Females								
Flat-rate benefit payable—total	16	311	325	349	331	359	250	278
Flat-rate benefit only	11	279	295	321	304	333	231	174.8
Flat-rate benefit and earnings-related supplement[2]	5	–	–	–	–	–	–	–
Flat-rate benefit, earnings-related supplement and supplementary allowance[2,5]	–	–	–	–	–	–	–	–
Flat-rate benefit and supplementary allowance[5]	1	32	30	28	27	26	19	18.6
Supplementary allowance only[5]	14	343	401	423	409	407	354	258
No flat-rate benefit or supplementary allowance[3,5]	3	149	162	186	209	225	184	138.3
Total	33	803	888	958	949	991	788	588.7

Note: Figures are based on a five per cent sample. For Northern Ireland figures are based on a twenty per cent sample.

1 1981 figures are for Northern Ireland only. Due to industrial action 1981 figures for Great Britain are not available.

2 Earnings related supplement was abolished from 2 January 1982, but continued in payment for certain transitional cases up to 30 June 1982, when it finally ceased.

3 Prior to November 1978 figures for non-recipients of benefit include non-claimants; from November 1978 only claimants for benefit or credit are included.

4 Figures are for Great Britain only. Due to industrial action November 1985 figures for Northern Ireland are not available.

5 Supplementary Benefit was replaced by Income Support from April 1988, therefore, all references to Supplementary Benefit should be treated as Income Support cases for the 1988 figures supplied.

Sources *Department of Social Security; Department of Health and Social Services (Northern Ireland)*

3.17 Sickness and invalidity benefit

Claimants analysed by age and duration of spell
At beginning of June/At end of statistical year[1]

Thousands

	1978	1979	1980	1981	1982	1983	1984	1985	1986	1987	1988
Age at 31 May/31 March[2]											
Males											
All durations: All ages	891	891	849	834	903	903	840	859	896	913	978.3
Under 20	24	26	22	14	18	13	7	6	6	7	4.2
20–29	88	80	73	64	73	65	43	42	42	37	41
30–39	118	99	99	94	102	95	73	72	78	73	75.5
40–49	144	145	134	132	142	133	123	125	127	128	138.4
50–59	260	276	255	253	269	272	256	259	270	273	295
60–64	222	224	219	228	246	268	277	279	284	282	290.8
65 and over	35	41	49	49	53	57	61	76	89	113	134.2
Over six months: All ages	447	493	502	528	571	613	655	686	726	769	821.7
Under 20	1	2	2	1	2	2	1	1	1	3	1
20–29	12	13	13	18	17	18	22	22	22	22	23.1
30–39	33	31	34	39	41	44	45	46	51	53	54.5
40–49	61	65	67	73	80	84	87	92	93	100	107.2
50–59	147	171	165	168	179	191	200	206	219	226	243.6
60–64	160	172	174	181	200	218	240	244	251	253	260
65 and over	33	39	47	48	52	56	60	75	89	112	133.2
Females											
All durations: All ages	243	254	261	249	297	286	246	258	283	294	347.3
Under 20	24	19	20	11	14	11	5	5	4	5	6.2
20–29	62	69	66	56	65	60	39	35	41	41	43.7
30–39	37	40	43	48	60	53	47	50	53	54	61.8
40–49	46	47	50	51	63	62	55	61	66	67	86
50–59	71	74	76	77	86	91	91	94	102	109	128.7
60 and over	5	6	6	6	8	7	10	13	16	18	22
Over six months: All ages	98	106	112	122	140	158	173	188	211	229	267
Under 20	2	2	1	1	1	1	1	1	1	1	1
20–29	10	13	14	15	17	20	20	18	22	24	24.4
30–39	12	14	17	19	24	26	31	36	39	41	44.7
40–49	20	21	22	27	33	36	39	43	49	55	68.2
50–59	50	51	52	55	59	69	72	77	85	90	107.8
60 and over	4	5	5	5	7	7	8	12	15	18	21.9

Note Figures for Great Britain are based on a 2 per cent sample from 1975/76 to 1977/78 and on a 1 per cent sample thereafter. Figures for Northern Ireland are based on a 20 per cent sample.

1 For Great Britain commencing on first Monday in June up to 1982 and first Monday in April thereafter.
2 From 1984 age at 5 April.

Sources *Department of Social Security; Department of Health and Social Services (Northern Ireland)*

3.18 Sickness and invalidity benefit[1]: days of certified incapacity

Analysis by age at end of period
Years starting on first Monday in June up to 1982 and from first Monday in April thereafter

Millions

	1977/78	1978/79	1979/80	1980/81	1981/82	1982/83	1983/84	1984/85	1985/86	1986/1987	1987/1988
Males: All ages	282.7	298.0	285.2	272.2	280.5	281.4	251.4	262.8	275.8	275.5	294.8
Under 20	6.9	7.2	6.4	5.0	4.8	4.3	1.6	1.7	1.5	1.6	1.1
20–29	29.2	30.3	26.5	23.5	23.0	20.7	12.3	13.1	12.7	11.1	11.7
30–39	37.1	36.2	34.7	32.4	31.9	30.0	21.5	21.7	23.1	21.7	22.1
40–49	46.0	48.2	45.5	42.3	44.1	42.8	35.6	37.2	37.6	37.7	40.3
50–59	79.5	87.8	81.4	76.9	79.3	80.7	73.5	74.9	80.0	78.2	84.8
60–64	65.6	68.3	67.7	68.4	73.9	79.0	81.6	82.9	85.6	83.5	86.6
65 and over	18.3	20.0	23.1	23.8	23.4	24.1	25.1	31.2	35.2	41.7	48.3
Females: All ages	83.4	87.3	87.6	86.3	91.7	93.9	73.5	78.6	85.2	86.9	101.9
Under 20	6.9	7.1	6.4	4.6	4.0	3.4	1.3	1.4	1.1	1.0	1.5
20–29	21.0	25.1	23.1	21.7	21.3	20.2	11.5	10.8	12.0	12.1	13.7
30–39	9.8	12.1	13.4	15.2	15.3	17.7	18.0	13.7	15.1	16.0	17.7
40–49	15.2	15.2	15.8	16.9	19.0	20.0	16.4	17.5	19.5	19.8	24.2
50–59	25.7	23.7	24.0	24.7	25.9	28.5	26.4	28.4	29.9	31.0	36.4
60 and over	2.5	2.8	3.2	3.1	3.8	3.8	4.2	5.4	6.2	7.0	8.4

See *note* to Table 3.17.

Sources *Department of Social Security; Department of Health and Social Services (Northern Ireland)*

3.19 Widow's benefit (excluding widow's allowance[1]: widow's payment[1])

United Kingdom
Number in payment analysed by type of benefit and age of widow
Prior to 1988 figures are for November

Thousands

	September										
	1978	1979	1980[2]	1981	1982	1983	1984[3]	1985	1986	1987	1988
All widow's benefit (excluding widow's allowance)											
All ages	473	467	15	433	426	420	414	398	389	380	388
Under 30	3	3	–	3	3	3	3	3	2	2	3
30 – 39	17	17	1	18	18	19	19	18	18	17	17
40 – 49	77	75	3	70	71	69	68	66	65	64	65
50 – 59	316	320	9	293	289	283	279	266	260	253	258
60 and over	61	54	2	50	46	47	46	45	44	44	46
Widowed mother's allowance – with dependent children											
All ages	95	91	5	84	79	75	78	66	61	57	59
Under 30	3	3	–	2	3	3	3	2	2	2	2
30 – 39	16	16	1	16	17	17	17	16	16	15	15
40 – 49	42	40	2	36	34	32	33	28	26	25	26
50 – 59	33	32	2	29	27	24	26	20	17	15	15
60 and over	–	1	–	1	–	1	–	–	–	–	–
Widowed mother's allowance – without dependent children											
All ages	33	33	1	34	35	35	29	32	31	29	20
30 – 39	1	1	–	1	2	2	2	2	2	2	2
40 – 49	10	11	–	11	12	12	10	12	11	11	8
50 – 59	21	21	1	20	21	19	16	17	16	15	9
60 and over	1	1	–	1	1	1	–	1	1	–	–
Widow's pension											
All ages	235	231	7	208	203	203	201	195	189	185	186
40 – 49	–	–	–	–	–	–	–	–	–	–	–
50 – 59	179	184	5	165	163	162	161	155	152	148	146
60 and over	55	47	2	43	40	41	40	40	38	38	40
Age-related widow's pension[4]											
All ages	110	111	3	109	109	108	107	107	108	108	124
40 – 49	25	24	1	24	25	26	26	26	28	28	31
50 – 59	82	83	2	80	79	77	77	75	75	75	88
60 and over	4	5	–	5	5	5	5	5	5	5	6

1 This is an especially high rate of benefit which is payable for the first 26 weeks of widowhood, provided that the widow is under pensionable age (age 60) or, if she is over that age, provided that her husband was not entitled to retirement pension. Widow's allowance was replaced by widow's payment on 11-4-88.

2 Northern Ireland data only, Great Britain figures not available due to computer error.

3 For 1984 Great Britain data as at March.

4 From 1975 figures for widow's basic pension are included in age-related widow's pension.

Sources *Department of Social Security; Department of Health and Social Services (Northern Ireland)*

3.20 Family allowances/Child benefits[1]

At 31 December

Thousands

	1978	1979	1980	1981	1982	1983	1984	1985	1986	1987	1988
Families receiving allowances:											
Total	7 390	7 409	7 397	7 352	7 261	7 175	7 097	7 035	6 979	6 928	6 923
With 1 child	2 887	2 951	2 987	2 996	2 986	2 979	2 970	2 963	2 962	2 948	2 956
2 children[2]	3 032	3 051	3 055	3 048	3 016	2 978	2 939	2 901	2 851	2 817	2 788
3 children[2]	1 059	1 032	1 005	977	947	918	898	882	874	871	878
4 children[2]	302	278	260	247	234	222	214	213	215	217	222
5 or more children[2]	110	98	90	84	79	78	76	76	75	76	79

1 From April 1977 Family allowance has been replaced by Child benefit which is payable for all children in the family, including the first or only child.

2 Until 1976 including the elder or eldest child for whom no allowance was payable, but excluding children over the age limit.

Sources *Department of Social Security; Department of Health and Social Services (Northern Ireland)*

3.21 Contributory and non-contributory retirement pensions

United Kingdom
Numbers in payment analysed by age group[1]

Thousands (percentages in italics)

	At 31 December			At 30 November		At 30 September[2]					
	1978	1979	1980	1981	1982	1983	1984[3]	1985	1986	1987	1988
Men:											
Age groups:											
65 – 69	1 171	1 171	1 170	1 157	1 130	1 072	1 046	1 066	1 102	1 143	1 178.5
Percentage	*37.3*	*36.5*	*36.0*	*35.2*	*34.4*	*32.6*	*32.0*	*31.7*	*32.3*	*33.1*	*67.4*
70 – 74	982	1 003	1 019	1 026	1 034	1 043	1 047	1 053	1 046	1 010	959.2
Percentage	*31.3*	*31.3*	*31.4*	*31.2*	*31.5*	*31.8*	*32.0*	*31.4*	*30.6*	*29.3*	*56.6*
75 – 79	587	614	629	653	661	684	688	710	720	723	748.2
Percentage	*18.7*	*19.2*	*19.4*	*19.9*	*20.1*	*20.8*	*21.0*	*21.1*	*21.1*	*21.0*	*42.4*
80 – 84	267	279	289	304	315	334	340	363	376	389	403
Percentage	*8.5*	*8.7*	*8.9*	*9.3*	*9.6*	*10.2*	*10.4*	*10.8*	*11.0*	*11.3*	*22.5*
85 – 89	103	105	109	113	113	117	116	127	133	142	152
Percentage	*3.3*	*3.3*	*3.4*	*3.4*	*3.4*	*3.6*	*3.5*	*3.8*	*3.9*	*4.1*	*8.6*
90 and over	31	32	32	34	34	35	36	39	40	42	44
Percentage	*1.0*	*1.0*	*1.0*	*1.0*	*1.0*	*1.1*	*1.1*	*1.2*	*1.2*	*1.2*	*2.5*
Total all ages	3 142	3 205	3 248	3 286	3 286	3 285	3 274	3 359	3 416	3 449	3 485.8
Women:											
Age groups:											
60 – 64	862	852	945	1 007	1 110	1 210	1 274	1 217	1 195	1 154	1 117.6
Percentage	*15.1*	*14.7*	*16.0*	*16.5*	*18.1*	*19.4*	*20.2*	*19.0*	*18.4*	*17.7*	*35.7*
65 – 69	1 421	1 423	1 417	1 410	1 367	1 293	1 260	1 339	1 412	1 488	1 565.3
Percentage	*24.9*	*24.6*	*24.0*	*23.3*	*22.2*	*20.7*	*20.0*	*20.9*	*21.7*	*22.8*	*48.1*
70 – 74	1 344	1 361	1 358	1 373	1 377	1 378	1 380	1 379	1 369	1 319	1 257.2
Percentage	*23.5*	*23.5*	*23.0*	*22.7*	*22.4*	*22.1*	*21.9*	*21.5*	*21.1*	*20.2*	*39.1*
75 – 79	1 009	1 040	1 055	1 085	1 095	1 122	1 127	1 149	1 151	1 160	1 161.2
Percentage	*17.7*	*18.0*	*17.8*	*17.9*	*17.8*	*18.0*	*17.9*	*17.9*	*17.7*	*17.8*	*34.7*
80 – 84	638	658	670	690	701	727	736	768	790	807	827.7
Percentage	*11.2*	*11.4*	*11.3*	*11.4*	*11.4*	*11.6*	*11.7*	*12.0*	*12.2*	*12.4*	*24.3*
85 – 89	314	326	336	348	351	362	365	388	398	415	432.4
Percentage	*5.5*	*5.6*	*5.7*	*5.8*	*5.7*	*5.8*	*5.8*	*6.0*	*6.1*	*6.4*	*12.5*
90 and over	124	130	130	144	146	155	156	171	177	186	194.6
Percentage	*2.2*	*2.2*	*2.2*	*2.4*	*2.4*	*2.5*	*2.5*	*2.7*	*2.7*	*2.8*	*5.5*
Total all ages	5 712	5 791	5 911	6 057	6 148	6 247	6 297	6 413	6 492	6 529	6 556

1 Including pensions payable to persons residing overseas.
2 Northern Ireland as at 30 November.
3 For 1984 Great Britain as at 31 March.

Sources *Department of Social Security; Department of Health and Social Services (Northern Ireland)*

3.22 Family income supplement[1]/Family credit

United Kingdom
At 31 December

Thousands

	1978	1979	1980	1981	1982	1983	1984	1985	1986[3]	1987[4]	1988[5,6]
Families receiving supplements:											
Total	89	89	105	143	179	215	218[2]	214[2]	218	235	298.3
Two-parent families: total	51	43	51	78	105	133	121[3]	117[3]	128	140	189.9
With 1 child	9	7	10	15	21	28	26[3]	25[3]	27	30	44.8
2 children	14	12	15	25	36	47	46[3]	45[3]	50	51	67.1
3 children	13	12	14	19	26	32	29[3]	28[3]	31	34	44.8
4 children	8	7	7	11	13	15	13[3]	12[3]	13	16	21.9
5 children	4	3	3	4	5	6	4[3]	4[3]	5	6	7.8
6 or more children	3	2	3	3	3	3	2[3]	2[3]	2	3	3.6
One-parent families: total	38	46	54	65	74	83	82[3]	82[3]	90	95	108.9
With 1 child	21	24	29	34	40	46	46[3]	46[3]	50	54	61.8
2 children	10	14	17	21	24	28	27[3]	27[3]	30	31	34.7
3 or more children	6	7	8	9	9	10	9[3]	9[3]	10	10	12.3

1 For weekly rates of Family income supplement see Table 3.13.
2 Provisional.
3 Great Britain only; Northern Ireland data unavailable.
4 Great Britain figures are for 30.4.87.
5 From April 1988 Family Income Supplement was replaced by Family Credit.
6 1988 Family Credit figures are at 1 November for Northern Ireland data.

Sources *Department of Social Security; Department of Health and Social Services (Northern Ireland)*

3.23 Income support: Number of beneficiaries receiving weekly payment[1]
Great Britain
On a day in May

Thousands

	1988
All income support	4 352
All aged 60 and over	1 719
Retirement pensioners	1 431
In receipt of other NI benefit	38
Others	250
All under 60	2 632
Unemployed with contributory benefit	133
Unemployed without contributory benefit	1 230
Disabled with contributory benefit	55
Disabled without contributory benefit	192
Lone parent premium not in other groups[2]	694
Others	327

1 Great Britain data is extracted from the Annual Statistical Enquiry undertaken in May 1988.

2 Figures relate to one-parent families headed by a man also.

Source Department of Social Security

3.24 Income support
Great Britain
On a day in May

Thousands

	1988
Number of regular weekly payments	4 352
Total number of persons provided for	7 388
Number of dependants	3 036
Partners	841
Total children under 16 years	2 092
Under 11	1 571
11–15 years	521
16–17 years	91
Other dependants 18 years and over	13

1 Great Britain data is extracted from the Annual Statistical Enquiry undertaken in May 1988.

Source: Department of Social Security

3.25 Income Support: average weekly amounts of benefit
Great Britain
May

Thousands

	1988
All income support	34.25
All aged 60 and over	20.16
Retirement pensioners	14.69
In receipt of other NI benefit	16.10
Others	52.06
All under 60	43.45
Unemployed with contributory benefit	16.15
Unemployed without contributory benefit	43.75
Disabled with contributory benefit	17.00
Disabled without contributory benefit	38.45
Lone parent premium not in other groups	49.09
Others	48.83

1 Great Britain data extracted from the Annual Statistical Enquiry undertaken in May 1988.

2 Figures relate to one parent families headed by a man also.

Source Department of Social Security

3.26 War pensions

Estimated number of pensioners
At 31 March in each year

Thousands

	1977	1978	1979	1980	1981	1982	1983	1984	1985	1986	1987	1988
Total	407.50	391.65	377.25	362.45	349.36	336.19	323.40	310.34	298.50	287.40	271.72	263.86
Disablement— 1914 war; 1939 war and later service	305.50	294.20	283.45	273.00	263.66	253.86	244.50	234.60	225.90	217.80	207.30	201.70
Widows and dependants— 1914 war; 1939 war and later service	102.00	97.45	93.80	89.45	85.70	82.34	78.90	75.74	72.60	69.60	64.42	62.16

Source *Department of Social Security*

3.27 Hospital and family practitioner services
England and Wales

	Unit	1979	1980	1981	1982	1983	1984		1985		1986		1987		1988	
							England	Wales	England	Wales	England	Wales	England	Wales	England	Wales
Hospital services																
In-patients:																
Average daily number of available beds	Thousands	388	383	380	378	372	335	22	326	22	316	22	297	21	..	20.7
Average daily occupation of beds:																
All departments	,,	311	307	304	298	294	269	18	264	17	255	17	..	16	..	15.8
Psychiatric departments	,,	129	125	122	119	116	106	6	101	6	96	6	..	6	..	5.3
Persons on waiting lists at 31 December	,,	726	678	658	787	743	692	40	680	43	676	42	679	41	..	42.5
Discharges or deaths	,,	5 750	6 036	6 135	6 090	6 412	6 178	413	6 354	426	6 414	434	6 619	449	..	459.6
Day case attendances	,,	623	706	751	741	851	903	36	963	45	1 050	62	881	77	..	83.2
Out-patients[1]																
New cases	,,	17 873	18 146	18 489	18 782	19 324	18 721	1 092	19 085	1 108	19 299	1 125	19 409	1 174	..	1 183.5
Total attendances	,,	49 921	50 994	51 656	51 950	53 068	50 812	3 030	51 244	3 080	51 503	3 113	51 552	3 164	..	3 196.8
Staff: at 30 September																
Medical, dental[2]	No. (WTE)	35 184	36 302	37 148	37 745	38 452	36 515	2 420	37 118	2 465	37 505	2 470	37 575	2 491	38 745	2 545
Professional and technical[2,3,14]	,,	63 758	65 630	69 049	71 258	72 852	72 656	4 466	74 298	4 649	76 083	4 771	78 975	4 993	..	5 711
Nursing and midwifery[3,14]	,,	381 478	394 445	417 128	422 990	423 106	397 488	26 448	401 151	27 014	402 690	27 187	404 041	27 764	..	27 920
Administrative: clerical[14]	,,	108 999	111 709	115 179	115 240	116 446	110 304	6 626	111 048	6 787	111 351	6 924	114 595	7 087	..	7 279
Other non medical[4,14]	,,	230 014	231 647	232 956	231 322	226 488	196 533	14 568	183 406	14 406	168 216	13 984	158 258	13 567	..	12 739
Family practitioner services																
Medical services:																
Doctors on the list[5]	Number	22 696	23 184	23 701	24 217	24 719	25 132		24 035	1 523	24 460	1 549	24 922	1 587	25 322	1 599[16]
Number of patients per doctor	,,	2 277	2 238	2 193	2 147	2 108	2 080		2 068	1 914	2 042	1 881	2 020	1 849	1 999	..
Paid to doctors	£ million	493.3	658.6	776.5	878.5	960.5	1019.4	58.0	1 114.9	63.9	1 195.9	68.6	1 314.4	74.5	1 466.7	83.4
Pharmaceutical services:																
Prescriptions dispensed	Million	328.2	327.0	323.4	335.3	339.9	320.5	25.0	318.7	25.0	322.5	25.1	335.3	26.0	3 465	27.1
Payments to pharmacists[6]	£ million	795.9	966.6	1 103.7	1 268.8	1 405.5	1408.7	104.6	1 517.7	111.6	1 643.2	120.3	1 830.7	133.6	2 045.7	149.1
Payment by patients	,,	35.0	62.5	81.3	94.5	102.6	103.3	7.2	114.4	6.8	125.4	7.3	138.1	9.0	131.0	8.1
Paid out of public funds	,,	760.9	904.1	1 022.4	1 174.3	1 302.8	1 305.4	97.4	1 403.3	104.8	1 517.5	113.0	1 692.6	124.6	1 914.7	141.0
Average total cost per prescription	£	2.43	2.96	3.41	3.78	4.14	4.40	4.19	4.76	4.52	5.09	4.80	5.460	5.13	5.90	5.50
Dental services:																
Dentists on the list[7] at 30 September	Number	12 750	13 039	13 473	13 936	14 374	14 066	714	14 334	742	14 516	740	14 765	780	15 070	798
Courses of treatment completed and emergency cases[8]	Thousands	28 538	30 072	30 502	31 468	32 087	30 971	1 637	31 385	1 667	32 279	1 786	32 108	1 788	33 595	1 901.3
Payments to dentists	£ million	320.2	410.5	478.3	536.5	582.6	604.7	31.2	634.9	32.8	698.7	37.5	773.3	40.3	881.8	48.8
Payments by patients	,,	66.5	93.8	115.9	141.9	161.0	167.7	7.5	189.7	8.4	216.9	9.8	233.9	10.3	270.2	14
Paid out of public funds	,,	253.7	316.7	362.4	394.6	421.6	437.0	23.7	445.2	24.4	481.8	27.7	539.4	30.1	611.6	34.8
Average gross cost per course and case	£	11.2	13.7	15.7	17.0	18.12	19.52	19.07	20.23	19.67	21.64	20.84	24.02	23.04	26.19	25.67
General ophthalmic services:																
Sight tests, given[9]	Thousands	8 593	8 795	8 932	9 192	9 558	9 747	561	10 247	597	10 502	623	..	651	..	733.5
Pairs of glasses dispensed/ vouchers issued	,,	4 975	5 148	5 226	5 200	5 176	4 939	344	3 323	233	2 214	161	..	176	..	..
Cost of services (gross)	£ million	79.5	89.6	103.2	126.7	231.8	157.5	9.9	129.6	9.4	127.4	..	141.6	9.1	163.4	10.5
Payments by patients	,,	28.4	30.6	33.1	38.9	44.1	44.1	2.8	21.4	2.4	0.9	..	–[13]	–[13]	..	—
Paid out of public funds:																
For sight testing	,,	33.6	40.8	45.4[11]	87.8[12]	187.7[12]	79.4	4.7	84.9	5.2	84.6	..	95.7	5.7	112.9	7.1
For dispensing	,,	17.5	18.2	24.7[11]			34.0	2.4	23.3	1.8	26.4	..	–[13]	–[13]	—	—
For cost of vouchers[10]											15.5	..	45.9	3.4	50.5	3.4

1 At consultant and general practitioner clinics and accident and emergency departments. Total attendances for England from 1977/88 includes ward attenders.
2 Whole-time equivalents (WTE). Excluding locums and general medical practitioners participating in Hospital Staff Fund.
3 Includes hospital and community staff and agency staff.
4 Including works, maintenance, ancillary and ambulance staff.
5 Principals providing unrestricted services as at 1 October.
6 The cost of prescriptions dispensed during the calendar year as certified by the Pricing authorities.
7 All assistants are included.
8 Number scheduled for payment.
9 Number of sight tests paid for by Family practitioner committees in the period and not those carried out.
10 NHS voucher scheme commenced 1 July 1986.
11 England figures contain an element of arrears payments.
12 Figures contain an element of arrears payments.
13 Dispensing fees ceased to be paid and charges payable with the introduction of the voucher scheme.
14 England 1987 figures include "other statutory authorities" (eg Public Health Laboratory Service and Health Education Authority). Figures for these authorities were not collected in the annual non-medical manpower census prior to 1987. Therefore figures for 1987 are not strictly comparable with those for previous years.
15 For England, from 1987 collection of data changed from year ended 31 Dec. to years ended 31 March. Changes in definition mean that these figures are not comparable with data for earlier years.
16 Provisional.

Sources Department of Health; Welsh Office

3.28 Hospital and primary care services
Scotland

	Unit	1977	1978	1979	1980	1981	1982	1983	1984	1985	1986	1987	1988
Hospital services													
In-patients:													
Average allocated staffed beds[1]	Thousands	59.1	58.8	58.3	57.9	57.9	57.6	57.1	57.2	56.6	56.0	55.3	54.5
Average occupied beds:[1]													
All departments	,,	49.8	49.5	48.7	48.4	48.1	47.8	46.7	47.0	46.6	46.0	45.1	44.4
Mental and mentally deficient	,,	22.7	22.3	21.8	21.3	21.0	20.7	20.0	20.1	19.8	19.3	18.8	18.2
Discharges or deaths[1, 2]	,,	737	749	738	774	793	794	791	810	822	837	843	871
Out-patients[1, 3]:													
New cases	,,	1 920	1 961	1 961	1 999	2 033	2 047	2 042	2 084	2 141	2 196	2 233	2 275
Total attendances	,,	5 128	5 183	5 203	5 321	5 434	5 440	5 422	5 589	5 586	5 668	5 693	5 767
Medical and dental staff[4, 5]:													
Whole-time	Number	4 220	4 293	4 446	4 456	4 479	4 584	4 657	4 696	4 647	4 545	4 565	4 769
Part-time	,,	1 221	1 218	1 280	1 267	1 465	1 362	1 415	1 415	1 428	1 440	1 421	1 505
Professional and technical staff[4,6]:													
Whole-time	,,	5 998	6 267	6 680	6 807	7 033	7 113	7 392	7 492	7 591	7 615	7 672	7 676
Part-time	,,	1 289	1 244	1 360	1 380	1 417	1 461	1 440	1 465	1 489	1 558	1 672	1 716
Nursing and midwifery staff[4]:													
Whole-time	,,	34 484	35 368	36 594	37 977	40 218	40 825	41 337	41 080	41 320	41 295	41 388	41 438
Part-time	,,	23 030	23 311	23 800	23 974	24 407	24 437	24 115	23 850	23 886	24 390	24 640	25 175
Administrative and clerical staff[4]:													
Whole-time	,,	5 105	5 027	5 106	5 158	5 310	5 410	5 535	5 591	5 653	5 612	5 726	6 683
Part-time	,,	1 846	1 838	1 894	1 927	2 066	2 156	2 285	2 408	2 584	2 716	2 903	3 075
Domestic, transport, etc. staff[4]:													
Whole-time	,,	19 804	18 970	17 522	17 289	17 235	17 101	16 604	15 568	14 791	14 089	14 062	13 162
Part-time	,,	14 535	14 914	14 943	15 209	15 659	16 150	16 310	16 298	16 487	16 913	17 235	16 483
Cost of services (gross)[7]	£ million	518.5	628.7	749.3	964.3	1 117.9	1 212.6	1 290.2	1 376.1	1 461.5	1 537.4	..	1 828.1
Payments by patients[7]	,,	0.9	0.8	0.9	1.0	1.2	1.1	1.3	1.2	1.1	1.3	..	1.4
Payments out of public funds[7]	,,	517.6	627.9	748.4	963.3	1 116.7	1 211.5	1 288.9	1 374.9	1 460.4	1 536.1	..	1 826.7
Primary care services													
Medical services													
Doctors on the list[8]:													
Principals	Number	2 839	2 884	2 921	2 959	3 001	3 040	3 106	3 169	3 224	3 271	3 305	3 355
Assistants	,,	40	34	22	28	29	32	31	25	22	21	14	13
Average number of patients per principal doctor	,,	1 905	1 875	1 857	1 835	1 804	1 778	1 739	1 704	1 668	1 653	1 626	1 602
Payments to doctors	£ million	43.7	49.0	59.3	76.7	90.7	102.2	110.8	123.0	133.4	140.5	156.5	165.7
Pharmaceutical services													
Prescriptions dispensed	Million	33.0	34.5	34.3	34.3	33.9	35.0	35.7	36.4	36.4	36.7	38.34	39.50
Payments to pharmacists (gross)[9]	£ million	62.8	81.1	90.1	111.1	126.7	144.4	161.1	172.2	180.2	196.2	217.70	244.02
Average gross cost per prescription	£	2.079	2.341	2.625	3.242	3.741	4.128	4.514	4.734	4.951	5.348	5.678	6.18
Dental services													
Dentists on list[10]	Number	1 164	1 188	1 207	1 251	1 294	1 362	1 407	1 449	1 407	1 488	1 515	1 523
Number of courses of treatment completed	Thousands	2 419	2 419	2 460	2 549	2 595	2 672	2 746	2 792	2 857	2 984	2 987	3 054
Payments to dentists (gross)	£ million	22.2	25.0	29.9	36.6	41.4	46.1	50.9	54.8	59.4	68.0	76.2	36.9
Payments by patients	,,	5.3	5.8	6.9	9.5	12.0	15.3	17.9	20.1	24.1	28.3	30.3	33.9
Payments out of public funds	,,	16.9	19.2	23.0	27.1	29.4	30.8	32.9	34.6	35.3	39.8	45.9	53.0
Average gross cost per course	£	9.2	10.4	12.2	14.3	15.9	17.3	18.5	19.6	20.8	22.7	25.5	28.5
General ophthalmic services													
Number of sight tests given	Thousands	673	688	722	727	736	761	816	857	918	949	1 022	1 141
Number of pairs of glasses supplied[11]	,,	522	489	522	546	552	568	570	604	438	305	338	322
Cost of services (gross)	£ million	6.9	7.4	8.7	10.0	12.1	18.3	17.5	17.8	15.7	13.9	15.9	
Payments by patients	,,	2.4	2.6	2.6	2.8	3.1	3.6	4.3	4.6	2.1	0.5	—	
Payments out of public funds:													
For sight testing and dispensing	,,	4.5	4.8	6.1	7.2	9.0	14.7	13.2	13.2	13.6	13.4	15.9	

1 In year to 30 September, from 1984 is to 31 March.
2 Includes transfers out from 1976 onwards.
3 At out-patient and accident and emergency departments.
4 At 30 September.
5 Figures exclude officers holding honorary and locum appointments. Part-time includes maximum part-time and GP hospital appointments.
6 From 1979 onwards, ODAs (Operating Department Assistants) are included in Professional and technical staff; previously ODAs were included in Ancillary staff.
7 Estimated from financial year figures.
8 At 1 October.
9 For prescriptions dispensed in calendar year by all general practice pharmacists and appliance suppliers.
10 Assistants are excluded.
11 Supply of spectacles restricted from 1 April 1985, include hospital eye service.

Source *Scottish Health Service Common Services Agency*

3.29 Hospital and general health services

Northern Ireland

	Unit	1977	1978	1979	1980	1981	1982	1983	1984	1985	1986	1987	1988
Hospital services													
In-patients:													
Beds available[1]	Number	17 221	17 093	17 126	17 060	17 023	[10]	16 976	16 715	16 595	15 962	15 411	14 686
Average daily occupation of beds	Per cent	*79.7*	*79.8*	*79.9*	*79.8*	*78.4*	[10]	*78.1*	*77.8*	*78.6*	*78.2*	*78.9*	*79.8*
Discharges or deaths	Thousands	231	237	241	246	249	[10]	259	261	274	269	267	267
Out-patients[2]:													
New cases	,,	592	608	618	628	637	[10]	685	720	739	756	770	755[12]
Total attendances	,,	1 590	1 639	1 670	1 736	1 746	[10]	1 893	1 975	2 028	2 025	2 049	1 949[12]
General health services													
Medical services													
Doctors (principals) on the list[3]	Number	734	735	747	764	790	813	838	851	880	908	917	927
Number of patients per doctor[4]	,,	2 163	2 189	2 165	2 097	2 032	1 981	1 951	1 925	1 865	1 823	1 835	1 808
Payments to doctors	£ thousand	11 146	12 310	14 392	19 325	22 923	24 854	28 539	30 668	33 860	35 856	38 935	43 235
Pharmaceutical services													
Prescription forms dispensed	Thousands	7 458	7 802	7 809	7 866	7 886	8 077	8 389	8 429	8 319	8 190	8 522	8 915
Number of prescriptions	,,	12 162	12 591	12 589	12 682	12 691	13 067	13 593	13 667	13 268	13 224	13 920	14 606
Payments to pharmacists (gross)	£ thousand	25 114	29 326	32 814	40 812	47 699	55 454	61 883	64 349	65 570	70 752	79 662	88 688
Payments by patients	,,	808	831	1 202	2 112	2 596	2 807	2 936	3 082	3 168	3 298	3 577	3 900
Payments out of public funds	,,	24 306	28 495	31 612	38 700	45 102	52 646	58 947	61 267	62 401	67 454	76 085	84 787
Average gross cost per prescription	£	2.065	2.329	2.607	3.22	3.76	4.24	4.55	4.71	4.94	5.35	5.72	6.07
Dental services													
Dentists on the list[5]	Number	310	309	319	336	342	363	377	394	420	428	437	460
Number of courses of treatment completed	Thousands	680	688	682	726	752	775	812	838	863	890	909	965
Payments to dentists (gross)	£ thousand	6 984	8 232	9 788	12 733	14 669	15 333	16 952	18 540	19 458	21 202	24 226	27 422
Payments by patients	,,	925	1 067	1 250	1 781	2 252	2 679	3 034	3 384	3 796	4 517	5 156	5 976
Payments out of public funds	,,	6 058	7 166	8 539	10 952	12 417	12 654	13 917	15 156	15 663	16 686	19 071	21 447
Average gross cost per course	£	10.3	12.0	14.3	17.5	19.5	19.8	20.9	22.1	22.5	23.8	26.7	28.4
Ophthalmic services													
Number of sight tests given[6]	Thousands	154	158	162	170	168	161	207	203	219	226	236	281
Number of optical appliances supplied	,,	129	132	135	146	144	143	168	167	115	52	5[11]	—
Cost of service (gross)[7]	£ thousand	1 786	1 902	2 146	2 688	3 085	3 315	6 242	4 892	4 287	3 789	4 484	5 135
Payments by patients	,,	552	620	655	716	756	908	1 210	1 244	524	32	0.40	—
Payments out of public funds	,,	1 234	1 281	1 491	1 971	2 329	2 407	5 031	3 648	3 763	3 758	4 425	5 135
Health and social services[8]													
Medical and dental staff													
Whole-time	Number	1 585	1 711	1 810	1 864	1 874	1 935	1 988	2 044	2 027	2 040	2 065	2 091
Part-time	,,	721	711	726	725	697	661	660	680	692	704	720	719
Nursing and midwifery staff													
Whole-time	,,	12 912	13 269	13 523	14 082	14 971	15 391	15 376	15 288	15 058	14 846	14 634	14 637
Part-time	,,	4 242	4 676	5 288	5 704	5 857	5 811	5 722	5 554	5 549	5 718	5 941	6 207
Administrative and clerical staff													
Whole-time	,,	4 171	4 416	4 586	4 661	4 786	4 833	4 933	5 003	5 079	5 051	5 051	5 175
Part-time	,,	760	867	952	971	1 009	1 071	1 113	1 157	1 208	1 317	1 378	1 445
Professional and technical staff													
Whole-time	,,	1 888	2 051	2 080	2 121	2 157	2 172	2 261	2 309	2 334	2 359	2 408	2 477
Part-time	,,	371	397	414	445	437	442	419	448	435	432	437	453
Social services staff (excluding casual home helps)													
Whole-time	,,	2 751	2 956	3 199	3 402	3 554	3 728	3 717	3 794	3 791	3 850	3 570	3 601
Part-time	,,	708	799	959	1 009	1 086	1 180	1 240	1 284	1 292	1 357	1 382	1 467
Ancillary and other staff													
Whole-time	,,	9 218	9 355	9 357	9 432	9 574	9 608	9 279	9 029	8 826	8 424	7 994	7 551
Part-time	,,	4 063	4 358	4 535	4 644	4 949	5 174	5 238	5 403	5 516	5 553	5 659	5 591
Cost of services (gross)	£ thousand	215 595	248 848	302 901	381 276	438 533	474 189	507 629	534 928	562 636	597 356	639 866[9]	695 515
Payments by recipients	,,	3 064	3 564	4 223	4 978	5 924	7 066	7 850	8 689	9 329	9 684	10 315	10 812
Payments out of public funds	,,	212 531	245 284	298 677	376 298	432 609	467 123	499 779	526 239	553 307	587 670	629 551	684 703

1 Average during year.
2 At out-patient and A & E departments.
3 At 31 September.
4 At 1 July.
5 At 31 December.
6 Excluding sight tests given in hospitals and under the school health service.
7 Figures from 1977 include payments superannuation.
8 Manpower figures refer to 31 December. From 1981, figures for medical and dental staff exclude some joint appointees, information for whom is not held on the computer payroll.
9 Figures relate to the cost of the hospital, community health, and personal social services, and have been estimated from financial year data.
10 Data not available due to industrial action.
11 The decrease in figures is due to legislation introduced on 1 July 1985 which allowed the issue of optical appliances by unregistered suppliers under the 'Voucher Scheme'.
12 Provisional.

Source *Department of Health and Social Services (Northern Ireland)*

3.30 Health and personal social services: manpower summary

Great Britain
At 30 September each year

Number or whole-time equivalent

	1977	1978	1979	1980	1981	1982	1983	1984	1985	1986	1987	1988[7]
Health service staff and practitioners: total	952 595	968 733	986 500	1 010 402	1 047 803	1 058 297	1 059 474	1 048 863	1 043 894	1 029 794	..	
Regional and area health authorities/boards and boards of governors staff: total	900 223	915 678	932 034	954 617	990 572	999 975	999 833	987 919	981 930	969 849	..	
Medical staff: total	40 184	41 261	42 648	43 784	44 706	45 351	46 114	46 375	47 040	47 355	47 119	
Hospital medical staff: total[1]	36 781	37 819	39 179	40 290	41 152	41 808	42 558	42 848	43 456	43 784	43 741	
Consultant and Senior hospital medical officer with allowance	12 400	12 726	13 004	13 482	13 777	14 017	14 349	14 699	14 978	15 281	15 512	
Associate specialist	1 069	1 013	1 020	1 039	1 014	1 035	1 019	995	935	884	865	
Senior registrar	2 639	2 688	2 808	2 933	3 046	3 079	3 187	3 142	3 254	3 326	3 322	
Registrar	6 266	6 479	6 613	6 764	6 787	6 995	7 099	7 054	7 014	7 108	7 097	
Senior house officer including post registration house officer	9 325	9 668	10 285	10 590	10 904	11 023	11 137	11 142	11 351	11 228	10 994	
Pre-registration house officer	3 022	3 149	3 291	3 355	3 419	3 411	3 553	3 483	3 518	3 493	3 478	
Other staff[2]	100	91	81	71	66	58	37	89	36	40	51	
Hospital Practitioner	58	134	165	210	242	251	252	262	257	262	249	
Part-time medical officer (clinical assistant)	1 902	1 871	1 912	1 846	1 898	1 940	1 924	1 982	2 113	2 162	2 170	
Community health medical staff[3]	3 403	3 442	3 469	3 494	3 554	3 543	3 557	3 527	3 586	3 571	3 377	
Dental staff: total	3 154	3 235	3 286	3 288	3 360	3 397	3 372	3 350	3 370	3 322	3 168	
Hospital dental staff: total[1]	1 253	1 288	1 350	1 366	1 408	1 440	1 433	1 487	1 498	1 492	1 470	
Consultant and Senior hospital dental officer with allowance	419	433	452	471	477	485	489	506	508	503	517	
Associate specialist	86	74	76	91	91	101	103	105	99	103	93	
Senior registrar	108	112	111	100	108	106	112	98	97	118	121	
Registrar	175	190	206	204	199	211	210	229	230	223	201	
Senior house officer	157	174	182	186	196	197	202	218	232	215	236	
Dental house officer	157	154	170	159	170	180	166	170	171	168	152	
Other staff[2]	16	16	12	10	10	8	5	5	3	4	5	
Hospital Practitioner	4	7	12	16	15	17	17	15	14	12	13	
Part-time medical officer (clinical assistant)	131	128	128	130	142	136	128	142	145	146	134	
Community health dental staff[3]	1 901	1 948	1 936	1 921	1 952	1 957	1 939	1 863	1 872	1 831	1 697	
Nursing and midwifery staff: (Excluding agency): total	415 694	424 304	433 490	448 824	474 497	481 873	483 061	482 215	486 607	487 273	397 902.5	
Qualified nurses and midwives	219 900	226 904	233 249	240 462	256 921	265 109	270 736	276 602	284 116	287 715	239 354.0	
Student and pupil nurses and midwives	94 939	92 433	91 043	91 983	96 255	97 044	94 167	91 369	86 485	83 148	64 563.8	
Other nursing and midwifery staff	99 675	104 154	108 582	115 808	120 991	119 504	118 063	114 200	115 985	116 404	93 979.5	
Nursing cadets	1 181	813	616	571	330	216	95	44	21	6	5.0	
Professional and technical (excluding works) staff[6]	65 405	68 650	72 097	74 153	77 887	80 299	82 084	86 776	88 839	90 913	77 394.4	
Works and maintenance staff	30 493	30 867	31 243	32 166	32 977	32 971	32 650	32 087	31 566	30 973	24 046.4	
Administrative and clerical staff[4,5]	113 757	115 107	118 078	120 492	124 426	124 863	126 220	126 652	127 594	128 439	110 699.7	
Ambulance officers, ambulancemen/women and other ambulance staff	20 383	20 707	20 223	20 934	21 435	21 590	21 697	21 441	21 595	22 465	19 010.2	
Ancillary staff[6]	211 153	211 547	210 969	210 976	211 284	209 631	204 635	189 023	175 319	159 109	114 497.6	

1 Whole-time equivalent. Figures exclude locums and general medical practitioners participating in Hospital Staff Fund.
2 Figures include Senior Hospital Medical/Dental Officers (SHMO) without an allowance and other ungraded staff.
3 Whole-time equivalent. Figures exclude locums and occasional seasonal staff.
4 Figures exclude ambulance officers.
5 Includes Family Practitioner Service administrative and clerical staff and General Managers.
6 From 1 April 1984, Operating Department Assistants (ODAs) were transferred from Ancillary to Professional and Technical 'B' Staffs Council. Therefore figures for these staff groups prior to September 1984 are not comparable with those for September 1984 onwards (accounting for approximately 3000 WTE in September 1984).
7 Figures for 1988 are not available.

Sources *Department of Health—Scottish Health Service Common Services Agency; Welsh Office*

3.30 Health and personal social services: manpower summary

(continued) Great Britain

At 30 September each year

Number or whole-time equivalent

	1977	1978	1979	1980	1981	1982	1983	1984	1985	1986	1987	1988
Family Practitioner Committee services:												
Practitioners: Total	48 283	48 988	50 310	51 381	52 897	54 136	55 397	56 688	57 755	55 689	..	..
General medical practitioners[7]: total	26 810	27 227	27 696	28 414	29 252	29 806	30 422	30 976	31 465	31 854	32 422	32 992[13]
Unrestricted principals	24 939	25 245	25 614	26 141	26 702	27 256	27 825	28 299	28 783	29 279	29 808	30 267[13]
Restricted principals	315	296	276	257	238	227	204	195	184	175	172	174[13]
Assistants	435	391	345	312	315	301	317	300	258	283	260	286[13]
Trainees	1 121	1 295	1 461	1 704	1 997	2 022	2 076	2 182	2 240	2 117	2 182	2 265[13]
General dental practitioners: total	13 564	13 740	13 989	14 316	14 803	15 305	15 769	16 185	16 483	16 744	17 083	17 440
Principals	13 359	13 573	13 845	14 173	14 671	15 181	15 646	16 069	16 375	16 640	16 969	17 144
Assistants	205	167	144	143	132	124	123	116	108	104	114	296
Ophthalmic medical practitioners[8]	949	913	918	938	963	957	951	972	981	1 007	963	..
Ophthalmic opticians[8]	5 235	5 246	5 680	5 511	5 540	5 608	5 697	5 830	6 011	6 084[12]	6 281	..
Dispensing opticians[8]	1 725	1 862	2 027	2 200	2 338	2 460	2 558	2 725	2 815	—	..	..
Dental Estimates Board staff:												
Total	1 588	1 577	1 565	1 682	1 626	1 603	1 679	1 698	1 691	1 720	1 469.8	..
Professional and technical staff (Ex works)	6	1	1	1	1	1	1	1	1	1	1.0	..
Administrative and clerical staff	1 538	1 533	1 521	1 639	1 579	1 556	1 632	1 653	1 647	1 676	1 424.5	..
Ancillary and maintenance staff	44	43	43	42	46	46	47	44	43	43	44.3	..
Prescription Pricing Authority/ Prescription Pricing Division staff/Welsh Pricing Committee[9]:												
Total	2 501	2 490	2 591	2 722	2 708	2 583	2 565	2 558	2 518	2 512	1 847.0	..
Professional and technical staff (works)	..	..	..	..	..	..	..	..	..	1	1.0	..
Administrative and clerical staff	2 448	2 434	2 534	2 661	2 645	2 526	2 506	2 499	2 454	2 446	1 784.3	..
Ancillary and maintenance staff	53	56	57	61	63	57	58	59	63	65	61.7	..
Other Statutory Authorities:[10]												
Total	..	..	..	..	..	..	..	..	..	..	2 862.3	..
Nursing and midwifery staff	..	..	..	..	..	..	..	..	..	..	6.0	..
Professional and technical (excluding works) staff	..	..	..	..	..	..	..	..	..	..	1 580.1	..
Professional and technical staff (works)	..	..	..	..	..	..	..	..	..	..	22.0	..
Administrative and clerical staff	..	..	..	..	..	..	..	..	..	..	686.3	..
Ancillary and maintenance staff	..	..	..	..	..	..	..	..	..	..	567.9	..
Personal social services staff[11]	187 930	192 160	193 614	199 534	200 945	203 344	209 993	212 856	217 013	223 898	232 019[13]	..

7 Figures relate to 1 October.
8 Figures relate to 31 December.
9 The Prescription Pricing Authority in England is synonymous with the Prescription Pricing Division in Scotland. Figures for the Prescription Pricing Division in Scotland relate to 30 November.
10 Prior to 1987 figures for "other statutory authories" (e.g. Public Health Laboratory service and Health Education Authority) were not collected in the annual non-medical manpower census.
11 Figures are for England only.
12 As from 1 July 1986 dispensing opticians no longer perform general ophthalmic services.
13 Provisional.

Source *Department of Health; Scottish Health Service Common Services Agency; Welsh Office*

3.31 NHS hospitals: selected diagnoses of in-patients treated in non-psychiatric departments (excluding maternity)

Great Britain

International Classification of Diseases (ICD), Injuries and Causes of Death Ninth Revision (1975), World Health Organisation

Thousands

	Code numbers	1979	1980	1981	1982	1983	1984	1985	1986[1]
Diagnostic group									
All causes: total	001 – 999	4 961.1	5 167.9	5 355.7	5 295.2	5 601.6	5 771.2	6 005.3	. .
Males		2 376.4	2 461.4	2 549.5	2 526.7	2 661.4	2 740.9	2 819.8	. .
Females		2 584.7	2 706.5	2 806.2	2 768.5	2 940.2	3 030.3	3 185.5	. .
Tuberculosis: total	010 – 018	10.9	10.3	9.2	7.5	7.9	6.3	5.7	. .
Males		6.6	6.5	5.7	4.3	4.5	3.6	3.2	. .
Females		4.3	3.8	3.5	3.2	3.4	2.7	2.5	. .
Malignant neoplasms: total	140 – 208	417.0	433.8	451.5	460.9	472.3	475.8	482.9	. .
Males		211.3	217.4	226.1	233.1	239.8	239.5	245.5	. .
Females		205.7	216.4	225.4	227.8	232.5	236.3	237.4	. .
Benign and unspecified neoplasms: total	210 – 239	95.3	96.7	97.8	93.0	99.5	102.5	106.4	. .
Males		26.8	27.0	28.6	26.9	28.3	28.7	28.2	. .
Females		68.5	69.7	69.2	66.1	71.2	73.8	78.2	. .
Endocrine, metabolic and nutritional diseases and immunity disorders: total	240 – 279	96.9	100.4	101.3	97.5	102.2	100.5	97.0	. .
Males		38.1	40.2	40.4	39.7	40.8	40.7	39.9	. .
Females		58.8	60.2	60.9	57.8	61.4	59.8	57.1	. .
Diseases of nervous system: total	320 – 359	103.5	109.5	114.9	114.0	119.4	122.2	125.1	. .
Males		48.9	52.0	55.0	54.3	56.5	59.1	59.7	. .
Females		54.6	57.5	59.9	59.7	62.9	63.1	65.4	. .
Diseases of the heart, including rheumatic fever and hypertensive disease: total	390 – 429	337.1	346.1	359.9	373.7	385.2	401.1	417.2	. .
Males		194.4	198.7	206.9	214.8	220.6	230.6	238.9	. .
Females		142.7	147.4	153.0	158.9	164.6	170.5	178.3	. .
Cerebrovascular disease and other diseases of circulatory system: total	430 – 459	248.7	262.3	271.3	260.6	285.5	293.5	298.5	. .
Males		124.4	128.4	131.1	127.6	138.4	140.6	143.2	. .
Females		124.3	133.9	140.2	133.0	147.1	152.9	155.3	. .
Diseases of respiratory system: total	460 – 519	410.4	444.1	459.3	467.2	489.6	507.8	550.1	. .
Males		232.8	249.4	260.7	261.3	274.3	283.8	305.2	. .
Females		177.6	194.7	198.6	205.9	215.3	224.0	244.9	. .
Diseases of digestive system: total	520 – 579	550.8	578.1	595.8	558.6	600.0	604.2	616.9	. .
Males		293.9	310.6	316.6	291.4	315.8	316.1	323.9	. .
Females		256.9	267.5	279.2	267.2	284.2	288.1	293.0	. .
Diseases of urinary system: total	580 – 599	96.3	101.5	106.4	110.5	116.9	120.6	126.0	. .
Males		52.0	55.8	57.9	62.0	64.2	67.1	55.9	. .
Females		44.3	45.7	48.5	48.5	52.7	53.5	70.1	. .
Complications of pregnancy, childbirth and puerperium: Females	630 – 676	157.2	159.1	159.6	159.8	160.1	161.9	162.7	. .
Diseases of musculo-skeletal system: total	710 – 739	239.0	271.8	292.2	277.1	312.8	326.1	334.2	. .
Males		107.8	123.1	130.4	123.9	137.7	145.3	148.7	. .
Females		131.2	148.7	161.8	153.2	175.1	180.8	185.5	. .
Fractures, dislocations and sprains: total	800 – 848	215.8	209.8	218.7	225.9	228.6	234.6	243.9	. .
Males		113.7	108.8	112.0	116.9	116.6	121.3	123.0	. .
Females		102.1	101.0	106.7	109.0	112.0	113.3	120.9	. .
Other injuries and reactions: total	850 – 999	419.0	412.4	428.4	423.8	417.0	420.5	421.3	. .
Males		237.1	232.5	243.0	241.9	241.1	243.9	244.6	. .
Females		181.9	179.9	185.4	181.9	175.9	176.6	176.7	. .
Other causes: total		1 563.2	1 632.0	1 689.4	1 665.1	1 804.6	1 893.6	1 966.5	. .
Males		688.5	711.0	735.1	728.6	782.8	820.6	845.6	. .
Females		874.7	921.0	954.3	936.5	1 021.8	1 073.0	1 120.9	. .

1 Later figures still not available.

Sources *Department of Social Security; Office of Population Censuses and Surveys; Welsh Office; Scottish Health Service*

3.32 Notifications of infectious diseases

Number

	1977	1978	1979	1980	1981	1982	1983	1984	1985	1986	1987	1988
United Kingdom												
Diphtheria	3	–	–	5	2	4	4	4	4	4	2	1
Typhoid and paratyphoid fevers	327	353	313	307	277	253	269	219	262	260	215	369
Scarlet fever	11 903	10 239	10 815	12 936	8 024	8 415	7 609	7 231	7 451	7 881	7 275	7 087
Measles	190 374	133 707	93 371	147 938	61 747	105 634	114 945	67 631	104 774	90 207	46 070	90 635
Whooping cough	18 729	70 508	33 200	22 873	21 459	70 868	21 589	6 219	24 244	39 939	17 354	5 879
Smallpox	–	2	–	–	–	–	–	–	–	–	–	–
Dysentery	8 332	5 486	4 037	3 595	3 674	3 256	6 039	8 734	6 111	5 096	3 979	3 946
Food poisoning	9 639	12 167	13 128	12 021	12 994	17 478	20 486	23 237	20 242	26 645	32 234	43 013
Tuberculosis: total	11 172	11 221	10 721	10 486	9 290	8 449	7 792	7 044	6 648	6 856	5 705	5 753
Respiratory	8 507	8 357	8 015	7 789	6 817	6 696	6 138	5 579	5 293	5 421	4 514	4 470
Other	2 665	2 864	2 706	2 697	2 473	1 906	1 764	1 512	1 404	1 489	1 181	1 221
Acute poliomyelitis[1]	18	3	8	3	2	4	5	–	5	4	3	2
England and Wales[2]												
Diphtheria	2	–	–	5	2	4	4	4	4	4	2	1
Typhoid and paratyphoid fevers	296	331	293	290	254	234	259	206	252	239	203	354
Scarlet fever	10 769	9 169	9 585	11 116	7 148	7 601	6 539	6 327	6 438	6 888	6 439	5 949
Measles	173 342	124 064	77 363	139 485	52 975	94 195	103 700	62 079	97 408	82 054	42 165	86 001
Whooping cough	17 475	65 956	30 816	21 131	19 395	65 810	19 340	5 517	22 046	36 506	15 203	5 117
Smallpox	–	2	–	–	–	–	–	–	–	–	–	–
Dysentery	6 202	4 332	2 786	2 708	3 398	2 850	5 003	6 844	5 334	4 774	3 617	3 692
Food poisoning	7 922	9 739	11 060	10 071	9 925	14 242	17 726	20 702	18 114	23 937	29 331	39 713
Ophthalmia neonatorum	239	228	235	278	210	201	208	247	258	298	300	374
Tuberculosis[3] total	9 520	9 682	9 266	9 142	8 128	7 406	6 800	6 141	5 857	5 992	5 046	5 164
Respiratory[4]	7 121	7 078	6 807	6 670	5 859	5 827	5 317	4 871	4 660	4 758	4 010	4 019
Other[4]	2 399	2 604	2 459	2 472	2 269	1 732	1 593	1 317	1 246	1 288	1 026	1 083
Acute poliomyelitis[1]	16	3	8	3	2	2	4	–	4	3	3	2
Acute encephalitis (infective and post infective)	103	154	79	91	58	71	56	37	39	51	57	65
Acute meningitis: total	1 339	1 697	1 427	1 796	1 393	1 271	1 226	1 230	1 345	2 172	2 542	2 987
Meningococcal	500	500	525	509	464	410	428	401	548	870	1 050	1 304
Scotland												
Diphtheria	1	–	–	–	–	–	–	–	–	–	–	–
Typhoid and paratyphoid fevers	29	20	18	17	20	18	10	13	10	20	11	14
Erysipelas	94	78	90	99	87	76	75	69	88	111	120	112
Scarlet fever	821	766	818	1 343	592	552	734	512	649	728	562	658
Measles	8 626	8 953	10 324	6 646	4 698	10 581	6 193	4 897	4 595	7 073	2 695	2 258
Whooping cough	943	3 500	1 885	1 366	1 385	4 224	1 870	271	1 118	2 943	1 588	356
Smallpox	–	–	–	–	–	–	–	–	–	–	–	–
Dysentery	2 015	1 076	1 052	854	204	261	871	1 554	512	286	344	196
Food poisoning	1 563	2 319	1 937	1 836	2 934	3 038	2 632	2 391	1 967	2 436	2 480	2 998
Ophthalmia neonatorum	37	33		27	38	45	86	87	61	101	56	9
Puerperal fever and pyrexia	11	10	5	2	9	4	6	6	5	9	5	2
Tuberculosis total[5]	1 465	1 322	1 224	1 138	972	902	829	738	707	756	560	534
Respiratory	1 226	1 093	1 014	943	799	762	692	586	560	578	425	406
Other	239	229	210	195	173	140	137	152	147	178	135	128
Acute poliomyelitis[1]	–	–	–	–	–	1	1	–	1	1	–	–
Cholera	–	–	–	–	–	–	–	3	–	1	–	–
Northern Ireland												
Diphtheria	–	–	–	–	–	–	–	–	–	–	–	–
Typhoid and paratyphoid fevers	2	2	2	–	3	1	–	–	–	1	1	1
Scarlet fever	313	304	412	477	284	262	336	392	364	265	274	480
Measles	8 406	690	5 684	1 807	4 074	858	5 052	655	2 771	1 080	1 210	2 376
Whooping cough	311	1 052	499	376	679	834	379	431	1 080	490	563	406
Smallpox	–	–	–	–	–	–	–	–	–	–	–	–
Dysentery	115	78	199	33	72	145	165	336	265	36	18	58
Food poisoning	154	109	131	114	135	198	128	144	158	272	423	302
Tuberculosis: total	187	217	231	206	190	141	163	162	83	108	99	86
Respiratory	160	186	194	176	159	107	129	118	72	85	79	71
Other	27	31	37	30	31	34	34	44	11	23	20	15
Acute poliomyelitis[1]	2	–	–	–	–	1	–	–	–	–	–	–
Acute meningitis	–	–	–	–	–	115	117	182	149	162	102	154
Acute encephalitis	–	–	–	–	–	5	4	2	1	5	2	2
Infective hepatitis	–	–	–	–	–	530	252	132	97	153	506	527
Gastro-enteritis (persons under 2 years of age only)	–	–	–	–	–	560	598	575	606	806	745	869
Rubella[6]												124
Mumps[6]												532

1 Including acute polioencephalitis.

2 The figures show the corrected number of notifications, incorporating revisions of diagnosis, either by the notifying medical practitioner or by the medical superintendent of the infectious diseases hospital. Cases notified in Port Health Districts are excluded.

3 Formal notifications of new cases only. The figures from 1982 exclude chemoprophylaxis.

4 From 1982 categories overlap and therefore cases will be included in respiratory and other tuberculosis.

5 Figures include cases of tuberculosis not notified before death.

6 From 1st July 1988 only.

Sources *Office of Population Censuses and Surveys; Scottish Health Service Common Services Agency; Department of Health and Social Services (Northern Ireland)*

3.33 Deaths due to occupationally related lung disease

	1978	1979	1980	1981	1982	1983	1984	1985	1986	1987
Asbestosis (without mesothelioma)	109	102	102	137	128	121	129	140	166	144
Mesothelioma[2]	390	434	458	472	504	573	624	615	700	806
Pneumoconiosis (other than asbestosis)	391	391	330	341	314	317	314	324	337	279
Byssinosis	19	24	17	26	22	33	24	25	29	25
Farmer's lung and other occupational allergic alveolitis		14	9	13	15	15	10	7	15	16
Total	909	965	916	989	983	1 059	1 101	1 111	1 247	1 270

1 The data in this table is derived from death certificates. For asbestosis and mesothelioma, the figure shown is the number of certificates mentioning the disease. For the other diseases the figure is the number of deaths coded to the disease as underlying cause.

2 Not all mesothelioma cases are related to occupational exposure to asbestos. The 'natural' rate for mesothelioma is probably about 2 per million per year, equivalent to approximately 100 deaths annually for GB.

Sources *Health and Safety Executive; Office of Population Censuses and Surveys*

3.34 New cases of occupational disease diagnosed under the Industrial Injuries and Pneumoconiosis, Byssinosis and Miscellaneous Diseases benefit schemes

	Disablement Benefit									
	1979	1980	1981	1982	1983	1984	1985	1986	1987	1988
A. Occupational lung diseases and deafness										
Pneumoconiosis (except asbestosis)	725	665	657	611	540	451	468	480	469	411
Asbestosis	135	150	153	185	212	200	301	329	282	225
Byssinosis	76	156[3]	113	135	74	63	37	27	25	15
Farmer's lung	10	14	12	11	8	4	6	11	8	15
Occupational asthma	–[4]	–[4]	–[4]	105	175	136	170	171	202[3]	222[3]
Mesothelioma	..	..	93	123	148	201	245	305	399	479
Lung cancer (asbestos)	–[4]	–[4]	–[4]	–[4]	–[4]	–[4]	8	34	55	59
Lung cancer (nickel)	1	2	0	0	1	5	2	3	0	0
Bilateral pleural thickening	–[4]	–[4]	–[4]	–[4]	–[4]	–[4]	61	111	115	114
Other occupational lung disease	5	9	3	9	6	1	2	5	10	5
Occupational deafness[1]	555	661[3]	1 022	680	447[3]	1 443[3]	1 464	1 179	1 381	1 515
Total: Occupational lung disease and deafness	1 507	1 657	2 053	1 859	1 611	2 504	2 764	2 655	2 946	3 060

	Injury and Disablement Benefit					Disablement Benefit				
	1978/79	1979/80	1980/81	1981/82	1982/83[5]	1983/84	1984/85	1985/86	1986/87[2]	1987/88[2]
B. Other diseases										
Dermatitis	7 004	5 816	3 960	3 452	2 110	611	619	785	464	368
Tenosynovitis	3 259	3 009	2 413	2 282	1 433	337	390	619	376	322
Vibration white finger	–[4]	–[4]	–[4]	–[4]	–[4]	–[4]	3	641	1 366	1 673
Beat conditions	765	734	621	525	324	131	180	220	57	171
Viral hepatitis	25	32	40	26	24	3	5	9	5	3
Tuberculosis	44	39	32	29	11	6	7	3	13	3
Leptospirosis	2	3	7	1	4	2	0	0	1	0
Other infections	28	11	9	2	3	2	0	1	5	0
Poisonings	37	29	23	30	14	2	4	3	9	2
Occupational cancers	19	21	15	6	5	8	6	12	27	29
Other conditions	130	84	73	55	35	22	15	27	58	39
Total: Other diseases	11 313	9 778	7 193	6 408	3 963	1 124	1 229	2 320	2 381	2 610

1 For occupational deafness figures to 1982 are for years ending in June; for 1983 ending December; from 1984, years ending September.

2 From October 1986 disablement benefit was paid only for cases with disability assessed at 14% or more; the figures for 1986–87 and 1987–88 include cases not qualifying for benefit but assessed at 1–13%.

3 Series affected by widening of prescription rules.

4 The following diseases were first prescribed during the period covered by the table:

	Benefit first payable in
Occupational asthmas	1982
Lung Cancer (asbestos)	1985
Bilateral pleural thickening	1985
Vibration white finger	1984/85

5 For year 1982/83 the figures are for 10 months (June 82 to March 83).

Sources *Health and Safety Executive; Department of Social Security*

3.35 Fatal injuries[1] at work

Standard Industrial Classification 1980

Number

		1982	1983	1984	1985	1986/87[7]	1987/88[7]
0	Agriculture, forestry and fishing	66	64	61	75	60	63
01	Agriculture and horticulture	61	54	56	68	54	59
02	Forestry	5	9	4	7	6	4
03	Fishing	–	1	1	–	–	–
1	Energy and water supply industries	78	55	71	63	37	35
11	Coal extraction and manufacture of solid fuels	45	31	20	30	19	15
12	Coke ovens	–	–	1	1	–	–
13	Extraction of mineral oil and natural gas[2]	14	10	13	8	4	9
14	Mineral oil processing	3	1	1	1	1	1
15	Nuclear fuels industry[3]	. .	. .	. .	. .	1	–
16	Production and distribution of electricity, gas and other forms of energy	11	9	15	20	9	9
17	Water supply industry	5	4	21	3	3	1
2	Extraction of minerals and ores other than fuels; manufacture of metals, mineral products and chemicals	57	32	61	45	45	43
21/23	Extraction and preparation of metalliferous ores/extraction of minerals nes.	13	6	18	20	15	13
22	Metal manufacture	26	11	23	13	10	16
24	Manufacture of non-metallic mineral products	11	4	15	6	12	8
25	Chemical industry	6	11	5	6	8	6
26	Man-made fibres industry	1	–	–	–	–	–
3	Metal goods, engineering and vehicles industries	53	39	52	46	41	36
31	Manufacture of metal goods nes.	13	6	15	6	6	9
32	Mechanical engineering	19	18	19	19	19	15
33	Manufacture of office machinery and data processing equipment	–	–	–	2	1	–
34	Electrical and electronic engineering	8	3	5	2	4	5
35	Manufacture of motor vehicles and of motor vehicles parts thereof	3	6	3	6	3	3
36	Manufacture of other transport equipment	10	6	10	10	7	4
37	Instrument engineering	–	–	–	1	1	–
4	Other manufacturing industries	34	63	37	38	29	24
41/42	Food, drink and tobacco industry	10	23	10	13	12	9
43	Textile industry	6	5	4	8	8	1
44	Leather and leather goods industry	–	–	1	–	1	–
45	Footwear and clothing industry	1	13	–	–	1	–
46	Timber and wooden furniture industries	9	9	14	6	2	4
47	Manufacture of paper and paper products; printing and publishing	6	6	5	7	1	5
48	Processing of rubber and plastics	1	4	2	2	2	5
49	Other manufacturing industries	1	3	1	2	2	–
2–4	Total manufacturing industries	144	134	150	129	115	103
5	Construction	131	151	124	139	139	158
6	Distributive trades, hotels and catering; repairs	43	45	42	38	35	41
7	Transport and communication	58	47	50	53	37	54
8	Banking and finance, insurance, business services and leasing	3	–	–	1	9	6
9	Other services	66	78	87	122	50	84
	Unclassified[4]	14	24	18	10	17	15
	Total reported to enforcement authorities	603	598	603	630	499	559
	Reported to other authorities under:						
	Merchant shipping regulations:[5]						
	(*a*) Seamen	49	19	14	7	13[8]	44[8]
	(*b*) Fishermen:						
	Deep sea trawlers (over 80 ft. in length)[6]	3	5	2	1	8[8]	4[8]
	Other fishing vessels	14	22	11	21	11[8]	12[8]
	Total fishermen	17	27	13	22	19[8]	16[8]
	Total merchant shipping, etc. regulations	66	46	27	29	32[8]	60[8]
	Civil aviation (various legislation)	6	4	3	2	4[8]	1[8]
	Total reported to other authorities	72	50	30	31	36[8]	61[8]
	Total reported to all authorities	675	648	633	661	535	620

See note and footnotes on page 73.

Sources *Health and Safety Executive (HSE); Department of Energy; Department of Transport; Civil Aviation Authority*

3.36 Private households with usual residents: Census 1981

Number of families and family type by selected tenures of households in permanent buildings and with no car

Figures are a ten per cent sample

Number of families in household and family type	All households	Selected tenures of households in permanent buildings: Owner occupied	Rented: From council or new town	Rented: Unfurnished	With no car
Great Britain					
All households	1 949 341	1 084 545	607 085	114 553	768 474
Households with no family	516 171	222 685	174 084	53 066	365 946
One person	423 980	178 732	152 025	44 603	322 613
Two or more persons	92 191	43 953	22 059	8 463	43 333
Households with one family	1 416 132	852 256	426 900	60 909	397 726
Married couple family	1 252 564	787 622	345 521	52 289	310 261
With no children	498 920	306 319	133 694	31 371	162 350
With at least one dependent child	595 088	387 713	158 577	15 342	117 754
With non-dependent child(ren) only	158 556	93 590	53 250	5 576	30 157
Lone parent family	163 568	64 634	81 379	8 620	87 465
With at least one dependent child	91 582	31 859	49 605	3 825	53 815
With non-dependent child(ren) only	71 986	32 775	31 774	4 795	33 650
Households with two or more families	17 038	9 604	6 101	578	4 802
England and Wales					
All households	1 770 745	1 022 529	509 678	107 279	681 914
Households with no family	469 089	208 665	148 560	49 763	329 447
One person	384 915	167 373	129 989	41 836	290 990
Two or more persons	84 174	41 292	18 571	7 927	38 457
Households with one family	1 286 201	804 662	356 095	56 972	348 387
Married couple family	1 139 273	743 572	286 554	48 887	271 792
With no children	458 406	290 246	113 575	29 478	145 770
With at least one dependent child	537 926	364 711	129 228	14 201	100 570
With non-dependent child(ren) only	142 941	88 615	43 751	5 208	25 452
Lone parent family	146 928	61 090	69 541	8 085	76 595
With at least one dependent child	83 057	30 327	43 270	3 613	47 667
With non-dependent child(ren) only	63 871	30 763	26 271	4 472	28 928
Households with two or more families	15 455	9 202	5 023	544	4 080
Scotland					
All households	178 596	62 016	97 407	7 274	86 560
Households with no family	47 082	14 020	25 524	3 303	36 499
One person	39 065	11 359	22 036	2 767	31 623
Two or more persons	8 017	2 661	3 488	536	4 876
Households with one family	129 931	47 594	70 805	3 937	49 339
Married couple family	113 291	44 050	58 967	3 402	38 469
With no children	40 514	16 073	20 119	1 893	16 580
With at least one dependent child	57 162	23 002	29 349	1 141	17 184
With non-dependent child(ren) only	15 615	4 975	9 499	368	4 705
Lone parent family	16 640	3 544	11 838	535	10 870
With at least one dependent child	8 525	1 532	6 335	212	6 148
With non-dependent child(ren) only	8 115	2 012	5 503	323	4 722
Households with two or more families	1 583	402	1 078	34	722

Sources *Office of Population, Censuses and Surveys; General Register Office (Scotland)*

Table 3.35
See *Note* on page 45.
1 Includes work related fatalities to employees and non-employees, ie the self employed and members of the public.
2 Includes figures for the oil and gas industry collected under the Mineral Workings (Offshore Installations) Act 1971.
3 Included with SIC80. Class 25, for the years 1982–85.
4 Mainly injuries reported to local authorities.
5 Includes deaths of the crew on board vessels registered in the United Kingdom from casualties to vessels and accidents on board (excluding homicide and suicide) and the presumed deaths of crew members missing at sea for 1980–82 reported under the Merchant Shipping (Returns of Births and Deaths) Regulations. The fatalities reported for 1983–87/8 are reported under the Merchant Shipping (SORADO) Regulations (SI-1982/876). They are those which occurred on board or on access equipment to all vessels registered in the UK.
6 From 1983 this should read 'over 24 metres in length'.
7 Data for year commencing 1st April 1986.
8 Calendar year 1987.

3.37 Parliamentary elections

Thousands

	23 Feb 1950	25 Oct 1951	26 May 1955	8 Oct 1959	15 Oct 1964	31 Mar 1966	18 June 1970[1]	28 Feb 1974	10 Oct 1974	3 May 1979	9 June 1983	11 June 1987
United Kingdom												
Number of electors	34 412	34 919	34 852	35 397	35 894	35 957	39 615	40 256	40 256	41 573	42 704	43 666
Average—electors per seat	55.1	55.9	55.3	56.2	57.0	57.1	62.9	63.4	63.4	65.5	65.7	67.2
Number of valid votes counted	28 771	28 597	26 760	27 863	27 657	27 265	28 345	31 340	29 189	31 221	30 671	32 530
As percentage of electorate	*83.6*	*81.9*	*76.8*	*78.7*	*77.1*	*75.8*	*71.5*	*77.9*	*72.5*	*75.1*	*71.8*	*74.5*
England and Wales												
Number of electors	30 177	30 626	30 591	31 109	31 610	31 695	34 931	35 509	35 509	36 695	37 708	38 568
Average—electors per seat	55.1	56.5	55.9	56.9	57.8	57.9	63.9	64.3	64.3	66.5	67.2	68.8
Number of valid votes counted	25 483	25 356	23 570	24 619	24 384	24 116	24 877	27 735	25 729	27 609	27 082	28 832
As percentage of electorate	*84.4*	*82.8*	*77.0*	*79.1*	*77.1*	*76.1*	*71.2*	*78.1*	*72.5*	*75.2*	*71.8*	*74.8*
Scotland												
Number of electors	3 370	3 421	3 388	3 414	3 393	3 360	3 659	3 705	3 705	3 837	3 934	3 995
Average—electors per seat	47.5	48.2	47.7	48.1	47.8	47.3	51.5	52.2	52.2	54.0	54.6	55.5
Number of valid votes counted	2 727	2 778	2 543	2 668	2 635	2 553	2 688	2 887	2 758	2 917	2 825	2 968
As percentage of electorate	*80.9*	*81.2*	*75.1*	*78.1*	*77.6*	*76.0*	*73.5*	*77.9*	*74.5*	*76.0*	*71.8*	*74.3*
Northern Ireland												
Number of eligible electors on day of election	865	872	873	875	891	902	1 025	1 027	1 037	1 028	1 050	1 090
Average—electors per seat	72.1	72.5	72.8	72.9	74.2	75.2	85.4	85.6	86.4	85.6	61.8	64.1
Number of valid votes counted	561	463	647	576	638	596	779	718	702	696	765	730
As percentage of electorate	*64.9*	*53.1*	*74.1*	*65.8*	*71.7*	*66.1*	*76.0*	*69.9*	*67.7*	*67.7*	*72.9*	*67.0*
Number of Members of Parliament elected:	625	625	630	630	630	630	630	635	635	635	650	650
Conservative	297	320	344	364	303	253	330	296	276	339	396	375
Labour	315	295	277	258	317	363	287	301	319	268	209	229
Liberal	9	6	6	6	9	12	6	14	13	11	17	17
Social Democratic Party	–	–	–	–	–	–	–	–	–	–	6	5
Scottish National Party	–	–	–	–	–	–	1	7	11	2	2	3
Plaid Cymru	–	–	–	–	–	–	–	2	3	2	2	3
Other[2]	4	4	3	2	1	2	6	15	13	13	18	18

1 The Representation of the People Act 1969 lowered the minimum voting age from 21 to 18 years with effect from 16 February 1970.

2 The Speaker is included in Other.

Source *Home Office; Scottish Home and Health Department; Northern Ireland Office*

3.38 Parliamentary by-elections

	June 1970 – Feb 1974	Previous[1] General Election June 1970	March 1974 – Oct 1974	Previous[1] General Election Feb 1974	Oct 1974 – May 1979	Previous[1] General Election Oct 1974	May 1979 – June 1983	Previous[1] General Election May 1979	June 1983 – June 1987	Previous[1] General Election June 1983
Number of by-elections	30		1		30		20		31	
Votes recorded										
By party (*percentages*)										
Conservative	*34.2*	*44.8*	*11.1*	*12.2*	*45.1*	*34.8*	*23.8*	*33.7*	*16.0*	*23.3*
Labour	*40.5*	*42.2*	*62.6*	*66.1*	*36.6*	*44.8*	*25.7*	*35.2*	*14.9*	*14.8*
Liberal[2]	*15.3*	*6.0*	*12.5*	*14.8*	*10.9*	*17.3*	*9.0*	*8.0*	*15.0*	*10.9*
Social Democratic Party[2]	–	–	–	–	–	–	*14.2*	–	*5.6*	*3.0*
Plaid Cymru	*1.2*	*0.3*	–	–	–	–	*0.5*	*0.4*	*0.3*	*0.3*
Scottish National Party	*3.5*	*1.1*	–	–	*2.7*	*2.6*	*1.7*	*1.4*	–	–
Other	*5.4*	*5.6*	*13.7*	*6.9*	*4.7*	*0.5*	*25.1*[3]	*21.2*[3]	*48.2*[4]	*47.6*[4]
Total votes recorded										
(*percentages*)	*100.0*	*100.0*	*100.0*	*100.0*	*100.0*	*100.0*	*100.0*	*100.0*	*100.0*	*100.0*
(thousands)	1 028	1 210	15	36	1 058	1 288	715	852	1 235	1 410

1 Votes recorded in the same seats in the previous General Election. Does not apply to June 1983 election in Northern Ireland.

2 The Social Democratic Party was launched on 26 March 1981. An SDP candidate contested a Parliamentary seat for the first time in the by-election held at Warrington on 16 July 1981. From that date, the Liberal and Social Democratic Parties contested 26 by-elections with only one of the parties putting up a candidate in each.

3 The proportions of votes recorded for 'other' is high because three of the 20 by-elections were in Northern Ireland. Two were in the same constituency, Fermanagh and South Tyrone, and as votes recorded at both by-elections have been included, votes recorded for the 1979 General Election have been included twice in the previous General Election column.

4 The proportion of votes recorded for 'other' is high because 15 of the 31 by-elections were in Northern Ireland.

Source *Home Office*

4 Law enforcement

There are differences in the legal and judicial systems of England and Wales, Scotland and Northern Ireland which make it impossible to provide tables covering the United Kingdom as a whole in this section. These differences concern the classification of offences, the meaning of certain terms used in the statistics, the effects of the several Criminal Justice Acts and recording practices.

Court proceedings and police cautions

The statistical basis of the tables of court proceedings is broadly similar in England and Wales, Scotland and Northern Ireland; the tables show the number of persons found guilty, recording a person under the heading of the principal offence of which he is found guilty, excluding additional findings of guilt at the same proceedings. A person found guilty at a number of separate court proceedings is included more than once.

The statistics on offenders cautioned cover only those who, on admission of guilt, were given a formal caution by, or on the instructions of, a senior police officer as an alternative to prosecution; written warnings by the police for motoring offences and persons paying fixed penalties for certain motoring offences are excluded. There are no statistics on cautioning available for Northern Ireland.

For England and Wales from 1979 a new offence classification and tabulation procedure was introduced to reflect the changes in the mode of trial introduced by Part III of the Criminal Law Act 1977 in July 1978. Figures for 1977 and 1978 are given on the new basis to enable comparisons to be made with 1979 to 1983. Indictable offences cover offences for which a defendant may be tried at the Crown Court; summary offences cover offences for which the defendant may only be tried at a Magistrates' Court. Since 29 March 1982 the courts have had the power to suspend between one quarter and three quarters of a sentence of imprisonment of six months for up to two years; from 31 January 1983 Section 30 of the Criminal Justice Act 1982 reduced the minimum period to three months and allowed a minimum of 28 days to be served. Part I of the Criminal Justice Act 1982, with effect from 24 May 1983, abolished borstal training and imprisonment for offenders aged under 21 and introduced youth custody.

Section 45 of the Criminal Justice (Scotland) Act 1980 was implemented on 15 November 1983; this introduced unified custodial sentencing for under 21 offenders and abolished borstal training.

In Northern Ireland non-indictable offences are dealt with at Magistrates' Courts where some indictable offences may also be tried. The majority of indictable offences are, however, tried at Crown Courts. The Crown Court system was introduced in Northern Ireland in April 1979; prior to this date the County Courts and Assizes system was equivalent to the Crown Court in England and Wales.

4.1 Notifiable[1] offences recorded by the police
England and Wales

Thousands

	1978	1979	1980[2]	1981[2]	1982[2]	1983[2]	1984[2]	1985[2]	1986[2]	1987[2]	1988
Violence against the person	87.1	95.0	97.2	100.2	108.7	111.3	114.2	121.7	125.5	141.0	158.2
Sexual offences[3]	22.4	21.8	21.1	19.4	19.7	20.4	20.2	21.5	22.7	25.2	26.5
Burglary	560.1	544.0	618.4	718.4	805.4	808.3	892.9	866.7	931.6	900.1	817.8
Robbery	13.1	12.5	15.0	20.3	22.8	22.1	24.9	27.5	30.0	32.6	31.4
Theft and handling stolen goods	1 441.3	1 416.1	1 463.5	1 603.2	1 755.9	1 705.9	1 808.0	1 884.1	2 003.9	2 052.0	1 931.3
Fraud and forgery	122.2	118.0	105.2	106.7	123.1	121.8	126.1	134.8	133.4	133.0	133.9
Criminal damage[3]	306.2	320.5	359.5	386.7	417.8	443.3	497.8	539.0	583.6	589.0	594.0
Other offences[4]	9.1	8.8	8.3	8.9	9.0	13.8	15.0	16.7	16.7	19.3	22.7
Total	2 561.5	2 536.7	2 688.2	2 963.8	3 262.4	3 247.0	3 499.1	3 611.9	3 847.4	3 892.2	3 715.8

1 These offences were referred to in 1978 and earlier years as 'Indictable offences recorded by the police'.
2 Figures for 1980 onwards are not comparable with those for previous years because of changes to improve the consistency of recording of multiple, continuous and repeated offences.
3 Includes from the beginning of 1983 offences of 'Gross indecency with a child'.
4 Includes from the beginning of 1983 offences of 'Trafficking in controlled drugs'.

Source Home Office

4.2 Police Forces: authorised establishment and strength

End of year

Number

	1978	1979	1980	1981	1982	1983	1984	1985	1986	1987	1988
England and Wales											
Regular police											
Authorised establishment[1]	117 668	118 322	118 930	120 008	120 125	120 447	120 679	120 903	121 785	122 648	123 551
Strength:											
Men	99 134	102 360	105 563	107 379	108 517	108 519	108 102	107 960	108 225	109 773	109 900
Women	8 477	9 394	10 355	10 702	10 935	10 995	11 001	11 213	11 600	12 492	13 007
Seconded[2]:											
Men	1 386	1 477	1 430	1 424	1 419	1 407	1 388	1 439	1 617	1 716	1 730
Women	78	78	75	70	80	82	82	90	108	121	122
Additional constables[3]:											
Men	85	114	96	90	89	84	83	79	88	70	69
Women	1	2	1	1	1	2	–	1	1	–	–
Special constables											
Enrolled strength:											
Men	14 636	13 513	12 438	11 813	11 932	11 743	11 749	11 550	11 140	10 927	10 578
Women	2 316	2 447	2 629	2 791	3 228	3 588	4 307	4 611	4 930	5 282	5 210
Scotland											
Regular police[4]											
Authorised establishment:											
Men / Women	13 162	13 148	13 187	13 195	13 205	13 261	13 283	13 377	13 489	13 569	13 707
Strength[5]:											
Men	11 477	12 280	12 419	12 379	12 433	12 435	12 415	12 455	12 504	12 470	12 498
Women	746	786	771	749	719	713	722	761	838	933	1 020
Central service[5, 6]:											
Men	51	56	60	54	55	65	61	69	70	73	65
Women	4	4	5	2	2	2	2	1	2	3	3
Seconded[5, 7]:											
Men	72	72	69	78	73	68	67	67	88	85	88
Women	5	3	2	5	4	3	3	3	4	5	7
Additional regular police											
Authorised establishment[4]	179	126	72	67	62	60	88	88	86	73	64
Strength	176	148	71	66	62	60	88	88	86	73	64
Part-time auxiliaries[8]											
Strength:											
Men	2 974	2 944	2 807	2 612	2 528	2 439	2 250	1 846	1 755	1 561	1 514
Women	164	184	198	202	208	204	203	200	209	216	233
Northern Ireland											
Royal Ulster Constabulary											
Strength:											
Men	5 495	5 938	6 224	6 622	7 017	7 328	7 487	7 610	7 581	7 591	7 568
Women	615	676	711	712	701	675	640	649	653	645	659
Royal Ulster Constabulary											
Reserve Strength:											
Men	3 904	3 823	4 123	4 350	4 385	4 105	4 102	4 199	4 127	4 319	4 268
Women	704	690	629	520	455	388	337	309	287	325	386

1 Total of establishments of individual forces *plus* the Metropolitan Regional Crime Squad and additional constables in the Metropolitan Police.
2 Regional Crime Squads, other inter-force units and officers on central service.
3 Excluding additional constables in the Metropolitan Police Force.
4 From 1976, officers employed at ports, airports and oil related industries are no longer included in 'Regular police' but included in 'Additional regular police'.
5 'Strength' includes central service and seconded police.
6 Instructors at Training Establishments, etc. formerly shown as secondments.
7 Scottish Crime Squad, Officers on courses, etc.
8 Including special constables (enrolled strength).

Sources Home Office; Scottish Home and Health Department; Northern Ireland Office

4.3 Offenders found guilty: by offence group

Magistrates' courts and the Crown Court
England and Wales

Thousands

	1978	1979	1980	1981	1982	1983	1984	1985	1986	1987	1988
Offenders[1] of all ages found guilty											
					Indictable offences						
Violence against the person:											
Murder	0.1	0.1	0.2	0.1	0.1	0.1	0.2	0.2	0.2	0.2	0.2
Manslaughter	0.2	0.3	0.3	0.3	0.2	0.2	0.2	0.3	0.3	0.3	0.3
Wounding	40.8	46.2	50.0	48.7	49.6	49.5	45.8	45.3	40.9	45.6	50.9
Other offences of violence against the person	1.5	1.9	1.9	1.7	1.7	1.6	1.6	1.7	1.5	1.8	2.1
Sexual offences	7.5	7.4	8.0	6.9	6.6	6.4	5.6	6.0	5.5	6.2	7.2
Burglary	69.0	59.1	68.1	76.4	76.5	72.7	72.7	69.4	56.3	54.2	48.4
Robbery	3.4	3.2	3.5	4.1	4.4	4.0	4.3	4.4	4.2	4.4	4.3
Theft and handling stolen goods	226.3	220.6	233.6	232.2	238.7	224.9	219.2	216.3	183.2	175.9	163.4
Fraud and forgery	19.9	20.9	24.9	25.7	24.9	25.6	25.7	25.5	22.8	22.5	22.7
Criminal damage	9.5	9.2	11.4	11.8	11.4	12.1	11.5	11.5	10.1	10.6	11.8
Other offences (excluding motoring)	15.8	21.6	27.9	29.0	31.2	33.4	33.5	34.3	29.1	35.6	43.7
Motoring offences	20.2	21.8	25.7	27.7	29.8	30.5	29.2	29.0	27.5	29.1	31.3
Total	414.2	412.3	455.4	464.6	475.1	461.0	449.4	443.9	381.5	386.4	386.3
					Summary offences						
Assaults	11.6	12.4	12.2	11.2	11.1	10.7	11.4	10.5	9.6	10.8	11.5
Betting and gaming	0.7	0.8	0.8	0.5	0.5	0.6	0.3	0.3	0.1	0.1	–[3]
Breach of local or other regulations	16.8	16.9	19.2	15.8	14.7	14.4	13.3	12.5	13.0	12.6	11.0
Intoxicating Liquor Laws:											
Drunkenness	98.0	105.6	109.5	97.2	96.4	96.2	60.5	49.2	38.0	42.3	45.3
Other offences	8.0	8.9	8.6	6.5	4.9	4.5	3.5	2.8	3.0	2.7	3.8
Education Acts	3.7	3.5	3.7	3.0	2.9	2.5	2.7	2.9	3.1	2.9	2.8
Game Laws	1.9	1.8	1.7	1.9	1.7	1.9	1.8	1.5	1.4	1.4	1.3
Labour Laws	0.8	0.6	0.4	0.4	0.3	0.2	0.3	0.2	0.2	0.1	0.1
Summary offences of criminal damage and malicious damages	33.3	36.2	38.6	37.8	36.6	38.6	39.0	38.5	34.2	35.4	35.2
Offences by prostitutes	3.7	3.0	3.4	4.1	5.8	10.4	8.6	9.2	9.1	8.2	8.8
Railway offences	15.1	15.0	18.1	17.4	15.4	15.9	13.3	11.9	9.7	8.3	9.2
Revenue Laws	62.2	63.6	83.3	73.6	72.7	107.8	108.7	114.3	121.9	107.4	113.4
Motoring offences (summary)	1 088.9	1 079.8	1 294.1	1 210.5	1 128.0	1 161.7	1 083.2	1 052.0	1 066.2	738.1	713.9
Vagrancy Acts	4.2	3.8	3.9	2.9	2.0	1.6	1.3	0.9	0.8	0.9	1.0
Wireless Telegraphy Acts	40.8	33.7	44.7	49.6	61.9	67.5	77.2	80.6	128.6	120.4	124.3
Other summary offences	72.8	100.2	114.2	107.5	100.7	99.7	88.3	79.7	72.8	76.6	87.6
Total	1 462.5	1 485.8	1 756.3	1 640.1	1 555.9	1 634.5	1 513.5	1 467.0	1 510.0	1 168.3	1 169.1
Persons aged under 17 found guilty[2]											
					Indictable offences						
Violence against the person	6.0	6.6	7.4	7.3	7.3	6.7	6.0	5.6	4.4	4.2	4.3
Sexual offences	0.6	0.7	0.7	0.6	0.6	0.6	0.5	0.5	0.4	0.4	0.4
Burglary	28.8	22.6	25.6	25.8	23.0	21.2	20.7	18.1	12.9	11.0	9.1
Robbery	0.9	0.7	0.8	1.0	1.0	0.8	1.0	0.9	0.8	0.8	0.8
Theft and handling stolen goods	47.8	45.2	48.3	44.6	42.9	38.0	36.1	32.7	25.1	21.4	17.6
Fraud and forgery	1.0	1.0	1.1	1.1	0.9	0.8	0.8	0.8	0.6	0.5	0.4
Criminal damage	2.8	2.6	3.3	3.1	2.8	2.9	2.6	2.4	1.8	1.6	1.5
Other offences (excluding motoring)	0.3	0.5	0.6	0.7	0.7	0.6	0.7	0.6	0.5	0.9	1.1
Motoring offences	1.5	2.0	2.5	2.4	2.5	1.9	1.9	1.6	1.4	1.2	1.2
Total	89.7	81.9	90.3	86.6	81.8	73.3	70.2	63.2	48.0	42.0	36.5
					Summary offences						
Highway Acts and motoring summary offences:											
Offences with pedal cycles	2.3	2.7	3.1	2.4	2.1	2.2	1.9	1.3	0.7	0.4	0.2
Other	14.4	13.1	15.0	15.5	11.2	10.9	9.1	7.8	7.4	4.5	3.8
Breach of local or other regulations	1.0	1.1	1.4	0.9	0.8	0.8	0.6	0.5	0.4	0.3	0.1
Summary offences of criminal damage and malicious damage	7.0	6.8	7.5	7.1	6.0	6.2	5.3	5.0	3.9	3.1	2.5
Railway offences	1.5	1.6	1.6	0.7	0.7	0.7	0.6	0.4	0.2	0.2	0.2
Other summary offences	8.9	9.2	9.2	5.1	7.5	6.5	5.6	4.5	2.1	3.2	3.6
Total	35.1	34.5	37.8	31.7	28.3	27.1	23.1	19.5	14.6	11.6	10.4

1 Includes 'Companies', etc. (see Tables 4.5 and 4.6).
2 Figures for persons aged under 17 are included in the totals for all offenders above.
3 Less than 50

Source Home Office

4.4 Offenders cautioned: by offence group

England and Wales

Thousands

	1978	1979	1980	1981	1982	1983	1984	1985	1986	1987	1988
Offenders[1] of all ages cautioned					Indictable offences						
Violence against the person	4.4	4.7	5.1	5.6	6.5	7.0	7.8	9.0	9.5	11.3	12.7
Sexual offences	3.0	2.8	2.9	2.8	2.7	2.9	2.8	2.9	2.9	3.2	3.6
Burglary	11.1	10.0	11.3	11.5	11.2	12.0	13.5	14.3	12.8	13.0	12.2
Robbery	0.1	0.1	0.1	0.1	0.2	0.2	0.2	0.2	0.2	0.2	0.2
Theft and handling stolen goods	79.1	75.0	77.0	79.2	85.9	86.9	92.3	109.0	100.3	106.5	92.6
Fraud and forgery	1.3	1.2	1.4	1.4	1.4	1.6	1.8	2.2	2.7	3.9	4.0
Criminal damage	2.1	2.0	2.0	2.1	1.9	2.4	2.6	3.1	3.0	3.5	4.3
Other offences (excluding motoring)	1.8	1.0	1.1	1.2	1.5	2.1	3.0	4.7	5.5	8.1	11.0
Total	103.0	96.8	100.9	103.9	111.3	114.9	124.1	145.4	136.9	149.8	140.7
					Summary offences						
Assaults	0.1	0.1	0.1	0.2	0.2	0.2	0.4	0.6	0.8	0.8	0.9
Betting and gaming	0.1	0.2	0.2	0.2	0.1	0.1	0.1	0.1	0.1	0.1	0.1
Breach of local or other regulations	1.1	1.1	1.2	1.3	1.2	1.2	2.1	3.3	3.4	2.0	2.0
Intoxicating Liquor Laws:											
Drunkenness	0.5	0.6	0.7	0.7	0.8	2.1	21.2	26.1	29.2	40.7	48.6
Other offences	2.4	2.5	3.0	3.0	2.8	2.2	2.0	2.2	0.5	3.3	4.0
Education Acts	[3]	[3]	[3]	[3]	[3]	[3]	[3]	[3]	[3]	[3]	[3]
Game Laws	0.2	0.2	0.2	0.1	0.2	0.2	0.2	0.2	0.2	0.2	0.2
Labour Laws	[3]	[3]	[3]	[3]	[3]	[3]	[3]	[3]	[3]	0.1	0.1
Summary offences of criminal damage and malicious damage	6.1	5.9	7.4	8.5	9.2	10.1	11.2	12.7	13.1	13.1	13.5
Offences by prostitutes	5.4	5.3	6.2	7.9	7.9	7.3	4.9	4.2	4.9	4.7	5.2
Railway offences	0.1	0.1	0.1	0.1	0.1	0.1	0.1	0.2	0.2	0.4	0.4
Revenue Laws	1.1	1.4	1.2	1.4	1.6	1.4	1.6	1.7	1.6	1.3	1.0
Highway Act offences	8.8	9.8	11.7	14.0	12.4	12.9	10.7	9.2	10.0	5.6	5.1
Vagrancy Acts	0.3	0.2	0.3	0.2	0.2	0.2	0.3	0.3	0.3	0.6	0.6
Wireless Telegraphy Acts	—	—	[3]	[3]	[3]	[3]	[3]	[3]	[3]	[3]	[3]
Other summary offences	11.8	12.3	12.7	12.4	12.5	12.7	11.6	12.6	12.4	13.7	13.1
Total	38.4	39.7	45.0	50.0	49.2	50.6	66.3	73.3	76.6	86.7	94.7
Persons aged under 17 cautioned[2]					Indictable offences						
Violence against the person	2.9	3.1	3.4	3.8	4.4	4.8	5.1	5.7	5.2	5.7	6.2
Sexual offences	1.3	1.3	1.4	1.4	1.4	1.5	1.4	1.5	1.2	1.3	1.5
Burglary	10.8	9.7	11.0	11.2	10.7	11.5	12.9	13.6	11.7	11.8	10.9
Robbery	0.1	0.1	0.1	0.1	0.1	0.2	0.2	0.2	0.2	0.2	0.2
Theft and handling stolen goods	69.2	65.2	66.6	68.2	73.2	73.2	75.6	86.8	70.8	71.1	57.9
Fraud and forgery	0.8	0.8	0.9	0.8	0.8	0.9	0.9	1.1	1.1	1.4	1.3
Criminal damage	2.0	1.9	1.8	1.9	1.8	2.2	2.4	2.8	2.5	2.8	3.4
Other offences (excluding motoring)	0.4	0.1	0.2	0.3	0.4	0.5	0.5	0.8	0.7	1.3	1.4
Total	87.5	82.2	85.5	87.6	93.0	94.6	99.1	112.5	93.5	95.7	82.8
					Summary offences						
Highway Acts offences:											
Offences with pedal cycles	4.3	4.7	5.3	5.4	4.8	5.0	4.2	3.1	2.3	1.6	1.5
Other	0.8	0.7	0.8	1.6	0.8	0.7	0.6	0.7	1.8	0.6	0.4
Breach of local or other regulations	0.6	0.6	0.7	0.6	0.6	0.6	0.8	1.0	1.0	0.7	0.6
Summary offences of criminal damage and malicious damage	5.2	5.0	6.5	7.5	8.0	8.7	9.4	10.5	9.7	8.5	8.5
Railway offences	0.1	0.1	0.1	0.1	0.1	0.1	0.1	0.1	0.1	0.2	0.2
Other summary offences	4.9	4.9	5.5	5.5	5.4	5.6	5.7	6.7	5.1	7.1	7.4
Total	15.9	16.0	18.9	20.6	19.8	20.8	20.8	22.1	20.0	18.7	18.6

1 Includes 'Companies', etc. (see Tables 4.5 and 4.6).
2 Figures for persons aged under 17 are included in the figures for all offenders above.
3 Less than 50.

Source Home Office

4.5 Offenders found guilty of offences: by sex and age

Magistrates' courts and the Crown Court

England and Wales

Thousands

	1978	1979	1980	1981	1982	1983	1984	1985	1986	1987	1988
Males						Indictable offences					
All ages	350.5	349.2	386.6	397.9	407.7	397.0	387.4	382.5	331.7	336.4	337.5
10 and under 14 years	18.6	16.1	16.9	15.1	13.6	11.6	10.9	9.1	6.1	4.3	3.7
14 and under 17 years	60.8	56.6	63.5	62.3	59.5	54.4	52.8	48.1	37.7	34.3	29.6
17 and under 21 years	91.5	93.8	106.1	113.9	119.6	115.3	114.0	114.0	98.9	99.9	97.2
21 years and over	179.6	182.7	200.0	206.6	215.1	215.8	209.6	211.3	189.0	198.0	207.1
						Summary offences					
All ages	1 294.7	1 314.8	1 547.3	1437.1	1 358.8	1 411.7	1 298.3	1 247.3	1 252.6	972.5	974.5
10 and under 14 years	3.2	3.2	3.2	2.7	2.2	2.2	1.8	1.5	1.0	0.7	0.6
14 and under 17 years	29.7	29.0	32.2	27.0	24.5	23.5	20.0	16.9	12.8	10.4	9.2
17 and under 21 years	181.6	193.0	227.7	215.8	213.2	212.2	192.3	183.1	171.5	148.9	145.6
21 years and over	1 080.2	1 089.6	1 284.3	1 191.6	1 118.9	1 173.8	1 084.2	1 045.7	1 067.3	812.6	819.1
Females						Indictable offences					
All ages	65.5	62.7	67.8	65.5	66.1	62.7	59.9	59.0	50.0	47.5	46.1
10 and under 14 years	2.3	2.0	2.0	1.8	1.7	1.3	1.0	0.9	0.5	0.3	0.3
14 and under 17 years	8.0	7.2	7.8	7.5	7.0	6.1	5.4	5.0	3.7	3.1	2.9
17 and under 21 years	12.6	13.0	14.7	14.6	15.1	14.8	14.4	14.8	12.7	12.2	11.5
21 years and over	42.6	40.5	43.3	41.6	42.3	40.5	39.0	38.4	33.1	31.9	31.4
						Summary offences					
All ages	144.0	145.9	181.0	175.6	169.4	190.4	183.0	189.3	227.4	175.2	176.4
10 and under 14 years	0.2	0.1	0.2	0.1	0.1	0.1	0.1	0.1	0.1	1	1
14 and under 17 years	2.0	2.1	2.2	1.8	1.5	1.4	1.2	1.0	0.7	0.6	0.5
17 and under 21 years	11.8	12.2	14.8	14.7	14.8	16.7	14.9	14.5	14.9	12.4	12.9
21 years and over	130.0	131.5	163.8	158.9	153.1	172.3	166.7	173.8	211.6	162.2	163.0
Companies, etc.											
Indictable offences	0.4	0.4	1.1	1.2	1.3	1.4	2.2	2.3	2.4	2.5	2.7
Summary offences	25.0	25.0	28.0	27.4	29.1	32.4	32.3	30.4	30.0	20.7	18.2

1 Less than 50.

Source *Home Office*

4.6 Offenders cautioned by the police: by sex and age

England and Wales

Thousands

	1978	1979	1980	1981	1982	1983	1984	1985	1986	1987	1988
Males						Indictable offences					
All ages	79.6	69.1	73.3	75.1	78.5	82.7	91.6	104.2	98.7	111.5	107.0
10 and under 14 years	36.3	31.1	31.9	32.2	31.6	32.0	33.2	34.4	26.3	26.0	22.9
14 and under 17 years	32.7	28.9	31.7	32.6	35.4	37.5	42.1	48.0	43.6	48.0	43.0
17 and under 21 years	3.5	3.0	3.2	3.4	3.8	4.4	5.7	7.5	10.5	14.3	15.0
21 years and over	7.1	6.1	6.5	6.9	7.7	8.7	10.6	14.4	18.3	23.2	26.1
						Summary offences					
All ages	23.4	30.2	33.8	36.8	36.2	38.2	54.6	62.0	64.3	73.8	80.6
10 and under 14 years	2.7	5.1	5.6	6.3	5.9	6.3	6.2	6.1	4.9	4.1	4.0
14 and under 17 years	7.0	9.5	11.4	12.4	12.0	12.4	12.5	13.9	13.2	12.6	12.5
17 and under 21 years	2.7	3.2	3.6	4.5	4.6	4.6	7.0	8.3	10.1	12.1	12.4
21 years and over	11.0	12.4	13.2	13.7	13.7	14.9	28.9	33.8	36.2	45.0	51.8
Females						Indictable offences					
All ages	29.4	27.6	27.7	28.8	32.9	32.2	32.4	41.1	38.2	38.3	33.7
10 and under 14 years	13.0	11.9	11.3	11.5	12.8	12.0	10.4	12.5	8.7	7.5	5.3
14 and under 17 years	10.7	10.3	10.6	11.3	13.2	13.1	13.3	17.6	14.9	14.2	11.7
17 and under 21 years	0.7	0.7	0.7	0.8	1.0	1.1	1.6	2.1	3.5	4.2	4.2
21 years and over	5.0	4.7	5.0	5.2	5.9	6.1	7.0	8.9	11.1	12.4	12.5
						Summary offences					
All ages	9.0	9.5	11.1	13.1	13.0	12.4	11.6	11.3	12.2	13.0	14.1
10 and under 14 years	0.2	0.4	0.5	0.5	0.5	0.6	0.6	0.5	0.4	0.4	0.4
14 and under 17 years	0.8	1.0	1.4	1.5	1.4	1.6	1.5	1.6	1.6	1.6	1.8
17 and under 21 years	2.9	2.8	3.3	3.9	3.7	3.1	2.5	2.2	2.6	2.8	2.9
21 years and over	5.1	5.3	5.9	7.3	7.3	7.1	7.0	7.0	7.7	8.2	9.1
Companies, etc.											
Indictable offences	—	—	1	1	1	1	1	1	1	1	1
Summary offences	0.1	0.1	0.1	0.1	0.1	0.1	0.1	0.1	0.1	1	1

1 Less than 50.

Source *Home Office*

4.7 Sentence or order passed on offenders sentenced for indictable offences: by sex

Magistrates' courts and the Crown Court
England and Wales

Percentages

	1978	1979	1980	1981	1982	1983	1984	1985	1986	1987	1988
Males											
Sentence or order											
Absolute discharge	0.6	0.6	0.6	0.6	0.6	0.6	0.5	0.5	0.5	0.5	0.6
Conditional discharge	9.8	9.1	9.3	9.9	10.2	10.5	11.2	11.0	11.3	11.4	11.1
Probation order	4.1	4.5	5.0	5.4	5.5	6.0	6.7	7.1	7.7	8.1	8.3
Supervision order	3.6	3.6	3.7	3.3	3.1	2.8	2.8	2.7	2.4	2.1	1.8
Fine	50.0	49.8	48.1	45.0	44.0	42.8	41.2	39.7	38.9	38.5	39.4
Community service order	3.2	3.6	4.7	5.9	6.5	7.5	8.2	8.4	8.6	8.7	8.5
Attendance centre order	2.9	2.9	3.2	3.4	3.5	3.6	3.4	3.3	2.8	2.5	2.2
Care order	1.3	1.0	1.0	0.8	0.7	0.5	0.4	0.3	0.3	0.2	0.1
Young offender institution	5.5	5.2	5.1	5.3	5.1	6.5	7.7	7.9	7.5	7.3	6.7
Imprisonment											
Fully suspended[2]	7.7	7.6	7.4	7.6	7.7	6.7	6.0	6.4	6.6	6.9	7.3
Partly suspended[3]					0.3	0.9	0.9	0.9	0.8	0.7	0.7
Unsuspended[4]	10.3	10.7	10.6	11.3	11.7	10.4	9.7	10.7	11.3	11.8	11.7
Other sentence or order	1.1	1.2	1.2	1.1	1.2	1.2	1.2	1.2	1.1	1.3	1.5
Total number of offenders (thousands) = 100 per cent	350.8	349.5	387.9	399.2	409.6	397.8	387.8	383.0	332.5	336.8	337.5
Females											
Sentence or order											
Absolute discharge	0.9	0.8	0.8	0.8	0.8	0.8	0.8	0.7	0.7	0.8	0.8
Conditional discharge	19.4	18.8	19.1	20.8	21.7	22.3	23.5	24.5	25.5	26.6	28.1
Probation order	11.4	12.6	14.0	14.9	15.2	15.8	16.4	16.7	18.0	18.2	18.1
Supervision order	3.6	3.7	3.7	3.5	3.2	2.5	2.4	2.1	1.6	1.4	1.2
Fine	53.5	52.0	49.8	46.2	45.0	44.0	41.7	40.0	37.4	35.6	34.4
Community service order	1.1	1.4	1.7	1.9	2.3	2.6	3.0	3.0	3.5	3.5	3.8
Attendance centre order	–	0.2	0.5	0.7	0.8	0.8	0.7	0.6	0.5	0.4	0.4
Care order	1.3	1.0	1.0	0.9	0.6	0.5	0.3	0.3	0.2	0.1	0.1
Young offender institution	0.5	0.5	0.6	0.4	0.3	0.9	1.4	1.5	1.5	1.4	1.3
Imprisonment											
Fully suspended[2]	4.9	5.1	5.0	5.3	5.7	5.0	4.9	5.3	5.4	5.5	5.7
Partly suspended[3]					0.2	0.6	0.7	0.6	0.6	0.7	0.6
Unsuspended[4]	2.7	2.9	3.0	3.4	3.5	3.2	3.3	3.7	3.9	4.5	4.2
Other sentence or order	0.7	1.0	0.9	0.9	0.9	1.0	1.1	1.0	1.1	1.2	1.4
Total number of offenders (thousands) = 100 per cent	65.5	62.7	67.8	65.4	66.0	62.7	59.9	59.1	59.1	47.5	46.1

1 Includes borstal training (abolished January 1983), detention centre orders and youth custody (both abolished October 1988).
2 Up until 1982 this was known as Suspended sentence.
3 Introduced on 29 March 1982.
4 Up until 1982 this was known as Immediate imprisonment.

Source Home Office

4.8 Receptions into prison[1]: by number of previous convictions

England and Wales

Number of receptions

	1978	1979	1980	1981	1982	1983[2,3]	1984	1985	1986	1987	1988
Number of previous convictions:											
Males:											
None	1 936	1 634	1 731	1 518	1 773	1 848	1 765	1 686	2 004	1 655	2 562
1–2 sentences	2 500	2 484	2 685	3 002	3 164	2 969	2 924	3 394	3 165	3 046	2 808
3–5 sentences	5 399	5 652	6 092	7 161	7 312	6 104	5 694	6 273	5 727	5 619	4 911
6–10 sentences	9 470	9 412	9 665	11 152	11 845	10 048	9 009	9 861	8 695	8 427	7 977
11 or more sentences	11 011	11 340	11 905	13 343	14 057	13 632	13 169	13 835	11 855	11 363	10 716
Previous conviction information not recorded	4 516	5 890	5 938	7 212	8 628	8 115	7 369	8 577	8 558	11 332	12 411
Total	34 832	36 412	38 016	43 388	46 779	42 716	39 930	43 626	40 004	41 442	41 385
Females:											
None	240	156	155	177	176	271	289	208	300	247	324
1–2 sentences	149	148	172	234	261	273	252	241	289	258	217
3–5 sentences	279	293	322	423	445	419	374	347	349	338	344
6–10 sentences	253	287	331	434	443	401	397	360	327	351	271
11 or more sentences	189	196	195	267	322	294	265	261	258	242	261
Previous conviction information not recorded	890	1 029	1 090	998	1 045	691	811	1 058	851	952	818
Total	2 000	2 109	2 265	2 533	2 692	2 349	2 388	2 475	2 374	2 388	2 235

1 Receptions into Prison Department custody under sentence of imprisonment without the option of a fine.
2 From 1983 data are not comparable with previous years because of the Criminal Justice Act 1982.
3 Youth custody for offenders aged 15 to 20 replaced imprisonment on 24 May 1983.

Source Home Office

4.9 Receptions and average population in custody
England and Wales

Number

	1978	1979	1980	1981	1982[4]	1983[4]	1984	1985	1986	1987	1988
Receptions											
Type of inmate											
Untried	39 757	41 394	40 145	47 169	48 474	47 719	51 900	54 718	55 398	59 165	58 219[6]
Convicted, unsentenced	21 071	22 565	21 771	24 085	23 268	20 155	18 560	18 523	16 595	18 430	17 185[6]
Remanded for medical examination[1]	1 810	2 003	1 760	1 568	1 357	..	..	..	..	..	..
Others	19 261	20 562	20 011	22 517	21 911	..	..	..	..	..	..
Sentenced											
Immediate imprisonment[2]	72 311	74 079	75 896	88 110	94 377	93 414	92 810	96 189	86 153	86 358	81 836
Up to 18 months	28 280	29 981	31 964	37 456	40 978	36 696	34 087	36 048	31 867	81 847	31 016
Over 18 months up to 4 years	7 164	7 114	6 929	7 039	6 849	6 772	6 704	8 101	8 177	9 149	9 731
Over 4 years (including life)	1 388	1 426	1 388	1 426	1 644	1 597	1 527	1 952	2 334	2 834	2 873
Imprisoned in default of payment of a fine	16 442	17 044	15 938	21 153	24 492	23 241	21 761	20 493	19 159	18 723	16 817
Youth custody[2, 7]	—	—	—	—	—	10 411	17 149	18 061	15 707	15 841	11 576
Borstal training[2]	7 399	6 912	7 357	7 459	7 219	2 839	—	—	—	—	—
Detention centre[7]	11 638	11 602	12 320	13 577	13 195	11 858	11 582	11 534	8 909	7 964	5 131
Detention in a young offender Institution[7]	—	—	—	—	—	—	—	—	—	—	—
Non-criminal prisoners	5 882	5 309	4 743	4 735	4 715	4 050	3 683	3 444	3 665	3 353	2 922
Immigration Act 1971	1 305	1 168	1 137	907	963	872	949	1 066	1 422	1 311	1 259
Others[3]	4 577	4 141	3 606	3 828	3 752	3 178	2 734	2 378	2 243	2 042	1 663
Average population											
Total	41 796	42 220	43 109[5]	43 436	43 754	43 772	43 349	46 278	46 889	48 963	49 949
Untried	3 849	4 019	3 921	4 804	5 362	6 002	7 173	8 132	8 530	9 074	8 797
Convicted, unsentenced	1 782	2 113	1 872	2 101	2 023	1 649	1 514	1 565	1 432	1 551	1 660
Remanded for medical examination[1]	130	139	129	138	173	118	77	71	46	37	32
Others	1 652	1 974	1 743	1 963	1 850	1 531	1 437	1 494	1 385	1 514	1 628
Police cells[8]	—	—	845	125	47	310	54	45	119	537	1 077
Sentenced	35 561	35 591	35 981	36 022	35 928	35 486	34 321	36 305	36 571	37 531	38 188
Imprisonment[2]											
Up to 18 months	12 679	12 729	12 940	13 380	13 857	12 941	10 972	11 302	10 292	9 609	8 705
Over 18 months up to 4 years	9 724	9 788	9 647	9 158	8 966	8 881	7 944	8 501	9 535	10 283	11 009
Over 4 years (including life)	5 576	5 707	5 794	5 643	5 704	5 878	6 311	6 920	7 789	9 076	10 338
Youth custody[2, 7]	—	—	—	—	—	4 389	7 632	8 156	7 858	7 694	5 696
Borstal training[2]	5 692	5 464	5 596	5 674	5 288	1 704	—	—	—	—	—
Detention centre[7]	1 890	1 903	2 004	2 167	2 113	1 693	1 461	1 426	1 098	870	483
Detention in a young offender institution[7]	—	—	—	—	—	—	—	—	—	—	1 957
Non-criminal prisoners	604	497	490	384	394	324	288	231	238	270	227
Immigration Act 1971	206	166	166	116	113	141	143	104	132	167	146
Others[3]	398	331	324	268	281	182	145	126	106	103	81

1 Under Section 26, Magistrates' Courts Act 1952 or Section 30, Magistrates' Courts Act 1980.
2 Youth custody for offenders aged 15 to 20 replaced borstal training and imprisonment on 24 May 1983.
3 Mainly persons failing to comply with money orders.
4 From 1983 data are not comparable because of the Criminal Justice Act 1982.
5 Including approved places.
6 Provisional.
7 Detention in a young offender institution replaced youth custody and detention centre orders on 1 October 1988.
8 Mostly untried prisoners.

Source *Home Office*

4.10 Prison population serving sentences: analysis by age and offence
England and Wales

Number

	Total	Age in years: 14–16	17–20	21–24	25–29	30–39	40–49	50–59	60 and over
At 30 June 1986									
Offence									
Males									
Total	35 239	767	7 783	7 985	6 638	7 448	3 229	1 090	299
Violence against the person	7 371	91	1 467	1 652	1 456	1 667	699	273	66
Sexual offences	1 886	9	158	260	283	556	406	152	62
Burglary	8 813	372	2 838	2 377	1 527	1 210	366	100	23
Robbery	3 365	57	801	877	746	639	202	34	9
Theft, handling, fraud and forgery	7 053	132	1 434	1 477	1 308	1 547	786	287	82
Other offences	6 323	95	999	1 232	1 242	1 744	731	226	54
Offence not known	428	11	86	110	76	85	39	18	3
Females									
Total	1 211	13	236	244	250	292	110	56	10
Violence against the person	206	5	51	33	28	55	19	12	3
Sexual offences	12	–	2	1	3	3	3	–	–
Burglary	91	3	31	29	13	11	4	–	–
Robbery	65	1	30	12	11	6	5	–	–
Theft, handling, fraud and forgery	466	2	75	93	109	104	47	30	6
Other offences	356	2	45	73	83	110	29	13	1
Offence not known	15	–	2	3	3	3	3	1	–
At 30 June 1987									
Offence									
Males									
Total	37 916	788	8 068	8 689	7 370	7 923	3 579	1 195	304
Violence against the person	8 073	97	1 499	1 897	1 625	1 777	811	306	61
Sexual offences	2 320	6	176	287	375	648	535	209	84
Burglary	8 904	359	2 934	2 426	1 535	1 157	378	89	26
Robbery	3 765	74	891	960	876	689	227	39	9
Theft, handling, fraud and forgery	6 851	160	1 406	1 512	1 235	1 437	773	271	57
Other offences	7 156	74	1 023	1 401	1 539	2 026	781	252	60
Offence not known	847	18	39	206	185	189	74	29	7
Females									
Total	1 387	10	200	306	303	369	137	51	11
Violence against the person	202	–	32	52	27	52	25	11	3
Sexual offences	12	–	1	–	4	6	1	–	–
Burglary	103	3	31	27	20	16	4	2	–
Robbery	83	6	20	24	13	14	4	2	–
Theft, handling, fraud and forgery	472	–	71	97	113	119	53	15	4
Other offences	502	1	43	103	125	159	46	21	4
Offence not known	13	–	2	3	1	3	4	–	–
At 30 June 1988									
Offence									
Males									
Total	37 292	547	7 171	8 668	7 748	8 058	3 569	1 198	333
Violence against the person	8 623	86	1 482	2 040	1 857	1 925	832	316	85
Sexual offences	2 679	10	185	318	414	801	604	242	105
Burglary	7 890	250	2 257	2 239	1 599	1 104	333	90	18
Robbery	3 917	42	829	1 034	967	759	227	51	8
Theft, handling, fraud and forgery	5 562	81	1 074	1 287	1 063	1 170	636	209	42
Other offences	7 459	60	1 134	1 454	1 610	2 063	830	249	59
Offence not known	1 162	18	210	296	238	236	107	41	16
Females									
Total	1 256	9	156	274	299	333	129	43	13
Violence against the person	247	6	42	49	44	61	28	12	5
Sexual offences	15	–	–	3	3	5	4	–	–
Burglary	58	–	17	13	14	9	4	1	–
Robbery	73	1	21	24	12	10	4	1	–
Theft, handling, fraud and forgery	320	1	32	69	88	75	38	13	4
Other offences	500	1	33	105	130	164	47	16	4
Offence not known	43	–	11	11	8	9	4	–	–

Source Home Office

4.11 Expenditure on prisons
England and Wales
Years ended 31 March

£ thousand

	1977/78	1978/79	1979/80	1980/81	1981/82	1982/83	1983/84[1]	1984/85	1985/86	1986/87	1987/88
Manpower costs[2]	..	..	..	..	..	..	397 558	433 851	451 619	475 871	538 398
Manpower related costs[6]	..	..	..	..	..	..	15 182	14 602	14 591	37 035	43 012
Establishment related costs	..	..	..	..	..	..	64 266	71 712	70 053	63 964	69 937
Inmate related costs[6]	..	..	..	..	..	..	52 871	54 583	58 917	40 776	47 065
Industries and farms:											
Materials	..	..	..	..	..	..	26 471	27 308	25 870	28 931	32 354
Income	..	..	..	..	..	..	− 40 259	− 40 556	− 41 719	− 45 891	− 48 890
Net income	..	..	..	..	..	..	− 13 788	− 13 248	− 15 849	− 16 960	− 16 536
Other activities	..	..	..	..	..	..	17 434	18 086	18 650	17 538	13 467
Total establishment operating costs	..	..	..	..	..	..	533 523	579 586	597 981	618 224	695 343
Headquarter/regional office costs	..	..	..	..	..	..	60 395	53 630	62 215	58 131	78 981
Total net operating costs[3]	215 536	259 195	318 420	404 313	466 509	526 440	593 918	633 216	660 196	676 355	774 324
Capital expenditure:[4]											
Expenditure	26 999	26 071	25 906	33 571	31 915	46 157	59 674	71 210	94 121	121 884	118 198
Receipts	–	–	–	–	–	–	− 16 474	− 17 309	− 11 088	− 11 789	− 10 181
Total net capital expenditure	26 999	26 071	25 906	33 571	31 915	46 157	43 200	53 901	83 033	110 095	108 017
Emergency arrangements[5]	–	–	–	17 220	4 201	–	–	–	–	–	–
Total net expenditure	242 535	285 266	344 326	455 104	502 625	572 597	637 118	687 117	743 229	786 450	882 341

1 The Prison Department introduced in 1983/84 a costing system designed to provide line managers in the Prison Service with better management and financial information. The present table classifies expenditure in the same way as the costing system but differently from in earlier years. It follows that the accounting records showing expenditure details from 1983/84 onwards are not comparable, except as regards capital expenditure, with those for previous years.

2 'Costs' differ from actual money spent as they include notional charges, ie superannuation and depreciation.

3 Total net operating costs for 1974/75 to 1982/83 have been calculated by adding maintenance, repairs, rentals, etc. costs, shown under capital expenditure in earlier volumes of the Annual Abstract, to the total net current expenditure for those years. This is consistent with the approach taken in the costing system.

4 Capital expenditure includes Property Services Agency expenditure on behalf of Prison Department.

5 This was the cost of setting up and maintaining camps during the Prison Officers' dispute from October 1980 to February 1981. These costs cannot be attributed to individual groups.

6 Manpower related costs for 1986/87 onwards include Education and Probation Salary costs previously charged to inmate related costs.

Source Home Office

4.12 Crimes and offences recorded by the police
Scotland

Thousands

	1978	1979	1980	1981	1982	1983	1984	1985	1986	1987	1988
Non-sexual crimes of violence against the person	9.9	10.0	11.1	12.2	12.1	13.0	13.7	15.1	15.7	18.4	17.9
Assault, etc.	3.4	3.5	4.4	4.5	4.5	5.0	5.3	6.0	6.4	7.6	7.7
Handling offensive weapons	1.8	2.0	2.3	2.9	2.7	3.1	3.0	3.6	3.9	4.7	4.5
Robbery	3.9	3.8	3.7	4.2	4.2	4.2	4.5	4.4	4.1	4.6	4.2
Other	0.9	0.7	0.7	0.6	0.7	0.8	1.0	1.0	1.3	1.5	1.5
Crimes involving indecency	4.7	4.7	5.2	4.8	5.0	5.5	5.7	5.7	5.4	5.3	5.1
Sexual assault	1.3	1.3	1.3	1.3	1.1	1.3	1.5	1.4	1.3	1.4	1.3
Lewd and libidinous practices	2.5	2.4	2.5	2.2	2.3	2.5	2.4	2.6	2.6	2.4	2.4
Other	0.9	1.0	1.5	1.3	1.6	1.8	1.8	1.7	1.5	1.4	1.4
Crimes involving dishonesty	262.6	269.2	279.8	320.0	340.1	342.5	359.2	342.3	342.5	356.5	344.5
Housebreaking	75.7	76.6	78.4	95.7	106.3	108.5	112.1	100.7	96.9	98.6	91.4
Theft by opening lockfast places	32.4	33.5	36.6	47.3	49.2	50.7	51.9	52.1	61.4	69.0	77.5
Theft of a motor vehicle	34.7	35.1	32.2	32.5	33.0	30.0	32.6	29.9	28.0	26.2	26.4
Shoplifting } Other theft }	103.6	105.9									
Shoplifting			24.1	22.6	24.3	24.0	24.8	25.4	26.3	28.4	25.5
Other theft			86.2	97.4	101.8	101.5	104.5	99.3	94.9	97.8	91.2
Fraud	10.1	12.0	15.9	16.9	17.2	17.3	19.6	22.3	23.1	23.5	22.4
Other	6.2	6.1	6.3	7.7	8.3	10.5	13.8	12.7	11.9	13.0	10.1
Fire-raising, vandalism, etc.	51.1	56.1	60.1	61.7	66.0	73.1	79.1	79.5	78.9	76.4	73.5
Fire-raising	2.5	2.6	2.8	3.0	3.4	3.7	4.2	4.1	3.9	3.8	3.7
Vandalism, etc.	48.7	53.5	57.3	58.7	62.6	69.4	74.8	75.4	75.0	72.6	68.9
Other crimes	6.8	6.7	8.3	9.5	11.9	14.3	17.3	19.2	21.4	24.6	29.0
Crimes against public justice	5.0	5.0	6.8	7.7	9.3	10.9	12.7	14.0	15.9	19.7	23.6
Drugs	1.6	1.6	1.4	1.6	2.5	3.2	4.4	5.1	5.3	4.7	5.2
Other	0.2	0.1	0.1	0.2	0.1	0.2	0.2	0.2	0.2	0.2	0.2
Total crimes	335.0	346.7	364.6	408.2	435.1	448.3	474.9	462.0	463.8	481.2	470.0
Miscellaneous offences	121.9	123.3	123.2	118.2	115.4	114.8	114.9	118.1	120.4	127.3	124.9
Petty assault	28.0	29.5	28.2	27.6	28.5	30.3	31.7	32.2	32.6	35.7	36.6
Breach of the peace	47.7	50.4	53.9	53.6	53.0	51.3	51.9	54.4	56.4	59.9	55.9
Drunkenness	17.9	18.6	18.2	16.5	15.8	15.0	13.8	12.6	12.4	12.4	12.2
Other	28.2	24.9	22.9	20.4	18.1	18.1	17.6	18.9	19.0	19.4	20.2
Motor vehicle offences	183.9	204.0	236.9	218.3	212.0	236.5	219.6	220.3	238.1	249.7	260.7
Reckless and careless driving	22.7	23.3	25.0	24.4	24.0	25.4	24.3	23.8	23.4	22.7	23.5
Drunk driving	14.7	15.5	15.9	13.8	14.0	15.4	15.0	15.4	14.6	13.5	11.4
Speeding	30.7	38.3	46.8	33.9	29.3	37.7	33.7	32.0	41.0	58.7	64.8
Unlawful use of a motor vehicle	58.3	64.5	76.0	79.3	86.6	90.7	82.6	84.7	87.0	78.9	68.7
Vehicle defect offences	20.6	22.0	24.4	25.1	26.1	29.4	29.4	29.3	33.4	37.5	47.7
Other	37.0	40.2	48.8	41.9	32.1	38.0	34.7	35.1	38.6	38.4	44.7
Total offences	305.8	327.3	360.1	336.5	327.4	351.3	334.5	338.4	358.5	377.0	385.6
Total crimes and offences	640.8	674.0	724.7	744.7	762.5	799.6	809.4	800.4	822.4	858.2	855.6

Source Scottish Home and Health Department

4.13 Persons proceeded against
Scotland

Number of persons

	1977	1978	1979	1980	1981	1982	1983	1984	1985	1986	1987
Non-sexual crimes of violence	2 804	3 190	2 876	3 491	3 299	4 740	4 878	4 052	3 984	4 161	4 394
Homicide	161	135	118	137	116	132	129	124	127	114	123
Serious assault, etc.	958	1 343	1 142	2 006	1 861	2 451	2 504	1 736	1 443	1 631	1 569
Handling offensive weapons	785	858	815	366	460	1 035	1 147	1 174	1 227	1 197	1 340
Robbery	595	571	494	657	610	843	776	733	902	883	981
Other Violence	305	283	307	325	252	279	322	285	285	336	381
Crimes of indecency	1 201	1 061	828	1 161	1 340	1 799	1 908	1 926	1 829	1 479	1 464
Sexual assault	198	221	180	189	182	178	198	183	226	234	227
Lewd and libidinous practices	447	462	417	455	439	420	437	404	469	426	484
Other indecency	556	378	231	517	719	1 201	1 273	1 339	1 134	819	753
Crimes of dishonesty	38 647	39 295	36 019	41 058	44 255	49 824	49 624	47 039	48 891	47 287	45 633
Housebreaking	7 952	8 074	6 744	8 061	8 847	11 297	10 871	10 803	10 686	9 543	9 076
Theft by opening lockfast places	1 792	1 869	1 633	2 275	2 510	3 351	3 259	3 133	3 726	3 844	3 867
Theft of or from motor vehicle	5 179	5 140	4 194	4 678	4 002	4 427	4 205	4 080	4 255	3 957	3 381
Shoplifting[1]	3 556	3 637	3 481	4 588	5 693	5 581	5 783	5 559	6 137	6 784	7 169
Other theft[1]	14 464	14 842	14 307	14 741	16 135	17 595	17 425	15 777	15 655	14 644	13 644
Fraud	3 241	3 074	3 162	3 254	3 586	4 005	4 501	3 728	3 789	3 945	3 881
Other dishonesty	2 463	2 659	2 498	3 461	3 482	3 568	3 580	3 959	4 643	4 570	4 615
Fire-raising, vandalism etc.	3 574	4 073	3 874	5 080	6 087	6 441	6 519	7 018	7 120	7 304	7 421
Fire-raising	135	149	118	170	185	194	158	248	278	253	279
Vandalism, etc.	3 439	3 924	3 756	4 910	5 902	6 247	6 361	6 770	6 842	7 051	7 142
Other Crime	2 500	2 853	2 865	3 584	3 786	5 818	8 124	8 534	9 942	9 907	10 041
Crime against public justice	1 577	1 634	1 472	2 052	2 507	4 031	5 984	5 854	6 823	6 739	7 120
Drugs offences	895	1 157	1 336	1 402	1 183	1 663	1 971	2 584	3 047	3 065	2 842
Other	28	62	57	130	96	124	169	96	72	103	79
Total crimes	48 726	50 472	46 462	54 374	58 767	68 622	71 053	68 569	71 766	70 138	68 953
Miscellaneous offences	79 595	83 027	79 440	87 540	84 127	75 182	74 700	68 857	67 912	67 301	64 440
Petty assault	12 027	13 085	12 874	13 394	13 231	12 639	12 356	12 939	13 387	13 660	14 353
Breach of the peace	35 031	36 554	34 335	37 663	39 697	36 798	35 171	31 838	32 652	31 338	30 826
Drunkenness	14 627	14 828	15 531	14 459	11 579	10 033	8 324	6 893	5 289	3 815	3 776
Other miscellaneous offences	17 910	18 560	16 700	22 024	19 620	15 712	18 849	17 187	16 584	18 488	15 485
Motor vehicle offences	84 515	94 643	97 348	122 930	103 401	91 648	100 374	72 804	71 070	67 494	66 561
Reckless and careless driving	12 083	12 156	10 509	12 380	10 470	8 955	9 125	7 575	7 702	7 040	6 701
Drunk driving	9 387	11 337	11 636	12 779	11 460	10 666	11 767	12 500	12 514	12 019	11 438
Speeding	20 804	24 161	24 797	37 557	27 296	20 466	22 210	5 692	5 519	6 976	9 803
Unlawful use of vehicle	18 812	21 472	23 404	29 363	27 066	28 291	33 434	29 306	28 477	27 596	26 639
Vehicle defect offences	9 415	9 299	9 571	10 526	10 024	8 356	8 491	5 269	5 115	5 355	4 740
Other motor vehicle offences	14 014	16 218	17 431	20 325	17 085	14 914	15 347	12 462	11 743	8 508	7 240
Total Offences	164 110	177 670	176 788	210 470	187 528	166 830	175 074	141 661	138 982	134 795	131 001
Total crimes and offences	212 836	228 142	223 250	264 844	246 295	235 452	246 127	210 230	210 748	204 933	199 954

1 Only since 1980 has shoplifting been distinguished from 'Other theft'. Figures for earlier years in this table are estimated.

Source Scottish Home and Health Department

4.14 Persons called to court
Scotland

Number of persons

	1977	1978	1979	1980	1981	1982	1983	1984	1985	1986	1987
Court procedure											
Solemn	3 737	3 399	3 129	4 097	3 443	4 357	4 011	4 067	4 450	4 868	4 556
High Court	493	461	422	576	467	576	557	689	1 036	1 056	1 113
Sheriff Court (remit to High Court)	111	68	96	101	85	94	122	76	150	127	139
Sheriff Court (other Solemn)	3 133	2 870	2 611	3 420	2 891	3 687	3 332	3 302	3 264	3 685	3 304
Summary	205 461	221 281	216 403	257 265	238 563	228 690	240 825	205 213	205 617	199 453	194 778
Sheriff Court	135 997	148 398	137 201	172 403	143 379	137 575	142 389	106 710	108 628	104 749	100 756
District Court	57 637	62 178	68 780	72 839	81 272	75 458	80 918	83 912	78 681	77 728	78 591
Stipendiary Magistrate Court	11 827	10 705	10 422	12 023	13 912	15 657	17 518	14 591	18 308	16 976	15 431
Total called to court	209 198	224 680	219 532	261 362	242 006	233 047	244 836	209 280	210 067	204 321	199 334

Source Scottish Home and Health Department

4.15 Persons with charge proved
Scotland

Number of persons

	1977	1978	1979	1980	1981	1982	1983	1984	1985	1986	1987
Main penalty											
Absolute discharge	1 204	1 203	1 036	1 078	939	792	717	512	527	465	457
Admonition or caution	20 434	20 498	20 040	23 568	23 101	22 010	22 115	18 422	17 805	16 687	16 500
Probation	2 364	2 654	2 090	2 410	2 639	2 682	2 757	2 985	3 136	2 931	3 131
Remit to children's hearing	183	128	91	90	99	49	55	121	135	97	68
Community service order	–	–	220	329	1 099	1 950	1 987	2 430	2 658	3 150	3 287
Fine	162 110	175 352	175 515	208 096	187 308	173 856	183 021	150 047	149 323	144 547	140 752
Compensation order	–	–	–	–	363	909	1 050	953	926	916	794
Guardianship order	5	7	5	6	3	4	4	2	13	8	6
Prison	6 562	7 195	6 014	7 053	7 060	8 995	9 280	8 965	10 066	9 859	9 293
Young offenders' institution	1 639	1 821	1 564	1 851	1 719	2 243	2 147	1 902	2 709	2 964	2 937
Borstal training	825	934	715	715	691	955	894	–	–	–	–
Detention centre	967	1 051	622	921	949	1 140	1 281	2 826	2 744	2 470	1 881
Detention of child	231	170	120	101	77	88	107	68	68	52	43
Insane and hospital order	97	108	53	45	48	45	83	95	130	130	127
Total persons with charge proved	196 621	211 121	208 085	246 263	226 095	215 718	225 498	189 328	190 240	184 276	179 276

Source *Scottish Home and Health Department*

4.16 Persons with charge proved
Scotland

Number of persons

	1977	1978	1979	1980	1981	1982	1983	1984	1985	1986	1987
Males	174 501	187 386	185 719	218 354	199 327	191 184	198 705	166 976	166 681	160 708	158 376
Under 16	1 412	1 353	887	924	822	642	645	463	495	367	307
16 to 20	50 509	54 601	52 159	61 683	60 013	59 423	59 162	52 072	52 586	50 548	48 160
21 to 30	51 361	54 870	55 228	65 121	60 583	60 513	64 856	55 973	57 493	57 282	58 568
Over 30	71 219	76 562	77 445	90 626	77 909	70 606	74 042	49 616	47 625	46 296	47 343
Not known[1]	–	–	–	–	–	–	–	8 852	8 482	6 215	3 998
Females	20 532	21 356	19 896	24 948	24 313	22 151	24 097	20 065	20 698	21 535	19 116
Under 16	104	90	60	93	73	25	45	40	21	25	23
16 to 20	3 618	3 999	3 589	4 316	4 595	4 170	4 444	3 611	3 894	3 952	3 690
21 to 30	5 564	5 751	5 492	7 024	7 047	6 794	7 383	6 286	6 423	6 865	6 830
Over 30	11 246	11 516	10 755	13 515	12 598	11 162	12 225	6 911	6 662	7 044	6 964
Not known[1]	–	–	–	–	–	–	–	3 217	3 698	3 649	1 609
Males and females	195 033	208 742	205 615	243 302	223 640	213 335	222 802	187 041	187 379	182 243	177 492
Under 16	1 516	1 443	947	1 017	895	667	690	503	516	392	330
16 to 20	54 127	58 600	55 748	65 999	64 608	63 593	63 606	55 683	56 480	54 500	51 850
21 to 30	56 925	60 621	60 720	72 145	67 630	67 307	72 239	62 259	63 916	64 147	65 398
Over 30	82 465	88 078	88 200	104 141	90 507	81 768	86 267	56 527	54 287	53 340	54 307
Not known[1]	–	–	–	–	–	–	–	12 069	12 180	9 864	5 607
Companies	1 588	2 379	2 470	2 961	2 455	2 383	2 696	2 287	2 861	2 033	1 784
Total persons with charge proved	196 621	211 121	208 085	246 263	226 095	215 718	225 498	189 328	190 240	184 276	179 276

1 Prior to 1984, 'Not known' was included in the over 30 total.

Source *Scottish Home and Health Department*

4.17 Penal establishments: average daily population and receptions
Scotland

Number

	1978	1979	1980	1981	1982	1983	1984	1985	1986	1987	1988
Average daily population											
Male	4 893	4 433	4 713	4 383	4 755	4 917	4 621	5 097	5 394	5 259	5 057
Female	169	152	147	135	136	135	132	177	194	187	172
Total	5 062	4 585	4 860	4 518	4 891	5 052	4 753	5 273	5 588	5 446	5 229
Analysis by type of custody											
Remand	728	691	705	746	844	863	942	1 092	1 017	938	844
Persons under sentence: total	4 331	3 891	4 152	3 769	4 044	4 183	3 807	4 178	4 570	4 509	4 385
Adult prisoners[1]											
direct sentence	2 559	2 318	2 441	2 379	2 539	2 673	2 545	2 904	3 181	3 262	3 223
in default of fine	256	236	309	177	179	176	207	235	266	210	209
in default of compensation order	–	–	–	–	1	2	1	1	1	1	2
Young offenders[1]											
direct sentence	628	597	610	547	587	528	556	705	850	768	751
in default of fine	53	57	77	54	54	50	51	73	63	77	66
in default of compensation order	–	–	–	–	–	–	–	–	–	–	–
Borstal inmates	608	508	521	451	493	568	175	2	–	–	–
Detention centre inmates[3]	157	99	140	122	142	136	217	210	161	143	85
Persons recalled from supervision/licence	29	44	34	33	42	42	36	34	35	31	28
Others	41	32	20	6	7	9	18	13	13	17	17
Persons sentenced by court martial	2	2	2	2	2	5	3	3	1	–	3
Civil prisoners	1	1	1	1	1	1	1	1	1	1	1
Receptions to penal establishments											
Total[2]											
Remand	16 640	14 400	13 864	13 550	16 072	15 286	16 048	18 985	18 107	17 111	15 000
Male	15 775	13 636	13 151	12 791	15 265	14 400	15 141	18 088	17 114	16 213	14 225
Female	865	764	713	759	807	886	907	897	993	898	775
Persons under sentence: total	17 592	14 447	16 933	15 539	20 522	20 183	19 955	24 532	23 220	22 186	20 540
Male	16 764	13 792	16 250	14 863	19 749	19 276	19 164	23 310	22 020	20 987	19 427
Female	828	655	683	676	773	907	791	1 222	1 200	1 199	1 113
Imprisoned:											
directly	7 179	5 905	6 763	6 311	7 992	7 925	7 634	8 864	8 598	7 975	7 984
in default of fine	5 775	5 072	6 125	5 635	7 773	7 572	6 941	8 626	8 139	8 049	7 234
in default of compensation order	–	–	–	1	8	2	1	1	24	2	46
Sentenced to young offenders institution:											
directly	1 578	1 315	1 329	1 221	1 542	1 463	1 733	2 359	2 593	2 064	2 160
in default of fine	1 376	955	1 264	1 120	1 679	1 757	1 903	2 779	2 398	2 882	2 466
in default of compensation order	–	–	–	–	1	1	1	2	2	3	6
Sentenced to borstal training	706	570	573	490	630	544	–	–	–	–	–
Sentenced to detention centre[3]	919	591	834	729	862	889	1 741	1 901	1 462	1 210	642
Recalled to Young Offenders Institutions/from Borstal supervision	59	39	44	31	33	28	1	–	1	1	1
Other sentences	–	–	1	1	2	2	–	–	1	–	1
Persons sentenced by court martial	6	3	8	10	10	12	5	6	4	11	10
Civil prisoners	20	11	15	14	13	15	17	21	13	18	8

1 From 1983 onwards persons detained under Section 205(2) of the Criminal Procedure (Scotland) Act 1975 are included as adults or young offenders according to the type of establishment in which they were held. For earlier years they are all included as young offenders.

2 Total receptions cannot be calculated by adding together receptions in each category because there is double counting. This arises because when a person is received on remand and then under sentence in relation to the same set of charges, he is counted in both categories.

3 From 1 November 1988 Detention centre sentences were no longer used.

Source Scottish Home and Health Department

4.18 Expenditure on penal establishments
Scotland
Years ended 31 March

£ thousand

	1977/78	1978/79	1979/80	1980/81	1981/82	1982/83	1983/84	1984/85	1985/86	1986/87	1987/88
Central charges and costs of staff	18 492	20 804	25 268	31 565	35 955	40 661	42 586	46 009	51 575	58 081	71 683
Inmate maintenance	2 407	1 686	2 043	4 267	4 630	5 048	5 686	5 825	6 934	6 295	7 112
Materials for production and training	1 432	2 034	2 194	2 605	2 076	2 627	2 372	2 210	2 565	2 459	2 651
Miscellaneous	1 222	2 135	2 823	1 490	1 807	2 139	2 355	2 746	3 117	3 362	3 935
Maintenance of establishments	1 112	1 622	1 898	2 469	3 273	3 971	4 568	5 065	5 720	5 684	5 413
Capital expenditure	2 049	1 963	2 010	4 410	5 339	4 752	7 227	12 641	12 761	7 182	9 721
Cost of central administration	1 192	1 185	1 453	1 547	1 865	1 954	2 006	2 106	2 141	2 248	3 693
Total	27 906	31 429	37 689	48 353	54 945	61 152	66 800	76 602	84 813	85 311	104 208
Receipts from sales, etc.	1 927	2 188	2 917	2 769	2 050	2 583	1 957	2 053	2 023	3 950	4 184
Net total	25 979	29 241	34 772	45 584	52 895	58 569	64 843	74 549	82 790	81 361	100 024
Average daily number of inmates	4 892	5 038	4 616	4 822	4 455	5 036	4 956	4 823	5 398	5 564	5 421

Source Scottish Home and Health Department

4.19 Offences known to police, proceedings taken and results of proceedings
Northern Ireland

Number

	1978	1979	1980	1981	1982	1983	1984	1985	1986	1987	1988
Offences known to police[1]	46 499	49 975	52 384	59 157	62 020	63 984	66 779	64 584	68 255	63 860	55 890
Indictable offences[1]											
Persons proceeded against	5 140	7 054	6 998	9 136	10 510	9 007	9 651	11 125	12 702	12 938	11 745
Tried in Courts of Summary Jurisdiction	3 308	5 150	5 469	7 368	8 518	7 138	8 023	9 094	10 843	11 015	10 276
Tried at Crown Courts	1 832	1 904	1 529	1 768	1 992	1 869	1 628	2 031	1 859	1 923	1 469
Results of proceedings:											
Found guilty	4 803	6 593	6 566	7 932	8 244	8 317	8 077	8 568	10 312	10 649	9 571
Absolute discharge	71	119	150	204	178	115	74	76	109	109	99
Probation order	325	502	571	638	600	580	547	649	775	668	740
Conditional discharge	850	1 070	1 026	1 289	1 403	1 461	1 322	1 409	1 713	1 717	1 581
Committed to training schools	164	274	262	270	181	187	179	161	246	210	154
Fine	1 009	1 540	1 692	1 811	1 904	2 000	2 083	2 044	2 830	2 696	2 555
Sentenced to:											
Borstal training[2]	122	160	56								
Imprisonment[3]	1 217	1 460	1 320	1 724	1 813	1 806	1 625	1 809	1 976	2 149	1 870
Suspended sentence	950	1 196	1 112	1 354	1 491	1 488	1 472	1 687	1 829	2 108	1 766
Otherwise dealt with	95	272	377	642	674	680	775	733	834	992	806
Non-indictable offences[1]											
Persons proceeded against	47 593	46 177	46 480	32 033	33 555	34 687	35 137	37 789	34 011	–	–
Tried in Courts of Summary Jurisdiction	47 593	46 177	46 480	32 033	33 555	34 687	35 137	37 789	34 011	36 589	36 949
Results of proceedings:											
Found guilty	44 296	42 036	40 608	30 181	31 505	32 444	33 171	35 601	32 103	34 273	34 624
Absolute discharge	1 321	1 345	1 647	1 482	1 555	1 290	1 166	1 521	1 359	1 551	1 562
Probation order	203	255	283	201	169	157	139	177	111	116	97
Conditional discharge	1 009	1 768	1 284	1 037	1 201	1 134	958	1 057	907	936	1 191
Committed to training schools	119	193	194	94	98	77	66	58	37		
Fine	39 675	35 423	34 888	20 029	21 072	22 220	23 953	25 303	23 605	25 122	25 490
Sentenced to:											
Training school	–	–	–	–	–	–	–	–	–	23	18
Borstal training[2]	27	32	47	–	–	–	–	–	–	–	–
Imprisonment[4]	1 714	1 943	1 526	1 745	1 704	1 844	1 601	1 998	1 194	1 777	943
Otherwise dealt with	228	1 077	739	5 593	5 706	5 722	5 288	5 487	4 890	5 348	5 323

1 Offences known to the police consist mainly of indictable offences and include some hybrid offences. From 1975 to 1981 hybrid offences were included under non-indictable offences; for 1982 onwards, they are included under indictable offences.

2 Borstal training ceased in October 1980.

3 Includes those awarded periods of detention in young offenders centres.

4 Includes those awarded periods of detention in the young offenders centre and those awarded suspended sentences.

Source Northern Ireland Office

4.20 Persons found guilty: analysis by type of offence
Northern Ireland

Number

	1978	1979	1980	1981	1982	1983	1984	1985	1986	1987	1988
All offences	49 093	48 629	47 174	38 113	39 749	40 762	41 248	44 169	43 249	44 922	44 197
Indictable offences[1]	4 797	6 593	6 566	8 291	8 244	8 318	8 077	8 568	10 312	10 649	9 573
Burglary and robbery	1 603	2 020	2 192	2 556	2 514	2 619	2 535	2 562	2 318	2 806	1 849
Fraud[2] and forgery	252	379	424	341	351	382	362	440	467	728	687
Handling stolen goods	205	334	324	390	390	406	476	419	413	417	347
Theft	1 520	2 132	2 273	2 901	3 023	2 962	2 944	3 426	3 697	3 690	3 267
Sexual offences	95	108	131	134	119	124	151	170	189	210	228
Offences against the person: total	479	717	573	642	769	771	772	818	1 362	1 534	1 491
Murder	46	59	23	34	21	15	10	39	25	45	30
Manslaughter	19	32	13	22	22	13	15	16	20	15	22
Wounding	385	620	521	555	681	698	705	723	491	81	94
Other offences against the person	29	6	16	31	45	45	42	40	826	1 393	1 345
Other offences	643	903	649	1 327	1 078	1 054	837	733	1 866	1 264	1 704
Non-indictable offences[1]	44 296	42 036	40 608	29 822	31 505	32 444	33 171	35 601	32 103	34 273	34 624
Assaults	1 450	1 484	1 386	1 230	1 454	1 555	1 501	1 608	943	985	1 015
Betting and gaming	49	69	41	21	81	104	54	40	23	31	71
Public order offences	2 912	3 113	2 833	3 017	3 038	3 212	3 072	3 391	3 205	2 962	3 034
Intoxicating Liquor Laws:											
Drunkenness	360	354	374	284	259	317	322	274	244	189	282
Other offences	725	642	541	474	538	567	454	437	381	541	558
Malicious damage	670	925	956	764	739	767	737	897	264	251	151
Offences by prostitutes	–	–	17	11	8	37	44	39	35	50	53
Traffic offences	29 266	28 140	28 640	22 585	23 459	24 145	25 417	27 255	26 010	28 201	28 553
Vagrancy Acts	45	17	40	27	25	22	10	4	7	9	11
Wireless Telegraphy Acts[3]	97	116	85	1	–	–	1	–	32	–	–
Education Acts[3]	436	199	341	–	–	–	–	–	–	–	–
Game Laws	1	2	–	2	7	15	12	2	10	5	13
Labour Laws[3]	147	218	87	3	5	1	5	–	–	–	–
Railway offences[3]	22	–	17	–	3	–	–	–	–	–	–
Revenue Laws[3]	2 905	2 344	2 055	45	65	71	27	17	–	–	–
Other offences	5 211	4 413	3 195	1 358	1 824	1 631	1 515	1 637	949	1 049	883

1 From 1975 to 1981 hybrid offences were included under non-indictable offences. From 1982 they are included under indictable offences.

2 Including offences in connection with bankruptcy.

3 These offence headings are brought to court by other government departments and are not collated by police.

Source *Northern Ireland Office*

4.21 Juveniles found guilty of offences[1]
Northern Ireland

Number

	1978	1979	1980	1981	1982	1983	1984	1985	1986	1987	1988
Juveniles found guilty											
All offences	2 432	2 646	2 580	2 176	2 052	1 784	1 616	1 523	1 866	1 373	1 199
Indictable offences	952	1 259	1 214	1 251	1 132	1 009	978	921	1 169	983	909
Handling stolen goods	29	63	51	57	49	45	41	28	43	14	40
Theft[2]	284	352	368	421	379	296	354	390	487	421	417
Burglary and robbery	514	693	709	657	518	532	469	404	385	285	270
Sexual offences	10	4	9	8	7	5	3	7	22	12	15
Fraud and forgery	13	12	15	20	12	12	17	12	10	21	6
Offences against the person	27	51	32	24	39	28	32	26	47	55	57
Other offences	75	84	30	64	128	91	62	54	175	189	144
Non-indictable offences	1 480	1 387	1 366	925	920	775	638	602	697	390	290
Assaults	137	137	110	80	100	124	113	105	94	78	80
Offences connected with motor vehicles	582	531	668	354	374	247	248	213	370	128	100
Malicious damage	175	295	176	158	123	139	77	120	28	29	9
Disorderly behaviour	296	229	199	225	258	168	127	103	123	90	49
Offences against the Education Act	109	48	91								
Other offences	181	147	122	108	65	97	73	61	82	65	52
Disposal by Courts											
Total dealt with	2 432	2 646	2 580	2 176	2 052	1 784	1 616	1 523	1 866	1 374	1 196
Absolute discharge	141	109	93	53	84	76	28	24	40	23	19
Conditional discharge	775	887	675	548	667	572	493	449	454	375	264
Placed on probation	301	389	400	412	354	275	291	294	304	221	249
Fine	714	539	667	395	306	310	307	282	548	270	202
Remand home order	19	40	46	47	10	23	18	21	16	3	3
Training school order	171	369	385	296	248	232	214	189	259	223	166
Borstal training[3]	99	68	22							–	–
Otherwise dealt with	212	245	292	425	383	296	265	264	245	259	293

1 Persons under 17 years of age.

2 Including unauthorised taking of motor vehicle and handling stolen goods.

3 Borstal institutions closed down in October 1980.

Source *Northern Ireland Office*

4.22 Prisons, Young Offenders Centres and Borstal institutions: receptions and average population[1]

Northern Ireland

Number

	1978	1979	1980	1981	1982	1983	1984	1985	1986	1987	1988
Receptions:											
Reception of untried prisoners	1 667	1 680	1 550	2 354	2 159	2 175	2 179	2 008	2 250	2 138	1 853
Reception of sentenced prisoners:											
Imprisonment without the option of a fine[2]	1 623	1 590	976	1 148	1 198	1 156	1 038	1 139	1 107	1 288	1 136
Imprisonment in default of payment of a fine	306	315	214	348	415	620	731	1 091	1 448	1 379	1 493
Total	1 929	1 905	1 190	1 496	1 613	1 776	1 769	2 230	2 555	2 667	2 629
Reception into Young Offenders Centres:[1]											
Detention without the option of a fine	–	–	533	755	632	651	600	605	583	577	437
Detention in default of payment of a fine	–	–	80	135	207	305	399	450	580	562	457
Total	–	–	613	890	839	956	999	1 055	1 163	1 139	894
Other receptions:											
Sentenced to Borstal training[3]	127	150	58					–		–	–
Civil committals	83	88	74	68	43	22	22	22	16	24	50
Persons detained or interned	–	–	–	–	–	–	–	–	–	–	–
Other receptions	–	–	–	–	–	–	–	–	–	–	–
Total	210	238	132	68	43	22	22	22	16	24	50
Daily average population:											
Total	2 813	2 691	2 489	2 521	2 481	2 453	2 248	2 043	1 900	1 947	1 901
Unconvicted[4]	603	400	361	424	428	430	404	338	310	283	270
Internees and detainees	–	–	–	–	–	–	–	–	–	–	–
Convicted	2 210	2 291	2 128	2 097	2 053	2 023	1 844	1 705	1 590	1 664	1 631

1 1980 is the first full year of operation of the Young Offenders Centres.
2 Includes those detained under Section 73 of the Children and Young Persons (NI) Act 1968.
3 Borstal institutions closed down in October 1980.
4 Prisoners on remand or awaiting trial and prisoners committed by civil process.

Source *Northern Ireland Office*

5 Education

In general the education services of the United Kingdom are not subject to detailed central control. Standards are maintained by an Inspectorate with advisory functions having access to all institutions except the universities and related bodies. Within this framework detailed control is exercised by local education authorities or by various forms of independent governing bodies, in association with the teaching staff. In all sectors, such matters as engaging teachers and selection of textbooks and curricula are part of these detailed local responsibilities.

The four government departments dealing with education statistics are:

Department of Education and Science:
which deals with all sectors of education in England, and with the Government's responsibilities towards universities in Great Britain.

Welsh Office, Education Department:
which deals with schools and (from April 1978) higher and further education in Wales, excluding matters connected with universities and with the qualifications, probation, remuneration, superannuation and misconduct of teachers.

Scottish Education Department:
schools and further education in Scotland.

Department of Education, Northern Ireland:
schools, further education and universities in Northern Ireland.

The Universities Funding Council (UFC) is responsible for administering funds made available to it by the Secretary of State for Education and Science to provide financial support for education and research in universities in Great Britain and for advising, when necessary, the Departments of Education and Agriculture in Northern Ireland on matters relating to universities in Northern Ireland.

The Polytechnics and Colleges Funding Council (PCFC) which came into being on 1 April 1989 has a remit for England only. It performs a similar function to the UFC with regard to those polytechnics and colleges which come within the PCFC sector. The PCFC also plans and funds certain courses in English colleges remaining under LEA control.

Statistics for the separate systems obtaining in England, Wales, Scotland and Northern Ireland are collected and processed separately in accordance with the particular needs of the responsible Departments and, particularly where there are structural differences, the assembly of statistics covering the United Kingdom as a single unit presents considerable problems and in some fields is impossible at present.

Stages of education

There are three main stages of education: primary, secondary, and further and higher education. The first two stages are compulsory for all children between the ages of five and sixteen years and the transition from primary to secondary education is usually made at the age of eleven. The third stage of education is voluntary and includes all education provided after full-time schooling ends.

Primary education

Primary education provides for pupils aged five to eleven. The great majority of public sector primary schools take both boys and girls in mixed classes.

Middle schools

In England middle schools take children from first schools and generally lead on, in turn, to comprehensive upper schools. They cover varying age ranges between eight and fourteen. Depending on their individual age range they are deemed either primary or secondary by Order of the Secretary of State for Education and Science or (for age range nine to thirteen) by choice of the local education authority.

Secondary education

Provision of secondary education in an area may include any combination of types of schools. The pattern is a reflection of historical circumstance and of the policy adopted by the local education authority. There is a growing trend to comprehensive schools, on a variety of patterns as to forms of organisation and the age range of the pupils attending. In their 'pure' form, comprehensive schools admit pupils without reference to ability and aptitude, and cater for all the children in a neighbourhood. In 1987, 8 per cent of secondary schools in England were comprehensive. Scotland has some schools which are part comprehensive/part selective; these are comprehensive in intake but selective as regards level of courses offered (typically not beyond 'O' grade).

Special schools, both day and boarding, provide education for handicapped children who cannot be educated satisfactorily in an ordinary school. Hospital special schools provide education for children who are spending a period in hospital.

Further education

The term 'further education' covers post-school education below higher education. It can include study of courses undertaken by those staying on in school, e.g. A-level GCE.

Higher education

The term higher education includes students on all courses provided by universities (including the Open University, but not the independent University of Buckingham), and courses at polytechnics, Scottish central institutions, and other institutions of further and higher education which lead to qualifications of a standard higher than A-level GCE, BTEC National Certificate/Diploma or Scottish Higher Certificate.

5.1 Number of schools[1] or departments by type and establishments of higher and further education

Academic years[2]

	1978/79	1979/80	1980/81	1981/82	1982/83	1983/84	1984/85	1985/86	1986/87	1987/88
United Kingdom: Public sector schools										
Nursery	1 213	1 236	1 251	1 254	1 259	1 260	1 257	1 262	1 271	1 298
Primary	26 850	26 764	26 504	26 072	25 755	25 326	24 993	24 756	24 609	24 482
Secondary	5 585	5 571	5 542	5 506	5 437	5 328	5 262	5 161	5 091	5 020
Non-maintained[3]	2 761	2 654	2 640	2 635	2 637	2 619	2 599	2 538	2 544	2 546
Special[4]	2 018	2 016	2 011	1 994	1 989	1 972	1 949	1 923	1 915	1 900
Universities (including Open University)	46	46	46	46	46	46	46	46	46	46
Polytechnics and other major establishments, vocational further education colleges and colleges of education										
Public sector[4]	751	746	744	729	729	728	693	697	677	673
Assisted[5]	67	63	62	58	57	57	56	56	52	51
Adult education centres (England and Wales)	5 303	4 926	4 628	4 318	4 542	4 513	4 227	2 874	2 523	2 632
England: Public sector schools										
Nursery	593	596	588	582	575	565	561	560	558	558
Primary	21 309	21 242	21 018	20 650	20 384	20 020	19 734	19 549	19 432	19 319
Secondary	4 694	4 680	4 654	4 622	4 553	4 444	4 382	4 286	4 221	4 153
Non-maintained	2 459	2 351	2 342	2 340	2 344	2 333	2 313	2 274	2 276	2 273
Special	1 599	1 597	1 593	1 571	1 562	1 548	1 529	1 493	1 470	1 443
Universities (including Open University)	35	35	35	35	35	35	35	35	35	35
Polytechnics	29	29	29	29	29	29	29	29	29	29
Other major establishments										
Maintained and assisted	488	481	468	459	450	439	437	436	422	417
Grant-aided	40	36	35	34	33	33	32	31	29	29
Adult education centres	4 527	4 309	4 067	3 747	3 958	3 938	3 684	2 616[7]	2 718	2 412
Wales: Public sector schools										
Nursery	70	69	69	64	64	65	61	59	59	58
Primary	1 930	1 925	1 908	1 873	1 844	1 821	1 796	1 774	1 762	1 753
Secondary	244	241	239	241	238	236	237	237	234	233
Non-maintained	71	71	72	71	73	70	67	69	69	67
Special	74	75	73	73	71	69	68	67	65	65
Universities	1	1	1	1	1	1	1	1	1	1
Polytechnics	1	1	1	1	1	1	1	1	1	1
Other major establishments										
Maintained and assisted	45	46	44	43	43	43	43	39	39	39
Grant-aided	1	1	1	1	1	1	1	1	1	1
Adult education centres	776	617	561	571	584	575	543	258[7]	205	220
Scotland: Public sector schools										
Nursery	489	503	515	527	537	546	551	559	568	596
Primary	2 532	2 530	2 522	2 499	2 489	2 461	2 443	2 425	2 417	2 418
Secondary	443	445	444	439	442	444	440	440	440	438
Non-maintained[3]	144	144	138	136	132	127	131	106	111	118
Special[3]	319	320	319	324	330	330	328	339	356	346
Universities	8	8	8	8	8	8	8	8	8	8
Vocational further education colleges										
Education authority										
Day	69	69	65	64	67	64	52	50	49	49
Evening	90	91	109	105	111	124	104	115	109	111
Central institutions	14	14	14	14	14	14	14	16	16	15
Voluntary bodies	–	–	–	–	–	–	–	–	–	–
Colleges of education	10	10	10	7	7	7	7	7	5	5
Northern Ireland: Public sector schools										
Nursery	61	68	79	81	83	84	84	84	86	86
Primary	1 079	1 067	1 056	1 050	1 038	1 024	1 020	1 008	998	992
Secondary	204	205	205	204	204	204	203	198	196	196
Non-maintained	87	88	88	88	88	89	88	89	87	88
Special	26	24	26	26	26	25	24	24	24	46[7]
Universities	2	2	2	2	2	2	2	2	2	2
Colleges of education	3	3	3	3	3	3	3	2	2	2
Polytechnics	1	1	1	1	1	1	–	–	–	–
Further education colleges	27	27	26	26	26	26	26	26	26	26

1 Schools (excluding independent) in Scotland and Northern Ireland with more than one department have been counted once for each department.

2 Schools are counted at January except for Scotland and Wales (1977–78 onwards) when the count is at September. Further education establishments are counted at 1 November–England and Wales, October–Scotland and Northern Ireland. University establishments at 31 December.

3 Including for Scotland grant-aided nursery, primary and secondary schools/departments and independent schools.

4 Polytechnics and maintained and assisted colleges in England and Wales, education authority colleges in Scotland, Stranmillis College of Education and education authority/education and library board colleges in Northern Ireland.

5 Direct grant colleges in England and Wales, central institutions, voluntary bodies and colleges of education in Scotland, voluntary colleges of education in Northern Ireland (St. Mary's College and St. Joseph's College).

6 Excludes youth clubs and centres; these were included in years prior to 1985–86.

7 Include 22 schools which were the responsibility of Northern Ireland Department of Health and Social Security up to 31 March 1987.

Source Education Departments

5.2 Pupils in school by age and sex: number and as a percentage of the population

United Kingdom
All schools
At January[1]

	1978	1979	1980[2]	1980[3]	1981	1982[4]	1983	1984	1985	1986[5]	1987[6]	1988
Age at the beginning of January												
Number (thousands)												
England	9 196	9 094	8 933	8 933	8 720	8 502	8 276	8 096	7 956	7 830	7 721	7 610
Wales	573	567	558	558	545	531	519	510	503	495	487	481
Scotland	1 081	1 059	1 034	1 034	1 005	975	945	918	894	..	..	840
Northern Ireland	372	371	367	367	363	359	354	351	349	346	343	341
United Kingdom	11 222	11 091	10 892	10 892	10 633	10 367	10 094	9 876	9 702	9 565	9 392	9 273
Boys and girls												
2–4[7]	557	573	585	804	792	794	823	887	915	917	900	912
5–10	5 247	5 090	4 908	4 959	4 752	4 542	4 302	4 140	4 085	4 096	4 134	4 180
11	936	921	908	919	903	869	879	825	774	737	692	668
12–14	2 857	2 853	2 808	2 822	2 777	2 727	2 660	2 631	2 565	2 487	2 314	2 199
Total 2–14	9 597	9 437	9 209	9 503	9 225	8 932	8 664	8 482	8 340	8 236	8 041	7 960
15	922	937	960	943	940	924	903	886	872	845	864	818
16	458	468	468	266	280	306	312	297	289	286	285	296
17	186	186	192	160	168	181	188	182	174	169	174	171
18 and over	60	63	63	19	21	24	27	28	28	28	27	27
Boys												
14	482	495	487	488	481	475	465	457	444	452	421	398
15	472	479	492	483	481	472	462	453	446	433	443	420
16	232	236	234	130	136	149	152	145	142	141	141	146
17	96	95	97	83	85	91	94	91	88	86	88	86
18 and over	34	35	34	12	13	14	15	16	16	16	15	15
Girls												
14	460	471	463	464	457	450	442	435	420	428	397	375
15	450	458	468	461	459	452	440	433	425	412	421	397
16	225	232	234	136	144	157	161	152	147	145	143	150
17	90	91	95	78	82	90	93	91	86	84	87	85
18 and over	26	28	28	8	8	10	12	12	12	12	12	12
As a percentage of population[8]												
Boys and girls												
2–4	*25.8*	*27.8*	*29.4*	*40.8*	*40.4*	*39.6*	*39.2*	*40.9*	*42.2*	*42.6*	*41.9*	*41.7*
5–10	*100.2*	*100.1*	*100.3*	*104.3*	*100.6*	*100.6*	*100.6*	*100.5*	*100.2*	*99.9*	*99.8*	*99.4*
11	*100.4*	*100.2*	*100.3*	*103.6*	*101.4*	*100.6*	*100.8*	*101.6*	*101.6*	*102.8*	*100.2*	*100.0*
12–14	*100.1*	*100.2*	*100.2*	*103.3*	*100.5*	*100.4*	*100.2*	*100.3*	*100.6*	*101.7*	*100.6*	*100.9*
15	*99.4*	*99.7*	*99.5*	*100.0*	*97.7*	*98.5*	*97.9*	*98.1*	*97.9*	*97.3*	*98.8*	*100.1*
16	*50.8*	*50.8*	*49.7*	*28.0*	*29.0*	*31.7*	*33.1*	*32.2*	*31.9*	*32.1*	*32.9*	*33.7*
17	*21.2*	*20.7*	*20.8*	*17.1*	*17.8*	*18.7*	*19.4*	*19.3*	*18.9*	*18.8*	*19.5*	*19.7*
18 and over[9]	*7.0*	*7.2*	*7.0*	*2.1*	*2.3*	*2.5*	*2.8*	*2.9*	*3.0*	*3.0*	*3.0*	*3.1*
Boys												
14	*100.0*	*100.1*	*100.2*	*102.7*	*100.0*	*100.1*	*100.4*	*100.2*	*100.0*	*100.6*	*100.2*	*100.6*
15	*99.2*	*99.7*	*99.4*	*99.8*	*97.3*	*97.9*	*97.2*	*97.7*	*97.7*	*97.4*	*98.6*	*100.6*
16	*50.3*	*49.9*	*48.5*	*26.7*	*27.4*	*30.0*	*31.4*	*30.5*	*30.5*	*30.9*	*31.7*	*32.5*
17	*21.3*	*20.5*	*20.5*	*17.3*	*17.6*	*18.3*	*18.8*	*18.8*	*18.5*	*18.5*	*19.2*	*19.4*
18 and over[9]	*7.6*	*7.7*	*7.3*	*2.5*	*2.8*	*2.9*	*3.0*	*3.2*	*3.3*	*3.3*	*3.2*	*3.3*
Girls												
14	*100.1*	*100.1*	*100.0*	*103.1*	*100.2*	*100.5*	*100.6*	*100.5*	*99.9*	*100.5*	*100.1*	*100.8*
15	*99.5*	*99.8*	*99.6*	*100.4*	*98.1*	*99.1*	*98.3*	*98.5*	*98.2*	*97.8*	*98.9*	*100.0*
16	*51.3*	*51.6*	*50.9*	*29.4*	*30.6*	*33.5*	*35.2*	*33.9*	*33.4*	*33.4*	*34.2*	*35.1*
17	*21.1*	*20.8*	*21.2*	*17.1*	*17.8*	*19.1*	*19.8*	*19.9*	*19.2*	*19.0*	*19.9*	*20.0*
18 and over[9]	*6.3*	*6.6*	*6.4*	*1.8*	*1.8*	*2.2*	*2.5*	*2.5*	*2.7*	*2.8*	*2.7*	*2.9*

1 In Wales from 1977 the school census date was advanced to September whereas that for the rest of the United Kingdom remains at January. From 1977 onwards in Scotland, figures are at the previous September (the same academic session).
2 Age at beginning of January for 1980.
3 Age at 31 August from 1980 onwards.
4 For non-maintained schools in England, pupils' ages have been estimated.
5 Estimated; these figures include 1984–85 data for Scotland.
6 Estimated; these figures include 1987–88 data for Scotland.
7 Each part-time pupil (aged 2–4, but also small numbers aged 5 in Scotland attending nursery schools) has been counted as one.
8 The Registrars General estimates of resident population have sometimes been slightly below the number of children found to have attended school.
9 As a percentage of the 18 years age-group.

Source Education Departments

5.3 Number of pupils and teachers: pupil/teacher ratios

United Kingdom
At January[1]

Thousands

	1976	1977	1978	1979	1980	1981	1982	1983	1984	1985	1986	1987	1988
All schools or departments[2]													
Total													
Pupils													
Full-time and full-time equivalent of part-time	10 575.9	10 586.2	10 490.2	10 353.9	10 770.9	10 525.3	10 234.7	9 949.7	9 724.7	9 544.3	9 384.8[5]	9 245.6[6]	9 100.7
Teachers[3]	531.6	537.4	538.7	543.4	590.2	579.1	568.1	559.6	554.1	546.0	540.3[5]	537.4[6]	531.1
Pupils per teacher:													
United Kingdom[3]	19.9	19.7	19.5	19.1	18.2	18.2	18.0	17.8	17.6	17.5	17.4[5]	17.2[6]	17.1
England	20.0	19.8	19.6	19.2	18.4	18.2	18.1	17.9	17.6	17.6	17.4	17.2	17.2
Wales	19.7	19.6	19.5	19.0	18.6	18.5	18.5	18.3	18.1	18.2	18.2	18.2	18.0
Scotland	18.7	18.4	18.3	17.7	16.8	16.7	16.7	16.6	16.4	16.2	..	..	15.8
Northern Ireland	22.1	20.9	19.9	19.6	19.0	18.9	18.9	18.7	18.7	18.6	18.5	18.4	18.4
Public sector schools or departments													
Nursery													
Pupils													
Full-time and full-time equivalent of part-time	47.1	50.2	53.2	54.7	54.9	55.5	55.8	56.3	57.2	57.3	56.9[5]	57.5[6]	57.6
Teachers[3]	2.1	2.3	2.4	2.5	2.5	2.6	2.6	2.6	2.6	2.6	2.6[5]	2.7[6]	2.7
Pupils per teacher	22.1	21.8	22.5	22.1	21.6	21.5	21.6	21.8	21.7	21.8	21.7[5]	21.2[6]	21.4
Primary													
Pupils													
Full-time and full-time equivalent of part-time	5 940.3	5 834.6	5 675.7	5 513.6	5 317.1	5 087.3	4 870.0	4 659.0	4 549.7	4 513.6	4 520.8	4 550.3	4 598.9
Teachers[3]	249.5	246.4	242.1	241.2	237.0	227.8	218.7	211.1	207.1	205.0	205.8	208.7	210.1
Pupils per teacher	23.8	23.7	23.4	22.9	22.4	22.3	22.3	22.1	22.0	22.0	22.0	21.8	21.9
Secondary													
Pupils													
Full-time and full-time equivalent of part-time	4 448.4	4 558.9	4 617.5	4 643.1	4 636.2	4 606.3	4 558.5	4 493.6	4 384.2	4 243.6	4 080.0	3 902.4	3 701.5
Teachers[3]	264.1	271.9	276.8	281.8	283.4	281.6	278.5	277.0	274.5	267.7	260.5	253.8	244.9
Pupils per teacher	16.8	16.8	16.7	16.5	16.4	16.4	16.4	16.2	16.0	15.9	15.7	15.4	15.1
Special Schools[4]													
Pupils													
Full-time and full-time equivalent of part-time	140.0	142.5	143.8	142.4	149.3	147.2	145.0	142.7	137.3	133.1	130.0	124.9	120.9
Teachers[3]	15.8	16.8	17.4	18.0	19.8	19.8	19.7	19.7	19.7	19.7	19.6	19.5	19.3
Pupils per teacher	8.9	8.5	8.3	7.9	7.5	7.4	7.4	7.3	7.0	6.8	6.6	6.4	6.3

1 In Scotland and in Wales from 1977 the school census date was advanced to September whereas that for the rest of the United Kingdom remains at January.
2 From 1980 onwards includes non-maintained schools or departments, including independent schools in Scotland.
3 Figures of teachers and of pupil/teacher ratios take account of the full-time equivalent of part-time teachers.
4 Public sector only up to and including 1979.
5 Includes 1984–85 data for Scotland.
6 Includes 1987–88 data for Scotland.

Source *Education Departments*

5.4 Pupils with special needs in public sector and assisted schools

United Kingdom
At January[1]

(i) Numbers of public sector and assisted special schools, full-time pupils and teachers

	1977	1978	1979	1980	1981	1982	1983	1984	1985	1986	1987	1988
Hospital schools[2]												
Schools:												
Public sector	154	150	145	145	141	132	125	117	111	98	88	79
Assisted	5	5	5	4	4	3	3	3	2	2	1	1
Total	159	155	150	149	145	135	128	120	113	100	89	80
Full-time pupils (thousands)	9.2	8.8	8.1	7.8	7.3	6.7	6.2	5.3	4.8	4.6	3.2	3.0
Teachers (thousands)[3]												
Full-time teachers	1.2	1.3	1.3	1.2	1.2	1.1	1.0	0.9	0.8	0.7	0.6	0.6
Other special schools or departments[4]												
Schools:												
Public sector	1 707	1 733	1 759	1 760	1 763	1 759	1 763	1 757	1 742	1 726	1 739	1 736
Assisted	119	118	116	115	112	109	107	104	103	95	96	92
Day	1 357	1 375	1 384	1 412	1 412	1 412	1 393	1 488	1 469	1 464	1 174[5]	1 500
Boarding	469	476	491	463	463	456	477	373	376	357	281[5]	328
Total	1 826	1 851	1 875	1 875	1 875	1 868	1 870	1 861	1 845	1 821	1 835	1 828
Full-time pupils (thousands):												
Blind and partially sighted	3.9	3.8	3.8	3.7	3.5	3.3	3.2	7	7	7	7	7
Deaf and partially hearing	6.6	6.4	6.1	5.6	5.3	5.0	4.7	7	7	7	7	7
Delicate and physically handicapped	19.0	18.8	18.6	18.0	17.3	16.8	16.2	7	7	7	7	7
Maladjusted	14.6	14.6	14.3	15.0	14.7	14.5	14.8	7	7	7	7	7
Educationally sub-normal and mentally handicapped[6]	90.8	93.5	94.2	92.1	92.8	92.9	92.2	7	7	7	7	7
Epileptic	2.2	2.0	2.0	1.9	1.8	1.6	1.6	7	7	7	7	7
Speech defect	4.8	4.1	3.7	3.5	3.1	2.5	2.3	7	7	7	7	7
Autistic[5]	0.6	0.6	0.6	0.6	0.7	0.6	0.6	7	7	7	7	7
Total	142.4	143.8	143.3	140.7	139.2	137.3	135.5	132.1	128.8	126.0	120.4	117.7
Teachers (thousands)												
Full-time teachers	16.2	16.9	17.4	17.6	17.7	17.7	17.8	17.9	17.8	17.7	17.7[8]	9
Full-time equivalent of part-time teachers	0.7	0.6	0.7	0.7	0.7	0.7	0.7	0.7	0.8	0.8	0.8[8]	18.7

1 In Wales from 1977 the school census date was advanced to September whereas that for the rest of the United Kingdom remains at January.
2 England, Wales and Northern Ireland only.
3 Excluding part-time teachers in hospital schools, full-time equivalent in 1988 was 36.
4 In the 1986 column, data for Scotland relate to 1984/85.
5 England and Wales only.
6 In 1975 a change was made in the method of recording the major handicap of pupils attending educationally sub-normal (severe) special schools in England and Wales and for the first time a number of them (6 908) were returned within a category other than 'educationally sub-normal'.
7 Information on individual handicaps ceased to be collected in 1984.
8 Including 1984–85 data for Scotland.
9 Data on full-time teachers no longer collected separately.

(ii) Pupils with statements of special needs in other public sector schools

	1985	1986	1987	1988
Public sector primary schools[10]	21.1[12]	22.8[12]	24.0	28.5
Public sector secondary schools[11]	12.5[12]	15.4[12]	17.4	21.8
Total	33.5	38.2	41.3	50.2

10 Including middle schools deemed primary.
11 Including middle schools deemed secondary.
12 Including estimated primary/secondary split for Wales.

Source Education Departments

5.5 Pupils leaving school by sex and highest qualification held

Academic years

Thousands

	1976/77	1977/78	1978/79	1979/80	1980/81[1]	1981/82	1982/83[1]	1983/84	1984/85[1]	1985/86	1986/87	1987/88
Boys and girls												
Leavers with GCE 'A' level/SCE 'H' grade passes												
2 or more 'A', 3 or more 'H'	113	117	117	121	122	133	131	136	127	127	129	131
1 'A', 1 or 2 'H'	33	32	31	33	32	36	37	37	34	34	34	33
Leavers with GCSE/GCE 'O' level/CSE/SCE 'O' grades alone												
5 or more A – C awards/CSE grade 1[2]	78	81	83	85	81	90	91	95	93	95	92	97
1 – 4 A – C awards/CSE grade 1[2]	228	232	241	242	228	240	244	243	232	231	233	210
No higher grades												
1 or more other grades[3]	416	427	427	434	284	293	293	295	283	283	284	241
No GCSE/GCE/SCE or CSE qualifications					119	121	105	108	98	101	95	86
Total school leavers	868	888	900	915	865	913	902	914	866	871	867	797
Boys												
Leavers with GCSE/GCE 'A' level/SCE 'H' grade passes												
2 or more 'A', 3 or more 'H'	63	64	64	64	65	69	68	70	67	66	66	67
1 'A', 1 or 2 'H'	16	15	15	16	15	17	17	17	15	16	16	16
Leavers with GCSE/GCE 'O' level/CSE/SCE 'O' grades alone												
5 or more A – C awards/CSE grade 1[2]	36	38	38	39	37	41	42	44	43	44	42	42
1 – 4 A – C awards/CSE grade 1[2]	110	110	116	115	109	115	116	114	108	108	109	100
No higher grades												
1 or more other grades	220	230	228	234	149	154	155	155	151	151	152	132
No GCSE/GCE/SCE or CSE qualifications					68	69	62	64	57	59	56	51
Total school leavers	445	457	461	469	442	466	460	464	441	444	442	409
Girls												
Leavers with GCSE/GCE 'A' level/SCE 'H' grade passes												
2 or more 'A', 3 or more 'H'	51	52	54	58	57	64	63	65	60	61	62	64
1 'A', 1 or 2 'H'	17	17	17	17	17	19	20	20	19	18	18	17
Leavers with GCSE/GCE 'O' level/CSE/SCE 'O' grades alone												
5 or more A – C awards/CSE grade 1[2]	42	43	45	45	44	49	49	50	50	51	50	55
1 – 4 A – C awards/SCE grade 1[2]	118	122	125	127	120	125	128	129	124	123	124	110
No higher grades												
1 or more other grades	196	198	199	200	135	139	138	140	131	132	132	108
No GCSE/GCE/SCE or CSE qualifications					51	51	44	45	42	43	39	35
Total school leavers	424	432	439	446	423	447	442	450	425	427	425	388

1 Great Britain only.

2 'O' grades in Scotland (from 1974) and 'O' levels in England, Wales and Northern Ireland (from 1975) have been awarded in bands A to E; awards in bands A to C can be regarded as equivalent to what were previously rated as passes.

3 The numbers of pupils who left school in Great Britain with no GCSE/GCE/SCE or CSE qualifications were as follows:

Thousands

1977/78	*1978/79*	*1979/80*	*1980/81*	*1981/82*	*1982/83*	*1983/84*	*1984/85*	*1985/86*	*1986/87*	*1987/88*
146	135	132	119	113	105	102	98	95	90	81

Source *Education Departments*

5.6 Numbers and percentages continuing education aged 16 and over by age, sex and type of course[1]

Men and women

1987 – 88

Home students

	All students	Total 16 – 18	16	17	18	19 – 20	21 – 24	25 and over
		Age at 31 August 1987						
Number in thousands								
Total population	–	2 638	877	868	892	1 835	3 851	–
Full-time and sandwich students								
Schools	489	486	293	170	23	3	–	–
Further education[2]	414	328	155	116	57	30	19	36
Higher education	566	95	1	8	86	228	164	79
Universities	275	52	–	5	47	118	77	28
Undergraduates	241	52	–	5	47	117	57	15
Postgraduates	34	–	–	–	–	–	20	14
Polytechnics[3]	184	28	–	2	25	71	56	29
Other advanced courses	106	15	–	1	14	39	30	22
Total full-time and sandwich students	1 468	908	449	293	166	262	183	115
Part-time students								
Further education[4]	3 080	539	205	182	153	215	459	1 867
Day students	777	327	128	125	74	73	62	315
Evening students[5]	2 303	212	77	56	79	142	397	1 552
Higher education[6]	354	12	–	1	10	38	69	235
Universities	40	–	–	–	–	1	6	33
Open University[7]	84	–	–	–	–	–	6	78
Other advanced courses, part-time day	175	11	–	1	9	32	44	87
part-time evening[8]	55	1	–	–	1	4	14	37
of which Polytechnics	77	2	–	–	2	8	20	47
Total part-time students	3 434	551	205	183	163	253	528	2 102
As percentage of population								
Full-time and sandwich students								
Schools	..	18.4	33.4	19.5	2.6	0.2	–	..
Further education	..	12.4	17.7	13.3	6.4	1.7	0.5	..
Higher education[2]	..	3.6	0.1	0.9	9.6	12.4	4.3	..
Universities	..	2.0	–	0.5	5.3	6.4	2.0	..
Undergraduates	..	2.0	–	0.5	5.3	6.4	1.5	..
Postgraduates	..	–	–	–	–	–	0.5	..
Polytechnics[3]	..	1.0	–	0.3	2.8	3.9	1.5	..
Other advanced courses	..	0.6	–	0.1	1.5	2.1	0.8	..
Total full-time and sandwich students	..	34.4	51.2	33.8	18.6	14.3	4.7	..
Part-time students								
Further education[4]	..	20.4	23.3	20.9	17.1	11.7	11.9	..
Day students	..	12.4	14.6	14.4	8.2	4.0	1.6	..
Evening students[5]	..	8.0	8.8	6.5	8.9	7.7	10.3	..
Higher education[6]	..	0.5	–	0.2	1.2	2.1	1.8	..
Universities	..	–	–	–	–	–	0.1	..
Open University[7]	..	–	–	–	–	–	0.1	..
Other advanced courses, part-time day	..	0.4	–	0.1	1.0	1.8	1.1	..
part-time evening[8]	..	–	–	–	0.1	0.2	0.4	..
of which Polytechnics	..	0.1	–	–	0.2	0.4	0.5	..
Total part-time students	..	20.9	23.4	21.1	18.3	13.8	13.7	..

1 Further and higher education data for Northern Ireland relate to 1986–87.
2 Including 2 600 students (1 100 men) (provisional) in Polytechnics (and Central Institutions in Scotland).
3 Including Central Institutions in Scotland.
4 Including 11 200 students (5 500 men) in Polytechnics.
5 Including estimated age detail for 1 578 thousand students aged 16 years or more in adult education centres; excluding youth clubs and centres. Excluding 539 thousand students on courses run by Responsible Bodies for whom age detail was not available. Responsible Bodies are the extramural departments of universities, the Workers' Educational Association and the Welsh Council of the Young Men's Christian Association.
6 Excluding 93 600 (provisional) students enrolled on nursing and paramedical courses at DHSS establishments.
7 Provisional. Excluding some 2 200 students for whom data by age are not available.
8 Including part-time evening students in Polytechnics in England (18 900 in 1987-88, 18 600 in 1986-87 and 19 400 in 1985-86).

Source Education Departments

5.7 Students in further education by mode of study[1]

Autumn term

Thousands

	1975	1976	1977	1978	1979[2]	1980	1981	1982	1983	1984	1985	1986	1987
Major establishments													
Full-time[3]	495	508	499	498	495	510	564	603	595	594	608	624	633
Sandwich	52	56	59	62	65	68	74	83	90	90	90	91	93
Part-time day	830	789	790	846	836	820	806	787	846	891	914	951	988
Evening	860	773	739	778	698	694	692	720	771	780	807	852	868
Total	2 237	2 126	2 087	2 184	2 094	2 092	2 136	2 193	2 302	2 354	2 419	2 518	2 581
Adult education centres (England and Wales only)	1 982	1 797	1 708	2 005	1 849	1 645	1 609	1 632	1 734	1 693	1 478[4]	1 519	1 439[5]

1 Excluding students on non-vocational courses in Scotland and Northern Ireland.

2 In previous years this time series was based on ages as at 31 December, from this year the basis has been changed to 31 August.

3 Including from 1977, teacher training colleges of education in Scotland and Northern Ireland.

4 From 1985 onwards, excludes students aged 18 and over in youth clubs and centres.

5 In 1986 contains 36 thousand men and 69 thousand women aged 18 years and under; and 349 thousand men and 985 thousand women aged 19 years and over.

Source *Education Departments*

5.8 Full-time students from abroad

(i) Enrolments by type of course, sex and country, in higher and further education.[1] Autumn 1987

Thousands

	Higher education			Further education			
	Postgraduate	First degree level or equivalent	Other		Men	Women	Total
Europe							
Belgium	0.1	0.3	–	–	0.3	0.2	0.5
Cyprus	0.2	0.9	0.2	0.1	0.9	0.5	1.4
Denmark	0.1	0.1	–	–	0.1	0.1	0.2
France	0.3	0.8	0.5	0.3	0.9	1.0	1.9
Germany, West	0.4	1.0	0.8	0.2	1.3	1.2	2.4
Greece	1.3	0.8	0.2	0.3	1.9	0.7	2.6
Ireland, Republic of	0.4	1.2	0.3	0.3	1.1	1.0	2.1
Italy	0.2	0.3	0.1	0.2	0.4	0.4	0.8
Netherlands	0.2	0.3	0.1	–	0.3	0.3	0.5
Norway	0.1	1.2	–	–	0.9	0.4	1.4
Spain	0.2	0.2	0.1	0.3	0.4	0.4	0.8
Sweden	–	0.1	–	–	0.1	0.1	0.2
Other	0.5	0.7	0.2	0.1	0.8	0.7	1.5
Australasia							
Australia	0.3	0.1	–	–	0.3	0.2	0.5
New Zealand	0.1	–	–	–	0.1	0.1	0.2
Other	0.1	–	–	–	0.1	–	0.1
Africa							
Algeria	0.8	–	–	–	0.8	0.1	0.9
Cameroon	0.2	0.3	–	–	0.4	0.1	0.5
Ghana	0.2	0.1	–	0.1	0.3	0.1	0.1
Kenya	0.4	0.5	0.1	0.1	0.8	0.3	1.1
Libya	0.1	0.1	0.3	–	0.5	–	0.5
Mauritius	–	0.2	–	–	0.2	0.1	0.3
Nigeria	0.8	0.5	0.2	0.2	1.1	0.5	1.7
South Africa	0.3	0.1	–	0.1	0.4	0.2	0.5
Tanzania	0.3	0.1	0.1	0.1	0.3	0.1	0.5
Zambia	0.3	0.3	0.1	0.1	0.6	0.2	0.7
Zimbabwe	0.1	0.1	–	0.1	0.3	0.1	0.4
Other	1.8	0.8	0.4	0.5	2.7	0.7	3.5
The Americas							
Brazil	0.5	–	–	–	0.4	0.2	0.5
Canada	0.7	0.2	0.1	–	0.6	0.4	1.0
USA	1.4	0.7	2.9	0.2	2.2	2.9	5.1
Venezuela	–	–	–	–	–	–	0.1
Other	0.8	0.5	0.1	0.2	1.1	0.6	1.6

1 Data for Northern Ireland relate to 1986–87.

Source *Education Departments*

5.8 (continued) Full-time students from abroad

(i) Enrolments by type of course, sex and country, in higher and further education. Autumn 1987

Thousands

	Higher education			Further education	Men	Women	Total
	Post-graduate	First degree level or equivalent	Other				
Asia							
Bangladesh	0.3	–	0.1	–	0.4	–	0.4
Brunei	0.1	0.5	0.2	0.1	0.6	0.3	0.9
China, People's Republic of	1.0	0.1	–	–	0.9	0.2	1.1
Hong Kong	1.1	4.9	0.4	1.0	5.1	2.3	7.4
India	0.6	0.2	0.1	0.2	0.9	0.2	1.1
Indonesia	0.3	0.1	0.1	–	0.5	0.1	0.6
Iran	0.8	0.3	0.1	0.2	1.1	0.2	1.3
Iraq	0.9	0.2	0.1	–	1.2	0.1	1.3
Japan	0.3	0.2	0.2	0.1	0.4	0.4	0.8
Jordan	0.2	0.2	–	0.1	0.5	0.1	0.6
Malaysia	1.1	4.9	0.5	0.3	4.3	2.4	6.8
Oman	–	0.3	0.1	0.3	0.6	0.1	0.7
Pakistan	0.7	0.1	0.1	0.1	1.0	0.1	1.1
Saudi Arabia	0.5	0.1	0.1	0.1	0.6	0.1	0.7
Singapore	0.4	1.5	0.1	–	1.3	0.7	2.0
Sri Lanka	0.2	0.2	0.1	0.1	0.5	0.1	0.6
Thailand	0.1	0.1	–	0.1	0.2	0.1	0.3
Turkey	0.2	–	–	0.1	0.3	0.1	0.4
Other	1.5	0.7	0.2	0.6	2.4	0.6	3.0
Stateless/Unknown	–	0.1	–	–	0.1	0.1	0.2
All countries	23.8	27.3	9.3	7.1	45.3	22.2	67.5
Foreign	15.6	10.8	6.6	4.2	24.6	12.7	37.3
Commonwealth	8.2	16.5	2.7	2.9	20.7	9.5	30.3

(ii) Entrants and enrolments by grouped country of domicile in higher and further education[1]

Thousands

	1975–76[2]	1977–78[2]	1978–79[2]	1979–80	1980–81	1981–82	1982–83	1983–84	1984–85	1985–86	1986–87	1987–88
Entrants												
European Community	2.0	1.9	2.0	1.9	3.0	3.0	3.6	3.7	4.5	5.6	6.3	7.6
Europe	. .	5.2	5.1	4.7	4.1	3.9	4.9	4.8	3.5	4.0	2.1	2.4
OPEC	11.6	14.1	12.6	10.8	9.4	8.0	6.9	6.0	5.7	6.4	5.9	3.5
Commonwealth	23.6	24.0	23.5	23.2	18.1	15.7	13.6	14.3	14.6	16.9	16.2	15.9
Non-commonwealth	23.1	24.8	24.6	21.6	17.3	14.9	14.7	14.7	16.9	21.6	22.9	23.1
Developing countries	39.3	40.1	38.9	37.5	29.5	24.5	22.0	22.4	21.0	24.1	24.3	23.6
All countries[3]	46.7	48.8	48.1	44.9	35.6	30.7	28.3	29.0	31.5	38.5	39.1	39.0
of which												
Higher education	26.8	29.1	28.7	26.4	23.8	24.5	23.0	23.7	26.5	31.0	32.8	33.6
Further education	19.9	18.8	18.9	18.5	11.8	6.2	5.3	5.3	5.0	7.5	6.3	5.4
Enrolments												
European Community	2.6	3.0	3.1	3.0	5.3	5.3	6.4	6.6	7.4	8.9	10.1	12.0
Europe	. .	9.1	9.0	8.6	8.3	7.5	8.8	9.0	6.6	7.0	3.9	4.3
OPEC	17.1	23.2	22.3	19.8	17.4	15.1	12.5	11.8	10.5	10.7	10.0	7.8
Commonwealth	39.8	44.0	44.5	43.0	38.7	32.7	28.0	27.4	28.1	30.2	30.2	30.3
Non-commonwealth	35.0	41.2	41.2	40.0	32.3	27.8	25.6	25.8	28.0	33.5	35.5	37.3
Developing countries	62.2	71.5	71.4	68.6	60.9	50.4	43.9	42.9	39.4	42.0	43.5	44.1
All countries[3]	74.8	85.1	85.8	82.9	71.2	60.6	53.8	53.2	56.1	63.7	65.6	67.5
of which												
Higher education	48.1	56.0	57.0	56.2	51.6	49.4	45.6	45.3	48.6	53.7	57.1	60.4
Further education	26.8	27.5	27.1	26.7	19.7	11.2	8.2	7.9	7.5	10.0	8.5	7.1

1 Data for Northern Ireland relate to 1986–87.
2 Great Britain data.
3 Numbers in grouped countries do not sum to all overall student numbers due to overlap.

Source *Education Departments*

5.9 Students in education by type of course, mode of study, sex and subject group[1]

Home and overseas students

Academic year 1987–88[2] | Thousands

	Postgraduate level		Undergraduate level or equivalent		Other higher education		Total higher education	Further education[3]		All students		
										Full-time[4]		Part-time[5]
	Full-time[4]	Part-time[5]	Full-time[4]	Part-time[5]	Full-time[4]	Part-time[5]		Full-time[4]	Part-time[5]	Home	Home and overseas	Home and overseas[6]
Male												
Subject group												
1. Education	5.7	6.0	6.3	1.8	1.5	6.5	27.8	3.6	5.0	15.7	17.0	19.4
2. Medicine, dentistry and health	2.4	2.2	16.1	0.4	1.0	2.4	24.5	1.2	6.4	18.5	20.8	11.3
3. Engineering and technology	8.7	4.3	57.5	5.2	17.4	54.5	147.6	52.0	281.2	121.0	135.5	345.2
4. Agriculture, forestry and veterinary science	0.9	0.3	2.8	–	1.3	0.1	5.5	4.4	19.8	8.5	9.5	20.2
5. Science	11.7	5.0	58.3	3.1	8.6	7.6	94.3	8.7	17.3	80.0	87.3	33.0
6. Administrative, business and social studies	9.6	12.9	57.9	5.8	13.3	49.0	148.6	21.8	72.3	92.1	102.6	140.0
7. Architecture and other professional and vocational subjects	2.2	1.3	9.0	0.6	3.9	2.3	19.5	19.9	40.6	32.4	35.0	44.9
8. Languages, literature and area studies	1.6	1.5	13.0	0.5	0.1	0.4	17.2	0.3	11.4	13.3	15.0	13.8
9. Arts other than languages	1.4	1.8	12.2	1.1	0.6	0.2	17.3	1.8	23.6	14.6	16.0	26.8
10. Music, drama, art and design	1.2	0.7	13.6	0.8	4.8	0.4	21.4	12.7	15.6	31.3	32.3	17.4
11. GCE, GCSE, SCE and CSE	–	–	–	–	–	–	–	47.9	106.5	46.7	47.9	106.5
12. Other	0.3	–	0.3	–	–	–	0.6	18.7	132.5	19.2	19.3	132.5
All subjects	45.6	36.0	247.1	19.3	52.7	123.4	524.1	193.0	732.2	493.2	538.4	910.9
Female												
Subject group												
1. Education	7.9	5.3	24.6	3.8	2.0	11.1	54.6	3.8	8.9	37.2	38.2	29.2
2. Medicine, dentistry and health	1.9	1.7	18.3	0.7	4.6	5.4	32.7	17.6	18.9	41.0	42.4	26.8
3. Engineering and technology	1.0	0.6	8.6	0.3	2.4	2.5	15.5	4.9	21.7	15.2	17.0	25.1
4. Agriculture, forestry and veterinary science	0.3	0.1	2.3	–	0.4	0.1	3.3	1.4	6.8	4.1	4.5	6.9
5. Science	3.8	2.0	34.2	1.4	2.9	4.0	48.3	4.3	16.2	41.5	45.3	23.6
6. Administrative, business and social studies	5.8	6.4	55.0	4.4	16.2	40.0	128.0	56.5	212.6	126.6	133.6	263.4
7. Architecture and other professional and vocational subjects	1.2	0.8	7.7	0.5	4.9	1.2	16.1	44.9	105.5	57.7	58.7	107.8
8. Languages, literature and area studies	1.5	1.6	27.4	1.4	0.6	0.9	33.6	1.4	17.6	28.4	30.9	21.6
9. Arts other than languages	0.6	1.0	13.7	2.1	1.1	0.4	18.8	2.2	41.6	16.3	17.7	45.0
10. Music, drama, art and design	1.2	0.7	20.0	1.0	5.4	0.5	28.8	16.7	23.0	41.7	43.3	25.3
11. GCE, GCSE, SCE and CSE	–	–	–	–	–	–	–	55.9	167.8	55.3	55.9	167.8
12. Other	0.5	–	2.2	–	–	–	2.8	18.8	252.5	21.5	21.6	252.5
All subjects	25.8	20.2	214.1	15.8	40.6	66.2	382.6	228.5	892.9	486.7	509.0	995.0
Persons												
Subject group												
1. Education	13.6	11.3	30.8	5.7	3.5	17.6	82.4	7.4	14.0	52.9	55.2	48.5
2. Medicine, dentistry and health	4.4	4.0	34.4	1.1	5.6	7.8	57.2	18.8	25.3	59.5	63.2	38.1
3. Engineering and technology	9.6	4.9	66.1	5.5	19.8	57.1	163.1	56.9	302.9	136.2	152.5	370.4
4. Agriculture, forestry and veterinary science	1.2	0.4	5.1	–	1.7	0.2	8.8	5.8	26.6	12.7	13.9	27.1
5. Science	15.5	7.0	92.6	4.5	11.5	11.6	142.6	13.1	33.5	121.6	132.6	56.5
6. Administrative, business and social studies	15.4	19.2	112.9	10.3	29.5	89.0	276.6	78.3	284.8	218.7	236.2	403.4
7. Architecture and other professional and vocational subjects	3.4	2.1	16.7	1.1	8.8	3.5	35.6	64.9	146.1	90.1	93.7	152.8
8. Languages, literature and area studies	3.2	3.1	40.5	2.0	0.7	1.4	50.9	1.6	29.0	41.7	46.0	35.4
9. Arts other than languages	2.1	2.8	25.9	3.2	1.8	0.6	36.1	4.0	65.2	31.0	33.7	71.7
10. Music, drama, art and design	2.4	1.4	33.6	1.8	10.2	0.9	50.3	29.4	38.6	73.0	75.5	42.7
11. GCE, GCSE, SCE and CSE	–	–	–	–	–	–	–	103.7	274.3	102.0	103.7	274.3
12. Other	0.8	–	2.5	–	0.1	–	3.4	37.6	384.9	40.7	40.9	384.9
All subjects	71.4	56.2	461.2	35.0	93.3	189.5	906.7	421.5	1,625.1	979.9	1,047.4	1,905.9

1 Excluding data for pupils at schools and for the Open University for which subject detail in this format is not available. Also, excluding 93 600 (provisional) students on nursing and paramedical courses at DHSS establishments.

2 Data for Northern Ireland (except for universities) relate to 1986–87.

3 Including 716.0 thousand students in all modes in England, Wales and Northern Ireland who are taking unspecified courses.

4 Including sandwich students.

5 Day and evening.

6 Including 8.9 thousand part-time students from abroad.

Source *Education Departments*

5.10 Students obtaining qualifications by subject of study,[1] sex and awarding body in the year ended 31 December 1987[2]

Thousands

	Education	Medicine, dentistry and health	Engineering and technology	Agriculture, forestry and veterinary science	Science	Administrative, business and social studies	Architecture and other professional and vocational studies	Language, literature and area studies	Arts other than languages[3]	Music, drama, art and design[3]	All students	Men
Higher degree												
University[4]	3.2	1.8	4.3	0.5	5.6	7.1	1.0	1.6	1.0	0.3	26.5	18.6
CNAA	0.2	0.1	0.5	–	0.6	0.6	0.2	–	0.1	0.3	2.5	1.8
Total	3.4	1.9	4.7	0.5	6.2	7.7	1.1	1.6	1.1	0.6	28.9	20.4
Higher diplomas and certificates												
University[5, 6]	6.3	0.5	0.5	0.1	0.6	2.9	0.7	0.1	–	0.2	12.0	6.1
CNAA	2.3	0.1	0.3	–	0.2	0.8	0.4	0.1	–	0.1	4.2	1.8
Total	8.6	0.6	0.8	0.1	0.8	3.7	1.1	0.2	0.1	0.3	16.2	7.9
First degree												
University[4]	1.5	6.3	9.8	1.3	17.6	18.5	1.3	8.8	5.1	1.5	71.6	41.1
CNAA[6]	4.5	1.1	6.6	0.1	8.5	10.7	3.1	1.4	3.3	6.5	45.8	24.5
University validated degrees (GB)[6]	2.9	0.1	–	–	1.1	0.6	0.2	0.4	1.4	0.6	7.3	2.2
Total	9.0	7.5	16.4	1.4	27.1	29.8	4.6	10.6	9.7	8.6	124.7	67.8
First university diplomas and certificates[6, 7]	0.3	0.4	0.3	–	1.8	1.2	0.1	0.6	0.5	0.4	5.6	2.6
CNAA diplomas and certificates[8, 11]	4.2	0.1	–	–	0.3	2.5	–	0.3	0.6	0.4	8.3[11]	4.6[11]
Professional qualifications (public sector)[10]	0.6	4.2	5.0	0.1	1.7	26.6	2.6	0.6	0.1	1.2	42.6	25.1
BTEC higher diploma	–	–	4.0	0.6	2.6	4.3	1.5	–	–	2.2	15.2	9.6
BTEC higher certificate	–	–	12.4	–	2.6	5.7	0.1	–	–	0.2	21.0	16.6
SCOTVEC higher diploma/certificate	–	–	1.3	0.1	0.6	3.2	0.5	–	–	–	5.7	3.2
Total[1]			17.7	0.7	5.7	13.2	2.2	13.9		2.4	41.9	29.3
Total higher education[1]	26.1	14.7	45.0	2.7	43.7	84.6	11.6	13.5	12.1	14.0	268.3[11,12]	157.6[11]
Further education												
BTEC ordinary diploma	–	–	6.4	0.9	2.7	11.5	2.7	–	–	5.5	29.8	16.3
BTEC ordinary certificate	–	–	17.0	–	2.7	17.2	1.5	–	–	0.8	39.2	25.2
Total further education[13]	–	–	23.5	0.9	5.4	28.7	4.2	–	–	6.4	69.0	41.5
Grand total	26.1	14.7	68.4	3.6	49.0	113.3	15.9	13.9	12.1	20.3	337.3[11,12]	199.2[11]
Men												
Higher degrees	2.1	1.1	4.3	0.4	4.6	5.3	0.7	0.8	0.8	0.2	20.4	20.4
Higher diplomas and certificates	3.4	0.3	0.7	0.1	0.6	2.0	0.5	0.1	–	0.2	7.9	7.9
First degrees (excluding university validated)	1.6	3.4	14.8	0.8	16.3	15.5	2.5	3.3	4.1	3.2	65.6	65.6
First university diplomas and certificates	0.1	0.1	0.3	–	0.9	0.5	0.1	0.1	0.4	–	2.6	2.6
CNAA diplomas and certificates[11]	1.9	–	–	–	0.1	1.8	–	0.1	0.3	0.2	4.6	4.6
Professional qualifications (public sector)[10]	0.3	1.0	4.7	–	1.1	15.3	1.9	0.2	–	0.5	25.1	25.1
BTEC higher diploma	–	–	3.8	0.4	1.7	2.0	0.5	–	–	0.1	9.6	9.6
BTEC higher certificate	–	–	12.0	–	1.5	2.9	0.1	–	–	0.1	16.6	16.6
BTEC ordinary diploma	–	–	6.2	0.7	1.8	4.5	0.7	–	–	2.4	16.3	16.3
BTEC ordinary certificate	–	–	16.4	–	1.4	6.5	0.5	–	–	0.4	25.2	25.2

1 Teacher training results are shown in table 5.12. However these overlap with results shown here.
2 Excluding qualifications from the private sector.
3 University and CNAA data for these subject groups have been estimated.
4 Excluding Open University degrees for which subject detail in this format is not available. These numbered 127 higher degrees, 1 610 honours degrees (828 men) and 6 424 ordinary degrees (3 226 men).
5 Including Postgraduate Certificates in Education (PGCEs).
6 Department of Education and Science (DES) estimates based on various sources.
7 Excluding students who successfully completed courses for which formal qualifications are not awarded.
8 Including Dip HE, Certificates of Education and PGCEs.
9 Including Diploma in Management studies, which is equivalent to First Degree. These numbered 2 089 students (1 635 men).
10 DES estimates based on final year of course data.
11 Including 335 students (141 men) awarded CNAA certificates for which subject detail is not available.
12 In addition, 38 200 students obtained nursing and paramedical qualifications at Department of Health and Social Security establishments.
13 Excluding about 90 500 students taking the new SCOTVEC National Certificate (48 200 men). Subject detail is not available.

Source Education Departments

5.11 Lecturers and teachers by type of establishment, sex and graduate status

Percentage trained

(i) Full-time

	1981–82		1982–83		1983–84		1984–85		1985–86		1986–87		1987–88		
	All 000s	% Graduate	All 000s	% Graduate	All 000s	% Graduate	All 000s	% Graduate	All 000s	% Graduate	All 000s	% Graduate	All 000s	% Graduate	% Graduates trained[1]
United Kingdom															
Males															
Schools[2]															
Public sector															
Primary[3]	46	25.6	45	27.5	43	29.5	42	31.3	41	33.2	41	35.5	40	37.3	96.7
Secondary	153	59.4	152	61.2	150	62.6	147	64.0	144	65.3	140	65.7	135	66.7	88.1
Non-maintained[4]	20	79.8	21	79.9	21	80.8	21	81.6	21	82.4	21	83.4	21	84.3	..
Special	6	26.9	6	29.3	6	31.6	6	33.4	6	35.4	6	36.4	6	37.9	94.8
All schools[2,4]	227	53.4	224	55.2	221	56.9	216	58.5	213	59.9	209	60.7	202	61.8	..
Establishments of further education[5]	70	43.5	71	43.7	71	44.3	70	45.2	69	45.9	69	46.6	69	47.0	50.9
Universities[6]	30	98.8	28	98.9	28	98.9	28	98.9	28	99.0	28	99.0	27	99.0	..
All establishments[2,7]	329	55.3	325	56.4	321	57.4	315	58.9	311	60.1	308	60.5	300	61.4	..
Females															
Schools[2]															
Public sector															
Primary[3]	167	16.0	162	17.4	160	19.4	159	21.1	160	22.8	162	23.8	166	26.6	96.5
Secondary	126	51.5	126	53.8	126	55.8	124	57.3	123	58.4	120	59.7	118	59.9	90.2
Non-maintained[4]	20	50.8	20	52.8	21	53.7	21	55.4	22	56.1	22	56.9	22	58.0	..
Special	13	22.8	13	24.9	13	26.7	13	28.5	13	30.1	13	30.9	13	31.2	94.3
All schools[2,4]	327	32.1	321	34.2	319	36.3	317	37.9	317	39.1	318	40.0	320	41.3	..
Establishments of further education[5]	20	42.2	21	43.0	22	44.2	23	45.3	23	46.7	24	47.1	25	47.8	62.3
Universities[6]	4	98.7	3	98.6	3	98.5	4	98.4	4	98.9	4	98.7	4	98.9	..
All establishments[2,7]	352	33.3	347	35.4	347	37.3	345	39.0	346	40.2	348	40.8	351	42.1	..
England and Wales															
All schools[2]															
Males	200	51.9	198	53.9	195	55.8	191	57.5	187	59.0	183	59.9	179	61.2	76.0
Females	280	32.1	276	34.3	275	36.4	273	38.2	274	39.6	274	40.5	277	42.0	83.1
Scotland															
All schools[4]															
Males	20	67.9	19	68.2	19	68.0	19	68.6	..	..	..	..	16	69.2	..
Females	35	31.3	34	32.3	33	33.8	32	34.3	..	..	..	..	32	34.2	..
Northern Ireland															
All schools[4]															
Males	7	55.6	7	56.8	7	57.9	7	58.8	7	59.9	7	60.7	7	60.7	..
Females	12	35.6	11	37.3	11	39.0	11	40.8	11	42.5	11	44.0	11	44.0	..

(ii) Part-time

	1981–82		1982–83		1983–84		1984–85		1985–86		1986–87		1987–88		
	All 000s	% Graduate	All 000s	% Graduate	All 000s	% Graduate	All 000s	% Graduate	All 000s	% Graduate	All 000s	% Graduate	All 000s	% Graduate	% Graduates trained
Great Britain[8]															
Persons	..	..	..	..	..	..	..	..	..	..	..	..	..	..	..
Persons—full-time equivalent	40	..	40	..	41	..	42	..	43[2]	..	45[2]	..	48	..	..
Schools[9]	18	..	17	..	18	..	19	..	18	..	19	..	21	..	..
Establishments of further education[10]	23	..	23	..	23	..	23	..	23	..	24	..	27	..	..

1 England and Wales only; partly estimated.
2 1985–86 and 1986–87 include 1984–85 schools data for Scotland; 1985–86 also includes estimated data for the maintained sector in England and Wales.
3 Including nursery schools.
4 Excluding independent schools in Scotland and Northern Ireland.
5 Excluding Ulster Polytechnic. Figures include teacher training.
6 Excluding 663 male and female professors and lecturers and 5 544 part-time tutorial and counselling staff employed by the Open University at January 1988.
7 Totals include a number of teachers in England and Wales classified as miscellaneous who are not shown above (about 1,800 men and 1,900 women in 1987–88).
8 Excluding universities.
9 Excluding independent schools. Figures include unqualified teachers in England and Wales up to 1984–85.
10 England and Wales only up to 1983–84.

Source Education Departments

5.12 Initial training of teachers by sex, type of course and stage
United Kingdom
Men and Women

Thousands

	1977	1978	1979	1980	1981	1982	1983	1984	1985	1986	1987
Admissions to courses of initial training[1]											
University Departments of Education											
Courses for graduates	5.2	5.2	5.1	5.7	5.7	4.9	4.8	4.5	4.3	5.1[2]	5.5[2]
Courses for non-graduates	0.3	0.7	0.6	0.6	0.5	0.7	0.6	0.7	0.6	0.6[2]	1.0[2]
Total	5.5	5.9	5.7	6.2	6.2	5.5	5.3	5.2	5.0	5.7[2]	6.5[2]
Other institutions											
Courses for graduates	5.6	6.1	6.4	7.0	6.8	5.2	4.6	4.6	4.8	5.3	6.0
Courses for non-graduates	16.7	13.1	11.2	8.7	9.1	9.7	9.9	9.1	9.5	9.7	10.5
Total	22.4	19.2	17.6	15.7	15.9	15.0	14.5	13.6	14.3	15.0	16.5
Students on initial training courses[3]											
University Departments of Education											
Courses for graduates	5.3	5.1	5.1	5.7	5.7	4.9	4.8	4.5	4.4	5.2[2]	5.6[2]
Courses for non-graduates	1.2	2.0	1.9	2.0	2.2	2.3	2.2	2.3	2.2	2.3[2]	2.6[2]
Total	6.5	7.1	7.0	7.7	7.9	7.2	7.0	6.9	6.6	7.5[2]	8.1[2]
Other institutions											
Courses for graduates	5.9	5.2	6.5	7.0	6.8	5.2	4.5	4.5	4.8	5.3	6.0
Courses for non-graduates	64.3	45.6	35.1	28.0	25.9	25.0	26.1	25.7	28.1	28.7	30.9
Total	70.2	50.8	41.6	35.1	32.7	30.3	30.7	30.3	33.0	34.0	36.9
Students successfully completing courses of initial training[4,5]											
University Departments of Education											
Courses for graduates	4.9	4.7	4.9	4.8	5.4	5.4	4.6	4.5	4.3	4.3	4.5
Courses for non-graduates	0.2	0.4	0.8	0.6	0.6	0.6	0.6	0.6	0.6	0.5	0.6
Total	5.1	5.0	5.7	5.5	6.0	6.0	5.2	5.1	4.9	4.8	5.0
Other institutions											
Courses for graduates	5.8	5.7	6.2	6.2	6.6	6.3	5.0	4.2	4.6	4.0	4.2
Courses for non-graduates	27.8	27.5	19.8	13.1	9.6	8.5	7.3	7.0	6.0	6.5	7.1
Total	33.5	33.2	26.0	19.4	16.2	14.8	12.3	11.2	10.6	10.5	11.4

1 Calendar year.
2 Including a small element of estimated data for England.
3 October/November of year shown.
4 Academic year ending in year shown.
5 Including students in England and Wales who failed their B.Ed. degree course but have received qualified teacher status, on the basis of a non-degree qualification obtained in an earlier year.

Source Education Departments

5.13 Full-time academic teaching and research staff at universities[1]
United Kingdom
Academic years

Number

	Professors	Readers and senior lecturers	Lecturers and assistant lecturers	Other	Total	Percentage annual change
1971/72	3 492	6 034	19 215	914	29 655	*3.5*
1972/73	3 649	6 475	19 651	969	30 744	*3.7*
1973/74	3 753	6 972	19 698	1 031	31 454	*2.3*
1974/75	3 906	7 398	19 883	914	32 101	*2.1*
1975/76	3 989	7 617	19 722	880	32 208	*0.3*
1976/77	4 124	7 877	20 022	712	32 735	*1.6*
1977/78	4 164	8 163	19 980	677	32 984	*0.8*
1978/79	4 225	8 454	20 302	714	33 695	*2.2*
1979/80	4 337	8 734	20 518	661	34 250	*1.6*
1980/81	4 382	8 809	20 460	646	34 297	*0.1*
1981/82	4 351	8 777	20 045	562	33 735	*−1.6*
1982/83	4 017	8 284	18 885	456	31 642	*−6.2*
1983/84	3 893	8 145	18 595	463	31 096	*−1.7*
1984/85[2]	3 807	7 942	18 737	557	31 043	*−0.2*
1985/86	3 959	8 025	18 850	578	31 412	*1.2*
1986/87	4 070	8 074	18 711	577	31 432	*0.1*
1987/88	4 160	8 291	18 268	542	31 261	*−0.5*

1 Full-time teaching and research staff in posts wholly financed from general university funds excluding the Open University.
2 Includes Ulster Polytechnic which merged with the University of Ulster in October 1984.

Source Universities Funding Council

5.14 Students at universities[1, 2]
United Kingdom
Academic years

Number

	1977/78	1978/79	1979/80	1980/81	1981/82	1982/83	1983/84	1984/85[3]	1985/86	1986/87	1987/88
Full-time students											
Total full-time students	288 135	295 923	300 526	306 614	308 394	303 965	300 593	305 008	310 145	316 290	320 920
of which											
Total overseas students	35 494	36 839	35 177	31 275	28 365	27 520	28 732	29 994	34 357	37 208	38 512
Total postgraduate students	49 674	49 990	48 536	48 439	47 674	46 232	48 355	50 189	53 805	56 199	56 117
Total women students	100 222	105 265	110 509	115 691	118 840	119 381	118 910	122 555	125 203	128 814	132 674
Overseas students as a percentage of total	*12.3*	*12.4*	*11.7*	*10.2*	*9.2*	*9.1*	*9.6*	*9.8*	*11.1*	*11.8*	*12.0*
Postgraduate students as a percentage of total	*17.2*	*16.9*	*16.2*	*15.8*	*15.5*	*15.2*	*16.1*	*16.5*	*17.3*	*17.8*	*17.5*
Women students as a percentage of total	*34.8*	*35.6*	*36.8*	*37.7*	*38.5*	*39.3*	*39.6*	*40.2*	*40.4*	*40.7*	*41.3*
At undergraduate level											
Total	238 461	245 933	251 990	258 175	260 720	257 733	252 238	254 819	256 340	260 091	264 803
Men	152 067	154 996	155 987	157 335	156 685	152 869	148 633	148 367	148 320	149 516	150 808
Women	86 394	90 937	96 003	100 840	104 035	104 864	103 605	106 452	108 020	110 575	113 995
From United Kingdom											
Total	221 125	227 708	234 379	242 771	246 965	244 506	238 751	240 918	240 401	242 546	246 122
Men	139 083	141 598	143 320	146 162	146 886	143 580	139 231	138 812	137 715	138 121	139 010
Women	82 042	86 110	91 059	96 609	100 079	100 926	99 520	102 106	102 686	104 425	107 112
From overseas											
Total	17 336	18 225	17 611	15 404	13 755	13 227	13 487	13 901	15 939	17 545	18 681
Men	12 984	13 398	12 667	11 173	9 799	9 289	9 402	9 555	10 605	11 395	11 798
Women	4 352	4 827	4 944	4 231	3 956	3 938	4 085	4 346	5 334	6 150	6 883
At postgraduate level											
Total	49 674	49 990	48 536	48 439	47 674	46 232	48 355	50 189	53 805	56 199	56 117
Men	35 846	35 662	34 030	33 588	32 869	31 715	33 050	34 086	36 622	37 960	37 438
Women	13 828	14 328	14 506	14 851	14 805	14 517	15 305	16 103	17 183	18 239	18 679
From United Kingdom											
Total	31 516	31 376	30 970	32 568	33 064	31 939	33 110	34 096	35 388	36 536	36 286
Men	21 356	20 885	20 120	21 072	21 354	20 527	21 172	21 502	22 125	22 599	22 124
Women	10 160	10 491	10 850	11 496	11 710	11 412	11 938	12 594	13 263	13 937	14 162
From overseas											
Total	18 158	18 614	17 566	15 871	14 610	14 293	15 245	16 093	18 417	19 663	19 831
Men	14 490	14 777	13 910	12 516	11 515	11 188	11 878	12 584	14 497	15 361	15 314
Women	3 668	3 837	3 656	3 355	3 095	3 105	3 367	3 509	3 920	4 302	4 517
Part-time students											
Total part-time students	28 679	29 553	31 412	33 311	34 613	34 942	36 319	40 752	42 274	44 519	46 062
At undergraduate level											
Total	4 169	4 086	4 381	4 779	5 258	5 450	6 159	8 806	9 172	9 441	9 927
Men	2 086	2 068	2 223	2 421	2 476	2 496	2 839	4 491	4 542	4 514	4 541
Women	2 083	2 018	2 158	2 358	2 782	2 954	3 320	4 315	4 630	4 927	5 386
From United Kingdom											
Total	3 550	3 379	3 703	4 281	4 909	5 056	5 551	8 168	8 576	8 596	9 405
Men	1 856	1 786	1 961	2 227	2 303	2 311	2 575	4 205	4 291	4 252	4 319
Women	1 694	1 593	1 742	2 054	2 606	2 745	2 976	3 963	4 285	4 704	5 086
From overseas											
Total	619	707	678	498	349	394	608	638	596	485	522
Men	230	282	262	194	173	185	264	286	251	262	222
Women	389	425	416	304	176	209	344	352	345	223	300
At postgraduate level											
Total	24 510	25 467	27 031	28 532	29 355	29 492	30 160	31 946	33 102	35 078	36 135
Men	18 156	18 638	19 373	20 143	20 352	20 072	20 270	21 203	21 720	23 037	23 030
Women	6 354	6 829	7 658	8 389	9 003	9 420	9 890	10 743	11 382	12 041	13 105
From United Kingdom											
Total	21 287	22 280	23 170	24 571	25 850	26 231	26 923	28 657	29 300	30 734	32 511
Men	15 774	16 263	16 525	17 228	17 823	17 729	17 948	18 815	18 914	19 745	20 554
Women	5 513	6 017	6 645	7 343	8 027	8 502	8 975	9 842	10 386	10 989	11 957
From overseas											
Total	3 223	3 187	3 861	3 961	3 505	3 261	3 237	3 289	3 802	4 344	3 624
Men	2 382	2 375	2 848	2 915	2 529	2 343	2 322	2 388	2 806	3 292	2 476
Women	841	812	1 013	1 046	976	918	915	901	996	1 052	1 148

1 Excluding the Open University.
2 Overseas students defined by fee-paying status. From 1980/81 most European Community students paid home fees and are therefore excluded from the overseas figures and shown as home students.
3 Includes Ulster Polytechnic which merged with the University of Ulster in October 1984.

Source Universities Funding Council

5.15 Students at universities[1]

United Kingdom

New admissions taking courses, and numbers of full-time students by country of home residence and university residence

Academic years

Number

		1977/78	1978/79	1979/80	1980/81	1981/82	1982/83	1983/84	1984/85[2]	1985/86[2]	1986/87	1987/88
New students admitted (full-time only)												
Men		52 359	52 870	51 997	52 214	50 646	48 387	46 939	50 280	49 108	49 569	49 907
Women		30 463	32 014	33 906	34 613	33 879	33 452	32 601	36 178	35 689	36 649	38 721
Students taking courses (full and part-time)												
Men		208 155	211 364	211 613	213 487	212 382	207 152	204 792	208 147	211 204	215 027	215 817
Women		108 659	114 112	120 325	126 438	130 625	131 755	132 120	137 613	141 215	145 782	151 165
Full-time students:												
Total	Men	187 913	190 658	190 017	190 923	189 554	184 584	181 683	182 453	184 942	187 476	188 246
	Women	100 222	105 265	110 509	115 691	118 840	119 381	118 910	122 555	125 203	128 814	132 674
Advanced	Men	35 846	35 662	34 030	33 588	32 869	31 715	33 050	34 086	36 622	37 960	37 438
	Women	13 828	14 328	14 506	14 851	14 805	14 517	15 305	16 103	17 183	18 239	18 679
First degree	Men	150 122	152 711	153 852	155 601	154 991	151 299	146 806	145 434	145 166	146 052	147 707
	Women	84 371	88 789	94 041	99 107	102 416	103 201	101 841	103 976	104 918	107 195	110 474
First diploma	Men	267	301	360	281	275	178	212	1 132	211	240	194
	Women	299	201	173	119	123	93	101	543	272	198	137
Others	Men	1 678	1 984	1 775	1 453	1 419	1 392	1 615	1 801	2 943	3 224	2 907
	Women	1 724	1 947	1 789	1 614	1 496	1 570	1 663	1 933	2 830	3 182	3 384
Part-time students:												
Total	Men	20 242	20 706	21 596	22 564	22 828	22 568	23 109	25 694	26 262	27 551	27 571
	Women	8 437	8 847	9 816	10 747	11 785	12 374	13 210	15 058	16 012	16 968	18 491
Advanced	Men	18 156	18 638	19 373	20 143	20 352	20 072	20 270	21 203	21 720	23 037	23 030
	Women	6 354	6 829	7 658	8 389	9 003	9 420	9 890	10 743	11 382	12 041	13 105
First degree	Men	1 440	1 392	1 503	1 644	1 699	1 770	1 896	2 694	2 740	2 770	2 883
	Women	1 143	1 095	1 200	1 378	1 751	1 972	2 199	2 785	3 192	3 298	3 638
First diploma	Men	80	30	61	84	70	52	70	824	392	175	155
	Women	93	43	52	64	48	26	31	263	113	63	79
Occasional	Men	566	646	659	693	707	674	873	973	1 410	1 569	1 503
	Women	847	880	906	916	983	956	1 090	1 267	1 325	1 566	1 669
Country of home residence:[3]												
United Kingdom		250 673	257 065	262 527	270 442	273 443	270 323	266 458	269 872	270 440	273 326	275 365
Foreign and Commonwealth countries		37 462	38 858	37 999	36 172	34 951	33 642	34 135	35 136	39 705	42 964	45 555
University residence[4, 5]												
Colleges and hostels:	Men	86 227	87 162	86 911	87 766	88 974	87 196	86 486	85 588	86 570	87 373	86 442
	Women	45 718	47 736	50 557	52 728	53 542	54 569	54 368	54 742	55 520	57 157	58 023
Lodgings:	Men	65 519	67 592	67 983	69 131	68 016	66 566	65 752	64 311	67 197	65 858	67 576
	Women	33 963	36 577	37 881	40 568	42 838	42 949	42 941	43 379	45 990	45 857	47 509
At home:	Men	29 065	28 947	28 173	27 758	26 156	25 340	23 423	23 356	22 950	23 061	23 280
	Women	16 257	16 658	17 343	18 029	17 674	17 715	16 680	17 209	17 447	18 134	19 045

1 Excluding the Open University.
2 Includes Ulster Polytechnic which merged with the University of Ulster in October 1984. Data for some courses in the categories first diploma and others have been re-coded in 1985/86.
3 Stateless and unknown domicile included in the overseas figure.
4 Including those students on courses 'not of university standard', but not those sandwich students undertaking the industrial part of their training away from the university or college at the time of the student count, which is the end of the autumn term (31 December).
5 Excludes students whose type of residence is other than those listed or unknown.

Source *Universities Funding Council*

5.16 Universities[1]: full-time students analysed by subject group of study

United Kingdom
Academic years

Thousands

	1981/82[2]	1982/83	1983/84	1984/85[3]	1985/86[4]	1986/87	1987/88
Medicine and dentistry:							
Men	26.4	26.5	26.5	26.8	15.2	14.9	14.8
Women					11.5	11.5	11.5
Subjects allied to medicine:							
Men	8.0	8.0	8.0	8.1	3.0	3.1	3.1
Women					5.7	5.8	5.9
Biological sciences:							
Men	20.1	20.0	20.0	20.3	10.1	10.4	10.5
Women					10.5	10.9	11.3
Agriculture and related subjects:							
Men	6.6	6.6	6.3	6.2	3.6	3.7	3.7
Women					2.6	2.7	2.6
Physical sciences:							
Men	26.7	26.7	26.7	27.1	20.9	20.9	20.5
Women					6.3	6.4	6.7
Mathematical sciences:							
Men	18.0	18.0	17.9	18.1	13.8	14.0	14.7
Women					4.7	4.6	4.6
Engineering and technology:							
Men	39.6	39.3	39.0	39.4	36.7	37.3	37.4
Women					3.6	4.0	4.3
Architecture, building and planning:							
Men	4.8	4.8	4.7	5.0	4.0	3.9	4.0
Women					1.3	1.4	1.5
Social studies:							
Men	43.0	42.2	41.7	42.9	24.1	24.6	24.7
Women					19.6	20.6	21.3
Business and administrative studies:							
Men	13.1	12.9	12.8	13.3	9.2	9.5	10.1
Women					5.3	5.9	6.5
Mass communications and documentation:							
Men	0.8	0.8	0.8	0.9	0.4	0.4	0.4
Women					0.7	0.7	0.6
Languages and related disciplines:							
Men	32.2	31.4	31.0	30.9	10.0	9.9	9.8
Women					21.2	21.2	21.5
Humanities:							
Men	18.8	18.3	17.4	17.8	9.4	9.8	9.9
Women					7.9	8.0	8.2
Creative arts:							
Men	4.3	4.2	4.0	4.1	1.9	1.9	2.0
Women					2.5	2.8	2.9
Education:							
Men	11.9	10.9	11.0	11.0	4.7	5.0	4.4
Women					6.4	6.6	6.6
Multidisciplinary:							
Men	34.1	33.6	32.9	33.3	17.8	18.2	18.4
Women					15.5	15.7	16.6

(For 1981/82 to 1984/85 a single figure is printed for men and women combined, bracketed across both rows.)

1 Excludes the Open University.
2 These estimates are based on a 'bridging' technique developed by the DES which did not incorporate a sex split.
3 Includes Ulster Polytechnic which merged with the University of Ulster in October 1984.
4 A new subject classification was introduced in 1985 when certain subjects were reclassified and combinations of subjects were classified separately for the first time.

Source Universities Funding Council

5.17 Universities[1]: degrees and diplomas obtained by full-time students

Calendar years

Number

		1977	1978	1979	1980	1981	1982	1983	1984[2]	1985[2]	1986	1987
Degrees												
First degrees—honours:	Men	31 195	33 095	34 085	35 127	36 018	36 696	37 103	36 940	36 119	35 823	35 845
	Women	17 685	19 004	20 193	21 344	22 563	24 273	25 636	25 577	26 122	25 988	26 601
First degrees—ordinary:	Men	7 496	7 631	7 611	7 704	7 743	7 387	7 520	7 031	6 057	5 405	5 518
	Women	4 008	3 927	4 093	3 975	4 218	4 272	4 659	4 293	3 911	3 696	3 853
Higher degrees:	Men	13 560	14 581	14 173	14 414	14 746	14 864	15 565	15 593	16 802	17 354	18 559
	Women	3 456	3 891	4 239	4 511	4 803	5 209	5 671	5 936	6 754	7 219	8 008
Total:	Men	52 251	55 307	55 869	57 245	58 507	58 947	60 188	59 564	58 978	58 582	60 059
	Women	25 149	26 822	28 525	29 830	31 584	33 754	35 966	35 806	36 787	36 903	38 475
Diplomas and certificates:	Men	7 576	7 238	7 379	7 044	7 260	7 572	6 853	6 613	6 447	5 867	6 800
	Women	5 597	5 290	5 509	5 754	6 015	6 208	5 547	5 587	5 751	5 706	6 303

1 Excluding the Open University.
2 Includes Ulster Polytechnic which merged with the University of Ulster in October 1984.

Source Universities Funding Council

5.18 Scientific research: postgraduate awards and special grants

At 1 October in each year

	1978	1979	1980[1]	1981	1982	1983	1984	1985	1986	1987	1988
Special research grants											
Number of new awards	2 492	2 645	4 394	2 462	2 355	2 609	2 493	2 901	2 988	3 372	2 219
Number current: total	4 434	7 023	5 056	5 024	5 056	5 476	5 389	5 350	5 824	6 230	5 037
Biological sciences	653	1 007	720	752	754	713	644	626	627	714	712
Biotechnology[2]	–	–	–	–	–	95	103	103	124	130	123
Chemistry/enzyme chemistry	563	982	670	668	618	572	525	506	535	542	489
Computing science	78	104					154	–	–	–	–
Mathematics	77	146	73	66	94	136	185	189	255	258	255
Science Board co-operative grants	–	–	–	–	–	–	–	33	38	45	51
Process engineering[3]	139	155	–	–	–	–	141	127	227	170	107
Control engineering	44	63	–	–	–	–	–	–	–	–	–
Electrical and systems engineering	185	217	–	–	–	–	–	–	–	–	–
Aeronautical and mechanical engineering	190	208	–	–	–	–	–	–	–	–	–
Civil and transport engineering	148	177	–	–	–	–	–	–	–	–	–
Manufacturing technology	91	118	–	–	–	–	–	–	–	–	–
Materials	302	462	344	381	346	335	300	266	310	301	246
Physics (other than nuclear)	308	497	357	339	331	508	427	412	415	413	375
Nuclear physics	102	202	98	117	143	143	127	118	101	192	70
Astronomy[5] Planetary Sciences	364	691	397	388	371	355	355	334	330	475	390
Information science	77	94	82	63	87	78	98	97	75	76	85
Geology and geophysics	171	181	186	183	178	167	119	123	113	152	156
Social sciences	542	578	506	319	324	381	420	522	454	473	563
Neutron beam	78	102	70	77	71	66	66	78	91	81	66
Polymer science/engineering	–	156	114	117	106	90	82	75	–	–	–
Laser facility	–	–	14	13	14	26	33	34	31	34	36
Science based archaeology	–	–	25	22	22	25	31	35	37	37	24
Synchroton radiation facility	–	–	51	73	77	98	103	114	117	126	113
Engineering processes	–	–	224	229	225	212	132	–	–	–	–
Environment	–	–	160	172	197	236	270	251	265	274	203
Information engineering	–	–	320	370	378	489	404	379	369	360	272
Alvey Directorate	–	–	–	–	–	–	–	163	361	351	305
Electro-Mechanical Engineering[6]	–	–	277	341	349	357	343	331	323	336	246
ACME	–	–	–	–	–	–	–	142	178	194	153
Marine technology	–	–	55	61	73	84	73	68	107	95	106
Teaching company	–	–	38	65	98	146	173	191	251	307	328
Energy	–	–	27	39	47	52	–	–	–	–	
Joint SERC/ESRC[4]	–	–	19	31	25	28	26	20	16	12	15
Other grants[2]	323	883	229	138	128	84	55	14	74	82	105
Total expenditure on grants (years beginning 1 April) (£ thousand)	38 057	52 438	67 567	73 769	80 082	88 494	95 958	106 747	116 813	141 527	142 389
Postgraduate awards											
Studentships:											
Number of new awards	5 849	5 295	5 207	4 791	4 501	5 814	5 602	5 960	6 001	5 927	6 129
Number current: total	11 726	11 405	11 173	10 622	10 132	11 278	11 349	11 809	12 036	12 072	12 276
Biological sciences/Biology	1 918	1 996	1 989	1 924	1 861	1 820	1 813	1 891	1 925	1 974	1 922
Biotechnology[2]	–	–	–	–	–	112	157	194	203	206	241
Chemical engineering	273	250	–	–	–	–	71	227	–	–	–
Chemistry/enzyme chemistry	1 476	1 523	1 534	1 488	1 456	1 464	1 507	1 552	1 595	1 599	1 498
Electrical engineering	458	437	–	–	–	–	–	–	–	–	–
Aeronautical and mechanical engineering	334	319	–	–	–	–	–	–	–	–	–
Civil and transport engineering	368	376	–	–	–	–	–	–	–	–	–
Manufacturing technology	111	125	–	–	–	–	–	–	–	–	–
Materials	395	401	412	434	477	515	509	468	454	435	460
Total technology	90	98	–	–	–	81	82	87	83	84	99
Geology and geophysics	479	462	473	498	499	496	477	1 104	484	485	–
Mathematics	655	640	614	587	531	562	551	525	629	673	684
Physics	1 031	993	572	521	519	534	535	–	569	584	631
Computing science	329	–	–	–	–	–	–	–	–	–	–
Social sciences	3 383	2 938	2 348	1 758	1 727	1 689	1 536	1 481	1 392	1 402	1 336
Control engineering	70	82	–	–	–	–	–	–	–	–	–
Polymer science/engineering	–	–	–	27	26	20	21	18	7	4	–
Information science	51	53	81	51	53	1 130	1 699	2 071	2 532	2 639	2 790
ACME	–	–	–	–	–	–	–	103	163	167	155

1 The Science Research Council became the Science and Engineering Research Council from mid – 1981, incorporating additional classifications.
2 Biotechnology was included in Other before 1983.
3 Until 1984 Chemical Engineering and Production Engineering were contained within the Engineering Processes Committee. In 1985 Engineering Processes reorganised, forming the Application of Computers to Manufacturing Engineering Directorate (ACME) and Process Engineering, which subsumed Chemical Engineering.
4 The Social Science Research Council became the Economic and Social Research Council on 1 January 1984.
5 Astronomy, Space and Radio became Astronomy & Planetary Sciences from September 1986.
6 Machines & Power became Electro-Mechanical Engineering from May 1987.

Sources *Science and Engineering Research Council; Natural Environment Research Council; Economic and Social Research Council; The British Library Research and Development Department; Department of Education and Science*

5.18 Scientific research: postgraduate awards and special grants

(continued)

At 1 October in each year

	1978	1979	1980[1]	1981	1982	1983	1984	1985	1986	1987	1988
Postgraduate awards *(continued)*											
Neutron beam	–	–	5	9	9	7	3	1	–	–	–
Science based archaeology	–	–	24	27	29	31	32	42	41	43	65
Astronomy, & Planetary Sciences[5]	–	–	248	246	232	249	246	253	257	251	258
Nuclear physics	–	–	179	176	178	180	184	186	194	191	194
Engineering processes[2]	–	–	370	368	349	360	188	–	–	–	–
Environment	–	–	261	535	323	316	318	351	350	324	321
Information engineering	–	–	770	829	731	667	360	310	19	–	–
Electro Mechanical Engineering[6]	–	–	583	415	406	398	384	367	355	320	309
Marine technology	–	–	76	92	95	107	105	113	100	71	85
Energy	–	–	42	42	43	58	66	37	11	–	–
Joint SERC/ESRC[3]	–	–	313	288	267	201	174	179	204	224	228
Other	343	383	279	307	321	281	236	231	204	210	324
Production	–	–	–	–	–	–	95	65	29	5	–
Process engineering	–	–	–	–	–	–	–	–	267	257	257
Fellowships:											
Number of new awards	105	108	109	118	96	128	159	51	56	70	133
Number current	224	234	264	291	275	282	344	227	227	203	185
Bursaries:											
Number of new awards	267	184	200	159	127	144	–	86	82	81	76
Number current	341	238	235	178	133	155	–	87	88	86	79
Total expenditure on awards (years beginning 1 April) (£ thousand)	34 656	37 914	54 930	47 064	49 083	55 322	60 355	64 729	67 837	70 896	73 617

1 The Science Research Council became the Science and Engineering Research Council from mid – 1981, incorporating additional classifications.
2 Biotechnology was included in Other before 1983.
3 Until 1984 Chemical Engineering and Production Engineering were contained within the Engineering Processes Committee. In 1985 Engineering Processes reorganised, forming the Application of Computers to Manufacturing Engineering Directorate (ACME) and Process Engineering, which subsumed Chemical Engineering.
4 The Social Science Research Council became the Economic and Social Research Council on 1 January 1984.
5 Astronomy, Space & Radio became Astronomy & Planetary Sciences from September 1986.
6 Machines & Power became Electro-Mechanical Engineering from May 1987.
7 All SERC I.T. provision is recorded under information science and includes, for this year, provision under the DES Engineering and Technology programme (The 'Switch').

Sources *Science and Engineering Research Council; Natural Environment Research Council; Economic and Social Research Council; The British Library Research and Development Department; Department of Education and Science*

5.19 Student awards

New and current, by type

Thousands

	1976–77	1977–78	1978–79	1979–80	1980–81	1981–82	1982–83	1983–84	1984–85	1985–86	1986–87	1987–88[6]
New awards												
All new awards[1]	227.2	223.7	235.2[5]	241.0[5]	243.4[5]	264.7[5]	267.4[5]	285.3	289.5	296.6	304.5	311.3
Postgraduate awards: Made by education departments and the research councils[1]	9.7[5]	10.2[5]	10.3[5]	10.5[5]	10.4[5]	9.3[5]	9.1[5]	9.0[6]	9.4[6]	9.5[6]	9.3	8.7
Local education authorities[2]	1.9	2.1	2.4	2.2	2.2	2.4	3.0	3.0	3.5	3.9	4.3	4.6
Undergraduate and non-graduate awards at university[1]	68.6	69.8[5]	71.7[5]	72.9[5]	74.5[5]	73.2[5]	70.4[5]	70.7	72.2	71.9	72.2	74.5
Teacher training awards[1]	36.7	26.5	24.0	23.5	21.2	21.5	19.7	18.9	18.9	18.9	19.5	21.2
Other awards: Including polytechnics and colleges first degree and comparable courses,[3] further and higher education courses, state scholarships and adult education bursaries[4]	70.3	70.2	71.7	73.7	79.6	91.6	96.5	102.4	102.0	102.1	104.7	105.9
Awards paid at 50 per cent or less of the mandatory rate	40.1	45.0	55.2[5]	58.3[5]	55.5[5]	66.7[5]	68.7[5]	81.3	83.5	90.2	94.5	96.4
Current awards												
All current awards[1]	520.1	521.5	529.4	536.8	545.7	586.2	604.4	637.3	656.0	664.3	676.1	690.0
Postgraduate awards: Made by education departments and the research councils	18.5	19.2	19.6	19.2	19.0	18.1	17.6	18.2[6]	18.2[6]	18.9[6]	17.3	16.0
Local education authorities[2]	2.1	2.3	2.6	2.4	2.3	2.5	3.1	3.1	4.0	4.4	7.0	7.3
Undergraduate and non-graduate awards at university	204.6	211.9	218.5	224.6	231.1	237.1	232.1	231.4	225.2	225.4	232.8	236.3
Teacher training awards	104.2	79.7	61.4	50.1	44.1	41.4	37.7	37.0	38.1	39.4	40.5	42.0
Other awards: Including polytechnics and other colleges first degree and comparable courses,[3] other further and higher education courses, state scholarships and adult education bursaries[4]	136.9	147.9	154.4	160.5	171.8	193.2	212.4	234.5	242.5	244.5	243.3	249.4
Awards paid at 50 per cent or less of the mandatory rate	53.8	60.5	72.9	80.1	77.3	93.8	101.5	113.1	127.9	131.6	135.2	139.0

1 Data refers to calendar year for 1974–75.

2 Postgraduate course awards made under Section 2 of the Education Act 1962 (excluding initial teacher training) in England and Wales (includes estimated numbers of new awards prior to 1975/76).

3 'Comparable courses' are courses at establishments of further and higher education which have been designated under the University and other Awards regulations, 1965, as comparable to first degree courses.

4 The adult education bursary scheme commenced in September 1975 and operates in England, Wales and Scotland.

5 United Kingdom estimate based upon data for England, Wales and Northern Ireland.

6 Includes estimated data for Scotland.

Sources Education Departments

6. Employment

6.1 Distribution of the workforce

At mid-June each year

Thousands

United Kingdom	1977	1978	1979	1980	1981	1982	1983	1984	1985	1986	1987	1988
Workforce[1]	26 224	26 358	26 627	26 839	26 741	26 677	26 610	27 265	27 714	27 791	27 979	28 211
Males	16 224	16 221	16 224	16 320	16 348	16 257	16 104	16 315	16 484	16 383	16 352	16 363
Females	10 000	10 137	10 404	10 520	10 393	10 421	10 506	10 950	11 230	11 408	11 628	11 848
Unemployed[2,3,4,5]	1 359	1 343	1 235	1 513	2 395	2 770	2 984	3 030	3 179	3 229	2 905	2 341
Males	1 021	986	888	1 072	1 775	2 043	2 145	2 120	2 197	2 217	2 023	1 632
Females	339	358	346	441	620	727	839	910	982	1 012	882	709
Workforce in employment[6]	24 865	25 014	25 393	25 327	24 346	23 908	23 626	24 235	24 536	24 561	25 074	25 870
Males	15 204	15 235	15 335	15 248	14 573	14 214	13 959	14 196	14 288	14 166	14 329	14 731
Females	9 661	9 779	10 057	10 078	9 773	9 694	9 667	10 040	10 248	10 396	10 745	11 140
HM Forces[7]	327	318	314	323	334	324	322	326	326	322	319	316
Males	313	303	299	307	317	309	306	310	309	305	302	300
Females	14	15	15	16	17	15	16	16	16	16	16	16
Self-employed persons (with or without employees)[8]	1 907	1 907	1 906	2 013	2 119	2 170	2 221	2 496	2 610	2 627	2 860	2 986
Males	1 519	1 534	1 550	1 622	1 694	1 700	1 705	1 903	1 975	1 989	2 152	2 257
Females	388	372	357	391	425	470	516	594	635	637	708	729
Employees in employment[9]	22 631	22 789	23 173	22 991	21 892	21 414	21 067	21 238	21 423	21 387	21 584	22 226
Males	13 372	13 398	13 487	13 319	12 562	12 205	11 940	11 888	11 903	11 744	11 698	11 970
Females	9 259	9 391	9 686	9 672	9 331	9 209	9 127	9 350	9 521	9 644	9 886	10 257
of whom												
Total, production and construction industries	9 240	9 197	9 213	8 906	8 061	7 610	7 217	7 062	6 974	6 760	6 669	6 745
Total, all manufacturing industries	7 317	7 281	7 253	6 937	6 222	5 863	5 525	5 409	5 362	5 227	5 152	5 215
Work Related Government Training Programmes[10]	–	–	–	–	–	–	16	175	176	226	311	343
Males	–	–	–	–	–	–	8	95	100	127	177	205
Females	–	–	–	–	–	–	8	80	76	99	134	138
Great Britain												
Workforce[1]	25 598	25 716	25 969	26 176	26 077	26 012	25 932	26 582	27 021	27 095	27 282	27 516
Males	15 831	15 824	15 823	15 916	15 942	15 853	15 693	15 903	16 067	15 966	15 935	15 951
Females	9 767	9 892	10 147	10 260	10 135	10 160	10 239	10 679	10 954	11 129	11 347	11 565
Unemployed[2,3,4,5]	1 303	1 282	1 175	1 444	2 299	2 664	2 871	2 911	3 057	3 103	2 780	2 225
Males	980	942	847	1 024	1 706	1 967	2 062	2 034	2 109	2 126	1 931	1 548
Females	323	340	328	420	593	697	809	877	948	978	848	677
Workforce in employment[6]	24 295	24 434	24 794	24 731	23 777	23 348	23 061	23 671	23 964	23 992	24 502	25 291
Males	14 851	14 882	14 976	14 892	14 236	13 886	13 631	13 869	13 958	13 841	14 003	14 403
Females	9 444	9 553	9 818	9 839	9 541	9 463	9 430	9 802	10 006	10 151	10 498	10 887
HM Forces[7]	327	318	314	323	334	324	322	326	326	322	319	316
Males	313	303	299	307	317	309	306	310	309	305	302	300
Females	14	15	15	16	17	15	16	16	16	16	16	16
Self-employed persons (with or without employees)[8]	1 843	1 843	1 842	1 950	2 058	2 109	2 160	2 435	2 550	2 567	2 801	2 926
Males	1 463	1 478	1 494	1 567	1 641	1 647	1 652	1 850	1 923	1 937	2 099	2 205
Females	380	364	348	383	417	462	508	586	628	630	701	721
Employees in employment[9]	22 126	22 273	22 638	22 458	21 386	20 916	20 572	20 741	20 920	20 886	21 080	21 714
Males	13 076	13 100	13 183	13 018	12 278	11 930	11 670	11 619	11 632	11 477	11 431	11 699
Females	9 050	9 173	9 455	9 440	9 107	8 985	8 901	9 123	9 288	9 409	9 650	10 015
of whom												
Total, production and construction industries	9 048	9 006	9 020	8 723	7 900	7 460	7 072	6 919	6 830	6 622	6 531	6 605
Total, all manufacturing industries	7 172	7 138	7 107	6 801	6 099	5 751	5 418	5 302	5 254	5 122	5 049	5 110
Work Related Government Training Programmes[10]	–	–	–	–	–	–	8	168	168	218	303	335
Males	–	–	–	–	–	–	3	91	94	122	171	199
Females	–	–	–	–	–	–	5	78	74	96	132	135

Note: Because the figures have been rounded independently totals may differ from the sum of the components. Also the totals may include some employees whose industrial classification could not be ascertained.

1 The workforce is the workforce in employment plus the claimant unemployed.

2 From October 1982 new basis (claimants); article in *Employment Gazette,* December 1982, page S 20 refers.

3 From October 1980 the figures are affected by the introduction in Great Britain of fortnightly payment of unemployment benefit. This is estimated to have resulted in an artificial increase of 20 000 (13 000 males and 7 000 females) in the count of the unemployed and therefore a corresponding reduction should be made when comparing the 1980 figures with those of earlier years.

4 From April 1983, the figures of unemployment reflect the effects of the provisions in the Budget for some men aged 60 and over who no longer have to sign on at an unemployment office. It is estimated that 132 500 men were affected over the period April to June 1983, and a further 29 300 were affected in July and August 1983, the total effect was a reduction in the coverage of the unemployment count of 161 800.

5 Due to a change in the compilation of the unemployment statistics to remove over-recording (see *Employment Gazette* March/April 1986, pp107 – 108), unadjusted figures from February 1986 are not directly comparable with earlier figures. It is estimated that the change reduced the total UK count by 50,000 on average.

6 The workforce in employment comprises employees in employment, the self-employed, HM Forces and work related government training programmes.

7 HM Forces figures, provided by the Ministry of Defence, represent the total number of UK service personnel, male and female, in HM Regular Forces, wherever serving and including those on release leave.

8 Estimates of the self-employed up to mid-1988 are based on the 1981 census of population and the results of the Labour Force Surveys. A detailed description of the current estimates is given in the article on p182 of the April 1989 edition of *Employment Gazette.*

9 Estimates of employees in employment for December 1984 and subsequent months include an allowance based on the Labour Force Survey to compensate for persistent undercounting in the regular sample enquiries (*Employment Gazette*, January 1987, p31). For all dates, individuals with two jobs as employees of different employers are counted twice.

10 Participants in the YTS except those who have contracts of employment (those who do have contracts of employment are included in employees in employment) plus participants in new JTS. Additionally for the UK this includes some participants on Northern Ireland schemes—those on: Youth Training Programme (excluding second year trainees in further education colleges); Job Training Programme; and Attachment Training Scheme participants and other management train scheme participants training with an employer.

Source *Department of Employment*

6.2 Employees in employment

Analysis by industry based on the Standard Industrial Classification 1980

At June in each year

Thousands

	SIC 1980	United Kingdom						Great Britain					
		1983	1984	1985	1986	1987	1988	1983	1984	1985	1986	1987	1988
All industries and services	0–9	21 067	21 238	21 423	21 387	21 584	22 226	20 572	20 741	20 920	20 886	21 080	21 714
Index of production and construction industries	1–5	7 217	7 062	6 974	6 760	6 669	6 745	7 072	6 919	6 830	6 622	6 531	6 605
Index of production industries	1–4	6 173	6 025	5 953	5 771	5 660	5 702	6 057	5 909	5 836	5 658	5 548	5 589
of which, manufacturing industries	2–4	*5 525*	*5 409*	*5 362*	*5 227*	*5 152*	*5 215*	*5 418*	*5 302*	*5 254*	*5 122*	*5 049*	*5 110*
Service industries	6–9	13 500	13 836	14 108	14 298	14 594	15 168	13 169	13 504	13 769	13 954	14 247	14 815
Agriculture, forestry and fishing	0	350	340	341	329	321	313	330	320	321	310	302	294
Agriculture and horticulture	01	331	321	323	311	303	295	312	302	304	293	285	276
Energy and water supply	1	648	616	591	545	508	487	639	607	582	536	499	479
Coal extraction and solid fuels	111	..	..	..	..	..	..	257	234	217	177	145	121
Electricity	161	..	..	..	..	..	..	155	150	146	143	142	143
Gas	162	..	..	..	..	..	..	99	95	91	88	84	82
Other mineral and ore extraction	2	817	799	779	729	694	687	807	788	768	720	685	678
Metal manufacturing and extraction of metal ores and minerals	21–23	253	231	217	194	177	168	251	228	215	192	175	166
Non-metallic mineral products	24	215	221	220	204	194	196	211	217	215	200	190	192
Chemical industry/man-made fibres	25/26	349	347	342	331	323	324	345	343	339	328	320	320
Basic industrial chemicals	251	..	..	..	..	..	..	125	124	123	119	115	115
Other chemical products and preparations	255–259/260	..	..	..	..	..	..	220	219	216	209	205	205
Metal goods, engineering and vehicles	3	2 549	2 469	2 443	2 372	2 331	2 364	2 515	2 436	2 410	2 340	2 299	2 332
Metal goods n.e.s.	31	346	334	329	320	323	335	344	332	327	318	321	333
Hand tools and finished metal goods including doors and windows	314–316	..	..	..	..	..	..	205	196	192	184	191	197
Other metal goods	311–313	..	..	..	..	..	..	140	136	135	133	130	137
Mechanical engineering	32	777	759	764	749	744	765	768	750	756	741	737	758
Industrial plant and steelwork	320	..	..	..	..	..	..	79	85	86	86	90	95
Machinery for agriculture, metal working, textile, food and printing etc. industries	321/322/324/326/327	..	..	..	..	..	..	211	205	203	195	190	192
Mining and construction machinery etc.	325	..	..	..	..	..	..	86	82	78	76	74	73
Other machinery and mechanical equipment incl. ordnance, small arms and ammunition	323/328/329	..	..	..	..	..	..	393	379	389	384	384	399
Office machinery, data processing equipment	33	81	84	88	83	82	85	81	84	88	83	82	85
Electrical and electronic engineering	34	612	607	596	573	563	561	605	600	589	567	556	554
Wires, cables, batteries and other electrical equipment	341/342/343	..	..	..	..	..	..	228	220	218	208	200	201
Telecommunication equipment	344	..	..	..	..	..	..	185	180	176	168	165	162
Other electronic and electrical equipment	345–348	..	..	..	..	..	..	191	200	195	192	191	191
Motor vehicles and parts	35	299	281	274	266	260	269	296	278	271	263	257	266
Motor vehicles and engines	351/352	..	..	..	..	..	..	165	157	157	156	155	162
bodies, trailers, caravans, motor vehicle parts	353	..	..	..	..	..	..	131	120	114	107	103	105
Other transport equipment	36	330	301	288	276	256	245	318	290	276	264	244	233
Shipbuilding and repairing	361	..	..	..	..	..	..	109	189	178	170	158	53
Aerospace and other transport equipment	362–365	..	..	..	..	..	..	209	201	198	194	186	180
Instrument engineering	37	104	104	105	106	103	104	102	102	103	105	102	103
Other manufacturing industries	4	2 159	2 142	2 140	2 126	2 128	2 164	2 096	2 078	2 075	2 063	2 065	2 100
Food, drink and tobacco	41/42	619	603	596	576	571	570	599	582	575	555	551	550
Meat and meat products, organic oils and fats	411/412	..	..	..	..	..	..	97	93	93	93	94	97
Bread, biscuits and flour confectionery	419	..	..	..	..	..	..	127	125	133	130	137	138

Sources *Department of Employment; Department of Manpower Services (Northern Ireland)*

6.2 Employees in employment

(continued)

Employees in employment

Analysis by industry based on the Standard Industrial Classification 1980

At June in each year

Thousands

	SIC 1980	United Kingdom 1983	1984	1985	1986	1987	1988	Great Britain 1983	1984	1985	1986	1987	1988
Alcoholic, soft drink and tobacco manufacture	424–429	..	..	..	..	..	..	183	128	119	108	101	97
All other food and drink manufacture	413–418/420–423	..	..	..	..	..	..	243	237	229	225	219	218
Textiles	43	250	245	245	249	240	242	239	234	235	238	229	231
Footwear and clothing	45	302	308	312	314	310	314	286	292	295	297	294	296
Clothing, hats, gloves and fur goods	453/4560	..	..	..	..	..	..	207	212	213	211	205	204
Timber and wooden furniture	46	206	206	210	220	227	240	201	201	205	215	222	235
Paper, printing and publishing	47	487	482	483	472	480	483	481	477	477	467	474	477
Pulp, paper, board and derived products	471/472	..	..	..	..	..	..	140	135	134	132	137	139
Printing and publishing	475	..	..	..	..	..	..	341	342	343	335	338	338
Rubber and plastics	48	190	196	196	198	203	218	185	192	192	194	199	214
Other manufacturing	49	83	79	77	76	76	76	83	79	77	76	76	76
Construction	5	1 044	1 037	1 021	189	1 009	1 043	1 015	1 010	994	964	983	1 017
Distribution, hotels, catering, repairs	6	4 118	4 244	4 295	4 298	4 310	4 427	4 037	4 163	4 213	4 213	4 223	4 340
Wholesale distribution	61	886	903	904	894	898	927	865	882	883	874	877	906
Agricultural and textile raw materials, fuels, ores, metals etc.	611/612	..	..	..	..	..	..	128	126	124	122	119	121
Timber and building materials	613	..	..	..	..	..	..	125	129	126	126	130	139
Machinery, industrial equipment, vehicles and parts	614	..	..	..	..	..	..	151	166	169	169	169	179
Food, drink and tobacco	617	..	..	..	..	..	..	235	235	234	231	233	232
Other wholesale distribution	615/616/618/619	..	..	..	..	..	..	227	225	230	226	227	236
Retail distribution	64/65	2 005	2 054	2 080	2 097	2 101	2 152	1 964	2 012	2 038	2 054	2 057	2 106
Food	641	..	..	..	..	..	..	544	572	584	585	586	597
Confectioners, tobacconists, etc.	642	..	..	..	..	..	..	138	131	123	119	113	104
Dispensing and other chemists	643	..	..	..	..	..	..	110	110	109	113	116	118
Clothing, footwear and leather goods	645/646	..	..	..	..	..	..	214	229	235	231	235	241
Household goods, hardware, ironmongery	648	..	..	..	..	..	..	187	201	212	212	214	230
Motor vehicles and parts, filling stations	651/652	..	..	..	..	..	..	244	233	230	235	231	243
Other retail distribution	653–656	..	..	..	..	..	..	506	516	523	533	533	544
Hotels and catering	66	963	1 010	1 042	1 042	1 046	1 080	949	995	1 027	1 026	1 028	1 063
Restaurants, cafes, snack bars etc.	661	..	..	..	..	..	..	198	213	223	229	240	258
Public houses and bars	662	..	..	..	..	..	..	237	252	266	260	263	265
Night clubs and licensed clubs	663	..	..	..	..	..	..	133	138	140	138	137	141
Canteens and messes	664	..	..	..	..	..	..	119	127	129	128	123	124
Hotel trade	665	..	..	..	..	..	..	221	230	234	238	231	238
Repair of consumer goods and vehicles	67	221	229	218	215	213	216	216	226	215	211	209	213
Motor vehicles	671	..	..	..	..	..	..	185	189	186	184	183	187
Transport and communication	7	1 345	1 341	1 327	1 298	1 285	1 324	1 326	1 321	1 308	1 279	1 266	1 304
Railways	71	161	156	148	143	140	136	161	155	147	142	139	135
Other inland transport	72	414	420	416	395	384	389	408	414	410	389	377	383
Scheduled road passenger transport	721	..	..	..	..	..	..	191	192	182	166	158	153
Other including road haulage	722–726	..	..	..	..	..	..	218	224	229	223	219	231
Sea transport	74	48	40	37	34	34	34	48	40	37	33	34	34
Air transport	75	44	47	50	52	53	64	43	46	49	51	52	63
Supporting services to transport	76	99	96	95	93	91	93	97	95	94	92	90	92

Sources *Department of Employment; Department of Manpower Services (Northern Ireland)*

6.2 (continued) Employees in employment

Analysis by industry based on the Standard Industrial Classification 1980

At June in each year

Thousands

	SIC 1980	United Kingdom 1983	1984	1985	1986	1987	1988	Great Britain 1983	1984	1985	1986	1987	1988
Miscellaneous transport and storage	77	146	150	154	160	162	173	144	148	152	159	160	171
Postal services and Telecommunications	79	433	432	427	420	422	436	424	424	419	412	413	428
Postal services	7901	..	..	..	..	..	..	194	194	192	188	192	198
Telecommunications	7902	..	..	..	..	..	..	230	230	227	224	222	230
Banking, finance, insurance etc.	8	1 875	1 969	2 068	2 166	2 280	2 467	1 848	1 941	2 039	2 136	2 250	2 435
Banking and finance	81	493	507	521	534	562	608	484	499	513	526	554	600
Banking and bill discounting	814	..	..	..	..	..	..	374	384	393	400	416	448
Other financial institutions	815	..	..	..	..	..	..	110	116	120	126	138	151
Insurance, except social security	82	223	224	227	228	236	254	220	221	224	225	233	251
Business services	83	953	1 020	1 097	1 174	1 253	1 368	942	1 008	1 085	1 160	1 239	1 353
Professional business services	831–837	..	..	..	..	..	..	606	641	673	713	752	810
Other business services	838/839	..	..	..	..	..	..	336	367	412	447	487	543
Renting of movables	84	96	101	103	108	107	110	95	100	102	107	106	109
Owning and dealing in real estate	85	111	118	119	122	122	127	108	114	116	118	118	123
Other services	9	6 163	6 282	6 418	6 536	6 719	6 949	5 958	6 078	6 209	6 326	6 508	6 736
Public administration and defence	91	1 606	1 602	1 587	1 595	1 633	1 672	1 553	1 548	1 532	1 539	1 577	1 616
National Government n.e.s./ social security	9111/9190	..	..	..	..	..	..	518	511	497	516	540	551
Local government services n.e.s.	9112	..	..	..	..	..	..	599	600	603	594	606	620
Justice, police, fire services	912–914	..	..	..	..	..	..	303	306	307	306	309	320
National defence	915	..	..	..	..	..	..	133	131	126	123	122	126
Sanitary services	92	312	335	334	333	337	350	309	331	330	329	333	345
Education	93	1 592	1 603	1 616	1 650	1 698	1 751	1 535	1 544	1 557	1 592	1 642	1 694
Research and development	94	106	112	114	112	110	115	105	111	113	111	109	114
Medical and other health services	95	1 294	1 298	1 347	1 359	1 383	1 436	1 247	1 252	1 301	1 312	1 337	1 389
Other services	96	650	699	744	804	870	921	619	669	713	772	837	888
Social welfare, etc.	9611	..	..	..	..	..	..	502	540	564	601	647	679
Recreational and cultural services	97	421	448	490	493	500	514	413	440	482	484	491	505
Personal services	98	180	186	186	191	187	190	176	182	182	187	183	186

Sources *Department of Employment; Department of Manpower Services (Northern Ireland)*

6.3 Males employed in engineering industries

Analysed by broad occupational category[1]

Great Britain

At April 1988

Thousands

Industry based on the Standard Industrial Classification 1980[2]	All employees	Managerial, adminis-trative, technical and clerical	Foremen[3]	Craftsmen (production and main-tenance)	All other production and other occupations	All appren-tices[5]	Craft appren-tices[5]	Others being trained[4, 5]
Metal manufacturing	39.10	7.60	2.48	5.34	23.68	0.21	0.20	0.72
Steel tubes	10.46	1.88	0.72	1.48	6.39	0.05	0.05	0.25
Drawing, cold rolling and cold forming of steel	0.81	0.23	0.04	0.08	0.46	–	–	0.01
Non-ferrous metals industry	27.82	5.49	1.72	3.78	16.84	0.15	0.14	0.45
Manufacturing of metal goods nes	223.61	43.38	13.64	42.96	123.63	1.71	1.38	4.60
Foundries	50.90	8.26	2.94	11.56	28.14	0.35	0.27	0.83
Forging, pressing, stamping	25.33	4.17	1.63	4.47	15.07	0.09	0.08	0.32
Bolts, nuts, etc, springs, non-precision chains, metals treatment	27.17	5.39	1.88	3.66	16.24	0.23	0.23	0.52
Metal doors, windows, etc	17.91	4.47	1.02	2.21	10.21	0.12	0.05	0.21
Hand tools and finished metal goods	102.31	21.10	6.17	21.07	53.96	0.92	0.75	2.73
Mechanical engineering	442.28	133.66	24.45	129.60	154.57	5.03	4.01	10.60
Industrial plant and steelwork	45.68	15.46	2.63	14.95	12.64	0.54	0.43	0.99
Agricultural machinery and tractors	17.27	4.27	0.83	2.66	9.51	0.14	0.08	0.30
Metal-working machine tools and engineers' tools	47.82	11.59	2.46	18.85	14.92	0.75	0.65	0.71
Textile machinery	6.46	1.57	0.34	2.56	1.99	0.03	0.03	0.10
Machinery for food, chemical and related industries; process engineering contractors	21.74	8.19	1.29	6.86	5.40	0.30	0.21	0.69
Mining machinery, construction and mechanical handling equipment	57.75	17.81	3.28	17.35	19.32	0.62	0.44	1.37
Mechanical power transmission equipment	18.11	4.08	1.10	3.98	8.94	0.28	0.25	0.89
Machinery for the printing, paper, wood, leather, rubber, glass and related industries, laundry and dry cleaning machinery	16.08	6.25	0.84	5.28	3.72	0.20	0.20	0.27
Other machinery and mechanical equipment	197.24	59.14	10.89	52.74	74.47	1.74	1.34	4.85
Ordnance, small arms and ammunition	14.13	5.32	0.79	4.36	3.67	0.44	0.40	0.43
Manufacture of office machinery and data processing equipment	63.91	46.60	2.18	3.62	11.52	0.41	0.07	1.63
Electrical and electronic engineering	321.54	151.71	18.38	41.47	109.99	3.73	1.49	11.15
Insulated wires and cables	21.37	6.35	1.30	2.29	11.44	0.19	0.09	0.42
Basic electrical equipment	59.83	24.24	3.29	13.14	19.17	0.81	0.44	1.71
Electrical equipment for industrial use, and batteries and accumulators	40.31	17.37	2.29	6.40	14.25	0.29	0.15	1.41
Telecommunications equipment, electrical measuring equipment, electronic capital goods and passive electronics components	122.90	73.84	7.07	12.59	29.40	1.74	0.49	5.17
Other electronic equipment	40.16	21.16	2.41	3.28	13.31	0.45	0.15	1.57
Domestic-type electric appliances	24.87	4.84	1.10	2.13	16.81	0.14	0.11	0.38
Electric lamps and other electric lighting equipment	11.84	3.79	0.93	1.55	5.58	0.11	0.06	0.48
Electrical equipment installation	0.26	0.13	0.01	0.08	0.05	0.01	–	0.01
Manufacture of motor vehicles and parts thereof	199.55	42.77	9.51	32.42	114.84	1.64	1.27	3.00
Motor vehicles and their engines	127.55	28.67	6.01	19.56	73.31	1.08	0.83	1.79
Motor vehicle bodies, trailers and caravans	12.74	1.87	0.59	3.20	7.08	–	–	0.24
Motor vehicle parts	59.25	12.23	2.91	9.66	34.45	0.55	0.44	0.97
Manufacture of other transport equipment	156.34	64.11	8.38	52.05	31.79	3.06	2.57	3.92
Shipbuilding and repairing	0.33	0.10	0.03	0.02	0.19	–	–	–
Railway and tramway vehicles	20.26	4.26	0.63	9.45	5.93	0.29	0.27	0.27
Cycles and motor cycles	2.26	0.41	0.10	0.12	1.63	–	–	0.01
Aerospace equipment manufacturing and repairing	133.12	59.29	7.59	42.41	23.82	2.76	2.30	3.63
Other vehicles	0.37	0.06	0.02	0.06	0.23	–	–	–
Instrument engineering	48.42	25.71	2.29	7.44	12.98	0.57	0.36	1.42
Measuring, checking and precision instruments and apparatus	28.58	16.53	1.42	4.26	6.37	0.32	0.16	0.83
Medical and surgical equipment and orthopaedic appliances	6.13	2.44	0.29	1.39	2.02	0.01	0.01	0.13
Optical precision instruments and photographic equipment	12.36	6.27	0.48	1.61	3.99	0.23	0.19	0.45
Clocks, watches and other timing devices	1.35	0.47	0.09	0.18	0.60	0.01	–	0.01
All other engineering industries nes	9.44	7.61	0.22	0.83	0.79	0.08	0.01	0.38
Total	1 504.17	523.15	81.51	315.73	583.78	16.43	11.35	37.40

1 This occupational survey is carried out by the EITB in April every year on a sample basis. All the figures in this table are estimates based on this survey and other EITB data. For information about the detailed methods used please contact the Statistics Section, EITB, 54 Clarendon Road, Watford, Herts: Watford (0923) 38441 Ext 143.

2 Only that part of each industry which is within the scope of the EITB is included in the figures.

3 Except works and other senior foremen and office supervisors, who are included in the preceding column.

4 Excluding canteen staff and seafarers.

5 Included in the previous columns.

Source Engineering Industry Training Board (EITB)

6.3 (*continued*) Females employed in engineering industries

Analysed by broad occupational category[1]
Great Britain
At April 1988

Thousands

Industry based on the Standard Industrial Classification 1980[2]	All employees	Managerial, adminis-trative, technical and clerical	Foremen[3]	Craftsmen (production and main-tenance)	All other production and other occupations	All appren-tices[5]	Craft appren-tices[5]	Others being trained[4, 5]
Metal manufacturing	6.61	3.21	0.12	0.03	3.25	–	–	0.10
Steel tubes	1.71	0.85	0.02	–	0.84	–	–	0.03
Drawing, cold rolling and cold forming of steel	0.13	0.09	–	0.02	0.02	–	–	0.01
Non-ferrous metals industry	4.77	2.27	0.10	0.01	2.40	–	–	0.06
Manufacturing of metal goods nes	61.06	22.59	0.80	0.24	37.42	0.01	0.01	1.38
Foundries	6.52	3.30	0.08	0.03	3.11	–	–	0.14
Forging, pressing, stamping	8.12	2.08	0.08	0.01	5.95	–	–	0.12
Bolts, nuts, etc springs, non-precision chains, metals treatment	9.04	3.43	0.11	0.10	5.40	–	–	0.28
Metal doors, windows, etc	3.59	2.38	0.06	–	1.15	–	–	0.04
Hand tools and finished metal goods	33.79	11.40	0.47	0.10	21.82	0.01	0.01	0.80
Mechanical engineering	73.70	47.85	1.25	0.42	24.18	0.09	0.04	2.03
Industrial plant and steelwork	4.81	4.08	0.09	–	0.64	0.01	–	0.15
Agricultural machinery and tractors	1.48	1.24	0.04	0.01	0.20	0.01	–	0.04
Metal-working machine tools and engineers' tools	7.55	4.81	0.10	0.05	2.59	–	–	0.29
Textile machinery	0.92	0.58	–	0.02	0.32	–	–	0.02
Machinery for food, chemical and related industries; process engineering contractors	3.75	2.96	0.07	0.01	0.72	–	–	0.14
Mining machinery, construction and mechanical handling equipment	7.18	6.29	0.11	0.03	0.76	0.02	0.01	0.28
Mechanical power transmission equipment	2.98	1.57	0.03	0.01	1.36	–	–	0.07
Machinery for the printing, paper, wood, leather, rubber, glass and related industries, laundry and dry cleaning machinery	2.54	2.11	0.05	0.01	0.38	0.01	–	0.05
Other machinery and mechanical equipment	39.10	22.72	0.69	0.20	15.49	0.03	0.01	0.90
Ordnance, small arms and ammunition	3.40	1.49	0.08	0.10	1.73	0.02	0.02	0.08
Manufacture of office machinery and data processing equipment	24.10	15.20	0.52	0.13	8.26	0.04	–	0.55
Electrical and electronic engineering	159.47	52.01	3.77	0.90	102.78	0.20	0.02	4.62
Insulated wires and cables	10.37	2.69	0.21	0.01	7.46	0.01	–	0.22
Basic electrical equipment	22.11	7.54	0.40	0.14	14.02	0.03	–	0.41
Electrical equipment for industrial use, and batteries and accumulators	16.06	6.34	0.36	0.06	9.30	0.02	–	0.47
Telecommunications equipment, electrical measuring equipment, electronic capital goods and passive electronics components	61.43	22.41	1.76	0.53	36.73	0.12	0.02	2.05
Other electronic equipment	26.80	7.22	0.69	0.08	18.81	0.03	–	1.01
Domestic-type electric appliances	11.63	3.81	0.16	0.01	7.64	–	–	0.22
Electric lamps and other electric lighting equipment	11.02	1.93	0.19	0.07	8.83	–	–	0.24
Electrical equipment installation	0.07	0.07	–	–	–	–	–	–
Manufacture of motor vehicles and parts thereof	23.04	10.69	0.33	0.07	11.95	0.04	0.03	0.61
Motor vehicles and their engines	9.97	5.79	0.18	0.04	3.96	0.03	0.02	0.31
Motor vehicle bodies, trailers and caravans	0.79	0.56	0.01	–	0.22	–	–	0.02
Motor vehicle parts	12.28	4.34	0.15	0.02	7.77	0.01	0.01	0.28
Manufacture of other transport equipment	19.83	15.07	0.55	0.16	4.04	0.08	0.05	0.72
Shipbuilding and repairing	0.02	0.02	–	–	–	–	–	–
Railway and tramway vehicles	1.68	1.15	0.04	–	0.50	–	–	0.03
Cycles and motor cycles	0.50	0.21	0.02	–	0.27	–	–	–
Aerospace equipment manufacturing and repairing	17.56	13.65	0.50	0.16	3.25	0.08	0.05	0.68
Other vehicles	0.07	0.05	–	–	0.02	–	–	–
Instrument engineering	16.61	8.37	0.36	0.18	7.70	0.03	–	0.53
Measuring, checking and precision instruments and apparatus	10.13	4.92	0.23	0.11	4.88	0.01	–	0.38
Medical and surgical equipment and orthopaedic appliances	1.96	1.07	0.04	0.05	0.80	–	–	0.01
Optical precision instruments and photographic equipment	3.48	2.12	0.07	0.02	1.27	0.01	–	0.14
Clocks, watches and other timing devices	1.04	0.27	0.02	–	0.75	–	–	–
All other engineering industries nes	1.90	1.70	0.02	0.01	0.18	–	–	0.13
Total	386.31	176.68	7.73	2.13	199.77	0.50	0.15	10.66

1 This occupational survey is carried out by the EITB in April every year on a sample basis. All the figures in this table are estimates based on this survey and other EITB data. For information about the detailed methods used please contact the Senior Statistician, EITB, 54 Clarendon Road, Watford, Herts: Telephone Watford (0923) 38441 Ext 143.
2 Only that part of each industry which is in scope to the EITB is included in the figures.
3 Except works and other senior foremen and office supervisors, who are included in the preceding column.
4 Excluding canteen staff and seafarers.
5 Included in the previous columns.

Source *Engineering Industry Training Board (EITB)*

6.4 Administrative, technical and clerical workers in manufacturing industries[1]

Analysis by industry based on Standard Industrial Classification 1980

Great Britain

Percentage

	Division/class SIC 1980	1983	1984	1985	1986	1987	1988
All manufacturing industries	2–4	28.7	25.9	26.3	27.3	26.4	26.7
Minerals and ores extraction other than fuels	2	31.6	27.3	27.6	28.6	26.5	..
Metal manufacturing	22	26.5	23.3	23.0	24.9	25.3	26.0
Non-metallic mineral products	24	23.3	20.4	21.6	21.2	21.2	21.8
Chemical industry	25	40.4	35.5	36.6	38.0	34.7	37.9
Metal goods, engineering and vehicles	3	32.6	29.1	30.0	31.8	30.9	..
Metal goods nes	31	23.1	19.7	20.5	19.5	20.0	19.3
Mechanical engineering	32	33.3	29.2	29.7	31.4	30.2	29.2
Office machinery, data processing equipment	33	46.9	43.0	48.0	49.5	53.4	45.0
Electrical and electronic engineering	34	37.5	31.1	33.7	36.5	34.9	34.4
Motor vehicles and parts	35	24.9	21.6	20.5	22.7	21.3	22.2
Other transport equipment	36	35.7	37.1	35.6	39.0	37.7	41.9
Instrument engineering	37	34.0	33.7	34.1	33.0	31.4	34.5
Other manufacturing industries	4	23.0	21.7	21.6	21.8	21.4	..
Food, drink and tobacco	41/42	21.9	21.6	20.8	20.3	19.4	20.3
Textiles	43	18.6	16.2	16.6	17.0	16.3	..
Footwear and clothing	45	14.4	12.3	14.0	12.6	13.2	..
Timber and wooden furniture	46	21.5	19.7	21.3	21.9	22.8	..
Paper, printing and publishing	47	32.7	31.2	29.6	30.7	31.0	..
Rubber and plastics	48	24.6	21.4	21.6	22.5	20.6	..
Other manufacturing	49	22.7	23.0	24.0	24.7	21.1	..

1 Expressed as percentage of total number of employees at September.

Source *Department of Employment*

6.5 Number of workers employed in agriculture[1,2,3]

United Kingdom

At June in each year

Thousands

	Regular workers					Seasonal or casual workers			All workers			Salaried managers[4]
		Whole-time		Part-time								
	Total	Male	Female Great Britain	Male	Female	Total	Male	Female	Total	Male	Female	
1980	244.1	162.6	17.3	32.3	31.9	100.7	57.2	43.4	344.7	252.1	92.7	8.0
1981	236.7	157.7	16.7	31.5	30.7	97.0	57.1	39.9	333.8	246.4	87.4	7.9
1982	232.2	154.6	16.0	31.9	29.7	98.7	57.3	41.5	331.0	243.8	87.2	7.9
1983	228.3	152.2	15.5	31.3	29.4	97.9	56.9	41.0	326.2	240.3	85.9	7.8
1984	220.8	145.6	15.2	30.7	29.4	96.0	57.1	38.9	316.8	233.3	83.5	7.8
1985	218.0	141.6	15.1	31.5	29.8	98.1	58.7	39.4	316.1	231.8	84.3	8.3
1986	210.3	134.1	14.8	32.2	29.1	96.6	58.2	38.4	306.9	224.5	82.4	8.2
1987	202.1	126.9	14.6	31.5	29.0	95.2	57.1	38.1	297.3	215.6	81.7	7.9
1988	195.5	120.3	14.5	31.4	29.2	94.9	57.7	37.2	290.4	209.5	80.9	7.9

See notes on page 109.

1 Figures exclude school children, farmers, partners and directors and their wives.
2 Figures include estimated figures for Scotland.
3 Includes estimates for minor holdings in England and Wales.
4 Great Britain only.

Source *Ministry of Agriculture, Fisheries and Food*

6.6 Rates of unemployment[1]

Analysis by standard regions

Seasonally adjusted[2]

Percentages

Annual averages	1978	1979	1980	1981	1982	1983	1984	1985	1986	1987	1988
United Kingdom	*4.3*	*4.0*	*5.1*	*8.1*	*9.5*	*10.5*	*10.7*	*10.9*	*11.1*	*10.0*	*8.0*
Great Britain	*4.3*	*3.9*	*5.0*	*8.0*	*9.4*	*10.4*	*10.6*	*10.8*	*10.9*	*9.8*	*7.8*
North	*6.4*	*6.5*	*8.0*	*11.8*	*13.3*	*14.6*	*15.3*	*15.4*	*15.2*	*14.0*	*11.9*
Yorkshire and Humberside	*4.2*	*4.1*	*5.3*	*6.9*	*10.4*	*11.4*	*11.7*	*12.0*	*12.4*	*11.3*	*9.5*
East Midlands	*3.6*	*3.3*	*4.5*	*7.4*	*8.4*	*9.5*	*9.8*	*9.9*	*9.9*	*9.0*	*7.2*
East Anglia	*3.5*	*3.1*	*3.8*	*6.3*	*7.4*	*8.0*	*7.9*	*8.0*	*8.1*	*6.8*	*4.8*
South East	*3.0*	*2.6*	*3.1*	*5.5*	*6.7*	*7.5*	*7.8*	*8.0*	*8.2*	*7.1*	*5.2*
South West	*4.6*	*4.0*	*4.5*	*6.8*	*7.8*	*8.7*	*9.0*	*9.3*	*9.5*	*8.2*	*6.3*
West Midlands	*4.0*	*4.0*	*5.5*	*10.0*	*11.9*	*12.9*	*12.7*	*12.7*	*12.6*	*11.1*	*8.5*
North West	*5.3*	*5.0*	*6.5*	*10.2*	*12.1*	*13.4*	*13.6*	*13.8*	*13.9*	*12.7*	*10.7*
Wales	*5.7*	*5.3*	*6.9*	*10.5*	*12.1*	*12.9*	*13.2*	*13.8*	*13.9*	*12.5*	*10.5*
Scotland	*5.9*	*5.7*	*7.0*	*9.9*	*11.3*	*12.3*	*12.6*	*12.9*	*13.3*	*13.0*	*11.2*
Northern Ireland	*8.1*	*7.9*	*9.4*	*12.7*	*14.4*	*15.5*	*15.9*	*16.1*	*17.6*	*17.6*	*16.4*

1 The number of claimants unemployed as a percentage of the estimated total work force (the sum of claimant employees in employment, unemployed, self-employed, participants on work related government training programmes and HM Forces) at mid-year.

2 Seasonally adjusted and excluding claimants under 18, consistent with current coverage.

Sources *Department of Employment; Department of Economic Development (Northern Ireland)*

6.7 Civil Service staff[1]

Analysis by ministerial responsibility

At 1 April in each year

Full-time equivalents[2] (thousands)

	1979	1980	1981	1982	1983	1984	1985	1986	1987	1988	1989
Agriculture, Fisheries and Food	14.5	14.3	13.6	13.1	12.7	12.1	12.1	11.7	11.3	11.1	10.9
Chancellor of the Exchequer's Departments:[3, 4, 5]	128.2	119.0	114.9	121.0	117.4	112.4	111.9	111.0	110.1	108.6	109.1
Customs and Excise	28.8	27.2	26.8	26.2	25.4	25.1	25.4	25.1	25.8	26.3	26.4
Inland Revenue	84.6	78.3	75.6	74.0	73.1	69.8	69.8	69.3	67.8	66.6	67.0
Department for National Savings	10.8	10.4	10.0	9.1	8.3	8.0	7.8	7.8	7.7	7.4	7.3
Treasury and others	4.0	3.1	2.5	11.7	10.6	9.5	8.9	8.8	8.8	8.3	8.3
Education and Science[6]	3.7	3.7	3.6	3.5	3.5	2.4	2.4	2.4	2.4	2.5	2.5
Employment	53.6	50.7	53.8	58.7	57.9	56.4	54.7	55.7	60.5	58.3	55.0
Energy[19]	1.3	1.3	1.2	1.1	1.1	1.1	1.1	1.0	1.0	1.0	1.1
Environment[7, 8, 9, 10]	56.0	51.7	47.0	42.1	39.4	36.6	35.8	34.9	34.2	33.0	30.6
Foreign and Commonwealth[11]	12.1	11.6	11.4	11.1	11.1	10.0	9.8	9.6	9.5	9.6	9.6
Home[11, 12]	33.5	34.1	35.4	34.6	35.1	36.4	36.6	37.5	37.6	39.2	40.8
Industry[13]	9.5	9.1	8.8	8.3	7.7	–	–	–	–	–	–
Scotland[14, 15]	13.7	13.6	13.6	13.4	13.1	12.8	13.0	12.9	13.0	13.0	12.3
Social Services[21]	100.9	98.9	100.1	98.0	96.4	92.6	94.9	94.9	97.7	102.3	94.3
Trade[13, 16]	9.6	9.4	9.3	8.9	8.9	–	–	–	–	–	–
Trade and Industry[12, 13, 17]	–	–	–	–	–	14.7	14.8	14.8	14.8	14.6	14.7
Transport[8, 16]	13.9	13.5	13.7	13.0	13.0	14.2	14.4	14.7	12.3	14.1	14.1
Wales	2.6	2.5	2.3	2.3	2.2	2.2	2.3	2.3	2.3	2.2	2.2
Other civil departments[3, 20]	31.4	31.7	31.3	20.2	20.5	20.9	21.2	21.5	25.1	26.7	30.7
Total Ministry of Defence[18]	247.7	239.8	229.6	216.9	208.9	199.2	174.0	169.5	164.0	143.4	141.3
Total civil and defence departments	732.3	704.9	689.6	666.4	648.9	624.0	599.0	594.4	597.8	579.6	569.2
of which Non-industrials	*565.8*	*547.5*	*539.9*	*528.0*	*518.5*	*504.3*	*498.0*	*498.2*	*507.5*	*506.6*	*499.8*
Industrials	*166.5*	*157.4*	*149.7*	*138.4*	*130.4*	*119.7*	*101.0*	*96.2*	*90.3*	*73.0*	*69.4*
Total civil departments	484.6	465.1	460.0	449.4	440.0	424.8	425.0	424.9	433.8	436.2	427.9

1 The figures include non-industrial and industrial staff but exclude casual or seasonal staff (normally recruited for short periods of not more than twelve months) and employees of the Northern Ireland Government
2 Part-time employees are counted as half units
3 The responsibilities for the Paymaster General's Office transferred from the Chancellor of the Exchequer's Departments to 'Other civil departments' on 1 July 1979 (868 staff) and are now included with 'Other civil departments'. The Treasury Solicitor was reclassified to 'Other civil departments' on 1 April 1981
4 Certain Civil Service Department (CSD) divisions, along with responsibility for CISCO, HMSO, COI and the Government Actuary's Department, were transferred to the Chancellor of the Exchequer (9 873 staff in all) on 7 December 1981. From the same date the Management and Personnel Office became responsible for CSD's work on efficiency and personnel management, recruitment and training (1 378 staff)
5 On 1 April 1982, responsibility for the HMSO binderies was transferred to the British Libraries Board, and in Scotland, to the National Library of Scotland. A total of 160 staff have been excluded from the manpower count
6 As of 1 April 1984 the Victoria and Albert Museum and the Science Museum became non-manpower count bodies, they have been accorded Trustee Status – around 1 100 staff are involved
7 From 1 October 1980, certain staff in Property Services Agency (1 276 involved) have been excluded from the manpower count
8 With effect from 1 April 1981, some 765 non-industrial Environment/Transport common services staff employed on work for the Department of Transport and previously counted in the Department of the Environment, were instead included in the former's figures
9 With effect from 1 April 1982, the Department of the Environment transferred to the Countryside Commission 96 staff formerly on secondment to it; and hived-off the Hydraulics Research Station with its 244 staff. A total of 340 staff have been excluded from the manpower count
10 From 1 April 1984 approximately 1 100 staff of the Directorate of Historic Monuments and Ancient Buildings have been transferred to a new Commission outside the manpower count
11 From 1 April 1984 responsibility for the Passport Office was passed to the Home Office from the Foreign and Commonwealth Office (around 950 staff involved)
12 279 non-industrial staff employed in the Radio Regulatory Department of the Home Office were transferred to the Department of Trade and Industry in June 1983
13 Following the general election in June 1983 the former Departments of Trade and Industry merged
14 Departments of the Secretary of State for Scotland and the Lord Advocate
15 The State Hospital, Carstairs was hived-off on 31 March 1984, around 400 staff were involved
16 Some 1 454 non-industrial staff employed in the Aviation and Shipping divisions of the Department of Trade were transferred in June 1983 to the Department of Transport
17 At 1 July 1984 a new department, the Office of Telecommunications, was formed under the responsibility of the Secretary of State for Trade and Industry
18 On 2 January 1985 the Royal Ordnance Factories were incorporated as a Companies Act company and are no longer included in the manpower count
19 On 18 August 1986 a new department, the Office of Gas Supply, was formed under the responsibility of the Secretary of State for Energy
20 On 20 July 1987 the Serious Fraud Office was formed with staff transferred from the Crown Prosecution Service
21 With effect from 25 July 1988 the Department of Health and Social Security was split into the Department of Health and the Department of Social Security

Source HM Treasury

6.8 Unemployment figures by region[1]

Seasonally adjusted

Thousands

		South East	Greater London[2]	East Anglia	South West	West Midlands	East Midlands	Yorkshire and Humberside	North West	North	Wales	Scotland	Great Britain	Northern Ireland	United Kingdom
1978	Jan	2 717	1 332	294	904	1 011	639	969	1 656	936	705	1 486	11 288	520	11 808
	Apr	2 580	1 269	292	867	1 006	635	966	1 644	933	714	1 439	11 073	539	11 612
	Jul	2 505	1 231	287	838	1 006	639	964	1 636	934	715	1 410	10 937	540	11 477
	Oct	2 420	1 197	276	810	998	622	963	1 605	947	699	1 406	10 748	529	11 277
1979	Jan	2 306	1 147	273	782	986	605	952	1 577	942	694	1 386	10 499	524	11 023
	Apr	2 235	1 120	264	759	992	580	942	1 561	942	684	1 410	10 365	526	10 891
	Jul	2 133	1 066	249	731	1 001	568	916	1 540	934	656	1 399	10 129	532	10 661
	Oct	2 051	1 024	244	705	1 006	573	903	1 551	933	639	1 405	10 009	530	10 539
1980	Jan	2 062	1 040	244	694	1 015	584	917	1 623	959	654	1 452	10 202	536	10 738
	Apr	2 247	1 125	269	743	1 137	659	1 057	1 800	1 069	731	1 577	11 288	571	11 859
	Jul	2 597	1 268	315	840	1 357	787	1 205	2 004	1 148	837	1 707	12 801	625	13 426
	Oct	3 175	1 538	385	981	1 720	969	1 449	2 348	1 274	1 000	1 945	15 244	720	15 964
1981	Jan	3 830	1 850	450	1 128	2 105	1 143	1 730	2 693	1 478	1 123	2 136	17 816	795	18 611
	Apr	4 382	2 107	502	1 269	2 410	1 279	1 907	2 960	1 587	1 210	2 326	19 843	837	20 680
	Jul	4 856	2 376	544	1 341	2 580	1 333	2 066	3 209	1 671	1 291	2 498	21 400	868	22 268
	Oct	5 186	2 520	562	1 396	2 750	1 407	2 167	3 372	1 758	1 334	2 596	22 529	893	23 422
1982	Jan	5 418	2 639	586	1 445	2 875	1 466	2 223	3 475	1 792	1 388	2 675	23 342	916	24 258
	Apr	5 614	2 739	604	1 467	2 913	1 469	2 260	3 560	1 823	1 413	2 711	23 833	944	24 777
	Jul	5 781	2 843	624	1 517	2 978	1 510	2 351	3 679	1 893	1 451	2 776	24 560	974	25 534
	Oct	6 011	2 940	660	1 590	3 063	1 571	2 442	3 797	1 938	1 489	2 857	25 398	1 016	26 414
1983	Jan	6 201	3 049	683	1 629	3 160	1 639	2 515	3 883	1 981	1 524	2 930	26 143	1 037	27 180
	Apr	6 354	3 183	692	1 648	3 223	1 679	2 555	3 959	2 003	1 541	2 960	26 615	1 053	27 668
	Jul	6 507	3 285	694	1 688	3 251	1 715	2 581	4 009	2 033	1 542	3 007	27 026	1 076	28 102
	Oct	6 583	3 340	703	1 709	3 207	1 719	2 574	4 035	2 052	1 546	3 007	27 134	1 086	28 220
1984	Jan	6 706	3 417	700	1 727	3 188	1 750	2 607	4 085	2 070	1 555	3 051	27 436	1 098	28 534
	Apr	6 772	3 456	703	1 757	3 199	1 778	2 641	4 093	2 105	1 585	3 051	27 685	1 102	28 787
	Jul	6 905	3 527	713	1 787	3 222	1 810	2 683	4 098	2 151	1 607	3 093	28 070	1 103	29 173
	Oct	7 068	3 618	722	1 844	3 264	1 860	2 753	4 148	2 191	1 649	3 131	28 626	1 096	29 722
1985	Jan	7 195	3 688	734	1 869	3 271	1 868	2 765	4 188	2 197	1 665	3 149	28 902	1 104	30 006
	Apr	7 282	3 745	748	1 902	3 278	1 885	2 812	4 220	2 219	1 682	3 225	29 254	1 118	30 372
	Jul	7 268	3 765	751	1 900	3 263	1 878	2 805	4 205	2 215	1 689	3 233	29 210	1 123	30 333
	Oct	7 320	3 808	757	1 917	3 263	1 874	2 838	4 221	2 224	1 696	3 253	29 364	1 143	30 507
1986	Jan	7 408	3 846	776	1 941	3 270	1 899	2 915	4 223	2 241	1 715	3 249	29 638	1 175	30 813
	Apr	7 573	3 940	786	1 967	3 290	1 905	2 941	4 250	2 227	1 716	3 275	29 932	1 214	31 146
	Jul	7 593	3 963	797	1 981	3 299	1 924	2 968	4 271	2 219	1 703	3 340	30 094	1 238	31 332
	Oct	7 454	3 914	784	1 949	3 255	1 915	2 942	4 196	2 182	1 659	3 377	29 710	1 253	30 963
1987	Jan	7 286	3 829	775	1 899	3 191	1 892	2 895	4 130	2 163	1 623	3 406	29 262	1 251	30 513
	Apr	6 935	3 673	737	1 822	3 065	1 845	2 836	4 016	2 120	1 553	3 376	28 303	1 236	29 539
	Jul	6 544	3 515	692	1 715	2 908	1 756	2 702	3 836	2 029	1 492	3 232	26 902	1 224	28 126
	Oct	2 787	3 338	641	1 597	2 736	1 657	2 562	3 653	1 948	1 426	3 094	25 436	1 203	26 639
1988	Jan	2 498	3 137	584	1 512	2 579	1 565	2 439	3 499	1 863	1 357	2 997	24 029	1 165	25 194
	Apr	5 286	3 022	539	1 417	2 438	1 503	2 360	3 339	1 800	1 317	2 884	22 884	1 145	24 029
	Jul	4 861	2 802	496	1 325	2 282	1 420	2 244	3 178	1 729	1 246	2 759	21 536	1 137	22 673
	Oct	4 553	2 672	457	1 229	2 117	1 346	2 145	3 072	1 656	1 196	2 701	20 473	1 106	21 579
1989	Jan	4 057	2 422	385	1 091	1 921	1 222	1 976	2 888	1 577	1 097	2 566	18 781	1 097	19 878
	Apr	3 743	2 232	355	1 016	1 741	1 129	1 838	2 720	1 492	1 012	2 434	17 482	1 082	18 564

1 The figures are based on the number of claimants at Unemployment Benefit Offices and are adjusted for seasonality and discontinuities to be consistent with current coverage.

2 Included in South East.

Source *Department of Employment*

6.9 Vacancies at jobcentres in the United Kingdom[1]

Seasonally adjusted

Thousands

	January	February	March	April	May	June	July	August	September	October	November	December
Numbers of vacancies remaining unfilled												
1980	193.4	183.9	174.5	160.9	152.6	138.3	122.1	112.4	104.7	92.3	86.6	89.0
1981	91.0	89.8	90.0	85.6	83.3	76.9	85.1	91.7	93.1	98.5	102.8	105.1
1982	111.0	114.7	113.6	114.2	112.9	112.9	113.8	114.4	110.3	113.5	116.1	119.1
1983	121.6	124.5	126.7	132.4	131.0	136.5	141.3	146.2	146.8	147.5	146.5	147.0
1984	148.0	147.5	149.1	147.3	152.5	151.2	152.2	149.4	151.2	149.0	150.4	154.3
1985	155.4	157.5	160.3	165.7	162.2	164.0	162.2	162.1	162.7	165.5	164.7	162.7
1986	164.7	171.4	174.8	175.1	172.7	185.2	193.7	200.8	201.2	207.0	209.9	209.0
1987	212.9	212.3	217.0	219.6	231.6	233.7	235.3	237.7	244.4	259.9	265.1	254.9
1988	250.8	249.6	249.4	255.9	254.5	255.1	249.7	242.8	240.3	251.2	245.2	238.3
1989	229.2	228.1	222.9	222.1	218.2	226.4						
Inflow of vacancies												
1980	200.6	209.4	209.4	193.6	192.8	177.9	169.9	162.3	163.1	150.6	145.0	145.2
1981	168.1	143.0	142.1	140.2	139.2	144.0	140.9	147.2	159.7	158.2	156.6	160.1
1982	174.3	166.7	169.0	167.2	167.1	167.4	166.6	159.9	161.7	162.3	162.2	167.0
1983	173.0	173.9	170.7	175.4	176.1	183.7	183.3	195.2	185.8	185.2	189.4	188.7
1984	187.0	188.3	188.2	195.8	197.3	191.6	195.8	191.4	195.3	196.1	198.8	201.3
1985	198.4	194.4	200.8	195.2	196.6	204.5	205.8	207.9	203.6	206.3	203.7	202.1
1986	186.6	206.0	196.8	211.9	213.1	208.1	218.5	220.0	220.4	220.7	223.1	221.1
1987	222.5	207.9	231.0	222.4	223.1	229.8	221.1	224.4	229.3	235.6	234.9	234.7
1988	227.3	234.7	236.0	230.6	231.2	230.8	230.3	227.0	227.7	232.8	234.0	230.8
1989	220.4	234.8	229.3	220.8	221.4	231.6						
Outflow of vacancies												
1980	206.0	219.9	220.5	205.0	204.1	191.0	189.1	170.9	171.0	164.0	148.9	142.8
1981	161.6	145.5	142.5	143.8	142.9	151.0	133.4	141.6	157.8	152.3	151.8	158.0
1982	165.6	163.5	170.7	168.2	168.1	167.1	166.8	159.5	166.0	160.1	160.4	164.1
1983	171.7	171.2	168.7	174.1	174.7	176.0	179.2	189.5	184.5	184.5	191.6	188.8
1984	187.3	189.7	186.8	194.3	195.8	193.2	195.1	194.0	194.3	198.9	198.4	196.2
1985	199.1	194.3	198.0	190.1	191.6	203.8	207.5	207.3	203.8	205.1	203.0	201.8
1986	188.5	202.8	193.1	211.1	212.3	198.0	208.7	211.7	218.2	217.9	219.5	218.2
1987	221.5	211.5	225.8	214.7	215.5	227.0	217.9	219.4	220.4	223.8	229.4	241.1
1988	233.4	239.2	236.1	227.3	228.0	229.7	231.8	232.6	229.0	229.3	242.5	233.4
1989	231.0	239.4	234.8	221.9	222.5	222.4						
Number of placings												
1980	148.8	153.4	153.6	145.3	145.0	137.5	133.3	122.1	124.5	119.3	111.5	108.9
1981	125.7	109.9	109.0	109.9	109.7	115.3	106.2	110.2	119.5	119.5	117.0	121.4
1982	130.7	127.4	131.0	129.8	130.1	129.6	130.1	122.7	127.4	123.0	123.7	126.9
1983	131.3	132.5	128.5	131.5	133.2	135.8	136.5	144.8	141.4	140.5	144.6	143.8
1984	143.2	143.4	142.7	150.9	152.0	148.4	151.8	150.0	151.3	155.2	155.7	153.0
1985	153.7	150.0	153.4	143.2	144.1	157.9	160.4	161.7	157.7	158.4	157.5	156.8
1986	144.6	155.9	148.1	161.8	162.3	149.8	157.6	158.6	161.8	162.1	163.8	162.4
1987	162.8	157.2	166.8	156.8	156.8	163.3	155.3	155.8	156.7	157.6	158.9	165.6
1988	165.7	165.3	163.0	158.1	157.9	156.3	156.4	156.8	155.4	153.4	162.3	157.6
1989	160.5	167.2	164.0	154.8	154.5	155.1						

Note: Vacancies notified to and placings made by jobcentres do not represent the total number of vacancies/engagements in the economy. Latest estimates suggest that about a third of all vacancies are notified to jobcentres: and about a quarter of all engagements are made through jobcentres. Inflow, outflow and placings figures are collected for four or five-week periods between count dates; the figures in this table are converted to a standard $4\frac{1}{3}$ week month.

[1] Excluding vacancies on government programmes (except vacancies on Enterprise Ulster and Action for Community Employment (ACE) which are included in the seasonally adjusted figures for Northern Ireland). Note that Community Programme vacancies handled by jobcentres were excluded from the seasonally adjusted series when the coverage was revised in September 1985. The coverage of the seasonally adjusted series is therefore not affected by the cessation of C.P. vacancies with the introduction of Employment Training in September 1988. For further details, see the October 1985 *Employment Gazette*, p 143.

Source *Department of Employment*

6.10 Vacancies unfilled in Northern Ireland[1]

Number

	January	February	March	April	May	June	July	August	September	October	November	December
Adults												
1978	1 757	1 907	1 929	1 810	1 863	1 941	1 713	1 604	1 608	1 460	1 366	1 155
1979	1 098	1 160	1 237	1 489	1 558	1 517	1 398	1 314	1 388	1 318	1 210	1 109
1980	1 054	1 177	1 289	1 228	1 284	1 334	1 001	993	825	759	669	639
1981	595	603	619	732	728	741	714	735	791	811	859	795
1982	752	847	875	900	937	957	1 022	1 079	1 123	1 207	1 072	1 019
1983	1 017	1 037	1 160	1 171	1 237	1 380	1 351	1 334	1 298	1 203	1 070	1 113
1984	1 109	1 203	1 294	1 331	1 543	1 779	1 756	1 746	1 628	1 701	1 776	1 419
1985	1 216	1 349	1 609	1 669	1 876	1 912	1 766	1 651	1 662	1 627	1 516	1 502
1986	1 545	1 836	1 924	2 206	2 160	2 202	2 151	2 180	2 097	2 100	2 005	1 723
1987	1 766	1 952	1 985	2 162	2 147	2 223	2 130	2 111	2 148	2 222	2 326	2 728
1988	2 891	2 848	2 824	3 003	2 800	2 795	2 836	2 646	2 562	2 667	2 741	2 781
1989	2 748	3 654	3 511	3 820	3 671	3 722						
Young Persons												
1978	364	359	303	349	344	338	307	316	505	406	341	278
1979	243	252	261	286	306	240	261	294	308	250	228	182
1980	170	187	165	164	163	164	149	135	182	123	109	64
1981	71	64	66	109	61	62	54	82	135	158	120	124
1982	136	190	167	158	170	190	157	162	221	206	214	210
1983	193	208	243	295	340	282	240	227	309	352	371	330
1984	309	330	377	400	469	595	542	576	574	673	744	746
1985	709	766	797	837	887	967	758	628	691	651	605	489
1986	445	480	530	576	592	695	572	589	662	675	662	567
1987	546	598	703	635	737	893	814	806	846	978	921	819
1988	777	787	812	996	1 196	1 096	1 005	993	1 038	1 238	1 235	1 140
1989	1 083	1 150	1 271	1 373	1 300	1 284						

1 The figures refer to vacancies notified to the Employment Service Jobmarkets of the Department of Economic Development, and remaining unfilled on the day of the count.

Source *Department of Economic Development (Northern Ireland)*

6.11 Industrial stoppages
United Kingdom

Thousands

	1983	1984	1985	1986	1987	1988
Working days lost through all stoppages in progress: total	3 754	27 135	6 402	1 920	3 546	3 702
Analysis by industry						
Coal extraction	484	22 483	4 142	143	217	222
Other energy and water	888	36	57	6	9	16
Metals, minerals and chemicals	229	185	167	192	60	70
Engineering and vehicles	1 242	1 965	481	744	422	1 409
Other manufacturing industries	302	510	261	135	115	151
Construction	68	334	50	33	22	17
Transport and communication	295	666	197	190	1 705	1 491
Public admin., sanitary services and education	115	764	957	449	939	254
Medical and health services	6	22	33	11	6	36
All other industries and services	124	170	54	20	53	30
Analysis by number of working days lost in each stoppage						
Under 250 days	57	49	39	48	48	33
250 and under 500 days	63	57	46	50	54	34
500 and under 1 000 days	121	116	100	89	88	78
1 000 and under 5 000 days	536	606	400	369	360	310
5 000 and under 25 000 days	678	993	499	381	388	325
25 000 and under 50 000 days	305	691	281	258	118	127
50 000 days and over	2 223	28 539	5 037	726	2 490	2 795
Working days lost per 1 000 employees all industries and services	178	1 278	298	89	162	164
Workers directly and indirectly involved: total	574	1 464	791	720	887	790
Analysis by industry						
Coal extraction	133	281	177	87	98	92
Other energy and water	41	7	6	2	2	2
Metals, minerals and chemicals	32	42	17	17	9	10
Engineering and vehicles	206	420	163	147	174	137
Other manufacturing industries	47	53	34	30	19	29
Construction	7	17	6	8	4	4
Transport and communication	48	192	104	72	207	321
Public admin., sanitary services and education	40	414	261	348	361	161
Medical and health services	1	17	10	4	4	31
All other industries and services	19	21	14	6	10	4
Analysis by duration of stoppage						
Not more than 5 days	282	684	335	369	308	381
Over 5 but not more than 10 days	69	123	67	47	66	280
Over 10 but not more than 20 days	75	130	40	24	153	19
Over 20 but not more than 30 days	37	33	170	58	25	22
Over 30 but not more than 50 days	67	212	13	17	23	57
Over 50 days	44	208	167	206	313	32
Numbers of stoppages in progress: total	1 364	1 221	903	1 074	1 016	781
Analysis by industry						
Coal extraction	356	79	160	351	296	154
Other energy and water	19	21	9	10	6	6
Metals, minerals and chemicals	110	139	86	62	36	50
Engineering and vehicles	307	368	198	202	209	162
Other manufacturing industries	201	200	104	85	98	75
Construction	46	31	27	26	24	16
Transport and communication	150	204	143	145	191	176
Public admin., sanitary services and education	82	99	107	132	99	104
Medical and health services	34	64	28	35	24	21
All other industries and services	68	68	45	34	41	31
Analysis of number of stoppages by duration						
Not more than 5 days	920	792	622	836	784	587
Over 5 but not more than 10 days	190	181	115	108	103	89
Over 10 but not more than 20 days	131	123	93	65	78	60
Over 20 but not more than 30 days	44	39	35	23	23	17
Over 30 but not more than 50 days	38	43	22	18	12	12
Over 50 days	29	28	16	24	16	16

Notes These figures exclude details of stoppages involving fewer than ten workers or lasting less than one day except any in which the aggregate number of working days lost exceeded 100.

There may be some under-recording of small or short stoppages; this would have much more effect on the total of stoppages than of working days lost.

Some stoppages which affected more than one industry group have been counted under each of the industries but only once in the totals.

Stoppages have been classified using Standard Industrial Classification 1980.

The figures have been rounded to the nearest 100 workers and 1 000 working days; the sums of the constituent items may not, therefore, agree precisely with the totals shown.

Classifications by size are based on the full duration of stoppages where these continue into the following year.

In the analyses for 1983 and 1984, figures are for stoppages beginning in the year, working days lost include those lost in the first two months of the following year.

Working days lost per thousand employees are based on the latest available mid-year (June) estimates of employees in employment.

Source Department of Employment

6.12 Economic activity: 1981[1]
Great Britain
All residents

Thousands

	Total	Age last birthday: Under 20	20–24	25–34	35–44	45–54	55–59	60–64	65 and over
Males: total population (aged 16 and over)	19 929	1 821	2 004	3 835	3 250	3 011	1 542	1 310	3 155
Total economically inactive (aged 16 and over)	4 430	645	218	110	71	109	130	333	2 815
Students	896	627	193	60	13	4	–	–	–
Retired	2 923	–	–	–	3	10	28	181	2 702
Permanently sick	512	8	13	31	43	86	98	147	85
Other	99	10	11	18	12	9	5	5	28
Total economically active	15 499	1 177	1 787	3 725	3 180	2 902	1 412	977	340
Self-employed (included above)	1 840	23	103	435	496	407	160	120	95
In employment	13 736	949	1 492	3 326	2 902	2 648	1 263	822	333
Working full-time	13 374	933	1 476	3 299	2 881	2 625	1 243	788	130
Working part-time	362	17	17	27	21	24	20	33	203
Out of employment	1 763	227	294	399	278	253	149	156	7
Seeking work	1 595	222	285	374	246	214	122	129	5
Temporarily sick	168	5	9	25	32	39	27	27	3
Females: total population (aged 16 and over)	21 687	1 746	1 954	3 797	3 223	3 039	1 625	1 474	4 830
Total economically inactive (aged 16 and over)	11 809	760	602	1 733	1 112	1 032	776	1 144	4 651
Students	862	672	139	34	13	4	–	–	–
Retired	1 785	–	–	–	3	10	38	298	1 437
Permanently sick	357	6	11	26	33	62	58	31	130
Other	8 806	82	451	1 673	1 064	958	680	815	3 083
Total economically active	9 878	986	1 352	2 064	2 110	2 007	849	330	179
Self-employed (included above)	457	5	23	100	128	107	43	26	26
In employment	9 146	814	1 196	1 909	2 014	1 912	802	324	174
Working full-time	5 602	776	1 092	1 163	975	1 013	417	117	50
Working part-time	3 543	38	104	746	1 039	899	385	207	125
Out of employment	732	172	157	155	96	95	47	6	5
Seeking work	645	165	147	139	79	72	36	4	3
Temporarily sick	88	7	10	16	17	22	11	2	2

1 During the week before the census (5 April 1981). For definition of terms used see *Census 1981, Definitions, Great Britain* (HMSO 1981).

Sources *Office of Population Censuses and Surveys; General Register Office (Scotland)*

6.13 Size of manufacturing units 1989

	Total	Analysis by number of employees							
		1–9	10–19	20–49	50–99	100–199	200–499	500–999	1 000 and over
Number of units									
All manufacturing industries	159 238	107 155	17 250	17 519	7 708	4 920	3 323	930	433
Extraction and preparation of metalliferous ores and metal manufacturing	1 615	690	205	298	164	114	97	29	18
Extraction of minerals not elsewhere specified and manufacture of non-metallic mineral products	7 395	4 687	995	870	386	239	169	40	9
Chemical industry and production of man-made fibres	4 147	2 164	506	564	346	255	178	90	44
Manufacture of metal goods not elsewhere specified	15 002	9 646	1 869	2 031	790	407	204	49	6
Mechanical engineering	25 662	17 617	2 886	3 037	1 026	575	360	119	42
Manufacture of office machinery and data processing equipment	1 346	967	112	119	54	44	28	15	7
Electrical and electronic engineering	11 183	7 274	1 074	1 190	607	423	376	158	81
Manufacture of motor vehicles and parts thereof	2 453	1 216	342	352	201	133	122	47	40
Manufacture of other transport equipment	2 509	1 597	247	258	147	88	78	33	61
Instrument engineering	2 825	1 683	347	410	178	125	69	9	4
Food, drink and tobacco manufacturing industries	10 930	6 433	1 402	1 270	648	495	462	153	67
Textile industry	5 427	3 072	551	701	474	373	212	37	7
Manufacture of leather and leather goods	1 374	973	164	136	65	27	9	–	–
Footwear and clothing industries	11 947	7 979	1 314	1 235	632	447	300	32	8
Timber and wooden furniture industries	15 268	11 529	1 450	1 359	518	283	112	16	1
Manufacture of paper and paper products; printing and publishing	24 553	18 103	2 410	2 310	828	495	309	69	29
Processing of rubber and plastics	5 684	3 040	716	895	485	321	196	23	8
Other manufacturing industries	9 918	8 485	660	484	159	76	42	11	1
Number of employees (thousands)									
All manufacturing industries	4 805.9	319.0	241.1	540.5	532.3	684.2	1 012.4	625.9	850.5
Extraction and preparation of metalliferous ores and metal manufacturing	129.5	2.4	2.9	9.7	11.5	15.9	30.3	20.0	36.8
Extraction of minerals not elsewhere specified and manufacture of non-metallic mineral products	204.3	14.6	13.7	27.0	26.6	32.7	51.3	26.5	11.9
Chemical industry and production of man-made fibres	284.3	6.9	7.1	18.0	24.5	35.7	56.2	61.1	74.8
Manufacture of metal goods not elsewhere specified	327.2	28.6	26.6	62.1	54.5	56.1	59.2	33.2	7.0
Mechanical engineering	589.1	52.0	40.6	93.2	70.0	79.2	109.0	80.7	64.4
Manufacture of office machinery and data processing equipment	48.1	2.6	1.6	3.7	3.9	5.9	8.1	10.2	12.2
Electrical and electronic engineering	536.4	19.8	15.0	36.8	42.3	59.2	116.7	108.5	138.2
Manufacture of motor vehicles and parts thereof	244.7	4.0	4.7	11.2	14.3	19.1	38.8	33.1	119.4
Manufacture of other transport equipment	277.6	4.2	3.4	7.8	10.3	11.9	23.9	24.0	192.0
Instrument engineering	86.0	5.3	5.0	12.8	12.1	17.3	21.2	6.5	5.8
Food, drink and tobacco manufacturing industries	548.7	24.2	19.6	39.1	45.0	69.4	144.4	100.7	106.2
Textile industry	223.6	10.0	7.6	22.2	33.6	52.2	65.0	23.9	9.1
Manufacture of leather and leather goods	19.5	2.7	2.2	4.0	4.4	3.6	2.5	–	–
Footwear and clothing industries	308.7	27.4	18.0	38.3	43.5	63.3	89.1	19.1	10.1
Timber and wooden furniture industries	209.2	30.4	20.3	41.7	35.1	38.4	31.9	10.4	1.0
Manufacture of paper and paper products; printing and publishing	460.1	51.1	33.6	69.7	56.2	69.4	92.0	44.7	43.4
Processing of rubber and plastics	220.3	10.0	10.1	28.3	33.8	44.8	60.6	15.7	17.1
Other manufacturing industries	88.6	22.7	9.1	14.9	10.7	10.2	12.2	7.6	1.1

Notes

(i) The analysis follows the Classes of the *Standard Industrial Classification 1980.*

(ii) The employment information is drawn from BSO production inquiries (in particular the Annual Census of Production and the quarterly inquiries into manufacturers' sales) and relates generally to 1987.

Source *Central Statistical Office*

6.14 Average weekly earnings and hours of manual workers

Great Britain

Standard Industrial Classification 1980

At October

Average weekly earnings[2](£)	All workers on adult rates Full-time	Males on adult rates Full-time	Males on other rates Full-time	Females on adult rates Full-time	Females on adult rates Part-time	Females on other rates Full-time
	Manufacturing and certain other industries[1]					
1984	148.69	159.30	80.33	97.34	50.91	61.27
1985	160.39	..	..	..	..	..
1986	171.02	..	..	..	..	..
1987	184.10	..	..	..	..	..
1988	198.57	..	..	..	..	..
	Manufacturing industries					
1984	143.09	157.50	80.38	96.30	51.54	61.17
1985	155.04	170.58	84.73	103.21	54.91	64.39
1986	164.74	182.25	88.68	110.48	59.04	70.59
1987	178.54	197.92	94.86	118.79	63.46	75.06
1988	192.55	213.59	101.30	128.82	68.36	77.22

Average weekly hours worked[3]	All workers on adult rates Full-time	Males on adult rates Full-time	Males on other rates Full-time	Females on adult rates Full-time	Females on adult rates Part-time	Females on other rates Full-time
	Manufacturing and certain other industries[1]					
1984	42.5	43.4	39.8	38.2	21.5	37.9
1985	42.8	..	..	..	..	..
1986	42.7	..	..	..	..	..
1987	43.1	..	..	..	..	..
1988	43.5	..	..	..	..	..
	Manufacturing industries					
1984	41.7	42.8	39.5	38.1	21.7	37.9
1985	41.8	43.0	39.7	38.1	21.7	37.9
1986	41.6	42.7	39.4	38.1	21.9	37.9
1987	42.2	43.5	39.7	38.4	22.0	38.0
1988	42.4	43.6	39.8	38.7	22.2	37.5

1 The coverage of the 'certain other industries' changed in 1984.

2 The figures represent the average earnings, including bonus, overtime, etc., and before deduction of income tax or insurance contributions, in one week in the month indicated. Administrative and clerical workers and other salaried persons have been excluded, together with short-time workers.

3 The figures include overtime and correspond with those for average earnings. A full account of the survey relating to October 1988 was published in *Employment Gazette,* April 1989.

Source *Department of Employment*

6.15 Average weekly and hourly earnings and hours of full-time employees on adult rates

Great Britain

New Earnings Survey

April of each year

	All industries					Manufacturing industries[1]				
	Average weekly earnings[2]		Average hours[3]	Average hourly earnings[2,3]		Average weekly earnings[2]		Average hours[3]	Average hourly earnings[2,3]	
				including overtime	excluding overtime				including overtime	excluding overtime
	including those whose pay was affected by absence[4]	excluding those whose pay was affected by absence[4]				including those whose pay was affected by absence[4]	excluding those whose pay was affected by absence[4]			
	£	£		p	p	£	£		p	p
All adults										
1983	144.5	147.4	40.1	362.6	360.0	142.2	147.0	41.4	351.5	347.3
1984	155.8	159.3	40.3	389.9	386.7	155.2	160.8	41.9	380.6	375.4
1985	167.4	171.0	40.4	416.8	412.7	169.2	174.7	41.9	411.8	404.8
1986	181.2	184.7	40.4	450.8	446.8	183.1	188.6	41.9	444.4	437.7
1987	194.9	198.9	40.4	484.7	481.1	196.0	202.0	42.0	474.1	467.6
1988	213.6	218.4	40.6	529.2	525.9	212.7	219.4	42.3	509.4	501.7
All men										
1983	161.1	164.7	41.4	392.6	391.2	156.4	161.2	42.2	378.1	375.0
1984	174.3	178.8	41.7	423.0	421.4	171.2	176.8	42.8	409.9	406.2
1985	187.9	192.4	41.9	452.5	449.9	187.2	192.6	42.9	444.3	438.6
1986	203.4	207.5	41.8	488.9	486.6	202.3	207.8	42.9	479.1	474.0
1987	219.4	224.0	41.9	527.3	526.2	217.0	222.3	43.0	511.0	506.5
1988	240.6	245.8	42.1	573.6	573.1	236.3	242.3	43.3	549.8	544.1
Manual men										
1983	138.4	141.6	43.8	322.7	315.2	141.0	145.5	43.6	333.0	325.5
1984	148.8	152.7	44.3	345.0	336.1	153.6	158.9	44.4	358.1	348.5
1985	159.8	163.6	44.5	368.0	356.8	167.5	172.6	44.6	386.8	373.8
1986	170.9	174.4	44.5	392.6	380.8	178.4	183.4	44.5	411.6	398.5
1987	182.0	185.5	44.6	416.5	404.3	191.2	195.9	44.7	437.6	423.8
1988	196.3	200.6	45.0	445.7	431.5	206.8	212.3	45.2	468.5	451.7
Non-manual men										
1983	190.6	191.8	38.4	494.8	494.2	191.4	192.9	39.1	487.3	486.6
1984	207.3	209.0	38.5	537.4	536.4	211.7	213.5	39.3	537.8	537.1
1985	223.5	225.0	38.6	574.7	573.2	230.7	232.0	39.3	582.0	580.7
1986	243.4	244.9	38.6	627.3	625.8	254.4	255.7	39.3	641.0	640.0
1987	263.9	265.9	38.7	679.9	679.3	271.9	273.7	39.4	684.1	684.0
1988	292.1	294.1	38.7	748.8	748.3	299.1	300.5	39.4	744.9	744.1
All women										
1983	107.6	109.5	37.2	290.6	289.5	94.7	97.9	38.6	252.7	251.0
1984	114.9	117.2	37.2	310.3	309.1	101.7	105.5	38.8	270.9	268.8
1985	123.9	126.4	37.3	334.0	332.4	110.6	114.7	38.8	294.4	291.5
1986	134.7	137.2	37.3	362.5	360.7	119.2	123.2	38.8	316.1	313.3
1987	144.9	148.1	37.5	388.4	386.2	128.2	133.4	39.0	339.2	335.9
1988	160.1	164.2	37.6	431.3	429.0	138.4	144.3	39.2	365.8	362.3
Manual women										
1983	85.8	88.1	39.3	224.9	222.6	86.7	90.4	39.7	227.7	225.3
1984	90.8	93.5	39.4	238.0	235.1	91.9	96.0	39.9	240.9	238.1
1985	98.2	101.3	39.5	256.9	252.9	100.1	104.5	40.0	261.7	257.3
1986	104.4	107.5	39.5	273.0	269.2	107.0	111.6	40.0	278.9	274.6
1987	111.4	115.3	39.7	292.0	287.4	113.8	119.6	40.3	297.2	291.9
1988	118.8	123.6	39.8	310.5	305.6	121.2	127.9	40.5	315.5	309.6
Non-manual women										
1983	115.1	116.1	36.5	312.9	311.9	106.2	107.0	37.2	285.4	284.0
1984	123.0	124.3	36.5	334.3	333.1	115.8	117.2	37.4	310.8	308.7
1985	132.4	133.8	36.6	359.1	357.6	125.5	126.8	37.4	336.5	334.7
1986	144.3	145.7	36.7	390.6	388.8	135.8	136.7	37.4	363.2	361.2
1987	155.4	157.2	36.8	418.0	415.9	147.7	149.1	37.5	391.6	389.4
1988	172.9	175.5	36.9	467.7	465.3	161.6	163.3	37.6	430.0	427.5

1 Results for manufacturing industries relate to Divisions 2, 3 and 4 of the 1980 SIC.

2 The figures are gross before deductions. Generally they exclude the value of earnings in kind, but include payment such as overtime (except where otherwise stated), bonus, commission and shift premiums for the pay period.

3 The estimates given relate only to employees for whom normal basic hours were reported.

4 Those whose pay was affected by absence included or excluded as indicated.

Source: Department of Employment

6.16 Average earnings index: all employees

Great Britain

Analysis by industry based on Standard Industrial Classification 1980

January 1985 = 100

Unadjusted

	Annual averages	January	February	March	April	May	June	July	August	September	October	November	December
Whole economy (Divisions 0 – 9)													
1982	80.2	76.4	77.4	78.4	78.4	79.5	80.6	82.0	80.9	80.8	81.3	83.0	83.7
1983	87.0	83.1	84.8	85.2	85.1	86.4	87.2	88.4	87.6	87.7	88.4	89.1	90.4
1984	92.2	89.0	89.6	89.9	90.1	90.7	91.8	93.0	92.8	93.1	95.6	94.8	96.2
1985	100.0	95.1	95.8	97.8	98.6	98.6	100.0	101.1	100.9	102.5	101.2	102.9	104.8
1986	107.9	102.9	103.5	106.2	107.1	106.1	108.1	109.4	109.0	108.7	109.6	111.2	112.5
1987	116.3	110.8	111.2	113.2	114.0	115.3	116.4	118.2	117.3	117.2	118.4	120.6	122.4
1988	126.4	120.4	120.3	124.0	124.3	124.1	125.9	128.3	126.8	127.3	128.9	131.2	135.7
Manufacturing industries (Revised definition Divisions 2 – 4)													
1982	77.4	73.8	74.2	75.7	76.0	77.5	78.2	78.4	77.5	77.7	78.9	80.3	80.7
1983	84.4	80.5	80.9	81.7	82.6	84.1	84.6	85.2	84.5	85.0	86.4	88.2	88.5
1984	91.7	87.8	88.7	89.7	89.0	90.5	92.2	92.7	91.7	92.7	94.2	95.3	95.7
1985	100.0	96.0	96.1	97.9	99.1	98.9	100.8	101.5	99.7	101.2	101.1	103.6	104.3
1986	107.7	103.7	103.9	105.3	106.6	106.1	108.6	108.4	107.4	108.2	109.2	111.7	113.0
1987	116.3	111.7	112.3	113.2	114.0	114.7	117.2	118.1	116.0	117.2	118.8	120.5	122.4
1988	126.2	121.1	120.3	123.3	124.7	124.9	126.6	127.9	125.6	126.4	128.7	130.8	133.5
Production industries (Revised definition Divisions 1 – 4)													
1982	78.2	74.5	75.7	76.6	76.6	78.0	79.9	79.3	78.4	78.6	79.2	81.4	81.5
1983	84.9	81.3	81.6	82.6	83.5	84.5	85.2	85.9	85.2	85.7	87.3	88.2	88.3
1984	89.8	87.7	88.7	87.4	86.9	88.2	89.7	90.3	89.3	90.4	91.9	93.1	93.4
1985	100.0	94.0	94.2	97.2	98.7	98.7	100.8	101.8	100.0	101.8	101.5	103.9	104.4
1986	108.0	104.2	104.4	105.7	106.7	106.3	108.4	108.8	108.0	108.6	109.6	112.0	113.1
1987	116.7	112.3	112.7	113.6	114.4	114.8	117.1	118.2	116.9	117.6	119.1	120.9	122.3
1988	126.5	121.3	119.9	123.4	125.4	125.5	126.8	128.4	126.4	127.1	129.2	131.2	133.4

Seasonally adjusted

	Annual averages	January	February	March	April	May	June	July	August	September	October	November	December
Whole economy (Divisions 0 – 9)													
1982	80.2	77.4	78.2	78.6	79.0	79.6	80.1	81.3	80.7	80.6	81.4	82.7	82.6
1983	86.9	84.1	85.6	85.4	85.8	86.5	86.7	87.5	87.5	87.6	88.5	88.7	89.4
1984	92.2	90.0	90.6	90.1	90.7	90.9	91.2	92.1	92.6	93.1	95.7	94.4	95.1
1985	100.0	96.2	96.9	97.9	99.0	98.7	99.4	100.2	100.7	102.4	101.4	102.5	103.5
1986	107.9	104.2	104.9	106.2	107.4	106.2	107.4	108.3	108.8	108.8	109.9	110.9	111.2
1987	116.2	112.1	112.8	113.2	114.2	115.4	115.7	117.0	117.1	117.4	118.8	120.2	121.0
1988	126.4	121.8	122.0	124.0	124.4	124.2	125.1	126.9	126.6	127.6	129.5	130.7	134.3
Manufacturing industries (Revised definition Divisions 2 – 4)													
1982	77.4	74.4	74.7	75.7	76.3	77.4	77.2	77.6	78.2	78.2	79.1	79.5	80.4
1983	84.4	81.1	81.5	81.7	83.0	84.0	83.5	84.3	85.2	85.7	86.7	87.5	88.1
1984	91.7	88.3	89.3	89.7	89.4	90.4	91.0	91.7	92.5	93.4	94.8	94.5	95.2
1985	100.0	96.5	96.8	97.9	99.5	98.9	99.5	100.4	100.5	101.9	102.0	102.7	103.6
1986	107.7	104.2	104.6	105.2	107.0	106.0	107.2	107.3	108.3	109.0	110.0	110.9	112.1
1987	116.3	112.2	113.1	113.2	114.4	114.7	115.7	116.9	117.0	118.2	119.4	119.8	121.4
1988	126.2	121.7	121.1	123.2	125.2	124.9	125.0	126.6	126.7	127.6	129.2	130.2	132.4
Production industries (Revised definition Divisions 1 – 4)													
1982	78.2	75.1	76.2	76.4	76.7	77.8	78.1	78.4	78.9	79.3	79.7	80.9	81.4
1983	84.9	81.8	82.2	82.5	83.6	84.4	84.1	85.0	85.8	86.5	87.7	87.6	88.1
1984	89.8	88.2	89.4	87.2	87.0	88.1	88.6	89.3	89.9	91.2	92.4	92.6	93.1
1985	100.0	94.4	95.0	97.1	98.9	98.6	99.6	100.7	100.7	102.6	102.1	103.3	103.9
1986	108.0	104.7	105.2	105.6	106.9	106.4	107.1	107.5	108.8	109.5	110.3	111.3	112.4
1987	116.7	112.7	113.5	113.4	114.6	115.2	115.7	116.9	117.7	118.6	119.9	120.1	121.5
1988	126.5	121.7	120.7	123.1	125.6	126.0	125.3	127.0	127.2	128.3	130.1	130.4	132.5

Note: The seasonal adjustment factors currently used for the SIC 1980 series are based on data up to January 1988.

Source *Department of Employment*

6.16 Average earnings index: all employees

(continued)

Great Britain

Analysis by industry based on Standard Industrial Classification 1980

1985 = 100

SIC 1980 Class	Agriculture and forestry[1] (01–02)	Coal and coke[2] (11–12)	Mineral oil and natural gas (14)	Electricity, gas, other energy and water supply (15–17)	Metal processing and manufacturing (21–22)	Mineral extraction and manufacturing (23–24)	Chemicals and man-made fibres (25–26)	Mechanical engineering (32)	Electrical and electronic engineering (33–34)	Motor vehicles and parts (35)	Other transport equipment (36)	Metal goods and instruments (31,37)	Food, drink and tobacco (41–42)	Textiles (43)
1982 Annual	78.2	89.1	76.0	80.9	75.6	79.4	77.6	75.8	76.4	74.2	80.3	78.8	78.2	77.7
1983 averages	85.4	99.6	82.8	87.2	83.0	86.1	84.9	82.6	83.9	82.1	83.8	85.5	85.5	84.6
1984	92.0	50.0	91.0	93.3	92.0	92.5	92.1	90.6	91.7	88.2	92.1	92.6	92.0	91.0
1985	100.0	100.0	100.0	100.0	100.0	100.0	100.0	100.0	100.0	100.0	100.0	100.0	100.0	100.0
1986	105.5	113.3	109.5	106.9	106.5	107.8	107.9	106.9	108.0	108.7	107.9	107.4	108.7	107.2
1987	112.2	121.6	120.0	115.0	116.5	116.9	116.9	114.7	117.6	118.0	115.7	116.0	116.9	116.1
1988	117.7	135.8	133.0	122.0	128.0	126.2	126.9	125.3	128.5	129.0	120.0	126.3	126.3	123.7
1988 January	106.1	128.1	127.0	116.0	126.2	120.6	121.3	120.2	124.6	120.0	118.8	120.7	121.2	119.6
February	105.0	116.8	125.8	115.6	115.7	121.3	120.3	121.4	125.7	102.5	119.0	123.2	121.2	120.0
March	108.0	131.9	126.9	116.0	117.6	123.5	120.5	124.6	126.1	132.9	119.9	122.7	121.2	122.6
April	112.4	141.9	129.6	120.2	136.5	123.9	125.1	122.9	128.5	127.1	118.9	124.3	124.8	122.6
May	112.1	134.2	138.8	123.5	120.1	126.3	125.1	124.3	126.5	129.9	119.0	125.7	126.6	123.7
June	115.2	133.1	128.2	122.5	124.0	127.9	126.8	123.9	129.1	137.0	112.5	126.3	128.6	125.8
July	118.7	139.7	134.2	125.5	141.7	127.9	126.0	126.7	128.7	135.8	114.3	128.0	125.7	124.8
August	128.8	138.5	131.2	125.8	129.8	124.8	125.9	124.9	127.1	129.5	111.6	127.1	125.0	123.6
September	134.4	140.9	131.4	124.0	123.4	127.4	126.1	125.4	128.0	128.5	121.8	127.3	126.0	123.9
October	136.9	141.8	134.6	124.9	142.9	126.1	128.4	127.4	130.7	129.0	124.5	128.2	127.0	124.5
November	116.1	142.1	147.2	125.3	124.2	127.9	139.2	129.5	131.7	136.3	126.1	131.3	133.2	128.0
December	119.2	140.7	141.0	124.2	134.1	136.3	138.5	132.6	135.1	139.4	134.0	130.5	135.2	125.4

SIC 1980 Class	Leather, footwear and clothing (44–45)	Timber and wooden furniture (46)	Paper products, printing and publishing (47)	Rubber, plastics and other manufacturing (48–49)	Construction (50)	Distribution and repairs (61–65, 67)	Hotels and catering (66)	Transport and communication[3] (71–72, 75–77, 79)	Banking, finance and insurance (81–82 83pt.–84pt.)	Public administration (91–92pt.)	Education and health (93,95)	Other services[4] (97pt.–98pt.)	Whole economy
1982 Annual	79.6	78.8	77.3	79.0	81.2	80.2	81.2	79.5	78.2	82.8	83.0	78.8	80.2
1983 averages	86.2	86.9	84.7	84.8	87.3	86.9	87.7	86.8	85.3	88.4	91.7	85.6	87.0
1984	92.4	93.3	92.0	92.6	92.5	93.2	94.1	92.7	92.2	94.3	95.5	92.9	92.2
1985	100.0	100.0	100.0	100.0	100.0	100.0	100.0	100.0	100.0	100.0	100.0	100.0	100.0
1986	107.4	107.1	107.5	107.9	107.9	107.0	107.3	106.5	110.1	105.6	110.1	107.9	107.9
1987	114.5	116.5	116.2	116.9	116.5	114.9	115.7	114.9	121.8	112.8	117.9	115.3	116.3
1988	123.9	131.9	124.0	126.5	129.1	125.1	126.0	122.0	131.8	124.2	130.2	123.1	126.4
1988 January	120.4	123.3	117.8	121.7	121.2	118.9	121.1	117.7	127.4	118.1	120.4	121.2	120.4
February	121.4	126.0	119.0	122.4	121.9	120.4	119.5	117.4	126.7	120.7	121.2	119.8	120.3
March	124.8	123.5	120.7	123.7	128.1	124.9	121.1	118.7	135.4	122.2	126.5	117.1	124.0
April	123.3	123.2	121.0	123.5	126.3	126.5	122.1	121.5	132.7	120.0	121.5	118.1	124.3
May	124.0	127.5	122.6	127.5	125.4	123.2	123.7	122.0	129.7	121.7	122.4	121.7	124.1
June	123.2	137.2	126.0	127.6	129.6	125.1	125.7	120.5	131.4	122.6	128.1	123.3	125.9
July	126.7	135.5	125.1	130.4	130.2	125.2	125.0	122.5	132.9	126.2	135.3	126.8	128.3
August	122.0	140.0	125.2	124.7	127.9	123.9	126.6	122.5	129.6	124.6	134.3	124.0	126.8
September	124.5	135.2	127.1	126.4	130.3	126.6	124.9	122.1	128.6	124.7	131.5	125.1	127.3
October	123.9	134.2	127.7	127.4	133.5	126.0	129.4	124.4	128.7	128.3	131.6	123.8	128.9
November	124.9	138.3	127.3	131.2	136.4	127.1	132.5	127.0	142.1	131.8	132.8	124.8	131.2
December	127.4	138.3	128.3	131.2	138.8	132.8	139.9	127.5	136.7	129.5	156.6	131.8	135.7

1 England and Wales only.

2 The index series for this group has been based on average 1985 excluding January and February figures which were seriously affected by a dispute in the coal mining industry.

3 Excluding sea transport.

4 Excluding private domestic and personal services.

Source *Department of Employment*

6.17 Gross weekly and hourly earnings of full-time adult employees[1]

Great Britain *New Earnings Survey* April of each year

		Gross weekly earnings[2]					Gross hourly earnings[2, 3]				
		Lowest decile	Lower quartile	Median	Upper quartile	Highest decile	Lowest decile	Lower quartile	Median	Upper quartile	Highest decile
		£	£	£	£	£	p	p	p	p	p
All men	1980	74.7	90.7	113.3	143.4	183.1	178.4	212.5	260.8	335.7	447.8
	1981	82.9	100.9	126.5	163.8	212.1	201.1	238.8	298.0	392.2	531.1
	1982	89.7	109.9	139.1	180.5	233.8	217.5	260.5	327.8	433.3	587.9
	1983	96.3	118.4	150.3	195.0	255.0	234.6	281.5	356.1	473.0	648.6
	1983	92.8	115.9	148.1	192.8	252.4	227.2	275.6	349.9	466.2	639.3
	1984	99.0	124.0	160.6	209.6	275.4	240.8	294.3	377.1	503.2	694.2
	1985	105.1	132.9	172.8	226.3	296.3	255.8	313.8	402.9	537.8	740.7
	1986	111.4	141.8	185.1	243.7	320.8	271.6	334.6	432.9	581.5	806.4
	1987	117.9	150.1	198.4	262.8	349.5	286.1	354.4	462.1	627.7	875.6
	1988	127.1	162.7	215.5	288.7	384.2	305.9	380.0	498.2	686.8	963.8
Manual men	1980	71.8	86.3	105.0	129.0	156.7	170.1	198.5	234.8	278.8	330.5
	1981	79.6	94.5	114.2	139.9	172.0	190.7	221.0	261.9	314.4	374.7
	1982	85.5	102.4	125.2	154.6	191.0	206.1	241.2	287.7	345.7	412.6
	1983	91.2	110.2	134.8	165.4	204.5	221.5	259.3	310.1	375.2	450.5
	1983	89.0	108.1	133.1	163.9	202.7	216.0	255.3	307.0	372.0	446.6
	1984	94.1	115.2	143.3	178.8	220.7	227.9	270.7	328.0	399.6	478.6
	1985	100.4	122.9	153.3	191.8	237.1	242.4	288.3	350.2	425.7	509.2
	1986	105.5	130.2	163.4	205.5	253.9	256.1	305.9	373.2	457.2	546.4
	1987	110.6	137.8	173.9	218.8	272.2	268.5	322.4	395.1	486.0	585.4
	1988	119.4	148.6	188.0	237.2	295.4	286.3	343.4	422.4	521.1	627.3
Non-manual men	1980	80.3	100.4	127.7	163.8	215.0	206.2	256.8	330.2	432.3	568.1
	1981	91.5	115.5	148.9	192.8	248.3	235.0	295.5	383.7	507.7	676.2
	1982	98.9	125.4	162.5	210.5	275.2	254.4	325.4	423.6	559.8	739.8
	1983	106.3	136.2	176.1	230.3	300.2	273.9	351.5	458.1	608.5	808.5
	1983	101.8	132.7	173.9	228.1	297.5	260.3	341.5	451.0	602.1	800.0
	1984	109.4	143.3	188.8	247.4	325.2	280.6	368.5	488.8	652.5	864.7
	1985	116.6	153.7	202.4	266.2	348.9	298.2	393.0	523.7	696.2	924.4
	1986	124.6	165.9	219.4	289.2	383.2	319.9	424.3	567.1	761.7	1 012.3
	1987	132.5	176.8	235.7	312.1	416.4	339.7	450.4	608.0	820.9	1 101.3
	1988	143.9	191.9	259.7	345.3	466.1	368.8	489.9	667.6	905.3	1 225.0
As percentages of the corresponding median						Percentage					
All men	1980	*65.9*	*80.1*	*100.0*	*126.5*	*161.6*	*68.4*	*81.5*	*100.0*	*128.7*	*171.7*
	1981	*65.6*	*79.8*	*100.0*	*129.5*	*167.7*	*67.5*	*80.1*	*100.0*	*131.6*	*178.2*
	1982	*64.5*	*79.0*	*100.0*	*129.8*	*168.1*	*66.4*	*79.5*	*100.0*	*132.2*	*179.4*
	1983	*64.1*	*78.8*	*100.0*	*129.8*	*169.7*	*65.9*	*79.1*	*100.0*	*132.8*	*182.2*
	1983	*62.7*	*78.2*	*100.0*	*130.2*	*170.4*	*64.9*	*78.8*	*100.0*	*132.2*	*182.7*
	1984	*61.6*	*77.2*	*100.0*	*130.6*	*171.5*	*63.9*	*78.0*	*100.0*	*133.5*	*184.1*
	1985	*60.8*	*76.9*	*100.0*	*131.0*	*171.5*	*63.5*	*77.9*	*100.0*	*133.5*	*183.9*
	1986	*60.2*	*76.6*	*100.0*	*131.6*	*173.3*	*62.7*	*77.3*	*100.0*	*134.3*	*186.3*
	1987	*59.4*	*75.7*	*100.0*	*132.5*	*176.2*	*61.9*	*76.7*	*100.0*	*135.8*	*189.5*
	1988	*59.0*	*75.5*	*100.0*	*134.0*	*178.3*	*61.4*	*76.3*	*100.0*	*137.9*	*193.5*
Manual men	1980	*68.4*	*82.2*	*100.0*	*122.9*	*149.2*	*72.4*	*84.5*	*100.0*	*118.7*	*140.7*
	1981	*69.7*	*82.8*	*100.0*	*122.5*	*150.6*	*72.8*	*84.4*	*100.0*	*120.1*	*143.1*
	1982	*68.3*	*81.8*	*100.0*	*123.5*	*152.6*	*71.6*	*83.8*	*100.0*	*120.2*	*143.4*
	1983	*67.7*	*81.8*	*100.0*	*122.7*	*151.7*	*71.4*	*83.6*	*100.0*	*121.0*	*145.3*
	1983	*66.9*	*81.2*	*100.0*	*123.1*	*152.3*	*70.4*	*83.2*	*100.0*	*121.2*	*145.5*
	1984	*65.7*	*80.4*	*100.0*	*124.8*	*154.0*	*69.5*	*82.6*	*100.0*	*121.8*	*145.9*
	1985	*65.5*	*80.1*	*100.0*	*125.1*	*154.6*	*69.2*	*82.3*	*100.0*	*121.5*	*145.4*
	1986	*64.5*	*79.7*	*100.0*	*125.8*	*155.4*	*68.6*	*82.0*	*100.0*	*122.5*	*146.4*
	1987	*63.6*	*79.2*	*100.0*	*125.8*	*156.5*	*67.9*	*81.6*	*100.0*	*123.0*	*148.2*
	1988	*63.5*	*79.1*	*100.0*	*126.2*	*157.1*	*67.8*	*81.3*	*100.0*	*123.4*	*148.5*
Non-manual men	1980	*62.9*	*78.6*	*100.0*	*128.2*	*168.3*	*62.4*	*77.8*	*100.0*	*130.9*	*172.0*
	1981	*61.4*	*77.6*	*100.0*	*129.5*	*166.8*	*61.2*	*77.0*	*100.0*	*132.3*	*176.3*
	1982	*60.9*	*77.2*	*100.0*	*129.6*	*169.4*	*60.1*	*76.8*	*100.0*	*132.2*	*174.7*
	1983	*60.4*	*77.3*	*100.0*	*130.8*	*170.4*	*59.8*	*76.7*	*100.0*	*132.8*	*176.5*
	1983	*58.6*	*76.3*	*100.0*	*131.2*	*171.1*	*57.7*	*75.7*	*100.0*	*133.5*	*177.4*
	1984	*57.9*	*75.9*	*100.0*	*131.1*	*172.3*	*57.4*	*75.4*	*100.0*	*133.5*	*176.9*
	1985	*57.6*	*75.9*	*100.0*	*131.6*	*172.4*	*57.0*	*75.1*	*100.0*	*132.9*	*176.5*
	1986	*56.8*	*75.6*	*100.0*	*131.8*	*174.7*	*56.4*	*74.8*	*100.0*	*134.3*	*178.5*
	1987	*56.2*	*75.0*	*100.0*	*132.4*	*176.6*	*55.9*	*74.1*	*100.0*	*135.0*	*181.1*
	1988	*55.4*	*73.9*	*100.0*	*133.0*	*179.5*	*55.2*	*73.4*	*100.0*	*135.5*	*183.5*

1 Results for 1980–82 inclusive and the first row of figures for 1983 relate to men aged 21 and over. The second row of figures for 1983 and figures for 1984 onwards relate to males on adult rates.

2 Of those whose pay for the survey pay period was not affected by absence. See also note 2 to Table 6.15.

3 Including overtime hours and overtime pay, of persons for whom normal basic hours were reported and for whom hourly earnings could, therefore, be calculated.

Source Department of Employment

6.17 (continued)

Gross weekly and hourly earnings of full-time adult employees[1]
Great Britain *New Earnings Survey* April of each year

		Gross weekly earnings[2]					Gross hourly earnings[2, 3]				
		Lowest decile	Lower quartile	Median	Upper quartile	Highest decile	Lowest decile	Lower quartile	Median	Upper quartile	Highest decile
		£	£	£	£	£	p	p	p	p	p
All women	1980	49.5	58.8	72.4	91.2	116.7	131.5	153.7	188.9	238.9	317.7
	1981	55.9	66.3	82.2	106.7	141.9	148.0	174.9	216.3	278.5	385.8
	1982	60.2	71.7	90.0	116.5	152.0	160.2	190.4	237.4	306.1	418.0
	1983	65.6	78.7	98.8	128.3	166.2	174.1	208.1	260.4	337.7	459.6
	1983	66.2	79.6	99.5	129.3	166.6	175.6	209.9	262.4	340.3	462.9
	1984	70.7	84.6	106.8	139.1	177.7	187.3	223.0	279.9	365.8	496.7
	1985	75.7	90.6	115.2	150.8	189.5	201.1	238.5	301.1	394.3	534.1
	1986	80.3	97.0	123.4	163.8	209.8	213.1	255.9	323.9	427.9	589.2
	1987	85.3	103.8	132.9	177.5	228.3	226.7	272.8	347.7	459.4	625.8
	1988	92.2	112.1	145.3	198.5	258.0	244.4	294.8	379.8	515.6	708.5
Manual women	1980	45.6	53.8	64.7	78.1	92.9	122.5	140.2	165.1	194.8	226.3
	1981	49.7	58.8	71.4	86.2	102.5	135.2	153.6	182.5	216.3	252.5
	1982	53.0	62.8	76.7	92.4	110.5	144.2	165.9	197.2	234.4	270.5
	1983	57.9	68.5	84.1	101.8	122.2	155.8	179.9	215.6	255.9	300.6
	1983	58.3	68.8	84.3	102.0	122.3	156.9	180.6	216.2	256.3	300.7
	1984	62.0	72.7	88.6	108.1	131.0	166.4	191.0	227.5	271.2	319.5
	1985	66.1	78.5	95.3	116.4	143.2	178.5	205.6	244.1	292.3	345.4
	1986	69.9	83.3	101.1	124.6	151.3	188.0	217.7	259.1	313.1	366.6
	1987	74.0	88.1	108.2	133.7	165.5	200.0	231.1	276.7	334.1	397.5
	1988	80.1	94.2	115.6	143.0	178.0	212.6	246.0	293.1	355.7	424.2
Non-manual women	1980	51.4	61.0	75.7	96.6	122.3	137.2	162.4	201.2	258.3	345.9
	1981	58.7	69.5	87.0	114.9	150.3	156.3	185.9	231.9	304.2	421.4
	1982	63.4	75.9	95.6	124.7	158.8	169.6	203.8	255.7	335.3	454.0
	1983	69.1	83.0	104.7	137.9	172.4	183.8	222.7	280.5	369.2	498.3
	1983	70.0	83.7	105.6	139.1	173.4	186.0	225.1	282.6	372.8	502.2
	1984	74.5	89.4	113.5	149.6	185.2	199.3	239.2	302.0	400.9	535.1
	1985	79.9	95.7	122.0	161.4	199.0	212.6	254.8	323.1	430.7	577.4
	1986	85.0	102.9	131.5	175.3	219.7	226.7	274.7	349.0	466.8	635.9
	1987	90.4	110.4	142.2	188.9	237.9	241.7	294.0	374.4	498.7	676.2
	1988	98.3	120.9	157.1	213.0	269.9	262.5	322.0	414.1	564.9	758.1
As percentages of the corresponding median		Percentage									
All women	1980	*68.4*	*81.3*	*100.0*	*126.1*	*161.3*	*69.6*	*81.4*	*100.0*	*126.5*	*168.2*
	1981	*68.0*	*80.6*	*100.0*	*129.8*	*172.6*	*68.5*	*80.9*	*100.0*	*128.8*	*178.4*
	1982	*66.9*	*79.7*	*100.0*	*129.4*	*169.0*	*67.5*	*80.2*	*100.0*	*128.9*	*176.1*
	1983	*66.4*	*79.7*	*100.0*	*129.9*	*168.3*	*66.9*	*79.9*	*100.0*	*129.7*	*176.5*
	1983	*66.5*	*79.9*	*100.0*	*129.9*	*167.4*	*66.9*	*80.0*	*100.0*	*129.7*	*176.5*
	1984	*66.2*	*79.2*	*100.0*	*130.2*	*166.3*	*66.9*	*79.7*	*100.0*	*130.7*	*177.5*
	1985	*65.8*	*78.7*	*100.0*	*130.9*	*164.5*	*66.8*	*79.2*	*100.0*	*131.0*	*177.4*
	1986	*65.1*	*78.6*	*100.0*	*132.7*	*170.0*	*65.8*	*79.0*	*100.0*	*132.1*	*181.9*
	1987	*64.2*	*78.1*	*100.0*	*133.5*	*171.7*	*65.2*	*78.5*	*100.0*	*132.2*	*180.0*
	1988	*63.4*	*77.2*	*100.0*	*136.6*	*177.5*	*64.3*	*77.6*	*100.0*	*135.7*	*186.5*
Manual women	1980	*70.5*	*83.1*	*100.0*	*120.7*	*143.6*	*74.2*	*84.9*	*100.0*	*118.0*	*137.0*
	1981	*69.6*	*82.4*	*100.0*	*120.7*	*143.6*	*74.1*	*84.1*	*100.0*	*118.6*	*138.3*
	1982	*69.2*	*81.9*	*100.0*	*120.5*	*144.1*	*73.1*	*84.1*	*100.0*	*118.8*	*137.2*
	1983	*68.8*	*81.5*	*100.0*	*121.1*	*145.3*	*72.3*	*83.4*	*100.0*	*118.7*	*139.4*
	1983	*69.2*	*81.6*	*100.0*	*120.9*	*145.1*	*72.6*	*83.5*	*100.0*	*118.6*	*139.1*
	1984	*70.0*	*82.1*	*100.0*	*122.0*	*147.9*	*73.1*	*84.0*	*100.0*	*119.2*	*140.5*
	1985	*69.4*	*82.4*	*100.0*	*122.2*	*150.4*	*73.1*	*84.2*	*100.0*	*119.8*	*141.5*
	1986	*69.2*	*82.4*	*100.0*	*123.3*	*149.7*	*72.6*	*84.0*	*100.0*	*120.8*	*141.5*
	1987	*68.3*	*81.4*	*100.0*	*123.5*	*152.9*	*72.3*	*83.5*	*100.0*	*120.8*	*143.7*
	1988	*69.2*	*81.4*	*100.0*	*123.7*	*153.9*	*72.6*	*83.9*	*100.0*	*121.4*	*144.7*
Non-manual women	1980	*67.9*	*80.6*	*100.0*	*127.6*	*161.6*	*68.2*	*80.7*	*100.0*	*128.4*	*172.0*
	1981	*67.5*	*79.9*	*100.0*	*132.1*	*172.7*	*67.4*	*80.2*	*100.0*	*131.2*	*181.7*
	1982	*66.4*	*79.4*	*100.0*	*130.5*	*166.2*	*66.3*	*79.7*	*100.0*	*131.2*	*177.6*
	1983	*66.1*	*79.3*	*100.0*	*131.7*	*164.8*	*65.5*	*79.4*	*100.0*	*131.6*	*177.7*
	1983	*66.3*	*79.3*	*100.0*	*131.7*	*164.2*	*65.8*	*79.6*	*100.0*	*131.9*	*177.7*
	1984	*65.7*	*78.8*	*100.0*	*131.8*	*163.1*	*66.0*	*79.2*	*100.0*	*132.7*	*177.2*
	1985	*65.5*	*78.5*	*100.0*	*132.3*	*163.1*	*65.8*	*78.9*	*100.0*	*133.3*	*178.7*
	1986	*64.6*	*78.2*	*100.0*	*133.3*	*167.1*	*65.0*	*78.7*	*100.0*	*133.8*	*182.2*
	1987	*63.6*	*77.6*	*100.0*	*132.8*	*167.3*	*64.6*	*78.5*	*100.0*	*133.2*	*180.6*
	1988	*62.6*	*77.0*	*100.0*	*135.6*	*171.8*	*63.4*	*77.8*	*100.0*	*136.4*	*183.1*

1 Results for 1980–82 inclusive and the first row of figures for 1983 relate to women aged 18 and over. The second row of figures for 1983 and figures for 1984 onwards relate to females on adult rates.

2 Of those whose pay for the survey pay period was not affected by absence. See also note 2 to Table 6.15.

3 Including overtime hours and overtime pay, of persons for whom normal basic hours were reported and for whom hourly earnings could, therefore, be calculated.

Source Department of Employment

6.18 Gross weekly and hourly earnings of full-time adults[1]

Northern Ireland

April of each year

		Gross weekly earnings[2]					Gross hourly earnings[2]				
		Lowest decile	Lower quartile	Median	Upper quartile	Highest decile	Lowest decile	Lower quartile	Median	Upper quartile	Highest decile
		£	£	£	£	£	p	p	p	p	p
All men	1979	53.7	65.5	84.3	112.7	145.3	130.6	153.6	190.7	239.3	318.6
	1980	64.8	79.1	103.5	134.3	176.6	158.7	188.6	234.0	304.9	379.1
	1981	73.4	90.1	114.8	152.9	210.3	178.5	212.3	264.3	347.0	439.6
	1982	79.6	97.5	125.5	163.5	225.8	193.3	229.8	291.8	385.4	507.9
	1983	83.9	102.3	133.2	175.6	240.0	208.7	246.4	307.1	410.9	518.3
	1984	85.4	107.3	144.6	194.9	273.3	210.1	258.6	332.4	447.1	587.3
	1985	91.9	115.7	153.7	205.1	279.4	222.8	274.6	347.6	465.8	617.1
	1986	95.5	119.1	160.6	216.6	297.5	234.4	289.1	363.8	506.6	663.5
	1987	103.3	130.4	176.3	242.0	324.8	253.6	313.6	404.9	551.0	714.5
	1988	105.6	138.2	189.5	263.7	359.4	262.7	328.4	426.1	595.8	759.7
Manual men	1979	52.5	61.9	77.5	97.3	124.8	127.7	144.0	174.4	208.3	243.6
	1980	63.2	75.1	92.0	120.1	147.6	153.9	178.0	213.8	257.3	318.1
	1981	71.3	83.7	103.4	128.5	157.0	175.2	203.3	241.4	294.7	348.1
	1982	75.6	90.4	111.0	137.1	164.8	187.4	218.2	262.1	308.9	371.1
	1983	80.5	94.8	117.4	146.4	174.6	201.1	232.0	276.5	334.7	392.1
	1984	80.8	98.0	123.6	160.4	199.2	202.1	236.6	292.2	352.4	427.4
	1985	88.5	105.7	131.6	168.6	208.2	214.9	256.8	307.1	378.6	451.1
	1986	90.4	110.3	137.1	177.5	220.6	226.5	267.9	322.6	387.6	482.0
	1987	98.4	119.1	151.6	191.8	236.7	244.4	296.4	349.2	423.3	511.4
	1988	99.8	123.1	156.5	206.6	259.6	250.7	300.1	367.5	450.3	552.4
Non-manual men	1979	58.6	72.3	96.4	128.8	163.9	146.8	179.9	232.5	303.3	387.8
	1980	69.6	91.1	119.1	161.8	210.6	172.5	222.7	291.6	366.4	472.1
	1981	78.8	105.9	143.3	196.8	262.9	200.2	257.3	348.6	445.8	573.4
	1982	91.1	118.4	154.5	210.2	305.9	224.8	293.0	392.9	501.7	694.0
	1983	97.0	124.2	165.6	225.0	290.7	241.1	305.1	419.3	514.7	680.3
	1984	100.6	133.2	181.0	250.6	328.5	247.6	329.0	450.3	569.3	725.8
	1985	102.4	140.1	187.4	250.6	327.7	255.5	340.4	460.4	593.4	744.5
	1986	104.6	149.1	198.5	274.7	348.0	253.9	357.4	497.3	628.7	809.0
	1987	116.7	166.7	226.9	302.6	381.8	292.4	411.5	552.5	690.6	859.1
	1988	126.7	177.2	245.2	326.6	429.8	309.0	429.8	601.3	732.0	922.8
As percentages of the corresponding median		Percentage					Percentage				
All men	1979	*63.7*	*77.8*	*100.0*	*133.7*	*172.4*	*68.5*	*80.6*	*100.0*	*125.5*	*167.1*
	1980	*62.6*	*76.5*	*100.0*	*129.7*	*170.7*	*67.8*	*80.6*	*100.0*	*130.3*	*162.0*
	1981	*63.9*	*78.5*	*100.0*	*133.2*	*183.2*	*67.5*	*80.4*	*100.0*	*131.3*	*166.3*
	1982	*63.4*	*77.7*	*100.0*	*130.2*	*179.9*	*66.2*	*78.8*	*100.0*	*132.1*	*174.1*
	1983	*63.0*	*76.8*	*100.0*	*131.8*	*180.2*	*68.0*	*80.2*	*100.0*	*133.8*	*168.8*
	1984	*59.1*	*74.2*	*100.0*	*134.8*	*189.0*	*63.2*	*77.8*	*100.0*	*134.5*	*176.7*
	1985	*59.8*	*75.3*	*100.0*	*133.5*	*181.8*	*64.1*	*79.0*	*100.0*	*134.0*	*177.5*
	1986	*59.5*	*74.2*	*100.0*	*134.9*	*185.2*	*64.4*	*79.5*	*100.0*	*139.3*	*182.4*
	1987	*58.6*	*74.0*	*100.0*	*137.3*	*184.2*	*62.6*	*77.5*	*100.0*	*136.1*	*176.5*
	1988	*55.7*	*72.9*	*100.0*	*139.2*	*189.7*	*61.7*	*77.1*	*100.0*	*139.8*	*178.3*
Manual men	1979	*67.7*	*79.8*	*100.0*	*125.5*	*161.0*	*73.2*	*82.6*	*100.0*	*119.5*	*139.7*
	1980	*68.7*	*81.6*	*100.0*	*130.6*	*160.4*	*72.0*	*83.2*	*100.0*	*120.3*	*148.8*
	1981	*69.0*	*81.0*	*100.0*	*124.3*	*151.8*	*72.6*	*84.2*	*100.0*	*122.1*	*144.2*
	1982	*68.1*	*81.5*	*100.0*	*123.5*	*148.5*	*71.5*	*83.3*	*100.0*	*117.9*	*141.6*
	1983	*68.5*	*80.7*	*100.0*	*124.7*	*148.7*	*72.7*	*83.9*	*100.0*	*121.0*	*141.8*
	1984	*65.4*	*79.3*	*100.0*	*129.8*	*161.2*	*69.2*	*81.0*	*100.0*	*120.6*	*146.3*
	1985	*67.3*	*80.4*	*100.0*	*128.2*	*158.3*	*70.0*	*83.6*	*100.0*	*123.3*	*146.9*
	1986	*65.9*	*80.5*	*100.0*	*129.5*	*160.9*	*70.2*	*83.0*	*100.0*	*120.1*	*149.4*
	1987	*64.9*	*78.6*	*100.0*	*126.5*	*156.1*	*70.0*	*84.9*	*100.0*	*121.2*	*146.4*
	1988	*63.8*	*78.7*	*100.0*	*132.0*	*165.9*	*68.2*	*81.7*	*100.0*	*122.5*	*150.3*
Non-manual men	1979	*60.7*	*75.0*	*100.0*	*133.6*	*169.9*	*63.2*	*77.4*	*100.0*	*130.5*	*166.8*
	1980	*58.4*	*76.4*	*100.0*	*135.8*	*176.8*	*59.2*	*76.4*	*100.0*	*125.7*	*161.9*
	1981	*54.9*	*73.9*	*100.0*	*137.3*	*183.4*	*57.4*	*73.8*	*100.0*	*127.9*	*164.5*
	1982	*58.9*	*76.6*	*100.0*	*136.0*	*198.0*	*57.2*	*74.6*	*100.0*	*127.7*	*176.6*
	1983	*58.6*	*75.0*	*100.0*	*135.9*	*175.5*	*57.5*	*72.8*	*100.0*	*122.7*	*162.3*
	1984	*55.6*	*73.6*	*100.0*	*138.4*	*181.5*	*55.0*	*73.1*	*100.0*	*126.4*	*161.2*
	1985	*54.7*	*74.8*	*100.0*	*133.8*	*174.9*	*55.5*	*73.9*	*100.0*	*128.9*	*161.7*
	1986	*52.7*	*75.1*	*100.0*	*138.4*	*175.3*	*51.1*	*71.9*	*100.0*	*126.4*	*162.7*
	1987	*51.4*	*73.5*	*100.0*	*133.4*	*168.2*	*52.9*	*74.5*	*100.0*	*125.0*	*155.5*
	1988	*51.7*	*72.3*	*100.0*	*138.2*	*175.3*	*51.4*	*71.5*	*100.0*	*121.7*	*153.5*

1 For 1978 to 1983 men aged 21 and over, women aged 18 and over. For 1984 onwards men and women on adult rates.

2 Those whose pay in the survey period was not affected by absence. Weekly earnings figures refer to April in each year and are gross before deductions excluding, generally, the value of incomes in kind, but including bonus and commission payments for the pay period.

Source Department of Economic Development (Northern Ireland)

6.18 Gross weekly and hourly earnings of full-time adults[1]

(*continued*)

Northern Ireland

April of each year

		Gross weekly earnings[2]					Gross hourly earnings[2]				
		Lowest decile	Lower quartile	Median	Upper quartile	Highest decile	Lowest decile	Lower quartile	Median	Upper quartile	Highest decile
		£	£	£	£	£	p	p	p	p	p
All women	1979	39.0	45.4	55.8	72.1	97.6	100.4	114.2	137.4	169.5	212.5
	1980	45.9	54.8	68.7	87.5	118.1	117.6	140.6	172.3	210.4	271.0
	1981	51.2	62.3	78.9	105.1	145.3	132.9	160.2	198.5	245.0	316.8
	1982	54.7	67.3	85.0	112.6	157.7	138.2	169.3	212.2	267.4	339.7
	1983	60.9	73.4	95.4	126.8	166.8	160.7	188.5	235.7	297.8	390.0
	1984	66.0	77.3	99.6	134.9	178.1	173.6	202.1	248.2	321.0	418.3
	1985	72.2	85.9	109.6	148.9	184.3	183.4	216.4	268.3	349.0	447.4
	1986	72.4	89.3	114.4	158.5	199.4	187.1	226.2	279.4	370.5	495.2
	1987	75.2	92.1	123.3	170.7	220.2	199.5	238.4	301.6	400.1	539.8
	1988	80.5	97.7	129.9	181.9	247.0	209.1	248.5	316.6	423.2	567.0
Manual women	1979	36.5	42.2	50.5	60.7	71.8	96.0	109.2	127.3	147.6	172.5
	1980	43.5	50.2	60.4	75.1	88.4	113.5	130.2	156.8	185.2	211.0
	1981	48.3	56.9	69.2	84.1	100.9	130.1	147.9	177.5	209.8	247.4
	1982	52.6	61.1	72.8	90.6	112.3	136.9	156.3	187.3	226.1	274.3
	1983	55.9	65.7	77.5	95.5	115.1	147.0	169.1	198.6	241.3	291.5
	1984	60.8	68.7	81.3	97.4	117.4	162.3	181.6	208.8	248.4	294.5
	1985	65.5	75.8	90.0	109.4	143.8	169.5	193.2	228.3	275.9	345.2
	1986	63.7	75.4	93.3	111.6	144.6	176.1	198.3	235.6	282.9	336.6
	1987	70.9	79.7	99.6	121.2	157.0	187.0	213.7	250.6	305.7	371.4
	1988	75.8	85.6	106.4	129.6	149.2	200.6	225.7	270.1	325.7	383.4
Non-manual women	1979	40.8	48.0	59.6	80.2	100.0	103.6	120.0	146.5	186.3	234.5
	1980	49.5	58.6	73.8	97.7	125.6	126.8	145.9	184.0	226.4	303.5
	1981	53.1	64.4	84.4	116.9	158.2	135.0	166.3	210.8	264.8	361.3
	1982	57.7	72.0	90.5	124.1	160.3	139.2	177.9	229.4	281.9	371.3
	1983	66.1	81.9	103.6	141.3	176.4	170.1	207.0	256.5	332.5	434.4
	1984	71.4	87.3	109.9	149.2	188.8	186.5	218.5	275.3	356.9	454.8
	1985	77.3	92.2	121.4	163.9	200.4	197.4	236.5	294.8	383.4	472.6
	1986	79.6	98.4	128.7	179.9	210.1	204.5	250.9	316.0	418.4	524.1
	1987	82.0	100.8	137.1	191.8	234.3	209.6	255.0	338.8	442.7	584.0
	1988	86.2	106.4	147.4	213.7	264.7	227.0	269.3	361.3	476.7	630.4
As percentages of the corresponding median		Percentage					Percentage				
All women	1979	*70.0*	*81.5*	*100.0*	*129.4*	*175.1*	*73.0*	*83.1*	*100.0*	*123.4*	*154.6*
	1980	*66.8*	*79.7*	*100.0*	*127.3*	*171.9*	*68.2*	*81.6*	*100.0*	*122.2*	*157.3*
	1981	*64.9*	*78.9*	*100.0*	*133.2*	*184.0*	*66.9*	*80.7*	*100.0*	*123.4*	*159.6*
	1982	*64.4*	*79.1*	*100.0*	*132.5*	*185.4*	*65.1*	*79.8*	*100.0*	*126.0*	*160.1*
	1983	*63.9*	*77.0*	*100.0*	*132.9*	*174.9*	*68.2*	*80.0*	*100.0*	*126.4*	*165.5*
	1984	*66.3*	*77.6*	*100.0*	*135.4*	*178.7*	*70.0*	*81.4*	*100.0*	*129.3*	*168.5*
	1985	*65.9*	*78.4*	*100.0*	*135.9*	*168.2*	*68.4*	*80.7*	*100.0*	*130.1*	*166.7*
	1986	*63.3*	*78.1*	*100.0*	*138.5*	*174.3*	*67.0*	*81.0*	*100.0*	*132.6*	*177.2*
	1987	*60.9*	*74.7*	*100.0*	*138.4*	*178.6*	*66.1*	*79.0*	*100.0*	*132.7*	*178.9*
	1988	*62.0*	*75.2*	*100.0*	*140.0*	*190.1*	*66.0*	*78.5*	*100.0*	*133.7*	*179.1*
Manual women	1979	*72.2*	*83.6*	*100.0*	*120.2*	*142.2*	*75.4*	*85.7*	*100.0*	*115.9*	*135.5*
	1980	*71.9*	*83.1*	*100.0*	*124.3*	*146.2*	*72.4*	*83.0*	*100.0*	*118.1*	*134.6*
	1981	*69.8*	*82.2*	*100.0*	*121.5*	*145.8*	*73.3*	*83.3*	*100.0*	*118.2*	*139.4*
	1982	*72.2*	*83.8*	*100.0*	*124.4*	*154.1*	*73.1*	*83.4*	*100.0*	*120.7*	*146.5*
	1983	*72.1*	*84.8*	*100.0*	*123.2*	*148.5*	*74.0*	*85.2*	*100.0*	*121.5*	*146.8*
	1984	*74.7*	*84.5*	*100.0*	*119.8*	*144.4*	*77.8*	*87.0*	*100.0*	*119.0*	*141.1*
	1985	*72.8*	*84.2*	*100.0*	*121.5*	*159.8*	*74.3*	*84.6*	*100.0*	*120.9*	*151.2*
	1986	*68.3*	*80.8*	*100.0*	*119.6*	*155.0*	*74.7*	*84.2*	*100.0*	*120.1*	*142.9*
	1987	*71.2*	*80.0*	*100.0*	*121.7*	*157.6*	*74.6*	*85.3*	*100.0*	*122.0*	*148.2*
	1988	*71.2*	*80.5*	*100.0*	*121.8*	*140.2*	*74.3*	*83.6*	*100.0*	*120.6*	*141.9*
Non-manual women	1979	*68.6*	*80.6*	*100.0*	*134.7*	*167.8*	*70.7*	*81.9*	*100.0*	*127.1*	*160.1*
	1980	*67.1*	*79.4*	*100.0*	*132.5*	*170.2*	*68.9*	*79.3*	*100.0*	*123.0*	*164.9*
	1981	*62.9*	*76.3*	*100.0*	*138.5*	*187.4*	*64.0*	*78.9*	*100.0*	*125.6*	*171.4*
	1982	*63.7*	*79.6*	*100.0*	*137.0*	*177.1*	*60.7*	*77.5*	*100.0*	*122.9*	*161.9*
	1983	*63.8*	*79.1*	*100.0*	*136.4*	*170.3*	*66.3*	*80.7*	*100.0*	*129.6*	*169.4*
	1984	*65.0*	*79.5*	*100.0*	*135.8*	*171.9*	*67.8*	*79.4*	*100.0*	*129.6*	*165.2*
	1985	*63.6*	*75.9*	*100.0*	*135.0*	*165.0*	*67.0*	*80.2*	*100.0*	*130.1*	*160.3*
	1986	*61.8*	*76.5*	*100.0*	*139.8*	*163.2*	*64.7*	*79.4*	*100.0*	*132.4*	*165.9*
	1987	*59.8*	*73.5*	*100.0*	*140.0*	*171.0*	*61.9*	*75.3*	*100.0*	*130.7*	*172.4*
	1988	*58.5*	*72.2*	*100.0*	*145.0*	*179.6*	*62.8*	*74.5*	*100.0*	*131.9*	*174.5*

See footnotes on page 129

Source *Department of Economic Development (Northern Ireland)*

6.19 Average earnings by age group of full-time employees whose pay for the survey pay-period was not affected by absence

Great Britain

New Earnings Survey April 1988

	Gross weekly earnings								Average weekly hours[1]		Average hourly earnings excluding overtime pay[1]
	Average		As percentage of the median		Median	As percentage of the median		Percentage earning under £120			
	Total	Overtime pay	Lowest decile	Lower quartile		Upper quartile	Highest decile		Total	Normal basic	
	£	£			£						p
All males											
Under 18	89.3	6.4	66.1	79.7	83.1	124.2	158.5	85.6	41.0	38.7	213.3
18 to 20	131.6	12.4	66.6	80.2	121.3	127.8	159.8	48.7	41.7	38.6	308.3
21 to 24	179.6	18.1	64.5	79.5	166.1	126.1	157.0	16.6	42.1	38.5	417.5
25 to 29	222.5	21.6	63.4	78.9	202.6	128.0	163.1	7.2	42.2	38.3	519.6
30 to 39	265.5	22.4	60.2	76.8	238.8	129.2	169.1	4.1	42.0	38.1	625.0
40 to 49	283.0	22.6	60.1	75.9	248.2	133.5	178.6	3.3	42.2	38.1	663.2
50 to 59	255.5	20.5	61.0	76.4	220.9	135.1	182.7	5.4	42.1	38.3	595.5
60 to 64	217.1	17.8	63.9	78.8	189.2	129.3	177.2	9.6	42.2	38.6	498.7
All ages	241.6	20.6	57.0	74.8	212.3	134.8	180.3	9.7	42.1	38.3	562.9
Manual males											
Under 18	87.4	7.3	65.6	79.3	81.0	125.2	159.1	86.9	42.0	39.4	201.8
18 to 20	132.1	15.3	65.3	80.1	121.9	129.4	160.9	48.3	43.2	39.2	297.8
21 to 24	173.2	23.7	64.9	79.6	162.1	125.8	155.5	18.1	44.2	39.3	381.2
25 to 29	196.7	30.2	65.4	80.0	183.1	125.8	157.0	10.2	45.0	39.2	423.1
30 to 39	213.4	35.0	65.3	79.9	200.3	125.3	155.9	6.6	45.5	39.1	453.7
40 to 49	219.1	36.2	65.6	79.8	205.7	124.6	154.4	5.2	45.7	39.1	464.9
50 to 59	203.0	31.0	66.0	80.2	190.1	125.1	154.7	7.8	44.9	39.1	438.5
60 to 64	184.5	25.2	67.1	80.8	173.7	123.2	151.8	11.6	44.1	39.1	407.2
All ages	196.6	30.3	60.7	77.8	185.0	126.9	158.2	12.9	44.9	39.1	423.2
Non-manual males											
Under 18	94.4	4.2	69.2	81.0	87.8	124.4	160.6	82.2	38.3	37.1	245.7
18 to 20	130.9	7.2	68.9	80.5	120.4	124.4	156.4	49.6	38.9	37.3	328.8
21 to 24	188.4	10.3	64.5	79.3	172.3	126.8	160.7	14.5	39.1	37.4	472.3
25 to 29	249.7	12.6	63.4	79.4	225.6	128.1	164.0	4.1	39.1	37.2	632.9
30 to 39	312.1	11.2	62.6	79.8	277.3	127.4	170.1	1.9	38.6	37.2	801.8
40 to 49	343.3	9.7	60.0	77.8	302.3	129.9	176.7	1.5	38.5	37.1	885.3
50 to 59	317.6	8.0	57.3	74.5	277.6	133.6	182.2	2.7	38.4	37.2	813.7
60 to 64	269.7	5.8	60.2	76.8	226.7	139.4	192.3	6.4	38.5	37.5	675.4
All ages	290.9	9.9	54.0	73.5	257.6	133.0	179.7	6.1	38.7	37.2	739.5
All females											
Under 18	87.4	2.7	69.5	82.1	81.1	127.4	157.8	86.3	38.0	37.2	228.5
18 to 20	110.3	3.4	72.6	85.4	103.9	121.6	148.9	69.3	38.1	37.2	287.4
21 to 24	143.2	5.0	68.2	80.7	134.6	123.7	150.2	35.8	38.1	37.1	371.8
25 to 29	177.3	5.4	62.9	77.5	163.0	127.5	162.1	20.2	37.7	36.8	464.9
30 to 39	186.3	4.7	58.1	73.8	170.1	135.4	165.9	21.6	37.2	36.3	494.1
40 to 49	173.3	4.6	62.9	77.0	152.3	141.0	179.1	26.8	37.3	36.4	454.2
50 to 59	166.5	3.6	63.9	78.1	144.7	139.5	184.5	30.7	37.2	36.4	435.8
60 to 64	160.3	3.5	60.8	79.2	139.2	133.2	187.6	34.8	37.3	36.4	423.0
All ages	161.6	4.5	62.5	76.7	143.2	136.7	178.4	32.8	37.6	36.7	421.8
Manual females											
Under 18	85.3	3.4	67.7	81.8	81.4	121.6	151.7	88.8	39.8	38.7	213.6
18 to 20	101.9	4.6	68.6	83.5	97.7	122.1	145.6	75.6	40.0	38.6	253.1
21 to 24	121.7	6.5	69.5	81.7	114.7	122.8	151.8	55.1	40.1	38.4	298.2
25 to 29	132.0	7.1	69.7	82.3	122.7	124.2	156.2	46.4	40.1	38.3	322.7
30 to 39	129.2	7.8	66.5	79.9	120.6	123.7	157.0	49.3	40.0	38.2	317.6
40 to 49	127.5	8.8	68.6	81.5	119.6	123.7	152.9	50.5	39.9	37.8	314.3
50 to 59	122.2	6.1	70.0	82.4	114.9	123.3	152.3	55.5	39.2	37.7	309.7
60 to 64	117.8	7.2	68.7	82.8	109.1	126.6	162.0	62.2	39.0	37.1	249.9
All ages	121.9	6.9	68.5	81.0	114.2	124.1	154.7	55.8	39.8	38.1	301.6

1 The estimates given relate to employees for whom normal basic hours were reported.

Source *Department of Employment*

6.19 (continued) Average earnings by age group of full-time employees whose pay for the survey pay-period was not affected by absence

Great Britain

New Earnings Survey April 1988

	Gross weekly earnings								Average weekly hours[1]		Average hourly earnings excluding overtime pay[1]
	Average		As percentage of the median		Median	As percentage of the median		Percentage earning under £120	Total	Normal basic	
	Total	Overtime pay	Lowest decile	Lower quartile		Upper quartile	Highest decile				
	£	£			£						*p*
Non-manual females											
Under 18	88.1	2.4	*70.2*	*82.2*	81.0	*130.5*	*162.6*	*85.3*	37.3	36.6	234.6
18 to 20	112.9	3.0	*73.2*	*86.0*	105.6	*121.9*	*150.0*	*67.3*	37.5	36.8	298.5
21 to 24	148.2	4.6	*69.1*	*81.0*	139.6	*122.4*	*150.0*	*31.2*	37.6	36.8	389.4
25 to 29	185.6	5.0	*63.9*	*79.0*	171.6	*125.2*	*159.1*	*15.3*	37.3	36.5	491.7
30 to 39	199.3	4.0	*58.1*	*74.1*	186.6	*130.4*	*157.7*	*15.3*	36.6	35.9	537.2
40 to 49	188.0	3.2	*62.0*	*76.4*	168.7	*140.4*	*168.2*	*19.2*	36.5	35.9	503.7
50 to 59	185.1	2.5	*63.0*	*77.1*	164.0	*141.8*	*175.7*	*20.4*	36.4	35.9	494.7
60 to 64	178.8	1.9	*64.5*	*79.7*	154.8	*136.2*	*181.8*	*22.9*	36.5	36.1	482.8
All ages	172.6	3.8	*61.7*	*76.0*	154.4	*136.6*	*173.8*	*26.4*	36.9	36.3	457.3

1 The estimates given relate to employees for whom normal basic hours were reported.

Source *Department of Employment*

6.20 Trade unions[1, 2]

United Kingdom

At end of year

per cent

	1977	1978	1979	1980	1981	1982	1983	1984	1985	1986	1987
Number of trade unions	481	462	453	438	414	408	394	375	370	335	330
Analysis by number of members:											
Under 100 members	15.4	15.6	16.1	15.8	17.1	19.1	17.8	17.6	16.8	18.5	16.1
100 and under 500	30.1	29.2	27.4	26.9	28.0	24.3	26.4	25.1	25.1	24.2	25.8
500 and under 1 000	9.4	10.4	10.4	10.3	9.9	11.8	10.7	10.1	10.0	9.0	7.9
1 000 and under 2 500	13.7	13.4	12.8	12.8	12.1	12.5	14.4	14.9	14.9	14.9	15.8
2 500 and under 5 000	8.5	8.0	9.5	8.9	8.9	9.3	7.9	8.8	7.3	6.6	6.7
5 000 and under 10 000	5.8	5.6	5.3	5.7	5.6	5.6	4.5	4.3	3.8	4.8	4.8
10 000 and under 15 000	2.1	1.9	1.5	1.6	1.0	0.7	0.5	0.8	1.1	1.5	1.8
15 000 and under 25 000	2.7	3.0	4.2	4.8	3.6	4.4	5.1	4.0	3.0	3.0	3.3
25 000 and under 50 000	3.7	4.1	3.3	4.3	4.1	3.7	3.8	5.1	6.2	7.5	7.3
50 000 and under 100 000	3.1	3.0	3.5	3.2	3.4	3.2	3.3	3.5	2.4	2.1	2.1
100 000 and under 250 000	3.1	3.2	3.5	3.4	3.4	2.7	3.0	3.5	3.8	4.5	3.9
250 000 and over	2.3	2.4	2.4	2.3	2.9	2.7	2.5	2.4	2.7	2.7	3.3
Membership unknown[3]	–	–	–	–	–	–	–	–	3.2	0.9	1.2
All sizes	100	100	100	100	100	100	100	100	100	100	100
Membership[4] (Thousands)											
Analysis by size of union:											
Under 100 members	–	–	–	–	–	–	–	–	–	–	–
100 and under 500	0.3	0.3	0.2	0.2	0.2	0.2	0.2	0.2	0.2	0.2	0.2
500 and under 1 000	0.2	0.3	0.3	0.2	0.3	0.3	0.2	0.2	0.2	0.2	0.2
1 000 and under 2 500	0.8	0.8	0.7	0.7	0.7	0.7	0.8	0.8	0.8	0.8	0.8
2 500 and under 5 000	1.1	1.0	1.2	1.1	1.0	1.1	1.0	1.0	0.9	0.7	0.8
5 000 and under 10 000	1.4	1.3	1.2	1.3	1.3	1.3	1.0	1.0	0.8	1.0	1.0
10 000 and under 15 000	1.0	0.9	0.6	0.6	0.4	0.4	0.2	0.3	0.4	0.6	0.7
15 000 and under 25 000	2.0	2.0	2.7	3.0	2.9	3.1	3.6	2.7	1.9	1.8	2.1
25 000 and under 50 000	5.0	5.4	4.2	5.6	5.0	4.7	4.9	6.0	7.5	8.6	8.4
50 000 and under 100 000	7.9	7.2	7.6	7.9	7.9	8.4	8.6	8.9	6.1	5.2	5.3
100 000 and under 250 000	17.1	17.3	18.0	19.4	17.9	16.1	18.6	22.3	22.8	25.2	20.3
250 000 and over	63.1	63.6	63.4	59.9	62.2	63.7	60.9	56.5	58.4	55.6	60.3
All sizes	100	100	100	100	100	100	100	100	100	100	100
Total	12 846	13 112	13 289	12 947	12 106	11 593	11 236	10 994	10 821	10 539	10 475

1 The statistics relate to all organisations of employees with head offices in the United Kingdom—including those of salaried and professional workers, as well as those of manual wage-earners—which are known to include among their functions that of negotiating with employers with the object of regulating the conditions of employment of their members.

2 Figures are confined to organisations which appear to satisfy the statutory definition of trade union in Section 28 of the Trade Union and Labour Relations Act 1974. This has had the effect of excluding 31 organisations which were previously regarded by the Department as trade unions e.g. organisations representing members of the police service which are specifically excluded from the statutory definition by Section 30 of the 1974 Act.

3 There were 4 unions in 1987 whose membership was not reported, one of which was newly formed in 1987.

4 The figures of membership include the membership of branches in the Irish Republic and overseas but wholly exclude the membership of unions whose headquarters are situated outside the United Kingdom. A small number of people who are members of more than one union are included more than once in the figures, but the effect on the aggregates is relatively insignificant.

Source *Department of Employment*

7 Defence

This section includes figures on Defence expenditure, on the size and role of the Armed Forces and on related support activities.

Much of the material in this section can be found in Volume 2 of the *Statement on the Defence Estimates 1989* (*Defence Statistics*) (CM. 675 – II) (HMSO 1989).

Formation of the Armed Forces (*Table 7.1*). This table shows the number of units which comprise the 'teeth' elements of the Armed Forces and excludes supporting units. Greater detail for the current year is given in Volume I of the *Statement on the Defence Estimates 1989* (CM. 675 – I).

Service personnel (*Tables 7.3 to 7.6 and 7.10*). The Regular Forces consist entirely of volunteer members serving on a whole-time basis. The figures for females consist of all members of the Women's Services (ie WRNS, WRAC and WRAF) and female members of the Nursing Services. Certain male members of the RAF Medical Branch were transferred to the Princess Mary's RAF Nursing Service on 1 April 1980 and certain members of the RN Medical specialisation were transferred to the Queen Alexandra's Royal Naval Nursing Service on 1 April 1983 as a result of reorganisations. They continue to be shown in the male figures in Table 7.3 and are now included in the Nursing Services figures in Table 7.10. Certain professionally qualified female officers are not commissioned in the Women's Service, but in the appropriate branch or corps (ie medical, dental, legal, veterinary) and are not accounted for in the female figures. There were 236 such officers on 1 January 1989.

Locally Entered Personnel are recruited outside the United Kingdom for whole-time service in special formations with special conditions of service and normally restricted locations. The Brigade of Gurkhas is an example.

The Regular Forces are supported by Reserves and Auxiliary Forces. There are both regular and volunteer Reserves. Regular Reserves consist of former Service personnel with a Reserve liability. Volunteer Reserves are open to both former Service personnel and civilians. The call out liabilities of the various reserve forces differ in accordance with their roles.

All three Services run cadet forces for young people and the Combined Cadet Force, which is found in certain schools where education is continued to the age of 17 or above, may operate sections for any or all of the Services.

Deployment of Service personnel (*Table 7.6*). The source from which the individual national totals are compiled is different from that used to obtain the total United Kingdom strength and consequently the figures for England, Wales, Scotland and Northern Ireland do not add up to the United Kingdom figure. Royal Navy and Royal Marines personnel on board ship are included in the United Kingdom figure if the ship was in home waters on the situation date or otherwise against the appropriate overseas area. The overseas figures include personnel who are on loan to countries in the areas shown.

Service married accommodation and Defence land holdings (*Table 7.7*). Accommodation is provided for Service families in the United Kingdom and abroad, partly by building to approved standards and partly by renting accommodation. Permanent holdings in the United Kingdom include a small number of unfurnished hirings taken on from local authorities which are not recorded separately. Multiple hirings relate to accommodation built by private developers and leased by the Federal German Authorities and the Government of Gibraltar on behalf of British Forces.

The table also presents statistics of land and foreshore in the United Kingdom owned by the Ministry of Defence or over which it has limited rights under grants or licences. Land declared as surplus to Defence requirements is also included. At 1 April 1988 about 2 277 hectares were awaiting disposal by the Property Services Agency.

Civilian personnel (*Table 7.8*). This table gives an analysis of the number of civilians employed in the various management areas, viz Centre (those authorities not in the Service Departments, the Procurement Executive (PE) or the Royal Ordnance Factories (ROFs)), Royal Dockyards, Other Navy, Army, Royal Air Force (including the Meteorological Office), PE and ROFs. The attribution of civilian staff can change according to circumstances so that figures for successive years may not always be comparable.

Attention is drawn to the fact that the Royal Ordnance Factories changed from being part of MoD to independent Companies Act status on 2 January 1985. Staff employed at the factories are excluded from the MoD strengths from that date.

Some civilians from the United Kingdom serve tours of duty overseas. There were 5 504 such civilians serving abroad on 1 April 1989. Other civilian staff are engaged overseas to work locally as circumstances demand.

In addition Department of the Environment staff directly engaged on the Defence programme totalled 16 376 on 1 April 1989.

Health (*Tables 7.9 to 7.11*). The Services operate a number of hospitals in this country and in areas abroad where there is a significant British military presence. These hospitals take as patients members of all three Services and their dependants; in addition the hospitals in the United Kingdom take civilian patients under arrangements agreed with the National Health Service. Medical support is also supplied by Service medical staff at individual units, ships and stations.

Sickness, medical discharges and deaths of UK Service personnel (*Table 7.11*). It should be noted that, whereas the Royal Navy and Royal Air Force content is for all episodes of bedded sickness lasting two days or more terminating in the year, that for the Army covers only those cases admitted to medical units (including hospitals) for two days or more.

Search and rescue (*Table 7.12*). This table covers incidents in which Rescue Co-ordinating Centres (RCCs) in the United Kingdom co-ordinated search and rescue (SAR) action in which elements of the Armed Forces were involved. The table also includes urgent medical incidents in which the Forces SAR facilities gave assistance (eg inter-hospital transfers).

Defence services and the civilian community (*Table 7.13*). The Ministry of Defence helps the civil community in a variety of ways, for example by providing assistance in time of natural disasters or other emergencies and by undertaking community projects which are of training value to the Services. In some cases facilities established primarily for defence purposes also provide benefits to the general public. Overall figures are not available, but the table presents information on a number of these activities and facilities.

Service assistance may be provided during an industrial dispute at the request of the civil ministries in order to maintain services essential to the life of the community (eg maintenance of emergency fire services in 1977/78).

The Royal Navy Fishery Protection squadron operates within the United Kingdom fishery limits on behalf of Fishery departments, who pay some of the running costs of the squadron.

The Hydrographer of the Navy is the national authority responsible for hydrographic and oceanographic surveys and nautical charting. The Admiralty chart series comprises some 3 400 basic charts and 600 latticed versions covering the whole world.

Defence energy consumption (*Table 7.14*). Consumption is expressed in terms of the System International (SI) unit of energy, the joule. The table has been re-designed to distinguish between fuels used for operational purposes and non-operational purposes.

7.1 Formation of the Armed Forces
At 1 April

Number

	Unit[1]	1979	1980	1981	1982	1983	1984	1985	1986	1987	1988	1989
Royal Navy[2]												
Submarines	Vessels	22	23	22	22	21	22	24	26	26	24	26
Carriers and assault ships	Vessels	3	4	3	3	4	4	4	4	3	3	4
Cruisers and destroyers	Vessels	11	10	12	11	13	13	46	47	46	42	39
Frigates	Vessels	42	39	36	38	42	39					
Mine counter-measure[3]	Vessels	35	35	32	33	36	34	32	39	36	35	36
Patrol ships and craft	Vessels	19	23	22	21	25	31	28	32	28	31	34
Fixed wing aircraft	Squadrons	–	2	3	3	3	3	3	3	3	3	3
Helicopters	Squadrons	13	14	14	15	13	12	14	14	14	14	14
Royal Marines	Commandos	4	4	3	3	3	3	3	3	3	3	3
Army[4, 5]												
Royal Armoured Corps	Regiments	19	19	19	19	19	19	19	19	19	19	19
Royal Artillery	Regiments	22	22	22	22	22	22	22	22	22	22	22
Royal Engineers[6]	Regiments	9	10	11	11	12	12	13	13	13	13	13
Infantry[6]	Battalions	56	56	56	57	56	56	56	56	55	55	55
Special Air Service	Regiments	1	1	1	1	1	1	1	1	1	1	1
Army Air Corps	Regiments	6	6	6	6	4	4	4	4	4	4	4
Royal Air Force[4]												
Strike/attack	Squadrons	14	15	15	12	10	11	11	11	11	11	11
Offensive support	Squadrons	5	5	5	5	5	5	5	5	5	5	5
Air defence	Squadrons	9	9	9	9	9	8	9	9	9	9	9
Maritime patrol	Squadrons	4	4	4	4	4	4	4	4	4	4	4
Reconnaissance	Squadrons	5	5	5	3	2	3	3	3	3	3	3
Airborne early warning	Squadrons	1	1	1	1	1	1	1	1	1	1	1
Transport[7]	Squadrons	10	10	9	10	11	10	11	12	12	12	12
Tankers	Squadrons	2	2	2	2	3	3	3	4	3	3	3
Search and rescue	Squadrons	3	3	3	3	3	2	2	2	2	2	2
Surface to air missiles	Squadrons	7	8	8	8	8	8	8	8	8	8	8
Ground defence	Squadrons	6	6	6	6	6	5	5	5	5	5	6

1 The number of personnel and the amount of equipment in each vessel, regiment, etc, varies according to the role currently assigned.
2 Excludes vessels undergoing major refit, conversion, or on stand-by, etc.
3 In 1981 four ex-inshore minesweepers used for training are excluded.
4 Regular forces only.
5 Combat Arm major units only.
6 Includes Gurkhas.
7 Includes helicopters.

Source *Ministry of Defence*

7.2 Defence expenditure[1, 2]

£ million

	1977/78	1978/79	1979/80	1980/81	1981/82	1982/83	1983/84	1984/85	1985/86	1986/87	1987/88
Total expenditure at outturn prices[3]	6 787	7 455	9 178	11 182	12 607	14 412	15 487	17 122	17 943	18 163	18 856
of which:											
Expenditure on personnel	3 021	3 293	3 912	4 556	5 058	5 455	5 726	5 983	6 379	6 890	7 212
of the Armed Forces	1 519	1 639	2 099	2 460	2 728	2 914	3 076	3 236	3 510	3 787	4 032
of the retired Armed Forces	361	432	459	503	624	680	777	828	899	980	1 079
of civilian staff	1 141	1 222	1 354	1 593	1 706	1 861	1 873	1 919	1 970	2 123	2 101
Expenditure on equipment	2 565	2 984	3 640	4 885	5 638	6 297	6 939	7 838	8 193	7 885	8 270
Sea systems[4]	672	878	1 110	1 513	1 624	1 730	1 849	2 228	2 499	2 494	2 797
Land systems	612	601	740	904	1 101	1 353	1 475	1 638	1 887	1 759	1 700
Air systems	1 010	1 214	1 427	2 059	2 458	2 640	3 057	3 474	3 296	3 090	3 230
Other	271	291	363	410	456	574	558	498	511	542	543
Other expenditure	1 201	1 178	1 625	1 741	1 910	2 659	2 822	3 302	3 370	3 387	3 374
Works, buildings and land[5]	462	405	599	623	664	832	1 067	1 271	1 413	1 498	1 453
Miscellaneous stores and services	739	773	1 026	1 118	1 246	1 827	1 754	2 031	1 958	1 889	1 921
Total expenditure at constant (1987/88) prices[3]	16 583	16 466	16 966	17 543	17 793	18 875	19 137	19 891	19 863	19 176	18 856

1 Expenditure as given in the annual Appropriation Accounts for the Defence Votes, Class I.
2 Including expenditure of government departments other than the Ministry of Defence in years when these contributed to the Defence budget.
3 Because of changes in the responsibilities of the Ministry of Defence, expenditures in successive years are not necessarily comparable.
4 Prior to 1976/77 the dockyard services element of the sea systems expenditure was included under other equipment. The contractorisation of the dockyards in April 1987 has the effect of increasing sea systems expenditure and decreasing expenditure on personnel and miscellaneous stores and services.
5 Including pay of civilian staff employed in works and building.

Source *Ministry of Defence*

7.3 Defence manpower strengths

At 1 April[1]

Thousands

	1978	1979	1980	1981	1982	1983	1984	1985	1986	1987	1988	1989
UK service personnel												
All services:												
Male	306.1	299.7	304.4	316.8	311.9	305.2	309.7	309.8	306.5	303.7	300.9	295.4
Female	14.6	15.3	16.2	16.9	15.7	15.4	16.2	16.4	16.0	16.2	15.9	16.3
Total	320.7	315.0	320.6	333.8	327.6	320.6	325.9	326.2	322.5	319.8	316.9	311.6
Royal Navy:												
Male	63.8	61.2	60.5	62.3	61.1	60.1	59.8	59.1	56.8	55.3	54.3	53.5
Female	4.0	3.8	3.8	4.1	4.0	3.9	3.9	3.7	3.4	3.4	3.3	3.5
Total	67.8	65.1	64.4	66.4	65.1	64.0	63.7	62.8	60.3	58.7	57.7	57.0
Royal Marines:												
Male	7.5	7.4	7.6	7.9	7.9	7.8	7.6	7.6	7.6	7.8	7.8	7.7
Total	7.5	7.4	7.6	7.9	7.9	7.8	7.6	7.6	7.6	7.8	7.8	7.7
Army:												
Male	155.1	150.4	152.8	159.4	157.2	152.9	155.0	155.6	154.8	153.2	151.8	149.1
Female	5.7	5.8	6.3	6.6	6.0	6.1	6.6	6.8	6.6	6.5	6.3	6.5
Total	160.8	156.2	159.0	166.0	163.2	159.1	161.5	162.4	161.4	159.7	158.1	155.6
Royal Air Force:												
Male	79.7	80.7	83.5	87.2	85.7	84.5	87.3	87.5	87.2	87.3	87.0	85.1
Female	4.9	5.6	6.1	6.3	5.8	5.4	5.7	6.0	6.0	6.3	6.3	6.3
Total	84.6	86.3	89.6	93.5	91.5	89.8	93.1	93.4	93.2	93.6	93.3	91.4
Personnel locally entered overseas:												
Total	8.4	8.4	8.2	9.7	10.1	10.1	10.1	10.2	10.1	9.8	9.4	9.1
Regular Reserves:[1]												
Royal Navy	26.3	28.4	27.0	26.8	24.8	23.9	23.5	23.3	24.2	24.5	24.7	25.1
Royal Marines	2.4	2.4	2.2	2.2	2.2	2.2	2.2	2.2	2.3	2.3	2.4	2.5
Army	118.5	127.0	133.1	137.5	140.2	138.3	143.2	150.2	153.9	160.4	167.7	175.3
Royal Air Force	32.3	30.8	30.3	30.1	29.3	28.9	29.0	29.8	31.5	33.7	35.4	37.5
Total	179.5	188.5	192.6	196.5	196.4	193.4	198.0	205.5	211.6	220.9	230.2	240.4
Volunteer Reserves and Auxiliary Forces:												
Royal Navy	5.5	5.4	5.1	5.4	5.4	5.4	5.2	5.2	5.5	5.7	5.6	5.6
Royal Marines	1.0	0.8	0.8	0.9	1.0	1.1	1.1	1.1	1.2	1.2	1.3	1.2
Territorial Army	60.6	59.4	63.3	69.5	72.1	72.8	71.4	73.7	77.7	78.5	74.7	72.5
Ulster Defence Regiment	7.9	7.6	7.4	7.5	7.1	7.1	6.8	6.4	6.6	6.5	6.4	6.3
Home Service Force	–	–	–	–	–	0.3	0.3	0.9	3.0	3.3	3.1	3.0
Royal Air Force	0.4	0.3	0.5	0.6	0.6	0.8	1.1	1.2	1.4	1.6	1.8	1.7
Total[1]	75.3	73.4	77.1	84.0	86.3	87.5	85.9	88.6	95.4	96.8	92.8	90.4
Cadet Forces:[1, 2]												
Royal Navy	25.0	23.9	29.1	31.1	28.7	29.4	28.4	28.4	28.0	27.5	27.1	26.5
Army	73.4	72.6	74.6	75.1	74.1	74.5	73.8	72.1	70.9	71.2	69.3	65.9
Royal Air Force	43.8	43.5	44.1	44.4	45.9	45.1	44.3	44.1	44.5	47.0	48.3	46.7
Total	142.2	140.0	147.8	150.6	148.7	149.0	146.5	144.7	143.4	145.7	144.6	139.2

1 A few of the figures for reserves and cadets were collected at irregular intervals and do not necessarily refer to 1 April; they are the latest figures available at that date.

2 Combined Cadet Force cadets are included under the relevant service.

Source Ministry of Defence

7.4 Recruitment of UK Service personnel to each Service

Number

	1978/79	1979/80	1980/81	1981/82	1982/83	1983/84	1984/85	1985/86	1986/87	1987/88	1988/89
All services:											
Male	38 774	46 206	46 693	21 188	19 342	33 760	32 076	30 407	31 147	31 215	30 862
Female	4 592	4 446	3 795	1 419	2 305	3 231	2 645	2 244	2 902	2 611	3 001
Total	43 366	50 652	50 488	22 607	21 647	36 991	34 721	32 651	34 049	33 826	33 863
Royal Navy:											
Male	5 978	7 701	8 130	3 353	3 078	4 223	4 231	3 987	4 791	4 601	4 598
Female	813	825	958	452	506	562	351	289	545	580	700
Total	6 791	8 526	9 088	3 805	3 584	4 785	4 582	4 276	5 336	5 181	5 298
Royal Marines:											
Male	1 282	1 676	1 674	699	447	447	954	1 093	1 233	991	937
Total	1 282	1 676	1 674	699	447	447	954	1 093	1 233	991	937
Army:											
Male	23 528	27 164	27 241	13 603	11 679	20 811	20 914	19 173	18 718	19 895	19 921
Female	1 726	2 025	1 630	601	1 392	1 537	1 364	1 095	1 200	1 146	1 427
Total	25 254	29 189	28 871	14 204	13 071	22 348	22 278	20 268	19 918	21 041	21 348
Royal Air Force:											
Male	7 986	9 665	9 648	3 533	4 138	8 279	5 977	6 154	6 405	5 728	5 406
Female	2 053	1 596	1 207	366	407	1 132	930	860	1 157	885	874
Total	10 039	11 261	10 855	3 899	4 545	9 411	6 907	7 014	7 562	6 613	6 280

Source Ministry of Defence

7.5 Outflow of UK Service personnel from each Service

Number

	1978/79	1979/80	1980/81	1981/82	1982/83	1983/84	1984/85	1985/86	1986/87	1987/88	1988/89
All Services:											
Male	45 369	41 465	34 438	26 799	26 108	29 468	32 095	33 881	34 194	34 054	36 556
Female	3 937	3 577	3 097	2 652	2 549	2 458	2 459	2 640	2 767	2 884	2 722
Total	49 306	45 042	37 535	29 451	28 657	31 926	34 554	36 521	36 961	36 938	39 278
Royal Navy:											
Male	8 828	8 314	6 563	5 131	4 085	4 514	5 011	6 356	6 295	5 603	5 382
Female	975	841	778	577	532	581	561	559	624	621	588
Total	9 803	9 155	7 341	5 708	4 617	5 095	5 572	6 915	6 919	6 224	5 970
Royal Marines:											
Male	1 348	1 568	1 347	781	625	701	913	1 088	1 068	1 007	1 095
Total	1 348	1 568	1 347	781	625	701	913	1 088	1 068	1 007	1 095
Army:											
Male	28 162	24 753	20 627	15 878	15 960	18 854	20 286	19 999	20 473	21 393	22 834
Female	1 645	1 595	1 292	1 216	1 218	1 105	1 162	1 302	1 288	1 356	1 222
Total	29 807	26 348	21 919	17 094	17 178	19 959	21 448	21 301	21 761	22 749	24 056
Royal Air Force:											
Male	7 031	6 830	5 901	5 009	5 438	5 399	5 885	6 438	6 358	6 051	7 245
Female	1 317	1 141	1 027	859	799	772	736	779	855	907	912
Total	8 348	7 971	6 928	5 868	6 237	6 171	6 621	7 217	7 213	6 958	8 157

Source *Ministry of Defence*

7.6 Deployment of Service personnel
At 1 July

Thousands

	1978	1979	1980	1981	1982	1983	1984	1985	1986	1987	1988
UK Service personnel, Regular Forces:											
In United Kingdom	230.2	232.2	238.1	245.0	215.2	228.8	230.4	229.6	228.3	228.1	226.2
England[1]	192.7	192.6	200.0	207.7	195.9	195.1	194.5	193.3	191.7	190.9	189.8
Wales[1]	6.3	6.3	6.9	6.3	6.1	6.1	6.2	6.3	6.3	6.1	5.8
Scotland[1]	19.3	19.0	18.1	18.9	19.0	18.7	20.6	20.1	19.7	19.6	19.3
Northern Ireland[2]	14.4	13.6	11.9	11.6	10.9	10.2	10.0	9.7	10.5	11.4	11.2
Overseas	91.7	84.9	87.6	91.3	109.8	94.0	96.1	96.9	94.1	91.3	90.4
Federal Republic of Germany[3]	65.7	64.6	65.3	70.4	69.8	67.0	66.7	67.3	66.7	66.8	65.6
Elsewhere in Continental Europe[4]	5.9	5.7	5.7	6.1	6.2	6.1	7.2	7.7	6.3	6.9	6.9
Gibraltar	2.7	2.0	3.2	2.2	2.7	2.0	2.1	2.4	2.3	2.1	1.8
Malta	1.3	–	–	–	–	–	–	–	–	–	–
Cyprus	4.6	4.0	4.7	4.9	4.8	4.9	4.8	4.7	4.9	4.6	4.5
Elsewhere in Mediterranean, Near East and Gulf	0.4	0.4	0.4	1.4	1.1	0.3	1.2	2.3	0.4	1.1	3.4
Hong Kong	2.4	2.4	2.5	2.5	2.5	2.4	2.5	2.4	2.4	2.3	2.3
Singapore	–	–	–	–	–	–	–	–	–	–	–
Elsewhere in the Far East	0.3	1.8	1.7	0.3	0.3	0.7	0.6	0.4	0.3	0.3	0.3
Other locations[1, 5]	8.4	3.9	4.1	3.5	22.4	10.5	11.3	9.8	10.9	7.0	5.6
Total	318.2	314.1	323.4	334.3	324.3	321.7	325.9	325.8	321.7	318.7	315.8
Locally entered service personnel:											
United Kingdom	0.7	0.7	0.9	1.3	0.6	1.2	1.2	1.2	1.3	1.2	1.3
Gibraltar	0.1	0.1	0.1	0.1	0.1	0.1	0.1	0.1	0.1	0.1	0.1
Malta	0.4	–	–	–	–	–	–	–	–	–	–
Hong Kong	5.4	5.8	6.4	6.7	6.6	6.6	6.7	6.7	6.4	6.0	5.8
Brunei	0.8	0.8	0.8	0.8	0.8	0.8	0.8	0.8	0.8	0.8	0.8
Nepal	1.0	1.0	1.1	1.2	1.3	1.4	1.3	1.3	1.4	1.5	1.4
Other locations[6]	–	–	–	–	0.6	–	–	–	–	–	–
Total	8.3	8.3	9.2	10.0	9.9	10.0	10.1	10.1	10.0	9.6	9.4

1 From 1982 the England, Wales and Scotland national figures include personnel who were UK based but temporarily deployed in the South Atlantic. These have been included also in the Overseas numbers against 'Other locations'.
2 The figures for Northern Ireland include all personnel from other parts of the United Kingdom and the British Army of the Rhine who are serving on emergency tours of duty, but exclude the Ulster Defence Regiment.
3 Army personnel serving in Northern Ireland on emergency tours of duty but remaining under the command of the Commander-in-Chief British Army of the Rhine are included in these figures.
4 These figures include personnel stationed in Berlin and Sardinia.
5 These figures include Defence Attaches/Advisers and their staffs.
6 The 1982 figures comprise Gurkha troops serving in the Falkland Islands.

Source *Ministry of Defence*

7.7 Service married accommodation and Defence land holdings

	1979	1980	1981	1982	1983	1984	1985	1986	1987	1988	1989
Married accommodation[1]	Thousand										
United Kingdom: total	95.4	92.7	88.7	87.5	87.0	85.9	85.3	84.3	82.5	81.0	78.5
Permanent holdings	94.7	92.4	88.3	87.2	86.6	85.7	85.0	84.0	82.4	80.9	78.5
Hirings	0.6	0.4	0.3	0.3	0.3	0.3	0.2	0.3	0.1	0.1	–
Overseas: total	46.7	46.5	46.4	46.0	46.0	46.0	47.6	50.3	50.6	47.1	49.3
Permanent holdings	21.2	21.1	21.4	21.4	21.4	21.4	21.5	21.6	21.5	21.1	22.8
Hirings[2]	25.6	25.4	25.0	24.5	24.6	24.6	26.1	28.7	29.1	26.0	26.5
Land holdings[3]	Thousand hectares										
United Kingdom											
Land: freehold	221.1	220.2	220.1	217.8	215.9	215.0	211.1	210.9	210.3	211.1	212.5
leasehold	11.9	11.9	11.9	11.9	11.9	11.6	11.4	10.9	10.9	10.8	10.8
Foreshore: freehold	13.3	13.2	13.2	13.2	13.1	13.1	13.1	13.1	13.1	13.1	13.0
leasehold	4.9	4.9	4.9	4.9	4.9	4.9	4.9	4.9	5.0	5.0	5.0
Rights[4]	31.3	31.1	36.7	36.7	36.7	36.0	36.0	36.2	36.2	99.9	101.1
Defence land (freehold and leasehold)											
Used for agricultural purposes	112.6	113.8	111.9	109.1	109.7	110.0	109.1	107.6	105.5	105.4	109.6
Used for grazing only	61.2	60.2	59.8	58.8	58.8	58.8	58.6	58.1	57.6	56.9	61.4
Full agricultural use	51.4	53.6	52.0	50.3	50.9	51.2	50.5	49.5	47.9	48.5	48.2

1 From 1978 to 1985 at 15 January each year. Before that the different Services collated information at different times, usually between 1 December in the preceding year and 1 March. Due to changes in reporting dates, figures from 1986 are taken as at 30 November of the previous year.
2 Includes multiple hirings.
3 At 1 April each year.
4 The 1988 figure includes the renewal of two leases granting long term rights when in previous years these were on a short term basis and were not included.

Sources Crown Suppliers; Ministry of Defence

7.8 Defence civilian manpower strengths
At 1 April

Thousands

	1979	1980	1981	1982	1983	1984	1985	1986	1987	1988	1989
Ministry of Defence civilians											
UK based[2]	247.7	239.8	229.6	216.9	208.9	199.1	174.1	169.5	164.0	143.3	141.3
Non-industrial	120.6	118.5	113.5	108.1	105.6	103.3	94.9	93.8	93.3	88.5	88.7
Industrial	127.0	121.2	116.1	108.8	103.3	95.8	79.1	75.6	70.7	54.8	52.5
of which											
Centre											
Non-industrial[5]	20.9	20.2	19.0	18.3	14.5	14.1	13.8	13.5	13.3	13.3	17.2
Industrial	0.6	0.6	0.6	0.6	0.6	0.5	0.5	0.5	0.5	0.2	0.3
Royal Dockyards[3]											
Non-industrial	9.1	9.0	8.4	7.6	7.0	6.3	5.6	5.6	5.4	–	–
Industrial	25.0	24.2	23.6	22.4	20.7	18.0	16.7	15.7	14.5	–	–
Other Navy											
Non-industrial	13.8	14.0	13.7	13.1	14.5	14.3	14.6	14.5	15.4	16.4	14.8
Industrial	22.0	21.3	20.3	19.0	18.4	17.2	17.1	16.4	15.8	17.5	17.1
Army											
Non-industrial	26.7	25.7	24.7	23.9	24.2	23.6	22.9	23.0	22.7	22.6	21.9
Industrial	32.0	30.3	28.4	26.3	25.2	24.0	23.3	22.6	20.8	19.1	17.8
Air Force											
Non-industrial	14.4	14.1	14.0	13.4	13.5	13.4	13.2	12.9	12.7	12.7	12.2
Industrial	12.3	11.7	11.5	10.7	10.1	9.5	8.7	8.4	8.1	7.8	7.8
Procurement Executive											
Non-industrial	29.9	29.6	27.8	26.4	26.8	26.3	24.9	24.3	23.9	23.5	22.6
Industrial	17.9	17.4	16.8	15.9	14.9	14.0	12.8	12.0	11.0	10.2	9.5
Royal Ordnance Factories											
Non-industrial	5.9	5.9	5.8	5.4	5.1	5.2	..[4]	..[4]	..[4]	..[4]	..[4]
Industrial	17.1	15.9	15.0	14.0	13.4	12.7	..[4]	..[4]	..[4]	..[4]	..[4]
Locally engaged overseas	38.2	36.4	35.3	34.8	33.8	33.4	32.4	32.2	32.1	31.8	31.2
Non-industrial	11.2	11.0	10.9	10.7	10.5	10.4	10.2	10.3	10.3	10.2	10.2
Industrial	27.1	25.5	24.4	24.1	23.3	23.0	22.2	22.0	21.8	21.6	21.1
Total[1]	285.9	276.2	264.9	251.7	242.7	232.5	206.5	201.7	196.1	175.1	172.5

1 Two part-time employees are counted as one whole-time employee.
2 Including UK-based civilians serving overseas.
3 From 1985 these figures exclude Gibraltar but still include Portsmouth, which is now classified as a Fleet Maintenance Repair Organisation establishment. Following the contractorisation of the Devonport and Rosyth Dockyards on 6 April 1987, staff employed in Naval Bases are now included in the 'Other Navy' figures.
4 See notes on page 133.
5 The 1988 figure includes MDP staff transferred from the rest of MOD and staff transferred from the PSA.

Source Ministry of Defence

7.9 Service hospitals

	1978	1979	1980	1981	1982	1983	1984	1985	1986	1987	1988[4,5]
Average number of beds[1]											
United Kingdom	2 352	2 297	2 287	2 286	2 195	2 113	1 956	1 986	1 959	1 846	1 766
Overseas	1 351	1 243	1 231	1 269	1 252	1 261	1 218	1 184	1 117	1 029	981
Average percentage of beds occupied[2]											
United Kingdom	*63.4*	*67.0*	*65.8*	*64.2*	*61.5*	*61.6*	*63.8*	*62.0*	*59.2*	*57.6*	*57.4*
Overseas	*56.4*	*58.5*	*60.8*	*58.2*	*56.6*	*55.1*	*54.3*	*50.6*	*48.6*	*47.9*	*48.2*
In-patient admissions (thousands)											
United Kingdom:	68.3	72.3	76.0	75.9	71.3	69.9	71.6	75.1	72.1	71.7	75.0
Service personnel	28.4	27.4	28.2	28.6	27.0	26.9	26.9	27.9	26.3	25.9	26.0
Service dependants	14.5	14.4	14.6	14.4	14.1	12.8	12.7	12.6	11.4	10.8	10.2
NHS/Other	25.4	30.5	33.2	32.9	30.2	30.1	32.0	34.6	34.4	35.2	38.9
Overseas:	43.5	42.1	43.8	42.3	42.7	43.6	43.5	41.7	40.6	39.2	38.6
UK Service personnel	12.6	12.4	13.2	12.7	13.6	14.3	14.5	13.8	13.6	12.9	12.8
Service dependants	23.3	20.8	21.8	21.5	23.2	22.9	22.2	22.1	22.2	22.1	21.7
Others	7.6	8.9	8.8	8.1	5.9	6.3	6.8	5.9	4.9	4.2	4.1
Average number of admissions per bed[2]											
United Kingdom	*29.1*	*31.5*	*33.2*	*33.1*	*32.5*	*33.1*	*36.6*	*37.8*	*36.8*	*38.3*	*42.5*
Overseas	*32.2*	*33.9*	*35.6*	*33.4*	*34.1*	*34.5*	*35.7*	*35.3*	*36.4*	*38.1*	*40.7*
Average days in hospital per patient											
United Kingdom	*8.0*	*7.8*	*7.2*	*7.1*	*6.9*	*6.8*	*6.4*	*6.0*	*5.9*	*5.6*	*5.1*
Overseas	*6.4*	*6.3*	*6.2*	*6.4*	*6.1*	*5.8*	*5.6*	*5.2*	*4.9*	*4.6*	*4.5*
Outpatient attendances (thousands)[3]											
United Kingdom	..	366.3	377.5	401.4	399.7	369.4	381.6	373.7	373.8	359.6	364.5
Service personnel	..	115.4	118.4	133.0	134.3	118.0	123.1	119.3	117.2	116.4	120.1
Service dependants	..	71.0	69.3	67.9	65.1	58.5	54.3	48.7	46.2	41.1	38.8
NHS/Others	..	179.9	189.8	200.5	200.2	192.8	204.3	205.7	210.3	202.1	205.6
Overseas	..	235.9	223.1	229.0	232.1	241.1	235.7	229.6	212.9	202.8	187.9
UK Service personnel	..	62.5	60.5	65.5	68.7	73.4	68.0	64.4	59.6	56.5	55.5
Service dependants	..	101.6	96.5	111.8	111.5	116.2	108.2	102.9	96.5	94.0	89.5
Others	..	71.8	66.1	51.7	51.9	51.5	59.5	62.3	56.8	52.2	43.0

1 Up to 1980, these are the numbers of approved beds. From 1981 they are the numbers of available beds.
2 Based on the numbers of beds as defined above.
3 In addition 24 500 patients were seen at outlying clinics of the hospitals and some 9 800 day patients were treated in the UK and 3 800 overseas in 1987.
4 Provisional.
5 Changes to the Statistical package producing 1988 figures have not been fully implemented in certain hospitals, therefore the latest year's figures are not fully comparable with those for earlier years.

Source *Ministry of Defence*

7.10 Strength of uniformed medical staff[1]

At 1 April

Number

	1979	1980	1981	1982	1983	1984	1985	1986	1987	1988	1989
Qualified doctors:											
Royal Navy	282	272	290	295	285	289	283	291	289	283	279
Army	504	496	507	493	507	515	539	549	560	570	547
Royal Air Force	395	408	388	392	373	367	377	370	363	360	350
Total	1 181	1 176	1 185	1 180	1 165	1 171	1 199	1 210	1 212	1 213	1 176
Qualified dentists:											
Royal Navy	91	95	98	101	101	92	92	80	81	80	81
Army	172	173	173	182	197	197	198	197	200	201	200
Royal Air Force	103	108	109	116	108	110	110	112	118	115	117
Total	366	376	380	399	406	399	400	389	399	396	398
Support staff:[2]											
Royal Navy	1 863	1 839	1 818	1 913	1 863	1 747	1 648	1 473	1 329	1 315	1 244
Army	4 420	4 295	4 549	4 688	4 859	5 089	5 121	4 912	4 856	4 716	4 696
Royal Air Force	2 210	2 358	2 300	2 183	2 134	2 081	2 070	2 004	2 020	2 102	2 032
Total	8 493	8 492	8 667	8 784	8 856	8 917	8 839	8 389	8 205	8 133	7 972

1 Includes staff employed at units (including ships) and in hospitals.
2 Includes all members of the Nursing Services /Nursing corps.

Source *Ministry of Defence*

7.11 Sickness, medical discharges and deaths of United Kingdom Service personnel[1]

	ICD codes[2]	1978	1979	1980	1981	1982	1983	1984	1985	1986	1987	1988[3]
Average strength: (Thousands)		318.5	316.2	325.2	333.8	325.0	322.4	326.3	325.5	322.2	319.1	315.7
Male		303.7	300.7	308.7	317.1	309.5	306.6	309.8	309.0	305.8	302.8	299.6
Female		14.8	15.5	16.5	16.7	15.5	15.8	16.5	16.5	16.4	16.3	16.1
Number of episodes of sickness[4]												
All causes	001–999	58 199	54 763	55 453	53 746	52 535	51 798	52 821	50 208	47 489	45 076	42 577
Male	and	53 101	49 749	50 362	49 013	48 232	47 540	48 275	45 830	43 508	41 328	39 043
Female	V01–V82	5 098	5 014	5 091	4 733	4 303	4 258	4 546	4 378	3 981	3 748	3 534
All diseases	001–799	45 516	42 569	42 807	41 114	39 524	40 114	41 868	39 448	37 380	35 693	33 902
Infective and parasitic diseases	001–139	5 273	4 038	3 806	3 252	2 963	3 245	3 360	3 148	3 127	3 052	2 700
Neoplasms	140–239	608	559	506	557	607	656	735	739	653	587	607
Endocrine, nutritional and metabolic	240–279	397	367	391	469	407	393	351	288	241	233	227
Diseases of blood and blood forming organs	280–289	114	114	118	76	90	89	88	70	72	62	64
Mental disorders	290–319	1 276	1 384	1 467	1 313	1 109	1 165	1 025	1 081	1 033	995	960
Diseases of the nervous system and sense organs	320–389	1 237	1 243	1 230	1 177	1 117	1 126	1 059	965	1 019	981	858
Diseases of the circulatory system	390–459	1 770	1 671	1 673	1 439	1 510	1 655	1 606	1 467	1 393	1 283	1 124
Diseases of the respiratory system	460–519	14 862	12 133	11 762	10 094	9 624	9 003	10 159	9 166	7 849	7 476	7 313
Diseases of the digestive system	520–579	6 221	7 451	7 982	8 208	7 840	7 709	7 651	7 278	7 214	6 842	6 590
Diseases of the genito-urinary system	580–629	1 979	2 249	2 247	2 371	2 401	2 493	2 474	2 287	2 254	2 265	2 213
Complications of pregnancy, childbirth and the puerperium	630–676	162	180	217	270	207	152	149	174	151	147	136
Diseases of skin and subcutaneous tissue	680–709	2 256	2 138	2 254	2 255	2 146	2 059	1 948	1 854	1 733	1 588	1 345
Diseases of the musculoskeletal system and connective tissue	710–739	5 561	5 971	6 130	6 763	6 974	7 682	8 381	8 251	8 038	7 882	7 512
Congenital anomalies	740–759	342	304	320	369	266	285	272	224	199	208	152
Symptoms and ill-defined conditions	780–799	3 458	2 767	2 704	2 501	2 263	2 402	2 610	2 456	2 404	2 092	2 101
All injuries[5]	800–999	9 979	9 845	10 410	10 357	10 725	9 585	9 049	8 855	8 619	8 033	7 516
Aircraft accident injuries		142	158	123	132	121	139	91	120	98	94	87
Training and exercise injuries		491	693	972	1 148	934	1 283	1 257	1 346	1 213	1 131	1 112
Road traffic accident injuries		1 601	1 595	1 799	1 813	1 702	1 340	1 141	1 114	941	903	818
Sports injuries		1 692	1 673	1 951	1 965	1 800	1 746	1 693	1 617	1 717	1 540	1 529
Accidents due to falls or jumps		1 717	1 777	1 762	1 626	1 734	1 745	1 710	1 741	1 570	1 494	1 294
Other injuries		4 336	3 949	3 803	3 673	4 434	3 332	3 157	2 917	3 080	2 871	2 676
Supplementary classifications[6]	V01–V82	2 704	2 349	2 236	2 275	2 286	2 099	1 904	1 905	1 490	1 350	1 159
Number of medical discharges												
All causes	001–999	1 651	1 388	1 010	882	800	794	1 071	1 393	1 343	1 112	1 305
Male		1 594	1 336	962	836	772	761	1 025	1 360	1 291	1 051	1 265
Female		57	52	48	46	28	33	46	33	52	61	40
All diseases	001–799	1 377	1 188	842	738	677	628	840	1 050	1 048	911	1 061
Mental disorders	290–319	193	182	163	125	107	114	106	123	102	93	95
Diseases of the nervous system and sense organs	320–389	277	273	196	178	152	160	177	169	147	140	125
Diseases of the musculoskeletal system	710–739	414	348	218	195	222	164	313	472	536	494	608
Other diseases	001–799 nes	493	385	265	240	196	190	244	286	263	184	233
All injuries	800–999	274	200	168	144	123	166	231	343	295	201	244
Number of deaths												
All causes	001–999	393	384	365	367	596	349	332	314	295	296	316
Male		387	378	362	361	592	345	325	309	292	294	310
Female		6	6	3	6	4	4	7	5	3	2	6
All diseases	001–799	125	133	118	137	119	129	120	112	118	105	110
Neoplasms	140–239	43	51	44	54	48	49	54	62	51	47	52
Heart and cerebrovascular diseases	390–438	57	59	56	65	56	63	56	44	56	51	47
Other diseases	001–799 nes	25	23	18	18	15	17	10	6	11	7	11
All injuries	800–999	268	251	247	230	477	220	212	202	177	191	206
Road traffic accident injuries		135	133	141	130	115	115	113	113	78	100	73
Other injuries		133	118	106	100	362	105	99	89	99	91	133

1 Regular Service personnel only. Includes all deaths whether occurring on or off duty.

2 Code numbers refer to the Ninth Revision (1975) of the *International Statistical Classification of Diseases, Injuries and Causes of Death.* Prior to 1979 the Eighth Edition was used and this may mean that some groups of diseases are not exactly comparable, the changes however are small.

3 Figures for the latest year are provisional.

4 Based upon spells of bedded sickness lasting two days or more terminating during the year except for the Army, where the coverage is for admissions to medical units for two days or more.

5 Where an injury could be classified under more than one cause it is shown under the first listed cause. Figures by cause for 1980 onwards are not directly comparable with those for previous years because of changes to improve the method of classification.

6 Used where no classifiable diagnosis is reported or where the person is not sick, eg admissions for investigation, preventive measures or elective surgery.

Source Ministry of Defence

7.12 Search and rescue operations at home

Number

	1977	1978	1979	1980	1981	1982	1983	1984	1985	1986	1987	1988
Call outs[1]												
of helicopters[2]	1 206	1 317	1 309	1 090	1 168	1 164	1 224	1 211	1 215	1 251	1 486	1 734
of other aircraft	67	113	98	68	58	59	73	56	62	74	80	81
of marine craft[3]	7	11	2	9	6	8	7	8	1	–	–	–
of mountain rescue teams[3]	47	60	55	45	43	58	46	56	33	73	79	80
Persons rescued[4]: total	713	1 030	986	859	859	898	969	1 061	883	811	950	1 234
by helicopters	692	945	974	837	840	834	948	1 028	869	797	929	1 194
by marine craft[3]	3	6	–	1	–	1	3	2	–	–	–	–
by mountain rescue teams[3]	18	79	12	21	19	63	18	31	14	14	21	40
Incidents: total	1 206	1 373	1 268	1 070	1 097	1 111	1 146	1 145	1 129	1 188	1 361	1 599

1 More than one element of the search and rescue services may be called out to a reported incident.
2 Prior to 1977 these figures are estimated numbers of journeys based on the reported flying hours and the average flight length.
3 Royal Air Force only.
4 Figures for persons rescued relate only to number of persons who were actually removed (alive) from a hazard or who were assisted in an urgent medical incident.

Source Ministry of Defence

7.13 Defence services and the civilian community

	1978	1979	1980	1981	1982	1983	1984	1985	1986	1987	1988
Military aid to civil ministries during industrial disputes											
(Manweeks of Service personnel deployed)[1]	1 550	–	17 000	3	305	–	–	–	389	256	14 762
Fishery protection											
Vessels boarded[2]	1 637	1 563	1 508	1 548	1 869	2 102	1 858	1 687	1 458	1 488	2 202
Hydrographic services											
New charts produced	207	236	226	143	163	226	198	152	118	144	212
New editions of charts	289	353	254	300	372	277	280	266	274	293	323
Charts printed (millions)	3.5	3.5	3.5	3.6	3.5	2.8	3.2	2.8	2.5	2.5	2.6

1 Data relates to financial years (1 April – 31 March) commencing in the year shown.
2 Boardings by RN Fishery Protection Squadron only.

Sources Ministry of Defence; Ministry of Agriculture, Fisheries and Food

7.14 Defence energy consumption
Financial years

Petajoules[1]

	1979/80	1980/1	1981/2	1982/3	1983/4	1984/5	1985/6	1986/7	1987/88	1988/89[6]
All fuels	149.2	135.8	136.5	154.2	150.9	139.3	131.1	137.2	127.7	120.8
Royal Navy }	44.7	39.8	40.8	54.6	52.2	42.1	36.6	39.9	33.1	33.3
Royal Dockyards[2] }						3.0	3.7	3.7	0.8	–
Army	27.1	24.9	24.4	23.6	24.3	24.9	24.8	24.0	22.4	21.0
Royal Air Force	62.9	57.8	56.9	63.0	60.5	59.8	59.0	63.7	65.3	61.4
Procurement Executive	8.3	7.7	7.7	7.2	7.4	5.9	7.0	5.9	6.1	5.1
Royal Ordnance Factories[3]	6.2	5.8	6.7	5.8	6.5	3.7	–	–	–	–
Operational fuels	92.2	81.6	81.7	102.2	98.1	92.4	86.1	93.6	88.5	86.3
Aviation fuels	51.4	47.1	46.7	54.0	51.3	50.4	49.8	54.4	56.1	52.5
Diesel	26.1	22.2	22.9	36.7	35.9	31.8	27.8	30.1	24.8	26.2
Petroleum	4.0	3.6	3.6	3.8	3.7	3.9	3.7	3.7	3.1	2.8
Other liquid fuels	10.7	8.7	8.5	7.7	7.2	6.3	4.8	5.4	4.5	4.8
Non-Operational fuels[4]	57.0	54.2	54.8	52.0	52.7	47.1	44.9	43.6	39.2	34.5
Furnace fuel oil[5]	33.1	30.8	31.1	28.4	27.1	23.9	22.2	19.4	16.6	15.3
Other liquid fuels	0.9	0.8	0.8	0.8	0.8	0.9	0.9	0.9	0.9	0.9
Electricity	8.6	8.6	8.7	8.6	9.2	8.6	8.7	9.1	8.5	8.1
Gas	8.5	8.6	8.4	8.8	9.9	9.5	9.7	11.1	10.2	9.2
Solid fuel	5.9	5.4	5.8	5.4	5.7	4.2	3.4	3.1	3.0	1.0

1 Petajoules = 10^{15} joules.
2 The Royal Dockyards came under Commercial Management during 1987/88 and are therefore excluded.
3 Up to January 1985 when the ROFs became a Companies Act company.
4 Non-operational energy is that energy used for domestic purposes, space heating, lighting and the operation of plant and machinery; it does not include energy used for the propulsion of vehicles, weapons, aircraft or ships.
5 Other than that used by the Fleet.
6 Provisional.

Source Ministry of Defence

8 Production

Censuses of Production (*Table 8.1*)

The Census of Production provides summary information about the structure of industry in the United Kingdom. The results meet a wide range of needs for government, economic analysts and the business community at large. In official statistics the censuses are an important source for the national accounts and input-output tables, but they also provide weights for use in compiling the indexes of production and producer prices. Census results also enable the United Kingdom to meet the statistical requirements of the European Community.

In 1970 the earlier series of quinquennial censuses was replaced by a new system of production statistics. This took the form of a simplified annual census supplemented by a quarterly inquiry into manufacturing sales and an occasional purchases inquiry. During its early years the annual census covered in general all establishments with 25 or more employees, but this was reduced to 20 employees for the 1973 and subsequent censuses. For the 1978 and 1979 Censuses in 68 selected manufacturing industries, coverage of establishments in the 20 to 49 employment size band were reduced to a 1 in 2 sample. A still wider use of sampling was applied for most industries in the 1980 to 1983 Censuses, with a 1 in 4 selection in the 20 to 49 employment size band and a 1 in 2 selection for the 50 to 99 employment size band. Sampling for the benchmark Census of 1984 followed the same pattern as 1979 i.e. a 1 in 2 sample for establishments in the 20 to 49 employment size band and the latest Census for 1985 follows the 1980–83 pattern. For industries with fewer records in the sample size bands, all establishments employing 20 or more receive a form.

Currently census results are published in the Business Monitor series and appear as 110 individual industry reports and a summary volume.

8.1 Censuses of production: summary table
Standard Industrial Classification Revised 1980

	Estimates for all firms							
	Gross output (production)[1]	Gross value added	Stocks and work in progress: At end of year	Stocks and work in progress: Change during year	Capital expenditure *less* disposals	Wages and salaries	Average number of persons employed[2]	Gross value added per person employed
	£ million						Thousands	£
Production and construction Divisions 1–5[3]								
1981	225 386	79 819	..	..	9 720	47 205	7 603	10 498
1982	241 903	84 613	..	..	10 491	48 876	7 129	11 869
1983	259 915	89 901	..	..	10 621	50 694	6 845	13 134
1984	284 381	91 906	..	..	12 453	52 140	6 786	13 544
1985	307 987	101 415	..	..	13 383	56 787	6 591	15 386
1986	311 772	107 141	..	–224	13 388	59 705	6 468	16 565
1987	345 812	117 216	..	..	14 440	..	6 448	18 177
Production industries (Revised definition) Divisions 1–4[3]								
1981	199 419	70 312	42 802	1 768	9 201	39 025	6 406	10 975
1982	212 640	74 329	43 192	936	9 876	40 154	5 971	12 449
1983	227 083	78 727	44 736	2 077	9 955	41 134	5 654	13 924
1984	248 376	79 892	47 481	3 116	11 863	42 723	5 604	14 254
1985	268 824	89 322	48 017	1 010	12 796	46 494	5 466	16 341
1986	268 313	93 958	47 028	–225	12 751	48 854	5 346	17 576
1987	297 798	102 748	49 501	2 113	13 661	52 040	5 309	19 354
Manufacturing (Revised definition) Divisions 2–4								
1981	165 471	57 935	37 501	1 260	5 493	34 191	5 778	10 027
1982	175 657	60 799	37 521	229	5 514	35 050	5 360	11 342
1983	189 200	65 753	39 219	2 255	6 061	36 008	5 078	12 947
1984	209 656	71 092	42 069	3 203	7 589	38 516	5 059	14 052
1985	226 636	76 499	43 188	1 523	8 742	41 256	4 976	15 375
1986	232 499	80 955	42 979	–515	8 705	43 426	4 878	16 595
1987	254 683	89 745	44 797	2 111	9 754	46 429	4 874	18 412
Energy and water supply industries Division 1[3,4]								
1981	33 948	12 376	5 301	508	3 708	4 834	629	19 688
1982	36 983	13 530	5 671	706	4 362	5 103	610	22 178
1983	37 883	12 974	5 517	–178	3 894	5 126	575	22 552
1984	38 719	8 800	5 412	–87	4 274	4 207	545	16 134
1985	42 188	12 823	4 830	–513	4 054	5 238	490	26 142
1986	35 814	13 003	4 049	–740	4 045	5 428	468	27 799
1987	43 116	13 003	4 704	2	3 907	5 611	435	29 916

See footnotes on page 145.

Source Central Statistical Office

8.1 Censuses of production: summary table

Standard Industrial Classification Revised 1980

(continued)

	Estimates for all firms							
	Gross output (production)[1]	Gross value added	Stocks and work in progress: At end of year	Stocks and work in progress: Change during year	Capital expenditure *less* disposals	Wages and salaries	Average number of persons employed[2]	Gross value added per person employed
	£ million						Thousands	£
Coal extraction, coke ovens and manufacture of solid fuels								
Classes 11 and 12								
1981	4 748	3 326	984	95	699	1 964	274	12 159
1982	4 958	3 398	1 012	25	730	2 018	262	12 988
1983	4 471	3 012	920	−86	611	1 902	241	12 498
1984	1 662	863	858	−54	339	925	222	3 892
1985	4 349	2 696	584	−277	559	1 816	176	15 280
1986	4 007	2 513	546	8	507	1 828	160	15 691
1987	3 859	2 266	468	−72	507	1 878	132	17 166
Extraction of mineral oil and natural gas								
Class 13[5]								
1981	13 495	11 904	..	−58	2 885	240	20	597 430
1982	16 012	13 900	..	135	3 016	283	22	514 811
1983	18 603	16 268	..	−68	2 865	345	28	580 986
1984	22 578	19 580	..	−1	3 149	407	31	631 626
1985	22 383	18 998	..	104	2 817	468	29	609 603
1986	11 861	9 000	..	−89	2 579	..	23	321 443
1987	12 666	10 102	..	54	2 042	..	28	360 792
Mineral oil processing								
Class 14								
1981	12 874	1 772	1 985	87	412	204	23	75 584
1982	13 850	1 401	1 771	−250	239	206	21	67 248
1983	14 318	1 548	1 672	−128	199	212	19	79 989
1984	16 720	1 252	1 833	171	189	212	18	71 680
1985	15 721	1 312	1 577	−182	264	215	16	83 229
1986	9 080	1 337	994	−541	301	199	14	93 139
1987	16 328	1 349	996	−20	223	226	15	91 198
Other energy and water supply								
Classes 15 to 17[4]								
1981	16 326	7 279	2 332	325	2 597	2 666	332	21 947
1982	18 176	8 732	2 888	931	3 393	2 880	328	26 649
1983	19 094	8 415	2 925	36	3 084	3 012	315	26 722
1984	20 337	6 684	2 720	−205	3 746	3 070	306	21 828
1985	22 117	8 814	2 668	−54	3 231	3 206	298	29 550
1986	22 727	9 153	2 509	−208	3 237	3 401	293	31 215
1987	22 929	9 388	3 240	94	3 177	3 508	287	32 711
Extraction of minerals and ores other than fuels; manufacture of metals, mineral products and chemicals								
Division 2								
1981	34 920	10 565	6 508	133	1 459	5 637	823	12 831
1982	36 348	10 838	6 294	−169	1 396	5 679	757	14 325
1983	40 455	12 757	6 576	404	1 544	5 716	700	18 217
1984	44 579	13 927	7 025	610	1744	5 931	682	20 430
1985	48 088	14 778	7 274	258	2 201	6 331	668	22 117
1986	46 618	15 700	7 068	−216	2 249	6 669	655	23 961
1987	51 645	18 427	7 505	470	2 680	7 226	653	28 223
Extraction and preparation of metalliferous ores								
Class 21								
1981	21	12	3	−1	1	9	1	8 866
1982	24	14	9	−2	1	10	1	11 619
1983	25	15	2	–	2	10	1	12 365
1984	42	25	3	–	3	15	1	17 797
1985	37	18	7	4	4	16	2	12 193
1986	25	4	6	–	6	12	1	4 486
1987	19	−1	12	6	11	11	1	−1 925
Metal manufacturing								
Class 22								
1981	9 751	2 167	2 214	−2	292	1 655	238	9 086
1982	9 505	1 950	1 924	−289	226	1 547	207	9 437
1983	10 281	2 532	2 006	179	256	1 460	178	14 259
1984	11 172	2 589	2 040	198	295	1 448	163	15 888
1985	12 066	2 810	2 055	−6	358	1 564	162	17 386
1986	11 134	2 956	2 008	−25	417	1 593	153	19 278
1987	12 368	3 539	2 055	120	461	1 622	142	24 848
Extraction of minerals nes								
Class 23								
1981	799	422	65	–	41	139	21	19 824
1982	923	486	71	1	52	149	21	23 655
1983	731	403	49	−1	48	102	13	30 531
1984	629	334	38	4	36	93	11	29 840
1985	660	352	45	6	43	92	10	34 596
1986	659	343	41	−3	30	98	10	34 578
1987	670	350	43	3	43	102	9	37 191
Manufacture of non-metallic mineral products								
Class 24								
1981	6 235	2 623	1 031	27	268	1 364	227	11 557
1982	6 886	2 814	1 038	9	286	1 419	211	13 334
1983	7 719	3 176	1 020	−36	365	1 524	208	15 229
1984	8 156	3 414	1 112	94	484	1 597	206	16 558
1985	8 587	3 517	1 178	98	524	1 693	203	17 324
1986	9 021	3 848	1 170	−13	431	1 780	200	19 274
1987	10 013	4 364	1 185	10	601	1 964	202	21 583

See footnotes on page 145.

Source *Central Statistical Office*

8.1 Censuses of production: summary table
Standard Industrial Classification Revised 1980

(continued)

	Estimates for all firms							
	Gross output (production)[1]	Gross value added	Stocks and work in progress: At end of year	Stocks and work in progress: Change during year	Capital expenditure *less* disposals	Wages and salaries	Average number of persons employed[2]	Gross value added per person employed
	£ million						Thousands	£
Chemical industry								
Class 25								
1981	17 473	5 196	3 077	99	837	2 330	318	16 321
1982	18 397	5 456	3 154	134	814	2 433	303	17 997
1983	20 960	6 454	3 396	257	853	2 499	288	22 442
1984	23 764	7 354	3 717	305	906	2 664	288	25 491
1985	25 869	7 842	3 881	164	1 237	2 847	281	27 918
1986	24 889	8 221	3 738	– 171	1 318	3 061	281	29 298
1987	27 620	9 814	4 099	324	1 504	3 392	287	34 166
Production of man-made fibres								
Class 26								
1981	642	146	117	10	20	140	17	8 566
1982	613	118	99	– 21	17	122	14	8 421
1983	739	178	103	4	19	122	12	14 558
1984	816	211	114	10	20	115	12	18 388
1985	869	239	109	– 8	36	119	11	21 781
1986	889	329	105	– 4	47	125	11	30 454
1987	956	362	112	6	59	135	11	33 113
Metal goods, engineering and vehicles industries								
Division 3								
1981	61 341	25 377	20 452	913	2 149	16 465	2 680	9 467
1982	65 802	26 968	20 542	131	2 091	16 831	2 468	10 927
1983	69 646	28 209	21 529	1 163	2 225	17 027	2 314	12 189
1984	76 582	30 359	22 898	1 570	2 919	18 082	2 261	13 429
1985	84 839	32 756	23 668	944	3 291	19 406	2 216	14 783
1986	87 583	34 104	23 855	879	3 183	20 242	2 156	15 821
1987	95 497	36 453	24 394	716	3 182	21 286	2 116	17 231
Manufacture of metal goods nes								
Class 31								
1981	7 826	3 205	1 459	– 69	220	2 138	400	8 020
1982	8 507	3 498	1 451	– 12	209	2 214	372	9 409
1983	8 808	3 562	1 462	69	222	2 221	344	10 367
1984	9 726	3 821	1 577	131	320	2 388	338	11 294
1985	10 123	4 034	1 565	36	332	2 455	324	12 463
1986	10 611	4 298	1 581	27	350	2 610	322	13 339
1987	11 331	4 560	1 653	100	407	2 750	316	14 428
Mechanical engineering								
Class 32								
1981	18 601	8 143	5 969	– 10	556	5 108	808	10 079
1982	19 668	8 340	6 025	69	559	5 192	732	11 385
1983	19 859	8 427	6 112	92	511	5 164	676	12 464
1984	21 132	8 823	6 316	523	637	5 338	647	13 642
1985	23 568	9 534	6 611	348	785	5 799	642	14 856
1986	23 541	9 651	5 886	– 62	711	5 958	615	15 681
1987	24 351	9 966	5 710	51	696	5 973	586	16 995
Electrical and electronic engineering and manufacture of office machinery and data processing equipment								
Classes 33 and 34								
1981	14 741	6 495	4 112	78	541	3 802	634	10 238
1982	16 304	7 256	4 213	157	562	3 943	593	12 241
1983	18 362	7 829	4 696	401	678	4 191	586	13 362
1984	22 050	9 080	5 451	578	969	4 729	604	15 037
1985	24 303	9 630	5 554	174	1 082	5 127	597	16 125
1986	24 729	9 914	5 676	135	950	5 389	590	16 795
1987	27 401	10 861	5 868	261	999	5 796	590	18 408
Manufacture of motor vehicles and parts thereof								
Class 35								
1981	10 164	3 207	2 268	– 110	474	2 397	369	8 680
1982	10 657	3 211	2 245	– 58	468	2 318	325	9 867
1983	12 050	3 580	2 549	300	498	2 353	302	11 839
1984	12 641	3 807	2 584	66	596	2 467	288	13 218
1985	14 282	4 273	2 718	162	659	2 634	277	15 441
1986	15 140	4 657	2 907	173	677	2 688	261	17 844
1987	17 629	5 112	2 925	82	612	2 804	258	19 814
Manufacture of other transport equipment								
Class 36								
1981	8 262	3 555	6 092	1 014	311	2 509	377	9 431
1982	8 556	3 722	5 998	– 64	235	2 597	356	10 462
1983	8 565	3 884	6 104	267	246	2 538	325	11 945
1984	8 849	3 819	6 332	208	305	2 574	304	12 562
1985	10 048	4 124	6 487	158	324	2 720	293	14 062
1986	10 889	4 401	7 055	599	387	2 871	284	15 485
1987	11 854	4 695	7 461	366	354	3 183	282	16 640

See footnotes on page 145.

Source *Central Statistical Office*

8.1 Censuses of production: summary table

Standard Industrial Classification Revised 1980

(continued)

	Estimates for all firms								
	Gross output (production)[1]	Gross value added	Stocks and work in progress: At end of year	Stocks and work in progress: Change during year	Capital expenditure *less* disposals	Wages and salaries	Average number of persons employed[2]	Gross value added per person employed
	£ million						Thousands	£
Instrument engineering								
Class 37								
1981	1 746	772	551	9	48	511	92	8 384
1982	2 110	942	610	39	59	568	90	10 496
1983	2 002	928	606	35	70	561	81	11 427
1984	2 183	1 009	638	65	92	586	80	12 652
1985	2 516	1 160	733	67	109	671	83	13 964
1986	2 674	1 183	750	7	109	726	82	14 350
1987	2 932	1 259	776	20	114	779	83	15 128
Other manufacturing industries								
Division 4								
1981	69 210	21 993	10 541	215	1 885	12 090	2 274	9 671
1982	73 507	22 994	10 684	268	2 027	12 539	2 136	10 765
1983	79 099	24 786	11 114	688	2 293	13 265	2 064	12 009
1984	88 496	26 806	12 146	1 022	2 926	14 503	2 117	12 663
1985	93 709	28 965	12 246	321	3 250	15 518	2 092	13 848
1986	98 298	31 151	12 056	−147	3 273	16 513	2 067	15 067
1987	107 540	34 865	12 897	926	3 892	17 917	2 106	16 556
Food, drink and tobacco manufacturing industries								
Classes 41/42								
1981	34 843	8 424	4 502	150	881	3 624	657	12 825
1982	37 425	8 958	4 677	223	1 015	3 786	626	14 299
1983	40 085	9 493	4 885	264	1 075	3 968	603	15 742
1984	44 205	9 673	5 234	245	1 255	4 264	613	15 785
1985	45 336	10 175	5 084	28	1 340	4 455	591	17 207
1986	47 023	10 801	4 808	−384	1 275	4 735	582	18 572
1987	49 272	11 696	4 844	66	1 453	5 082	594	19 692
Textile industry								
Class 43								
1981	4 918	1 794	1 021	−3	113	1 157	267	6 711
1982	5 068	1 812	1 014	–	128	1 170	248	7 313
1983	5 439	1 978	1 046	80	140	1 210	235	8 421
1984	6 140	2 169	1 189	134	191	1 316	236	9 177
1985	6 648	2 342	1 238	94	228	1 392	230	10 186
1986	6 788	2 503	1 207	−4	265	1 504	229	10 929
1987	7 571	2 873	1 338	125	271	1 623	228	12 596
Footwear and clothing industries and manufacture of leather and leather goods								
Classes 44 and 45								
1981	5 070	2 050	1 088	23	83	1 328	360	5 692
1982	5 207	2 040	1 059	7	92	1 334	328	6 209
1983	5 501	2 200	1 089	69	116	1 386	320	6 883
1984	6 223	2 497	1 205	136	148	1 534	333	7 493
1985	6 940	2 759	1 340	116	168	1 675	341	8 058
1986	7 143	2 864	1 342	45	174	1 798	341	8 399
1987	7 800	3 104	1 509	198	194	1 904	341	9 103
Timber and wooden furniture industries								
Class 46								
1981	5 190	1 761	971	−35	108	1 159	216	8 149
1982	5 598	1 848	966	11	114	1 207	206	8 953
1983	6 330	2 100	1 068	145	162	1 299	202	10 394
1984	6 294	2 025	1 054	69	196	1 298	193	10 514
1985	6 761	2 240	1 094	19	208	1 417	194	11 544
1986	7 112	2 393	1 119	51	197	1 513	193	12 428
1987	8 335	2 884	1 230	155	271	1 647	198	14 544
Manufacture of paper and paper products; printing and publishing								
Class 47								
1981	12 422	5 384	1 673	89	462	3 257	484	11 133
1982	13 307	5 654	1 644	−11	424	3 438	458	12 338
1983	14 096	6 074	1 692	98	496	3 700	447	13 598
1984	16 353	6 974	1 956	282	701	4 112	458	15 233
1985	18 174	7 659	1 964	18	845	4 461	455	16 832
1986	19 396	8 364	1 982	91	870	4 653	439	19 065
1987	21 914	9 327	2 156	169	1 070	5 051	446	20 908
Processing of rubber and plastics								
Class 48								
1981	5 379	2 093	863	–	201	1 250	221	9 467
1982	5 562	2 177	873	24	204	1 286	205	10 618
1983	6 183	2 417	903	24	267	1 393	200	12 063
1984	7 054	2 617	1 008	106	365	1 515	203	12 867
1985	7 535	2 894	1 042	41	388	1 617	200	14 492
1986	8 379	3 274	1 125	44	419	1 777	204	16 084
1987	9 869	3 876	1 280	135	549	2 011	214	18 075

See footnotes on page 145.

Source *Central Statistical Office*

8.1 Censuses of production: summary table
(*continued*)

Standard Industrial Classification Revised 1980

	Estimates for all firms							
	Gross output (production)[1]	Gross value added	Stocks and work in progress: At end of year	Stocks and work in progress: Change during year	Capital expenditure *less* disposals	Wages and salaries	Average number of persons employed[2]	Gross value added per person employed
	£ million						Thousands	£
Other manufacturing industries								
Class 49								
1981	1 388	487	424	− 10	36	315	69	7 063
1982	1 340	505	452	13	49	319	64	7 949
1983	1 465	524	430	8	36	310	58	9 122
1984	2 228	850	500	51	70	465	81	10 545
1985	2 315	895	485	4	73	500	80	11 165
1986	2 458	952	475	11	73	534	81	11 747
1987	2 778	1 106	540	78	86	597	84	13 223
Construction								
Division 5								
1981	25 966	9 507	..	..	519	8 180	1 196	7 946
1982	29 264	10 284	..	..	615	8 723	1 158	8 879
1983	32 831	11 174	..	..	666	9 561	1 191	9 384
1984	36 005	12 014	..	..	590	9 106	1 181	10 171
1985	39 164	12 094	..	..	587	10 293	1 125	10 749
1986	43 459	13 183	..	..	637	10 851	1 122	11 751
1987	48 013	14 168	..	..	779	11 948	1 140	12 696

1 Figures for gross output include a substantial amount of duplication represented by the total value of partly manufactured goods sold by one industrial establishment to another. The extent of duplication varies from one census industry to another.
2 The figures include working proprietors but exclude outworkers.
3 Figures for mineral oil and natural gas not included.
4 Figures for stocks and work in progress exclude water undertakings and work in progress in the gas industry.
5 Figures for stocks and work in progress exclude goods on hand for sale.

Source *Central Statistical Office*

8.2 Total inland energy consumption
Heat supplied basis

Million therms[1]

	1978	1979	1980	1981	1982	1983	1984	1985	1986	1987	1988
Inland energy consumption of primary fuels and equivalents	84 023	87 766	81 109	78 740	77 315	77 673	77 352	81 050	83 269	84 037	84 677
Coal[2]	29 107	31 288	29 084	28 926	26 978	27 229	19 348	25 734	27 790	28 472	27 621
Petroleum[3]	35 073	35 016	30 710	28 117	28 189	27 046	33 924	29 167	28 711	27 953	29 661
Primary electricity[4]	3 567	3 678	3 536	3 677	4 218	4 708	4 958	5 583	5 859	6 138	7 017
Natural gas[5]	16 276	17 784	17 779	18 020	17 930	18 690	19 122	20 565	20 907	21 473	20 378
less Energy used by fuel producers and losses in conversion and distribution	24 896	26 071	24 572	23 819	23 036	23 630	23 462	24 731	25 424	25 360	25 206
Total consumption by final users	59 127	61 695	56 537	54 921	54 279	54 043	53 890	56 319	57 845	58 677	59 471
Analysed by type of fuel											
Coal (direct use)	5 738	6 004	5 103	4 748	4 831	4 640	3 840	4 814	4 902	4 451	4 280
Coke and breeze	2 652	2 889	1 578	2 039	1 850	1 945	1 983	2 118	1 933	2 121	2 225
Other solid fuel[6]	652	627	597	523	512	502	316	439	422	436	381
Coke oven gas	357	388	255	264	240	252	213	305	309	326	306
Natural gas (direct use)[7]	15 025	16 417	16 562	16 631	16 691	16 797	17 186	18 253	18 517	19 383	18 665
Electricity	7 676	8 028	7 653	7 521	7 371	7 486	7 654	7 987	8 243	8 520	8 724
Petroleum (direct use)	26 996	27 323	24 775	23 191	22 772	22 412	22 691	22 397	23 519	23 440	24 890
Other fuels (direct use)[8]	31	19	14	4	12	9	7	6	1	–	–
Analysed by class of consumer											
Agriculture	732	732	594	557	558	566	550	564	565	544	536
Iron and steel industry	4 662	5 025	2 867	3 249	2 934	2 972	2 935	3 048	2 801	3 052	3 235
Other industries	17 711	18 145	16 263	14 893	14 502	13 748	13 376	13 469	13 443	13 557	13 607
Railways	504	495	485	466	420	441	423	428	424	408	416
Road transport	10 697	10 925	11 042	10 722	11 035	11 372	11 912	12 142	12 944	13 522	14 384
Water transport	518	543	501	437	472	480	527	498	457	438	460
Air transport	2 005	2 074	2 081	1 993	1 982	2 022	2 137	2 216	2 432	2 572	2 741
Domestic	15 359	16 501	15 816	15 750	15 569	15 488	15 044	16 698	17 348	17 253	16 737
Public administration	3 657	3 792	3 546	3 504	3 441	3 497	3 497	3 540	3 547	3 408	3 287
Miscellaneous	3 282	3 463	3 342	3 350	3 366	3 446	3 490	3 714	3 895	3 921	4 067

1 Estimates of the gross calorific values used for converting the statistics for the various fuels to therms are given in the *Digest of United Kingdom Energy Statistics 1989.*
2 Including net trade and stock change in other solid fuels.
3 Refinery throughput of crude oil, *plus* net foreign trade and stock change in petroleum products. Liquid fuels derived from coal (which are included in coal consumption) and petroleum products not used as fuels (chemical feedstock, industrial and white spirits, lubricants, bitumen and wax) are excluded.
4 Primary electricity comprises UK produced nuclear and hydro-electricity plus net imports of electricity. The figures represent the notional thermal input of fossil fuel that would have been needed to produce the same quantities of electricity at the efficiency of contemporary UK conventional steam power stations.
5 Natural gas includes both indigenous and imported natural gas and colliery methane piped to the surface and consumed at collieries or sold.
6 Including briquettes, ovoids, Phurnacite, Coalite, Rexco, etc.
7 Figures for Natural gas include Town gas. For 1988 consumption of Town gas was 3m therms. Data for consumption of Town gas in previous years may be found in earlier editions of this publication.
8 Liquid fuels derived from coal.

Source *Department of Energy*

8.3 Coal: supply and demand

Million tonnes

	1978	1979	1980	1981	1982	1983	1984	1985	1986	1987	1988
Supply											
Production of deep-mined coal	107.5	107.8	112.4	110.5	106.2	101.7	35.2	75.2	90.4	85.9	83.5
Production of opencast coal	14.2	12.9	15.8	14.8	15.3	14.7	14.3	15.6	14.3	15.8	17.9
Total	121.7	120.7	128.2	125.3	121.5	116.4	49.5	90.8	104.6	101.6	101.4
Recovered slurry, fines, etc.	1.9	1.7	1.9	2.2	3.3	2.8	1.6	3.3	3.5	2.8	2.4
Imports	2.4	4.4	7.3	4.3	4.1	4.5	8.9	12.7	10.6	9.8	12.0
Total	126.0	126.8	137.4	131.8	128.8	123.7	60.1	106.8	118.6	114.2	115.8
Change in colliery stocks	+1.6	−1.9	+5.3	+4.3	+0.2	+1.2	−7.9	−5.3	+0.3	−1.1	+0.7
Change in stocks at opencast sites	+1.1	−0.8	+2.4	+0.5	−0.4	+0.8	+4.7	−6.3	−0.8	−1.5	+0.5
Total supply	123.3	129.5	129.7	127.0	128.9	121.7	63.2	118.3	119.2	116.8	114.6
Home consumption											
Electricity supply industry[1]	80.6	88.8	89.6	87.2	80.2	81.6	53.4	73.9	82.6	86.2	82.5
Coke ovens	15.0	15.1	11.6	10.8	10.4	10.4	8.2	11.1	11.1	10.9	10.9
Low temperature carbonization plants	1.9	1.7	1.9	1.3	1.2	1.2	1.1	1.4	1.0	1.0	0.8
Manufactured fuel plants	1.2	1.2	1.1	1.1	1.1	0.9	0.2	0.8	1.0	1.0	1.2
Railways	0.1	0.1	0.1	0.1	0.1	–	–	–	–	–	–
Collieries	1.0	0.8	0.7	0.6	0.5	0.5	0.2	0.3	0.3	0.2	0.2
Industry:											
Iron and steel	0.2	0.3	0.2	0.2	0.1	0.1	0.1	–	–	–	–
Other industries[2,3]	8.4	8.9	7.6	6.8	7.0	7.1	6.0	7.4	8.1	7.9	8.0
Domestic:											
House coal[3,4]	6.9	7.1	5.5	5.2	5.2	4.8	4.1	5.3	5.6	4.7	4.3
Anthracite and dry steam coal[4,5,6]	1.5	1.6	1.7	1.6	1.8	1.7	1.6	2.1	1.5	1.5	1.5
Miners' coal	1.8	1.8	1.7	1.6	1.6	1.5	0.8	1.2	1.3	1.0	0.8
Public services	1.6	1.7	1.5	1.4	1.4	1.4	1.3	1.3	1.3	1.2	1.0
Miscellaneous	0.3	0.3	0.3	0.4	0.5	0.4	0.5	0.4	0.2	0.2	0.2
Total home consumption	120.5	129.4	123.5	118.4	111.0	111.4	77.3	105.4	114.2	115.9	111.5
Overseas shipments and bunkers	2.3	2.2	3.8	9.1	7.4	6.6	2.3	2.4	2.7	2.4	1.8
Total consumption and shipments	122.8	131.6	127.3	127.5	118.4	118.0	79.6	107.8	116.9	118.2	113.3
Change in distributed stocks[7]	+0.3	−2.5	+2.1	−0.2	+10.3	+3.5	−18.2	+10.0	+4.0	−2.8	+1.7
Balance[8]	+0.2	+0.4	+0.3	−0.3	+0.2	–	+1.9	+0.5	−1.8	+1.3	−0.4
Stocks at end of year[9]											
Distributed[7]	22.0	18.2	20.4	20.1	30.4	34.0	15.8	25.8	29.8	27.0	28.7
At collieries	9.9	7.8	13.1	17.4	17.7	18.9	11.0	5.7	6.0	4.9	5.6
At opencast sites	2.6	1.8	4.2	4.7	4.3	5.1	9.8	3.5	2.7	1.2	1.7
Total stocks	34.5	27.8	37.7	42.3	52.4	58.0	36.5	35.0	38.5	33.2	36.0

TIME SERIES. Figures relate to periods of 52 weeks.

1 Includes quantities used in the production of steam for sale.
2 Colliery and opencast disposals to industry.
3 From 1984 includes estimated proportions of steam coal imports.
4 Colliery and opencast disposals to merchants.
5 Including disposals of imported anthracite.
6 Anthracite is also consumed under other categories, including miners' coal and manufactured fuel plants.
7 Great Britain. Stock change excludes industrial and domestic stocks.
8 This is the balance between supply and consumption, shipments and changes in known distributed stocks.
9 Figures for stocks at end of year for 1978 relate to position at 23 December. Stock change in 1979 is calculated on stocks at 30 December 1978. Figures for stocks at end of year for 1983 relate to position at 24 December.

Source *Department of Energy*

8.4 Coal: production[1]
Great Britain
Years ended March

Million tonnes

	1978/79	1979/80[2]	1980/81	1981/82	1982/83	1983/84	1984/85[3]	1985/86[4]	1986/87	1987/88	1988/89
Scottish	8.09	8.03	7.74	7.22	6.62	5.27	0.30	4.26	3.43	2.59	1.90
North East	12.93	13.98	14.09	13.41	12.42	10.91	0.38	9.50	10.17	10.22	10.30
North Yorkshire[4]	8.20	8.15	8.50	8.26	8.39	7.55	0.32	13.90	14.24	14.30	15.85
Barnsley[4]	7.39	8.00	8.32	8.40	8.13	6.19	0.12				
Doncaster[4]	6.96	7.49	7.16	7.12	6.78	5.82	0.01	12.48	12.49	11.55	13.23
South Yorkshire[4]	7.59	7.56	7.38	7.23	7.33	6.57	0.17				
North Derbyshire	7.38	7.65	8.26	8.48	8.15	6.29	1.44	6.21	6.04	10.57[5]	10.87[5]
North Nottingham[4]	11.01	11.86	11.97	12.26	12.36	11.60	9.16	18.67	18.06	17.61	17.15
South Nottingham[4]	8.60	8.65	8.83	8.54	8.25	6.97	5.59				
South Midlands and Kent	8.54	8.54	8.45	8.64	8.17	6.65	4.98	6.74	6.14	0.35[6]	0.44[6]
Western	10.94	11.10	11.19	11.08	10.78	9.08	4.82	9.38	10.09	9.55	9.73
South Wales	7.75	7.63	7.67	7.56	6.88	6.58	0.29	6.63	6.48	5.01	4.98
Total—Saleable mined coal	105.38	108.64	109.56	108.20	104.26	89.48	27.58	87.76	87.14	81.75	84.44

TIME SERIES. Figures relate to periods of 52 weeks.

1 Collieries operated by the British Coal Corporation (B.C.C.). Excludes coal extracted in work on capital account (0.64 million tonnes in 1987/88).
2 See footnote 2 to Table 8.7.
3 Production was affected by a national overtime ban from 1st November 1983 and by wider industrial action from 12th March 1984.
4 With effect from 1985/86 the B.C.C. altered their regional structure and incorporated Barnsley into North Yorkshire Area, Doncaster into South Yorkshire Area and merged North and South Nottingham into Nottinghamshire Area.
5 From 1987/88 figures relate to B.C.C.'s new Central Area (previously North Derbyshire and South Midlands).
6 From 1987/88 figures relate to B.C.C.'s new Kent Area only. See also footnote 5 above.

Source *Department of Energy*

8.5 Coal: average number of wage-earners on colliery books[1]
Great Britain
Years ended March

Thousands

	1978/79	1979/80	1980/81	1981/82	1982/83	1983/84	1984/85	1985/86[2]	1986/87	1987/88	1988/89
Scottish	21.1	21.0	20.5	18.3	16.9	14.5	12.3	8.8	6.0	4.3	3.3
North East	34.4	33.5	32.9	30.4	27.6	24.5	22.2	19.7	15.9	12.9	11.5
North Yorkshire[2]	15.6	15.8	15.4	14.8	14.4	13.6	12.7	22.8	19.0	16.5	12.9
Barnsley[2]	15.9	15.8	15.6	15.1	15.0	14.3	13.6				
Doncaster[2]	16.6	16.7	16.7	15.9	15.0	13.9	12.8	22.0	16.9	15.5	13.7
South Yorkshire[2]	17.3	17.1	16.9	16.3	15.5	14.7	13.7				
North Derbyshire	12.3	12.1	12.3	12.0	11.8	11.1	10.1	9.7	8.2	12.7[3]	10.8[3]
North Nottingham[2]	18.0	18.1	18.4	18.1	17.8	17.1	16.5	27.2	24.5	20.3	16.4
South Nottingham[2]	15.9	15.9	15.8	15.3	14.8	13.7	11.7				
South Midlands and Kent	16.2	16.5	16.8	16.1	15.2	13.6	12.6	11.4	9.3	0.8[4]	0.7[4]
Western	23.6	23.0	22.7	21.5	20.3	19.1	17.5	16.3	13.5	11.5	10.3
South Wales	28.0	27.0	25.8	24.8	23.4	21.5	19.7	16.7	12.1	9.9	7.4
Total	234.9	232.5	229.8	218.5	207.7	191.5	175.4	154.6	125.4	104.4	86.9

1 Collieries operated by the British Coal Corporation: See footnote 6 to Table 8.4.
2 See footnote 4 to Table 8.4.
3 See footnote 5 to Table 8.4.
4 See footnote 6 to Table 8.4.

Source *Department of Energy*

8.6 Coal: output per manshift[1]
Great Britain
Years ended March

Tonnes

	1978/79	1979/80[2]	1980/81	1981/82	1982/83	1983/84	1984/85	1985/86[3]	1986/87	1987/88	1988/89
Total	2.24	2.31	2.32	2.40	2.44	2.43	2.08	2.72	3.29	3.62	4.14
Scottish	1.96	1.98	1.92	2.00	1.97	1.95	0.37	2.21	2.54	2.71	2.45
North East	1.86	2.07	2.07	2.07	2.09	2.23	0.47	2.23	2.98	3.51	3.81
North Yorkshire[3]	2.57	2.50	2.68	2.80	3.01	3.13	1.29	3.04	3.89	4.45	5.26
Barnsley[3]	2.44	2.56	2.62	2.71	2.64	2.36	0.51				
Doncaster[3]	2.27	2.29	2.18	2.27	2.30	2.31	0.04	2.90	3.57	3.61	4.31
South Yorkshire[3]	2.25	2.24	2.17	2.22	2.35	2.47	0.50				
North Derbyshire	2.90	2.99	3.21	3.33	3.30	2.90	2.13	3.04	3.48	3.81[4]	4.31[4]
North Nottingham[3]	2.92	3.08	3.04	3.17	3.25	3.35	3.11	3.21	3.45	3.89	4.35
South Nottingham[3]	2.60	2.64	2.68	2.68	2.69	2.55	2.62				
South Midlands and Kent	2.50	2.45	2.36	2.52	2.51	2.41	2.62	2.82	3.12	1.93[5]	2.90[5]
Western	2.24	2.35	2.35	2.45	2.53	2.44	2.09	2.74	3.36	3.58	3.91
South Wales	1.41	1.40	1.46	1.47	1.47	1.57	0.39	1.87	2.47	2.30	2.88

1 Collieries operated by the British Coal Corporation (B.C.C.).
2 From April 1980 the B.C.C. have reclassified certain drivages from revenue account (on which the calculation of output per manshift is based) to capital account. The figures for 1979/80 have been adjusted to this new basis. Figures on this basis prior to 1979/80 are not available.
3 See footnote 4 to Table 8.4.
4 See footnote 5 to Table 8.4.
5 See footnote 6 to Table 8.4.

Source *Department of Energy*

8.7 Fuel input and gas output; gas sales

Public supply

	1978	1979	1980	1981	1982	1983	1984	1985	1986	1987	1988
Fuel input to gas industry:	million tonnes										
Petroleum	0.1	0.1	0.1	0.1	0.1	0.1	0.1	0.1	–	–	–
	million therms										
Petroleum gases[1]	86	80	79	71	52	33	30	28	36	6	1
Natural gas	8	–	–	–	–	–	–	–	–	–	–
Coke oven gas	–	–	–	–	–	–	–	–	–	–	–
Total to gas works	145	114	106	100	85	61	56	57	55	20	6
Natural gas for direct supply	15 777	17 238	17 012	17 044	16 667	17 153	17 739	18 988	19 215	20 198	19 083
Total fuel input	15 922	17 352	17 118	17 144	16 752	17 214	17 794	19 046	19 270	20 218	19 089
Fuel input to gas industry	million tonnes of coal or coal equivalent										
Petroleum	0.2	0.1	0.1	0.1	0.1	0.1	0.1	0.1	0.1	0.1	–
Petroleum gases[1]	0.3	0.3	0.3	0.2	0.2	0.1	0.1	0.1	0.1	–	–
Natural gas	–	–	–	–	–	–	–	–	–	–	–
Coke oven gas	–	–	–	–	–	–	–	–	–	–	–
Total to gas works	0.5	0.4	0.4	0.3	0.3	0.2	0.2	0.2	0.2	0.1	–
Natural gas for direct supply	63.1	68.9	68.0	68.2	66.7	68.6	71.0	76.0	76.9	80.8	76.3
Total fuel input	63.6	69.3	68.4	68.5	67.0	68.8	71.2	76.2	77.1	80.9	76.3
Gas output and sales	million therms										
Gas output:											
Town gas	55	40	35	31	26	23	21	20	18	13	4
Natural gas supplied direct[2]	15 858	17 303	17 076	17 108	16 719	17 186	17 764	19 017	19 243	20 205	19 083
Gross total available	15 913	17 343	17 111	17 139	16 745	17 209	17 785	19 038	19 261	20 218	19 087
Own use[3]	106	128	134	139	126	–121	–129	–140	–152	–137	–120
Statistical difference[4]	–499	–624	–347	–378	+38	–243	–351	–531	–613	–708	–328
Total sales	15 308	16 591	16 630	16 622	16 657	16 845	17 305	18 367	18 496	19 373	18 639
Analysis of gas sales	million therms										
Fuel producers											
Power stations	338	239	140	78	76	77	178	197	75	79	83
Coal extraction and manufacture of solid fuels[5]	..	..	..	..	..	9	13	12	14	13	14
Coke ovens[5]	..	..	..	..	..	10	10	11	3	1	1
Petroleum refineries[5]	..	..	..	..	..	76	29	8	10	11	11
Nuclear fuel production[5]	..	..	..	..	..	18	18	18	17	23	15
Production and distribution of other energy	..	..	..	..	..	6	4	11	5	8	4
Total final producers	338	239	140	78	76	196	252	257	124	135	128
Final users:											
Iron and steel industry[6]	446	538	451	409	365	390	449	449	419	468	449
Other industries[5]	5 519	5 622	5 539	5 261	5 319	5 040	5 249	5 310	4 804	5 275	4 811
Domestic	7 261	8 225	8 439	8 764	8 719	8 871	8 933	9 684	10 242	10 500	10 255
Public administration	814	908	948	966	1 003	1 100	1 095	1 184	1 286	1 326	1 242
Agriculture[7]	..	..	..	..	..	11	13	20	24	29	30
Miscellaneous[7]	930	1 059	1 113	1 144	1 175	1 237	1 314	1 463	1 597	1 636	1 725
Total final users	14 970	16 352	16 490	16 544	16 581	16 649	17 053	18 110	18 372	19 234	18 512
Total sales	15 308	16 591	16 630	16 622	16 657	16 845	17 305	18 367	18 496	19 369	18 639

Note: The breakdown of consumption by industrial users is made according to the 1980 Standard Industrial Classification, though only data for the years 1984 and 1985 are available on this basis.

1 Butane, propane, ethane and refinery tail gases.
2 Including substitute natural gas.
3 Used in works, offices, showrooms, etc.
4 Supply greater than recorded demand (–). Includes losses in distribution.
5 Prior to 1984, included in Other industries under Final users.
6 Prior to 1984, as reported by the Iron and Steel Statistics Bureau.
7 Prior to 1984, included in Miscellaneous.

Source Department of Energy

8.8 Electricity: production and fuel used[1]

	1978	1979	1980	1981	1982	1983	1984	1985	1986	1987	1988
Electricity generated: total	267 491	280 177	267 087	260 422	256 090	261 082	266 645	280 602	282 913	283 320	289 220
England and Wales	231 411	242 127	230 940	224 315	220 505	226 324	227 010	242 248	246 895	246 521	250 303
South of Scotland Electricity Board	25 577	26 907	25 565	25 331	23 276	20 332	22 938	25 771	23 748	25 814	23 942
North of Scotland Hydro-Electric Board	4 176	4 471	4 205	4 640	6 312	8 395	10 451	6 015	5 611	4 204	7 933
Northern Ireland	5 627	5 977	5 673	5 445	5 346	5 384	5 591	5 938	6 018	6 157	6 366
Railway and transport authorities	700	695	704	691	651	647	655	630	641	625	677
Method of generation											
Steam plant (nuclear): total	33 339	34 604	33 462	34 043	40 001	45 776	49 498	56 354	54 005	50 282	58 867
England and Wales	28 459	29 669	26 552	26 706	30 970	35 534	38 764	44 868	42 431	39 241	45 759
South of Scotland Electricity Board	4 880	4 935	6 910	7 337	9 031	10 242	10 733	11 487	11 574	11 041	13 108
Steam plant (other): total	228 762	239 875	228 577	220 849	210 545	209 116	209 711	216 830	221 981	226 957	223 527
England and Wales	202 079	211 538	203 714	196 847	188 768	189 422	185 017	194 276	202 089	205 137	202 339
South of Scotland Electricity Board	20 398	21 657	18 309	17 663	13 896	9 811	11 925	13 992	11 846	14 450	10 465
North of Scotland Hydro-Electric Board	156	200	291	321	1 956	3 907	6 595	2 062	1 487	663	3 749
Northern Ireland	5 560	5 922	5 659	5 428	5 337	5 374	5 584	5 925	5 969	6 132	6 322
Railway and transport authorities	569	558	604	590	588	601	590	575	590	575	651
Gas turbines and oil engines: total	819	895	551	610	580	401	2 012	1 138	609	562	533
England and Wales	312	355	106	150	187	89	1 678	799	220	204	175
South of Scotland Electricity Board	6	4	2	3	7	1	1	1	1	1	1
North of Scotland Hydro-Electric Board	303	344	329	339	314	256	260	271	287	283	288
Northern Ireland	67	55	14	17	9	10	7	13	50	25	43
Railway and transport authorities	131	137	100	101	63	46	65	55	51	49	26
Hydro-electric plant other than pumped storage plant: total	3 388	3 628	3 309	3 917	3 884	3 892	3 368	3 447	3 925	3 313	3 973
England and Wales	210	243	234	258	221	217	167	215	199	225	211
South of Scotland Electricity Board	292	311	344	328	342	279	279	290	327	322	368
North of Scotland Hydro-Electric Board	2 886	3 074	2 731	3 331	3 321	3 397	2 923	2 942	3 400	2 766	3 393
Pumped storage plant: total	1 183	1 175	1 188	1 003	1 080	1 897	2 055	2 831	2 394	2 207	2 320
England and Wales	351	322	334	354	359	1 062	1 383	2 091	1 957	1 715	1 818
North of Scotland Hydro-Electric Board	832	853	854	649	721	835	672	740	437	492	501
	Thousand tonnes										
Fuel used											
Coal: total	80 627	88 539	89 348	87 038	79 816	81 437	53 411	73 940	82 652	86 177	82 470
England and Wales	71 928	79 562	80 546	78 439	72 833	76 314	49 866	68 060	77 338	79 208	77 572
South of Scotland Electricity Board	8 195	8 440	8 236	8 103	6 456	4 566	3 328	5 357	4 980	6 399	4 549
Northern Ireland	504	537	566	496	527	557	216	523	334	570	349
Coke and coke breeze: total	131	158	117	82	69	33	19	–	–	–	–
England and Wales	131	158	117	82	69	33	19	–	–	–	–
Oil: total	11 475	10 670	6 573	5 075	6 232	4 746	21 313	10 638	6 097	4 812	5 391
England and Wales	9 365	8 294	5 016	3 568	4 427	2 579	17 261	8 278	4 009	3 128	2 884
South of Scotland Electricity Board	755	925	202	150	127	75	1 135	591	288	155	127
North of Scotland Hydro-Electric Board	107	126	157	162	543	981	1 589	533	412	217	920
Northern Ireland	1 240	1 300	1 193	1 181	1 126	1 107	1 325	1 219	1 371	1 306	1 458
Railway and transport authorities	8	25	5	14	9	3	3	16	16	7	2
Natural gas[2]: total	1 352	955	557	313	304	311	712	762	285	298	332
England and Wales	1 012	644	218	–	1	1	395	479	4	5	7
Railway and transport authorities	340	311	339	313	303	309	317	283	281	294	325

1 Public electricity supply and railway and transport authorities.

2 Expressed in thousand tonnes of coal equivalent.

Sources *Department of Energy; Scottish Economic Planning Department; Department of Economic Development (Northern Ireland)*

8.9 Electricity: generating capacity of plant and demand[1]
Great Britain

	1978	1979	1980	1981	1982	1983	1984	1985	1986	1987	1988
Capacity of generating plant installed at end of year (Megawatt)	69 911	71 426	70 886	68 382	68 106	67 022	68 632	69 763	70 087	69 704	69 637
Simultaneous maximum load on generating stations during the year[2] (Megawatt)	50 144	49 582	48 284	48 561	47 333	47 396	51 710	50 943	53 980	52 490	51 335
Electricity generated (GWh)	261 164	273 505	260 710	254 286	250 093	255 052	260 399	274 034	276 254	276 539	282 178
Electricity supplied net (GWh)	242 723	254 232	242 377	237 045	232 817	236 296	241 189	252 745	255 536	256 104	260 991
System load factor[3] (Percentage)	*56.1*	*59.4*	*58.0*	*56.0*	*57.1*	*58.0*	*54.1*	*57.8*	*56.1*	*59.4*	*62.1*

1 Public supply stations only.
2 Maximum occurring near the end of the year, or early in the following year.
3 The system load factor is the average hourly quantity of electricity sent out during the year (including purchases from other sources) expressed as a percentage of the maximum potential demand nearest the end of the year or early the following year.

Source *Department of Energy*

8.10 Electricity: sales[1]
Great Britain

GWh

	1978	1979	1980	1981	1982	1983	1984	1985	1986	1987	1988
Total	225 346	235 644	225 053	221 621	217 096	220 532	224 660	235 570	242 969	250 927	256 317
Domestic and farm premises	87 662	91 506	87 907	86 201	84 601	84 713	85 667	90 068	93 496	94 927	93 951
Domestic and commercial[2]	2 426	2 144	2 197	2 129	2 014	1 980	1 987	1 712	1 417	1 408	1 395
Shops, offices and other commercial premises	41 183	44 114	44 539	45 359	46 134	49 055	51 113	55 459	59 242	62 012	65 164
Factories and other industrial premises	89 349	93 167	85 539	83 078	79 806	80 034	81 105	83 419	83 870	87 531	90 687
Public lighting	2 177	2 160	2 252	2 240	2 243	2 261	2 296	2 335	2 316	2 345	2 381
Traction	2 549	2 553	2 619	2 614	2 298	2 488	2 492	2 577	2 627	2 704	2 739

1 Public supply system.
2 Premises used for domestic and commercial purposes having a combined tariff.

Source *Department of Energy*

8.11 Indigenous production, refinery receipts, arrivals and shipments of oil[1]

Thousand tonnes

	1978	1979	1980	1981	1982	1983	1984	1985	1986	1987	1988
Total indigenous petroleum production[2]	54 006	77 854	80 468	89 480	103 219	115 045	126 065	127 642	127 053	123 306	114 406
Crude petroleum[3]:											
Refinery receipts total	96 759	98 325	87 405	76 616	76 705	76 344	78 450	78 653	79 666	80 363	83 796
Indigenous[4]	28 609	38 493	39 844	37 769	40 294	44 815	45 304	43 231	38 780	38 794	40 453
Other[5]	916	606	2 005	2 486	3 162	2 366	2 196	1 095	1 006	939	730
Net foreign arrivals[6]	67 234	59 226	45 556	36 361	33 249	29 163	30 950	34 327	39 880	40 630	42 613
Foreign trade											
Arrivals[6]	68 144	60 380	46 717	36 855	33 754	30 324	32 272	35 576	41 209	41 541	44 272
Shipments											
Indigenous	23 948	39 044	38 531	51 149	60 195	67 397	77 271	79 335	83 341	80 318	69 926
Other[7]	910	1 154	1 161	494	505	1 161	1 363	1 416	1 635	1 113	1 967
Petroleum products											
Foreign trade											
Arrivals[6]	11 586	12 035	9 246	9 402	12 524	9 907	23 082	13 101	11 767	8 570	8 455
Shipments[6]	13 536	13 359	14 598	12 793	13 585	14 674	14 234	17 038	17 726	17 056	17 176
Net arrivals[6]	–1 950	–1 324	–5 352	–3 391	–1 061	–4 767	+8 848	–3 937	–5 959	–8 486	–8 721
Bunkers[8]	2 623	2 671	2 457	2 073	2 583	2 019	2 248	2 118	2 091	1 668	1 831

1 The term indigenous is used in this table for convenience to include oil from the UK Continental Shelf as well as the small amounts produced on the mainland.
2 Crude oil *plus* condensates and petroleum gases derived at onshore treatment plants.
3 Includes process (partly refined) oils.
4 Includes condensate for distillation.
5 Mainly recycled products.
6 Foreign trade as recorded by the petroleum industry and may differ from figures published in *Overseas Trade Statistics.*
7 Re-exports of imported crude which may include some indigenous oil in blend.
8 International marine bunkers.

Source *Department of Energy*

8.12 Throughput of crude and process oils and output of refined products from refineries[1]

Thousand tonnes

	1978	1979	1980	1981	1982	1983	1984	1985	1986	1987	1988
Throughput of crude and process oils	96 319	97 806	86 341	78 287	77 130	76 876	79 117	78 431	80 155	80 449	85 662
less: Refinery fuel[2]:	6 352	6 490	6 265	5 445	5 549	5 297	5 350	5 179	5 404	5 216	5 484
Losses	811	733	849	836	834	652	579	348	662	577	340
Total output of refined products	89 156	90 583	79 227	72 006	70 747	70 927	73 187	72 904	74 089	74 656	79 837
Gases:											
Butane and propane	1 613	1 604	1 366	1 391	1 400	1 482	1 578	1 436	1 328	1 422	1 581
Other petroleum	147	168	92	75	75	56	78	60	93	52	68
Naphtha and other feedstock	4 626	5 242	3 541	3 406	3 492	3 550	3 206	2 883	2 652	2 014	1 856
Aviation spirit	37	67	60	57	44	–	1	4	–	–	–
Wide-cut gasoline	76	87	6	–	–	–	–	–	–	–	–
Motor spirit	15 958	16 111	16 609	17 140	19 134	21 053	22 236	22 254	23 360	24 680	26 409
Industrial and white spirits	81	89	73	115	115	134	142	140	104	117	112
Kerosene:											
Aviation turbine fuel	4 783	5 236	5 198	4 559	4 457	4 723	5 352	5 257	5 813	6 063	6 725
Burning oil	2 602	2 709	2 034	1 904	1 851	1 770	2 066	2 307	2 147	2 270	2 289
Vaporising oil	12	–	–	–	–	–	–	–	–	–	–
Gas/diesel oil	24 024	25 450	22 153	20 411	20 581	21 029	21 547	21 701	22 409	21 424	23 925
Fuel oil	30 518	28 600	23 700	19 069	15 808	13 483	13 071	12 896	12 523	12 797	12 495
Lubricating oils	1 203	1 330	1 250	1 063	990	936	1 108	1 188	909	886	970
Bitumen	1 886	2 065	1 928	1 735	1 862	1 798	1 795	1 764	1 887	2 056	2 296
Petroleum wax	91	98	86	82	71	56	80	71	58	57	63
Petroleum coke	413	452	481	505	492	499	506	517	514	517	541
Other products	1 086	1 275	650	494	375	358	422	426	293	300	509

1 Crude and process oils comprise all feedstocks, other than distillation benzines, for treatment at refinery plants. Refinery production does not cover further treatment of finished products for special grade such as in distillation plant for the preparation of industrial spirits.
2 Comprising 2 252 thousand tonnes gases, 1 962 thousand tonnes fuel oil and 1 002 thousand tonnes other products in 1987.

Source *Department of Energy*

8.13 Deliveries of petroleum products for inland consumption

Thousand tonnes

	1978	1979	1980	1981	1982	1983	1984	1985	1986	1987	1988
Total (including refinery fuel)	90 493	91 044	77 442	71 701	72 795	69 761	86 785	74 960	74 631	72 917	77 037
Total (excluding refinery fuel)	84 141	84 554	71 177	66 256	67 246	64 464	81 435	69 781	69 227	67 701	71 553
Gases:											
Butane and propane:											
For gas works	28	32	31	34	39	35	41	41	44	41	35
Other uses	1 223	1 317	1 160	1 116	1 312	1 522	1 438	997	1 014	1 090	1 052
Other gases											
For gas works	154	160	156	137	97	63	58	50	66	8	–
Other uses	–	–	–	5	154	307	313	45	57	55	59
Feedstock:											
For petroleum chemical plants	5 847	5 880	3 741	4 492	4 165	4 513	4 695	5 032	5 652	5 537	5 942
Naptha (LDF) for gasworks[1]	66	70	71	74	71	56	52	51	46	30	10
Aviation spirit	46	44	40	32	27	28	27	28	29	28	28
Wide-cut gasoline	5	3	3	2	3	2	2	1	–	1	–
Dealers:											
5 star	161	21	–	–	–	–	–	–	–	–	–
4 star	14 101	14 872	15 393	15 041	15 656	16 107	16 990	17 361	18 621	19 520[3]	20 846[5]
3 star	1 112	859	590	410	257	166	111	77	48	29	17
2 star	2 052	2 023	2 181	2 286	2 483	2 431	2 331	2 188	2 052	1 877	1 669
Commercial consumers:											
5 star	37	5	–	–	–	–	–	–	–	–	–
4 star	601	645	706	719	616	621	561	552	535	582[4]	559[6]
3 star	103	101	132	118	103	99	90	86	77	62	51
2 star	181	159	143	144	132	142	143	139	136	115	109
Motor spirit: total	18 348	18 685	19 145	18 718	19 247	19 566	20 226	20 403	21 470	22 184	23 249
Industrial and white spirits	195	200	170	174	175	196	220	214	206	218	246
Kerosene:											
Aviation turbine fuel	4 506	4 666	4 685	4 495	4 474	4 566	4 828	5 007	5 497	5 815	6 200
Burning oil	2 652	2 695	2 103	1 906	1 745	1 663	1 710	1 870	2 020	2 034	1 992
Vaporising oil	8	3	–	–	–	–	–	–	–	–	–
Gas/diesel oil:											
Derv fuel	5 875	6 057	5 854	5 549	5 731	6 183	6 755	7 106	7 866	8 469	9 370
Other	13 600	13 804	11 771	10 994	10 552	9 944	9 967	9 732	9 241	8 608	8 456
Fuel oil	28 233	27 487	19 157	15 645	16 191	12 512	27 843	15 969	12 514	9 935	11 102
Lubricating oils	1 021	1 030	896	837	827	818	818	816	803	828	849
Bitumen	1 887	1 977	1 826	1 666	1 956	1 987	1 900	1 887	2 019	2 162	2 342
Petroleum wax	84	79	71	64	56	57	59	58	60	59	67
Petroleum coke[2]	115	115	100	98	128	142	104	96	268	260	136
Miscellaneous products[2]	248	250	197	218	296	306	379	379	355	339	419

1 Including a small quantity supplied for use as fuel by other consumers.
2 Prior to 1978 estimated.
3 Includes 14 thousand tonnes unleaded petrol.
4 Includes 4 thousand tonnes unleaded petrol.
5 Includes 247 thousand tonnes unleaded petrol.
6 Includes 11 thousand tonnes unleaded petrol.

Source *Department of Energy*

8.14 Iron and steel
Summary of steel supplies, deliveries and stocks

	1977	1978	1979	1980	1981	1982	1983	1984	1985	1986	1987	1988
	Finished product weight—thousand tonnes											
Supply, disposal and consumption												
UK producers' home deliveries	12 202	12 320	12 824	8 224	9 175	8 790	8 757	9 036	8 917	8 337	9 197	10 780
Imports excl steelworks receipts	3 089	3 243	3 330	3 977	2 738	2 988	2 760	2 691	2 924	3 409	3 595	4 228
Total deliveries to home market (a)	15 291	15 563	16 154	12 201	11 913	11 978	11 517	11 727	11 841	11 745	12 792	15 007
Total exports (producers, consumers, merchants)	4 176	4 164	4 326	2 553	3 718	3 281	3 812	3 843	4 562	4 922	6 057	6 168
Exports by UK producers	3 921	3 850	3 992	2 165	3 514	3 045	3 502	3 527	4 156	4 804	5 815	5 902
Derived consumers and merchants exports (b)	255	314	334	388	204	236	310	316	406	118	242	266
Net home disposals (a)—(b)	15 036	15 249	15 820	11 813	11 541	11 542	11 207	11 411	11 435	11 628	12 549	14 742
Consumers and merchants stock change[1]	−325	−394	+222	−674	−713	−370	−300	+170	−180	−310	+100	+30
Estimated home consumption	15 361	15 643	15 598	12 487	12 164	11 912	11 507	11 241	11 615	11 938	12 449	14 712
Stocks												
Producers—ingots and semi-finished steel	2 021	1 716	1 963	1 196	1 243	1 056	1 072	1 130	1 629	1 121	1 198	1 311
—finished steel	1 960	1 901	1 879	1 655	1 560	1 488	1 548	1 633	1 604	1 657	1 701	1 633
Consumers	4 147	3 814	3 640	2 870	2 330	2 110	1 800	1 830	1 640	1 380	1 430	1 480
Merchants	982	921	1 317	1 413	1 240	1 090	1 100	1 240	1 250	1 200	1 250	1 230
	Crude steel equivalent—million tonnes											
Estimated home consumption												
Crude steel production[2]	20.41	20.31	21.46	11.28	15.57	13.70	14.99	15.12	15.72	14.72	17.41	18.95
Producers stock change[1]	+0.19	−0.42	+0.25	−1.12	−0.06	−0.33	+0.10	+0.18	+0.60	−0.69	+0.20	+0.06
Re-usable material	0.08	0.07	0.09	0.09	0.06	0.08	0.10	0.07	0.08	0.08	0.10	0.08
Total supply from home sources	20.68	20.80	21.30	12.49	15.69	14.11	14.99	15.01	15.20	15.49	17.31	11.97
Total imports	4.89	4.79	4.95	5.99	4.30	4.74	4.07	4.34	4.54	4.95	5.06	5.95
Total exports	5.60	5.57	5.80	3.31	4.83	4.45	4.73	4.80	5.62	6.01	7.26	7.39
Net home disposals	19.97	20.02	20.45	15.17	15.16	14.70	14.33	14.55	14.12	14.43	15.11	17.53
Consumers and merchants stock change[1]	−0.55	−0.51	+0.29	−0.88	−0.93	−0.48	−0.38	+0.22	−0.23	−0.39	+0.13	+0.04
Estimated home consumption	20.52	20.53	20.16	16.05	16.09	15.18	14.71	14.33	14.35	14.82	14.98	17.49

TIME SERIES. The figures relate to periods of 52 weeks (53 weeks in 1981).

Note: Figures in the above table have been amended to reflect the Iron and Steel Statistics Bureau's revised definition of the iron and steel industry.

1 Increases in stock are shown as + and decreases in stock (i.e. deliveries from stock) as −.

2 Includes liquid steel for castings.

Sources *Department of Trade and Industry: Iron and Steel Statistics Bureau*

8.15 **Iron and steel**

Iron ore, manganese ore, pig iron and iron and steel scrap

Thousand tonnes

	1977	1978	1979	1980	1981	1982	1983	1984	1985	1986	1987	1988
Iron ore												
Jurassic	3 629	4 131	4 156	874	729	468	382	377	272	288	261	222
Hematite	116	108	113	42	2	2	3	2	3	1	2	2
Production: total	3 745	4 239	4 269	916	731	470	384	379	274	289	263	224
Home produced	3 973	4 477	4 268	875	923	527	449	403	326	352	305	237
Imported	16 026	15 379	16 919	8 475	12 854	11 125	12 756	13 273	14 812	13 991	17 330	19 233
Consumption: total	19 999	19 856	21 188	9 350	13 777	11 652	13 205	13 676	15 138	14 343	17 635	19 470
Manganese ore												
Consumption	352	277	495	168	259	188	262	252	291	309	292	307
Pig iron (and blast furnace ferro-alloys)												
Average number of furnaces in blast during period	*32*	*29*	*26*	*9*	*11*	*10*	*11*	*11*	*11*	*11*	*11*	*11*
Production												
Steelmaking iron	11 533	10 942	12 432	6 099	9 395	8 279	9 400	9 365	10 167	9 632	11 916	12 943
Foundry iron	602	423	329	165	75	48	77	122	214	53	101	113
Spiegeleisen and ferro-manganese	97	69	137	52	84	61	83	75	77	100	92	107
In blast furnaces: total	12 232	11 434	12 898	6 316	9 554	8 388	9 560	9 562	10 458	9 785	12 110	13 163
In steel works and steel foundries	11 753	11 152	12 494	6 065	9 473	8 160	9 468	9 271	10 125	9 613	11 922	13 022
In iron foundries	838	704	709	308	178	152	182	190	160	141	139	145
Consumption of pig iron: total	12 591	11 856	13 203	6 373	9 651	8 312	9 650	9 461	10 285	9 754	12 061	13 167
Pig iron stocks (end of period)	704	473	410	408	94	202	112	106	157	110	98	95
Iron and steel scrap												
Steelworks and steel foundries												
Circulating scrap	6 362	5 835	6 019	3 232	4 146	3 772	3 849	3 558	2 942	2 816	2 652	2 846
Purchased receipts	5 137	5 490	5 663	3 231	3 948	3 976	3 750	4 475	4 270	4 147	4 438	4 654
Consumption	11 858	11 826	11 739	6 756	8 216	7 463	7 670	7 866	6 994	6 660	7 060	7 700
Stocks (end of period)	1 903	1 401	1 284	858	618	742	467	439	438	552	582	382
Iron foundries												
Arisings	1 301	1 273	1 251	848	773	701	697	626	549	453	407	416
Consumption	3 632	3 509	3 473	2 416	2 093	2 035	1 891	1 698	1 402	1 166	1 143	1 159
Stocks (end of period)	356	223	240	173	158	160	108	75	68	89	67	57

TIME SERIES. The figures relate to periods of 52 weeks (53 weeks in 1981).

Sources *Department of Trade and Industry; Iron and Steel Statistics Bureau*

8.16 Iron and steel
Number of furnaces and production of steel

	1977	1978	1979	1980	1981	1982	1983	1984	1985	1986	1987	1988
Steel furnaces (Number in existence at end of period)[1]												
Total	512	471	431	399	400	353	321	310	297	283	268	259
Open hearth	63	21	2	–	–	–	–	–	–	–	–	–
Oxygen converters	23	21	21	16	14	14	14	14	14	14	14	14
Electric	408	414	396	380	384	339	307	296	283	269	254	248
Stock and tropenas	18	15	12	3	2	–	–	–	–	–	–	–
Production of crude steel (thousand tonnes)												
Total	20 411	20 311	21 464	11 277	15 573	13 705	14 986	15 121	15 722	14 725	17 414	18 950
by process												
Open hearth	3 279	1 764	1 163	–	–	–	–	–	–	–	–	–
Oxygen converters	10 843	11 336	12 894	6 689	10 535	9 036	10 496	10 295	11 185	10 560	12 957	14 008
Electric	6 269	7 200	7 385	4 579	5 038	4 669	4 490	4 826	4 537	4 165	4 457	4 942
Stock and tropenas	20	11	22	9	–	–	–	–	–	–	–	–
by cast method												
Cast to ingot	17 382	16 722	17 442	7 845	10 306	8 020	7 754	7 015	6 863	5 573	5 896	5 361
Continuously cast	2 554	3 149	3 627	3 059	4 959	5 341	6 986	7 858	8 620	8 903	11 293	13 356
Steel for castings	475	441	395	373	308	344	247	248	239	249	225	233
by quality												
Non alloy steel	18 529	18 416	19 553	10 041	14 088	12 500	13 887	13 890	14 502	13 587	16 149	15 000
Stainless and other alloy steel	1 882	1 895	1 911	1 236	1 485	1 205	1 100	1 231	1 220	1 138	1 265	1 170
Production of finished steel products (all qualities)[2] (thousand tonnes)												
Rods and bars for reinforcement (in coil and lengths)	948	1 037	982	709	711	675	814	846	916	879	914	1 168
Wire rods and other rods and bars in coil	1 676	1 708	1 779	1 004	1 169	1 011	1 040	1 125	1 136	1 149	1 273	1 349
Hot rolled bars in lengths	1 608	1 608	1 638	1 082	1 020	913	795	834	836	781	836	950
Bright steel bars[3]	558	522	486	353	331	300	292	347	319	307	315	342
Light sections other than rails	351	311	351	268	246	175	177	175	236	283	272	335
Heavy and light rails and accessories	262	233	257	176	219	209	260	227	226	172	237	395
Other heavy sections	1 815	1 907	1 907	1 336	1 856	1 621	1 712	1 594	1 770	1 836	2 060	2 100
Hot rolled plates and sheets in coil and lengths	6 945	6 816	7 525	3 863	6 181	5 506	6 080	6 357	6 135	6 166	7 106	7 853
Cold rolled plates and sheets in coil and lengths	3 852	3 734	3 928	1 873	3 081	2 964	3 208	3 357	3 418	3 342	3 730	3 952
Hot rolled strip	1 134	1 126	1 113	414	249	267	300	320	306	273	301	314
Cold rolled strip[3]	461	455	429	306	297	287	286	315	300	302	329	394
Tinplate	1 176	1 126	1 108	605	886	894	916	963	899	953	1 041	1 018
Other coated sheet	709	779	1 012	556	838	921	1 027	1 111	1 135	1 153	1 373	1 603
Tubes and pipes[3]	1 407	1 478	1 503	1 049	1 269	1 227	1 201	1 348	1 357	1 209	1 317	1 482
Forged bars[3]	11	14	17	15	19	23	12	17	20	13	15	17

TIME SERIES. The figures relate to periods of 52 weeks (53 weeks in 1981).

1 Includes steel furnaces at steel foundries.

2 Includes material for conversion into other products listed in the table.
3 Based on producers' deliveries.

Sources Department of Trade and Industry; Iron and Steel Statistics Bureau.

8.17 Non-ferrous metals

Thousand tonnes

	1977	1978	1979	1980	1981	1982	1983	1984	1985	1986	1987	1988
Copper												
Production of refined copper:												
Primary	44.4	46.2	48.5	68.3	59.8	63.2	67.5	69.5	63.9	62.4	54.0	49.3
Secondary	77.8	79.4	73.2	93.0	76.3	71.0	76.8	67.4	61.6	63.2	68.3	74.7
Home consumption:												
Refined	512.0	501.6	498.8	409.2	333.1	355.4	358.0	352.9	346.5	339.6	327.7	327.7
Scrap (metal content)	131.0	146.8	117.6	121.2	128.0	128.4	109.6	132.5	131.5	135.3	137.7	132.1
Stocks (end of period)[1, 2]	118.7	120.9	92.5	82.0	62.0	69.3	75.8	43.4	37.6	31.6	11.7	13.8
Analysis of home consumption (Refined and scrap):[3] total	643.0	648.4	616.4	530.4	461.1	483.8	467.6	485.4	477.9	474.9	465.4	459.8
Wire[4]	305.5	300.4	288.3	255.7	215.2	226.0	227.0	226.9	225.4	229.6	220.3	217.8
Rods, bars and sections	91.3	93.3	86.6	65.7	56.3	58.8	58.9	67.9	64.6	61.4	62.5	57.3
Sheet, strip and plate	108.4	108.5	102.1	80.1	63.4	69.2	59.9	67.7	66.9	62.4	62.5	66.3
Tubes	83.9	90.8	88.0	78.1	77.2	80.8	80.1	81.3	79.6	80.4	79.1	77.5
Castings and miscellaneous	53.9	55.4	51.3	50.8	48.9	49.0	41.7	41.5	41.4	41.2	41.0	40.9
Zinc												
Slab zinc:												
Production	81.5	73.6	76.7	86.7	81.7	79.3	87.7	85.6	74.3	85.9	81.4	92.8
Home consumption	244.8	247.6	238.8	181.3	185.4	181.6	177.2	182.2	189.3	181.9	188.1	192.8
Stocks (end of period)	22.2	23.8	22.0	19.7	16.1	16.0	19.3	15.9	15.5	15.3	14.0	13.2
Other zinc (metal content):												
Consumption	70.3	72.1	72.9	62.3	56.1	57.8	54.4	54.0	53.3	53.4	52.6	51.7
Analysis of home consumption (slab and scrap): total	315.1	319.7	311.7	243.6	241.5	239.3	231.6	236.2	242.6	235.3	240.7	244.4
Brass	87.5	86.7	81.6	66.7	56.8	59.3	56.6	61.8	58.3	55.1	55.8	54.0
Galvanized products	80.9	85.1	89.1	69.1	80.1	83.5	86.6	90.5	90.5	87.2	95.8	101.4
Zinc sheet and strip	23.4	23.2	20.6	19.1	15.9	14.1	8.6	5.7	5.8	4.6	4.0	4.1
Zinc alloy die castings	62.7	65.9	62.1	37.7	40.1	37.5	39.7	34.9	43.2	44.8	44.0	43.5
Zinc oxide	32.4	29.8	29.9	26.6	21.5	18.7	20.6	19.6	23.4	23.7	22.8	23.2
Other products	28.2	29.1	28.3	24.4	27.2	26.1	19.6	23.8	21.4	20.1	18.3	18.2
Refined lead												
Production[5, 6]	351.1	345.8	368.3	324.8	333.4	306.2	322.2	338.4	327.2	328.6	347.0	373.8
Home consumption[6, 7]												
Refined lead	317.7	336.5	333.2	295.5	265.8	271.9	292.9	295.3	274.3	282.1	287.5	302.5
Scrap and remelted lead[6]	2.4	2.4	2.7	10.0	8.2	9.9	14.3	19.8	29.0	27.0	36.6	37.0
Stocks (end of period)[8]												
Lead bullion	38.9	53.4	68.4	115.7	94.6	13.6	14.8	18.0	13.4	16.1	26.1	18.6
Refined lead at consumers	20.9	24.1	23.4	19.7	21.3	25.7	28.1	28.2	29.5	28.3	24.4	26.7
In LME Warehouses (UK)	26.7	10.9	16.4	19.0	39.5	53.7	60.3	34.2	27.5	18.5	2.8	. .
Analysis of home consumption (refined and scrap): total	320.1	338.9	335.9	305.5	274.0	281.8	307.1	315.4	303.6	309.1	324.1	339.4
Cables	31.1	31.0	26.6	21.7	19.4	20.9	19.2	15.1	13.1	13.0	10.0	11.0
Batteries (excluding oxides)	49.5	54.2	58.1	49.3	41.5	43.7	43.3	46.9	47.4	47.6	48.0	49.2
Oxides and compounds:												
Batteries	47.8	53.6	55.8	49.3	37.7	45.0	44.4	43.9	49.6	46.7	49.0	51.4
Other uses[9]	86.3	96.3	91.8	81.9	75.9	73.5	74.7	75.1	72.1	72.4	82.7	76.8
Sheets and pipes	47.2	47.9	47.1	50.9	51.7	53.6	77.2	84.3	77.6	84.5	86.1	102.4
White lead	1.4	0.9	1.2	0.9	0.7	0.7	0.5	0.4	0.4	. .	. .	. .
Solder	13.8	12.6	11.9	9.7	9.6	9.0	8.4	7.7	7.9	7.6	7.4	9.0
Alloys	13.4	13.4	12.6	11.9	7.1	7.9	11.2	10.9	11.2	11.5	13.6	13.5
Other uses	29.6	29.0	30.8	29.9	30.4	27.6	28.3	31.1	27.0	26.0	27.3	26.1
Tin												
Tin ore (metal content):												
Production	3.8	2.8	2.4	3.0	3.9	4.2	4.1	5.0	5.2	4.3	3.6	3.4
Stocks (end of period)	. .	. .	. .	. .	. .	. .	. .	. .	. .	. .	. .	. .
Tin metal[10]:												
Production[11]	13.9	11.2	11.4	11.4	12.9	13.6	13.3	13.8	14.8	14.9	17.0	13.8
Home consumption[11]	14.9	13.9	13.2	9.9	10.9	10.4	10.2	10.0	9.4	9.7	9.8	10.2
Exports and re-exports[12]	6.8	7.0	6.2	7.0	6.3	5.4	1.0	11.1	7.3	13.6	14.8	14.0
Stocks (end of period):												
Consumers	1.5	1.5	1.2	1.1	1.1	0.9	0.9	1.0	1.0	1.0	1.0	1.0
Merchants and others	. .	. .	. .	. .	. .	. .	. .	. .	. .	. .	. .	. .
Analysis of home consumption (excluding scrap): total	14.9	13.9	13.2	9.9	10.9	10.4	10.2	10.0	9.4	9.7	9.8	10.2
Tinplate	6.4	6.0	5.7	3.1	4.3	4.0	3.8	3.7	3.4	3.3	3.6	3.4
Alloys	4.7	4.7	4.2	3.6	3.4	3.4	3.2	3.1	3.1	3.1	3.2	3.4
Solder	1.1	0.8	1.0	0.9	1.0	0.8	0.9	0.8	0.8	0.9	0.9	1.0
Other uses	2.7	2.4	2.3	2.3	2.2	2.2	2.2	2.4	2.1	2.5	2.1	2.3
Primary aluminium[13]												
Production	349.7	346.2	359.5	374.4	339.2	240.8	252.5	287.9	275.4	275.9	294.4	300.2
Despatches to consumers	526.6	523.8	563.7	520.9	446.2	399.2	418.3	448.3	436.0	451.2	461.6	541.3

See footnotes page 158.

Sources *Department of Trade and Industry; World Bureau of Metal Statistics*

8.17 Non-ferrous metals

(continued)

Thousand tonnes

	1977	1978	1979	1980	1981	1982	1983	1984	1985	1986	1987	1988
Secondary aluminium												
Production	200.8	193.7	176.7	162.1	148.0	114.6	128.3	143.9	127.6	116.4	116.7	105.8
Despatches to consumers	201.7	195.1	179.4	161.0	148.8	114.9	127.5	142.1	126.6	117.2	120.9	
Exports	..	..	..	..	59.2	40.0	37.7	42.1	40.7	42.2	36.7	45.0
Fabricated aluminium												
Total despatches[14]	539.1	542.4	573.9	521.1	444.3	455.4	460.5	473.8	466.0	..	..	..
Rolled products[15]	203.8	189.4	209.5	199.4	165.8	173.7	174.9	191.2	194.6	215.5	224.4	225.7
Extrusions and tubes[16]	176.6	183.8	205.3	183.6	161.2	169.6	177.7	174.5	168.9	..	..	..
Wire products	34.8	35.0	38.2	33.3	31.6	31.9	29.2	28.9	29.9	27.3	27.0	20.9
Castings	121.6	131.9	118.9	101.9	83.3	78.3	77.0	77.5	72.6	73.3	74.8	..
Forgings	2.3	2.3	2.0	2.9	2.3	1.9	1.7	1.7	..	..	..	..
Foil products (Aluminium content)	39.0	39.7	41.3	40.4	37.8	[19]	[19]	[19]	[19]	[19]	..	..
Magnesium and magnesium alloys												
Production[17]	2.7	2.7	2.7	2.8	1.9	1.8	[19]	[19]	[19]	[19]	[19]	[19]
Consumption: total[18]	6.5	6.3	6.0	5.4	4.1	4.1	[19]	[19]	[19]	[19]	[19]	[19]
Refined nickel												
(including ferro-nickel) Production	23.2	21.4	18.9	19.3	25.4	6.9	23.2	22.3	17.8	30.9	29.5	27.7

1 Unwrought copper (electrolytic, fire refined and blister).
2 Reported stocks of refined copper held by consumers and those held in London Metal Exchange (LME) warehouses in the United Kingdom.
3 Copper content.
4 Consumption for high-conductivity copper and cadmium copper wire represented by consumption of wire rods, production of which for export is also included.
5 Lead reclaimed from secondary and scrap material and lead refined from bullion and domestic ores.
6 From 1975, figures for production and consumption of refined lead include antimonial lead, and for scrap and remelted lead, exclude secondary antimonial lead.
7 Including toll transactions involving fabrication.
8 Excluding government stocks.
9 Includes values for White Lead w.e.f. 1986.
10 Including production from imported scrap and residues refined on toll.
11 Primary and secondary metal.
12 Including re-exports on toll transactions.
13 Including primary alloys.
14 Includes wrought, cast and forged products, and excludes foil products.
15 Includes foil stock and excludes foil products.
16 Excluding forging bars, wirebars, and almost two-thirds of despatches of hot rolled rod.
17 Primary and remelt alloys.
18 Despatches to consumers of primary metal, primary and remelt alloys.
19 Data no longer obtainable.

Sources *Department of Trade and Industry; World Bureau of Metal Statistics; Aluminium Federation*

8.18 Cotton, man-made fibres and wool

	Unit	1977	1978	1979	1980	1981	1982	1983	1984	1985	1986	1987	1988
Raw cotton[1]													
Imports	Thousand	104	101	99	69	48	54	50	48	54	52	55	48
Home consumption: total	tonnes	103	92	96	69	46	45	45	44	44	47	51	43
Stocks (end of period)	,,	23	21	17	9	6	5	5	4	4	3	4	4
Cotton waste													
Imports	,,	20.3	24.7	29.0	26.5	22.6	30.2	28.9	27.0	28.7	24.3	28.1	28.4
Cotton linters													
Imports	,,	33.0	33.8	35.7	29.9	25.7	37.8	24.8	31.7	38.4	23.1	23.6	13.6
Man-made fibres[2]													
Production: total	,,	551.8	607.2	596.3	449.7	394.7	333.6	389.3	383.3	330.2	288.0	276.7	280.1
Continuous filament yarn	,,	239.3	240.6	230.6	162.6	126.3	89.3	102.6	102.5	99.1	100.8	99.0	105.3
Staple fibre	,,	312.5	366.6	365.7	287.2	268.4	244.3	286.6	280.9	231.1	187.2	177.7	174.9

Footnotes see page 159.

Source *Department of Trade and Industry*

8.18 Cotton, man-made fibres and wool

(continued)

	Unit	1978	1979	1980	1981	1982	1983	1984	1985	1986	1987	1988
Cotton and man-made fibre yarn	Thousand tonnes											
Production of single yarn:												
Cotton[3]	,,	79.0	79.0	61.3	42.5	42.3	40.9	38.0	38.6	39.8	41.8	35.4
Cotton mixture yarn	,,	26.8	27.4	18.4	15.5	15.6	17.1	17.2	16.5	15.9	16.4	16.5
Spun man-made fibre yarn	,,	43.7	41.9	31.2	25.5	26.5	28.2	28.9	30.1	31.3	33.1	30.0
Cotton waste yarn[4]	,,	12.3	11.8	10.8	8.5	8.7	9.0	9.3	9.5	8.6	9.0	8.3
Other waste yarn	,,	4.8	4.3	2.3	1.9	1.7	2.1	2.6	3.8	3.9	4.1	3.9
Production of doubled yarn	,,	60.6	58.0	49.1	39.8	34.1	30.6	29.8	32.6	31.8	31.4	31.1
Spindle activity[5]:												
Single yarn spindles:												
total (ring equivalent)	Millions	1.96	1.86	1.53	1.17	1.04	0.96	0.95	0.93	0.90	0.86	0.82
Doubling spindles	,,	0.29	0.27	0.22	0.17	0.12	0.11	0.10	0.09	0.09	0.08	0.08
Yarn consumed in cotton and man-made fibre weaving:												
Cotton and waste yarns	Thousand	58.5	58.6	45.5	35.9	35.8	36.2	39.0	39.5	37.0	37.0	31.4
Mixtures yarn[6]	tonnes	—	—	—	—	15.4	16.7	15.1	15.9	17.2	15.9	17.2
Man-made fibres: total	,,	82.2	82.0	62.5	50.3	45.0	41.7	45.7	50.4	51.6	52.4	49.8
Continuous filament yarn	,,	63.5	62.6	50.7	39.4	35.0	31.9	35.0	37.5	38.2	37.2	34.5
Spun yarn	,,	18.7	19.4	11.8	10.9	10.0	9.8	10.7	12.9	13.4	15.2	15.3
Cotton and man-made fibre weaving												
Production of woven cloth:	Million linear											
Cotton	metres	380	365	314	278	261	255	265	274	275	245	219
Man-made fibres	,,	377.8	385.6	298.9	229.9	204.8	176	182.7	206.6	217.7	214.7	212.5
Cotton/man-made fibre mixtures	,,	80.6	81.4	51.2	42.9	45.7	52.3	55.9	48.1	44.7	44.6	44.6
Loom activity												
Average number of looms running on cotton and man-made fibres	Thousands	34.4	32.9	26.2	19.8	16.9	14.7	14.0	13.3	12.6	11.6	11.6
Wool												
Virgin wool (clean weight):	Million kilo-											
Production[7]	grammes	32	32	34	33	33	33	37	40	40	42	44
Imports	,,	105	86[7]	67	76[7]	71[7]	77	82	90	83	98	89
Exports[8]	,,	23	26[7]	25	27[7]	24[7]	26	28	28	31	34	34
Stocks at 31 August	,,	54	49	42	39	21	19	20	23	22	22	21
Consumption:												
Wool	,,	109.0	106.0	92.3	88.2	88.1	90.0	94.9	96.6	100.2	104.0	104.5
Hair	,,	8.6	7.6	6.4	6.6	5.9	6.6	7.2	7.9	7.5	8.3	7.0
Man-made fibres	,,	84.2	73.8	53.1	51.6	48.8	51.5	50.4	53.9	57.6	56.2	53.9
Other fibres[9]	,,	21.0	21.0	15.0	11.5	10.1	10.1	9.0	9.3	8.8	9.8	10.0
Tops												
Production: total	,,	91.8	78.9	65.8	70.1	66.5	70.3	76.0	81.8	83.6	83.1	80.0
Wool and hair	,,	48.7	43.6	39.1	38.7	37.3	38.5	42.9	44.5	43.8	43.8	42.8
Man-made fibres	,,	43.1	35.3	26.7	31.4	29.2	31.8	33.2	37.3	39.8	39.3	37.2
Worsted yarns[10]:												
Production	,,	69.0	60.5	52.8	51.6	53.4	55.6	59.6	61.8	64.8	66.3	60.2
Semi-worsted yarns[10]:												
Production	,,	8.7	8.5	7.1	7.2	8.1	9.4	6.5	7.5	10.2	12.5	13.5
Woollen yarn[7]:												
Production	,,	106	105	81.2	72.0	53.4	56.2	60.5	64.3	72.9	76.7	78.3
Woven woollen and worsted fabrics[11]:	Million square											
Deliveries	metres	144.1	137.8	118.2	96.7	100.3	94.0	90.7	90.9	93.1	90.3	89.0
Blankets:												
Deliveries	,,	22.0	18.2	15.0	9.9	9.4	8.3	9.3	8.9	6.9	6.7	7.2

TIME SERIES. Figures for consumption of raw cotton, and production and consumption of cotton and man-made fibre yarn are for periods of 52 weeks (53 weeks in 1975, 1980 and 1986).

1 From 1978 figures for consumption of raw cotton are for calendar months.
2 Figures are based on returns from producers (excluding waste) and include all man-made fibres in commercial production.
3 Excluding waste yarns.
4 Yarns wholly of cotton waste, cotton yarn spun on condenser system and mixture yarns of cotton and cotton waste.
5 Average of numbers running in last week of each month. Waste spinning spindles are excluded.
6 Figures prior to 1982 are not provided.
7 Estimated.
8 Including imported wool and wool from imported skins, scoured, etc. in the United Kingdom.
9 Including noils, broken tops, wastes, mungo and shoddy.
10 Including all yarn spun on the worsted system.
11 Includes mixture and man-made fibre fabrics classified as wool or worsted, but excludes blankets.

Sources *Department of Trade and Industry; British man-made Fibres Federation; Wool Industry Bureau of Statistics; Textile Statistics Bureau*

8.19 Packaging products of paper and board: manufacturers' sales[1]
United Kingdom

£ million

	1978	1979	1980	1981	1982	1983	1984	1985	1986	1987	1988
Rigid boxes	72.4	79.3	63.5	59.8	60.2	67.0	81.8	88.1	88.7	97.8	91.5
Cartons	406.1	456.5	449.5	451.6	490.7	505.4	516.6	582.5	633.2	697.3	745.6
Fibreboard packing cases:											
Solid	33.2	36.5	34.4	31.0	29.0	27.2	27.6	23.8	..	..	..
Corrugated	442.7	525.0	512.0	513.8	529.4	558.8	653.7	695.7	709.1	768.5	852.3
Paper bags	65.0	74.0	58.1	55.8	57.1	49.1	49.8	53.7	53.0	53.8	54.6
Paper carrier bags	4.3	3.6	2.8	2.3	3.6	6.8	7.2	6.7	6.4	8.2	8.1
Paper sacks	109.8	131.3	116.0	114.7	121.0	119.7	112.5	120.2	108.3	113.4	109.2

1 Up to 1979 sales are by manufacturers employing 25 or more people, and from 1980 by those employing 75 or more in the case of board products or 100 or more in the case of paper products.

Source *Department of Trade and Industry*

8.20 Woodpulp, paper and paper-making materials
United Kingdom

Thousand tonnes

	1978	1979	1980	1981	1982	1983	1984	1985	1986	1987	1988
Woodpulp[1]											
Consumption	1 707.9	1 706.9	1 517.2	1 357.4	1 254.7	1 277.2	1 467.4	1 409.9	1 488.5	1 552.2	1 539.0
Stocks (end of period)	250.3	220.9	160.3	171.6	127.0	154.4	155.4	121.3	133.7	127.0	150.7
Other paper-making materials											
Total (paper equivalent):											
Consumption	2 090.7	2 266.8	2 052.2	1 815.3	1 772.0	1 751.8	1 946.1	2 075.5	2 241.8	2 400.6	2 541.9
Stocks at pulp and paper mills only (end of period)	274.5	224.8	177.2	145.9	148.3	129.1	105.0	208.9	213.5	197.6	216.0
Homegrown pulpwood (including wood waste, chippings and rejected pitprops)											
Consumption	970.0	1 020.6	863.0	397.3	426.0	479.9	606.4	809.9	1 055.5	1 132.6	1 187.0
Stocks at pulp and paper mills only (end of period)	136.5	118.4	89.1	73.0	28.4	27.9	39.5	103.3	89.9	65.6	116.9
Other vegetable fibre (including straw and esparto grass)											
Consumption	11.8	11.2	12.6	24.9	22.0	18.6	19.9	21.0	18.7	21.2	17.4
Stocks at pulp and paper mills only (end of period)	7.7	7.3	3.0	5.9	4.5	3.5	4.0	6.9	6.0	2.7	3.5
Rags, waste ropes, etc.											
Consumption	32.3	25.8	16.3	3.0	6.1	8.1	9.7	8.6	8.1	9.5	11.7
Stocks at pulp and paper mills only (end of period)	7.7	6.1	2.4	1.4	3.0	2.5	3.1	2.9	1.7	1.7	2.6
Waste paper											
Consumption	2 109.1	2 190.6	2 014.5	1 945.4	1 880.9	1 833.6	2 004.3	2 067.1	2 156.0	2 306.4	2 448.9
Stocks at pulp and paper mills only (end of period)	252.8	203.8	165.8	135.4	157.4	135.8	101.7	194.3	207.1	200.8	198.7
Paper and board (excluding building board)											
Production: total	4 164.8	4 222.2	3 788.2	3 378.4	3 226.3	3 296.4	3 587.2	3 684.8	3 923.6	4 178.7	4 343.1
Paper: total[3]	3 194.1	3 278.5	3 050.2	2 699.1	2 585.9	2.651.5	2 928.3	3 022.7	3 254.9	3 498.0	3 577.0
Newsprint	319.0	363.7	363.2	113.1	86.4	79.8	235.7	349.4	458.3	496.7	540.8
Other printings and writings[3,4]	1 059.1	1 055.1	962.6	921.5	866.8	918.2	964.6	965.0	1 081.1	1 183.6	1 229.2
Paper and board for corrugated board[5]	1 020.8	1 035.1	941.9	913.0	914.4	937.4	1 000.6	1 027.7	1 043.4	1 105.7	1 135.6
Other papers mainly used for packaging[5]	178.6	179.0	149.9	120.6	119.4	114.8	104.9	85.8	78.6	79.8	101.8
Toilet or facial tissue stock, towel etc. stock and cellulose wadding[6]	401.8	418.8	434.4	440.4	419.8	425.7	441.6	412.6	416.9	443.9	439.7
Other paper[4,6]	214.8	226.8	198.2	190.5	179.2	175.5	180.9	182.2	176.5	188.3	129.9
Board (excluding building board): total[7]	970.7	943.7	738.0	679.3	640.4	644.9	659.0	662.2	668.7	680.7	766.1
Boards mainly used for packaging	749.2	746.5	586.3	546.1	503.5	511.5	535.9	537.6	537.9	542.4	600.5
Other board[7]	221.5	197.2	151.7	133.2	136.9	133.4	123.0	124.6	130.7	138.3	165.6
Stocks (end of period): total[2]	215.8	212.7	190.5	210.5	191.3	187.7	205.0	233.5	231.9	197.9	199.5
Paper	176.5	169.3	161.3	176.5	161.1	152.4	172.7	200.7	194.8	166.5	165.6
Board (excluding building board)	39.3	43.4	29.2	34.0	30.2	35.4	32.3	32.8	37.1	31.4	33.9

TIME SERIES. The figures relate to periods of 52 weeks (53 weeks in 1982 and 1988).

1 For paper-making and manufacture of cellulose wadding; woodpulp for manufacture of rayon and transparent cellulose film is not included.
2 Stocks held by paper and board makers.
3 Including printing and writing board.
4 Up to 1987, base papers for wallpaper and for heat, light and pressure sensitive papers (including photographic, carbonising and self-copy base) were included with 'Other paper'. From 1988, these papers are included with 'Other printings and writings'.
5 Up to 1987, a small amount of imitation Kraft and sulphite wrapping paper was included with 'Paper and board for corrugated board'. From 1988 these papers are included with 'Other papers mainly used for packaging'.
6 Up to 1987, cigarette paper was included with 'Toilet or facial tissue stock etc'. From 1988, cigarette paper is included with 'Other paper'.
7 Excluding printing and writing board.

Source *Department of Trade and Industry*

8.21 Timber
United Kingdom

Thousand cubic metres

	1977	1978	1979	1980	1981	1982	1983	1984	1985	1986	1987	1988
Softwood												
Deliveries:												
Imported	6 369	6 709	7 053	6 131	5 649	6 237	6 895	6 650	6 441	7 010	..	..
Home grown[1, 2]	309	299	302	388	428	595	618	594	641	781	819	910
Stocks (end of period):												
Imported	2 040	1 798	1 959	1 846	1 646	1 494	1 729	1 765	1 435	1 429	..	..
Total	6 678	7 008	7 355	6 519	6 077	6 832	7 513	7 244	7 082	7 788	..	..
Hardwood												
Deliveries:												
Imported	813	842	964	766	717	740	951	841	830	855	..	..
Home grown[1, 2]	160	170	149	108	85	74	78	47	63	89	63	59
Stocks (end of period):												
Imported	282	270	300	228	223	232	272	271	249	241	..	..
Total	973	1 012	1 113	874	802	814	1 029	888	893	944	..	..
Imported plywood												
Deliveries	892	1 059	1 159	830	972	920	1 068	1 019	1 090	1 119	..	..
Stocks (end of period)	197	196	216	142	209	130	191	212	163	247	..	..
Mining timber												
Production:												
Sawn	355.2	373.5	372.3	407.6	407.2	428.3	415.2	135.6	306.8	335.9	300.2	281.7
Round	143.9	140.4	137.1	152.6	149.7	136.3	124.2	45.8	94.9	87.9	65.3	48.8
Total	499.1	513.8	509.5	560.2	556.9	564.6	539.4	181.4[4]	401.7	423.8	365.5	330.5
Consumption:												
Sawn	365.2	384.0	382.2	424.4	415.8	429.4	415.5	135.6	306.8	335.9	300.2	281.7
Round[5]	233.0	215.1	202.0	214.6	198.1	175.9	149.6	48.2	101.0	94.2	68.9	48.8
Stocks (end of period):												
Sawn	58.7	55.2	57.2	70.3	54.2	64.7	61.2	62.0	43.4	43.2	30.2	37.7
Round	169.8	134.7	103.5	45.2	96.1	62.6	39.9	27.7	21.0	18.0	10.5	10.4
Wood chipboard												
Production[3]	369.8	366.5	597.9	606.7	524.7	514.6	518.5	541.4	728.0	..	..	..
Stocks (end of period)[3]	23.0	37.2	32.6	55.4	24.1	45.5	39.4	38.5	47.8	..	..	..

TIME SERIES. Figures for wood chipboard relate to periods of 52 weeks (53 weeks in 1976 and 1982).

1 Up to and including 1979 sales of home-grown timber and of plywood are by firms employing 25 or more people and from 1980 by firms employing 35 or more people.
2 Home-grown excludes mining timber and relates to sawn and planed only. From 1976, home-grown hardwood also excludes planed timber.
3 Up to and including 1978 woodchip board figures are in thousand tonnes.
4 Reduction due to the miners' strike.
5 As from 02/88 imported materials no longer used for mining purposes.

Sources *Department of Trade and Industry; Timber Trade Federation; British Coal*

8.22 Synthetic rubber, carbon black and rubber products[1]
United Kingdom

	Unit	1978	1979	1980	1981	1982	1983	1984	1985	1986	1987	1988
Synthetic rubber	Thousand tonnes											
UK manufactures sales												
Synthetic rubber: total	,,	..	..	..	220.7	202.8	209.8	237.0	220.7	242.4	245.2	295.8
Solid	,,	..	..	..	139.6	139.0	145.3	165.9	162.4	182.8	178.5	204.3
Latex	,,	..	..	..	81.1	63.8	64.5	71.1	58.3	59.6	66.7	91.5
Carbon black												
Production[2]	,,	198.9	199.9	172.3	152.5	..[3]	..[3]	..[3]	..[3]	..[3]	..[3]	..
Rubber products	£ million											
UK manufactures sales												
Rubber products: total	,,	1 551.3	1 718.9	1 637.8	1 483.1	1 445.9	1 509.8	1 538.8	1 682.1	1 815.3	2 026.5	2 153.1
New tyres	,,	558.4	611.8	650.9	588.3	574.5	608.7	609.0	662.4	742.3	871.3	922.7
Retreads	,,	52.0	54.8	43.0	40.7	38.0	47.3	53.6	56.1	57.9	63.4	68.6
Tubes[4]	,,	24.5	26.3	27.8	24.2	26.5	22.1	22.9	19.6	10.6	11.1	14.1
Belting	,,	90.1	104.5	118.9	103.1	114.0	104.4	88.0	89.1	89.2	89.2	94.2
Hose/tubing	,,	126.8	142.6	131.9	127.1	126.9	122.6	125.9	144.6	152.6	163.5	170.7
Other products	,,	699.5	778.9	665.6	599.7	566.0	604.7	639.4	710.3	762.7	828.0	882.8

1 Figures prior to 1981 for synthetic rubber/carbon black and rubber products relate to establishments with minimum employment levels of 25 persons. From 1981 minimum employment levels for carbon black and rubber products are 75 and 100 respectively; except for those establishments producing new tyres and tubes whose minimum employment level is 300 persons.
2 Including lamp and vegetable black; excluding acetylene and bone black.
3 Data no longer published.
4 Figures include Repair Kits/materials and moulded solid rubber tyres with or without metallic bondings.

Source *Department of Trade and Industry*

8.23 Fertilisers
Years ended 31 May

Thousand tonnes

	1976	1977	1978	1979	1980	1981	1982	1983	1984	1985	1986	1987	1988
Deliveries to UK agriculture													
N (nitrogen):—nutrient content													
Straight	..	581	579	638	701	695	785	896	857	903	850	883	674
Compounds	..	509	538	522	544	468	476	529	476	471	445	472	482
P_2O_5 (phosphate)	355	377	388	394	394	372	379	407	395	404	367	355	331
K_2O (potash)	414	385	393	395	425	388	407	467	465	477	454	446	425
Compounds—total weight	2 746	3 077	3 062	3 024	3 120	2 819	2 922	3 260	3 082	3 167	3 022	2 997	3 013

Sources *Department of Trade and Industry; Fertiliser Manufacturers Association*

8.24 Synthetic dyestuffs, colours, paint, varnish and allied products[1]

	Unit	1976	1977	1978	1979	1980	1981[1]	1982	1983	1984	1985	1986	1987	1988
Dyestuffs and pigments	Thousand tonnes													
Finished synthetic dyestuffs	,,	52.0	53.7	48.3	53.2	46.2	42.6	42.4	42.1	43.5	42.9	46.0	51.3	53.8
Synthetic organic pigments	,,	16.7	16.9	15.8	15.7	13.0	10.5	9.8	11.9	..[4]	..[4]	..[4]	..[4]	..[4]
Inorganic pigment colours	,,	22.3	21.3	19.7	20.3	17.0	13.2	11.9	13.6	12.8	12.2	11.1	12.1	12.9
Ochres and mineral colours	,,	22.8	26.6	27.9	21.5	16.0	..[4]	..[4]	..[4]	..[4]	..[4]	..[4]	..[4]	..[4]
Titanium dioxide	,,	191.4	198.1	205.3	192.9	186.7	169.6	172.3	194.9	206.0	219.1	229.9	255.6	266.3
White lead	,,	1.1	0.9	0.8	0.5	0.4	..[4]	..[4]	..[4]	..[4]	..[4]	..[4]	..[4]	..[4]
Paint, varnish and allied products														
Sales by larger establishments	Million litres													
All paints and varnishes: total		585.2	612.0	630.4	660.0	596.0	523.0	533.1	541.5[5]	560.7	573.2	599.9	849.8	904.7
Emulsion paints	,,	170.1	174.4	184.9	183.1	173.4	158.2	171.5	178.2	186.4	202.3	210.7	234.9	245.4
Other aqueous paints	,,	25.7	27.3	27.0	21.6	23.7	33.9	38.0	39.3	41.4	45.1	47.1	49.5	35.7
Cellulose based varnishes, lacquers and clear solutions and pigmented cellulose paints	,,	42.4	48.7	46.6	51.4	40.2	32.2	26.2	28.9	29.4	26.8	31.7	35.3	36.5
Varnishes, lacquers and stains (other than cellulose)	,,	5.5	6.5	7.8	10.5	8.9	9.2	9.4	10.0	9.6	10.1	11.1	9.8	10.7
Others[2]	,,	341.5	355.1	364.1	393.4	349.8	289.5	287.9	285.0[5]	293.9	288.9	299.3	317.4	365.5
Manufactured thinners (solvent mixtures), removers and strippers[3]	,,	52.3	54.7	58.8	71.8	66.3	60.2	57.0	61.0	63.4	61.1	63.4	63.3	69.1
Mastics and putty	Mn. kilogrammes	65.0	57.4	65.9	64.3	65.1	64.6	73.5	76.8	85.5	100.2	119.8	139.6	141.8

1 Figures relate to sales by manufacturers in the United Kingdom employing 25 or more persons and from 1981 those with a minimum employment of 50.
2 Including oil and/or synthetic based non-aqueous products, marine paints, and bituminous paints. Figures prior to 1981 include paste fillers.
3 Removers and strippers are excluded from 1975 to 1978 data.
4 Data no longer published.
5 1983 is an estimated figure.

Source *Department of Trade and Industry*

8.25 Inorganic chemicals

Thousand tonnes

	1976	1977	1978	1979	1980	1981	1982	1983	1984	1985	1986	1987	1988
Materials used for the manufacture of sulphuric acid													
Zinc concentrates:													
Consumption	129.3	208.4	178.5	215.8	242.6	188.7	210.1	238.1	243.6	237.3	242.8	220.8	195.6
Spent oxide:													
Consumption	12.0	11.1	12.5	9.3	10.6	7.6	6.1	6.6	1.3	..	..	..	..
Stocks (end of period)	7.3	7.8	4.7	3.1	0.9	0.8	8.1	4.7	4.7	..	..	..	..
Sulphur:													
Consumption (for acid production)[1]	1 056.4	1 078.6	1 104.0	1 106.9	1 058.6	926.0	805.0	824.2	828.1	775.2	713.1	670.3	709.2
Stocks (end of period)[1]	55.6	44.1	53.2	41.0	48.7	50.5	36.7	32.1	45.8	31.0	18.8	21.1	22.3
Sulphuric acid[2]													
Production	3 271.2	3 404.9	3 453.1	3 498.1	3 380.7	2 888.9	2 587.3	2 628.7	2 654.2	2 525.1	2 329.8	2 157.7[2]	2 270.3
Consumption[3]: total	3 561.2	3 536.6	3 450.5	3 504.3	3 241.2	2 899.2	2 586.6	2 809.7	2 786.4	2 667.0	2 479.6	2 335.3	2 439.2
Fertilisers	1 097.4	1 057.1	1 096.3	1 072.0	1 042.8	901.2	749.3	857.1	739.4	661.3	508.4	335.8	246.5
All other chemical uses[4]	1 691.5	1 780.5	1 652.4	1 719.3	1 571.7	1 998.0	1 837.3	1 952.6	2 047.0	2 005.7	1 971.1	1 999.5	2 192.5
Metallurgy	83.8	79.1	74.4	69.0	50.4	..	..	..	..	..	..	..	
Other (incl. Textiles)	688.5	619.9	627.4	644.0	576.3	..	..	..	..	..	..	..	
Stocks (end of period)	172.3	162.2	174.8	139.3	145.0	151.2	122.3	113.0	118.8	106.9	91.5	72.7	79.7

1 Filter cake and boiler bottom are included.
2 As 100 per cent acid.
3 Including recovered and imported acid.
4 Figures from 1981 include Metallurgy and other (incl. Textiles).

Sources Department of Trade and Industry; National Sulphuric Acid Association

8.26 Organic chemicals: production[1]

Thousand tonnes[2]

	1976	1977	1978	1979	1980	1981	1982	1983	1984	1985	1986	1987	1988
Ethylene[3]	1 286.1	1 137.5	1 095.7	1 233.6	1 094.9	1 235.5	1 115.4	1 154.6	1 324.3	1 446.5	1 740.1	1 797.9	2 005.2
Propylene[3]	747.5	659.6	670.8	765.8	572.7	736.6	824.2	831.9	975.8	973.2	864.2	874.9	847.9
Butadiene[3]	230.2	221.7	209.4	227.1	191.9	207.9	228.8	237.7	259.2	297.6	192.9	231.4	239.7
Benzene[4]	928.0	844.6	790.7	1 056.3	825.5	751.9	569.5	725.9	754.7	834.9	852.8	911.6	941.7
Toluene[5]	273.1	212.9	199.5	293.7	170.1	179.0	[8]	[8]	[8]	164.8	..	..	..
Formaldehyde[6]	132.7	146.1	131.6	137.8	123.9	113.0	107.2	97.8	103.6	123.7	103.2	113.5	111.6
Propyl alcohols	130.9	154.3	145.2	135.7	61.4	[9]							
Acetone	149.0	143.7	145.6	146.9	122.6	111.2	135.3	121.8	161.5	146.8	123.2	117.9	127.5
Phenol (synthetic)	184.6	168.1	169.1	178.6	..	109.7	140.0	143.2	184.4	117.5	52.9	..	..
Phthalic anhydride	..	98.2	90.9	94.4	46.3	61.1	73.0	[9]					
Ethyl alcohol[7] (Thousand hectolitres of alcohol)	2 496.1	2 710.8	2 982.6	2 808.7	1 810.6	1 839.4	2 071.5	2 398.1	3 043.3	2 509.5	2 538.0	2 980.1	2 968.1

1 Figures relate to total production i.e. 'captive use' is included.
2 Except for Ethyl alcohol which is measured in thousand hectolitres of alcohol.
3 Produced from oil base, other than for use as fuel.
4 Includes production obtained by dealkylation of toluene (excludes production from coal).
5 Includes that used for the production of benzene, but excludes production from coal.
6 Including paraformaldehyde (expressed as 100 per cent formaldehyde).
7 Industrial alcohol made from molasses and derived from other processes. The figures include a small quantity of beverage spirits produced by rectification of spirits distilled from molasses. In the financial year ended 31 March 1985 this amounted to about 13.21 thousand hectolitres of alcohol a month.
8 Figures suppressed for disclosure reasons.
9 No longer published in the *Business Monitor* series.

Sources Department of Trade and Industry; HM Customs and Excise

8.27 Production of synthetic resins[1]

Thousand tonnes

	1977	1978	1979	1980	1981[2]	1982	1983	1984	1985	1986	1987	1988
All synthetic resins	2 571.3	2 614.9	2 646.5	2 259.3	1 972.8[4]	1 664.4[4]	1 411.7[4]	1 559.2[4]	1 698.9[4]	1 080.9[4]	1 555.2	1 564.1
Products of condensation, polycondensation and polyaddition	864.7	895.7	880.1	729.9	673.3	617.0	466.5[4]	595.5[4]	608.0[4]	382.2[4]	652.8[4]	461.2
Alkyds (including styrenated alkyds and unsaturated polyesters):												
Solid and liquid alkyd resins including solutions, emulsions and dispersions (net resin content including oil but excluding solvent)	132.0	123.1	129.8	111.8	102.5	99.1	98.0	97.8	79.2	78.5	82.0	97.1
Unsaturated polyester resins (including reactive monomer, but excluding filler)	59.0	60.8	59.6	48.4	51.0	48.6	50.2	52.1	55.0	58.7	66.8	79.9
Aminoplastics: Alkylated resin solutions (actual weight including solvent); Solid resins; Other liquid resins and solutions (actual weight including solvent)	178.4	167.2	164.5	164.8	155.1	139.4	143.7	161.0	157.2	167.6	184.3	202.7
Phenolics:												
Straight liquid resins, including aqueous solutions and dispersions (actual weight including water)	29.5	25.0	26.9	15.9	17.1	17.3	18.5	15.7	15.6	14.5	14.5	16.3
Straight resins, solid or in organic solution	22.5	22.3	21.6	20.7	18.3	20.2	21.5	18.4	19.3	18.4	27.2	26.5
Modified resins, including those in solution	5.9	5.7	6.2	4.6	4.1	3.8	3.6	4.6	4.1	..[5]		
Polyurethanes	78.9	81.5	85.2	73.2	75.0	83.9	93.3	..[5]	..[5]	..[5]	..[5]	..[5]
Epoxide resins (net resin content excluding added non-reactive solvent and/or filler)	21.4	24.1	27.0	27.0	28.4	27.7	37.7	36.3	43.7	44.5	42.9	38.7
Other[3]	337.1	386.0	359.3	263.5	222.0	177.0	..[5]	209.6	233.9	..[5]	235.1	..[5]
Products of polymerisation and co-polymerisation	1 597.2	1 611.1	1 665.2	1 323.4	1 207.7[4]	972.8[4]	884.8[4]	893.2[4]	1 019.5[4]	627.2[4]	902.4[4]	1 102.9
Acrylics: Lattices, dispersions and solutions; Moulding and extrusion compounds, cast sheet, cast rod and cast tube (based on methyl methacrylic monomer)	60.9	68.3	71.3	58.7	50.3	63.7	59.3	67.8	69.0	75.8	102.6	113.0
Polyolefines:												
Polyethylene	489.4	428.4	483.6	434.8	454.4	425.8	407.2	406.1	520.1	427.4	398.0	461.4
Polypropylene	248.2	292.3	263.4	190.4	197.5	221.4	229.9	258.2	269.0	..[5]	277.7	314.6
Polyvinyl acetate, including solutions and dispersions (net resin content excluding plasticiser)	105.3	116.5	113.4	93.9	94.8	92.8	91.6	100.2	103.2	117.4	128.7	127.0
Polyvinyl chloride (including lattices, solutions and dispersions)	386.4	410.1	440.2	349.7	314.8	..[5]	..[5]	..[5]	..[5]	..[5]	..[5]	..[5]
Styrene polymers and co-polymers:												
Non-toughened straight polystyrene resins, moulding and extrusion compounds	59.4	53.3	48.9	39.5	36.9	22.0	29.8	..[5]	..[5]	..[5]	..[5]	23.1
Toughened grades of resins, moulding and extrusion compounds	102.0	109.6	100.8	67.0	59.0	61.2	67.0	60.9	58.2	..[5]	..[5]	63.8
Other, including solutions, emulsions and dispersions, co-polymer resins and non-toughened co-polymer moulding and extrusion compounds but excluding styrene-butadiene co-polymers	67.5	46.2	66.8	50.6	..[5]	..[5]	..[5]	..[5]	..[5]	..[5]	..[5]	..[5]
Other	78.1	86.4	76.8	38.8	..[5]	85.9	..[5]	..[5]	..[5]	..[5]	..[5]	..[5]
Cellulosics and other plastics and modified natural resins	109.4	108.1	101.2	93.6	91.8	74.6	57.0[4]	70.5	71.4	71.5	68.7	..[5]
Regenerated cellulose film	77.7	79.8	73.8	78.8	76.7	62.6	57.0	54.6	55.0	52.9	49.3	..[5]
Other cellulosics and other plastics and modified natural resins (including casein, alginates and resin ester gums)	31.7	28.3	27.4	14.8	15.1	12.0	..[5]	15.9	16.4	18.6	18.2	19.9

1 Unless separately specified, all figures are in terms of net resin content and co-polymers are recorded against the heading for resins made from the major monomeric ingredient of the co-polymer.
2 From 1981 figures relate to establishments with a minimum employment level of 75. Previous figures were based on a minimum of 25 persons.
3 Includes production of polymers and co-polymers of polyamide and polyester by firms classified to man-made fibre industry.
4 Totals do not include suppressed figures.
5 Data suppressed for disclosure reasons.

Source Department of Trade and Industry

8.28 Minerals: production

Great Britain

Thousand tonnes

	1978	1979	1980	1981	1982	1983	1984	1985	1986	1987	1988
Limestone[1]	83 839	86 655	72 423	62 850	69 114	75 753	75 533	77 567	81 207	93 617	103 410
Sandstone	10 026	10 519	9 788	9 611	10 803	12 199	12 529	10 870	11 337	13 804	16 031
Igneous rock	27 807	29 098	28 497	25 323	29 987	30 733	29 969	31 720	34 038	39 529	44 636
Clay/shale	25 473	21 644	19 825	18 799	20 323	22 403	17 817	18 909	17 169	17 862	18 534
Industrial sand	6 224	5 829	5 708	4 451	4 123	4 026	4 328	4 178	4 108	4 029	4 340
Chalk	16 321	15 945	13 732	11 756	11 616	12 430	12 022	12 023	12 511	13 444	14 516
Fireclay	1 404	1 710	1 217	992	850	689	757	831	940	900	1 057
Barium sulphate	54.4	45.5	53.9	63.3	81.1	36.0	62.7	107.3	86.8	76.8	76.2
Calcium fluoride	189.3	153.6	186.1	255.5	200.8	131.3	136.7	167.4	133.4	120.4	103.7
Copper	0.1	..	0.2	0.6	0.6	0.7	0.7	0.6	0.6	0.8	0.7
Lead	4.6	4.7	3.6	7.0	4.0	3.8	2.4	4.0	0.6	0.7	1.2
Tin	3.2	2.7	3.3	3.7	4.2	4.0	5.2	4.3	3.8	3.7	3.4
Zinc	2.7	0.6	4.4	10.9	10.2	8.9	7.5	5.3	5.7	6.6	5.5
Iron ore: crude	4 254	4 272	960	703	392	262	246	147	291	246	227
Iron ore: iron content	1 116	1 130	225	162	85	57	53	31	77	56	50
Calcspar	13	21	18	20	18	10	7	6	10	..	23
China clay (including ball clay)	4 199	4 444	3 964	3 508	3 358	3 346	3 607	3 762	3 780	4 054	4 352
Chert and flint	52	47	14	10	..	174	17	22	14	16	11
Fuller's earth	218	..	..	205	243	267	286	292	248	..	277
Lignite	8	..	..	..	..	1	2	5	7	6	18
Rock salt	1 311	1 590	1 746	1 350	2 209	1 316	1 569	2 030	2 040	1 855	877
Salt from brine	1 760	1 915	1 608	1 454	1 554	1 394	1 423	1 552	1 510	1 554	1 426
Salt in brine	4 239	4 315	3 800	3 916	3 874	3 601	4 134	3 563	3 305	3 672	3 827
Anhydrite	92	..	76	47	67	51	56	59	53	..	..
Dolomite[2]	..	2 937	14 060	13 936	13 727	14 983	14 228	14 953	15 851	17 037	19 861
Gypsum	3 230	..	3 371	2 897	2 674	2 916	3 082	3 130	3 363	..	..
Slate[3]	945	513	225	350	785	494	157	158	242	322	708
Soapstone and talc	18	17	17	18	19	16	19	20	12	12	14
Sand and gravel (land-won)	90 196	89 267	83 624	77 951	79 287	88 002	87 092	87 813	90 215	95 409	110 516
Sand and gravel (marine dredged)	12 159	13 488	12 534	11 501	11 919	12 797	12 582	13 792	15 284	16 220	19 638

1 Prior to 1980, includes dolomite for constructional uses.

2 Prior to 1980, figures relate to dolomite and high magnesium limestone for special uses only.

3 Includes waste used for constructional fill, and powder and granules used in manufacturing.

Source *Central Statistical Office*

Northern Ireland

Thousand tonnes

	1978	1979	1980	1981	1982	1983	1984	1985	1986	1987	1988
Chalk	410	320	317	..	..	..	..	..	..	..	..
Clay and shale	..	..	..	..	..	..	..	..	397	409	..
Sand and gravel	4 127	4 300	3 807	3 738	3 665	3 207	3 506	3 627	4 226	3 634	3 871
Basalt and igneous rock (other than granite)	7 443	7 080	6 179	5 449	6 151	6 140	6 856	6 717	6 731	6 380	7 324
Limestone	2 465	2 602	2 290	2 281	2 609	3 249	3 707	3 057	3 436	3 041	2 409
Grit and conglomerate	3 364	3 025	2 809	2 622	2 524	2 532	2 578	2 307	2 693	2 573	2 870
Diatomite	..	..	..	..	..	..	..	..	..	..	..
Granite	..	..	..	..	..	..	..	..	189	107	..
Sandstone	..	..	..	..	..	..	..	..	..	..	..
Rock salt	..	..	..	..	..	..	..	..	..	..	..

Source *Department of Economic Development (Northern Ireland)*

8.29 Building materials and components: production[1]

Great Britain

	Unit	1977	1978	1979	1980	1981	1982	1983	1984	1985	1986	1987	1988
Building bricks (excluding refractory and glazed)	Millions	5 067	4 842	4 887	4 562	3 725	3 517	3 806	4 012	4 100	3 971	4 222	4 682
Cement[2]	Thousand tonnes	15 457	15 916	16 140	14 805	12 729	12 962	13 396	13 481	13 339	13 413	14 311	..
Building sand[3, 4]	,,	18 608	18 510	18 983	18 005	15 675	17 044	19 151	18 187	18 346	20 423	20 620	23 927[11]
Concreting sand[4]	,,	27 483	29 164	29 455	26 699	25 427	25 242	26 720	28 172	28 694	30 347	32 823	36 707[11]
Gravel[4, 5]	,,	53 138	54 426	54 056	51 454	48 351	48 920	54 929	53 316	54 564	54 729	38 185	67 493[11]
Crushed rock aggregates:[6]	Thousand tonnes												
used as roadstone (coated)		14 374	13 910	14 413	14 366	13 179	17 739	18 562	17 424	18 188	19 239	22 599	..
roadstone (uncoated)	,,	35 756	37 807	41 785	42 896	35 949	35 259	38 522	36 660	41 168	44 185	50 784	..
fill and ballast	,,	29 227	31 131	31 722	31 619	31 049	37 129	40 416	42 234	42 426	45 227	53 411	..
concrete aggregate	,,	15 259	15 872	15 588	13 653	11 205	12 721	14 582	14 360	13 214	13 715	15 443	..
Ready mixed concrete[2]	Million m^3	23.5	23.8	24.4	22.4	19.9	20.7	21.5	20.8	21.6	21.5[12]	24.4	28.8
Fibre cement products	Thousand tonnes	449.9	428.8	405.5	352.2	265.6	261.7	239.5	255.5	252.6	217.4	205.4	251.0
Clay roofing tiles[2, 7]	Thousand m^2	1 192	1 207	2 265	1 698	1 635	1 632	2 206	205.1	2 143	2 587	3 019	..
Concrete roofing tiles	,,	24 151	27 899	28 263	28 813	23 345	25 551	33 243	34 685	27 870	30 843	34 707	38 818
Concrete building blocks:[2]													
dense aggregate	,,	19 206	20 780	22 298	21 014	18 911	23 918	29 186	31 907	30 431	33 483	36 348[12]	44 404
lightweight aggregate	,,	27 118	29 937	28 407	23 779	20 896	23 395	25 544	24 378	21 867	27 515	31 121	33 530
aerated concrete	,,	20 542	20 343	22 385	22 027	15 758	16 372	20 912	25 358	22 147	26 156	29 328[12]	32 095
Concrete pipes[2, 7]	Thousand tonnes	1 111	1 158	1 063	692	648	694	744	701	571	630[12]	533	687
Roofing slates[8]	,,	14.3	15.0	14.5	17.7	16.3	22.7	18.4	22.0	34.0	34.7	45.6	40.9
Slates (damp-proof course)[8]	,,												
Gypsum (excluding anhydrite)	,,	3 136	3 144	3 396	3 264	2 667	2 566	2 978	3 155	3 074	3 253	..[10]	..
Plaster	,,	988	975	949	960	775	764	855	912	876	912	..[10]	..
Plasterboard	Thousand m^2	101 827	114 120	113 961	111 132	101 987	107 867	120 819	127 668	122 599	134 501	..[10]	..
Unglazed floorquarries[2, 7]	Thousand m^2	1 155	1 273	1 220	1 123	1 007	949	1 013	1 000	900	932	1 078	..
Unglazed tiles[2, 7]	,,	1 900	2 025	2 099	2 332	2 085	1 357	1 146	1 277	1 263	1 350	1 175	..
Copper tubing[2, 9]	Thousand tonnes	73	80	79	69	68	72	74	..[10]	..	..	..	..

1 The figures are summaries of returns made by manufacturers and producers. They represent total production and not merely the quantities available for building purposes.
2 United Kingdom.
3 Including sand used in the production of sand lime bricks.
4 From 1979 figures represent volume sold, not production.
5 Figures include hoggin, concrete aggregate, other purposes (excluding fill) and fill.
6 From 1979 figures represent volume sold, not production.
7 Figures represent volume sold, not production.
8 From 1985 figures refer to slates used for architectural and cladding uses, roofing and damp proof courses.
9 Figures relate to the production of copper tubes for all purposes including those used in the construction industry.
10 Series discontinued.
11 Provisional.
12 Revised.

Sources *Department of the Environment; Central Statistical Office; Department of Trade and Industry; World Bureau of Metal Statistics*

8.30 Construction: value of output in Great Britain

£ million

	1978	1979	1980	1981	1982	1983	1984	1985	1986	1987	1988
All work: total	15 702	18 871	22 052	21 547	22 540	24 343	26 203	27 850	30 123	34 580	40 546
New work: total	10 313	11 722	13 055	12 354	12 629	13 396	14 192	14 921	16 286	19 066	23 420
New housing: total	4 124	4 384	4 296	3 738	3 920	4 849	4 908	4 766	5 539	6 745	8 469
For public sector	1 749	1 711	1 711	1 222	1 021	1 120	1 077	918	842	933	922
For private sector	2 375	2 673	2 585	2 516	2 899	3 729	3 831	3 848	4 697	5 812	7 547
Other new work: total	6 189	7 338	8 760	8 616	8 709	8 546	9 285	10 154	10 747	12 321	14 951
For public sector	2 764	3 068	3 524	3 572	3 671	3 729	3 833	3 786	3 888	3 870	4 318
For private sector: total	3 425	4 270	5 236	5 044	5 038	4 817	5 452	6 368	6 859	8 451	10 633
Industrial	1 802	2 351	2 806	2 382	2 087	1 850	2 342	2 848	2 632	3 204	4 023
Commercial	1 623	1 919	2 430	2 662	2 951	2 967	3 110	3 520	4 226	5 247	6 610
Repair and maintenance: total	5 389	7 148	8 997	9 193	9 911	10 948	12 011	12 930	13 837	15 515	17 125
Housing	2 571	3 601	4 480	4 568	4 970	5 622	6 251	6 809	7 427	8 360	9 327
Public other work	1 854	2 269	2 920	3 026	3 285	3 548	3 746	3 800	3 768	4 042	4 251
Private other work	964	1 278	1 597	1 599	1 656	1 777	2 014	2 321	2 642	3 112	3 547

Note:
(i) Output by contractors, including unrecorded estimates by small firms and self-employed workers, and by the public sector's direct labour departments classified to construction in the *Standard Industrial Classification, Revised 1980.*

Source Department of the Environment

8.31 Construction: value of new orders obtained by contractors[1]
Great Britain

£ million

	1978	1979	1980	1981	1982	1983	1984	1985	1986	1987[3]	1988
New work: total	8 927	10 024	10 110	10 722	11 443	13 518	14 630	15 343	17 108	22 119	26 299
New housing: total	3 231	3 321	2 702	2 685	3 912	5 063	4 877	5 290	6 193	7 344	8 776
From public sector	1 271	1 056	758	672	984	985	876	734	772	903	882
From private sector	1 960	2 265	1 944	2 013	2 928	4 078	4 001	4 555	5 421	6 441	7 894
Other new work: total	5 696	6 703	7 408	8 037	7 531	8 455	9 753	10 054	10 916	14 775	17 523
From public sector: total	2 618	2 920	3 243	3 689	3 432	4 175	4 150	3 877	4 142	4 513	5 107
Gas, electricity, coalmining	247	291	390	431	280	287	161	253	229	301	234
Railways and air transport	120	78	173	275	82	136	222	195	348	204	138
Schools	231	305	292	239	219	326	338	297	305	317	435
Universities	26	26	38	42	32	34	31	45	59	52	66
Health	261	287	320	478	467	444	619	491	430	492	712
Offices, factories, etc.	585	582	589	519	584	691	750	617	638	688	845
Roads	424	466	562	781	770	799	849	802	853	894	1 029
Harbours and waterways	108	111	97	95	95	122	100	109	132	233	134
Water	78	82	67	129	110	128	117	104	160	155	153
Sewerage	184	196	227	211	221	304	256	257	268	251	313
Miscellaneous	354	497	487	489	574	905	706	709	720	925	1 048
From private sector: total[2]	3 078	3 783	4 165	4 348	4 099	4 280	5 603	6 176	6 774	10 262	12 407
Industrial: total	1 447	1 864	1 803	1 554	1 327	1 543	2 203	2 149	1 993	3 660	3 128
Commercial: total	1 631	1 919	2 362	2 794	2 772	2 737	3 400	4 028	4 781	6 602	9 279
Offices	678	821	1 045	1 451	1 414	1 209	1 601	1 775	2 256	3 110	4 585
Shops	380	414	536	531	521	549	702	1 022	1 102	1 616	2 048
Entertainment	248	308	342	388	382	363	564	577	739	991	1 356
Garages	99	114	125	98	134	166	171	133	190	228	375
Schools and colleges	35	60	44	48	48	67	65	85	72	87	182
Miscellaneous	191	202	270	278	273	384	296	435	422	570	734

1 Classified to construction in the *Standard Industrial Classification, Revised 1980.*
2 Figures for private sector include work to be carried out by contractors on their own initiative for sale.
3 Orders for 1987 include the Channel Tunnel project in the private industrial sector.

Source Department of the Environment

8.32 Metal goods, engineering and vehicles industries

Estimated total sales of UK manufactured goods[1, 2]
Standard Industrial Classification 1980

£ millions

	Activity heading	1978	1979	1980	1981	1982	1983	1984	1985	1986	1987	1988[7]
Division 3												
Manufacture of metal goods not elsewhere specified[3]												
Class 31												
Forging, pressing and stamping	3120	962	1 073	1 054	885	935	1 014	1 158	1 167	1 209	1 311	1 569
Bolts, nuts, washers, rivets, springs and non-precision chains	3137	479	471	450	410	424	470	515	532	553	587	651
Heat and surface treatment of metals, (including sintering)	3138	305	331	331	273	339	372	446	515	495	561	–
Metal doors, windows, etc.	3142	277	351	486	502	532	600	675	573	631	669	773
Hand tools and implements	3161	167	178	172	191	190	211	215	236	229	258	266
Cutlery, spoons, forks and similar tableware; razors	3162	74	74	79	80	81	89	101	109	105	104	116
Metal storage vessels (mainly non-industrial)	3163	60	66	66	68	71	77	64	63	71	77	104
Packaging products of metal	3164	1 085	1 212	1 132	1 108	1 202	1 311	1 462	1 539	1 600	1 660	1 804
Domestic heating and cooking appliances (non-electrical)	3165	200	223	226	242	251	279	291	319	350	366	412
Metal furniture and safes	3166	293	376	373	356	370	413	457	483	539	571	735
Domestic utensils of metal	3167	207	214	220	171	166	176	183	192	216	199	222
Miscellaneous finished metal products	3169	1 282	1 474	1 425	1 632	1 859	2 000	2 199	2 363	2 509	2 838	3 249
Total		5 391	6 043	6 014	5 918	6 420	7 012	7 766	8 095	8 507	9 201	9 901
Mechanical engineering[4]												
Class 32												
Fabricated constructional steelwork	3204	773	957	916	1 013	1 286	1 370	1 395	1 513	1 474	1 791	1 951
Boilers and process plant fabrications	3205	914	1 053	1 097	1 251	1 598	1 864	1 621	1 577	1 784	1 810	1 654
Agricultural machinery	3211	297	308	277	247	277	322	279	302	256	277	292
Wheeled tractors	3212	806	973	908	914	882	916	1 016	982	894	1 033	1 231
Metal-working machine tools	3221	601	664	705	565	598	562	683	822	840	877	1 119
Engineers' small tools	3222	545	617	698	580	566	556	649	770	790	818	882
Textile machinery	3230	282	294	255	256	230	219	306	307	324	321	362
Food, drink and tobacco processing machinery; packaging and bottling machinery	3244	391	429	457	430	493	521	521	538	619	656	727
Chemical industry machinery; furnaces and kilns; gas, water and waste treatment plant	3245	351	380	395	357	388	397	395	439	478	497	518
Mining machinery	3251	501	599	643	599	720	630	507	631	788	678	665
Construction and earth moving equipment	3254	869	954	941	1 023	940	839	876	1 011	1 006	996	1 265
Mechanical lifting and handling equipment	3255	1 044	1 163	1 218	1 038	1 166	1 422	1 586	1 747	1 758	1 826	2 236
Precision chains and other mechanical power transmission equipment	3261	420	449	524	508	474	472	552	648	684	780	843
Ball, needle and roller bearings	3262	195	214	248	214	210	195	206	229	254	272	320
Machinery for working wood, rubber, plastics, leather and making paper, glass, bricks and similar materials; laundry and dry cleaning machinery	3275	321	349	354	259	328	351	380	458	485	524	591
Printing, bookbinding and paper goods machinery	3276	297	346	342	351	363	364	433	580	639	680	762
Industrial (including marine) engines	3281	751	663	786	879	904	764	920	876	778	783	877
Compressors and fluid power equipment	3283	538	549	623	549	593	598	713	778	803	828	942
Refrigerating, space-heating, ventilating and air-conditioning equipment	3284	771	867	858	801	961	1 118	1 181	1 267	1 322	1 481	1 599
Scales, weighing machinery and portable power tools	3285	181	230	248	249	222	237	233	268	271	342	415
Miscellaneous industrial and commercial machinery	3286	458	515	555	539	608	630	650	767	854	1 040	975
Pumps	3287	335	352	387	394	409	384	409	474	473	477	598
Industrial valves	3288	290	332	360	406	432	414	401	456	475	447	470
Miscellaneous mechanical marine and precision engineering	3289	632	680	724	777	749	1 158	1 538	1 553	1 508	1 512	1 814
Ordnance, small arms and ammunition	3290	563	533	575	622	742	847	835	806	788	828	926
Total		13 126	14 470	15 094	14 821	16 139	17 150	18 285	19 799	20 346	21 574	24 034
Manufacture of office machinery and data processing equipment												
Class 33												
Office machinery	3301	116	123	121	113	114	120	139	169	218	279	267
Electronic data processing equipment	3302	761	984	1 053	1 047	1 278	1 535	2 519	3 459	2 954	4 328	5 175
Total		877	1 107	1 174	1 160	1 392	1 653	2 656	3 628	3 199	4 591	5 442

See footnotes on page 169.

Source *Department of Trade and Industry*

8.32 (*continued*)

Metal goods, engineering and vehicles industries
Estimated total sales of UK manufactured goods[1, 2]
Standard Industrial Classification 1980

£ million

	Activity heading	1978	1979	1980	1981	1982	1983	1984	1985	1986	1987	1988[7]
Electrical and electronic engineering[5] Class 34												
Insulated wires and cables	3410	666	795	904	910	966	1 051	1 141	1 256	1 268	1 420	1 639
Basic electrical equipment	3420	1 758	1 799	2 040	1 949	2 186	2 193	2 342	2 367	2 743	2 656	2 919
Batteries and accumulators	3432	302	329	343	309	335	298	324	367	361	410	482
Alarms and signalling equipment	3433	139	171	191	188	184	237	246	301	338	402	425
Electrical equipment for motor vehicles, cycles and aircraft	3434	462	495	480	416	456	514	613	711	710	796	831
Miscellaneous electrical equipment for industrial use	3435	205	238	238	225	252	241	299	339	320	299	346
Telegraph and telephone apparatus and equipment	3441	591	693	944	1 128	1 275	1 418	1 475	1 668	1 753	1 674	1 978
Electrical instruments and control systems	3442	522	598	667	737	837	974	1 081	1 301	1 354	1 489	1 595
Radio and electronic capital goods	3443	988	1 173	1 481	1 760	1 962	2 311	2 633	2 853	2 961	3 153	3 358
Components other than active components, mainly for electronic equipment	3444	509	617	748	664	754	831	1 064	1 128	1 154	1 229	1 483
Gramophone records and pre-recorded tapes	3452	143	154	135	130	129	148	194	236	304	394	394
Active components and electronic sub-assemblies	3453	664	758	712	655	676	868	1 092	1 139	1 150	1 167	1 334
Electronic consumer goods and miscellaneous equipment	3454	545	551	523	545	586	735	873	885	959	1 089	1 196
Domestic-type electric appliances	3460	799	890	936	915	920	1 083	1 140	1 208	1 327	1 540	1 816
Electric lamps and other electric lighting equipment	3470	409	452	483	524	559	635	700	726	798	877	1 022
Total		8 702	9 713	10 825	11 055	12 077	13 537	15 017	16 485	17 500	18 595	20 828
Manufacture of motor vehicles and parts thereof Class 35												
Motor vehicles and their engines	3510	4 425	4 761	4 603	4 420	4 854	4 786	5 505	6 762	7 229	9 535	10 928
Motor vehicle bodies and vehicle parts	3521 and 3530	3 107	3 353	3 338	3 051	3 179	3 509	3 705	3 858	4 078	4 433	5 533
Trailers, semi-trailers and caravans	3522/3	432	483	408	332	340	417	486	509	545	683	–
Total		7 964	8 597	8 349	7 803	8 373	8 712	9 696	11 129	11 852	14 657	17 347
Manufacture of other transport equipment[6] Class 36												
Railway and tramway vehicles	3620	216	308	341	355	344	286	247	242	273	264	462
Aerospace equipment manufacturing, repairing and modification	3640	2 182	2 528	3 701	4 288	4 698	4 757	5 167	5 934	6 841	8 306	8 150
Baby carriages and wheelchairs	3650	41	49	48	45	57	62	77	88	87	99	114
Total		2 439	2 885	4 090	4 688	5 099	5 105	5 491	6 264	7 201	8 669	8 726
Instrument engineering Class 37												
Measuring, checking and precision instruments and apparatus	3710	636	735	840	817	928	1 088	1 239	1 433	1 507	1 569	1 702
Medical and surgical equipment and orthopaedic appliances	3720	165	198	215	243	293	307	341	355	370	406	469
Spectacles and unmounted lenses	3731	68	77	92	98	95	117	140	143	124	127	171
Optical precision instruments	3732	67	71	84	91	107	140	148	166	180	182	200
Photographic and cinematographic equipment	3733	233	265	261	212	215	199	193	180	244	271	352
Clocks, watches and other timing devices	3740	143	120	105	97	134	111	117	100	92	89	83
Total		1 312	1 466	1 597	1 558	1 772	1 962	2 178	2 377	2 517	2 644	2 977

Note More detailed information can be found in the PQ series of Business Monitors for the activities listed above.

1 These figures represent the total sales of principal products of each activity excluding waste products and work done. Estimates of the sales of principal products of establishments falling below the employment threshold of the Quarterly Sales Inquiries are included
2 The total may differ from the sum of its constituent parts due to rounding
3 Excluding ferrous and non-ferrous metal foundries AH 3111/2
4 Excluding process engineering contractors AH 3246
5 Excluding electrical equipment installation AH 3480
6 Excluding shipbuilding and repairing AH 3610
7 Information not available.

Source *Department of Trade and Industry*

8.33 Volume index numbers of sales and orders for the engineering industries
United Kingdom

	Total			Home			Export		
	Orders on hand end of period	Net orders[1]	Sales	Orders on hand end of period	Net orders[1]	Sales	Orders on hand end of period	Net orders[1]	Sales
	1985 Average = 100	1985 Average monthly sales = 100		1985 Average = 100	1985 Average monthly sales = 100		1985 Average = 100	1985 Average monthly sales = 100	
Engineering industries combined									
SIC 1980 Class 32, 33, 34, 37									
1984	100	100	93	104	100	95	95	98	89
1985	97	98	100	96	96	100	100	103	100
1986	97	99	100	97	100	99	97	99	100
1987	100	105	104	102	105	102	96	106	107
1988	109	120	115	111	115	111	106	129	122
Percentage change 1988 on 1987[2]	*+9.0*	*+14.5*	*+10.5*	*+9.0*	*+9.5*	*+9.0*	*+10.5*	*+21.5*	*+14.0*
Mechanical engineering									
SIC 1980 Class 32									
1984	101	99	95	107	103	97	93	92	91
1985	95	97	100	94	94	100	98	102	100
1986	90	95	98	88	95	98	93	94	97
1987	93	99	98	96	102	98	87	95	98
1988	93	106	106	99	108	107	84	103	105
Percentage change 1988 on 1987[2]	–	*+7.0*	*+8.0*	*+3.0*	*+6.0*	*+9.0*	*−3.5*	*+8.5*	*+7.0*
Electrical and instrument engineering									
SIC 1980 Class 33, 34 and 37									
1984	100	101	92	102	99	95	96	105	88
1985	99	99	100	98	98	100	100	103	100
1986	102	103	101	104	103	100	100	103	103
1987	105	110	108	107	107	105	102	116	115
1988	120	131	122	120	121	115	121	153	138
Percentage change 1988 on 1987[2]	*+14.5*	*+19.0*	*+13.0*	*+12.0*	*+13.0*	*+9.5*	*+18.5*	*+32.0*	*+20.0*

1 Net of cancellations.

2 The percentage changes have been rounded to the nearest half percentage point.

Source *Department of Trade and Industry*

8.34 Merchant shipbuilding[1]
United Kingdom

	1978	1979	1980	1981	1982	1983	1984	1985	1986	1987	1988
Total Gross new orders[2]											
Number	70	52	61	72	57	45	90	58	61	37	41
Thousand gross tonnes[3,4]	301	325	517	482	355	172	127	291	146	163	26
£ million	253	260	312	383	313	279	224	330	280	277	84
For Overseas Registration											
Number	38	5	12	26	21	12	3	8	28	10	1
Thousand gross tonnes[3,4]	201	28	108	386	123	80	1	77	97	112	1
£ million	170	16	59	251	151	82	6	59	102	78	..
Total Orders on hand[5]											
Number	157	108	78	99	88	63	97	65	74	65	56
Thousand gross tonnes[3,4]	1 164	772	855	1 117	990	562	301	387	426	305	265
£ million	818	670	601	783	720	563	444	515	609	622	562
For Overseas Registration											
Number	59	33	10	26	35	24	10	8	31	31	18
Thousand gross tonnes[3,4]	459	236	102	386	384	195	95	73	140	160	123
£ million	306	194	57	271	339	194	85	64	135	144	102
Total Completions											
Number	96	95	88	51	67	68	56	86	48	43	41
Thousand gross tonnes[3,4]	1 135	707	431	217	453	540	411	225	106	247	31
£ million	404	412	363	194	408	390	311	259	175	278	106
For Overseas Registration											
Number	27	27	33	10	12	22	18	10	5	10	5
Thousand gross tonnes[3,4]	396	243	232	101	104	276	141	101	29	53	4
£ million	134	122	168	57	57	200	128	81	30	47	10

1 Merchant registered ships of 100 gross tonnes and over built in the United Kingdom (including drilling ships but excluding floating platform drilling rigs).
2 Includes vessels which may have been cancelled at a late stage.
3 From 1984, tonnages conform to the 1969 IMO Convention on the tonnage measurement of ships. Earlier years relate to gross registered tonnes.
4 Tonnages are only accurately measured on completion: earlier figures are estimates.
5 Includes both vessels under construction and those not yet commenced.

Source *Department of Trade and Industry*

8.35 Motor vehicle production
United Kingdom

Number

	1978	1979	1980	1981	1982	1983	1984	1985	1986	1987	1988
Motor vehicles											
SIC 1980, Group 351											
Passenger cars: total	1 222 949	1 070 452	923 744	954 650	887 679	1 044 597	908 906	1 047 973	1 018 962	1 142 683	1 226 835
1 000 c.c. and under	145 271	127 157	156 735	229 189	197 153	194 064	161 884	183 383	162 090	153 2141	129 446
Over 1 000 c.c. but not over 1 600 c.c.	696 658	616 105	521 933	526 498	547 676	723 289	637 868	694 876	665 093	718 046	764 289
Over 1 600 c.c. but not over 2 800 c.c.	314 138	277 199	209 635	153 957	97 536	77 504	56 587	109 437	134 802	205 067	260 231
Over 2 800 c.c.	66 882	49 991	35 441	45 006	45 314	49 740	52 567	60 277	56 977	66 356	72 869
Commercial vehicles: total	384 518	408 440	389 170	229 555	268 798	244 514	224 825	265 973	228 685	246 728	318 013
Of which:											
Light commercial vehicles	243 756	261 974	261 143	157 744	189 094	175 338	157 963	195 475	175 825	188 858	250 053
Trucks:											
Under 7.5 tonnes	23 336	32 970	24 199	14 294	16 367	12 792	13 057	14 601	12 451	15 697	19 732
Over 7.5 tonnes	82 532	77 807	74 890	41 152	43 469	34 850	31 945	33 716	22 718	22 834	25 057
Motive units for articulated vehicles	11 852	9 778	7 366	3 921	6 761	5 918	5 361	6 154	5 351	5 343	6 671
Buses, coaches and mini buses:											
Single deck buses	20 583	23 407	19 007	9 903	11 518	13 870	14 811	14 842	11 180	13 397	15 836
Double deck buses	2 459	2 504	2 565	2 541	1 589	1 746	1 688	1 185	1 160	599	664

TIME SERIES. Figures for motor vehicles relate to periods of 52 weeks (53 weeks in 1983 and 1988).

Source *Department of Trade and Industry*

8.36 Alcoholic drink
United Kingdom

	Unit	1977	1978	1979	1980	1981	1982	1983	1984	1985	1986	1987	1988
Spirits[1]													
Production	Thousand hectolitres of alcohol	4 322	5 211	5 207	4 907	3 251	3 021	2 898	2 986	3 124	3 148	3 316	3 568
Released for home consumption													
Imported:													
Rum	,,	76	90	99	86	80	73	73	75	77	78	81	93
Brandy	,,	57	69	77	71	64	66	69	70	77	79	82	93
Other	,,	41	52	62	57	58	59	65	71	72	74	86	91
Home produced:													
Whisky (mature)[3]	,,	403	488	525	502	477	448	445	434	461	456	446	452
Gin	,,	124	141	158	144	130	124	137	133	139	131	128	139
Other	,,	92	117	133	136	136	122	127	129	148	151	161	166
Total[2]	,,	794	957	1 055	996	945	891	916	912	974	971	983	1 034
Beer[4]													
Production	Thousand hectolitres	65 239	66 418	67 419	64 830	61 721	59 786	60 324	60 105	59 655	59 439	59 895	60 156
Released for home consumption													
Home produced	,,	63 531	65 416	65 688	63 188	60 024	58 668	59 586	59 241	58 431	57 911	58 519	59 981
Imported	,,	2 360	2 386	2 558	2 302	2 293	2 252	2 646	2 841	3 076	3 302	3 454	3 610
Total	,,	65 891	67 802	68 248	65 490	62 317	60 920	62 232	62 082	61 507	61 213	61 973	63 591
Imported wine/wine of fresh grapes													
Released for home consumption													
Heavy	,,	1 140	1 364	1 356	1 257	1 191	1 074	1 079	1 022	861	559	489	448
Light	,,	1 744	2 095	2 428	2 581	2 941	3 132	3 512	4 152	4 525	5 061	5 474	5 416
Sparkling	,,	138	161	179	183	196	193	218	224	257	281	315	352
Total	,,	3 021	3 620	3 962	4 022	4 328	4 399	4 810	5 398	5 644	5 902	6 278	6 217
British wine/made-wine													
Released for home consumption	,,	534	566	572	515	539	509	549	492	538	528	561	579
Cider and perry													
Released for home consumption	,,	2 215	2 222	2 324	2 255	2 409	2 899	3 258	3 259	3 174	3 233	3 205	3 125

1 Potable spirits distilled including spirits produced from molasses.
2 Includes a small amount of spirits unclassified by origin and/or tariff code number.
3 Before April 1983, the figures represent quantities of all mature home produced spirits.
4 From January 1976 the figures take account of brewing at high gravity with the addition of some brewing liquor after fermentation.

Source *HM Customs and Excise*

8.37 Tobacco products
United Kingdom

	Unit	1978	1979	1980	1981	1982	1983	1984	1985	1986	1987	1988
Released for home consumption												
Cigarettes:	Thousand million											
Home produced	,,	124.2	122.7	120.0	108.3	100.6	100.6	93.4	88.6	83.3	89.9	87.9
Imported	,,	1.4	1.9	2.0	1.5	1.8	2.0	6.4	10.5	11.7	11.0	9.4
Total	,,	125.7	124.5	122.0	109.8	102.3	102.6	99.9	99.1	95.0	100.9	97.3
Cigars:	Million kg.											
Home produced	,,	2.4	2.5	2.5	2.2	2.3	2.4	2.4	2.3	2.3	2.4	2.4
Imported	,,	0.7	0.8	0.7	0.7	0.4	0.2	0.2	0.2	0.2	0.2	0.2
Total	,,	3.1	3.3	3.2	2.9	2.7	2.7	2.5	2.5	2.5	2.6	2.6
Hand-rolling tobacco:												
Home produced	,,	6.1	5.7	5.8	6.2	6.2	5.9	5.4	5.1	4.8	4.8	4.5
Imported	,,	–	–	–	–	–	–	–	–	–	–	–
Total	,,	6.1	5.7	5.8	6.2	6.3	5.9	5.4	5.1	4.8	4.8	4.5
Other smoking and chewing tobacco:												
Home produced	,,	4.2	3.8	3.6	3.5	3.3	3.1	3.0	2.9	2.7	2.6	2.5
Imported	,,	0.1	0.2	0.1	–	–	–	–	–	–	–	–
Total	,,	4.3	4.0	3.7	3.5	3.3	3.1	3.0	2.9	2.7	2.6	2.5

Source *HM Customs and Excise*

9 Agriculture, fisheries and food

Agricultural censuses and surveys *(Tables 6.5, 9.3 and 9.5)*

The data in these tables vary between the different countries of the United Kingdom as follows:

The coverage from 1976 to 1979 includes all holdings in the United Kingdom with 40 standard man days or more (a standard man day (smd) represents 8 hours productive work by an adult male worker under average conditions). All holdings with less than 40 smd in Scotland are excluded but in England and Wales and Northern Ireland holdings with less than 40 smd are excluded only if they have less than 4 hectares of crops and grass and no regular whole-time worker.

From 1977 (table 9.4 from 1980) figures for England and Wales relate to all known agricultural holdings including minor holdings. Data on minor holdings in Scotland and Northern Ireland are excluded but see footnote 2 to table 9.4.

From 1981 the figures included for Northern Ireland relate to all holdings with one European Size Unit (ESU) or more; or 6 hectares or more of total area; or one or more whole-time workers (excluding the owner). This revised threshold resulted in the deletion of 7 000 holdings.

The estimated yields of sugar beet and hops (table 9.4) are obtained from production figures supplied by British Sugar plc, and English Hops Ltd. In Great Britain potato yields are estimated in consultation with the Potato Marketing Board.

Average weekly earnings and hours of agricultural workers *(Tables 9.7 and 9.8)*

Data on the earnings and hours of agricultural workers have been collected since 1945 through a series of investigations known as the Wages and Employment Enquiry. Appointed officers of the Ministry of Agriculture, Fisheries and Food, the Department of Agriculture and Fisheries for Scotland and the Welsh Office Agricultural Department undertake this series of investigations in the course of their duties as Wages Inspectors. Under the Agricultural Wages Act 1948, these officers monitor minimum wages determined by the Agricultural Wages Board. They visit a random sample of farms each year (approximately 4 000 in 1987) and collect information on workers' earnings, hours, overtime, bonuses, perquisites, etc.; the analysed results of which are published in quarterly press notices and annual reports. Summary tables of earnings and hours are also published by the Department of Employment, the Welsh Office Agricultural Department and the Department of Agriculture and Fisheries for Scotland. The enquiry also provides data used by the Agricultural Wages Board when considering wage claims and by the Ministry in estimating the cost of labour in agriculture for the Annual Review and similar purposes.

Fisheries *(Tables 9.12–9.14)*

Data relating to the weight and value of landings of fish in United Kingdom (table 9.12) is generally obtained from sales notes completed at fish market auctions.

Fishing fleet information (tables 9.13 and 9.14) is obtained from vessel registers maintained by the Ministry of Agriculture, Fisheries and Food in England and Wales and the Department of Agriculture and Fisheries for Scotland.

Estimated food consumption by all households in Great Britain—National Food Survey *(Table 9.18)*

The Sample

In the course of a year the National Food Survey investigates the food budgets of about 7 500 households throughout Great Britain. Fieldwork takes place in 52 local authority districts selected so as to be representative of Great Britain as a whole and, from the beginning of 1986, a proportion of the local authorities used are replaced for sampling purposes at the end of each calendar quarter. A description of the sampling methods used in the National Food Survey is given in the respective Annual Reports: for example, *Household Food Consumption and Expenditure 1987* (HMSO 1989).

Household

A group of persons living in the same dwelling and sharing common catering arrangements. The size of household is defined in terms of the number of persons who spend at least four nights in the household during the week of the Survey *and* also have at least one meal a day from the household food supply on at least four days. The head of the household and the housewife are regarded as persons in *all* cases.

Adult—A person aged 18 years or over.

Child—A person under 18 years of age.

Food purchased

Quantities of all foods purchased during the week for consumption in the home (but including *purchases* of milk at school). The Survey excludes food eaten outside the home (except packed meals prepared at home), chocolate and sugar confectionery, soft drinks, alcoholic drinks, vitamin preparations, and food obtained specifically for consumption by domestic pets. For a few minor miscellaneous items, expenditure is recorded, but not the quantity (e.g. artificial sweeteners, flavourings, colourings, etc.).

Free food

Quantity of food entering the household without payment, for consumption during the Survey week. Milk supplied under the Milk in Schools Scheme is included although it does not actually enter the household. Food grown or produced by the household and stored in bulk is recorded only when it is withdrawn from store.

Consumption

Averaged over a sufficiently large number of households and a sufficiently long period, the average quantity of food purchased *plus* the quantity of 'free' food will equal the average consumption if there is no general change in the level of larder stocks.

9.1 Outputs, inputs and net product at current prices

Calendar years

£ million

	1978	1979	1980	1981	1982	1983	1984	1985	1986	1987	1988[17]
Output[1]											
Cereals											
Wheat	449	605	786	855	1 137	1 115	1 460	1 409	1 366	1 264	1 158
Barley	550	557	651	811	894	851	930	842	776	745	689
Oats	19	19	24	25	28	28	26	28	30	30	30
Other[2]	2	2	2	2	2	3	3	2	2	2	2
1. Total cereals	1 019	1 184	1 462	1 693	2 062	1 996	2 420	2 281	2 174	2 041	1 879
Other crops											
Oilseed rape	28	43	69	87	157	174	254	244	270	298	242
Sugar beet	159	206	195	192	252	218	251	232	227	219	234
Hops	13	17	23	25	28	27	26	15	11	12	12
Peas and beans for stockfeed	9	16	15	32	28	34	51	64	111	109	124
Hay and dried grass	15	15	15	14	15	19	22	26	35	38	44
Grass and clover seed	8	20	19	18	19	22	21	16	20	16	14
Other minor crops[3]	13	9	10	8	8	10	18	20	9	10	12
2. Total other crops	245	325	346	374	507	503	642	616	683	703	682
Potatoes											
3. Total potatoes	260	385	312	392	451	495	585	318	447	534	422
Horticulture											
Vegetables[4]	477	556	574	607	610	729	814	804	807	927	945
Fruit[4]	152	158	169	187	212	230	242	231	256	242	264
Ornamentals	133	156	179	188	204	217	232	251	280	323	385
Other[5]	4	4	4	4	3	4	3	4	6	6	6
4. Total horticulture	767	874	927	987	1 029	1 179	1 292	1 290	1 348	1 503	1 600
Livestock											
Finished cattle and calves	1 258	1 420	1 498	1 601	1 674	1 834	1 968	1 958	1 816	1 968	1 919
Finished sheep and lambs	295	314	403	459	512	567	555	608	596	646	714
Finished pigs	676	730	778	817	907	896	977	958	924	928	871
Poultry	444	488	508	515	604	626	674	702	759	794	815
Other[6]	71	71	85	87	91	92	91	104	106	115	122
5. Total Livestock	2 744	3 023	3 272	3 510	3 787	4 015	4 267	4 330	4 201	4 450	4 439
Livestock products											
Milk	1 591	1 730	1 925	2 064	2 341	2 453	2 297	2 355	2 460	2 379	2 423
Milk products (farm mfr only)	29	34	35	37	43	40	40	44	52	55	60
Eggs	383	462	489	509	510	467	537	492	439	511	465
Clip wool	33	35	36	35	34	37	37	42	41	43	47
Other[7]	12	16	14	20	20	32	28	26	30	33	35
6. Total livestock products	2 047	2 276	2 498	2 664	2 949	3 029	2 939	2 959	3 022	3 022	3 029
Own account capital formation[8]											
Breeding livestock	15	−34	−35	3	28	−7	−29	13	5	−29	2
Other assets	50	57	82	91	109	112	122	116	103	98	115
7. Total own account capital formation	65	24	47	94	137	105	93	128	108	69	117
8. Total output (1+2+3+4+5+6+7)	7 148	8 091	8 864	9 714	10 922	11 322	12 237	11 923	11 982	12 322	12 169
Compensation payments and sundry receipts											
Annual Ewe Premium	–	–	–	28	34	32	98	100	113	106	134
Milk outgoers and quota cuts	–	–	–	–	–	–	–	9	10	21	69
Other payments	31	29	33	32	28	38	29	31	54	27	35
9. Total compensation payments and sundry receipts	31	29	33	60	62	70	127	140	177	154	238
Production grants											
Aid to less favoured areas	53	59	76	88	90	91	91	98	110	114	116
Suckler cow premium	–	–	12	19	22	16	24	26	27	32	38
Other	37	25	42	34	38	34	31	18	10	7	8
10. Total production grants	90	84	130	141	150	141	146	142	147	153	162
11. Total receipts (8+9+10)	7 269	8 204	9 026	9 914	11 134	11 533	12 510	12 205	12 305	12 628	12 569
Value of physical increase in:											
Work-in-progress[9]	1	−23	−42	−15	47	−15	−17	−73	−32	−86	−34
Output stocks	15	−6	12	−73	−20	56	121	−156	12	−32	−10

See footnotes on page 176.

9.1 Outputs, inputs and net product at current prices

Calendar years

(continued)

£ million

	1978	1979	1980	1981	1982	1983	1984	1985	1986	1987	1988[17]
12. Total value of physical increase	15	– 29	– 29	– 89	28	42	104	– 230	– 20	– 118	– 44
13. Gross output (11 + 12)	7 285	8 175	8 999	9 825	11 162	11 575	12 615	11 975	12 285	12 510	12 525
Intermediate Output[10]											
Feed	393	539	586	564	728	813	767	700	726	630	642
Seed	91	99	94	102	111	129	122	120	126	134	147
14. Total intermediate output	484	638	680	665	839	942	889	820	852	764	789
15. Final output (13–14)	6 800	7 537	8 318	9 160	10 323	10 633	11 725	11 156	11 433	11 746	11 736
Inputs											
Expenditure (net of reclaimed VAT)[11]											
Feedingstuffs: compounds	1 302	1 535	1 588	1 689	1 916	2 119	1 984	1 836	1 852	1 774	1 836
straights	409	472	505	496	590	634	745	771	722	805	827
other	63	82	95	97	109	111	129	83	175	173	170
16. Total feedingstuffs	1 774	2 089	2 188	2 282	2 615	2 864	2 858	2 690	2 749	2 752	2 833
Seeds: cereals	75	87	95	107	110	119	126	125	122	127	145
other	117	125	121	109	126	155	134	130	146	159	168
17. Total seeds	193	212	216	216	236	274	260	255	268	286	313
Livestock: imported	97	49	51	48	53	66	71	68	61	46	62
inter-farm expenses	79	88	100	117	131	136	131	138	139	138	150
18. Total livestock (imported and inter-farm expenses)	175	137	151	165	184	202	202	206	200	184	212
Fertilisers and lime: straights	166	175	224	271	298	348	402	372	318	285	257
compounds	285	333	380	437	419	456	478	462	414	342	370
lime	24	22	28	32	37	43	44	37	38	38	38
other	15	18	19	21	22	25	27	30	28	28	28
19. Total fertilisers and lime	490	548	651	762	777	873	951	901	797	693	693
20. Pesticides	96	169	175	159	246	260	269	313	318	334	386
Machinery: repairs	244	274	307	336	370	398	427	467	492	520	560
fuel and oil	202	265	299	337	388	430	432	476	374	372	376
licences	16	17	19	22	26	26	28	31	33	34	34
insurances	24	30	34	39	40	40	42	44	50	59	69
other	7	8	9	9	10	11	12	13	14	15	16
21. Total machinery	493	593	668	743	833	906	942	1 032	963	1 000	1 055
Farm maintenance: occupier	119	135	143	148	169	178	200	212	209	242	232
landlord	27	31	36	42	46	51	55	59	62	63	62
22. Total farm maintenance[12]	147	166	179	190	215	229	255	271	271	305	294
Miscellaneous expenditure											
Veterinary expenses and medicines	70	77	88	99	110	118	122	133	146	153	157
Power and fuel (mainly electricity)	81	93	111	125	137	137	139	151	152	153	161
Containers	58	67	65	70	82	89	98	97	103	110	119
Sundry equipment	59	63	71	78	81	90	96	101	105	108	114
Other[13]	215	241	269	310	344	367	389	424	452	478	467
23. Total miscellaneous expenditure[12]	483	540	603	682	755	800	843	906	958	1 002	1 018
24. Total expenditure	3 852	4 453	4 831	5 200	5 861	6 410	6 581	6 572	6 524	6 555	6 804
Value of usage of:											
Purchase feed	7	– 10	31	– 36	– 9	5	29	– 16	– 40	25	13
Fertilisers	16	– 17	– 8	– 20	10	55	– 18	30	– 34	38	30
25. Total value of physical usage of input stocks	23	– 27	23	– 56	2	60	10	14	– 74	63	43
26. Gross input (24 + 25)	3 875	4 427	4 854	5 144	5 862	6 470	6 591	6 586	6 450	6 618	6 846
27. Net input (26–14)	3 391	3 788	4 174	4 479	5 024	5 528	5 702	5 767	5 598	5 854	6 058

See footnotes on page 176.

9.1 Outputs, inputs and net product at current prices
Calendar years

(continued)

£ million

	1978	1979	1980	1981	1982	1983	1984	1985	1986	1987	1988[17]
28. **Gross product (13–26) or (15–27)**	3 410	3 748	4 144	4 681	5 299	5 105	6 024	5 389	5 836	5 892	5 679
Depreciation											
Buildings and works: landlord[12]	44	54	71	77	74	73	73	76	80	83	86
other	196	246	336	373	375	383	397	431	466	491	522
Plant, machinery and vehicles	581	658	726	752	820	856	886	921	907	937	982
29. Total depreciation	821	957	1 133	1 203	1 269	1 312	1 356	1 428	1 453	1 510	1 590
30. **Net product (28–29)**	2 588	2 791	3 012	3 478	4 030	3 793	4 668	3 961	4 382	4 382	4 088
Comprising											
Hired labour											
Wages and salaries	717	809	906	974	1 051	1 149	1 180	1 277	1 258	1 266	1 297
Insurance	78	99	115	124	124	126	124	118	104	103	106
Other	2	1	2	3	4	4	6	7	7	7	7
31. Total hired labour	796	910	1 023	1 100	1 180	1 279	1 309	1 401	1 369	1 375	1 410
Families, partners, directors											
Wages and salaries	271	306	371	415	456	496	528	587	624	629	639
Insurance	33	42	51	58	59	59	60	61	62	62	63
32. Total family, partners and director labour[14]	304	347	422	472	515	556	588	649	685	691	702
33. Total labour	1 100	1 257	1 445	1 573	1 695	1 834	1 897	2 050	2 054	2 066	2 112
Interest[15]	184	318	464	468	501	494	569	704	700	639	684
Net rate[12]	55	66	69	88	105	126	141	154	159	160	157
Farming income[16]	1 249	1 149	1 033	1 349	1 730	1 339	2 061	1 053	1 470	1 517	1 136

1 Output is net of VAT collected on the sale of non-edible products. Figures for total output include subsidies (but not compensation payments) and some are net of levies.
2 Mixed corn, maize and rye.
3 Root and fodder crop seed, straw, mustard and other minor crops.
4 Includes the value of the produce of gardens and allotments.
5 Seeds, hedgerow fruits and nuts.
6 Horses, breeding animals exported, poultry for export, rabbits and game, knacker animals and other minor livestock.
7 Honey, goats' milk, exports of eggs for hatching and minor livestock products.
8 This comprises the cost of that part of investment in buildings and works which is physically undertaken by the farmer or farm labour and the value of the physical increase in breeding livestock.
9 Work in progress is livestock other than breeding livestock. Output stocks comprise cereals, potatoes and some fruits.
10 Sales included in output but subsequently re-purchased and so reappearing as input.
11 Expenditure is net of VAT reclaimed in the normal way but each heading includes VAT paid without recovery by, for example, producers not registered for VAT.
12 Landlords expenses are included within farm maintenance, miscellaneous expenditure and depreciation on buildings and works. Net rent is the rent paid on tenanted land less these landlords' expenses and the benefit value of dwellings on that land.
13 Including drainage, water and general rates, fees, insurance and telephones.
14 Including employers national insurance contributions. The estimate in respect of family workers (except spouses), non-principal partners and directors is calculated on the basis of the earnings of hired labour.
15 Interest charges on loans for current farming purposes and buildings and works less interest on money held on short term deposit.
16 The return to farmers and spouses for their labour, management skills and own capital invested after providing for depreciation.
17 Provisional.

Source Agricultural Departments

9.2 Outputs, inputs and net product at constant (1985) prices

United Kingdom

Calendar years

£ million

	1978	1979	1980	1981	1982	1983	1984	1985	1986	1987	1988[13]
Output[1]											
Cereals											
Wheat	589	707	888	881	1 121	1 004	1 430	1 409	1 379	1 278	1 239
Barley	752	668	751	864	879	764	880	842	771	755	714
Oats	26	22	24	26	28	24	21	28	30	26	28
Other[2]	3	2	2	2	2	2	2	2	2	2	2
1. Total cereals	1 367	1 398	1 665	1 771	2 030	1 795	2 334	2 281	2 182	2 061	1 984
Other crops											
Oilseed rape	42	54	82	93	159	154	253	244	261	371	284
Sugar beet	209	230	222	213	300	225	271	232	244	240	255
Hops	22	24	22	21	24	20	18	15	12	12	12
Peas and beans for stockfeed	14	22	19	35	28	33	49	64	88	96	139
Hay and dried grass	25	23	20	20	20	20	20	16	17	17	17
Grass and clover seed	19	20	20	19	17	28	18	20	8	8	9
Fodder and other minor crops[3]	20	18	18	17	17	17	20	26	33	40	47
2. Total other crops	354	391	404	420	566	487	649	617	663	784	763
Potatoes											
3. Total potatoes	283	299	286	305	286	286	282	318	312	308	316
Horticulture											
Vegetables[4]	769	729	736	736	768	732	800	804	682	841	899
Fruit[4]	237	263	242	216	234	238	250	232	226	222	207
Ornamentals	210	222	231	240	242	242	250	251	222	232	250
Other[5]	7	6	6	6	6	5	3	4	5	4	4
4. Total horticulture	1 222	1 218	1 215	1 200	1 251	1 216	1 303	1 290	1 134	1 300	1 360
Livestock											
Finished cattle and calves	1 841	1 891	1 895	1 795	1 696	1 807	1 966	1 958	1 839	1 927	1 662
Finished sheep and lambs	464	465	563	528	535	576	579	608	584	603	668
Finished pigs	863	921	917	921	953	1 001	932	958	969	982	1 001
Poultry	573	594	602	596	651	646	680	702	748	806	871
Other[6]	109	108	109	110	107	102	100	104	103	107	112
5. Total livestock	3 848	3 982	4 081	3 950	3 948	4 133	4 257	4 330	4 242	4 425	4 315
Livestock products											
Milk	2 334	2 335	2 343	2 327	2 458	2 539	2 385	2 355	2 384	2 254	2 192
Milk products (farm MFR only)	40	42	44	44	46	42	40	44	49	51	54
Eggs	644	645	602	575	564	529	491	492	493	515	516
Clip wool	36	36	40	40	39	42	40	42	42	45	48
Other[7]	20	24	21	25	22	32	27	26	22	26	26
6. Total livestock products	3 075	3 081	3 051	3 010	3 131	3 183	2 983	2 959	2 990	2 889	2 836
Own account capital formation											
Breeding livestock	22	−42	−40	4	28	−6	−29	13	5	−28	2
Other assets	107	104	126	126	139	129	133	116	100	91	101
7. Total own account capital formation[8]	139	48	73	133	179	122	104	128	105	63	103
8. Total output (1+2+3+4+5+6+7)	10 256	10 415	10 777	10 796	11 405	11 222	11 911	11 923	11 626	11 830	11 678
9. Total compensation payments and sundry receipts	44	37	40	67	64	69	124	140	174	147	228
10. Total production grants	130	108	157	156	156	140	142	142	144	147	155
11. Total receipts (8+9+10)	10 430	10 560	10 973	11 019	11 625	11 431	12 178	12 205	11 944	12 124	12 061
Value of physical increase in:											
Work-in-progress[9]	1	−32	−51	−17	49	−16	−17	−73	−33	−91	−34
Output stocks	16	7	16	−72	−21	62	142	−157	15	−30	−10
12. Total value of physical increase	17	−36	−31	−86	24	47	125	−230	−19	−121	−44
13. Gross output (11+12)	10 444	10 516	10 936	10 921	11 647	11 478	12 302	11 975	11 925	12 003	12 017

See footnotes on page 178.

9.2 (continued) Outputs, inputs and net product at constant (1985) prices

United Kingdom
Calendar years

£ million

	1978	1979	1980	1981	1982	1983	1984	1985	1986	1987	1988[13]
Intermediate output[10]											
Feed	532	627	656	585	708	722	725	700	749	671	689
Seed	110	112	99	110	116	123	116	120	117	120	131
14. Total intermediate output	643	739	755	695	823	846	840	820	867	790	819
15. Final output (13–14)	9 814	9 780	10 186	10 237	10 827	10 632	11 462	11 157	11 059	11 212	11 197
Inputs											
Expenditure (net of reclaimed VAT)[11]											
Feedingstuffs	2 554	2 690	2 612	2 548	2 764	2 816	2 705	2 690	2 814	2 776	2 754
Seeds	253	271	229	235	246	262	246	255	250	254	278
Livestock (imported and interfarm expenses)	286	200	218	200	206	210	207	206	205	194	215
Fertilisers and lime	730	780	786	871	852	907	962	901	910	876	855
Pesticides	144	230	212	179	266	280	281	313	318	313	344
Machinery: repairs	506	491	467	469	474	471	467	467	466	467	474
fuel and oil	616	604	516	483	485	487	478	476	469	448	434
other	89	90	89	89	89	89	89	89	88	86	86
Total machinery	1 205	1 178	1 070	1 041	1 048	1 048	1 033	1 032	1 022	1 001	994
Farm maintenance[12]	302	295	271	258	268	263	269	271	258	275	252
Miscellaneous expenditure[12]	912	897	898	893	895	890	896	906	901	907	877
16. Total expenditure	6 291	6 490	6 251	6 190	6 531	6 675	6 599	6 572	6 678	6 595	6 569
17. Total value of physical usage of input stocks	32	−35	26	−58	−2	57	16	14	−91	72	46
18. Gross input (16+17)	6 321	6 443	6 274	6 117	6 525	6 733	6 615	6 586	6 587	6 667	6 615
19. Net input (18–14)	5 707	5 717	5 525	5 435	5 701	5 887	5 775	5 767	5 720	5 876	5 796
20. Gross product (13–18) or (15–19)	4 150	4 110	4 644	4 766	5 081	4 745	5 687	5 389	5 339	5 336	5 401
21. Total depreciation[12]	1 307	1 325	1 353	1 370	1 393	1 408	1 415	1 428	1 433	1 437	1 402
22. Net product (20–21)	2 849	2 794	3 288	3 392	3 679	3 337	4 272	3 961	3 906	3 899	4 000

1 Output is net of VAT collected on the sale of non-edible products. Figures for total output include subsidies (but not compensation payments) and some are net of levies.
2 Mixed corn, maize and rye.
3 Root and fodder crop seed, straw, mustard and other minor crops.
4 Includes the value of the produce of gardens and allotments.
5 Seeds, hedgerow fruits and nuts.
6 Horses, breeding animals exported, poultry for export, rabbits and game, knacker animals and other minor livestock.
7 Honey, goats' milk, exports of eggs for hatching and minor livestock products.
8 This comprises the cost of that part of investment in buildings and works which is physically undertaken by the farmer or farm labour and the value of the physical increase in breeding livestock.
9 Work-in-progress is livestock other than breeding livestock. Output stocks comprise cereals, potatoes and some fruits.
10 Sales included in output but subsequently re-purchased and so reappearing as input.
11 Expenditure is net of VAT reclaimed in the normal way, but each heading includes VAT paid without recovery by, for example, producers not registered for VAT.
12 Landlords' expenses are included within farm maintenance, miscellaneous expenditure and depreciation on buildings and works. Net rent is the rent paid on tenanted land less these landlords' expenses and the benefit value of dwellings on that land.
13 Provisional.

Source Agricultural Departments

9.3 Agriculture—land use

United Kingdom

Area at the June census[1]

Thousand hectares

	1978	1979	1980	1981	1982	1983	1984	1985	1986	1987	1988
Cereals											
Wheat	1 258	1 372	1 441	1 491	1 663	1 695	1 939	1 902	1 997	1 994	1 886
Barley	2 352	2 347	2 330	2 327	2 222	2 143	1 978	1 965	1 916	1 830	1 878
Oats	180	136	148	144	129	108	106	133	97	99	120
Mixed corn	17	16	13	11	10	8	8	7	7	6	5
Rye	9	7	6	6	6	7	6	8	7	7	7
Potatoes											
Early crop	29	26	27	24	25	24					
Main crop	185	178	179	167	167	171	198	191	178	177	180
Fodder crops											
Field beans[2]	38	42	48	45	40	34	32	45	60	91	154
Turnips and swedes[3]	91	87	84	79	71	66	64	62	59	56	54
Fodder beet and mangolds[3]	6	6	6	5	5	5	8	12	13	13	12
Maize for threshing or stockfeeding	26	25	22	18	16	15	16	20	23	23	24
Kale, cabbage, savoys, kohl rabi, Rape for stockfeeding	70	61	54	49	43	40	39	37	33	30	28
Peas harvested dry[4]	..	..	..	..	..	29	56	92	91	117	107
Other crops for stockfeeding	30	25	29	26	31	25	22	20	20	15	14
Horticultural crops[5]											
Orchards and small fruit	65	67	65	62	60	58	56	54	53	52	52
Vegetables grown in the open:											
Brussels sprouts	15	14	14	13	13	11	11	11	11	10	10
Cabbage (all kinds), kale, cauliflower and broccoli[6]	29	29	26	26	27	25	25	24	26	25	26
Carrots	21	18	16	14	14	13	14	14	14	13	15
Parsnips				2	3	2	3	3	3	3	3
Turnips and swedes[7]	4	4	4	3	3	..	..	..	..	..	..
Beetroot	3	2	2	2	2	2	2	2	2	2	2
Onions, salad and dry bulb	9	7	8	8	9	8	8	9	9	9	9
Beans (broad, runner and French)	18	18	13	11	12	11	10	11	10	10	10
Green peas	59	60	59	55	56	47	46	53	52	42	46
Peas, for harvesting dry[8]	36	36	34	28	27	18	..	..	..	..	..
Celery	1	1	1	1	1	1	1	1	1	1	1
Lettuce	4	4	4	4	4	4	4	4	4	4	5
Sweet corn	..	..	..	..	..	1	1	1	1	1	1
Other vegetables	12	10	10	10	9	10	10	12	12	13	13
Hardy nursery stock bulbs and other flowers grown in the open:											
Hardy nursery stock	7	7	7	7	7	7	7	7	7	7	8
Bulbs	4	5	4	5	5	4	4	4	4	4	5
Other flowers	1	1	1	1	1	1	1	1	1	1	1
Area under glass	2	2	2	2	2	2	2	2	2	2	2
Other crops											
Sugar beet	210	214	213	210	204	199	199	205	205	202	201
Rape grown for oilseed	64	74	92	125	174	222	269	296	299	388	347
Hops	6	6	6	6	6	6	5	5	4	4	4
Other crops not for stockfeeding	11	8	7	7	6	7	6	11	18	19	24
Bare fallow	68	73	59	76	55	97	42	41	48	42	58
Total tillage	4 943	4 986	5 031	5 071	5 127	5 124	5 196	5 265	5 287	5 312	5 311
All grasses under five years old	2 071	1 922	1 965	1 911	1 859	1 846	1 794	1 796	1 723	1 691	1 613
Total arable	7 014	6 909	6 996	6 982	6 986	6 970	6 990	7 061	7 010	7 003	6 924
All grasses five years old and over	5 065	5 191	5 140	5 103	5 097	5 107	5 105	5 019	5 077	5 112	5 161
Total crops and grass	12 079	12 100	12 136	12 085	12 083	12 078	12 095	12 080	12 088	12 115	12 085
Rough grazings											
Sole rights	5 193	5 140	5 119	5 021	4 984	4 927	4 895	4 872	4 829	4 743	4 712
Common (estimated)	1 206	1 212	1 214	1 214	1 214	1 212	1 212	1 216	1 216	1 214	1 216
Woodland on agricultural holdings	260	264	271	277	285	292	299	312	316	322	333
All other land on agricultural holdings	214	221	214	211	217	227	218	223	227	225	229
Total area of agricultural land	18 953	18 936	18 953	18 808	18 783	18 735	18 720	18 703	18 676	18 619	18 575
Total area of the United Kingdom	24 100	24 098	24 088	24 089	24 088	24 088	24 088	24 085	24 086	24 086	24 086

1 Figures from 1977 onwards include estimates for minor holdings not surveyed at the June census in England and Wales. See notes on page 173.
2 Prior to 1986 collected as 'Beans for stockfeeding' in England and Wales.
3 See footnote 5 to table 9.4.
4 Includes 'Peas for harvesting dry for both human consumption and stockfeeding' from 1984 onwards.
5 Figures relate to land usage at 1 June and are not necessarily good indicators of production as for some crops more than one crop may be obtained in each season or a crop may overlap two seasons.
6 Excludes kale from 1983 which is included with 'Other vegetables'.
7 From 1983 included with 'Other vegetables.'
8 Following a change in definition in 1986 'Peas for harvesting dry for human consumption' is now included with 'Peas harvested dry for stockfeeding'. Data from 1984 reflect this change.

Source Agricultural Departments

9.4 Estimated quantity of crops and grass harvested[1,2]

United Kingdom

Thousand tonnes

	1977	1978	1979	1980	1981	1982	1983	1984	1985	1986	1987	1988
Cereals												
Wheat	5 275	6 615	7 170	8 470	8 710	10 320	10 800	14 970	12 050	13 910	11 940	[8]
Barley	10 530	9 850	9 525	10 320	10 230	10 960	9 980	11 070	9 740	10 010	9 225	[8]
Oats	790	705	540	600	620	575	465	515	615	505	452	[8]
Mixed corn for threshing	95	65	60	59	44	39	35	35	31	29	26	[8]
Rye for threshing	35	30	25	24	25	27	24	28	35	32	32	[8]
Maize for threshing[3]	2	2	[4]	[4]	[4]	[4]	[4]	[4]	[4]	[4]	..	
Potatoes												
Early crop[4]	406	422	362	453	388	432	322	397	403	363	395	420
Main crop[4]	6 215	6 909	6 124	6 657	5 802	6 498	5 535	7 001	6 489	6 083	6 365	6 479
Fodder crops												
Beans for stockfeeding	112	130	128	150	125	120	105	125	155	230	294	[8]
Turnips, swedes[5]	5 869	5 565	5 370	5 065	4 795	4 575	3 655	3 960	3 300	3 855	3 451	[8]
Fodder beet and mangolds[5]	457	425	385	370	320	370	295	570	815	845	782	[8]
Maize for threshing or stock-feeding[3]	1 196	1 015	895	785	635	635	550	580	770	915	782	[8]
Rape for stockfeeding	578	625										
Kale, cabbage, savoys and kohl rabi	2 450	2 206	1 825	2 115	2 195	1 985	1 660	1 805	1 555	1 380	1 320	[8]
Peas harvested dry for stock-feeding	..	..	..	..	..	..	85	170	215	330	310	[8]
Other crops												
Sugar beet[6]	6 382	7 081	7 659	7 380	7 395	10 005	7 495	9 015	7 715	8 120	7 992	[8]
Rape grown for oilseed	142	155	198	300	325	580	565	925	895	965	1 326	[8]
Hops[7]	7	9	10	10	9	10	9	8	6	5	5	5
Hay[8]												
From all grasses under five years old	4 530											
From all grasses five years old and over	4 104	8 109	8 028	6 975	6 775	6 550	6 000	5 700	4 650	4 675	..	[8]
Horticultural crops												
Vegetables grown in the open												
Brussels sprouts	226	223	224	228	197	223	154	169	152	168	161	170
Cabbage (including savoys and spring greens)	779	573	594	576	546	610	518	670	683	688	692	691
Cauliflowers	348	367	348	367	325	353	298	344	356	360	373	373
Carrots	854	753	684	553	711	725	554	572	600	634	568	663
Parsnips	66	65	56	54	53	55	51	57	62	68	62	66
Turnips and swedes	223	196	170	163	109	145	135	142	140	163	166	177
Beetroot	110	109	98	109	97	105	94	115	114	95	101	96
Onions, Dry Bulb	306	231	214	224	232	231	175	238	268	247	286	309
Onions, Salad	23	28	26	26	25	27	25	22	25	30	31	30
Leeks	42	35	38	40	40	43	44	53	60	71	71	66
Broad beans	21	28	28	18	17	19	17	21	19	14	11	11
Runner beans including French	112	100	109	62	69	92	65	77	65	67	51	48
Peas, Green for market	38	34	38	18	25	28	23	27	26	20	12	13
Peas, Green for processing	267	210	229	223	277	238	198	241	206	239	182	183
Celery	70	66	64	54	50	51	46	57	53	65	55	59
Lettuce	145	133	127	135	134	161	155	153	166	160	176	204
Rhubarb	40	45	46	43	41	39	29	26	26	28	27	26
Protected crops												
Tomatoes	126	129	143	129	125	121	121	129	125	131	130	135
Cucumbers	52	58	53	57	54	56	61	68	71	76	79	87
Lettuce	36	36	35	36	37	45	49	48	49	50	52	54
Fruit crops												
Total Dessert Apples	136	211	222	178	152	216	186	184	161	163	165	134
Total Culinary Apples	134	180	141	179	80	147	126	163	145	139	125	124
Pears	36	27	73	44	49	40	54	48	51	47	66	32
Plums	43	41	49	47	16	34	36	34	24	33	36	24
Cherries	3	4	6	7	3	7	3	5	5	4	4	2
Soft Fruit	79	106	109	110	105	109	124	114	111	109	106	105

1 UK gross production in calendar years; for horticultural crops and potatoes it is in crop years.
2 Except for sugar beet and hops, the production area for England and Wales is the area returned at the June census together with estimates for very small holdings (known as minor holdings). In Scotland and Northern Ireland the area returned at June is also the production area except that estimates for minor holdings are included in Scotland for potatoes and in Northern Ireland for barley, oats and potatoes.
3 From 1979 maize for threshing is included with maize for stockfeeding.
4 Revised basis of calculation adopted in 1984 which prevents direct comparison with earlier years.
5 Before 1977 fodder beet was included with turnips and swedes for stockfeeding. In 1977, as a result of changes in the census categories, fodder beet was included with mangolds in England and Wales but continued to be included with turnips and swedes for stockfeeding in Scotland and Northern Ireland. Scotland collected fodder beet separately for the first time in 1986.
6 The production area for sugar beet is provided by British Sugar plc.
7 The production of hay in England and Wales is calculated from the area cut for hay and actually harvested and does not include the area mown for silage, drying or seed; the production of hay in Scotland and Northern Ireland is calculated from the area cut for hay only and does not include grass mown for silage or drying.
8 Not available.

Source *Agricultural Departments*

9.5 Cattle, sheep, pigs and poultry on agricultural holdings

United Kingdom

At June in each year

Thousands

	1978	1979	1980	1981	1982	1983	1984	1985	1986	1987	1988
Cattle and calves:											
Dairy herd	3 274	3 292	3 228	3 191	3 250	3 333	3 281	3 150	3 138	3 042	2 911
Beef herd	1 588	1 543	1 478	1 420	1 389	1 358	1 351	1 333	1 308	1 343	1 373
Heifers in calf (first calf)	859	864	838	863	851	847	811	874	879	774	834
Bulls for service	92	90	86	84	84	83	80	78	76	74	75
Other cattle:											
Two years old and over	1 029	1 033	1 005	963	937	904	905	852	769	732	726
One year old and under two	3 251	3 123	3 153	3 041	3 057	3 059	3 069	3 012	2 819	2 749	2669
Six months old and under one year	1 766	1 839	1 866	1 876	1 890	1 924	1 949	1 905	1 876	1 844	1 702
Under six months old	1 812	1 804	1 770	1 699	1 786	1 783	1 768	1 707	1 668	1 599	1 581
Total	13 670	13 589	13 426	13 138	13 244	13 290	13 213	12 911	12 533	12 158	11 872
Sheep and lambs:											
Breeding ewes	11 475	11 709	12 178	12 528	12 909	13 310	13 648	13 893	14 252	14 780	15 461
Rams for service	333	342	353	358	366	383	393	406	419	437	461
Other sheep	3 681	3 843	3 672	3 584	3 748	3 764	3 680	3 763	3 961	4 107	4 433
Lambs under one year old	14 282	14 051	15 243	15 628	16 044	16 612	17 080	17 566	18 384	19 377	20 587
Total	29 772	29 946	31 446	32 097	33 067	34 069	34 802	35 628	37 016	38 701	40 942
Pigs:											
Breeding herd	845	851	831	836	864	856	800	828	824	820	804
Boars for service	42	43	42	43	45	45	42	44	44	44	43
Gilts not yet in pig	90	82	84	87	89	82	77	80	79	81	73
Barren sows for fattening[2]	12	14	12	11	12	15	12	12	12	11	12
Other pigs:											
110 Kg and over[2]	105	112	102	90	117	100	91	89	80	67	62
80 Kg and under 110 Kg	671	695	657	638	630	605	599	589	603	615	621
50 Kg and under 80 Kg	1 777	1 770	1 772	1 776	1 824	1 868	1 787	1 813	1 863	1 890	1 898
20 Kg and under 50 Kg	2 221	2 258	2 240	2 227	2 281	2 362	2 198	2 260	2 270	2 253	2 263
Under 20 Kg	1 965	2 040	2 074	2 119	2 163	2 241	2 082	2 151	2 163	2 160	2 204
Total	7 728	7 864	7 815	7 828	8 023	8 174	7 689	7 865	7 937	7 942	7 980
Poultry:											
Fowls:											
Growing pullets	17 343	15 504	14 457	14 219	14 766	11 828	12 536	12 503	12 502	12 230	11 236
Laying flock	50 985	48 120	46 012	44 473	44 792	41 127	40 573	39 538	38 096	38 498	37 389
Breeding flock	6 447	6 657	6 678	6 117	6 457	6 012	6 396	6 104	6 334	7 146	6 879
Table birds	56 340	57 153	59 917	57 830	60 075	58 887	59 341	61 311	63 807	70 754	75 305
Total	131 116	127 433	127 063	122 639	126 091	117 854	118 846	119 456	120 740	128 628	130 809
Ducks[3]	1 343	1 552	1 390	1 333	1 443	1 566	1 527	1 648	1 747	1 744	1 821
Geese[3]	139		133	148	157						
Turkeys	5 376	6 359	6 519	8 167	7 672	8 198	7 134	7 864	..	..	..
Total	137 973	135 345	135 105	132 286	135 363	127 618	127 507	128 968	..	..	..

1 Figures from 1977 onwards include estimates for minor holdings not surveyed at the June census in England and Wales. See notes on page 173. Excludes Scotland except for years 1979, 1983 and 1984.

2 Barren sows for fattening in Northern Ireland are included with 'All other pigs weighing 110 kg and over'.

3 Excludes data for Scotland except for the years 1979 and 1983 to 1986.

Source Agricultural Departments

9.6 Forestry
End of period

Area—thousand hectares
Volume—million cubic metres

	1977/ 1978	1978/ 1979	1979/ 1980	1980/ 1981	1981/ 1982	1982/ 1983	1983/ 1984	1984/ 1985	1985/ 1986	1986/ 1987	1987/ 1988	1988/ 1989
	Years ending 31 March											
Forest area[1]												
United Kingdom	2 061	2 079	2 102	2 121	2 142	2 233	2 258	2 277	2 301	2 328	2 368	..
Great Britain	1 997	2 014	2 036	2 054	2 075	2 165[6]	2 189	2 207	2 230	2 256	2 285	2 291
Northern Ireland[2]	64	65	66	67	67	68	69	70	71	72	73	73
Forestry Commission (Great Britain)												
Productive woodland	856	868	884	896	905	909	902	892	889	890	888	888
Plantations and plantable land acquired during year[3]	6.0	4.7	6.9	1.1	2.1	−3.0	−13.7	−15.3	−7.3	−3.7	−4.7	−3.7[7]
Total area planted during year[4]	17.2	15.4	21.5	16.6	16.5	14.8	15.1	11.1	11.6	13.3	13.1	12.6
Volume of timber removed[5]	2.0	2.0	2.3	2.5	2.7	2.8	3.0	2.9	3.1	3.2	3.4	3.6
Area lost by fire during year	0.5	0.8	0.4	1.3	0.3	0.6	0.1	1.9	0.6	0.1	0.3	0.1
Total estates	1 253	1 256	1 263	1 264	1 259	1 251	1 209	1 181	1 166	1 157	1 148	1 143
Private forestry (Great Britain)												
Productive woodland	851	858	865	873	886	1 084[6]	1 116	1 145	1 171	1 195	1 227	1 231
Total area planted during year	8.3	10.8	11.2	11.4	15.9	15.6	19.7	19.1	23.4	23.6	28.7	29.8
Volume of timber removed[5]	2.1	2.1	2.3	2.3	2.0	2.2	1.8	2.0	2.2	2.4	2.6	3.0
	1977	1978	1979	1980	1981/82[2]	1982/83	1983/84	1984/85	1985/86	1986/87	1987/88	1988/89
State afforestation in Northern Ireland												
Land under plantation	51.2	52.2	53.0	53.9	54.4	55.2	56.3	56.6	57.3	57.9	58.4	58.3
Plantable land acquired during year	0.7	2.6	1.0	0.8	0.3	0.6	0.4	0.1	0.2	0.5	0.4	0.4
Total area planted during year[4]	1.0	1.0	1.0	1.1	1.1	1.2	1.1	1.0	1.2	1.0	0.9[7]	1.0[7]
Area lost by fire during year	0.5	0.2	0.02	0.8	0.01	0.14	0.06	0.09	0.02	0.05	0.02	0.09
Total estates	69.1	69.5	70.5	71.5	71.9	72.5	73.2	73.3	73.5	73.9	74.1	74.3

1 Includes unproductive woodland.
2 The figures for Northern Ireland refer to year ending 31 December up to and including 1980, and thereafter to year ending 31 March.
3 Net area acquired.
4 Including areas replanted.
5 Calendar year ending previous December.
6 The apparent increase in 1982/83 is a result of data from the Census of Woodlands and Trees becoming available. The change is entirely in the private sector of the industry.
7 Provisional.

Sources *Forestry Commission; Department of Agriculture (Northern Ireland)*

9.7 Average weekly earnings[1] and hours of agricultural workers
Great Britain

	1977	1978	1979	1980	1981	1982	1983	1984	1985	1986	1987	1988
Men[2]												
Earnings	54.77	61.99	72.04	86.26	96.52	106.87	117.02	123.11	134.67	141.32	148.61	154.62
Hours	45.9	45.9	46.4	46.4	46.9	46.7	46.7	46.2	46.9	46.8	46.6	47.10
Youths[3]												
Earnings	37.10	42.04	47.25	56.66	62.15	69.40	76.02	80.20	85.81	89.83	95.34	98.20
Hours	44.7	44.4	44.3	44.8	44.9	45.0	45.5	44.7	44.8	45.5	45.9	44.80
Females												
Earnings	43.54	49.19	54.87	65.53	70.35	80.36	87.70	93.47	102.06	107.77	121.78	124.82
Hours	42.1	42.5	41.6	42.1	41.7	42.9	42.6	41.7	42.7	42.6	42.6	42.80

1 Total earnings of hired regular whole-time workers, including payments-in-kind valued, where applicable, in accordance with Agricultural Wages Orders.
2 Twenty years and over.
3 Under twenty years.

Source *Agricultural Departments*

9.8 Distribution of hired regular full-time men in agriculture by earnings band in Great Britain 1988

	General farm workers	Foremen and grieves	Dairy cowmen	All other stockmen	Tractor drivers	Horticultural workers	All Hired men
Less than £100.00	1.0	0.0	0.0	0.0	0.0	1.2	0.4
£100.00–109.99	10.9	0.0	0.0	1.5	1.7	13.2	6.6
£110.00–119.99	9.5	0.1	0.0	4.1	4.6	11.7	6.5
£120.00–129.99	15.9	0.5	0.8	5.7	8.1	8.9	11.0
£130.00–139.99	11.8	5.2	5.1	9.2	10.2	10.8	10.8
£140.00–159.99	22.4	18.3	9.3	20.1	24.4	22.4	21.6
£160.00–179.99	11.9	20.0	14.9	24.7	12.5	12.3	14.3
£180.00–199.99	6.7	16.7	18.7	15.3	11.0	11.1	10.1
£200.00 and over	9.8	39.3	51.3	19.4	27.5	8.4	18.9
Average weekly earnings (£)	145.15	190.18	195.85	165.64	168.20	142.50	157.41

Source *Agricultural Departments*

9.9 Sales for food of agricultural produce and livestock
United Kingdom

	Unit	1977	1978	1979	1980	1981	1982	1983	1984	1985	1986	1987	1988
Cereals:													
Wheat[1]	Thousand tonnes	2 170	2 234	2 867	2 628	3 222	3 196	3 398	3 698	3 606	3 265	3 931	3 408
Barley	,,	2 213	4 123	2 903	3 530	5 142	4 316	4 399	5 584	4 486	5 679	4 902	4 573
Oats[2]	,,	111	128	102	121	139	136	116	125	145	162	166	196
Potatoes[3]	,,	4 671	5 136	5 016	5 105	5 183	5 025	5 193	5 083	5 481	5 572	5 486	5 617[5]
Milk:													
For consumption as liquid milk	,,	7 484	7 381	7 305	7 196	7 082	7 001	6 978	6 958	6 898	6 851	6 812	6 796
For manufacture[4]	,,	6 921	7 713	7 811	7 986	7 992	8 928	9 449	8 472	8 350	8 597	7 806	7 426
Total	Million litres	14 406	15 094	15 116	15 182	15 084	15 943	16 442	15 446	15 263	15 460	14 630	14 236
Eggs in shell including duck eggs	Million dozens	1 160	1 192	1 184	1 104	1 068	1 071	1 030	1 003	1 002	1 002	1 022	1 031[5]
Animals slaughtered:													
Cattle and calves:													
Cattle	,,	3 847	3 876	3 913	4 110	3 929	3 536	3 811	4 180	4 156	3 864	4 047	3 341
Calves	,,	264	155	145	145	120	94	117	133	100	79	66	35
Total	Thousands	4 111	4 030	4 057	4 255	4 049	3 629	3 928	4 313	4 256	3 943	4 114	3 376
Sheep and lambs	,,	11 356	11 591	11 884	14 316	13 978	13 894	15 068	14 953	15 762	15 473	15 762	17 098
Pigs:													
For bacon:													
Used wholly	,,	2 449	2 124	2 056	2 042	1 811	1 786	1 866	1 788	1 720	1 726	1 491	1 388
Used in part	,,	3 628	3 998	4 052	4 046	4 053	3 686	3 966	4 040	4 095	4 087	4 238	4 106
Other uses	,,	7 726	7 311	8 244	8 208	8 673	9 230	9 717	8 791	9 117	9 454	9 740	9 909
Sows and boars	,,	391	354	365	328	329	353	440	319	328	342	339	384
Total	,,	14 194	13 787	14 717	14 624	14 865	15 055	15 989	14 938	15 260	15 609	15 807	15 787
Poultry: total (fowls, ducks, geese, turkeys)	Millions	431	432	445	441	442	473	460	484	501	523	555	606[5]

TIME SERIES. The figures for cereals and for animals slaughtered relate to periods of 52 weeks (53 weeks in 1981 and 1987).

1 Flour millers' receipts of home-grown wheat.
2 Oatmeal millers' receipts of home-grown oats.
3 Human consumption of UK produced potatoes.
4 The method of calculating liquid milk has been revised from April 1981 to include a measurement adjustment. Therefore the totals of liquid and manufactured milk do not add up to the total.
5 Provisional.

Source *Ministry of Agriculture, Fisheries and Food*

9.10 Stocks of food and feedingstuffs[1]
United Kingdom
At end-December in each year

Thousand tonnes

	1977	1978	1979	1980	1981	1982	1983	1984	1985	1986	1987	1988
Wheat and flour (as wheat)	1 238	1 148	1 246	1 164	927	813	909	931	1 033	1 263	1 043	916
Barley	1 112	1 144	1 237	1 151	1 157	1 003	971	1 118	975	1 143	1 165	1 082
Maize	261	209	256	202	145	142	122	93	83	58	69	95
Oilcake and meal[2]	94	95	133	119	83	170	77	158	179	175	191	148
Oilseeds and nuts (crude oil equivalent)	24	22	19	23	23	27	29	23	37	39	36	26
Vegetable oil (as crude oil)	58	64	70	81	64	79	63	63	71	75	95	86
Marine oil (as crude oil)	40	47	25	48	40	54	44	51	42	22	16	12
Butter[3]	127	129	148	90	75	111	177	231	264	323	220	82
Imported meat and offal[4]	70	75	61	50	34	60	110	131	182	144	136	110
Raw coffee[5]	9	8	10	6	9	8	5	11	11	8	8	8
Tea[6]	109	94	89	92	72	67	55	62	56	66	51	50
Sugar	881	932	931	1 114	1 010	1 013	917	1 015	869	908	899	978
Chocolate and sugar confectionery[7]	62.1	74.8	78.4	70.4	68.5	67.8	70.6	73.7	62.5	64.5	63	

1 Recorded stocks, including stocks in bond or held by the main processors.
2 Excluding castor meal, cocoa cake and meal.
3 In addition to stocks in public cold stores surveyed by MAFF, closing stocks include all intervention stocks in private cold stores.
4 For meat and offals, from 1983 the figure represents imported and home-produced stocks.
5 Including manufacturers' stocks and additional public warehouses.
6 Including stocks held by primary wholesalers.
7 Manufacturers' stocks only.

Source *Ministry of Agriculture, Fisheries and Food*

9.11 Processed food and animal feedingstuffs: production

United Kingdom

Thousand tonnes

	1978	1979	1980	1981	1982	1983	1984	1985	1986	1987	1988
Flour milling:											
Wheat milling: total	5 159	5 053	4 809	4 753	4 616	4 478	5 044	4 749	5 308	4 917	5 166
Home produced	2 116	2 775	2 746	3 178	3 172	3 256	3 948	3 614	3 354	3 825	3 366
Imported	3 043	2 278	2 063	1 575	1 444	1 222	1 096	1 135	1 954	1 092	1 800
Flour produced	3 848	3 785	3 702	3 596	3 504	3 426	3 608	3 647	4 060	3 874	3 998
Offals produced	1 307	1 259	1 231	1 174	1 121	1 050	1 076	1 092	1 215	1 167	1 157
Oat milling:											
Oats milled by oatmeal millers	147	144	147	144	138	144	144	148	174	178	
Products of oat milling	85	84	83	85	82	81	87	89	103	107	
Seed crushing:											
Oilseeds and nuts processed	1 658	1 597	1 829	1 724	1 706	1 342	1 188	1 213	1 272	1 526	1 870
Crude oil produced, including production of maize oil	408	432	479	449	431	398	383	407	431	561	659
Oilcake and meal produced, excluding castor meal, cocoa cake and meal	1 221	1 139	1 337	1 241	1 240	945	790	841	823	923	1 162
Production of home-killed meat: total including meat subsequently canned	2 034	2 125	2 226	2 188	2 107	2 264	2 318	2 358	2 260	2 364	2 215
Beef	1 022	1 042	1 097	1 053	961	1 046	1 146	1 142	1 058	1 115	946
Veal	6	5	6	5	5	6	6	5	4	3	2
Mutton and lamb	228	231	277	263	264	287	288	304	290	293	321
Pork	630	694	684	710	728	763	708	735	747	783	793
Offal	148	152	162	157	149	161	170	171	162	167	156
Production of poultry meat	727	751	754	745	812	804	845	874	925	995	1 080
Production of bacon and ham, including meat subsequently canned	217	212	210	200	197	212	208	203	206	199	
Production of milk products:											
Butter	164	161	170	172	216	241	206	202	222	176	140
Cheese (including farmhouse)	216	234	238	242	244	245	246	256	259	266	300
Condensed milk excluding skim concentrate and condensed milk used in manufacture of chocolate crumb	159	145	129	124	118	110	104	103	93	98	100
Milk powder: excluding buttermilk and whey powder											
Full cream	20	20	27	29	34	35	53	61	57	94	104
Skimmed	272	233	237	251	296	302	223	241	268	194	136
Cream, fresh and sterilised; including farm cream[1]	84	87	85	77	75	74	59	48	39	36	38
Sugar: production from home-grown sugar-beet (as refined sugar)	1 022	1 154	1 106	1 092	1 418	1 062	1 314	1 210	1 318	1 226	1 307[3]
Production of compound fats:											
Margarine and other table spreads[4]	368	359	383	398	399	387	382	378	460	464	469
Solid cooking fats	131	131	130	153	157	153	115	108	104	107	104
Production of other processed foods:											
Jam and marmalade	169	168	155	173	177	168	174	182	174	185[3]	180[3]
Syrup and treacle	71	71	61	60	52	52	56	56	52	53	53
Canned vegetables[2]	850	821	778	753	810	811	789	786	782	723	701
Canned and bottled fruit[2]	59	56	30	29	39	42	42	39	35	41	36
Soups, canned and powdered	297	295	282	261	286	301	302	333	314	329[3]	313
Canned meat	115	136	115	95	86	93	98	98	86	93[3]	87[3]
Canned fish	13	12	9	6	5	4	7	9	7	6	8[3]
Biscuits, total disposals of home produced	645	626	629	632	622	698	643	704	709	699	724
Breakfast cereals, other than oatmeal and oatmeal flakes	229	208	229	219	229	233	248	249	264	259	273
Chocolate confectionery	424	425	407	409	451	464	489	492	483	501	
Sugar confectionery, excluding medicated confectionery	404	362	325	317	311	298	313	325	327	340	
Glucose	540	492	473	434	446	449	472	460	472	460	499
Production of soft drinks (million litres):											
Concentrated	426	478	489	503	523	570	602	511	544	559[3]	558[3]
Unconcentrated	2 131	2 351	2 233	2 231	2 458	2 642	2 690	2 899	3 417	3 713[3]	3 691[3]
Compound feedingstuffs: total	10 973	11 645	11 108	10 943	11 855	12 234	10 743	10 420	11 187	10 625	10 539[3]
Cattle food	4 516	4 936	4 556	4 538	5 012	5 456	4 382	4 116	4 486	3 826	3 771[3]
Calf food	423	455	428	436	478	504	422	401	402	352	334[3]
Pig food	2 303	2 380	2 267	2 169	2 317	2 292	2 099	2 142	2 186	2 189	2 140[3]
Poultry food	3 432	3 483	3 492	3 445	3 640	3 532	3 331	3 229	3 473	3 589	3 555[3]
Other compounds	299	391	365	355	408	450	509	532	640	670	739[3]

TIME SERIES. The figures relate to periods of 52 weeks (53 weeks in 1981 and 1987) with the following exceptions which are on a calendar year basis: butter, cheese, cream, canned meat, soft drinks, condensed milk and milk powder, canned vegetables, canned and bottled fruit, jam and marmalade and soups.

1 Excludes cream made from the residual fat of low fat milk production.
2 From 1981 the method of collecting these figures has changed. They are therefore not comparable with previous years.
3 Provisional figures.
4 Table spreads are only included from 1986 onwards.

Source *Ministry of Agriculture, Fisheries and Food*

9.12 Food and animal feedingstuffs: disposals

Thousand tonnes

	1978	1979	1980	1981	1982	1983	1984	1985	1986	1987	1988
Flour	3 854	3 777	3 706	3 041	3 547	3 492	3 626	3 640	3 657	3 892	3 917
Sugar (as refined sugar): total disposals	2 545	2 495	2 278	2 215	2 341	2 258	2 287	2 249	2 257	2 297	2 316
For food in the United Kingdom[1]	2 459	2 425	2 254	2 188	2 317	2 234	2 261	2 220	2 226	2 277	2 282
Syrup and treacle	71	71	61	60	52	52	56	56	52	53	53
Meat and fish:											
Fresh and frozen meat and offal, including usage for canning:											
Beef and veal	1 310	1 329	1 328	1 263	1 141	1 215	1 259	1 263	1 321	1 367	1 233
Mutton and lamb	444	444	469	432	457	472	449	450	441	447	458
Pork	668	732	724	746	756	801	747	770	779	831	854
Offal	271	270	277	275	270	277	283	284	262	261	249
Poultry-meat	757	775	778	785	837	854	910	941	1 008	1 062	1 159
Bacon and ham, including usage for canning	520	519	512	505	482	483	474	467	464	458	453
Fresh, frozen and cured fish (landed weight, excluding shellfish, including usage for canning):											
Total disposals	1 275	1 126	1 104	1 034	1 063	1 008	1 012	1 060	1 464	1 172	1 045[5]
For food in the United Kingdom	706	640	715	703	706	607	694	712	711	791	717[5]
Dairy products:											
Butter	458	435	398	400	382	368	309	324	328	394	368
Cheese	341	365	353	366	372	374	399	408	423	437	466
Condensed milk[2]	160	151	142	119	126	116	107	119	105	108	107
Milk powder, excluding buttermilk and whey powder:											
Full cream	27	25	30	30	35	38	54	71	71	103	106
Skimmed	305	258	227	262	298	333	246	253	288	210	142
Eggs in shell	839	847	798	773	762	734	743	745	723	729	
Oils (as crude oil):											
Vegetable oil	873	931	891	883	936	990	933	1 032	1 195	1 412	1 555
Marine oil for the manufacture of margarine and compound fat	182	206	212	216	203	182	200	196	178	167	129
Potatoes: total disposals[3]	6 003	5 942	5 883	6 290	6 040	6 285	6 022	6 740	6 531	6 587	6 745
For food in the United Kingdom[4]	5 592	5 532	5 733	5 861	5 994	6 018	5 858	6 166	6 439	6 494	6 545
Other foods:											
Chocolate and sugar confectionery, excluding medicated confectionery	896	797	764	764	801	803	845	872	850	884	
Tea excluding re-exports	163	176	184	178	174	168	177	161	161	158	164
Raw coffee	79	94	76	89	91	98	106	104	105	113	103
Cocoa beans excluding re-exports	72	67	66	86	88	77	90	91	87	95	101
Barley:											
For brewing and distilling and for food	4 078	2 893	3 706	5 056	4 279	4 435	5 403	4 739	5 667	4 941	4 563
Maize (including maize meal): total disposals	3 394	3 101	2 868	2 315	2 123	1 819	1 595	1 577	1 530	1 497	1 341
Animal feed	1 647	1 310	1 083	815	592	357	319	435	369	500	291
Oilcake and meal	1 990	2 189	2 380	2 505	2 837	2 889	2 695	2 721	2 640	3 014	2 330
Wheat milling offals	1 351	1 316	1 298	1 258	1 270	1 194	1 156	1 225	1 240	1 218	1 395
Fish and meat meal for animal feed, figures relate to sales	296	311	365	275	255	291	289	273	293	330	

TIME SERIES. The figures relate to periods of 52 weeks (53 weeks in 1981 and 1987) with the following exceptions which are on a calendar year basis: fish and potatoes; condensed milk; milk powder; and butter.

1 Including sugar used in the manufacture of other foods subsequently exported. Excluding sugar in imported manufactured foods.

2 Excluding skim concentrate and condensed milk used in manufacture of chocolate crumb.

3 Disposals (excluding seed and chats) of home-grown and imported potatoes for human consumption, processing, export and sales for stockfeed through schemes for implementing the Agricultural Act, 1947.

4 Disposals of home-grown and imported potatoes for human consumption in the United Kingdom.

5 Provisional.

Sources Ministry of Agriculture, Fisheries and Food; Central Statistical Office

9.13 Landings of fish of British taking: landed weight and value
United Kingdom

	Landed weight (Thousand tonnes)							Value (£ thousand)						
	1982	1983	1984	1985	1986	1987	1988	1982	1983	1984	1985	1986	1987	1988
Total all fish	774.6	748.4	733.7	762.1	716.9	790.4	742.0	260 624	280 263	297 863	323 825	361 680	435 162	402 893
Total wet fish	709.7	676.2	661.0	687.2	629.3	679.3	645.5	218 129	229 233	240 587	258 904	284 161	339 223	310 412
Demersal:														
Catfish	1.1	1.3	1.3	1.4	1.5	1.6	1.6	398	494	589	755	1 035	1 318	1 223
Cod	114.3	112.6	90.9	90.0	76.5	93.4	77.7	71 623	72 466	65 258	69 945	69 140	86 312	74 849
Dogfish	10.8	10.6	12.3	13.8	11.6	13.6	13.0	3 206	3 287	3 547	4 550	6 376	7 201	7 066
Haddock	129.0	122.6	107.5	132.2	131.0	102.4	97.6	50 311	57 361	64 204	67 757	79 019	78 079	68 708
Hake	3.2	2.3	2.5	2.7	3.0	3.3	3.6	4 126	2 519	2 794	3 851	4 549	5 540	6 389
Halibut	0.1	0.2	0.1	0.1	0.1	0.1	0.1	363	360	319	365	372	446	482
Lemon sole	5.0	5.9	5.7	5.7	5.0	5.3	5.4	5 061	5 493	5 972	7 137	8 265	9 018	8 788
Plaice	24.3	21.0	21.5	20.4	21.3	25.7	27.3	13 822	13 774	14 097	13 821	16 048	22 541	22 348
Redfish	0.4	0.3	0.4	0.2	0.1	0.2	0.2	96	73	98	75	56	62	71
Saithe (Coalfish)	16.6	12.8	12.1	14.4	17.7	15.2	14.4	4 776	3 520	2 759	3 874	6 361	7 077	5 657
Skate and ray	6.1	6.5	6.8	7.0	6.9	8.6	8.4	2 744	2 881	2 792	2 992	3 908	4 742	4 796
Sole	2.1	2.3	2.4	2.7	3.2	3.1	3.0	5 553	5 877	6 717	9 093	14 500	16 991	14 067
Turbot	0.5	0.5	0.5	0.5	0.6	0.7	0.7	1 298	1 426	1 660	1 976	2 607	3 612	3 690
Whiting	50.7	57.0	60.7	50.2	41.1	51.9	45.6	13 448	17 715	23 006	18 997	18 460	25 198	21 143
Livers[1]	0.1	..	..	..	..	..	..	4	..	..	1	1	..	..
Roes	0.6	0.5	0.6	0.5	0.5	0.5	0.5	345	275	321	390	348	499	473
Other demersal	83.1	71.1	69.7	60.5	63.1	55.0	66.9	13 710	14 563	17 580	21 596	25 660	35 690	37 198
Total	448.0	427.5	395.0	402.3	383.2	381.3	366.0	190 884	202 084	211 713	227 175	256 705	304 326	276 948
Pelagic:														
Herring	47.9	54.2	71.5	95.4	106.1	100.3	93.2	5 903	6 994	9 076	11 493	11 881	12 213	11 244
Mackerel[2]	185.7	175.5	186.3	174.2	132.1	189.4	176.1	19 332	18 649	18 768	18 694	14 766	21 484	20 791
Other pelagic	28.1	19.0	8.2	15.4	7.9	8.3	10.2	2 010	1 506	1 030	1 543	809	1 200	1 429
Total	261.7	248.7	266.0	285.0	246.1	298.0	279.5	27 245	27 149	28 874	31 730	27 456	34 897	33 464
Total shell fish	64.9	72.2	72.6	74.8	87.6	111.1	96.5	42 495	51 030	57 274	64 920	77 519	95 939	92 481
Cockles	8.3	5.8	5.4	7.8	19.4	39.0	24.6	458	327	311	476	1 165	4 285	3 276
Crab	8.6	11.3	14.0	13.5	12.6	13.5	15.2	4 246	6 373	8 422	8 557	9 599	11 400	13 908
Lobster	0.8	1.0	1.2	1.1	1.0	1.1	1.3	4 251	5 748	7 696	8 030	7 680	9 346	10 163
Mussels	4.4	5.9	4.3	5.8	6.3	4.9	6.9	461	468	314	467	541	543	906
Nephrop (Norway lobster)	19.9	22.1	22.2	24.8	25.4	24.2	27.4	21 289	24 061	24 545	31 548	39 119	43 007	44 585
Oysters[3]	0.4	0.3	0.4	0.5	0.6	0.1	0.1	925	636	770	734	845	241	225
Shrimps[4]	1.6	1.1	0.7	0.8	1.4	3.3	1.7	1 147	739	566	711	1 254	2 346	1 785
Whelks	1.6	1.3	2.2	1.6	2.0	2.7	2.0	380	226	456	355	418	665	473
Other shell fish	19.3	23.4	22.2	18.9	18.9	22.3	17.3	9 338	12 452	14 194	14 042	16 898	24 106	17 165

1 Including the raw equivalent of any liver oils landed.
2 Includes transhipments of mackerel or herring ie caught by British vessels but not actually landed at British ports. These quantities are transhipped to foreign vessels and are later recorded as exports.
3 The weight of oysters is calculated on the basis of one tonne being equal to 15 748 oysters in England and Wales.
4 1986 data may include some prawn data.

Sources *Ministry of Agriculture, Fisheries and Food; Department of Agriculture and Fisheries for Scotland*

9.14 Fishing fleet[1]
England and Wales
At 31 December in each year

Number

	1978	1979	1980	1981	1982	1983	1984	1985	1986	1987[2]	1988
By size:											
Under 40 ft.	3 044	3 288	2 917	3 504	3 126	3 662	4 079	4 482	4 919	4 793	4 623
40 ft.—79.9 ft.	892	934	967	969	931	853	834	764	572	614	624
80 ft.—109.0 ft.	56	53	53	64	76	82	89	91	95	109	123
110 ft.—139.9 ft.	77	72	60	63	63	57	55	37	48	52	53
140 ft.+	77	58	50	37	32	26	10	7	5	8	10
Total	4 146	4 405	4 047	4 637	4 228	4 680	5 067	5 381	5 639	5 576	5 433
By normal method of fishing:											
Trawlers	1 560	1 741	1 573	1 750	1 759	1 757	1 686	1 285	1 561	1 730	1 711
Seine nets	218	234	230	227	216	195	181	150	83	63	71
Lines	678	723	697	794	469	499	629	534	802	810	656
Purse seine	1	6	6	4	3	5	3	2	1	–	–
Other nets[3]	91	92	88	133	89	111	114	99	257	183	104
Other and unknown[4]	1 598	1 609	1 453	1 729	1 692	2 113	2 454	3 311	2 935	2 790	2 891

1 Changes in the numbers of vessels (especially those under 40 ft.) are due partly to changes in the definitions used.
2 Provisional figures.
3 Gill and cod nets, drift and ring nets.
4 Includes shellfishing.

Source Ministry of Agriculture, Fisheries and Food

9.15 Scottish fishing vessels
At 31 December in each year

Number

	1978	1979	1980	1981	1982	1983	1984	1985	1986	1987	1988
By size											
Under 40 ft.	1 510	1 412	1 417	1 288	1 189	1 191	1 184	1 216	1 216	1 275	1 342
40 ft.—59.9 ft.	553	541	536	530	514	496	469	461	435	440	441
60 ft.—79.9 ft.	462	476	479	477	468	467	469	461	465	469	471
80 ft.—109.9 ft.	55	57	57	51	40	38	35	32	33	38	35
110 ft.—139.9 ft.	35	31	25	24	22	20	20	21	22	26	27
140 ft. +	1	–	–	–	–	2	3	7	12	15	18
Total	2 616	2 517	2 514	2 370	2 233	2 214	2 180	2 198	2 183	2 263	2 334
By normal method of fishing											
Demersal trawl	364	365	359	339	315	291	244	253	235	253	288
Demersal pair trawl	9	26	38	72	70	76	104	116	122	132	129
Industrial trawl	15	9	6	9	19	17	12	10	6	6	6
Seine net	336	316	320	308	296	302	291	291	283	277	251
Lines	322	296	235	208	147	112	94	83	70	69	63
Purse seine	32	40	46	43	45	42	44	45	47	47	46
Pelagic trawl	82	50	42	35	34	26	23	20	12	7	6
Other nets[1]	13	11	15	22	27	43	48	46	43	32	31
Nephrops trawl	274	313	306	303	302	317	337	335	383	412	446
Other shellfishing[2]	1 169	1 091	1 147	1 031	978	988	983	999	982	1 028	1 068

1 Gill and cod nets, drift and ring nets.
2 All shellfishing methods except nephrops trawl.

Source Department of Agriculture and Fisheries for Scotland

9.16 Estimated food and drink supplies per head of population

	Kg per head per year										
	1977	1978	1979	1980	1981	1982	1983	1984	1985	1986	1987[1]
Grain products: Total	74.1	72.2	71.4	70.0	69.0	67.3	64.7	67.6	68.1	69.9	71.8
of which:											
Flour	65.3	63.7	63.2	61.4	60.5	58.6	55.9	58.4	58.7	60.0	61.6
Breakfast cereals	3.9	3.9	3.6	3.6	3.5	3.8	3.7	4.0	3.9	3.8	4.0
Rice	2.1	1.9	1.8	2.2	2.2	2.3	2.5	2.6	2.8	3.4	3.2
Sugar, honey and glucose (sugar content)[2]	48.0	48.5	46.9	43.4	42.6	44.9	43.3	44.2	43.2	43.5	43.9
Meat: Total (edible weight)	56.5	58.2	59.5	56.7	55.5	53.8	54.4	53.9	54.8	55.4	56.9
of which:											
Beef (bone-in)[3]	21.2	22.0	22.5	20.9	19.7	18.1	18.4	18.5	19.0	19.4	19.9
Lamb[3]	7.0	7.0	7.1	7.5	6.7	7.3	7.1	6.8	6.9	6.4	6.3
Pork[3]	11.5	11.7	12.7	12.6	12.9	13.2	13.3	12.5	12.7	12.8	13.9
Bacon and ham	9.0	9.2	9.3	9.0	8.8	8.4	8.4	8.3	8.1	8.1	7.9
Poultry[3]	12.1	12.9	13.1	13.4	13.3	14.4	14.7	15.4	16.0	17.2	17.8
Imported meat products	3.9	3.9	4.1	3.4	3.7	3.1	3.3	3.6	3.7	3.7	3.8
Fish: Total (edible weight)	7.4	6.6	6.7	7.7	7.2	6.8	7.1	7.7	7.5	8.3	8.0
Dairy products: Total supplies of											
Butterfat	14.5	14.3	13.8	13.2	12.7	12.2	12.3	12.0	11.9	11.4	11.7
Solids-not-fat	18.0	18.0	18.4	17.3	17.8	17.5	17.8	18.5	18.4	17.4	17.7
of which:											
Liquid milk and cream[4]	158.3	156.9	156.4	152.8	149.2	146.7	146.2	141.9	137.6	134.8	133.1
Liquid skimmed milk (as such)[5]	0.0	0.8	0.8	0.9	1.9	2.5	3.7	7.4	10.0	12.2	12.0
Butter	7.8	7.5	6.8	6.3	5.8	5.4	5.4	5.1	5.0	4.6	4.9
Cheese	5.5	5.8	6.2	6.0	6.1	6.2	6.0	6.5	6.6	6.5	7.0
Whole milk used in products n.e.s.	5.6	5.4	5.4	5.2	5.3	6.3	6.4	6.3	6.2	7.0	6.4
Skimmed milk used in products n.e.s.	8.1	9.6	10.2	10.6	9.7	11.6	13.0	11.9	10.8	10.2	10.4
Whey used in products n.e.s.	11.7	13.4	14.9	14.3	16.2	15.4	14.8	14.7	15.6	12.4	12.3
Eggs and egg products (equiv. no. of eggs)	247	249	248	235	227	228	224	224	224	220	228
Oils and fats: Total (fat content)	20.3	17.4	18.5	19.2	20.2	21.3	22.0	22.1	22.9	23.4	22.7
of which:											
Margarine (net)	5.4	5.9	6.2	6.7	7.2	7.7	7.7	7.9	8.3	8.6	8.5
Lard and cooking fat	6.5	5.9	5.8	5.4	5.4	5.5	5.2	4.7	4.3	4.0	3.9
Other edible oils	6.2	6.2	5.7	6.2	6.8	7.5	7.9	7.8	9.5	10.6	10.6
Other fats including cocoa butter	3.3	2.4	2.1	2.4	2.5	2.6	3.1	3.7	3.0	2.7	2.1
Potatoes and potato products:											
Total (as raw equiv.)	95.6	101.6	105.8	99.3	103.4	105.5	106.1	103.0	107.6	112.0	113.1
of which:											
For distribution unprocessed	71.0	78.3	79.2	77.4	79.1	77.8	76.5	74.7	77.6	81.5	81.5
Fruit: Total[6]	65.1	65.9	72.4	72.3	77.4	75.8	79.7	84.9	84.1	89.8	94.2
of which:											
Citrus	8.7	9.1	8.9	10.1	9.7	9.2	8.9	9.4	8.4	9.7	9.8
Tropical fruit	5.6	5.8	5.8	6.3	6.2	6.4	6.5	6.7	7.1	7.4	7.8
Other fresh fruit	16.1	19.0	19.8	19.8	18.7	20.3	20.1	20.7	20.8	21.2	21.5
Imported fruit juices (natural strength)	9.4	9.1	11.8	11.6	14.7	13.1	15.6	16.7	16.2	18.0	19.4
Other imported processed fruit	9.2	7.8	8.6	7.4	7.8	8.2	8.1	8.3	8.1	8.1	8.7
Vegetables: Total (as fresh equiv.)[6]	79.6	70.2	69.5	71.7	72.2	77.9	77.0	81.8	82.2	86.6	86.5
of which:											
Tomatoes and leafy salads	9.2	9.2	9.1	9.2	9.9	10.1	9.9	10.9	11.0	11.1	11.2
Cabbage, carrots, peas and beans	34.6	37.4	31.4	32.0	31.9	33.1	29.5	32.0	30.3	33.1	30.4
Beetroots, parsnips and onions	12.7	13.0	13.4	12.4	11.9	11.3	11.7	12.0	12.9	12.0	13.5
Other vegetables	7.8	8.1	7.3	6.9	6.9	7.8	8.0	9.0	9.8	10.6	11.2
Imported canned tomatoes[7]	4.1	3.1	4.5	4.0	4.5	4.5	4.6	4.8	4.7	5.6	5.6
Other imported processed vegetables	1.8	0.3	0.6	0.8	1.5	3.3	3.5	3.5	4.1	4.8	4.5
Pulses and nuts: Total[8]	4.9	4.1	5.1	4.6	4.6	4.5	5.0	5.0	4.6	5.3	4.5
Tea	3.2	2.9	3.1	3.3	3.2	3.1	3.0	3.1	2.8	2.8	2.6
Coffee and cocoa	2.7	2.6	3.2	2.9	3.3	3.1	3.2	3.3	3.2	3.2	3.3
Alcoholic drink:											
Spirit (litres at 40% alcohol content)	3.5	4.3	4.7	4.4	4.2	4.0	4.1	4.0	4.3	4.3	4.3
Beer (litres)	117.8	121.4	122.0	116.4	110.6	109.0	110.4	110.0	108.7	107.9	109.0
Wine (litres)	6.4	7.5	8.1	8.1	8.6	8.7	9.5	10.4	10.9	11.4	12.0
Cider and perry (litres)	3.9	4.0	4.1	4.0	4.3	5.2	5.8	5.8	5.6	5.7	5.6

Footnotes on page 189

Source *Ministry of Agriculture, Fisheries and Food*

9.16 Estimated food and drink supplies per head of population

(continued)

	Kg per head per year											
	1976	1977	1978	1979	1980	1981	1982	1983	1984	1985	1986	1987[1]
Nutritional value of supplies per head per day												
Protein (grammes)	84.2	84.2	84.3	85.2	83.8	84.2	83.5	83.5	84.3	84.7	85.4	86.6
Fat (grammes)	135	141	136	137	132	134	134	136	134	137	138	138
Carbohydrate (grammes)[9]	388	390	387	382	360	358	364	355	362	363	371	378
Energy (kilocalories):												
from Food	3 002	3 061	2 988	2 980	2 851	2 863	2 883	2 872	2 891	2 919	2 970	2 992
from Alcoholic drink	152	147	158	163	156	152	150	155	157	156	155	158

Note: For further details contact MAFF (Telephone: 01-270 8559)
1 Provisional.
2 Includes estimated sugar content of manufactured food products but excludes sugar used to produce alcoholic drink.
3 Dressed carcase weight.
4 Supplies of liquid milk for resale as milk and for making cream.
5 Liquid slimmed milk for consumption as such derived as a by-product of cream and butter production.
6 Home grown products include those used for processing (e.g. canning, freezing).
7 Includes tomato juice, puree and paste.
8 Includes dried peas and beans for canning.
9 Available carbohydrate expressed as monosaccharides.

Source Ministry of Agriculture, Fisheries and Food

9.17 Self-sufficiency in food and the cost of food processing and distribution in the United Kingdom

£ million

	1977	1978	1979	1980	1981	1982	1983	1984	1985	1986	1987[1,7]
At current prices											
Home production of food	5 602	5 824	6 610	7 076	7 547	8 373	8 616	9 223	8 914	9 079	9 305
Net deficit/surplus in production of intermediate agricultural products[2]	−525	−521	−535	−357	−166	−218	−244	+327	−186	−248	−353
Adjusted home production	5 077	5 303	6 075	6 719	7 382	8 155	8 372	9 550	8 728	8 831	8 952
Home production for home consumption[3]	4 944	5 155	5 948	6 184	6 679	7 221	7 264	7 738	7 459	7 534	7 629
Indigenous type food imports	2 528	2 705	2 961	2 869	3 016	3 404	3 498	3 817	3 929	4 289	4 412
All indigenous type food consumed in the United Kingdom[4]	7 472	7 860	8 909	9 053	9 695	10 624	10 762	11 555	11 388	11 823	12 041
Net imports of non-indigenous type food	2 305	2 229	2 488	2 339	2 378	2 643	2 914	3 618	3 692	3 732	3 626
All food consumed in the United Kingdom[4]	9 777	10 089	11 397	11 392	12 073	13 267	13 676	15 173	15 080	15 555	15 667
Self-sufficiency (as a percentage of consumption of)											
(i) Indigenous type food	*67.9*	*67.5*	*68.2*	*74.2*	*76.1*	*76.8*	*77.8*	*82.6*	*76.7*	*74.7*	*74.3*
(ii) All food	*51.9*	*52.6*	*53.3*	*59.0*	*61.1*	*61.5*	*61.2*	*62.9*	*57.9*	*56.8*	*57.1*
Cost of processing and distributing all food in the United Kingdom[5]	8 825	10 410	11 876	14 585	15 360	15 700	17 325	17 422	19 152	21 516	22 500
Total final expenditure on food	18 602	20 499	23 273	25 977	27 433	28 967	31 001	32 595	34 232	37 071	38 167
Cost of processing and distributing all food as a percentage of total expenditure[6]	*47.4*	*50.8*	*51.0*	*56.1*	*56.0*	*54.2*	*55.9*	*53.4*	*55.9*	*58.0*	*59.0*
At constant (1980) prices											
Home production of food	6 576	6 757	6 892	7 076	6 801	7 074	7 127	7 334	7 257	7 243	7 323
Net deficit/surplus in production of intermediate agricultural products[2]	−561	−586	−629	−357	−144	−275	−233	+427	−14	−9	−12
Adjusted home production	6 015	6 171	6 263	6 719	6 657	6 798	6 894	7 761	7 243	7 234	7 311
Home production for home consumption[3]	5 743	5 935	6 118	6 184	6 055	6 117	6 009	6 216	6 175	6 016	6 057
Indigenous type food imports	3 064	3 016	3 159	2 869	2 932	2 951	2 895	2 988	3 025	3 265	3 221
All indigenous type food consumed in the United Kingdom[4]	8 807	8 951	9 277	9 053	8 987	9 068	8 904	9 203	9 200	9 281	9 278
Net imports of non-indigenous type food	2 224	2 265	2 458	2 339	2 484	2 513	2 485	2 597	2 626	2 798	2 898
All food consumed in the United Kingdom[4]	11 031	11 216	11 735	11 392	11 471	11 581	11 389	11 800	11 826	12 079	12 176
Self-sufficiency (as a percentage of consumption of)											
(i) Indigenous type food	*68.2*	*68.9*	*67.5*	*74.2*	*74.1*	*75.0*	*77.4*	*84.3*	*78.7*	*78.0*	*78.8*
(ii) All food	*54.5*	*55.0*	*53.4*	*59.0*	*58.0*	*58.7*	*60.5*	*65.8*	*61.2*	*59.9*	*60.0*
Cost of processing and distributing all food in the United Kingdom[5]	13 743	14 247	14 311	14 585	14 289	13 991	14 774	14 269	14 722	15 608	15 405
Total final expenditure on food	24 774	25 463	26 046	25 977	25 760	25 572	26 163	26 069	26 548	27 687	27 581
Cost of processing and distributing all food as a percentage of total expenditure[6]	*55.5*	*56.0*	*54.9*	*56.1*	*55.5*	*54.7*	*56.5*	*54.7*	*55.5*	*56.4*	*55.9*

Note: For further details contact MAFF (Telephone: 01-270 8559)
1 Provisional.
2 The value of exports of feed, seed and livestock, plus the changes in stocks of feed and seed held on-farm and by the Intervention Board for Agricultural Produce, less the value of imports of feed, seed and livestock.
3 The value of home production of food, less the value of changes in stocks of food both on and off farms, and less the value of exports of indigenous type food.
4 At farmgate or landed value.
5 The difference between "Total final expenditure on food" and "All food consumed in the United Kingdom".
6 Taxes on food have been deducted and the value of subsidies added.
7 1988 figures not available.

Source Ministry of Agriculture, Fisheries and Food

9.18 Estimated household food consumption by all households in Great Britain

Ounces per person per week

	1978	1979	1980	1981	1982	1983	1984	1985	1986	1987	1988
Liquid wholemilk[1] (pints)	4.44	4.31	4.16	4.01	3.95	3.80	3.61	3.32	3.04	2.88	2.66
Other milk (pints or equivalent pints)	0.35	0.41	0.40	0.42	0.43	0.49	0.67	0.79	1.08	1.19	1.35
Cheese	3.72	3.84	3.89	3.89	3.80	4.01	3.84	3.91	4.16	4.09	4.13
Butter	4.55	4.45	4.05	3.69	3.17	3.27	2.87	2.83	2.27	2.14	2.00
Margarine	3.54	3.63	3.83	4.11	4.33	4.08	4.08	3.76	4.10	3.98	3.78
Lard and compound cooking fat	1.91	1.86	1.81	1.80	1.76	1.70	1.51	1.44	1.36	1.15	1.00
Eggs (number)	3.96	3.88	3.69	3.68	3.51	3.53	3.21	3.15	3.01	2.89	2.67
Preserves	2.15	2.17	2.05	2.08	1.99	2.05	1.95	1.87	1.98	1.88	1.85
Sugar	11.89	11.55	11.17	11.08	10.31	9.84	9.15	8.41	8.04	7.48	6.94
Beef and veal	8.27	8.27	8.13	6.96	7.06	6.57	6.27	6.51	6.58	6.77	6.35
Mutton and lamb	3.92	4.28	4.51	4.25	3.59	3.87	3.32	3.27	3.01	2.65	2.78
Pork	3.34	3.63	4.13	3.82	4.02	3.53	3.29	3.45	3.64	3.17	3.29
Bacon and ham, uncooked	4.31	4.35	4.20	4.14	3.95	4.02	3.58	3.69	3.68	3.46	3.48
Bacon and ham, cooked (including canned)	1.08	1.11	1.07	1.13	1.15	1.09	1.11	1.14	1.13	1.15	1.13
Poultry and cooked chicken	6.15	6.82	6.67	7.30	6.85	6.99	7.24	6.90	7.30	8.14	8.09
Other cooked and canned meats	2.66	2.64	2.40	2.42	2.51	2.65	2.45	2.60	2.59	2.45	2.62
Offals	1.11	1.04	1.03	1.04	0.97	0.84	0.83	0.79	0.74	0.69	0.63
Sausages, uncooked	3.54	3.49	3.25	3.41	3.33	3.33	3.00	2.97	2.73	2.66	2.48
Other meat products	4.46	4.57	4.70	4.81	5.19	5.18	5.44	5.42	5.67	5.84	5.72
Fish, fresh and processed	2.56	2.74	2.78	2.81	2.75	2.81	2.64	2.53	2.66	2.62	2.60
Canned fish	0.51	0.54	0.64	0.69	0.63	0.77	0.70	0.71	0.84	0.91	0.90
Fish and fish products, frozen	1.18	1.26	1.40	1.42	1.65	1.55	1.56	1.67	1.64	1.57	1.56
Potatoes (excluding processed)	44.05	43.59	40.95	41.87	41.11	39.88	39.82	40.96	38.76	37.68	36.43
Fresh green vegetables	13.45	10.88	12.42	11.98	11.24	10.78	10.83	9.78	11.11	9.97	10.42
Tomatoes, fresh	3.67	3.85	3.79	3.92	3.98	3.84	3.78	3.61	3.77	3.59	3.75
Other fresh vegetables and frozen vegetables	15.72	15.76	16.66	11.83	16.92	16.79	16.68	18.05	19.32	19.81	19.60
Canned tomatoes	1.16	1.27	1.43	1.52	1.38	1.44	1.34	1.61	1.82	1.51	1.62
Canned peas	2.46	2.67	2.25	2.36	2.53	2.30	2.19	2.31	2.17	1.98	1.87
Canned beans	3.92	4.09	4.00	4.12	4.16	4.45	4.45	4.43	4.79	4.59	4.64
Apples	7.02	7.88	7.85	7.28	7.02	7.08	6.84	6.93	7.26	7.05	7.17
Oranges	2.93	3.14	3.23	3.05	2.70	2.82	2.70	2.48	3.10	2.70	3.13
Other citrus fruit	1.84	1.87	2.04	1.92	1.72	1.97	1.85	1.60	1.97	2.11	1.98
All other fresh fruit	6.37	6.75	7.70	7.72	7.31	7.76	7.61	7.52	8.00	8.40	8.74
Canned fruit	3.05	2.84	2.79	2.61	2.65	2.42	2.28	2.05	2.22	2.06	2.15
Dried fruit, nuts and fruit and nut products	1.32	1.28	1.31	1.25	1.21	1.43	1.27	1.23	1.38	1.49	1.30
Flour	5.96	5.75	5.67	5.96	5.28	4.97	4.34	4.05	4.14	3.93	3.59
Bread	32.13	31.38	31.12	31.23	31.03	30.74	30.57	30.99	30.79	30.60	30.28
Buns, scones and teacakes	1.10	1.15	0.96	0.96	1.02	0.97	0.98	1.01	1.05	1.09	1.11
Cakes and pastries	2.67	2.86	2.77	2.81	2.74	2.62	2.58	2.48	2.55	2.61	2.56
Biscuits	5.45	5.54	5.40	5.39	5.66	5.47	5.29	5.22	5.42	5.32	5.28
Breakfast cereals	3.45	3.38	3.50	3.53	3.54	3.83	4.13	4.04	4.38	4.42	4.47
Oatmeal and oat products	0.47	0.45	0.42	0.46	0.37	0.45	0.42	0.49	0.55	0.49	0.63
Tea	1.99	2.11	2.05	1.98	2.02	2.04	1.80	1.74	1.74	1.71	1.65
Instant coffee	0.44	0.51	0.54	0.52	0.51	0.53	0.54	0.54	0.55	0.52	0.53
Canned soups	2.76	2.98	2.77	2.81	2.66	2.69	2.68	2.70	2.54	2.81	2.78
Pickles and sauces	1.74	1.83	1.81	2.01	1.97	2.15	2.10	2.14	2.18	2.09	2.30

Note: Page 173 contains a description of the National Food Survey
1 Including also school and welfare milk.

Source Ministry of Agriculture, Fisheries and Food (National Food Survey)

10 Transport and Communications

10.1 Goods transport in Great Britain

	1978	1979	1980	1981	1982	1983	1984	1985	1986	1987	1988[1]
Road	99.3	102.3	92.4	92.9	93.8	95.1	99.4	102.9	105.4	113.3	130.2
Rail[2]	20.0	19.9	17.6	17.5	15.9	17.1	12.7	15.4	16.5	17.3	18.0
Water:[3] Coastwise oil	29.9	34.0	38.2	38.0	39.8	40.2	41.3	39.5	34.4	31.7	35.7
Water:[3] Other	17.7	21.5	15.9	14.7	18.9	20.1	18.9	18.1	20.4	22.4	25.2
Pipelines[4]	9.8	10.3	10.1	9.3	9.3	9.9	10.4	11.2	10.4	10.5	10.8
Total tonne kilometres (thousand millions)	176.7	188.0	174.2	172.4	177.7	182.4	182.7	187.1	187.1	195.2	219.9
Road	1 491	1 487	1 383	1 286	1 376	1 344	1 390	1 445	1 471	1 542	1 758
Rail[2]	171	169	154	154	142	145	78	122	140	141	150
Water:[3] Coastwise oil	49	52	54	52	54	53	53	50	46	43	46
Water:[3] Other	83	88	83	77	83	90	87	92	99	100	106
Pipelines[4]	83	85	83	75	78	82	88	89	79	83	85
Total (million tonnes)	1 877	1 881	1 757	1 644	1 733	1 714	1 696	1 797	1 835	1 909	2 145

1 Water figures are provisional for 1987.
2 British Rail only. Traffic was affected by ASLEF industrial action in 1982 and by the miners' strike and associated action by BR staff in 1984 and 1985.
3 Revised series. Oil comprises crude oil and all Petroleum products. 'Coastwise' includes all sea traffic within the UK, Isle of Man and Channel Islands. 'Other' means other coastwise plus inland waterway traffic and one-port traffic (largely crude oil direct from rigs).
4 Excluding movements of gases by pipelines.

Source *Department of Transport*

10.2 Passenger transport in Great Britain: estimated passenger kilometres

Thousand million passenger kilometres

	1978	1979	1980	1981	1982	1983	1984	1985	1986	1987	1988[5]
Air[1]	3	3	3	3	3	3	3	4	4	4	5
Rail[2]	35	35	35	34	31	34	35	36	37	39	41
Road:											
Public service vehicles[3]	50	48	45	42	41	42	42	42	41	41	41
Cars and taxis[4]	372	373	394	400	409	412	432	439	463	498	517
Motorcycles[4]	6	7	8	10	10	9	9	8	8	7	6
Pedal cycles	5	5	5	5	6	6	6	6	5	6	5
Total	471	471	490	494	500	506	527	535	558	595	615

1 Domestic scheduled and non-scheduled services, including Northern Ireland, Isle of Man and Channel Islands.
2 British Rail, London Regional Transport and Passenger Transport Executive railway systems. The basis of calculating London Regional Transport railways' passenger kilometres has been revised from passenger kilometres paid for to passenger kilometres travelled. During 1982, British Rail traffics were affected by industrial action which took place on 34 days.
3 Calculated from operators' returns of numbers of passengers carried, using estimates for average length of journey.
4 Based on statistics of vehicle mileage derived from the traffic counts and estimates of average numbers of persons per vehicle, derived from the National Travel surveys.
5 Provisional figures.

Source *Department of Transport*

10.3 Length of public roads in Great Britain
At 1 April in each year

Kilometres

	1978	1979	1980	1981	1982	1983	1984	1985	1986	1987	1988
Motorway[1]	2 394	2 455	2 556	2 646	2 692	2 741	2 786	2 813	2 920	2 975	2 992
Trunk	12 426	12 350	12 282	12 269	12 209	12 231	12 271	12 201	12 439	12 419	12 480
Principal	34 199	34 430	34 298	34 656	34 700	34 819	34 753	34 800	34 868	34 987	34 939
Other[2]	287 245	288 743	290 497	292 749	294 341	295 985	297 779	298 885	299 849	302 314	303 904
Total	336 264	337 978	339 633	342 320	343 942	345 776	347 589	348 699	350 076	352 695	354 315

1 Including local authority motorways, the percentage of which is small, less than 5%.
2 Excluding unsurfaced roads and green lanes.

Source *Department of Transport*

10.4 Estimated traffic on all roads in Great Britain

Billion vehicle kilometres

	1978	1979	1980	1981	1982	1983	1984	1985	1986	1987	1988[1]
All motor vehicles	256.49	255.87	271.42	276.33	283.88	288.02	303.07	309.59	325.23	350.47	363.13
Cars and taxis[2]	202.39	201.45	215.17	219.62	227.50	231.45	244.30	250.46	264.44	284.63	295.44
Two-wheeled motor vehicles	6.15	6.39	7.69	8.90	9.25	8.31	8.16	7.37	7.07	6.71	5.44
Buses and coaches	3.30	3.33	3.50	3.47	3.49	3.65	3.81	3.66	3.69	4.08	4.20
Light vans[3]	22.60	22.38	23.14	23.39	23.18	23.15	24.48	25.17	26.49	28.98	31.05
Other goods vehicles	22.05	22.32	21.93	20.95	20.46	21.45	22.33	22.94	23.53	26.06	27.00
Total goods vehicles	44.65	44.70	45.07	44.34	43.64	44.60	46.81	48.11	50.02	55.04	58.05
Pedal cycles	5.11	4.58	5.10	5.46	6.41	6.40	6.41	6.08	5.48	5;74	4.97

1 Provisional.
2 This category includes three-wheeled cars; excludes all vans whether licensed for private or for commercial use.
3 Not exceeding 30 cwt. unladen weight.

Source *Department of Transport*

10.5 Motor Vehicles Currently Licensed[1, 2]
Great Britain

Thousands

	1978	1979	1980	1981	1982	1983	1984	1985	1986	1987	1988
Total	17 758	18 616	19 200	19 347	19 762	20 209	20 765	21 157	21 699	22 152	23 302
Private cars[3]	13 801	14 307	14 772	14 943	15 303	15 543	16 055	16 454	16 981	17 421	18 432
Other vehicles[3]	1 365	1 415	1 461	1 478	1 513	1 615	1 666	1 708	1 771	1 828	1 951
Private and light goods[3]	15 166	15 722	16 233	16 421	16 816	17 158	17 721	18 161	18 753	19 249	20 383
Up to 50 c.c.	458	466	473	472	489	474	449	423	389	352	312
Other	736	826	899	899	881	816	776	725	676	626	600
Motor cycles, etc: total	1 194	1 292	1 372	1 371	1 370	1 290	1 225	1 148	1 065	978	912
Public road passenger vehicles: total	110	111	110	110	111	113	116	120	125	129	132
Buses, coaches, taxis, etc.											
Not over 8 passengers	37	37	39	40	43	46	49	53	57	58	59
Over 8 passengers	74	73	71	70	68	68	67	67	68	71	73
Goods[4, 5]	606	624	575	558	549	565	576	582	593	609	647
Agricultural tractors, etc.[6]	394	402	397	365	371	376	375	374	371	374	383
Other licensed vehicles[7]	111	106	100	95	91	86	82	78	73	68	83
Crown vehicles	33	35	37	37	37	39	39	39	39	39	38
All other exempt vehicles	143	324	375	390	417	582	631	656	681	706	722
Exempt from licence duty: total[8]	177	359	412	427	454	621	670	695	720	744	761

1 Since 1978, censuses have been taken annually on 31 December and are obtained from a full count of licensing records held at DVLC Swansea. Prior to this, figures were compiled from a combination of DVLC data and records held at Local Taxation offices.
2 Excludes vehicles officially registered by the armed forces.
3 Includes taxis also used privately.
4 As a result of changes in the taxation system since October 1982, about 970 000 vans and light goods vehicles previously licensed as Goods vehicles, have now been regrouped, together with 14 000 newly licensed goods vehicles under the heading Private and light goods; which has replaced the old Private category. Figures for previous years have been estimated to provide a continuous series of data.
5 Includes agricultural vans and lorries, showmen's goods vehicles licensed to draw trailers.
6 Includes combine harvesters, mowing machines, digging machines, mobile cranes and works trucks.
7 Includes three wheelers, pedestrian controlled vehicles and showmen's haulage and recovery vehicles. New tax class introduced January 1988.
8 From 1979 includes exempt tax classes 61 and 62 not previously included and from 1980 includes electric vehicles which are now exempt from licence duty.

Source *Department of Transport*

10.6 New vehicle registrations by taxation class
Great Britain

Thousands

	1978	1979	1980	1981	1982	1983	1984	1985	1986	1987	1988
Total[1]	2 151.4	2 369.9	2 155.8	2 030.3	2 103.9	2 307.5	2 238.9	2 309.3	2 333.7	2 473.9	2 723.5
Private and light goods[2]											
Private Cars	1 519.9	1 625.4	1 436.8	1 434.8	1 527.0	1 773.3	1 721.6	1 804.0	1 839.3	1 962.7	2 154.7
Other vehicles	225.9	266.1	242.7	192.4	201.0	197.5	191.6	202.9	207.9	221.6	248.9
Total	1 745.8	1 891.5	1 679.5	1 627.2	1 728.0	1 970.9	1 913.2	2 006.9	2 047.2	2 184.3	2 403.6
Motor cycles, etc.											
Up to 50 c.c.	56.2	86.5	96.4	94.8	94.0	67.4	55.4	48.3	37.5	29.7	24.7
Other	169.1	199.4	216.3	177.1	137.6	107.1	89.8	77.5	68.9	61.1	65.4
Total	225.3	285.9	312.7	271.9	231.6	174.5	145.2	125.8	106.4	90.8	90.1
Public road passenger vehicles											
Buses, coaches, taxis, etc.											
Not over 8 seats	3.0	2.8	2.5	2.6	2.8	3.0	3.3	3.1	3.4	3.6	4.2
Over 8 seats	6.1	6.3	6.3	4.9	4.3	4.3	3.9	3.7	5.5	5.1	5.0
Total	9.1	9.1	8.8	7.5	7.1	7.3	7.2	6.8	8.9	8.7	9.2
Heavy general goods[2] and farmers'[3] goods vehicles: by weight	79.8	91.3	74.7	56.3	58.8	64.9	69.1	74.2	74.9	82.2	96.9
Privately owned agricultural tractors and engines[4]	50.0	47.7	36.7	32.6	38.9	42.1	40.1	40.1	34.8	37.7	45.2
Other licensed vehicles[5]	6.8	6.0	4.9	3.4	3.9	3.8	3.3	3.0	3.0	2.6	8.5
Exempt from licence duty											
Crown vehicles	4.7	4.4	5.9	4.6	4.6	5.0	5.1	5.8	5.3	4.6	4.1
All other exempt vehicles[1,6]	29.9	34.0	32.5	26.8	31.1	39.1	55.7	46.7	53.2	63.0	66.0
Total	34.6	38.4	38.5	31.4	35.7	44.1	60.8	52.5	58.5	67.5	70.1

1 Including personal and direct export vehicles.
2 Estimates of the total of vehicles within the Private and light goods taxation class, and within the Other goods class were estimated by assuming that all goods vehicles less than 1.5 tons unladen weight would have been registered in the Private and light goods class if it had existed prior to October 1982 when it first became effective.
3 Owned by a farmer and available for hauling produce and requisites for his farm.
4 Agricultural tractors are excluded unless driven on public roads.
5 Includes three wheelers, pedestrian controlled vehicles, general haulage and showmen's tractors and recovery vehicles new tax class introduced January 1988.
6 From 1980 includes electric vehicles which are now exempt from licence duty.

Source Department of Transport

10.7 Driving tests
Great Britain
Applications and results

Thousands

	1978	1979	1980	1981	1982	1983	1984	1985	1986	1987	1988
Applications received	1 908.9	1 786.4	1 800.5	1 837.3	1 891.6	1 917.0	1 955.7	1 935.2	1 968.7	1 990.4	2 241.4
Tests conducted	1 632.2	1 569.6	1 962.0	2 031.3	2 005.3	1 892.3	1 784.1	1 841.8	1 999.7	1 981.0	2 046.9
Tests passed	757.3	742.1	927.8	966.8	965.0	921.0	875.4	895.9	972.1	989.7	1 064.6
Percentage of passes	*46*	*47*	*47*	*48*	*48*	*49*	*49*	*49*	*49*	*50*	*52*

Source Department of Transport

10.8 Vehicles with licences current[1]
Northern Ireland

Number

	1977	1978	1979[2]	1980	1981	1982	1983	1984	1985	1986	1987[5]	1988[6]
Private cars, etc.	337 890	347 091	358 010	364 590	365 000	388 030	411 780	430 660	405 090	415 050	434 237	443 081
Cycles and tricycles	16 826	17 006	14 860	14 720	14 550	15 500	14 790	15 700	12 360	10 820	8 946	8 957
Public road passenger vehicles: total	2 224	1 888	2 110	2 270	2 510	2 210	2 200	2 780	2 460	2 450	3 258	3 333
Taxis up to 4 seats	771	386	410	710	840	720	940	1 240	860	940	1 087	1 128
Buses, coaches, over 4 seats	1 453	1 502	1 700	1 560	1 670	1 490	1 260	1 540	1 600	1 510	2 171	2 205
General (HGV) Goods vehicles: total	39 190	39 708	41 810	38 900	33 760	34 060	29 450	34 510	26 650	23 610	22 789	22 547
Unladen weight:												
Not over 1525 kgs	18 123	17 936	18 820	16 720	13 190	15 490	10 530	15 440	8 850	7 830	29 009	
Over 1525 and not over 12000 kgs [7]	6 149	6 971	6 780	6 710	6 140	5 730	9 690	9 310	8 070	7 690	17 521	17 524
Over 12000 kgs [7]	10 795	11 519	12 350	10 740	10 510	11 660	7 740	8 230	7 960	6 880	7 318	
Farmers Goods Vehicles[3]	4 054	3 222	3 710	4 620	3 770	1 090	1 440	1 430	1 630	1 090	5 101	4 858
Tractors for general haulage	59	50	130	80	130	70	50	90	120	100	148	144
Tower wagons	10	10	20	30	20	20	–	10	20	20	19	21
Agricultural tractors and engines, etc.[4]	11 329	13 980	11 040	9 580	7 660	9 150	9 870	9 840	8 370	7 310	6 806	7 640
Vehicles exempt from duty: total	8 598	9 283	11 119	12 288	13 215	13 610	13 764	13 208	13 681	13 615	13 308	15 427
Government owned	6 534	7 088	7 756	7 978	9 395	9 390	9 604	10 258	11 071	11 115	4 458	5 021
Other:												
Ambulances	–	10	50	70	10	290	342	358	203	324	41	49
Fire engines	49	59	–	60	110	140	40	50	80	50	14	210
Other	2 015	2 126	3 313	4 180	3 700	3 790	3 778	2 542	2 327	2 126	8 795	10 147
Total	416 057	428 956	438 949	442 348	436 695	462 560	481 854	506 698	468 611	472 855	489 344	500 985

1 Licences current at any time during the September quarter.
2 Licences current at any time during the quarter ended December.
3 Owned by a farmer and available for hauling produce and requisites for his farm.
4 Agricultural tractors are excluded unless driven on public roads.
5 Licences current at 31 March 1988.
6 Licences current at 31 December 1988.
7 General goods total applicable 1987 onwards.

Source *Department of the Environment for Northern Ireland*

10.9 New vehicles registrations
Northern Ireland

Number

	1977	1978	1979	1980	1981	1982	1983	1984	1985	1986	1987	1988
Private cars, etc.	50 287	56 728	56 053	47 228	44 427	54 793	64 493	68 627	66 629	60 591	62 480	66 153
Cycles and tricycles	4 813	4 133	3 471	3 543	3 533	3 111	2 814	2 815	2 286	1 893	1 447	1 870
Public road passenger vehicles: total	209	140	151	171	150	141	273	308	316	286	314	597
Taxis	35	21	27	26	32	38	153	182	163	142	34	61
Buses, coaches, etc.	174	119	124	145	118	103	120	126	153	144	280	536
Goods vehicles: total	6 522	6 705	7 226	5 917	4 631	5 482	5 961	7 617	7 996	6 537	6 833	8 246
General haulage vehicles: total	6 079	6 287	6 843	5 617	4 288	5 136	5 701	7 329	7 635	6 196	6 501	7 758
Unladen weight:												
Not over 1½ tons	3 529	3 839	4 324	3 590	2 561	3 225	3 466	4 782	4 898	3 698	3 829	3 847
Over 1½ and not over 3 tons [3]	837	853	755	815	722	638	1 061	1 227	1 394	1 245	1 264	
Over 3 tons	1 713	1 595	1 764	1 212	1 005	1 273	1 174	1 320	1 343	1 253	1 408	3 911
Agricultural vans and lorries[1]	439	407	370	282	339	343	249	271	336	340	322	476
Tractors for general haulage	4	11	13	18	4	3	11	17	25	1	10	12
Agricultural tractors and engines, etc.[2]	3 230	2 626	2 222	1 489	1 158	1 324	1 894	2 139	2 511	1 565	1 394	1 731
Vehicles exempt from duty: total	972	859	1 042	1 308	1 000	1 145	1 232	1 256	1 209	1 243	1 233	1 940
Ambulances	6	3	5	1	34	10	13	51	3	9	10	–
Fire engines	–	10	16	2	7	8	1	8	10	–	3	2
Road construction vehicles	32	14	25	10	24	38	24	27	5	6	23	4
Other	934	832	996	1 295	935	1 089	1 194	1 170	1 191	1 228	1 197	1 934
Total	66 033	71 191	70 165	59 656	54 899	65 996	76 667	82 762	80 947	72 115	73 701	80 537

1 Owned by a farmer and available for hauling produce and requisites for his farm.
2 Agricultural tractors are excluded unless driven on public roads.
3 Goods vehicles 1½–3 tons from 1988.

Source *Department of the Environment for Northern Ireland*

10.10 Buses and Coaches
Great Britain

	1977	1978	1979	1980	1981	1982	1983	1984	1985/6	1986/7	1987/88
Number of vehicles[1]	73.5	73.8	72.9	69.1	69.9	70.7	70.2	68.8	67.9	69.5	71.7
Single deck	46.5	47.1	47.1	43.6	44.7	44.8	44.9	43.2	42.9	45.1	47.7
Double deck	27.1	26.7	25.9	25.6	25.2	25.9	25.3	25.6	25.0	24.5	24.1
London Buses Ltd[2]	6.3	6.3	6.2	6.2	5.9	6.2	5.6	5.7	5.2	5.1	5.0
Passenger Transport Authority companies[3]	10.9	10.9	10.7	10.3	10.1	9.9	9.6	9.5	9.1	8.6	8.4
Municipal companies	6.0	5.9	5.9	5.7	5.5	5.3	5.3	5.3	5.2	5.1	5.4
National Bus Company & ex-NBC operators	18.8	18.2	17.8	16.0	15.3	15.0	14.6	14.5	14.7	16.4	16.4
Scottish Bus Group	4.1	3.9	3.8	3.6	3.4	3.3	3.1	3.1	3.4	3.4	3.1
Private operators	27.4	28.6	28.6	27.4	29.7	31.0	31.9	30.8	30.3	30.9	33.5
Vehicle kilometres (millions)	3 451	3 404	3 338	3 280	3 227	3 206	3 280	3 314	3 323	3 407	3 665
London Buses Ltd[2]	289	278	265	279	282	265	264	268	262	251	245
Passenger Transport Authority companies[3]	524	517	505	510	487	485	482	486	488	458	485
Municipal companies	250	246	242	241	233	232	231	235	233	237	257
National Bus Company & ex-NBC operators	1 110	1 075	1 045	1 026	973	972	969	981	979	1 042	1 045
Scottish Bus Group	216	212	208	203	206	200	202	201	210	210	204
Private operators	1 062	1 077	1 073	1 020	1 048	1 051	1 131	1 142	1 152	1 216	1 429
Passenger journeys (millions)	7 505	7 305	7 100	6 783	6 278	6 097	6 210	6 237	6 176	5 905	5 936
London Buses Ltd[2]	1 374	1 302	1 234	1 183	1 081	1 043	1 089	1 163	1 147	1 129	1 202
Passenger Transport Authority companies[3]	2 091	2 012	1 993	1 973	1 814	1 765	1 796	1 826	1 847	1 605	1 504
Municipal companies	1 077	1 052	1 019	952	886	854	854	837	799	761	714
National Bus Company & ex-NBC operators	1 858	1 825	1 795	1 669	1 529	1 479	1 460	1 440	1 453	1 415	1 396
Scottish Bus Group	358	351	350	339	322	314	319	311	320	307	287
Private operators	746	764	709	666	647	642	691	659	609	688	833
Passenger receipts (£ million)	1 144	1 265	1 404	1 637	1 745	1 908	2 024	2 085	2 219	2 269	2 388
London Buses Ltd[2]	147	157	163	207	209	254	266	264	292	288	288
Passenger Transport Authority companies[3]	234	255	282	328	334	364	379	389	406	417	431
Municipal companies	113	127	137	160	173	181	196	210	220	220	228
National Bus Company & ex-NBC operators	363	396	430	491	520	543	573	593	629	636	640
Scottish Bus Group	74	82	93	109	117	127	134	136	140	138	130
Private operators	213	248	300	342	393	437	476	494	532	571	670

1 1976–84 End of year; 1985/6 & 1986/7 Annual average. Includes trams.
2 1976–83 London Transport Executive; 1984 London Regional Transport.
3 1976–85/6 Passenger Transport Executives.

Source *Department of Transport*

10.11 Indices of local (stage) bus service fares
Index 1985=100
Great Britain

	1978	1979	1980	1981	1982	1983	1984	1985	1986/87	1987/88
London Regional Transport[1]	47.3	53.7	74.2	79.1	98.1	100.0	91.6	100.0	107.8	113.1
Passenger Transport Authority	56.6	63.6	81.3	88.4	97.4	99.4	98.5	100.0	124.6	135.7
Municipal companies[2]	45.7	50.3	62.5	74.8	83.2	89.1	95.4	100.0	105.2	111.1
Municipal and Passenger Transport Authority companies	52.3	58.4	73.9	83.1	91.8	95.4	97.5	100.0	117.5	126.7
Other operators[3]	47.4	53.1	66.5	76.4	84.9	90.9	95.9	100.0	106.9	110.1
All operators	47.5	53.2	68.1	96.7	96.7	93.8	95.8	100.0	110.8	116.4
Retail prices index[4]	52.8	59.9	70.7	79.0	85.9	89.8	94.3	100.0	104.4	108.6

1 Figures before 1984 refer to the London Transport Executive.
2 Formerly Passenger Transport Executives.
3 National Bus Company, Scottish Bus Group and private operators.
4 The published retail prices index has been rescaled to 1985=100 for comparability.

Source *Department of Transport*

10.12 Road accidents, vehicles involved and casualties

Great Britain

Number

	1978	1979	1980	1981	1982	1983	1984	1985	1986	1987	1988
Road accidents[1]	264 769	254 967	252 300	248 276	255 980	242 876	253 183	245 645	247 854	239 063	246 994
Vehicles involved:											
Pedal cycles	23 113	24 792	25 884	26 496	29 428	31 824	32 210	27 953	27 039	27 010	26 561
Motor vehicles	414 573	397 595	391 870	390 736	401 460	377 289	396 735	389 473	397 671	387 521	405 199
Two-wheeled motor vehicles	71 382	69 173	73 054	70 949	73 033	65 962	65 340	57 822	53 562	47 024	44 279
Cars and taxis	275 098	265 327	262 979	265 531	275 507	261 714	279 954	278 517	290 560	287 636	303 693
Light goods vehicles[2]	25 798	24 715	22 319	22 106	21 704	19 853	20 911	23 113	23 434	22 651	24 671
Heavy goods vehicles[3]	18 795	18 194	15 343	14 554	14 688	13 504	14 197	14 452	14 773	15 107	16 376
Buses and coaches	15 443	14 808	13 814	13 083	12 911	12 763	12 302	12 468	12 137	11 766	12 086
Other motor vehicles	8 057	5 378	4 361	4 513	3 617	3 493	3 531	3 101	3 205	3 337	4 094
Vehicles involved per hundred million kilometres travelled											
Pedal cycles	452	541	508	485	459	497	502	459	493	471	548
All two-wheeled motor vehicles	1 161	1 083	950	797	789	794	801	779	752	701	841
Cars and taxis	136	132	122	121	121	113	115	111	110	101	105
Light goods vehicles[2]	114	110	96	95	94	86	85	92	89	78	81
Heavy goods vehicles[3]	85	82	70	69	72	63	64	63	64	58	62
Total casualties	349 795	334 513	328 600	324 840	334 296	308 584	324 314	317 524	321 451	311 473	322 305
Killed[4]:											
Total	6 831	6 352	6 010	5 846	5 934	5 445	5 599	5 165	5 382	5 125	5 052
Pedestrians	2 427	2 118	1 941	1 874	1 869	1 914	1 868	1 789	1 841	1 703	1 753
Pedal cycles	316	320	302	310	294	323	345	286	271	280	227
All two-wheeled motor vehicles	1 163	1 160	1 163	1 131	1 090	963	967	796	762	723	670
Cars and taxis	2 569	2 429	2 278	2 287	2 443	2 019	2 179	2 061	2 231	2 206	2 142
Others	356	325	326	244	238	226	240	233	277	213	260
Killed and seriously injured[5]:											
By age group[6]											
0 – 4	1 552	1 464	1 351	1 286	1 345	1 403	1 435	1 429	1 289	1 277	1 339
5 – 9	4 906	4 576	4 203	3 909	3 717	3 586	3 740	3 579	3 254	3 219	3 122
10 – 14	5 366	5 151	5 255	5 162	5 474	5 450	5 541	4 903	4 426	3 988	3 871
15 – 19	21 609	20 859	21 501	21 848	21 413	18 456	18 484	16 582	15 591	13 752	12 866
20 – 24	13 433	13 555	13 243	13 682	14 522	12 575	13 214	13 282	13 058	12 041	11 629
25 – 29	7 206	7 270	6 741	6 466	6 964	6 072	6 549	6 647	6 916	6 854	7 026
30 – 39	9 518	9 437	9 045	8 973	9 366	8 102	8 391	8 276	8 455	8 029	7 999
40 – 49	6 752	6 608	6 236	6 161	6 250	5 441	5 765	5 911	5 698	5 915	5 892
50 – 59	6 738	6 569	6 027	5 771	5 784	4 980	5 027	5 038	4 827	4 566	4 620
60 and over	11 801	10 870	10 806	10 399	10 464	10 003	10 512	9 850	10 017	9 081	9 517
By type of road user:											
Child pedestrians[7]	7 925	7 359	6 893	6 547	6 695	6 640	6 823	6 663	5 992	5 472	5 471
Adult pedestrians	13 309	12 969	12 004	11 817	12 169	12 139	12 638	12 576	12 880	11 978	12 207
Child pedal cyclists[7]	1 875	2 085	2 135	2 096	2 058	2 287	2 269	1 704	1 396	1 458	1 322
Adult pedal cyclists	2 854	3 135	3 386	3 393	3 893	4 109	4 326	3 910	3 814	3 638	3 526
Moped riders	3 347	2 908	2 933	2 903	3 109	3 241	3 188	2 919	2 571	2 221	1 940
Motor scooter riders	402	356	500	515	608	647	748	715	606	499	380
Motor scooter passengers	43	36	51	62	106	95	100	93	66	71	46
Motor cycle riders	15 510	15 797	16 926	16 398	16 296	14 260	14 109	12 838	11 819	9 989	9 364
Motor cycle passengers	2 142	2 133	2 246	2 400	2 514	2 021	1 805	1 547	1 370	1 086	924
Car and taxi drivers	20 441	19 970	18 932	19 149	19 460	15 472	16 530	16 722	17 132	17 167	17 576
Car and taxi passengers	15 950	14 993	14 309	14 476	14 525	11 574	12 467	12 385	12 554	11 919	11 770
Users of buses and coaches	1 200	1 071	952	961	962	969	929	1 036	859	826	912
Users of goods vehicles	3 744	3 530	3 093	2 891	2 797	2 283	2 354	2 454	2 552	2 590	2 485
Users of other vehicles	405	367	305	308	312	278	313	254	263	229	255
All severities											
Total	349 795	334 513	328 600	324 840	334 296	308 584	324 314	317 524	321 451	311 473	322 305
Pedestrians	70 295	66 714	63 299	60 750	61 419	61 674	63 474	61 390	60 875	57 453	58 843
Vehicle users	279 500	267 799	265 301	264 090	272 877	246 910	260 840	256 134	260 576	254 020	263 462
Breath tests on car drivers involved in accidents											
all drivers	275 098	265 327	262 979	265 531	275 507	261 714	279 959	278 517	290 560	287 633	303 693
tested	31 531	32 447	32 735	32 640	34 472	33 769	35 192	36 655	49 559	52 760	60 798
failed test[8]	10 543	11 329	10 777	10 121	11 145	10 200	10 422	10 432	10 014	9 222	8 549

1 Accidents on public roads, involving injury, which are reported to the police.
2 $1\frac{1}{2}$ tons unladen weight and under.
3 Over $1\frac{1}{2}$ tons unladen weight.
4 Died within 30 days of accident.
5 Hospital in-patients plus casualties with any fracture, internal injury, concussion, crushing, severe general shock, etc. *plus* deaths after 30 days.
6 These figures may not add up to total fatal and serious figures, due to the exclusion of road users whose age was not reported.
7 Age 0 – 14.
8 Positive result, or refused to provide a specimen.

Sources *Department of Transport; Scottish Development Department; Welsh Office*

10.13 Road accident casualty rates: by type of road user and severity
Great Britain

Rate per 100 million vehicle kilometres

	1978	1979	1980	1981	1982	1983	1984	1985	1986	1987	1988
Pedal cyclists:											
Killed	6.2	7.0	5.9	5.7	4.6	5.0	5.4	4.7	4.9	4.9	4.7
Killed or seriously injured	93	114	109	101	93	100	103	93	96	89	101
All severities	434	516	486	463	439	478	483	444	477	457	534
Two-wheel motor vehicle riders											
Killed	16	16	13	11	10	10	10	9	9	10	12
Killed or seriously injured	313	298	265	223	216	218	221	223	211	189	221
All severities	1 014	943	826	692	687	695	707	696	675	628	753
Car drivers:											
Killed	0.8	0.7	0.6	0.6	0.6	0.5	0.5	0.5	0.5	0.5	0.4
Killed or seriously injured	10	10	9	9	9	7	7	7	6	6	6
All severities	43	41	37	37	37	32	33	34	34	32	34
Bus and coach drivers:											
Killed	0.2	0.1	0.1	0.1	0.1	0.1	0.1	0.0	0.0	0.0	0.1
Killed or seriously injured	3	3	2	2	2	2	2	1	2	1	1
All severities	21	20	15	15	14	13	12	15	14	13	14
Light Goods Vehicle drivers:											
Killed	0.4	0.5	0.5	0.4	0.3	0.3	0.3	0.3	0.3	0.3	0.3
Killed or seriously injured	7	7	6	6	5	4	4	4	4	4	4
All severities	30	30	25	24	23	19	19	21	22	20	21
Heavy Goods Vehicle drivers:											
Killed	0.4	0.4	0.3	0.2	0.3	0.2	0.3	0.2	0.3	0.2	0.2
Killed or seriously injured	4	4	3	3	3	3	3	3	3	3	2
All severities	16	15	12	11	12	11	12	12	12	11	12
All road users:[1]											
Killed	2.6	2.4	2.2	2.1	2.0	1.8	1.8	1.6	1.6	1.4	1.4
Killed or seriously injured	34	33	31	30	30	26	25	24	22	19	19
All severities	134	128	119	115	115	105	105	101	97	87	89

1 Includes other road users and road user not reported.

Source *Department of Transport*

10.14 Road goods transport: analysis by mode of working and by gross weight of vehicle[1,2]
Great Britain

	1978	1979	1980	1981	1982	1983	1984	1985	1986	1987	1988
Estimated tonne kilometres (Thousand million)											
Total	96.4	99.3	89.7	90.2	91.1	92.3	96.6	99.1	101.1	108.6	124.8
Own account	35.9	37.9	35.0	34.4	34.3	33.5	34.2	32.5	32.4	31.5	37.2
Public haulage	60.5	61.4	54.7	55.8	56.8	58.8	62.3	66.6	68.7	77.1	87.6
By gross weight of vehicle— (Billion tonne kilometres)											
Not over 25 tonnes	33.7	32.2	29.0	27.1	29.0	27.9	28.0	26.4	25.6	25.8	30.1
Over 25 tonnes	62.6	67.0	60.7	63.1	62.1	64.3	68.6	72.7	75.5	82.8	94.7
Estimated tonnes carried (Millions)											
Total	1 420	1 416	1 317	1 225	1 310	1 280	1 319	1 367	1 386	1 450	1 653
Own account	686	686	659	591	651	616	642	619	618	600	696
Public haulage	734	730	658	635	659	664	678	748	769	850	957
By gross weight of vehicle— (Million tonnes)											
Not over 25 tonnes	793	742	677	594	655	622	637	625	604	613	682
Over 25 tonnes	627	674	640	632	655	658	682	743	783	838	971

1 From 1978 onwards includes the small amount of work performed in Northern Ireland by British registered goods vehicles.

2 Excludes work done by small goods vehicles under 3.5 tonnes gross vehicle weight.

Source *Department of Transport*

10.15 British Rail: assets and privately-owned freight vehicles operated
Great Britain

	Unit	1978	1979	1980	1981	1982	1983	1984	1985[1]	1986[1]	1987[1]	1988[1]
Rolling stock												
Tractive units: total	Number	8 413	8 506	8 358	7 947	7 690	7 374	7 153	7 101	7 032	6 768	6 636
Locomotives: total	,,	3 580	3 571	3 379	3 131	3 016	2 850	2 756	2 581	2 441	2 270	2 180
Diesel[2]	,,	3 268	3 261	3 078	2 864	2 750	2 603	2 512	2 338	2 201	2 040	1 920
Electric	,,	312	310	301	267	266	247	244	243	240	230	260
Power cars: total	,,	4 833	4 935	4 979	4 816	4 674	4 524	4 397	4 520	4 591	4 498	4 456
Advanced passenger train	,,	2	5	6	6	6	6	6	6	4	2	–
High speed train	,,	109	136	142	181	197	197	197	197	197	197	197
Diesel[3]	,,	1 981	1 962	1 955	1 836	1 734	1 641	1 616	1 787	1 851	1 790	1 836
Electric[4]	,,	2 741	2 832	2 876	2 793	2 737	2 680	2 578	2 530	2 539	2 509	2 423
Coaching vehicles: total	,,	21 458	21 511	21 068	18 962	17 628	16 963	16 489	16 164	15 336	14 648	14 258
Passenger carriages: total	,,	17 028	17 175	17 042	16 166	15 400	14 807	14 362	14 062	13 677	13 013	12 924
Locomotive-hauled	,,	5 967	5 885	5 567	5 070	4 468	4 059	3 865	3 582	3 276	2 891	2 595
Advanced passenger train	,,	6	15	30	30	30	30	30	30	30	6	–
High speed train	,,	421	533	630	664	709	709	713	722	712	712	712
Diesel multiple unit[5]	,,	3 293	3 284	3 257	3 096	2 917	2 703	2 627	2 744	2 625	2 382	2 361
Electric multiple unit[6]	,,	7 341	7 458	7 558	7 306	7 276	7 306	7 127	6 984	7 034	7 022	7 256
Non-passenger-carrying vehicles[7]	,,	4 430	4 336	4 026	2 796	2 228	2 156	2 127	2 102	1 659	1 635	1 334
Seats or berths in passenger carriages	Thousands	1 080	1 090	1 090	1 040	1 000	970	940	930	900	870	880
Freight wagons operated: total	Thousands	168.8	157.0	138.6	105.6	87.9	70.4	61.7	54.4	48.4	44.2	40.2
Wagons owned by British Rail: total	,,	148.2	136.3	117.8	86.2	69.4	52.4	44.7	37.9	32.4	28.4	25.3
Air-braked wagons	,,	15.9	17.5	18.8	20.0	20.1	19.8	19.5	19.4	19.4	20.0	20.7
Vacuum-braked wagons	,,	70.7	66.3	59.8	50.1	40.2	28.3	21.9	15.6	10.8	7.6	4.2
Unbraked wagons	,,	61.6	52.5	39.2	16.1	9.1	4.3	3.3	2.9	2.2	0.8	0.4
Wagons owned by Freightliners Ltd	,,	2.1	2.1	2.1	2.1	2.1	2.1	2.0	2.0	1.9	1.7	1.6
Wagons owned by customers of British Rail	,,	18.4	18.7	18.8	17.2	16.4	15.9	15.0	14.5	14.1	14.1	13.3
Permanent way and stations												
Route open for traffic: total	Kilometres	17 901	17 735	17 645	17 431	17 229	16 964	16 879	16 752	16 670	16 633	16 599
Electrified	,,	3 716	3 718	3 718	3 729	3 753	3 750	3 798	3 809	4 154	4 207	4 376
Non-electrified	,,	14 185	14 017	13 927	13 702	13 476	13 214	13 081	12 943	12 516	12 426	12 223
Route open for passenger traffic	,,	14 396	14 412	14 394	14 394	14 371	14 375	14 304	14 310	14 304	14 302	14 309
Track open for traffic: total	,,	45 579	44 405	43 883	42 760	42 012	41 302	40 000	39 448	38 053	37 911	37 868
Running lines	,,	35 628	35 307	35 101	34 705	34 289	33 778	33 312	33 027	32 728	32 665	32 628
Sidings	,,	9 951	9 098	8 782	8 055	7 723	7 524	6 688	6 421	5 325	5 246	5 240
Stations: total[8]	Number	2 837	2 821	2 787	2 742	2 711	2 619	2 523	2 526	2 530	2 541	2 561
Passenger	,,	2 364	2 365	2 366	2 361	2 369	2 363	2 375	2 385	2 405	2 426	2 435
Parcel	,,	15	14	12	3	3	3	3	4	2	1	1
Freight	,,	458	442	409	378	339	253	145	137	123	114	125

1 Figures at 31 March of the following year.
2 Includes shunting locomotives (477 in 1988/89).
3 Diesel multiple unit power cars including a small number of non-passenger-carrying power cars (32 in 1988/89).
4 Electric multiple unit power cars including a small number of non-passenger-carrying power cars (23 in 1988/89).
5 Includes Diesel multiple unit power cars (1 804 in 1988/89, also included under Tractive units—Power cars—Diesel).
6 Includes Electric multiple unit power cars (2 400 in 1988/89, also included under Tractive units—Power cars—Electric).
7 Includes Advanced Passenger Train and High Speed Train power cars; also includes non-passenger-carrying power cars (32 diesel, 23 electric in 1988/89 which are also shown under Tractive units, Power cars); also includes brake vans (636 in 1988/89).
8 Combined passenger and freight stations have been reclassified as single purpose stations over the period.

Source Department of Transport

10.16 British Rail: passenger and freight receipts and traffic
Great Britain

	Unit	1978	1979	1980	1981	1982[1]	1983	1984[1]	1985[1]	1986	1987	1988
Traffic receipts: total[2]	£ million	1 224.3	1 383.1	1 555.0	1 646.3	1 494.9	1 763.0	1 633.8	1 882.4	2 065.5	2 209.1	2 524.6
Passenger: total[2, 3]	£ million	701.8	799.7	954.0	1 022.7	924.1	1 129.6	1 195.6	1 286.2	1 410.1	1 539.0	1 750.6
Full fares	,,	292.0	336.4	394.5	419.1	358.0	842.1	889.2	943.2	1 026.8	1 106.8	1 248.8
Reduced fares	,,	250.4	284.9	339.6	347.7	335.4						
Season tickets	,,	159.4	178.4	219.9	255.9	230.7	287.6	305.9	339.5	383.3	432.2	501.8
Freight: total	,,	503.9	562.9	601.0	623.6	570.8	633.4	438.2	596.2	655.4	670.1	774.0
Coal and coke	,,	192.0	218.0	248.0	274.1	270.5	280.4	84.9	226.5	283.2	282.5	287.7
Iron and steel	,,	59.4	67.5	46.8	65.0	51.9	57.5	50.8	52.8	59.0	68.5	78.2
Other	,,	133.0	146.6	165.0	164.6	155.8	180.4	184.9	191.1	195.5	198.0	281.5
Merchandise by coaching train	,,	82.6	89.9	91.4	119.9	92.6	115.1	117.6	125.8	117.7	121.1	126.6
Postal parcels and letter mails by coaching train	,,	36.8	40.9	49.8								
Miscellaneous receipts[4]	,,	18.6	20.5	..	..	..	..	..	..	..	..	..
Traffic												
Passenger journeys: total[3]	Million	723.8	748.2	760.2	718.5	630.1	693.7	702.4	697.4	699.1	710.5	824.5
Full fares	,,	203.2	211.1	201.5	184.4	159.0	386.4	394.7	374.3	381.9	398.8	422.7
Reduced fares	,,	227.0	227.8	227.5	211.6	202.9						
Season tickets[5]	,,	293.6	309.3	331.2	322.5	268.2	307.3	307.7	323.1	317.2	311.7	401.7
Passenger kilometres: (estimated) total[3]	,,	30 000	30 700	30 300	29 700	27 200	29 500	29 800	29 700	30 800	32 200	34 400
Full fares	,,	10 100	10 500	10 200	10 100	8 300	21 800	21 800	21 900	21 900	22 600	23 300
Reduced fares	,,	11 800	11 900	11 700	11 400	11 600						
Season tickets[5]	,,	8 100	8 200	8 300	8 200	7 300	7 800	7 900	8 100	8 800	9 600	11 100
Freight traffic originating: total[6]	Million tonnes	171.8	170.5	154.7	155.1	142.6	146.0	79.3	122.9	140.3	141.7	150.2
Coal and coke	,,	94.0	93.5	94.1	95.2	88.4	87.9	25.5	65.9	79.7	77.7	78.8
Iron and steel	,,	24.7	25.1	12.9	18.2	14.2	15.9	12.4	14.1	16.8	19.1	20.5
Other	,,	51.8	50.7	46.5	40.8	39.3	41.3	40.5	42.0	43.1	43.5	50.2
Merchandise by coaching train	,,	0.9	0.8	0.8	0.9	0.7	0.9	0.9	0.9	0.7	0.7	0.7
Postal parcels and letter mails by coaching train	,,	0.4	0.4	0.4								
Tonne kilometres: (estimated) total[6, 7]	Millions	19 982	19 893	17 640	17 505	15 880	17 144	12 700	15 400	16 600	17 300	18 000
Coal and coke	,,	6 832	6 788	6 455	6 544	5 741	5 875	1 600	4 100	5 100	4 700	4 600
All other freight train traffic	,,	13 150	13 105	11 185	10 961	10 139	11 269	11 100	11 300	11 500	12 600	13 400

1 British Rail traffic was affected by industrial action by ASLEF in 1982 and by the miners' strike and associated action by British Rail staff in 1984 and 1985.
2 Grants received by British Rail in respect of certain subsidised passenger services are not included in passenger receipts.
3 The receipts and passenger kilometres include an appropriate proportion in respect of through bookings with the railways of London Regional Transport and other administrations. Passenger journeys in respect of such through bookings are included. In 1985, 697 million journeys originated on British Rail only. From 1979 season ticket journeys include those in respect of West Midlands travel cards.
4 Miscellaneous receipts include charges for platform tickets, seat reservations, demurrage, provision of shunting services, etc. From 1980 Miscellaneous receipts are apportioned between the sectors.
5 All season ticket journeys and passenger kilometres were calculated on a rate of 480 journeys per year per annual season ticket and 540 journeys for shorter period tickets. Return tickets have been counted as two journeys.
6 Excluding free-hauled traffic on freight trains.
7 Excluding freight carried by coaching trains. In 1978 the method of estimating tonne-kilometres was changed to reflect the changing pattern in the operational working of freight trains. Pre-1978 figures have been re-estimated to bring them approximately onto the same basis as 1978 and subsequent years and rounded to the nearest 100 million.

Source Department of Transport

10.17 British Rail: operations
Great Britain

	Unit	1978	1979	1980	1981	1982[1]	1983	1984[1]	1985	1986/87	1987/88	1988/89
Loaded train kilometres												
Coaching: total[2]	Millions	335.3	333.4	344.3	336.2	298.1	325.4	324.0	327.7	327.7	340.6	351.7
High speed trains	,,	9.7	16.4	21.0	23.3	26.2	32.3	33.5	34.7	34.3	35.9	36.1
Diesel: locomotives	,,	80.9	74.9	73.0	69.0	57.9	62.0	61.2	59.1	54.1	47.1	37.2
multiple units	,,	88.4	87.2	88.5	86.7	74.5	78.4	76.5	79.3	82.5	91.1	107.6
Electric: locomotives	,,	31.2	32.1	32.5	30.9	26.4	27.2	28.2	30.0	30.1	32.9	32.7
multiple units	,,	125.2	122.8	129.3	126.3	113.0	125.5	124.5	124.6	126.7	133.6	138.2
of which, Non-passenger[3]	,,	*19.7*	*18.1*	*17.5*	*13.7*	*11.6*	*14.5*	*14.9*	*16.2*	*16.0*	*15.4*	*12.3*
Freight: total[4]	,,	60.4	58.0	52.3	49.0	43.4	45.4	38.7	36.8	50.0	50.4	51.8
Diesel locomotives	,,	51.9	49.6	44.2	41.6	37.0	38.5	31.7	30.2	43.9	44.5	45.6
Electric locomotives	,,	8.5	8.4	8.1	7.3	6.4	6.9	7.0	6.6	6.1	5.9	6.2

1 British Rail traffic was affected by industrial action by ASLEF in 1982 and by the miners strike in 1984.
2 Train kilometres worked by British Rail trains over all lines including certain London Regional Transport lines.
3 Non-passenger trains consist of vehicles for the conveyance of freight at coaching train rates.
4 Excludes free-hauled traffic on freight trains. From 1978, figures have been revised to reflect a change in the calculation of loaded train kilometres for 'Merry-Go-Round' coal traffic to power stations. From 1986/87 figures include unladen freight trains.

Source Department of Transport

10.18 London Regional Transport railways: receipts, operations and assets

	Unit	1978	1979	1980	1981	1982	1983	1984	1985	1986	1987	1988[1]
Receipts[2]												
Passenger: total	£ million	177.2	204.4	253.0	251.1	276.5	285.4	287.8	330.7	360.8	391.9	417.2
Ordinary	,,	104.5	123.1	145.4	137.4	161.5	158.0	171.8	185.1	198.1	206.3	220.1
Reduced rate	,,	16.4	19.6	25.4	28.8	31.2	27.4					
Season tickets	,,	56.4	61.6	82.2	85.0	83.8	100.0	116.0	145.6	162.7	185.6	197.1
Traffic[2]												
Passenger journeys: total	Million	568	594	559	541	498	563	650	724	761	804	799
Ordinary	,,	340	353	318	296	289	273	354	351	353	373	371
Reduced rate	,,	45	51	52	63	49	77					
Season tickets	,,	184	190	189	182	159	212	296	373	408	431	428
Passenger kilometres (estimated)	,,	4 510	4 460	4 250	4 090	3 660	4 350	5 210	5 860	6 170	6 330	6 300
Operations[3]												
Loaded train kilometres	Million	47	46	47	49	46	46	46	48	48	49	50
Place kilometres	,,	41 042	39 578	40 928	41 638	39 479	39 685	41 200	40 500	41 200	43 600	43 600
Rolling stock												
Railway cars	Number	4 223	4 228	4 353	4 267	4 069	3 885	3 918	3 875	3 877	3 905	3 950
Seating capacity	Thousand	172.0	170.0	174.0	165.7	169.0	165.0	167.7	166.2	166.2	167.2	169.8
Permanent way and stations												
Route kilometres open for traffic	Kilometres	383	388	388	388	388	388	388	388	394	394	394
Stations	Number	249	248	248	247	247	247	247	247	248	248	248

1 1988 figures are provisional.
2 The receipts and passenger kilometres include an appropriate proportion in respect of through bookings from British Rail. Passenger journeys in respect of such through bookings are included.
3 Train and place kilometres include kilometres run by London Regional Transport trains over British Rail lines.

Source Department of Transport

10.19 Accidents on railways
Great Britain

Number

	1978	1979	1980	1981	1982	1983	1984	1985	1986	1987	1988
Train accidents											
Number of accidents: total[1]	1 044	1 035	930	1 014	998	1 255	1 359	1 240	1 172	1 166	1 359
Collisions	283	256	290	280	250	315	300	282	266	290	293
Derailments	176	183	138	148	173	220	230	229	192	192	231
Running into level-crossing gates and other obstructions	336	323	286	353	284	363	471	440	452	392	515
Fires	166	186	151	165	163	165	168	191	174	191	229
Miscellaneous	83	87	65	68	128	192	190	98	88	101	91
Persons killed	22	20	7	7	11	10	30	6	27	11	40
Passengers	13	8	–	4	–	2	18	–	8	3	34
Railway staff	3	8	4	1	8	1	6	–	5	1	2
Others	6	4	3	2	3	7	6	6	14	7	4
Persons injured	233	422	447	195	264	218	475	380	511	396	693
Passengers	176	354	387	127	150	88	386	261	342	310	603
Railway staff	48	60	45	34	92	93	68	88	137	65	68
Others	9	8	15	34	22	37	21	31	32	21	22
Other accidents through movement of railway vehicles											
Persons killed	76	74	52	58	40	53	41	55	41	57	53
Passengers	32	42	25	31	18	25	21	31	24	36	34
Railway staff	33	24	20	21	17	24	14	16	8	11	11
Others	11	8	7	6	5	4	6	8	9	10	8
Persons injured	2 352	2 221	2 265	2 450	1 946	2 459	2 486	2 489	2 443	2 777	2 809
Passengers	1 959	1 887	1 945	2 218	1 822	2 341	2 400	2 383	2 346	2 689	2 721
Railway staff	383	325	309	219	121	97	73	96	80	85	85
Others	10	9	11	13	3	21	13	10	17	3	3
Other accidents on railway premises											
Persons killed	16	13	10	11	6	6	5	13	4	35	5
Passengers	2	2	1	4	2	2	–	2	1	30	2
Railway staff	9	11	8	5	2	3	5	9	3	4	3
Others	5	–	1	2	2	1	–	2	–	1	–
Persons injured	8 942	8 878	8 138	7 379	6 490	6 590	6 267	6 295	6 528	6 627	7 351
Passengers	2 842	2 805	2 977	2 657	2 571	3 381	3 473	3 518	3 577	3 650	4 035
Railway staff	5 726	5 737	4 848	4 530	3 740	2 981	2 530	2 533	2 691	2 781	3 142
Others	374	336	313	192	179	228	264	244	260	196	174
Trespassers and suicides											
Persons killed	345	314	360	369	296	358	339	318	325	316	318
Persons injured	121	136	141	127	141	153	128	128	120	101	70

1 The figures from 1982 onwards include accidents to non-passenger trains on non-passenger lines not previously reported.

Source Department of Transport

10.20 Railways: permanent way and rolling stock
Northern Ireland
At end of year

Number

	1978	1979	1980	1981	1982	1983	1984	1985	1986	1987	1988
Length of road open for traffic[1]											
(Km)	332	332	332	332	332	332	332	332	332	332	332
Length of track open for traffic											
(Km)											
Total	575	575	575	575	575	575	575	575	575	553	553
Running lines	521	521	521	521	521	521	521	521	521	500	500
Sidings (as single track)	53	53	53	53	53	53	53	53	53	53	53
Locomotives											
Diesel-electrics	6	6	8	8	8	8	9	9	13	12	12
Passenger carrying vehicles											
Total	116	107	113	114	115	105	106	108	112	112	115
Rail motor vehicles:											
Diesel-electric, etc.	39	36	35	35	35	30	30	28	31	31	31
Trailer carriages:											
Total locomotive hauled	23	21	33	33	33	32	28	28	25	27	28
Ordinary coaches	22	20	32	32	32	30	26	26	23	25	26
Restaurant cars	1	1	1	1	1	2	2	2	2	2	2
Rail car trailers	54	50	45	46	47	43	48	52	56	56	56
Non-passenger carrying vehicles											
Post Office and luggage vans, etc.	27	27	27	27	27	20	9	6	–	–	–
Trucks and wagons owned											
Total	144	144	139	123	119	111	21	20	17	17	17
Merchandise wagons:											
Open	82	82	82	82	78	74	3	3	–	–	–
Covered	6	6	6	6	6	6	–	–	–	–	–
Rail and timber trucks	2	2	2	2	2	2	–	–	–	–	–
Brake vans	1	1	1	1	1	–	–	–	–	–	–
Special wagons	53	53	48	32	32	29	18	17	17	17	17
Containers	10	10	10	10	10	10	10	10	–	–	–
Rolling stock for maintenance and repair	151	151	162	170	158	115	60	64	54	44	46

1 The total length of railroad open for traffic irrespective of the number of tracks comprising the road.

Source *Department of the Environment for Northern Ireland*

10.21 Operating statistics of railways
Northern Ireland

	Unit	1978	1979	1980	1981	1982	1983	1984	1985	1986	1987	1988
Maintenance of way and works												
Material used:												
Ballast	Thousand m^3	29.0	24.4	28.4	25.7	19.8	15.0	17.0	19.8	17.7	25.5	28.3
Rails	Thousand tonnes	2.33	3.65	1.02	1.38	1.70	1.06	1.86	1.95	2.20	0.73	1.72
Sleepers	Thousands	28.5	69.0	13.3	16.5	21.1	13.7	21.1	24.0	17.0	17.0	23.2
Track renewed	Km	21.7	48.2	9.0	12.5	16.09	9.6	16.09	16.9	5.0	15.3	17.2
Engine kilometres												
Total[1]	Thousand Km	3 532	3 632	3 730	3 712	3 683	3 579	3 410	3 558	3 579	3 576	3 572
Train kilometres:												
Total	,,	3 035	3 130	3 200	3 105	3 102	3 392	3 405	3 411	3 401	3 398	3 394
Coaching	,,	2 893	3 001	3 065	3 001	3 086	3 373	3 402	3 407	3 396	3 394	3 391
Freight	,,	142	129	135	105	16[2]	19	3	4	4	4	4

1 Including shunting, assisting, light, departmental, maintenance and repair.

2 The reduction in mileage from 1982 is a result of changes in C.I.E./N.I.R. freight contract.

Source *Department of the Environment for Northern Ireland*

10.22 Main output[1] of UK airlines

	1978	1979	1980	1981	1982	1983	1984	1985	1986	1987	1988
All services: total	11 970	12 751	13 212	13 087	11 848	12 011	13 155	13 408	14 306	15 853	17 225
Percentage growth on previous year	*13.9*	*6.5*	*3.6*	*−0.9*	*−9.5*	*1.4*	*9.5*	*1.9*	*6.7*	*10.8*	*8.7*
Scheduled services: total	8 095	8 841	9 829	9 936	9 068	8 989	9 854	10 166	10 655	11 430	12 405
Percentage growth on previous year	*18.5*	*9.2*	*11.2*	*1.1*	*−8.7*	*−0.9*	*9.6*	*3.2*	*4.8*	*7.3*	*8.5*
Non-scheduled services: total	3 875	3 910	3 383	3 151	2 780	3 022	3 301	3 242	3 651	4 423	4 820
Percentage growth on previous year	*5.6*	*0.9*	*−13.5*	*−6.9*	*−11.8*	*8.7*	*9.2*	*−1.8*	*12.6*	*21.1*	*9.0*

Mean rates of growth

Percentage

	1946 to 50	1951 to 55	1956 to 60	1961 to 65	1966 to 70	1971 to 75	1976 to 80	1981 to 85	Last 20 years	Last 10 years	Last 5 years
All services	..	..	..	*13.8*	*10.8*	*5.1*	*8.4*	*1.5*	*5.4*	*3.0*	*7.3*
Scheduled services	*27.1*	*11.9*	*16.2*	*13.9*	*8.5*	*6.1*	*11.1*	*1.3*	*5.9*	*3.0*	*5.9*
Non-scheduled services	..	..	..	*13.5*	*17.5*	*3.1*	*2.3*	*2.3*	*4.1*	*3.1*	*11.2*

1 Available million tonne-kilometres.

Source *Civil Aviation Authority*

10.23 Air traffic between the United Kingdom and abroad[1]

Aircraft flights and passengers carried

Thousands

	1978	1979[2]	1980	1981	1982	1983	1984	1985	1986	1987	1988
Flights											
United Kingdom airlines											
Scheduled services	165.9	172.9	166.1	149.7	143.5	141.9	151.3	170.8	177.5	188.5	216.9
Non-scheduled services	115.1	121.8	153.9	162.2	176.3	184.9	214.0	196.2	198.8	219.2	225.5
Overseas airlines[3]											
Scheduled services	150.7	155.8	157.8	152.0	154.3	155.2	160.9	172.8	195.8	222.8	249.8
Non-scheduled services	27.7	29.2	29.1	31.9	37.3	36.5	40.2	39.5	43.6	45.2	43.0
Total	459.3	479.6	506.9	495.8	511.4	518.5	566.3	579.3	615.8	675.7	735.2
Passengers carried											
United Kingdom airlines:											
Scheduled services	12 620.6	13 634.6	13 901.0	13 559.0	12 214.7	12 140.0	13 174.2	14 854.3	15 082.9	17 473.8	19 237.6
Non-scheduled services	9 340.1	9 997.9	11 195.3	12 128.9	13 216.6	14 661.9	16 643.7	15 529.0	12 929.7	22 250.5	23 062.1
Overseas airlines[3]											
Scheduled services	14 284.3	15 113.0	14 900.9	15 398.8	15 520.5	16 065.6	17 623.0	18 815.6	19 409.5	22 441.5	25 029.3
Non-scheduled services	2 667.1	2 858.3	2 647.4	2 645.4	3 180.1	3 417.4	3 713.9	3 663.8	4 186.0	4 412.8	4 086.5
Total	38 912.1	41 603.8	42 644.6	43 732.0	44 131.9	46 284.9	51 154.8	52 862.7	51 608.1	66 578.6	71 415.5

1 Excludes travel to and from the Channel Islands.
2 1979 figures do not include Sumburgh.
3 Includes airlines of overseas UK Territories.

Source *Civil Aviation Authority*

10.24 UK airlines[1]

Operations and traffic on scheduled services: revenue traffic

	Unit	1978	1979	1980	1981	1982	1983	1984	1985	1986	1987	1988
All services												
Aircraft stage flights:												
Number	Number	411 314	441 653	440 651	410 115	414 167	431 615	447 336	470 989	475 263	499 764	546 386
Average length	Kilometres	843	845	872	878	801	752	784	787	809	813	811
Aircraft-kilometres flown	Millions	346.7	373.4	384.4	359.9	331.7	324.6	350.9	370.6	384.7	406.3	443.2
Passengers uplifted	,,	20.3	22.3	22.2	21.4	20.6	20.4	22.6	24.8	25.0	28.5	31.4
Seat-kilometres used	,,	40 441.6	47 084.8	50 163.8	52 209.6	46 404.3	43 887.4	48 235.3	51 436.9	51 400.9	59 887.2	63 868.1
Cargo and Mail uplifted: total	Tonnes	278 016	294 380	294 692	294 866	263 798	294 247	363 461	358 927	376 023	405 419	435 071
Tonne-kilometres used: total	Millions	4 872.0	5 550.0	5 894.8	6 188.4	5 593.2	5 521.8	6 337.3	6 466.5	6 606.4	7 586.0	8 106.3
Passenger	,,	3 710.3	4 300.9	4 503.2	4 674.5	4 223.7	4 004.0	4 405.1	4 700.6	4 708.9	5 497.6	5 869.8
Cargo	,,	988.5	1 070.3	1 214.8	1 343.5	1 200.4	1 338.1	1 736.2	1 563.1	1 698.1	1 885.6	2 057.3
Mail	,,	173.2	178.7	176.8	170.5	169.1	179.7	196.0	202.8	199.3	202.8	179.2
Domestic services												
Aircraft stage flights:												
Number	Number	176 628	199 101	201 227	188 534	201 887	221 560	254 064	258 502	255 764	266 226	277 682
Average length	Kilometres	283	279	287	282	279	274	265	268	278	276	279
Aircraft-kilometres flown	Millions	50.0	55.5	57.7	53.1	56.2	60.7	67.3	69.3	71.1	73.6	77.4
Passengers uplifted	,,	6.4	7.2	7.2	6.6	7.1	7.2	8.3	9.0	9.1	10.1	11.2
Seat-kilometres used	,,	2 444.6	2 763.9	2 770.3	2 600.7	2 752.7	2 791.4	3 237.8	3 494.3	3 566.9	3 926.5	4 381.1
Cargo and Mail uplifted: total	Tonnes	44 608	39 339	31 005	35 212	37 993	39 739	45 529	46 337	47 550	50 783	48 794
Tonne-kilometres used: total	Millions	220.8	248.7	242.6	229.7	237.3	240.7	278.4	299.9	305.9	335.6	371.5
Passenger	,,	206.5	235.2	231.8	218.1	224.7	227.1	262.8	283.8	289.5	318.5	355.2
Cargo	,,	11.4	10.2	7.1	7.3	7.5	7.7	10.2	10.2	10.5	10.7	10.1
Mail	,,	2.9	3.2	3.8	4.3	5.2	5.9	5.4	6.0	5.9	6.4	6.3
International services												
Aircraft stage flights:												
Number	Number	234 686	242 552	239 424	221 581	212 280	210 055	193 272	212 487	219 499	233 537	268 704
Average length	Kilometres	1 264	1 310	1 365	1 385	1 298	1 256	1 467	1 418	1 428	1 425	1 361
Aircraft-kilometres flown	Millions	296.7	317.9	326.7	306.8	275.5	263.9	283.6	301.3	313.5	332.8	365.8
Passengers uplifted	,,	13.9	15.0	15.0	14.8	13.5	13.2	14.3	15.8	15.9	18.5	20.2
Seat-kilometres used	,,	37 997.0	44 320.9	47 393.5	49 608.9	43 651.6	41 096.1	44 997.5	47 942.7	47 834.0	55 960.7	59 487.1
Cargo and Mail uplifted: total	Tonnes	233 407	255 039	263 687	259 654	225 806	254 507	317 932	312 589	328 473	354 636	386 277
Tonne-kilometres used: total	Millions	4 651.2	5 301.2	5 652.2	5 958.7	5 355.9	5 281.1	6 058.9	6 166.6	6 300.4	7 250.4	7 734.8
Passenger	,,	3 503.8	4 065.7	4 271.5	4 456.3	3 998.9	3 776.9	4 142.3	4 416.8	4 419.4	5 179.1	5 514.6
Cargo	,,	977.1	1 060.1	1 207.7	1 336.2	1 193.0	1 330.4	1 726.0	1 552.9	1 687.6	1 875.0	2 047.2
Mail	,,	170.2	175.4	173.1	166.2	164.0	173.8	190.7	196.9	193.4	196.3	172.9

1 Includes services of British Airways and other UK private companies (including operations performed by Cathay Pacific Airways on their Scheduled Service London—Hong Kong from May, 1981 until December 1984).

Source *Civil Aviation Authority*

10.25 Non-scheduled services by UK airlines[1]

	Unit	1978	1979	1980	1981	1982	1983	1984	1985	1986	1987	1988
All non-scheduled services[2] Total	Tonne km available (millions)	3 875.2	3 909.8	3 383.4	3 151.3	2 780.0	3 022.2	3 301.1	3 242.1	3 650.8	4 423.3	4,820.2
Percentage of all UK services		*32.4*	*30.7*	*25.6*	*24.1*	*23.5*	*25.2*	*25.1*	*24.2*	*25.5*	*27.9*	*28.0*
Inclusive tours[3] Total	Tonne km available (millions)	1 234.7	1 546.4	1 813.2	1 950.1	2 180.1	2 371.8	2 635.6	2 477.6	3 100.0	3 786.9	4 012.4
Percentage of all UK services		*10.3*	*12.1*	*13.7*	*14.9*	*18.4*	*19.7*	*20.0*	*18.5*	*21.7*	*23.9*	*23.3*
Other separate fare and advance booking charters[3] Total	Tonne km available (millions)	616.1	352.3	344.9	335.9	184.5	240.4	291.1	327.7	264.9	308.4	403.0
Percentage of all UK services		*5.1*	*2.8*	*2.6*	*2.6*	*1.6*	*2.0*	*2.2*	*2.4*	*1.9*	*1.9*	*2.3*
Other charters Total	Tonne km available (millions)	2 024.4	2 011.1	1 225.3	864.8	415.4	410.0	374.3	436.8	285.9	328.0	404.8
Percentage of all UK services		*16.9*	*15.8*	*9.3*	*6.6*	*3.5*	*3.4*	*2.8*	*3.3*	*2.0*	*2.1*	*2.4*
						Load factors and distances						
Inclusive tours[3]												
Seat-kilometres available (A)	Millions	14 229	17 635	20 345	21 710	24 561	26 480	30 095	28 073	35 130	42 995	45 328
Seat-kilometres used (B)	,,	12 571	14 921	17 117	18 516	20 775	22 731	25 855	24 996	32 091	38 700	40 830
(B) as a percentage of (A)		*88.3*	*84.6*	*84.1*	*85.3*	*84.6*	*85.8*	*85.9*	*89.0*	*91.4*	*90.0*	*90.1*
Passengers uplifted	Millions	7.673	8.750	9.663	10.156	11.902	13.038	14.616	13 631	17 374	20 723	21 251
Stage flights	Number	68 608	80 441	86 298	87 689	104 700	108 173	116 404	102 674	121 747	140 143	139 478
Aircraft-kilometres flown	Millions	107.8	130.8	147.1	154.3	178.5	181.9	197.0	177.6	213.1	248.9	255.1
Average distance per stage flight	Kilometres	1 571	1 626	1 705	1 760	1 705	1 682	1 692	1 730	1 750	1 776	1 829
Average distance per passenger	,,	1 638	1 705	1 771	1 823	1 746	1 743	1 769	1 834	1 847	1 867	1 921
Other separate fare and advance booking charters[3]												
Seat-kilometres available (C)	Millions	6 312	3 732	3 729	3 715	2 104	2 526	3 203	3 684	2 978	3 461	4 122
Seat-kilometres used (D)	,,	5 068	2 872	2 943	3 071	1 759	2 189	2 789	3 090	2 507	2 882	3 476
(D) as a percentage of (C)		*80.3*	*77.0*	*78.9*	*82.7*	*83.6*	*86.6*	*87.1*	*83.9*	*84.2*	*83.3*	*84.3*
Passengers uplifted	,,	1.535	1.069	1.161	1.457	0.685	0.677	0.825	1.018	0.728	0.907	1.211
Stage flights	Number	15 143	10 933	12 655	13 058	6 353	5 914	7 938	8 687	6 036	7 602	10 914
Aircraft-kilometres flown	Millions	33.2	20.8	21.8	22.8	12.1	13.9	15.8	17.0	13.5	15.6	20.4
Average distance per stage flight	Kilometres	2 193	1 903	1 724	1 746	1 905	2 344	1 990	1 954	2 238	2 057	1 872
Average distance per passenger	,,	3 303	2 687	2 534	2 108	2 568	3 232	3 381	3 035	3 446	3 176	2 870

1 Includes services of the British Airways and other UK companies.
2 Excludes Air Taxi operations.
3 Inclusive tours performed under Class 4 licences are included with Other separate fare and advance booking charters.

Source Civil Aviation Authority

10.26 Trends in major United Kingdom airlines

Operating costs and revenues 1978–1987

All airlines	1978	1979	1980	1981	1982	1983	1984	1985[1]	1986[1]	1987[2]
Costs										
Comparison with 1980 (1980 = 100)										
Aircraft fuel and oil	46.2	74.7	100.0	105.5	109.5	106.5	126.2	122.4	82.6	84.5
Crew salaries and expenses	84.1	87.8	100.0	114.4	107.1	113.7	125.5	133.4	160.2	177.3
Aircraft depreciation and rental	83.0	90.8	100.0	113.8	100.3	106.8	149.3	194.4	217.2	279.4
Other costs	75.4	86.9	100.0	97.4	104.3	115.1	136.9	158.2	180.0	203.0
Total Operating Costs	68.1	83.7	100.0	101.5	105.7	112.1	134.1	149.0	153.7	172.8
Comparison with Total—Percentage distribution										
Aircraft fuel and oil	19.1	25.2	28.2	29.3	29.2	26.8	26.5	23.2	15.1	13.8
Crew salaries and expenses	6.2	5.3	5.0	5.7	5.1	5.1	4.7	4.5	5.3	5.2
Aircraft depreciation and rental	7.2	6.4	5.9	6.6	5.6	5.6	6.5	7.7	8.3	9.5
Other costs	67.5	63.2	60.9	58.4	60.1	62.5	62.2	64.6	71.3	71.5
Total Operating costs	100.0	100.0	100.0	100.0	100.0	100.0	100.0	100.0	100.0	100.0
Revenues										
Comparison with 1980 (1980 = 100)										
Scheduled services	74.8	88.5	100.0	103.6	114.4	124.4	147.3	160.1	161.1	183.8
Non-Scheduled services	68.6	80.8	100.0	114.8	133.8	147.2	170.5	171.1	186.2	216.9
Incidental Revenues	91.8	116.0	100.0	86.7	79.7	97.1	120.3	206.4	196.3	218.1
Total Operating Revenues	74.0	87.6	100.0	105.3	117.4	128.1	151.1	163.0	166.4	190.5
Comparison with Total—Percentage distribution										
Scheduled services	80.6	80.5	79.7	78.3	77.7	77.4	77.7	78.3	77.1	76.8
Non-Scheduled services	17.1	17.0	18.5	20.1	21.1	21.2	20.8	19.4	20.7	21.0
Incidental Revenues	2.3	2.5	1.9	1.5	1.3	1.4	1.5	2.4	2.2	2.1
Total Operating Revenues	100.0	100.0	100.0	100.0	100.0	100.0	100.0	100.0	100.0	100.0

Revenues, expenses and profits of major United Kingdom airlines 1978–1987

£ million

	1978	1979	1980	1981	1982	1983	1984	1985[1]	1986[1]	1987[3]
Total Operating Revenues	1 936.4	2 291.9	2 616.5	2 756.0	3 070.5	3 351.6	3 953.2	4 265.7	4 353.3	4 984.8
Total Operating Expenses	1 830.6	2 252.1	2 690.0	2 730.2	2 842.5	3 015.3	3 606.2	4 007.0	4 135.1	4 647.5
Operating profit (or loss)	105.8	39.8	(73.4)	25.8	228.0	336.3	346.9	258.7	218.2	319.1
Non-operating items (net)	12.1	(6.0)	(52.7)	(131.7)	(126.7)	(103.4)	(132.9)	(38.4)	(22.5)	(13.0)
Profit (or loss) before Tax	117.8	33.8	(126.1)	(105.9)	101.3	232.9	214.0	220.3	195.7	306.0

1 Excludes Virgin Atlantic whose Financial Report covers 18 months.
2 Excludes British Air Ferries.
3 Excludes British Air Ferries.
Operating profit (or loss), non-operating items (net) and profit (or loss) before tax include British Caledonian Airways for the months of January 1988–March 1988.

Source Civil Aviation Authority

10.27 United Kingdom airlines[1]

Accidents on scheduled fixed wing passenger-carrying services[2]

	Number of fatal accidents	Passenger casualties: Killed	Passenger casualties: Seriously injured	Crew casualties: Killed	Crew casualties: Seriously injured	Thousand aircraft stage flights per fatal accident	Million aircraft-Kms. flown per fatal accident	Thousand passengers carried per passenger killed	Million passenger Kms. flown per passenger killed	Fatal accidents: per 100,000 aircraft stage flights	Fatal accidents: per hundred million aircraft-Kms.	Passengers killed per hundred million passenger-Kms.
1950–54	7	194	9	28	4	107.4	61.8	46.1	50.0	0.93	1.62	1.99
1955–59	7	123	28	29	8	158.3	92.1	155.2	158.5	0.63	1.09	0.63
1960–64	5	104	35	21	6	303.7	182.3	373.4	390.6	0.33	0.55	0.25
1965–69	6	273	2	32	2	282.7	194.9	222.2	255.2	0.35	0.52	0.39
1970–74	2	167	5	14	2	897.4	737.6	466.3	657.7	0.11	0.14	0.15
1975–79	1	54	6	9	–	1 797.2	1 481.6	1 697.0	3 240.0	0.06	0.07	0.03
1980–84	–	–	4	–	–	–	–	–	–	–	–	–
1984	–	–	–	–	–							
1985	–	–	–	–	–	2 196.3	1 708.8	–	–	0.05	0.06	–
1986	1	–	10	1	1							
1987	–	–	–	–	–							
1988	–	–	–	–	–	2 286.0	1 890.6	–	–	0.04	0.05	–

1 Including services of UK Airways Corporations (reconstituted as the British Airways Board in 1973) and private companies.

2 Excluding accidents involving the deaths of third parties only.

Source *Civil Aviation Authority*

10.28 Activity at civil aerodromes

United Kingdom

	1978	1979	1980	1981	1982	1983	1984	1985	1986	1987	1988
Movement of civil aircraft (thousands)	1 981	2 170	2 181	2 103	2 113	2 238	2 363	2 354	2 439	2 614	2 868
Commercial: total	905	987	1 046	1 028	1 072	1 243	1 179	1 205	1 238	1 312	1 402
Transport	827	903	954	927	974	1 019	1 079	1 097	1 125	1 193	1 279
Other[1]	78	84	92	101	98	224	100	108	113	118	123
Non-commercial[2]	1 076	1 183	1 135	1 075	1 041	995	1 184	1 149	1 201	1 303	1 466
Passengers handled (thousands): total	53 369	57 848	58 942	58 979	60 033	62 301	68 830	71 812	76 593	87 517	94 640
Terminal	52 160	56 615	57 823	57 771	58 778	61 099	67 572	70 434	75 161	86 041	93 162
Transit	1 208	1 233	1 119	1 208	1 255	1 202	1 258	1 377	1 432	1 476	1 479
Commercial freight handled[3] (tonnes): total	746 103	795 315	744 244	723 709	692 693	725 897	860 629	850 268	881 202	975 879	1 088 151
Set down	325 531	364 662	352 133	341 932	320 604	332 162	388 292	377 127	419 275	485 468	572 426
Picked up	420 572	430 653	392 111	381 777	372 088	393 737	472 335	473 140	461 927	490 412	515 725
Mail handled (tonnes): total	71 109	86 097	98 336	106 497	118 406	124 080	136 640	145 770	153 467	155 199	153 308
Set down	29 404	36 675	44 978	50 063	55 200	56 943	61 461	64 138	67 802	67 758	66 978
Picked up	41 705	49 422	53 358	56 434	63 206	67 138	75 179	81 632	85 665	87 441	86 330

1 Local pleasure flights and non-transport charter flights for reward (for example: aerial survey work, crop dusting and delivery of empty aircraft).

2 Test and training flights, scheduled service positioning flights, private, aero-club and official flights, etc.

3 Figures include weight of vehicles carried on vehicle ferry services.

Source *Civil Aviation Authority*

10.29 United Kingdom and Crown Dependency registered trading vessels of 500 gross tons and over[1]

Summary of tonnage by type
End of year

	1978	1983	1986
Number			
Passenger[2]	102	89	79
Cargo liners	404	186	115
Tramps	283	178	132
Bulk carriers[3]	234	109	50
Tankers	398	304	169
All vessels	1 421	866	545
Thousand gross tons			
Passenger[2]	614	602	588
Cargo liners	4 374	2 642	1 932
Tramps	743	372	244
Bulk carriers[3]	7 174	3 911	1 864
Tankers	15 173	8 367	3 083
All vessels	28 078	15 894	7 711
Thousand deadweight tonnes			
Passenger[2]	189	168	156
Cargo liners	5 215	2 896	2 031
Tramps	1 161	588	395
Bulk carriers[3]	12 520	6 851	3 321
Tankers	27 988	14 357	5 499
All vessels	47 068	24 858	11 402

	1986	1988
Number		
Passenger[4]	8	9
Container	66	54
Other dry cargo[5]	234	214
Bulk carriers[6]	73	49
Tankers	165	156
All vessels	546	482
Thousand gross tons		
Passenger[4]	259	260
Container	1 677	1 548
Other dry cargo[5]	858	833
Bulk carriers[6]	2 003	1 301
Tankers	3 249	2 661
All vessels	8 046	6 603
Thousand deadweight tonnes		
Passenger[4]	47	47
Container	1 709	1 506
Other dry cargo[5]	842	686
Bulk carriers[6]	3 569	2 318
Tankers	5 908	4 787
All vessels	12 073	9 344

1 In 1986 a new classification of ship types was introduced. This is based on ship descriptions used by Lloyd's Register of Shipping from which the Department of Transport has been taking figures data since 1986. Because of this change, figures for 1986 in Table 10.29 have been given on both bases.
2 All vessels with passenger certificates.
3 Bulk carriers of 10,000 deadweight tons and over or approximately 6,000 gross tons and over including combination—ore/oil and ore/bulk/oil-carriers.
4 Cruise liner and other passenger.
5 General cargo roll-on/roll-of and lift-on/lift-off vessels, specialised dry cargo vessels and passenger ro-ro vessels.
6 Bulk carriers (large and small) including combination-ore/oil and ore/bulk/oil-carriers.

Source *Department of Transport*

10.30 United Kingdom and Crown Dependency registered trading vessels of 100 gross tons and over

Age distribution by type of vessel
End of year

Per cent

	1987						1988					
	Passenger[1]	Container	Other dry cargo[2]	Bulk carriers[3]	Tankers	All vessels	Passenger[1]	Container	Other dry cargo[2]	Bulk carriers[3]	Tankers	All vessels
Percentage of vessels in each age group												
Age (years)												
Under 5	8	12	11	23	3	9	9	11	12	29	3	11
5–9	–	25	14	41	30	21	–	26	14	44	31	21
10–14	17	27	21	24	18	21	9	26	22	21	18	21
15–19	34	34	17	7	26	20	37	37	17	4	27	20
20–24	8	2	13	3	13	12	9	–	12	–	11	10
25 and over	33	–	24	2	10	17	36	–	23	2	10	17
Total	100	100	100	100	100	100	100	100	100	100	100	100
No of vessels	12	59	432	58	202	763	11	54	412	52	191	720
Percentage of deadweight tonnage in each age group												
Age (years)												
Under 5	10	13	15	22	1	9	10	11	16	25	1	10
5–9	–	18	19	41	28	29	–	18	20	41	30	30
10–14	6	30	34	35	54	44	6	30	36	33	51	42
15–19	53	38	11	1	8	11	53	41	11	–	9	12
20–24	12	1	16	1	6	5	12	–	13	–	7	5
25 and over	19	–	5	–	3	2	19	–	4	1	2	1
Total	100	100	100	100	100	100	100	100	100	100	100	100
Total deadweight tonnes	47	1 623	799	2 354	5 489	10 311	47	1 506	767	2 321	4 802	9 442

1 All vessels with passenger certificates.
2 General cargo roll-on/roll-off and lift-on/lift-off vessels, specialised dry cargo vessels and passenger ro-ro vessels.
3 Bulk carriers (large and small) including combination ore/oil and ore/bulk/oil carriers.

Source *Department of Transport*

10.31 United Kingdom and Crown Dependency registered trading vessels of 100 gross tons and over[1]

End of year

Analysis by deadweight tonnage (dwt) and type of vessel

Size group (thousand dwt)	1981		1987		1988	
	Percentage of vessels	Percentage of deadweight tonnage	Percentage of vessels	Percentage of deadweight tonnage	Percentage of vessels	Percentage of deadweight tonnage
All vessels						
Under 10	48	4	77	10	77	10
10 and under 20	15	7	5	5	5	5
20 and under 50	23	21	12	29	12	30
50 and under 100	5	11	3	15	3	14
100 and under 250	6	27	2	21	2	25
250 and over	3	30	1	20	1	16
Total	100	100	100	100	100	100
Number/tonnes	..	..	763	10 311	720	9 442
Passenger[1]						
Under 10	98	83	92	66	91	66
10 and over	2	17	8	34	9	34
Total	100	100	100	100	100	100
Number/tonnes			12	47	11	47
Container						
Under 10	..	..	19	4	20	4
10 and under 20	..	..	8	5	4	2
20 and over	..	..	73	91	76	94
Total	..	..	100	100	100	100
Number/tonnes	..	..	59	1 623	54	1 506
Other dry cargo[2]						
Under 10	..	..	96	68	96	68
10 and over	..	..	4	28	4	29
20 and over	..	..	–	4	–	3
Total	..	..	100	100	100	100
Number/tonnes	..	..	432	799	412	767
Bulk carriers[3]						
Under 10	..	–	40	4	35	2
10 and under 20	9	2	17	6	17	6
20 and under 50	53	26	21	15	23	16
50 and under 100	14	16	5	10	6	10
100 and under 250	23	54	17	65	19	66
250 and over	1	2	–	–	–	–
Total	100	100	100	100	100	100
Number/tonnes	..	..	58	2 354	52	2 321
Tankers						
Under 10	37	2	64	5	65	5
10 and under 20	6	2	3	2	3	2
20 and under 50	31	16	18	20	18	22
50 and under 100	10	11	9	23	8	23
100 and under 250	6	19	2	12	3	16
250 and over	10	50	4	38	3	32
Total	100	100	100	100	100	100
Number/tonnes	..	..	202	5 489	191	4 802

1 Cruise liner and other passenger.
2 General cargo roll-on/roll-off and lift-on/lift-off vessels, Specialised dry cargo vessels and passenger ro-ro vessels.
3 Bulk carriers (large and small) including combination-ore/oil and ore/bulk/oil-carriers.

Source *Department of Transport*

10.32 International seaborne trade of the United Kingdom

Weight of cargo: analysis by area of consignment and proportion carried by UK registered vessels

	Dry cargo				Tanker cargo				All cargo			
	1987		1988		1987		1988		1987		1988	
	Total	UK flag	Total	UK flag	Total	UK flag	Total	UK flag	Total	UK flag	Total	UK flag
	Million tonnes	*Per cent*	Million tonnes	*Per cent*	Million tonnes	*Per cent*	Million tonnes	*Per cent*	Million tonnes	*Per cent*	Million tonnes	*Per cent*
Exports and re-exports												
Near and short sea:												
EC[1]	26.5	*34*	26.1	*29*	64.5	*23*	52.2	*25*	90.9	*27*	78.3	*26*
Scandinavia[2] and Baltic	8.1	*8*	6.6	*8*	8.6	*32*	2.8	*23*	16.7	*20*	9.4	*12*
Rest of Europe and Mediterranean	2.7	*21*	2.6	*20*	0.5	*1*	0.4	*1*	3.1	*19*	3.0	*17*
All[3]	37.3	*27*	35.2	*25*	73.5	*24*	55.5	*24*	110.8	*25*	90.7	*25*
Deep sea:												
Central and West Africa	0.5	*31*	0.4	*27*	0.1	*9*	0.1	*65*	0.6	*29*	0.6	*37*
South and East Africa	0.7	*6*	0.8	*4*	–	*6*	–	*3*	0.8	*6*	0.8	*4*
Gulf and Indian Ocean	2.9	*7*	2.4	*9*	0.1	*5*	0.1	*3*	3.0	*7*	2.5	*9*
Far East	3.0	*12*	3.0	*13*	–	*9*	0.1	*2*	3.1	*12*	3.0	*12*
Australasia	0.6	*41*	0.6	*36*	–	*20*	–	*32*	0.6	*41*	0.6	*36*
North America	3.4	*20*	3.5	*17*	24.7	*8*	26.6	*5*	28.2	*9*	30.1	*6*
Central and South America	0.6	*7*	0.5	*10*	–	*13*	0.1	*1*	0.7	*8*	0.5	*9*
West Indies	0.3	*30*	0.2	*34*	0.2	–		*4*	0.4	*18*	0.2	*33*
All	12.1	*15*	11.3	*15*	25.2	*8*	27.0	*5*	37.3	*10*	38.3	*8*
All trades	49.4	*24*	46.6	*22*	98.7	*20*	82.5	*18*	148.1	*22*	129.1	*20*
Imports												
Near and short sea:												
EC[1]	42.9	*34*	48.5	*30*	11.4	*28*	10.7	*29*	54.3	*33*	59.2	*30*
Scandinavia[2] and Baltic	14.9	*15*	16.3	*11*	17.7	*4*	17.9	*6*	32.5	*9*	34.2	*8*
Rest of Europe and Mediterranean	3.6	*19*	4.1	*15*	8.7	*13*	9.6	*11*	12.3	*15*	13.7	*12*
All[3]	61.3	*29*	69.0	*24*	37.7	*13*	38.2	*14*	99.1	*23*	107.1	*21*
Deep sea:												
Central and West Africa	1.4	*35*	1.4	*17*	1.2	*2*	1.1	*4*	2.6	*21*	2.5	*12*
South and East Africa	3.5	*30*	4.3	*27*	0.2	*6*	0.1	*66*	3.7	*29*	4.7	*30*
Gulf and Indian Ocean	0.9	*4*	0.9	*6*	5.5	*12*	5.2	*23*	6.3	*11*	6.1	*21*
Far East	3.1	*14*	3.6	*13*	0.4	*2*	0.6	*3*	3.5	*13*	4.2	*12*
Australasia	7.5	*15*	8.7	*13*	0.2	*9*	0.2	*8*	7.7	*15*	8.8	*13*
North America	15.9	*26*	17.7	*25*	0.3	*9*	0.4	*21*	16.3	*26*	18.1	*24*
Central and South America	5.9	*27*	5.2	*29*	3.6	*10*	2.5	*12*	9.6	*21*	7.7	*24*
West Indies	1.0	*23*	0.9	*23*	0.2	*2*	0.4	*19*	1.1	*20*	1.4	*22*
All	39.2	*23*	42.8	*21*	11.5	*10*	10.7	*19*	50.7	*20*	53.4	*21*
All trades	100.6	*27*	111.7	*23*	49.3	*13*	48.8	*14*	149.8	*22*	160.5	*21*

1 Figures for European Community (EC) relate to the eleven member countries.
2 Excluding Denmark.
3 Total near and short sea imports for tanker cargo includes imports from the Continental Shelf (foreign) not separately identified.

Sources Department of Transport; HM Customs and Excise

10.33 International seaborne trade of the United Kingdom

Total and proportion carried by UK registered vessels

	Total seaborne trade						Percentage carried by UK registered vessels						
	1983	1984	1985	1986	1987	1988	1982	1983	1984	1985	1986	1987	1988
Exports[1] *plus* Imports by sea													
Weight (million tonnes)													
All cargo	247.1	274.1	286.1	298.4	297.9	289.6	*28*	*24*	*23*	*23*	*21*	*22*	*21*
Dry bulk cargo	64.8	69.9	73.4	72.0	76.3	76.6	*33*	*28*	*24*	*26*	*22*	*24*	*22*
Other dry cargo	60.0	63.0	66.1	70.9	73.6	81.7	*32*	*29*	*31*	*31*	*27*	*27*	*24*
Tanker cargo	122.3	141.2	146.6	155.5	148.0	131.3	*24*	*20*	*19*	*18*	*18*	*18*	*17*
Value (£ hundred million)													
All cargo	996.0	1 160.9	1 279.2	1 219.2	1 332.6	1 416.2	*35*	*35*	*36*	*36*	*36*	*37*	*32*
Dry bulk cargo	62.0	73.6	74.2	66.4	64.2	69.3	*25*	*23*	*22*	*22*	*19*	*19*	*16*
Other dry cargo	750.7	858.0	960.3	1 023.8	1 136.8	1 254.7	*38*	*39*	*41*	*42*	*40*	*40*	*34*
Tanker cargo	183.3	229.3	244.7	128.9	131.7	92.2	*24*	*20*	*20*	*19*	*19*	*18*	*18*

1 Including re-exports.

Sources Department of Transport; HM Customs and Excise

10.34 International seaborne trade of the United Kingdom

Proportion of trade carried by the principal flags

Percentage

	Dry cargo				Tanker cargo				All cargo			
	1987		1988		1987		1988		1987		1988	
	Weight	Value	Weight	Value	Weight	Value	Weight	Value	Weight	Value	Weight	Value
Exports[1]												
United Kingdom	24.5	39.8	22.3	34.4	20.0	20.3	18.1	19.0	21.5	36.9	19.6	32.9
Germany (Federal Republic)[2]	15.0	12.8	13.7	11.5	2.1	2.7	2.1	3.2	6.4	11.3	6.3	10.7
Bahamas	2.8	2.2	3.9	2.6	19.2	18.3	21.1	19.8	13.7	4.6	14.9	4.3
Greece	2.9	0.6	2.4	2.4	6.8	6.8	5.4	4.9	5.5	1.5	4.3	0.9
Liberia	2.7	1.0	2.1	1.1	21.6	20.5	17.8	16.3	15.3	3.9	12.1	2.6
Panama	4.2	2.3	3.2	2.3	4.7	5.4	4.7	4.7	4.6	2.8	4.2	2.5
Other European Community flags[3]	20.3	20.4	22.0	23.8	8.7	8.8	10.2	10.8	12.6	18.9	14.4	22.6
All other flags	29.6	20.7	30.4	21.9	16.9	17.2	20.6	21.3	20.4	20.1	24.2	23.5
All	100.0	100.0	100.0	100.0	100.0	100.0	100.0	100.0	100.0	100.0	100.0	100.0
Imports												
United Kingdom	26.5	38.9	23.3	33.1	12.6	13.4	14.7	15.6	21.9	37.4	20.6	32.4
Liberia	4.7	0.8	4.1	0.9	12.2	10.7	13.1	11.8	7.2	1.4	6.9	1.4
Norway	2.4	1.1	3.8	1.4	23.5	22.5	23.4	21.7	9.3	2.4	9.7	2.2
Panama	4.6	2.1	5.1	2.6	4.4	5.5	3.1	4.0	4.6	2.3	4.5	2.6
Germany (Federal Republic)[2]	13.2	14.2	12.5	13.4	1.8	3.0	1.4	2.9	9.5	13.6	9.1	13.0
Netherlands	6.1	4.6	5.9	4.6	0.8	1.5	1.4	2.7	4.4	4.4	4.5	4.4
Other European Community flags[3]	13.7	18.2	14.8	20.9	15.9	15.5	13.4	12.8	14.4	18.0	14.3	20.6
All other flags	28.7	20.0	30.5	23.1	28.8	27.9	29.5	28.5	28.7	20.6	30.4	23.4
All	100.0	100.0	100.0	100.0	100.0	100.0	100.0	100.0	100.0	100.0	100.0	100.0

1 Including re-exports.
2 Federal Republic of Germany.
3 European Community.

Sources *Department of Transport; HM Customs and Excise*

10.35 Seaport traffic of Great Britain

Analysis of all foreign and domestic[1] traffic by mode of appearance

Million gross tonnes[2]

	1977	1978	1979	1980	1981	1982	1983	1984	1985	1986	1987	1988
Foreign traffic												
Imports												
Bulk fuel traffic	83.4	78.7	76.9	63.8	53.7	49.1	42.0	60.0	57.2	61.7	57.3	62.9
Other bulk traffic	40.0	37.4	40.3	29.4	32.8	31.8	34.3	34.6	36.7	37.3	42.0	45.0
Container and roll-on traffic	16.4	18.4	20.4	20.4	21.9	23.4	26.0	28.1	29.8	31.1	34.0	38.0
Semi-bulk traffic	13.5	14.0	14.7	13.6	12.3	14.1	14.6	14.6	14.5	15.8	16.9	18.9
Conventional traffic	4.9	4.3	4.8	4.0	3.0	2.3	2.3	2.3	1.7	1.5	1.6	1.6
All imports	158.2	152.8	157.1	131.2	123.7	120.7	119.1	139.6	139.9	147.4	151.8	166.4
Exports												
Bulk fuel traffic	43.1	53.3	72.0	79.9	86.9	92.0	96.0	97.3	103.1	101.9	100.2	91.1
Other bulk traffic	12.0	13.1	13.2	14.7	16.2	15.3	16.3	18.7	17.7	21.1	20.4	18.5
Container and roll-on traffic	14.5	15.8	16.0	16.7	16.5	17.1	18.6	20.3	21.3	22.1	23.9	26.5
Semi-bulk traffic	3.9	3.6	3.4	2.7	3.6	3.0	3.5	3.6	4.1	4.0	5.1	4.6
Conventional traffic	4.2	4.9	3.0	3.3	2.7	2.9	2.1	1.8	1.6	1.2	1.2	1.0
All exports	77.7	90.7	107.5	117.1	125.8	130.3	136.5	141.7	147.8	150.4	150.7	141.7
Domestic traffic[1]												
Bulk fuel traffic	97.7	110.6	122.8	124.3	118.3	129.0	130.7	123.2	119.9	112.2	108.1	115.3
Other bulk traffic	28.5	29.5	30.4	31.6	29.6	30.3	31.7	31.0	31.7	32.7	34.8	40.4
Container and roll-on traffic	4.6	5.1	5.4	4.6	4.5	5.1	5.4	5.4	5.9	6.2	7.3	7.6
Semi-bulk traffic	0.6	0.6	0.5	0.3	0.3	0.2	0.2	0.4	0.3	0.2	0.2	0.3
Conventional traffic	2.8	3.2	3.1	1.0	0.7	0.4	0.3	0.2	0.3	0.3	0.3	0.3
Non-oil traffic with UK offshore installations[3]	..	..	..	1.9	2.1	2.1	2.2	3.2	3.6	2.9	3.1	3.5
All domestic traffic	134.3	149.0	162.2	163.7	155.6	167.2	170.4	163.5	161.6	154.5	153.8	167.5
Total foreign and domestic traffic	370.2	392.4	426.8	412.0	405.1	418.3	426.0	444.7	449.3	452.3	456.2	475.6

1 Domestic traffic refers to traffic, through the ports of Great Britain only, to all parts of the United Kingdom, Isle of Man and the Channel Islands. Traffic to and from offshore installations, landing of sea dredged aggregates and material shipped for dumping at sea are included.
2 Including crates and immediate packaging.
3 Previous to 1980 included in conventional traffic.

Note
The mode of appearance classification was introduced by the Department of Transport and the British Ports Federation (Formerly British Ports Association) from 1982 onwards and corresponds with similar classifications used in other countries including the Statistical Office of the European Communities. It refers to the way cargoes are presented for loading/unloading at ports. Primarily, it distinguishes between bulk and break-bulk cargoes but the latter are further sub-divided into categories which are more meaningful to ports, shipping and inland transport from an operational point of view. Further details of this new classification are provided in *Port Statistics 1988* available from the British Ports Federation, London.

Source *Department of Transport*

10.36 United Kingdom international passenger movement by sea and air

Arrivals plus departures by country of embarkation or landing

Thousands

	1978	1979	1980	1981	1982	1983	1984	1985	1986	1987	1988
All passenger movements											
By sea	19 927	21 289	23 621	25 222	26 359	26 776	26 205	26 287	26 797	26 103	24 994
By air	38 492	41 195	42 068	42 965	43 511	45 233	49 991	51 770	56 554	65 734	70 506
Irish Republic:											
By sea	2 316	2 342	2 502	2 422	2 621	2 761	2 875	2 866	2 628	2 581	2 434
By air	1 933	2 015	1 861	1 806	1 726	1 645	1 714	1 807	2 107	2 721	3 517
Total	4 249	4 357	4 363	4 228	4 347	4 406	4 589	4 673	4 735	5 302	5 941
European continent and Mediterranean Sea area[5]											
By sea: total	17 400	18 732	20 893	22 603	23 628	23 856	23 172	23 241	24 026	23 357	22 399
Belgium	4 428	4 421	5 192	4 714	4 678	4 415	4 608	4 411	3 792	3 328	3 231
France[6]	9 805	11 112	12 621	14 734	15 747	16 140	15 353	15 645	16 867	16 826	15 977
Netherlands	2 056	2 044	1 940	1 958	1 968	2 210	2 191	2 207	2 258	2 092	2 218
Other European Community[7]	704	734	748	772	808	705	656	589	649	671	596
Other countries	407	421	392	425	427	386	364	389	459	440	377
By air: total	26 285	27 926	28 206	28 635	30 140	31 676	34 510	36 239	41 239	47 665	50 069
Belgium and Luxembourg	937	934	874	816	807	884	1 014	1 080	1 092	1 236	1 360
Denmark	621	626	558	510	490	548	592	613	622	670	698
Federal Republic of Germany	2 882	3 081	3 136	2 948	2 998	3 006	3 384	3 644	3 820	4 347	4 493
France	3 026	3 102	3 070	3 105	3 193	3 275	3 537	3 736	3 667	4 236	4 889
Italy	2 279	2 550	2 692	2 335	2 378	2 494	2 582	2 583	2 714	3 065	3 097
Netherlands	1 994	1 959	1 903	1 813	1 843	1 808	2 014	2 227	2 311	2 660	2 900
Norway	564	550	557	543	585	616	647	721	706	725	850
Portugal[1]	580	702	828	954	1 050	1 152	1 329	1 649	2 043	2 263	2 157
Sweden	524	500	449	450	433	454	502	511	566	644	753
Switzerland	1 372	1 413	1 444	1 469	1 576	1 711	1 875	2 016	2 112	2 325	2 490
Greece	1 162	1 562	1 839	2 095	2 123	2 006	2 301	2 875	3 349	3 981	3 796
Spain[2]	6 209	6 412	6 308	7 159	8 635	9 571	11 217	9 513	12 678	14 809	14 861
Yugoslavia	428	508	414	492	476	480	605	813	899	1 070	1 046
Eastern Europe	418	534	532	454	361	409	476	591	542	628	752
Middle East countries[4]	1 762	1 617	1 528	1 491	1 514	1 557	1 563	1 596	1 609	1 638	1 636
Austria	237	241	235	228	240	258	300	364	381	528	707
Rest of other Western Europe[3]	1 290	1 635	1 839	1 773	1 438	1 447	1 572	1 707	2 128	2 840	3 584
Rest of world											
By sea: total	52.0	40.3	45.9	35.4	22.5	35.4	36.0	42.4	36.1	40.9	33.6
United States of America	34.0	27.1	33.3	27.5	16.9	28.7	28.8	35.1	31.3	36.0	30.7
Canada	3.3	2.4	2.5	2.0	1.4	1.7	1.1	1.5	1.5	2.4	0.0
Australia	7.6	5.7	4.2	2.0	1.7	1.3	1.6	1.9	0.9	1.0	1.1
New Zealand	1.5	1.4	0.7	0.6	0.4	0.2	0.3	0.0	0.4	0.3	0.3
South Africa	0.2	0.4	2.0	0.6	0.3	1.4	2.3	2.4	0.8	0.2	0.6
West Africa	0.1	0.4	0.6	0.4	0.3	0.3	0.2	0.2	0.2	0.1	0.3
British West Indies and Bermuda	0.6	0.4	0.2	0.1	0.1	0.1	0.1	0.0	0.0	0.1	0.0
Other countries	4.6	2.5	2.4	2.3	1.5	1.6	1.6	1.2	0.9	0.8	0.6
By air: total	10 274	11 254	12 001	12 523	11 645	11 912	12 767	13 724	13 207	15 348	16 919
United States of America	5 128	5 388	5 914	6 142	5 334	5 739	6 521	6 970	6 336	7 734	8 539
Canada	1 505	1 637	1 496	1 451	1 369	1 366	1 392	1 528	1 501	1 692	1 878
Australasia	429	618	596	509	538	500	507	510	495	531	573
North Africa	509	633	729	765	687	684	648	715	734	872	931
Rest of Africa	1 007	1 040	1 163	1 257	1 284	1 269	1 231	1 303	1 254	1 182	1 245
South America	120	132	133	123	101	82	83	95	106	122	151
Latin America and Caribbean	328	384	415	454	433	361	374	397	419	524	642
Indian sub-continent	491	563	604	636	656	609	594	636	666	714	810
Japan	216	257	235	253	265	264	302	337	356	460	549
Rest of Asia	541	602	716	933	978	1 038	1 115	1 233	1 340	1 517	1 601
Pleasure cruises beginning and/or ending at United Kingdom seaports	158	175	180	162	86	124	121	137	107	125	127

1 Include Azores and Madeira.
2 Includes Canary Islands
3 Includes Cyprus, Faroes, Finland, Gibralter, Iceland, Malta, Turkey, Indian Ocean Islands
4 Includes Israel, Iran, Iraq, Jordan, Kuwait, Lebanon, Gulf States, Saudi Arabia, United Arab Emirates, Yemeni Arab Republic, Yemeni Peoples Republic.
5 Includes North Africa and Middle East Mediterranean countries.
6 Includes hovercraft passengers.
7 Greece, Portugal and Spain have been included in this grouping from 1977 onwards even though they joined the EC in 1981 and 1986 respectively.
8 Cruise passengers, like other passengers, are included at both departure and arrival if their journeys begin and end at United Kingdom seaports.

Sources Department of Transport; Civil Aviation Authority

10.37 Postal services and television licences

Years ended 31 March[1]
United Kingdom

	Unit	1978	1979	1980	1981	1982	1983	1984	1985	1986	1987	1988	1989
Letters and parcel post													
Letters, etc. posted[2]	Millions	9 485	9 965	10 208	10 072	9 985	10 255	10 665	11 439	11 721	12 535	13 568	..
of which:													
Registered and insured	,,	*37.4*	*37.1*	*36.7*	*36.6*	*33.5*	*33.5*	*32.5*	*33.5*	*33.2*	*33.2*	*33.1*	..
Airmail (Commonwealth and foreign)[3]	,,	511	503	493.4	436.8	393.0	378.0	379.3	417.8	383.1	377.7	427.2	..
Business reply and freepost items	,,	215.7	225.3	305.1	309.2	308.2	336.2	356.9	352.6	365.4	370.0	371.1	..
Parcels posted[4]	,,	156.6	168.3	176.8	168.8	179.6	189.6	194.9	202.5	186.5	192.2	197.1	
of which:..													
Registered and insured[5]	,,	*5.0*	*5.3*	*4.7*	*4.2*	*3.8*	*3.6*	*3.8*	*3.9*	*3.7*	*3.5*	*3.2*	..
Inward and transit parcels handled	,,	3.3	3.2	3.4	3.6	3.4	3.2	3.1	3.0	2.6	2.8	2.6	..
Postal orders													
Total issued[6]	,,	180 308	169 989	153 947	121 636	87 154	68 605	63 511	58 553	56 466	54 779	50 656	45 541
Telegrams and telephones													
Telegrams: total	Thousands	17 312	16 601	15 546	13 662	11 521	7 694[10]	5 710					
Inland	,,	3 259	3 347	3 372	2 963	2 276	901[10]						
Foreign (via Post Office system)[7]	,,	14 053	13 254	12 174	10 699	9 245	6 793	5 710					
Telex connections	Number	71 586	79 503	85 752	89 930	92 378	92 622	95 115					
Telephone calls (Inland): total	Millions	17 303	19 122	19 857	20 175	20 806	21 403	22 686					
Local	,,	14 600	16 100	16 600	16 840	17 360	17 800	18 750					
Trunk	,,	2 703	3 022	3 257	3 335	3 446	3 603	3 936					
Telephone calls (International): total	Thousands	70 537	86 930	106 427	116 533	132 255	148 478	172 746	[11]				
Continental	,,	52 689	62 998	75 287	79 467	86 352	93 109	104 065					
Intercontinental	,,	17 767	23 850	31 045	36 971	45 806	55 265	68 574					
Maritime	,,	81	82	95	95	97	104	107					
Telephone stations[8]: total	Thousands	23 016	24 760	26 807	27 870	28 450	28 882	29 336					
Public call offices	,,	77	77	77	77	77	77	77					
Private stations	,,	22 939	24 683	26 730	27 793	28 373	28 805	29 259					
Telephone exchanges[9]: total	Number	6 231	6 231	6 300	6 338	6 318	6 296	..					
Automatic	,,	6 231	6 231	6 300	6 338	6 318	6 296	..					
Manual	,,												
Television licences													
in force on 31 March	Thousands	18 149	18 381	18 285	18 667	18 554	18 494	18 632	18 716	18 705	18 953	19 354	19 396
of which:													
Colour	,,	*11 049*	*12 131*	*12 902*	*13 780*	*14 261*	*14 699*	*15 370*	*15 819*	*16 025*	*16 539*	*17 134*	*17 469*

1 Years ended 31 March for letter and parcel post, postal orders and telegrams sent. For all other items figures relate to 31 March in each year.
2 Including printed papers, newspapers, postcards and sample packets.
3 Including letters without special charge for air transport.
4 Includes Irish Republic inward traffic.
5 Includes compensation fee parcels.
6 Excluding those issued on HM ships, in many British possessions and in other places abroad. For 1980, 1981, 1984, 1986, 1987 and 1988 includes Overseas and Army.
7 Excluding those sent abroad via the private cable companies system.
8 A station is a telephone provided for the use of a customer or renter.
9 Excluding auto-manual and trunk exchanges.
10 Inland telegram service ceased from 1 October 1982, 1983 figures are therefore not comparable with earlier years.
11 Any enquiries should now be referred to: British Telecom plc, 81 Newgate Street, London EC1A 7AJ.

Sources Home Office; Post Office

11 Distributive Trades, Research and Development

Annual retailing inquiries *(Table 11.1)*

The retailing inquiry covers businesses which operate in Great Britain and are engaged in retail distribution. It is undertaken on a sample basis from a register of businesses which the Business Statistics Office (BSO) maintains largely from information obtained by Customs and Excise in the administration of value added tax (VAT). The inquiry is addressed to businesses classified to the retail headings in the VAT trade classification (other than opticians) and also businesses outside retailing which are believed to undertake retailing activity. The inquiry does not cover those businesses that are not registered for VAT, nor those retailers who are registered but with a VAT turnover beneath the mandatory threshold for VAT registration.

The results of the inquiries are presented using a 'kind of business' classification which is consistent with the Standard Industrial Classification 1980. Following a review of the retailing inquiry, two important changes to the inquiry procedures were introduced with effect from the 1986 inquiry. The main change concerns the collection of information in the retailing inquiry, which is now directed much more towards retail businesses. In this context retail businesses are defined as businesses whose main activity is retailing, as opposed to non-retail businesses who are only engaged in retailing as a subsidiary activity. Previously in each full inquiry the complete range of information relating only to the retailing activity of the business (eg stocks for retail trading) was collected from both retail and non-retail businesses. From the 1986 inquiry retail businesses are asked to provide the complete range of information, but relating to their total and not their retail activity. Non-retail businesses are asked to provide only retail turnover and employment, instead of the complete range of information on their retailing activity.

The other change concerns the coverage of the inquiry. Previously no allowance had been made for voluntary VAT registrations, that is businesses who are registered for VAT but with a VAT turnover beneath the mandatory threshold for VAT registration. There are just over 20 000 such retail businesses, accounting for an estimated 0.3 per cent of total retail turnover. From the 1986 inquiry the grossing-up procedure used for the inquiry has been adjusted to allow for voluntary VAT registrations.

These changes have led to a small discontinuity in the inquiry results. In order to facilitate comparisons with previous data, the 1982 and 1984 inquiry results have been re-worked onto the new basis and these data are included in Table 11.1. However, the change to the range of information collected in the inquiry has led to one discontinuity for which it has not been possible to make an adjustment. More precisely the inquiry forms were re-designed for the 1986 inquiry with a view to clarifying, amongst other things, the distinction between retail and non-retail turnover. This has led to an improvement in the quality of the returned data for retail and non-retail turnover in 1986, but suggests that a significant amount of non-retail turnover was mis-reported as retail turnover in the 1984 inquiry. This problem seems most severe for food retailers, where it is thought that retail turnover in 1984 may have been overstated by around £400 to £600m. For the 1986 inquiry Booksellers have been shown separately instead of being included with stationers and newsagents.

Retail trade: index numbers of value and volume *(Table 11.2)*

The retail sales index is based on monthly returns provided voluntarily by a panel of contributors. In its calculation, receipts under the National Health Service are excluded.

Full account has been taken of the results of the 1984 retailing inquiry, and the index has been re-referenced onto 1985 in line with economic series forming parts of the national accounts.

The series for 'All other non-food retailers' includes photographic goods retailers, florists, nurserymen and seedsmen, and other non-food retailers not elsewhere specified.

Motor Trades and Catering inquiries *(Tables 11.3 and 11.4)*

The motor trades and catering inquiries are conducted on a sample basis from the BSO's VAT-based register of businesses. In general the inquiries are addressed solely to businesses classified to these trades, in that businesses who may be engaged in the catering or motor trades as a subsidiary activity are excluded. (An exception is that the catering inquiry includes certain large groups of managed public houses owned by breweries.) The results generally relate to the total activity of all businesses registered for VAT, including those with a VAT turnover beneath the mandatory registration threshold.

Research and Development

Research and development (R & D) in the United Kingdom is financed and carried out mainly by the Government, industry, universities and further education institutions, and various non-profit making bodies. Until 1981, large scale surveys of industrial R & D were held every third year, but there is now a four-year cycle, with a large scale (benchmark) survey every fourth year, and smaller-scale (sample) inquiries in the other three years. The latest benchmark survey related to 1985. Surveys of government expenditure and employment on R & D are carried out every year. Information from these surveys is used to build up the total expenditure on R & D in the UK, which in 1985 was £7.9 billion and in 1987, £9.2 billion, both figures excluding social science research.

In line with international recommendations, research and experimental development is defined for statistical purposes as 'creative work undertaken on a systematic basis in order to increase the stock of knowledge, including knowledge of man, culture and society, and the use of this stock of knowledge to devise new applications'.

Definitions of the sectors surveyed and notes on the survey procedures employed are given in an article which appeared in *Economic Trends* (HMSO) August 1985.

For the 1985 inquiry, industrial firms were asked to provide figures relating to the calendar year 1985, or the business year ending on a date between 6 April 1985 and 5 April 1986.

Returns from government departments relate to financial years ended 31 March. Further details of trends in Government R & D expenditure are given in *Economic Trends*, and the *Annual Review of Government Funded R & D.*

Table 11.5

This table covers R & D in the natural and medical sciences and engineering, and excludes research in the social sciences and humanities. The totals of both sections of the table are the amounts of R & D performed in the United Kingdom and exclude R & D performed abroad which is financed from within this country. No surveys of R & D performed by local authorities have been carried out since 1972, but estimates of local authorities' expenditure in these years have been included in the all-sector figures.

The figures of government financing of R & D as returned by the government and as returned by the sectors carrying out the work vary, largely because of differences in timing.

Tables 11.6 and 11.7

Central government expenditure on R & D, including that of research councils, is surveyed annually and covers R & D in the social sciences as well as R & D in the natural sciences. The distinction between social science and other R & D has been retained in the accompanying tables, though it has been found difficult to make in practice. The borderline between research and other related activities, such as information services and general purpose data collection, is also difficult to define, especially for the social sciences. The figures for social science research are therefore considered to be less reliable than those for government R & D as a whole. The series which appeared in earlier editions of this publication has been amended by taking into account recently developed estimates for government expenditure on R & D in universities. These now include payments through the Treasury Grant for the research costs of postgraduate students, and also expenditure on research in the fields of the social services and humanities.

Table 11.6, as distinct from Table 11.7, includes money spent by the government to finance R & D work performed overseas. It shows the

continued on page 217

11.1 Retail trades by form of organisation and kind of business

Standard Industrial Classification 1980

Great Britain

	1984[2]				1986[2]				1987[3]			
	Businesses	Outlets	Persons engaged	Retail turnover (inclusive of VAT)	Businesses	Outlets	Persons engaged	Retail turnover (inclusive of VAT)	Businesses	Outlets	Persons engaged	Retail turnover (inclusive of VAT)
	Number	Number	Thousand	£ million	Number	Number	Thousand	£ million	Number	Number	Thousand	£ million
Total retail trade	246 931	349 728	2 317	80 128	244 006	343 387	2 334	93 669	240 941	345 424	2 189	101 403
Single outlet retailers[1]	218 700	218 700	840	24 028	217 247	217 247	832	26 943	213 488	213 488	673	28 924
Small multiple retailers[1]	27 399	70 235	331	9 935	25 898	65 783	325	11 311	26 587	69 310	300	11 677
Large multiple retailers[1]	832	60 793	1 146	46 165	861	60 356	1 177	55 414	866	62 627	1 216	60 802
of which Co-operative societies accounted for	*111*	*5 569*	*103*	*4 124*	*98*	*4 859*	*99*	*4 043*	*90*	*4 691*	*100*	*4 198*
Food retailers	81 680	105 953	816	30 131	77 137	99 751	818	33 386	73 792	98 340	772	35 892
Large grocery retailers	98	9 742	421	20 235	94	8 873	457	23 546				
Other grocery retailers	34 053	37 636	140	3 929	30 116	32 942	128	3 919				
Dairymen	7 954	8 786	51	1 457	8 543	9 700	37	1 106				
Butchers, poulterers	16 295	21 767	92	2 640	15 033	20 721	84	2 680				
Fishmongers	2 638	2 969	8	186	2 572	3 158	8	226				
Greengrocers, fruiterers	15 119	17 889	64	1 240	14 187	16 805	63	1 318				
Bread and flour confectioners	5 523	7 174	40	444	5 792	7 553	42	591				
Drink, confectionery and tobacco retailers	43 226	56 499	252	8 322	44 344	56 511	268	9 704	47 226	59 362	258	10 221
Retailers of confectionery, tobacco and newsagents	38 813	47 418	220	6 452	39 633	47 774	234	7 557				
Off-licences	4 413	9 081	32	1 870	4 711	8 736	34	2 148				
Clothing, footwear and leather goods retailers	32 000	58 552	292	7 382	32 656	59 286	294	9 347	31 183	58 517	268	9 902
Men's and boys' wear retailers	3 540	8 176	43	1 477	3 836	7 669	34	1 307				
Women's, girls', children's and infants' wear retailers	17 534	27 191	110	2 629	17 791	27 135	102	2 974				
General clothing businesses	5 802	9 188	48	1 324	5 940	11 282	73	2 856				
Footwear retailers	3 596	11 942	85	1 806	3 790	11 447	80	2 065				
Leather and travel goods retailers	1 528	2 055	6	146	1 299	1 753	5	145				
Household goods retailers	42 916	60 104	283	11 721	43 002	60 676	305	14 670	42 771	60 402	283	16 982
Household textiles retailers	3 220	4 441	17	457	3 458	5 199	22	611				
Carpet retailers	3 701	4 589	17	732	4 158	5 152	21	967				
Furniture retailers	10 603	14 428	69	3 151	10 950	14 639	73	3 789				
Electrical, gas, and music goods retailers	10 931	18 057	91	4 537	9 476	16 304	89	5 402				
Hardware, china and fancy goods retailers	8 744	10 632	46	1 170	8 966	11 051	41	1 174				
Do-it-yourself retailers	5 717	7 957	43	1 674	5 992	8 331	60	2 727				
Other non-food retailers	38 617	50 858	219	6 700	39 110	50 915	234	7 882	38 984	52 442	213	8 799
Chemists	8 603	12 218	67	2 435	8 535	12 538	77	3 005				
Newsagents and stationers / Booksellers (combined, 1984)	5 823	7 606	36	1 050								
Newsagents and stationers					3 418	4 308	21	545				
Booksellers					2 567	3 175	16	596				
Photographic goods retailers	781	1 011	4	218	682	980	4	218				
Jewellers	4 596	7 215	34	1 168	5 133	8 096	38	1 306				
Toys, hobby, cycle and sports goods retailers	8 385	10 287	34	985	7 840	9 408	32	1 100				
Florists, nurserymen and seedsmen	5 213	6 467	28	507	5 674	6 645	31	684				
Non-food retailers (nes)	5 216	6 054	16	337	5 261	5 764	17	428				
Mixed retail businesses	5 644	11 231	415	14 759	4 921	10 395	380	17 356	4 939	11 344	365	18 320
Large mixed businesses	39	4 142	335	11 191	33	4 254	308	13 267				
Other mixed businesses	5 581	7 032	38	831	4 873	6 050	40	924				
General mail order houses	24	57	42	2 737	14	91	32	3 165				
Hire and repair businesses	2 848	6 531	39	1 113	2 839	5 853	34	1 323	2 044	5 017	31	1 287
Television hire businesses	1 534	4 970	33	1 020	1 524	4 039	28	1 192				
Other hire or repair	1 314	1 561	6	93	1 314	1 813	6	131				

1 The terms 'single outlet retailers', 'small multiple retailers' and 'large multiple retailers' are used in the table to denote retail businesses with 1, 2–9 and 10 or more retail outlets respectively.

2 Revised figures.

3 Provisional figures. The 1987 retailing inquiry is the first of a new style of 'intermediate' inquiries.

Source *Central Statistical Office*

11.2 Retail trade: index numbers of value and volume of sales[1]

	Weekly average 1985=100							Sales in 1985 £m	Weekly average 1985=100		
	1978	1979	1980	1981	1982	1983	1984		1986	1987	1988
Value											
All kinds of business: all retailers total	150.4	59.0	66.3	71.8	177.6	84.8	91.7	879.20	108.8	118.3	130.4
Small retailers	..	..	75	79	84	88	94	29 294	106	113	124
Large retailers	..	..	62	68	75	83	90	58 626	110	121	134
Food retailers: total	50.4	57.9	68.1	74.7	80.9	86.8	93.3	32 986	106.9	114.3	124.3
Small retailers	..	..	87	91	95	95	98	8 601	103	106	110
Large retailers	..	..	62	69	76	84	92	24 385	108	117	129
Grocery retailers including co-operative societies	48	55	65	72	79	85	92	25 895	108	116	128
of which co-operative societies	*66*	*75*	*84*	*88*	*89*	*93*	*96*	*3 955*	*103*	*108*	*116*
Dairymen	60	73	81	89	94	98	100	1 843	100	102	102
Butchers	65	73	81	85	89	93	99	2 749	101	102	104
Fishmongers			73	79	83	86	89	210	119	123	131
Greengrocers and fruiterers			67	74	81	89	100	1 285	105	109	111
Bread and flour confectioners	54	67	77	78	78	84	94	1 004	116	123	129
Clothing and footwear retailers: total	50	58	63	65	69	79	88	8 677	112	124	137
Small retailers			74	73	76	84	91	3 510	107	114	124
Large retailers			56	60	65	75	85	5 167	116	132	146
Men's and boys' wear retailers	65	72	78	77	81	87	93	1 267	107	114	121
Women's, girls', children's and infants' wear retailers; general clothing businesses; leather and travel goods retailers	..	..	61	62	65	75	85	5 323	115	130	147
Footwear retailers	..	..	60	63	70	80	90	2 087	108	117	123
Household goods retailers (including hire and repair businesses): total	48	57	63	67	72	82	90	14 717	113	125	142
Small retailers	..	..	73	77	80	86	93	6 586	109	120	136
Large retailers	..	..	55	59	66	79	87	8 131	116	130	148
Furniture, carpets and household textiles retailers	52	63	69	72	76	84	89	4 902	112	126	149
Electrical and music goods retailers, gas showrooms	..	..	56	60	67	83	93	4 338	109	116	124
Hardware, china and fancy goods retailers	44	54	{ 89	90	89	89	90	1 194	113	126	141
DIY retailers			47	55	60	71	83	2 357	122	143	175
Electricity showrooms	47	53	57	59	65	80	91	673	113	124	136
Television and other hire and repair businesses	63	65	75	82	88	92	92	1 253	114	120	123
Other non-food retailers (including off licences, confectioners, tobacconists and newsagents): total	50	57	65	72	79	85	92	15 675	107	117	129
Small retailers	..	..	67	73	80	85	93	10 055	107	115	127
Large retailers	..	..	61	70	77	84	91	5 620	108	120	134
Retailers of confectionery, tobacco and newspapers	54	58	65	75	82	86	92	7 161	108	115	127
Off licences	49	58	64	72	77	83	92	2 287	107	115	122
Booksellers, stationers and specialist newsagents	42	50	60	67	75	87	95	1 208	105	117	133
Chemists	46	50	54	63	72	78	86	1 445	111	121	139
Jewellers	53	66	68	72	78	86	94	1 246	106	125	149
Toys, hobby and sports goods, and cycle retailers	47	60	{ 76	75	77	86	95	1 054	106	117	125
All other non-food retailers			62	69	76	83	89	1 274	108	115	130
Mixed retail businesses: total	53.4	63.2	68.9	73.1	79.2	85.8	91.5	15 865	108.4	118.2	129.5
Mixed businesses with turnover exceeding £11 million in 1986	52	60	66	72	78	86	91	11 965	109	118	131
Other mixed businesses	53	59	71	74	82	88	92	928	109	117	131
General mail order houses	60	74	78	77	81	86	92	2 972	107	118	125
Volume											
All retailers	82.7	86.3	85.8	85.9	87.6	92.0	95.5	87 920	105.3	111.5	119.2
Food retailers	83.4	86.6	90.3	91.0	91.7	94.8	96.6	32 986	103.4	107.4	112.8
Clothing and footwear retailers	74	78	77	75	77	85	92	8 677	109	119	127
Household goods retailers	69	75	73	74	77	86	93	14 717	111	121	135
Other non-food retailers	110	102	95	94	94	95	98	15 675	102	107	114
Mixed retail businesses	85.0	89.0	86.2	86.5	89.6	93.3	95.9	15 865	105.0	111.8	118.6

1 Please see notes on page 214.

Source *Central Statistical Office*

11.3 Motor trades
Great Britain

£m exclusive of VAT

6148, 6510, 6520 and 6710 SIC 1980	Number of businesses	Turnover	Stocks		Capital expenditure				
			Beginning of year	End of year	New building work	Vehicles[1]	Plant and machinery	Net capital expenditure	Land and existing buildings
Total motor trades									
1980	65 707	32 658[1]	3 627	3 764	110	82	114	304	64
1981	67 166	33 096[1]	3 701	3 431	88	72	88	248	35
1982	67 289	33 089	3 337	3 524	88	101	93	281	27
1983	68 573	36 556	3 398	3 833	78	99	124	301	28
1984	69 156	39 448	3 723	3 941	97	148	141	387	42
1985	67 704	40 195	3 831	4 117	109	142	136	387	44
1986	68 109	46 793	4 136	4 655	155	128	148	431	96
1987	69 660	54 206	4 653	5 354	158	163	200	520	114
Distribution, repair and service of motor vehicles (including caravans, tyres, motor accessories and spares)									
1980	57 319	28 522[1]	3 481	3 587	99	69	102	270	61
1981	58 819	28 091[1]	3 533	3 237	81	66	79	226	31
1982	59 198	28 149	3 149	3 337	75	91	77	242	20
1983	60 749	31 057	3 226	3 644	68	87	111	266	28
1984	61 043	33 425	3 544	3 745	85	143	127	355	33
1985	59 764	33 647	3 628	3 896	92	130	123	345	34
1986	60 046	39 983	3 923	4 444	133	117	130	381	81
1907	61 640	47 187	4 441	5 128	132	149	177	458	92
Petrol filling stations									
1980	8 387	4 136[1]	146	177	10	12	11	33	2
1981	8 348	5 005[1]	167	195	6	7	9	22	4
1982	8 090	4 940[2]	187	186	13	10	16	39	7
1983	7 824	5 500[2]	172	188	10	12	14	35	−1
1984	8 113	6 023	179	195	12	5	14	31	9
1985	7 941	6 548	203	221	17	12	13	42	10
1986	8 063	6 810	213	211	22	11	17	50	16
1987	8 021	7 019	212	226	25	14	24	63	21

1 Inclusive of VAT.

Motor trades: commodity analysis of 1982—1986 sales
Great Britain

£m exclusive of VAT

		Turnover	*of which* Motor trades turnover	Retail sales		Sales to other dealers		Used motor vehicles and motor cycles	Petrol and oil	Other sales and receipts
				New cars	Other new motor vehicles and motor cycles	New cars	Other new motor vehicles and motor cycles			
Total motor trades	1982	33 089	32 772	6 497	1 386	3 306	633	5 696	6 951	8 303
	1983	36 556	36 268	7 670	1 582	3 784	709	6 185	7 461	8 876
	1984	39 448	38 912	7 927	1 663	3 947	773	7 329	7 883	9 390
	1985	42 196	41 578	8 371	1 786	4 159	779	7 812	8 218	10 453
	1986	46 793	46 211	9 862	1 929	4 923	847	9 418	8 113	11 119
	1987	54 206	53 478	11 263	2 325	6 065	940	11 626	8 332	12 928
Distribution repair and servicing of motor vehicles (including caravans, tyres, motor accessories and spares)	1982	28 149	27 903	6 362	1 376	3 298	632	5 561	2 740	7 934
	1983	31 057	30 849	7 536	1 577	3 772	709	6 027	2 725	8 502
	1984	33 425	33 045	7 764	1 649	3 932	773	7 179	2 731	9 018
	1985	35 647	35 206	8 187	1 779	4 149[r]	779	7 577	2 728	10 007
	1986	39 983	39 677	9 658	1 912	4 893	847	9 190	2 500	10 677
	1987	47 187	46 745	11 049	2 310	6 053	940	11 380	2 581	12 432
Petrol filling stations	1982	4 940	4 869	135	11	9	1	135	4 210	369
	1983	5 500	5 419	134	5	12	–	158	4 736	374
	1984	6 023	5 867	163	13	15	–	150	5 152	373
	1985	6 548	6 372	185	8	10	–	235	5 489	446
	1986	6 810	6 534	204	17	30	–	228	5 613	442
	1987	7 019	6 733	214	15	11	–	245	5 751	496

Source *Business Statistics Office*

continued from page 214

gross expenditure of government on R & D: 'gross' in that any receipts used to finance the expenditure are not deducted. Money spent on R & D work done by government itself (intra-mural expenditure) is distinguished from money passed to other sectors to fund R & D work (extra-mural expenditure). Table 11.6 shows natural and social science R & D separately, the former being analysed by functional groups of expenditure.

Table 11.7 relates to net government expenditure on R & D, that is, gross expenditure *less* receipts allocated directly towards financing the expenditure. The table shows total expenditure broken down according to the Statistical Office of the European Communities' objectives classification of budgeted expenditure on R & D.

Table 11.8

The trend in the 'volume' of R & D performed can be shown by means of estimates of expenditure at constant prices, using the most appropriate price indices which can be prepared to revalue the current price figures. Work on constructing price indices specifically for R & D expenditure has been undertaken by the Department of Trade and Industry and by international organisations only in recent years. Table 11.8 shows figures for each of the industrial survey years from 1981 to 1987 at constant (1985) prices for total R & D in the natural sciences performed in the United Kingdom and the amounts performed by the government and industry, the latter being analysed by major product group. An article giving broad details of the method used in producing

(continued on page 219)

11.4 Catering and allied trades 1980 – 1987

Great Britain

£m exclusive of VAT

	Year	No of businesses	Turnover (inclusive of VAT)	Stocks: Beginning of year	Stocks: End of year	Capital expenditure: New building work	Capital expenditure: Land and existing buildings	Capital expenditure: Vehicles	Capital expenditure: Plant and machinery	Capital expenditure: Net capital expenditure[2]
Total catering	1980	109 471	12 424	423	467	343	88	63	238	733
	1981	111 532	13 627	447	490	316	118	63	266	769
	1982	113 333	14 926	487	501	337	74	43	262	716
	1983	114 563	15 871	494	517	330	45	46	314	734
	1984	117 715	17 284	513	542	374	145	36	346	902
	1985	117 788	19 271	529	580	454	232	47	425	1 157
	1986	119 889	20 971	571	610	610	405	48	531	1 594
	1987	121 050	23 111	600	659	834	757	57	499	2 146
Hotels and other residential establishments	1980	14 281	2 483	63	71	146	6	9	63	224
	1981	13 929	2 752	71	74	91	33	11	62	198
	1982	13 385	2 880	72	74	83	31	9	61	184
	1983	12 902	2 986	73	76	83	18	6	72	179
	1984	12 934	3 374	75	79	112	56	4	96	268
	1985	12 767	4 050	79	88	168	89	10	141	408
	1986	12 855	4 279	83	94	225	187	11	187	610
	1987	12 960	4 781	92	102	388	427	12	204	1 031
Holiday camps, camping and holiday caravan sites	1980	1 587	405	17	19	22	6	2	18	49
	1981	1 565	421	16	18	19	6	3	13	41
	1982	1 542	390	15	14	21	2	2	11	37
	1983	1 620	418	18	18	11	6	2	15	34
	1984	1 605	456	20	20	14	5	1	20	41
	1985	1 562	503	21	20	17	16	4	24	61
	1986	1 621	567	21	24	16	12	3	28	59
	1987	1 615	590	25	26	43	73	3	37	156
Restaurants, cafes, snack bars, etc. selling food for consumption on the premises only	1980	11 512	1 431	44	50	22	28	5	26	81
	1981	11 735	1 529	43	47	37	5	8	25	75
	1982	11 817	1 639	48	50	27	3	4	31	65
	1983	12 119	1 742	47	52	23	.. [3]	5	41	.. [3]
	1984	12 692	1 900	50	56	28	14	7	40	90
	1985	13 362	2 194	55	62	41	23	6	37	107
	1986	14 348	2 260	59	62	48	28	4	40	120
	1987	15 184	3 064	81	95	100	48	10	68	225
Fish and chip shops, sandwich and snack bars and other establishments selling food partly or wholly for consumption off the premises	1980	22 715	1 103	19	20	17	10	18	19	66
	1981	24 980	1 284	22	24	24	10	7	29	70
	1982	26 256	1 497	24	26	34	5	4	36	78
	1983	27 049	1 664	24	27	45	.. [3]	5	38	.. [3]
	1984	29 205	1 869	29	32	14	5	5	41	65
	1985	28 274	2 063	30	34	20	14	9	47	90
	1986	28 436	2 435	35	36	59	37	7	49	152
	1987	28 686	2 826	37	41	21	19	7	65	111
Public houses[1]	1980	40 608	4 857	196	214	84	20	24	88	216
	1981	40 145	5 273	203	228	104	40	23	104	271
	1982	41 457	6 002	229	238	134	15	18	102	269
	1983	41 868	6 424	232	242	142	30	24	125	321
	1984	42 010	6 888	233	249	156	47	16	114	333
	1985	42 294	7 336	238	263	165	70	17	145	397
	1986	42 901	8 043	258	273	213	126	19	191	549
	1987	42 873	8 274	249	277	250	171	19	93	534
Clubs (excluding sports clubs and gaming clubs)	1980	17 571	1 570	75	84	51	17	2	19	89
	1981	17 873	1 718	81	88	40	21	12	28	101
	1982	17 568	1 776	89	89	34	16	4	13	67
	1983	17 636	1 847	88	87	22	12	1	15	50
	1984	17 786	1 948	92	91	46	18	–	28	93
	1985	17 963	2 128	90	94	41	18	–2	23	80
	1986	18 002	2 203	97	101	46	13	–1	26	84
	1987	17 821	2 288	96	97	30	13	1	21	64
Catering contractors	1980	1 196	575	9	9	–	1	3	5	9
	1981	1 304	650	11	11	1	3	4	5	13
	1982	1 308	743	10	10	3	1	3	8	15
	1983	1 367	790	12	15	3	–	3	9	15
	1984	1 483	849	14	15	2	1	3	7	13
	1985	1 566	998	16	20	1	1	3	7	12
	1986	1 727	1 183	18	20	3	2	4	10	19
	1987	1 912	1 288	20	22	2	6	6	11	25

1 The figures include, besides those businesses registered as public houses, brewers known to operate managed public houses. These businesses account for about one-third of the total activity of public houses.

2 Includes net capital expenditure on land and existing buildings.

3 Figures suppressed for disclosure reasons.

Source Central Statistical Office

11.5 Cost of research and development[1]: analysis by sector

Work performed within each sector

	1981		1983		1985		1986		1987	
	£ million	Per cent	£ million	Per cent	£ million	Per cent	£ million	Per cent	£ million	Per cent
Sector carrying out the work										
Central government										
Defence	557.7	*9.4*	654.9	*9.9*	752.7	*9.5*	801.2	*9.3*	820.3	*8.9*
Civil:										
Research councils	250.2	*4.2*	279.0	*4.2*	313.0	*4.0*	363.4	*4.2*	378.1	*4.1*
Other	526.5	*8.9*	552.9	*8.4*	537.2	*6.8*	194.4	*2.2*	205.0	*2.2*
Local government[2]	5.0	*0.1*	7.0	*0.1*	8.1	*0.1*	7.3	*0.1*	8.0	*0.1*
Total	1 339.4	*22.6*	1 493.8	*22.7*	1 611.0	*20.3*	1 366.3	*15.8*	1 411.4	*15.3*
Universities and further education establishments	629.6	*10.6*	749.5	*11.4*	906.2	*11.4*	1 021.1	*11.8*	1 119.9	*12.2*
Public corporations	384.8	*6.5*								
Research associations	88.1	*1.5*	526.2	*8.0*	5 145.8	*65.0*	5 950.7	*68.8*	6 337.0	*68.9*
Private industry	3 319.5	*56.1*	3 637.1	*55.2*						
Other	159.6	*2.7*	176.4	*2.7*	256.2	*3.2*	315.0	*3.6*	3 28.5	*3.6*
Total cost of research and development performed	5 921.1	*100.0*	6 583.0	*100.0*	7 919.2	*100.0*	8 653.1	*100.0*	9 196.8	*100.0*

Finance provided by each sector

	1981		1983		1985		1986		1987	
	£ million	Per cent	£ million	Per cent	£ million	Per cent	£ million	Per cent	£ million	Per cent
Sector providing the funds										
Central government[3]										
Defence	1 666.7	*24.8*	1 884.3	*25.7*	2 263.7	*21.8*	2 262.6	*19.4*	2 235.7	*19.0*
Civil:										
Research councils	363.5	*5.4*	408.3	*5.6*	553.8	*5.3*	537.7	*4.6*	593.9	*5.1*
Other	1 161.3	*17.3*	1 265.4	*17.3*	1 534.0	*14.8*	1 552.0	*13.3*	1 543.0	*13.1*
Local government[2]	20.0	*0.3*	25.5	*0.3*	27.0	*0.3*	30.0	*0.3*	32.0	*0.3*
Total as returned by Government	3 211.5	*47.7*	3 583.5	*48.9*	4 378.5	*42.2*	4 382.3	*37.6*	4 404.6	*37.5*
Total as returned by sectors carrying out work	2 825.9	*47.7*	3 217.9	*48.9*	3 340.4	*42.2*	3 257.3	*37.6*	3 445.2	*37.5*
Universities	58.0	*1.0*	25.0	*0.4*	35.0	*0.4*	40.0	*0.5*	41.0	*0.4*
Public corporations	449.2	*7.6*								
Private industry[4]	2 080.1	*35.1*	2 869.4	*43.6*	3 752.4	*47.4*	4 402.2	*50.9*	4 689.3	*51.0*
Overseas	411.4	*6.9*	347.9	*5.3*	647.1	*8.2*	798.9	*9.2*	859.6	*9.3*
Other	96.6	*1.6*	122.8	*1.9*	144.3	*1.8*	154.7	*1.8*	161.7	*1.8*
Total	5 921.1	*100.0*	6 583.0	*100.0*	7 919.2	*100.0*	8 653.1	*100.0*	9 196.8	*100.0*

1 Excluding social science research.
2 Estimated.
3 The percentages applying to the government sector have been calculated using the figures returned by the sectors carrying out the work and these percentages have been apportioned *pro rata* over those subdivisions of the government sector shown here.
4 Including research associations.

continued from page 217

figures of R & D expenditure at constant prices was published in *Trade and Industry* (HMSO) on 6 April 1979.

Table 11.9

The table gives the results of the full-scale survey of industrial R&D relating to 1985 and the sample surveys for 1986 and 1987.

Firms covered in the surveys were asked to provide figures for each product group in which they had incurred research and development expenditure. Product groups generally correspond quite closely to industry groups, since manufacturing industries are defined in terms of the products they make and a high proportion of the output of a particular product usually comes from a single industry group. Fuller details for 1985 are given in Business Monitor *MO14 Industrial Research and Development Expenditure and Employment 1985* (HMSO).

Source *Department of Trade and Industry*

11.6 Gross central government expenditure on research and development

£ million

	1984/85		1985/86		1986/87		1987/88		1988/89	
	Intra-mural	Extra-mural	Intra-mural	Extra-mural	Intra-mural	Extra-mural	Intra-mural	Extra-mural	Intra-mural	Extra-mural
R & D in the natural sciences:										
Defence	690.1	1 523.7	752.7	1 629.8	801.2	1 516.2	820.3	1 558.4	893.9	1 623.3
Civil:										
Aerospace	0.6	209.6	0.6	258.6	0.7	286.8	0.8	201.2	0.9	208.2
Energy	346.5	37.3	366.3	43.1	1.9	184.4	2.6	174.1	2.6	193.5
Research councils	295.1	295.9	313.0	309.0	363.4	288.9	378.1	333.5	408.5	346.2
Universities	–	469.4	–	517.0	–	580.0	–	620.0	–	625.0
Other programmes	179.5	264.5	178.4	318.9	191.8	324.8	201.6	412.5	210.3	416.5
Total	1 511.8	2 800.5	1 611.0	3 076.4	1 359.0	3 181.1	1 403.4	3 299.7	1 516.2	3 412.7
Social science R & D	13.1	210.0	12.3	213.5	13.0	222.9	14.4	229.6	16.9	262.6
Total expenditure on R & D	1 524.9	3 010.5	1 623.3	3 289.9	1 372.0	3 404.0	1 417.8	3 529.3	1 533.1	3 675.3
	4 535.4		4 923.2		4 776.0		4 947.2		5 208.4	

Source *Department of Trade and Industry*

11.7 Net central government expenditure on research and development, using European Community objectives for R&D expenditure

£ million

	1982/83	1983/84[1]	1984/85[1]	1985/86[1]	1986/87	1987/88[1]	1988/89[2]	1989/90[2]
Exploration and exploitation of the earth	67.7	69.3	74.5	77.5	79.8	85.2	101.3	135.7
Infrastructure and general planning of land-use	61.1	57.3	60.3	54.1	65.5	66.8	69.6	73.4
Control of environmental pollution	49.0	44.0	51.6	53.4	48.8	56.1	59.0	65.0
Protection and promotion of human health	141.7	151.9	158.1	163.0	190.0	203.9	223.4	259.6
Production, distribution and rational utilization of energy	224.2	220.6	207.8	204.9	187.6	170.4	189.5	168.7
Agricultural production and technology	202.0	206.9	205.5	203.5	198.1	196.1	214.2	224.5
Industrial production and technology	218.1	257.9	288.0	435.3	443.6	411.8	388.6	500.3
Social structures and relationships	25.9	33.0	43.9	55.8	62.3	70.5	101.9	116.3
Exploration and exploitation of space	73.2	74.1	80.8	127.9	123.9	129.8	149.1	140.7
Research financed from General University Funds	600.0	616.0	630.1	669.0	716.1	760.0	770.0	780.0
Non-oriented research	210.6	268.2	281.0	183.8	196.7	219.5	224.7	230.1
Other civil research	58.0	11.1	11.4	12.4	14.2	13.6	13.0	15.6
Defence	1 758.2	1 976.6	2 169.6	2 335.0	2 258.6	2 232.1	2 356.6	2 428.9
Total	3 689.8	3 986.9	4 262.7	4 575.6	4 585.3	4 615.7	4 860.9	5 138.9

1 Revised.
2 Provisional.

Source *Department of Trade and Industry*

11.8 Intra-mural expenditure on research and development at 1985 prices

£ million

	1981	1983	1985	1986[3]	1987[3]
All product groups	4 745.2	4 604.6	5 121.6	5 745.0	5 834.6
All products of manufacturing industry	4 393.9	4 280.1	4 673.2	4 895.2	4 944.0
Chemicals industries	772.5	812.9	941.9	1 002.0	1 199.7
Mechanical engineering[1]	292.8	276.0	262.6	259.1	263.0
Electronics[2]	1 545.6	1 630.1	1 758.6	1 882.3	1 707.7
Other electrical engineering	151.1	130.2	125.6	147.2	130.9
Aerospace	954.6	796.3	818.0	800.9	801.8
Motor vehicles	225.7	264.9	371.6	380.6	414.8
Other manufactured products	451.8	369.7	394.9	423.0	426.1
Non-manufactured products	351.3	324.6	448.4	849.9	890.6

1 Including office machinery.
2 Including electronic data processing equipment.
3 From 1986, figures include UKAEA which became a public corporation in April 1986.

Source *Department of Trade and Industry*

11.9 Industrial expenditure on R&D in 1985, by source of finance and in 1986 and 1987[2]

£ million

Product group	1985 All R&D performed intra murally	1985 R&D financed by industry	1985 R&D financed from overseas	1985 R&D financed by the UK government	1986[2,3] All R&D performed intramurally	1987[2,3] All R&D performed intramurally
Total	5 121.6	3 377.1	569.0	1 175.5	5 950.7	6 337.0
Products of manufacturing industry: Total	4 673.2	3 033.6	[1]	[1]	5 070.4	5 369.7
Chemical industry: Total	941.9	789.2	144.9	7.8	1 037.9	1 303.0
Synthetic resins and plastics	44.2	42.9			48.9	62.3
Paint	19.0	18.2	67.1	1.3	17.7	28.0
Pharmaceutical products	469.3	403.0			520.6	666.9
Other chemical products	409.4	325.1	77.8	6.4	450.8	545.8
Mechanical engineering: Total	262.6	161.1	18.3	83.1	268.4	285.6
Industrial plant and steelwork	24.7	22.4	0.6	1.7	27.3	21.0
Metal working machine tools	10.4	8.6	0.5	1.2	14.0	16.0
Construction and earth-moving equipment	20.4	18.5	0.6	1.3	22.6	23.6
Other machinery and equipment	207.1	111.6	16.6	78.9	204.5	225.0
Office machinery	6.7	6.5	[1]	[1]	7.4	7.8
Electronic data-processing equipment	350.9	173.0	128.2	49.7	359.8	377.7
Electronic engineering: Total	1 401.0	848.5	108.5	444.0	1 949.7	1 854.7
Telegraph and telephone apparatus	393.8	380.6	2.2	11.0	353.6	335.0
Electrical instruments and control systems	252.9	129.0	18.6	105.3	259.9	259.0
Radio and electronic capital goods	530.8	198.3	69.8	262.7	713.5	664.2
Components other than active	41.5	31.2	17.2	64.4	35.0	25.3
Active components and sub-assemblies	165.0	93.7			204.5	175.1
Electronic consumer goods	17.0	15.6	0.7	0.7	16.0	10.6
Electrical engineering: Total	125.6	101.0	5.8	18.8	152.5	142.2
Insulated wires and cables	20.1	16.4	3.6	5.4	22.8	17.0
Basic electrical equipment	55.0	49.7			66.1	69.8
Other electrical goods	50.5	45.9	2.2	13.4	63.6	55.4
Aerospace	818.0	256.8	70.8	515.3	829.6	870.9
Motor vehicles and parts	371.6	339.0	18.6	14.0	394.2	450.5
Other manufacturing industry: Total	394.9	326.5	39.6	28.8	438.1	462.8
Iron and steel	36.2	31.0	2.6	2.6	38.3	47.0
Non-ferrous metals	18.1	12.4	3.9	1.8	20.1	21.1
Brick, cement, building materials	19.8	19.1	0.6	0.2	15.3	19.6
Pottery, china and glass	22.5	21.3	[1]	[1]	22.5	20.0
Metal goods	16.2	13.5	1.1	1.5	21.8	26.2
Shipbuilding and repairs	1.8	1.0	[1]	[1]	1.3	0.9
Instruments engineering	57.3	34.0	[1]	[1]	86.3	87.0
Food and drink	97.4	90.5			104.1	103.3
Tobacco	25.8	19.4	9.2	4.1	21.2	17.5
Textiles other than man-made fibres	16.0	14.1			16.6	11.0
Leather, footwear and clothing	5.7	3.7			6.3	6.0
Timber and wooden furniture	3.3	2.2			3.4	3.0
Paper and paper products; printing, publishing	21.0	18.3	5.0	9.9	25.8	33.0
Processing rubber and plastics	38.3	33.0			31.6	36.2
Other manufactured goods	15.5	13.6			23.4	31.0
Non-manufacturing	448.4	376.1	[1]	[1]	880.3	967.3
Extractive industries	105.1	93.2	[1]	[1]	103.7	117.0
Mineral oil refining	16.7	[1]	[1]	[1]	20.2	17.0
Other treatment of petrochemical products (excluding petrochemical manufacture)	38.2	[1]	[1]	[1]	43.2	39.0
Construction	21.3	17.8	0.7	2.8	25.6	25.0
Utilities	267.0	232.5	5.6	29.0	687.7	769.3
Expenditure not allocated separately	–	32.7	51.3	8.9	–	–

1 Figures removed due to disclosure reasons.
2 Sources of funds were collected for individual industries in respect of 1985 (benchmark survey) but not for 1986 and 1987 (sample surveys).
3 From 1986, figures include UKAEA which became a public corporation in April 1986.

Source *Department of Trade and Industry*

12 External Trade

The tables covering external trade have been compiled from the annual and monthly *Overseas Trade Statistics of the United Kingdom* from 1976. United Kingdom is defined as Great Britain, Northern Ireland, the Isle of Man, the Channel Islands and the Continental Shelf (United Kingdom part). The grouping of the commodities, previously shown in the sections and divisions of the Standard International Trade Classification (Revised), is currently based on those of the SITC (Revision 2) or SITC (R2) which was introduced into the *Overseas Trade Statistics* from January 1978. A new classification was introduced in January 1988—SITC (R3). There are only minor changes from SITC (R2)—See footnote to table 12.3. The statistics in Table 12.1 are on a balance of payments basis; all other statistics in this section are on an *Overseas Trade Statistics* basis. For more detailed figures, notes and definitions relating to external trade, reference should be made to these volumes and also to the annual publication *United Kingdom Balance of Payments* (the CSO Pink Book) and *Monthly Digest of Statistics, Supplement of Definitions and Explanatory Notes*.

Changes in the coverage of the overseas trade statistics are made from time to time but as far as possible figures in these tables have been adjusted to the current basis. For latest data reference should be made to the *Monthly Review of External Trade Statistics*, available from the Department of Trade and Industry.

The value of UK trade with selected areas, analysed by commodity divisions, is obtainable from the annual edition of the *Overseas Trade Statistics of the United Kingdom.*

Import penetration and export sales ratios *(Table 12.2)*

The ratios were first introduced in the August 1977 edition of *Economic Trends* in an article 'The Home and Export Performance of United Kingdom Industries' . The article described the conceptual and methodological problems involved in measuring such variables as import penetration. The industries are currently grouped according to the 1980 Standard Industrial Classification. The latest ratios for the full detail within manufacturing (over 200 activity headings) are shown in Business Monitor MQ12, *'Import Penetration and Export Sales Ratios for Manufacturing Industry'*.

12.1 Visible trade of the United Kingdom

On a balance of payments basis[1]

	1978	1979	1980	1981	1982	1983	1984	1985	1986	1987	1988
Value (£ million)											
Exports	34 981	40 470	47 147	50 668	55 330	60 698	70 263	77 988	72 656	79 421	80 602
Imports (fob)	36 574	43 814	45 792	47 418	53 422	62 207	75 432	81 120	82 020	90 350	101 428
Visible balance	−1 593	−3 344	+1 355	+3 250	+1 908	−1 509	−5 169	−3 132	−9 364	−10 929	−20 826
Unit value index numbers											
1985=100											
Exports (fob)	55.5	61.4	70.0	76.2	81.4	88.0	95.0	100.0	90.4	94.2	94.5
Imports (fob)	58.0	61.8	67.8	73.7	79.9	87.6	95.3	100.0	95.7	98.5	97.6
Terms of trade[2]	95.6	99.4	103.2	103.4	101.9	100.5	99.7	100.0	94.5	95.6	96.8
Volume index numbers											
1985=100											
Exports	79.6	83.1	84.1	83.3	85.6	87.6	94.7	100.0	104.0	109.1	110.7
Imports	76.1	83.5	79.0	75.9	80.1	87.0	96.9	100.0	107.1	114.6	129.5

1 Statistics of visible trade on a balance of payments basis are obtained by making certain adjustments in respect of valuation and coverage to the statistics recorded in the *Overseas Trade Statistics.* These adjustments are described in detail in *United Kingdom Balance of Payments 1987 Edition* (HMSO).

2 Export unit value index as a percentage of the import unit value index.

Source *Department of Trade and Industry*

12.2 Import penetration and export sales ratios for products of manufacturing industry
United Kingdom

	1980 SIC Class	1977	1978	1979	1980	1981	1982	1983	1984	1985	1986	1987	1988[2]
Ratio 1 Imports/Home demand													
Div 2–4 Manufacturing industries[1]	21–49	25.1	26.0	26.9	26.2	27.8	29.0	31.1	33.4	34.3	34.3	35.2	35.2
Class:													
Metals	21–22	32	31	32	33	30	33	36	43	45	..	..	..
Other minerals and mineral products	23–24	12	12	13	12	12	12	13	15	15	15	18	18
Chemicals and man-made fibres	25–26	27	28	30	29	31	34	36	39	41	41	43	42
Metal goods n.e.s.	31	9	10	10	11	11	12	13	14	16	16	18	19
Mechanical engineering	32	30	32	29	29	32	32	32	34	36	37	38	40
Office machinery and data processing equipment	33	84	92	92	96	96	105	106	105	100	100	93	91
Electrical and electronic engineering	34	30	31	31	31	36	39	42	44	47	47	49	48
Motor vehicles and their parts	35	35	35	41	39	42	47	52	51	50	51	48	48
Other transport equipment	36	45	41	38	38	41	39	42	51	45	45	42	..
Instrument engineering	37	51	52	53	52	58	56	55	57	57	56	58	..
Food, drink and tobacco	41–42	17	18	18	16	16	16	17	18	18	18	18	..
Textile industry	43	27	31	33	34	39	39	41	44	44	45	47	48
Leather and leather goods	44	32	34	40	40	42	42	44	44	49	46	49	49
Clothing and footwear	45	25	26	29	29	33	33	33	36	35	30	39	39
Timber and wooden furniture	46	28	27	29	27	29	29	32	32	30	31	31	30
Paper, printing and publishing	47	21	19	19	19	20	19	20	21	21	21	22	22
Rubber and plastics processing	48	17	18	18	18	21	22	24	25	26	27	28	26
Other manufacturing industries	49	34	35	36	41	48	38	38	39	38	39	46	44
Ratio 2 Imports/Home demand and Exports													
Div 2–4 Manufacturing industries[1]	21–49	19.9	20.6	21.6	20.7	21.8	22.9	24.9	26.4	26.7	26.9	27.5	27.8
Class:													
Metals	21–22	27	26	27	29	26	27	30	34	35	..	..	..
Other minerals and mineral products	23–24	10	10	11	10	10	11	12	13	13	13	15	16
Chemicals and man-made fibres	25–26	19	20	21	20	22	23	25	26	26	27	28	28
Metal goods n.e.s.	31	8	9	9	10	10	11	12	13	14	14	16	17
Mechanical engineering	32	19	21	19	19	20	20	22	24	24	25	26	28
Office machinery and data processing equipment	33	51	54	53	52	57	61	63	60	54	56	52	52
Electrical and electronic engineering	34	21	22	23	23	27	29	31	32	33	33	35	35
Motor vehicles and their parts	35	23	25	31	28	30	35	40	39	39	41	38	40
Other transport equipment	36	30	27	26	26	25	24	25	28	27	26	24	..
Instrument engineering	37	34	35	35	33	36	35	38	39	40	40	40	..
Food, drink and tobacco	41–42	16	16	16	14	15	15	15	17	17	17	17	..
Textile industry	43	21	25	26	26	30	31	33	35	35	36	38	38
Leather and leather goods	44	25	27	32	31	34	33	34	34	37	36	37	38
Clothing and footwear	45	21	22	25	25	28	29	29	32	31	31	33	34
Timber and wooden furniture	46	26	26	27	26	27	28	31	31	29	30	30	29
Paper, printing and publishing	47	19	17	18	17	18	18	18	20	19	19	20	20
Rubber and plastics processing	48	14	14	15	14	17	18	20	21	22	22	23	22
Other manufacturing industries	49	25	25	27	31	36	31	31	32	31	31	36	35

1 Certain sectors are excluded since they are inappropriate for this analysis. They are the following activity headings: 2396 (pt) unworked precious stones, 2436 ready-mixed concrete, 3138 heat and surface treatment of metals, 3246 process engineering contractors, 3480 electrical equipment installation, 4121 slaughterhouses, 4370 textile finishing, 4560 fur goods, 4672 shop and office fitting, 4820 retreading and specialist repairing of rubber tyres, 4910 jewellery and coins, 4930 photographic and cinematographic processing laboratories.

2 Provisional.

Source *Department of Trade and Industry*

12.2 Import penetration and export sales ratios for products of manufacturing industry

United Kingdom

(continued)

	1980 SIC Class	1977	1978	1979	1980	1981	1982	1983	1984	1985	1986	1987	1988[2]
Ratio 3 Exports/ Manufacturers' sales													
Div 2–4 Manufacturing industries[1]	21–49	25.7	26.1	25.1	26.5	27.3	27.2	26.6	28.4	30.2	29.4	30.3	28.9
Class:													
Metals	21–22	22	22	23	21	23	23	25	32	35	..	..	..
Other minerals and mineral products	23–24	17	16	15	16	15	14	14	14	15	15	16	16
Chemicals and man-made fibres	25–26	35	36	36	38	39	41	42	45	48	48	47	46
Metal goods n.e.s.	31	14	13	12	14	14	14	12	13	14	13	13	13
Mechanical engineering	32	44	44	42	45	47	45	40	42	43	42	42	40
Office machinery and data processing equipment	33	80	90	90	96	94	108	110	107	100	100	91	90
Electrical and electronic engineering	34	37	37	33	34	36	38	37	39	43	43	43	41
Motor vehicles and their parts	35	42	38	36	38	41	38	37	37	37	34	34	30
Other transport equipment	36	47	45	43	42	50	53	55	63	55	59	57	..
Instrument engineering	37	50	51	53	55	59	57	51	52	50	48	52	..
Food, drink and tobacco	41–42	9	11	10	10	10	11	10	10	11	11	12	..
Textile industry	43	27	27	27	30	30	29	28	30	31	30	32	32
Leather and leather goods	44	27	26	29	32	30	33	33	35	38	36	40	38
Clothing and footwear	45	19	18	18	19	20	18	18	18	19	18	21	19
Timber and wooden furniture	46	7	7	6	7	6	6	6	6	6	5	5	5
Paper, printing and publishing	47	11	11	10	10	10	10	10	10	11	11	11	10
Rubber and plastics processing	48	22	21	20	23	24	22	22	22	22	21	22	20
Other manufacturing industries	49	37	38	36	36	38	28	28	28	28	28	34	31
Ratio 4 Exports/ Manufacturers' sales and Imports													
Div 2–4 Manufacturing industries[1]	21–49	20.6	20.7	19.7	21.0	21.4	21.0	20.0	20.9	22.1	21.5	21.8	20.9
Class:													
Metals	21–22	16	16	17	15	17	17	18	21	23	..	..	..
Other minerals and mineral products	23–24	15	15	14	14	13	12	12	12	13	13	14	14
Chemicals and man-made fibres	25–26	29	29	28	31	31	31	32	33	35	35	34	34
Metal goods n.e.s.	31	13	12	11	13	12	12	11	11	12	11	11	11
Mechanical engineering	32	36	35	33	36	38	36	31	32	33	32	31	29
Office machinery and data processing equipment	33	39	42	42	45	40	42	41	43	46	44	43	44
Electrical and electronic engineering	34	29	28	26	27	27	27	26	26	29	28	28	27
Motor vehicles and their parts	35	32	28	25	28	29	25	22	23	22	20	21	18
Other transport equipment	36	33	33	32	31	38	40	41	45	40	44	43	..
Instrument engineering	37	33	33	34	37	38	37	32	31	30	29	32	..
Food, drink and tobacco	41–42	7	9	9	9	9	9	9	9	9	9	10	..
Textile industry	43	21	20	20	22	21	20	19	19	20	19	20	20
Leather and leather goods	44	20	19	20	22	20	22	22	23	24	23	25	24
Clothing and footwear	45	15	14	14	14	14	13	12	13	13	13	14	13
Timber and wooden furniture	46	5	5	4	5	4	5	4	4	4	4	3	4
Paper, printing and publishing	47	9	9	8	9	8	8	8	8	9	9	9	8
Rubber and plastics processing	48	19	18	17	19	20	18	17	17	17	17	17	16
Other manufacturing industries	49	28	28	26	25	25	20	19	19	20	19	21	20

1 Certain sectors are excluded since they are inappropriate for this analysis. They are the following activity headings: 2396 (pt) unworked precious stones, 2436 ready-mixed concrete, 3138 heat and surface treatment of metals, 3246 process engineering contractors, 3480 electrical equipment installation, 4121 slaughterhouses, 4370 textile finishing, 4560 fur goods, 4672 shop and office fitting, 4820 retreading and specialist repairing of rubber tyres, 4910 jewellery and coins, 4930 photographic and cinematographic processing laboratories.

2 Provisional.

Source *Department of Trade and Industry*

12.3 Value of United Kingdom exports (fob)[1]

Analysis by sections and divisions

£ million

	1978	1979	1980	1981	1982	1983	1984	1985	1986	1987	1988[2]
Total UK exports	35 380.3	40 637.0	47 357.1	50 998.1	55 557.8	60 684.3	70 488.3	78 391.8	72 987.7	79 848.7	81 476.2
0. Food and live animals chiefly for food	1 827.2	1 745.2	2 050.8	2 338.5	2 508.3	2 754.6	3 114.8	3 252.4	3 745.8	3 730.3	3 461.4
00. Live animals chiefly for food	130.7	170.9	139.9	175.6	179.1	187.4	191.0	262.0	299.9	325.8	254.8
01. Meat and meat preparations	282.3	275.4	327.2	328.9	347.5	495.7	491.1	497.4	521.9	625.9	590.4
02. Dairy products and birds' eggs	221.8	226.2	298.4	307.2	325.6	308.1	246.6	281.3	331.5	314.1	389.6
03. Fish, crustaceans and molluscs, and preparations thereof	144.0	146.3	145.6	150.2	162.3	203.2	224.4	260.3	328.9	407.2	384.4
04. Cereals and cereal preparations	364.8	264.4	455.7	697.8	773.9	740.9	992.7	833.0	1 177.5	831.2	676.7
05. Vegetables and fruit	132.8	148.5	152.5	152.2	154.0	163.2	190.8	205.3	251.7	300.3	222.3
06. Sugar, sugar preparations and honey	106.9	103.6	112.2	116.4	121.1	145.1	165.7	220.8	170.4	218.6	196.4
07. Coffee, tea, cocoa, spices, and manufactures thereof	292.9	268.2	261.1	245.2	252.2	291.4	363.4	390.8	364.0	377.5	363.4
08. Feeding stuff for animals (not including unmilled cereals)	58.4	56.9	63.6	60.9	69.0	78.9	96.8	121.8	139.3	155.8	176.4
09. Miscellaneous edible products and preparations	92.7	85.0	94.6	104.0	123.8	140.8	152.3	179.7	160.6	173.9	207.1
1. Beverages and tobacco	1 084.3	1 195.3	1 205.9	1 311.7	1 451.5	1 486.2	1 577.9	1 719.1	1 737.9	1 861.4	2 075.5
11. Beverages	805.1	854.3	897.9	951.6	1 060.1	1 051.2	1 157.0	1 253.7	1 331.6	1 411.6	1 575.5
12. Tobacco and tobacco manufactures	279.1	341.0	308.0	360.1	391.4	435.0	420.9	465.4	406.3	449.8	500.0
2. Crude materials, inedible, except fuels	940.8	1 215.3	1 378.5	1 247.6	1 293.7	1 527.7	1 898.1	2 032.1	1 940.9	1 926.4	2 032.0
21. Hides, skins and furskins, raw	161.0	221.5	189.9	173.9	180.5	200.2	280.3	288.5	260.2	311.5	254.8
22. Oil seeds and oleaginous fruit	5.7	3.1	2.9	4.5	7.9	37.8	54.0	90.4	155.5	86.2	41.7
23. Crude rubber (including synthetic and reclaimed)	69.9	79.2	75.6	108.1	122.8	141.7	166.9	173.9	183.0	180.0	193.0
24. Cork and wood	11.2	13.5	16.0	27.2	28.6	24.1	25.5	25.7	22.9	26.0	26.2
25. Pulp and waste paper	7.7	13.8	22.8	13.9	11.6	15.8	27.2	24.7	25.0	33.9	46.4
26. Textile fibres (other than wool tops) and their wastes (not manufactured into yarn or fabric)	282.2	315.7	312.9	298.3	314.2	375.1	427.9	419.4	373.0	397.0	439.5
27. Crude fertilisers and crude minerals (excluding coal, petroleum and precious stones)	139.2	217.7	235.3	227.0	224.2	223.8	249.1	269.2	271.9	340.6	339.3
28. Metalliferous ores and metal scrap	222.4	307.0	474.4	347.8	346.6	444.2	591.4	645.8	538.9	451.6	593.4
29. Crude animal and vegetable materials	41.6	43.8	48.6	46.9	57.3	64.9	75.6	94.3	110.4	99.7	97.6
3. Mineral fuels, lubricants and related materials	2 374.6	4 323.6	6 428.8	9 616.5	11 237.1	13 102.7	15 308.4	16 795.5	8 671.9	8 769.0	5 817.8
33. Petroleum, petroleum products and related materials	2 235.0	4 157.5	6 133.2	9 107.5	10 685.7	12 501.2	14 851.8	16 133.9	8 207.9	8 465.8	5 575.9
32, 34 and 35. Coal, coke, gas and electric current	139.6	166.0	295.6	508.9	551.4	601.5	456.6	661.6	464.0	303.1	241.9
4. Animal and vegetable oils, fats and waxes	56.6	65.7	71.0	65.1	46.5	59.1	91.0	95.9	105.3	263.5	88.7
5. Chemicals and related products	4 198.9	4 910.9	5 286.2	5 550.1	6 119.3	6 933.0	8 216.8	9 411.7	9 676.8	10 518.6	11 332.7
51. Organic chemicals	913.3	1 237.3	1 297.6	1 496.3	1 592.3	1 930.2	2 381.7	2 742.8	2 571.0	2 830.6	3 138.3
52. Inorganic chemicals	560.9	681.8	619.9	586.5	694.9	699.6	811.1	979.6	1 123.3	1 099.6	1 105.6
53. Dyeing, tanning and colouring materials	347.7	392.0	432.5	433.6	464.1	568.8	633.3	692.0	763.2	878.9	938.8
54. Medicinal and pharmaceutical products	654.1	638.8	744.8	851.9	978.0	1 073.4	1 222.4	1 427.0	1 532.7	1 620.7	1 735.3
55. Essential oils and perfume materials; toilet, polishing and cleansing materials	382.2	408.2	464.7	483.3	525.1	574.5	690.5	767.9	807.7	886.4	943.5
56. Fertilisers, manufactured	57.9	58.2	52.3	62.3	48.8	69.7	64.4	74.8	67.4	85.4	90.0
57. Explosives and pyrotechnic products	31.1	31.1	36.6	39.4	36.8	40.1	47.6	45.7	42.8	45.7	1 113.9
58. Artificial resins and plastic materials, and cellulose esters and ethers	648.3	777.0	874.4	810.7	875.3	980.5	1 179.8	1 330.7	1 401.1	1 553.1	616.1
59. Chemical materials and products, not elsewhere specified	603.5	686.4	763.4	786.2	904.1	996.4	1 186.0	1 351.3	1 367.5	1 518.1	1 651.1

Note: The statistics are on an overseas trade statistics basis (see footnote 1 to Table 12.1).

1 The numbers on the left hand side of the table refer to the Section and Division code numbers of the *Standard International Trade Classification (Revision 2)*. CHANGED TO REV. 3 FROM 1st JANUARY 1988.
The broad structure of SITC (R3) follows that of SITC (R2) but *one major* change should be noted: EXPLOSIVES AND PYROTECHNIC PRODUCTS: Div. 57 in SITC (R2) forms part of Div. 59 in SITC (R3).
Div. 58 in SITC (R2) has been split into Div. 57 and 58 in SITC (R3).

2 Provisional.

Source *Department of Trade and Industry*

12.3 Value of United Kingdom exports (fob)[1]

Analysis by sections and divisions

(continued)

£ million

	1978	1979	1980	1981	1982	1983	1984	1985	1986	1987	1988[2]
6. Manufactured goods classified chiefly by material	6 840.4	7 761.7	8 754.0	7 719.3	7 940.5	9 016.4	10 010.6	10 430.2	10 977.8	11 875.8	12 708.6
61. Leather, leather manufactures, n.e.s., and dressed furskins	187.9	223.6	212.2	207.2	202.1	233.3	312.5	295.2	321.5	372.9	311.4
62. Rubber manufactures, n.e.s.	340.2	363.4	447.1	464.6	417.9	451.6	481.8	554.4	611.8	678.0	715.5
63. Cork and wood manufactures (excluding furniture)	76.6	76.0	84.4	86.4	83.2	85.5	104.6	84.1	77.2	85.6	82.7
64. Paper, paperboard, and articles of paper pulp, of paper or of paperboard	390.6	435.6	475.0	461.5	503.1	543.1	678.6	767.6	824.3	971.2	1 093.7
65. Textile yarn, fabrics, made-up articles, n.e.s., and related products	1 237.8	1 339.4	1 363.0	1 202.7	1 192.0	1 285.0	1 484.8	1 709.1	1 711.5	1 886.2	1 934.9
66. Non-metallic mineral manufactures, n.e.s.	1 494.7	1 713.7	2 110.2	1 538.2	1 609.9	1 995.5	2 298.7	2 164.5	2 549.3	2 654.3	2 971.1
67. Iron and steel	1 105.8	1 277.6	983.4	1 239.4	1 291.8	1 330.7	1 528.9	1 856.2	1 866.5	2 185.8	2 391.2
68. Non-ferrous metals	834.7	1 140.4	1 770.6	1 244.1	1 244.7	1 766.6	1 656.7	1 379.6	1 551.3	1 502.2	1 648.6
69. Manufactures of metal, n.e.s.	1 172.0	1 192.1	1 308.0	1 275.2	1 395.6	1 325.1	1 464.1	1 619.6	1 464.5	1 539.7	1 559.6
7. Machinery and transport equipment	13 407.5	14 235.5	16 267.3	16 784.1	18 100.9	18 324.8	21 520.5	24 667.5	25 351.2	28 802.8	31 886.4
71. Power generating machinery and equipment	1 769.0	1 789.2	2 230.8	2 642.2	2 809.1	2 472.7	2 709.0	3 061.3	3 251.1	3 241.5	3 884.8
72. Machinery specialised for particular industries	2 169.4	2 312.7	2 573.6	2 557.9	2 601.3	2 335.0	2 676.8	3 077.6	3 101.1	3 300.5	3 288.4
73. Metalworking machinery	385.7	383.9	486.4	510.8	522.4	416.2	503.8	521.1	581.2	691.1	780.1
74. General industrial machinery and equipment, n.e.s., and machine parts, n.e.s.	1 837.6	1 960.3	2 316.8	2 305.7	2 411.8	2 334.2	2 577.1	2 937.5	3 037.2	3 097.5	3 577.5
75. Office machines and automatic data processing equipment	918.6	1 163.7	1 345.5	1 291.8	1 599.5	2 048.8	3 046.6	3 746.7	3 561.9	4 483.2	5 296.6
76. Telecommunications, sound recording and reproducing apparatus and equipment	742.1	734.4	712.5	820.5	897.2	991.6	1 117.0	1 295.1	1 401.6	1 567.6	1 758.3
77. Electrical machinery, apparatus and appliances, n.e.s., and electrical parts thereof (including non-electrical counterparts, n.e.s., of electrical household type equipment)	1 398.6	1 457.4	1 798.6	1 758.7	2 117.0	2 292.3	2 805.3	3 380.1	3 382.6	3 785.7	4 343.4
78. Road vehicles (including air cushion vehicles)	3 070.3	3 148.1	3 158.0	3 170.5	3 109.0	3 092.2	3 318.8	3 910.6	3 953.5	4 876.8	4 992.3
79. Other transport equipment	1 116.2	1 285.8	1 645.1	1 726.2	2 033.5	2 341.9	2 766.1	2 737.4	3 080.9	3 758.9	3 964.9
8. Miscellaneous manufactured articles	3 581.8	3 961.4	4 503.7	4 844.6	5 151.8	5 813.0	6 955.0	7 996.8	8 574.7	9 839.6	10 107.6
81. Sanitary, plumbing, heating and lighting fixtures and fittings, n.e.s.	93.7	89.9	109.0	113.0	107.0	108.4	118.9	135.0	126.3	133.0	199.4
82. Furniture and parts thereof	234.6	231.2	239.2	222.1	240.9	257.9	282.0	357.7	356.3	394.7	377.6
83. Travel goods, handbags and similar containers	14.4	16.7	19.5	20.1	19.1	19.3	22.4	29.4	30.6	34.8	43.9
84. Articles of apparel and clothing accessories	669.6	751.2	807.5	846.6	840.0	865.2	996.3	1 171.7	1 228.2	1 428.7	1 414.3
85. Footwear	98.1	113.3	130.4	121.2	114.9	123.4	142.7	159.2	167.2	186.6	210.4
87. Professional, scientific and controlling instruments and apparatus, n.e.s.	691.0	785.3	948.3	1 107.5	1 255.4	1 472.1	1 777.6	2 151.7	2 283.7	2 328.5	2 531.6
88. Photographic apparatus, equipment and supplies and optical goods, n.e.s., watches and clocks	409.7	437.0	519.5	504.6	551.9	573.4	694.2	817.3	843.3	976.2	1 004.1
89. Miscellaneous manufactured articles, n.e.s.	1 370.7	1 536.9	1 730.4	1 909.4	2 022.7	2 393.4	2 920.8	3 174.9	3 539.2	4 357.1	4 326.2
5–8. Manufactured goods	28 028.6	30 869.5	34 811.2	34 898.0	37 312.6	40 087.2	46 703.0	52 506.1	54 580.5	61 036.8	66 035.3
9. Commodities and transactions not classified elsewhere	1 068.3	1 222.4	1 411.0	1 520.7	1 708.2	1 666.9	1 795.3	1 990.7	2 205.5	2 261.3	1 965.5

Note: The statistics are on an overseas trade statistics basis (see footnote 1 to Table 12.1).

1 The numbers on the left hand side of the table refer to the Section and Division code numbers of the *Standard International Trade Classification (Revision 2)*. CHANGED TO REV. 3 FROM 1st JANUARY 1988. (See the full note on page 225).

2 Provisional.

Source *Department of Trade and Industry*

12.4 Value of United Kingdom imports (cif)[1]

Analysis by sections and divisions

£ million

	1978	1979	1980	1981	1982	1983	1984	1985	1986	1987	1988[2]
Total UK imports	39 533.0	46 924.9	49 772.9	51 168.6	56 978.2	66 101.1	78 967.4	85 027.0	86 175.5	94 026.2	106 412.9
0. Food and live animals chiefly for food	5 327.9	5 688.5	5 477.8	5 785.2	6 414.1	6 907.2	7 820.4	8 106.5	8 718.6	8 723.9	9 064.3
00. Live animals chiefly for food	136.9	88.3	102.1	109.5	133.1	170.3	196.8	238.3	293.4	236.4	287.1
01. Meat and meat preparations	1 139.0	1 258.0	1 225.5	1 260.0	1 370.9	1 313.4	1 342.2	1 400.9	1 465.3	1 562.2	1 646.3
02. Dairy products and birds' eggs	510.0	534.4	493.7	592.2	567.9	629.2	604.6	606.3	653.2	617.8	761.2
03. Fish, crustaceans and molluscs, and preparations thereof	260.6	323.7	348.8	403.5	404.2	505.2	537.8	600.4	747.8	759.1	785.8
04. Cereals and cereal preparations	674.6	668.4	603.2	565.9	549.9	593.5	629.0	713.2	769.3	740.8	751.3
05. Vegetables and fruit	1 041.3	1 174.6	1 238.9	1 389.4	1 608.3	1 718.5	1 930.3	2 037.1	2 184.4	2 394.0	2 462.4
06. Sugar, sugar preparations and honey	450.7	402.4	391.7	393.8	429.5	443.2	524.3	508.1	530.3	521.2	556.9
07. Coffee, tea, cocoa, spices and manufactures thereof	758.5	790.8	676.6	579.5	722.4	799.9	1 291.4	1 205.7	1 220.6	997.2	932.0
08. Feedingstuff for animals (not including unmilled cereals)	212.3	276.8	248.9	328.7	446.6	523.6	501.5	487.4	527.3	506.5	557.7
09. Miscellaneous edible products and preparations	143.9	171.3	148.4	162.8	181.1	210.4	262.6	309.0	326.9	388.5	323.7
1. Beverages and tobacco	813.4	828.4	674.8	752.1	836.7	962.0	1 112.5	1 230.8	1 346.7	1 433.2	1 521.9
11. Beverages	359.4	477.5	439.8	482.7	517.5	617.4	705.5	843.6	1 007.9	1 105.4	1 196.3
12. Tobacco and tobacco manufactures	454.0	350.9	235.0	269.5	319.2	344.6	407.1	387.2	338.7	327.9	325.7
2. Crude materials, inedible, except fuels	3 316.2	3 865.3	3 788.5	3 736.8	3 612.9	4 416.1	4 884.9	4 856.8	4 622.4	5 183.9	5 619.7
21. Hides, skins and furskins, raw	196.0	224.6	227.6	192.5	189.5	184.9	235.3	238.9	216.4	264.1	194.2
22. Oil seeds and oleaginous fruit	253.8	260.4	264.8	305.3	259.6	268.6	234.8	238.8	271.3	255.0	227.5
23. Crude rubber (including synthetic and reclaimed)	160.8	185.2	182.8	171.5	182.9	197.4	223.5	228.3	203.5	227.1	236.3
24. Cork and wood	599.6	743.0	683.1	603.7	673.8	937.8	1 009.3	895.3	1 000.3	1 198.6	1 355.9
25. Pulp and waste paper	348.7	388.8	398.7	438.5	412.0	428.0	611.7	505.9	523.3	657.2	725.3
26. Textile fibres (other than wool tops) and their wastes (not manufactured into yarn or fabric)	480.0	475.5	376.1	376.0	410.8	475.9	596.7	662.8	546.9	633.5	686.4
27. Crude fertilisers and crude minerals (excluding coal, petroleum and precious stones)	197.3	312.3	302.8	255.9	263.5	285.8	312.6	354.1	317.1	286.6	354.0
28. Metalliferous ores and metal scrap	905.7	1 077.5	1 168.6	1 185.0	977.5	1 357.8	1 343.8	1 371.8	1 139.5	1 223.1	1 372.9
29. Crude animal and vegetable materials	174.4	198.0	183.9	208.4	243.3	279.7	317.3	361.0	404.1	438.6	465.2
3. Mineral fuels, lubricants and related materials	4 805.2	5 782.2	6 875.4	7 166.4	7 408.6	7 076.3	10 333.8	10 663.6	6 400.4	6 117.0	5 058.3
33. Petroleum, petroleum products and related materials	4 503.7	5 228.2	6 072.7	6 235.6	6 276.9	5 743.3	8 219.8	8 316.2	4 461.3	4 493.3	3 495.2
32, 34 and 35. Coal, coke, gas and electric current	301.6	554.0	802.7	930.8	1 131.6	1 333.1	2 114.0	2 347.4	1 939.1	1 623.7	1 563.1
4. Animal and vegetable oils, fats and waxes	278.4	314.6	260.9	263.3	317.0	358.8	533.2	531.5	365.1	427.0	372.2
5. Chemicals and related products	2 756.7	3 402.2	3 146.9	3 596.6	4 179.1	5 118.9	6 322.1	6 900.8	7 345.3	8 329.8	9 312.7
51. Organic chemicals	791.0	1 020.1	897.4	1 062.4	1 171.9	1 456.3	1 874.4	1 893.8	1 830.7	2 025.7	2 352.9
52. Inorganic chemicals	431.6	452.7	432.9	454.4	539.3	560.8	709.8	897.0	951.4	987.3	910.8
53. Dyeing, tanning and colouring materials	148.0	167.9	145.7	170.7	198.0	235.1	269.7	310.9	396.5	448.1	543.5
54. Medicinal and pharmaceutical products	201.1	229.3	222.6	298.3	374.6	470.2	542.3	590.4	679.7	786.3	875.9
55. Essential oils and perfume materials; toilet, polishing and cleansing materials	139.5	177.1	174.7	203.6	242.2	305.3	377.1	443.3	480.3	554.5	615.1
56. Fertilisers, manufactured	75.9	96.6	89.9	104.9	127.1	171.7	219.4	217.3	213.2	210.6	203.6
57. Explosives and pyrotechnic products	5.6	6.9	7.5	7.7	10.9	14.1	19.0	20.0	22.0	24.1	1 935.3
58. Artificial resins and plastic materials, and cellulose esters and ethers	630.1	828.1	763.2	862.9	1 017.7	1 323.5	1 609.4	1 763.5	1 985.2	2 415.6	910.7
59. Chemical materials and products, not elsewhere specified	333.8	423.5	413.1	431.7	497.4	581.9	700.8	764.6	786.4	877.5	964.9

1 See *Note* and footnotes on page 228.

2 Provisional

Source Department of Trade and Industry

12.4 Value of United Kingdom imports (cif)[1]
Analysis by sections and divisions

(continued)

£ million

	1978	1979	1980	1981	1982	1983	1984	1985	1986	1987	1988[2]
6. Manufactured goods classified chiefly by material	7 652.8	9 291.9	10 333.8	8 936.3	9 852.5	11 846.6	13 447.4	14 342.3	15 328.1	16 968.7	19 586.1
61. Leather, leather manufactures, nes, and dressed furskins	133.0	196.8	137.1	140.7	154.6	183.9	245.1	250.3	247.9	299.4	245.3
62. Rubber manufactures, nes	215.2	259.2	263.5	281.0	326.2	419.6	457.1	527.4	589.2	682.4	798.8
63. Cork and wood manufactures (excluding furniture)	382.7	464.9	368.9	443.0	436.3	578.5	622.1	632.0	687.8	784.6	964.7
64. Paper, paperboard, and articles of paper pulp, of paper or of paperboard	1 054.9	1 240.3	1 286.7	1 536.9	1 675.1	1 905.8	2 280.4	2 532.0	2 702.8	3 237.8	3 622.7
65. Textile yarn, fabrics, made-up articles, nes, and related products	1 453.9	1 691.1	1 543.7	1 761.6	1 927.6	2 320.2	2 705.4	3 032.0	3 162.4	3 497.3	3 635.6
66. Non-metallic mineral manufactures, nes	1 569.5	1 889.4	1 938.0	1 443.4	1 520.3	2 085.4	2 269.3	2 242.6	2 661.7	2 747.4	3 301.0
67. Iron and steel	1 056.4	1 215.2	1 448.0	1 089.5	1 367.3	1 260.3	1 487.2	1 715.5	1 796.2	1 889.9	2 367.4
68. Non-ferrous metals	1 144.0	1 564.4	2 487.4	1 425.3	1 495.7	1 985.0	1 996.2	1 903.4	1 835.7	1 942.3	2 504.2
69. Manufactures of metal, nes	643.2	770.7	860.5	815.1	949.5	1 107.8	1 384.4	1 507.2	1 644.5	1 887.5	2 146.4
7. Machinery and transport equipment	10 198.8	12 226.4	12 565.6	13 399.2	16 464.2	20 260.7	23 781.7	26 937.5	28 765.7	32 808.9	40 043.1
71. Power generating machinery and equipment	811.2	853.6	961.1	1 272.8	1 482.7	1 568.7	1 782.4	1 997.5	2 237.3	2 513.3	3 047.0
72. Machinery specialised for particular industries	1 083.0	1 271.1	1 205.2	1 183.3	1 485.9	1 735.6	2 078.6	2 327.3	2 362.7	2 856.2	3 476.1
73. Metalworking machinery	320.6	412.8	408.4	346.4	380.6	342.3	432.7	525.1	645.7	567.7	800.8
74. General industrial machinery and equipment, nes, and machine parts, nes	1 186.7	1 351.6	1 414.7	1 394.9	1 634.4	1 845.2	2 249.9	2 603.9	2 757.2	3 014.2	3 544.9
75. Office machines and automatic data processing equipment	1 103.0	1 330.4	1 393.4	1 631.7	2 121.9	3 017.5	4 102,7	4 510.0	4 542.1	5 431.1	6 278.6
76. Telecommunications and sound recording and reproducing apparatus and equipment	617.3	796.5	823.6	1 291.4	1 586.2	1 915.9	1 848.3	2 130.6	2 401.6	2 800.8	3 176.7
77. Electrical machinery, apparatus and appliances, nes, and electrical parts thereof (including non-electrical counter-parts, nes, of electrical household type equipment)	1 210.6	1 410.5	1 518.5	1 759.6	2 179.1	2 805.8	3 846.7	4 276.9	4 445.9	5 051.7	5 813.5
78. Road vehicles (including air cushion vehicles)	2 796.9	3 943.2	3 351.6	3 408.1	4 489.6	5 753.8	5 957.6	6 800.6	7 938.8	8 807.4	11 247.9
79. Other transport equipment	1 069.7	856.6	1 488.9	1 111.1	1 103.8	1 275.9	1 482.9	1 765.6	1 434.5	1 766.4	2 657.7
8. Miscellaneous manufactured articles	3 813.2	4 768.1	5 130.7	6 061.1	6 618.4	7 710.4	9 459.5	10 131.6	11 386.1	12 887.8	14 422.2
81. Sanitary, plumbing, heating and lighting fixtures and fittings, nes	54.9	81.1	78.1	81.8	103.5	126.7	151.2	177.2	216.6	254.5	336.2
82. Furniture and parts thereof	194.5	253.8	283.2	349.2	400.1	490.4	591.6	662.8	776.0	877.7	988.9
83. Travel goods, handbags and similar containers	65.1	92.3	94.9	117.7	108.6	131.1	161.9	174.9	199.9	230.9	250.7
84. Articles of apparel and clothing accessories	920.5	1 194.1	1 230.7	1 438.4	1 500.0	1 601.3	2 011.7	2 090.1	2 386.1	2 777.7	3 108.1
85. Footwear	252.2	352.5	354.0	415.6	468.3	542.0	642.0	671.1	734.4	799.3	907.7
87. Professional, scientific and controlling instruments and apparatus, nes	555.4	634.4	743.5	865.6	1 052.1	1 301.3	1 593.8	1 761.5	1 790.0	1 903.2	2 024.6
88. Photographic apparatus, equipment and supplies and optical goods, nes, watches and clocks	538.3	608.9	655.0	749.0	761.0	862.2	1 068.7	1 173.0	1 285.6	1 357.4	1 465.1
89. Miscellaneous manufactured articles, nes	1 232.3	1 551.0	1 691.3	2 043.8	2 224.9	2 655.5	3 238.7	3 420.9	3 997.5	4 687.2	5 340.9
5–8. Manufactured goods	24 421.4	29 688.7	31 177.0	31 993.2	37 114.2	44 936.5	53 010.7	58 312.2	62 825.3	70 995.1	83 364.1
9. Commodities and transactions not classified elsewhere	570.4	757.2	1 518.5	1 471.6	1 274.8	1 444.3	1 271.8	1 325.7	1 897.0	1 146.2	1 412.3

Note The statistics are on an overseas trade statistics basis (see footnote 1 to Table 12.1).

1 The numbers on the left hand side of the table refer to the Section and Division code numbers of the *Standard International Trade Classification (Revision 2)*. CHANGED TO REV 3 FROM 1st JANUARY 1988. The broad structure of SITC(R3) follows that of SITC(R2) but *one major* change should be noted: EXPLOSIVES AND PYROTECHNIC PRODUCTS: Div. 57 in SITC (R2) forms part of Div. 59 in SITC (R3).
Div. 58 in SITC (R2) has been split into Div. 57 and 58 in SITC (R3).

2 Provisional.

Source *Department of Trade and Industry*

12.5 Value of United Kingdom exports (fob)
Analysis by destination

£ million

	1978	1979	1980	1981	1982	1983	1984	1985	1986	1987	1988[4]
Total trade	35 380.3	40 637.0	47 357.1	50 998.1	55 557.8	60 684.3	70 488.3	78 391.8	72 987.7	79 848.7	81 476.2
European Community[5]											
Total	13 620.8	17 479.4	20 542.6	21 119.1	23 123.6	26 508.8	31 506.7	36 233.8	34 996.3	39 414.9	40 932.0
France	2 495.6	3 026.6	3 594.5	3 625.9	4 491.8	5 650.8	6 996.3	7 771.4	6 210.5	7 781.4	8 270.4
Belgium and Luxembourg	1 605.1	1 890.6	2 258.9	2 092.0	2 309.6	2 574.5	3 051.9	3 347.7	3 832.9	3 857.4	4 252.0
Netherlands	2 251.3	3 061.3	3 838.7	4 019.4	4 642.8	5 441.1	6 127.0	7 344.8	5 441.7	5 855.8	5 583.3
Germany, Federal Republic	3 086.5	4 217.6	5 067.4	5 516.0	5 412.5	6 068.7	7 484.2	8 966.1	8 549.1	9 404.2	9 521.9
Italy	1 121.8	1 463.1	1 896.9	1 742.5	2 024.3	2 279.1	2 903.5	3 466.2	3 463.5	4 145.7	4 106.4
Irish Republic	2 024.1	2 544.9	2 639.0	2 813.0	2 889.4	3 055.3	3 393.8	3 631.1	3 553.5	3 831.6	4 057.0
Denmark	830.6	1 015.3	1 024.6	1 056.1	1 098.2	1 159.2	1 195.5	1 371.1	1 211.6	1 230.0	1 170.9
Greece	205.7	260.1	222.5	254.2	255.1	280.2	354.3	335.4	356.0	444.5	468.0
Rest of Western Europe[5]											
Total	4 424.7	5 559.1	6 749.8	6 341.3	6 680.9	7 506.2	8 752.9	9 430.6	6 961.1	7 621.3	7 411.5
Norway	637.8	773.2	790.6	877.0	933.9	829.1	972.9	1 140.7	1 147.6	1 220.7	1 053.6
Sweden	1 169.7	1 536.9	1 624.7	1 601.2	1 935.6	2 387.7	2 893.9	3 025.3	2 307.8	2 322.2	2 195.0
Finland	349.0	410.6	525.6	525.0	513.3	539.7	699.5	705.4	664.1	797.2	825.0
Switzerland	870.8	1 249.2	1 953.2	1 458.6	1 195.7	1 385.8	1 549.5	1 306.6	1 575.2	1 835.8	1 854.9
Austria	237.5	257.3	278.8	246.9	250.8	273.8	320.9	381.0	403.0	463.2	510.0
Portugal	284.1	305.4	390.0	360.1	428.5	397.0	386.4	439.6	472.1	699.9	810.5
Spain	470.6	567.3	700.4	740.7	871.4	1 128.4	1 234.3	1 552.6	1 905.5	2 164.3	2 691.7
Yugoslavia	158.8	173.8	176.3	194.8	158.8	147.8	163.9	177.5	188.4	206.9	203.1
Turkey	110.5	135.6	147.1	159.6	218.1	243.8	331.4	459.8	433.3	513.5	477.5
Other countries	135.9	149.8	163.1	169.4	174.8	173.1	200.3	242.1	241.7	261.7	292.4
North America											
Total	4 249.3	4 791.4	5 329.2	7 130.9	8 353.3	9 495.8	11 416.3	13 331.5	12 118.5	12 992.4	12 623.0
Canada	736.6	767.2	751.8	845.0	852.1	973.8	1 183.6	1 693.6	1 698.2	1 938.2	2 038.4
United States	3 485.0	4 003.1	4 553.6	6 258.2	7 474.8	8 485.8	10 159.2	11 519.4	10 369.9	11 013.4	10 544.1
Other countries[1]	27.7	21.1	23.8	27.7	26.4	36.3	73.4	118.6	50.4	40.7	40.5
Other developed countries											
Total	2 323.0	2 474.8	2 661.8	2 939.2	3 235.4	3 136.7	3 687.9	3 791.1	3 614.0	4 045.7	4 495.6
South Africa	659.1	715.7	998.4	1 220.0	1 190.7	1 110.7	1 204.1	1 009.2	849.5	948.6	1 074.8
Japan	541.8	606.2	596.5	620.3	680.9	799.2	926.6	1 012.3	1 193.7	1 495.1	1 742.7
Australia	854.2	840.8	815.8	863.6	1 041.5	940.6	1 189.0	1 373.0	1 227.7	1 223.7	1 378.0
New Zealand	267.8	312.1	251.1	235.4	322.3	286.1	368.3	396.6	343.2	378.4	300.0
Oil exporting countries											
Total	4 664.9	3 648.1	4 777.0	5 931.6	6 445.1	6 127.9	5 806.3	5 952.1	5 498.8	5 222.6	5 020.8
Algeria	121.4	108.9	140.4	173.0	199.2	233.9	272.4	176.6	129.6	73.1	86.6
Libya	214.2	248.7	288.4	530.4	261.0	274.1	246.5	237.2	263.8	220.6	236.0
Nigeria	1 121.1	627.2	1 191.5	1 428.0	1 225.8	800.3	768.8	961.0	565.4	481.6	390.5
Gabon	6.2	6.5	9.2	12.1	14.2	18.8	20.5	30.7	16.6	12.0	18.8
Saudi Arabia	729.7	808.3	945.2	1 133.9	1 361.5	1 480.2	1 386.7	1 249.0	1 508.2	1 978.4	1 713.4
Kuwait	307.8	224.8	250.8	281.2	333.1	333.5	301.5	347.9	300.6	225.2	237.5
Bahrain	116.7	110.8	95.1	102.3	152.0	150.3	138.7	161.5	131.0	125.2	138.2
Qatar	91.8	101.7	102.0	135.7	245.4	216.5	133.8	142.1	112.1	105.1	88.9
Abu Dhabi	124.9	154.9	214.6	246.7	272.9	219.3	215.9	246.7	168.1	150.0	128.8
Dubai	272.5	303.2	268.5	230.4	253.9	313.3	298.8	345.3	379.5	306.8	306.7
Sharjah, etc.	37.1	23.5	17.5	15.0	32.1	35.5	27.0	29.3	34.2	22.2	27.8
Oman	121.2	122.3	121.0	170.8	265.2	449.1	390.4	489.9	399.6	249.9	344.9
Iraq	216.7	201.2	322.1	623.9	873.7	399.9	343.1	444.7	443.8	271.7	412.1
Iran	751.2	231.8	392.7	402.8	333.6	630.7	703.4	525.6	399.4	307.9	247.8
Brunei	16.3	22.8	23.1	24.2	41.8	106.5	122.7	71.5	154.1	204.3	171.6
Indonesia	83.6	75.8	112.2	139.2	212.1	193.6	186.7	175.3	196.5	236.0	203.3
Trinidad and Tobago	110.7	104.6	120.4	121.5	158.4	149.0	113.5	93.9	79.0	57.0	39.9
Venezuela	188.9	137.7	131.5	126.3	148.6	88.3	101.5	165.3	170.1	157.8	177.8
Ecuador	33.0	33.5	30.9	34.1	60.8	35.0	34.3	58.6	47.1	37.9	50.4

1 Greenland, Puerto Rico and St. Pierre and Miquelon.
2 See page 230.
3 See page 230.
4 Provisional.
5 With effect from 1 January 1986 European Community figure includes Portugal and Spain, Rest of Western Europe figure excludes both countries.

Source *Department of Trade and Industry*

12.5 Value of United Kingdom exports (fob)

Analysis by destination

(continued)

£ million

	1978	1979	1980	1981	1982	1983	1984	1985	1986	1987	1988[4]
Other developing countries											
Total	4 927.4	5 353.8	5 847.5	6 279.8	6 607.8	6 664.6	7 550.1	7 923.5	7 647.6	8 514.4	8 612.0
Egypt	205.1	253.1	324.0	325.1	338.8	370.9	427.7	470.5	371.0	342.3	289.3
Ghana	115.1	87.8	88.2	87.8	66.7	82.2	82.9	116.9	113.2	138.1	126.1
Kenya	192.8	170.3	257.0	173.7	153.7	111.4	176.1	160.6	170.7	199.0	202.1
Tanzania	112.2	121.4	110.9	83.0	71.9	62.1	60.4	88.6	62.9	91.9	88.7
Zambia	68.4	85.5	96.3	68.2	61.2	55.5	66.7	85.9	77.9	75.2	85.7
Cyprus	90.3	97.6	108.4	115.6	111.8	127.9	146.8	151.2	140.5	141.1	159.8
Lebanon	57.9	65.7	70.7	61.9	67.6	81.4	76.2	52.8	55.9	40.7	55.6
Israel	243.4	270.8	230.6	212.0	264.1	354.6	393.0	434.5	462.4	523.6	487.3
Pakistan	112.0	139.9	139.8	149.4	199.1	191.9	282.5	255.4	227.0	253.0	263.3
India	348.4	455.8	529.2	638.9	805.0	805.2	780.7	895.1	941.2	1 090.1	1 111.7
Thailand	86.4	94.4	97.0	91.5	104.8	132.3	149.7	157.7	158.2	206.6	279.7
Malaysia	186.4	187.5	223.3	196.2	210.6	248.3	283.1	281.7	226.9	258.0	310.5
Singapore	255.7	270.9	327.6	355.0	406.0	469.4	556.5	612.9	547.4	602.6	632.5
Taiwan	92.5	103.1	92.4	120.0	125.2	128.4	150.6	164.8	192.5	292.3	355.8
Hong Kong	361.7	439.5	559.2	618.5	730.7	727.3	897.4	949.2	961.0	1 013.0	1 030.7
South Korea	129.1	145.2	101.4	155.8	167.7	169.0	219.6	247.8	288.4	427.2	450.9
Philippines	111.9	104.3	86.2	85.7	97.7	102.9	92.0	94.4	79.8	113.8	124.0
Jamaica	48.6	44.7	33.3	42.9	55.9	116.2	48.1	44.3	43.4	54.6	48.9
Mexico	108.6	134.8	188.1	209.6	162.9	95.7	150.2	203.4	162.3	198.9	190.0
Chile	37.5	43.1	55.8	62.2	56.9	43.5	75.0	73.9	67.5	105.8	80.9
Brazil	221.0	285.8	220.2	174.4	158.8	158.4	238.7	211.5	299.8	347.9	304.7
Argentina	114.6	128.4	172.9	161.2	37.3	4.5	5.2	3.8	10.1	10.3	13.0
Other countries	1 627.8	1 624.2	1 734.9	2 091.2	2 153.4	2 025.6	2 190.9	2 166.5	1 987.6	1 988.4	1 920.8
Centrally planned economies											
Total	1 070.0	1 185.6	1 308.3	1 130.4	974.2	1 113.3	1 629.6	1 587.2	1 710.3	1 538.7	1 614.1
Soviet Union	422.9	416.2	449.2	408.3	356.1	445.4	734.8	536.5	542.5	491.6	511.7
German Democratic Republic	47.4	57.0	93.0	83.0	63.7	61.0	92.3	63.8	81.9	81.5	113.2
Poland	266.0	260.1	296.2	175.7	133.2	151.7	170.0	184.2	167.1	181.5	175.7
Czechoslovakia	73.2	73.8	81.0	70.7	70.1	69.5	78.1	100.5	108.8	114.1	130.4
Romania	74.9	70.3	99.1	150.3	115.2	82.2	71.6	78.5	82.0	55.6	50.1
Other countries[2]	185.6	308.2	289.8	242.4	235.9	303.5	483.0	623.8	727.9	614.4	633.0
Low value trade[3]	100.1	144.9	140.9	125.8	137.5	131.0	138.5	141.9	441.1	498.7	767.1

2 Hungary, Albania, Bulgaria, China, North Korea, Vietnam and Mongolia.

3 Items valued at less than £50 (raised to £100 with effect from 1 September 1973; to £150 from 1 January 1977; to £200 from 1 January 1979 and to £475 from 1 January 1986) have not been allocated to specific countries and areas. The threshold was increased to £600 with effect from 1st January 1988.

4 Provisional.

Source *Department of Trade and Industry*

12.6 Value of United Kingdom imports (cif)

Analysis by source

£ million

	1978	1979	1980	1981	1982	1983	1984	1985	1986	1987	1988[4]
Total trade	39 533.0	46 924.9	49 772.9	51 168.6	56 978.2	66 101.1	78 967.4	85 027.0	86 175.5	94 026.2	106 412.9
European Community											
Total	16 547.1	20 887.6	20 574.2	21 718.0	25 269.0	30 104.1	35 159.3	39 004.8	44 576.8	49 555.4	55 784.6
France	3 198.1	4 015.8	3 848.7	3 978.6	4 266.9	5 042.2	5 885.7	6 635.8	7 387.1	8 381.5	9 390.2
Belgium and Luxembourg	1 757.2	2 272.9	2 380.7	2 448.6	2 857.5	3 129.0	3 688.1	4 015.2	4 084.3	4 361.9	4 956.0
Netherlands	2 518.4	3 442.8	3 397.9	3 895.5	4 512.0	5 103.8	6 115.2	6 553.2	6 623.0	7 148.4	8 279.7
Germany, Federal Republic	4 498.3	5 778.1	5 654.1	5 941.1	7 405.9	9 665.7	11 088.1	12 655.3	14 137.8	15 783.0	17 667.1
Italy	1 926.8	2 478.8	2 291.2	2 330.4	2 736.6	3 196.6	3 809.0	4 293.1	4 666.0	5 216.6	5 817.4
Irish Republic	1 601.3	1 681.4	1 769.4	1 782.1	2 003.4	2 289.4	2 635.1	2 817.2	3 054.0	3 488.2	3 878.6
Denmark	954.5	1 079.6	1 100.6	1 179.1	1 335.3	1 512.4	1 659.2	1 714.8	1 756.8	1 873.4	2 028.1
Greece	92.5	138.0	131.5	162.6	151.3	164.9	278.9	320.1	309.1	355.3	357.0
Rest of Western Europe											
Total	5 998.3	7 192.0	7 265.0	7 798.8	8 390.4	10 457.4	13 432.3	14 571.5	11 886.8	12 883.5	13 942.7
Norway	1 438.2	1 316.9	1 439.5	1 943.2	2 019.2	2 833.8	3 999.4	4 444.3	3 253.7	3 290.3	3 074.3
Sweden	1 337.5	1 600.2	1 466.3	1 533.6	1 672.9	2 053.5	2 416.8	2 467.4	2 760.4	2 952.3	3 366.5
Finland	637.0	792.2	793.4	844.4	921.8	996.0	1 248.2	1 324.0	1 346.0	1 551.7	1 813.0
Switzerland	1 304.6	1 835.1	1 893.8	1 708.1	1 664.5	2 153.2	2 490.1	2 370.9	3 020.1	3 299.4	3 840.6
Austria	322.9	345.2	307.0	348.0	402.4	438.3	529.5	630.2	705.3	782.0	874.4
Portugal[5]	254.3	338.1	334.4	333.4	379.9	475.6	644.8	695.7	768.4	848.0	928.0
Spain[5]	496.3	706.4	795.2	788.6	941.0	1 110.2	1 603.7	1 773.4	1 790.2	2 099.0	2 482.4
Yugoslavia	37.7	51.3	48.2	42.4	52.1	84.0	108.4	122.2	145.1	175.2	197.3
Turkey	62.6	65.8	49.3	128.2	207.8	184.9	237.2	538.5	406.6	579.4	509.6
Other countries	107.2	140.8	137.9	128.9	128.8	128.2	154.3	205.0	249.5	253.3	266.4
North America											
Total	5 313.7	6 197.2	7 464.2	7 587.8	8 095.0	9 082.9	11 067.4	11 709.1	10 028.3	10 781.0	12 899.5
Canada	1 134.0	1 272.2	1 411.7	1 508.8	1 436.2	1 523.3	1 618.1	1 653.0	1 470.4	1 569.2	2 038.2
United States	4 149.0	4 883.6	6 019.2	6 048.3	6 624.1	7 497.2	9 367.7	9 925.5	8 471.5	9 134.5	10 767.8
Other countries[1]	30.7	41.4	33.3	30.7	34.7	62.5	81.7	130.6	86.4	77.3	93.5
Other developed countries											
Total	2 997.9	3 042.7	3 367.5	3 678.1	4 436.1	5 170.6	5 620.5	6 379.3	6 865.3	7 282.9	8 505.5
South Africa	911.2	648.9	752.4	649.2	745.7	764.5	725.6	989.8	829.6	658.2	807.7
Japan	1 283.0	1 488.2	1 707.2	2 206.4	2 658.8	3 355.4	3 771.9	4 115.5	4 936.9	5 464.0	6 509.1
Australia	369.6	489.7	498.8	395.4	492.7	564.1	640.1	741.0	643.2	673.5	745.6
New Zealand	434.1	415.9	409.0	427.2	538.9	486.4	482.9	533.0	455.7	487.3	443.1
Oil exporting countries											
Total	3 326.2	3 212.7	4 253.1	3 666.9	3 453.4	2 832.7	2 934.2	2 814.7	2 103.0	1 699.7	2 087.2
Algeria	37.9	83.4	113.8	159.5	176.3	157.7	274.1	262.1	140.9	172.9	159.7
Libya	96.5	58.4	46.2	74.8	342.5	223.6	164.8	311.8	136.4	133.6	111.8
Nigeria	275.8	176.3	144.3	95.1	356.8	388.0	434.6	663.0	329.0	159.4	128.1
Gabon	2.9	10.9	10.6	36.7	27.6	66.1	67.5	48.3	36.6	5.4	5.1
Saudi Arabia	798.0	1 000.6	1 874.3	1 892.6	1 447.8	897.7	545.6	496.3	659.6	383.1	614.1
Kuwait	589.7	736.9	646.8	477.3	104.7	67.3	141.5	161.5	62.7	81.5	72.3
Bahrain	30.1	9.3	13.1	16.7	35.5	36.8	28.2	45.1	19.0	60.7	75.8
Qatar	29.8	40.5	44.7	10.7	34.0	10.1	28.2	32.6	29.6	13.8	3.9
Abu Dhabi	121.9	90.3	246.3	274.7	184.3	59.0	21.9	25.2	14.6	13.8	25.6
Dubai	148.3	141.7	235.2	116.0	57.5	211.6	60.6	44.4	56.2	77.3	55.8
Sharjah, etc.	0.8	1.1	0.8	2.7	25.2	48.6	4.7	27.3	3.3	4.0	2.9
Oman	30.4	26.0	19.2	40.5	46.4	90.6	80.9	68.4	85.5	49.5	146.8
Iraq	496.6	393.5	532.3	72.6	79.6	30.3	69.0	44.1	66.1	33.9	43.4
Iran	526.8	242.7	107.2	154.4	225.9	100.6	368.6	63.3	100.3	187.6	140.2
Brunei	0.4	0.4	0.8	2.7	2.4	27.2	27.3	23.3	71.6	34.1	142.5
Indonesia	33.4	56.1	57.0	73.8	90.7	169.4	181.5	156.5	141.2	144.8	233.8
Trinidad and Tobago	31.6	41.2	35.0	37.2	65.1	52.7	164.7	83.7	41.6	38.6	35.7
Venezuela	71.3	97.3	116.9	124.0	141.9	184.4	257.5	238.9	97.4	91.7	76.6
Ecuador	4.1	6.2	8.6	5.1	9.3	11.0	13.0	19.0	11.3	14.0	13.1

1 Greenland, Puerto Rico and St. Pierre and Miquelon.
2 See page 232.
3 See page 232.
4 Provisional.
5 With effect from 1 January 1986, European Community figure includes Portugal and Spain, Rest of Western Europe figure excludes both countries.

Source *Department of Trade and Industry*

12.6 Value of United Kingdom imports (cif)

Analysis by source

(continued)

£ million

	1978	1979	1980	1981	1982	1983	1984	1985	1986	1987	1988[4]
Other developing countries											
Total	4 186.8	5 104.4	5 679.9	5 599.9	5 895.8	6 798.4	8 579.3	8 512.0	8 439.8	9 284.5	10 470.9
Egypt	99.0	237.7	333.9	414.6	412.8	79.8	179.9	162.0	87.7	127.3	163.0
Ghana	110.7	89.9	100.0	61.2	78.4	58.1	61.5	99.4	103.5	113.9	106.3
Kenya	111.1	115.4	103.1	95.2	104.3	128.5	203.1	185.6	163.7	129.2	142.5
Tanzania	41.5	40.4	34.6	25.3	19.5	46.5	42.2	46.6	40.3	26.4	26.4
Zambia	67.9	101.4	88.9	41.4	40.0	50.2	48.1	27.9	27.3	30.3	24.8
Cyprus	75.7	87.3	97.7	80.6	89.9	87.4	94.3	93.7	124.1	118.2	121.8
Lebanon	8.1	9.4	9.1	7.5	24.2	11.5	6.9	7.9	9.8	9.5	14.2
Israel	176.4	219.3	232.7	255.9	276.1	313.7	392.7	404.0	385.2	437.0	460.3
Pakistan	54.9	68.0	58.3	63.2	81.5	80.3	93.1	119.9	131.3	167.3	175.3
India	322.1	365.5	318.0	294.3	378.7	366.8	571.0	434.5	440.6	536.5	559.7
Thailand	37.3	49.9	51.0	56.3	76.5	87.8	112.4	131.8	182.7	239.4	321.2
Malaysia	200.1	221.7	186.9	188.3	185.2	222.5	319.5	383.9	349.9	397.1	525.0
Singapore	116.8	185.3	535.5	207.0	245.5	403.1	488.4	441.3	463.0	473.8	579.4
Taiwan	147.0	213.5	230.5	321.1	335.3	458.1	585.2	582.6	705.6	1 006.9	1 150.4
Hong Kong	528.1	689.3	849.8	896.6	870.8	1 177.3	1 266.2	1 175.6	1 537.0	1 531.6	1 788.6
South Korea	214.5	263.6	242.5	325.5	321.6	440.3	444.1	480.4	660.9	935.9	1 135.1
Philippines	57.1	81.3	99.4	105.5	127.0	160.7	199.7	180.0	182.8	202.7	223.6
Jamaica	100.1	82.1	99.0	114.2	92.8	94.0	77.9	89.7	84.5	85.7	89.7
Mexico	41.3	35.5	111.6	108.8	106.1	161.0	175.4	236.8	116.1	244.7	144.9
Chile	82.2	131.2	128.6	87.9	111.2	107.6	108.4	134.7	127.9	112.8	179.6
Brazil	282.2	399.3	296.4	369.9	443.9	560.2	637.8	610.9	552.1	636.7	742.1
Argentina	153.2	144.2	116.2	136.9	58.3	0.2	0.0	2.0	28.6	64.6	66.3
Other countries	1 159.5	1 273.2	1 355.9	1 342.7	1 416.2	1 702.8	2 470.6	2 480.6	1 935.2	1 657.3	1 730.5
Centrally planned economies											
Total	1 099.7	1 196.0	1 069.7	1 014.6	1 327.2	1 535.1	2 042.7	1 893.2	1 863.9	2 097.5	2 038.2
Soviet Union	488.8	491.6	422.0	426.7	645.4	729.9	855.3	726.5	702.1	875.4	732.1
German Democratic Republic	88.4	109.7	88.2	93.6	133.9	167.6	198.1	204.2	195.5	180.3	153.0
Poland	211.9	227.4	193.7	133.6	151.9	177.1	266.7	321.7	308.6	303.5	328.0
Czechoslovakia	85.8	96.8	87.8	70.5	82.0	101.4	117.5	120.0	126.1	141.5	148.2
Romania	51.7	65.9	64.8	46.5	51.5	58.9	226.1	99.2	86.7	92.5	100.9
Other countries[2]	173.1	204.6	213.1	243.7	262.5	300.2	378.9	421.6	444.9	504.3	576.0
Low value trade[3]	63.3	92.3	99.3	104.7	111.3	119.9	131.7	142.5	411.7	441.8	684.3

2 Hungary, Albania, Bulgaria, China, North Korea, Vietnam and Mongolia.

3 Items valued at less than £50 (raised to £100 with effect from 1 September 1973; to £150 from 1 January 1977; to £200 from January 1979 and to £475 from 1 January 1986) have not been allocated to specific countries and areas. The threshold was increased to £600 with effect from 1st January 1988.

4 Provisional.

Source *Department of Trade and Industry*

13 Balance of Payments

Tables 13.1, 13.2 and 13.3 in this section are derived from *United Kingdom Balance of Payments 1989 Edition*—the CSO Pink Book and Tables 13.4 and 13.5 are based on the annual publication *British Aid Statistics,* the latest edition of which covers the period 1983 to 1987.

The following general notes and footnotes to the tables provide brief definitions and explanations of the figures and terms used. Further notes are included in the publications named above. As far as possible transactions have been included in the balance of payments at the rate of exchange at which the transactions took place.

CURRENT ACCOUNT

In principle, transactions are recorded when the ownership of goods or assets changes and when services are rendered.

Visible trade

The *Overseas Trade Statistics of the United Kingdom* are the basis of the balance of payments figures, with certain adjustments in respect of valuation and coverage.

Invisibles: Services

General government covers all UK government current expenditure and receipts not appropriate to other items in the current account.

Transport—sea transport covers both dry and wet cargo transactions of UK operators with overseas residents, and of overseas operators with UK residents. The figures relate to freight, charter hire, port disbursements and passage money.

Transport—civil aviation covers overseas transactions of British airlines, and the transactions of overseas airlines with UK residents. Figures relate to passenger fares, freight, charter hire and airport disbursements.

Travel covers personal expenditure by overseas residents in the United Kingdom and by UK residents in overseas countries.

Financial and other services comprises the earnings, net of expenses, of UK financial and allied institutions for services and all services transactions not included elsewhere.

Invisibles: Interest, profits and dividends

Includes all interest, profits and dividends accruing to UK residents from non-residents or payable overseas by UK residents (after deduction of local taxes and depreciation) and includes profits retained for re-investment.

Invisibles: Transfers

General government transfers includes principally grants to overseas countries and contributions and subscriptions to and grants from international organisations (including European Community institutions).

Private transfers. Value of private assets passing from non-resident to resident ownership or *vice versa* without a *quid pro quo* including transfers of assets by migrants other than their personal or household belongings.

TRANSACTIONS IN EXTERNAL ASSETS AND LIABILITIES

Overseas investment by and in the United Kingdom

Direct investment
Comprises mainly net investment by overseas companies in their United Kingdom affiliates, including the re-investment of retained profits, and by United Kingdom companies in their overseas branches, subsidiaries and associates. Government departments are excluded but outward investment includes public corporations.

Also included are identified transactions in real estate and outward investment includes transactions in non-bank financial institutions' loans and mortgages.

Portfolio investment
United Kingdom portfolio investment overseas consists of purchases (net of sales) of overseas government, municipal and company securities.
Overseas investment in the United Kingdom comprises net investment by overseas residents in:

- UK company securities, including securities issued abroad;
- British government stocks;
- British government foreign currency bonds and notes; and local authorities' and public corporations' securities.

Net foreign currency transactions of UK banks

This item consists of changes in deposits of foreign currencies made with UK resident banks by non-residents and loans by the banks in those currencies to non-residents.

It covers the financing of UK banks' net foreign currency business with UK residents *plus* any switching by the banks between foreign currencies and sterling.

Prior to 1979 data on foreign currency lending (apart from certain export credit) and borrowing are not available separately. Net transactions are shown under borrowing.

Net sterling transactions of UK banks

This item consists of sterling advances and overdrafts (net of repayments) provided to overseas residents (including banks abroad) by UK banks, sterling commercial bills discounted, acceptances, and sterling borrowing and deposit liabilities abroad.

Deposits with and lending to banks abroad by UK non-bank private sector

Consist of UK residents' deposits with banks in the International Monetary Fund (IMF) reporting area supplemented by fiduciary accounts with Swiss banks and deposits with branches of US banks in Panama.

Borrowing from banks abroad

Covers predominately borrowing from commercial banks in the IMF reporting area, the European Investment Bank and the United States Export-Import Bank.

Official reserves

Consists of the sterling equivalent, at current rates of exchange, of drawings on or additions to the gold, convertible currencies and special drawing rights held in the reserves and of changes in the reserve position with the IMF.

Other external assets

Includes identified trade credit between unrelated companies (advance and progress payments on imports and until end-1982 export credit), inter-government loans by the United Kingdom and subscriptions to international lending bodies.

Other external liabilities

Includes identified trade credit between unrelated companies (advance on progress payments on exports and import credit), inter-government loans to the United Kingdom, transactions with the IMF and overseas holdings of Treasury bills.

Allocation of special drawing rights

The distribution of reserve assets created by the IMF.

Balancing item

Represents the net total of errors and omissions in other items in the current and capital accounts.

LEVELS OF UK EXTERNAL ASSETS AND LIABILITIES

(Table 13.3)

The figures in this table show the levels of the stocks of identified external financial assets and liabilities at the end of each calendar year. Changes in these levels reflect not only the capital transactions during the year but also, in many instances, revaluations and other changes. In particular some items may be valued in foreign currency terms and most investments are recorded at either book or market values; in such instances revaluations will usually occur regardless of whether transactions take place.

Because of the very varied data sources used to derive the estimates there are many inconsistencies in the figures resulting particularly from different methods of valuation, which wherever possible, are at market value. The balance between the estimates of identified external assets and liabilities has always been an imperfect measure of the UK's debtor/creditor position with the rest of the world and the persistence of a substantial positive balancing item in the balance of payments accounts in recent years has undoubtedly increased the uncertainty of the estimates. To the extent that the balancing item reflects unrecorded or misrecorded capital transactions, the external balance sheet will tend to fail to capture the corresponding levels of assets and liabilities, although much will depend on the categories of assets and liabilities concerned.

Identified assets include direct and portfolio investment overseas by UK residents, lending to overseas residents by UK banks, deposits and lending overseas by other UK residents and the official reserves. Identified liabilities include overseas residents' direct and portfolio investment in the United Kingdom, borrowing, etc. from overseas residents by UK banks and borrowing from overseas by other UK residents.

General government comprises UK central government and local authorities.

For a more detailed explanation and analysis of the figures see Section 9 of the 1989 Pink Book.

OVERSEAS AID

(Tables 13.4 and 13.5)

The United Kingdom aid programme is administered by the Overseas Development Administration (ODA) to promote the economic development of developing countries. It is managed within financial years, the money being voted annually by Parliament. However the statistics relating to the programme are published for the calendar year as this basis is used both for international aid comparisons and for national purposes such as the balance of payments. Fluctuations may thus occur in the calendar year figures which are not reflected in the financial year figures. This has been particularly true in the case of India, the largest bilateral recipient, whose aid receipts in 1976, 1979 and 1981 were abnormally high, while its receipts in 1980 and 1982 were abnormally low.

Aid flows can be measured before (gross) or after (net) deduction of repayments of principal on past loans. These tables show only the gross figures.

Aid is provided in two main ways: *bilateral,* that is directly to governments of developing countries or to institutions in the United Kingdom for work on behalf of such countries, or *multilateral,* that is to international institutions for their economic development programmes. Table 13.4 shows the three main groups of multilateral agencies, the International Development Association being the largest in the World Bank Group.

Bilateral aid takes various forms. *Project aid* is finance for the establishment of new, or expansion of existing, production and infrastructure facilities. The bulk is provided by the ODA, either from country programmes or from the Aid and Trade Provision (a special allocation to soften the terms of credits to developing countries by mixing aid funds with private export credits). The Commonwealth Development Corporation invests in productive public or private sector projects in developing countries. *Non-project aid* includes programme aid (for import finance not related to specific projects), debt relief, budgetary aid, food aid and disaster relief. *Technical Co-operation* is used to provide experts to work overseas, training for developing country nationals, consultancies, small items of equipment, to fund research and development in the United Kingdom of benefit to developing countries and support to voluntary organisations. Most of the aid not allocable by country in Table 13.5 is for technical co-operation provided through organisations in the United Kingdom.

Fuller statistics of Britain's aid effort are published annually in *British Aid Statistics* (obtainable from the Library, ODA, Abercrombie House, East Kilbride, Glasgow G75 8EA). International comparisons are available in the OECD Development Assistance Committee's annual report. The latest is *1987 Report: Development co-operation* (available from HMSO).

13.1 Balance of payments of the United Kingdom

£ million

	1978	1979	1980	1981	1982	1983	1984	1985	1986	1987	1988
Current account											
Visible trade											
Exports (fob)	34 981	40 470	47 147	50 668	55 330	60 698	70 263	77 988	72 656	79 421	80 602
Imports (fob)	36 574	43 814	47 792	47 418	53 422	62 207	75 432	81 120	82 020	90 350	101 428
Visible balance	−1 593	−3 344	1 355	3 250	1 908	−1 509	−5 169	−3 132	−9 364	−10 929	−20 826
Invisibles											
Credits	24 889	33 330	41 249	57 322	65 412	65 887	77 665	80 583	77 421	80 037	87 233
Debits	22 360	30 535	39 785	53 944	62 733	60 619	70 611	74 248	67 991	72 779	81 024
Invisibles balance	2 529	2 794	1 465	3 378	2 679	5 267	7 054	6 335	9 430	7 258	6 209
of which:											
Services balance	*3 514*	*3 799*	*3 653*	*3 715*	*2 971*	*3 995*	*4 339*	*6 606*	*6 247*	*5 682*	*4 165*
Interest, profits and dividends balance	*806*	*1 205*	*−204*	*1 210*	*1 449*	*2 857*	*4 449*	*2 763*	*5 364*	*4 987*	*5 619*
Transfers balance	*−1 791*	*−2 210*	*−1 984*	*−1 547*	*−1 741*	*−1 585*	*−1 734*	*−3 034*	*−2 181*	*−3 411*	*−3 575*
Current balance	936	−550	2 820	6 628	4 587	3 758	1 885	3 203	66	−3 671	−14 617
Transactions in external assets and liabilities[1]											
Investment overseas by UK residents											
Direct	−3 520	−5 889	−4 867	−6 005	−4 091	−5 417	−6 033	−8 799	−11 304	−18 615	−15 219
Portfolio	−1 073	−887	−3 310	−4 467	−7 565	−7 194	−9 870	−19 435	−23 068	2 702	−9 718
Total UK investment overseas	−4 593	−6 776	−8 175	−10 474	−11 656	−12 612	−15 903	−28 234	−34 379	−15 913	−24 937
Investment in the United Kingdom by overseas residents											
Direct	1 962	3 030	4 355	2 932	3 027	3 386	−181	3 784	4 846	8 108	7 346
Portfolio	−139	1 549	1 499	323	225	1 888	1 419	7 121	8 135	10 440	4 639
Total overseas investment in the United Kingdom	1 823	4 579	5 854	3 255	3 252	5 274	1 238	10 905	12 981	18 548	11 985
Foreign currency lending abroad by UK banks[2]	−163	−30 104	−29 836	−36 900	−16 521	−16 162	−9 439	−20 200	−47 885	−45 684	−14 692
Foreign currency borrowing abroad by UK banks[2]	−850	30 752	30 505	36 763	19 904	17 192	18 648	25 306	58 361	44 283	20 300
Net foreign currency transactions of UK banks	−1 013	648	669	−137	3 383	1 030	9 209	5 106	10 476	−1 401	5 608
Sterling lending abroad by UK banks	−1 030	210	−2 778	−3 019	−4 019	−2 232	−4 933	−1 635	−5 955	−4 638	−4 569
Sterling borrowing and deposit liabilities abroad of UK banks	57	2 788	3 044	2 497	4 421	3 945	6 149	4 155	5 605	8 547	13 556
Net sterling transactions of UK banks	−973	2 998	266	−522	402	1 713	1 216	2 520	−350	3 909	8 987
Deposits with and lending to banks abroad by UK non-bank private sector	−280	−1 138	−2 502	−1 864	−598	863	−3 239	−1 253	−2 782	−5 311	−3 035
Borrowing from banks abroad by:											
UK non-bank private sector	527	693	472	1 042	985	73	−2 176	2 598	3 735	2 069	3 830
Public corporations	182	246	−15	−178	−35	−35	−47	64	−31	−166	−253
General government	−7	46	−40	−192	58	78	49	87	100	104	−10
Official reserves (additions to −, drawings on +)	2 329	−1 059	−291	2 419	1 421	607	908	−1 758	−2 891	−12 012	−2 761
Other external assets of:											
UK non-bank private sector and public corporations	−459	−1 184	−209	−1 026	126	−161	1 281	533	1 933	433	812
General government	−181	−137	351	93	−161	−478	−743	−730	−509	−796	−891
Other external liabilities of:											
UK non-bank private sector and public corporations	472	605	301	224	119	−55	517	728	539	1 402	2 089
General government	−698	−263	−553	−14	351	−661	−89	−64	+78	1 466	912
Net transactions in assets and liabilities	−2 871	−742	−3 873	−7 370	−2 353	−4 366	−7 780	−9 497	−11 091	−7 667	2 334
Allocation of special drawing rights	–	195	180	158	–	–	–	–	–	–	–
Balancing item	1 935	1 097	873	584	−2 234	608	5 895	6 294	11 025	11 338	12 283

1 Assets: increase −/decrease +. Liabilities: increase +/decrease −.

2 See notes on page 233.

Source *Central Statistical Office*

13.2 Current account

£ million

	1978	1979	1980	1981	1982	1983	1984	1985	1986	1987	1988
Credits											
Exports (fob)	34 981	40 470	47 147	50 688	55 330	60 698	70 263	77 988	72 656	79 421	80 602
Services:											
General government	254	265	315	401	404	470	474	481	507	517	520
Private sector and public corporations											
Sea transport	3 149	3 804	3 816	3 784	3 267	3 054	3 253	3 271	3 230	3 302	3 551
Civil aviation	1 455	1 755	2 210	2 359	2 471	2 665	2 931	3 078	2 786	3 159	3 192
Travel	2 507	2 797	2 961	2 970	3 188	4 003	4 614	5 442	5 553	6 260	6 085
Financial and other services	5 130	5 803	6 373	7 487	8 283	9 467	10 655	12 379	13 716	14 425	14 583
Interest, profits and dividends											
General government	692	816	946	971	979	765	818	735	765	933	1 458
Private sector and public corporations	10 489	16 689	22 735	36 559	43 419	41 716	50 897	51 578	47 035	47 545	54 068
Transfers											
General government	439	550	958	1 675	2 154	2 235	2 392	1 870	2 138	2 271	2 119
Private sector	774	850	935	1 117	1 248	1 512	1 631	1 749	1 693	1 626	1 657
Total invisibles	24 889	33 330	41 249	57 322	65 412	65 887	77 665	80 583	77 421	80 037	87 233
Total credits	59 870	73 800	88 396	107 990	120 742	126 585	147 928	158 571	150 077	159 458	167 835
Debits											
Imports (fob)	36 574	43 814	45 792	47 418	53 422	62 207	75 432	81 120	82 020	90 350	101 428
Services:											
General government	986	1 073	1 165	1 264	1 754	1 522	1 655	1 780	1 907	2 117	2 353
Private sector and public corporations											
Sea transport	3 163	3 766	3 802	3 974	3 704	3 832	3 847	3 727	3 701	3 896	4 127
Civil aviation	1 175	1 450	1 827	1 979	2 172	2 345	2 694	2 925	3 200	3 778	4 054
Travel	1 549	2 109	2 738	3 272	3 640	4 090	4 663	4 871	6 083	7 280	8 127
Financial and other services	2 108	2 227	2 490	2 797	3 372	3 875	4 729	4 742	4 654	4 910	5 105
Interest, profits and dividends											
General government	650	682	895	940	1 091	1 188	1 328	1 478	1 667	2 023	2 296
Private sector and public corporations	9 725	15 618	22 991	35 380	41 858	38 434	45 939	48 072	40 768	41 467	47 612
Transfers											
General government	2 103	2 566	2 738	3 282	3 943	4 165	4 491	5 202	4 371	5 559	5 388
Private sector	901	1 044	1 139	1 057	1 200	1 167	1 266	1 451	1 641	1 749	1 963
Total invisibles	22 360	30 535	39 785	53 944	62 733	60 619	70 611	74 248	67 991	72 779	81 024
Total debits	58 934	74 349	85 577	101 362	116 155	122 826	146 043	155 368	150 011	163 129	182 452
Balances											
Visible balance	−1 593	−3 344	1 355	3 250	1 908	−1 509	−5 169	−3 132	−9 364	−10 929	−20 826
Services:											
General government	−732	−808	−850	−863	−1 350	−1 502	−1 181	−1 299	−1 400	−1 600	−1 833
Private sector and public corporations											
Sea transport	−14	38	14	−190	−437	−778	−594	−456	−471	−594	−576
Civil aviation	280	305	383	380	299	320	237	153	−414	−619	−862
Travel	958	688	223	−302	−452	−87	−49	571	−530	−1 020	−2 042
Financial and other services	3 022	3 576	3 883	4 690	4 911	5 592	5 926	7 637	9 062	9 515	9 478
Interest, profits and dividends											
General government	42	134	52	31	−113	−425	−511	−743	−902	−1 091	−837
Private sector and public corporations	764	1 071	−255	1 179	1 561	3 282	4 959	3 505	6 266	6 078	6 456
Transfers											
General government	−1 664	−2 016	−1 780	−1 607	−1 789	−1 930	−2 099	−3 332	−2 233	−3 288	−3 269
Private sector	−127	−194	−204	60	48	345	365	298	52	−123	−306
Invisibles balance	2 529	2 794	1 465	3 378	2 679	5 267	7 054	6 335	9 430	7 258	6 209
of which: private sector and public corporations: services and interest, profits and dividends	*5 010*	*5 678*	*4 248*	*5 757*	*5 882*	*8 329*	*10 479*	*11 410*	*13 913*	*13 360*	*12 454*
Current balance	936	−550	2 820	6 628	4 587	3 758	1 885	3 203	66	−3 671	−14 617

Source *Central Statistical Office*

13.3 Levels of UK external assets and liabilities

End of year

£ million

	1978	1979	1980	1981	1982	1983	1984	1985	1986	1987	1988
Assets											
General government	15 263	18 181	17 978	17 109	19 214	19 555	21 267	21 630	26 373	35 666	37 991
Public corporations	715	775	734	660	867	947	1 234	827	926	828	718
Private sector	151 227	180 360	212 244	312 587	395 984	466 587	604 394	579 180	704 089	669 803	732 295
Total	167 205	199 316	230 955	330 356	416 064	487 088	626 895	601 637	731 387	706 297	771 005
Liabilities											
General government	8 385	8 634	9 256	9 598	12 181	12 616	13 651	16 306	19 824	24 495	26 085
Public corporations	4 444	4 503	4 129	3 876	4 197	4 532	4 767	3 990	4 114	3 090	2 722
Private sector	140 961	172 773	199 769	284 658	357 051	414 907	527 171	498 418	594 663	588 591	648 181
Total	153 790	186 910	213 154	298 132	373 430	432 056	545 589	518 713	618 601	616 175	676 988
Net											
General government	6 878	9 547	8 722	7 511	7 032	6 938	7 616	5 324	6 549	11 171	11 906
Public corporations	−3 729	−3 728	−3 395	−3 216	−3 330	−3 586	−3 533	−3 163	−3 188	−2 261	−2 003
Private sector	10 266	6 587	12 474	27 929	38 933	51 680	77 223	80 763	109 426	81 212	84 114
Total	13 415	12 406	17 801	32 224	42 635	55 032	81 306	82 924	112 786	90 122	94 016

Source *Central Statistical Office*

13.4 United Kingdom public expenditure on overseas aid

Gross aid—analysis by major components[1]

£ million

	1977	1978	1979	1980	1981	1982	1983	1984	1985	1986	1987	1988
Total public expenditure on overseas aid	611.7	752.0	939.4	966.5	1 150.7	1 085.3	1 174.3	1 315.6	1 324.5	1 349.6	1 298.0	1 657.4
Bilateral: total	405.8	564.2	682.6	702.6	804.4	673.9	693.5	784.2	830.5	839.9	775.1	998.7
Project aid: total	137.3	188.7	270.0	288.8	425.1	308.0	325.6	405.3	368.4	391.2	259.2	337.3
Overseas Development Administration excluding ATP	101.4	155.3	189.3	219.7	323.8	194.2	236.9	239.8	238.3	249.4	163.9	169.9
Aid and Trade Provision (ATP)	–	1.3	36.8	24.0	33.3	62.6	32.6	51.5	42.4	78.2	29.2	55.8
Commonwealth Development Corporation	35.9	32.2	44.0	45.1	68.0	51.1	56.0	114.0	87.7	63.7	66.1	111.6
Non-project aid	124.9	202.3	202.9	160.4	130.9	121.5	103.7	104.4	148.3	119.6	140.9	193.7
Technical co-operation	126.6	153.2	185.7	223.3	216.4	211.4	231.2	239.5	277.6	292.8	330.0	411.5
Administrative costs	17.0	20.0	24.0	30.0	32.0	33.0	33.0	35.0	36.0	36.0	45.0	46.4
Multilateral: total	205.9	187.8	256.8	263.9	346.3	411.4	480.8	531.3	494.0	509.6	522.9	658.7
European Community	55.2	44.5	117.8	120.4	158.1	173.8	188.7	225.6	234.1	223.3	222.0	273.8
World Bank Group	88.9	64.5	43.9	73.4	115.5	153.7	205.5	197.4	128.1	153.7	157.3	228.8
UN Agencies	42.8	53.8	68.9	48.0	48.6	58.0	57.3	65.8	83.9	81.2	99.6	110.2
Other multilateral	18.9	25.1	26.1	22.1	24.1	25.9	29.3	42.6	47.9	51.5	43.9	45.8

1 See introductory notes on page 233.

Source *Overseas Development Administration*

13.5 United Kingdom public expenditure on overseas aid

Gross bilateral aid-analysis by main recipient countries

£ million

	1978	1979	1980	1981	1982	1983	1984	1985	1986	1987	1988
Total bilateral aid	564.2	682.6	702.6	804.4	673.9	694.3	784.2	830.5	839.9	775.1	998.7
Africa: total	176.7	230.7	257.0	266.8	247.2	237.6	268.0	315.4	284.7	304.7	421.9
Botswana	5.6	8.0	11.5	10.2	7.6	13.3	16.0	8.8	12.3	12.2	8.3
Cameroon	1.0	1.1	5.2	3.5	3.1	3.1	5.6	7.5	3.7	6.8	5.4
Ethiopia	2.8	2.9	1.9	0.6	5.6	3.4	7.0	28.1	9.6	8.6	19.2
Egypt	3.7	17.8	12.2	8.1	7.5	10.6	15.4	19.1	15.7	7.9	18.7
Gambia	3.6	2.5	2.3	2.3	2.5	2.4	3.6	3.6	9.9	7.2	6.5
Ghana	4.5	11.2	15.6	7.5	7.0	6.7	3.8	11.7	19.5	20.0	32.9
Kenya	31.3	33.1	31.7	39.7	37.4	31.9	38.3	34.4	33.8	28.5	49.4
Malawi	16.0	24.9	16.5	16.0	17.0	14.6	13.0	22.4	15.3	24.9	46.5
Mauritius	1.4	2.6	2.7	2.8	1.7	1.3	1.4	2.2	5.8	8.1	6.4
Mozambique	5.8	6.4	4.6	5.4	1.9	2.4	4.2	8.4	7.4	22.8	30.5
Nigeria	9.8	5.1	4.9	4.2	4.9	5.5	5.6	6.2	5.6	6.6	7.5
St. Helena and Dependencies	3.7	3.9	3.8	4.1	5.8	6.5	7.5	9.4	9.2	12.2	15.2
Somalia	1.0	1.3	2.8	2.4	2.5	2.5	2.1	1.7	3.9	7.3	6.7
Sudan	7.1	13.9	22.6	32.7	39.4	32.2	27.4	42.3	26.0	20.3	25.8
Swaziland	8.7	8.4	6.5	4.1	6.4	5.7	5.6	3.5	6.4	3.5	5.1
Tanzania	10.4	24.1	32.1	30.0	27.3	30.4	33.0	18.0	12.7	28.8	33.5
Uganda	1.1	2.2	2.9	15.1	10.6	6.1	7.1	9.2	8.6	12.2	28.6
Zambia	33.3	29.2	20.7	24.1	14.2	15.5	32.9	25.6	35.4	25.6	16.7
Zimbabwe	3.5	5.1	36.4	17.1	21.5	19.5	15.1	23.6	12.5	12.5	23.9
Other Countries	22.6	28.2	28.3	40.9	37.7	24.1	23.5	29.9	31.4	28.8	35.2
America: total	53.4	42.4	36.5	49.0	92.2	67.9	58.4	70.3	58.0	61.4	69.7
Barbados	0.3	0.7	0.6	3.6	2.5	0.4	0.3	0.3	0.4	0.5	0.5
Belize	3.9	7.5	4.4	4.8	2.9	6.1	6.0	5.7	3.2	2.1	3.2
Brazil	0.7	1.0	1.0	0.6	10.0	5.6	7.8	4.0	0.9	0.8	1.4
Costa Rica	0.5	0.6	0.6	0.6	0.5	1.8	1.7	12.7	10.0	2.8	1.6
Ecuador	1.8	1.9	0.9	0.8	1.0	0.8	0.9	0.9	0.8	2.6	1.5
Falkland Islands	2.1	0.9	1.0	1.1	4.0	9.1	6.0	10.7	10.3	8.2	4.3
Guyana	6.4	2.6	2.4	2.5	1.7	1.6	0.4	0.4	0.5	0.6	0.5
Honduras	0.3	0.2	0.3	5.0	2.3	6.7	3.4	3.7	1.3	0.8	1.2
Jamaica	19.6	6.4	4.8	8.7	8.9	8.9	15.2	8.0	3.8	16.1	20.0
Mexico	0.8	1.2	1.6	1.5	34.3	2.8	0.5	0.8	0.8	0.6	1.2
St. Lucia	0.6	0.8	1.2	2.2	1.6	2.6	0.5	0.5	1.0	3.2	2.8
Turks and Caicos Islands	1.4	1.0	1.3	3.4	5.7	4.2	3.9	3.6	5.4	5.4	4.2
Other countries	11.3	12.1	11.4	10.1	12.7	17.3	11.6	19.1	19.7	17.7	27.1
Asia: total	218.7	292.3	264.0	317.4	182.2	244.8	306.2	255.3	315.6	216.1	298.5
Bangladesh	44.0	33.8	66.2	33.4	23.5	24.7	35.7	41.2	38.3	34.8	42.0
Burma	1.4	2.8	6.5	5.3	3.4	1.8	0.8	1.0	2.9	4.7	2.2
China	–	–	0.0	0.1	0.0	0.2	0.6	1.2	2.2	4.0	28.4
India	118.9	153.3	86.1	168.6	54.2	127.6	146.5	106.5	143.5	78.5	101.0
Indonesia	6.5	13.1	11.2	15.3	17.2	12.4	28.3	33.6	8.9	12.2	17.4
Jordan	3.1	13.6	4.7	7.1	3.3	2.7	6.1	2.3	5.6	4.8	4.1
Malaysia	1.5	1.6	10.5	10.1	6.4	3.9	5.0	7.5	55.5	9.8	10.1
Nepal	4.4	11.2	6.8	8.0	9.6	7.4	8.6	9.7	9.9	10.0	10.8
Pakistan	18.2	27.7	22.2	24.6	18.7	16.6	18.0	16.6	20.7	22.5	23.3
Philippines	0.2	0.8	3.2	3.3	1.2	3.7	3.8	1.8	0.2	0.3	1.0
Sri Lanka	8.3	14.1	32.9	26.3	33.3	29.5	26.2	17.3	16.0	18.7	21.7
Thailand	1.3	5.0	4.7	7.8	4.0	5.6	20.0	7.4	4.2	5.4	23.2
Yemen North (YAR)	1.3	1.8	2.7	2.5	2.8	3.8	3.1	3.1	3.8	5.2	6.6
Other countries	8.0	11.8	5.0	3.3	3;7	5.0	3.5	6.1	3.8	5.2	6.6
Europe: total	17.1	8.6	14.2	37.3	19.6	8.8	9.6	33.5	19.4	13.1	12.6
Gibraltar	1.9	3.2	4.9	4.0	1.9	2.4	8.2	22.5	14.3	9.0	9.2
Malta	3.8	0.3	0.2	0.2	0.2	0.2	0.1	0.1	0.1	0.1	0.1
Turkey	0.6	4.3	8.0	32.1	16.9	5.4	0.4	10.3	4.6	3.0	2.5
Other countries	10.8	0.8	1.1	1.0	0.6	0.9	0.9	0.7	0.4	1.0	0.7
Oceania: total	30.4	28.6	36.3	33.0	31.6	24.7	27.3	22.2	26.1	28.7	35.6
Fiji	5.1	6.9	5.3	7.0	8.7	4.0	4.7	4.0	7.1	2.0	1.2
Kiribati and Tuvalu	4.5	3.7	7.1	6.0	7.3	7.4	6.5	4.9	3.9	9.5	7.5
Papua New Guinea	2.4	3.1	3.7	7.0	3.8	0.1	–	2.3	4.9	6.6	14.6
Solomon Islands	10.4	7.4	10.0	7.3	6.3	6.8	7.3	4.1	3.7	4.2	5.2
Vanuatu	7.6	6.7	8.7	4.6	4.3	5.9	8.1	6.0	5.4	5.5	5.6
Other countries	0.4	0.8	1.5	1.1	1.2	0.5	0.6	1.0	1.0	0.9	1.4
Unallocated: total	48.0	56.0	64.6	68.9	68.1	77.5	79.8	97.8	100.1	106.2	114.2
Administrative costs	20.0	24.0	30.0	32.0	33.0	33.0	35.0	36.0	36.0	45.0	46.4

1 See introductory notes on page 233.

Source *Overseas Development Administration*

14 National Income and Expenditure

The tables which follow are taken from those in *United Kingdom National Accounts 1989 Edition,* (the *CSO Blue Book*) published by Her Majesty's Stationery Office (September 1989). Some of the figures are provisional and may have to be revised later; this applies particularly to the figures for 1987 and 1988. The 1983 and earlier editions were called *National Income and Expenditure*.

From the 1987 edition, *The Blue Book* contains a brief introduction to the UK system of national accounts outlining some of the main concepts and principles of measurement used. This shows how the aggregate figures describing the whole economy are related to one another and to figures in the sector accounts. A more detailed description of the statistics, together with a detailed description of the sources, methods and definitions used in making the estimates, is given in *United Kingdom National Accounts: Sources and Methods Third Edition* (HMSO 1985). Further information on the structure and inter-relationships of the tables in the national accounts is given in *The National Accounts—A short guide* (HMSO 1981).

In the tables in this section, analyses by industry are based, as far as possible, on the Standard Industrial Classification 1980.

The first aggregate measured in these tables is the **Gross domestic product** (GDP).

This is a concept of the value of the total economic activity taking place in UK territory. It can be viewed as incomes earned, as expenditures incurred, or as production. Adding net property income from abroad produces **Gross national product** (GNP). This is a concept of the value of all incomes earned by UK residents. **National income,** or Net national product, is GNP net of depreciation (that is, after deducting what is required to keep real capital intact).

The definitive estimate of GDP, which is recommended for assessing levels and medium and long-term changes is the average estimate, GDP(A). GDP(A) is derived using three broadly independent measures: the expenditure-based measure, GDP(E); the income-based measure, GDP(I); and the output-based measure, GDP(O). Such measures as GNP, National income, and Gross national disposable income (GNDI), can then be derived from GDP(A) as the best central estimates.

From the 1988 *CSO Blue Book,* constant price series are expressed in 1985 prices, rather than, as formerly, in 1980 prices.

Gross national product (*Table 14.1*). The upper half of this table shows the various money flows which generate the gross domestic product and the gross national product. These include expenditure by UK final buyers—that is, expenditure on goods and services other than for use in current production and resale—and expenditure on British exports by overseas purchasers. The sum of these two items overstates the amount of income generated in the United Kingdom by the value of imports of goods and services; this item is therefore subtracted to produce gross domestic product at market prices. Deducting taxes on expenditure and adding subsidies produces the expenditure-based measure of the gross domestic product at factor cost, which is equivalent to the sum of the incomes of the factors of production before deduction of depreciation (capital consumption).

The lower half of the table shows the contribution to the gross national product of the different factors of production. The profit items in the table—income from self-employment, trading profits of companies, trading surpluses of public corporations and of other public enterprises—are shown before any deduction for depreciation and before providing for stock appreciation. (Stock appreciation is the change in value of stocks due to the change, if any, in the prices at which stocks are valued in the reckoning of profits.) This element of stock appreciation is deducted in reckoning the total of the gross national product.

Personal income and expenditure (*Table 14.2*). 'Persons' are here defined as including unincorporated businesses and private non-profit-making bodies serving persons. Income is shown gross before providing for depreciation or stock appreciation. Employers' national insurance contributions (but not the surcharge) are treated as employee income taxed at source and therefore appear under both income and expenditure. Personal income also includes employers' contributions to pension funds. Personal saving before providing for depreciation or stock appreciation is estimated as a residual and is subject to a wide margin of error.

Corporate sector appropriation account (*Table 14.3*). This table covers companies and public corporations. Trading profits earned in the United Kingdom are shown both before and after providing for stock appreciation but before deduction of depreciation allowances. Profits from operations outside the United Kingdom are included under income earned abroad. Dividends paid by one company to another are excluded both from dividends and from non-trading income.

Current account of general government (*Table 14.4*). This table is a consolidation of central government and local authorities' transactions on current account.

Summary capital account (*Table 14.5*). This table brings together the saving and investment of the several sectors of the economy and shows the total investment at home and overseas.

The index of output of the production industries (*Table 14.6*) (index of production), which accounts for 34½ per cent of the output measure of gross domestic product shown in the same table, provides a general measure of changes in the volume of industrial production in the United Kingdom. Production industries comprise Division 1, energy and water supply (coal mining, oil and gas extraction, production of other fuels and water) and Divisions 2 to 4, manufacturing. The index of production is prepared by the Central Statistical Office in collaboration with the statistics divisions of other government departments and is published monthly, approximately six weeks after the end of the month to which it relates. The indices are calculated currently with 1985 as the base year, with the volume of production in other periods expressed as a percentage of the average monthly production in 1985. Annual series for broad industry groups from 1948, and quarterly series from 1952, are published in *Economic Trends Annual Supplement* (HMSO) and for more recent periods, along with monthly data, in *Economic Trends* (HMSO). More detailed monthly index of production series are published in the *Monthly Digest of Statistics* (HMSO).

The index of production is a weighted average of 291 indicators, each representing the 'value added' by an individual industry or part of an industry as its contribution to total output of the United Kingdom. The weight given to each industry is proportional to its contribution to gross domestic product at factor cost in 1985; that is to say, the value the industry adds to its purchased materials, fuels and services. This is equal to the sum of income from employment *plus* profits after the deduction of stock appreciation. The weights are derived from the Annual Census of Production for that year, constrained to the aggregates shown in Table 2.1 of *United Kingdom National Account 1989 Edition* (HMSO). The weights shown in the table are those used in the compilation of the index from 1983 onwards. The 1985-based data were linked to the figures for earlier years on the basis of the annual figures for 1983 (see notes on rebasing below).

The gross output (that is, the total production) of an industry is the most frequently used proxy indicator for assessing change in value added, since the latter is difficult to measure in the short-term. In some cases the volume of production can be measured and such indicators make up about two-fifths of the index of production. About three-fifths of the index of production is derived from the volume of sales or deliveries or their value deflated by the relevant producer prices indices: however, adjustments for changes to stocks and work done in the industries represented by these indicators are made at a more aggregate level. A very small proportion of the index of production is derived from work done or input of labour or materials indicators. For further notes on the general method of constructing the index on the 1980 base see Industry Statistics: Occasional Paper No 18 *Series and weights used in the index of output of the production industries—1980 base* (CSO 1983), which is obtainable from the Central Statistical Office, Branch C3, Room 131/2, Great George Street, London SW1P 3AQ, price £20.00 (cheques payable to *Central Statistical Office*). An updated paper, to reflect the 1985-based series and weights is now available.

The index of production along with the national accounts is rebased at five-yearly intervals. Regular rebasing is required because the rate of growth in relative prices of net output of the various sectors may vary over time. In addition, the relative importance of each sector may change because of advances of technology, or variations in the pattern of demand for its goods. Index numbers for 1983 onwards were recalculated when the index was rebased onto 1985 = 100 in August 1988. The index numbers up to 1983 (on a 1980 = 100 base) were linked to the later figures by a simple rescaling of series, using the two sets of index numbers for 1983. An article describing the effect of rebasing for 1989 appeared in *Economic Trends* in February 1989.

Industrial classification. The industrial analysis of the index of production is in conformity with the *Standard Industrial Classification Revised 1980* (HMSO) to which reference should be made for the details of the composition of each industrial group.

Market sector classification. These groupings combine the output of industries which meet broadly similar categories of demand: consumer goods, investment goods and intermediate goods (materials and fuels). Because the index of production measures the output of an industry and not of commodities, each market sector group will include some output from the other sector. The industrial composition of the market sectors on the 1980 base is set out in Industry Statistics: Occasional Paper No 21 *Supplementary analyses of series used in the index of output of the production industries 1980 base* (CSO 1983) which is obtainable from the Central Statistical Office, price £20.00 (address shown above). An updated paper, to reflect the 1985-based detail is now available.

Gross domestic product by industry (*Table 14.7*). This table shows the contribution of each industry to the gross domestic product, measured as the sum of incomes, before providing for depreciation, arising in the industry. This is also equal to the 'value added' by the industry, that is, the excess of the value of its current output over the value of goods and services purchased from outside the industry and used in production.

Expenditure and output at constant prices (*Tables 14.6 and 14.8*). These tables contain two virtually independent estimates of the gross domestic product of the United Kingdom at 1985 prices. The estimates in Table 14.6 are based on the index of industrial production and other statistics relating to the volume of output; those in Table 14.8 have been derived by revaluing estimates of final expenditure on goods and services at average 1985 prices. With full and accurate information the two methods would in theory lead to the same result. In practice, because there are numerous imperfections and gaps in the data, the two methods produce different results. Table 14.8 is expressed in £ million at 1985 prices, whereas Table 14.6 is expressed in index form, taking 1985 = 100. For a general account of the methods of compiling the output index numbers, see *United Kingdom National Accounts: Sources and Methods Third Edition*. See also *Series and weights used in estimating the gross domestic product at constant factor cost, 1980 = 100*, Industry Statistics: Occasional Paper No 20 (CSO 1984) for a list of series and weights currently used outside the production and construction industries, in compiling the index numbers, which is obtainable from the Central Statistical Office, price £20.00 (address shown above).

Consumers' expenditure at current and constant prices (*Table 14.9*). Consumers' expenditure is a major component of final expenditure contributing to gross domestic product calculated by the expenditure method, at current prices (*Table 14.1*) and at constant prices (*Table 14.8*).

Consumers' expenditure consists of personal expenditure on goods and services for current use. It is now classified in two ways, first in certain commodity groups which are also available on a quarterly basis in the *Monthly Digest of Statistics* and secondly (in more detail) according to purpose. It includes the value of income-in-kind; imputed rent of owner-occupied dwellings; and final expenditure by private non-profit-making bodies serving persons. It excludes business expenditure allowed as deductions in computing income for tax purposes of both employed and self-employed persons.

It includes expenditure on durable goods, for instance motor cars, which from the point of view of the individual might more appropriately be treated as capital expenditure. The only exceptions are the purchase of land and dwellings and costs incurred in connection with the transfer of their ownership and expenditure on major improvements by occupiers, which are treated as personal capital expenditure.

The estimates of consumers' expenditure include purchases of second-hand as well as new goods, *less* the proceeds of sales of used goods.

Table 14.12: **National accounts aggregates**, gives two different kinds of information. The first part deals with National disposable income, which measures the total disposable income of the country's residents, that is, the command they have over resources. The second part gives volume indices at 1985 prices for the main estimates of total UK economic activity, and for the components of the expenditure-based estimate.

Value of physical increase in stocks and work in progress (*Table 14.13*). This table gives a broad analysis by industry, and, for manufacturing industry, by asset, of the physical increase in stocks and work in progress. For most industries, the physical increase at current prices equals the change in the book value of stocks *less* stock appreciation.

Gross domestic fixed capital formation (*Table 14.14*). Fixed capital formation comprises expenditure on the replacement of, and additions to, the stock of fixed capital assets located in the United Kingdom, including all ships and aircraft of UK ownership.

Gross capital stock (*Table 14.15*). The table shows estimates of the value of the reproducible capital assets (buildings, plant and machinery, vehicles, ships and aircraft) owned by various industry groups, without allowance for depreciation during the expended proportions of asset lives. The estimates are expressed at 1985 replacement cost. Leased assets are mainly included under 'distributive trades and other service industries' on the basis of ownership. A rough analysis of these assets, which still constitute only a small proportion of total gross capital stock, appears in *United Kingdom National Accounts 1989 Edition*.

14.1 National product: categories of expenditure and factor incomes

£ million

	1978	1979	1980	1981	1982	1983	1984	1985	1986	1987	1988
Categories of expenditure at current market prices:											
Consumers' expenditure	100 847	119 516	139 016	154 701	169 816	185 895	198 895	217 023	239 156	261 698	293 569
General government final consumption	33 404	38 883	49 018	55 452	60 440	65 866	69 857	73 879	79 645	85 540	91 847
of which: Central government	*20 146*	*23 401*	*29 989*	*33 879*	*37 000*	*40 654*	*43 142*	*45 879*	*48 806*	*52 059*	*55 721*
Local authorities	*13 258*	*15 482*	*19 029*	*21 573*	*23 440*	*25 212*	*26 715*	*28 000*	*30 839*	*33 481*	*36 126*
Gross domestic fixed capital formation	31 060	36 925	41 561	41 304	44 824	48 615	54 960	60 343	64 399	73 570	88 751
Value of physical increase in stocks and work in progress	1 804	2 162	−2 572	−2 768	−1 188	1 465	1 287	615	696	1 276	4 371
Total domestic expenditure	167 115	197 486	227 023	248 689	273 892	301 841	324 999	351 860	383 896	422 084	478 538
Exports of goods and services	47 476	54 894	62 822	67 669	72 943	80 357	92 190	102 639	98 448	107 084	108 533
of which: Goods	*34 981*	*40 470*	*47 147*	*50 668*	*55 330*	*60 698*	*70 263*	*77 988*	*72 656*	*79 421*	*80 602*
Services	*12 495*	*14 424*	*15 675*	*17 001*	*17 613*	*19 659*	*21 927*	*24 651*	*25 792*	*27 663*	*27 931*
Total final expenditure	214 591	252 380	289 845	316 358	346 835	382 198	417 189	454 499	482 344	529 168	587 071
less Imports of goods and services[1]	−45 555	−54 439	−57 814	−60 704	−68 064	−77 871	−93 020	−99 165	−101 565	−112 331	−125 194
of which: Goods	*−36 574*	*−43 814*	*−45 792*	*−47 418*	*−53 422*	*−62 207*	*−75 432*	*−81 120*	*−82 020*	*−90 350*	*−101 428*
Services	*−8 981*	*−10 625*	*−12 022*	*−13 286*	*−14 642*	*−15 664*	*−17 588*	*−18 045*	*−19 545*	*−21 981*	*−23 766*
Gross domestic product (expenditure-based)[2]	169 036	197 941	232 031	255 654	278 771	304 327	324 169	355 334	380 779	416 837	461 877
Statistical discrepancy (expenditure adjustment)[3]	−913	−110	−759	−1 361	−365	−695	271	−5	−156	941	2 056
Gross domestic product (average estimate)[2]	168 123	197 831	231 272	254 293	278 406	303 632	324 440	355 329	380 623	417 778	463 933
Net property income from abroad	806	1 205	−204	1 210	1 449	2 857	4 449	2 763	5 364	4 987	5 619
Gross national product (average estimate)[4]	168 929	199 036	231 068	255 503	279 855	306 489	328 889	358 092	385 987	422 765	469 552
Factor cost adjustment											
Taxes on expenditure	22 756	29 670	36 474	42 465	46 467	49 502	52 595	56 672	62 743	68 349	75 029
Subsidies	3 775	4 643	5 719	6 369	5 811	6 269	7 538	7 202	6 151	6 126	5 883
Factor cost adjustment (taxes less subsidies)	18 981	25 027	30 755	36 096	40 656	43 233	45 057	49 470	56 592	62 223	69 146
Factor incomes											
Income from employment	98 843	115 866	137 614	149 573	158 622	169 586	180 145	194 865	209 830	225 945	249 775
Income from self-employment[5]	13 539	15 811	17 928	19 937	22 076	24 314	27 382	29 466	33 600	38 044	42 617
Gross trading profits of companies[5, 6]	22 382	29 240	27 918	27 295	31 460	39 837	44 967	52 572	48 327	61 281	70 242
Gross trading surplus of public corporations[4]	5 393	5 594	6 162	7 821	9 347	9 847	8 204	7 025	7 953	6 713	7 286
Gross trading surplus of general government enterprises[4]	216	180	180	236	216	50	−117	243	145	−58	−70
Rent	10 036	11 951	14 243	16 365	17 699	18 763	19 807	21 646	23 406	25 258	27 464
Imputed charge for consumption of non-trading capital	1 445	1 707	2 103	2 334	2 403	2 465	2 578	2 776	3 005	3 214	3 408
Total domestic income[5]	151 854	180 349	206 148	223 561	241 823	264 862	282 966	308 593	326 266	360 387	400 722
less Stock appreciation	−4 228	−8 837	−6 391	−5 974	−4 276	−4 204	−4 509	−2 739	−1 766	−4 746	−6 116
Gross domestic product (income-based)	147 626	171 512	199 757	217 587	237 547	260 658	278 457	305 854	324 500	355 651	394 606
Statistical discrepancy (income adjustment)[3]	1 516	1 292	760	610	203	−259	926	5	−469	−96	181
Gross domestic product (average estimate) at factor cost	149 142	172 804	200 517	218 197	237 750	260 399	279 383	305 859	324 031	355 555	394 787
Net property income from abroad	806	1 205	−204	1 210	1 449	2 857	4 449	2 763	5 364	4 987	5 619
Gross national product (average estimate)[4]	149 948	174 009	200 313	219 407	239 199	263 256	283 832	308 622	329 395	360 542	400 406
less Capital consumption	−19 378	−22 827	−27 952	−31 641	−33 653	−36 150	−38 725	−41 886	−45 178	−48 366	−54 769
Net national product at factor cost (average estimate): "National income"[4]	130 570	151 182	172 361	187 766	205 546	227 106	245 107	266 736	284 217	312 176	345 637
Value indices, at current prices (1985=100)											
Gross domestic product (expenditure-based)											
At market prices	47.6	55.7	65.3	71.9	78.5	85.6	91.2	100.0	107.2	117.3	130.0
At factor cost	49.1	56.5	65.8	71.8	77.8	85.4	91.3	100.0	106.0	115.9	128.4
Gross domestic product (income-based) at factor cost	48.3	56.1	65.3	71.1	77.7	85.2	91.0	100.0	106.1	116.3	129.0
Gross domestic product (average estimate)											
At market prices ("money GDP")	47.3	55.7	65.1	71.6	78.4	85.5	91.3	100.0	107.1	117.6	130.6
At factor cost	48.8	56.5	65.6	71.3	77.7	85.1	91.3	100.0	105.9	116.2	129.1

1 Excluding taxes on expenditure levied on imports.
2 Including taxes on expenditure levied on imports.
3 The Statistical discrepancies (expenditure adjustment and income adjustment) are each part of the Residual error.
4 Expenditure-based estimates of Gross national product and of National income can be derived as in previous issues of this publication. The derivation is shown in 'United Kingdom National Accounts' 1989 Edition Methodology notes.
5 Before providing for depreciation and stock appreciation.
6 Including financial institutions.

Source Central Statistical Office

14.2 Personal income and expenditure

£ million

	1978	1979	1980	1981	1982	1983	1984	1985	1986	1987	1988
Income before tax											
Income from employment:											
Wages and salaries	84 001	98 424	116 544	125 184	133 341	142 355	151 870	165 247	179 048	194 108	215 287
Pay in cash and kind of HM Forces	1 645	2 020	2 436	2 689	2 905	3 121	3 288	3 590	3 833	4 093	4 335
Total	85 646	100 444	118 980	127 873	136 246	145 476	155 158	168 837	182 881	198 201	219 622
Employers' contributions:											
Social security	6 069	6 889	8 210	8 814	9 344	10 536	11 269	12 248	13 386	14 504	16 511
Other	7 128	8 533	10 424	12 886	13 032	13 574	13 718	13 780	13 563	13 240	13 642
Total income from employment	98 843	115 866	137 614	149 573	158 622	169 586	180 145	194 865	209 830	225 945	249 775
Income from self-employment:											
After deducting stock appreciation	13 092	15 035	17 209	19 311	21 714	23 764	27 057	28 992	33 438	37 546	41 895
Stock appreciation	447	776	719	626	362	550	325	474	162	498	722
Total[1]	13 539	15 811	17 928	19 937	22 076	24 314	27 382	29 466	33 600	38 044	42 617
Rent, dividends and net interest:											
Receipts by life assurance and pension schemes	4 766	6 406	7 790	8 762	10 505	11 785	14 017	15 872	17 497	20 307	22 739
Imputed rent of owner-occupied dwellings	5 403	6 522	7 830	9 114	10 160	11 181	11 917	12 783	13 653	14 463	15 504
Other receipts, net	2 528	3 696	3 622	3 233	3 260	2 825	1 169	965	382	−745	2 635
Total	12 697	16 624	19 242	21 109	23 925	25 791	27 103	29 620	31 532	34 025	40 878
Social security benefits and other current grants from general government	17 871	20 917	25 524	31 242	36 584	39 856	43 020	46 792	50 850	52 580	54 207
Current transfers from overseas	774	850	935	1 117	1 248	1 512	1 631	1 749	1 693	1 626	1 657
Current transfers to charities from companies	45	51	52	62	69	86	105	119	145	160	179
Imputed charge for capital consumption of private non-profit making bodies	266	308	368	403	409	416	431	458	485	502	514
Total personal income[1]	144 035	170 427	201 663	223 443	242 933	261 561	279 817	303 069	328 135	352 882	389 827
Deductions from income											
UK taxes on income	19 460	21 586	25 683	28 969	31 396	33 230	34 551	37 599	40 834	43 650	48 655
Social security contributions	10 101	11 526	13 939	15 916	18 095	20 780	22 322	24 213	26 069	28 188	31 686
Current transfers abroad	901	1 044	1 139	1 057	1 200	1 167	1 266	1 451	1 641	1 749	1 963
Miscellaneous current transfers	151	134	169	177	187	222	215	225	258	329	353
Personal disposable income[2]	113 422	136 137	160 733	177 324	192 055	206 162	221 463	239 581	259 333	278 966	307 170
Expenditure											
Consumers' expenditure	100 847	119 516	139 016	154 701	169 816	185 895	198 895	217 023	239 156	261 698	293 569
Balance: saving[2]	12 575	16 621	21 717	22 623	22 239	20 267	22 568	22 558	20 177	17 268	13 601
Total	113 422	136 137	160 733	177 324	192 055	206 162	221 463	239 581	259 333	278 966	307 170
Memorandum items											
Saving ratio (per cent)[3]	*11.1*	*12.2*	*13.5*	*12.8*	*11.6*	*9.8*	*10.2*	*9.4*	*7.8*	*6.2*	*4.4*
Real personal disposable income[4]:											
At 1985 prices	210 047	221 999	225 532	223 715	222 857	227 887	232 945	239 581	248 434	257 309	269 867
1985 = 100	87.7	92.7	94.1	93.4	93.0	95.1	97.2	100.0	103.7	107.4	112.6

1 Before providing for depreciation and stock appreciation.
2 Before providing for depreciation, stock appreciation and additions to tax reserves.
3 Saving as a percentage of personal disposable income.
4 Personal disposable income revalued by the implied consumers' expenditure deflator (1985 = 100).

Source *Central Statistical Office*

14.3 Corporate sector appropriation account[1]

£ million

	1978	1979	1980	1981	1982	1983	1984	1985	1986	1987	1988
Income											
Income arising in the United Kingdom:											
Gross trading profits of companies and trading surplus:											
After deducting stock appreciation	23 994	26 773	28 408	29 768	36 893	46 030	48 987	57 332	54 676	63 746	72 134
Stock appreciation	3 781	8 061	5 672	5 348	3 914	3 654	4 184	2 265	1 604	4 248	5 394
Total[2]	27 775	34 834	34 080	35 116	40 807	49 684	53 171	59 597	56 280	67 994	77 528
Rent and non-trading income	9 076	12 637	16 968	18 867	20 517	20 528	24 059	29 962	31 591	33 892	37 594
Total	36 851	47 471	51 048	53 983	61 324	70 212	77 230	89 559	87 871	101 886	115 122
Income from abroad[3,4]	4 522	7 096	7 230	8 962	9 235	11 297	14 371	15 369	15 943	18 490	21 109
Total income	41 373	54 567	58 278	62 945	70 559	81 509	91 601	104 928	103 814	120 376	136 231
Allocation of income											
Dividends and interest payments[5]	10 278	15 121	19 463	20 396	22 872	22 732	25 303	32 537	34 088	37 611	45 857
Current transfers to charities from companies	45	51	52	62	69	86	107	123	158	184	208
Profits due abroad, net of UK tax[3]	2 229	3 992	4 769	4 695	4 659	5 258	6 271	7 499	5 204	6 601	7 370
UK taxes on income[6]	4 099	5 064	6 665	8 657	10 569	12 118	14 230	10 540	14 286	15 208	17 200
Royalties and licence fees on oil and gas production	286	531	1 156	1 362	1 600	1 887	2 459	2 366	941	1 151	820
Balance: undistributed income after taxation[7]	24 436	29 808	26 173	27 773	30 790	39 428	43 231	45 863	49 137	59 621	64 776
Total	41 373	54 567	58 278	62 945	70 559	81 509	91 601	104 928	103 814	120 376	136 231

1 The sum of two subsectors, namely public corporations plus companies and financial institutions. Flows between the two constituent subsectors are not netted out.
2 Before providing for depreciation and stock appreciation.
3 After deducting depreciation allowances but before providing for stock appreciation.
4 Includes net receipts of interest by UK banks and other financial institutions on their foreign currency lending to and borrowing from overseas residents.
5 Excludes dividends and debenture interest payments by UK subsidiaries to their overseas parents. After 6 April 1973 figures are net of advance corporation tax.
6 From April 1973 figures reflect change to imputation system of corporation tax.
7 Before providing for depreciation, stock appreciation and additions to tax reserves.

Source *Central Statistical Office*

14.4 General government current account

£ million

	1978	1979	1980	1981	1982	1983	1984	1985	1986	1987	1988
Receipts											
Taxes on income	22 624	25 239	31 002	36 249	40 392	43 484	46 789	51 685	52 183	55 403	61 123
Taxes on expenditure	22 756	29 670	36 474	42 465	46 467	49 502	52 595	56 672	62 743	68 349	75 029
Social security contributions	10 101	11 526	13 939	15 916	18 095	20 780	22 322	24 213	26 069	28 188	31 686
Gross trading surplus[1]	216	180	180	236	216	50	–117	243	145	–58	–70
Rent, dividends and interest, etc	5 368	6 525	8 206	9 171	10 149	9 933	10 502	11 769	10 003	10 414	10 308
Miscellaneous current transfers	151	134	169	177	187	222	217	229	271	353	382
Imputed charge for consumption of non-trading capital	1 179	1 399	1 735	1 931	1 994	2 049	2 147	2 318	2 520	2 712	2 894
Total	62 395	74 673	91 705	106 145	117 500	126 020	134 455	147 129	153 934	165 361	181 352
Expenditure											
Final consumption	33 404	38 883	49 018	55 452	60 440	65 866	69 857	73 879	79 645	85 540	91 847
Subsidies	3 775	4 643	5 719	6 369	5 811	6 269	7 538	7 202	6 151	6 126	5 883
Social security benefits	15 417	18 122	21 813	27 002	31 677	32 336	34 350	37 609	40 860	42 176	43 331
Other current grants to personal sector	2 454	2 795	3 711	4 240	4 907	7 520	8 670	9 183	9 990	10 404	10 876
Current grants paid abroad (net)	1 664	2 016	1 780	1 607	1 789	1 930	2 099	3 332	2 233	3 288	3 269
Debt interest	7 093	8 669	10 873	12 703	13 975	14 188	15 754	17 455	17 129	17 758	18 027
Total current expenditure	63 807	75 128	92 914	107 373	118 599	128 109	138 268	148 660	156 008	165 292	173 233
Balance: current surplus[1]	–1 412	–455	–1 209	–1 228	–1 099	–2 089	–3 813	–1 531	–2 074	69	8 119
Total	62 395	74 673	91 705	106 145	117 500	126 020	134 455	147 129	153 934	165 361	181 352

1 Before providing for depreciation.

Source *Central Statistical Office*

14.5 Summary capital account[1]

£ million

	1978	1979	1980	1981	1982	1983	1984	1985	1986	1987	1988
Receipts											
Saving[2]											
Personal sector	12 575	16 621	21 717	22 623	22 239	20 267	22 568	22 558	20 177	17 268	13 601
Industrial and commercial companies	17 952	21 774	17 377	18 224	20 075	25 469	30 885	32 350	30 573	40 356	43 310
Financial companies and institutions	2 756	4 342	4 668	4 114	4 236	6 573	6 344	8 261	12 565	14 172	15 700
Public corporations	3 728	3 692	4 128	5 435	6 479	7 386	6 002	5 252	5 999	5 093	5 766
Central government	−3 008	−1 854	−2 275	−3 750	−4 067	−4 315	−6 033	−3 549	−4 318	−2 631	6 550
Local authorities	1 596	1 399	1 066	2 522	2 968	2 226	2 220	2 018	2 244	2 700	1 569
Total saving	35 599	45 974	46 681	49 168	51 930	57 606	61 986	66 890	67 240	76 958	86 496
Capital transfers (net receipts):											
Personal sector	301	196	253	136	446	1 109	1 359	404	−32	−319	−1 336
Industrial and commercial companies	398	353	429	557	491	322	217	112	52	−371	−210
Financial companies and institutions	14	−107	−142	−315	−148	−61	−64	−118	−219	−283	−403
Public corporations[3]	500	412	472	532	473	602	568	634	456	676	787
Central government[3]	−1 246	−946	−1 092	−952	−1 088	−1 197	−1 129	−949	−531	−70	793
Local authorities	33	92	80	42	−174	−775	−951	−83	274	367	369
Total transfers[4]	–	–	–	–	–	–	–	–	–	–	–
Residual error[5]	2 429	1 402	1 519	1 971	568	436	655	10	−313	−1 037	−1 875
Total	38 028	47 374	48 200	51 138	52 499	58 042	62 641	66 900	66 927	75 921	84 621
Expenditure											
Gross domestic fixed capital formation:											
Personal sector[6]	6 209	8 158	9 284	9 716	11 897	13 796	14 581	15 282	17 860	21 425	25 496
Industrial and commercial companies	12 051	14 038	14 893	14 716	15 292	15 890	19 614	24 876	26 682	32 285	40 308
Financial companies and institutions	3 203	3 943	5 232	5 514	6 206	5 338	7 024	7 829	7 301	8 250	12 277
Public corporations	4 944	5 641	6 653	6 780	7 114	7 884	7 247	5 772	5 455	4 512	4 882
Central government	1 290	1 557	1 757	1 863	2 224	2 490	2 719	3 115	3 321	3 319	3 675
Local authorities	3 363	3 588	3 742	2 715	2 091	3 217	3 775	3 469	3 780	3 779	2 113
Total	31 060	36 925	41 561	41 304	44 824	48 615	54 960	60 343	64 399	73 570	88 751
Increase in book value of stocks and work in progress[7]:											
Personal sector	760	1 164	479	415	420	698	513	426	526	823	1 105
Industrial and commercial companies	4 969	9 277	2 794	2 531	1 845	4 316	5 357	2 374	2 524	5 821	9 428
Financial companies and institutions	−10	−17	6	9	4	38	24	–	–	–	–
Public corporations	282	610	497	344	664	371	−378	104	−351	−124	276
Central government	31	−35	43	−93	155	246	280	450	−237	−498	−322
Total	6 032	10 999	3 819	3 206	3 088	5 669	5 796	3 354	2 462	6 022	10 487
Net investment abroad[8]	936	−550	2 820	6 628	4 587	3 758	1 885	3 203	66	−3 671	−14 617
Total investment	38 028	47 374	48 200	51 138	52 499	58 042	62 641	66 900	66 927	75 921	84 621
Financial surplus/deficit:											
Personal sector	5 907	7 495	12 207	12 628	10 368	6 882	8 833	7 254	1 759	−5 299	−14 336
Industrial and commercial companies	1 330	−1 188	119	1 534	3 429	5 585	6 131	5 212	1 419	1 879	−6 636
Financial companies and institutions	−423	309	−712	−1 724	−2 122	1 136	−768	314	5 045	5 639	3 020
Public corporations	−998	−2 147	−2 550	−1 157	−826	−267	−299	10	1 351	1 381	1 395
Central government	−5 575	−4 322	−5 167	−6 472	−7 534	−8 248	−10 161	−8 063	−7 933	−5 522	3 990
Local authorities	−1 734	−2 097	−2 596	−151	703	−1 766	−2 506	−1 534	−1 262	−712	−175
Total	−1 493	−1 950	1 301	4 658	4 018	3 322	1 230	3 193	379	−2 634	−12 742
Net investment abroad[8]	936	−550	2 820	6 628	4 587	3 758	1 885	3 203	66	−3 671	−14 617
less Residual error[5]	−2 429	−1 402	−1 519	−1 971	−568	−436	−655	−10	313	1 037	1 875

1 Figures for companies and public corporations are affected by privatisation.
2 Before providing for depreciation, stock appreciation and additions to dividend and tax reserves.
3 Excluding financial transactions on writing-off debt.
4 "Total capital transfers for the domestic sectors" equals capital transfers paid abroad.
5 Residual error is the difference between the expenditure-based and the income-based estimates of Gross domestic product.
6 Gross and net fixed capital formation by the personal sector excludes that by life assurance and pension funds: this is included with that of financial companies and institutions.
7 Equal to stock appreciation plus value of physical increase in stocks and work in progress.
8 Net investment abroad is equal, but opposite in sign, to the Overseas sector's financial surplus or deficit.

Source Central Statistical Office

14.6 Gross domestic product: output-based measure by industry at constant factor cost

1985 = 100

	Weight per 1 000[1]	1978	1979	1980	1981	1982	1983	1984	1985	1986	1987	1988
Agriculture, forestry and fishing	*19*	78.0	76.8	85.3	87.5	94.8	89.7	105.4	100.0	98.9	99.3	100.5
Production:												
Energy and water supply:												
Coal and coke	*12*	136.6	136.6	139.9	136.2	130.4	125.3	55.9	100.0	114.2	110.8	109.8
Extraction of mineral oil and natural gas	*62*	45.6	65.3	66.2	73.0	83.2	91.1	97.4	100.0	101.2	98.6	90.1
Mineral oil processing	*4*	114.4	115.5	101.6	94.5	94.2	96.7	99.6	100.0	100.9	102.2	109.1
Other energy and water supply	*28*	89.3	92.9	92.4	94.6	93.9	97.2	82.4	100.0	109.9	112.9	114.3
Total energy and water supply	*106*	69.8	82.5	82.6	86.5	91.6	96.8	88.8	100.0	105.0	103.9	99.4
Manufacturing:												
Metals	*9*	113.4	118.2	89.7	95.1	92.5	93.9	93.6	100.0	99.9	108.6	121.5
Other minerals and mineral products	*12*	115.1	114.2	102.9	91.6	93.5	96.6	100.4	100.0	101.3	106.8	117.2
Chemicals	*24*	90.5	93.0	84.2	84.2	84.8	91.1	96.5	100.0	101.8	109.0	114.2
Man-made fibres	*1*	184.2	176.4	128.8	109.4	87.5	100.6	105.0	100.0	103.5	110.0	106.9
Metal goods nes	*13*	124.6	122.6	101.2	93.3	93.9	96.3	104.4	100.0	99.4	103.1	110.4
Mechanical engineering	*29*	121.5	117.4	107.7	96.2	97.6	93.8	96.0	100.0	96.6	97.4	105.7
Electrical and instrument engineering	*34*	79.5	79.2	77.5	72.7	76.1	84.1	94.3	100.0	100.4	106.6	118.8
Motor vehicles and parts	*13*	136.3	132.6	114.6	95.1	91.8	96.3	94.7	100.0	98.0	105.4	116.8
Other transport equipment	*13*	103.3	99.8	107.9	111.7	108.8	102.5	99.8	100.0	103.8	111.1	107.1
Food	*23*	94.5	95.9	95.5	94.6	97.9	99.1	100.1	100.0	101.6	103.0	105.3
Drink and tobacco	*8*	106.8	109.0	107.7	104.0	101.4	102.3	102.7	100.0	99.2	104.2	106.0
Textiles	*7*	128.8	123.6	102.1	93.8	91.5	93.6	96.2	100.0	100.3	104.5	102.1
Clothing, footwear and leather	*9*	106.8	108.5	94.1	88.1	87.3	91.6	95.7	100.0	101.2	102.2	102.1
Paper, printing and publishing	*24*	105.3	109.4	101.0	95.9	92.5	93.1	97.8	100.0	104.3	114.3	125.1
All other manufacturing (including timber, furniture, rubber and plastics)	*19*	113.4	113.9	98.2	89.5	88.2	93.8	99.1	100.0	104.9	115.3	128.0
Total	*238*	106.0	105.9	96.7	90.9	91.1	93.7	97.6	100.0	101.0	106.6	114.0
Total production	*344*	95.3	99.0	92.5	89.6	91.3	94.7	94.9	100.0	102.2	105.8	109.5
Construction	*59*	93.6	94.2	89.1	82.1	88.6	94.3	98.6	100.0	101.1	109.0	117.0
Service industries:												
Distribution, hotels and catering; repairs	*134*	89.8	92.4	86.7	85.4	87.1	90.9	95.7	100.0	103.6	110.6	118.0
Transport and communication:												
Transport	*43*	95.5	98.9	95.4	94.5	91.4	93.5	96.3	100.0	102.5	112.0	118.1
Communication	*27*	75.8	80.8	83.0	84.8	87.4	90.8	97.6	100.0	107.8	113.4	120.8
Total	*70*	88.7	92.2	90.5	90.7	89.8	92.5	96.8	100.0	104.6	112.5	119.1
Banking, finance, insurance, business services and leasing	*155*	65	70	72	75	80	86	94	100	110	123	134
Ownership of dwellings	*59*	92	93	94	96	97	98	99	100	102	102	103
Public administration, national defence and compulsory social security	*71*	101	101	102	102	101	101	101	100	100	101	102
Education and health services	*85*	91	94	95	96	97	98	99	100	101	103	107
Other services[2]	*59*	81	84	89	87	87	91	97	100	105	114	119
Adjustment for financial services	*−55*	59	64	68	72	76	82	93	100	113	127	138
Total services	*578*	87.1	89.6	89.2	89.6	90.8	93.8	97.1	100.0	103.8	109.7	115.3
Gross domestic product	*1000*	90.2	92.9	90.3	89.0	91.0	94.0	96.6	100.0	103.0	108.1	113.1

1 The weights are proportional to the distribution of net output in 1985 and are used to combine the indices from 1983 onwards. For the method of calculation in earlier years see paragraph 5.19 of *United Kingdom National Accounts: Sources and Methods, Third Edition*.

2 Comprising classes 92, 94, 96–99 and 00 of the Standard Industrial Classification Revised 1980.

Source Central Statistical Office

14.6 Gross domestic product: output-based measure by industry at constant factor cost

(continued)

1985 = 100

	Weight per 1 000[1]	1978	1979	1980	1981	1982	1983	1984	1985	1986	1987	1988
Consumer goods industries:												
Cars, etc.	*20*	140.9	121.1	100.3	95.4	86.6	98.7	95.1	100.0	97.8	105.8	116.3
Other durables	*24*	115.2	111.6	95.8	89.3	88.6	92.0	96.3	100.0	104.2	109.0	121.6
Clothing and footwear, etc.	*28*	106.1	107.6	94.6	89.0	88.2	91.6	95.8	100.0	100.2	100.5	98.9
Food, drink and tobacco[2]	*84*	98.1	100.0	99.2	97.5	98.6	99.7	100.9	100.0	100.9	103.6	105.4
Other	*86*	99.1	100.7	92.9	90.3	89.2	92.5	97.3	100.0	103.0	110.8	119.0
Total	*242*	104.4	104.4	96.4	93.0	92.4	95.3	98.1	100.0	101.6	106.5	112.0
Investment goods industries:												
Electrical	*59*	73.5	73.3	75.2	70.1	74.3	82.6	93.8	100.0	98.5	103.8	117.5
Transport	*56*	118.7	117.7	113.0	103.3	101.7	99.1	98.1	100.0	101.4	108.7	110.6
Other	*80*	118.6	115.9	106.5	96.2	96.5	93.5	95.7	100.0	97.8	98.8	107.6
Total	*195*	105.0	103.5	98.8	90.3	91.3	91.8	95.8	100.0	99.0	103.2	111.5
Intermediate goods industries:												
Fuels	*299*	67.6	80.5	81.1	86.0	90.9	96.8	88.5	100.0	105.1	104.0	99.4
Materials	*264*	107.6	108.9	94.5	89.3	89.6	93.8	98.5	100.0	101.8	109.0	117.3
Total	*563*	86.4	93.9	87.5	87.6	90.4	95.4	93.2	100.0	103.5	106.3	107.8

1 These sum to the total of 1000 for the production industries.

2 This does not include certain activities classified to intermediate goods industries: materials.

Source *Central Statistical Office*

14.7 Gross domestic product by industry[1]

£ million

	1978	1979	1980	1981	1982	1983	1984	1985	1986	1987	1988
Agriculture, forestry and fishing	3 371	3 677	4 019	4 520	5 117	4 902	5 892	5 197	5 706	5 791	5 625
Energy and water supply[2]	10 079	13 838	19 356	23 475	26 091	30 071	30 026	32 381	23 681	23 981	21 845
Manufacturing	43 512	48 714	52 872	53 987	58 658	61 299	65 984	72 226	76 485	83 013	93 433
Construction	9 126	10 617	12 220	13 007	14 098	15 647	16 990	17 849	20 309	22 683	25 745
Distribution; hotels and catering; repairs	19 968	22 863	25 755	27 257	30 190	33 133	35 960	40 428	44 990	48 610	55 131
Transport and communication	11 754	13 203	14 333	15 897	17 201	18 243	19 772	21 323	23 323	25 741	28 657
Banking, finance, insurance, business services and leasing	16 680	20 776	25 053	27 285	30 949	36 444	40 603	48 511	57 127	65 580	76 922
Ownership of dwellings	8 598	10 307	12 147	13 895	15 044	15 944	16 734	17 963	19 170	20 180	21 407
Public administration, national defence and compulsory social security	9 942	11 438	14 520	16 244	17 367	18 806	20 175	21 598	23 066	24 795	27 023
Education and health services	12 377	14 140	17 995	20 618	21 308	23 305	24 487	26 101	28 928	31 609	35 237
Other services[2]	8 031	9 224	10 677	12 005	13 305	15 072	16 463	18 371	20 560	22 872	25 785
Total	153 438	178 797	208 947	228 190	249 328	272 866	293 086	321 948	343 345	374 855	416 810
Adjustment for financial services	5 812	7 285	9 190	10 603	11 781	12 208	14 629	16 094	18 845	19 204	22 204
Statistical discrepancy (income adjustment)	1 516	1 292	760	610	203	−259	926	5	−469	−96	181
Gross domestic product (average estimate)	149 142	172 804	200 517	218 197	237 750	260 399	279 383	305 859	324 031	355 555	394 787

1 The contribution of each industry to the gross domestic product before providing for depreciation but after providing for stock appreciation.

2 Comprising classes 92, 94, 96 and 00 of the Standard Industrial Classification, Revised 1980.

Source *Central Statistical Office*

14.8 Gross national product by category of expenditure at 1985 prices[1]

£ million

	1978	1979	1980	1981	1982	1983	1984	1985	1986	1987	1988
At 1985 market prices											
Consumers' expenditure	186 759	194 895	195 060	195 173	197 051	205 484	209 207	217 023	229 105	241 382	257 918
General government final consumption	68 394	69 870	70 984	71 184	71 762	73 193	73 902	73 879	75 454	76 346	76 678
of which: Central government	*41 798*	*42 435*	*43 690*	*44 108*	*44 421*	*45 281*	*45 741*	*45 879*	*46 729*	*46 819*	*46 929*
Local authorities	*26 577*	*27 410*	*27 272*	*27 074*	*27 318*	*27 912*	*28 161*	*28 000*	*28 725*	*29 527*	*29 749*
Gross domestic fixed capital formation	54 914	56 450	53 416	48 298	50 915	53 476	58 058	60 343	61 478	66 894	75 680
Value of physical increase in stocks and work in progress	2 867	3 328	−3 371	−3 200	−1 281	1 357	1 112	615	677	1 051	3 578
Total domestic expenditure	313 492	325 135	315 944	310 888	318 186	333 510	342 279	351 860	366 714	385 673	413 854
Exports of goods and services	85 720	88 943	88 966	88 307	89 048	90 971	96 892	102 639	106 906	112 355	113 186
of which: Goods	*62 051*	*64 816*	*65 575*	*64 956*	*66 789*	*68 343*	*73 889*	*77 988*	*81 076*	*85 108*	*86 332*
Services	*23 851*	*24 282*	*23 488*	*23 458*	*22 267*	*22 628*	*23 003*	*24 651*	*25 830*	*27 247*	*26 854*
Total final expenditure	399 209	414 074	404 872	399 148	407 203	424 481	439 171	454 499	473 620	498 028	527 040
less Imports of goods and services[2]	−76 593	−83 956	−81 134	−78 878	−82 721	−88 116	−96 735	−99 165	−105 829	−113 905	−127 833
of which: Goods	*−61 760*	*−67 735*	*−64 078*	*−61 531*	*−64 983*	*−70 597*	*−78 631*	*−81 120*	*−86 884*	*−92 920*	*−105 037*
Services	*−14 827*	*−16 214*	*−17 070*	*−17 371*	*−17 758*	*−17 519*	*−18 104*	*−18 045*	*−18 945*	*−20 985*	*−22 796*
Gross domestic product (expenditure-based)[3]	322 579	330 106	323 721	320 247	324 471	336 365	342 436	355 334	367 791	384 123	399 207
Statistical discrepancy (expenditure adjustment)[4]	−1 688	−180	−1 050	−1 711	−429	−772	286	−5	−152	873	1 792
Gross domestic product (average estimate)[3]	320 883	329 931	322 668	318 527	324 045	335 593	342 722	355 329	367 639	384 996	400 999
Net property income from abroad	1 355	1 858	−286	1 572	1 761	3 233	4 627	2 763	5 589	5 057	5 737
Gross national product (average estimate)[3,5]	322 247	331 795	322 399	320 106	325 812	338 826	347 349	358 092	373 228	390 053	406 736
At 1985 factor cost											
Gross domestic product at market prices (expenditure-based)[3]	322 579	330 106	323 721	320 247	324 471	336 365	342 436	355 334	367 791	384 123	399 207
Statistical discrepancy (expenditure adjustment)[4]	−1 688	−180	−1 050	−1 711	−429	−772	286	−5	−152	873	1 792
Gross domestic product at market prices (average estimate)	320 883	329 931	322 668	318 527	324 045	335 593	342 722	355 329	367 639	384 996	400 999
less Factor cost adjustment[6]	−45 203	−46 610	−45 305	−44 246	−44 895	−46 355	−48 377	−49 470	−52 020	−55 164	−56 890
Gross domestic product at factor cost (average estimate)	275 734	283 384	277 408	274 296	279 158	289 238	294 345	305 859	315 619	329 832	344 109
Net property income from abroad	1 355	1 858	−286	1 572	1 761	3 233	4 627	2 763	5 589	5 057	5 737
Gross national product at factor cost[5] (average estimate)	277 112	285 259	277 166	275 887	280 937	292 471	298 972	308 622	321 208	334 889	349 846
less Capital consumption	−34 327	−35 200	−36 417	−37 625	−38 744	−39 872	−40 917	−41 886	−42 864	−43 706	−45 918
Net national product at factor cost (average estimate): 'National income'	243 035	250 327	240 848	238 261	242 160	252 599	258 055	266 736	278 344	291 183	303 928

1 For the years before 1983, totals differ from the sum of their components.
2 Excluding taxes on expenditure levied on imports.
3 Including taxes on expenditure levied on imports.
4 The difference between the average estimate of gross domestic product and expenditure-based measure at 1985 prices.
5 Expenditure-based estimates of Gross national product and of Net national product (National Income) can be derived as in previous issues of this publication. The derivation is shown in *'United Kingdom National Accounts'*, 1989 Edition Table 1.6.
6 This represents taxes on expenditure *less* subsidies valued at constant rates.

Source Central Statistical Office

14.9 Consumers' expenditure at current prices classified by function

£ million

	1978	1979	1980	1981	1982	1983	1984	1985	1986	1987	1988
Food (household expenditure):											
Bread and cereals	2 424	2 752	3 175	3 426	3 598	3 768	3 954	4 165	4 592	4 862	5 357
Meat and bacon	5 151	5 920	6 624	6 851	7 466	7 455	7 540	7 884	8 199	8 437	8 798
Fish	556	635	748	782	821	921	945	1 055	1 194	1 200	1 374
Milk, cheese and eggs	2 717	3 126	3 550	3 799	3 993	4 135	4 229	4 385	4 591	4 644	4 957
Oils and fats	802	893	942	949	955	965	1 001	1 043	1 025	950	986
Fruit	1 003	1 096	1 300	1 337	1 381	1 613	1 614	1 706	1 959	2 082	2 272
Potatoes	570	744	785	897	1 052	1 157	1 360	1 251	1 361	1 575	1 502
Vegetables	1 232	1 463	1 657	1 779	1 811	2 061	2 146	2 328	2 601	2 746	3 017
Sugar	271	299	330	357	362	374	358	331	320	317	335
Confectionery	1 466	1 611	1 800	1 953	2 129	2 242	2 460	2 692	2 834	2 956	3 083
Coffee, tea and cocoa	724	743	787	762	771	920	1 085	1 179	1 236	1 190	1 208
Soft drinks	815	1 019	1 183	1 202	1 254	1 459	1 580	1 697	1 993	2 223	2 504
Other manufactured food[1]	642	687	774	852	897	989	1 032	1 010	1 154	1 218	1 294
Total	18 373	20 988	23 655	24 946	26 490	28 059	29 304	30 726	33 059	34 400	36 687
Alcoholic drink:											
Beer	3 974	4 571	5 320	5 971	6 450	7 138	7 734	8 416	8 849	9 206	9 793
Spirits	1 999	2 454	2 720	2 908	3 003	3 265	3 471	3 831	3 946	4 153	4 564
Wine, cider and perry	1 310	1 640	1 915	2 273	2 550	2 867	3 111	3 404	3 555	3 901	4 151
Total	7 283	8 665	9 955	11 152	12 003	13 270	14 316	15 651	16 350	17 260	18 508
Tobacco											
Cigarettes	3 362	3 693	4 218	4 762	5 048	5 352	5 739	6 112	6 552	6 729	7 001
Other	523	541	603	753	833	857	883	894	919	924	944
Total	3 885	4 234	4 821	5 515	5 881	6 209	6 622	7 006	7 471	7 653	7 945
Clothing and footwear:											
Men's and boys' wear	2 229	2 587	2 705	2 751	2 933	3 274	3 620	3 989	4 705	5 207	5 693
Women's, girls' and infants' wear	4 253	4 962	5 408	5 562	5 924	6 550	7 115	8 309	9 000	9 811	10 735
Footwear	1 348	1 621	1 762	1 844	2 068	2 296	2 525	2 766	3 009	3 230	3 363
Total	7 830	9 170	9 875	10 157	10 925	12 120	13 260	15 064	16 714	18 248	19 791
Housing:											
Rents, rates and water charges:											
Imputed rent of owner-occupied dwellings	5 403	6 522	7 830	9 114	10 160	11 181	11 917	12 783	13 653	14 463	15 504
Other rents	2 978	3 367	3 841	4 998	5 989	6 352	6 508	6 988	7 415	7 938	8 588
Rates, sewerage and water charges	2 977	3 464	4 377	5 333	6 274	6 182	6 587	7 151	8 031	8 845	10 057
Maintenance, etc. by occupiers											
Do-it-yourself goods	1 073	1 305	1 594	1 800	1 927	2 230	2 486	2 911	3 349	3 815	4 509
Contractors' charges and insurance	728	916	1 183	1 335	1 573	1 805	2 084	2 392	3 015	3 701	4 335
Total	13 159	15 574	18 825	22 580	25 923	27 750	29 582	32 225	35 463	38 762	42 993
Fuel and power:											
Electricity	2 396	2 703	3 370	3 973	4 264	4 450	4 551	4 860	5 196	5 068	5 545
Gas	1 359	1 567	1 852	2 458	3 063	3 530	3 671	4 046	4 372	4 466	4 548
Coal and coke	521	617	677	789	829	840	765	1 033	898	820	811
Other	337	405	456	507	540	579	588	718	682	728	658
Total	4 613	5 292	6 355	7 727	8 696	9 399	9 575	10 657	11 148	11 082	11 562
Household goods and services:											
Furniture, pictures, etc.	1 752	2 216	2 345	2 420	2 522	2 677	2 727	2 982	3 092	3 342	3 828
Carpets and other floor coverings	857	1 032	1 049	1 068	1 093	1 206	1 290	1 409	1 462	1 582	1 810
Major appliances	1 436	1 794	2 001	2 128	2 356	2 778	2 996	3 101	3 603	3 827	4 073
Textiles and soft furnishings	938	1 027	1 119	1 145	1 142	1 202	1 235	1 513	1 624	1 880	2 221
Hardware	1 003	1 129	1 198	1 325	1 383	1 481	1 657	1 941	2 234	2 546	3 009
Cleaning materials; matches	584	666	798	886	970	1 050	1 140	1 261	1 327	1 391	1 454
Household and domestic services	963	1 107	1 373	1 550	1 638	1 784	1 965	2 224	2 378	2 556	2 768
Total	7 533	8 971	9 883	10 522	11 104	12 178	13 010	14 431	15 720	17 124	19 163
Transport and communication:											
Cars, motorcycles and other vehicles	4 811	6 493	6 510	6 557	7 407	9 105	9 004	9 989	11 604	13 776	17 437
Petrol and oil	2 610	3 554	4 646	5 695	6 331	6 913	7 450	7 972	7 327	7 721	8 038
Vehicle excise duty	590	601	726	840	1 022	1 184	1 289	1 482	1 566	1 612	1 672
Other running costs of vehicles	2 730	3 193	3 797	4 195	4 439	4 831	4 942	5 444	6 058	6 817	7 615
Rail travel	773	884	1 063	1 123	1 093	1 287	1 348	1 474	1 618	1 770	1 988
Buses and coaches	1 154	1 282	1 492	1 572	1 697	1 789	1 833	1 971	1 952	2 047	2 178
Air travel	1 026	1 337	1 818	2 060	2 323	2 498	2 688	2 784	3 179	3 692	4 044
Other travel	448	572	727	814	798	939	1 041	1 185	1 333	1 572	1 776
Postal services	224	240	309	379	423	467	485	494	535	553	567
Telecommunications	1 246	1 448	1 938	2 413	2 678	2 846	3 108	3 495	3 983	4 465	5 083
Total	15 612	19 604	23 026	25 648	28 211	31 859	33 188	36 290	39 155	44 025	50 398

1 This category now includes estimates for preserves which were formerly combined with estimates for confectionery.

Source *Central Statistical Office*

14.9 (continued) Consumers' expenditure at current prices classified by function

£ million

	1978	1979	1980	1981	1982	1983	1984	1985	1986	1987	1988
Recreation, entertainment and education:											
Radio, television and other durable goods	1 312	1 552	1 590	1 769	2 061	2 477	2 752	2 755	3 203	3 410	3 638
Television and video hire charges, licence fees and repairs	1 183	1 351	1 578	1 692	1 951	2 034	2 113	2 327	2 441	2 578	2 775
Sports goods, toys, games and camping equipment	888	1 124	1 273	1 339	1 454	1 638	1 801	1 944	2 274	2 564	2 760
Other recreational goods	1 699	2 069	2 471	2 443	2 656	2 802	3 071	3 427	3 786	4 197	4 741
Betting and gaming	1 131	1 283	1 520	1 626	1 776	1 842	1 972	2 117	2 257	2 439	2 613
Other recreational and entertainment services	1 093	1 291	1 529	1 778	1 761	1 907	2 082	2 360	2 735	3 161	3 707
Books	315	367	458	529	556	620	665	708	810	922	984
Newspapers and magazines	990	1 108	1 332	1 686	1 907	1 967	2 096	2 347	2 442	2 621	2 753
Education	783	883	1 135	1 337	1 442	1 432	1 510	1 623	1 763	1 931	2 125
Total	9 394	11 028	12 886	14 199	15 564	16 719	18 062	19 608	21 711	23 823	26 096
Other goods and services:											
Pharmaceutical products and medical equipment	403	502	615	689	787	930	1 123	1 213	1 258	1 311	1 417
NHS payments and other medical expenses	430	509	676	857	1 055	1 214	1 236	1 414	1 590	1 842	2 147
Toilet articles; perfumery	1 006	1 209	1 387	1 567	1 803	1 979	2 250	2 663	2 882	3 136	3 577
Hairdressing and beauty care	557	668	793	860	910	1 022	1 129	1 310	1 439	1 580	1 744
Jewellery, silverware, watches and clocks	828	1 019	1 083	1 094	1 169	1 281	1 413	1 433	1 633	1 924	2 299
Other goods	883	1 058	1 273	1 300	1 458	1 610	1 787	1 858	2 191	2 481	2 852
Catering (meals and accommodation)	5 840	6 874	8 288	8 820	9 461	10 936	12 491	13 831	16 031	18 545	23 557
Administrative costs of life assurance and pension schemes	1 227	1 497	1 778	2 092	2 475	2 935	3 393	3 765	4 438	5 134	5 939
Other services	1 334	1 557	1 841	2 088	2 516	3 070	3 538	4 275	5 493	7 005	7 316
Total	12 508	14 893	17 734	19 367	21 634	24 977	28 360	31 762	36 955	42 958	50 848
Total household and tourist expenditure in the United Kingdom	100 190	118 419	137 015	151 813	166 431	182 540	195 279	213 420	233 746	255 335	283 991
less Expenditure by foreign tourists, etc. in the United Kingdom	-2 891	-3 207	-3 436	-3 513	-3 792	-4 661	-5 344	-6 282	-6 456	-7 212	-7 065
Household expenditure abroad	1 592	2 079	2 648	3 131	3 483	3 855	4 275	4 540	5 651	6 689	7 542
Total household expenditure on goods and services	98 891	117 291	136 227	151 431	166 122	181 734	194 210	211 678	232 941	254 812	284 468
Final expenditure by private non-profit-making bodies	1 956	2 225	2 789	3 270	3 694	4 161	4 685	5 345	6 215	6 886	7 601
National accounts statistical adjustment	..	..	..	..	..	..	..	..	..	..	1 500
Total consumers' expenditure	100 847	119 516	139 016	154 701	169 816	185 895	198 895	217 023	239 156	261 698	293 569

14.9 Consumers' expenditure at 1985 prices classified by function[1]

(continued)

£ million

	1978	1979	1980	1981	1982	1983[1]	1984	1985	1986	1987	1988
Food (household expenditure):											
Bread and cereals	3 922	3 949	3 950	3 989	4 014	4 139	4 152	4 165	4 350	4 455	4 495
Meat and bacon	8 214	8 481	8 476	8 219	8 157	8 066	7 779	7 884	7 929	7 935	7 871
Fish	876	908	1 000	1 023	1 024	1 057	1 034	1 055	1 130	1 067	1 110
Milk, cheese and eggs	4 693	4 710	4 639	4 527	4 455	4 522	4 433	4 385	4 431	4 293	4 356
Oils and fats	1 201	1 193	1 179	1 139	1 095	1 101	1 051	1 043	1 061	1 018	1 016
Fruit	1 626	1 720	1 839	1 800	1 705	1 844	1 741	1 706	1 846	1 907	2 014
Potatoes	932	963	975	1 015	1 037	1 083	1 114	1 251	1 217	1 307	1 268
Vegetables	1 943	2 004	2 076	2 111	2 053	2 117	2 078	2 328	2 375	2 307	2 410
Sugar	466	453	439	434	403	384	359	331	315	295	285
Confectionery	2 473	2 371	2 251	2 343	2 488	2 535	2 633	2 692	2 637	2 681	2 742
Coffee, tea and cocoa	1 135	1 248	1 262	1 237	1 222	1 271	1 202	1 179	1 204	1 169	1 168
Soft drinks	1 149	1 254	1 254	1 268	1 346	1 544	1 608	1 697	1 926	2 083	2 088
Other manufactured food[2]	911	933	907	921	921	995	987	1 010	1 078	1 104	1 088
Total	29 714	30 380	30 419	30 217	30 299	30 658	30 171	30 726	31 499	31 621	31 911
Alcoholic drink:											
Beer	9 499	9 568	9 109	8 561	8 261	8 412	8 447	8 416	8 407	8 485	8 568
Spirits	3 774	4 168	3 923	3 693	3 503	3 597	3 641	3 831	3 814	3 881	4 097
Wine, cider and perry	2 320	2 500	2 515	2 692	2 780	3 050	3 275	3 404	3 478	3 661	3 763
Total	15 371	16 069	15 408	14 875	14 503	15 059	15 363	15 651	15 699	16 027	16 428
Tobacco											
Cigarettes	7 969	7 983	7 768	7 109	6 525	6 480	6 259	6 112	5 940	5 902	5 935
Other	1 133	1 083	1 045	1 059	1 014	976	942	894	873	861	845
Total	9 098	9 060	8 806	8 167	7 541	7 456	7 201	7 006	6 813	6 763	6 780
Clothing and footwear:											
Men's and boys' wear	3 203	3 292	3 094	3 035	3 202	3 456	3 808	3 989	4 590	4 959	5 207
Women's, girls' and infants' wear	5 772	6 344	6 519	6 564	6 669	7 096	7 395	8 309	8 779	9 466	10 068
Footwear	2 258	2 402	2 293	2 195	2 358	2 519	2 661	2 766	2 902	3 038	3 043
Total	11 239	12 038	11 903	11 795	12 227	13 071	13 864	15 064	16 271	17 463	18 318
Housing:											
Rents, rates and water charges:											
Imputed rent of owner-occupied dwellings	10 593	10 886	11 162	11 490	11 899	12 259	12 584	12 783	13 027	13 206	13 387
Other rents	7 506	7 532	7 491	7 377	7 201	7 043	6 945	6 988	6 997	7 085	7 175
Rates, sewerage and water charges	6 572	6 694	6 794	6 818	6 912	6 974	7 061	7 151	7 245	7 342	7 440
Maintenance, etc. by occupiers											
Do-it-yourself goods	1 947	2 101	2 171	2 240	2 234	2 468	2 625	2 911	3 198	3 540	4 005
Contractors' charges and insurance	1 590	1 687	1 820	1 807	1 886	2 019	2 186	2 392	2 864	3 466	3 869
Total	27 890	28 625	29 207	29 562	30 034	30 763	31 401	32 225	33 331	34 639	35 876
Fuel and power:											
Electricity	4 712	4 887	4 809	4 728	4 618	4 628	4 681	4 860	5 082	4 978	5 171
Gas	3 102	3 464	3 534	3 704	3 712	3 788	3 817	4 046	4 276	4 403	4 485
Coal and Coke	1 237	1 248	1 058	1 042	1 023	980	809	1 033	872	792	777
Other	1 088	1 069	836	754	685	663	651	718	703	748	661
Total	10 214	10 714	10 282	10 246	10 047	10 059	9 958	10 657	10 933	10 921	11 094
Household goods and services:											
Furniture pictures, etc.	2 700	3 037	2 839	2 797	2 827	2 912	2 822	2 982	2 972	3 133	3 460
Carpets and other floor coverings	1 320	1 417	1 270	1 234	1 224	1 310	1 334	1 409	1 403	1 479	1 631
Major appliances	2 076	2 347	2 329	2 341	2 501	2 859	3 070	3 101	3 581	3 806	3 869
Textiles and soft furnishings	1 372	1 323	1 256	1 256	1 266	1 326	1 321	1 513	1 562	1 781	2 050
Hardware	1 845	1 805	1 632	1 650	1 604	1 639	1 750	1 941	2 131	2 358	2 668
Cleaning materials; matches	1 061	1 069	1 105	1 137	1 162	1 180	1 209	1 261	1 298	1 323	1 310
Household and domestic services	1 926	1 907	2 003	2 028	1 972	2 009	2 095	2 224	2 255	2 296	2 360
Total	12 244	12 885	12 389	12 389	12 525	13 235	13 601	14 431	15 202	16 176	17 348
Transport and communication:											
Cars, motorcycles and other vehicles	7 113	8 054	7 623	7 754	8 005	10 073	9 477	9 989	10 792	11 618	13 340
Petrol and oil	6 734	6 823	7 005	7 096	7 369	7 517	7 838	7 972	8 427	8 736	9 220
Vehicle excise duty	1 130	1 151	1 226	1 190	1 274	1 367	1 409	1 482	1 525	1 571	1 625
Other running costs of vehicles	4 858	4 914	4 939	5 047	5 060	5 163	5 067	5 444	5 810	6 226	6 577
Rail travel	1 387	1 411	1 375	1 344	1 257	1 402	1 451	1 474	1 547	1 607	1 685
Buses and coaches	2 385	2 352	2 166	2 020	1 935	1 926	1 918	1 971	1 824	1 835	1 862
Air travel	1 614	1 929	2 204	2 404	2 496	2 456	2 670	2 784	3 213	3 804	4 247
Other travel	902	972	1 053	1 063	981	1 063	1 108	1 185	1 286	1 481	1 604
Postal services	456	454	453	469	487	479	490	494	529	525	528
Telecommunications	2 396	2 757	2 900	2 931	2 921	3 133	3 311	3 495	3 781	4 148	4 621
Total	28 676	30 623	30 674	31 091	31 563	34 579	34 739	36 290	38 734	41 551	45 309

1 For the years before 1983, totals differ from the sum of their components due to the method of rebasing used.

2 This category now includes estimates for preserves which were formerly combined with estimates for confectionery.

Source Central Statistical Office

14.9 Consumers' expenditure at 1985 prices classified by function[1]

(*continued*)

£ million

	1978	1979	1980	1981	1982	1983[1]	1984	1985	1986	1987	1988
Recreation, entertainment and education:											
Radio, television and other durable goods	1 281	1 476	1 485	1 668	1 975	2 402	2 709	2 755	3 406	3 727	4 068
TV and video hire charges, licence fees and repairs	1 795	1 878	1 905	1 993	2 069	2 189	2 279	2 327	2 403	2 530	2 704
Sports goods, toys, games and camping equipment	1 345	1 501	1 548	1 510	1 576	1 712	1 865	1 944	2 190	2 448	2 544
Other recreational goods	2 702	2 905	3 069	2 914	3 057	3 105	3 193	3 427	3 633	3 905	4 324
Betting and gaming	2 252	2 211	2 228	2 102	2 078	2 044	2 080	2 117	2 155	2 234	2 277
Other recreational and entertainment services	2 496	2 474	2 501	2 351	2 146	2 140	2 198	2 360	2 441	2 701	2 880
Books	829	865	923	909	846	790	742	708	747	776	768
Newspapers and magazines	2 306	2 325	2 303	2 449	2 346	2 270	2 295	2 347	2 353	2 383	2 345
Education	1 680	1 682	1 778	1 883	1 740	1 625	1 610	1 623	1 663	1 681	1 696
Total	15 991	16 734	17 144	17 250	17 565	18 277	18 971	19 608	20 991	22 385	23 606
Other goods and services:											
Pharmaceutical products and medical equipment	830	884	931	918	955	1 029	1 172	1 213	1 199	1 192	1 227
NHS payments and other medical expenses	884	915	992	1 103	1 237	1 343	1 305	1 414	1 539	1 686	1 751
Toilet articles; perfumery	1 910	2 018	1 954	2 054	2 176	2 269	2 444	2 663	2 749	2 902	3 165
Hairdressing and beauty care	1 210	1 221	1 206	1 169	1 120	1 172	1 211	1 310	1 352	1 394	1 429
Jewellery, silverware, watches and clocks	1 889	1 786	1 302	1 367	1 499	1 392	1 512	1 433	1 583	1 825	2 176
Other goods	1 959	1 950	1 927	1 839	1 908	1 947	1 984	1 858	2 078	2 303	2 480
Catering (meals and accommodation)	12 763	12 826	12 904	12 261	12 002	12 723	13 290	13 831	14 974	16 254	19 309
Administrative costs of life assurance and pension schemes	2 268	2 439	2 491	2 630	2 864	3 234	3 568	3 765	4 253	4 738	5 237
Other services	2 883	2 996	3 049	3 095	3 275	3 583	3 890	4 275	4 970	5 811	5 957
Total	26 676	27 098	26 691	26 425	27 080	28 692	30 376	31 762	34 697	38 105	42 731
Total household and tourist expenditure in the United Kingdom	186 150	193 454	192 248	191 521	193 141	201 849	205 645	213 420	224 170	235 651	249 401
less Expenditure by foreign tourists, etc. in the United Kingdom	−5 866	−5 664	−5 134	−4 646	−4 602	−5 323	−5 730	−6 282	−6 054	−6 376	−5 993
Household expenditure abroad	2 562	3 225	4 038	4 277	4 267	4 344	4 354	4 540	5 064	5 825	6 623
Total household expenditure on goods and services	183 019	191 124	191 164	191 115	192 767	200 870	204 269	211 678	223 180	235 100	250 031
Final expenditure by private non-profit-making bodies	3 740	3 776	3 899	4 060	4 283	4 614	4 938	5 345	5 925	6 282	6 569
National accounts statistical adjustment	..	..	..	..	..	..	..	..	..	..	1 318
Total consumers' expenditure	186 759	194 895	195 060	195 173	197 051	205 484	209 207	217 023	229 105	241 382	257 918

1 For the years before 1983, totals differ from the sum of their components due to the method of rebasing used. See notes on page 131 of *United Kingdom National Accounts 1989 Edition.* (HMSO)

Source Central Statistical Office

14.10 Consumers' expenditure at current prices classified by commodity

£ million

	1978	1979	1980	1981	1982	1983	1984	1985	1986	1987	1988
Durable goods:											
Cars, motorcycles and other vehicles	4 811	6 493	6 510	6 557	7 407	9 105	9 004	9 989	11 604	13 776	17 437
Furniture and floor coverings	2 609	3 248	3 394	3 488	3 615	3 883	4 017	4 391	4 554	4 924	5 638
Other durable goods	2 748	3 346	3 591	3 897	4 417	5 255	5 748	5 856	6 806	7 237	7 711
Total	10 168	13 087	13 495	13 942	15 439	18 243	18 769	20 236	22 964	25 937	30 786
Other goods:											
Food (household expenditure)	18 373	20 988	23 655	24 946	26 490	28 059	29 304	30 726	33 059	34 400	36 687
Beer	3 974	4 571	5 320	5 971	6 450	7 138	7 734	8 416	8 849	9 206	9 793
Other alcoholic drink	3 309	4 094	4 635	5 181	5 553	6 132	6 582	7 235	7 501	8 054	8 715
Tobacco	3 885	4 234	4 821	5 515	5 881	6 209	6 622	7 006	7 471	7 653	7 945
Clothing other than footwear	6 482	7 549	8 113	8 313	8 857	9 824	10 735	12 298	13 705	15 018	16 428
Footwear	1 348	1 621	1 762	1 844	2 068	2 296	2 525	2 766	3 009	3 230	3 363
Energy products	7 223	8 846	11 001	13 422	15 027	16 312	17 025	18 629	18 475	18 803	19 600
Other goods	10 610	12 583	14 601	15 803	17 212	18 790	20 724	23 219	25 810	28 788	32 576
Services:											
Rents, rates and water charges	11 358	13 353	16 048	19 445	22 423	23 715	25 012	26 922	29 099	31 246	34 149
Other services[1]	24 117	28 590	35 565	40 319	44 416	49 177	53 863	59 570	69 214	79 363	92 027
National accounts statistical adjustment	–	–	–	–	–	–	–	–	–	–	1 500
Total consumers' expenditure	100 847	119 516	139 016	154 701	169 816	185 895	198 895	217 023	239 156	261 698	293 569

1 Including the adjustments for international travel, etc. and final expenditure by private non-profit-making bodies serving persons.

14.11 Consumers' expenditure at 1985 prices classified by commodity[1]

£ million at 1985 prices

	1978	1979	1980	1981	1982	1983	1984	1985	1986	1987	1988
Durable goods:											
Cars, motorcycles and other vehicles	7 113	8 054	7 623	7 754	8 005	10 073	9 477	9 989	10 792	11 618	13 340
Furniture and floor coverings	4 020	4 454	4 109	4 031	4 051	4 222	4 156	4 391	4 375	4 612	5 091
Other durable goods	3 301	3 763	3 757	3 973	4 461	5 261	5 779	5 856	6 987	7 533	7 937
Total	14 337	16 169	15 417	15 707	16 504	19 556	19 412	20 236	22 154	23 763	26 368
Other goods:											
Food (household expenditure)	29 714	30 380	30 419	30 217	30 299	30 658	30 171	30 726	31 499	31 621	31 911
Beer	9 499	9 568	9 109	8 561	8 261	8 412	8 447	8 416	8 407	8 485	8 568
Other alcoholic drink	6 049	6 615	6 397	6 363	6 273	6 647	6 916	7 235	7 292	7 542	7 860
Tobacco	9 098	9 060	8 806	8 167	7 541	7 456	7 201	7 006	6 813	6 763	6 780
Clothing other than footwear	8 989	9 643	9 610	9 593	9 869	10 552	11 203	12 298	13 369	14 425	15 275
Footwear	2 258	2 402	2 293	2 195	2 358	2 519	2 661	27 660	2 902	3 038	3 043
Energy products	16 912	17 489	17 259	17 319	17 410	17 576	17 796	18 629	19 360	19 657	20 314
Other goods	19 992	20 523	20 036	20 128	20 586	21 127	22 112	23 219	24 721	26 736	29 062
Services:											
Rents, rates and water charges	24 404	24 872	25 244	25 539	25 943	26 276	26 590	26 922	27 269	27 633	28 002
Other services[2]	47 150	49 384	51 843	52 536	52 759	54 705	56 698	59 570	65 319	71 719	79 417
National accounts statistical adjustment	–	–	–	–	–	–	–	–	–	–	1 318
Total consumers' expenditure	186 759	194 895	195 060	195 173	197 051	205 484	209 207	217 023	229 105	241 382	257 918

1 For the years before 1983, totals differ from the sum of their components; see notes on page 239.

2 Including the adjustments for international travel, etc. and final expenditure by private non-profit-making bodies serving persons.

Source Central Statistical Office

14.12 National accounts aggregates: national disposable income and volume indices

	1978	1979	1980	1981	1982	1983	1984	1985	1986	1987	1988
National disposable income (£ million): Average estimates											
Gross national disposable income at current market prices	167 138	196 826	229 084	253 956	278 114	304 904	327 155	355 058	383 806	419 354	465 977
Real national disposable income at 1985 market prices	313 391	324 150	318 850	317 745	323 320	336 990	344 525	355 058	366 631	382 824	400 721
Volume indices at 1985 prices (1985 = 100)											
Average estimates											
At market prices											
Gross domestic product	90.3	92.9	90.8	89.6	91.2	94.4	96.5	100.0	103.5	108.3	112.9
Gross national product	90.0	92.7	90.0	89.4	91.0	94.6	97.0	100.0	104.2	108.9	113.6
Gross national disposable income ('RNDI')	88.3	91.3	89.8	89.5	91.1	94.9	97.0	100.0	103.3	107.8	112.9
At factor cost											
Gross domestic product	90.2	92.7	90.7	89.7	91.3	94.6	96.2	100.0	103.2	107.8	112.5
Gross national product	89.8	92.4	89.8	89.4	91.0	94.8	96.9	100.0	104.1	108.5	113.4
Net national product ('National income')	91.1	93.8	90.3	89.3	90.8	94.7	96.7	100.0	104.4	109.2	113.9
Categories of expenditure:											
At market prices											
Consumers' expenditure	86.1	89.8	89.9	89.9	90.8	94.7	96.4	100.0	105.6	111.2	118.8
General government final consumption	92.6	94.6	96.1	96.4	97.1	99.1	100.0	100.0	102.1	103.3	103.8
of which: Central government	91.1	92.5	95.2	96.1	96.8	98.7	99.7	100.0	101.9	102.0	102.3
Local authorities	94.9	97.9	97.4	96.7	97.6	99.7	100.6	100.0	102.6	105.5	106.2
Gross domestic fixed capital formation	91.0	93.5	88.5	80.0	84.4	88.6	96.2	100.0	101.9	110.9	125.4
Total domestic expenditure	89.1	92.4	89.8	88.4	90.4	94.8	97.3	100.0	104.2	109.6	117.6
Exports of goods and services	83.5	86.7	86.7	86.0	86.8	88.6	94.4	100.0	104.2	109.5	110.3
of which: Goods	79.6	83.1	84.1	83.3	85.6	87.6	94.7	100.0	104.0	109.1	110.7
Services	96.8	98.5	95.3	95.2	90.3	91.8	93.3	100.0	104.8	110.5	108.9
Total final expenditure	87.8	91.1	89.1	87.8	89.6	93.4	96.6	100.0	104.2	109.6	116.0
Imports of goods and services	77.2	84.7	81.8	79.5	83.4	88.9	97.5	100.0	106.7	114.9	128.9
of which: Goods	76.1	83.5	79.0	75.9	80.1	87.0	96.9	100.0	107.1	114.5	129.5
Services	82.2	89.9	94.6	96.3	98.4	97.1	100.3	100.0	105.0	116.3	126.3
Gross domestic product (expenditure-based) at market prices	90.8	92.9	91.1	90.1	91.3	94.7	96.4	100.0	103.5	108.1	112.3
Factor cost adjustment	91.4	94.2	91.6	89.4	90.8	93.7	97.8	100.0	105.2	111.5	115.0
Expenditure-based measure											
Gross domestic product at factor cost	90.7	92.7	91.0	90.2	91.4	94.8	96.1	100.0	103.2	107.6	111.9
Income-based measure[1]											
Gross domestic product at factor cost	89.2	92.0	90.4	89.4	91.2	94.7	95.9	100.0	103.3	107.9	112.5
Output-based measure											
Gross domestic product at factor cost	90.2	92.9	90.3	89.0	91.0	94.0	96.6	100.0	103.0	108.1	113.1

1 Income data deflated by the implied GDP deflator at factor cost, based on expenditure data.

Source *Central Statistical Office*

14.13 Value of physical increase in stocks and work in progress

£ million

	1978	1979	1980	1981	1982	1983	1984	1985	1986	1987	1988
At current prices											
Energy and water supply	29	-29	212	-446	-15	199	-661	-14	-279	-114	-20
Manufacturing[1]	348	228	-2 321	-1 565	-1 291	129	1 010	-443	-381	-262	870
Materials and fuels	137	16	-1 251	-1 033	-543	-259	323	139	-117	112	20
Work in progress	124	-260	-714	-42	-561	386	352	-667	-88	-252	360
Finished goods	87	472	-357	-491	-187	1	335	86	-176	-123	489
Retail distribution	660	774	-467	-20	9	144	512	403	927	1 120	1 184
Wholesale distribution	671	1 162	-409	-607	14	267	1	-122	351	636	526
Other industries	96	27	413	-130	95	726	425	791	78	-104	311
National accounts statistical adjustment[2]	0	0	0	0	0	0	0	0	0	0	1 500
Total	*1 804*	*2 162*	*-2 572*	*-2 768*	*-1 188*	*1 465*	*1 287*	*615*	*696*	*1 276*	*4 371*
Revalued at 1985 prices											
Energy and water supply	95	-203	335	-566	68	41	-985	9	-216	-205	-104
Manufacturing[1]	621	365	-3 048	-1 989	-1 461	135	1 057	-443	-403	-223	744
Materials and fuels	221	16	-1 593	-1 260	-618	-293	323	139	-106	103	20
Work in progress	242	-357	-982	-66	-651	423	381	-667	-123	-220	305
Finished goods	159	665	-452	-606	-196	3	354	86	-174	-108	419
Retail distribution	1 051	1 122	-604	-18	27	147	540	403	906	1 039	1 059
Wholesale distribution	1 130	1 891	-555	-730	94	274	24	-122	371	578	455
Other industries	143	55	834	-571	65	760	476	768	19	-138	194
National accounts statistical adjustment[2]	0	0	0	0	0	0	0	0	0	0	1 230
Total	*2 867*	*3 328*	*-3 371*	*-3 200*	*-1 281*	*1 357*	*1 112*	*615*	*677*	*1 051*	*3 578*

1 Differences between totals and the sum of constituent parts of manufacturing at 1985 prices for 1983 onwards and for all current prices are due to rounding. Differences between totals and components at 1985 prices before 1983 arise from the method of rebasing these years on to 1985 prices.

2 The National accounts statistical adjustment applies to the Value of the physical increase in stocks held by Industrial and Commercial Companies.

Source Central Statistical Office

14.14 Gross domestic fixed capital formation
At current prices

£ million

	1978	1979	1980	1981	1982	1983	1984	1985	1986	1987	1988[5]
By type of asset											
Buses and coaches	157	173	175	153	132	153	126	121	125	167	140
Other road vehicles	2 955	3 718	3 208	2 971	3 710	3 676	4 294	5 318	6 533	6 091	8 167
Railway rolling stock	98	126	163	136	123	101	75	106	95	126	203
Ships	533	308	355	221	326	284	502	332	168	236	109
Aircraft	261	359	665	365	−6	316	668	907	511	633	834
Plant and machinery[1]	11 446	13 539	14 958	15 067	16 296	17 935	20 255	23 865	24 608	26 924	32 495
Dwellings	6 325	7 649	8 674	8 138	8 920	10 447	11 725	11 859	13 607	15 640	18 509
Other new buildings and works	8 182	9 637	11 802	12 471	13 386	13 306	14 642	15 211	16 501	19 261	21 762
National Accounts statistical adjustment	–	–	–	–	–	–	–	–	–	–	1 000
By industry group											
Agriculture, forestry and fishing[1]	953	959	1 023	940	1 129	1 259	1 208	982	1 048	1 061	1 135
Extraction of mineral oil and natural gas	2 151	2 056	2 399	2 892	3 021	2 901	3 151	2 819	2 577	2 046	2 117
All other energy and water supply	2 119	2 546	3 290	3 679	3 790	4 127	3 591	3 925	4 180	4 231	4 386
Manufacturing[2]	5 624	6 515	6 478	5 323	5 486	5 859	7 382	8 735	8 831	9 950	11 431
Construction	407	484	586	468	440	543	597	520	531	537	..
Distribution, hotels and catering; repairs	2 329	3 040	3 239	3 223	3 579	3 776	4 514	5 188	5 755	7 167	..
Transport	2 188	2 383	2 426	1 896	1 721	2 100	2 756	2 301	2 574	2 892	..
Communication	965	1 142	1 456	1 465	1 491	1 605	1 858	2 301	2 572	2 881	..
Banking, finance, insurance business services and leasing[2]											
Leased assets	1 146	1 734	2 157	2 240	2 699	2 483	3 523	4 931	4 169	4 840	..
Other assets	2 176	2 748	3 383	4 096	4 452	4 661	5 060	5 687	6 745	9 198	..
Other services	3 497	4 151	5 007	5 190	6 056	6 323	6 999	7 632	8 328	8 780	9 185
Dwellings	6 325	7 649	8 674	8 138	8 920	10 447	11 725	11 859	13 607	15 640	18 509
Transfer costs of land and buildings	1 103	1 416	1 561	1 782	1 937	2 397	2 673	2 972	3 466	4 050	5 532
National Accounts statistical adjustment[4]	–	–	–	–	–	–	–	–	–	–	1 000
Total	31 060	36 925	41 561	41 304	44 824	48 615	54 960	60 343	64 399	73 570	88 751

Revalued at 1985 prices[3]

£ million

	1978	1979	1980	1981	1982	1983	1984	1985	1986	1987	1988[5]
By type of asset											
Buses and coaches	281	273	238	190	155	183	125	121	117	143	115
Other road vehicles	5 350	6 087	4 411	3 808	4 338	4 223	4 689	4 970	4 908	5 587	6 420
Railway rolling stock, ships and aircraft	1 328	1 225	1 663	901	530	771	1 318	1 345	726	874	967
Plant and machinery[1]	18 313	19 736	19 660	18 269	18 478	19 401	21 220	23 865	23 977	25 334	30 117
Dwellings	12 913	13 363	12 379	10 247	10 899	12 247	12 571	11 859	12 885	13 815	14 802
Other new buildings and works	14 147	13 790	13 086	12 527	13 815	13 878	15 169	15 211	15 799	17 854	18 798
National Accounts statistical adjustment	–	–	–	–	–	–	–	–	–	–	850
By industry group											
Agriculture, forestry and fishing[1]	1 548	1 358	1 213	1 043	1 229	1 338	1 246	982	996	974	979
Extraction of mineral oil and natural gas	3 681	3 010	2 860	3 196	3 283	3 086	3 260	2 819	2 479	1 921	1 852
All other energy and water supply	3 747	3 945	4 250	4 263	4 235	4 426	3 751	3 925	4 033	3 966	3 882
Manufacturing[2]	9 763	10 136	8 761	6 579	6 360	6 422	7 818	8 735	8 489	9 107	10 112
Construction	803	875	607	537	607	659	552	531	524	669	..
Distribution, hotels and catering; repairs	3 993	4 547	4 093	3 760	4 019	4 153	4 809	5 181	5 437	6 545	..
Transport	3 747	3 618	3 149	2 234	1 973	2 309	2 896	2 788	2 447	2 627	..
Communication	1 693	1 749	1 916	1 749	1 670	1 877	1 977	2 301	2 471	2 652	..
Banking, finance, insurance, business services and leasing[2]											
Leased assets	1 752	2 411	2 686	2 594	2 962	2 651	3 670	4 931	4 069	4 536	..
Other assets	3 247	3 573	3 741	4 229	4 589	4 839	5 241	5 687	6 524	8 554	..
Other services	6 024	6 091	5 950	5 557	6 448	6 696	7 301	7 632	8 058	8 241	8 016
Dwellings	12 913	13 363	12 379	10 247	10 899	12 247	12 562	11 859	12 883	13 815	14 802
Transfer costs of land and buildings	2 505	2 303	2 170	2 295	2 521	2 773	2 975	2 972	3 068	3 287	3 611
National Accounts statistical adjustment[4]	–	–	–	–	–	–	–	–	–	–	850
Total	54 914	56 405	53 416	48 298	50 915	53 476	58 058	60 343	61 478	66 894	75 680

1 Including changes in the stock of breeding animals.
2 Leased assets are classified, on the basis of ownership rather than use, to the finance industry.
3 For the years before 1983, totals differ from the sum of their components due to the method of rebasing used. See notes on page 130 of *United Kingdom National Accounts, 1989 Edition* (HMSO).
4 For explanation of adjustment see Methodological notes on page 130 of the 1989 CSO Blue Book.
5 For explanation of unavailability of estimates for the year 1988 see page 137 of the 1989 CSO Blue Book.

Source *Central Statistical Office*

14.15 Gross capital stock at 1985 replacement cost by industry[1]
United Kingdom

£ billion at 1985 prices

	1978	1979	1980	1981	1982	1983	1984	1985	1986	1987	1988
Agriculture, forestry and fishing	28.5	28.9	29.0	29.0	29.1	29.2	29.3	29.1	28.9	28.7	28.5
Extraction of mineral oil and natural gas	18.8	21.6	24.1	26.6	28.9	30.8	32.8	34.3	35.3	35.7	35.7
All other energy and water supply	139.1	140.3	141.9	143.5	145.0	146.7	147.6	148.6	149.5	150.3	150.8
Manufacturing (revised definition)	241.1	246.5	250.3	251.5	252.4	253.1	254.6	256.7	258.4	260.2	262.7
Construction	14.9	15.4	15.5	15.5	15.6	15.7	15.7	15.6	15.5	15.5	..
Distribution, hotels and catering; repairs	66.0	69.4	72.2	74.7	77.3	79.9	83.1	86.6	90.3	95.1	..
Transport	83.8	83.2	83.4	80.9	78.2	76.0	75.0	73.7	70.9	69.3	..
Communication	34.4	35.4	36.5	37.4	38.2	39.0	39.7	40.8	41.8	42.9	..
Banking, finance, insurance, business services and leasing	65.3	70.9	76.9	83.2	90.1	96.8	104.7	114.1	123.2	134.4	..
Other services[2]	188.0	192.8	197.4	201.6	206.6	211.9	217.7	223.7	230.1	236.6	242.8
Dwellings	427.2	439.3	450.5	459.7	469.4	480.2	490.7	501.0	512.3	524.5	537.6
Total[3, 4]	1 307.1	1 343.6	1 377.6	1 403.6	1 430.8	1 459.4	1 490.8	1 524.2	1 556.3	1 593.3	1 637.9

1 For an account of the principles of valuation, see paragraphs 12.104 – 124 of *United Kingdom National Accounts, Sources and Methods, Third Edition,* (HMSO). Figures relate to end of year. Assets are classified to industry on the basis of ownership, not use.

2 Comprising classes 91–99 of the Standard Industrial Classification Revised 1980.

3 Differences between totals and sums of components are due to rounding.

4 Includes the National accounts statistical adjustment to gross domestic fixed capital formation in 1988.

Source Central Statistical Office

15 Personal Income, Expenditure and Wealth

Family Expenditure Survey *(Tables 15.3 – 15.5)*

The Family Expenditure Survey, introduced in 1957, covers all types of private households in the United Kingdom. It is a continuous enquiry in which a total set sample of about 13 000 addresses is selected annually, from which an effective sample of some 10 400 households is obtained, of which about 70 per cent co-operate. The main purpose of the survey is to provide a source of the weighting pattern for the Index of Retail Prices and so it is primarily concerned with household expenditure on a wide range of goods and services.

The income information the survey collects is basically to enable households to be classified into income groups and although most of the income information obtained is on a current basis, incomes from investment and self-employment are estimated over a twelve-month period. As income and expenditure figures relate to different periods, the difference between expenditure and income as measured in the survey should not be regarded as savings or dis-savings.

Although the survey is primarily concerned with the expenditure of private households, much additional information is collected about the characteristics of co-operating households. Consequently the survey provides a unique fund of important economic and social data.

Like all surveys based on a sample of the population, its results are subject to sampling error, and to some bias due to non-response. The sampling error is smallest in relation to the average expenditure of large groups of households or items purchased frequently when expenditure does not vary greatly between households. Conversely, it is largest in relation to small groups of households, and for items purchased infrequently for which expenditure varies considerably between households. However, comparison of the survey results over successive years justifies confidence in their reliability.

The results of the survey are published in an annual report, the latest being *Family Expenditure Survey 1987* (HMSO). This includes a list of definitions used in the survey, items on which information is collected and a brief account of the field work procedure.

15.1 Average incomes of households before and after taxes and benefits[1, 2]
United Kingdom

£ per year

	1977	1978	1979	1980	1981	1982	1983	1984	1985	1986
1 adult—non-pensioner										
Original income	2 060	2 299	2 653	3 019	3 673	3 800	4 055	4 123	4 703	5 711
Disposable income	2 038	2 326	2 690	3 165	3 777	3 927	4 255	4 419	4 903	5 770
Income after all taxes and benefits	1 830	2 129	2 398	2 843	3 293	3 390	3 730	3 880	4 196	4 886
1 adult—pensioner[3]										
Original income	48	50	56	70	104	109	98	109	138	203
Disposable income	1 132	1 287	1 447	1 723	2 081	2 308	2 454	2 582	2 750	2 824
Income after all taxes and benefits	1 374	1 552	1 772	2 121	2 461	2 662	2 860	3 083	3 257	3 281
2 adults—non-pensioner										
Original income	4 196	4 869	5 519	6 876	7 747	7 821	8 707	8 735	10 040	11 482
Disposable income	3 698	4 375	5 078	6 261	7 026	7 235	8 003	8 255	9 327	10 523
Income after all taxes and benefits	3 246	3 875	4 360	5 374	6 014	6 139	6 787	6 936	7 884	8 818
2 adults—pensioner[3]										
Original income	123	124	163	194	224	234	304	270	295	396
Disposable income	1 736	1 991	2 258	2 687	3 160	3 447	3 870	3 981	4 214	4 439
Income after all taxes and benefits	2 029	2 320	2 629	3 170	3 649	3 857	4 284	4 466	4 791	4 819
2 adults, 1 child										
Original income	4 627	5 223	5 874	7 327	8 260	9 062	9 353	9 316	10 505	12 165
Disposable income	3 865	4 499	5 203	6 411	7 167	7 923	8 322	8 570	9 512	10 932
Income after all taxes and benefits	3 626	4 239	4 776	5 840	6 579	7 159	7 616	7 893	8 676	9 995
2 adults, 2 children										
Original income	4 887	5 761	6 795	8 094	8 459	9 115	10 198	10 936	11 166	12 766
Disposable income	4 105	4 942	5 978	7 033	7 466	8 028	9 026	9 723	10 561	11 493
Income after all taxes and benefits	4 170	5 006	5 876	6 991	7 528	7 938	8 819	9 488	10 415	11 223
2 adults, 3 children										
Original income	5 378	5 230	6 337	7 773	8 086	8 500	8 928	9 773	10 175	11 376
Disposable income	4 575	4 906	5 921	7 072	7 623	8 179	8 571	9 466	10 023	11 093
Income after all taxes and benefits	5 082	5 615	6 535	7 773	8 535	9 115	9 624	10 355	11 094	11 801
3 adults										
Original income	5 961	6 920	8 126	9 198	10 495	10 749	11 075	12 402	13 494	15 142
Disposable income	5 094	6 041	7 237	8 216	9 292	9 685	10 022	11 081	12 128	12 978
Income after all taxes and benefits	4 538	5 363	6 407	7 200	8 059	8 325	8 634	9 319	10 341	10 818
3 adults, 1 child										
Original income	6 285	7 815	8 233	9 975	10 633	11 466	11 879	12 710	15 476	15 776
Disposable income	5 421	6 629	7 227	8 654	9 235	10 020	10 541	11 207	13 647	13 690
Income after all taxes and benefits	5 408	6 504	6 959	8 331	8 930	9 759	10 181	10 805	13 247	13 189
4 adults										
Original income	8 205	9 771	11 315	13 021	15 153	14 597	15 626	17 555	19 168	19 971
Disposable income	6 783	8 211	9 463	11 031	12 474	12 505	13 575	15 047	16 282	17 185
Income after all taxes and benefits	6 135	7 503	8 423	9 869	10 994	11 027	11 951	12 991	13 962	14 891
1 adult with child(ren)[4]										
Original income	1 472	1 894	2 269	2 692	3 375	2 189	2 276	2 601	2 345	2 478
Disposable income	2 189	2 787	3 186	3 601	4 644	4 047	4 352	4 661	4 800	5 013
Income after all taxes and benefits	2 746	3 456	3 881	4 425	5 617	5 004	5 296	5 681	5 751	5 862
Other households										
Original income	6 480	7 510	8 728	10 681	11 296	12 432	12 183	12 640	14 884	16 042
Disposable income	5 914	6 953	8 081	9 765	10 544	11 987	11 912	12 471	14 526	15 683
Income after all taxes and benefits	6 492	7 496	8 546	10 389	11 055	12 607	12 671	12 944	14 710	16 282
All households in the sample										
Original income	4 037	4 618	5 217	6 353	7 132	7 376	7 757	8 133	9 068	9 786
Disposable income	3 690	4 312	4 967	5 992	6 749	7 106	7 544	7 975	8 832	9 498
Income after all taxes and benefits	3 573	4 175	4 714	5 682	6 371	6 646	7 058	7 375	8 141	8 701

1 Original income is the total income in cash and kind of the household before the deduction of taxes or the addition of state benefits. The addition of cash benefits (retirement pensions, child benefit, etc.) and the deduction of income tax and employees' national insurance contributions give disposable income. By further allowing for taxes paid on goods and services purchased (such as VAT) and benefits in kind received from public expenditure (housing subsidies, education, health, etc.) an estimate of 'final' income is derived.

2 These income figures are derived from estimates made by the Central Statistical Office, based largely on information from the Family Expenditure Survey, and published each year in *Economic Trends.* **As a result of changes in the coverage of taxes and benefits and the method of allocating them to households, these figures are not exactly comparable from year to year.**

3 A pensioner household is one in which the head is over state retirement pension age and when more than three quarters of the household's income consists of national insurance retirement and similar state pensions, or related supplementary benefit.

4 Due to the smaller sample size of this household type, the figures may be subject to greater than average year to year variation.

Source Central Statistical Office

15.2 Distribution of total incomes before and after tax

Years ended 5 April

Lower limit of range of income	1983/84 Annual Survey			
	Thousands	£ million		
	Number of incomes	Total income before tax	Tax[4]	Total income after tax
All incomes[1,2,3]	22 000	178 000	35 200	143 000
Income before tax £				
1 500	509	955	11	944
2 000	1 230	2 760	89	2 670
2 500	1 070	2 930	193	2 740
3 000	1 200	3 900	306	3 600
3 500	1 220	4 600	491	4 110
4 000	1 240	5 260	668	4 600
4 500	1 130	5 350	773	4 570
5 000	1 140	5 950	917	5 040
5 500	1 100	6 380	1 040	5 350
6 000	1 890	12 200	2 090	10 100
7 000	1 710	12 800	2 340	10 500
8 000	2 810	25 000	4 780	20 200
10 000	2 040	22 200	4 410	17 800
12 000	1 740	23 200	4 900	18 300
15 000	1 120	19 000	4 290	14 700
20 000	645	15 200	3 990	11 200
30 000	169	6 200	2 060	4 140
50 000	44	2 840	1 200	1 640
100 000 and over	8	1 290	694	597
Income after tax £				
1 550	635	1 220	21	1 190
2 000	1 470	3 460	166	3 290
2 500	1 410	4 230	372	3 850
3 000	1 670	6 130	712	5 420
3 500	1 670	7 220	965	6 250
4 000	1 530	7 680	1 180	6 510
4 500	1 490	8 480	1 400	7 070
5 000	1 280	8 080	1 380	6 700
5 500	1 170	8 130	1 420	6 710
6 000	2 110	16 800	3 110	13 700
7 000	1 760	16 200	3 070	13 100
8 000	2 560	28 500	5 650	22 900
10 000	1 400	19 300	4 060	15 300
12 000	956	16 500	3 750	12 700
15 000	616	14 100	3 660	10 500
20 000 and over	280	12 000	4 320	7 630

Lower limit of range of income	1984/85 Annual Survey			
	Thousands	£ million		
	Number of incomes	Total income before tax	Tax[4]	Total income after tax
All incomes[1,2,3]	21 900	191 000	37 300	154 000
Income before tax £				
2 000	1 340	2 990	54	2 930
2 500	1 000	2 730	139	2 590
3 000	1 060	3 440	241	3 200
3 500	1 090	4 080	379	3 700
4 000	1 210	5 160	565	4 590
4 500	1 090	5 170	660	4 510
5 000	1 060	5 530	774	4 750
5 500	985	5 680	865	4 810
6 000	1 910	12 400	2 020	10 400
7 000	1 690	12 700	2 200	10 500
8 000	2 930	26 100	4 820	21 300
10 000	2 090	22 900	4 400	18 500
12 000	1 990	26 600	5 380	21 200
15 000	1 340	22 900	4 990	17 900
20 000	780	18 500	4 570	13 900
30 000	246	9 010	2 830	6 180
50 000	62	3 980	1 580	2 390
100 000 and over	11	1 710	846	860
Income after tax £				
2 000	1 580	3 630	98	3 530
2 500	1 280	3 760	271	3 490
3 000	1 480	5 360	537	4 820
3 500	1 480	6 350	784	5 560
4 000	1 490	7 270	973	6 300
4 500	1 400	7 840	1 210	6 620
5 000	1 290	8 060	1 290	6 770
5 500	1 170	8 130	1 380	6 750
6 000	2 230	17 600	3 110	14 500
7 000	1 740	15 900	2 910	13 000
8 000	2 690	29 600	5 640	24 000
10 000	1 670	22 800	4 560	18 200
12 000	1 180	20 000	4 310	15 600
15 000	769	17 300	4 170	13 100
20 000 and over	433	17 900	6 060	11 800

1 The distributions cover only incomes as computed for tax purposes and above a level which for each year corresponds approximately to the single person's allowance. Incomes below these levels are not shown because the information about them is incomplete.
2 The reporting of investment income in the Survey is incomplete; investment income from which basic rate tax has been deducted at source and upon which there is no higher rate liability, investment income surcharge or restricting age allowance is under-recorded. This is because this type of investment income has no operational significance as all liability to tax has been satisfied.
3 All figures have been independently rounded.
4 Where relief at basic rate is given at source, eg under the MIRAS scheme, income tax is calculated without any deduction for such relief (but after allowance for any basic rate relief due at higher rates). The provision of basic rate relief at source on most mortgage interest from 1983–84 thus produces higher estimates of tax due than in previous years.

Source Board of Inland Revenue

15.2 Distribution of total incomes before and after tax

Years ended 5 April

(continued)

Lower limit of range of income	1985/86 Annual Survey			
	Thousands	£ million		
	Number of incomes	Total income before tax	Tax[4]	Total income after tax
All incomes[1,2,3]	21 900	209 000	40 500	168 000
Income before tax £				
2 000	672	1 580	18	1 560
2 500	1 070	2 920	95	2 820
3 000	969	3 140	193	2 950
3 500	1 020	3 810	294	3 520
4 000	1 100	4 660	470	4 190
4 500	1 040	4 930	582	4 350
5 000	1 080	5 670	731	4 930
5 500	1 010	5 790	784	5 010
6 000	1 840	11 900	1 850	10 100
7 000	1 710	12 800	2 180	10 600
8 000	3 010	27 000	4 810	22 200
10 000	2 100	22 900	4 270	18 600
12 000	2 130	28 500	5 520	23 000
15 000	1 770	30 200	6 250	24 000
20 000	975	23 200	5 460	17 700
30 000	307	11 300	3 410	7 920
50 000	87	5 650	2 180	3 460
100 000 and over	17	2 810	1 390	1 430
Income after tax £				
2 000	840	2 010	38	1 970
2 500	1 320	3 820	187	3 630
3 000	1 280	4 560	401	4 160
3 500	1 480	6 250	689	5 560
4 000	1 340	6 520	838	5 680
4 500	1 420	7 840	1 100	6 750
5 000	1 230	7 580	1 150	6 430
5 500	1 260	8 590	1 390	7 200
6 000	2 170	17 000	2 960	14 100
7 000	1 910	17 400	3 110	14 300
8 000	2 660	29 100	5 300	23 800
10 000	1 820	24 700	4 730	19 900
12 000	1 570	26 300	5 350	20 900
15 000	1 000	22 100	5 020	17 100
20 000 and over	453	14 700	4 120	10 600
30 000	119	6 750	2 450	4 300
50 000	23	2 570	1 130	1 440
100 000	3	992	511	481

Lower limit of range of income	1986/87 Annual Survey			
	Thousands	£ million		
	Number of incomes	Total income before tax	Tax[4]	Total income after tax
All incomes[2,3,4]	22 200	240 000	43 300	197 000
Income before tax £				
2 330	266	642	2	640
2 500	933	2 550	56	2 500
3 000	937	3 020	154	2 860
3 500	855	3 200	210	2 990
4 000	1 060	4 510	348	4 160
4 500	912	4 320	411	3 910
5 000	1 010	5 280	608	4 670
5 500	881	5 060	587	4 480
6 000	1 760	11 400	1 480	9 930
7 000	1 490	11 200	1 580	9 630
8 000	2 830	25 400	3 900	21 500
10 000	2 360	25 800	4 150	21 700
12 000	2 450	32 800	5 370	27 400
15 000	2 330	40 000	7 130	32 900
20 000	1 430	34 200	7 000	13 100
30 000	1 490	18 000	4 920	5 290
50 000	129	8 490	3 190	
100 000 and over	28	4 590	2 230	2 360
Income after tax £				
2 330	309	749	5	744
2 500	1 250	3 570	134	3 430
3 000	1 060	3 690	251	3 440
3 500	1 160	4 800	438	4 360
4 000	1 390	6 620	698	5 920
4 500	1 130	6 060	726	5 330
5 000	1 140	6 910	912	6 000
5 500	1 090	7 240	957	6 280
6 000	1 190	15 200	2 260	13 000
7 000	1 710	15 200	2 360	12 800
8 000	2 960	31 300	4 940	26 400
10 000	2 110	27 500	4 410	23 000
12 000	2 180	35 100	6 000	29 100
15 000	1 610	34 000	6 460	27 500
20 000	824	25 600	6 250	19 400
30 000	200	11 000	3 790	7 230
50 000	39	4 320	1 880	2 440
100 000	5	1 650	848	798

Footnotes on page 259.

Source *Board of Inland Revenue*

15.3 Sources of household income[1]
United Kingdom

	1976	1977	1978	1979	1980	1981	1982	1983	1984	1985	1986	1987
Number of households supplying data[2]	7 203	7 198	7 001	6 777	6 944	7 525	7 428	6 973	7 081	7 012	7 178	7 396
Average weekly household income[3] by source (£)												
Wages and salaries	60.23	66.92	76.10	86.27	104.78	114.22	118.50	121.56	131.00	141.26	150.32	162.70
Self-employment	4.38	5.47	5.29	5.63	8.16	10.24	10.59	12.26	12.07	14.65	17.96	21.53
Investments	2.51	2.81	2.95	3.28	4.49	6.35	6.94	6.77	7.07	8.42	9.78	12.44
Annuities and pensions (other than social security benefits)	2.15	2.29	3.03	3.14	3.79	5.20	5.26	7.39	7.72	9.58	10.14	11.87
Social security benefits[3]	8.68	10.57	12.50	14.88	17.60	21.87	24.58	28.03	27.45	28.90	30.30	31.09
Imputed income from owner/rent-free occupancy[4]	3.46	3.93	4.93	5.65	6.75	7.79	8.57	9.70	10.23	11.86	12.57	12.95
Other sources[5]	0.89	0.99	1.33	1.59	1.61	1.93	2.24	2.15	1.84	2.21	2.61	3.72
Total	82.30	92.98	106.13	120.45	147.18	167.60	176.67	187.86	197.37	216.86	233.68	256.31
Sources of household income as a percentage of total household income[3] (per cent)												
Wages and salaries	*73.2*	*72.0*	*71.7*	*71.6*	*71.2*	*68.1*	*67.1*	*64.7*	*66.4*	*65.1*	*64.3*	*63.5*
Self-employment	*5.3*	*5.9*	*5.0*	*4.7*	*5.5*	*6.1*	*6.0*	*6.5*	*6.1*	*6.8*	*7.7*	*8.4*
Investments	*3.1*	*3.0*	*2.8*	*2.7*	*3.0*	*3.8*	*3.9*	*3.6*	*3.6*	*3.9*	*4.2*	*4.9*
Annuities and pensions (other than social security benefits)	*2.6*	*2.5*	*2.9*	*2.6*	*2.6*	*3.1*	*3.0*	*3.9*	*3.9*	*4.4*	*4.3*	*4.6*
Social security benefits[3]	*10.5*	*11.4*	*11.8*	*12.4*	*12.0*	*13.1*	*13.9*	*14.9*	*13.9*	*13.3*	*13.0*	*12.1*
Imputed income from owner/rent-free occupancy[4]	*4.2*	*4.2*	*4.6*	*4.7*	*4.6*	*4.6*	*4.8*	*5.2*	*5.2*	*5.5*	*5.4*	*5.1*
Other sources[5]	*1.1*	*1.0*	*1.2*	*1.3*	*1.1*	*1.2*	*1.3*	*1.2*	*0.9*	*1.0*	*1.1*	*1.5*
Total	*100.0*	*100.0*	*100.0*	*100.0*	*100.0*	*100.0*	*100.0*	*100.0*	*100.0*	*100.0*	*100.0*	*100.1*

1 Information derived from the Family Expenditure Survey.
2 In 1979 and 1983 data were not collected for a few weeks at the time of the General Elections.
3 Because of the introduction of the Housing Benefit Scheme figures for 1983 and 1984 are not on a comparable basis, nor are those for 1983 consistent with earlier years.
4 Imputed income is the weekly equivalent of the rateable value: this is adjusted to allow for general increases in rents since date of valuation, and is also included in income of households living rent-free. From 1976 the method of calculating this adjustment is changed. 1985 assessments of rateable values in Scotland were used from 1 April 1985 in the calculation of imputed income and housing expenditure of owner-occupiers and those living rent-free (1987 FES definitions 14(h), (g)).
5 From 1982 'Other sources' includes very small amounts of income previously classified under self-employment.

Source *Family Expenditure Surveys*

15.4 Availability in households of certain durable goods[1]
United Kingdom

	1976	1977	1978	1979	1980	1981	1982	1983	1984	1985	1986	1987
Number of households supplying data[2]	7 203	7 198	7 001	6 777	6 944	7 525	7 428	6 973	7 081	7 012	7 178	7 396
	Percentage											
Car	*55.2*	*57.2*	*57.6*	*57.9*	*60.3*	*61.8*	*61.4*	*62.1*	*61.3*	*62.8*	*62.4*	*63.4*
One	*44.5*	*46.2*	*45.2*	*44.3*	*45.0*	*46.3*	*46.6*	*45.4*	*44.8*	*45.2*	*44.3*	*44.8*
Two	*9.6*	*9.7*	*10.9*	*11.7*	*13.1*	*13.4*	*12.7*	*14.4*	*13.5*	*14.6*	*14.9*	*15.5*
Three or more	*1.1*	*1.3*	*1.5*	*1.9*	*2.2*	*2.1*	*2.0*	*2.3*	*3.0*	*2.9*	*3.2*	*3.1*
Central heating, full or partial	*47.1*	*50.8*	*53.8*	*55.0*	*59.1*	*60.5*	*62.8*	*63.9*	*66.4*	*69.0*	*70.1*	*74.4*
Washing machine	*72.3*	*74.6*	*75.0*	*76.6*	*78.7*	*80.7*	*81.1*	*81.3*	*81.9*	*83.0*	*82.9*	*84.6*
Refrigerator or Fridge/Freezer	..	..	..	..	..	..	..	..	..	*97.6*	*96.9*	*97.6*
Freezer or Fridge/Freezer	..	..	..	..	..	..	..	..	..	*67.3*	*69.2*	*72.6*
Refrigerator	*88.1*	*89.9*	*91.6*	*92.9*	*94.8*	*96.1*	*96.4*	*97.0*	*97.2*	—	—	—
Television	*95.6*	*96.0*	*95.6*	*95.8*	*96.9*	*96.6*	*96.8*	*96.9*	*97.2*	*97.6*	*97.1*	*97.9*
Telephone	*52.6*	*56.8*	*62.0*	*67.2*	*71.6*	*75.8*	*75.7*	*77.3*	*78.3*	*80.5*	*80.9*	*82.5*
Home computer	..	..	..	..	..	..	..	..	..	*12.6*	*15.1*	*16.6*
Video recorder	..	..	..	..	..	..	..	..	..	*30.1*	*36.3*	*43.5*

1 Information derived from Family Expenditure Survey.
2 In 1979 and 1983 data were not collected for a few weeks at the time of the General Elections.

Source *Family Expenditure Surveys*

15.5 Households and their expenditure[1]
United Kingdom

	1976	1977	1978	1979	1980	1981	1982	1983	1984	1985	1986	1987
Number of households supplying data[2]	7 203	7 198	7 001	6 777	6 944	7 525	7 428	6 973	7 081	7 012	7 178	7 396
Total number of persons	19 793	19 885	19 019	18 314	18 844	20 535	20 022	18 532	18 557	18 206	18 330	18 735
Total number of adults[3]	13 978	14 072	13 581	13 021	13 408	14 685	14 386	13 401	13 618	13 401	13 554	13 902
Household percentage distribution by tenure												
Rented unfurnished	43.0	44.1	41.9	41.2	40.9	41.6	39.0	35.8	35.4	34.9	33.9	32.5
Rented furnished	4.4	2.9	3.5	2.7	2.6	2.5	2.7	2.9	2.7	2.5	3.0	3.3
Rent-free	2.6	2.2	2.8	2.6	2.2	2.2	2.0	2.2	1.8	2.1	2.0	2.1
Owner-occupied	50.0	50.8	51.8	53.5	54.3	53.7	56.3	59.2	60.1	60.5	61.1	62.2
Average number of persons per household												
All persons	2.748	2.763	2.717	2.702	2.714	2.729	2.695	2.658	2.621	2.596	2.554	2.553
Males	1.346	1.338	1.314	1.300	1.307	1.329	1.317	1.289	1.266	1.258	1.236	1.223
Females	1.402	1.425	1.403	1.403	1.407	1.400	1.378	1.369	1.355	1.339	1.317	1.310
Adults[3]	1.941	1.955	1.940	1.921	1.931	1.951	1.937	1.922	1.923	1.911	1.888	1.880
Persons under 65	1.570	1.592	1.579	1.550	1.563	1.585	1.584	1.562	1.572	1.552	1.526	1.512
Persons 65 and over	0.370	0.363	0.361	0.371	0.368	0.366	0.353	0.360	0.351	0.359	0.362	0.368
Children[3]	0.807	0.808	0.777	0.781	0.783	0.777	0.759	0.736	0.698	0.685	0.665	0.653
Children under 2	0.073	0.075	0.073	0.086	0.076	0.078	0.081	0.080	0.068	0.077	0.073	0.078
Children 2 and under 5	0.127	0.128	0.117	0.118	0.116	0.109	0.119	0.123	0.114	0.114	0.118	0.118
Children 5 and under 18	0.607	0.604	0.587	0.577	0.591	0.591	0.559	0.533	0.516	0.495	0.474	0.457
Persons working[4]	1.338	1.352	1.348	1.334	1.357	1.363	1.221	1.172	1.179	1.164	1.160	1.161
Persons not working[4]	1.410	1.410	1.369	1.369	1.356	1.366	1.474	1.485	1.442	1.433	1.394	1.372
Men 65 and over, women 60 and over	0.387	0.388	0.377	0.386	0.386	0.396	0.383	0.403	0.399	0.407	0.403	0.408
Others	1.023	1.022	0.992	0.983	0.971	0.970	1.092	1.082	1.043	1.026	0.991	0.965
Average weekly household expenditure on commodities and services (£)[7]												
Housing[5]	9.21	10.31	11.87	13.72	16.56	19.76	22.29	23.99	24.06	26.63	29.92	34.35
Fuel, light and power	3.53	4.38	4.76	5.25	6.15	7.46	8.35	9.22	9.42	9.95	10.43	10.55
Food	15.36	17.74	19.31	21.83	25.15	27.20	28.19	29.56	31.43	32.70	34.97	35.79
Alcoholic drink	3.11	3.51	3.92	4.56	5.34	6.06	6.13	6.91	7.25	7.95	8.21	8.70
Tobacco	2.29	2.60	2.72	2.85	3.32	3.74	3.85	4.21	4.37	4.42	4.55	4.67
Clothing and footwear	4.99	5.78	6.78	7.79	8.99	9.23	9.69	10.00	11.10	11.92	13.46	13.32
Durable household goods	4.06	4.99	5.66	7.05	7.70	9.40	9.65	10.26	11.57	11.61	13.83	13.48
Household services	–	–	–	–	–	–	–	–	–	–	–	8.23
Personal goods and services	–	–	–	–	–	–	–	–	–	–	–	7.02
Other goods	4.49	5.33	5.99	7.28	8.75	9.45	10.06	10.81	11.89	12.59	13.87	–
Transport and vehicles	8.14	9.71	10.90	13.13	16.15	18.70	19.79	20.96	22.77	24.56	25.43	23.80
Fares and other travel costs	–	–	–	–	–	–	–	–	–	–	–	4.60
Services	6.19	6.93	7.66	9.74	11.96	13.84	15.37	16.09	17.41	19.48	22.67	–
Leisure goods												9.03
Leisure services												18.11
Miscellaneous[6]	0.32	0.56	0.69	0.97	0.53	0.58	0.53	0.58	0.64	0.68	0.74	0.88
Total	61.70	71.84	80.26	94.17	110.60	125.41	133.92	142.59	151.92	162.50	178.10	–
Expenditure on commodity or service as a percentage of total expenditure (per cent)[7]												
Housing[5]	14.9	14.4	14.8	14.6	15.0	15.8	16.6	16.8	15.8	16.4	16.8	–
Fuel, light and power	5.7	6.1	5.9	5.6	5.6	5.9	6.2	6.5	6.2	6.1	5.9	5.6
Food	24.9	24.7	24.1	23.2	22.7	21.7	21.1	20.7	20.7	20.1	19.6	19.0
Alcoholic drink	5.1	4.9	4.9	4.8	4.8	4.8	4.6	4.8	4.8	4.9	4.6	4.6
Tobacco	3.7	3.6	3.4	3.0	3.0	3.0	2.9	3.0	2.9	2.7	2.6	2.5
Clothing and footwear	8.1	8.0	8.4	8.3	8.1	7.4	7.2	7.0	7.3	7.3	7.5	7.1
Durable household goods	6.6	6.9	7.0	7.5	7.0	7.5	7.2	7.2	7.6	7.2	7.8	7.1
Household services	–	–	–	–	–	–	–	–	–	–	–	4.4
Personal goods and services	–	–	–	–	–	–	–	–	–	–	–	3.7
Other goods	7.3	7.4	7.5	7.7	7.9	7.5	7.5	7.6	7.9	7.8	7.8	–
Transport and vehicles	13.2	13.5	13.6	13.9	14.6	14.9	14.8	14.7	15.0	15.1	14.3	–
Fares and other travel costs	–	–	–	–	–	–	–	–	–	–	–	2.4
Services	10.0	9.7	9.5	10.4	10.8	11.0	11.5	11.3	11.5	12.0	12.7	12.6
Leisure goods	–	–	–	–	–	–	–	–	–	–	–	4.8
Leisure services	–	–	–	–	–	–	–	–	–	–	–	9.6
Miscellaneous[6]	0.5	0.8	0.9	1.0	0.5	0.5	0.4	0.4	0.4	0.4	0.4	0.5
Total	100.0	100.0	100.0	100.0	100.0	100.0	100.0	100.0	100.0	100.0	100.0	–

1 Information derived from the Family Expenditure Survey.

2 In 1979 and 1983 data were not collected for a few weeks at the time of the General Elections.

3 Adults and children are:
Adults = all persons 18 and over and married persons under 18
Children = all unmarried persons under 18.

4 From 1982, figures for persons working (and persons not working) are on a revised basis: see *Family Expenditure Survey Report* for 1982 for details.

5 Excludes mortgage payments but includes imputed expenditure from owner-occupancy and from rent-free occupancy. Imputed expenditure is the weekly equivalent of the rateable value which is adjusted to allow for general increase in rents since date of valuation. From 1976 the method of calculating this adjustment is changed. Because of the introduction of the Housing Benefit Scheme, figures for expenditure on housing for 1983 and 1984 are not on a comparable basis. Nor are those for 1983 consistent with earlier years. 1985 assessments of rateable values in Scotland were used from 1 April 1985 in the calculation of imputed income and housing expenditure of owner—occupiers and those living rent-free (1987 definition 14(h), (g)) *to CSO*: definition in the FES Report.

6 Miscellaneous expenditure was greater before 1980 when changes in classifying credit card expenditure were introduced.

7 The component/service groupings used to categorise FES expenditure have been revised to align with the categories recommended for the Retail Price Index (RPI) by the RPI Advisory Committee. The 11 commodity groups have been extended to 14.

Source *Family Expenditure Surveys*

16 Home Finance

Public sector

In Table 16.1 the term public sector describes the consolidation of central government, local authorities and public corporations. The table sets out the relationship between the public sector financial surplus or deficit and the public sector borrowing requirement, (PSBR). A financial surplus or deficit represents the extent to which a sector's gross savings—that is, the balance of receipts and expenditure on current transactions—*plus* net capital transfers are more than sufficient or insufficient to finance the sector's expenditure on physical assets.

In recent years the public sector has usually been in deficit and has had to borrow. The surplus or deficit is not a complete indication of the borrowing requirement because it does not take into account lending to the private sector and overseas and other non-borrowing financial transactions. The borrowing requirement equals the financial surplus or deficit *plus* the net increase or decrease in these financial assets. A revised definition of the PSBR was announced by the Chancellor of the Exchequer on 10 February 1984. Under this definition changes in public sector bank deposits and holdings of other liquid assets are regarded as financing the PSBR rather than contributing to it.

Details of public sector borrowing and the contributions to the PSBR are given in Table 16.2. The PSBR indicates the extent to which the public sector borrows from other sectors of the economy and overseas to finance the balance of expenditure and receipts arising from its various activities. A considerable part of the central government borrowing requirement is needed to finance central government on-lending to local authorities and public corporations. Their additional 'contributions' to the PSBR are therefore equal to their borrowing requirements *less* their direct borrowing from central government.

General government borrowing requirement (GGBR) is the sum of the borrowing requirements of central government and local authorities *less* direct borrowing by local authorities from central government. The PSBR is the GGBR *plus* public corporations borrowing requirement *less* their direct borrowing from central government.

The borrowing requirements are measured from the financing items rather than as the difference between receipts and payments because for local authorities and public corporations, this information comes to hand more quickly and is regarded as more reliable.

Central government

The central government embraces all bodies for whose activities a Minister of the Crown, or other responsible person, is accountable to Parliament. It includes, in addition to the ordinary government departments, a number of bodies administering public policy but without the substantial degree of financial independence which characterises the public corporations; it also includes certain extra-budgetary funds and accounts controlled by departments.

The government's financial transactions are handled through a number of statutory funds, or accounts. The most important of these is the Consolidated Fund which is the government's main account with the Bank of England. Up to 31 March 1968 the Consolidated Fund was virtually synonymous with the term 'Exchequer' which was then the government's central cash account. From 1 April 1968 the National Loans Fund, with a separate account at the Bank of England, was set up by the National Loans Act, 1968. The general effect of this Act was to remove from the Consolidated Fund most of the government's domestic lending and the whole of the government's borrowing transactions and to provide for them to be brought to account in the National Loans Fund.

Revenue from taxation and miscellaneous receipts, including interest and dividends on loans made from Votes, continue to be paid into the Consolidated Fund. After meeting the ordinary expenditure on Supply Services and the Consolidated Fund Standing Services, the surplus or deficit on the Consolidated Fund (Table 16.4), is payable into or met by the National Loans Fund.

Table 16.4 also provides a summary of the transactions of the National Loans Fund. The service of the National Debt, previously borne on the Consolidated Fund, is now met from the National Loans Fund which receives (a) interest payable on loans to the nationalised industries, local authorities and other bodies, whether the loans were made before or after 1 April 1968 and (b) the profits of the Issue Department of the Bank of England, mainly derived from interest on government securities, which were formerly paid into the Exchange Equalisation Account. The net cost of servicing the National Debt after applying these interest receipts and similar items is a charge on the Consolidated Fund as part of the standing services. Details of National Loans Fund loans outstanding are shown in Table 16.7.

Details of borrowing and repayments of debt, other than loans from the National Loans Fund, are shown in Table 16.6.

16.1 Public sector financial account

£ million

	1977/78	1978/79	1979/80	1980/81	1981/82	1982/83	1983/84	1984/85	1985/86	1986/87	1987/88	1988/89
Financial surplus or deficit												
Public sector total	−6 574	−8 337	−8 093	−11 609	−5 455	−8 498	−11 692	−13 369	−7 658	−8 315	−1 899	7 625
Transactions in financial liabilities												
Total	6 652	10 855	12 959	14 603	9 184	10 546	12 146	13 389	6 505	4 605	−2 072	−12 131
Public sector borrowing requirement: total	5 381	9 174	9 926	12 519	8 617	8 937	9 718	10 101	5 659	3 394	−3 485	−14 424
Contributions by												
Central government	4 522	7 910	8 262	12 732	7 597	12 734	12 178	10 164	10 962	10 452	882	−6 898
Local authorities	357	974	2 152	819	941	−2 667	−2 224	−942	−4 067	−5 734	−2 860	−4 579
Public corporations	502	290	−488	−1 032	79	−1 130	−236	879	−1 236	−1 324	−1 507	−2 947
Other financial liabilities	1 271	1 681	3 033	2 084	567	1 609	2 428	3 288	846	1 211	1 413	2 293
Transactions in financial assets												
Total	617	2 945	4 093	2 893	4 051	1 841	494	112	−1 796	−4 314	−4 690	−6 030
Net lending, etc. to private sector and overseas												
Central government	−679	629	−374	1 437	545	503	−938	−1 734	−2 641	−3 586	−5 057	−6 227
Local authorities	−35	52	452	300	504	352	−233	−301	−393	−390	−141	−160
Public corporations	499	356	355	−1 102	245	79	65	−42	−41	95	−178	32
Other financial assets	832	1 908	3 660	2 258	2 757	907	1 600	2 189	1 279	−433	686	325
Total financial transactions	−6 035	−7 910	−8 866	−11 710	−5 133	−8 705	−11 652	−13 277	−8 301	−8 919	−2 618	6 101
Balancing item	−539	−427	773	101	−322	207	−40	−92	643	604	719	1 524

Source *Central Statistical Office*

16.2 Public sector borrowing and contributions to the public sector borrowing requirement

£ million

	1977/78	1978/79	1979/80	1980/81	1981/82	1982/83	1983/84	1984/85	1985/86	1986/87	1987/88	1988/89
Central government borrowing requirement	4 522	7 910	8 262	12 732	7 597	12 734	12 178	10 164	10 962	10 452	882	−6 898
of which: own account	*2 757*	*5 832*	*4 364*	*9 391*	*6 552*	*7 769*	*8 040*	*6 500*	*4 271*	*4 502*	*−3 244*	*−12 845*
Local authorities:												
Direct borrowing from central government[1]	1 063	337	817	1 301	−1 172	2 757	3 431	3 329	5 742	5 884	4 097	4 963
Net borrowing from other sources	357	981	2 117	853	1 094	−2 794	−2 219	−907	−4 059	−5 731	−2 831	−4 530
less Transactions in other public sector debt:												
Central government	–	7	9	7	11	5	23	9	3	–	30	10
Public corporations	–	–	−44	27	142	−132	−18	26	5	3	−1	39
Borrowing requirement	1 420	1 311	2 969	2 120	−231	90	1 207	2 387	1 675	150	1 237	384
General government borrowing requirement	4 879	8 884	10 414	13 551	8 538	10 067	9 954	9 222	6 895	4 718	−1 978	−11 477
Public corporations:												
Direct borrowing from central government[1]	702	1 741	3 081	2 040	2 217	2 208	707	335	949	66	29	984
Net borrowing from other sources	597	266	−433	−715	382	−927	323	619	−953	−1 669	−976	−2 508
less Transactions in other public sector debt:												
Central government	128	97	190	165	339	155	482	−171	179	−120	475	459
Local authorities	−33	−121	−135	152	−36	48	77	−89	104	−225	56	−20
Borrowing requirement	1 204	2 031	2 593	1 008	2 296	1 078	471	1 214	−287	−1 258	−1 478	−1 963
Public sector borrowing requirement	5 381	9 174	9 926	12 519	8 617	8 937	9 718	10 101	5 659	3 394	−3 485	−14 424

1 Excluding market transactions of central government in public sector debt; these transactions are included in 'Net borrowing from other sources.'

Source *Central Statistical Office*

16.3 Debt of the public sector: nominal amount outstanding[1]

At 31 March in each year

£ million

	1977	1978	1979	1980	1981	1982	1983	1984	1985	1986	1987	1988
Central government												
National debt[2]												
Sterling debt	62 796	74 550	82 597	91 366	109 953	116 030	125 326	140 329	155 119	167 506	179 899	192 737
Foreign currency debt[3]	4 370	4 630	4 288	3 949	3 083	2 360	2 601	2 555	2 909	3 861	5 912	4 721
less Official holdings[4,5]	14 418	18 363	17 741	18 161	18 277	14 506	14 096	12 201	12 381	13 517	17 603	19 404
equals Market holdings	52 748	60 817	69 144	77 154	94 759	103 884	113 831	130 683	145 647	157 824	168 208	178 054
Other liabilities:												
Net indebtedness of the central government to the Bank of England banking department	1 397	2 193	653	599	650	725	676	474	–	–	319	583
Deposits with:												
National Savings Bank: ordinary accounts	1 548	1 719	1 849	1 821	1 740	1 703	1 735	1 758	1 734	1 691	1 666	1 679
Trustee Savings Banks: ordinary department[6]	1 626	1 735	1 665									
Fund for banks for savings' liability to Trustee Savings Banks[6]				1 266	1 116	937	745	638	318	105	–	
Accrued interest, etc. on national savings[7]	653	844	1 087	1 430	1 954	2 493	3 002	3 795	4 629	5 508	6 076	6 237
Notes and coin in circulation[8]	7 346	8 628	9 657	10 667	11 203	10 867	12 162	12 438	13 239	13 888	13 675	15 534
Market holdings of Northern Ireland Government debt	116	121	170	168	201	238	250	279	235	255	230	168
Other stocks issued by government funds[9]	70	58	58	57	56	55	55	54	53	52	52	51
Consolidated fund liability to Post Office Superannuation Fund[10]	901	792	662	530	370	168	–	–	–	–		
Funds lodged in the Supreme Court and County Courts	112	126	148	172	210	253	300	369	503	497	537	636
Public corporations' balancer with the Paymaster General	61	114	101	74	55	134	149	150	134	72	53	65
Total central government liabilities	66 578	77 147	85 194	93 938	112 314	121 457	132 905	150 638	166 492	179 892	190 816	203 007
Government guaranteed stocks of nationalised industries[11]	808	808	794	254	224	224	224	224	224	224	10	10
Total held by other sectors	67 386	77 955	85 988	94 192	112 538	121 681	133 129	150 862	166 716	180 116	190 826	203 017
of which:												
Local authorities	*31*	*32*	*50*	*51*	*56*	*61*	*74*	*86*	*96*	*96*	*98*	*120*
Public corporations	*402*	*521*	*619*	*880*	*1 140*	*1 232*	*1 347*	*1 850*	*1 561*	*1 740*	*1 181*	*1 669*
Domestic private sector[12]	*57 493*	*66 778*	*75 967*	*82 816*	*99 241*	*108 098*	*119 216*	*133 658*	*148 903*	*159 695*	*167 548*	*177 097*
Overseas	*9 460*	*10 624*	*9 352*	*10 445*	*12 101*	*12 290*	*12 492*	*15 268*	*16 156*	*18 585*	*21 999*	*24 131*
Local authorities												
Sterling debt	28 624	30 083	31 326	34 551	36 842	36 897	37 482	38 783	41 498	43 776	46 381	49 100
less debt held by other local authorities	747	715	717	671	652	794	874	1 002	1 040	1 029	1 058	882
equals debt held outside local authority sector	27 877	29 368	30 609	33 880	36 190	36 103	36 608	37 781	40 458	42 747	45 323	48 218
Foreign currency debt[3]	779	759	572	233	192	222	359	444	504	614	719	768
Total held by other sectors	28 656	30 127	31 181	34 113	36 382	36 325	36 967	38 225	40 962	43 361	46 042	48 986
of which:												
Central government	*12 950*	*13 948*	*14 456*	*15 577*	*16 711*	*15 769*	*18 207*	*21 391*	*24 618*	*30 042*	*35 933*	*39 934*
Public corporations	*334*	*219*	*202*	*231*	*262*	*279*	*326*	*405*	*316*	*356*	*195*	*251*
Domestic private sector[12]	*14 816*	*15 386*	*15 944*	*17 882*	*18 959*	*19 785*	*17 791*	*15 741*	*15 306*	*12 125*	*9 173*	*7 822*
Overseas	*556*	*574*	*579*	*423*	*450*	*492*	*643*	*688*	*722*	*835*	*741*	*979*

See footnotes on page 266.

Source *Central Statistical Office*

16.3 Debt of the public sector: nominal amount outstanding[1]

At 31 March in each year

(continued)

£ million

	1977	1978	1979	1980	1981	1982	1983	1984	1985	1986	1987	1988
Public corporations												
Sterling debt	19 482	20 678	21 847	25 503	27 120	26 841	27 139	27 842	26 142	25 771	23 726	24 373
Foreign currency debt[3]	5 392	5 794	5 222	4 523	4 158	4 762	5 291	5 609	5 498	5 149	4 548	3 001
Total held by other sectors	24 874	26 472	27 069	30 026	31 278	31 603	32 430	33 451	31 640	30 920	28 274	27 374
of which:												
Central government	*17 492*	*18 502*	*19 632*	*22 901*	*24 689*	*23 676*	*24 834*	*25 551*	*22 797*	*23 837*	*22 120*	*22 549*
Local authorities	*1 420*	*1 429*	*1 380*	*1 369*	*1 369*	*1 469*	*1 172*	*1 108*	*1 086*	*1 022*	*949*	*898*
Domestic private sector[12]	*2 282*	*2 072*	*1 740*	*1 655*	*1 512*	*2 505*	*2 306*	*2 332*	*3 704*	*2 218*	*1 713*	*1 028*
Overseas	*3 680*	*4 469*	*4 317*	*4 101*	*3 708*	*3 953*	*4 118*	*4 460*	*4 053*	*3 863*	*3 492*	*2 899*
Public sector debt held outside the public sector												
Total	88 287	99 903	107 899	117 322	135 971	147 123	156 566	172 147	188 844	197 324	204 666	213 958
Sterling debt held by:												
Domestic private sector	70 257	80 183	90 355	99 801	117 884	129 309	137 926	150 380	166 300	171 321	174 300	183 074
Overseas	7 489	8 537	7 462	8 816	10 654	10 470	10 389	13 159	13 633	16 405	19 187	22 392
Foreign currency debt held by:												
Domestic private sector	4 334	4 053	3 296	2 552	1 828	1 079	1 387	1 351	1 613	2 717	4 134	2 873
Overseas	6 207	7 130	6 786	6 153	5 605	6 265	6 864	7 257	7 298	6 881	7 045	5 617
Contingent liabilities of central government[13]												
Export credit guarantees	16 380	19 046	21 058	24 337	25 585	30 838	50 901	42 790	42 298	38 389	37 213	36 128
Assistance to industry, guaranteed loans	1 223	1 201	1 552	1 492	1 652	2 116	1 917	2 140	2 536	2 053	1 801	1 788
Overseas Development and Co-operation Act, 1980, guaranteed loans	39	29	30	25	54	53	61	56	66	40	64	5
Other identified	7	7	8	7	8	9	10	9	10	10	12	13
Total	17 649	20 283	22 648	25 861	27 299	33 016	52 889	44 995	44 910	40 492	39 090	37 349
Public sector debt ratios												
Percentage of total debt held outside public sector	*73*	*74.2*	*74.8*	*74.1*	*75.5*	*77.6*	*77.3*	*77.4*	*78.9*	*77.6*	*77.2*	*76.6*
Debt held outside sector as a percentage of GDP (at current market prices)	*62.9*	*61.6*	*62.3*	*56.5*	*57.5*	*56.5*	*55.0*	*56.0*	*57.3*	*54.6*	*53.0*	*50.4*
Debt held overseas as a percentage of debt held outside public sector	*15.5*	*15.7*	*13.2*	*12.8*	*12.0*	*11.4*	*11.0*	*11.9*	*11.1*	*11.8*	*12.8*	*13.1*
Debt held overseas as a percentage of GDP (at current market prices)	*9.8*	*9.7*	*8.2*	*7.2*	*6.9*	*6.4*	*6.2*	*6.6*	*6.3*	*6.4*	*6.8*	*6.6*
Foreign currency debt as a percentage of debt held outside public sector	*11.9*	*11.2*	*9.3*	*7.4*	*5.5*	*5.0*	*5.3*	*5.0*	*4.7*	*4.9*	*5.5*	*4.0*

1 An article describing these statistics was published in *Economic Trends* No. 283, May 1977.

2 Comprises the total liabilities of the National Loans Fund, full details of which are given in Section 3 of *Consolidated Fund and National Loans Fund; Supplementary Statements* each year.

3 Total foreign currency debt for each sub-sector is valued at middle closing spot exchange rates on the last working day of March of each year. Much of the foreign currency debt of local authorities and public corporations has been contracted through the exchange cover scheme under which the Treasury guarantees the debt against depreciation of sterling *vis-a-vis* the currency in which the debt is denominated. Thus the market exchange rate valuation used will overstate the liability of these authorities when sterling depreciates, but not the liability of the public sector as a whole.

4 Including sterling stocks of nationalised industries guaranteed by the British government.

5 Official holdings at 31 March 1988 were made up as follows: Treasury bills—£3 692 million, marketable securities—£6 852 million, ways and means advances—£8 034 million, other (longstanding) debt to the Bank of England Issue Department—£11 million, and non-marketable stocks issued to the National Debt Commissioners—£815 million.

6 From November 1979 Trustee savings banks' ordinary department and new department were amalgamated. The deposit liabilities of the former are now shown as a diminishing claim on the fund for banks for savings.

7 Includes accrued interest, index-linking and bonus as applicable on national savings certificates and SAYE contracts and, from 1981, National Savings Bank investment accounts.

8 Excluding notes and coin held by the Bank of England.

9 For details see Section 4 of *Consolidated Fund and National Loans Fund: Supplementary Statements* for each year.

10 The nominal amount outstanding. The Consolidated Fund's actual liability to the Post Office Superannuation Fund has been up to 1982 to make quarterly payments partly to meet interest at 2½ per cent on the nominal debt and partly to reduce it in the form of a holding of consols. The amount of this nominal reduction therefore depended upon the price of consols at the time of payment.

11 These stocks are liabilities of public corporations but cannot be distinguished from British government securities in the sector analysis of holdings.

12 Holdings by the domestic private sector are obtained as a residual and may contain some unidentified holdings by public sector bodies.

13 Where data are readily available and other than guarantees of loans to the public sector. Further details are given in *Consolidated Fund and National Loans Fund Accounts: Supplementary Statements* for each year.

Source *Central Statistical Office*

16.4 Consolidated Fund: revenue and expenditure
Years ended 31 March

£ million

	1978/79	1979/80	1980/81	1981/82	1982/83	1983/84	1984/85	1985/86	1986/87	1987/88	1988/89
Revenue											
Inland Revenue	24 080.1	28 153.4	32 981.8	40 318.3	43 793.7	45 926.0	50 350.1	55 438.1	57 114.9	64 508.5	68 812.7
Customs and Excise	13 835.0	18 031.9	22 095.2	25 247.8	27 895.5	31 434.3	35 502.2	37 397.9	41 094.0	44 737.5	49 565.3
Motor vehicle duties	1 113.0	1 148.9	1 418.7	1 640.2	1 823.4	2 036.1	2 219.4	2 432.3	2 576.3	2 644.7	2 810.8
Selective employment tax and national insurance surcharge[1]	1 914.4	2 987.0	3 541.9	3 596.3	2 831.3	1 670.5	924.1	34.7	1.0	–	1.5
Miscellaneous receipts	2 145.4	4 010.3	6 175.9	5 952.4	6 927.5	7 297.0	9 250.9	10 828.8	10 424.7	11 078.0	12 402.5
Total revenue	43 087.9	54 331.5	66 213.5	76 755.0	83 271.4	88 363.9	98 246.7	106 131.8	111 210.9	122 968.7	133 592.8
Expenditure											
Supply services	45 762.4	53 774.0	67 997.4	74 090.8	80 456.4	86 749.3	93 412.1	97 961.7	102 358.7	104 875.5	110 713.9
Debt interest[2]	3 222.4	4 143.2	5 043.8	6 503.5	5 392.7	6 485.1	7 520.1	7 567.5	8 893.4	9 598.5	10 263.0
Payments to Northern Ireland	765.2	986.8	1 236.5	1 475.2	1 607.1	1 603.0	1 647.5	1 808.2	2 030.8	2 218.7	2 383.3
Payments to the European Community, etc.	1 669.2	2 007.5	1 905.6	2 642.0	2 804.6	2 618.4	2 915.9	2 587.4	3 327.3	3 789.3	3 899.5
Other expenditure[3]	50.2	95.9	−13.2	73.9	210.0	−4.8	121.4	201.8	−149.7	79.0	177.8
Total expenditure	51 469.4	61 007.4	76 170.1	84 785.5	90 470.8	97 451.0	105 617.0	110 126.6	116 460.5	120 561.0	127 437.5
Deficit met from the National Loans Fund	8 381.5	6 675.9	9 956.6	8 030.5	7 199.4	9 087.1	7 370.3	3 994.8	5 249.6	−2 407.7	−6 155.3

National Loans Fund: summary of receipts and payments

£ million

	1978/79	1979/80	1980/81	1981/82	1982/83	1983/84	1984/85	1985/86	1986/87	1987/88	1988/89
Receipts											
Interest on loans, and profits of Issue Department of the Bank of England	3 235.9	4 256.4	4 810.0	4 702.1	5 430.9	5 347.4	5 405.0	6 645.0	6 721.1	6 807.0	7 411.1
Service of the National Debt—balance met from the Consolidated Fund	3 222.4	4 143.2	5 043.8	6 503.5	5 392.7	6 485.1	7 520.1	7 567.5	8 893.4	9 598.5	10 263.0
	6 458.3	8 399.6	9 853.8	11 205.6	10 823.6	11 832.5	12 925.1	14 212.5	15 614.5	16 405.5	17 674.1
Exchange Equalisation Account—sterling capital[4]	1 850.0	200.0	1 400.0	3 600.0	2 800.0	600.0	1 000.0	−2 300.0	−3 650.0	−10 250.0	–
Net borrowing[5]	6 796.4	8 530.9	12 617.8	4 833.6	7 906.9	13 372.7	13 964.8	9 008.1	13 279.7	12 071.8	–
International Monetary Fund—maintenance of sterling holdings	35.1	228.5	152.2	44.4	–	–	–	–	151.3	–	234.7
Reduction of National Debt Commissioners Liability in respect of the National Savings Bank Investment Account	–	–	179.2	315.5	1 215.9	46.9	19.5	14.1	–	–	–
Change in balances and other items	−0.1	–	–	–	2.0	−8.1	−4 929.2	3 840.9	1 096.4	–	–
	15 139.7	17 359.0	24 203.0	19 999.1	22 748.4	25 844.0	22 980.2	24 775.6	26 491.9	18 227.3	17 908.8
Payments											
Service of the National Debt:											
Interest	6 369.4	8 290.5	9 732.7	11 075.5	10 687.3	11 692.2	12 773.2	14 046.4	15 441.1	16 232.9	17 501.1
Management and expenses	88.9	109.1	121.1	130.1	136.3	140.3	151.9	166.1	173.4	172.6	173.0
	6 458.3	8 399.6	9 853.8	11 205.6	10 823.6	11 832.5	12 925.1	14 212.5	15 614.5	16 405.5	17 674.1
Consolidated Fund deficit met from the National Loans Fund	8 381.5	6 675.9	9 956.6	8 030.5	7 199.4	9 087.1	7 370.3	3 994.8	5 249.6	−2 407.7	−6 155.3
Net repayment[5]	–	–	–	–	–	–	–	–	–	–	2 411.5
Net lending	216.2	2 283.5	3 557.0	763.0	4 463.8	3 413.3	2 501.1	6 378.6	5 627.8	4 132.0	3 978.5
International Monetary Fund—maintenance of value of sterling holding	–	–	–	–	261.6	188.5	183.7	189.7	–	97.5	–
International Monetary Fund—additional subscription	83.7	–	835.6	–	–	1 322.6	–	–	–	–	–
	15 139.7	17 359.0	24 203.0	19 999.1	22 748.4	25 844.0	22 980.2	24 775.6	26 491.9	18 227.3	17 908.8

1 Actual receipts in the year are shown gross, and payments of refunds and premiums are included in expenditure on supply services, national insurance surcharge from April 1977.
2 Payment to National Loans Fund representing its payments for the service of the National Debt *less* its receipts of interest on loans outstanding, etc.
3 Includes net issues to Contingences Fund.
4 Minus sign indicates a net issue.
5 See Table 16.6.

Source HM Treasury

16.5 Central government borrowing requirement (net balance)[1]

United Kingdom
Years ended 31 March

£ million

	1978/79	1979/80	1980/81	1981/82	1982/83	1983/84	1984/85	1985/86	1986/87	1987/88	1988/89
National Loans Fund:											
Net lending	216	2 283	3 557	745	4 464	3 412	2 501	6 378	5 637	4 132	3 978
less Surplus from Consolidated Fund[2]	8 381	6 676	9 957	8 049	7 200	9 086	7 370	3 995	5 240	−2 407	−6 155
Other items	–	–	–	–	–	–	–	–	–	–	–
Borrowing required[2]	8 597	8 959	13 514	8 794	11 664	12 498	9 871	10 373	10 877	1 725	−2 177
Surplus of National Insurance Funds[2]	−341	−381	25	604	216	−520	−203	−396	−410	−1 385	−3 162
Departmental balances and miscellaneous	−409	−318	−828	−1 801	824	277	473	976	168	554	−1 553
Northern Ireland central government debt	63	2	33	17	33	34	−41	−15	−7	−12	−3
Central government borrowing requirement (net balance)	7 910	8 262	12 732	7 597	12 734	12 178	10 164	10 962	10 452	882	−6 895
Borrowing requirement analysed by investment											
Liabilities											
Notes and coin	1 030	1 008	552	189	1 206	323	900	744	−290	1 873	802
Marketable debt:											
Treasury bills[3]	−840	56	−1 025	−111	195	126	−185	124	670	793	460
British government securities	6 256	8 977	13 107	5 959	5 140	11 677	10 223	5 675	6 132	7 119	−13 254
Non-marketable debt:											
National savings	1 604	985	2 140	4 321	3 028	3 258	3 115	2 142	3 326	2 138	637
Tax instruments[4]	1 119	−953	490	558	1 035	−235	771	376	−682	−21	−635
Other	−9	−16	−68	−99	−173	300	−498	−201	−440	323	−29
Net indebtedness to Bank of England, Banking Department	−1 568	−26	50	55	−69	−143	−4 855	3 803	805	229	371
Northern Ireland central government debt[5]	48	2	28	17	33	34	−40	−15	−7	−12	−3
Exchange cover scheme: payment of claims	−160	−118	59	21	−94	−79	−356	−168	−229	64	136
Government foreign currency debt	−810	−632	−762	−1 394	−276	–	75	1 569	2 684	−272	67
Other government overseas financing	144	51	100	−75	−87	100	−105	−86	−86	−69	−73
Assets											
Overseas official financing:											
Net change in official reserves[6]	1 328	−561	−153	2 749	2 062	32	921	−2 428	−3 834	−11 142	−1 606
Public sector debt and commercial bills[6] and government guaranteed stock	−90	−562	−1 667	−4 505	658	−2 934	118	−568	2 519	−268	6 296
Bank deposits	−142	51	−119	−98	76	−82	80	3	−71	−12	−67

1 This is equal to National Loans Fund borrowing and special transactions (net) *less* receipts from other central government funds, etc.
2 A negative item represents a surplus, a positive item a deficit.
3 Excluding bills held as the sterling counterpart of assistance from overseas central banks, which are part of Overseas official financing.
4 Includes tax reserve certificates, tax deposit accounts, and certificates of tax deposit from October 1975.
5 Excluding foreign currency borrowed under the exchange cover scheme which is included in Overseas official financing: net official financing.
6 Market transactions by the Issue department, Bank of England and by the National Debt Commissioners.

Sources HM Treasury; Central Statistical Office

16.6 Borrowing and repayment of debt
Years ended 31 March

£ million

	1978/79	1979/80	1980/81	1981/82	1982/83	1983/84	1984/85	1985/86	1986/87	1987/88	1988/89
Borrowing											
Marketable securities: new issues	7 845.1	14 925.3	16 083.7	10 997.6	10 704.6	15 888.4	16 057.3	11 897.6	15 182.7	16 735.6	4 045.6
National savings securities:											
National savings certificates	1 507.0	1 458.5	2 081.9	4 116.2	2 077.8	1 631.4	2 208.1	961.8	1 303.7	395.5	641.0
Capital bonds	–	–	–	–	–	–	–	–	–	–	190.1
Income bonds	–	–	–	–	878.1	1 115.4	1 073.0	1 209.9	2 206.0	2 109.9	1 741.9
Deposit bonds	–	–	–	–	–	106.3	137.1	130.2	236.0	230.2	143.7
British savings bonds	94.6	24.0	–	–	–	–	–	–	–	–	–
Premium savings bonds	193.0	121.2	167.3	144.5	179.8	186.9	207.9	186.4	211.7	290.3	320.0
Save As You Earn	109.6	120.6	128.7	136.7	138.0	123.9	116.9	91.5	66.5	62.0	66.9
Yearly plan	–	–	–	–	–	–	28.6	106.0	126.1	132.3	114.2
National savings stamps and gift tokens	1.8	1.3	1.2	1.2	1.2	1.2	1.2	1.2	3.2	3.0	2.8
National Savings Bank deposits	–	–	486.7	1 096.7	1 413.8	1 506.5	1 261.0	1 225.5	1 408.3	1 811.1	1 596.7
Certificate of tax deposit	2 408.2	893.7	1 921.6	2 777.5	2 499.9	2 359.9	4 523.2	4 413.0	3 339.6	2 060.8	891.1
Nationalised industries', etc. temporary deposits	–	–	–	–	–	2 894.0	4 297.0	8 319.0	7 076.0	11 087.0	12 708.0
British Gas Corporation deposits	–	200.0	100.0	–	–	–	–	–	–	–	–
Treasury bills (net receipt)	–	–	–	–	8.2	160.2	–	358.8	358.7	1 122.0	588.4
ECU Treasury Bills (net receipt)	–	–	–	–	–	–	–	–	–	–	1 562.1
Ways and means (net receipt)	1 951.8	–	1 178.6	–	658.7	–	555.6	–	3 319.2	1 214.7	2 329.6
Other debt: payable in sterling:											
Interest free notes	97.1	13.0	624.6	–	–	1 312.1	313.8	368.2	259.2	373.0	142.2
Other debt: payable in external currencies	696.9	242.3	–	–	261.5	–	236.7	1 743.0	2 720.7	–	–
Total receipts	14 905.1	17 999.9	22 774.3	19 270.4	18 821.6	27 286.2	31 017.4	31 012.1	37 817.6	37 627.4	27 084.3
Repayment of debt											
Marketable securites: redemptions	2 102.3	2 859.4	3 645.5	6 119.3	6 266.0	4 600.1	4 666.8	6 097.7	9 299.1	8 295.3	8 537.0
Statutory sinking funds	4.8	4.5	4.2	4.0	3.8	3.6	3.4	3.2	3.1	3.0	2.8
Terminable annuities:											
National Debt Commissioners	9.4	2.6	–	–	–	–	–	–	–	–	–
National savings securities:											
National savings certificates	275.8	591.6	756.7	922.1	1 331.6	1 144.3	1 298.5	1 220.7	1 495.9	1 483.8	1 580.6
Income bonds	–	–	–	–	1.8	60.1	233.0	305.7	382.2	626.6	940.3
Deposit bonds	–	–	–	–	–	–	16.6	43.6	66.2	105.3	135.3
Yearly Plan	–	–	–	–	–	–	–	2.2	8.4	10.9	17.0
British savings bonds	138.1	176.3	191.9	153.4	90.3	99.2	82.1	18.7	0.7	2.9	–
Premium savings bonds	74.1	119.0	110.1	102.3	100.0	102.6	110.1	117.0	125.8	130.9	134.0
Save As You Earn	69.6	70.5	83.9	67.7	184.2	110.0	117.6	159.1	130.0	86.9	94.1
National savings stamps and gift tokens	3.7	9.6	1.2	1.2	1.2	1.2	1.2	1.2	2.5	2.8	2.3
National Savings Bank deposits (repayments)	–	–	102.0	722.0	874.3	1 127.8	1 367.4	1 315.2	1 344.2	1 509.5	1 858.4
Certificates of tax deposit	1 288.1	1 846.6	1 431.4	2 219.7	1 465.0	2 595.2	3 802.2	3 987.3	4 022.0	2 082.1	1 526.3
Tax reserve certificates	0.9	0.3	0.2	0.1	0.2	0.1	–	–	–	–	–
Nationalised industries', etc. temporary deposits	–	–	–	–	–	2 489.0	4 554.0	8 187.0	6 987.0	10 776.0	12 770.0
British Gas Corporation (Repayment of Deposits)	–	–	–	–	–	–	–	–	300.0	–	–
Treasury bills (net repayment)	2 503.7	250.4	2 550.2	80.8	–	–	291.9	–	–	–	–
Ways and means (net repayment)	–	2 148.1	–	2 393.7	–	1 394.5	–	226.6	–	–	–
Other debt: payable in sterling:											
Interest free notes	1 066.7	1 031.7	593.1	341.8	394.8	89.0	61.1	39.4	205.6	97.2	330.0
Other	0.2	0.1	0.1	0.1	–	0.1	0.1	0.1	0.1	0.1	0.1
Other debt: payable in external currencies	571.4	358.3	686.0	1 308.6	201.5	96.7	446.6	279.3	165.1	342.3	1 567.6
Total payments	8 108.8	9 469.0	10 156.5	14 436.8	10 914.7	13 913.5	17 052.6	22 004.0	24 537.9	25 555.6	29 495.8
Net borrowing	6 796.3	8 530.9	12 617.8	4 833.6	7 906.9	13 372.7	13 964.8	9 008.1	13 279.7	12 071.8	–
Net repayment	–	–	–	–	–	–	–	–	–	–	2 411.5

Source *HM Treasury*

16.7 Consolidated Fund and National Loans Fund: assets and liabilities

At 31 March in each year

£ million

	1978	1979	1980	1981	1982	1983	1984	1985	1986	1987	1988
Consolidated Fund											
Total estimated assets	7 229.3	8 659.0	10 786.9	9 853.8	7 562.3	7 239.1	7 924.8	8 719.4	9 477.1	9 879.8	9 918.3
Subscriptions and contributions to international financial organisations	702.1	760.2	815.4	881.4	1 063.4	1 248.3	1 491.9	1 715.6	1 899.7	2 176.3	2 378.0
International Bank for Reconstruction and Development	116.8	114.9	114.1	113.5	117.7	119.8	150.2	157.3	180.0	197.7	193.2
International Finance Corporation	7.7	18.3	17.5	16.9	21.3	25.6	26.3	30.8	25.6	31.2	29.8
International Development Association	449.8	484.6	512.8	562.7	713.4	871.1	1 046.4	1 199.2	1 312.1	1 475.2	1 629.4
African Development Fund	1.0	2.5	3.1	6.0	7.8	9.8	14.4	25.1	30.3	40.5	52.1
Asian Development Bank	26.2	30.6	35.2	37.9	40.9	45.4	53.4	66.2	81.7	92.2	105.0
Caribbean Development Bank	6.2	8.5	11.2	12.0	12.1	12.3	12.7	12.9	13.1	15.3	17.8
European Investment Bank	68.6	85.8	100.5	104.1	115.2	120.6	136.5	157.6	175.0	227.5	242.6
Inter-American Development Bank	7.8	13.2	19.2	25.7	30.1	36.1	41.5	50.8	62.0	73.5	82.1
International Fund for Agricultural Development	18.0	1.8	1.8	2.6	4.8	7.6	10.5	15.7	19.9	23.2	26.0
Amounts due from overseas governments	115.2	117.0	118.3	118.3	98.7	84.1	81.6	79.1	29.2	26.6	6.5
War of 1939–45	83.5	83.7	83.8	84.0	64.3	64.5	64.6	64.8	17.4	17.5	–
Other	31.7	33.3	34.5	34.3	34.4	19.6	17.0	14.4	11.8	9.1	6.5
Loans from Votes	3 818.1	4 017.4	3 589.4	3 007.7	2 558.6	2 050.0	1 953.1	1 942.1	1 794.9	1 845.3	1 816.2
Issues of public dividend capital:	2 327.8	3 557.0	5 704.1	5 576.4	3 513.5	3 369.2	4 053.5	4 532.6	5 134.0	5 388.9	5 502.3
British Airways Board	300.0	310.0	320.0	170.0	180.0	180.0	180.0	–	–	–	–
British Steel Corporation	1 824.0	2 674.0	3 579.0	4 812.0	2 618.0	2 361.0	2 757.0	3 424.0	3 980.0	3 980.0	3 980.0
Royal Ordnance Factories	35.0	35.0	35.0	35.0	35.0	35.0	35.0	–	–	–	–
National Enterprise Board	110.4	470.7	1 432.3	179.7	187.7	224.2	232.0	64.0	32.0	–	–
Royal Mint	7.0	7.0	7.0	7.0	7.0	7.0	7.0	7.0	7.0	7.0	7.0
Post Office	13.0	17.0	17.0	17.0	22.0	22.0	22.0	22.0	22.0	22.0	22.0
Scottish Development Agency	9.6	11.5	12.1	6.8	6.8	11.4	15.2	16.3	17.1	19.2	21.5
Welsh Development Agency	1.8	4.8	5.7	2.9	4.0	5.6	7.4	12.4	14.0	14.3	17.2
British Aerospace	27.0	27.0	60.0	–	–	–	–	–	–	–	–
British Shipbuilders	–	–	236.0	346.0	453.0	523.0	797.9	986.9	1 061.9	1 346.4	1 454.6
Contingencies Fund—capital	94.0	126.0	176.0	138.0	186.0	346.0	277.0	337.0	482.0	222.0	202.0
Balance on revenue accounts	172.0	81.4	383.7	132.0	142.2	141.6	67.7	112.9	137.1	220.7	13.3
Total liabilities	39 737.3	48 208.0	55 723.4	70 213.0	78 512.9	86 580.4	96 534.7	108 238.6	113 431.4	121 862.8	121 375.2
Liability to balance National Loans Fund	39 113.4	47 396.1	54 836.6	69 147.4	77 187.7	84 742.1	94 623.3	106 084.0	111 448.6	119 976.2	118 809.6
Payment from Votes:	75.2	74.8	74.1	73.2	72.8	72.4	71.9	71.9	70.8	70.3	69.7
Married quarters for armed forces	75.2	74.8	74.1	73.2	72.8	72.4	71.9	71.9	70.8	70.3	69.7
Liability to Post Office Superannuation Fund	173.2	152.6	103.3	75.8	33.3	–	–	–	–	–	–
Post-war credits outstanding and interest due—estimated	66.0	64.0	62.0	62.0	62.0	62.0	47.0	46.9	46.8	46.7	46.4
Revenue paid over in advance of collection	5.5	6.9	–	63.5	11.8	29.8	85.4	69.1	39.7	–	74.2
Inland Revenue	–	–	–	–	–	–	85.0	23.0	–	–	51.2
Customs and Excise	–	–	–	–	–	–	–	–	0.8	–	23.0
Broadcast receiving licences	5.4	5.5	–	0.7	3.5	4.8	–	–	–	–	–
Vehicle Excise Duty	–	–	–	–	7.9	–	–	–	–	–	–
National insurance surcharge—Great Britain	–	–	–	62.8	–	24.3	–	46.1	38.9	–	–
National insurance surcharge—Northern Ireland	0.1	1.4	–	–	0.4	0.7	0.4	–	–	–	–

Source *HM Treasury*

16.7 Consolidated Fund and National Loans Fund: assets and liabilities

(continued)

At 31 March in each year

£ million

	1978	1979	1980	1981	1982	1983	1984	1985	1986	1987	1988
Consolidated Fund *(continued)*											
Promissory notes issued by Minister of Overseas Development	304.0	513.6	803.9	791.1	1 145.3	1 674.1	1 707.1	1 966.7	1 825.5	1 769.6	2 375.3
International Development Association	245.4	377.6	510.4	552.9	680.9	709.3	673.0	610.0	629.9	630.3	475.3
African Development Fund	1.6	10.0	9.4	18.8	23.2	29.3	34.9	34.5	41.9	44.1	45.1
Asian Development Bank	3.2	3.0	2.7	3.5	3.5	3.5	3.5	3.5	3.5	3.5	4.2
Asian Development Fund	17.4	21.0	33.0	45.6	57.5	67.8	79.0	85.4	89.0	87.5	99.8
Caribbean Development Bank	–	–	–	0.1	0.3	0.5	0.8	1.0	0.8	0.7	0.3
European Community/International Development Association Special Action Account	–	63.0	61.0	37.0	24.5	7.2	–	–	–	–	–
European Investment Bank	–	–	47.3	31.8	87.9	86.1	70.6	51.7	149.1	147.8	117.7
Inter-American Development Bank	18.4	22.7	1.2	2.6	3.8	6.7	7.9	8.8	7.7	5.5	3.9
Fund for special operations	–	–	13.5	22.9	32.6	47.8	49.4	48.4	38.5	30.5	24.5
International Fund for Agricultural Development	–	16.2	16.2	15.4	13.2	14.7	16.1	15.3	11.0	17.8	21.1
International Bank for Reconstruction and Development	–	–	–	–	–	–	27.6	25.8	20.2	–	–
Special Development Fund	–	–	–	–	–	–	–	–	1.7	1.7	6.6
Other contributions and instalments due in respect of international subscriptions, etc.	–	–	109.2	60.5	217.9	701.2	744.3	1 082.3	832.2	800.2	1 576.8
National Loans Fund											
Total assets	79 179.9	86 884.9	95 314.2	113 036.0	118 390.4	127 927.3	142 885.2	158 028.5	171 367.2	185 814.3	197 461.5
Total National Loans Fund loans outstanding	29 348.2	29 511.4	31 399.1	34 799.7	35 023.4	39 411.0	42 794.7	42 503.8	48 861.2	52 804.9	56 936.8
Loans to nationalised industries:											
Post Office	3 305.5	3 323.6	3 139.1	3 148.4	190.6	178.6	174.4	172.3	170.1	170.1	170.1
National Coal Board	622.6	845.3	1 084.3	1 656.8	2 588.9	2 989.1	3 407.8	3 531.8	3 243.1	3 276.5	3 374.3
Electricity Council	3 286.5	3 279.8	4 116.7	4 413.0	3 963.7	3 988.3	3 276.3	2 578.5	3 275.4	2 617.5	1 698.5
North of Scotland Hydro-Electric Board	247.4	279.6	293.1	440.1	369.6	419.1	393.8	373.7	339.5	329.7	394.9
South of Scotland Electricity Board	474.4	436.4	503.3	457.6	670.5	739.7	843.6	768.1	732.4	638.4	881.0
British Gas Corporation	882.6	217.0	97.0	–	–	40.0	–	–	–	–	–
British Steel Corporation	929.0	767.5	558.9	509.3	–	–	–	–	–	–	–
British Airways Board	60.6	46.2	40.2	34.3	41.3	42.4	–	–	–	–	–
Civil Aviation Authority	63.7	76.0	80.8	82.9	73.8	73.8	69.3	59.5	78.7	78.0	69.4
British Airports Authority	63.5	62.8	62.2	61.5	62.3	57.6	52.9	48.2	43.5	–	–
British Railways Board	332.2	348.1	374.1	457.9	471.4	449.2	427.6	406.3	437.0	365.9	254.5
British Transport Docks Board	110.6	89.5	89.5	81.3	81.3	–	–	–	–	–	–
British Waterways Board	11.0	10.5	13.2	17.3	19.6	21.3	22.3	23.0	23.3	24.6	25.0
National Freight Corporation	153.1	100.0	100.0	–	–	–	–	–	–	–	–
National Bus Company	133.0	138.0	150.0	163.0	161.0	151.2	143.3	128.3	96.4	79.4	23.0
Scottish Transport Group	14.8	14.8	16.8	14.8	12.8	10.8	0.8	–	–	–	–
British National Oil Corporation	–	–	–	–	–	1.7	–	–	–	–	–
British Aerospace	17.1	15.3	35.5	32.6	28.6	–	–	–	–	–	–
British Shipbuilders	–	55.0	–	–	–	–	–	17.8	–	–	–
British Telecommunications	–	–	–	–	3 056.1	2 943.7	2 789.9	–	–	–	–
Regional water authorities	792.4	1 060.7	1 424.4	1 859.8	2 224.5	2 680.4	2 959.9	2 829.9	2 709.5	3 103.6	3 858.6
Loans to other public corporations:											
New Towns—Development Corporations and Commission	2 369.7	2 713.3	3 144.1	3 612.2	3 940.9	4 271.5	4 453.8	4 653.3	4 742.3	3 057.3	2 975.0
Scottish Special Housing Association	311.9	343.6	380.5	424.7	451.3	476.7	503.4	533.3	558.1	571.5	606.7
Housing Corporation	444.0	481.7	568.6	892.1	1 104.0	1 620.8	1 591.7	1 414.4	1 619.0	1 680.2	1 756.2
Covent Garden Market Authority	25.8	25.1	23.2	23.1	23.1	21.1	19.7	18.9	18.3	17.6	2.0
National Enterprise Board	931.4	624.9	84.5	34.2	3.3	1.4	2.0	–	–	–	–
Land Authority for Wales	4.8	5.5	6.4	7.2	7.5	8.6	7.3	7.2	8.0	7.0	7.5
Scottish Development Agency	2.0	4.5	9.4	7.6	6.5	8.7	9.7	9.6	9.5	8.7	6.7
Welsh Development Agency	3.2	4.7	6.3	5.2	5.7	5.1	4.6	4.2	4.5	4.9	3.5
Development Board for Rural Wales	3.3	7.5	12.2	16.5	20.7	25.2	29.3	34.6	41.0	8.3	8.3
Royal Mint	7.1	6.7	6.3	5.5	4.6	3.7	2.7	1.6	0.9	0.7	0.5
Royal Ordnance Factories	39.9	28.6	21.8	15.2	10.5	6.3	2.1	–	–	–	–
The Crown Suppliers	18.1	16.5	25.5	22.5	16.5	15.7	12.0	20.0	20.3	23.7	23.7
Crown Agents	–	–	30.0	30.0	20.8	20.3	19.8	19.1	18.3	17.4	16.6
Her Majesty's Stationery Office	–	–	–	75.1	75.9	69.8	63.0	56.3	49.6	41.2	34.4
Urban Development Corporations	–	–	–	–	0.7	1.0	0.6	0.4	1.0	1.1	0.8
Harbour authorities	162.6	171.1	172.7	175.9	167.0	158.9	120.5	112.5	80.7	69.9	60.4
Commonwealth Development Corporation	–	–	–	–	–	–	15.0	29.7	35.1	28.5	–
UK Atomic Energy Authority	–	–	–	–	–	–	–	–	–	85.0	79.0

Source *HM Treasury*

16.7 (*continued*) Consolidated Fund and National Loans Fund: assets and liabilities

United Kingdom
At 31 March in each year

£ million

	1978	1979	1980	1981	1982	1983	1984	1985	1986	1987	1988
National Loans Fund (*continued*)											
Loans to local authorities	12 950.7	13 254.8	14 015.3	15 272.4	14 126.6	16 866.6	20 294.3	23 612.8	29 374.3	35 305.1	39 368.4
Loans to private sector:											
Shipbuilding Industry Board	3.5	3.5	3.5	3.5	3.5	2.2	2.2	–	–	–	–
Shipowners (Ship credit scheme)	–	–	–	–	–	–	–	–	–	–	–
Housing associations	23.8	23.7	23.7	23.5	23.3	21.2	20.0	19.4	18.9	18.5	17.8
Building societies	11.5	8.2	4.6	2.2	–	–	–	–	–	–	–
British Nuclear Fuels Ltd	8.9	8.9	8.5	8.1	7.6	7.1	6.5	5.9	5.1	4.3	3.4
British Aerospace plc	–	–	–	–	–	24.6	20.6	16.6	12.6	8.6	5.5
Loans within central government:											
Northern Ireland Exchequer	450.8	537.7	598.8	639.2	653.8	707.7	798.5	924.7	1 024.1	1 091.4	1 141.4
Married quarters for armed forces	75.2	74.8	74.1	73.2	72.8	72.4	71.9	71.9	70.8	70.3	69.7
Town and country planning compensation	–	–	–	–	–	–	–	–	–	–	–
Redundancy Fund	–	–	–	–	260.8	207.5	161.6	–	–	–	–
Other assets:											
Exchange Equalisation Account—capital	8 650.0	6 800.0	6 600.0	5 200.0	1 600.0	–	–	–	2 300.0	5 950.0	16 200.0
Subscriptions and contributions to international financial organisations:											
International Monetary Fund	2 044.9	2 128.6	2 128.6	2 964.3	2 539.1	2 800.7	4 311.8	4 495.5	4 685.3	4 533.9	4 631.4
Borrowing included in national debt but not brought to account by 31 March	21.4	1 046.6	347.9	2 022.6	755.2	893.1	1 113.7	−6.1	2 975.6	2 549.3	883.7
National Debt Commissioners' liability in respect of the National Savings Banks Investment Fund	–	–	–	1 611.9	1 285.6	80.5	33.6	14.1	–	–	–
Other	2.0	2.1	2.0	2.0	2.0	–	8.1	4 937.2	1 096.4	–	–
Consolidated Fund liability	39 113.4	47 396.1	54 836.6	66 435.5	77 185.1	84 742.1	94 623.3	106 084.0	111 448.6	119 976.2	118 809.6
Total liabilities											
National Loans Fund—national debt outstanding	79 179.9	86 884.9	95 314.2	113 036.0	118 390.4	127 927.3	142 885.2	158 028.5	171 367.2	185 814.3	197.461.5

Source *HM Treasury*

16.8 British government and government guaranteed marketable securities[1]

Nominal values of official and other holdings by maturity[2]
At 31 March in each year

£ million

	1978	1979	1980	1981	1982	1983	1984	1985	1986	1987	1988
Total holdings	52 112	59 340	70 985	86 475	91 150	96 414	108 589	120 057	130 073	136 519	144 106
Up to 5 years	19 209	21 574	24 233	25 484	25 470	27 635	34 513	41 753	43 666	40 678	41 481
Over 5 and up to 15 years	9 022	12 473	16 772	27 574	34 297	36 490	46 892	47 648	50 701	56 289	64 534
Over 15 years (including undated)	23 881	25 293	29 980	33 417	31 383	32 289	27 184	30 656	35 706	39 552	38 091
Official holdings:											
Total	8 616	7 815	10 688	10 939	9 616	8 739	7 994	6 861	8 312	9 590	9 544
Up to 5 years	4 091	4 033	5 796	4 528	3 106	3 520	2 749	2 483	4 285	3 979	3 771
Over 5 and up to 15 years	2 101	2 272	2 859	4 932	5 213	3 670	4 296	3 550	3 061	3 324	4 527
Over 15 years (including undated)	2 404	1 492	2 014	1 458	1 275	1 524	921	797	935	2 251	1 246
Other holdings:											
Total	43 496	51 525	60 297	75 536	81 534	87 675	100 595	113 196	121 761	126 929	134 562
Up to 5 years	15 118	17 541	18 437	20 956	22 364	24 115	31 764	39 270	39 381	36 699	37 710
Over 5 and up to 15 years	6 921	10 201	13 913	22 642	29 084	32 820	42 596	44 098	47 642	52 965	60 007
Over 15 years (including undated)	21 477	23 801	27 966	31 959	30 108	30 765	26 263	29 859	34 771	37 301	36 845

1 The government guaranteed securities of nationalised industries only. A relatively small amount of other government guaranteed securities is excluded.

2 Securities with optional redemption dates are classified according to the final redemption date.

Source *Bank of England*

16.9 National savings
Year ended 31 March

£ million

	1978/79	1979/80	1980/81	1981/82	1982/83	1983/84	1984/85	1985/86	1986/87[9]	1987/88	1988/89
Department for National Savings											
Receipts											
Total[1]	2 942.7	2 804.4	3 913.9	5 898.4	5 211.8	5 302.5	5 701.2	4 517.3	6 521.8	6 063.5	6 992.4
Capital Bonds	–	–	–	–	–	–	–	–	–	–	199.5
National savings certificates:											
Fixed interest	1 243.7	798.3	1 074.2	2 054.8	1 380.9	1 451.0	2 107.8	731.0	1 309.6	457.8	1 382.6
Index-linked	244.4	632.7	1 173.8	1 990.3	638.3	186.3	106.5	217.7	171.1	253.7	785.2
Yearly plan	–	–	–	–	–	–	27.7	106.9	126.9	128.8	115.8
Save as you earn:											
Fixed interest (1st, 2nd and 4th issues)	3.6	1.4	0.1	4.7	11.5	18.0	23.7	34.4	42.0	52.6	63.3
Index-linked (3rd issue)	100.1	114.8	127.6	131.3	123.8	106.6	90.2	56.4	23.8	8.8	2.9
Income bonds	–	–	–	–	893.1	1 126.4	1 081.1	1 201.5	2 202.3	2 101.2	1 729.7
Investment account[2]	386.5	440.3	803.2	992.5	1 346.3	1 447.9	1 255.8	1 204.2	1 517.4	1 880.9	1 628.1
Premium savings bonds	191.2	124.5	165.0	148.5	178.1	190.2	204.3	184.9	216.9	298.0	313.5
Ordinary account	669.6	661.7	569.8	576.3	639.8	667.8	667.0	645.1	645.2	649.5	637.0
Deposit bonds	–	–	–	–	–	108.3	137.1	130.3	247.2	225.8	134.8
Indexed-income bonds	–	–	–	–	–	–	–	4.9	19.4	6.4	–
British savings bonds	103.6	30.7	0.2	–	–	–	–	–	–	–	–
Repayments											
Total[1]	2 009.5	2 191.0	2 485.2	3 012.1	3 698.2	3 777.5	4 649.3	4 718.2	5 341.0	6 043.5	8 510.8
Capital bonds	–	–	–	–	–	–	–	–	–	–	–
National savings certificates:											
Fixed interest – Principal	239.4	522.4	632.4	722.6	513.8	453.3	776.6	713.7	971.7	1 296.9	2 117.3
– Accrued interest	93.7	183.5	251.8	305.2	201.1	210.6	341.1	371.3	563.7	842.5	1 578.5
Index-linked – Principal	44.0	57.9	111.8	208.0	821.2	672.6	527.6	521.8	618.6	369.4	409.4
– Accrued interest/ index-linking, bonuses and supplements	7.3	16.7	47.8	89.1	276.5	199.7	216.9	283.4	350.6	246.7	329.0
Yearly plan:											
Principal	–	–	–	–	–	–	0.1	3.3	7.6	10.8	16.6
Interest	–	–	–	–	–	–	–	–	–	0.5	1.3
Save as you earn:											
Fixed interest – Principal	36.2	33.2	10.4	8.8	1.7	1.5	4.7	7.5	26.5	20.8	38.3
– Accrued interest	17.3	15.5	4.7	4.0	0.5	0.1	0.6	1.3	6.6	4.5	10.8
Index-linked – Principal	5.2	6.2	56.9	50.8	157.5	118.1	120.3	155.4	99.5	65.7	51.3
– Accrued interest/ index-linking	0.5	0.8	22.9	18.0	87.2	54.4	49.7	51.2	33.4	27.4	28.5
Income bonds	–	–	–	–	1.8	60.7	243.2	311.6	381.9	621.6	943.0
Investment account[2]	750.4	312.5	334.3	670.8	770.3	1 085.4	1 391.1	1 343.8	1 349.0	1 560.5	1 984.8
Premium savings bonds	76.6	119.0	108.7	103.9	98.6	102.2	110.5	119.6	124.2	131.1	133.5
Ordinary account	623.1	776.6	733.7	695.6	678.2	722.8	770.1	772.1	741.8	735.8	723.1
Deposit bonds	–	–	–	–	–	0.1	17.3	44.3	63.2	104.0	142.4
Indexed-income bonds	–	–	–	–	–	–	–	–	1.3	4.1	3.0
British savings bonds:											
Before maturity	82.4	117.6	77.6	32.9	16.0	6.3	2.0	–		–	–
On maturity	33.4	29.1	92.3	102.4	73.8	89.7	77.5	17.9	1.4	1.2	–
Trustee Savings Bank (not included in above figures)											
Receipts											
Total	2 786.0	1 334.6	–	–	–	–	–	–	–	–	–
Save as you earn:											
Fixed interest (1st and 2nd issues only)	4.5	2.8	–	–	–	–	–	–	–	–	–
Ordinary department[3]	2 781.5	1 331.8[3]	–	–	–	–	–	–	–	–	–
British savings bonds	–	–	–	–	–	–	–	–	–	–	–

1 Excludes Ulster Savings Certificates.
2 Investment Account contributes to the funding of PSBR/CGBR from January 1981.
3 From 21 November 1979 the Ordinary and New departments of the Trustee Savings Banks amalgamated and will no longer be part of National Savings.
4 Including National Savings stamps and gift tokens and securities on the National Savings register, which (except for British savings bonds) do not appear in the first part of the table.
5 Nominal value held in National Savings section.
6 Including accrued interest to date.
7 From September 1979 excludes £7.7 million deemed to be outstanding National Savings stamps written off on 15 August 1979.
8 Nominal value held (until 1979) in Trustee Savings Banks section.
9 From 1 April 1986 onwards the data series have been revised. The revisions, notably those for the estimates of accrued interest, coincided with the adoption of an improved transaction accounting system for National Savings.

Source Department for National Savings

16.9 National savings
Year ended 31 March

(continued)

£ million

	1978/79	1979/80	1980/81	1981/82	1982/83	1983/84	1984/85	1985/86	1986/87[9]	1987/88	1988/89
TSB not included above (contd.)											
Repayments											
Save as you earn:											
Fixed interest – Principal	28.0	32.1	11.5	10.1	2.1	–	–	–	–	–	–
– Accrued interest	12.3	13.8	4.7	4.6	0.4	–	–	–	–	–	–
Ordinary department	2 911.6	1 460.6	–	–	–	–	–	–	–	–	–
British savings bonds:											
Before maturity	13.1	13.7	2.5	0.1	–	–	–	–	–	–	–
On maturity	15.7	18.6	17.3	12.2	–	–	–	–	–	–	–
Total	2 980.7	1 538.8	36.0	27.0	2.5	–	–	–	–	–	–
Department for National Savings											
Interest accruing											
Capital bonds	–	–	–	–	–	–	–	–	–	–	–
National savings certificates:											
Fixed interest	260.6	351.6	428.9	483.2	648.1	815.3	1 000.4	1 137.8	1 095.3	1 124.9	810.0
Index-linking (including bonuses and supplements)	74.8	190.8	270.8	401.9	332.1	364.1	361.3	389.3	314.4	267.5	365.8
Yearly plan	–	–	–	–	–	–	–	3.9	12.0	23.2	33.1
Save as you earn:											
Fixed interest (1st, 2nd and 4th issues)	10.6	5.2	1.6	2.0	0.8	1.9	3.7	5.5	8.7	9.3	11.5
Index-linked (3rd issue)	13.5	20.7	81.7	41.9	93.0	52.4	46.1	44.1	28.3	31.2	33.7
Investment account[2]	119.9	174.4	246.0	353.1	380.2	438.6	509.7	608.1	640.0	655.4	696.9
Ordinary account	83.0	87.0	83.0	81.2	70.5	78.6	79.6	78.8	78.7	76.2	61.5
Deposit bonds	–	–	–	–	–	1.5	17.8	37.8	49.7	73.7	87.0
Total[1]	562.4	829.7	1 112.0	1 363.3	1 524.7	1 752.4	2 018.6	2 305.3	2 227.1	2 261.4	2 099.5
Amounts remaining invested											
Capital bonds	–	–	–	–	–	–	–	–	–	–	199.5
National savings certificates											
Fixed interest – Principal	3 782.9	4 058.8	4 500.6	5 832.8	6 699.9	7 697.6	9 028.8	9 046.1	9 318.1	8 479.0	7 744.3
– Accrued interest	844.7	1 012.8	1 189.9	1 367.9	1 814.9	2 419.6	3 078.9	3 845.4	4 112.4	4 394.8	3 626.3
Index-linked – Principal	817.4	1 392.2	2 454.2	4 236.5	4 053.6	3 567.3	3 146.2	2 842.1	2 422.9	2 307.2	2 683.0
– Bonuses and supplements/index-linking	186.0	360.1	583.1	895.9	951.5	1 115.9	1 260.3	1 366.2	1 317.4	1 338.2	1 375.0
Yearly plan:											
Capital	–	–	–	–	–	–	27.6	133.9	258.5	380.7	483.4
Interest	–	–	–	–	–	–	–	1.2	9.4	27.9	56.2
Save as you earn:											
Fixed interest – Principal	52.5	20.7	10.4	6.3	16.1	32.6	51.6	78.5	92.8	124.6	149.6
– Accrued interest	16.0	5.7	2.6	0.6	0.9	2.7	5.8	10.0	12.0	16.8	17.5
Index-linked – Principal	261.6	370.2	440.9	521.4	487.7	476.2	446.1	347.1	266.3	209.4	161.0
– Accrued interest/index linking	23.6	43.5	102.3	126.2	132.0	130.0	126.4	119.3	112.4	116.2	121.4
Stock on the National savings register (DNS only)[5]	389.3	706.0	755.1	842.1	812.5	818.1	891.7	872.3	836.0	811.2	846.4
Income bonds	–	–	–	–	891.3	1 957.0	2 794.9	3 684.8	5 494.6	6 974.2	7 760.9
Investment account[6]	1 303.2	1 605.4	2 320.3	2 995.1	3 951.3	4 752.4	5 126.8	5 595.3	6 403.7	7 379.5	7 719.7
Premium savings bonds	1 399.8	1 405.3	1 461.6	1 506.2	1 585.7	1 673.7	1 767.5	1 832.8	1 924.1	2 091.0	2 271.0
Ordinary account[6]	1 848.9	1 821.0	1 740.1	1 702.0	1 734.1	1 757.7	1 734.2	1 686.0	1 668.1	1 658.0	1 633.4
Deposit bonds	–	–	–	–	–	109.7	247.3	371.1	605.0	800.5	879.9
Indexed-income bonds	–	–	–	–	–	–	–	4.9	23.0	25.3	22.3
British savings bonds	706.8	590.8	421.1	285.8	196.0	100.0	20.5	2.6	1.2	–	–
National savings stamps and gift tokens[7]	8.0	1.2	1.2	1.2	1.3	1.3	1.3	1.3	1.8	2.1	2.4
Total administered by DNS[4]	11 640.7	13 393.7	15 983.4	20 320.0	23 328.8	26 611.8	29 755.9	31 840.9	34 879.7	37 136.6	37 753.2
Trustee Savings Bank											
Interest accruing											
Save as you earn:											
Fixed interest (1st and 2nd issues only)	15.2	4.4	0.1	1.8	0.2	–	–	–	–	–	–
Ordinary department	59.7	25.6	–	–	–	–	–	–	–	–	–
Total	74.9	30.0	0.1	1.8	0.2	–	–	–	–	–	–
Amounts remaining invested											
Save as you earn:											
Fixed interest – Principal	53.0	23.7	12.2	2.1	–	–	–	–	–	–	–
– Interest	17.0	7.6	3.0	0.2	–	–	–	–	–	–	–
Ordinary department[6]	1 664.8	–	–	–	–	–	–	–	–	–	–
British savings bonds	64.4	32.1	12.3	–	–	–	–	–	–	–	–
TSB stock register[8]	318.8	–	–	–	–	–	–	–	–	–	–
Total Trustee Savings Bank	2 118.0	63.4	27.5	2.3	–	–	–	–	–	–	–

See footnotes on page 273

Source *Department for National Savings*

16.10 Income tax: allowances and reliefs

	1979/80	1980/81	1981/82	1982/83	1983/84[1]	1984/85	1985/86	1986/87	1987/88	1988/89	1989/90
Personal allowances											
Married man's allowance[1]	£1 815	£2 145	£2 145	£2 445	£2 795	£3 155	£3 455	£3 655	£3 795	£4 095	£4 375
Single person's allowance	£1 165	£1 375	£1 375	£1 565	£1 785	£2 055	£2 205	£2 335	£2 425	£2 605	£2 785
Wife's earned income allowance[2]	£1 165	£1 375	£1 375	£1 565	£1 785	£2 055	£2 205	£2 335	£2 425	£2 605	£2 785
Age allowance[3]:											
Married (either partner over 65 but neither partner over 80)	£2 455	£2 895	£2 895	£3 295	£3 755	£3 955	£4 255	£4 505	£4 675	£5 035	£5 385
Married (either partner over 80)	£2 455	£2 895	£2 895	£3 295	£3 755	£3 955	£4 255	£4 505	£4 845	£5 205	£5 565
Single (over 65 but under 80)	£1 540	£1 820	£1 820	£2 070	£2 360	£2 490	£2 690	£2 850	£2 960	£3 180	£3 400
Single (over 80)	£1 540	£1 820	£1 820	£2 070	£2 360	£2 490	£2 690	£2 850	£3 070	£3 310	£3 540
Income limit	£5 000	£5 900	£5 900	£6 700	£7 600	£8 100	£8 800	£9 400	£9 800	£10 600	£11 400
Marginal fraction	2/3	2/3	2/3	2/3	2/3	2/3	2/3	2/3	2/3	2/3	1/2
Child allowance[4]:											
Aged under 11	–	–	–	–	–	–	–	–	–	–	–
Aged 11–15	–	–	–	–	–	–	–	–	–	–	–
Aged 16 and over	–	–	–	–	–	–	–	–	–	–	–
Limits of child's income:	–	–	–	–	–	–	–	–	–	–	–
Family allowance deduction[5]	–	–	–	–	–	–	–	–	–	–	–
Additional personal allowance[6]	£650	£770	£770	£880	£1 010	£1 150	£1 250	£1 320	£1 370	£1 490	£1 590
Widow's bereavement allowance[7]	–	£770	£770	£880	£1 010	£1 150	£1 250	£1 320	£1 370	£1 490	£1 590
Dependent relative allowance[8,14]:											
Maintained by single woman	£145	£145	£145	£145	£145	£145	£145	£145	£145	–	–
Other cases	£100	£100	£100	£100	£100	£100	£100	£100	£100	–	–
Limit of relative's income	£1 090	£1 284	£1 458	£1 601	£1 708	£1 804	£1 901	£1 901	£1 901	–	–
Daughter's or son's services allowance[9,14]	£55	£55	£55	£55	£55	£55	£55	£55	£55	–	–
Housekeeper allowance[10,14]	£100	£100	£100	£100	£100	£100	£100	£100	£100	–	–
Blind person's allowance[11]:											
Single or married (one spouse blind)	£180	£180	£360	£360	£360	£360	£360	£360	£540	£540	£540
Married (both spouses blind)	£360	£360	£720	£720	£720	£720	£720	£720	£720	£720	£720

Life assurance relief[12]	1978/79
Total allowable premiums	Amount of premiums upon which tax relief at basic rate allowed
Not over £10	All
Over £10 but not over £20	£10
Over £20	1/2

Life assurance relief[13]	1979/80	1980/81	1981/82	1982/83	1983/84	1984/85	1985/86	1986/87	1987/88	1988/89	1989/90
(Percentage of gross premium)	*17.5*	*17.5*	*15.0*	*15.0*	*15.0*	*15.0 or Nil*	*15.0 or Nil*	*15.0 or Nil*	*15.0 or Nil*	*15.0 or Nil*	*15.0 or Nil*

1 The married man's allowance is that for a full year. In the year of marriage the allowance is reduced by one twelfth of the difference between the married and single personal allowances for each complete month (beginning on the sixth day of each calendar month) prior to the date of marriage. From 1989–90 Age Allowance will be over 65 and under 75.

2 The wife's earned income allowance has as its maximum value the amount shown. Where the earned income is less, the allowance is reduced to the actual amount of earned income.

3 The age allowance. It replaces the single or married allowances, provided the taxpayer's income is below the limit shown. For incomes in excess of the limit, the allowance is reduced by £2 for each additional £3 of income until the ordinary single or married allowance is reached. From 1989–90 the marginal fraction is changed to $\frac{1}{2}$.

4 The child allowance depends upon the age of the child at the start of the tax year (6 April). Where the child's income exceeds the limit shown, the child allowance is reduced by the excess. For unmarried children under 18, there is a further limit of £115 investment income. From 1978–79, special rules apply in respect of certain students and certain children resident overseas. All child allowances were discontinued from 1982–83.

5 The family allowance deduction was a reduction in personal allowances for each child for whom a family allowance was received. Where the family allowance was payable for only part of the year, the family allowance deduction was reduced accordingly.

6 The additional personal allowance may be claimed by a single parent (or by a married man if his wife is totally incapacitated) who maintains a resident child at his or her own expense.

7 Widow's bereavement allowance is due to a widow in the year of her husband's death and in the following year provided the widow has not remarried before the beginning of that year.

8 The dependent relative allowance is due to a taxpayer who maintains, wholly or partially, either (a) an aged or infirm relative, or (b) his or his wife's separated, divorced or widowed mother. The relative's income must be below the limits shown in order for the full allowance to be given (the limit is equal to the basic National Insurance Retirement Pension). The allowance is reduced by the excess of the relative's income over the income limit.

9 The daughter's or son's services allowance may be claimed by an aged or infirm taxpayer who maintains a daughter or son (before 1978–79 a daughter only) on whose services the taxpayer or his wife are dependent.

10 The housekeeper allowance may be claimed by a widow or widower who has a resident housekeeper (before 1978–79 a female housekeeper only). For 1978–79 and earlier years this allowance could also have been claimed by an unmarried person who maintained a resident relative (before 1978–79 a female relative only) to look after a brother or sister for whom child allowance was given.

11 The blind person's allowance is due to a registered blind taxpayer and up to 1980/81 was reduced by the amount of any tax-free blindness disability pension which was receivable.

12 From 1979–80 relief on life assurance premiums is given by deduction from the premium payable.

13 From 1984–85 life assurance relief is confined to policies made before 14 March, 1984.

14 From 1988–89 the following allowances were abolished: Dependent Relative Allowance, Daughter's or Son's Allowance, Housekeeper Allowance.

Source Board of Inland Revenue

16.11 Rates of income tax

	1980/81		1981/82		1982/83		1983/84		1984/85	
	Slice of taxable income	Rate per cent	Slice of taxable income	Rate per cent	Slice of taxable income	Rate per cent	Slice of taxable income	Rate per cent	Slice of taxable income	Rate per cent
	£		£		£		£		£	
Lower rate[1]	–	–	–	–	–	–	–	–	–	–
Basic rate	1–11 250	30	1–11 250	30	1–12 800	30	1–14 600	30	1–15 400	30
Higher rates	11 251–13 250	40	11 251–13 250	40	12 801–15 100	40	14 601–17 200	40	15 401–18 200	40
	13 251–16 750	45	13 251–16 750	45	15 101–19 100	45	17 201–21 800	45	18 201–23 100	45
	16 751–22 250	50	16 751–22 250	50	19 101–25 300	50	21 801–28 900	50	23 101–30 600	50
	22 251–27 750	55	22 251–27 750	55	25 301–31 500	55	28 901–36 000	55	30 601–38 100	55
	over 27 750	60	over 27 750	60	over 31 500	60	over 36 000	60	over 38 100	60
Investment Income surcharge[2]	Slice of net investment income	Rate per cent	Slice of net investment income	Rate per cent	Slice of net investment income	Rate per cent	Slice of net investment income	Rate per cent	Slice of net investment income	Rate per cent
	£		£		£		£		£	
Non-aged persons										
Exempt slice	1–5 500	–	1–5 500	–	1–6 250	–	1–7 100	–	–	–
	over 5 500	15	over 5 500	15	over 6 250	15	over 7 100	15	–	–
Aged persons										
Exempt slice	1–5 500	–	1–5 500	–	1–6 250	–	1–7 100	–	–	–
	over 5 500	15	over 5 500	15	over 6 250	15	over 7 100	15	–	–

	1985/86		1986/87		1987/88		1988/89		1989/90	
	Slice of taxable income	Rate per cent	Slice of taxable income	Rate per cent	Slice of taxable income	Rate per cent	Slice of taxable income	Rate per cent	Slice of taxable income	Rate per cent
	£		£		£		£		£	
Lower rate[1]	–	–	–	–	–	–	–	–		
Basic rate	1–16 200	30	1–17 200	29	1–17 900	27	0–19 300	25	0–20 700	25
Higher rates	16 201–19 200	40	17 201–20 200	40	17 901–20 400	40				
	19 201–24 400	45	20 201–25 400	45	20 401–25 400	45				
	24 401–32 300	50	25 401–33 300	50	25 401–33 300	50				
	32 301–40 200	55	33 301–41 200	55	33 301–41 200	55				
	over 40 200	60	over 41 200	60	over 41 200	60	over 19 300	40	over 20 700	40
Investment Income surcharge[3]	Slice of net investment income	Rate per cent	Slice of net investment income	Rate per cent	Slice of net investment income	Rate per cent	Slice of net investment income	Rate per cent	Slice of net investment income	Rate per cent
	£		£		£		£		£	
Non-aged persons										
Exempt slice	–	–	–	–	–	–	–	–	–	–
	–	–	–	–	–	–	–	–	–	–
Aged persons										
Exempt slice	–	–	–	–	–	–	–	–	–	–
	–	–	–	–	–	–	–	–	–	–

1 The lower rate slice applies additionally to wife's earned income, but any increase is deducted from the slice of total income chargeable at the basic rate.

2 Chargeable in addition to any basic or higher rates of tax where an individual's investment income exceeded the limits shown.

3 Investments income surcharge was abolished from 1984/85 onwards.

Source *Board of Inland Revenue*

16.12 **Rateable values**

England and Wales
At April in each year

	1978	1979	1980	1981	1982	1983	1984	1985	1986	1987	1988
Number of properties (Thousands)											
Total—all classes	21 634.9	21 876.3	22 102.5	22 291.1	22 463.1	22 621.6	22 827.7	23 032.3	23 243.4	23 456.1	23 667.8
Domestic: total	17 984.9	18 199.0	18 405.5	18 578.4	18 736.7	18 873.8	19 055.6	19 238.3	19 429.1	19 621.2	19 817.8
Houses and flats with rateable values:											
Not over £75	1 459.5	1 408.2	1 366.2	1 323.5	1 291.5	1 267.8	1 249.6	1 234.1			
Over £75 but not over £100	1 290.1	1 288.4	1 287.0	1 286.2	1 285.5	1 288.3	1 292.2	1 295.8	19 102.6[1]	19 301.9	19 503.2[1]
Over £100	14 873.8	15 143.3	15 396.6	15 618.1	15 814.3	15 976.6	16 177.4	16 376.3			
Agricultural dwelling-houses, etc.	361.6	359.1	355.7	350.6	345.3	341.2	336.4	332.0	326.5	319.4	314.6
Commercial: total	3 039.2	3 062.5	3 079.7	3 092.3	3 102.9	3 120.7	3 138.2	3 156.0	3 171.8	3 187.0	3 200.2
Shops and cafes	585.3	580.2	574.9	570.1	567.2	566.2	566.5	567.3	567.9	569.0	569.2
Offices	172.5	174.0	175.3	177.3	179.7	182.9	186.6	191.3	197.1	202.9	209.0
Other	2 281.4	2 308.3	2 329.5	2 344.9	2 355.9	2 371.7	2 385.1	2 397.4	2 406.8	2 415.3	2 421.9
On-licensed premises: total	55.3	55.1	55.0	54.9	54.8	54.8	55.1	54.9	54.8	54.9	54.8
Entertainment and recreational: total	72.9	73.6	74.1	74.7	75.3	76.1	76.8	77.3	77.8	78.2	78.6
Cinemas	1.2	1.2	1.1	1.1	1.0	1.0	1.0	0.9	0.8	0.8	0.7
Theatres and music-halls	0.4	0.4	0.4	0.4	0.4	0.4	0.4	0.5	0.5	0.5	0.5
Other	71.3	72.0	72.6	73.2	73.9	74.7	75.4	75.9	76.5	77.0	77.4
Public utility: total	39.0	39.0	39.0	38.8	38.5	38.6	38.5	38.7	38.6	38.5	38.3
Educational and cultural: total	42.3	42.3	42.3	42.2	42.1	41.8	41.6	41.3	41.0	40.8	40.5
Miscellaneous: total	297.2	300.4	301.7	302.9	304.9	306.6	311.2	313.6	316.7	320.9	322.9
Industrial: total	104.1	104.4	105.2	106.9	107.9	109.1	110.7	112.3	113.6	114.7	114.8
Value of assessments (£ million)											
Total—all classes	7 058.0	7 181.9	7 317.8	7 441.5	7 552.6	7 641.4	7 730.7	7 822.2	7 915.1	8 025.2	8 121.0
Domestic: total	3 459.2	3 519.7	3 578.5	3 630.7	3 678.2	3 719.2	3 766.6	3 814.5	3 864.6	3 916.4	3 969.1
Houses and flats with rateable values:											
Not over £75	82.4	79.8	77.6	75.4	73.8	72.7	71.8	71.0			
Over £75 but not over £100	114.1	114.0	114.0	113.7	113.8	114.0	114.4	114.7	3 793.2[1]	3 845.3[1]	3 899.7[1]
Over £100	3 187.8	3 251.2	3 312.4	3 367.5	3 417.4	3 459.7	3 507.9	3 557.0			
Agricultural dwelling-houses, etc.	74.8	74.7	74.5	74.1	73.3	72.8	72.5	71.9	71.4	71.1	69.7
Commercial: total	1 654.8	1 698.8	1 746.6	1 792.8	1 847.6	1 897.3	1 946.2	1 988.8	2 037.5	2 078.7	2 120.6
Shops and cafes	590.5	594.4	600.8	607.4	615.2	621.1	628.1	634.1	638.5	644.6	648.6
Offices	570.9	595.2	618.7	637.2	660.3	681.7	702.8	722.1	748.1	768.0	789.9
Other	493.4	509.2	527.1	548.2	572.1	594.5	615.3	632.6	650.9	666.0	682.1
On-licensed premises: total	63.5	63.6	64.0	65.1	65.8	65.5	64.4	63.8	63.9	64.5	65.0
Entertainment and recreational: total	72.8	74.1	75.7	77.3	79.4	81.3	83.6	85.0	86.4	88.2	89.5
Cinemas	4.3	4.1	4.0	3.9	3.8	3.8	3.6	3.4	3.3	3.1	3.0
Theatres and music-halls	1.6	1.7	1.7	1.8	1.9	1.9	2.1	2.1	2.1	2.1	2.1
Other	66.9	68.3	70.0	71.6	73.7	75.6	77.9	79.5	81.0	82.9	84.4
Public utility: total	391.0	392.8	398.3	407.7	406.1	406.7	407.6	412.6	409.8	423.1	428.3
Educational and cultural: total	233.3	238.9	242.2	244.3	244.6	243.9	242.0	240.4	239.2	237.9	236.3
Miscellaneous: total	402.8	413.6	428.6	436.4	444.2	450.0	455.4	462.3	468.9	478.2	480.1
Industrial: total	780.6	780.4	784.0	787.2	786.8	777.5	764.8	754.7	744.8	738.8	732.1

1 The detailed breakdown of the various rateable value bands for houses and flats is no longer available.

Source: Board of Inland Revenue

16.13 Local authorities: gross loan debt outstanding[1]

At 31 March in each year[2]

£ million

	1978	1979	1980	1981	1982	1983	1984	1985	1986	1987	1988
United Kingdom											
Total debt[3]	31 831	33 586	36 715	38 810	41 607	44 392	..	..	..	..	..
Public Works Loan Board	12 931	13 214	13 994	15 259	14 111	16 846	20 250	23 527	29 288	35 252	39 356
Northern Ireland Consolidated Fund[3]	238	229	238	238	225	215	204	199	198	195	190
Other debt	18 662	20 143	22 483	23 313	27 271	27 331	..	..	..	..	..
England and Wales											
Total debt	27 694	29 112	31 802	33 796	35 862	38 116	40 816	42 266	42 540	45 548	45 176
of which Public Works Loan Board	*11 285*	*11 434*	*12 100*	*13 124*	*12 129*	*14 331*	*17 310*	*20 141*	*24 887*	*29 901*	*33 379*
Scotland											
Total debt	4 096	4 430	4 864	5 465	5 878	6 201	6 658	7 009	7 378	7 783	8 199[4]
of which Public Works Loan Board	*1 646*	*1 780*	*1 894*	*2 135*	*1 982*	*2 515*	*2 940*	*3 386*	*4 401*	*5 351*	*5 970*
Northern Ireland											
Total debt[3]	41	44	49	58	66	67	71	74	75	82	84

1 The sums shown exclude inter-authority loans and debt transfers, and temporary loans and overdrafts obtained for the purpose of providing for current expenses. No deduction has been made in respect of sums held in sinking funds for the repayment of debt.

2 At 15 May for Scotland up to 1975.

3 The Northern Ireland Loans Fund was abolished on 1 April 1983 and its functions transferred to the Northern Ireland Consolidated Fund.

4 Provisional.

Sources *Department of the Environment; Scottish Office, Central Statistics Unit; Public Works Loan Board; Department of the Environment for Northern Ireland; Welsh Office*

16.14 Expenditure and income of local authorities: summary

Years ended 31 March

£ million

	1977/78	1978/79	1979/80	1980/81	1981/82	1982/83	1983/84	1984/85	1985/86	1986/87	1987/88
United Kingdom											
Total expenditure:											
On capital works	4 552.0	4 787.4	5 517.4	5 861.0	5 637.1	6 911.0	7 868.0	..	..	..	..
Other	20 948.9	23 917.4	28 332.4	34 109.8	37 633.8	40 715.6	43 468.6	..	..	..	..
Total income[1]	25 841.7	28 747.5	33 524.1	40 121.4	44 189.6	47 899.0	50 409.6	..	..	..	..
England and Wales											
Total expenditure:											
On capital works	4 039.3	4 229.8	4 837.6	5 176.0	4 903.3	6 111.8	6 918.0	7 228.7	6 443.1	6 666.3	7 103.5
Other	18 768.2	21 409.8	25 264.9	30 337.5	33 441.0	36 142.3	38 573.3	40 544.5	42 138.3	44 783.4	48 992.3
Total income[1]	23 155.2	25 734.8	29 979.7	35 915.8	39 311.2	42 617.6	44 718.7	46 602.7	48 581.4	49 873.3	52 734.6
Scotland											
Total expenditure:											
On capital works	499.3	542.4	658.5	660.9	707.3	763.6	918.8	840.0	777.1	912.2	1 079.4
Other	2 123.2	2 442.3	2 985.9	3 675.5	4 082.2	4 241.1	4 566.5	4 794.1	5 048.2	5 352.0	5 726.8
Total income[1]	2 617.0	2 934.4	3 449.8	4 085.5	4 742.2	5 146.1	5 559.6	5 585.6	6 048.2	6 236.1	6 934.2
Northern Ireland											
Total expenditure:											
On capital works	13.4	15.2	21.3	24.1	25.1	24.1	29.2	25.2	33.3	25.0	31.0
Other	57.4	65.3	81.6	96.8	110.6	121.9	133.1	143.3	153.2	154.1	166.9
Total income[1]	69.5	78.3	94.6	120.1	136.2	151.1	165.3	168.8	151.6	142.8	170.2

1 Including government grants.

Sources *Department of the Environment; Scottish Office, Central Statistics Unit; Department of the Environment for Northern Ireland; Welsh Office*

16.15 Revenue account expenditure of local authorities[1]
England and Wales
Years ended 31 March

£ thousand

	1977/78	1978/79	1979/80	1980/81	1981/82	1982/83	1983/84	1984/85	1985/86	1986/87	1987/88
Education	7 031 701	7 965 754	9 117 703	10 959 016	12 067 947	12 694 348	13 315 708	13 847 423	14 543 279	15 830 234	17 167 558
Libraries, museums and art galleries	225 313	253 864	292 225	348 875	383 711	418 829	449 830	476 978	511 738	546 860	584 453
Local authority port health	2 342	2 541	2 995	3 359	3 752	3 950	4 107	4 281	4 492	4 290	4 182
Personal social services	1 267 077	1 441 032	1 755 420	2 155 468	2 387 807	2 609 425	2 805 816	2 975 712	3 179 720	3 473 265	3 879 120
Sheltered employment and workshops	20 593	23 678	27 153	27 590	30 077	34 498	39 567	44 252	47 845	51 969	57 334
Police including school crossing patrols	1 129 410	1 272 409	1 639 616	1 979 491	2 343 472	2 600 177	2 852 148	3 336 832	3 269 169	3 653 573	3 687 531
Fire service	252 334	305 880	378 473	451 336	515 080	573 469	624 376	677 370	730 910	783 013	858 089
Administration of justice	129 583	146 351	179 827	233 629	269 498	295 782	319 827	343 968	372 339	408 616	434 960
Refuse collection and disposal	373 342	428 142	532 309	632 169	667 880	704 935	718 788	739 527	792 951	815 216	882 340
Agriculture and fisheries	70 980	77 758	90 209	100 023	123 398	132 687	144 871	153 078	150 286	186 780	198 412
Local transport	1 300 338	1 472 100	1 708 626	2 086 930	2 353 479	2 574 827	2 679 754	2 766 627	2 690 078	2 789 027	2 860 313
Parks and open spaces[2]	458 355	527 278	648 079	770 001	832 813	935 228	1 019 267	1 105 067	1 219 350	1 292 082	1 407 677
Environmental health[2]	185 159	213 404	270 513	332 638	353 124	383 218	407 269	425 828	444 906	477 735	832 086
Cemeteries and crematoria	38 310	42 835	51 791	62 435	67 662	73 292	77 808	80 831	84 998	90 353	151 222
Town and country planning	271 980	301 549	383 700	494 567	537 104	573 639	649 960	683 829	736 779	712 303	777 955
Housing to which the Housing Revenue Account relates	2 589 771	3 048 656	3 787 707	4 564 027	4 840 523	5 087 065	5 197 414	5 472 814	5 921 884	5 943 738	5 985 596
Other housing	699 287	761 268	836 368	933 627	904 599	926 476	1 422 253	1 832 746	1 922 983	2 428 967	2 481 296
Trading services:											
Passenger transport[3]	99 916	108 910	135 402	162 365	172 819	182 556	193 970	201 750	207 770	..	..
Harbours, docks and piers	29 783	36 498	43 360	47 390	51 788	51 888	52 245	45 853	47 601	49 143	50 880
Other trading services	303 698	436 894	410 288	503 706	570 818	658 182	744 595	773 012	905 900	804 272	814 134
Other rate fund services	460 688	507 726	591 058	679 419	816 105	900 665	1 047 593	1 135 816	1 309 794	1 339 875	1 434 994
Expenditure on general administration and all other expenditure and transfers[4]	1 828 176	2 035 260	2 382 053	2 809 467	3 147 558	3 727 135	3 806 176	3 420 927	3 043 590	3 102 087	3 720 456
Total loan charges included in expenditure above	3 209 299	3 643 648	4 428 819	5 132 094	5 360 460	5 281 623	5 038 198	5 031 808	5 331 273	5 533 395	5 817 368
Allocated to:											
Rate fund services	1 460 936	1 611 855	1 873 994	2 132 841	2 257 041	2 178 073	1 997 302	2 201 900	1 962 944	2 550 690	2 644 233
Housing revenue	1 663 204	1 940 889	2 448 960	2 876 539	2 953 678	2 911 281	2 859 447	2 632 679	3 168 914	2 789 490	2 980 441
Trading services	85 159	90 904	105 865	122 714	149 741	192 269	181 449	197 229	199 415	193 215	192 694
Debt repayments included in Table 16.16	367 661	413 756	346 961	425 926	587 906	669 533	588 438	499 807	373 394	348 813	486 297
Total	18 768 136	21 409 787	25 264 875	30 337 528	33 441 014	36 142 271	38 573 342	40 544 521	42 138 362	44 783 398	48 270 588

1 Expenditure of superannuation and statutory special funds is not included.
2 Baths and laundries are included with parks and open spaces, and from 1978/79 swimming baths are included with parks and open spaces; and other public baths and public laundries are included with environmental health.
3 Due to deregulation of Passenger Transport Services this information was not supplied for 1986/87 and 1987/88.
4 Rate fund contributions to the Housing Revenue Account are included.

Sources Department of the Environment; Welsh Office

16.16 Capital account expenditure of local authorities[1]

England and Wales

Years ended 31 March

£ thousand

	1978/79	1979/80	1980/81	1981/82	1982/83	1983/84	1984/85	1985/86	1986/87	1987/88[2]
Total	4 229 785	4 837 638	5 176 038	4 903 289	6 111 775	6 918 015	7 228 696	6 437 079	6 666 333	7 103 769
Education	332 811	367 542	477 762	431 177	474 214	486 234	538 909	569 803	604 588	656 388
Libraries, museums and art galleries	11 991	15 122	24 743	20 504	29 248	40 993	56 218	50 469	44 091	47 016
Local authority port health	80	3	62	16	17	213	96	5	7	0
Personal social services	61 598	77 801	101 437	99 751	104 002	110 958	122 318	124 879	133 514	153 685
Sheltered employment and workshops	1 046	1 304	1 136	1 362	2 685	2 029	1 972	2 843	3 567	..
Police including school crossing patrols	44 204	42 120	36 267	58 877	80 519	94 909	99 833	108 186	110 932 }	
Fire service	10 321	11 736	17 493	21 426	32 238	37 966	36 874	34 749	29 763 }	195 037[3]
Administration of justice	8 901	8 926	11 365	9 126	9 928	14 896	18 564	19 242	28 459 }	
Refuse collection and disposal	28 869	40 890	60 082	55 240	64 192	62 950	60 670	53 098	55 429	..
Agriculture and fisheries	61 850	96 113	90 983	116 209	112 083	61 701	40 231	44 799	49 841	45 894
Local transport	368 846	459 415	610 937	606 653	700 783	794 341	829 967	757 331	740 469	860 555[4]
Parks and open spaces[5]	82 868	116 370	169 385	140 858	202 835	243 756	274 294	223 710	250 664	..
Environmental health[5]	8 521	13 283	16 227	10 912	18 499	13 159	13 275	13 224	15 438	..
Cemeteries and crematoria	2 016	2 765	3 629	3 490	6 464	5 987	4 994	4 904	6 339	..
Town and country planning	132 392	178 258	236 453	199 936	297 993	324 062	359 578	391 168	372 291	..
Housing to which the Housing Revenue Account relates	1 890 746	2 055 639	1 868 996	1 707 558	2 106 908	2 251 937	2 537 721	2 268 944	2 301 576	2 679 506
Other housing	897 721	999 972	976 741	942 139	1 201 398	1 736 308	1 519 019	1 071 788	1 055 738	1 005 446
Trading services:										
Passenger transport[6]	13 512	13 345	16 437	15 377	11 963	12 259	7 933	8 919	25 422 }	..
Harbours, docks and piers	6 626	9 697	16 125	12 313	12 012	10 601	8 318	13 941	10 340 }	251 539
Other trading services	97 907	144 895	221 860	225 339	268 211	280 150	291 468	282 032	208 398 }	
Other rate fund services	86 698	94 602	86 352	89 122	126 339	144 446	166 451	142 727	301 492	1 208 703
General administration	80 261	87 840	131 566	135 904	249 244	188 160	239 993	250 320	317 981	..

1 Expenditure met out of loans, government grants for capital works, sales of property, etc. and sums repaid to lenders or transferred to sinking funds out of unexpected balances of loans and other capital receipts.

2 Due to extensive revisions to the means of obtaining capital information, those services denoted as 'not available' in 1987/88 have been grouped as one total in the 'Other rate fund services' row.

3 Includes Civil Defence.

4 Includes Public Transport Companies.

5 Baths and laundries are included with parks and open spaces and from 1978/79 swimming baths are included with parks and open spaces; and other public baths and public laundries are included with environmental health.

6 From 1986/87 grants and advances to Public Transport Companies are included.

Sources *Department of the Environment; Welsh Office*

16.17 Water authority expenditure

England and Wales

£ million (current prices)

	1977/78	1978/79	1979/80	1980/81	1981/82	1982/83	1983/84	1984/85	1985/86	1986/87	1987/88[2]	1988/89[3,4]
Revenue expenditure[1]												
Water resources	24.9	30.5	36.9	45.2	48.0	50.4	51.1	52.4	54.4	57.1	48.3	52.9
Water supply	283.3	326.3	382.4	452.6	492.9	529.6	553.8	576.8	594.8	629.4	705.02	757.6
Sewerage	68.9	81.2	100.8	122.6	135.7	151.0	156.6	158.7	163.0	162.5	170.7	626.6
Sewage treatment/disposal	177.7	204.2	248.7	293.2	321.3	343.9	357.8	363.1	378.1	392.0	390.3	..
Environmental services:												
Water quality regulation	8.3	9.8	11.9	14.0	15.8	15.8	17.2	17.1	17.5	18.9 }		
Pollution alleviation	1.2	1.2	1.8	2.1	2.5	3.2	3.4	4.0	4.3	4.9 }		
Recreation and amenity	2.6	3.5	4.3	5.1	5.9	5.7	6.2	6.3	6.4	8.6 }	49.8	54.1
Navigation	1.9	2.3	2.6	3.2	3.7	3.9	4.5	4.1	4.4	4.5 }		
Fisheries	3.7	4.3	5.3	6.3	6.9	7.2	7.8	8.1	8.3	8.7 }		
Land drainage and flood protection	28.7	33.0	39.0	44.2	48.7	51.7	56.4	53.9	55.6	63.4	67.7	70.0
Capital expenditure												
Water resources	55.6	56.3	49.2	55.9	41.2	38.7	35.3	27.5	30.4	25.7	26.5	30.2
Water supply	136.4	148.8	164.1	177.5	194.0	212.8	266.0	260.0	290.9	346.0	420.8	459.0
Sewerage	150.3	162.0	171.8	204.5	191.6	216.3	233.4	237.3	268.7	297.8	307.8	300.5
Sewage treatment/disposal	109.2	110.4	126.5	143.1	148.4	153.5	153.4	147.0	165.2	188.7	214.4	274.5
Land drainage	40.8	52.5	72.2	80.9	84.1	74.1	68.2	57.8	49.8	67.3	71.9	68.2
Environmental services	2.4	3.7	4.8	5.0	4.8	4.2	4.0	3.2	5.5	6.7	10.8	8.3
Other	19.2	17.5	17.0	26.2	32.6	46.4	64.1	65.0	78.8	114.3	134.4	181.9

1 Excludes depreciation and interest charges.

2 From 1987/88 Environmental services are no longer available in diaggregated format.

3 From 1988/89 Sewage treatment/disposal and Sewerage are aggregated.

4 Capital Expenditure in 1989 includes expenditure on infrastructure assets charged to profit.

Source *Water Authorities Association*

16.18 Income of local authorities: classified according to source[1]

England and Wales

Years ended 31 March

£ thousand

	1977/78	1978/79	1979/80	1980/81	1981/82	1982/83	1983/84	1984/85	1985/86	1986/87	1987/88
Capital income: total	4 132 824	4 341 816	5 001 245	5 555 754	5 488 790	7 306 638	7 708 054	7 360 997	7 007 915	7 559 298	8 061 504
Loans	2 815 850	2 751 052	3 135 903	3 050 494	2 668 918	3 572 576	3 806 320	3 632 215	3 206 909	3 061 905	3 237 846
Government grants	213 975	380 089	412 140	524 812	508 922	456 845	424 148	374 296	401 810	372 767	333 752
Sales and other sources	1 102 999	1 210 675	1 453 202	1 980 448	2 310 950	3 277 217	3 477 586	3 354 486	3 399 208	4 124 626	4 489 906
Revenue income: total	19 022 414	21 393 037	24 978 451	30 360 050	33 822 423	35 310 980	37 010 684	39 241 728	38 090 360	42 314 045	44 673 230
Rates	4 686 733	5 166 634	6 122 518	7 845 479	9 450 945	10 693 917	10 907 676	11 792 986	13 768 154	14 821 223	15 786 563
Government grants	9 138 334	10 103 779	11 684 364	13 784 425	13 998 687	14 246 491	16 106 399	17 165 363	16 385 455	18 831 610	19 614 008
Miscellaneous income including rents, tolls, fees and interest	5 197 347	6 122 624	7 171 569	8 730 146	10 372 791	10 370 572	9 996 609	10 283 379	7 936 751	8 661 212	1 272 659
Total income	23 155 238	25 734 853	29 979 696	35 915 804	39 311 213	42 617 618	44 718 738	46 602 225	45 098 275	49 873 343	52 734 734

1 Expenditure of superannuation and statutory special funds is not included.

Sources Department of the Environment; Welsh Office

16.19 Income of local authorities from government grants including grants for capital works

England and Wales

Years ended 31 March

£ thousand

	1977/78	1978/79	1979/80	1980/81	1981/82	1982/83	1983/84	1984/85	1985/86	1986/87	1987/88[1]
Allocated to specific services:											
Education	395 356	459 663	534 881	665 279	769 811	694 028	752 147	783 066	775 367	1 000 617	1 140 791
Libraries, museums and art galleries	730	1 190	1 643	1 914	2 689	2 878	3 426	3 729	4 328	5 048	4 804
Personal social services	13 790	16 236	21 682	27 417	29 187	33 791	40 825	40 575	37 641	45 969	52 794
Sheltered employment and workshops[2]	4 508	5 872	6 015	6 847	7 672	9 342	9 795	11 193	12 724	13 841	12 250
Police including school crossing patrols[2]	503 483	554 951	717 714	859 959	1 033 595	1 130 067	1 227 906	1 504 499	1 400 283	1 598 631	1 691 824
Fire service[2]	3	9	9	42	55	128	119	151	98	391	523
Administration of justice[2]	93 068	105 098	129 161	172 863	196 957	216 088	228 708	249 171	270 477	271 443	322 828
Refuse collection and disposal[1]	958	1 130	602	621	797	550	492	460	2 222	408	275
Agriculture and fisheries	25 238	44 377	58 986	65 026	73 576	66 113	14 207	10 694	15 404	17 518	13 459
Local transport[3]	300 921	292 045	369 527	458 834	436 285	515 440	468 500	328 025	226 975	133 367	151 728
Parks and open spaces[1,4]	7 741	13 545	17 461	22 162	23 968	27 128	29 761	32 957	41 073	47 638	36 515
Environmental health[1,4]	1 562	2 530	3 870	4 313	2 817	3 255	3 008	3 611	2 747	2 983	1 732
Cemeteries and crematoria[1]	12	53	59	75	47	96	99	141	42	19	32
Town and country planning[1]	22 755	33 553	35 332	43 344	43 436	68 831	91 848	112 858	132 100	120 522	48 522
Housing to which the Housing Revenue Account relates[5]	1 141 639	1 322 009	1 637 489	1 867 979	1 273 442	1 058 408	2 000 853	2 105 541	2 057 350	2 528 408	2 491 003
Other housing	215 232	377 591	390 355	483 535	461 646	520 486	1 041 986	1 427 574	1 630 417	1 661 198	1 819 333
Trading services:											
Passenger transport[1,6]	5 769	7 331	7 714	8 341	7 369	4 146	4 359	3 913	9 802	..	..
Harbours, docks and piers[7]	606	964	862	837	291	245	1 151	130	223	741	63
Other trading services[7]	4 718	9 835	13 177	16 735	24 331	37 088	25 085	21 582	20 315	18 129	20 420
Other services[1]	18 775	17 285	27 092	31 067	39 907	48 478	76 677	68 192	57 533	86 347	263 722
Not allocated to specific services:											
Local Government Acts grants	6 595 196	7 218 301	8 122 377	9 571 553	10 079 109	10 265 908	10 853 748	10 830 612	10 088 913	11 677 705	11 874 254
Local taxation licence duties	249	300	496	494	622	842	948	985	960	972	888
Total	9 352 309	10 483 868	12 096 504	14 309 237	14 507 609	14 703 336	16 875 648	17 539 659	16 787 246	19 231 895	19 947 760

1 For 1987/88, the capital account data supplied for each of these services is grouped as one total (of 84 452) in the 'Other services' row total.

2 For 1987/88, the capital account data for police including school crossing patrols, fire service and administration of justice has been grouped as one total (of 1 785) in the 'Administration of justice' row. This total also includes Civil Defence.

3 Includes Public Transport Companies.

4 Baths and laundries are included with parks and open spaces and from 1978/79 swimming baths are included with parks and open spaces, and other public baths and public laundries are included with environmental health.

5 Includes the rent rebate subsidy.

6 Due to deregulation of Passenger Transport Services this information was not supplied for 1986/87.

7 For 1987/88 the capital account data for 'Harbours, docks and piers' and 'Other trading services' is grouped as one total (of 8 111) in the 'Other trading services' row total.

Sources Department of the Environment; Welsh Office.

16.20 Expenditure of local authorities

Scotland

Year ended 31 March

Out of revenue[1]

£ thousand

	1976/77	1977/78	1978/79	1979/80	1980/81	1981/82	1982/83	1983/84	1984/85	1985/86	1986/87	1987/88
Total	1 892 140	2 049 118	2 369 475	2 881 365	3 536 791	3 926 170	4 241 068	4 566 462	4 794 090	5 048 188	5 351 981	5 721 849
Rate Fund Services	1 467 035	1 593 182	1 860 261	2 276 196	2 799 715	3 131 773	3 385 945	3 580 249	3 744 950	3 862 915	4 097 987	4 380 607
Education	674 604	721 565	830 182	975 555	1 190 993	1 331 560	1 423 903	1 487 339	1 535 138	1 588 425	1 691 333	1 817 823
Libraries, museums and galleries	19 448	21 563	26 603	32 282	40 263	45 639	49 423	53 745	57 390	61 907	64 161	69 410
Social work	119 799	129 846	156 542	196 210	249 554	277 681	299 742	319 029	338 848	369 017	383 840	433 590
Law, order and protective services	134 434	141 053	166 171	213 441	254 434	294 266	325 742	359 383	388 309	402 458	437 168	480 487
Roads[2]	124 448	153 237	180 185	229 117	299 278	320 862	359 423	368 793	385 018	404 427	425 932	439 473
Environmental services[3]	112 995	125 292	153 591	189 645	228 933	237 974	246 121	261 484	274 190	289 276	297 278	317 334
Planning	35 504	36 112	39 617	49 851	58 948	60 008	64 592	71 706	72 907	79 500	92 444	111 731
Leisure and recreation	67 373	74 193	91 371	114 378	133 956	146 218	157 651	167 269	173 643	182 057	195 626	217 527
Central administration	71 748	74 359	92 127	114 370	143 483	163 741	161 549	172 563	170 818	178 696	207 347	205 176
Other services[3]	35 256	41 832	50 999	56 782	79 123	103 451	124 774	131 925	142 681	152 215	160 991	170 891
Other rate fund expenditure[4]	71 426	74 130	72 873	104 565	120 750	150 373	173 025	187 013	206 008	154 937	141 867	117 165
Housing	404 299	431 536	469 851	578 271	689 972	745 431	819 026	941 484	1 025 160	1 098 802	1 166 619	1 257 988
Trading Services	92 232	98 530	112 236	131 463	167 854	205 016	209 122	231 742	229 988	241 408	229 242	200 419
Water supply	57 628	59 111	65 817	79 243	101 395	117 672	119 561	122 508	127 685	134 660	135 237	142 223
Passenger transport	20 912	23 034	28 917	30 249	36 682	36 836	39 703	43 488	45 876	47 017	27 833	149
Ferries	745	812	898	1 504	2 090	2 283	2 485	2 890	3 037	3 542	3 594	3 577
Harbours, docks and piers	1 099	1 436	8 602	11 497	14 822	33 297	31 225	37 332	41 291	43 433	47 689	38 879
Airports	131	170	323	404	1 216	1 364	1 632	1 793	1 543	1 366	1 315	951
Road bridges	2 338	3 187	2 621	2 936	3 275	5 672	4 321	4 873	4 819	5 057	5 179	7 378
Slaughterhouses	2 382	2 538	3 001	3 492	4 152	3 937	4 659	10 608	4 068	3 789	4 438	3 169
Markets	833	937	975	1 107	1 213	1 630	1 822	1 777	1 717	1 744	1 878	2 193
Other trading services[3]	6 164	7 305	1 082	1 031	3 009	2 325	3 714	6 473	−48	800	2 079	1 900
Loan Charges (included above): total	496 778	514 770	577 199	713 930	846 434	898 174	935 023	940 254	1 011 951	1 093 108	1 105 995	1 130 636
Allocated to:												
Rate fund services	195 914	204 572	233 458	293 982	349 889	365 594	388 838	393 532	423 245	466 597	478 185	502 383
Housing	272 872	281 667	308 015	379 867	445 701	467 086	478 552	470 701	513 030	544 053	541 880	558 172
Trading services	27 992	28 531	35 726	40 081	50 844	65 494	67 633	76 021	75 676	82 458	85 930	72 081

On capital works[5]

	1976/77	1977/78	1978/79	1979/80	1980/81	1981/82	1982/83	1983/84	1984/85	1985/86	1986/87	1987/88
Total	532 022	499 287	542 109	658 485	660 868	707 305	763 625	929 438	839 994	777 147	912 229	1 079 366
Rate Fund Services	263 721	228 699	243 955	299 614	293 966	320 396	336 346	358 684	360 236	402 025	401 338	424 624
Education	88 294	75 789	58 241	56 761	58 857	66 545	60 827	55 282	53 274	58 612	54 226	60 201
Libraries, museums and galleries	3 854	4 617	6 007	7 602	8 927	10 513	8 427	4 894	4 330	4 834	4 518	3 555
Social work	10 971	8 119	8 724	11 688	12 244	13 314	14 397	18 959	22 471	21 827	18 028	18 846
Law, order and protective services	10 253	9 973	10 308	11 908	12 795	10 541	12 956	15 485	15 723	20 324	21 286	27 121
Roads	52 108	46 487	58 123	77 724	78 479	96 348	107 328	112 128	111 310	134 684	144 324	127 768
Environmental services[3]	43 084	40 331	48 374	64 347	61 024	61 329	55 326	64 576	64 637	64 285	68 858	67 476
Planning	25 827	20 553	24 910	28 578	23 761	21 718	29 661	29 687	24 528	32 873	26 762	34 600
Leisure and recreation	15 946	12 201	13 810	20 663	19 766	19 237	20 304	25 433	22 748	28 188	26 104	29 032
Central administration	11 455	8 386	6 830	12 633	10 539	10 111	16 919	16 374	23 088	21 346	22 788	39 239
Other services[3]	1 929	2 243	8 628	7 710	7 574	10 740	10 201	15 866	18 127	15 052	14 444	16 786
Housing	234 734	229 413	243 956	293 763	311 010	329 276	373 464	519 266	431 703	325 511	461 099	603 511
Trading Services	33 567	41 175	54 198	65 108	55 892	57 633	53 815	51 488	48 055	49 611	49 792	51 231
Water supply	20 500	21 317	27 803	37 968	35 757	37 664	38 492	39 422	37 412	38 352	41 583	42 989
Passenger transport	3 495	1 990	3 658	3 238	4 700	5 264	5 575	5 636	4 489	1 160	1 414	–
Ferries	36	71	221	881	843	1 925	879	745	1 999	1 841	639	564
Harbours, docks and piers	5 842	14 768	21 140	20 373	8 646	7 730	6 404	3 334	2 159	6 701	3 917	4 155
Airports	253	215	64	294	268	123	161	314	455	193	123	86
Road bridges	425	727	21	121	371	1 929	398	878	478	962	1 633	998
Slaughterhouses	1 941	1 165	860	1 979	3 725	2 587	426	380	342	127	17	85
Markets	447	326	31	21	7	–	117	81	216	2	171	171
Other trading services[3]	628	596	400	233	1 575	411	1 363	698	505	273	295	2 183

1 Gross expenditure *less* inter-authority and inter-account transfers.
2 Including rate fund support for transport (LA and non-LA).
3 Burial grounds and Crematoria were treated as trading services for 1976/77 and 1977/78, and were included amongst 'Other trading services'. In 1978/79, 1979/80 and 1980/81 they were included amongst 'Environmental services'. From 1981/82 they were included amongst 'Other services'.
4 Rate fund contributions to Housing and Trading Services (excluding transport) and public water requisitions, and therefore included in the expenditure figures for these services.
5 Expenditure out of loans, government grants and other capital receipts.
6 Provisional.

Source *Scottish Office, Central Statistics Unit*

16.21 Income of local authorities: classified according to source

Scotland

Year ended 31 March

£ thousand

	1976/77	1977/78	1978/79	1979/80	1980/81	1981/82	1982/83	1983/84	1984/85	1985/86	1986/87	1987/88
Revenue account												
Rates[1]	470 905	544 656	616 555	716 966	938 618	1 255 542	1 427 243	1 377 275	1 420 354	1 609 148	1 717 558	1 942 864
Government grants												
RSG: Needs element	665 600	705 900	822 400	946 400	1 256 300	1 376 300	1 434 600	1 493 150	1 442 300	1 391 300	1 380 800	1 509 400
Resources element	167 800	177 300	204 900	234 900	180 900	152 900	207 900	210 800	215 000	205 900	184 200	196 200
Domestic element	42 200	49 700	13 400	13 500	13 800	14 100	14 300	14 300	14 400	102 900	91 300	90 800
Rate rebate grant	18 480	21 548	19 063	24 511	28 786	52 790	55 000	145 550	160 820	223 129	220 527	248 045
Specific grants and subsidies	238 738	242 017	265 572	345 136	412 348	375 039	387 857	471 892	521 332	582 653	631 343	758 538
Sales	21 840	31 125	25 968	33 027	35 491	46 433	42 009	41 931	44 185	42 190	49 327	60 769
Fees and charges[4]	85 898	98 895	125 306	146 217	182 892	217 037	233 440	255 272	768 420	823 112	882 645	936 928
Other income[4]	210 846	246 089	298 161	329 379	372 407	469 548	571 607	617 713	155 832	173 616	163 297	110 219
Capital account												
Sale of fixed assets	6 016	8 416	21 936	22 616	38 022	75 042	128 482	144 719	138 345	130 831	133 988	191 620
Loans	489 460	453 664	481 862	583 444	566 914	574 655	562 501	693 851	608 797	656 869	694 680	790 368
Government grants	8 773	12 941	10 837	18 673	31 628	32 726	32 139	35 518	37 242	36 476	47 595	44 974
Revenue contributions to capital	8 888	8 392	10 678	16 217	12 392	11 635	13 157	17 688	9 358	6 722	10 781	19 365
Transfers from special funds	761	1 932	1 343	1 234	709	1 094	1 319	3 442	945	1 473	1 881	6 184
Other receipts	18 920	14 445	16 479	17 580	14 323	15 918	34 536	36 512	48 311	61 838	26 197	27 906
Total income	2 455 125	2 617 020	2 934 460	3 449 800	4 085 530	4 670 759	5 146 090	5 559 613	5 585 641	6 048 157	6 236 119	6 934 180

1 Excluding Government grants towards rate rebates and domestic element of rate support grant (RSG) but including payments in lieu of rates under Part V of The Local Government Act 1948 for years to 1977/78. Including domestic water rate receipts.

2 Excluding certificated rate rebates paid in respect of supplementary benefit recipients. In prior years such sums were included with rate income, but are now part of rate rebate grant.

3 Provisional.

4 Prior to 1984/85 rents are treated as other income from 1984/85 onwards rents are included with fees and charges.

Source Scottish Office

16.22 Income of local authorities from government grants[1]

Scotland

Year ended 31 March

£ thousand

	1976/77	1977/78	1978/79	1979/80	1980/81	1981/82	1982/83	1983/84	1984/85	1985/86	1986/87	1987/88
Rate fund services	63 840	72 833	82 411	107 875	135 668	153 343	167 318	182 062	190 594	202 313	249 871	278 888
Education	134	696	3 174	1 776	2 247	2 564	3 549	3 208	4 170	4 365	8 453	13 323
Libraries, museums and galleries	3	35	200	905	2 371	2 827	2 030	39	150	286	210	233
Social work	902	680	934	797	1 169	1 553	2 265	2 295	2 968	3 427	3 738	3 228
Law, order and protective services	47 704	51 225	59 708	75 173	90 443	105 695	117 032	125 194	137 232	140 796	156 133	173 228
Roads and transport	3 346	4 781	2 902	7 871	13 727	8 735	13 349	18 302	11 200	17 261	28 246	30 178
Environmental services	987	2 889	2 550	5 235	6 030	9 174	6 213	6 270	6 233	6 615	5 725	5 615
Planning	6 287	6 377	6 331	7 139	7 167	7 215	7 305	7 323	8 223	7 173	3 264	4 555
Leisure and recreation	1 685	1 391	1 767	1 584	1 220	1 538	1 682	1 025	582	1 321	3 743	2 950
Central administration	3	7	57	13	20	7	42	10	28	15	246	357
Other rate fund services	2 789	4 752	4 788	7 382	11 274	14 035	13 851	18 396	19 808	21 054	40 113	45 221
Housing	178 853	176 626	188 085	248 184	299 990	248 456	227 874	317 241	360 162	408 637	444 131	506 342
Trading services	4 812	5 499	5 912	8 095	8 298	7 911	6 103	8 107	7 812	8 140	11 327	10 485
Water supply	2 802	3 951	3 700	6 321	6 352	4 874	2 671	5 714	6 336	4 981	7 737	8 001
Ferries	–	60	257	243	250	450	10	264	690	953	597	213
Other trading services	2 010	1 488	1 955	1 531	1 696	2 587	3 422	2 129	786	2 206	2 993	2 271
Grants not allocated to specific services[2]	894 080	954 448	1 059 763	1 219 311	1 479 786	1 595 500	1 711 800	1 863 800	1 832 520	1 923 229	1 876 827	2 044 445
Total	1 141 585	1 209 406	1 336 171	1 583 465	1 923 742	2 005 210	2 113 095	2 371 210	2 391 088	2 542 319	2 582 156	2 840 160

1 Including grants for capital works.

2 Rate support grant and rate rebates grant.

Source Scottish Office

16.23 Expenditure of local authorities

Northern Ireland

Years end 31 March

Out of revenue and special funds

£ thousand

	1976/77	1977/78	1978/79	1979/80	1980/81	1981/82	1982/83	1983/84	1984/85	1985/86	1986/87	1987/88
Total	50 593	57 366	65 267	81 599	96 828	110 557	121 856	133 056	143 346	153 223	154 142	166 911
Libraries, museums and art galleries	22	28	44	50	113	218	271	321	493	485	517	678
Environmental health services:												
Refuse collection and disposal	7 618	9 086	10 295	12 337	14 932	15 871	17 986	19 463	20 360	21 854	22 733	25 599
Public baths	2 410	3 006	3 114	3 191	3 762	3 957	4 630	3 980	3 705	3 503	3 649	3 145
Parks, recreation grounds, etc.	8 072	10 390	12 928	16 739	20 834	25 274	30 338	35 397	40 059	45 336	49 491	56 478
Other sanitary services	6 319	6 741	7 352	8 593	10 467	11 619	12 980	14 053	15 389	16 834	18 210	19 758
Housing (grants and small dwellings acquisition)[1]	1 111	1 122	1 094	1 241	1 466	1 369	1 345	1 825	1 593	1 498	1 354	1 265
Trading services:												
Gas supply	13 313	13 835	16 363	21 789	23 061	25 337	25 773	25 338	26 105	24 613	18 896	15 529
Cemeteries	1 072	1 231	1 348	1 640	2 065	2 418	2 508	2 622	2 816	3 089	3 221	3 674
Other trading services (including markets, fairs and harbours)	1 852	2 056	1 990	2 495	3 681	4 047	4 313	5 024	5 570	6 051	5 589	5 242
Miscellaneous	8 804	9 871	10 739	13 524	16 447	20 447	21 712	25 033	27 256	29 960	30 482	35 543
Total loan charges	5 292	5 526	5 757	7 018	9 068	10 236	11 538	11 257	12 111	13 836	12 484	12 583
Loan charges included in terms of expenditure above:												
Allocated to rate fund services	2 513	2 865	3 216	3 793	4 963	6 113	7 071	7 484	8 749	10 628	9 869	10 001
Allocated to trading services	2 239	2 137	2 024	2 643	3 401	3 437	3 717	2 519	2 335	2 280	1 825	1 820
Not allocated	540	524	517	582	704	686	750	1 254	1 027	928	790	762

On capital works[1]

	1976/77	1977/78	1978/79	1979/80	1980/81	1981/82	1982/83	1983/84	1984/85	1985/86	1986/87	1987/88
Total	11 879	13 377	15 163	21 318	24 079	25 078	24 073	29 192	25 176	33 102	24 226	28 958
Libraries, museums and art galleries	6	17	1	–	94	120	65	88	232	585	411	129
Environmental health services:												
Refuse collection and disposal	1 611	892	737	1 233	1 337	1 964	2 170	2 801	1 231	1 954	1 490	3 551
Public baths	744	450	354	787	1 205	811	454	1 249	596	556	359	75
Parks, recreation grounds, etc.	5 051	6 824	8 080	9 957	11 675	11 395	11 985	16 155	16 103	21 443	15 406	8 986
Other sanitary services	343	275	642	689	554	742	719	829	739	766	499	891
Housing (including small dwellings acquisition)[1]	1 004	850	1 100	1 815	965	639	211	484	262	242	264	438
Trading services:												
Gas supply	782	528	757	419	421	282	648	646	391	214	4	(112)
Cemeteries	78	61	58	28	139	280	103	343	470	402	388	645
Other trading services (including markets, fairs and harbours)	319	563	1 149	2 983	3 215	3 113	2 679	2 864	1 403	2 204	1 506	2 520
Miscellaneous	1 941	2 917	2 285	3 407	4 474	5 732	5 041	3 733	3 749	4 736	3 907	11 835

1 Expenditure met out of loans, government grants for capital works, sales of property and other capital receipts.

Source *Department of the Environment for Northern Ireland*

16.24 Income of local authorities: classified according to source

Northern Ireland

Years ended 31 March

£ thousand

	1976/77	1977/78	1978/79	1979/80	1980/81	1981/82	1982/83	1983/84	1984/85	1985/86	1986/87	1987/88
Total income	68 907	69 565	78 285	94 584	120 114	136 219	151 064	165 348	168 786	190 145	179 700	203 851
Capital receipts: total	11 441	11 428	12 631	15 214	19 420	21 676	23 502	23 274	22 114	29 701	23 656	27 308
Loans	3 970	3 279	3 871	5 831	9 616	9 533	8 296	7 854	8 028	11 724	11 124	8 815
Government grants	4 712	5 049	6 192	6 824	6 778	7 604	9 878	9 022	8 854	11 073	6 407	7 534
Other sources	2 759	3 100	2 568	2 559	3 026	4 539	5 328	6 398	5 232	6 904	6 125	10 959
Other income: total	39 634	37 947	41 675	48 826	61 513	73 019	83 684	95 758	98 374	103 047	112 368	130 110
Rates	25 397	27 130	30 376	35 532	45 579	54 261	60 924	67 382	68 353	71 453	79 882	96 475
Government grants	9 292	10 267	10 754	12 695	15 196	18 045	17 844	22 445	28 993	30 711	31 499	32 950
Housing[1]												
Grants and small dwellings acquisition	596	550	545	599	738	713	729	1 237	1 028	883	987	685
Miscellaneous income	4 349	4 671	5 304	7 147	7 963	9 415	11 306	12 501	15 228	17 521	18 652	21 871
Trading services[2]												
Total (capital and revenue)	17 832	15 519	18 675	23 397	31 218	32 109	32 572	33 815	33 070	39 876	25 024	24 562
Gas: total	15 423	12 601	15 118	18 275	24 342	24 666	26 056	25 016	25 604	31 840	18 110	16 564
Loans	616	701	451	174	272	308	392	56	9	150	4	9
Government grants	2 404	494	3 374	5 774	9 712	8 887	10 916	11 118	11 419	17 637	6 368	9 951
Miscellaneous	12 403	11 406	11 293	12 327	14 358	15 471	14 748	13 842	14 176	14 153	11 756	6 601
Cemeteries: total	297	298	317	359	507	830	637	919	1 049	1 046	1 023	1 507
Loans	59	38	28	10	78	170	20	294	150	173	284	497
Government grants	3	–	–	–	–	4	15	85	50	42	33	16
Miscellaneous	235	260	289	349	429	656	602	540	849	831	706	994
Other trading: total	2 112	2 620	3 240	4 763	6 369	6 613	5 879	7 880	6 417	6 990	5 891	6 491
Loans	155	436	888	2 153	1 700	1 522	824	948	307	598	343	674
Government grants	140	52	556	307	1 346	1 551	1 453	1 970	755	189	257	916
Miscellaneous	1 817	2 132	1 796	2 303	3 323	3 540	3 602	4 962	5 355	6 203	5 291	4 901

1 Including annuity repayments made by borrowers under the Small Dwellings Acquisition scheme.

2 Reclassified in 1975/76.

Source *Department of the Environment for Northern Ireland*

16.25 Income of local authorities from government grants[1]: classified according to services

Northern Ireland

Years ended 31 March

£ thousand

	1976/77	1977/78	1978/79	1979/80	1980/81	1981/82	1982/83	1983/84	1984/85	1985/86	1986/87	1987/88
Total	16 551	15 862	20 586	25 600	33 032	36 091	44 293	49 334	50 071	59 552	44 554	51 372
Allocated to specific services:												
Environmental health services	5 873	6 602	7 353	8 027	8 118	8 951	12 190	11 838	11 820	14 123	9 225	6 537
Housing	672	560	546	539	438	318	16	–	–	–	–	–
Other services	2 871	1 135	4 529	7 136	12 329	12 420	14 072	15 051	14 013	19 670	8 536	16 015
Not allocated to specific services[2]	7 135	7 565	8 158	9 898	12 147	14 402	18 015	22 445	24 238	25 759	26 793	28 820

1 Including grants for capital works.

2 Assistance to local authorities under various Local Government Acts.

Source *Department of the Environment for Northern Ireland*

17 Banking, Insurance, etc.

Public sector borrowing requirement
Table 17.7

Net non-deposit sterling liabilities

This comprises changes in the sterling component of capital and internal funds and reserves of all monetary sector institutions, *less* their sterling investments in UK banks and other non-financial sterling assets, together with residual errors arising from the exclusion of sterling transactions between institutions within the sector. This item replaces 'Net non-deposit liabilities' which comprised changes in both sterling and foreign currency items. Total net non-deposit liabilities (in sterling and foreign currency) are shown in Table 17.4.

External and foreign currency counterparts

This now includes changes in the foreign currency component of capital, internal funds and reserves of all monetary sector institutions, *less* their foreign currency investments in UK banks and other non-financial assets in currencies other than sterling: these items were formerly included in 'Net non-deposit liabilities'. Changes in these items are calculated in transactions terms, that is after an adjustment has been made for the estimated effect of changes in the sterling value of foreign currencies.

17.1 Bank of England

£ million

	1978 Dec 13	1979 Dec 12	1980 Dec 10	1981 Dec 9	1982 Dec 8	1983 Dec 14	1984 Dec 12	1985 Dec 11	1986 Dec 10	1987 Dec 9	1988 Dec 14
Issue Department											
Liabilities:											
Notes in circulation	9 122	10 089	10 611	11 001	11 271	12 152	12 610	12 612	13 259	13 901	15 418
Notes in Banking Department	28	11	14	24	4	8	10	8	11	9	12
Assets:											
Government securities[1]	8 085	8 635	8 430	6 329	3 217	4 699	1 888	938	1 890	9 545	10 711
Other securities	1 065	1 465	2 195	4 696	8 058	7 461	10 732	11 682	11 380	4 365	4 719
Banking Department											
Liabilities:											
Total[2]	2 250	1 999	1 162	2 039	2 754	2 356	2 595	2 328	2 157	3 053	3 385
Public deposits[3]	25	20	33	40	41	44	99	83	83	88	96
Special deposits[4]	1 099	805	–	–	–	–	–	–	–	–	–
Bankers deposits[5]	423	462	487	482	647	650	787	848	949	1 044	1 249
Reserves and other accounts	689	697	627	1 503	2 051	1 647	1 694	1 382	1 572	1 907	2 025
Assets:											
Total	2 251	2 000	1 162	2 039	2 754	2 356	2 595	2 328	2 618	3 053	3 385
Government securities	1 848	1 462	447	433	456	383	460	579	614	599	766
Advances and other accounts	206	161	175	1 026	1 283	947	894	719	900	815	587
Premises, equipment and other securities	169	365	526	556	1 011	1 018	1 231	1 022	1 093	1 630	2 020
Notes and coin	28	12	15	24	4	8	10	8	11	9	12

1 Including the historic liability of the Treasury of £11 million.
2 The only liability not shown separately is the Bank's capital (held by the Treasury) which has been constant at £14.6 million.
3 Excluding local authorities' and public corporations' deposits, which are included under Reserves and other accounts.
4 Deposits called from institutions are not at their free disposal. Until 19 August 1981, all banks and finance houses which observed the common reserve ratio were liable for calls to lodge special deposits. With effect from 20 August 1981 only reporting institutions with eligible liabilities of £10 million or more are liable for special deposit calls. This item also includes deposits under the supplementary special deposits scheme which was in force on three occasions before 1980.
5 Up to 19 August 1981 these constituted the current accounts held at the Bank by the banks and discount houses. From the introduction of new arrangements for monetary control on 20 August, they consist of operational deposits held mainly by the clearing banks and non-operational cash ratio deposits for which recognised banks and licensed deposit takers are liable.

Source Bank of England

17.2 Bank clearing[1]

£ million

	1978	1979	1980	1981	1982	1983	1984	1985	1986	1987	1988
Credit clearing: total	36 887	43 497	51 808	61 480	62 563	67 978	69 478	72 616	80 426	91 980	103 404
Debit clearing: total	2 847 030	3 616 555	4 458 326	4 835 414	5 771 350	6 800 818	7 544 555	8 143 884	8 939 234	9 184 717	8 646 156
Bankers' clearing house: total	2 845 901	3 615 313	4 456 893	4 835 414	5 771 350	6 800 818	7 544 555	8 143 884	8 939 234	9 184 717	8 646 156
Town	2 544 254	3 258 830	4 051 203	4 403 794	5 291 926	6 257 551	6 922 420	7 463 677	8 173 039	8 324 927	7 692 868
General	301 647	356 483	405 690	431 620	479 424	543 267	622 135	680 207	766 195	859 790	953 288
Provincial clearing houses: total	1 129	1 242	1 433	[2]	[2]	[2]	[2]	[2]	[2]	[2]	[2]

1 Figures are not strictly comparable throughout owing to changes in the composition of the clearings. This table includes only inter-bank clearings.
2 Data no longer collected.

Source Bankers' Clearing House

17.3 UK monetary sector: liabilities and assets outstanding[1]

End-year

£ million

	1977	1978	1979	1980	1981[2]	1982	1983	1984	1985	1986	1987	1988
Liabilities												
Total	144 850	167 408	199 591	233 403	332 039	411 602	480 369	604 477	589 880	704 182	728 649	816 592
Public sector deposits												
Sterling	1 424	1 313	1 258	1 606	2 063	3 159	3 220	3 987	5 067	6 672	7 796	9 626
Other currencies[3]	124	102	117	154	202	282	308	431	287	306	304	191
Private sector deposits												
Sterling	36 313	41 846	47 719	57 571	73 825	80 892	90 443	100 414	114 905	138 323	172 031	208 918
Other currencies[3]	4 151	4 799	5 202	6 189	9 849	12 717	16 376	20 947	20 144	28 602	30 778	33 635
Overseas sector deposits												
Sterling	5 615	5 476	8 475	11 477	14 413	18 892	23 369	29 661	33 923	39 488	47 925	61 561
Other currencies	89 558	105 046	127 347	145 684	217 904	279 510	327 338	423 955	382 072	453 913	426 286	450 124
Non-deposit liabilities (net)	7 665	8 826	9 473	10 722	13 783	16 150	19 315	25 082	33 482	36 838	43 529	52 537
Assets												
Total	144 850	167 408	199 591	233 403	332 039	411 602	480 369	604 477	589 880	704 158	728 649	816 592
Lending to public sector												
Sterling	13 633	13 478	14 980	17 325	22 650	20 322	18 389	19 299	17 274	16 242	15 984	14 719
Other currencies	3 751	3 151	2 325	1 485	1 000	1 170	1 399	2 011	1 938	1 860	1 037	442
Lending to private sector												
Sterling	31 922	36 759	45 280	54 907	68 322	82 910	97 521	112 206	131 888	161 711	203 997	260 641
Other currencies	7 422	8 088	8 326	8 852	15 616	20 038	24 735	38 028	35 505	44 611	46 859	56 733
Lending to overseas sector												
Sterling	4 232	5 094	5 073	7 853	11 196	14 339	17 257	23 108	25 653	31 450	37 203	41 483
Other currencies	83 890	100 838	123 607	142 981	213 255	272 823	321 068	409 825	377 622	448 284	423 569	442 574

1 At end-1981, in the quarterly series, the old banking sector was replaced by the new monetary sector. The UK monetary sector comprises the UK offices of institutions either recognised as banks or licensed to take deposits under the Banking Act 1979, together with the National Girobank, the Banking Department of the Bank of England, and those institutions (including branches of mainland banks) in the Channel Islands and the Isle of Man which have opted to participate in the new monetary control arrangements introduced in August 1981. Inter-bank items are excluded and adjustments made to allow for transit items. Figures for other currencies are affected by changes in exchange rates.

2 The introduction of the new monetary sector at end-1981 added about £9 850 to total assets and liabilities.

3 Before the introduction of new statistical returns during 1975 all UK residents' deposits in foreign currency were allocated to the private sector.

Source *Bank of England*

17.4 Banks: summary of monthly reporting institutions

£ million

	Second Wednesday in Dec. 1980
Liabilities	
Notes outstanding	554
Sterling deposits: total	90 354
Sight deposits	
UK banking sector	2 299
UK Public sector	659
UK Private sector	21 000
Overseas	2 946
Time deposits	
UK banking sector	15 377
UK Public sector	303
UK Private sector	34 108
Overseas	7 936
Certificates of deposit (CD)	5 727
Other currency deposits: total	193 374
Sight and time deposits	
UK banking sector	42 727
Other United Kingdom	5 574
Overseas	124 125
Certificates of deposit	20 947

	Second Wednesday in Dec.				End Dec.			
	1981[1]	1982	1983[2]	1984	1985	1986	1987	1988
Liabilities								
Notes outstanding	625	716	836	917	995	1 145	1 266	1 407
Sterling deposits: total	109 906	134 649	156 794	180 119	208 572	253 557	304 220	368 952
Sight deposits								
UK monetary sector	3 458	5 887	7 637	7 789	9 746	11 298	9 306	9 652
UK Public sector	823	992	1 118	1 078	1 244	1 927	2 314	2 447
UK Private sector	23 023	26 662	32 532	39 318	48 471	63 263	79 101	90 708
Overseas	3 137	3 748	4 699	5 392	6 770	8 067	10 533	10 653
Time deposits								
UK monetary sector	20 728	28 542	28 358	35 450	40 540	45 838	52 573	63 309
UK Public sector	460	1 119	1 245	1 237	1 790	2 699	4 097	6 704
UK Private sector	41 124	44 796	53 843	55 735	61 491	70 441	80 683	99 111
Overseas	10 458	14 377	17 570	22 890	25 703	30 195	35 916	48 669
Certificates of deposit	6 695	8 525	9 792	11 230	12 818	19 829	29 697	37 700
Other currency deposits: total	288 379	376 259	439 301	534 136	499 530	591 173	543 860	568 204
Sight and time deposits								
UK monetary sector	64 614	84 887	87 389	98 692	92 656	101 033	85 675	83 550
Other United Kingdom	9 663	12 081	15 483	19 041	19 019	27 893	30 264	33 086
Overseas	173 678	221 993	265 972	336 754	323 730	384 874	356 645	391 747
Certificates of deposit	40 424	57 299	70 457	79 648	64 125	77 373	71 276	77 822

1 From 1981 this table relates to the business of the United Kingdom offices of those members of the monetary sector which report on a monthly basis, other than members of the London Discount Market Association (LDMA), the Trustee savings banks and the Banking Department of the Bank of England. For a description of the background of these changes see the December 1981 *Bank of England Quarterly Bulletin,* page 531.

2 From 1983, the Trustee savings banks and the Banking Department of the Bank of England are included.

3 From 1983, market loans to UK public corporations and the UK private sector are included as advances.

Source *Bank of England*

17.4 Banks: summary of monthly reporting institutions

(continued)

£ million

	Second Wednesday in Dec. 1980
Sterling and other currencies	
Items in suspense and transmission	3 966
Capital and other funds	15 032
Total liabilities/assets	303 279
of which Sterling Liabilities	*108 043*
Sterling Assets	*108 022*
Sterling assets	
Notes and coin	1 591
Reserve assets: total	9 084
Balances with Bank of England	485
Money at call	
Discount market	4 601
Other	295
UK and Northern Ireland Treasury bills	1 168
Other bills	
Local authority	502
Commercial	1 251
British government stocks up to one year	782
Special and supplementary deposits	–
Market loans (other than reserve assets): total	28 908
Banks in United Kingdom	17 403
Loans to discount market	206
Certificates of deposit	3 510
UK local authorities	3 939
UK public corporations	229
UK private sector	804
Overseas	2 817
Bills (other than reserve assets)	435
Advances: total	52 939
UK public sector	1 885
UK private sector	46 469
Overseas	4 586
Investments	
British government stocks	
Over 1 year and up to 1½ years	198
Over 1½ years and up to 5 years	1 890
Over 5 years and undated	1 152
Other	
Public sector	470
Other	2 291
Sterling	
Miscellaneous assets	
Items in suspense and collections	5 705
Assets leased	396
Other	2 963
Other currency	
Items in suspense and collections	314
Assets leased	13
Other	1 291
Other currency assets	
Market loans and advances: total	189 871
of which Advances	*45 833*
Banks in United Kingdom and discount market	41 484
Certificates of deposit	3 931
UK public sector	1 523
UK private sector	8 675
Overseas	134 259
Bills	592
Investments: total	3 176
United Kingdom	154
Overseas	3 022
Acceptances	
Sterling	5 106
Other currencies	454

	Second Wednesday in Dec.				End Dec.			
	1981[1]	1982	1983[2]	1984	1985	1986	1987	1988
Sterling and other currencies								
Items in suspense and transmission	6 140	6 107	7 198	10 702	10 738	12 100	14 199	14 460
Capital and other funds	19 056	22 343	27 425	33 749	41 916	49 206	54 859	64 404
Total liabilities/assets	424 105	540 074	631 554	759 622	761 751	907 181	918 405	101 728
of which Sterling Liabilities	*131 270*	*158 561*	*185 575*	*213 369*	*242 912*	*295 847*	*352 826*	*425 689*
Sterling Assets	*131 257*	*159 595*	*185 673*	*215 322*	*242 348*	*296 762*	*353 493*	*426 871*
Sterling assets								
Notes and coin	1 612	1 586	1 938	2 006	2 313	2 640	2 994	3 405
Balances with Bank of England:								
Cash ratio deposits	321	434	497	577	667	732	906	1 124
Special deposits	–	–	–	–	–	–	–	–
Other	159	209	147	187	83	281	159	154
Market loans[3]								
LDMA—secured	4 317	4 685	5 764	6 070	6 367	6 819	7 947	7 992
LDMA—unsecured	21	20	37	45	47	57	50	75
Other UK monetary sector	21 658	30 695	32 830	39 099	45 517	54 863	58 479	68 317
UK monetary sector CDs	4 094	4 573	4 980	5 847	6 210	7 735	10 318	12 533
Building Society CDs and time deposits	–	–	365	775	766	1 401	1 407	1 660
UK local authorities	5 386	5 172	5 085	4 824	3 565	2 514	1 780	1 452
UK public corporations	320	61	–	–	–	–	–	–
UK private sector	1 129	1 160	–	–	–	–	–	–
Overseas	4 060	4 441	4 634	6 837	8 891	14 012	19 200	24 248
Bills:								
Treasury bills	707	313	333	286	300	292	776	1 632
Eligible local authority	278	226	351	413	581	462	433	388
Eligible bank bills	1 389	1 335	2 286	2 848	2 806	4 166	5 741	6 856
Other	278	253	258	275	297	428	664	566
Advances: total	66 772	83 905	100 067	114 369	131 994	158 828	197 630	250 771
UK public sector	3 053	3 033	2 613	2 616	2 067	1 334	1 670	1 906
UK private sector	58 266	73 126	87 475	100 723	117 658	144 660	182 814	234 357
Overseas	5 453	7 746	9 979	11 031	12 269	12 834	13 146	13 552
Banking Dept lending to central government (net)	–	–	387	461	574	525	820	956
Investments								
British government stocks								
Up to 1 year	505	567						
Over 1 year and up to 5	2 355	2 469	6 618	6 696	7 171	8 617	7 702	5 371
Over 5 years and undated	1 287	1 196						
Other								
Public sector	520	361	366	442	425	403	501	207
Other	3 229	3 797	5 264	7 688	7 573	11 557	13 402	12 214
Sterling								
Miscellaneous assets								
Items in suspense and collections	6 143	7 023	7 373	8 879	8 870	12 667	13 967	14 583
Assets leased	1 292	1 076	1 195	1 302	1 426	1 432	1 278	1 065
Other	3 424	4 038	4 898	5 396	5 904	6 332	7 339	8 731
Other currency								
Items in suspense and collections	1 829	1 782	2 172	3 567	5 086	3 553	4 180	4 043
Assets leased	12	20	17	16	10	10	1	0
Other	1 405	3 265	2 613	1 930	1 589	2 414	2 732	2 107
Other currency assets								
Market loans and advances: total	283 400	365 773	426 195	513 290	478 474	558 587	520 211	544 209
of which Advances	*68 849*	*91 389*	*109 186*	*134 784*	*120 287*	*128 052*	*115 953*	*127 311*
UK monetary sector	61 325	80 013	83 714	95 010	89 171	97 225	78 826	78 138
UK monetary sector CDs	5 407	7 200	10 615	11 621	11 610	12 999	9 252	7 392
UK public sector	902	1 028	1 376	1 864	1 632	1 527	925	70
UK private sector	15 287	19 946	24 187	35 762	33 837	42 877	45 238	54 809
Overseas	200 480	257 585	306 304	369 033	342 225	403 959	385 969	403 794
Bills	822	1 070	1 242	1 562	1 717	3 144	2 399	3 837
Investments: total	5 380	8 570	13 642	23 935	32 527	42 711	35 396	36 306
United Kingdom	315	308	436	617	1 949	3 923	2 678	2 396
Overseas	5 065	8 262	13 205	23 318	30 578	38 788	32 718	33 910
Acceptances								
Sterling	7 921	12 198	13 385	16 335	18 251	21 013	18 303	18 743
Other currencies	827	1 261	1 524	2 718	2 987	3 309	3 172	3 514

See footnotes on page 287.

Source *Bank of England*

17.5 Analysis of bank lending to UK residents[1]

Amounts outstanding

£ million

	Third Wednesday in Nov			End Nov	End Nov
	1984	1985	1986	1987	1988
Total to UK residents	150 793	168 280	203 010	242 964	302 877
Loans and advances	139 315	154 919	189 467	230 818	287 409
of which in sterling	*103 027*	*119 819*	*141 358*	*183 737*	*236 702*
Acceptances	11 478	13 361	13 543	12 146	15 468
of which in sterling	*10 579*	*12 407*	*12 913*	*11 706*	*15 006*
Agriculture, Forestry and Fishing					
Total	5 495	5 878	6 088	6 081	6 530
of which in sterling	*5 469*	*5 859*	*6 048*	*6 041*	*6 461*
Energy and water supply					
Total	6 314	4 888	4 424	4 197	3 977
of which in sterling	*3 020*	*2 107*	*1 416*	*1 804*	*1 953*
Oil and extraction of natural gas	3 996	3 072	2 726	2 731	3 155
Other energy industries	2 168	1 310	1 090	988	723
Water supply	150	506	608	478	99
Manufacturing industry					
Total	26 390	27 433	29 599	28 950	39 925
of which in sterling	*20 810*	*22 353*	*23 289*	*23 396*	*30 448*
Extraction of minerals and ores	770	805	648	650	719
Metal manufacturing	1 660	1 268	1 100	1 111	1 450
Mineral products	926	960	1 073	926	1 096
Chemical industry	2 010	2 016	2 117	2 046	2 094
Mechanical engineering	1 837	2 162	2 152	2 136	2 603
Electrical engineering	3 071	3 628	3 547	3 424	4 596
Motor vehicles	1 120	1 352	1 736	928	1 269
Other transport equipment	1 569	1 474	1 518	743	955
Other engineering and metal goods	2 009	1 989	1 979	1 811	2 527
Food, drink and tobacco	4 810	4 595	5 974	5 961	9 272
Textiles, leather, clothing and footwear	1 546	1 796	1 722	2 022	2 500
Other manufacturing	5 062	5 388	6 026	7 192	10 839
Construction					
Total	4 609	5 074	5 675	7 175	10 721
of which in sterling	*4 243*	*4 614*	*5 253*	*6 677*	*9 810*
Garages, distribution, hotels and catering					
Total	19 746	22 388	24 359	27 412	32 730
of which in sterling	*14 792*	*17 057*	*18 572*	*20 812*	*25 287*
Retail motor trades	2 006	2 246	2 488	2 794	3 172
Other retail distribution	5 715	6 621	7 192	8 256	10 061
Wholesale distribution	8 946	9 973	10 609	10 654	12 343
Hotels and catering	3 079	3 548	4 070	5 707	7 154
Transport					
Total	3 571	3 509	3 569	4 099	4 843
of which in sterling	*2 127*	*2 356*	*2 396*	*3 144*	*3 575*
Air transport	760	502	457	416	543
Other transport	2 811	3 007	3 112	3 683	4 300
Postal services and telecommunications					
Total	283	339	304	419	984
of which in sterling	*133*	*177*	*162*	*252*	*668*
Financial					
Total	31 644	32 574	55 477	69 992	78 799
of which in sterling	*13 822*	*18 072*	*30 032*	*41 175*	*53 893*
Building societies	1 420	2 064	3 355	4 660	4 977
Investment and unit trusts	2 369	3 462	3 725	6 474	6 776
Insurance companies and pension funds	2 248	2 370	2 912	3 892	3 319
Leasing companies	4 508	6 660	7 799	10 179	11 281
Other financial	21 099	18 018	25 024	29 998	37 204
Securities dealers, stockbrokers, jobbers, etc.[2]	..	..	12 662	14 789	15 242
Business and other services					
Total	18 694	25 094	25 194	31 765	46 087
of which in sterling	*15 233*	*18 644*	*21 905*	*28 667*	*41 614*
Central and local government	2 108	2 144	1 380	1 299	1 554
Property companies	5 420	7 109	9 341	13 333	21 287
Hiring of movables	687	771	919	1 063	1 070
Other services	10 479	15 070	13 554	16 070	22 177
Persons					
Total (loans and advances only)	34 048	41 102	48 322	62 859	78 260
of which in sterling	*33 956*	*40 991*	*48 145*	*62 629*	*77 999*
Bridging finance for house purchase	828	832[3]	} 25 291	34 865	44 677
Other house purchase	16 092	20 167	}		
Other advances to persons	17 128	20 103	23 031	27 994	33 583

1 This is a series of statistics based on the Standard Industrial Classification 1980 and comprises loans, advances and acceptances by all monthly reporting institutions other than members of the London Discount Market Association (LDMA). The table includes lending under the Department of Trade and Industry special scheme for domestic shipbuilding, secured money placed with money brokers and gilt-edged jobbers, time deposits placed with and certificates of deposit issued by building societies.

2 From end November 1986 lending to securities dealers, stockbrokers and stock jobbers (including money placed with the stock exchange money brokers and gilt-edged market makers) is shown separately within the Financial sector. Such lending was previously included in the Other services line of Business and other services.

3 Now published as Home Purchase.

Source Bank of England

17.6 Discount market[1, 2]
Mid-December

£ million

	1978	1979	1980	1981	1982	1983	1984	1985	1986	1987	1988
Assets											
Total	4 308	4 909	5 305	5 084	5 459	6 953	8 096	8 713	9 539	11 566	12 015
Treasury bills	845	709	556	99	70	31	222	50	240	261	647
Other bills[3]:											
Sterling	2 038	2 638	2 485	2 892	2 394	3 577	3 589	3 474	4 073	5 351	4 205
Other currencies	16	12	22	34	24	13	77	135	30	25	40
British government securities	454	754	956	742	555	364	401	292	22	33	9
UK monetary sector CDs:											
Sterling	333	84	613	642	1 468	2 044	2 179	2 729	3 022	3 705	4 354
Other currencies	75	109	50	198	149	70	302	148	124	38	33
Building Society CDs and time deposits	–	–	–	–	–	280	522	550	348	747	897
Local authority securities	282	373	377	243	216	154	127	37	13	2	–
Other assets[4]:											
Sterling	262	220	234	212	574	410	673	1 241	1 501	1 328	1 744
Other currencies	3	10	12	22	9	10	4	57	168	119	136
Borrowed funds[5]											
Total	4 111	4 704	5 140	4 926	5 286	6 738	7 818	8 457	9 246	11 312	11 727
Bank of England, Banking Dept.	–	–	–	20	–	55	48	80	–	45	35
Other UK monetary sector:											
Sterling	3 425	4 228	4 804	4 360	4 733	5 838	6 124	6 409	6 984	8 064	8 182
Other currencies	41	85	16	157	136	49	293	121	129	59	68
Other sources:											
Sterling	597	340	296	327	391	774	1 263	1 632	1 988	3 019	3 294
Other currencies	48	51	24	62	26	21	90	215	146	125	148

1 Between 1975 and November 1981 these figures include the members of the London Discount Market Association (LDMA), two discount brokers (who became members of the LDMA in 1980) and the money trading departments of five banks carrying on an essentially similar type of business. Since November 1981 this group has again comprised members of the LDMA.
2 Securities, etc, are generally reported at the value standing in the reporting institution's books.
3 Including local authority and public corporation bills.
4 Including funds lent to the United Kingdom monetary sector and in the local authority market.
5 Excluding capital and reserves.

Source *Bank of England*

17.7 Public sector borrowing requirement and other counterparts to changes in money stock during the year

£ million

	1978	1979	1980	1981	1982	1983	1984	1985	1986	1987	1988
Public sector borrowing requirement (surplus–)	+8 340	+12 551	+11 786	+10 507	+4 880	+11 604	+10 283	+7 474	+2 439	–1 427	–11 630
Sales (–) of public sector debt to UK private sector (other than banks)	–6 033	–10 958	–9 435	–11 213	–10 590	–11 175	–11 147	–7 790	–3 530	–1 322	–5 176
Sterling lending to the private sector[1]	+4 698	+8 585	+10 025	+11 405	+17 556	+12 903	+16 541	+20 968	+30 449	+38 692	+57 282
External and foreign currency finance of the public sector	–987	+640	–11	–1 069	–1 323	–1 569	–1 616	–3 142	–2 022	+6 959	+3 149
External and foreign currency transactions of UK banks[2,3]	+1 561	–3 527	–637	+906	–1 592	–719	–1 987	+500	–444	–3 677	–10 072
Net non-deposit liabilities (increase–)[3]	–972	–768	–1 169	–1 211	–1 460	–1 592	–2 182	–3 013	–3 767	–4 662	–6 052
Money stock (M3)	+6 607	+6 523	+10 559	+9 325	+7 471	+9 452	+9 892	+14 997	+23 125	+34 563	+37 853

1 Bank lending, *plus* holdings of commercial bills by the Issue Department of the Bank of England.
2 Including sterling lending to overseas sector.
3 With effect from the third quarter 1975 the external and foreign currency transactions of UK banks include net non-deposit currency liabilities. From this date 'Net non-deposit liabilities' comprise sterling components only. See note on page 286.

Source *Bank of England*

17.8 Money stock and liquidity

£ million

	1978	1979	1980	1981[1]	1982	1983	1984	1985	1986	1987	1988
Amounts outstanding at end-year											
Notes and coin in circulation with the public[2]	8 291	8 939	9 631	10 189	10 599	11 216	11 542	12 069	12 824	13 592	14 756
UK private sector sterling sight deposits[3, 4]	18 631	20 345	20 805	25 766	29 436	33 324	40 017	48 889	61 870	78 274	90 292
Money stock (M1)	26 922	29 284	30 436	35 955	40 035	44 540	51 559	60 958	74 694	91 866	105 048
UK private sector sterling time deposits[3, 5]	23 215	27 374	36 766	48 059	51 456	57 119	60 397	66 016	76 453	93 757	118 626
Money stock (M3)	50 137	56 658	67 202	84 014	91 491	101 659	111 956	126 974	151 147	185 623	223 674
UK private sector deposits in other currencies[3, 5, 6]	4 799	5 202	6 189	9 849	12 717	16 376	20 947	20 144	28 602	30 778	33 635
Money stock (M3c)	54 936	61 860	73 391	93 863	104 208	118 035	132 903	147 118	179 749	216 401	257 309
Money stock M(4)	85 792	98 155	114 959	138 404	154 951	174 760	197 526	222 794	261 190	303 941	357 488
Money stock M(5)	99 599	114 539	130 683	148 286	166 139	187 777	212 579	239 365	276 320	319 400	372 649
Changes during year[7]											
Notes and coin in circulation with the public[2]	+1 074	+648	+707	+615	+410	+642	+326	+527	+768	+768	+1 164
UK private sector sterling sight deposits[3, 4]	+2 671	+1 714	+460	+2 823	+3 668	+3 860	+6 593	+8 860	+12 381	+16 339	+12 013
Money stock (M1)	+3 745	+2 362	+1 167	+3 438	+4 078	+4 502	+6 919	+9 387	+13 149	+17 107	+13 177
UK private sector sterling time deposits[3, 5]	+2 862	+4 161	+9 392	+5 887	+3 393	+4 950	+2 973	+5 610	+9 976	+17 456	+24 676
Money stock (M3)	+6 607	+6 523	+10 559	+9 325	+7 471	+9 452	+9 892	+14 997	+23 125	+34 563	+37 853
UK private sector deposits in other currencies[3, 5, 6]	+648	+403	+987	+3 668	+2 733	+3 378	+4 533	−815	+8 421	+2 311	+2 977
Money stock (M3c)	+7 255	+6 926	+11 546	+12 993	+10 204	+12 830	+14 425	+14 182	+31 546	+36 874	+40 830
Money Stock M(4)	+11 256	+12 365	+16 819	+15 958	+16 541	+19 093	+22 361	+25 247	+34 453	+42 461	+53 349
Money stock M(5)	+13 455	+14 950	+16 303	+16 389	+17 911	+20 917	+24 401	+26 735	+35 215	+43 663	+53 012

1 The stock figures for end-1981 are on the basis of the new monetary sector; changes during the years, up to and including 1981, are on the basis of the old banking sector.
2 The estimates of levels of coin in circulation include allowance for wastage, hoarding, etc.
3 Deposits are confined to those with institutions included in the United Kingdom monetary sector (see Table 17.3).
4 After deducting 60 per cent of transit items.
5 Including UK residents' holdings of certificates of deposit.
6 The figures include changes in the sterling value of the deposits caused by changes in exchange rates.
7 As far as possible the changes exclude the effect of changes in the number of contributors to the series, and also of the introduction of new statistical returns in 1975.

Source *Bank of England*

17.9 Money and bill rates

London clearing banks' base rates[1]
Percentage rates operative between dates shown

Rate

Date	Per cent	Date	Per cent	Date	Per cent	Date	Per cent	Date	Per cent	Date	Per cent
1979		1982		1984		1985		1987		1988	
Feb. 14	*13½*	Jan. 22	*14*	Mar. 7	*8¾ – 9*	Mar. 29	*13 – 13½*	Mar 10	*10½*	June 29	*9½*
Mar. 6	*13*	Feb. 25	*13½*	Mar. 15	*8½ – 8¾*	Apr. 2	*13 – 13¼*	Mar 19	*10*	July 5	*10*
Apr. 6	*12*	Mar. 12	*13*	May 10	*9 – 9¼*	Apr. 12	*12¾ – 13*	Apr 29	*9½*	July 19	*10½*
June 15	*14*	June 8	*12½*	June 27	*9¼*	Apr. 19	*12½ – 12¾*	May 11	*9*	Aug. 8	*10½-11*
Nov. 16	*17*	July 13	*12*	July 9	*10*	June 12	*12½*	Aug 7	*10*	Aug. 9	*11*
		Aug. 2	*11½*	July 12	*12*	July 15	*12 – 12½*	Oct 26	*9½*	Aug. 25	*11–12*
1980		Aug. 18	*11*	Aug. 9	*11½*	July 16	*12*	Nov 5	*9*	Aug. 26	*12*
July 4	*16*	Aug. 31	*10½*	Aug. 10	*11*	July 29	*11½ – 12*	Dec 4	*8½*	Nov. 25	*13*
Nov. 24	*14*	Oct. 7	*10*	Aug. 20	*10½*	July 30	*11½*				
		Oct. 14	*9½*	Nov. 7	*10*			1988		1989	
1981		Nov. 4	*9*	Nov. 20	*9¾ – 10*	1986		Feb 2	*9*	May 24	*14*
Mar. 11	*12*	Nov. 26	*10 – 10¼*	Nov. 23	*9½ – 9¾*	Jan. 9	*12½*	Mar 17	*8½*		
Sept. 16	*14*					Mar. 19	*11½*	Apr 11	*8*		
Oct. 1	*16*	1983		1985		Apr. 8	*11 – 11½*	May 18	*7½*		
Oct. 14	*15½*	Jan. 12	*11*	Jan. 11	*10½*	Apr. 9	*11*	June 3	*8*		
Nov. 9	*15*	Mar. 15	*10½*	Jan. 14	*12*	Apr. 21	*10½*	June 6	*8–8½*		
Dec. 3	*14½*	Apr. 15	*10*	Jan. 28	*14*	May 27	*10*	June 7	*8½*		
		June 15	*9½*	Mar. 20	*13½ – 14*	Oct 10	*11*	June 22	*9*		
		Oct. 4	*9*	Mar. 21	*13½*						

1 See footnote 1 on page 292.

Source *Bank of England*

17.9 Money and bill rates

(continued)

Rate per cent

	1978	1979	1980	1981	1982[1]	1983	1984	1985	1986	1987	1988	1989
Treasury bills:[2]												
January	5.810	11.862	15.793	12.824	14.205	10.593	8.868	10.550	11.977	10.524	8.374	12.45
February	5.957	12.637	16.143	12.088	13.564	10.739	8.854	12.691	12.017	10.290	8.785	12.39
March	5.924	11.348	16.181	11.534	12.489	10.465	8.433	12.935	11.055	9.346	8.273	12.41
April	6.735	11.317	16.166	11.327	12.864	9.841	8.375	11.925	9.993	9.430	7.737	12.51
May	8.402	11.347	16.091	11.347	12.633	9.696	8.815	11.935	9.704	8.456	7.543	12.54
June	9.170	12.566	15.799	12.088	12.227	9.471	8.863	11.889	9.318	8.540	8.882	13.59
July	9.217	13.325	14.548	13.150	11.580	9.367	10.974	11.385	9.452	8.837	10.051	
August	8.897	13.320	14.864	13.416	10.335	9.342	10.213	10.962	9.392	9.788	11.132	
September	8.982	13.380	14.404	13.962	9.909	9.157	10.020	11.060	9.605	9.693	11.528	
October	9.860	13.377	14.294	15.549	9.140	8.841	9.850	11.052	10.252	9.448	11.542	
November	11.515	15.330	13.945	14.075	8.937	8.842	9.225	11.107	10.632	8.433	12.070	
December	11.568	15.895	13.070	14.443	9.897	8.870	9.103	11.153	10.659	8.186	12.532	
Three months bank bills:[3]												
January	6.01	12.34	16.63	13.38	14.35	10.69	8.93	11.03	12.27	10.64	8.42	12.62
February	6.42	12.93	17.36	12.34	13.66	10.84	8.88	13.16	12.14	10.47	8.88	12.52
March	6.45	11.68	17.57	11.71	12.66	10.50	8.49	13.06	11.36	9.58	8.52	12.55
April	7.40	11.54	17.13	11.53	12.92	9.82	8.39	12.10	10.21	9.46	7.89	12.63
May	8.86	11.55	15.74	11.56	12.67	9.82	8.98	11.99	9.85	8.55	7.69	12.64
June	9.63	12.83	16.24	12.08	12.36	9.54	8.99	11.91	9.45	8.66	8.65	13.62
July	9.83	13.74	15.18	13.11	11.68	9.48	10.90	11.52	9.61	8.85	10.15	
August	9.39	13.87	15.58	13.52	10.53	9.44	10.47	11.01	9.52	9.72	10.88	
September	9.23	14.10	15.15	14.04	10.09	9.23	10.13	11.09	9.78	9.38	11.70	
October	10.29	14.10	15.04	15.54	9.31	8.88	10.05	11.11	10.58	9.58	11.62	
November	11.86	15.93	15.05	14.30	8.89	8.88	9.31	11.15	10.72	8.62	11.81	
December	12.06	16.65	13.90	14.50	10.09	8.90	9.13	11.18	10.70	8.38	12.62	
Three months inter-bank deposits:[4, 5]												
January	6.26	12.70	17.17	14.28	15.13	11.22	9.45	11.66	12.87	11.05	8.97	13.14
February	6.87	13.32	17.78	13.04	14.48	11.31	9.38	13.76	12.66	10.85	9.27	13.02
March	6.82	12.06	18.11	12.65	13.57	10.94	8.95	13.64	11.72	9.96	8.87	13.05
April	7.62	11.69	17.64	12.33	13.77	10.27	8.88	12.75	10.48	9.78	8.30	13.13
May	9.30	11.82	17.06	12.41	13.35	10.27	9.40	12.66	10.22	8.81	8.03	13.14
June	10.04	13.12	16.77	12.67	13.00	9.93	9.45	12.45	9.77	8.89	8.93	14.15
July	10.18	13.98	15.88	13.79	12.37	9.89	11.51	12.05	9.97	9.21	10.55	
August	9.45	14.12	16.53	14.18	11.11	9.87	11.06	11.50	9.85	10.04	11.39	
September	9.37	14.17	16.00	14.78	10.89	9.69	10.83	11.54	10.12	10.16	12.15	
October	10.57	14.22	15.99	16.33	9.79	9.38	10.66	11.55	11.04	9.96	12.04	
November	12.07	16.24	15.84	15.06	9.39	9.30	9.93	11.57	11.17	8.94	12.31	
December	12.36	16.82	14.73	15.44	10.16	9.42	9.82	11.76	11.35	8.76	13.13	
Three months local authority deposits:[4, 6]												
January	6.459	11.942	17.935	14.382	14.791	10.900	9.000	11.363	12.090	11.000	8.265	13.05
February	6.104	13.439	17.996	14.304	14.369	11.050	9.000	14.000	12.850	11.000	8.323	12.95
March	6.361	13.260	18.325	13.668	13.907	11.043	9.000	14.381	12.578	10.545	8.551	12.94
April	6.651	12.279	18.090	12.356	13.303	10.421	9.000	13.050	11.227	10.000	8.074	13.04
May	8.309	12.201	17.698	11.994	13.262	10.000	8.476	13.000	10.250	8.736	7.376	13.13
June	9.938	13.227	17.391	11.766	12.925	10.000	8.904	13.000	10.000	9.000	7.689	14.08
July	10.351	14.418	17.153	12.833	12.508	9.381	11.090	12.652	10.000	8.956	9.443	
August	9.391	14.331	16.970	13.307	11.418	9.272	11.318	11.857	10.000	9.250	10.440	
September	8.962	14.285	16.575	14.085	10.890	9.818	10.950	11.714	9.545	9.681	11.081	
October	9.518	14.283	17.028	16.015	10.162	9.047	10.782	11.782	10.260	9.727	11.735	
November	11.556	15.933	16.082	15.529	9.360	9.000	10.045	11.476	10.850	9.000	11.848	
December	12.079	16.968	14.489	15.139	10.567	9.000	9.157	11.700	11.000	8.238	12.627	

1 Each bank has a single base rate, which may sometimes differ from those of other banks. The rates of interest charged by the London clearing banks for their advances to customers and their discounting of trade bills are, in general, linked to their own individually declared base rates. The rates charged for advances depend on the nature and status of the customer; most lending is between 1 per cent and 5 per cent higher than base rate. Some lending is related to market rates instead of base rates.
Between 11 September 1973 and 28 February 1975 the banks were not allowed to pay more than 9½ per cent on deposits under £10 000.
Since February 1975 the margin between base rate and that on deposit accounts has fluctuated between 2 per cent and 4½ per cent.

2 Weighted averages of discount rates at the weekly allotments of 91 day bills.

3 The mean of the discount market's buying rates (discount rates per cent per annum). Averages of working days.

4 Figures are averages of working days.

5 The mean of the lowest bid and highest offer rates over the day. The yield on a three-month sterling certificate of deposit is usually close to that for a three-months inter-bank deposit.

6 For a minimum term of three months and thereafter at seven days notice. The mean of the daily range. From June 1982 the rates are for 10.30 a.m.

Source *Bank of England*

17.10 Security yields and prices

	1978	1979	1980	1981	1982	1983	1984	1985	1986	1987	1988	1989
British government securities												
Short-dated[1]:												
(5 years)	11.32	12.64	13.84	14.65	12.79	11.19	11.29	11.13	10.01	9.37	9.66	..
Medium-dated[1]:												
(10 years)	12.12	12.93	13.91	14.88	13.08	11.27	11.27	11.06	10.05	9.57	9.67	..
Long-dated[1]:												
(20 years)	12.47	12.99	13.79	14.74	12.88	10.80	10.69	10.62	9.87	9.47	9.36	..
$2\frac{1}{2}$ per cent Consols[2]:												
Average net price	21.0	22.1	21.1	19.3	21.4	24.5	24.7	24.8	26.4	27.7	27.4	..
Average flat yield	11.93	11.39	11.88	13.01	11.90	10.24	10.16	10.11	9.47	9.31	9.12	..
January	10.67	12.51	11.41	12.12	13.72	10.73	9.83	10.26	10.14	9.82	9.33	9.05
February	11.21	12.63	11.76	12.05	13.01	10.87	9.93	10.44	9.92	9.64	9.23	8.77
March	11.18	11.36	12.62	12.02	12.41	10.34	9.83	10.30	9.10	9.07	8.93	8.56
April	11.65	10.68	12.35	12.11	12.92	10.09	9.93	10.14	8.54	9.04	8.96	8.91
May	12.07	11.02	12.18	12.70	12.66	10.19	10.29	10.38	8.64	8.80	9.06	9.12
June	12.31	11.39	11.98	12.96	12.48	9.83	10.48	10.28	8.73	8.85	9.12	9.42
July	12.20	10.88	11.55	13.44	12.22	10.24	10.88	10.04	9.01	9.12	9.28	..
August	12.15	10.54	11.80	13.46	11.61	10.42	10.42	9.90	9.18	9.67	9.16	..
September	12.17	10.75	11.64	13.72	10.87	10.18	10.27	9.92	9.63	9.77	9.27	..
October	12.42	11.07	11.55	14.16	10.29	10.09	10.17	9.88	10.16	9.70	9.03	..
November	12.63	11.86	11.54	13.53	9.92	9.97	9.88	9.92	10.36	8.89	9.00	..
December	12.38	11.85	11.94	13.63	10.65	9.90	9.94	9.89	10.28	9.31	9.10	..
Industrial securities[3]												
Debentures[4]:												
Price index	58.3	56.27	52.42	77.33	92.25	103.37	107.13	110.25	116.34	111.71	118.48	..
Average yield	12.75	13.23	14.16	15.44	13.95	12.14	11.83	11.50	10.82	10.62	10.80	..
Preference shares:												
Price index	72.7	69.48	64.60	63.93	69.41	79.04	77.14	79.31	83.43	85.50	89.56	..
Average dividend yield	12.68	13.21	13.91	15.28	14.46	12.50	12.75	12.39	11.31	10.74	10.10	..
Ordinary shares[5]:												
Price index	235.3	267.31	285.68	322.16	373.31	471.23	560.52	692.02	858.57	1 050.18	1 019.76	..
Average dividend yield	5.48	5.78	6.59	5.96	5.47	4.60	4.46	4.38	3.93	3.41	4.25	..
January	5.39	5.66	6.86	6.46	5.80	4.90	4.30	4.26	4.32	3.77	4.09	4.45
February	5.73	5.70	6.46	6.22	5.63	4.78	4.33	4.22	4.07	3.45	4.15	4.10
March	5.78	5.08	6.83	6.06	5.75	4.72	4.20	4.28	3.76	3.29	4.10	4.08
April	5.68	4.85	7.07	5.64	5.71	4.50	4.24	4.38	3.65	3.35	4.11	4.18
May	5.42	4.90	7.07	5.61	5.56	4.61	4.35	4.31	3.80	3.09	4.15	4.08
June	5.49	5.17	6.85	5.74	5.67	4.40	4.59	4.47	3.81	2.98	4.10	4.13
July	5.50	5.71	6.49	5.87	5.74	4.52	4.88	4.69	3.91	2.87	4.14	..
August	5.15	5.93	6.49	5.56	5.61	4.41	4.66	4.48	3.93	3.03	4.22	..
September	5.14	6.14	6.38	6.00	5.25	4.56	4.59	4.47	3.90	3.02	4.46	..
October	5.34	6.20	6.27	6.43	5.03	4.71	4.58	4.43	4.04	3.40	4.33	..
November	5.62	6.94	6.04	6.01	4.87	4.59	4.40	4.22	3.93	4.36	4.41	..
December	5.56	7.02	6.25	5.91	4.99	4.54	4.41	4.32	4.02	4.36	4.72	..

1 Gross redemption yields derived from yield-maturity curves fitted mathematically. The figures are averages of Wednesday yields until 1979. From 1980 the average is of all observations (usually 3 per week); from January 1982 figures are the average of working days. The method of calculation is described in the *Bank of England Quarterly Bulletin,* December 1972, September 1973, June 1976 and June 1982.

2 Averages of working days, based, up to and including March 1982, on the mean of the middle opening and middle closing prices each day; thereafter the figures are based on closing prices only. Gross accrued interest is excluded; tax is ignored.

3 The series are arithmetic averages of daily figures from the *Financial Times*—Actuaries share indices. Price indices (using weighted arithmetic averages) are based on 10 April 1962 = 100.

4 Up to and including 1980, series are based on 15 redeemable debentures, weighted to give average term to maturity of 20 years. The yields used are redemption yields. The *Financial Times* published a new rebased series of debenture and preference share indices from 17 March 1981. The series from 1981 relate to the price index and redemption yield on 25 year stocks.

5 Based on 500 shares.

Sources *Bank of England; Financial Times; Institute of Actuaries; Faculty of Actuaries*

17.11 Securities quoted on the Stock Exchange[1]

At last working day in March

£ million

	1979	1980	1981	1982	1983	1984	1985	1986	1987	1988	1989
Total of all securities at market values	328 331	280 793	375 931	455 995	688 493	832 098	1 107 548	1 247 580	1 547 845	1 427 397	1 861 091
British government and government guaranteed stocks[2]											
Nominal values	59 256	70 959	85 384	91 106	96 039	107 932	118 115	128 850	138 777	142 857	133 780
Market values	54 850	57 766	76 079	81 087	97 001	111 060	117 616	138 417	147 550	151 207	137 195
Other securities at market values:											
Irish government stocks	3 095	3 015	2 690	2 457	4 732	5 013	5 891	8 398	9 727	11 026	10 730
Corporation stocks, public boards, etc.	2 967	2 678	2 609	2 425	2 364	2 237	1 629	1 149	912	644	763
Dominion and foreign government and corporation stocks	6 151	6 067	10 062	20 071	35 976	42 802	75 121	83 656	104 460	102 703	142 501
Company securities											
Total	261 268	211 267	284 491	349 955	548 420	670 986	907 302	1 015 960	1 285 196	1 161 817	1 569 902
Loan capital	4 750	3 803	4 144	4 905	6 320	8 256	8 680	9 004	12 013	11 820	13 621
Preference and preferred capital	1 596	1 836	1 916	1 860	3 070	6 416	5 510	8 259	22 438	26 887	35 459
Ordinary and deferred capital[3] Shares of no par value[3]	254 922	205 628	278 431	343 190	539 030	656 314	893 112	998 697	1 250 745	1 123 110	1 520 822

1 The stock exchanges of the United Kingdom and the Republic of Ireland form one exchange (The Stock Exchange).
2 Excluding marketable unlisted securities; including all outstanding amounts of 4 per cent Victory Bonds and 4 per cent Funding Loan, 1960–90 (that is, amounts for death duties and held by the National Debt Commissioners are included).
3 From 1978 shares of no par value are no longer distinguished separately.

Source *Council of The Stock Exchange*

Footnotes to Table 17.12 on page 295.

1 The estimates relate to new money raised on the main stock market by issues of ordinary, preference and loan capital (public issues, offers for sale, issues by tender, placings, and issues to shareholders and employees) by listed public companies and local authorities in the United Kingdom; and by overseas borrowers split between central government, state and local governments and companies. The estimates include UK local authority negotiable bonds (of not less than one year) issues to or through the agency of banks, discount houses, issuing houses or brokers. Mortgages, bank advances and any other loans redeemable in less than twelve months are excluded; so also are loans from UK government funds (including the former Industrial Reorganisation Corporation and the National Enterprise Board) but not government subscriptions to company issues made *pari passu* with the market. Issues to shareholders are included only if the sole or principal share register is maintained in the United Kingdom. Estimates of issues are based on the prices at which securities are offered to the market. Subscriptions are recorded under the periods in which they are due to be paid. Redemptions relate to fixed interest securities of the kinds included as issues; conversion issues in lieu of cash repayment are included in the gross figures of both issues and redemptions. These figures include issues of debentures and loan stock carrying the right of conversion into, or subscription to, equity capital. Estimates for these issues *less* redemptions are: 1977 –5; 1978 –21; 1979 23; 1980 178; 1981 194; 1982 8; 1983 47; 1984 101; 1985 320. The division between United Kingdom and overseas company borrowers is determined by the location of the registered office. The industrial classification of companies is according to the primary occupation of the borrowing company or group and is based up to 1982 on the former Standard Industrial Classification 1968 and from 1983 on the Revised Standard Industrial Classification 1980.
2 The estimates exclude issues on the unlisted securities market which was launched by the Stock Exchange in November 1980. These issues are mainly of ordinary shares by industrial and commercial companies. Estimates of new money raised are 1980 88; 1981 54; 1982 87; 1983 163; 1984 159; 1985 180; 1986 322; 1987 961; 1988 631.
3 The figures for 1978 and 1979 include £449 m. and £149 m. respectively for rights issues by BL Ltd. Over 99 per cent of both issues was taken up by the National Enterprise Board. However, the figures for 1980 exclude £375 m. issued by BL Ltd to the Government via the National Enterprise Board.
4 Overseas companies including public corporations.
5 Prior to the introduction of the Monetary sector in November 1981 statistics relate to issues by the banking sector.
6 'Other' includes special finance agencies (listed public companies engaged in the provision of medium and long-term finance to industry e.g. ICFC) and those finance houses and other consumer credit grantors not covered by the Monetary sector.

Source *Bank of England*

17.12 Capital issues and redemptions in the United Kingdom[1, 2]

£ million

	1979[3]	1980[3]	1981	1982		1983	1984	1985	1986	1987	1988
Total issues and redemptions											
Gross issues	1 743	2 083	3 311	2 907		4 675	3 562	6 238	10 053	17 181	8 572
Gross redemptions	1 005	1 310	1 341	1 351		1 347	1 224	1 063	748	1 737	1 008
Issues *less* redemptions: total	738	773	1 970	1 556		3 328	2 338	5 175	9 305	15 444	7 544
Loan capital	−276	−209	67	582		980	874	527	1 185	−178	946
Preference shares	54	29	68	9		59	42	414	66	703	964
Ordinary shares	960	953	1 835	965		2 289	1 422	4 234	7 804	14 919	5 634
United Kingdom borrowers: total	762	767	1 675	993		2 746	1 463	4 500	8 520	15 256	7 141
Local authorities	−170	−166	−157	−174		−66	−258	−566	−202	−177	−34
Listed public companies: total	932	933	1 832	1 167		2 812	1 721	5 066	8 722	15 433	7 175
Overseas borrowers: total	−24	6	295	563		582	875	675	535	188	403
Central government	−23	9	124	201		246	351	250	164	–	90
State, local government	–	−1	6	85		−13	106	–	–	–	–
Companies[4]	−1	−2	165	277		349	418	425	371	188	313
United Kingdom listed public companies											
All companies: total	932	933	1 832	1 167		2 812	1 721	5 066	8 722	15 433	7 175
Loan capital	−82	−50	−72	195		565	281	442	905	1	795
Preference shares	54	30	68	8		59	42	414	66	704	744
Ordinary shares	960	953	1 836	964		2 188	1 398	4 210	7 751	14 728	5 636
Financial companies: total	75	−7	123	296		684	498	1 016	2 924	2 327	1 733
Loan capital	−6	−62	−83	278		219	74	53	433	300	172
Preference shares	–	−6	−8	–		–	19	5	90	10	280
Ordinary shares	81	61	214	18		465	405	958	2 401	2 017	1 281
Other companies: total	857	940	1 709	871		2 128	1 223	4 050	5 798	13 106	5 442
Loan capital	−76	12	11	−83		346	207	389	472	−299	623
Preference shares	54	36	76	8		59	23	409	−24	694	464
Ordinary shares	879	892	1 622	946		1 723	993	3 252	5 350	12 711	4 355
United Kingdom listed public companies											
Financial companies: total	75	−7	123	296		684	498	1 016	2 924	2 327	1 733
Monetary sector[5]	79	−34	–	298		549	278	729	743	829	458
Insurance companies	–	−2	198	2		5	−7	7	606	−2	–
Investment trust companies	7	33	9	18		92	135	157	374	324	143
Other[6]	−11	−4	−84	−22		38	92	123	1 201	1 176	1 132
Other companies: total	857	940	1 709	871		2 128	1 223	4 050	5 798	13 106	5 442
Manufacturing industries: total	446	211	632	407		1 386	498	2 365	2 625	5 284	2 305
Food, drink and tobacco	−8	39	50	102	Minerals and Metal Manufacture	253	29	221	301	286	97
Chemicals and allied industries	17	6	85	111	Chemicals and allied industries	314	−3	308	541	98	196
Metal manufacture	–	−6	−1	1	Metal goods, engineering and vehicles	157	33	329	177	1 616	415
Engineering, shipbuilding and electrical goods	32	23	302	194	Electrical and electronic engineering	200	156	355	158	514	63
Vehicles	154	−4	97	−2	Food, Drink and Tobacco	200	105	183	557	288	748
Textiles	11	–	1	4	Other manufacturing	262	178	969	891	2 482	786
Clothing and footwear	1	–	1	−5	Energy	192	57	158	151	933	771
Paper, printing and publishing	16	6	4	–	Water	30	2	34	49	46	16
Other	223	147	93	2	Construction	53	7	112	513	445	268
Public utilities, transport and communication	17	38	83	6	Distribution, hotels and repairs	172	107	597	748	2 770	378
Distributive trades	111	89	50	15	Transport and communications	9	26	177	−129	−232	5
Property companies	79	147	97	258	Property companies	78	232	344	705	1 649	457
Rest	204	455	847	185	Services, Agriculture, Forestry and Fishing	208	294	263	1 136	2 211	1 242

See footnotes 1 – 6 on page 294.

Source Bank of England

17.13 Building societies[1]

Great Britain (Until 1985)
United Kingdom (From 1986)

Number and balance sheets

	1977	1978	1979	1980	1981	1982	1983	1984	1985	1986[2]	1987	1988
Societies on register (Number)	339	316	287	273	253	227	206	190	167	151	138	130
Share Investors (Thousands)	22 536	24 999	27 878	30 636	33 388	36 607	37 711	39 380	39 996	40 559	41 967	43 816
Depositors (Thousands)	760	781	797	915	995	1 094	1 200	1 550	2 149	2 850	3 648	4 306
Borrowers (Thousands)	4 836	5 108	5 251	5 383	5 490	5 645	5 928	6 314	6 657	7 023	7 182	7 369
Liabilities (£ million):												
Shares	31 109.7	36 185.9	42 023.1	48 914.6	55 463.4	64 968.0	75 197.3	88 087.0	102 331.8	115 550.8	129 954.3	149 791.1
Deposits and loans	1 238.3	1 264.2	1 289.8	1 762.0	2 576.9	3 531.6	5 601.4	8 425.6	10 751.5	16 862.2	20 571.8	26 528.5
Taxation and other	676.1	611.7	835.2	1 228.5	1 495.3	1 729.6	1 583.1	2 067.1	2 767.5	2 250.4	2 569.1	2 953.4
General reserves	1 264.3	1 476.6	1 640.9	1 887.9	2 279.0	2 803.3	3 487.0	4 109.1	4 912.6	5 939.0	7 001.7	8 466.0
Subordinates Debt	–	–	–	–	–	–	–	–	–	–	–	1 105.1
Assets (£ million): total	34 288.4	39 538.4	45 789.1	53 792.9	61 814.6	73 032.5	85 868.8	102 688.8	120 763.4	140 602.5	160 096.9	188 844.2
Mortgages	26 426.5	31 598.3	36 800.5	42 437.0	48 874.8	56 695.7	67 473.5	81 881.9	96 764.5	115 669.4	130 870.4	153 015.4
Investments	6 158.1	6 395.7	7 436.9	8 878.0	10 106.4	12 430.4	13 641.1	15 746.8	16 177.4	16 353.9	17 689.6	20 964.9
Cash	1 251.3	1 019.1	928.0	1 728.1	1 949.9	2 925.2	3 676.3	3 861.2	6 507.4	7 105.0	9 590.4	11 748.1
Other	452.4	525.2	623.8	749.8	883.6	981.2	1 077.9	1 198.9	1 314.1	1 474.2	1 946.4	3 115.7

Current transactions

£ million

	1977	1978	1979	1980	1981	1982	1983	1984	1985	1986[2]	1987	1988
Shares:												
Received	13 549.3	15 684.6	18 849.4	21 916.5	26 126.9	32 434.8	40 204.5	54 251.7	76 151.5	83 866.9	97 503.5	111 716.9
Interest thereon	1 985.2	2 172.9	3 297.7	4 699.4	4 795.7	5 298.6	5 095.6	6 318.8	8 269.5	8 498.5	9 141.7	9 852.6
Withdrawn (including interest)	10 183.9	12 769.4	16 313.6	19 726.1	24 373.0	28 218.0	34 813.3	47 759.0	70 444.9	79 262.9	92 024.6	100 991.8
Deposits:												
Received	783.4	670.1	678.4	1 091.2	1 571.5	2 029.3	4 801.4	11 244.2	17 924.9	28 100.8	38 325.7	58 637.2
Interest thereon	63.5	70.7	97.2	148.2	186.6	273.2	327.4	581.5	853.7	1 263.7	1 683.7	2 170.0
Withdrawn (including interest)	470.3	710.1	749.0	785.2	964.1	1 389.2	3 001.2	8 966.1	16 244.5	23 239.2	35 957.5	54 924.7
Mortgages:												
Advances	6 745.1	8 807.8	9 002.3	9 503.4	12 005.3	15 036.4	19 346.5	23 770.9	26 530.8	35 913.2	36 034.0	47 374.9
Repayments of principal	2 882.2	3 614.8	3 805.4	3 867.9	5 566.9	7 214.0	8 316.8	9 345.2	11 650.8	16 976.3	19 864.6	25 002.8
Interest[3]	2 706.1	2 770.1	4 082.5	5 912.9	6 398.1	7 030.7	6 845.9	8 843.5	12 027.6	12 820.0	14 306.7	15 965.1
Management expenses	296.8	363.5	449.3	589.6	731.6	874.6	1 002.2	1 109.9	1 264.9	1 437.4	1 668	2 074.7
Percentage rate of interest[4]												
Paid on shares	*6.98*	*6.46*	*8.43*	*10.34*	*9.19*	*8.80*	*7.27*	*7.74*	*8.69*	*7.80*	*7.45*	*7.04*
Paid on deposits	*6.13*	*5.70*	*7.67*	*9.77*	*8.71*	*9.12*	*7.24*	*8.30*	*8.92*	*9.15*	*9.00*	*9.21*
Received on mortgage advances	*11.05*	*9.55*	*11.94*	*14.92*	*14.01*	*13.32*	*11.03*	*11.84*	*13.47*	*12.07*	*11.61*	*11.25*

1 The figures for each year relate to accounting years ending on dates between 1 February of that year and 31 January of the following year.
2 1986 and subsequent years include Northern Ireland societies, responsibility for which was acquired under the Building Societies Act 1986.
3 Includes amounts recoverable from HM Government under Option Mortgage Scheme and MIRAS (Mortgage interest relief at source).
4 Based on the mean of the amounts outstanding at the end of the previous and the current year.

Source *Building Societies Commission*

Footnotes to Table 17.14 on page 297.

1 Prior to 1987 excludes bank loans on personal accounts.
2 Finance houses, check traders, money lenders and pawnbrokers. Up to 1985 covers only agreements regulated under the Consumer Credit Act, 1974.
3 Self financed credit advanced by clothing retailers, household goods retailers, mixed business retailers (other than co-operative societies) and general mail order houses.
4 Class 3 loans advanced under the terms of the Building Societies Act, 1986. For 1987 new credit advanced on these agreements is included under finance houses and other specialist credit grantors.
5 Loans by banks on personal accounts, not exceeding £15,000, excluding bridging loans and house purchase finance. There are no data for these agreements before end-1986.
6 Prior to 1985 includes only policy loans.
7 End year, seasonally adjusted.
8 A high proportion of credit advanced in certain types of agreement, notably on bank credit cards and by mail order houses, is repaid within a month, reflecting the use of such agreements as a method of payment rather than as a means of obtaining credit.
9 There is a break at the end of 1985. Before this running-account agreements were excluded.

Sources *Department of Trade and Industry; Committee of London and Scottish Bankers*

17.14 Consumer Credit

£ million

	1978	1979	1980	1981	1982	1983	1984	1985	1986	1987	1988
Total change in amounts outstanding owing[1]	1 070	1 376	1 209	975	1 544	2 194	2 133	3 117	2 457	5 667	5 916
To finance houses and other specialist credit grantors[2]	662	893	839	551	972	1 481	1 432	2 099	1 452	2 619	2 853
On bank credit cards	231	271	239	365	427	542	573	761	838	889	708
To retailers[3]	181	220	100	31	127	132	116	195	95	359	260
To building societies on class 3 loans[4]										69	214
On bank loans on personal accounts[5]										1 711	1 797
To insurance companies on loans to individuals[6]	−4	−8	31	28	18	39	12	62	72	20	84
Total amount outstanding[7]	4 553	5 929	7 138	8 113	9 657	11 851	13 984	17 416	19 910	36 412	42 086
Total new credit advanced[8]	6 395	7 724	9 148	10 083	12 126	14 550	16 980	20 941	28 057	34 764	42 134
By finance houses and other specialist credit grantors[2,9]	2 156	2 611	3 006	3 146	3 780	4 470	5 092	6 168	10 276	12 837	15 604
On bank credit cards	1 541	2 093	2 883	3 726	4 898	6 396	8 043	10 504	12 916	16 641	20 310
By retailers[3]	2 698	3 020	3 259	3 211	3 448	3 684	3 845	4 269	4 865	5 286	5 732
By building societies on class 3 loans	–	–	–	–	–	–	–	–	–	–	488

See footnotes 1 to 9 on page 296.

17.15 Finance houses and other credit companies in Great Britain: assets and liabilities

End-year

£ million

	1979	1980	1981	1981[1]	1982	1983	1984	1985	1986	1987	1988
Assets											
Cash in hand and balances with UK monetary sector[2]	152	157	204	49	30	43	54	58	60	78	214
Amounts outstanding on loans and advances: on agreements block discounted by retailers and financial institutions	37	42	38	3	3	3	3	3	1	1	1
on finance leases[3]	..	..	..	..	..	..	..	..	575	648	889
on other loans and advances[4]:											
to individuals (including unincorporated businesses)	2 441	2 767	3 039	1 183	1 317	1 842	2 204	2 815	3 561	4 307	4 619
to UK financial institutions outside the monetary sector	286	238	262	–	–	–	–	–	–	–	–
to UK industrial and commercial companies	1 296	1 487	1 537	464	597	862	891	1 041	897	1 042	1 341
to overseas residents	10	–	–	–	–	–	–	–	–	–	–
Other current assets:											
Certificates of deposit	26	11	17	7	8	6	6	7	6	5	6
Other	103	101	81	48	83	115	143	146	255	362	512
Real assets:											
for own use	57	72	73	29	34	25	24	40	53	62	70
for leasing under operating leases, hiring or renting out[3]	602	705	823	391	503	496	494	488	26	36	100
Company and government securities	201	131	104	30	25	25	24	30	33	33	33
Other assets	98	96	117	30	20	18	15	20	42	76	82
Total	5 309	5 807	6 295	2 234	2 620	3 435	3 858	4 648	5 509	6 650	7 867
Liabilities											
Borrowing (including deposits by and borrowing from other group companies):											
Commercial bills	756	693	944	339	452	557	658	772	750	682	587
Short term borrowing from UK monetary sector (excl. deposits)	547	450	415	845	900	1 197	1 364	1 646	1 833	2 647	3 601
Deposits and medium and long term borrowing from UK monetary sector	917	1 429	1 465	279	374	609	667	937	1 272	1 634	1 498
Borrowing from other UK financial institutions	993	827	888	33	25	28	28	33	36	143	180
Other borrowing:											
UK	853	931	890	99	113	190	209	170	345	231	235
Overseas	135	146	165	21	22	21	22	26	27	27	23
Other current liabilities	202	249	295	135	132	174	190	252	334	288	751
Issued capital	258	320	585	111	106	106	108	106	109	112	134
Reserves and provisions	648	762	648	372	496	553	612	706	803	886	858
Total	5 309	5 807	6 295	2 234	2 620	3 435	3 858	4 648	5 509	6 650	7 867

1 Many companies included in these statistics became part of the new monetary sector at end-1981. See table 17.3. The new coverage excludes such companies, with the 1981 figures showing the position immediately after the transfer.

2 Data up to end-1981 were collected on a different return and in some cases have been estimated.

3 Prior to 1986, amounts outstanding on finance leases are included with real assets for leasing, hiring or renting out.

4 Net of unearned credit charges.

Source Department of Trade and Industry

17.16 End-year assets and liabilities of investment trust companies, unit trusts and property unit trusts[1, 2]

£ million

	1977	1978	1979	1980	1981	1982	1983	1984	1985	1986	1987	1988
Investment trust companies												
Short-term assets and liabilities (net):	223	314	202	230	283	249	154	404	365	438	1 517	614
Cash and UK bank deposits	159	210	163	187	210	186	273	366	429	447	1 386	627
Other short-term assets	146	176	213	216	221	269	244	381	722	583	602	315
Short-term liabilities	-82	-72	-174	-173	-148	-206	-363	-343	-786	-592	-471	-328
Medium and long-term liabilities and capital:	..	..	-7 194	-8 546	-9 188	-10 241	-13 419	-15 826	-18 385	-21 055	-21 282	-18 211
Issued share and loan capital	..	..	-1 951	-2 013	-2 211	-2 087	-2 258	-2 445	-2 713	-3 237	-4 206	-3 973
Foreign currency borrowing	..	..	-342	-280	-228	-361	-538	-608	-592	-406	-625	-466
Other borrowing	..	..	-12	-24	-69	-88	-100	-94	-89	-178	-398	-281
Reserves and provisions, etc.	..	..	-4 889	-6 229	-6 680	-7 705	-10 523	-12 679	-14 991	-17 234	-16 053	-13 491
Investments:	6 341	6 460	6 996	8 352	8 904	10 051	13 371	15 251	18 085	20 692	19 835	17 685
British government securities	321	232	320	266	183	199	310	306	464	311	619	329
UK company securities:												
Loan capital and preference shares	177	172	134	132	136	129	172	136	279	378	514	804
Ordinary and deferred shares	3 729	3 734	4 160	4 620	4 673	4 604	5 306	6 322	8 069	8 957	9 513	8 081
Overseas company securities:												
Loan capital and preference shares	82	87	75	98	203	344	396	400	507	725	495	532
Ordinary and deferred shares	1 891	2 067	2 139	3 042	3 514	4 256	6 570	7 259	7 820	9 356	7 784	7 438
Other investments	141	168	168	194	195	519	617	828	946	965	910	501
Unit trusts												
Short-term assets and liabilities:	324	400	209	179	254	348	569	901	1 179	1 392	3 321	2 066
Cash and UK bank deposits	293	427	178	126	210	189	475	651	1 141	1 115	3 650	2 032
Other short-term assets	93	100	89	90	90	204	205	420	462	792	663	472
Short-term liabilities	-62	-127	-58	-37	-46	-45	-111	-170	-424	-515	-992	-438
Foreign currency borrowing	..	..	-35	-12	-3	-58	-123	-128	-475	-190	994	498
Investments:	3 109	3 474	3 600	4 629	5 369	7 309	10 843	13 997	18 433	30 308	33 202	41 462
British government securities	32	32	52	72	175	322	415	566	512	537	664	502
UK company securities:												
Loan capital and preference shares	78	102	76	64	106	154	225	283	505	961	1 520	1 738
Ordinary and deferred shares	2 572	2 732	2 758	3 357	3 566	4 457	5 954	8 201	10 884	16 424	20 524	24 103
Overseas company securities:												
Loan capital and preference shares	12	10	6	14	31	49	58	109	249	424	398	557
Ordinary and deferred shares	411	594	688	1 081	1 454	2 229	4 091	4 689	6 179	11 747	9 727	14 167
Other assets	4	4	20	41	37	98	100	149	104	215	369	395
Property unit trusts												
Short-term assets and liabilities (net)	..	..	135	152	158	146	180	147	67	85	49	84
Property	..	..	757	951	1 271	1 321	1 426	1 364	928	987	672	683
Other assets	..	..	49	166	259	216	333	439	341	200	186	174
Long-term borrowing	..	..	-60	-50	-69	-67	-77	-81	-40	-29	-16	-

Note: Assets are shown as being positive: liabilities as being negative.

1 Investments are at market value.

2 From end-1979 revised reporting forms for investment trust companies and for unit trusts, giving additional information, were introduced and their reported figures have been grossed up to cover non-contributors to the series. Also from end-1979 annual balance sheet returns were introduced for property unit trusts.

Source *Bank of England*

17.17 Self-administered pension funds: market value of assets

United Kingdom

£ million, end-year

	1977	1978	1979	1980	1981	1982	1983	1984	1985	1986	1987
Total pension funds[1,2,3]											
Total net assets	29 936	35 447	42 348	55 791	65 682	86 907	111 375	134 402	156 395	190 044	196 282
Short-term assets	1 926	2 075	2 716	2 571	2 694	3 190	4 809	6 739	7 112	9 157	12 609
British government securities	6 829	7 945	9 511	12 011	13 022	18 984	22 631	24 505	27 233	28 723	29 119
UK local authority long-term debt[4]	299	252	248	198	156	189	234	211	205	204	162
Overseas government securities	17	70	46	102	120	422	518	714	1 063	1 127	1 248
UK company securities	14 791	17 180	19 690	26 005	30 129	39 257	50 990	66 047	80 580	101 001	106 937
Overseas company securities	1 178	1 674	2 026	4 325	6 321	9 742	15 566	17 998	21 862	30 709	25 615
Local authorities mutual investment trust	85	74	104	116	141	79	89	124	90	111	55
Loans and mortgages	246	611	591	402	450	480	493	513	448	381	273
UK land and property and ground rents[5]	4 268	4 927	6 242	8 305	9 782	10 654	11 293	12 359	12 929	13 822	15 842
Property unit trusts	776	948	1 240	1 441	1 678	2 076	2 308	2 424	2 357	1 988	1 374
Other assets[5,6]	..	417	682	1 124	2 000	2 737	3 732	4 543	4 448	4 922	5 038
Long-term borrowing[7]	−242	−422	−409	−365	−447	−451	−525	−615	−486	−342	−261
Short-term liabilities[7]	−237	−304	−339	−444	−364	−452	−763	−1 160	−1 446	−1 759	−1 729
Private sector[3]											
Total net assets	17 970	21 295	24 949	33 102	38 831	51 310	66 591	80 036	100 076	120 668	129 621
Short-term assets	1 297	1 300	1 672	1 542	1 628	1 962	2 965	3 889	4 611	6 078	8 079
British government securities	4 207	5 047	5 870	7 603	8 039	11 397	13 639	14 899	17 777	18 184	19 129
UK local authority long-term debt[4]	135	138	130	98	76	80	73	60	67	73	98
Overseas government securities	16	61	40	56	91	247	318	494	618	554	627
UK company securities	8 876	10 456	11 645	15 526	17 896	23 333	30 370	39 347	51 442	64 456	71 096
Overseas company securities	765	1 005	1 198	2 388	3 774	6 047	9 657	11 128	13 877	19 260	17 312
Loans and mortgages	147	293	269	210	205	217	204	202	170	163	158
UK land and property and ground rents[5]	2 171	2 423	3 279	4 415	5 143	5 282	5 846	6 445	7 646	8 267	9 829
Property unit trusts	527	638	830	980	1 080	1 380	1 634	1 677	1 624	1 288	792
Other assets[5,6]	..	302	423	714	1 336	1 869	2 579	2 842	3 206	3 670	3 588
Long-term borrowing[7]	−129	−181	−239	−224	−247	−222	−239	−257	−236	−176	−116
Short-term liabilities[7]	−42	−187	−168	−206	−190	−282	−455	−690	−726	−1 149	−971
Local authorities											
Total net assets	3 849	4 304	4 942	6 891	8 167	11 268	14 316	17 982	20 765	25 401	26 470
Short-term assets	138	205	279	263	304	306	446	755	949	1 046	1 624
British government securities	1 169	1 227	1 411	1 845	1 977	2 925	3 249	3 221	3 446	3 792	3 702
UK local authority long-term debt[4]	118	102	94	85	66	68	71	68	48	38	58
Overseas government securities	1	1	1	2	5	21	27	93	159	137	128
UK company securities	1 970	2 240	2 436	3 479	4 180	5 686	7 482	9 854	11 569	14 290	15 559
Overseas company securities	151	134	168	530	720	1 179	1 824	2 553	3 187	4 467	3 515
Local authorities mutual investment trust	85	74	104	116	141	79	89	124	90	111	55
Loans and mortgages	2	3	3	4	2	1	—	—	—	1	2
UK land and property and ground rents[5]	140	210	287	387	493	613	692	833	893	997	1 358
Property unit trusts	106	123	160	172	258	363	400	452	474	493	415
Other assets[5,6]	4	15	20	47	52	74	102	132	138	188	233
Long-term borrowing[7]	—	—	—	—	—	—	—	—	−2	—	—
Short-term liabilities[7]	−35	−30	−21	−39	−31	−47	−66	−103	−186	−159	−179
Other public sector[1,2,3]											
Total net assets	8 117	9 848	12 457	15 798	18 684	24 329	30 468	36 384	35 554	43 975	40 191
Short-term assets	491	570	765	766	762	922	1 398	2 095	1 552	2 033	2 906
British government securities	1 453	1 671	2 230	2 563	3 006	4 662	5 743	6 385	6 010	6 747	6 288
UK local authority long-term debt[4]	46	12	24	15	14	41	90	83	90	93	6
Overseas government securities	—	8	5	44	24	154	173	127	286	436	493
UK company securities	3 945	4 484	5 609	7 000	8 053	10 238	13 138	16 846	17 569	22 255	20 282
Overseas company securities	262	535	660	1 407	1 827	2 516	4 085	4 317	4 798	6 982	4 788
Loans and mortgages	97	315	319	188	243	262	289	311	278	217	113
UK land and property and ground rents	1 892	2 294	2 676	3 503	4 146	4 759	4 755	5 081	4 390	4 558	4 655
Property unit trusts	143	187	250	289	340	333	274	295	259	207	167
Other assets[6]	61	100	239	363	612	794	1 051	1 569	1 104	1 064	1 217
Long-term borrowing[7]	−113	−241	−170	−141	−200	−229	−286	−358	−248	−166	−145
Short-term liabilities[7]	−160	−87	−150	−199	−143	−123	−242	−367	−534	−451	−579

1 These figures cover funded schemes only and therefore exclude the main superannuation arrangements in the central government sector.
2 Prior to 1978 no adjustment has been made for funds representing some 42 per cent (other public sector) of total assets which have an accounting year other than end-December (usually end-March).
3 Funds where the parent has been privatised are included in the private sector from the year in which privatisation took place if that occurred by the end of September, or from the following year if privatisation was in October or later.
4 From 1982 including UK public corporation securities.
5 Other assets are included with UK land, property and ground rent prior to 1978.
6 Including overseas land and property.
7 Liabilities are shown negative.

Source *Central Statistical Office*

17.18 Insurance companies: balance sheet
Market values

£ million, end-year

	1977	1978	1979	1980	1981	1982	1983	1984	1985	1986	1987
Assets											
Long-term business assets:											
Total current assets (gross)	1 075	1 341	1 389	1 394	1 955	2 382	2 677	4 264	4 363	5 369	7 767
Agents' and reinsurance balances (net)[1]	561	205	246	269	309	313	382	172	214	303	306
Other debtors[2]	. .	394	468	537	641	761	935	1 096	1 161	1 638	1 898
British government securities	8 834	9 260	11 340	14 632	15 249	22 782	25 794	27 608	30 456	31 448	34 690
UK local authority long-term debt[3]	601	558	541	664	627	658	691	854	726	1 073	890
UK company securities[4]	12 358	13 122	13 820	17 978	20 464	27 127	35 126	45 134	55 315	74 516	81 333
Overseas company securities	940	1 162	1 155	2 059	3 110	5 051	7 711	10 130	12 278	16 319	13 264
Overseas government securities	98	151	112	128	226	738	1 148	1 836	1 803	2 142	2 093
Loans and mortgages	2 961	3 008	3 161	3 472	3 678	3 691	3 968	4 056	4 342	4 806	5 629
UK land, property and ground rents	6 637	8 446	10 330	12 362	14 490	15 993	17 169	18 693	20 162	21 993	26 979
Other investments[5]	191	156	164	183	265	401	495	616	538	583	557
Total assets	34 256	38 164	42 727	53 678	61 014	79 897	96 096	114 459	131 358	160 190	175 406
Other than long-term business assets:											
Total current assets (gross)	989	1 075	1 235	1 171	1 370	1 325	1 720	2 185	2 634	3 767	4 261
Agents' and reinsurance balances (net)[1]	1 158	1 313	1 649	1 839	2 003	2 432	2 828	2 342	2 726	3 025	3 158
Other debtors[2]	. .	131	224	281	359	402	473	528	656	486	546
British government securities	1 724	1 806	2 177	2 777	3 221	4 269	4 909	4 709	4 860	5 873	6 725
UK local authority long-term debt[3]	185	209	185	180	113	119	76	96	70	70	75
UK company securities[4]	1 963	2 048	2 162	2 755	3 029	3 704	4 405	5 085	5 931	7 176	7 477
Overseas company securities	424	475	525	658	885	1 149	1 326	2 055	2 210	3 022	2 380
Overseas government securities	154	274	307	322	417	843	1 001	1 704	1 575	2 334	2 127
Loans and mortgages	251	224	255	297	327	379	462	418	412	667	925
UK land, property and ground rents	516	797	952	1 280	1 450	1 568	1 640	1 691	1 616	1 795	2 013
Other investments[5]	11	49	61	105	118	162	140	189	269	241	300
Total assets	7 375	8 401	9 729	11 665	13 292	16 352	18 980	21 002	22 959	28 456	29 987
Net value of direct investment in:											
Non-insurance subsidiaries and associate companies in the United Kingdom								1 382	1 618	2 124	2 089
UK associate and subsidiary insurance companies and insurance holding companies								1 204	1 218	1 405	1 734
Overseas subsidiaries and associates								4 703	5 234	6 907	6 435
Total assets								142 750	162 387	199 082	215 651
Liabilities											
Borrowing:											
Borrowing from UK monetary sector institutions						333	511	1 766	1 741	2 266	2 942
Other UK borrowing			524	444	542	421	618	215	326	447	900
Borrowing from overseas								644	434	666	694
General business technical reserves								12 858	14 481	17 351	19 273
Long-term business:											
Funds								86 167	100 174	118 884	134 109
Claims admitted but not paid								346	402	572	609
Provision for taxation net of amounts receivable:											
UK authorities								–31	671	730	298
Overseas authorities								33	43	45	31
Provision for recommended dividends								491	418	595	654
Other creditors and liabilities								1 305	1 515	2 086	2 231
Excess of assets over above liabilities:											
Excess of value of assets over liabilities in respect of long-term funds								26 675	29 159	38 531	38 057
Minority interests in UK subsidiary companies								3	2	3	10
Shareholders' capital and reserves in respect of general business								11 263	11 464	14 755	13 635
Other reserves including profit and loss account balances								1 015	1 557	2 151	2 208
Total liabilities								142 750	162 387	199 082	215 651

1 Prior to 1978 agents' and reinsurance balances include outstanding interest, dividends and rents. Up to 1983, agents' and reinsurance balances are shown gross of amounts payable by insurance companies.
2 Including outstanding interest, dividends and rents (net) which, up to 1983 are shown gross of amounts payable by insurance companies. Amounts receivable from Inland Revenue are included up to 1983.
3 From 1984 including UK public corporation securities.
4 Including authorised unit trust units.
5 Including overseas land and property.

Source *Central Statistical Office*

17.19 Industrial and provident societies[1]
Great Britain

	1977	1978	1979	1980	1981	1982	1983	1984	1985	1986	1987
Number of societies	9 279	9 321	9 390	9 664	9 736	9 601	9 662	9 799	9 940	10 207	10 486
Number of members (thousands)	14 092	13 995	13 798	13 558	13 547	12 961	12 460	11 948	11 267	11 883	11 232
Assets (£ thousand)	4 439 155	5 342 578	6 311 910	7 456 987	8 837 347	10 400 488	11 761 990	13 330 091	14 937 025	15 645 308	18 660 066

1 The annual returns from which these figures are derived are mainly made up to dates varying between September of the year shown and January of the following year.

Source *Registry of Friendly Societies*

17.20 Co-operative trading societies[1]
Great Britain

	1977	1978	1979	1980	1981	1982	1983	1984	1985	1986	1987
Number of societies											
General trading societies:											
Retail societies	296	294	280	270	251	243	237	229	217	213	203
Principal wholesale societies[2]	2	2	2	2	2	2	2	2	2	2	2
Other wholesale and productive societies	97	111	118	148	163	187	203	219	225	232	243
Agricultural and fishing trading societies	524	536	539	541	550	584	597	611	623	636	641
Number of members (thousands)											
General trading societies:											
Retail societies	10 422.6	10 325.3	10 117.3	9 752.9	9 426.4	8 849.4	8 359.3	7 857.1	7 186.1	7 805.4	7 429.0
Principal wholesale societies[2]	0.4	0.3	0.3	0.3	0.3	0.3	0.3	0.3	0.2	0.2	0.2
Other wholesale and productive societies	40.3	41.3	42.6	153.1	43.9	44.3	45.9	50.9	53.7	52.7	53.0
Agricultural and fishing trading societies	315.8	318.8	316.0	312.2	309.4	304.3	305.9	305.9	300.8	294.6	294.6[5]
Sales (£ million)											
General trading societies:											
Retail societies[3]	2 548.0	2 798.3	3 078.5	3 446.9	3 644.3	3 771.2	3 913.7	4 125.6	3 994.7	3 989.4	4 408.9
Principal wholesale societies[2]	1 391.0	1 500.5	1 613.0	1 755.6	1 833.9	1 933.6	2 080.6	2 087.0	2 248.7	2 308.7	2 308.7
Other wholesale and productive societies	213.5	266.7	284.1	407.0	432.6	512.8	561.9	609.7	694.9	687.9	853.5[5]
Agricultural and fishing trading societies	913.0	1 005.4	1 118.6	1 228.7	1 365.3	1 541.9	1 596.6	1 700.7	1 697.8	1 683.3	1 670.5
Share and loan capital[4] (£ thousand)											
General trading societies:											
Retail societies	417 327	471 215	524 073	630 210	658 657	680 818	654 553	676 951	638 742	695 144	756 917
Principal wholesale societies[2]	184 621	189 705	231 658	250 084	269 645	301 194	313 668	292 194	301 294	299 127	299 127[5]
Other wholesale and productive societies	30 782	38 442	44 555	53 784	56 186	57 924	62 377	67 863	71 151	69 540	105 030
Agricultural and fishing trading societies	92 454	104 481	117 109	130 938	154 999	161 590	186 614	188 028	190 541	198 501	206 441

1 These societies are registered under the Industrial and Provident Societies Acts and are included in Table 17.19. See also footnote 1 to that table.
2 Co-operative Wholesale Society Ltd., Scottish Co-operative Society Ltd., and Co-operative Tea Society Ltd. During 1973 the businesses of the last two mentioned societies were transferred to the Co-operative Wholesale Society Ltd. Only in respect of the Scottish Co-operative Society Ltd. has the registry been cancelled.
3 These figures include the sale of goods purchased from the wholesale societies which are also included in the sales of those societies in this table.
4 Including net balance disposable and reserves but excluding loans from non-members.
5 1986 figure.

Source *Registry of Friendly Societies*

17.21 Collecting societies
Great Britain

£ thousand

	1977	1978	1979	1980	1981	1982	1983	1984	1985	1986	1987
Income: total	143 220	159 392	189 667	218 639	251 204	266 778	293 096	355 638	341 834	379 674	410 927
Premiums	84 231	92 766	112 398	129 242	138 529	151 193	164 353	173 476	177 466	186 838	195 417
Interest	57 690	65 721	76 157	88 188	99 263	113 971	124 373	142 087	158 191	173 618	185 474
Miscellaneous[1]	1 299	905	1 112	1 209	13 412	1 614	4 370	40 076	6 178	19 218	30 036
Expenditure: total	100 379	108 831	117 211	135 051	147 430	172 724	190 483	196 417	208 377	235 503	270 370
Claims	46 418	49 047	52 822	57 111	55 343	57 956	65 971	70 931	78 187	94 073	107 876
Cash bonuses	894	885	964	1 045	1 052	1 383	1 126	1 156	1 143	1 039	
Surrenders	11 789	10 984	12 145	15 848	23 828	29 602	35 918	39 166	42 469	43 636	40 863
Expenses of management	39 996	45 757	49 919	57 784	64 676	72 496	74 288	77 688	79 058	86 074	93 202
Miscellaneous	1 283	2 158	1 362	3 263	2 532	11 287	13 179	7 476	7 519	10 681	28 181
Funds at end of year	671 062	721 514	793 492	877 246	980 971	1 075 063	1 177 384	1 336 582	1 470 102	1 613 759	1 754 332

1 Including accrued interest.

Source *Office of the Industrial Assurance Commissioner*

17.22 Friendly societies[1]
Great Britain

	1977	1978	1979	1980	1981	1982	1983	1984	1985	1986	1987
Number of societies, orders and branches[2]	4 793	4 587	4 455	4 242	4 069	3 927	3 814	3 659	3 478	3 350	3 193
Number of members[2] (Thousands) total	3 957	3 744	3 651	3 596	3 431	3 349	3 246	3 213	3 095	2 968	2 987
Societies without branches	3 262	3 073	3 021	2 987	2 830	2 766	2 687	2 673	2 581	2 491	2 501
Orders and branches	695	671	630	608	601	583	560	540	514	477	486
Benefits paid (£ thousand)											
Sickness pay: total	6 254	6 852	6 841	6 578	7 109	7 982	7 639	8 396	9 280	10 671	11 526
Societies without branches	5 344	5 908	5 929	5 747	6 290	7 193	6 841	7 660	8 558	9 995	10 841
Orders and branches	910	944	912	831	819	789	798	736	722	676	685
Sums at death: total	3 183	3 542	3 663	4 039	4 364	4 982	5 321	5 726	6 932	6 984	9 256
Societies without branches	2 812	3 165	3 313	3 700	4 034	4 610	4 903	5 371	6 526	6 592	8 852
Orders and branches	371	377	350	339	330	372	418	355	406	392	404
Other benefits: total	28 201	27 750	31 920	37 384	48 320	48 364	54 503	62 468	76 810	100 857	101 137
Societies without branches	25 629	25 793	29 726	35 205	45 532	44 971	50 966	58 768	72 840	96 712	96 892
Orders and branches	2 572	1 956	2 194	2 179	2 788	3 393	3 537	3 700	3 970	4 145	4 245
Total funds[2] (£ thousand)	407 640	444 635	488 986	545 915	613 817	719 040	851 790	1 023 990	1 227 190	1 233 799	1 657 264

1 Excluding collecting societies.
2 At end of year.

Source *Registry of Friendly Societies*

17.23 Life assurance[1]

Industrial business
Great Britain

£ thousand

	1977	1978	1979	1980	1981	1982	1983	1984	1985	1986	1987
Companies established in Great Britain											
Income: total	790 715	854 562	1 080 735	1 296 551	1 430 365	1 685 658	1 812 348	2 138 229	2 199 242	2 314 009	2 490 070
Premiums	447 251	501 687	657 172	781 168	841 217	902 175	972 028	1 076 709	1 084 091	1 132 260	1 183 331
Interest, etc. (gross)	267 548	306 000	375 872	439 128	484 959	564 385	592 598	667 168	730 495	795 900	829 293
Miscellaneous[2]	75 916	46 875	47 692	76 254	104 189	219 098	247 722	394 352	384 656	385 849	477 446
Expenditure: total	557 806	608 959	699 425	829 058	961 773	1 119 894	1 228 631	1 403 906	1 562 315	1 711 128	1 826 814
Claims paid and outstanding	235 075	249 587	273 719	317 357	364 321	424 544	480 377	568 452	676 695	748 272	855 680
Surrenders	84 389	85 276	98 217	135 862	189 519	243 322	256 393	288 729	314 143	338 248	334 101
Expenses of management	195 830	225 014	267 812	312 322	339 157	357 047	378 058	407 967	425 031	448 848	469 562
Shareholders' surplus	9 363	10 745	13 060	15 954	20 829	25 140	30 245	45 797	45 150	49 091	53 064
Miscellaneous (including income tax)	33 149	38 337	46 617	47 564	47 946	69 842	83 557	92 961	101 296	126 669	114 407
Industrial assurance funds at end of year	2 814 851	3 081 954	3 463 264	3 930 757	4 400 480	4 969 117	5 552 834	6 287 156	6 924 083	7 527 524	8 190 872

1 The 'year' is, for each company included, its accounting year which ended between 1 September of the year shown and 31 August of the following year.

2 In 1975 includes £99 million transferred from investment and other reserves by five companies and £10 million written up by two companies on their investments. In 1977 includes £53 million transferred from investment reserves by two companies.

Source *Office of the Industrial Assurance Commissioner*

17.24 Returns of industrial assurances taken up and discontinued

Great Britain

Thousands

	1977	1978	1979	1980	1981	1982	1983	1984	1985	1986	1987
Industrial assurance companies[1]											
Paying:											
Assurances taken up during year	3 288	3 269	3 354	3 445	3 314	3 330	3 203	3 375	3 235	3 019	2 876
Assurances discontinued during year:											
Claims on death	768	757	776	724	696	688	656	628	612	583	541
Claims on maturity	999	985	975	967	1 017	1 054	1 076	1 192	1 168	1 076	1 035
Surrender for cash	1 750	1 628	1 609	1 807	2 051	2 217	2 084	2 044	1 940	1 858	1 695
Conversion to free policies:											
For full sums assured	412	429	420	418	462	421	450	424	455	528	399
For reduced sums assured	286	240	284	284	293	296	274	257	237	210	216
Forfeiture without grant of free policy or cash surrender value	580	546	472	484	536	536	514	536	564	735	487
Assurances in force at end of year	47 282	45 935	44 753	43 514	41 772	39 888	38 040	37 119	35 376	33 401	31 899
Free:											
Assurances converted to free policies during year	697	669	704	702	755	717	725	676	691	731	608
Assurances discontinued during year:											
Claims on death	483	473	568	522	521	519	512	502	513	515	483
Claims on maturity	35	36	111	76	84	86	91	97	100	96	101
Surrender for cash	180	158	155	176	192	193	197	183	201	178	179
Assurances in force at end of year	15 416	15 384	15 254	15 177	15 135	15 055	14 987	14 881	14 758	14 700	14 545
Collecting societies[2]											
Paying:											
Assurances taken up during year	594	563	521	516	463	440	417	370	356	343	336
Assurances discontinued during year:											
Claims on death	237	227	225	218	206	211	199	183	182	172	157
Claims on maturity	122	117	117	118	117	127	129	118	107	118	121
Surrender for cash	335	271	290	336	491	500	500	462	431	382	322
Conversion to free policies:											
For full sums assured	213	202	192	178	171	165	161	154	149	136	121
For reduced sums assured	203	185	178	162	93	80	77	69	64	66	53
Forfeiture without grant of free policy or cash surrender value	96	82	69	73	69	65	61	64	66	64	65
Assurances in force at end of year	14 192	13 667	13 117	12 541	11 847	11 137	10 419	9 741	9 108	8 519	8 011
Free:											
Assurances converted to free policies during year	416	388	370	340	264	245	239	222	212	201	174
Assurances discontinued during year:											
Claims on death	198	198	223	222	216	423	228	220	222	219	206
Claims on maturity	2	2	2	3	3	52	10	16	30	7	17
Surrender for cash	183	158	140	118	61	53	50	47	45	43	36
Assurances in force at end of year	7 910	7 941	7 943	7 945	7 935	7 653	7 595	7 535	7 452	7 381	7 296

1 Industrial assurance companies incorporated in Great Britain.

2 Collecting societies registered in Great Britain.

Source *Office of the Industrial Assurance Commissioner*

17.25 Acquisitions and mergers of companies

Analysis of expenditure by industry group of acquiring company

	Expenditure (£ million)[1]								Number of companies acquired							
	1981	1982	1983	1984	1985	1986	1987	1988	1981	1982	1983	1984	1985	1986	1987	1988
Industrial and commercial companies[2]																
Manufacturing industries:																
Food	99	48	92	536	277	356	449	2 970	17	14	19	22	24	45	36	40
Drink	13	34	8	209	473	4 173	331	311	7	8	3	21	14	11	12	16
Tobacco	39	–	–	51	662	–	–	–	2	–	–	1	1	–	–	–
Chemicals and man-made fibres	17	49	25	25	167	88	71	172	19	20	13	9	17	13	16	21
Mineral and ore extraction			–	17	62	–	2	270			–	1	1	–	2	6
Metals	13	61	31	23	52	123	73	326	16	19	22	9	3	31	30	35
Mechanical and instruments engineering	49	25	108	96	104	362	848	1 374	36	31	45	44	36	55	132	124
Electrical and electronic engineering																
Office machinery, etc.	84	31	91	762	158	214	1 374	592	36	22	29	44	40	61	92	69
Shipbuilding and vehicles	1	–	45	38	4	23	78	305	5	3	6	9	2	4	8	12
Metal goods nes	59	7	5	56	95	448	183	278	10	7	11	38	31	26	31	37
Textiles	21	9	8	32	249	909	104	38	22	15	9	15	14	21	28	16
Leather footwear and clothing	48	5	43	37	45	42	155	298	26	8	12	10	8	11	34	36
Non-metallic mineral products	16	180	31	34	98	212	167	887	10	7	7	7	9	14	20	18
Timber and furniture	5	33	24	23	4	54	801	93	7	8	7	7	3	9	31	32
Paper, printing and publishing	40	60	66	378	635	870	1 235	1 694	20	32	29	33	35	59	78	73
Other manufacturing	25	7	20	23	84	77	79	171	2	8	9	9	6	24	28	40
Mixed activity (mainly manufacturing)			972	1 220	85	2 730	822	439			14	4	7	18	31	23
Total manufacturing	529	549	1 568	3 558	3 256	10 681	6 771	10 218	235	202	235	283	251	402	609	598
Agriculture; forestry and fishing	107	270	3	4	4	4	37	2	17	20	2	3	2	3	5	3
Energy industries			172	121	185	106	137	3 794			18	17	14	11	14	26
Construction	90	140	193	262	94	469	281	424	31	39	31	35	9	20	46	70
Wholesaling (excluding petroleum)	41	210	43	305	59	218	375	781	19	34	39	48	29	48	93	130
Retailing	54	581	69	559	2 016	1 326	2 130	2 004	17	17	20	35	40	44	71	73
Hotels and catering			24	66	13	219	78	15			6	10	7	16	13	9
Transport and communication	24	9	55	97	33	62	369	657	9	13	7	13	12	8	7	12
Real estate	108	185	37	112	293	382	1 968	589	29	51	24	29	25	29	63	43
Services	76	243	141	220	403	620	784	2 159	59	61	53	86	64	95	163	232
Mixed activities (mainly non-manufacturing)			38	170	735	849	2 433	1 479			12	9	21	19	41	28
Mixed activities	114	20	[3]	[3]	[3]				36	26	[3]	[3]	[3]			
Total all industrial and commercial companies	1 143	2 206	2 343	5 474	7 090	14 935	15 363	22 123	452	463	447	568	474	695	1 125	1 224

1 A merger (which takes place when two companies combine to form a new company) is reckoned as the acquisition of the smaller company by the larger and is valued at the market value of the smaller company's share in the newly formed company.

2 The headings relate to the 1983 and later figures which are based on the 1980 Standard Industrial Classification. There are changes in coverage in nearly all headings. The major ones being the transfer of:
(a) man-made fibres from textiles to chemicals
(b) office machinery from mechanical to electrical engineering
(c) marine engineering from shipbuilding to mechanical engineering
(d) mineral and ore extraction from energy to form a new heading
(e) coal and petroleum products, nuclear fuel from chemicals to energy
(f) distribution of motor vehicles and parts, retail distribution of petroleum products and repair of motor vehicles from services to wholesaling and retailing (repairs with retailing)
(g) estate agents from real estate to services
(h) hotels and catering from services to form a new heading
(i) mixed activities have been split between manufacturing and non-manufacturing
(j) the definition of total manufacturing in 1983 and in subsequent years is not comparable with earlier years

3 Not applicable for 1983 and onwards.

Source *Central Statistical Office*

17.26 Income and finance of large companies[1,2]

Balance sheet summary

£ million

Balance sheet at end of accounting 'year'[3]	1986	1987	1988[4]
Estimated number of companies	*1 720*	*1 640*	*1 633*
Fixed assets:			
Net tangible assets	163 781	185 258	225 717
Intangible assets	7 606	9 658	16 788
Investments[5]	19 502	22 156	27 403
Total net fixed assets	190 889	217 072	269 910
Current assets and investments:			
Stocks and work-in-progress	67 877	69 859	82 257
Total debtors and Government grants receivable	78 134	88 142	105 867
Investments	11 657	11 610	12 509
Cash at bank and in hand	27 010	33 050	34 547
Total current assets and investments	184 678	202 661	235 184
Current liabilities:			
Total creditors and accruals falling due within one year	103 736	117 524	140 939
Dividends and interest due	6 267	7 605	8 799
Current taxation[6]	17 330	19 447	22 474
Total current liabilities	127 333	144 576	172 210
Net current assets	57 345	58 085	62 974
Total net assets	248 234	275 157	332 885
Financed by:			
Shareholders' interest	163 385	187 192	227 021
Minority shareholders' interest	9 571	6 714	8 009
Provisions[7]	20 640	19 845	21 496
Total creditors and accruals falling due after more than one year	54 639	61 406	76 357

Income and appropriation account

Accounts for 'year'[3]	1986	1987	1988[4]
Estimated number of companies	*1 720*	*1 640*	*1 633*
Income from trading and other activities:			
Gross trading profit[8]	47 148	58 801	71 347
Total income	53 522	65 701	79 153
Less:			
Interest on bank and short-term loans	5 420	6 095	8 612
Gross income	48 102	59 607	70 540
Appropriation of gross income:			
Depreciation and amounts written-off	15 666	15 292	17 279
Taxation	10 277	13 395	15 656
Dividends	9 647	11 392	14 416
Interest on long-term loans	2 289	2 018	1 730
Minority shareholders' interest	836	1 123	1 158
Retained income	9 387	16 386	20 299
Total appropriation of gross income	48 102	59 607	70 540

See *Note* and footnotes on page 306.

Source *Department of Trade and Industry*

17.26 Income and finance of large companies[1, 2]

(continued)

Sources and uses of funds

Accounts for 'year'[3]	1986	1987	1988[4]
Estimated number of companies	*1 720*	*1 640*	*1 633*
Receipts from issues of share and loan capital	11 826	17 989	17 846
Increase in amount owing to banks, short-term lenders and creditors	8 747	14 461	24 709
Gross income	48 102	59 607	70 540
Other sources (including exchange differences)	617	−3 613	409
Total sources of funds	69 293	88 443	113 503
Payments out of income	20 822	24 898	28 338
Expenditure on fixed assets, etc.	33 870	50 832	59 328
Increase in current assets and investments	14 601	12 713	25 837
Total uses of funds	69 293	88 443	113 503

Supplementary information

Accounts for 'year'[3]	1986	1987	1988[4]
Estimated number of companies	*1 720*	*1 640*	*1 633*
Capital employed[9]	244 800	271 800	331 500
Turnover (where reported)[10]	467 980	514 341	589 670
Ratio of net income to average net assets (per cent)	14.2	17.0	17.2
Ratio of gross trading profit to turnover (per cent)	10.1	11.4	12.1
Ratio of current assets less stock to current liabilities (per cent)	91.7	91.8	88.8
Estimated number of overseas owned companies	283	260	260

Note: The figures are based on an analysis of company accounts and full details are given in Business Monitor *MA3 Company finance* (HMSO).

1 Listed and unlisted limited companies registered in Great Britain excluding companies whose main activity is insurance, banking or finance. The figures relate to limited companies only and are based on the consolidated annual accounts of independent companies registered in Great Britain. Please note that revisions made in the format of analysis to accord with the Companies Act, 1985, mean that some balance sheet items cannot be compared directly with their predecessors in previous editions of *Annual Abstract of Statistics.*
2 There may be a slight discrepancy between a total and the sum of its constituent items due to rounding.
3 The figures for a particular year relate to companies' accounting years ending between 1 April of the year shown and 31 March of the following year. 75 per cent of the larger companies have accounting periods ending in the fourth quarter of the calendar year or in the first quarter of the following year.
4 Provisional.
5 Includes shares in and loans to Group and Related companies, other investments other than loans, other loans and own shares.
6 Includes all corporation tax, irrespective of the date on which it is payable, but is net of advance corporation tax recoverable.
7 Includes Pensions and similar obligations, deferred taxation and other taxation and Provisions.
8 Relates to the position after charging directors' fees and emoluments, pensions to past directors, superannuation payments, compensation for loss of office, auditors' fees and any exceptional expenditure (e.g. on reorganisation or closure) but excluding any profit or loss on disposal of assets and before allowing for depreciation provisions, all interest on loans, and hire charges for plant and machinery.
9 Defined for the purpose of this analysis, as shareholders' interest (issued share capital and reserves), minority shareholders' interest, deferred taxation, long-term loans (including debentures and mortgages)—i.e. all the items which finance net assets—*plus* bank loans and overdrafts, short-term loans and indebtedness to directors and group members, *less* amounts due from group members.
10 Excludes VAT but includes excise duties.

Source Department of Trade and Industry

17.27 Individual insolvencies

Number

	1977	1978	1979	1980	1981	1982	1983	1984	1985	1986	1987	1988
England and Wales												
Bankruptcies[1, 2]	4 403	3 826	3 456	3 986	5 075	5 654	6 981	8 178	6 730	7 093	6 994	7 717
Individual voluntary arrangements[3]	–	–	–	–	–	–	–	–	–	–	404	779
Deeds of arrangement	82	70	44	52	76	46	51	51	48	62	29	11
Total	4 485	3 896	3 500	4 038	5 151	5 700	7 032	8 229	6 778	7 155	7 427	8 507
Scotland												
Sequestrations[4]	132	127	106	150	181	213	282	292	298	437	818	1 401
Northern Ireland												
Bankruptcies[5, 6]	49	44	37	41	70	78	103	114	150	193	134	164
Deeds of arrangement	–	–	–	–	–	–	–	–	–	–	–	–
Total	49	44	37	41	70	78	103	114	150	193	134	164

1 Comprises receiving and administration orders under the Bankruptcy Act 1914 and bankruptcy orders under the Insolvency Act 1986.
2 Orders later consolidated or rescinded are included in these figures.
3 Introduced under the Insolvency Act 1986.
4 Sequestrations awarded but not brought into operation are included in these figures.
5 Comprises bankruptcy adjudication orders, arrangement protection orders and orders for the administration of estates of deceased insolvents.
6 Orders later set aside or dismissed are included in these figures.

Source *Department of Trade and Industry*

17.28 Company insolvencies

Number

	1977	1978	1979	1980	1981	1982	1983	1984	1985	1986	1987	1988
England and Wales												
Compulsory liquidations	2 425	2 265	2 064	2 935	2 771	3 745	4 807	5 260	5 761	5 204	4 116	3 667
Creditors' voluntary liquidations	3 406	2 821	2 473	3 955	5 825	8 322	8 599	8 461	9 137	9 201	7 323	5 760
Total	5 831	5 086	4 537	6 890	8 596	12 067	13 406	13 721	14 898	14 405	11 439	9 427
Scotland												
Compulsory liquidations	67	78	56	135	158	177	263	272	306	299	253	228
Creditors' voluntary liquidations	204	196	182	244	280	326	258	251	231	212	203	168
Total	271	274	238	379	438	503	521	523	537	511	456	396
Northern Ireland												
Compulsory liquidations	1	8	7	8	16	10	15	19	36	56	59	60
Creditors' voluntary liquidations	31	45	27	66	83	111	96	64	75	108	91	63
Total	32	53	34	74	99	121	111	83	111	164	150	123

Source *Department of Trade and Industry*

17.29 Industry analysis: bankruptcies and deeds of arrangement[1]
England and Wales

	1984	1985	1986	1987	1988
Industry					
Self-employed					
Agriculture and horticulture	155	136	130	172	162
Manufacturing:					
Food, drink and tobacco	36	26	16	17	25
Chemicals	3	4	–	2	3
Metals and engineering	99	84	92	147	158
Textiles and clothing	72	50	41	63	73
Timber and furniture	61	46	48	83	94
Paper, printing and publishing	32	30	36	39	60
Other manufacturing	84	55	44	35	30
Total manufacturing	387	295	277	386	443
Construction	901	788	801	1 123	1 590
Transport and communication	475	347	407	464	527
Wholesaling:					
Food, drink and tobacco	89	65	57	45	53
Motor vehicles	9	1	–	–	6
Other	89	69	41	61	69
Retailing:					
Food	499	421	452	468	447
Motor vehicles and filling stations	198	153	141	138	163
Other	815	714	755	620	459
Financial institutions	28	13	3	99	86
Business services	226	186	194	486	325
Hotels and catering	602	520	506	594	625
All other industries/businesses	1 444	1 220	1 249	462	646
Total: self-employed	5 917	4 928	5 013	5 118	5 601
Other individuals					
Employees	527	419	504	591	686
No occupation and unemployed	550	393	492	597	652
Directors and promoters of companies	568	486	524	441	345
Occupation unknown	215	180	229	276	444
Total: other individuals	1 860	1 478	1 749	1 905	2 127
Total	7 777	6 406	6 762	7 023	7 728

1 The total is not the same as in Table 17.27 because from 1983 to 1986 bankruptcies were analysed by industry after cases consolidated or rescinded during the year had been excluded. From 1987 individual voluntary arrangements are not included because they cannot be analysed by industry.

Source Central Statistical Office

17.30 Industry analysis: company insolvencies
England and Wales

	1984	1985	1986	1987	1988
Industry					
Agriculture and horticulture	77	102	128	126	73
Manufacturing:					
Food, drink and tobacco	132	129	133	140	88
Chemicals	115	138	112	97	75
Metals and engineering	1 338	1 376	1 371	1 035	708
Textiles and clothing	1 330	1 408	1 502	1 041	811
Timber and furniture	382	495	427	378	242
Paper, printing and publishing	479	494	497	380	326
Other manufacturing	681	797	734	557	480
Total manufacturing	4 457	4 837	4 776	3 628	2 730
Construction	1 831	1 975	1 914	1 490	1 471
Transport and communication	730	757	765	657	548
Wholesaling:					
Food, drink and tobacco	249	303	261	238	125
Motor vehicles	129	131	165	134	91
Other	838	813	624	511	487
Retailing:					
Food	206	238	262	216	170
Motor vehicles and filling stations	352	369	325	173	121
Other	1 538	1 552	1 383	1 047	795
Financial institutions	186	222	251	212	159
Business services	930	869	935	781	843
Hotels and catering	382	378	374	380	359
All other industries/businesses	1 816	2 352	2 242	1 846	1 455
Total	13 721	14 898	14 405	11 439	9 427

Source Department of Trade and Industry

18 Prices

Producer price index numbers (*Table 18.1 – 18.4*)

The producer price indices were published for the first time in August 1983, replacing the former wholesale price indices. Full details of the differences between the two indices were given in an article published in *British business,* 15 April 1983.

The producer price indices are calculated using the same general methodology as that used by the wholesale price indices. A comprehensive guide to the collection and calculation of the wholesale price indices entitled *Wholesale price index: principles and procedures* is published by the Government Statistical Service and is available from HMSO, price £5.60.

The index numbers in Tables 18.1 and 18.2 are constructed on a net sector basis. That is to say, they are intended to measure only transactions between the sector concerned and other sectors: within sector transactions are excluded. Index numbers for the whole of manufacturing are thus not weighted averages of sector index numbers.

All the index numbers are compiled exclusive of value-added tax. Revenue duties on cigarettes, manufactured tobacco and alcoholic liquor are included as is the duty on hydrocarbon oils.

The indices relate to the average prices for a year.

Purchasing power of the pound (*Table 18.5*)

Changes in the internal purchasing power of a currency may be defined as the 'inverse' of changes in the levels of prices; when prices go up, the amount which can be purchased with a given sum of money goes down. Movements in the internal purchasing power of the pound are based on the consumers' expenditure deflator (CED) prior to 1962 and on the General index of retail prices (RPI) from January 1962 onwards. The CED shows the movement in prices implied by the national accounts estimates of consumers' expenditure valued at current and at constant prices, whilst the RPI is constructed directly by weighting together monthly movements in prices according to a given pattern of household expenditure derived from the Family Expenditure Survey. If the purchasing power of the pound is taken to be 100p in a particular month (quarter, year), the comparable purchasing power in a subsequent month (quarter, year) is

$100 \times \frac{\text{earlier period price index}}{\text{later period price index}}$, where the price index used is the CED for years 1946–1961 and the RPI for periods after 1961.

A long series on the purchasing power of the pound back to 1914, the latest information and a detailed explanation of the estimation of changes in the purchasing power of the pound are given in 'The Internal Purchasing Power of the Pound', a leaflet obtainable from the Press Office, Room 65c/3, Central Statistical Office, Government Offices, Great George Street, London, SW1P 3AQ.

Index of retail prices (*Table 18.6*)

The retail prices index measures the change from month to month in the average level of prices of goods and services purchased by most households in the United Kingdom. The expenditure pattern on which the index is based is revised each year using information from the Family Expenditure Survey. The expenditure of certain higher income households and households of retired people dependent mainly on social security benefits is excluded.

The index covers a large and representative selection of more than 600 separate goods and services, for which price movements are regularly measured in more than 180 towns throughout the country. Approximately 130 000 separate price quotations are used in compiling the index.

The index of retail prices replaced the interim index from January 1956 (indices of the interim index of retail prices for the period 1952 to January 1956 were last published in *Annual Abstract of Statistics* No. 103, 1965). A new set of weights was introduced, based on ascertained expenditure in 1953–54, valued at January 1956 prices. Between January 1962 and 1974 the weights have been revised each January on the basis of ascertained expenditure in the three years ended in the previous June, valued at prices obtaining at the date of revision. From 1975 the weights have been revised on expenditure for the latest available year.

Following the recommendations of the Retail Prices Index Advisory Committee, the index has been re-referenced to make January 13, 1987 = 100. Calculations of price changes which involve periods spanning the new reference date are made as follows:

$$\%\ \text{change} = \frac{\dfrac{\text{Index for later month}}{(\text{Jan 1987}=100)} \times \dfrac{\text{Index for Jan 1987}}{(\text{Jan 1974}=100)}}{\text{Index for earlier month (Jan 1974}=100)} - 100$$

Tax and price index (TPI) (*Table 18.7*)

The purpose and methodology of the TPI were described in an article in the August 1979 issue (No. 310) of *Economic Trends* (HMSO). The TPI measures the increase in *gross* taxable income needed to compensate taxpayers for any increase in retail prices. The RPI measures changes in retail prices; the TPI also takes account of the changes to direct taxes (and employees' National Insurance contributions) facing a representative cross-section of taxpayers. It is thus an additional, more comprehensive, index.

When direct taxation or employees' National Insurance contributions change the TPI will rise by less than or more than the RPI according to the type of changes made. Between Budgets the monthly increase in the TPI is normally slightly larger than that in the RPI, since all the extra income needed to offset any rise in retail prices is fully taxed. However, the focus of attention should be the changes over twelve months.

Index numbers of agricultural prices (*Tables 18.8 and 18.9*)

The indices of agricultural prices for the United Kingdom are based on the calendar year 1980 are designed to provide an indication of movements in the purchase prices of the means of agricultural production and of the prices received by producers for their agricultural products. The methodology is compatible with that used for the other member states of the European Community and enables the compilation of indices for the Twelve, which appear in the Communities Eurostat series of publications.

18.1 Producer price index numbers of materials and fuel purchased
United Kingdom
Annual averages

1985=100

	1980 SIC Division, class or group	1985	1986	1987	1988
Materials and fuel purchased by manufacturing industry	2 to 4	100.0	92.4	95.3	98.4
Materials		100.0	93.6	97.4	101.5
Fuel		100.0	87.2	85.5	84.3
Materials and fuel purchased by manufacturing industry other than the food, drink and tobacco manufacturing industries	2 to 4 excluding 41/42	100.0	89.5	94.0	98.4
Materials		100.0	90.1	96.5	102.6
Fuel		100.0	87.7	86.0	84.9
Materials and fuel purchased by the food, drink and tobacco manufacturing industries	41/42	100.0	98.8	99.5	100.9
Materials and fuel purchased by selected broad sectors of industry					
Metal manufacturing	22	100.0	95.3	99.2	110.3
Extraction of minerals not elsewhere specified	23	100.0	89.2	91.4	91.7
Non-metallic mineral products	24	100.0	95.2	98.0	101.2
Chemical industry	25	100.0	82.9	86.8	85.7
Man-made fibres	26	100.0	91.2	97.8	100.0
Metal goods, engineering and vehicles industries	3	100.0	98.4	101.6	110.0
Metal goods not elsewhere specified	31	100.0	97.9	101.0	111.4
Mechanical engineering	32	100.0	101.4	104.4	111.6
Electrical and electronic engineering	34	100.0	99.4	104.1	113.0
Motor vehicles and parts	35	100.0	102.3	106.8	113.0
Other transport equipment	36	100.0	101.6	105.1	112.1
Instrument engineering	37	100.0	101.7	105.8	112.6
Food manufacturing industries	411 to 423	100.0	99.1	99.5	101.6
Materials		100.0	99.9	100.4	102.0
Fuel		100.0	84.4	83.3	81.2
Textile industry	43	100.0	97.4	103.2	107.9
Footwear and clothing industries	45	100.0	100.0	104.5	106.9
Timber and wooden furniture industries	46	100.0	99.6	105.5	109.4
Paper and paper products; printing and publishing	47	100.0	100.1	108.1	113.5
Processing of rubber and plastics	48	100.0	98.2	104.8	111.1
Other manufacturing industries	49	100.0	98.6	104.9	109.4
Construction materials	5	100.0	103.6	109.3	115.4
Housebuilding materials	Part of 5	100.0	103.8	110.1	116.2

Source *Central Statistical Office*

18.2 Producer price index numbers of output (home sales)
United Kingdom
Annual averages

1985=100

	1980 SIC[1]	1985	1986	1987	1988
Output of manufactured products	2 to 4	100.0	104.3	108.3	113.2
Products of manufacturing industries other than the food, drink and tobacco manufacturing industries	2 to 4 excluding 41/42	100.0	104.1	108.6	113.8
Products of the food, drink and tobacco manufacturing industries	41/42	100.0	104.4	107.5	111.5
Output of selected broad sectors of industry					
Metal manufacturing	22	100.0	98.7	101.3	109.8
Extraction of minerals not elsewhere specified	23	100.0	105.8	109.8	115.2
Non-metallic mineral products	24	100.0	103.4	108.9	114.4
Chemical Industry	25	100.0	101.7	105.8	111.5
Man-made fibres	26	100.0	104.7	105.7	106.9
Metal goods, engineering and vehicles industries	3	100.0	104.3	108.6	113.7
Metal goods not elsewhere specified	31	100.0	103.9	107.9	114.0
Mechanical engineering	32	100.0	104.4	109.0	114.8
Electrical and electronic engineering	34	100.0	104.2	108.2	111.9
Motor vehicles and parts	35	100.0	106.5	114.3	122.7
Instrument engineering	37	100.0	105.0	109.3	114.3
Food manufacturing industries	411 to 423	100.0	102.8	105.5	109.5
Textile industry	43	100.0	104.5	109.4	115.2
Footwear and clothing industries	45	100.0	104.7	108.3	113.5
Timber and wooden furniture industries	46	100.0	104.1	110.6	115.8
Paper and paper products; printing and publishing	47	100.0	103.7	109.3	113.6
Processing of rubber and plastics	48	100.0	104.4	108.8	114.4
Other manufacturing industries	49	100.0	105.7	111.5	115.6

1 Division, class or group.

Source *Central Statistical Office*

18.3 Producer price index numbers of products manufactured in the United Kingdom (home sales)
United Kingdom
Annual averages

1985=100

	1980 SIC[1]	1985	1986	1987	1988
Energy and water supply industries	**1**				
Coal mining	1113	100.0	101.3	100.7	104.5
Coke ovens	1200				
Foundry coke		100.0	101.6	101.6	101.6
Mineral oil refining (including duty)	1401				
Petroleum products (including duty)		100.0	79.6	79.6	76.6
Motor spirit (including duty)		100.0	86.6	87.2	87.0
Kerosene (including duty)		100.0	80.5	79.6	78.6
Gas oil/derv (including duty)		100.0	75.0	72.0	66.4
Gas oil fuel (including duty)		100.0	64.0	60.3	50.2
Derv (including duty)		100.0	84.9	82.4	80.8
Fuel oil (including duty)		100.0	55.3	60.8	46.9
Light fuel oil (including duty)[2]		100.0	71.4	80.8	84.4
Medium fuel oil (including duty)[2]		100.0	70.3	78.0	77.0
Heavy fuel oil (including duty)		100.0	52.8	58.0	41.8
Petroleum bitumen[2]		100.0	75.0	80.3	88.9
Other treatment of petroleum products (excluding petrochemical manufacture)	1402				
Lubricating oils and greases		100.0	95.4	95.2	92.5
Water supply industry	1700				
Water for industrial use[3]		100.0	107.7	114.8	122.6
Metal manufacturing	**22**				
Iron and steel	2210	100.0	101.1	102.1	106.8
Foundry pig iron		100.0	97.3	97.3	97.3
Ordinary steel		100.0	101.8	102.3	106.2
Finished rolled products		100.0	102.5	103.0	107.7
Rails and accessories		100.0	103.8	108.2	109.2
Sheet piling		100.0	103.2	109.0	114.0
Heavy sections		100.0	103.2	103.7	106.0
Hot rolled narrow strip (less than 600 mm)		100.0	105.7	109.3	115.2
Hot rolled coil, plate and sheet		100.0	102.8	105.1	110.3
3 mm thick and over		100.0	103.2	105.4	110.6
Less than 3 mm thick		100.0	101.6	103.8	109.4
Cold rolled sheets		100.0	102.3	103.5	111.0
End products		100.0	99.8	100.8	103.0
Tinplate and other tinned sheet		100.0	99.6	100.7	104.2
Black plate		100.0	102.4	104.7	108.5
Zinc coated, lead coated and other coated sheet		100.0	100.0	100.0	100.0
Electrical sheet (including hot rolled electrical strip)		100.0	100.0	106.6	111.9
Grain non-orientated		100.0	100.0	107.1	112.6
Grain orientated		100.0	100.0	105.5	110.4
Special steels		100.0	97.9	101.2	110.4
Semis for direct use		100.0	100.6	103.5	108.4
Other alloy steel		100.0	100.8	102.6	104.0
Semis for direct use		100.0	101.2	103.1	104.9
Finished flat products		100.0	102.2	102.7	107.3
Plate 3 mm and over		100.0	102.2	102.7	107.3
Merchant bars, sections and other products		100.0	100.4	103.3	104.0
Stainless and heat resisting steels		100.0	91.3	97.0	122.0
Semis for direct use		100.0	96.0	97.8	121.6
Finished flat products—Sheet and strip		100.0	90.4	102.6	122.2
Steel for reinforcement; cut, bent and delivered		100.0	98.3	93.5	105.6
Light re-rolled bars and sections		100.0	99.8	94.2	101.7
Steel tubes	2220	100.0	103.6	109.2	117.8
Drawing and manufacture of steel wire and steel wire products	2234	100.0	103.3	106.0	109.4
Single drawn wire of iron and steel whether covered or not (excluding insulated electric wire)		100.0	104.7	108.5	111.1
Single drawn wire of iron and steel whether covered or not (excluding insulated electric wire) of high carbon steel		100.0	106.0	109.6	110.0
Woven wire cloth, gauze, fabric etc. of iron and steel (excluding netting, fencing and similar iron and steel manufactures and fabric reinforcements of concrete) in squares or rectangular mesh		100.0	105.2	109.9	116.7
Stainless steel		100.0	108.2	114.6	124.3
Other than stainless steel		100.0	103.6	107.6	112.9
Fabric reinforcement manufacture to BS 4483 and rods and bars cut and/or bent, sold for use as concrete reinforcements to BS 4449 or BS 4461		100.0	101.2	103.3	111.2

1 Division, class or activity heading.
2 This index is based on list prices rather than prices actually charged.
3 This index is based on volumetric charges and does not reflect fixed or standing charges.

Source *Central Statistical Office*

18.3 (*continued*) Producer price index numbers of products manufactured in the United Kingdom (home sales)
United Kingdom
Annual averages

1985 = 100

	1980 SIC[1]	1985	1986	1987	1988
Metal manufacturing (*continued*)					
Other drawing, cold rolling and cold forming of steel	2235	100.0	101.8	102.2	107.0
Other drawing, cold rolling and cold forming of non-alloy steel		100.0	102.5	102.7	108.1
Over 0.25% carbon		100.0	107.2	111.3	115.8
Other drawing, cold rolling and cold forming of other alloy steels		100.0	98.5	100.4	106.2
Bright bars		100.0	98.5	100.4	106.2
Aluminium and aluminium alloys	2245				
Plate, sheet, strip circles and blanks		100.0	94.5	97.8	105.4
Strip		100.0	95.4	101.2	108.7
Plate, sheet, blanks and circles		100.0	93.7	94.5	102.3
Extrusions and tubes (bars, rods, sections etc.)		100.0	99.3	100.1	114.1
Copper, brass and other copper alloys	2246				
Primary and secondary copper and copper based alloys unwrought		100.0	86.4	78.3	86.2
Brass and other copper alloys, unwrought (i.e. alloys in which copper is the largest constituent by weight, excl. cadmium copper)		100.0	86.4	78.3	86.2
Copper rods		100.0	86.8	97.2	128.8
Copper tubes		100.0	99.2	112.5	131.7
Wire and wire manufactures of copper, brass and other copper alloys (incl. nickel silver and cupro-nickel but excl. all other nickel alloys)		100.0	90.2	99.2	125.2
Single drawn wire, uninsulated of copper (including cadmium copper)		100.0	89.6	98.8	126.0
Copper, brass and other copper alloy scrap		100.0	82.3	89.0	119.0
Other non-ferrous metals and their alloys	2247				
Titanium		100.0	90.2	88.5	95.2
Extraction of minerals not elsewhere specified	**23**				
Extraction of stone, clay, sand and gravel unprocessed before sale	2310	100.0	106.2	110.5	116.9
Sand, gravel and pebbles (excluding sand for foundry purposes, glassmaking or other industrial uses)		100.0	105.4	110.2	117.9
Sand and gravel delivered		100.0	105.6	110.2	117.7
Salt extraction and refining	2330	100.0	106.3	108.2	112.0
Rock salt		100.0	108.1	111.8	122.6
White salt		100.0	105.6	106.6	107.3
Non-metallic mineral products	**24**				
Structural clay products	2410	100.0	105.4	115.6	127.9
Common, facing and engineering bricks		100.0	104.9	115.3	127.7
Common bricks		100.0	102.2	118.7	136.1
Fletton (delivered)		100.0	105.4	118.8	127.7
Facing bricks		100.0	105.8	114.2	123.8
Non-fletton (ex-works) facings		100.0	108.9	118.9	131.0
Fletton (delivered)		100.0	101.2	107.1	113.0
Clay roofing tiles (plain and single lap) excl. fittings		100.0	109.5	122.0	137.9
Cement, lime and plaster	2420	100.0	..	..	105.5
Calcareous cement		100.0	..	..	103.5
Ready-mixed concrete	2436	100.0	100.0	100.2	105.2
Other building products of concrete, cement or plaster	2437	100.0	104.0	108.7	112.8
Plaster products		100.0	100.1	104.6	108.3
Gypsum plaster products incl. coving		100.0	101.3	104.0	108.4
Plasterboard		100.0	100.0	104.7	108.3
Precast concrete goods		100.0	104.0	108.4	112.9
Concrete blocks, bricks, kerbs and edgings etc.		100.0	104.5	109.4	114.2
Concrete blocks (all types)		100.0	103.8	109.1	114.3
Flagstones and paving stones		100.0	106.1	110.4	114.2
Kerbs, edgings, channels, quadrants to BS 340		100.0	105.4	109.2	113.1
Concrete pipes to BS 5911		100.0	102.1	104.6	108.5
Asbestos goods	2440	100.0	104.6	108.5	112.0
Working of stone and other non-metallic minerals not elsewhere specified	2450	100.0	101.4	106.3	111.0
Ground and processed minerals		100.0	101.3	105.7	109.6
Limestone and dolomite		100.0	102.6	107.3	111.0
Processed dry limestone and dolomite, ground agriculture and industrial limestone		100.0	109.1	115.8	119.5
Limestone and dolomite coated macadam		100.0	94.0	96.0	99.7
Granite		100.0	101.9	107.9	113.8
Processed granite (classified in accordance with BS group classification as granite, basalt etc.)		100.0	103.8	107.4	115.1
Granite coated macadam		100.0	100.8	108.2	113.4
Building, ornamental and funerary stonework (excl. sculpture)		100.0	122.5	131.6	151.8
Clays, kaolin, marl		100.0	105.6	111.0	121.8
Processed ball and china clays (kaolin)		100.0	105.6	111.0	121.8
Abrasive products	2460	100.0	106.3	113.3	118.4
Diamond type abrasive wheels		100.0	104.5	107.4	110.9

1 Division, class or activity heading.

Source *Central Statistical Office*

18.3 (continued) Producer price index numbers of products manufactured in the United Kingdom (home sales)

United Kingdom

Annual averages

1985=100

	1980 SIC[1]	1985	1986	1987	1988
Non-metallic mineral products *(continued)*					
Glass containers	2478	100.0	99.3	99.6	102.2
Other glass products	2479	100.0	102.8	106.0	111.2
Domestic and ornamental glassware		100.0	106.8	110.9	116.8
Other table, toilet, ornamental and stationery glassware and kitchenware (excl. heat resisting glassware for cooking purposes)		100.0	107.0	114.0	117.9
Glass envelopes, tubes and illuminating glassware		100.0	106.4	106.8	110.6
Refractory goods	2481	100.0	107.1	113.1	115.3
Firebricks and blocks		100.0	104.4	109.6	112.7
Miscellaneous refractory goods nes		100.0	105.8	112.3	115.4
Ceramic goods	2489	100.0	105.7	109.9	116.5
Sanitary ware of vitreous china		100.0	103.8	105.3	112.1
Domestic china and other pottery		100.0	106.2	111.8	119.1
China or porcelain		100.0	105.9	111.8	120.6
Table and kitchenware		100.0	105.7	112.3	121.4
Electrical ware wholly or mainly of ceramic material (incl. insulators and insulator fittings)		100.0	106.8	109.5	113.7
Chemical industry	**25**				
Inorganic chemicals except industrial gases	2511	100.0	101.6	104.7	110.5
Chemical elements excluding elemental gases		100.0	95.1	102.0	105.6
Inorganic acids and oxygen compounds of non-metals		100.0	101.6	101.5	104.3
Sulphuric acid and oleum		100.0	96.7	90.4	88.6
Metallic salts and peroxy salts of inorganic acids		100.0	104.4	107.1	111.8
Soda ash		100.0	105.5	106.2	110.9
Metallic salts and peroxy salts of inorganic acids other than soda ash		100.0	103.9	107.5	112.2
Basic organic chemicals except specialised pharmaceutical chemicals	2512				
Carboxylic acids and specified derivatives		100.0	94.4	98.9	108.5
Fertilisers	2513	100.0	89.2	80.4	82.9
Synthetic resins and plastics materials	2514	100.0	97.8	107.7	118.4
Products of polymerisation and co-polymerisation		100.0	94.4	105.8	118.7
Dyestuffs and pigments	2516	100.0	107.4	117.1	128.7
Paints, varnishes and painters' fillings	2551				
Non-aqueous building, structural, preservation and decorative products		100.0	106.4	110.1	116.9
Emulsion paints		100.0	103.4	105.0	111.2
Paint removers and strippers, and filling and sealing compounds of all types		100.0	107.7	108.9	117.1
Chemical treatment of oil and fats	2563	100.0	71.6	69.4	71.3
Formulated pesticides	2568	100.0	102.6	106.5	110.4
Herbicides		100.0	104.8	112.9	121.3
Herbicides containing phenoxy derivatives of acetic, propionic or butyric acids		100.0	105.0	115.5	125.3
Herbicides other than those containing phenoxy derivatives of acetic, propionic or butyric acids		100.0	104.5	104.6	108.2
Adhesive film, cloth and foil adhesive film, tape etc. of plastics or cellulose, adhesive cloth and foil	2569	100.0	95.2	100.1	101.8
Pharmaceutical products	2570	100.0	106.3	110.4	115.6
Medical preparations as specified		100.0	101.7	104.8	109.4
Central nervous system		100.0	101.9	107.2	110.3
Analgesics—antipyretics		100.0	103.2	108.5	113.3
Cardiovascular system		100.0	102.5	104.8	103.8
Plain hypotensives		100.0	100.0	100.4	101.9
Plain diuretics		100.0	100.0	100.8	101.6
Cough and cold preparations		100.0	108.4	118.3	127.1
Preparations for the alimentary tract and nutrition		100.0	102.4	104.8	109.1
Antacids and anti-ulcerants		100.0	100.8	101.6	105.5
Vitamins and mineral supplements		100.0	102.1	106.8	112.1
Muscular and skeletal systems (systemic)		100.0	100.4	101.4	103.2
Topical cortiso-steroids		100.0	101.4	101.4	107.2
Antibiotics		100.0	99.8	100.7	117.6
Preparations for genito-urinary system (incl. sex hormones)		100.0	104.3	119.2	122.7
Surgical bandages etc.		100.0	107.2	113.8	121.8
Adhesive plasters, bandages and self adhesive first-aid dressings		100.0	103.9	107.4	114.6
Soap and synthetic detergents	2581	100.0	103.5	107.9	114.0
Soap (excluding scouring preparations)		100.0	100.6	101.2	106.8
Toilet soap in tablet form		100.0	99.7	99.2	104.2
Liquid finished synthetic detergents		100.0	105.6	111.5	116.7
Perfumes, cosmetics and toilet preparations	2582				
After shave, cologne and pre-shave lotions		100.0	107.8	119.6	129.8
Perfumes, cosmetics and toilet preparations other than specifically for men		100.0	104.4	107.8	112.5
Talc and dusting powders and bath preparations		100.0	105.5	111.3	114.8
Talc and dusting powders		100.0	105.9	110.0	115.7
Make-up preparations		100.0	105.8	110.0	115.4
Lipsticks and lipglosses, including lipsalve		100.0	103.4	107.0	112.7
Face powders		100.0	106.4	109.3	115.7
Liquid and cream make-up for the face		100.0	104.4	111.8	121.4
Deodorants, anti-perspirants and depilatories		100.0	102.7	106.5	111.0
Toothpaste and dental powders		100.0	103.4	108.0	116.2
Photographic materials and chemicals	2591	100.0	103.4	108.1	113.0

1 Division, class or activity heading.

Source Central Statistical Office

18.3 (*continued*) Producer price index numbers of products manufactured in the United Kingdom (home sales)

United Kingdom
Annual averages

1985=100

	1980 SIC[1]	1985	1986	1987	1988
Man-made fibres	**26**				
Man-made fibres	2600	100.0	104.7	105.7	106.9
Manufacture of metal goods not elsewhere specified	**31**				
Ferrous foundry products	3111	100.0	104.3	106.4	113.9
Iron castings in the rough or machined		100.0	104.6	107.0	111.7
Engineers castings		100.0	106.0	109.0	114.4
Vehicle iron castings		100.0	107.0	110.4	115.6
Industrial and marine machinery and plant		100.0	105.0	107.7	113.2
Light engineering		100.0	106.3	108.5	114.3
Steel castings		100.0	101.4	100.4	136.1
Non-alloy steel castings		100.0	101.3	99.5	136.3
Stainless and heat resisting alloy steel castings		100.0	102.6	119.2	126.5
Other alloy steel castings		100.0	101.6	107.3	135.9
Forging, pressing and stampings	3120				
Steel forgings		100.0	106.2	111.2	116.2
Bolts, nuts, washers, springs and non-precision chains	3137	100.0	103.7	107.2	111.0
Bolts, nuts, screws, washers, rivets, etc. of iron or steel		100.0	103.5	107.2	110.4
All bolt products including machine screws, studs and socket screws		100.0	103.7	106.0	109.8
All bolt products of high tensile steel		100.0	104.7	107.1	111.1
All bolt products of mild steel		100.0	101.9	104.2	107.8
Metal doors, windows etc.	3142	100.0	105.6	112.8	121.4
Metal windows and doors (excl. strongroom doors and doors for motor vehicles) door frames, window frames, casements and curtain walling		100.0	105.6	112.8	121.4
Hand tools and implements	3161	100.0	105.2	109.7	115.4
Agricultural hand tools		100.0	105.1	109.9	113.4
Other hand tools		100.0	105.2	109.7	116.1
Hacksaw blades		100.0	104.4	107.4	111.1
Bolt cutters, pliers, pincers, nippers and snips		100.0	105.4	111.6	118.3
Spanners and wrenches		100.0	106.1	109.8	115.9
Hammers		100.0	101.7	106.7	112.6
Cutlery, spoons, forks and similar tableware: razors	3162				
Scissors and tailors' shears including pinking shears		100.0	104.4	109.4	114.6
Metal storage vessels (mainly non-industrial)	3163	100.0	103.8	109.7	122.5
Packaging products of metal	3164	100.0	102.0	103.8	107.1
Cans and boxes, covers and components of steel (incl. tinplate and blackplate) and aluminium		100.0	101.4	102.3	..
New metal kegs, drums and barrels of wrought iron and steel with a capacity exceeding 20 litres		100.0	107.5	112.1	118.9
Reconditioned metal kegs, drums and barrels		100.0	101.5	105.8	109.1
Domestic heating and cooking appliances (non-electrical)	3165	100.0	105.5	109.2	114.8
Gas cookers		100.0	106.3	110.7	115.5
Gas fires and space heaters (excluding gas central heating equipment)		100.0	103.9	105.7	112.8
Metal furniture and safes	3166	100.0	105.5	109.9	115.5
Office furniture wholly or mainly of metal		100.0	104.3	107.4	112.5
Seating		100.0	104.6	108.7	115.7
Adjustable office seating		100.0	104.4	108.6	116.4
Filing cabinets and other filing containers		100.0	104.1	106.4	112.0
Shelving and racking including lateral and library shelving		100.0	105.6	110.8	116.7
Domestic and similar utensils of metal	3167	100.0	105.1	110.6	113.5
Kettles (non-electric) and teapots (excluding electro-plated and precious metal teapots)		100.0	102.0	106.1	..
Bakeware, including baking pans, sheets, tins etc.		100.0	103.2	104.6	108.8
Finished metal products nes	3169	100.0	104.7	110.1	117.5
Locks, padlocks, latches, keys and blanks including bicycle locks (excluding for motor vehicles and time locks)		100.0	105.6	111.4	118.5
Needles, pins and other metal smallwares		100.0	106.5	111.9	118.6
Builders' and cabinet makers ironmongery and hardware		100.0	103.3	106.6	112.5
Base metal fittings and mountings for door and door frames		100.0	104.8	108.0	113.6
Windows and shutters		100.0	101.8	106.7	114.3
Sanitary ware and plumbing fixtures and fittings for domestic and similar use		100.0	104.5	110.3	118.0
Domestic cocks and taps		100.0	104.7	109.2	118.8
Fire extinguishers (hand operated chemical type)		100.0	111.1	123.0	133.9
Mechanical engineering	**32**				
Agricultural machinery	3211				
Harvesting and threshing machinery		100.0	107.0	115.0	..
Grain and grass dryers		100.0	103.5	107.4	..
Agricultural elevators and conveyors (including grain augers)		100.0	101.9	108.5	124.2
Wheeled tractors	3212				
Wheeled tractors, complete (including KD tractors of a minimum value of 50 per cent of a corresponding complete tractor)		100.0	104.7	105.3	109.5
Metal working machine tools	3221	100.0	104.7	108.1	113.8
Metal cutting machine tools		100.0	104.7	108.0	114.2
Numerically controlled machine tools complete		100.0	103.3	106.9	113.0
Machining centres		100.0	101.2	108.1	115.0
Non numerically controlled metal cutting machine tools complete		100.0	106.5	109.8	118.0
Non numerically controlled grinding machines		100.0	105.7	110.2	116.0
Non numerically controlled turning machines		100.0	106.3	113.5	119.8

1 Division, class or activity heading.

Source *Central Statistical Office*

18.3 (continued) Producer price index numbers of products manufactured in the United Kingdom (home sales)

United Kingdom

Annual averages

1985 = 100

	1980 SIC[1]	1985	1986	1987	1988
Mechanical engineering *(continued)*					
Engineers' small tools	3222	100.0	106.5	112.2	..
Hard tipped and other metal cutting tools		100.0	104.7	110.0	116.6
Hard metal tipped tools		100.0	106.7	114.6	119.9
Hard metal tips and die pellets sold separately		100.0	103.3	107.9	110.3
Diamond tipped tools and diamond dies		100.0	103.8	106.9	111.1
Threading dies and taps		100.0	107.0	111.5	120.4
Saws and saw blades		100.0	102.7	109.4	116.2
Bandsaws and blades for metal		100.0	102.4	106.2	113.3
Reamers, end mills and similar shank tools		100.0	104.0	107.0	113.0
Milling cutters		100.0	102.2	107.5	109.2
Lathe and planer tools		100.0	106.6	110.5	120.6
Food, drink and tobacco processing machinery; packaging and bottling machinery	3244	100.0	105.2	111.8	116.4
Food and drink processing machinery		100.0	104.1	108.9	112.3
Bakery and confectionery machinery (including parts)		100.0	101.4	102.1	103.5
Drink processing machinery including parts		100.0	103.7	108.6	112.2
Grain milling machinery and plant (including parts)		100.0	101.8	109.3	..
Other machinery and parts for the preparation, processing and sterilisation of food (incl. oil or fat machinery for food industry)		100.0	109.0	116.2	120.9
Machines for filling, closing, sealing, capsulating or labelling containers		100.0	105.3	112.0	117.6
Filling, closing, sealing, etc. machines for cans		100.0	109.4	118.4	127.0
Mining machinery	3251	100.0	103.1	105.0	108.6
Mineral transport machinery		100.0	101.1	102.4	106.4
Construction and earth moving equipment	3254				
Wheeled tractor shovels		100.0	103.6	107.5	110.0
Dumpers and dump trucks		100.0	103.7	105.9	..
Equipment for concrete, crushing and screening and road works		100.0	104.7	110.1	..
Concrete mixing and placing machinery and parts		100.0	106.4	107.9	..
Asphalt, bitumen, tar and tarmacadam plants and parts		100.0	102.5	105.2	..
Mechanical lifting and handling equipment	3255	100.0	103.2	106.2	..
Cranes and transporters		100.0	107.4	111.8	119.1
Lifting and winding devices		100.0	105.6	111.7	117.9
Lifting jacks, vehicle jacks and lifts		100.0	107.8	116.4	124.5
Capstans, winches, windlasses		100.0	103.1	107.1	112.1
Precision chains and other mechanical power transmission equipment	3261	100.0	106.1	112.6	118.9
Transmission chains		100.0	106.0	109.4	115.0
Bearings and bushes other than ball roller and needle roller bearings and parts and plain bearings		100.0	105.2	110.0	115.5
Helical, spur and bevel gears		100.0	106.5	111.7	115.6
Ball, needle and roller bearings	3262	100.0	104.9	105.2	111.2
Machinery for working wood, rubber, plastics, leather and making paper, glass, bricks and similar materials; laundry and dry cleaning machinery	3275				
Woodworking machinery		100.0	..	..	123.5
Leather work and footwear making and repairing machinery		100.0	105.7	112.3	121.8
Boot and shoe-making and repairing machinery		100.0	105.7	112.3	121.8
Laundry and dry cleaning machinery		100.0	100.5	109.4	113.2
Internal combustion engines (except for road vehicles, wheeled agricultural tractors and aircraft) and other prime movers	3281				
Compression ignition IC engines		100.0	103.5	106.2	110.0
Compressors and fluid power equipment	3283	100.0	105.4	111.8	118.6
Compressors		100.0	106.4	112.6	119.4
Oil hydraulic pumps		100.0	104.7	110.6	116.2
Oil hydraulic control valves		100.0	106.6	114.8	124.1
Pneumatic control equipment		100.0	104.2	109.1	115.7
Directional control, flow control, check and non-return valves, and moving and non-moving fluidic devices		100.0	102.9	108.3	113.4
Other pneumatic control equipment (including pressure control valves)		100.0	105.0	109.5	117.0
Refrigerating machinery, space heating, ventilating and air conditioning equipment	3284				
Space heating equipment		100.0	104.0	108.1	113.4
Boilers for central heating		100.0	104.1	110.1	115.3
Other heat emitters		100.0	105.7	109.6	114.0
Ventilating equipment		100.0	103.8	108.9	..
Scales, weighing machinery and portable power tools	3285	100.0	101.7	105.7	111.7
Scales and weighing machinery complete and parts		100.0	99.5	98.9	101.5
Portable power tools		100.0	102.7	109.0	116.7
Pneumatic, petrol, hydraulic and other tools for civil engineering, mining and quarrying		100.0	104.1	109.9	118.3
Portable power tools (electric)		100.0	101.4	107.1	114.2
Other industrial and commercial machinery	3286	100.0	104.6	108.6	113.6
Industrial and commercial machinery and service equipment		100.0	104.4	108.2	113.3
Lawn mowers powered, incl. electrically		100.0	104.6	109.6	115.4
Garage equipment and plant n.e.s.		100.0	105.3	110.7	117.1

1 Division, class or activity heading.

Source *Central Statistical Office*

18.3 (continued) Producer price index numbers of products manufactured in the United Kingdom (home sales)

United Kingdom

Annual averages

1985 = 100

	1980 SIC[1]	1985	1986	1987	1988
Mechanical engineering *(continued)*					
Pumps	3287	100.0	105.7	110.6	117.2
Centrifugal pumps		100.0	105.9	110.8	116.9
Centrifugal pumps with stuffing box or mechanical seal		100.0	105.7	110.7	118.5
Positive displacement pumps		100.0	105.0	111.4	116.5
Rotary pumps		100.0	105.5	111.8	117.9
Manufacture of office machinery and data processing equipment	**33**				
Office machinery	3301	100.0	103.7	104.5	107.6
Electrical and electronic engineering	**34**				
Insulated wires and cables	3410	100.0	100.1	101.8	108.3
Mains (power distribution) cables 600/1000 volts and over		100.0	96.4	96.2	97.4
General wiring cables (incl. building wires, ship wiring and trailing cables)		100.0	101.1	104.7	115.6
Winding wires and strips		100.0	92.1	89.1	105.7
Batteries and accumulators	3432	100.0	104.2	110.3	114.7
Electrical equipment for motor vehicles, cycles and aircraft	3434	100.0	107.4	124.0	128.8
Electrical instruments and control systems	3442	100.0	102.7	106.3	110.0
Electricity supply meters incl. prepaid		100.0	102.9	105.8	108.7
Instruments and equipment for integrated process control schemes		100.0	102.7	104.0	104.3
Electrical measuring, testing and controlling instruments and apparatus		100.0	104.3	108.9	115.3
Ammeters, voltmeters, wattmeters		100.0	106.3	113.4	122.6
Signal and waveform generators		100.0	103.3	104.4	109.4
Other electrical measuring, testing and controlling instruments and appliances, including telemetering instruments, other than for motor vehicles or aircraft		100.0	104.9	110.5	117.0
Radio and electronic capital goods	3443				
Electro medical apparatus		100.0	111.3	112.9	115.4
Domestic-type electric appliances	3460	100.0	104.3	104.9	106.9
Electric cooking apparatus		100.0	104.0	107.7	110.6
Electric kettles		100.0	103.9	105.4	106.8
Electric heating apparatus		100.0	103.4	105.8	108.2
Electric water heaters		100.0	105.1	108.6	116.4
Deep-freeze units		100.0	104.4	108.0	112.1
Electric lamps and other electric lighting equipment	3470				
Electric lamp bulbs and tubes		100.0	105.2	110.4	..
Discharge lamps, complete		100.0	105.0	110.7	..
Electric lamp bulbs, filament type complete		100.0	105.4	110.2	..
Lamp and lighting fittings and parts thereof		100.0	106.6	110.2	115.5
For tubular fluorescent lamps		100.0	105.4	108.1	112.1
Other fittings and parts		100.0	106.8	111.8	120.1
Motor vehicles and parts thereof	**35**				
Motor vehicles and their engines	3510	100.0	106.8	114.7	123.2
Passenger cars		100.0	106.9	116.1	126.2
Goods vehicles not exceeding 3.5 tons gvw		100.0	106.7	114.4	123.1
Goods vehicles exceeding 16 tons gvw		100.0	107.5	115.1	122.3
Passenger cars (inclusive of VAT and car tax)		100.0	106.9	116.1	126.2
Trailers and semi-trailers (incl. freight containers)	3522				
Trailers and semi-trailers		100.0	104.7	111.3	116.4
Motor vehicle parts	3530				
Fuel pumps (not electric)		100.0	103.7	108.8	112.0
Instrument engineering	**37**				
Measuring, checking and precision instruments and apparatus	3710	100.0	105.4	109.7	115.9
Process measuring and control instruments and equipment		100.0	106.4	111.6	116.9
Level indicating recording or controlling instruments		100.0	106.0	114.3	118.9
Temperature measuring and control instruments		100.0	107.2	113.2	119.2
Thermostats and temperature indicators and controllers		100.0	108.6	115.6	122.0
Pressure measuring and control instruments		100.0	108.4	113.6	121.0
Pressure gauges and switches		100.0	105.4	111.8	118.1
Other pressure measuring and control instruments		100.0	114.9	117.2	127.2
Analytical instruments		100.0	104.6	107.6	109.5
Ultrasonic instruments and equipment		100.0	111.2	116.8	117.9
Counting, and velocity measuring instruments		100.0	104.7	108.0	111.9
Engineers gauges and measuring instruments		100.0	107.8	114.2	124.2
Static gauges		100.0	108.8	122.3	128.7
Mechanical measuring instruments		100.0	107.2	111.6	122.6
Medical and surgical equipment and orthopaedic appliances	3720	100.0	105.2	111.1	114.5
Medical, surgical and veterinary equipment		100.0	105.2	112.6	116.1
Other medical, surgical, veterinary and dissecting instruments		100.0	102.6	106.7	113.4
Aseptic hospital furniture		100.0	104.3	107.7	111.7
Orthopaedic appliances and artificial limbs etc.		100.0	105.9	109.3	112.5
Photographic and cinematographic equipment	3733	100.0	104.1	109.7	110.3
Clocks, watches and other timing devices	3740				
Time switches etc.		100.0	104.0	107.9	113.2

1 Division, class or activity heading.

Source *Central Statistical Office*

18.3 (continued) Producer price index numbers of products manufactured in the United Kingdom (home sales)

United Kingdom

Annual averages

1985 = 100

	1980 SIC[1]	1985	1986	1987	1988
Food, drink and tobacco manufacturing industries	41/42				
Margarine and compound cooking fats	4115	100.0	90.7	87.6	91.6
Processing organic oils and fats (other than crude animal fat production)	4116	100.0	60.6	57.8	66.5
Slaughterhouses	4121	100.0	101.0	101.7	109.7
Bacon curing and meat processing	4122	100.0	101.1	101.2	104.8
Poultry slaughter and processing	4123	100.0	101.6	102.4	102.8
Animal by-product processing	4126	100.0	84.7	95.8	91.8
Preparation of milk and milk products	4130	100.0	101.6	105.3	110.8
Processing of fruit and vegetables	4147	100.0	104.8	111.0	110.2
Fish processing	4150	100.0	105.5	109.6	111.0
Grain milling	4160	100.0	109.3	109.8	114.4
Starch	4180	100.0	101.1	100.0	98.6
Bread and flour confectionery	4196	100.0	106.8	111.3	118.2
Biscuits and crispbread	4197	100.0	103.6	106.7	112.2
Sugar and sugar by-products	4200	100.0	100.9	106.2	111.5
Ice cream	4213	100.0	104.3	111.8	112.7
Cocoa, chocolate and sugar confectionery	4214	100.0	103.8	106.3	106.7
Compound animal feeds	4221	100.0	100.3	100.3	106.1
Pet foods and non-compound animal feeds	4222	100.0	101.5	101.9	102.4
Miscellaneous foods	4239	100.0	103.7	106.0	108.5
Wines, cider and perry	4261	100.0	105.6	110.0	116.3
Brewing and malting	4270				
Beer		100.0	105.0	108.6	113.7
Soft drinks	4283	100.0	105.3	109.4	116.1
Tobacco industries	4290	100.0	110.4	113.8	117.4
Cigarettes		100.0	110.7	114.0	117.6
Standard cigarettes—sold duty paid		100.0	110.3	113.8	117.9
Tipped cigarettes—sold duty paid		100.0	110.7	114.0	117.6
Manufactured tobacco not elsewhere specified—sold duty paid		100.0	108.2	111.2	114.1
Textile industry	**43**				
Woollen and worsted industry	4310	100.0	101.1	107.3	117.7
Yarns of all wool spun on the woollen system		100.0	100.6	107.1	118.5
Worsted yarns, wholly or predominantly of wool, spun on the worsted and semi-worsted systems		100.0	101.1	109.3	121.0
All wool		100.0	100.4	109.9	124.7
Worsted yarns of man-made fibres, spun on the worsted and semi-worsted systems		100.0	104.8	108.5	112.5
Wholly of man-made fibres		100.0	104.4	107.2	110.3
Weaving		100.0	104.4	109.1	121.0
Woven woollen fabrics (excl. blankets)		100.0	105.0	108.7	119.5
Apparel cloths containing 50 per cent or more by weight of wool or fine animal hair		100.0	104.5	108.4	118.1
Woven worsted fabrics containing 50% or more by weights of wool or fine animal hair		100.0	103.9	109.8	123.5
Spinning and doubling on the cotton system	4321	100.0	98.2	107.8	106.2
Spinning		100.0	97.9	110.8	103.9
Single yarns of mm staple fibre nes		100.0	102.2	106.5	108.5
Finished thread for sewing, embroidery, etc., doubling and winding		100.0	106.9	112.2	122.5
For industrial uses, of man-made fibre		100.0	105.1	110.6	118.1
Man-made continuous filament yarns, textured, bulked or crimped					
Of synthetic fibres	4336	100.0	106.1	108.1	110.5
Jute and polypropylene yarns and fabrics	4350	100.0	94.1	94.7	98.3
Woven cloth of polypropylene		100.0	98.3	97.8	100.9
Hosiery and other weft knitted goods and fabrics	4363				
Hosiery including tights and panti-hose		100.0	107.5	112.8	118.9
Tights and panti-hose		100.0	107.7	113.6	120.7
Underwear, nightwear and swimwear		100.0	105.6	108.2	117.0
Men's knitted underwear		100.0	107.8	109.9	117.1
Women's knitted underwear of cotton		100.0	102.1	104.2	113.7
Men's fully fashioned outerwear of wool		100.0	109.6	113.1	122.7
Pile carpets, carpeting and rugs	4384	100.0	105.5	112.2	119.0
Woven carpets, carpeting and carpet type rugs		100.0	106.0	112.6	119.4
Containing 50 per cent or more of wool yarn		100.0	106.1	112.5	119.0
Figured and plain Brussels and Wilton		100.0	106.7	113.0	117.0
Spool and gripper Axminster		100.0	105.8	112.2	120.0
Tufted carpets, carpeting and carpet type rugs containing 50 per cent or more by weight of acrylic and polyamide fibres		100.0	105.5	113.5	119.8
Containing more than 50% by weight of wool		100.0	106.3	110.4	117.4
Rope, twine and net	4396	100.0	103.6	106.8	116.2
Twines, cords, ropes, cables and lines of textile materials other than agricultural twine		100.0	104.1	109.7	116.8

1 Division, class or activity heading.

Source *Central Statistical Office*

18.3 Producer price index numbers of products manufactured in the United Kingdom (home sales)

(continued)

United Kingdom

Annual averages

1985=100

	1980 SIC[1]	1985	1986	1987	1988
Textile industry *(continued)*					
Narrow fabrics	4398				
Non-elastic and non-elastomeric goods not exceeding 30 cms in width –					
Petersham, galloons and ribbons		100.0	104.5	108.8	113.2
Miscellaneous textiles nes	4399	100.0	102.8	108.3	112.6
Felt (and bonded fibre fabrics)		100.0	102.8	108.3	112.6
Leather and leather goods	**44**				
Leather (tanning and dressing) and fellmongery	4410				
Fellmongery		100.0	89.0	114.9	110.9
Footwear and clothing industries	**45**				
Footwear	4510	100.0	106.3	110.4	115.4
Outdoor footwear		100.0	106.0	110.2	115.5
With uppers wholly or mainly of leather					
Men's		100.0	105.6	110.3	115.8
Women's		100.0	106.4	109.9	116.1
With uppers wholly or mainly of plastics including poromeric –					
other than sandals or sandalised shoes					
Women's		100.0	104.6	109.1	112.9
Weatherproof outerwear	4531				
Raincoats (excluding infants)		100.0	108.8	119.2	..
Raincoats other than of plastic materials		100.0	108.8	119.2	..
Men's and boy's tailored outerwear	4532				
Men's trousers (sold separately)		100.0	104.2	106.4	109.0
Work clothing and men's and boys' jeans	4534				
Cotton boilersuits, men's and boys'		100.0	99.5	102.1	108.2
Men's and boys' shirts, underwear and nightwear	4535				
Shirts (other than industrial shirts)		100.0	104.2	108.6	114.6
Woven		100.0	104.2	108.6	114.6
Gloves	4538	100.0	107.4	112.3	119.4
Fabric gloves, mittens and mitts (fabric content exceeding 50 per cent value)		100.0	106.4	113.4	120.2
Dresswear – other than children's		100.0	108.9	112.9	118.6
Household textiles	4557	100.0	102.8	103.5	104.7
Sheets		100.0	102.3	108.8	117.5
Bedspreads other than tufted		100.0	107.9	109.8	..
Tea towels, cleaning and polishing cloths, etc.		100.0	102.7	104.7	104.2
Tea towels		100.0	103.7	106.9	109.4
Hand and bath towels of cotton, terry		100.0	99.8	101.8	107.2
Timber and wooden furniture industries	**46**				
Sawmilling, planing, etc. of wood	4610				
Sawnwood planed wood – homegrown oak		100.0	105.6	111.8	116.6
Builders' carpentry and joinery	4630	100.0	103.6	109.8	112.7
Builders' woodwork and prefabricated building structures		100.0	103.6	109.7	112.5
Doorsets, leaves and frames and window frames		100.0	103.7	109.7	112.7
Doorsets, leaves and frames		100.0	103.4	110.0	112.6
Door leaves flush		100.0	103.7	110.9	114.4
Window frames		100.0	104.0	109.3	112.8
Other wooden articles (except furniture)	4650				
Domestic woodware		100.0	107.4	100.1	106.3
Wooden and upholstered furniture	4671				
Upholstered furniture		100.0	106.0	111.4	118.3
Lounge suites and settees, fireside, easy and reclining chairs		100.0	105.9	111.1	117.9
With frames of wood		100.0	105.9	111.1	117.9
Desks and desking		100.0	104.3	110.0	..
Fully finished interior spring matresses – 120 cm in width or over		100.0	104.3	109.2	..
Paper and paper products: printing and publishing	**47**				
Pulp, paper and board	4710	100.0	100.8	106.5	112.5
Writing and printing papers other than newsprint		100.0	101.0	109.9	115.9
Wrapping and packaging papers		100.0	100.2	101.1	105.8
Flutings and liners for corrugated board		100.0	100.3	99.4	103.2
Industrial and special purpose papers		100.0	100.2	106.9	112.4

1 Division, class or activity heading.

Source *Central Statistical Office*

18.3 (*continued*) Producer price index numbers of products manufactured in the United Kingdom (home sales)

United Kingdom

Annual averages

1985=100

	1985 SIC[1]	1985	1986	1987	1988
Household and personal hygiene products of paper	4722	100.0	104.2	113.0	117.2
Toilet paper		100.0	103.8	113.8	117.9
Sanitary towels and tampons		100.0	106.6	112.7	119.1
Stationery	4723	100.0	103.6	110.5	116.4
Commercial envelopes		100.0	107.4	114.2	120.2
Stationery and scholastic books and ruled paper		100.0	108.4	120.1	126.7
Loose-leaf supplies		100.0	104.6	107.9	115.8
Filing supplies		100.0	107.7	113.4	119.4
Packaging products of paper and pulp	4724				
Paper sacks		100.0	98.2	104.7	103.9
Packaging products of board	4725	100.0	103.1	107.3	111.4
Fibre-board packing cases		100.0	103.2	107.0	111.8
Printing and publishing of newspapers	4751				
Sales of newspapers by printer/publisher		100.0	102.5	107.8	114.2
National morning		100.0	101.3	107.3	114.0
National Sunday		100.0	103.3	108.1	119.7
Regional morning, evening and Sunday		100.0	103.7	108.3	111.9
Printing and publishing other than of newspapers, periodicals and books	4754				
Atlases, maps, charts and globes		100.0	108.0	120.5	127.4
Processing of rubber and plastics	**48**				
Rubber tyres and inner tubes	4811				
New tyre covers		100.0	105.3	108.1	113.1
Commercial vehicles		100.0	104.6	107.4	111.9
Other rubber products	4812	100.0	106.0	108.6	..
Rubber and plastic hose and tubing		100.0	106.8	111.8	116.3
Rubber or plastics belting		100.0	105.1	107.9	103.1
Rubber products nes including reclaimed rubber		100.0	106.0	108.1	..
Moulded, bonded, extruded, handbuilt, dipped and cast products nes		100.0	107.4	108.2	..
Footwear components		100.0	104.0	108.7	113.5
Rubber linings and rubber flooring		100.0	106.2	112.7	118.9
Rubber floorings		100.0	106.2	112.7	118.9
Plastics – semi manufactures	4832	100.0	105.0	111.7	116.2
Plastics floorcoverings	4833	100.0	104.0	107.6	111.9
Linoleum or plastic (excluding plastic floor covering on a textile base) but including printed felt base		100.0	104.0	107.6	111.9
Plastics building products	4834	100.0	103.8	110.3	116.5
Pipes and fittings		100.0	104.9	112.9	121.0
Soil waste pipes and fittings		100.0	105.7	116.9	129.9
Rainwater pipes and fittings		100.0	102.7	111.8	120.8
Sanitary ware		100.0	104.6	112.6	115.6
Plastics packaging products	4835				
Pots and jars		100.0	101.8	103.0	104.8
Plastics products nes	4836				
Haberdashery (including slide and zip fasteners)		100.0	102.6	107.5	111.3
Other manufacturing industries	**49**				
Photographic and cinematographic processing laboratories	4930				
Development and printing of cinematographic film		100.0	107.6	116.8	129.5
Colour 16 mm		100.0	106.9	116.2	127.5
Toys and games	4941	100.0	105.2	111.2	118.3
Toys, wholly or mainly of metal, excluding wheeled toys and construction models		100.0	104.1	110.6	..
Other plastic toys		100.0	107.4	114.3	..
Sports goods	4942	100.0	101.8	106.5	112.7
Miscellaneous stationers goods	4954	100.0	105.8	113.8	..
Pens and pencils		100.0	106.6	113.0	122.0
Fountain pens, stylographic pens, markers and refills		100.0	108.1	113.5	120.5
Pencils including coloured pencils		100.0	108.2	110.2	116.1

1 Division, class or activity heading.

Source Central Statistical Office

18.4 Producer price index numbers of commodities wholly or mainly imported into the United Kingdom

United Kingdom
Annual averages

1985 = 100

	1985	1986	1987	1988
Hides, skins and fur skins, raw				
Hides[1]	100.0	93.9	103.0	107.9
Wet[1]	100.0	94.7	104.0	108.7
Dry[1]	100.0	82.5	88.5	95.7
Calf skins[1]	100.0	79.2	71.6	72.1
Oilseeds and oleaginous fruit				
Soya beans, US, cif UK[1]	100.0	65.8	49.6	57.2
Copra, Philippine/Indonesian cif N. Europe[1]	100.0	43.0	58.9	70.8
Palm nuts and palm kernels, West African, cif Europe[1]	100.0	41.4	47.2	63.4
Linseed, Canadian No. 1, cif. Rotterdam[1]	100.0	64.4	48.1	52.2
Crude rubber				
Natural rubber (other than latex)[1]	100.0	93.2	102.3	113.0
Wood and cork				
Wood sawn lengthwise	100.0	97.1	105.0	107.9
Softwood (delivered to consumers)	100.0	96.7	105.4	110.2
Hardwood (ex yard or wharf)	100.0	98.6	103.6	99.7
Mahogany	100.0	101.8	114.8	105.1
Meranti	100.0	92.8	100.7	91.6
Lauan	100.0	102.8	100.8	91.8
Oak	100.0	94.2	96.6	101.4
Beech	100.0	104.0	107.9	111.5
Pulp and waste paper				
Woodpulp	100.0	95.8	113.8	120.0
Soda or Sulphate chemical wood pulp	100.0	96.9	120.2	128.6
Textile fibres and their wastes	100.0	91.6	97.8	105.6
Raw cotton[1]	100.0	69.5	96.6	75.6
Raw jute[1]	100.0	45.3	49.9	47.6
Vegetable textile fibres	100.0	82.8	84.9	82.0
Wool and other animal hair	100.0	97.4	105.2	122.1
Crude fertilisers and crude minerals	100.0	94.7	89.7	86.5
Clay[1]	100.0	99.2	95.0	95.0
Asbestos, Canadian, fob. Quebec[1]	100.0	86.0	80.8	80.0
Quartz, mica, felspar, etc[1]	100.0	100.0	100.0	120.2
Mineral substances not elsewhere specified[1]	100.0	106.5	107.6	107.6
Metalliferous ores				
Aluminium ores and concentrates (including alumina)	100.0	104.0	104.5	98.7
Manganese ore, 48 – 50% Mn grade max. 0.1% P, cif. Europe[1]	100.0	87.1	73.0	85.9
Ores and concentrates of other non-ferrous base metals	100.0	105.9	113.8	119.2
Chromium ores and concentrates[1]	100.0	73.8	66.2	70.6
Tungsten ore, min. 65%, cif. Europe[1]	100.0	61.0	56.2	59.2
Titanium ore[1]	100.0	110.2	119.9	125.5
Crude animal and vegetable materials not elsewhere specified				
Gum arabic[1]	100.0	104.1	98.6	77.2
Petroleum, petroleum products and related materials				
Crude oil[2]	100.0	48.0	52.0	40.4
Naphtha	100.0	46.7	52.3	42.3
Fixed vegetable oils and fats	100.0	49.3	50.0	60.4
Fixed vegetable oils 'soft' crude, refined or purified	100.0	52.1	44.7	55.7
Soyabean oil, Dutch, ex-mill, fob[1]	100.0	51.0	44.4	56.9
Groundnut oil, any origin ⅔% ffa, cif Rotterdam[1]	100.0	58.7	45.3	49.1
Sunflower seed oil, any origin ex-tk Rotterdam[1]	100.0	52.6	45.2	55.1
Other fixed vegetable oils fluid or solid, crude, refined or purified[1]	100.0	46.5	55.6	65.4
Palm oil, crude, cif Liverpool[1]	100.0	45.9	54.8	63.6
Coconut oil, Philippine, cif. Europe[1]	100.0	41.4	54.4	63.9
Palm kernel oil, Malaysian, cif. Rotterdam[1]	100.0	43.8	57.6	67.3
Organic chemicals	100.0	95.1	100.9	101.4
Carboxylic acids and their halogenated, sulphonated, nitrated or nitrosated derivatives	100.0	96.5	95.8	97.7
Monocarboxylic acids and derivatives	100.0	93.7	86.3	88.2
Amine-function compounds	100.0	106.1	102.8	95.5
Heterocyclic compounds and nucleic acids	100.0	99.3	104.1	101.5

1 Source of information: trade publications.

2 Includes imported oil and North Sea oil; the imported oil component is based on unit value of imports at their time of entry.

Source *Central Statistical Office*

18.4 (*continued*) Producer price index numbers of commodities wholly or mainly imported into the United Kingdom

United Kingdom
Annual averages

1985 = 100

	1985	1986	1987	1988
Inorganic chemicals				
Mercury, min. 99.99%, cif Europe[1]	100.0	58.5	67.5	75.9
Other inorganic bases and metallic ores, hydroxides and peroxides	100.0	99.6	99.6	106.3
Metallic salts and peroxysalts of inorganic acids	100.0	100.6	103.7	106.3
Inorganic chemical products not elsewhere specified	100.0	106.4	101.0	103.2
Dyeing, tanning and colouring materials	100.0	111.6	131.3	150.9
Essential oils and perfume materials; toilet, polishing and cleansing preparations				
Essential oils, terpenic by-products[1]	100.0	78.8	91.1	110.1
Mint oil[1]	100.0	51.6	48.6	76.9
Other essential oils[1]	100.0	84.3	101.0	119.6
Artificial resins and plastic materials, and cellulose esters and ethers				
Polymerisation and copolymerisation products	100.0	96.3	106.7	117.8
Polyethylene in primary forms	100.0	84.8	95.6	121.1
Polypropylene in primary forms	100.0	91.6	106.0	112.4
Polyvinyl choride	100.0	107.9	120.1	128.0
Chemical materials and products, not elsewhere specified				
Chemical products and preparations not elsewhere specified	100.0	113.5	126.7	122.9
Cork and wood manufactures (excluding furniture)				
Plywood and blockboard (delivered to consumers)	100.0	97.6	103.1	109.3
Paper, paperboard, and articles of paper pulp, of paper or of paperboard				
Paper and paperboard	100.0	103.6	112.4	116.9
Non-ferrous metals				
Silver, gold and platinum and other metals of the platinum group[1]	100.0	91.1	100.4	88.1
Silver, refined and partly refined[1]	100.0	78.1	89.6	77.1
Platinum and platinum alloys (unwrought)[1]	100.0	140.1	150.4	131.6
Other metals of platinum group and alloys thereof (unwrought)[1]	100.0	95.2	89.6	77.5
Gold, refined and partly refined[1]	100.0	101.6	110.4	99.5
Copper, LME settlement price[1]	100.0	84.8	97.4	131.9
Unwrought nickel, free market price[1]	100.0	69.8	76.2	195.4
Lead, LME settlement price[1]	100.0	91.1	119.5	120.9
Zinc, producers' price[1]	100.0	81.5	76.6	100.2
Zinc, LME settlement price[1]	100.0	85.7	81.3	116.2
Tin, free market price[1]	100.0	59.8	58.6	56.5
Magnesium[1]	100.0	100.6	100.6	100.6

1 Source of information: trade publications.

Source Central Statistical Office

18.5 Internal purchasing power of the pound[1] (based on RPI)

pence

	Year in which purchasing power was 100p																	
	1971	1972	1973	1974	1975	1976	1977	1978	1979	1980	1981	1982	1983	1984	1985	1986	1987	1988
1970	109	117	128	148	184	215	249	270	306	361	404	438	458	481	511	528	550	577
1971	100	107	117	136	168	196	228	246	279	330	369	400	419	440	467	482	503	527
1972	93	100	109	127	157	183	212	230	261	308	344	374	391	411	435	450	469	492
1973	86	92	100	116	144	168	195	211	239	282	316	343	358	376	399	413	430	451
1974	74	79	86	100	124	145	168	182	206	243	272	295	309	324	344	356	371	389
1975	59	64	69	80	100	117	135	146	166	196	219	238	249	261	277	286	298	313
1976	51	55	60	69	86	100	116	125	142	168	188	204	213	224	238	246	256	268
1977	44	47	51	60	74	86	100	108	123	145	162	176	184	193	205	212	221	232
1978	41	43	47	55	68	80	92	100	113	134	150	163	170	178	189	196	204	214
1979	36	38	42	49	60	70	81	88	100	118	132	143	150	157	167	173	180	189
1980	30	32	35	41	51	60	69	75	85	100	112	122	127	133	142	146	152	160
1981	27	29	32	37	46	53	62	67	76	89	100	109	114	119	127	131	136	143
1982	25	27	29	34	42	49	57	62	70	82	92	100	105	110	116	120	125	132
1983	24	26	28	32	40	47	54	59	67	79	88	96	100	105	111	115	120	126
1984	23	24	27	31	38	45	52	56	64	75	84	91	95	100	106	110	114	120
1985	21	23	25	29	36	42	49	53	60	71	79	86	90	94	100	103	108	113
1986	21	22	24	28	35	41	47	51	58	68	76	83	87	91	97	100	104	109
1987	20	21	23	27	34	39	45	49	56	66	74	80	84	88	93	96	100	105
1988	19	20	22	26	32	37	43	47	53	63	70	76	79	83	88	92	95	100

Note To find the purchasing power of the pound in 1980, given that it was 100 pence in 1970, select the column headed 1970 and look at the 1980 row. The result is 28 pence.

1 These figures are calculated by taking the inverse ratio of the respective annual averages of the General Index of Retail Prices. See table 18.6.

Source Central Statistical Office

18.6 Index of retail prices

Indices for main groups[1]

	All items	Food	Alcoholic drink	Tobacco	Housing	Fuel and light	Durable household goods	Clothing and footwear	Transport and vehicles	Miscellaneous goods	Services	Meals bought and consumed outside the home
15 January 1974 = 100												
Weights												
1974	*1 000*	*253*	*70*	*43*	*124*	*52*	*64*	*91*	*135*	*63*	*54*	*51*
1975	*1 000*	*232*	*82*	*46*	*108*	*53*	*70*	*89*	*149*	*71*	*52*	*48*
1976	*1 000*	*228*	*81*	*46*	*112*	*56*	*75*	*84*	*140*	*74*	*57*	*47*
1977	*1 000*	*247*	*83*	*46*	*112*	*58*	*63*	*82*	*139*	*71*	*54*	*45*
1978	*1 000*	*233*	*85*	*48*	*113*	*60*	*64*	*80*	*140*	*70*	*56*	*51*
1979	*1 000*	*232*	*77*	*44*	*120*	*59*	*64*	*82*	*143*	*69*	*59*	*51*
1980	*1 000*	*214*	*82*	*40*	*124*	*59*	*69*	*84*	*151*	*74*	*62*	*41*
1981	*1 000*	*207*	*79*	*36*	*135*	*62*	*65*	*81*	*152*	*75*	*66*	*42*
1982	*1 000*	*206*	*77*	*41*	*144*	*62*	*64*	*77*	*154*	*72*	*65*	*38*
1983	*1 000*	*203*	*78*	*39*	*137*	*69*	*64*	*74*	*159*	*75*	*63*	*39*
1984	*1 000*	*201*	*75*	*36*	*149*	*65*	*69*	*70*	*158*	*76*	*65*	*36*
1985	*1 000*	*190*	*75*	*37*	*153*	*65*	*65*	*75*	*156*	*77*	*62*	*45*
1986	*1 000*	*185*	*82*	*40*	*153*	*62*	*63*	*75*	*157*	*81*	*58*	*44*
Annual averages												
1974	108.5	106.1	109.7	115.9	105.8	110.7	107.9	109.4	111.0	111.2	106.8	108.2
1975	134.8	133.3	135.2	147.7	125.5	147.4	131.2	125.7	143.9	138.6	135.5	132.4
1976	157.1	159.9	159.3	171.3	143.2	182.4	144.2	139.4	166.0	161.3	159.5	157.3
1977	182.0	190.3	183.4	209.7	161.8	211.3	166.8	157.4	190.3	188.3	173.3	185.7
1978	197.1	203.8	196.0	226.2	173.4	227.5	182.1	171.0	207.2	206.7	192.0	207.8
1979	223.5	228.3	217.1	247.6	208.9	250.5	201.9	187.2	243.1	236.4	213.9	239.9
1980	263.7	255.9	261.8	290.1	269.5	313.2	226.3	205.4	288.7	276.9	262.7	290.0
1981	295.0	277.5	306.1	358.2	318.2	380.0	237.2	208.3	322.6	300.7	300.8	318.0
1982	320.4	299.3	341.4	413.3	358.3	433.3	243.8	210.5	343.5	325.8	331.6	341.7
1983	335.1	308.8	366.5	440.9	367.1	465.4	250.4	214.8	366.3	345.6	342.9	364.0
1984	351.8	326.1	387.7	489.0	400.7	478.8	256.7	214.6	374.7	364.7	357.3	390.8
1985	373.2	336.3	412.1	532.5	452.3	499.3	263.9	222.9	392.5	392.2	381.3	413.3
1986	385.9	347.3	430.6	584.9	478.1	506.0	266.7	229.2	390.1	409.2	400.5	439.5
1987 Jan 13	394.5	354.0	440.7	602.9	502.4	506.1	265.6	230.8	399.7	413.0	408.8	454.8

13 January 1987 = 100

	All items	Food	Catering	Alcoholic drink	Tobacco	Housing	Fuel and light	Household goods*	Household services*	Clothing and footwear	Personal goods & services*	Motoring expenditure	Fares and other travel*	Leisure goods*	Leisure services*
Weights															
1987	*1 000*	*167*	*46*	*76*	*38*	*157*	*61*	*73*	*44*	*74*	*38*	*127*	*22*	*47*	*30*
1988	*1 000*	*163*	*50*	*78*	*36*	*160*	*55*	*74*	*41*	*72*	*37*	*132*	*23*	*50*	*29*
Annual Averages															
1987	101.9	101.1	102.8	101.7	100.1	103.3	99.1	102.1	101.9	101.1	101.9	103.4	101.5	101.6	101.6
1988	106.9	104.6	109.6	106.9	103.4	112.5	101.6	105.9	106.8	104.4	106.8	108.1	107.5	104.2	108.1
1988 March 15	104.1	103.9	107.5	104.6	101.6	104.7	97.8	104.5	105.4	102.9	105.1	105.6	105.6	103.3	103.8
June 14	106.6	104.8	109.5	106.8	103.6	109.8	102.4	105.6	106.2	105.3	106.6	108.2	106.9	104.2	108.4
September 13	108.4	104.8	111.1	108.4	103.7	116.5	103.6	107.2	107.8	104.8	107.8	109.7	108.8	104.5	110.6
December 13	110.3	106.5	112.4	108.9	105.2	122.5	104.1	107.9	108.8	107.9	109.1	109.8	109.6	105.0	111.7

See note on page 309.

1 Following the recommendations of the Retail Price Index Advisory Committee the Index has been re-referenced to Jan 13 1987 = 100. The published groups (marked *) were restructured and these have no direct counterparts in the series.

Source Central Statistical Office

18.7 Tax and price index

	January 1978=100											January 1987=100		
	1977	1978	1979	1980	1981	1982	1983	1984	1985	1986	1987	1987	1988	1989
January	95.3	100.0	106.1	123.2	140.4	162.3	170.7	177.9	184.7	192.9	198.0	100.0	101.4	107.1
February	96.4	100.7	107.2	125.3	141.9	162.4	171.6	178.8	186.4	193.7	..	100.5	101.8	108.0
March	97.5	101.5	108.2	127.2	144.3	164.0	171.9	179.4	188.4	194.0	..	100.7	102.3	108.5
April	96.4	98.4	110.5	130.8	151.3	166.0	171.8	178.8	190.2	192.5	..	99.7	101.4	109.8
May	97.3	99.1	111.6	132.2	152.4	167.4	172.6	179.6	191.2	192.9	..	99.8	101.9	110.5
June	98.5	100.0	113.8	133.6	153.5	168.0	173.1	180.1	191.7	192.8	..	99.8	102.3	110.9
July	98.6	100.5	113.8	134.9	154.2	169.0	174.2	179.9	191.3	192.1	..	99.7	102.4	
August	99.2	101.3	114.9	135.3	155.5	169.0	175.1	181.8	191.8	192.9	..	100.0	103.7	
September	99.9	101.8	116.2	136.3	156.6	168.9	176.0	182.2	191.7	194.0	..	100.4	104.3	
October	100.4	102.4	117.6	137.3	158.2	169.9	176.7	183.5	191.4	194.3	..	100.9	105.4	
November	98.7	103.2	118.8	138.5	160.1	170.9	177.5	184.1	192.1	196.3	..	101.5	106.0	
December	99.3	104.3	119.8	139.4	161.2	170.5	178.0	183.9	192.4	197.1	..	101.4	106.3	
Percentage changes on one year earlier														
Tax and price index														
January	*+18.5*	*+4.9*	*+6.1*	*+16.1*	*+14.0*	*+15.6*	*+5.2*	*+4.2*	*+3.8*	*+4.4*	*+2.6*	..	*+1.4*	*+5.6*
February	*+18.1*	*+4.5*	*+6.5*	*+16.9*	*+13.2*	*+14.4*	*+5.7*	*+4.2*	*+4.3*	*+3.9*	..	*+2.7*	*+1.3*	*+6.1*
March	*+18.6*	*+4.1*	*+6.6*	*+17.6*	*+13.4*	*+13.7*	*+4.8*	*+4.4*	*+5.0*	*+3.0*	..	*+2.8*	*+1.6*	*+6.1*
April	*+16.3*	*+2.1*	*+12.3*[1]	*+18.4*[1]	*+15.7*	*+9.7*	*+3.5*	*+4.1*	*+6.4*	*+1.2*	..	*+2.5*	*+1.7*	*+8.3*
May	*+15.8*	*+1.8*	*+12.6*[1]	*+18.5*[1]	*+15.3*	*+9.8*	*+3.1*	*+4.1*	*+6.5*	*+0.9*	..	*+2.4*	*+2.1*	*+8.4*
June	*+16.6*	*+1.5*	*+13.8*[1]	*+17.4*[1]	*+14.9*	*+9.4*	*+3.0*	*+4.0*	*+6.4*	*+0.6*	..	*+2.5*	*+2.5*	*+8.4*
July	*+16.4*	*+1.9*	*+13.2*	*+18.5*	*+14.3*	*+9.6*	*+3.1*	*+3.3*	*+6.3*	*+0.4*	..	*+2.8*	*+2.7*	
August	*+15.2*	*+2.1*	*+13.4*	*+17.8*	*+14.9*	*+8.7*	*+3.6*	*+3.8*	*+5.5*	*+0.6*	..	*+2.6*	*+3.7*	
September	*+14.2*	*+1.9*	*+14.1*	*+17.3*	*+14.9*	*+7.9*	*+4.2*	*+3.5*	*+5.2*	*+1.2*	..	*+2.4*	*+3.9*	
October	*+12.3*	*+2.0*	*+14.8*	*+16.8*	*+15.2*	*+7.4*	*+4.0*	*+3.8*	*+4.3*	*+1.5*	..	*+2.9*	*+4.5*	
November	*+8.6*	*+4.6*	*+15.1*	*+16.6*	*+15.6*	*+6.7*	*+3.9*	*+3.7*	*+4.3*	*+2.2*	..	*+2.4*	*+4.4*	
December	*+7.5*	*+5.0*	*+14.9*	*+16.4*	*+15.6*	*+5.8*	*+4.4*	*+3.3*	*+4.6*	*+2.4*	..	*+1.9*	*+4.8*	
Retail prices index														
January	*+16.6*	*+9.9*	*+9.3*	*+18.4*	*+13.0*	*+12.0*	*+4.9*	*+5.1*	*+5.0*	*+5.5*	*+3.9*	..	*+3.3*	*+7.5*
February	*+16.2*	*+9.5*	*+9.6*	*+19.1*	*+12.5*	*+11.0*	*+5.3*	*+5.1*	*+5.4*	*+5.1*	..	*+3.9*	*+3.3*	*+7.8*
March	*+16.7*	*+9.1*	*+9.8*	*+19.8*	*+12.6*	*+10.4*	*+4.6*	*+5.2*	*+6.1*	*+4.2*	..	*+4.0*	*+3.5*	*+7.9*
April	*+17.5*	*+7.9*	*+10.1*	*+21.8*	*+12.0*	*+9.4*	*+4.0*	*+5.2*	*+6.9*	*+3.0*	..	*+4.2*	*+3.9*	*+8.0*
May	*+17.1*	*+7.7*	*+10.3*	*+21.9*	*+11.7*	*+9.5*	*+3.7*	*+5.1*	*+7.0*	*+2.8*	..	*+4.1*	*+4.2*	*+8.3*
June	*+17.7*	*+7.4*	*+11.4*	*+21.0*	*+11.3*	*+9.2*	*+3.7*	*+5.1*	*+7.0*	*+2.5*	..	*+4.2*	*+4.6*	*+8.3*
July	*+17.6*	*+7.8*	*+15.6*	*+16.9*	*+10.9*	*+8.7*	*+4.2*	*+4.5*	*+6.9*	*+2.4*	..	*+4.4*	*+4.8*	
August	*+16.5*	*+8.0*	*+15.8*	*+16.3*	*+11.5*	*+8.0*	*+4.6*	*+5.0*	*+6.2*	*+2.4*	..	*+4.4*	*+5.7*	
September	*+15.6*	*+7.8*	*+16.5*	*+15.9*	*+11.4*	*+7.3*	*+5.1*	*+4.7*	*+5.9*	*+3.0*	..	*+4.2*	*+5.9*	
October	*+14.1*	*+7.8*	*+17.2*	*+15.4*	*+11.7*	*+6.8*	*+5.0*	*+5.0*	*+5.4*	*+3.0*	..	*+4.5*	*+6.4*	
November	*+13.0*	*+8.1*	*+17.4*	*+15.3*	*+12.0*	*+6.3*	*+4.8*	*+4.9*	*+5.5*	*+3.5*	..	*+4.1*	*+6.4*	
December	*+12.1*	*+8.4*	*+17.2*	*+15.1*	*+12.0*	*+5.4*	*+5.3*	*+4.6*	*+5.7*	*+3.7*	..	*+3.7*	*+6.8*	

1 These figures are affected by the late timing of the 1979 Budget; the changes introduced by that Budget are included in the Tax and price index from July 1979.

Source *Central Statistical Office*

18.8 Index of purchase prices of the means of agricultural production

United Kingdom

Annual averages

1985 = 100

	Weights	1979	1980	1981	1982	1983	1984	1985	1986	1987	1988
Goods and services currently consumed	*100*	67.40	75.47	83.02	88.91	95.09	98.72	100.00	98.30	98.80	103.20
Seeds	*3.9*	96.20	100.10	101.10	108.71	116.62	122.22	100.00	92.50	100.60	100.70
Animals for rearing and production	*1.1*	61.00	53.94	70.60	78.48	92.07	101.35	100.00	98.80	102.60	111.90
Energy, lubricants	*9.6*	45.19	59.07	71.29	81.22	89.31	91.55	100.00	79.40	77.70	78.70
Fuels for heating	*1.6*	40.70	53.91	65.66	75.80	86.36	92.24	100.00	65.00	63.10	54.50
Motor fuel	*5.5*	40.77	54.29	66.02	76.87	86.21	88.76	100.00	73.70	71.70	65.80
Electricity	*2.1*	60.36	75.08	90.02	97.67	101.43	100.30	100.00	102.60	101.50	106.00
Lubricants	*0.4*	50.99	68.35	75.94	80.25	84.28	90.12	100.00	95.50	95.20	92.50
Fertilisers and soil improvers	*13.8*	66.95	78.31	86.30	90.37	91.46	94.05	100.00	90.40	82.90	85.40
Straight fertilisers	*5.7*	64.59	73.31	81.23	89.59	92.74	95.09	100.00	85.40	77.20	84.20
Compound fertilisers	*7.1*	67.77	80.97	89.31	90.69	89.96	93.04	100.00	91.90	82.90	81.60
Lime	*1.0*	72.79	83.47	88.65	92.65	96.99	97.16	100.00	109.10	115.80	119.50
Plant protection products	*4.8*	71.52	82.78	88.91	92.30	92.96	95.78	100.00	102.60	106.40	110.40
Animal feedingstuffs	*41.0*	76.43	81.57	88.09	92.90	100.90	103.59	100.00	101.20	101.30	106.90
Straight feedingstuffs	*12.3*	77.07	81.30	88.05	91.87	99.84	101.14	100.00	105.10	106.10	109.60
Wheat	*3.3*	77.71	81.63	89.47	93.06	102.04	101.39	100.00	103.40	110.40	106.90
Whole barley	*3.1*	77.61	79.68	84.70	91.16	98.41	100.56	100.00	112.20	114.60	112.20
Flaked maize	*0.1*	72.86	81.50	86.88	93.89	97.80	99.51	100.00	101.20	104.00	100.10
Whole oats	*0.3*	..	..	..	..	..	..	100.00	100.10	119.90	119.70
Oilcake	*2.9*	78.48	80.00	89.04	90.00	98.56	102.40	100.00	100.90	88.90	106.10
White fish meal	*0.5*	76.38	82.58	90.42	88.77	100.25	103.96	100.00	105.70	103.30	126.20
Sugar beet pulp	*2.0*	77.27	87.41	91.23	93.88	100.79	103.23	100.00	103.40	108.60	109.80
Compound feedingstuffs	*28.6*	76.16	81.63	88.08	93.22	101.22	104.41	100.00	99.50	99.20	105.70
for calves	*1.2*	78.10	84.89	89.64	97.62	104.07	104.24	100.00	99.00	100.60	106.30
cattle	*10.1*	79.06	85.47	90.26	95.56	103.93	106.23	100.00	98.80	97.60	101.60
pigs	*6.1*	72.93	79.62	87.42	92.03	99.28	103.34	100.00	99.70	100.00	107.40
poultry	*9.8*	74.40	77.82	85.53	90.74	98.91	102.72	100.00	100.10	99.50	108.80
sheep	*1.3*	82.75	89.37	92.76	97.82	104.38	109.12	100.00	98.80	104.10	105.30
Material and small tools	*3.6*	64.37	75.02	80.12	84.77	88.60	93.85	100.00	103.80	108.60	114.90
Maintenance and repair of plant	*7.2*	56.79	65.88	71.61	78.06	84.52	91.57	100.00	106.10	111.00	117.70
Maintenance and repair of buildings	*4.2*	58.25	69.01	75.64	82.26	87.99	93.58	100.00	105.20	108.20	113.20
Veterinary services	*2.1*	58.75	69.20	80.35	86.64	90.93	95.36	100.00	106.60	106.80	112.30
General expenses	*8.7*	56.93	66.27	76.34	84.10	88.87	94.17	100.00	104.90	109.40	119.50
Goods and services contributing to investment in agriculture	*100*	61.63	71.99	77.83	84.02	88.91	94.60	100.00	106.80	113.90	120.80
Machinery and other equipment	*57.8*	63.53	72.94	78.56	84.54	88.77	94.38	100.00	105.20	110.10	116.10
Machinery and plant for cultivation	*7.8*	69.85	81.70	85.46	88.24	90.52	93.71	100.00	112.10	115.50	123.10
Machinery and plant for harvesting	*13.5*	57.66	70.57	76.76	84.05	91.60	96.97	100.00	103.20	109.30	115.40
Farm machinery and installations	*10.2*	67.28	76.45	82.80	90.98	90.75	94.50	100.00	103.20	108.20	113.30
Tractors	*16.8*	62.17	69.54	74.62	79.14	85.54	93.25	100.00	105.80	108.40	113.60
Other vehicles	*9.4*	64.57	72.46	78.91	83.77	87.46	93.12	100.00	103.80	111.80	118.80
Buildings	*42.2*	58.48	70.37	76.57	83.25	89.16	95.07	100.00	108.90	119.10	127.20
Farm buildings	*22.5*	58.25	69.01	75.64	82.19	87.99	93.58	100.00	104.20	108.70	114.50
Engineering and soil improvement operations	*19.7*	58.78	72.87	78.01	84.91	91.15	97.39	100.00	114.20	181.00	141.70

The movement of Price Indices between 1985 and 1988 differ from those published previously because of the different selection of Indicators and weighting patterns.

Source *Ministry of Agriculture, Fisheries and Food*

18.9 Index of producer prices of agricultural products

United Kingdom
Annual averages

1985 = 100

	Weights	1979	1980	1981	1982	1983	1984	1985	1986	1987	1988
All products	*100*	76.53	80.65	89.44	96.45	101.45	101.61	100.00	102.30	104.10	108.40
All crop products	*37.4*	82.69	82.44	92.66	99.84	113.03	108.82	100.00	106.90	109.30	102.90
Cereals	*19.9*	84.54	86.36	95.25	102.50	113.64	105.01	100.00	101.90	102.00	99.30
Wheat— for breadmaking	*4.4*	..	..	..	..	..	..	100.00	102.30	104.30	98.90
other milling	*0.5*	83.22	85.62	94.09	98.54	109.42	100.17	100.00	100.40	101.40	97.00
for feeding	*7.5*	87.11	89.53	98.57	103.58	114.95	104.39	100.00	101.00	100.00	98.10
Barley— for-feeding	*5.0*	84.70	86.43	93.17	100.69	110.46	105.19	100.00	101.50	98.40	96.70
for malting	*2.3*	82.08	82.58	93.56	106.11	117.92	108.59	100.00	105.50	110.30	108.80
Oats— for milling	*0.1*	91.86	98.04	99.12	102.75	115.78	123.43	100.00	97.70	117.70	111.30
for feeding	*0.1*	87.76	96.34	96.53	100.39	113.01	124.57	100.00	100.00	116.40	108.70
Root crops	*4.9*	107.94	94.52	116.16	132.23	161.25	157.09	100.00	145.00	152.60	121.10
Potatoes—early	*0.3*	123.71	91.91	166.08	128.13	152.57	217.19	100.00	142.50	156.90	129.30
main crop	*2.5*	123.50	100.00	130.70	158.80	213.60	196.80	100.00	184.00	196.20	137.60
Sugar beet	*2.0*	88.21	88.65	93.00	102.75	103.19	103.99	100.00	97.10	97.70	99.30
Fresh vegetables	*6.4*	72.27	70.92	78.16	80.43	94.04	92.62	100.00	93.50	104.60	101.90
Cauliflowers	*0.6*	63.90	66.36	78.57	77.24	86.39	82.22	100.00	65.60	86.60	71.20
Lettuce	*0.6*	82.93	69.40	78.49	76.27	100.49	92.23	100.00	100.40	121.60	105.50
Tomatoes	*0.5*	80.22	102.99	93.82	86.20	106.90	109.58	100.00	101.80	112.80	113.70
Carrots	*0.4*	57.14	62.38	84.03	73.24	89.39	87.27	100.00	84.70	106.50	106.70
Cabbage	*0.6*	78.10	52.91	64.13	84.44	93.23	86.08	100.00	89.40	101.40	105.30
Beans	*0.3*	56.78	70.27	74.56	78.43	100.84	88.97	100.00	96.10	125.50	111.30
Onions	*0.5*	81.85	75.93	82.23	82.16	102.05	112.38	100.00	94.30	121.40	94.30
Mushrooms	*0.9*	85.09	89.85	86.25	94.61	97.30	100.90	100.00	101.70	101.60	112.20
Fresh fruit	*1.9*	63.98	65.62	82.68	87.34	93.37	94.42	100.00	117.50	108.30	114.20
Dessert apples	*0.5*	49.39	63.98	86.95	88.42	90.85	95.77	100.00	110.50	96.30	111.40
Dessert pears	*0.1*	69.58	69.93	83.29	100.07	99.02	97.06	100.00	110.00	100.90	97.10
Cooking apples	*0.3*	57.49	69.69	96.24	93.94	93.59	100.35	100.00	117.70	107.20	130.00
Strawberries	*0.5*	74.07	63.86	72.09	89.46	101.72	94.76	100.00	108.00	100.50	104.60
Raspberries	*0.2*	74.44	57.84	60.50	65.53	82.13	85.95	100.00	161.10	158.50	126.70
Seeds	*1.0*	102.60	108.46	109.54	118.33	118.54	135.36	100.00	109.70	124.30	115.20
Flowers and plants	*1.1*	66.34	69.83	72.42	77.65	82.89	85.68	100.00	99.20	105.50	110.00
Other crop products	*2.2*	73.94	82.99	91.37	97.59	110.87	109.05	100.00	99.70	88.50	79.00
Animals and animal products	*62.6*	73.50	79.81	87.87	94.89	95.85	98.08	100.00	99.60	100.90	103.80
Animals for slaughter	*36.9*	75.60	79.74	88.36	95.61	97.21	100.24	100.00	99.80	100.40	103.40
Calves	*0.2*	..	..	..	..	..	..	100.00	106.70	126.00	160.80
Clean cattle	*13.4*	74.05	77.94	86.28	95.25	100.94	100.94	100.00	99.80	101.50	114.40
Cows & bulls	*3.5*	75.88	82.03	96.06	104.51	99.34	94.34	100.00	93.10	96.30	113.86
Clean pigs	*8.1*	79.19	84.60	91.37	94.33	89.85	104.91	100.00	96.20	95.00	88.70
Sows & boars	*0.3*	69.60	80.65	89.27	102.02	84.92	102.50	100.00	96.70	85.70	82.40
Sheep	*4.9*	63.11	69.74	83.89	94.21	100.70	94.49	100.00	109.30	112.50	101.70
Ewe & ram	*0.4*	62.86	58.21	80.79	89.12	82.01	86.03	100.00	96.80	94.50	105.30
Poultry	*6.1*	81.72	83.47	85.64	93.57	96.58	98.50	100.00	101.10	98.30	93.40
Chickens	*4.5*	82.59	86.21	88.88	95.78	98.79	102.24	100.00	99.50	97.90	93.10
Turkeys	*1.4*	79.56	76.28	77.19	87.95	90.85	88.56	100.00	105.70	98.00	92.60
Cows milk	*21.0*	67.51	76.45	84.25	91.97	94.34	92.97	100.00	103.00	103.80	109.90
Eggs	*4.3*	84.47	95.88	101.92	103.36	92.33	106.52	100.00	81.50	91.40	77.50
Other animals products:	*0.4*	96.26	88.97	88.17	87.9	88.70	92.70	100.00	100.40	99.30	98.90
Wool (Clip)	*0.4*	96.26	88.97	88.17	87.9	88.70	92.70	100.00	100.40	99.30	98.90

The movement of Price Indices between 1985 and 1988 differ from those published previously because of the different selection of Indicators and weighting patterns.

Source Ministry of Agriculture, Fisheries and Food

18.10 Commodity price trends[1]
United Kingdom
Calendar years

		1977	1978	1979	1980	1981	1982	1983	1984	1985	1986	1987	1988
Wheat *£ per tonne*	Average ex-farm price[2]	83.34	85.69	95.92	99.30	108.92	113.74	124.69	114.59	112.25	111.18	111.00	104.83
Barley *£ per tonne*	Average ex-farm price[2]	77.95	78.35	89.60	92.84	100.45	108.65	119.29	112.36	106.05	105.89	105.39	103.43
Oats *£ per tonne*	Average ex-farm price[2]	74.84	73.92	88.90	97.52	97.42	101.22	113.20	123.01	99.19	100.87	114.74	107.01
Rye *£ per tonne*	Average ex-farm price[2]	70.4	76.2	89.0	101.78	100.97	108.43	120.65	117.15	110.53	106.78	110.24	106.13
Hops *£ per tonne*	Average farm-gate price[3]	1 390	1 431	1 578	2 184	2 636	2 740	3 140	3 306	2 297	2 270	2 352	2 428
Potatoes *£ per tonne*	Average farm-gate price[4]	69.9	40.0	58.9	51.2	63.0	78.1	81.9	102.1	48.1	72.8	87.7	66.8[17]
Sugar beet *£ per tonne*	Producer price[5]	21.93	23.72	28.28	27.93	27.74	27.15	31.06	30.71	32.81	29.66	30.31	28.30[17]
Oilseed rape	Average market price[6]	162	182	215	230	255	270	310	275	274	284	221	234
Apples	Average market price[7]												
£ per tonne	Dessert	304	224	193	259	335	301	363	369	369	391	368	424
	Culinary	242	105	171	207	270	279	280	318	299	327	316	385
Pears *£ per tonne*	Average market price[7]	275	260	200	232	281	331	315	314	325	352	326	321
Tomatoes *£ per tonne*	Average market price[7]	411	440	389	504	475	466	632	560	502	601	684	571
Cauliflowers *£ per tonne*	Average market price[7]	143	133	163	186	207	214	243	217	268	203	275	247
Cattle (rearing)	1st quality Hereford/ cross bull calves[8]	65	88	103	100	108	125	124	124	130	133	136	183.5
£ per head	1st quality yearling steers beef/dairy cross[8, 16]	174	213	236	243	275	313	326	330	343	347	358	..
Cattle (fat) *p per kg liveweight*	Clean cattle[9]	56.94	66.26	75.21	76.65	88.72	98.30	95.88	95.87	94.72	94.42	96.05	109.21
Sheep (store) *£ per head*	1st quality lambs, hoggets and tegs[8]	24.0	25.9	26.0	25.9	30.2	33.0	33.4	35.3	36.4	36.7	37.5	41.3
Sheep (fat)[10]		124.5	137.4	139.2	125.7	153.3	152.7[13]	146.5	166.5	167.1	175.3	186.1	172.2
p per kg estimated dressed carcase weight							173.0[14]	180.5	179.3	177.5	200.1	214.6	200.4
Pigs *£ per kg deadweight*	Average market price clean pigs	72.64	80.08	81.35	86.64	93.70	97.09	92.31	108.43	103.89	98.12	97.28	90.49
Broilers *p per kg*	Average wholesale price	76.0	81.1	82.1	91.1	91.6	92.8	99.5	104.2	98.9	99.7	98.1[15]	..
Milk *p per litre*	Average net return to producers[11]	10.18	10.61	11.55	12.77	13.79	14.81	15.02	14.99	15.56	16.07	16.44[15]	17.22
Eggs *p per dozen*	Average producer price[12]	31.2	27.0	32.8	37.4	40.7	38.8	35.5	44.7	40.0	32.6	36.6	31.1[17]
Wool *p per kg*	Average producer price for clip paid to producers by the British Wool Marketing Board	93.2	93.8	97.7	91.3	89.5	89.2	90.0	94.03	100.04	97.71	97.41	96.85

1 This table gives indications of the movement in commodity prices at the first point of sale. The series do not always show total receipts by farmers; for some commodities additional premiums or deficiency payments are made to achieve support price levels.
2 Weighted average ex-farm prices of United Kingdom cereals.
3 Average farm-gate prices paid by English Hops Ltd to growers in England. Hops are not grown elsewhere in the United Kingdom.
4 Weighted average price paid to growers by registered merchants for early and main crop potatoes in the United Kingdom. The 1986 figure is provisional.
5 Average price paid to growers in the United Kingdom by British Sugar plc for sugar beet of average sugar content. The 1986 figure is provisional.
6 Typical contract price adjusted to delivered basis and 42 per cent oil content.
7 Weighted average wholesale prices for England and Wales. From 1982, for England only.
8 Average prices at representative markets in England and Wales.
9 Based on Meat and Livestock Commission all clean cattle prices.
10 UK weighted average market price for animals certified under the Fat Sheep Guarantee Scheme/Sheep Variable Premium Scheme.
11 Derived by dividing total value of output by the total quantity of output available for human consumption.
12 Average price of all Class A eggs weighted according to quantity in each grade.
13 Great Britain weighted average market price for animals certified under the Sheep Variable Premium Scheme from 1982.
14 Northern Ireland unweighted average market price for clean sheep from 1982.
15 Figures forecasted.
16 Due to change in definition, no direct comparisons are available from 1988.
17 Provisional.

Source *Ministry of Agriculture, Fisheries and Food*

Index of sources

This index of sources gives the titles of official publications or other sources containing statistics allied to those in the tables of this *Annual Abstract*. These publications provide more detailed analyses than are shown in the *Abstract*. This index includes publications to which reference should be made for short-term (monthly or quarterly) series. No entry is made in this index for items where the data have been obtained from departmental records.

Subject	Table number in *Abstract*	Government department or other organisation	Official publication or other source
1. Area and climate			
Area	1.1	Ordnance Survey	Central Statistical Office: Regional Trends
Climate	1.2–1.4	Meteorological Office	Monthly Weather Report Central Statistical Office: Monthly Digest of Statistics
2. Population and vital statistics			
Population census	2.1–2.3, 2.5, 2.8	Office of Population Censuses and Surveys	*England and Wales:* Census reports, 1911, 1921, 1931, 1951, 1961, 1971 and 1981 Sample census 1966; Registrar General's statistical review of England and Wales, Part II, Tables Census 1971, Great Britain, Summary tables Census 1981, National Report, Great Britain Part 1 Census 1981, Key statistics for urban areas: Great Britain Welsh Office: Digest of Welsh Statistics (annual)
		General Register Office for Scotland	*Scotland:* Census reports 1951, 1961, 1971 and 1981 Sample census 1966 Census 1971 Census 1981 Key statistics for urban areas: Scotland
		General Register Office (Northern Ireland)	*Northern Ireland:* Census of population 1951, 1961, 1966 and 1971 The Northern Ireland Census 1981. Summary Report
Mid-year estimates	2.1, 2.4, 2.6, 2.9	Office of Population Censuses and Surveys	*England and Wales:* Series FM (Family statistics), DH (Deaths), MB (Morbidity), PP (Population estimates and projections), MN (Migration) and VS (Local authority vital statistics) Population Trends (quarterly) Series PP1, Population estimates: The Registrar General's estimates of the population of regions and local government areas of England and Wales
		General Register Office for Scotland	*Scotland:* Registrar General Scotland Annual Report Quarterly return of births, deaths and marriages Annual estimate of the population of Scotland
		General Register Office (Northern Ireland)	*Northern Ireland:* Annual report of the Registrar General Quarterly return of births, deaths and marriages
Projections	2.7	Government Actuary's Department	Series PP2, Population projections—national figures
Migration	2.10, 2.11	Office of Population Censuses and Surveys	Series MN (Migration) Population Trends (quarterly)
	2.12	Home Office	Control of immigration statistics United Kingdom (annual)
Vital statistics	2.13, 2.14, 2.16–2.22	Office of Population Censuses and Surveys	*England and Wales:* Series FM (Family statistics), DH (Deaths), MB (Morbidity), PP (Population estimates and projections), MN (Migration) and VS (Local authority vital statistics) Population Trends (quarterly)
		General Register Office for Scotland	*Scotland:* Registrar General Scotland, Annual Report Quarterly return of births, deaths and marriages
		General Register Office (Northern Ireland)	*Northern Ireland:* Annual report of the Registrar General Quarterly return of births, deaths and marriages
	2.15	Lord Chancellor's Department	Judicial statistics, England and Wales (annual)
		Scottish Courts Administration	Judicial statistics, Scotland; Civil judicial statistics (annual)
	2.23	Office of Population Censuses and Surveys; General Register Office for Scotland; General Register Office (Northern Ireland) and Government Actuary's Department	*England and Wales:* Registrar General's Decennial Supplement, England and Wales, 1981–83, Interim Life Table *Scotland:* Life Table: 1982–84, Registrar General Scotland, Annual Report, Supplement *Northern Ireland:* Interim Life Table 1981–83

Subject	Table number in *Abstract*	Government department or other organisation	Official publication or other source
3. Social conditions			
Social services	3.1–3.6	Central Statistical Office	Civil Appropriation Accounts (annual) Northern Ireland Annual Abstract of Statistics
	3.7, 3.8, 3.9	Department of the Environment	Housing and Construction Statistics (quarterly) Housing return for Scotland (quarterly)
	3.10	Department of the Environment	Housing and Construction Statistics (quarterly) Welsh Office: Welsh housing statistics (annual)
		Scottish Development Department	Housing return for Scotland (quarterly)
		Department of the Environment for Northern Ireland	Digest of Housing Statistics for Northern Ireland (annual)
Social security pensions, benefits and allowances	3.11, 3.12, 3.15	Department of Health and Social Security	National Insurance Fund Account (annual)
		Department of Health and Social Services, Northern Ireland	Northern Ireland National Insurance Fund Account (annual)
	3.13 3.15–3.27	Department of Health and Social Security Department of Health and Social Security Northern Ireland	Social Security Statistics (annual) Health and Personal Social Services Statistics for England (annual) Welsh Office: Health and Personal Social Services Statistics for Wales (annual)
National health service	3.27	Department of Health and Social Security; Welsh Office	Civil Appropriation Accounts (annual) Health and Personal Social Services Statistics for England (annual) Health and Personal Social Services Statistics for Wales (annual)
	3.28	Scottish Health Service, Common Services Agency	
	3.29	Department of Health and Social Services, Northern Ireland	Parliament of Northern Ireland Estimates (annual) Summary of Health and Personal Social Services Accounts (annual)
	3.30–3.31	Department of Health and Social Security	Health and Personal Social Services Statistics for England (annual)
Public health	3.32	Office of Population Censuses and Surveys	Communicable Disease Statistics Series MB2 (annual) Population Trends (quarterly)
		Scottish Health Service, Common Services Agency	Scottish Health Statistics (annual)
		General Register Office (Northern Ireland)	Annual report of the Registrar General Quarterly return of births, deaths and marriages
	3.33, 3.35	Health and Safety Executive	Health and Safety statistics Manufacturing and service industries (annual) Agriculture Mines (annual) Quarries (annual) Department of Energy: Digest of United Kingdom Energy Statistics (annual)
		Department of Trade and Industry	Casualties to vessels and accidents to men. Vessels registered in the United Kingdom (annual)
		Department of Transport	Railway accidents (annual)
		Civil Aviation Authority	Accidents to aircraft on the British Register
	3.36	Office of Population Censuses and Surveys; General Register Office for Scotland	Census 1981 National Report Great Britain Part II
Elections	3.37	Home Office; Scottish Home and Health Department	Office of Population Censuses and Surveys Electoral statistics (series EL) Return of election expenses Vachers Parliamentary Companion
	3.38	Home Office	Central Statistical Office: Social Trends
4. Law enforcement	4.2	Home Departments	*England and Wales:* Report of Her Majesty's Chief Inspector of Constabulary (annual) *Scotland:* Report of Her Majesty's Chief Inspector of Constabulary for Scotland (annual)
		Northern Ireland Office	*Northern Ireland:* Chief Constable's Report (Royal Ulster Constabulary)

Subject	Table number in *Abstract*	Government department or other organisation	Official publication or other source
Law enforcement *(contd)*	4.1, 4.3–4.11	Home Office	Central Statistical Office: Monthly Digest of Statistics Criminal statistics, England and Wales (annual) Prison statistics, England and Wales (annual) Prison Department Financial Report (annual) Welsh Office: Digest of Welsh Statistics (annual) Offences relating to motor vehicles, England and Wales (annual bulletin)
	4.12–4.16	Scottish Home and Health Department	Criminal statistics, Scotland (annual)
	4.17, 4.18	Scottish Home and Health Department	Prisons in Scotland (annual)
	4.19–4.22	Northern Ireland Office	Chief Constable's Report (Royal Ulster Constabulary)
5. Education	5.1–5.12	Education Departments	Scottish Educational Statistics (annual) Education in Northern Ireland (half-yearly) Education Statistics for the United Kingdom (annual) Northern Ireland Annual Abstract of Statistics Welsh Office: Statistics of Education in Wales (annual)
	5.18	Engineering & Research Council British Library Department of Education and Science	
	5.13–5.19	University Grants Committee	University statistics (volumes 1 and 3) (annual) Open University Digest of Statistics, Vol. 1, Students and courses (annual)
6. Employment	6.1, 6.2, 6.4, 6.6, 6.8, 6.10, 6.11, 6.14, 6.17	Department of Employment Department of Economic Development (Northern Ireland)	Employment Gazette (monthly) Central Statistical Office: Monthly Digest of Statistics Welsh Office: Digest of Welsh Statistics (annual)
	6.3	Engineering Industries Training Board	Employment Gazette (monthly) Annual Report of the Engineering Industries Training Board
	6.9	Department of Manpower Services (Northern Ireland)	Northern Ireland Annual Abstract of Statistics
	6.5	Ministry of Agriculture, Fisheries and Food	Agricultural Statistics, United Kingdom (annual)
	6.7	HM Treasury	Civil Service Statistics (annual) Central Statistical Office: Monthly Digest of Statistics
	6.12	Office of Population Censuses and Surveys	Census 1981, Definitions Great Britain
	6.13	Business Statistics Office	Analyses of United Kingdom manufacturing (local) units by employment size (Business Monitor PA 1003)
	6.15–6.19	Department of Employment	Employment Gazette (monthly) New Earnings Survey (annual) Central Statistical Office: Monthly Digest of Statistics
	6.18	Department of Manpower Services (Northern Ireland)	New Earnings Survey Northern Ireland (annual)
	6.20	Department of Employment	Employment Gazette (monthly)
7. Defence	7.1–7.14	Ministry of Defence	Volume II (Defence Statistics) of the Statement on the Defence Estimates (annual)
8. Production			
Census of production	8.1	Business Statistics Office	Report on the Census of Production (Business Monitor PA 1002.1) (annual)
Fuel and power	8.2–8.13	Department of Energy	Digest of United Kingdom Energy Statistics (annual) Energy Trends (monthly)

Subject	Table number in *Abstract*	Government department or other organisation	Official publication or other source
Iron and steel	8.14–8.16	Department of Trade and Industry; Iron and Steel Statistics Bureau	Iron and steel industry: Annual Statistics published by the British Steel Corporation on behalf of the Iron and Steel Statistics Bureau Regional Trends (annual)
Industrial materials	8.17	World Bureau of Metal Statistics Department of Trade and Industry	World Metal Statistics (monthly)
Industrial materials *(contd)*	8.18–8.27	Department of Trade and Industry	British Business (weekly) Business Monitor (monthly and quarterly) Central Statistical Office: Monthly Digest of Statistics
	8.28	Business Statistics Office	Minerals (Business Monitor PA 1007) Natural Environment Research Council: United Kingdom Mineral Statistics (annual)
		Department of Economic Development (Northern Ireland)	Northern Ireland Annual Abstract of Statistics
Building and construction	8.29	Department of Trade and Industry; Department of the Environment; World Bureau of Metal Statistics	Business Monitor (quarterly) Housing and Construction Statistics (quarterly) Central Statistical Office: Monthly Digest of Statistics
	8.30, 8.31	Department of the Environment	Housing and Construction Statistics (quarterly)
Manufactured goods	8.32–8.35	Department of Trade and Industry	Business Monitor (monthly and quarterly) British Business (weekly) Central Statistical Office: Monthly Digest of Statistics
	8.36, 8.37	HM Customs and Excise	Annual report of the Commissioners of HM Customs and Excise
9. Agriculture, Fisheries and Food			
	9.1, 9.2	Agricultural Departments	Agricultural Statistics: England and Wales (annual) Output and utilization of farm produce in the United Kingdom (annual) Scotland: Agricultural Statistics (annual)
	9.3–9.5	Agricultural Departments	Agricultural Statistics, United Kingdom (annual) Scottish Agricultural Economics (annual) Welsh Office: Welsh Agricultural Statistics (annual)
Forestry	9.6	Forestry Commission	*Great Britain:* Annual report and Accounts of the Forestry Commission
		Department of Agriculture for Northern Ireland	Northern Ireland Annual Abstract of Statistics
Agriculture	9.7	Agricultural Departments	Employment Gazette (monthly)
Food	9.9–9.12	Ministry of Agriculture, Fisheries and Food	Central Statistical Office: Monthly Digest of Statistics
Fisheries	9.13–9.15	Ministry of Agriculture, Fisheries and Food; Department of Agriculture and Fisheries for Scotland	*England and Wales:* Sea fisheries statistical tables (annual) *Scotland:* Fisheries of Scotland report (annual) Scottish sea fisheries statistical tables (annual)
Food supplies		Ministry of Agriculture, Fisheries and Food	MAFF Food Facts British Business (weekly)
	9.17	Ministry of Agriculture, Fisheries and Food	MAFF Food Facts
	9.18–9.19	National Food Survey Committee	Annual Report of the National Food Survey Committee: Household Food Consumption and Expenditure
10. Transport and communications			
Road transport	10.1–10.7, 10.11	Department of Transport	Transport Statistics Great Britain (annual) Central Statistical Office: Monthly Digest of Statistics
	10.12–10.14	Department of Transport	Road accidents in Great Britain Business Monitor (monthly) Central Statistical Office: Monthly Digest of Statistics Welsh Office: Road accidents Wales (annual)
	10.8, 10.9	Department of the Environment for Northern Ireland	Northern Ireland Annual Abstract of Statistics
Rail transport	10.15–10.18	Department of Transport	Transport Statistics Great Britain (annual)

Subject	Table number in *Abstract*	Government department or other organisation	Official publication or other source
	10.19	Department of Transport	Health and Safety Executive: Industry and Services (annual)
	10.20, 10.21	Department of the Environment for Northern Ireland	Northern Ireland Annual Abstract of Statistics
Air transport	10.22–10.27	Civil Aviation Authority	Central Statistical Office: Monthly Digest of Statistics Civil Aviation Authority; Annual and Monthly Statistics Accidents to aircraft on the British Register (annual)
Shipping	10.29–10.31	Department of Transport	Central Statistical Office: Monthly Digest of Statistics
	10.32–10.35	Department of Transport	British Business (weekly) Port Statistics (annual) Transport Statistics Great Britain (annual)
		HM Customs and Excise	Nationality of vessels in seaborne trade (Business Monitor M8)
Passenger movement	10.36	Department of Transport; Civil Aviation Authority	Central Statistical Office: Monthly Digest of Statistics
Communications	10.37	Home Office Post Office	Central Statistical Office: Monthly Digest of Statistics Post Office report and accounts (annual)
11. Distributive trades and services n.e.s.			
	11.1	Business Statistics Office	Retailing 1982 Business Monitor SDO 25 (biennially) Business Monitor SDA 25
	11.2	Business Statistics Office	British Business (weekly) Business Monitor SDM 28 (monthly) Central Statistical Office: Monthly Digest of Statistics
	11.3	Business Statistics Office	British Business (weekly) Business Monitor SDO 24
	11.4	Business Statistics Office	British Business (weekly) Business Monitor SDO 29
Scientific research and development	11.5–11.9	Department of Trade and Industry	British Business (weekly) Industrial Research and Development Expenditure and Employment Business Monitor MO14 Central Statistical Office: Economic Trends, August 1981, August 1982, September 1983, August 1984, August 1985 and August 1986
12. External trade	12.1–12.6	Department of Trade and Industry	Monthly Review of External Trade Statistics Overseas Trade Statistics of the United Kingdom, (Annual Supplement) Central Statistical Office: Monthly Digest of Statistics
13. Balance of payments			
	13.1–13.3	Central Statistical Office	United Kingdom Balance of Payments (annual) Quarterly figures: Economic Trends
	13.3	Bank of England; HM Treasury	United Kingdom Balance of Payments (annual) Quarterly figures: Financial Statistics
Overseas aid	13.4,13.5	Overseas Development Administration	British Aid Statistics (annual), Statistics of UK Economic Aid to Developing Countries
14. National income and expenditure			
	14.1–14.15	Central Statistical Office	United Kingdom National Accounts (annual) Monthly Digest of Statistics Economic Trends (monthly)
15. Personal income, expenditure and wealth			
	15.1	Central Statistical Office; Department of Employment	Economic Trends, December 1982
	15.2	Board of Inland Revenue	Inland Revenue Statistics (annual) Central Statistical Office: Economic Trends, February 1981
	15.3–15.5	Department of Employment	Family Expenditure Survey (annual)
16.Home finance			
Central government	16.1, 16.2	Central Statistical Office	Financial Statistics (monthly)
	16.3–16.7, 16.11	HM Treasury; Central Statistical Office; Bank of England	Consolidated Fund and National Loans Fund Accounts Financial Statistics (monthly)

Subject	Table number in *Abstract*	Government department or other organisation	Official publication or other source
Saving	16.9	Department for National Savings	Annual report of the Inspection Committee of Trustee savings banks Accounts of National Savings Bank; Investment Deposit Accounts (annual) Ordinary Deposit Accounts (annual) Accounts of Savings Banks Funds (annual) Accounts of Trustee savings banks (annual)
Central government	16.10, 16.11	Board of Inland Revenue	Inland Revenue Statistics (annual)
Rateable values	16.12	Board of Inland Revenue	Rates and Rateable values in England and Wales (annual)
Local authorities	16.13, 16.14	Department of the Environment	Local government financial statistics (England and Wales) (annual) Welsh Office: Welsh local government financial statistics (annual)
		Public Works Loan Board	Annual report of the Public Works Loan Board
		Scottish Office, Central Statistics Unit	Local financial returns (Scotland) (annual)
		Department of the Environment for Northern Ireland Welsh Office	District Council—Summary of Statements of Accounts (annual)
	16.15, 16.16	Department of the Environment Wolsh Office	Local government financial statistics (England and Wales) (annual)
	16.17	Water Authorities Association	Digest of environmental protection and water statistics (annual) Water Facts
	16.18, 16.19	Department of the Environment Welsh Office	Local government financial statistics (England and Wales) (annual)
	16.20–16.22	Scottish Office, Central Statistics Unit	Local financial returns (Scotland) (annual)
	16.23–16.25	Department of the Environment for Northern Ireland	Local authority financial returns (Northern Ireland) (annual) District Council—Summary of Statement of Accounts (annual)
17. Banking, Insurance, etc.			
Banking	17.1 17.3–17.6	Bank of England	Bank of England Annual Report and Accounts Bank of England Quarterly Bulletin
	17.2	Bankers' Clearing House	Annual report of the Bankers' Clearing House
	17.7	Bank of England; Central Statistical Office	Financial Statistics (monthly)
	17.8 17.9	Bank of England Bank of England	Bank of England Quarterly Bulletin Bank of England Quarterly Bulletin Central Statistical Office: Monthly Digest of Statistics Central Statistical Office: Financial Statistics (monthly)
Capital markets	17.10	Bank of England	Central Statistical Office: Financial Statistics (monthly)
	17.11	Council of The Stock Exchange	Stock Exchange Fact Book (quarterly)
	17.12	Bank of England	Central Statistical Office: Financial Statistics (monthly)
Other financial institutions	17.13	Registry of Friendly Societies	Report of the Chief Registrar of Friendly Societies, incorporating the Report of the Industrial Assurance Commissioner (annual)
	17.14, 17.15	Department of Trade and Industry	British Business (weekly) Business Monitor (monthly)
	17.16	Bank of England	Central Statistical Office: Financial Statistics (monthly)
	17.17, 17.18	Central Statistical Office; Department of Trade and Industry	Financial Statistics (monthly) Business Monitor M25 (quarterly)
	17.19, 17.20	Registry of Friendly Societies	Report of the Chief Registrar of Friendly Societies, incorporating the Report of the Industrial Assurance Commissioner (annual)
	17.21	Office of the Industrial Assurance Commissioner	Report of the Chief Registrar of Friendly Societies, incorporating the Report of the Industrial Assurance Commissioner (annual)
	17.22	Registry of Friendly Societies	Report of the Chief Registrar of Friendly Societies, incorporating the Report of the Industrial Assurance Commissioner (annual)
Insurance	17.23, 17.24	Office of the Industrial Assurance Commissioner	Report of the Chief Registrar of Friendly Societies, incorporating the Report of the Industrial Assurance Commissioner (annual)

Subject	Table number in *Abstract*	Government department or other organisation	Official publication or other source
Companies	17.25	Department of Trade and Industry	Business Monitor MQ7 (quarterly) British Business (weekly) Central Statistical Office: Financial Statistics (monthly)
	17.26	Department of Trade and Industry Business Statistics Office	Business Monitor MA3 (annual)
Insolvency	17.27, 17.28, 17.29, 17.30	Department of Trade and Industry	British Business (weekly) Bankruptcy, General annual report Companies in (annual) Central Statistical Office: Financial Statistics (monthly) Civil judicial statistics, Scotland (annual) Ulster Yearbook
18. Prices			
	18.1–18.4	Business Statistics Office	British Business (weekly) Central Statistical Office: Monthly Digest of Statistics
	18.5, 18.7	Central Statistical Office	Monthly Digest of Statistics
	18.6	Department of Employment	Employment Gazette (monthly)
	18.8, 18.9	Ministry of Agriculture, Fisheries and Food	Agricultural Statistics, United Kingdom (annual) Central Statistical Office: Monthly Digest of Statistics
	18.10	Ministry of Agriculture, Fisheries and Food	Annual Review of Agriculture (annual)

Index

Figures indicate Table numbers

G

H

I

W

Y

Z

Printed in the United Kingdom for Her Majesty's Stationery Office
Dd289990 1/90 C56 G443 10170

CENTRAL STATISTICAL OFFICE PUBLICATIONS

ANNUAL

Annual Abstract of Statistics — has some 350 tables generally giving data for the last 11 years covering just about every aspect of economic, social and industrial life.

Social Trends — provides a valuable insight into the changing patterns of life in Britain. The chapters provide analyses and breakdowns of statistical information on population, households and families, education and employment, income and wealth, resources and expenditure, health and social services, and many other aspects of British life and work.

Regional Trends — with over 130 tables and 50 maps and charts, brings together a wide range of government statistics on the various countries and regions of the United Kingdom.

United Kingdom National Accounts — The CSO Blue Book is the essential data source for everyone concerned with macro-economic policies and studies and shows how the nation makes and spends its money. It is issued in early September and covers all aspects of the United Kingdom economy giving data for the last eleven years or longer.

United Kingdom Balance of Payments — The CSO Pink Book is the basic reference book for balance of payments statistics, presenting all the statistical information, for the last eleven years or more, needed by analysts who seek to assess UK transactions with the rest of the world.

Key Data — with over 130 tables, maps and coloured charts covers a very wide range of social and economic data. Each table and chart is accompanied by a reference to sources.

MONTHLY

Economic Trends — a compilation of all the main economic indicators liberally illustrated with charts and diagrams. The largest section gives time series and graphs over the last five years or so. It is the primary publication for quarterly articles on national accounts and the balance of payments as well as others commenting on and analysing economic statistics. The *Economic Trends Annual Supplement* contains long runs of annual and quarterly figures for the key series of economic indicators.

Financial Statistics — gives data on the key financial and monetary statistics of the United Kingdom. Table usually contain at least 18 monthly and 12 quarterly or 5 annual figures. The annual *Financial Statistics Explanatory Handbook* contains comprehensive notes and definitions for the tables.

Monthly Digest of Statistics — provides basic information on 20 subjects. Tables contain mostly runs of monthly and quarterly estimates for at least two years and annual figures for several more. The annual *Monthly Digest of Statistics Supplement of Definitions and Explanatory Notes* gives definitions for items and units in the *Digest*. It also applies to corresponding items in the *Annual Abstract* and *Regional Trends.*

OTHERS

Guide to Official Statistics (fifth edition) — an indispensible reference book for all users of statistics. Vital information about sources of government and important non-government statistics for the United Kingdom over the last five years are given.

United Kingdom National Accounts: Sources and Methods (third edition) — an essential reference book for everyone who makes use of national accounts data. It contains details of the concepts, definitions, statistical sources, methods of compilation and reliability of the various statistical sources which comprise the national accounts.

Statistical News — a quarterly journal providing a comprehensive account of current developments in British official statistics.

Standard Industrial Classification Revised 1980 — is a system of classification of establishments according to industry covering all economic activity.

Indexes to the Standard Industrial Classification Revised 1980 contains lists of characteristic activities for each heading of the classification as well as an alphabetical index of activities. The publication is also indexed to the previous 1968 classification and to the European standard industrial classification (NACE).